12th Joint Conference on Lexical and Computational Semantics (*SEM 2023)

Toronto, Canada
13 - 14 July 2023

ISBN: 978-1-7138-8234-3

Printed from e-media with permission by:

Curran Associates, Inc.
57 Morehouse Lane
Red Hook, NY 12571

Some format issues inherent in the e-media version may also appear in this print version.

Printed with permission by Curran Associates, Inc. (2024)

For permission requests, please contact the Association for Computational Linguistics at the address below.

Association for Computational Linguistics
209 N. Eighth Street
Stroudsburg, Pennsylvania 18360

Phone: 1-570-476-8006
Fax: 1-570-476-0860

acl@aclweb.org

Additional copies of this publication are available from:

Curran Associates, Inc.
57 Morehouse Lane
Red Hook, NY 12571 USA
Phone: 845-758-0400
Fax: 845-758-2633
Email: curran@proceedings.com
Web: www.proceedings.com

StarSEM 2023

The 12th Joint Conference on Lexical and Computational Semantics

Proceedings of the Conference (*SEM 2023)

July 13-14, 2023

The StarSEM organizers gratefully acknowledge the support from the following sponsors.

Sponsored by

Order copies of this and other ACL proceedings from:

Association for Computational Linguistics (ACL)
209 N. Eighth Street
Stroudsburg, PA 18360
USA
Tel: +1-570-476-8006
Fax: +1-570-476-0860
acl@aclweb.org

Preface by the Conference Organizers

We are excited to welcome you to *SEM 2023, the 12th Joint Conference on Lexical and Computational Semantics! We are pleased to present this volume containing the accepted long and short papers. *SEM 2023 follows a hybrid format (remote and in-person) and will be held on July 13th-14th 2023, co-located with ACL 2023 in Toronto, Ontario, Canada.

Since its first edition in 2012, *SEM has become a major venue to present recent advances in all areas of lexical and computational semantics, including semantic representations, theoretical semantics, multilingual semantics, and others. *SEM is sponsored by SIGLEX, the ACL Special Interest Group on the Lexicon.

*SEM 2023 accepted both papers submitted directly through the START system and those already reviewed through ARR (ACL Rolling Review). In total, we received 95 submissions in 9 areas:

- Commonsense reasoning and natural language understanding
- Discourse, dialogue, and generation
- Lexical semantics
- Multilinguality
- Psycholinguistics, cognitive linguistics, and semantic processing
- Resources and evaluation
- Semantic composition and sentence-level semantics
- Semantics in NLP applications
- Theoretical and formal semantics

We compiled an exciting and wide-ranging program, accepting a total of 45 papers – 29 long papers and 16 short papers. In addition, 8 papers accepted to ACL Findings will be presented as part of the *SEM poster session.

The submitted papers were carefully evaluated by a program committee led by 13 area chairs, who coordinated a panel of 140 reviewers. Because the number of submissions was almost double our expectation, we recruited a number of late reviewers and emergency reviewers. The reviews were almost all of very high quality, and for that we are extremely grateful! All but a handful of papers were reviewed by three reviewers, who were encouraged to discuss any divergence in evaluations. Area chairs then added meta-reviews to explain their accept/reject suggestions. The final selection was made by the program co-chairs after a check of the reviews, meta-reviews, and discussions with the area chairs.

We are also very excited to have three excellent keynote speakers: Jessy Li (University of Texas at Austin) presents recent work on how we might better model discourse in the age of large language models, Hinrich Schütze (University of Munich) talks about massively multilingual language models and issues related to their semantic evaluation, and finally Danushka Bollegala (Amazon and University of Liverpool) discusses the topic of lexical semantics over time.

We are honored to serve as the organizing committee for *SEM 2023, and we absolutely could not have made this happen without a huge amount of help. First, tremendous thanks to all area chairs and reviewers for their invaluable help in selecting the program, for their engagement in thoughtful discussions, and for providing valuable feedback to the authors. Second, thanks to our Publicity chair Malihe Alikhani (University of Pittsburgh) who took care of website and social media updates. Next, thanks to our Publication chair Luis Espinosa-Anke (Cardiff University and AMPLYFI) for being the mastermind and driving force behind compilation of the proceedings, and finally the ACL 2023 workshop organizers for help and support with all organizational aspects of the conference. Finally, thank you to the authors and presenters for making *SEM 2023 such an engaging and exciting event! We hope that you, dear audience, will find the content of these proceedings as engaging as we do, and we hope to see you at future iterations of *SEM!

Jose Camacho-Collados and Alexis Palmer, Program co-chairs
Mohammad Taher Pilehvar, General chair

Organizing Committee

General Chair

Mohammad Taher Pilehvar, Tehran Institute for Advanced Studies

Program Chairs

Alexis Palmer, University of Colorado Boulder
Jose Camacho-Collados, Cardiff University

Publication Chair

Luis Espinosa-Anke, Cardiff University / AMPLYFI

Publicity Chairs

Malihe Alikhani, University of Pittsburgh
Mert Inan, University of Pittsburgh

Program Committee

Area Chairs

Chenghua Lin, Department of Computer Science, University of Sheffield
Steven Schockaert, Cardiff University
Lucia Donatelli, Vrije Universiteit Amsterdam
Montse Cuadros, Vicomtech
Valerio Basile, University of Turin
Sebastian Schuster, Saarland University
Mahmoud El-haj, Lancaster University
Christina Niklaus, University of St. Gallen
Asad Sayeed, University of Gothenburg
Guy Emerson, University of Cambridge
Alessandro Raganato, University of Milano-Bicocca
Ghazaleh Kazeminejad, University of Colorado Boulder

Program Committee

Rodrigo Agerri, HiTZ Center - Ixa, University of the Basque Country UPV/EHU
Ameeta Agrawal, Portland State University
Shafiuddin Rehan Ahmed, University of Colorado Boulder
Marianna Apidianaki, University of Pennsylvania
Yuki Arase, Osaka University
Nicholas Asher, CNRS Institut de Recherche en Informatique de Toulouse
Timothy Baldwin, MBZUAI
Forrest Sheng Bao, Iowa State Univerity
Mohamad Hardyman Barawi, University of Malaysia, Sarawak
Tilman Beck, UKP Lab, Technical University of Darmstadt
Farah Benamara, University of toulouse
Gábor Berend, University Of Szeged
Steven Bethard, University of Arizona
Abhidip Bhattacharyya, University of Colorado Boulder
Eduardo Blanco, University of Arizona
Michael Bloodgood, The College of New Jersey
Joanne Boisson, Cardiff University
Marianna Bolognesi, University of Bologna
Johan Bos, University of Groningen
Trung Bui, Adobe Research
Paul Buitelaar, University of Galway
Davide Buscaldi, LIPN, Université Sorbonne Paris Nord
Elena Cabrio, Université Côte d'Azur, Inria, CNRS, I3S
Aoife Cahill, Dataminr
Santiago Castro, University of Michigan
Thiago Castro Ferreira, Federal University of Minas Gerais
Akshay Chaturvedi, Institut de Recherche en Informatique de Toulouse
Aditi Chaudhary, Google Research
Pinzhen Chen, University of Edinburgh
Emmanuele Chersoni, Hong Kong Polytechnic University
Patricia Chiril, University of Chicago

Hyunsoo Cho, Seoul National University
Gabriella Chronis, The University of Texas at Austin
Philipp Cimiano, Univ. Bielefeld
Robin Cooper, University of Gothenburg
Bonaventura Coppola, University of Trento
Walter Daelemans, University of Antwerp, CLiPS
Maksym Del, University of Tartu
Jakub Dotlacil, Utrecht University
Jad Doughman, Mohamed bin Zayed University of Artificial Intelligence
Yo Ehara, Tokyo Gakugei University
Katrin Erk, University of Texas at Austin
Francis Ferraro, University of Maryland, Baltimore County
Mark Fishel, University of Tartu
Meaghan Fowlie, Utrecht University
Diego Frassinelli, University of Konstanz
Simona Frenda, Università degli Studi di Torino
Richard Futrell, University of California, Irvine
Voula Giouli, Institute for Language
Speech Processing, ATHENA Research
Innovation Centre
Colin Gordon, Drexel University
Venkata Subrahmanyan Govindarajan, University of Texas at Austin
Jonas Groschwitz, University of Amsterdam (UvA)
Ivan Habernal, Technical University of Darmstadt
Michael Hahn, Saarland University
Udo Hahn, Friedrich-Schiller-Universitaet Jena
Siegfried Handschuh, University of St. Gallen
Yoshihiko Hayashi, Waseda University
Jena D. Hwang, Allen Institute for AI
Nancy Ide, Vassar College/Brandeis University
Joseph Marvin Imperial, National University
Sk Mainul Islam, IIT Kharagpur
Mikaela Keller, Universite de Lille
Najoung Kim, Boston University
Thomas Kober, Zalando SE
Valia Kordoni, Humboldt-Universität zu Berlin
Kenneth Lai, Brandeis University
Dan Lassiter, University of Edinburgh
John Lee, City University of Hong Kong
Patrick Lee, Montclair State University
Els Lefever, LT3, Ghent University
Junyi Jessy Li, University of Texas at Austin
Zongxi Li, Hong Kong Metropolitan University
Chunhua Liu, The University of Melbourne
Renze Lou, Pennsylvania State University
Qing Lyu, University of Pennsylvania
Alda Mari, http://www.institutnicod.org/
Eugenio Martínez Cámara, University of Jaén
Sahisnu Mazumder, University of Illinois at Chicago
Yisong Miao, National University of Singapore
Timothee Mickus, University of Helsinki

Koji Mineshima, Keio University
Amita Misra, Amazon
Richard Moot, CNRS
Gaku Morio, Research
Development Group, Hitachi America, Ltd.
Larry Moss, Indiana University, Bloomington
Tomáš Musil, Charles University
Skatje Myers, University of Colorado at Boulder
Nona Naderi, University of Applied Sciences HES-SO Genève, Swiss Institute of Bioinformatics (SIB)
Martha Palmer, University of Colorado
Emerson Paraiso, Pontificia Universidade Catolica do Parana - PUCPR
Lucia Passaro, University of Pisa
Naiara Perez, Vicomtech
Sandro Pezzelle, University of Amsterdam
Jakob Prange, Hong Kong Polytechnic University
Sara Rajaee, University of Amsterdam
Giulia Rambelli, University of Bologna
Carlos Ramisch, Aix Marseille University, CNRS, LIS
Michael Regan, University of Washington
Christian Retoré, University of Montpellier
Kiamehr Rezaee, Cardiff University
Juan Diego Rodriguez, The University of Texas at Austin
Alla Rozovskaya, Queens College, City University of New York
Irene Russo, ILC CNR
Farig Sadeque, BRAC University
Mehrnoosh Sadrzadeh, University College London
Ryohei Sasano, Nagoya University
Dominik Schlechtweg, University of Stuttgart
Sabine Schulte Im Walde, University of Stuttgart
Vered Shwartz, University of British Columbia
Melanie Siegel, Hochschule Darmstadt - University of Applied Sciences
Katharina Stein, Saarland University
Egon Stemle, Eurac Research
Kevin Stowe, Educational Testing Services (ETS)
Sara Stymne, Uppsala University
Yoshi Suhara, Grammarly
Elior Sulem, Ben-Gurion University of the Negev
Aarne Talman, University of Helsinki
Andon Tchechmedjiev, IMT Mines Alès
Samia Touileb, University of Bergen
Enrica Troiano, Vrije Universiteit
Thinh Hung Truong, The University of Melbourne
Shyam Upadhyay, Google
L. Alfonso Ureña-lópez, University of Jaen
Rossella Varvara, University of Fribourg
Eva Maria Vecchi, Universitat Stuttgart, Institut fur Maschinelle Sprachverarbeitung
Serena Villata, Université Côte d'Azur, CNRS, Inria, I3S
Ekaterina Vylomova, University of Melbourne
Shira Wein, Georgetown University
Genta Winata, Bloomberg

Tak-lam Wong, Department of Computing Studies and Information Systems, Douglas College
Shijie Wu, Bloomberg
Hanzi Xu, Temple University
Huiling You, University of Oslo
Alessandra Zarcone, Hochschule für angewandte Wissenschaften
Jie Zhao, Microsoft
Yi Zhou, Cardiff University

Table of Contents

Program

Thursday, July 13, 2023

09:00 - 09:15 *Opening remarks*

09:15 - 10:30 *Invited Talk - Jessy Li*

10:30 - 11:00 *Morning break*

11:00 - 12:20 *Applications*

Evaluating Factual Consistency of Texts with Semantic Role Labeling
Jing Fan, Dennis Aumiller and Michael Gertz

CRAPES:Cross-modal Annotation Projection for Visual Semantic Role Labeling
Abhidip Bhattacharyya, Martha Palmer and Christoffer Heckman

Robust Integration of Contextual Information for Cross-Target Stance Detection
Tilman Beck, Andreas Waldis and Iryna Gurevych

Generative Data Augmentation for Aspect Sentiment Quad Prediction
An Wang, Junfeng Jiang, Youmi Ma, Ao Liu and Naoaki Okazaki

Estimating Semantic Similarity between In-Domain and Out-of-Domain Samples
Rhitabrat Pokharel and Ameeta Agrawal

How Are Idioms Processed Inside Transformer Language Models?
Ye Tian, Isobel James and Hye Son

12:30 - 14:00 *Lunch break*

14:00 - 15:30 *Semantic composition and sentence-level semantics*

Arithmetic-Based Pretraining Improving Numeracy of Pretrained Language Models
Dominic Petrak, Nafise Sadat Moosavi and Iryna Gurevych

Functional Distributional Semantics at Scale
Chun Hei Lo, Hong Cheng, Wai Lam and Guy Emerson

Syntax and Semantics Meet in the Middle": Probing the Syntax-Semantics Interface of LMs Through Agentivity
Lindia Tjuatja, Emmy Liu, Lori Levin and Graham Neubig

Monolingual Phrase Alignment as Parse Forest Mapping
Sora Kadotani and Yuki Arase

Semantically-informed Hierarchical Event Modeling
Shubhashis Roy Dipta, Mehdi Rezaee and Francis Ferraro

Does Character-level Information Always Improve DRS-based Semantic Parsing?
Tomoya Kurosawa and Hitomi Yanaka

Query Generation Using GPT-3 for CLIP-Based Word Sense Disambiguation for Image Retrieval
Xiaomeng Pan, Zhousi Chen and Mamoru Komachi

15:30 - 16:00 *Afternoon break*

16:00 - 17:30 *In-person poster session*

Robust Integration of Contextual Information for Cross-Target Stance Detection
Tilman Beck, Andreas Waldis and Iryna Gurevych

Estimating Semantic Similarity between In-Domain and Out-of-Domain Samples
Rhitabrat Pokharel and Ameeta Agrawal

Query Generation Using GPT-3 for CLIP-Based Word Sense Disambiguation for Image Retrieval
Xiaomeng Pan, Zhousi Chen and Mamoru Komachi

Scalable Performance Analysis for Vision-Language Models
Santiago Castro, Oana Ignat and Rada Mihalcea

Thursday, July 13, 2023 (continued)

Friday, July 14, 2023

08:30 - 10:30 *Virtual poster session*

Not All Counterhate Tweets Elicit the Same Replies: A Fine-Grained Analysis
Abdullah Albanyan, Ahmed Hassan and Eduardo Blanco

KGLM: Integrating Knowledge Graph Structure in Language Models for Link Prediction
Jason Youn and Ilias Tagkopoulos

Are Language Models Sensitive to Semantic Attraction? A Study on Surprisal
Yan Cong, Emmanuele Chersoni, Yu-yin Hsu and Alessandro Lenci

Language models are not naysayers: an analysis of language models on negation benchmarks
Thinh Hung Truong, Timothy Baldwin, Karin Verspoor and Trevor Cohn

JSEEGraph: Joint Structured Event Extraction as Graph Parsing
Huiling You, Lilja Vrelid and Samia Touileb

Testing Paraphrase Models on Recognising Sentence Pairs at Different Degrees of Semantic Overlap
Qiwei Peng, David Weir and Julie Weeds

Can Sequence-to-Sequence Transformers Naturally Understand Sequential Instructions?
Xiang Zhou, Aditya Gupta, Shyam Upadhyay, Mohit Bansal and Manaal Faruqui

Can Pretrained Language Models Derive Correct Semantics from Corrupt Subwords under Noise?
Xinzhe Li, Ming Liu and Shang Gao

True Detective: A Deep Abductive Reasoning Benchmark Undoable for GPT-3 and Challenging for GPT-4
Maksym Del and Mark Fishel

09:30 - 10:30 *Invited Talk - Hinrich Schütze*

10:30 - 11:00 *Morning break*

Friday, July 14, 2023 (continued)

11:00 - 12:00 *Invited Talk - Danushka Bollegala*

12:00 - 12:30 *Oral presentations*

Limits for learning with language models
Nicholas Asher, Swarnadeep Bhar, Akshay Chaturvedi, Julie Hunter and Soumya Paul

JSEEGraph: Joint Structured Event Extraction as Graph Parsing
Huiling You, Lilja Vrelid and Samia Touileb

12:30 - 14:00 *Lunch break*

14:00 - 15:35 *Generation and understanding*

Including Facial Expressions in Contextual Embeddings for Sign Language Generation
Carla Viegas, Mert Inan, Lorna Quandt and Malihe Alikhani

Is Shortest Always Best? The Role of Brevity in Logic-to-Text Generation
Eduardo Cal, Jordi Levy, Albert Gatt and Kees Van Deemter

Empirical Sufficiency Lower Bounds for Language Modeling with Locally-Bootstrapped Semantic Structures
Jakob Prange and Emmanuele Chersoni

Event Semantic Knowledge in Procedural Text Understanding
Ghazaleh Kazeminejad and Martha Palmer

Improving Toponym Resolution with Better Candidate Generation, Transformer-based Reranking, and Two-Stage Resolution
Zeyu Zhang and Steven Bethard

Probing neural language models for understanding of words of estimative probability
Damien Sileo and Marie-francine Moens

Friday, July 14, 2023 (continued)

15:30 - 16:00 *Afternoon break*

16:00 - 16:50 *Lexical semantics*

Leveraging Active Learning to Minimise SRL Annotation Across Corpora
Skatje Myers and Martha Palmer

Seeking Clozure: Robust Hypernym extraction from BERT with Anchored Prompts
Chunhua Liu, Trevor Cohn and Lea Frermann

Leverage Points in Modality Shifts: Comparing Language-only and Multimodal Word Representations
Lisa Bylinina, Denis Paperno and Alexey Tikhonov

16:40 - 16:50 *Closing Remarks*

Including Facial Expressions in Contextual Embeddings for Sign Language Generation

Carla Viegas[1,2] and **Mert Inan**[3] and **Lorna Quandt**[4] and **Malihe Alikhani** [3]
[1]Stella AI, Pittsburgh, USA
[2]Language Technologies Institute, Carnegie Mellon University, Pittsburgh, USA
[3] Computer Science Department, School of Computing and Information, University of Pittsburgh, Pittsburgh, USA
[4] Educational Neuroscience Program, Gallaudet University, Washington, D.C, USA

Abstract

State-of-the-art sign language generation frameworks lack expressivity and naturalness which is the result of only focusing on manual signs, neglecting the affective, grammatical, and semantic functions of facial expressions. The purpose of this work is to augment semantic representation of sign language through grounding facial expressions. We study the effect of modeling the relationship between text, gloss, and facial expressions on the performance of the sign generation systems. In particular, we propose a Dual Encoder Transformer able to generate manual signs as well as facial expressions by capturing the similarities and differences found in the text and sign gloss annotation. We take into consideration the role of facial muscle activity to express intensities of manual signs by being the first to employ facial action units in sign language generation. We perform a series of experiments showing that our proposed model improves the quality of automatically generated sign language.

1 Introduction

Communication between the Deaf and Hard of Hearing (DHH) people and hearing non-signing people may be facilitated by emerging language technologies. DHH individuals are medically underserved worldwide (McKee et al., 2020; Masuku et al., 2021) due to the lack of doctors who can understand and use sign language. Also, educational resources that are available in sign language are limited especially in STEM fields (Boyce et al., 2021; Lynn et al., 2020). Although the Americans with Disabilities Act (United States Department of Justice, 2010) requires government services, public accommodations, and commercial facilities to communicate effectively with DHH individuals, the reality is far from ideal. Sign language interpreters are not always available, and communicating through text is not always feasible as written languages are completely different from signed languages.

In contrast to Sign Language Recognition (SLR) which has been studied for several decades (Rastgoo et al., 2021) in the computer vision community (Yin et al., 2021), Sign Language Generation (SLG) is a more recent and less explored research topic (Quandt et al., 2021; Cox et al., 2002; Glauert et al., 2006).

Missing a rich, grounded semantic representation, the existing SLG frameworks are far from generating understandable and natural sign language. Sign languages use spatiotemporal modalities and encode semantic information in manual signs and facial expressions. A major focus in SLG has been put on manual signs, neglecting the affective, grammatical, and semantic roles of facial expressions. In this work, we bring insights from computational linguistics to study the role of and include facial expressions in automated SLG. Apart from using facial landmarks encoding the contours of the face, eyes, nose, and mouth, we are the first to explore using facial Action Units (AUs) to learn semantic spaces or representations for sign language generation.

In addition, with insights from multimodal Transformer architecture design, we present a novel application of the Dual Encoder Transformer model for SLG, which takes as input spoken text and glosses, computes the correlation between both inputs and generates skeleton poses with facial landmarks and facial AUs. Previous work used either gloss or text to generate sign language or used text-to-gloss (T2G) prediction as an intermediary step (Saunders et al., 2020). Our model architecture, on the other hand, allows us to capture information otherwise lost when using gloss only and captures differences between text and gloss, which is especially useful for highlighting adjectives otherwise lost in gloss annotation. We perform several experiments using the PHOENIX14-T

*Proceedings of the The 12th Joint Conference on Lexical and Computational Semantics (*SEM 2023)*, pages 1–10
July 13-14, 2023 ©2023 Association for Computational Linguistics

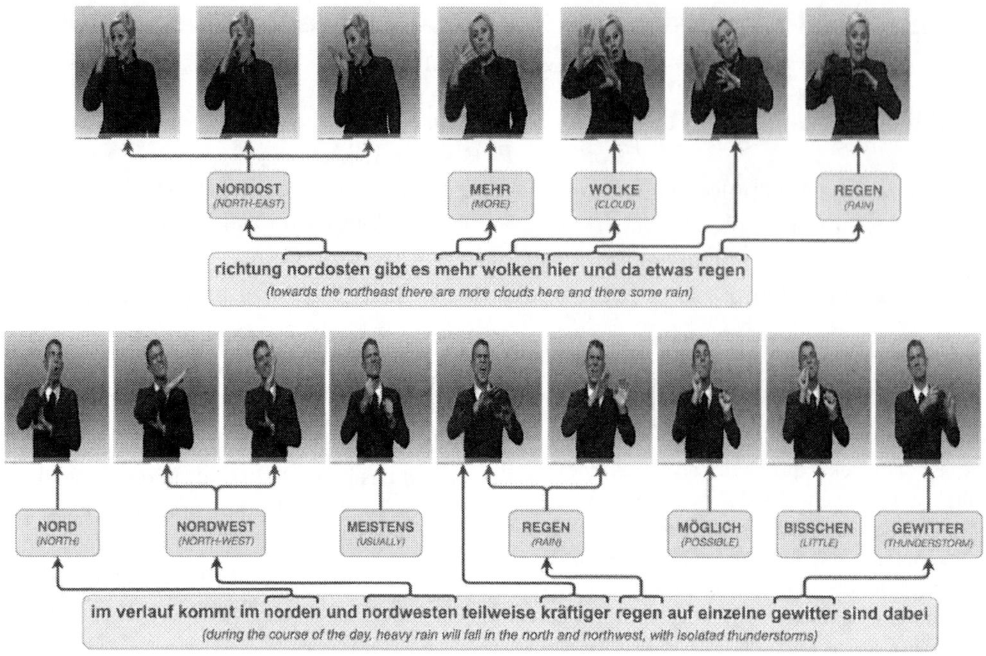

Figure 1: Sign Language uses multiple modalities, such as hands, body, and facial expressions to convey semantic information. Although gloss annotation is often used to transcribe sign language, the above examples show that meaning encoded through facial expressions are not captured. In addition, the translation from text (blue) to gloss (red) is lossy even though sign languages have the capability to express the complete meaning from text. The lower example shows lowered brows and a wrinkled nose to add the meaning of `kräftiger(heavy)` (present in text) to the RAIN sign.

weather forecast dataset and show that our model performs better than baseline models using only gloss or text.

In summary, our main contributions are the following:

- Novel Dual Encoder Transformer for SLG captures information from text and gloss, as well as their relationship to generate continuous 3D sign pose sequences, facial landmarks, and facial action units.

- Use of facial action units to ground semantic representation in sign language.

2 Background and Related Work

More than 70 million Deaf and Hard of Hearing worldwide use one of 300 existing sign languages as their primary language (Kozik, 2020). In this section, we explain the linguistic characteristics of sign languages, the importance of facial expressions to convey meaning, and elaborate on prior work in SLG.

2.1 Sign Language Linguistics

Sign languages are spatiotemporal and are articulated using the hands, face, and other parts of the body, which need to be visible. In contrast to spoken languages, which are oral-aural, sign languages are articulated in front of the top half of the body and around the head. No universal method, such as the International Phonetic Alphabet (IPA), exists to capture the complexity of signs. Gloss annotation is often used to represent the meaning of signs in written form. Glosses do not provide any information about the execution of the sign, only about its meaning. Even more, as glosses use written language rather than sign language, they are a mere approximation of the sign's meaning, representing only one possible transcription. For that reason, glosses do not always represent the full meaning of signs, as shown in Figure 1.

Every sign can be broken into four manual characteristics: shape, location, movement, and orientation. Non-manual components such as mouth movements (mouthing), facial expressions, and body movements are other aspects of sign language phonology. In contrast to spoken languages,

	NOUN	VERB	ADV	ADJ
gloss	20927	6407	17718	648
TEXT	25952	7638	24755	5628

Table 1: Occurrence of different Part-of-Speech (POS) in the sign gloss annotation and the German transcripts computed with Spacy (Honnibal and Montani, 2017). Although gloss annotations show fewer samples for all POS, the difference in the occurrence of adjectives is statistically significant with $p < 0.05$.

signing occurs simultaneously, while vowels and consonants occur sequentially. Although the vocabulary size of ASL in dictionaries is around 15,000 (Spread the Sign, 2017) compared to approximately 170,000 in spoken English, the simultaneity of phonological components allows for a wide range of signs to describe slight differences of the same gloss.

While in English various words describe largeness (big, large, huge, humongous, etc.), in ASL, there is one main sign for "large": BIG. However, through modifications of facial expressions, mouthing, and the size of the sign, different levels of largeness can be expressed just as in a spoken language (Grushkin, 2017). To communicate spoken concepts without a corresponding fingerspelling—a manual alphabet—is sometimes used. (Baker et al., 2016)

2.2 Grammatical Facial Expressions

Facial expressions are grammatical components of sign languages that encode semantic representations, which, when excluded leads to loss of meaning. Facial expressions in particular have an important role in distinguishing different types of sentences such as WH-questions, Yes/No questions, doubt, negations, affirmatives, conditional clauses, focus and relative clauses (da Silva et al., 2020). The following example shows how the same gloss order can present a question or an affirmation (Baker et al., 2016):

Example 1
Indopakistani Sign Language
a) FATHER CAR EXIST.
"(My) father has a car."

b) FATHER CAR EXIST?
"Does (your/his) father have a car."

In this example, what makes sentence b) a question are raised eyebrows and a forward and/or downward movement of the head/chin in parallel to the manual signs.

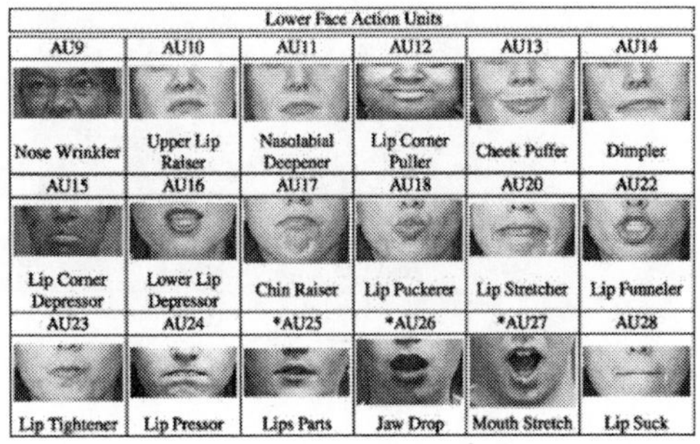

Figure 2: Examples from different facial Action Units (AUs) (Friesen and Ekman, 1978) from the lower face relevant to the generation of mouthings in sign languages. AUs can occur with different intensity values between 0 and 5. AUs have been used in psychology and in affective computing to understand emotions expressed through facial expressions. Image from (De la Torre and Cohn, 2011).

In addition, facial expressions can differentiate the meaning of a sign assuming the role of a determiner. Figure 1 shows different signs for the same gloss, REGEN (rain). We can observe from the text transcript (in blue) that the news anchor says "rain" in the upper example but "heavy rain" in the lower. This example shows how gloss annotations are not perfect transcriptions of sign languages as they only convey the meaning of manual aspect of the signs. Information conveyed through facial expressions to show intensities are not represented in gloss annotation. To view the loss of information that occurs in gloss annotation we used Spacy (Honnibal and Montani, 2017) to compute the Part-of-Speech (POS) annotation for text and gloss. In Table 1 the occurrence of nouns, verbs, adverbs, and adjectives are shown for text and gloss over the entire dataset. We can see that although gloss annotations have lower occurrence for all POS, the difference is statistically significant for adjectives with $p < 0.05$. To calculate this significance, we performed hypothesis testing with two proportions by computing the Z score. We used t-tests to determine statistical significance of our model's performance.

2.3 Sign Language Generation

Several advances in generating sign poses from text have been recently achieved in SLG, however there is limited work that considers the loss of semantic

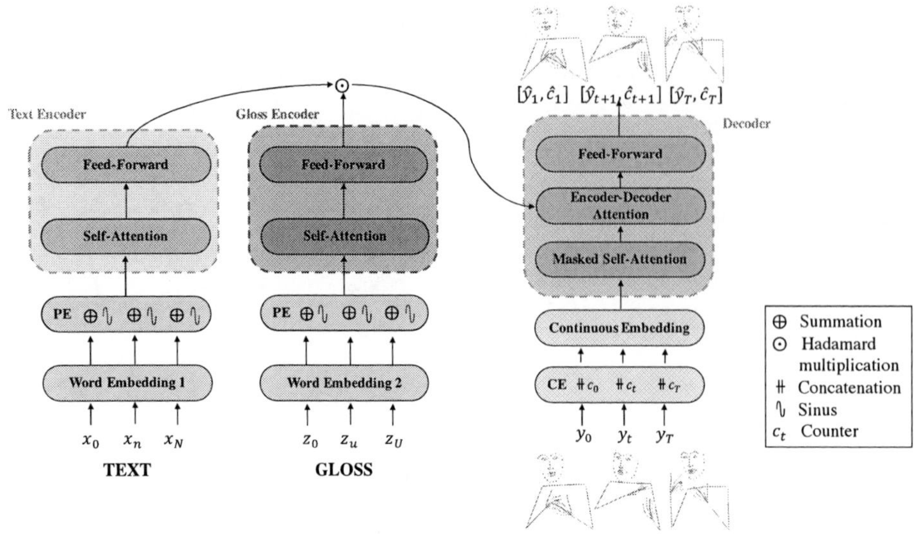

Figure 3: Our proposed model architecture, the Dual Encoder Transformer for Sign Language Generation. Our architecture is characterized by using two encoders, one for text and one for gloss annotation. The use of two encoders allows to multiply the outputs of both emphasizing the differences and similarities. In addition we to using skeleton poses and facial landmarks, we include facial action units (Friesen and Ekman, 1978).

information when using gloss to generate poses and aligned facial expressions. Previous work has generated poses by translating text-to-gloss (T2G) and then gloss-to-pose (G2S) or by using either text or gloss as input (Stoll et al., 2020; Saunders et al., 2020). We propose a Dual Encoder Transformer for SLG which trains individual encoders for text and gloss, and combines the encoder's output to capture similarities and differences.

In addition, the majority of previous work on SLG has focused mainly on manual signs (Stoll et al., 2020; Saunders et al., 2020; Zelinka and Kanis, 2020; Saunders et al., 2021b). (Saunders et al., 2021a) are the first to generate facial expressions and mouthing together with hand poses. The representation used for the non-manual channels is the same as for the hand gestures, namely coordinates of facial landmarks. In this work we explore the use of facial Action Units (AUs) (see Figure 2) which represent intensities of facial muscle movements (Friesen and Ekman, 1978). Although AUs have been primarily used in tasks related to emotion recognition (Viegas et al., 2018), recent works have shown that AUs help detect WH-questions, Y/N questions, and other types of sentences in Brazilian Sign Language (da Silva et al., 2020).

3 Sign Language Dataset

In this work, we use the publicly available PHOENIX14T dataset (Camgoz et al., 2018), frequently used as a benchmark dataset for SLR and SLG tasks. The dataset comprises a collection of weather forecast videos in German Sign Language (DGS), segmented into sentences and accompanied by German transcripts from the news anchor and sign-gloss annotations. PHOENIX14T contains videos of 9 different signers with 1066 different sign glosses and 2887 different German words. The video resolution is 210 by 260 pixels per frame and 30 frames per second. The dataset is partitioned into training, validation, and test sets with respectively 7,096, 519, and 642 sentences.

4 Methods: Dual Encoder Transformer for Sign Language Generation

In this section, we present our proposed model, the Dual Encoder Transformer for Sign Language Generation. Given the loss of information that occurs when translating from text-to-gloss, our novel architecture takes into account the information from text and gloss as well as their similarities and differences to generate sign language in the form of skeleton poses and facial landmarks shown in Figure 3. For that purpose, we learn the conditional probability $p = (Y|X, Z)$ of producing a sequence of signs $Y = (y_1, \ldots, y_T)$ with T frames, given the text of a spoken language sentence $X_T = (x_1, \ldots, x_N)$ with N words and the corresponding glosses $Z = (z_1, \ldots, z_U)$ with U glosses.

Our work is inspired by the Progressive Transformer (Saunders et al., 2020), which allows translation from a symbolic representation (words or glosses) to a continuous domain (joint and face landmark coordinates) by employing positional encoding to permit the processing of inputs with varied lengths. In contrast to the Progressive Transformer, which uses one encoder to use either text or glosses to generate skeleton poses, we employ two encoders, one for text and one for glosses, to capture information from both sources and create a combined representation from the encoder outputs to represent correlations between text and glosses. In the following, we will describe the different components of the dual-encoder transformer.

4.1 Embeddings

As our input sources are words, we must convert them into numerical representations. Similar to transformers used for text-to-text translations, we use word embeddings based on the vocabulary in the training set. As we are using two encoders to represent similarities and differences between text and glosses, we use one word embedding based on the vocabulary of the text and one using the vocabulary of the glosses. We also experiment by using text word embedding for both encoders. Given that our target is a sequence of skeleton joint coordinates, facial landmark coordinates, and continuous values of facial AUs with varying lengths we use counter encoding (Saunders et al., 2020). The counter c varies between [0,1] with intervals proportional to the sequence length. It allows the generation of frames without an end token. The target joints are then defined as:

$$\begin{aligned} m_t &= [y_t, c_t] \text{ with} \\ y_t &= [y_{hands+body}, y_{face}, y_{facialAUs}] \end{aligned}$$

The target joints m_t are then passed to a continuous embedding which is a linear layer.

4.2 Dual Encoders

We use two encoders, one for text and one for gloss annotations. Both encoders have the same architecture. They are composed of L layers, each with one Multi-head Attention (MHA) and a feed-forward layer. Residual connections (He et al., 2016) around each of the two sublayers with subsequent layer normalization (Ba et al., 2016). MHA uses multiple projections of scaled dot-products which permits the model to associate each word of the input with each other. The scaled dot-product attention outputs a vector of values, V, which is weighted by queries, Q, keys, K, and dimensionality, d_k:

$$Attention(Q, K, V) = softmax(\frac{QK^T}{\sqrt{d_k}}) \quad (1)$$

Different self-attention heads are used in MHA, allowing parallel mappings of the Q, V, and K with different learned parameters.

The outputs of MHA are then fed into a non-linear feed-forward projection. In our case, where we employ two different encoders, their outputs can be formulated as follows:

$$\begin{aligned} H_n &= E_{text}(\hat{w}_n, \hat{w}_{1:N}) \\ H_u &= E_{gloss}(\hat{w}_u, \hat{w}_{1:U}) \end{aligned} \quad (2)$$

with h_n being the contextual representation of the source sequence, N being the number of words, and U being the number of glosses in the source sequence.

As we want to use not only the information encoded in text and gloss but also their relationship, we combine the output of both encoders with a Hadamard multiplication. As the $N \neq U$, we stack h_n vertically for U times and stack h_u vertically for N times to have two matrices with the same dimensions. Then we multiply both matrices with the Hadamard multiplication. Hadamard multiplication is a concatenation of every element in two matrices, where $a_{i,j}$ and $b_{i,j}$ are multiplied together to get $a_{i,j}b_{i,j}$. This represents concatenating the output vectors from the text encoder with the output of the vectors from the gloss encoder.

$$H_{text,gloss} = \begin{bmatrix} H_{n0} \\ H_{n1} \\ \vdots \\ H_{nU} \end{bmatrix} \odot \begin{bmatrix} H_{u0} \\ H_{u1} \\ \vdots \\ H_{uN} \end{bmatrix} \quad (3)$$

4.3 Decoder

Our decoder is based on the progressive transformer decoder (DPT), an auto-regressive model that produces continuous sequences of sign pose and the previously described counter value (Saunders et al., 2020). In addition to producing sign poses and facial landmarks, our decoder also produces 17 facial AUs. The counter-concatenated joint embeddings, which include manual and facial features (facial landmarks and AUs), $\hat{j}_u$, are used to represent the sign pose of each frame. Firstly, an initial MHA sub-layer is applied to the joint embeddings, similar to the encoder but with an extra masking operation. The masking of future frames is necessary to prevent the model from attending to future time steps. A further MHA mechanism is then used to map the symbolic representations from the encoder to the continuous domain of the decoder. A final feed-forward sub-layer follows, with each sub-layer followed by a residual connection and layer normalization as in the encoder. The output of the progressive decoder can be formulated as:

$$[\hat{y}_u, \hat{c}_u] = D(\hat{j}_{1:u-1}, h_{1:T}) \quad (4)$$

where $\hat{y}_u$ corresponds to the 3D joint positions, facial landmarks, and AUs, representing the produced sign pose of frame u, and $\hat{c}_u$ is the respective counter value. The decoder learns to generate one frame at a time until the predicted counter value, $\hat{c}_u$, reaches 1. The model is trained using the mean squared error (MSE) loss between the predicted sequence, $\hat{y}_{1:U}$, and the ground truth, $y^*_{1:U}$:

$$L_{MSE} = \frac{1}{U}(y^*_{1:U} - \hat{y}_{1:U})^2 \quad (5)$$

5 Computational Experiments

5.1 Features

We extract three different types of features from the PHOENIX14T dataset: skeleton joint coordinates, facial landmark coordinates, and facial action unit intensities. We use OpenPose (Cao et al., 2019) to extract skeleton poses from each frame and use for our experiments the coordinates of 50 joints which represent the upper body, arms, and hands, which we will start referring to as "manual features". We also use OpenFace (Baltrusaitis et al., 2018) to extract 68 facial landmarks as well as 17 facial action units (AUs) shown in Figure 2 to describe "facial features".

5.2 Baseline Models

We will compare the performance of our proposed model (TG2S) with two Progressive Transformers (Saunders et al., 2020), one using gloss only to produce sign poses (G2S), and one that uses text only (T2S). We train each model only with manual features and also with the combination of manual and facial features through concatenation.

5.3 Evaluation Methods

In order to automatically evaluate the performance of our model and the baseline models, we use back translation suggested by (Saunders et al., 2020). For that purpose, we use the Sign Language Transformer (SLT) (Camgoz et al., 2020) which translates sign poses into text and computes BLEU and ROUGE scores between the translated text and the original text. As the original SLT was designed to receive video frames as input, we modified the architecture by removing the convolutional layers that were used for image feature extraction, and then we replaced skeletal pose and facial features as input.

6 Results

6.1 Quantitative Results

Table 2 shows how well the SLT model performs the translation from ground truth sign poses to text when trained and evaluated with the PHOENIX14T dataset. The results show the highest BLEU scores are achieved when training the SLT model only with skeleton joints from the hands and upper body, presenting a BLEU-4 score of 11.32 for the test set. When facial AUs are added to the hands, body, and face features, the difference from using manual data only is slightly lower, being BLEU-4 of 10.61.

In Table 3, the results of using hands and body joint skeleton as sole input to the baseline models and our proposed model are shown. We can see that our proposed model TG2S shows the highest BLEU-4 scores of 8.19 in the test set, compared to 7.84 for G2S and 7.56 for T2S.

Table 4 presents the results of including facial landmarks as well as facial AUs with body and hands skeleton joints as input. Also, here we can see that our proposed model outperforms the baseline models showing a BLEU-4 score of 5.76 in the test set. G2S obtained a BLUE-4 score of 6.37 and T2S 5.53.

We see in Tables 3 and 4 that G2S obtained higher scores than T2S. Given that gloss annotations fail to encode the richness of meaning in signs, it appears the smaller vocabulary helps the model achieve higher scores by neglecting information otherwise described in the text. Our proposed model is able to obtain better results than G2S by making a compromise of using information from gloss, text, and their similarities and differences. We also can see in both tables that the inclusion of facial information reduces the overall scores. We

Components	Dev Set					Test Set				
	$Bleu_1$	$Bleu_2$	$Bleu_3$	$Bleu_4$	ROUGE	$Bleu_1$	$Bleu_2$	$Bleu_3$	$Bleu_4$	ROUGE
Manual	30.15	20.58	15.41	12.22	30.41	27.76	18.86	14.11	11.32	27.44
Manual and Facial	29.46	20.30	15.31	12.10	29.25	26.75	17.88	13.29	10.61	26.54

Table 2: Translation results of the SLT model (Camgoz et al., 2020) used for backtranslation when trained and evaluated with ground truth hand and body skeleton joints (manual) and facial landmarks and AUs (facial).

Model	Dev Set					Test Set				
	$Bleu_1$	$Bleu_2$	$Bleu_3$	$Bleu_4$	ROUGE	$Bleu_1$	$Bleu_2$	$Bleu_3$	$Bleu_4$	ROUGE
G2S	24.51	15.71	11.19	8.70	**24.84**	**23.26**	14.54	10.21	7.84	22.89
T2S	22.90	14.55	10.42	8.14	23.42	22.14	13.88	9.85	7.56	22.50
TG2S (Ours)	**24.60**	**16.20**	**11.68**	**8.97**	24.82	22.97	**14.71**	**10.59**	**8.19**	**23.45**

Table 3: Back translation results obtained from the generative models when using only manual features. Our proposed model has the highest scores in almost all metrics compared to the models using only gloss or text.

Model	Dev Set					Test Set				
	$Bleu_1$	$Bleu_2$	$Bleu_3$	$Bleu_4$	ROUGE	$Bleu_1$	$Bleu_2$	$Bleu_3$	$Bleu_4$	ROUGE
G2S	16.11	8.77	5.97	4.49	16.19	16.29	9.20	6.37	4.93	16.73
T2S	15.65	8.35	5.76	4.44	15.65	14.12	7.76	5.53	4.39	14.82
TG2S	**17.25**	**10.17**	**7.04**	**5.32**	**17.85**	**17.18**	**10.39**	**7.39**	**5.76**	**17.64**

Table 4: Back translation results obtained from the generative models when using manual features and facial landmarks and AUs. Our proposed model has the highest scores in all metrics compared to the models using only gloss or text.

believe that this might be the case due to the diverse range of facial expressions possible. We cannot directly compare the results of Table 3, and 4 as two SLT models pretrained on different domains were used to compute the BLEU scores.

6.2 Qualitative Results

Figure 4 shows the visual quality of our model's prediction when using manual and facial information. Both examples show that the predictions captured the hand shape, orientation, and movement from the ground truth. In the bottom example for RAIN, the predictions were even able to capture the repetitive hand movement symbolizing falling rain. What can also be noted is that the ground truth is not perfect. In both examples unnatural finger and head postures can be seen. In addition, ground truth is not displaying movements of the eyebrows and mouth in the expected intensities.

Figure 5 shows situations in which the predictions failed to represent the correct phonology of signs. In the first example, we see that hand shape, orientation, and position are incorrect. The predictions of our models also fail to capture pointing hand shapes as shown in example 2.

7 Discussion and Conclusion

In this work, for the first time, we attempt to augment contextual embeddings for sign language by learning a joint meaning representation that includes fine-grained facial expressions. Our results show that the proposed semantic representation is richer and linguistically grounded.

Although our proposed model helped bridge the loss of information by taking into account text, gloss, and their similarities and differences, there are still several challenges to be tackled by a multidisciplinary scientific community.

Complex hand shapes with pointing fingers are very challenging to generate. The first step to improving the generation of the fingers is in improving methods to recognize finger movements more accurately. Similarly, we need tools that are more robust in detecting facial expressions even in situations of occlusion. We also realize that SLG models are overfitting specific sign languages instead of learning generalized representations of signs.

We chose to work with a German sign language since that is the only dataset with gloss annotation that could help us study our hypotheses. The How2Sign dataset (Duarte et al., 2021) is a feasible dataset for ASL, but it does not allow any model

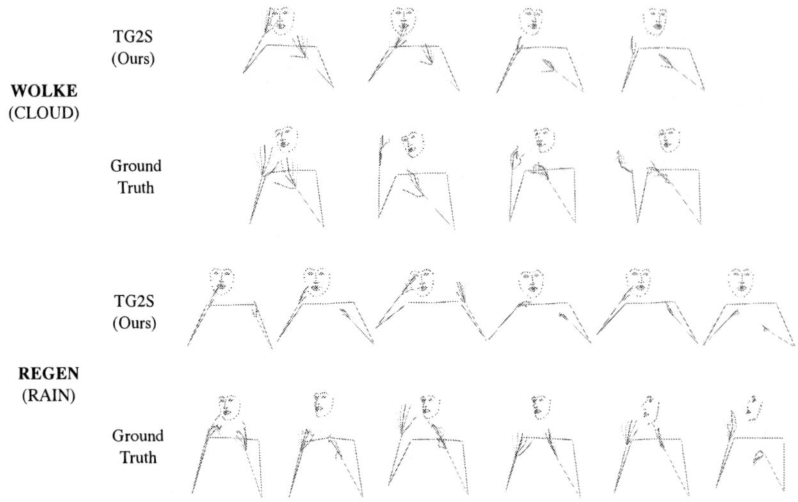

Figure 4: Comparison of the ground truth and the generated poses with our proposed dual encoder model for the gloss annotations CLOUD and RAIN. The upper example shows that the predictions captured the correct hand shape, orientation, and movement of the sign CLOUD. In the lower example, it is visible that the predictions captured the repeating hand movement meaning RAIN. Although at first glance the hand orientation seems not correct, it is a slight variation which still is correct.

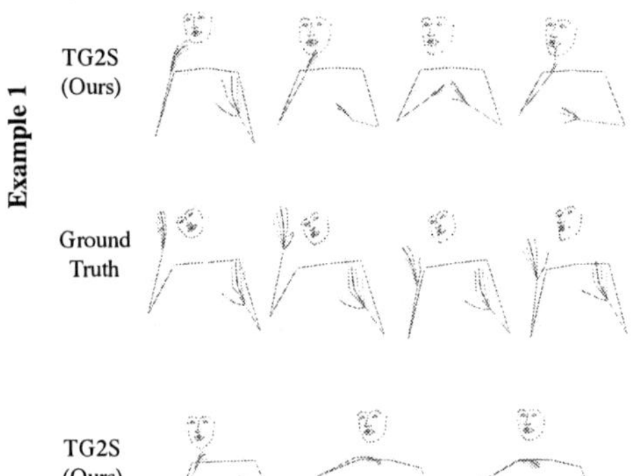

Figure 5: Examples in which our model failed to generate the correct phonology of signs. Example 1 depicts inaccuracies in hand shape, orientation, and movement. Example 2 shows the difficulty of the model to capture pointing hand shapes.

to extract facial landmarks, facial action units, or facial expressions from the original video frames since the faces are blurred. In the future, we hope to see new datasets with better and more diverse annotations for different sign languages that would allow the design of a natural and usable sign language generation system.

Acknowledgements

We want to thank Stella AI LLC for supporting Carla Viegas with computational resources and funding. This project was partly supported by the University of Pittsburgh Momentum Fund for research towards reducing language obstacles that Deaf students face when developing scientific competencies. We also acknowledge the Center for Research Computing at the University of Pittsburgh for providing part of the required computational resources. Lorna Quandt from Gallaudet University was partly supported by NSF Award IIS-2118742.

References

Jimmy Lei Ba, Jamie Ryan Kiros, and Geoffrey E Hinton. 2016. Layer normalization. *arXiv preprint arXiv:1607.06450*.

Anne Baker, Beppie van den Bogaerde, Roland Pfau, and Trude Schermer. 2016. *The linguistics of sign languages: An introduction*. John Benjamins Publishing Company.

Tadas Baltrusaitis, Amir Zadeh, Yao Chong Lim, and Louis-Philippe Morency. 2018. Openface 2.0: Facial behavior analysis toolkit. In *2018 13th IEEE international conference on automatic face & gesture recognition (FG 2018)*, pages 59–66. IEEE.

Richard Boyce, Malihe Alikhani, Sheila Pratt, David Boone, and Kenneth De Haan. 2021. Reducing language obstacles that deaf students face when developing scientific competencies. In *Pitt Momentum Fund 2021*.

Necati Cihan Camgoz, Simon Hadfield, Oscar Koller, Hermann Ney, and Richard Bowden. 2018. Neural sign language translation. In *Proceedings of the IEEE Conference on Computer Vision and Pattern Recognition*, pages 7784–7793.

Necati Cihan Camgoz, Oscar Koller, Simon Hadfield, and Richard Bowden. 2020. Sign language transformers: Joint end-to-end sign language recognition and translation. In *Proceedings of the IEEE/CVF conference on computer vision and pattern recognition*, pages 10023–10033.

Z. Cao, G. Hidalgo Martinez, T. Simon, S. Wei, and Y. A. Sheikh. 2019. Openpose: Realtime multi-person 2d pose estimation using part affinity fields. *IEEE Transactions on Pattern Analysis and Machine Intelligence*.

Stephen Cox, Michael Lincoln, Judy Tryggvason, Melanie Nakisa, Mark Wells, Marcus Tutt, and Sanja Abbott. 2002. Tessa, a system to aid communication with deaf people. In *Proceedings of the fifth international ACM conference on Assistive technologies*, pages 205–212.

Emely Pujólli da Silva, Paula Dornhofer Paro Costa, Kate Mamhy Oliveira Kumada, José Mario De Martino, and Gabriela Araújo Florentino. 2020. Recognition of affective and grammatical facial expressions: a study for brazilian sign language. In *European Conference on Computer Vision*, pages 218–236. Springer.

Fernando De la Torre and Jeffrey F Cohn. 2011. Facial expression analysis. *Visual analysis of humans*, pages 377–409.

Amanda Duarte, Shruti Palaskar, Lucas Ventura, Deepti Ghadiyaram, Kenneth DeHaan, Florian Metze, Jordi Torres, and Xavier Giro-i Nieto. 2021. How2sign: a large-scale multimodal dataset for continuous american sign language. In *Proceedings of the IEEE/CVF Conference on Computer Vision and Pattern Recognition*, pages 2735–2744.

E Friesen and Paul Ekman. 1978. Facial action coding system: a technique for the measurement of facial movement. *Palo Alto*, 3(2):5.

JRW Glauert, Ralph Elliott, SJ Cox, Judy Tryggvason, and Mary Sheard. 2006. Vanessa–a system for communication between deaf and hearing people. *Technology and Disability*, 18(4):207–216.

Don Grushkin. 2017. How large is the vocabulary of asl.

Kaiming He, Xiangyu Zhang, Shaoqing Ren, and Jian Sun. 2016. Deep residual learning for image recognition. In *Proceedings of the IEEE conference on computer vision and pattern recognition*, pages 770–778.

Matthew Honnibal and Ines Montani. 2017. spaCy 2: Natural language understanding with Bloom embeddings, convolutional neural networks and incremental parsing. To appear.

Karolina Kozik. 2020. Without sign language, deaf people are not equal.

Matthew A Lynn, David C Templeton, Annemarie D Ross, Austin U Gehret, Morgan Bida, Timothy J Sanger, and Todd Pagano. 2020. Successes and challenges in teaching chemistry to deaf and hard-of-hearing students in the time of covid-19. *Journal of Chemical Education*, 97(9):3322–3326.

Khetsiwe P Masuku, Nomfundo Moroe, and Danielle van der Merwe. 2021. 'the world is not only for hearing people–it's for all people': The experiences of women who are deaf or hard of hearing in accessing healthcare services in johannesburg, south africa. *African Journal of Disability*, 10.

Michael McKee, Christa Moran, and Philip Zazove. 2020. Overcoming additional barriers to care for deaf and hard of hearing patients during covid-19. *JAMA Otolaryngology–Head & Neck Surgery*, 146(9):781–782.

Lorna C Quandt, Athena Willis, Melody Schwenk, Kaitlyn Weeks, and Ruthie Ferster. 2021. Attitudes toward signing human avatars vary depending on hearing status, age of signed language exposure, and avatar type.

Razieh Rastgoo, Kourosh Kiani, and Sergio Escalera. 2021. Sign language recognition: A deep survey. *Expert Systems with Applications*, 164:113794.

Ben Saunders, Necati Cihan Camgoz, and Richard Bowden. 2020. Progressive transformers for end-to-end sign language production. In *European Conference on Computer Vision*, pages 687–705. Springer.

Ben Saunders, Necati Cihan Camgoz, and Richard Bowden. 2021a. Continuous 3d multi-channel sign language production via progressive transformers and mixture density networks. *International Journal of Computer Vision*, pages 1–23.

Ben Saunders, Necati Cihan Camgoz, and Richard Bowden. 2021b. Mixed signals: Sign language production via a mixture of motion primitives.

Spread the Sign. 2017. About us.

Stephanie Stoll, Necati Cihan Camgoz, Simon Hadfield, and Richard Bowden. 2020. Text2sign: towards sign language production using neural machine translation and generative adversarial networks. *International Journal of Computer Vision*, 128(4):891–908.

United States Department of Justice. 2010. Ada requirements: Effective communication.

Carla Viegas, Shing-Hon Lau, Roy Maxion, and Alexander Hauptmann. 2018. Towards independent stress detection: A dependent model using facial action units. In *2018 International Conference on Content-Based Multimedia Indexing (CBMI)*, pages 1–6. IEEE.

Kayo Yin, Amit Moryossef, Julie Hochgesang, Yoav Goldberg, and Malihe Alikhani. 2021. Including signed languages in natural language processing. *arXiv preprint arXiv:2105.05222*.

Jan Zelinka and Jakub Kanis. 2020. Neural sign language synthesis: Words are our glosses. In *Proceedings of the IEEE/CVF Winter Conference on Applications of Computer Vision*, pages 3395–3403.

Leverage Points in Modality Shifts: Comparing Language-only and Multimodal Word Representations

Aleksey Tikhonov
Inworld.AI
altsoph@gmail.com

Lisa Bylinina*
Center for Language and Cognition
University of Groningen
e.g.bylinina@rug.nl

Denis Paperno*
Institute for Language Sciences
Utrecht University
d.paperno@uu.nl

Abstract

Multimodal embeddings aim to enrich the semantic information in neural representations of language compared to text-only models. While different embeddings exhibit different applicability and performance on downstream tasks, little is known about the systematic representation differences attributed to the visual modality. Our paper compares word embeddings from three vision-and-language models (CLIP, OpenCLIP and Multilingual CLIP, Radford et al. 2021; Ilharco et al. 2021; Carlsson et al. 2022) and three text-only models, with static (FastText, Bojanowski et al., 2017) as well as contextual representations (multilingual BERT Devlin et al. 2018; XLM-RoBERTa, Conneau et al. 2019). This is the first large-scale study of the effect of visual grounding on language representations, including 46 semantic parameters. We identify meaning properties and relations that characterize words whose embeddings are most affected by the inclusion of visual modality in the training data; that is, points where visual grounding turns out most important. We find that the effect of visual modality correlates most with denotational semantic properties related to concreteness, but is also detected for several specific semantic classes, as well as for valence, a sentiment-related connotational property of linguistic expressions.

1 Introduction

Linguistic representations developed by recent large pre-trained language models (LMs) (Devlin et al., 2018; Liu et al., 2019; Radford et al., 2019 a.o.) proved to be very useful across a variety of practical applications. This success has given a new life to the debate around extractability and quality of semantic information in representations trained solely on textual input. According to the widely supported argument, unless the textual data is grounded in a separate space (say, visual), the linguistic representations are bound to be semantically deficient (see Bender and Koller, 2020 a.o.).

We aim to shed new empirical light on the discussion of grounding in computational models by comparing language-only text representations to visually informed text representations. Recent advances produced empirically successful large models pre-trained on a combination of textual and visual data (Li et al., 2019; Tan and Bansal, 2019, 2020; Radford et al., 2021). While these multimodal systems have already given rise to a plethora of applications for language-and-vision (L&V) downstream tasks, there is still little work that directly compares textual representations of language-only models to those of multimodal ones (however, see Davis et al., 2019; Lüddecke et al., 2019; Pezzelle et al., 2021). In contrast to previous related work that focuses on model evaluation with respect to specific benchmarks, we look at the impact of visual grounding from a somewhat different, non-evaluation-based perspective. We do not aim to measure the representation quality with respect to some gold standard, but compare language-only and L&V models to each other intrinsically. Our **goal** is to identify the areas in which *the contrasts between the two kinds of models* tend to lie, independent of the models' fitness for specific tasks.

To do so, we focus on a set of 13k word pairs and compare cosine distances within these pairs in the embedding spaces of language-only vs. L&V models. Fixing the word pairs and comparing the models allows us to measure how the change in model modality stretches the embedding space, with the word pairs as indirect reference points.

The pairs are characterized along 46 different semantic parameters. This information makes it possible to identify the meaning aspects for which

*Equal contribution.

*Proceedings of the The 12th Joint Conference on Lexical and Computational Semantics (*SEM 2023)*, pages 11–17
July 13-14, 2023 ©2023 Association for Computational Linguistics

the change in model modality matters the most.

Our **contributions** are:

1. a methodology for measuring the influence of grounding on semantic representations;
2. a dataset characterizing a large number of word pairs along various semantic parameters and embedding distances in the models that we study.

Our **results** are the following:

• The semantic parameter that makes the highest contribution into explaining the impact of modality on word representation is **concreteness**. This aligns with previous results that visual modality improves representations of concrete nouns but not abstract ones (Pezzelle et al., 2021).

• Representations of particular semantic groups of nouns are affected the most.

• Semantic relations between nouns only have small interaction with modality across the models we tested, with variation from model to model.

• Connotational meanings from the VAD (valence, arousal, dominance) repertoire (Mohammad, 2018) – specifically, valence – play a role in representational shifts relating to modality. This is a somewhat surprising result since visual grounding is expected to relate to the denotational aspects of representations. This result is in line with recent discussion in semantics about the inter-relatedness of denotational and connotational meanings (Ruytenbeek et al., 2017; Terkourafi et al., 2020; Van Tiel and Pankratz, 2021; Beltrama, 2021; Gotzner and Mazzarella, 2021).

We now discuss our data, analysis and results.

2 Data[1]

The dataset consists of word pairs. To collect them, we start with 1000 most frequent words in FastText (Bojanowski et al., 2017). For each of them, we take 100 closest words, by cosine distance over FastText embeddings. This gives 1M pairs to work with. We filter this list of pairs in several ways. First, we only keep those pairs where both words are nouns, according to both NLTK[2] and SpaCy[3] POS labels. Second, we filter out pairs where one of the words is a substring of the other or where the two words have the same lemma. This helps against some FastText artifacts.

One of the goals of our filtering strategy was to balance representation quality of the words (the frequency filter) and the chance for the pair to stand in a WordNet relation (the similarity filter). This gives us a set of pairs like the following:

⟨ page, article ⟩
⟨ people, politicians ⟩
⟨ city, hometown ⟩

Each of the resulting pairs was characterized along a set of properties of interest, collected over a variety of available sources of human-annotated semantic information. The properties we look at come in two big blocks: 1) the ones that characterize individual words (assigned to each word in the pair); 2) the ones that characterize a semantic relation between the words in the pair.

Properties for individual words included:

• **Concreteness**, a continuous score on the abstractness-concreteness scale, the Ghent concreteness norms (Brysbaert et al., 2014);

• 26 **WordNet supersenses** of nouns (ACT, ANIMAL, FEELING, FOOD etc.), implemented as boolean labels (Miller, 1995);

• 3 NRC VAD continuous scores for **valence**, **arousal** and **dominance** (Mohammad, 2018).

Relational semantic properties included:

• 6 **WordNet semantic relations** (Miller, 1995): ANTONYMS, SYNONYMS, SAME_HYPONYMS, SAME_HYPERNYMS, HYPONYMS, HYPERNYMS.

• 10 **ConceptNet semantic relations** (Speer et al., 2017): ANTONYM, SYNONYM, ATLOCATION, DERIVEDFROM, DISTINCTFROM, FORMOF, ISA, PARTOF, RELATEDTO, SIMILARTO.

The relations were implemented as boolean labels.

This is the most comprehensive list of semantic parameters for which human annotations exist on a large scale. It covers both denotational and connotational aspects of meaning of both individual words and relation within pairs. Connotational meanings are represented with three sentiment-related meaning aspects only, as these are the only ones represented in a large human-annotated dataset (Mohammad, 2018).

Additionally, word count based on Wikipedia

[1]Our code and data are available on GitHub: https://github.com/altsoph/modality_shifts

[2]https://github.com/nltk/nltk

[3]https://github.com/explosion/spacy-models

(accessed via `Textacy`) is included for each word in all pairs as a non-semantic baseline parameter.

We leave only those word pairs for which all the above mentioned parameters are defined. This gives us 13k word pairs in total, each of the pairs gets characterized along 30 individual semantic parameters (*2, for the first and the second noun in the pair) and 16 relational parameters; plus, word count for each of the words in the pair.

We collect the distances between the words in each pair for their embeddings from the models of interest. As **text-only models**, we use fastText (Bojanowski et al., 2017) and two contextualized embedding models: multilingual BERT (mBERT, Devlin et al., 2018) and XLM-RoBERTa (XLMR, Conneau et al., 2019). For each contextualized model, we extract three kinds of word type embeddings known to show systematic differences (Vulić et al., 2020); average of all token embeddings, including separator tokens, from the final encoding layer of a word presented in isolation (**iso**); the average encoding over the bottom 6 layers across a sample of 10 usage contexts (**avg-bottom**), amd the average encoding from the final layer across a sample of 10 usage contexts (**avg-last**). As multimodal models, we use CLIP, OpenCLIP and Multilingual CLIP (Radford et al., 2021; Ilharco et al., 2021; Carlsson et al., 2022). For each multimodal model, we extract two different types of word type embeddings, one by encoding the word in isolation and one by averaging over sentence embeddings of 10 usage examples.

The goal is to find a common ground of different models depending on their modality. In this way we hope to be able to distinguish between model-specific idiosyncrasies and general properties of text-based representations.

3 Analysis

We run a series of regression analyses with semantic features and relations as predictors, along with word frequency as baseline.

We analyze the shift in distances within word pairs between two embedding models. To measure it, we rank all word pairs in our dataset by the ratio between the cosine distance values of the pair in the two embedding models. Using ratios and ranks rather than absolute differences serves as a normalization strategy because the vector spaces have significantly different structures (see Appendix A). The resulting rank of the pair is then used as the dependent variable in a regression analysis.

The baseline regression model includes as predictors word frequencies in the Wikipedia corpus and concreteness scores from the Ghent concreteness norms dataset (Brysbaert et al., 2014). To estimate the contribution of different groups of semantic features, we add them to the regression as additional predictors. This is done separately for

1. taxonomic features of the two words formalized as their WordNet supersenses (Miller, 1995);
2. sentiment/connotation-related features of the two words extracted from NRC VAD (Mohammad, 2018);
3. relation within the word pair according to Princeton WordNet (Miller, 1995);
4. relation within the word pair according to ConceptNet (Speer et al., 2017).

All numeric parameters (concreteness scores, word frequencies, and VAD values) were normalized by converting numeric values into ranks.

To calculate regression, we used a standard implementation of ordinary least squares regression from the statsmodels python package. We compute adjusted R-squared values to avoid a bias from the different numbers of parameters. Each fitted regression showed high significance ($p < 0.0001$).

4 Results

The results of regression analysis for several models are illustrated in Table 1. Our main observations are:

• **Baselines**. Concreteness plays a major role in explaining modality shifts, in line with results of previous studies (Pezzelle et al., 2021).

• Combined **WordNet supersenses**. We find a significant effect for many pairs of text vs. multimodal models, although different subsets of taxonomic features prove significant in different pairs of models.

• **WordNet and ConceptNet relations** tend to be significant when aggregated, although no individual relation has a systematic effect across model pairs.

• **VAD** features produce varied effects, with valence showing the most consistent modality difference. VAD features explain only a small percentage of variance in all models.

CLIP-iso vs.	XLMR-iso	mBERT-iso	BERT-avg-last	fastText
Baselines				
concreteness	9.5	11.68	2.27	8.71
frequency	5.43	7.81	1.91	0.45
concreteness+frequency	16.73	17.16	3.65	9.54
+taxonomic	21 (+4.27)	20.35 (+3.19)	5.43 (+1.78)	19.50 (+9.96)
+VAD	17.36 (+0.63)	17.49 (+0.33)	4.62 (+0.97)	10.78 (+1.24)
+WordNet relations	18.47 (+1.74)	17.36 (+0.2)	10.05 (+6.4)	10.34 (+0.8)
+ConceptNet relations	19.8 (+3.07)	17.47 (+0.31)	8.84 (+5.19)	10.26 (+0.72)

Table 1: Illustration of our method: Embedding space in CLIP-iso vs. four of the text-only models. Table reports percentage of variance (adjusted R^2) in cosine distance ratio explained by different groups of semantic factors. We take the number in parentheses as an estimate of the *effect* of the factor (e.g. the effect of all taxonomic features from WordNet combined) on the difference between two embedding spaces (e.g. fastText vs. CLIP).

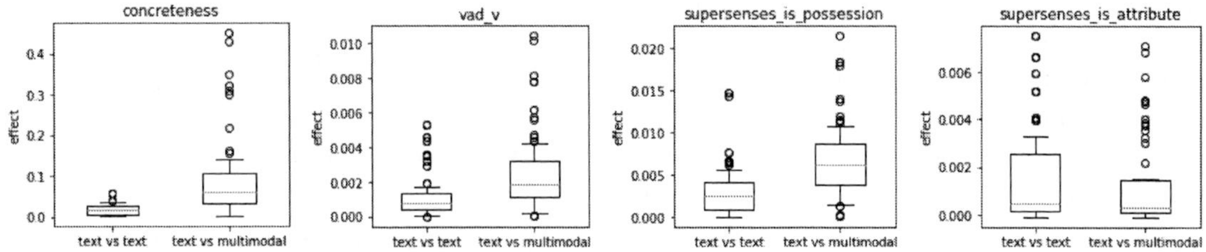

Figure 1: Comparing semantic features' contributions to contrasts between text models vs. other text models, on the one hand, and text models vs. L&V models, on the other hand. Explanatory contributions of concreteness, VAD valence and Wordnet supersense 'Is Possession' are sensitive to model modality, unlike supersense 'Is Attribute'. (Here and in Appendix B, whiskers in the boxplots are set to 0.5 IQR.)

Figure 1 illustrates the effect of specific features: concreteness, valence and possession WordNet supersense, vs. the attribute supersense that has no consistent effect on modality shifts. For more plots, see Appendix B.

5 Conclusion and discussion

The goal of our paper was to investigate what semantic factors contribute to the difference in representational spaces of language-only models vs. multimodal models.

Our regression analysis confirmed previous findings that concreteness plays a major role in this difference (Pezzelle et al., 2021). This is natural since imageability, the measurable manifestation of concreteness, is directly related to whether useful information about a concept can be inferred form visual data.

However, other factors beyond abstractness contribute to the modality-based space contrasts as well. The most important factor here is taxonomical, as measured by the effect of WordNet lexicographer files. Wordnet supersenses consistently affect semantic similarities in text-only models vs. L&V models: in particular, we found this for artifacts, quantities, possessions and communication lexical classes.

Lastly, sentiment-related lexical properties, most clearly valence, also affect the semantic similarity in language-only vs. multimodal spaces. Recently, several studies in semantics and pragmatics have indicated interactions of connotational content with denotational meanings (Ruytenbeek et al., 2017; Terkourafi et al., 2020; Van Tiel and Pankratz, 2021; Beltrama, 2021; Gotzner and Mazzarella, 2021). Our results can be interpreted as pointing in that direction too. Still, the effect of sentiment is overall much smaller than the core denotational properties of the words in the lexical pair, as illustrated by the comparison of the combined VAD to combined taxonomic features in Table 1.

We contribute to the understanding of different embedding spaces by demonstrating systematic differences between text-only vs. L&V models. Many questions are however left for future research. For example, do the distinct properties of multimodal embeddings make them better suited for specific tasks, as Pezzelle et al. (2021) argued for the relatedness judgments of concrete nouns?

In the light of Kruszewski's finding (Kruszewski and Baroni, 2015) that taxonomic information interacts strongly with referential compatibility between concepts, our findings on the role of taxonomic status on vector space structure suggests that the choice of multimodal vs. textual representations can be crucial for inference, especially for the difficult case of the neutral vs. contradiction distinction.

Finally, we note that the semantic factors we considered only explain a small part of the discrepancy between textual and L&V models. The rest must be attributed to other factors, such as random differences in the textual data used for model training as well as semantic phenomena outside the scope of our study.

We hope that our study inspires further exploration of systematic differences between embedding models, both for visual grounding and beyond.

Acknowledgements

This work was funded by the European Research Council (ERC) under the European Union's Horizon 2020 research and innovation programme (grant agreement No 742204).

References

Andrea Beltrama. 2021. Just perfect, simply the best: an analysis of emphatic exclusion. *Linguistics and Philosophy*, pages 1–44.

Emily M Bender and Alexander Koller. 2020. Climbing towards nlu: On meaning, form, and understanding in the age of data. In *Proceedings of the 58th Annual Meeting of the Association for Computational Linguistics*, pages 5185–5198.

Piotr Bojanowski, Edouard Grave, Armand Joulin, and Tomas Mikolov. 2017. Enriching word vectors with subword information. *Transactions of the Association for Computational Linguistics*, 5:135–146.

Marc Brysbaert, Amy Beth Warriner, and Victor Kuperman. 2014. Concreteness ratings for 40 thousand generally known english word lemmas. *Behavior research methods*, 46(3):904–911.

Fredrik Carlsson, Philipp Eisen, Faton Rekathati, and Magnus Sahlgren. 2022. Cross-lingual and multilingual CLIP. In *Proceedings of the Thirteenth Language Resources and Evaluation Conference*, pages 6848–6854, Marseille, France. European Language Resources Association.

Alexis Conneau, Kartikay Khandelwal, Naman Goyal, Vishrav Chaudhary, Guillaume Wenzek, Francisco Guzmán, Edouard Grave, Myle Ott, Luke Zettlemoyer, and Veselin Stoyanov. 2019. Unsupervised cross-lingual representation learning at scale. *CoRR*, abs/1911.02116.

Christopher Davis, Luana Bulat, Anita Lilla Verő, and Ekaterina Shutova. 2019. Deconstructing multimodality: visual properties and visual context in human semantic processing. In *Proceedings of the Eighth Joint Conference on Lexical and Computational Semantics (* SEM 2019)*, pages 118–124.

Jacob Devlin, Ming-Wei Chang, Kenton Lee, and Kristina Toutanova. 2018. BERT: pre-training of deep bidirectional transformers for language understanding. *CoRR*, abs/1810.04805.

Nicole Gotzner and Diana Mazzarella. 2021. Face management and negative strengthening: The role of power relations, social distance, and gender. *Frontiers in psychology*, 12.

Gabriel Ilharco, Mitchell Wortsman, Ross Wightman, Cade Gordon, Nicholas Carlini, Rohan Taori, Achal Dave, Vaishaal Shankar, Hongseok Namkoong, John Miller, Hannaneh Hajishirzi, Ali Farhadi, and Ludwig Schmidt. 2021. Openclip. If you use this software, please cite it as below.

Germán Kruszewski and Marco Baroni. 2015. So similar and yet incompatible: Toward the automated identification of semantically compatible words. In *Proceedings of the 2015 Conference of the North American Chapter of the Association for Computational Linguistics: Human Language Technologies*, pages 964–969.

Liunian Harold Li, Mark Yatskar, Da Yin, Cho-Jui Hsieh, and Kai-Wei Chang. 2019. Visualbert: A simple and performant baseline for vision and language. *arXiv preprint arXiv:1908.03557*.

Yinhan Liu, Myle Ott, Naman Goyal, Jingfei Du, Mandar Joshi, Danqi Chen, Omer Levy, Mike Lewis, Luke Zettlemoyer, and Veselin Stoyanov. 2019. Roberta: A robustly optimized bert pretraining approach. *arXiv preprint arXiv:1907.11692*.

Timo Lüddecke, Alejandro Agostini, Michael Fauth, Minija Tamosiunaite, and Florentin Wörgötter. 2019. Distributional semantics of objects in visual scenes in comparison to text. *Artificial Intelligence*, 274:44–65.

George A Miller. 1995. Wordnet: a lexical database for english. *Communications of the ACM*, 38(11):39–41.

Saif Mohammad. 2018. Obtaining reliable human ratings of valence, arousal, and dominance for 20,000 english words. In *Proceedings of the 56th Annual Meeting of the Association for Computational Linguistics (Volume 1: Long Papers)*, pages 174–184.

Sandro Pezzelle, Ece Takmaz, and Raquel Fernández. 2021. Word Representation Learning in Multimodal Pre-Trained Transformers: An Intrinsic Evaluation.

Transactions of the Association for Computational Linguistics, 9:1563–1579.

Alec Radford, Jong Wook Kim, Chris Hallacy, Aditya Ramesh, Gabriel Goh, Sandhini Agarwal, Girish Sastry, Amanda Askell, Pamela Mishkin, Jack Clark, et al. 2021. Learning transferable visual models from natural language supervision. In *International Conference on Machine Learning*, pages 8748–8763. PMLR.

Alec Radford, Jeff Wu, Rewon Child, David Luan, Dario Amodei, and Ilya Sutskever. 2019. Language models are unsupervised multitask learners.

Nicolas Ruytenbeek, Steven Verheyen, and Benjamin Spector. 2017. Asymmetric inference towards the antonym: Experiments into the polarity and morphology of negated adjectives. *GLOSSA-A JOURNAL OF GENERAL LINGUISTICS*, 2(1).

Robyn Speer, Joshua Chin, and Catherine Havasi. 2017. Conceptnet 5.5: An open multilingual graph of general knowledge. In *Thirty-first AAAI conference on artificial intelligence*.

Hao Tan and Mohit Bansal. 2019. Lxmert: Learning cross-modality encoder representations from transformers. *arXiv preprint arXiv:1908.07490*.

Hao Tan and Mohit Bansal. 2020. Vokenization: Improving language understanding with contextualized, visual-grounded supervision. *arXiv preprint arXiv:2010.06775*.

Marina Terkourafi, Benjamin Weissman, and Joseph Roy. 2020. Different scalar terms are affected by face differently. *International Review of Pragmatics*, 12(1):1–43.

Bob Van Tiel and Elizabeth Pankratz. 2021. Adjectival polarity and the processing of scalar inferences. *Glossa: a journal of general linguistics*, 6(1).

Ivan Vulić, Edoardo Maria Ponti, Robert Litschko, Goran Glavaš, and Anna Korhonen. 2020. Probing pretrained language models for lexical semantics. *arXiv preprint arXiv:2010.05731*.

A Properties of embedding spaces

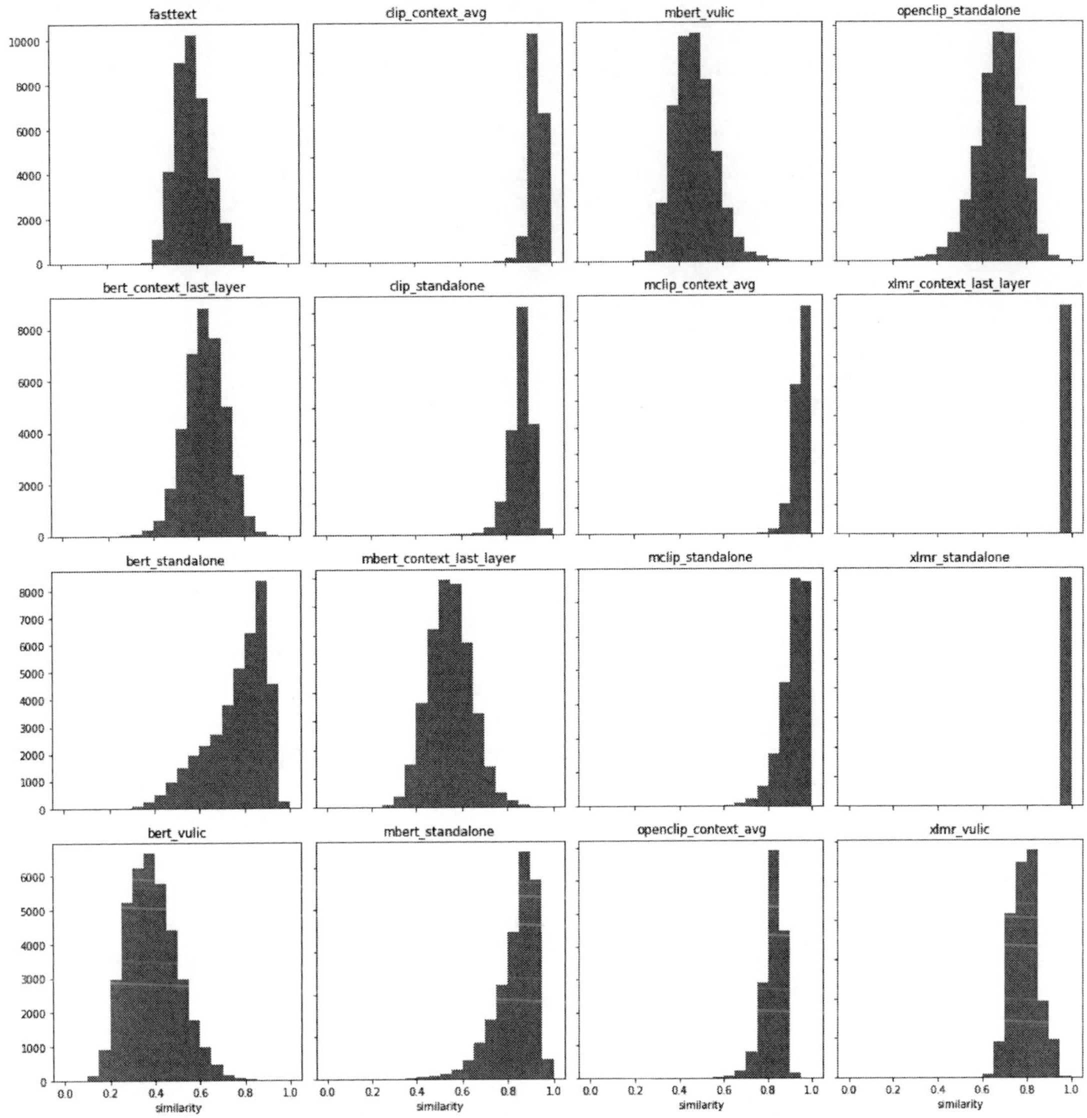

Distributions of similarities between lexical pairs per model and embedding type

B Plots for more factors

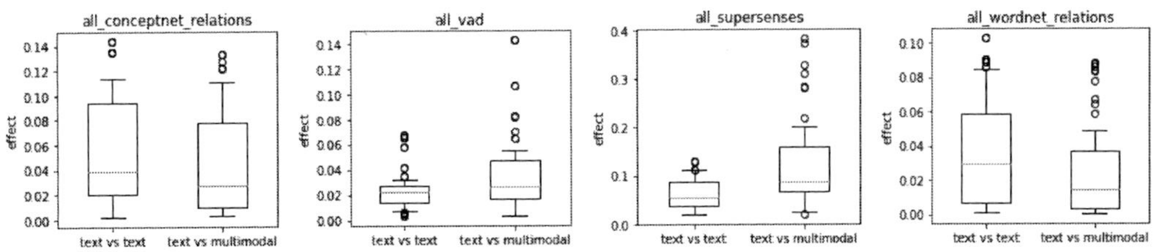

Comparing semantic features' contributions to contrasts between text models vs. other text models, on the one hand, and text models vs. L&V models, on the other hand. Explanatory contributions of ConceptNet relations, combined VAD features, combined WordNet supersenses, and combined WordNet relations.

Revisiting Syntax-Based Approach in Negation Scope Resolution

Asahi Yoshida[1], **Yoshihide Kato**[2], **Shigeki Matsubara**[1,2]
[1]Graduate School of Informatics, Nagoya University
[2]Information and Communications, Nagoya University
Furo-cho, Chikusa-ku, Nagoya, 464-8601, Japan
yoshida.asahi.y7@s.mail.nagoya-u.ac.jp

Abstract

Negation scope resolution is the process of detecting the negated part of a sentence. Unlike the syntax-based approach employed in previous researches, state-of-the-art methods performed better without the explicit use of syntactic structure. This work revisits the syntax-based approach and re-evaluates the effectiveness of syntactic structure in negation scope resolution. We replace the parser utilized in the prior works with state-of-the-art parsers and modify the syntax-based heuristic rules. The experimental results demonstrate that the simple modifications enhance the performance of the prior syntax-based method to the same level as state-of-the-art end-to-end neural-based methods.

1 Introduction

Negation is a common linguistic phenomenon that frequently appears in natural language. Consequently, its detection is crucial for various NLP applications, including sentiment analysis, relation extraction and medical data mining. Typically, the negation detection task is broken down into two subtasks: (i) detecting negation cues (words, affixes, or phrases that express negations) and (ii) resolving their scopes (parts of a sentence affected by the negation cue). In example (1) below, the word "not" is the negation cue (marked in bold) and word sequences "He did" and "go to school" form the scope (underlined parts).

(1) He did **not** go to school and stayed home.

This work addresses the second subtask: negation scope resolution. Prior works used syntactic features for resolving the scope of negations (Read et al., 2012; Carrillo de Albornoz et al., 2012; Abu-Jbara and Radev, 2012; White, 2012). Read et al. (2012) tackled this issue with syntax-based approach and obtained the best performance on the token-level evaluation in *SEM2012 shared task (Morante and Blanco, 2012). Recently, many studies treat this task as a sequence labeling problem and use deep-learning techniques (Fancellu et al., 2016; Khandelwal and Sawant, 2020; Truong et al., 2022). Without explicitly utilizing syntactic structure, they argued that end-to-end neural approaches can outperform earlier syntax-based ones. However, the prior works proposed in *SEM2012 shared task used the parser of that time[1]. The performances of parsers have considerably improved since. The effectiveness of the syntax-based approach will increase with the usage of accurate parsers. Furthermore, syntax-based methods have an advantage over deep-learning techniques: high interpretability.

Motivated by the point mentioned above, this work revisits the syntax-based approach for negation scope resolution. We use state-of-the-art parsers to re-evaluate the earlier syntax-based approach. We also modify the syntactic-based heuristic rules used in the prior syntax-based method. Our experimental results demonstrate that the prior method, based on heuristics for syntax structure, can obtain the same level of performance as state-of-the-art methods based on end-to-end neural networks.

2 Related Work

This section describes the syntax-based method proposed by Read et al. (2012), based on which we re-evaluate the usefulness of syntax for negation scope resolution. Their approach assumes that the scope of negation corresponds to a constituent. As an example, let us consider the sentence (2).

(2) I know that he is **not** a student.

[1]The syntactic information provided by the parser is annotated on the datasets utilized in *SEM2012 shared task. Participants in the shared task applied this syntactic information.

*Proceedings of the The 12th Joint Conference on Lexical and Computational Semantics (*SEM 2023)*, pages 18–23
July 13-14, 2023

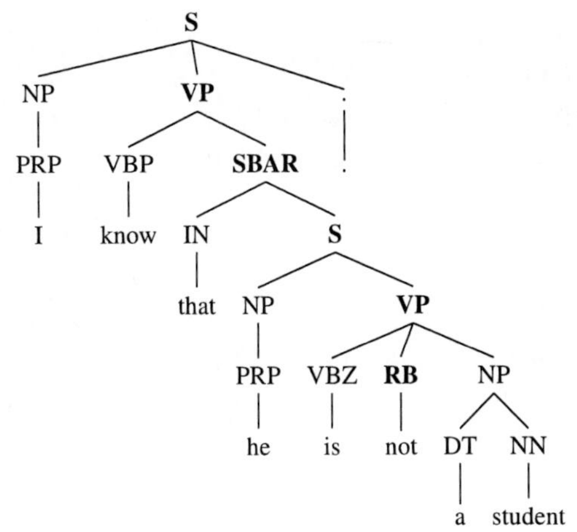

Figure 1: Constituent parse tree of sentence (2), highlighting candidate scope constituents.

```
RB//VP/SBAR if SBAR\WH*   (#)
RB//VP/S
RB//S
DT/NP if NP/PP
DT//SBAR if SBAR\WHADVP
DT//S
JJ//ADJP/VP/S if S\VP\VB* [@lemma="be"]
JJ/NP/NP if NP\PP
JJ//NP
UH
IN/PP
NN/NP//S/SBAR if SBAR\WHNP
NN/NP//S
CC/SINV
```

Figure 2: Scope resolution heuristics. Each row displays one rule, which is presented in the order that they should be applied. Each rule is represented as a path pattern. A/B denotes that B is the parent of A, A//B implies B is an ancestor of A, and A\B means B is a child of A. (#) is the rule we modify in this work.

Figure 1 shows the constituent parse tree of the sentence. In this sentence, the scope of the negation cue "not" corresponds to the constituent S whose left end is "he" and whose right end is "student". This method resolves the scope of the negation cue according to the following steps:

1. Parse the sentence and select the constituents on the path from the cue to the root as candidates (The candidates are marked in bold in Figure 1).

2. Select one constituent corresponding to the scope using heuristics or the Support Vector Machine classifier.

3. Adjust the scope by removing certain elements from the constituent selected in the second step.

In the first step, the sentence is parsed and all the constituents that dominate the negation cue are considered as scope candidates. For example, in sentence (2), six constituents highlighted in Figure 1 are selected as candidates. In the second step, one constituent is selected from the candidates using heuristics or a classifier. We describe the heuristic method, which we use in this work. This method selects one constituent from the candidates using *scope resolution heuristics* shown in Figure 2. The 14 rules that form the heuristics are applied in order from top to bottom; the rules are listed in a specific-to-general order. Each rule is represented as a path pattern and some rules have additional constraints (if part). For example, the fifth rule "`DT//SBAR if SBAR\WHADVP`" will be activated and the constituent SBAR is selected when the negation cue is a determiner (DT), provided that it has an ancestor SBAR if the SBAR has a child WHADVP. If no rule is activated, it uses a *default scope*, which expands the scope to the left and the right of the negation cue until either a sentence boundary or a punctuation is found.

The alignment of the constituent and the scope is not always straightforward. Sentence (1) is one of such illustration. In this sentence, the scope of the negation cue "not" does not cross the coordination boundary: the coordinating conjunction "and", its following conjunct "stayed home" and the punctuation "." are not included in the scope. To deal with such a case, Read et al. (2012) adopted some heuristics to remove certain elements from the constituent in the following way:

- Remove the constituent-initial and -final punctuations from the scope.

- Remove certain elements at the beginning or the end of the constituent using *slackening rules*, which consist of five heuristics.

- Apply two post-processing heuristics to handle discontinuous scopes:

  - Remove previous conjuncts from the scope if the cue is in a conjoined phrase.
  - Remove sentential adverbs from the scope.

For sentence (1), the scope "He did, go to school" is correctly resolved using the series of process.

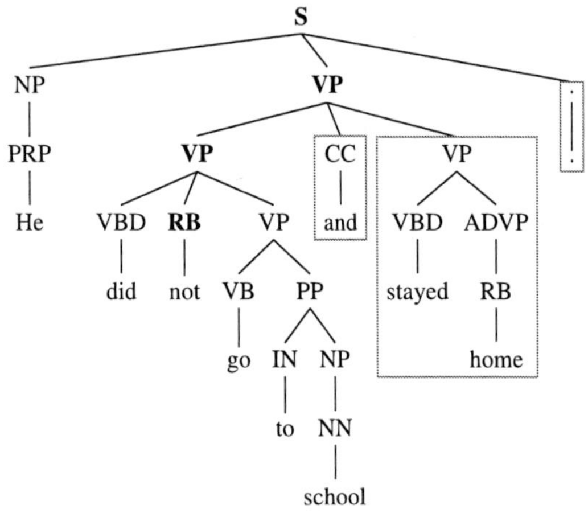

Figure 3: Constituent parse tree of sentence (1), enclosing removed parts in boxes.

The constituent S is selected as the scope of the cue according to the first and second steps. In the third step, the coordinating conjunction "and", and its conjunct "stayed home" are removed by the first heuristic rule for discontinuous scope, and the punctuation "." is removed by the above first heuristic rule (removed parts are enclosed in Figure 3).

3 Revisiting the Syntax-Based Method

In this section, we revise the method described in the previous section to re-evaluate the syntax-based approach in negation scope resolution. Section 3.1 describes the parsers we use in this work. Sections 3.2 and 3.3 discuss the modifications we made for the second and the third steps of Read et al. (2012)'s method, respectively.

3.1 Replacement of the Parser

The dataset used in *SEM2012 shared task (Morante and Daelemans, 2012), also known as the Conan Doyle dataset, is one of the primary datasets used for negation scope resolution. This dataset also contains syntactic information, which was assigned using the reranking parser of Charniak and Johnson (2005). As Read et al. (2012) mentioned, syntactic information contains parse errors. They suspected that parse errors cause scope resolution errors in their method. To mitigate this issue, we parse the sentences in the dataset using state-of-the-art, high-accuracy parsers. We use two parsers: Berkeley Neural Parser (Kitaev and Klein, 2018; Kitaev et al., 2019) with BERT (Devlin et al., 2019), and Attach Juxtapose Parser (Yang and Deng, 2020) with XLNET (Yang et al., 2019). Table 1 shows the performances of the parsers on Penn Treebank (Marcus et al., 1993).

Parser	F_1 score (%)
Reranking Parser (2005)	91.02
Berkeley Neural Parser (2018)	95.77
Attach Juxtapose Parser (2020)	96.34

Table 1: Performances of the parsers in Penn Treebank Section 23.

3.2 Modification of *Scope Resolution Heuristics*

Read et al. (2012) used *scope resolution heuristics* shown in Figure 2 to detect the constituent corresponding to the scope of the negation cue. The first rule of Read et al. (2012) (denoted with (#) in Figure 2) is considered to extract relative clauses, but this rule does not work properly. In relative clauses in Penn Treebank, SBAR directly dominates not VP but S (and the S has a child VP). To accurately capture this structure, we modify the rule as follows:

(3) `RB//VP/S/SBAR if SBAR\WHNP`

This modification is based on the preliminary experiment conducted on the training data.

3.3 Modification of Scope Adjustment

As indicated in Section 2, Read et al. (2012)'s method adjusts the constituent in the third step. This work partially modifies *slackening rules* and post-processing.

In the case of *slackening rules*, we present the following additional rule to the original five rules:

- Remove initial PP (prepositional phrase) if delimited by a comma.

This modification was motivated by the annotation guideline of the Conan Doyle dataset (Morante et al., 2011). According to this guideline, discourse markers are excluded from the scope. Comma-delimited prepositional phrases often function as discourse markers, such as "In my opinion" in example (4). In this case, we should remove them from the scope.

(4) In my opinion, he should **not** go.

For the post-processing, we modify the second processing: removing sentential adverbs from the

Parser	Scope-level			Token-level		
	Pre. (%)	**Rec.** (%)	**F$_1$** (%)	**Pre.** (%)	**Rec.** (%)	**F$_1$** (%)
Reranking Parser	97.21	69.88	81.31	86.87	93.07	89.86
	(97.14)	(68.27)	(80.19)	(85.48)	(93.63)	(89.37)
Berkeley Neural Parser	98.91	72.69	83.80	89.78	92.96	91.34
	(98.88)	(70.68)	(82.43)	(87.88)	(93.57)	(90.64)
Attach Juxtapose Parser	98.94	74.70	**85.13**	90.62	94.68	**92.61**
	(98.90)	(72.29)	(83.53)	(88.70)	(95.24)	(91.85)

Table 2: Scope resolution performances for gold cues using the three different parsers. The upper figure in each row demonstrates the result with modified rules discussed in Sections 3.2 and 3.3; the lower figure shows the result without modifications. Note that in the case of the rule to remove sentential adverbs from the scope in the third step, we were not able to reproduce the Read et al. (2012)'s method because the sentential adverb list is not publicly available. Thus, both the upper and the lower figures describe the results of our modified rule.

scope. Read et al. (2012) compiled a list of sentential adverbs from the training data and used it for this processing. Instead, in this work, we simply remove "comma-delimited ADVP (adverbial phrase) or INTJ (interjection)" from the scope along with the commas. This is a generalization of Read et al. (2012)'s processing. As an example of a comma-delimited ADVP that functions as a discourse-level adverbial and should be excluded from the scope, see sentence (5) below.

(5) There was **no** trace, however, of anything.

Again, this modification of scope adjustment rules is based on the training data.

4 Experiment

To re-evaluate the syntax-based approach to negation scope resolution, we conducted an experiment[2]. This section describes the detail of the experiment. We explain the dataset, settings and results in Sections 4.1, 4.2 and 4.3, respectively.

4.1 Dataset

To evaluate the performance of our work, we used the Conan Doyle dataset, which was employed in *SEM2012 shared task. The dataset is divided into training data, development data and evaluation data. The training data contains 848 sentences including negation, the development data 144 and the evaluation data 235. Note that there can be more than one negation cue in a sentence. Each data contains 984, 173 and 264 negation cues, respectively.

4.2 Experimental Settings

We conducted an experiment using the evaluation data of Conan Doyle dataset. We created new constituent parse trees for the sentences in the dataset using Berkeley Neural Parser and Attach Juxtapose Parser. We did not perform cue detection, that is, we report performance using gold cues. Other experimental setups are similar to those of *SEM2012 shared task, with the scope-level F$_1$ score and the token-level F$_1$ score as the evaluation metrics. Among the evaluation metrics, the following points should be noted:

- Punctuation tokens are excluded from the evaluation.
- If a sentence contains two or more negation cues, scope predictions for each negation cue are evaluated separately.
- For the scope-level evaluation, a predicted scope is counted as TP if all tokens corresponding to the scope of a negation cue are predicted correctly. Partial matches are counted as FN.

We used the official script distributed in the shared task[3] for evaluation.

4.3 Experimental Results

Table 2 shows the experimental results with three different parsers to provide the constituent parse trees. The results demonstrate that the use of accurate parsers leads to an increase in performance in negation scope resolution for both scope-level and

[2]The code is available at `https://github.com/asahi-y/revisiting-nsr`.

[3]`https://www.clips.ua.ac.be/sem2012-st-neg/data.html`

Method	Token-level F_1 (%)	
	Including punctuations	Excluding punctuations
This work	91.74	92.61
Fancellu et al. (2016)	88.72	-
Li and Lu (2018)	-	89.4
Khandelwal and Sawant (2020)	92.36	-
Truong et al. (2022)	91.24	-

Table 3: Comparison to previous methods. The results of this work are the ones obtained by using syntactic information generated by Attach Juxtapose Parser, and by applying modified rules. Note that the results are for negation scope resolution using gold cues.

token-level metrics. We also verified that the rule modifications introduced in this work contributed to the performance improvement.

Several previous works, including state-of-the-art methods, incorporate punctuation tokens for evaluation, which were omitted in *SEM2012 shared task. To compare our results with these methods, we also assessed F_1 score including punctuation tokens. Table 3 shows the results. The performance of the syntax-based method tested in this work obtained 91.74% in F_1 score including punctuations, which is only 0.62% behind values reported by the state-of-the-art method (92.36%), obtained by Khandelwal and Sawant (2020). This result shows that the prior method based on heuristics for syntax, with the use of a high-performance parser, can obtain performance close to the results obtained by the best-performing deep learning methods.

5 Conclusion

This work re-evaluated the syntax-based approach in negation scope resolution. We replaced the parser used in the prior works with the state-of-the-art parsers. We also slightly modified the syntax-based heuristic rules designed in the prior work. The experimental results demonstrate that the prior syntax-based approach can obtain high performance comparable to those of state-of-the-art methods. This work gives a strong baseline for the negation scope resolution task and opens up the possibility of accurate and interpretable negation scope resolution.

In future work, we will introduce a tree-based neural model into the constituent selection process to enhance the performance of the scope prediction. It would also be interesting to apply the syntax-based approach to the scope resolution of other linguistic phenomena, for example, speculation or quantifier.

Acknowledgements

This research was partially supported by the Grant-in-Aid for Scientific Research (C) (No. 22K12148) of JSPS.

References

Amjad Abu-Jbara and Dragomir Radev. 2012. UMichigan: A conditional random field model for resolving the scope of negation. In **SEM 2012: The First Joint Conference on Lexical and Computational Semantics – Volume 1: Proceedings of the main conference and the shared task, and Volume 2: Proceedings of the Sixth International Workshop on Semantic Evaluation (SemEval 2012)*, pages 328–334, Montréal, Canada. Association for Computational Linguistics.

Jorge Carrillo de Albornoz, Laura Plaza, Alberto Díaz, and Miguel Ballesteros. 2012. UCM-I: A rule-based syntactic approach for resolving the scope of negation. In **SEM 2012: The First Joint Conference on Lexical and Computational Semantics – Volume 1: Proceedings of the main conference and the shared task, and Volume 2: Proceedings of the Sixth International Workshop on Semantic Evaluation (SemEval 2012)*, pages 282–287, Montréal, Canada. Association for Computational Linguistics.

Eugene Charniak and Mark Johnson. 2005. Coarse-to-fine n-best parsing and MaxEnt discriminative reranking. In *Proceedings of the 43rd Annual Meeting of the Association for Computational Linguistics (ACL'05)*, pages 173–180, Ann Arbor, Michigan. Association for Computational Linguistics.

Jacob Devlin, Ming-Wei Chang, Kenton Lee, and Kristina Toutanova. 2019. BERT: Pre-training of deep bidirectional transformers for language understanding. In *Proceedings of the 2019 Conference of the North American Chapter of the Association for Computational Linguistics: Human Language Technologies, Volume 1 (Long and Short Papers)*, pages 4171–4186, Minneapolis, Minnesota. Association for Computational Linguistics.

Federico Fancellu, Adam Lopez, and Bonnie Webber. 2016. Neural networks for negation scope detection. In *Proceedings of the 54th Annual Meeting of the Association for Computational Linguistics (Volume 1: Long Papers)*, pages 495–504, Berlin, Germany. Association for Computational Linguistics.

Aditya Khandelwal and Suraj Sawant. 2020. NegBERT: A transfer learning approach for negation detection and scope resolution. In *Proceedings of the Twelfth Language Resources and Evaluation Conference*, pages 5739–5748, Marseille, France. European Language Resources Association.

Nikita Kitaev, Steven Cao, and Dan Klein. 2019. Multilingual constituency parsing with self-attention and pre-training. In *Proceedings of the 57th Annual Meeting of the Association for Computational Linguistics*, pages 3499–3505, Florence, Italy. Association for Computational Linguistics.

Nikita Kitaev and Dan Klein. 2018. Constituency parsing with a self-attentive encoder. In *Proceedings of the 56th Annual Meeting of the Association for Computational Linguistics (Volume 1: Long Papers)*, pages 2676–2686, Melbourne, Australia. Association for Computational Linguistics.

Hao Li and Wei Lu. 2018. Learning with structured representations for negation scope extraction. In *Proceedings of the 56th Annual Meeting of the Association for Computational Linguistics (Volume 2: Short Papers)*, pages 533–539, Melbourne, Australia. Association for Computational Linguistics.

Mitchell P. Marcus, Beatrice Santorini, and Mary Ann Marcinkiewicz. 1993. Building a large annotated corpus of English: The Penn Treebank. *Computational Linguistics*, 19(2):313–330.

Roser Morante and Eduardo Blanco. 2012. *SEM 2012 shared task: Resolving the scope and focus of negation. In **SEM 2012: The First Joint Conference on Lexical and Computational Semantics – Volume 1: Proceedings of the main conference and the shared task, and Volume 2: Proceedings of the Sixth International Workshop on Semantic Evaluation (SemEval 2012)*, pages 265–274, Montréal, Canada. Association for Computational Linguistics.

Roser Morante and Walter Daelemans. 2012. ConanDoyle-neg: Annotation of negation cues and their scope in conan doyle stories. In *Proceedings of the Eighth International Conference on Language Resources and Evaluation (LREC'12)*, pages 1563–1568, Istanbul, Turkey. European Language Resources Association (ELRA).

Roser Morante, Sara Schrauwen, and Walter Daelemans. 2011. Annotation of negation cues and their scope : Guidelines v1.0. Technical report, University of Antwerp.

Jonathon Read, Erik Velldal, Lilja Øvrelid, and Stephan Oepen. 2012. UiO1: Constituent-based discriminative ranking for negation resolution. In **SEM 2012: The First Joint Conference on Lexical and Computational Semantics – Volume 1: Proceedings of the main conference and the shared task, and Volume 2: Proceedings of the Sixth International Workshop on Semantic Evaluation (SemEval 2012)*, pages 310–318, Montréal, Canada. Association for Computational Linguistics.

Thinh Truong, Timothy Baldwin, Trevor Cohn, and Karin Verspoor. 2022. Improving negation detection with negation-focused pre-training. In *Proceedings of the 2022 Conference of the North American Chapter of the Association for Computational Linguistics: Human Language Technologies*, pages 4188–4193, Seattle, United States. Association for Computational Linguistics.

James Paul White. 2012. UWashington: Negation resolution using machine learning methods. In **SEM 2012: The First Joint Conference on Lexical and Computational Semantics – Volume 1: Proceedings of the main conference and the shared task, and Volume 2: Proceedings of the Sixth International Workshop on Semantic Evaluation (SemEval 2012)*, pages 335–339, Montréal, Canada. Association for Computational Linguistics.

Kaiyu Yang and Jia Deng. 2020. Strongly incremental constituency parsing with graph neural networks. In *Neural Information Processing Systems (NeurIPS 2020)*.

Zhilin Yang, Zihang Dai, Yiming Yang, Jaime Carbonell, Russ R Salakhutdinov, and Quoc V Le. 2019. Xlnet: Generalized autoregressive pretraining for language understanding. In *Advances in Neural Information Processing Systems (NeurIPS 2019)*.

When Truth Matters – Addressing Pragmatic Categories in Natural Language Inference (NLI) by Large Language Models (LLMs)

Reto Gubelmann
University of St. Gallen
reto.gubelmann@unisg.ch

Aikaterini-Lida Kalouli
CIS - LMU Munich
katerina.kalouli@hotmail.com

Christina Niklaus
University of St. Gallen
christina.niklaus@unisg.ch

Siegfried Handschuh
University of St. Gallen
siegfried.handschuh@unisg.ch

Abstract

In this paper, we focus on the ability of large language models (LLMs) to accommodate different pragmatic sentence types, such as questions, commands, as well as sentence fragments for natural language inference (NLI). On the commonly used notion of logical inference, nothing can be inferred from a question, a command, or an incomprehensible sentence fragment. We find MNLI, arguably the most important NLI dataset, and hence models fine-tuned on this dataset, insensitive to this fact. Using a symbolic semantic parser, we develop and make publicly available, fine-tuning datasets designed specifically to address this issue, with promising results. We also make a first exploration of ChatGPT's concept of entailment.

1 Introduction: "I didn't say that!'

Committing oneself to the truth of a certain claim always implies or suggests one's commitment to the truth of a number of other claims, and it precludes one's commitment to the truth of a second set of claims. This is the essence of the logical notion of entailment (here used synonymously with inference) and contradiction. For instance, somebody who claims "Loral did harm national security" is also committed to the less specific claim "Something or somebody did harm national security".

The concept of inference is itself quite complex. As Gubelmann et al. (2022) detail, valid inferences can be divided into deductively valid inferences, where it is not logically (see Plantinga 1974) possible that the premise is true while the conclusion is false, and inductively valid inferences (also called abductions), where it is possible that the premise is true while the conclusion is false, but where the truth of the premise is in general a good reason for the truth of the conclusion.

For two utterances to be able to (deductively or inductively) entail or contradict each other, they have to be of the correct pragmatic category. While assertions or claims are able to stand in these logical relationships, the same does not hold for other pragmatic kinds of utterances, such as questions or commands, as they do not involve making a claim that could be true or false and hence commit their author to the truth of certain claims that could then entail or contradict other claims. For instance, uttering (P) in example (1) does not commit the speaker to Loral's harming of national security – she's simply asking a question, not making a claim. Hence if, after uttering (P) from (1), somebody replies with "So you claim that somebody did harm national security", the appropriate response would be "I didn't say that!".

Neither does she commit herself to everybody's, as a matter of fact, having a happy Hanukkah when uttering (P) in (2), that is, wishing everyone a happy Hanukkah: Rather, she is expressing the wish that everyone is going to have a happy Hanukka. Committing oneself to some state of affairs, i.e., to express a claim that can be true or false, is not the kind of thing one does when uttering a question or a command (which is not to dispute that questions and commands come with specific presuppositions, including factual presuppositions, that need to be fulfilled for the speech act in question to succeed).

(1) (P) Did Loral harm national security? (H) National security was not in danger. (contradiction)

(2) (P) Happy Hanukkah, everybody! (H) Everyone, have a happy Hanukkah! (entailment)

Properly distinguishing between pragmatic kinds of utterances that can and cannot stand in logical relations is important in several areas of application. First, we can consider the legal context, where fact and claim verification is of critical importance. In the setting of the automatic extraction of claims from testimonies, a system should be able to dis-

*Proceedings of the The 12th Joint Conference on Lexical and Computational Semantics (*SEM 2023)*, pages 24–39
July 13-14, 2023

tinguish between claims and statements with other pragmatic functions such as questions, which do not commit their speakers to the truth of any claims (see, e.g., the overview in Ashley (2018)). Additionally, an essential application area is education: Using large language models (LLMs) to give formative feedback on students' arguments requires that the LLMs be able to distinguish between claims made in the text, which can be used to infer other claims, and questions and commands, which cannot (see Rapanta et al. (2013) for an illustration of the importance for this logical concept of entailment in education science).

Most recently, the introduction of general-domain, openly-available conversational systems such as ChatGPT (OpenAI) shows the need for such a distinction even more clearly: a chatbot, which collects its information from web resources but does not perform any reasoning steps itself, can falsely spread non-claims as claims if it cannot differentiate between the two.

Current NLP research conceives natural language inference (NLI) as a three-way classification task between two sentences (or sentence-fragments), called premise (P) and hypothesis (H). LLMs are trained to predict *contradiction* (P and H cannot both be correct), *entailment* (If P is correct, then H must be correct as well), or *neutral* (neither of the two). While much of the very early research focused on deductively valid inferences, more recent research has also taken into account inductive inference, which are called applied entailments (Dagan et al., 2005) or informal reasoning (MacCartney, 2009).

The Multi-Genre Natural Language Inference Dataset (MNLI) Williams et al. (2018) has arguably become the most widely used dataset for fine-tuning LLMs for NLI. This means that many (perhaps the majority of) LLMs that are fine-tuned for the task of NLI are fine-tuned using MNLI and thereby pick up MNLI's concept of inference. The instructions given to the crowdworkers who worked to create the dataset as well as explicit comments by the authors support the conclusion that MNLI's target notion of entailment dovetails with the one detailed here, applicable to claims but not to questions and commands.

However, MNLI contains prompts that are questions, such as in (1), or commands, such as in (2), as well as fragments such as (3), which are entirely incomprehensible if they are presented, as in MNLI, without any context. In fact, all examples are from MNLI's training split with their respective gold-labels in brackets. Hence, there seems to be a conceptual gap between the notion of entailment as explicitly embraced by the authors of MNLI and the pragmatic kinds of some of the prompts used to create the dataset.

(3) (P) The kids. (H) The adults. (contradiction)

In this paper, we study the extent of the phenomenon, the consequences that this set-up of MNLI has for LLMs that are fine-tuned on MNLI, and we explore ways to acquaint the LLMs with these core pragmatic categories. Our paper makes three contributions. First, after detailing the notion of inference as well as the conceptual gap in MNLI on a theoretical level (section 3), we empirically assess the extent of the phenomenon of non-assertive premises in MNLI (section 4). Second, relying on the existing semantic parser GKR, we show a promising path towards acquainting LLMs with these pragmatic categories (section 5). Third, we publish both an expert-curated gold-standard evaluation dataset as well as 7 different fine-tuning datasets to further research in this field.[1] Additionally, we also take the very first steps toward exploring ChatGPT's concept of entailment.

2 Related Research

2.1 Inference in Logic and Semantics

Both deductive and inductive inferences require claims with determinate truth-values for their functioning. This means that it is necessary for any relationship of inference to be possible that both relata are constituted by a claim with determinate truth conditions: it needs to be clear in which situations premise and hypothesis are true. Otherwise, it would be impossible to assess whether the truth of the premise guarantees/makes reasonable the truth of the hypothesis, which is the essence of both deductive and inductive inferences. We propose that only sentences fulfilling the following conditions C1 and C2 can express such determinate claims.

C1 Only sentences whose pragmatic force is assertive can express determinate claims.

C2 Only assertions which are sensible (that is, where it is clear what has to be the case for

[1] To access the datasets, please consult: `https://github.com/retoj/whentruthmatters`.

the claim to be true) can express determinate claims.

C1 is violated by questions and commands, such as the premises in examples (1) and (2). The question "Did Loral harm national security?" lacks determinate truth conditions because questions cannot be true or false, but rather sensible or nonsensical. Similarly, uttering a command like "Happy Hanukkah!" does not aim to make a determinate claim about the state of affairs but rather aims to bring about a certain state of affairs.

We owe the insight that one can do different things with different types of sentences (the theory of so-called "speech acts") to Austin (1962, 1975) and Searle (1969, 1985), continuing a basically Wittgensteinian outlook Wittgenstein (2006/1953, §43).[2] For a more recent survey of this approach, see Levinson (2017). Speech acts, like any actions, can succeed or fail to reach the goal that the agent intends with it. If some presuppositions for an act are not met, then it cannot possibly succeed.

With regard to fulfilling C2, the bare minimum needed for a sentence to express a claim with determinate truth conditions is some entity that is identified with sufficient precision (call it "subject") as well as something, again sufficiently precise, that is predicated of that entity (call it "predicate"). This conception of a minimal claim as consisting of some specific entity of which something is said is a standard in logical textbooks, see, e.g., Smullyan (1968, 43) or Garson (2006, 29), but also in everyday human communications. For an overview, see Shapiro and Kouri Kissel (2021, sec. 2.2). For an influential contemporary statement of this minimal notion of a determinate claim, see Burge (2010, 537-547). For example, C2 is clearly violated by the premise of (3). Without any further context, *and MNLI does not provide any such context*, it is not clear whether the fragment "the kids" is intended as subject or predicate, but it is clear that one of the two is missing.

To see that nothing can be inferred from anything that violates C1 and C2, it is crucial to be aware of the distinction between *inference* and *presupposition*. For instance, one might be tempted to say that from the question (1), it can be inferred that Loral potentially endangers national security, which would contradict the hypothesis of this example. This, however, would be to confuse inference with presupposition (the subtleties of the notion of presupposition, going back to Russell 1905 are still lively discussed in linguistics, see Dryer 1996 for a more recent influential contribution).

To claim that national security was never in danger would not, as the gold label for example (1) suggests, contradict the question: questions can be answered, rejected, ridiculed, etc., but not contradicted in the relevant logical sense. Rather, the claim would (at least on some readings of the question) show that the question fails to make proper sense, as one of its presuppositions, that national security was ever endangered, is not met.

A phenomenon similar to presuppositions has been described by Grice (1975) as conventional implicature.[3] Roughly, conventional implicatures, unlike presuppositions, do not affect the sensibility of the utterance in question (this follows (Potts, 2015, 31), who argues that an implicature, unlike a presupposition, is independent from the primary content of the utterance.[4] Consider example (4).

(4) (a) Bern, the capital of Switzerland, is the largest city of the country. (b) This is not true.

On a first level, the claim expressed by sentence (a) in example (4) is simply wrong: Zurich, not Bern, is the largest city of Switzerland. On the second level, however, it is also not the case that Bern is the capital of Switzerland: The founders of Switzerland deliberately avoided designating an official capital city due to existing rivalries between the candidates for such a role. This second level is beyond the reach of the challenge (b), it only reaches the actual claim being made about the relative population of Bern.

In fact, this availability for direct challenge is what helps to clearly identify the determinate, claimed content in an utterance – and it also helps to establish whether there is any such claimed content in the first place. With commands such as the one in example (2), you cannot respond with "This is not true", nor can you do so in response to a question such as in (1), or in response to an incomprehensible fragment such as in (3). In contrast, to

[2] Mastery of this multitude of language games in a flexible and adaptive manner is a key challenge for AI systems to come to really understand language, see Gubelmann (2023).

[3] See Davis (2019) for an overview. For more recent discussions of the concept, see Potts (2004); Lepore and Stone (2010). For an original perspective on the concept from formal semantics, see Peters (1979).

[4] Karttunen and Peters 1979, in contrast, use the two concepts almost equivalently.

access and reject the presuppositions behind some of these utterances, one has to do more linguistic work. For instance, you could reject a possible presupposition of the question in example (1) with: "Your question is beside the point because Loral has newer produced anything else than toilet paper; therefore, the very idea that it could have been even a potential danger for national security is misguided."

The second important distinction that we want to point out is that between inference and meaning-preserving paraphrase. The two relationships are orthogonal: If one claim with determinate truth-conditions is the meaning-preserving paraphrase of another such claim, than they can be mutually inferred from each other. If, in contrast, what is being paraphrased is a question, a command, or an incomprehensible fragment, then no relationship of inference exists between the original and the paraphrase – regardless of how synonymous they are.

We would, finally, like to note that we recognize the usefulness of a broader, non-truth-functional notion of entailment for uses beyond NLI. For instance, Groenendijk and Stokhof (1984, p.47f.,p481f.) define entailment between questions by resorting to a very general, non-truth-functional notion of entailment as a kind of semantic inclusion. Such a notion is very useful for question-answering or information retrieval tasks, but it is not how the NLI task was originally defined Dagan et al. (2005); MacCartney (2009), nor what the MNLI instructions to the crowdworkers specify, as we shall see.

2.2 Inference in NLP

LLMs based on the transformer architecture (Vaswani et al., 2017) have become the *de facto* standard in a variety of NLP tasks, including NLI. Highly successful architectures, starting with BERT (Devlin et al., 2019) and followed by others such as RoBERTa (Liu et al., 2019), XLNet (Yang et al., 2019), DeBERTa (He et al., 2020) as well as smaller versions such as DistilBERT (Sanh et al., 2019) and Albert (Lan et al., 2019), but also sequence-to-sequence architectures, e.g., T5 (Raffel et al., 2019) and BART (Lewis et al., 2020), have shown state-of-the-art performance on NLI.

Thanks to their sheer size, SNLI (Bowman et al., 2015), 570k premise-hypothesis pairs from image captions, and MNLI (Williams et al., 2018), 433k premise-hypothesis-pairs from 10 genres, written and spoken, dominate the field, as their size is suitable for fine-tuning large LLMs. There is a number of studies that critically assess SNLI and MNLI for their bias. Williams et al. (2018) themselves note that their dataset contains a negation bias: if the hypothesis contains a negation, then it is more likely to be part of a contradiction pair (this bias is most likely due to the fact that simply negating the premise provides an efficient way for crowdworkers to create contradiction pairs). Poliak et al. (2018) systematically investigate the prospects of hypothesis-only approaches (methods that only consider the hypothesis for predicting the label) to NLI in different datasets, finding better-than-random performance at most of them, which suggests the broad presence of statistical irregularities. Gururangan et al. (2018) show that SNLI and, to a lesser extent, MNLI, contain clues that make hypothesis-only approaches quite successful. Chien and Kalita (2020) focus on syntactic bias for LLMs fine-tuned on SNLI and MNLI, also finding that these bias are strong. Bernardy and Chatzikyriakidis (2019) argue that both SNLI and MNLI only cover a part of the entire range of human reasoning. In particular, they suggest that they do not cover quantifiers, nor strict logical inference. Furthermore, Pavlick and Kwiatkowski (2019), Zhang and de Marneffe (2021), and Jiang and de Marneffe (2022) all address the topic of disagreement among annotators. Jiang and de Marneffe (2022) focus on MNLI and suggest using a fourth category, namely "complicated", along with the known ones of entailment, contradiction, and neutral. Similarly, Kalouli et al. (2019, 2023) discuss the annotation artifacts and quality of such datasets, especially concerning the distinction between neutral and contradiction pairs, and propose a refinement of the task.

We contribute to this ongoing research by focusing on the pragmatic categories of sentences (questions, commands, claims) which determine whether they can stand in the logical relationships introduced above (section 2.1). We use GKR (Kalouli and Crouch, 2018; Kalouli, 2021) to automatically categorize premises from MNLI that violate C1 or C2. GKR (Graphical Knowledge Representation) is the semantic representation generated by the corresponding parser. In GKR the sentence information is split into six subgraphs: a) the dependency graph holding the syntactic dependencies, b) the lexical graph holding lexical information such as synonyms and antonyms of the words of the sentence, c) the properties graph holding morpho-syntactic information such as the numerus of nouns and quantifiers, d) the concept graph holding the basic predicate-argument-structure of the sentence, the "who-is-doing-what-to-whom" information, e) the context graph making existential commitments over the concepts of the concept graph, e.g., for the sentence "the dog is not eating the bone" it says not only that there is the concept of *eating* involved in the sentence, but it also commits to its non-existence, its non-*instantiation* (due to the negation) and f) the coreference graphs capturing coreference links between entities.

In addition to its performance, what makes this parser particularly suitable for our goal is that it also identifies the type of sentence that is being parsed (assertion, question, or command). By default, the parser also categorizes subject-less sentences as imperatives (which helps to identify incomprehensible sentence fragments).

3 Analyzing MNLI's Concept of Inference

After describing how current research in linguistics and logic conceives inference and separates it from presupposition, implicature, and paraphrase, and after situating MNLI in the current way how NLP approaches the task of NLI, we now detail the tension that we see in MNLI's concept of inference.

Given how Williams et al. (2018, 1114) specify the tasks for the crowdworkers creating MNLI, the goal seems to be premise-hypothesis pairs that are deductively valid. We give the part of the instruction that is relevant for entailment in bold (for the full instructions, see the Appendix, section A):

> [...] The line will describe a situation or event. Using only this description and what you know about the world: **Write one sentence that is definitely correct about the situation or event in the line**.

According to this passage, the hypothesis to be written should be such that it is definitively correct about the situation or event described in the premise. World knowledge is allowed to be used, presumably to make room for implicit but uncontroversial premises. From a logical point of view, this means that whenever the state of affairs described in the premise obtains, the one described in the hypothesis must obtain as well. Hence, MNLI seems indeed to follow earlier NLI research and aim at inference in the deductive or inductive sense detailed above (sections 1 and 2.1). This also agrees with the stated goal of Williams et al. (2018), according to which they are aiming at pairs where the hypothesis is "necessarily true or appropriate whenever the premise is true".

However, a manual inspection of the collected examples shows a different picture: the dataset contains entailment and contradiction pairs with premises that are non-assertive because they express commands or questions, or because they are fragmentary beyond comprehension (see examples above (1), (2), and (3)). Note that these examples are not resulting from cherry-picking: The creators of MNLI deliberately selected bits of text at random from 10 different genres, emphasizing that they only applied minimal pre-processing (e.g., removing sentences with less than eight characters, mathematical formulae, bibliographical references, see (Williams et al., 2018, 114f.)). No grammaticality checks or parsing of sentence types are done. Hence, including incomprehensible fragments as well as questions and commands results from an explicit design decision by the authors.

Unfortunately, this design decision seems to be in tension with the instructions to the crowdworkers as well as with the stated goal to find premises that are true or appropriate whenever the premise is true. The examples (1), (2), and (3) do not contain premises that can be true or false, making it exceedingly difficult for the crowdworkers to follow the instructions and write a sentence that is definitively correct about the situation or event in the line: Commands and Questions do not aim to describe situations, incomprehensible fragments cannot describe such situations.

The crowdworkers did their best. Sometimes, as in (1), they developed a hypothesis that contradicts one of the presuppositions of a question (see, for example, (1)), developed a largely synonymous command for a premise containing a command (see example (2)), or just wrote down a concept that differs from the concept in the premise (see (3)). None of this, of course, amounts to developing entailment or contradiction pairs.

In our pre-study, we try to quantitatively assess the extent of this problem and develop a solution for it.

4 Pre-Study: Non-Assertive Premises in MNLI

With this pre-study, we pursue two goals. First, we would like to obtain a more reliable estimate for the amount of non-assertive premises (that is, premises that do not express a determinate claim because they violate C1 or C2 from section 2.1 above) in MNLI. Second, our main experiment relies on GKR correctly categorizing premises from MNLI that violate C1 or C2 (for details, see section 2.1) or that don't violate them and thus represent assertive sentences. Thus, before starting with the main experiment, we conduct a pre-study to evaluate our choice of using GKR.

We randomly select 1000 premise-hypothesis-pairs from MNLI and submit the premises of each of the samples to the parser. The output of GKR (more specifically its context graph, where the type of sentence is specified) is then compared to our gold-standard annotations. The precision (P) and recall (R) results of this pre-study are shown in Table 1. The table also compares the results to a simplistic baseline approach, where we only count as non-assertive all premises that end with a question mark (?) or an exclamation mark (!).

	Assertive		Non-Assertive		Total	
	P	R	P	R	P	R
GKR	**93.6**	**97.7**	**83.6**	**63.3**	**88.6**	**80.5**
?, !	88.4	96.5	54.6	22.8	71.5	59,6

Table 1: The P(precision) and R(recall) results from the evaluation of 1000 MNLI premises.

Table 1 shows that GKR's precision is at 83.6% and its recall at 63.3%, when it comes to identifying non-assertive premises that cannot stand in a logical relationship. Identifying assertive premises is achieved with an even higher precision and recall (93.6% and 97.7%, respectively). These results heavily outperform the simplistic baseline approach, in which both the precision and the recall for non-assertive premises do not overcome chance. This is not surprising though. First, in MNLI, questions and commands are not always marked with question and exclamation marks, respectively, so this is no reliable method. Second, many questions do have a question mark, but are direct speech embedded in indirect speech, e.g., *How much? asked the northerner.* In these cases, the premises are indeed assertions (with an embedded non-assertive content). Third, there are premises with exclamation marks, which are no commands, e.g., *You were just wonderful!*. Finally, this simplistic approach cannot capture any cases of fragmentary premises. These results confirm the quality of the GKR parser and the need for such a tool.

With our pre-study we find that 153 of the 1000 samples are non-assertive (based on their gold label). This suggests that approximately 15% of all pairs in MNLI are indeed not assertions, meaning that they cannot entail or contradict any other assertions[5]. This however also means that any of these pairs having an entailment or a contradiction label (assuming a balanced dataset, this would mean around 10%) is indeed mislabeled as there can only be the neutral relation for non-assertions. Note that even if we do not consider the gold labels but only the true positives of GKR (since GKR's output is what will be considered in the main experiment), the percentage of non-assertions in MNLI only drops to 10% (97 out of 1000 samples are true positives). This would again mean that around 2/3 of these 10%, that is, some 6.6%, of MNLI is incorrectly annotated.

5 Main Experiment: Probing LLMs for Pragmatic Understanding

For our main experiment, based on the tension found in MNLI's concept of inference (see above, section 3), we hypothesize that *models fine-tuned on MNLI lack any sensitivity to the fact that non-assertive premises cannot entail or be contradicted by other premises* (research hypothesis 1), and that *this deficit can be amended using properly composed fine-tuning datasets* (research hypothesis 2). Finally, we hypothesize that *this does not significantly harm performance on the original MNLI evaluation dataset* (research hypothesis 3). To empirically test these hypotheses, we compile a number of fine-tuning datasets and evaluate LLMs fine-tuned on them both on a specific, hand-corrected dataset that only contains neutral premises as well as on the original MNLI-matched evaluation dataset.

5.1 Models

We use three transformer-based models that are already fine-tuned on MNLI, delivering very good performance on this dataset, and that differ substantially in their architecture. We deliberately choose

[5] Since this was tested on a random sample, we can expect that this percentage will be similar for any other random sample.

models based on different architectures, sizes and fine-tuning methods.

The reason why we fine-tune models that are already fine-tuned on MNLI is that we assume that our non-assertive dataset is not large enough on its own for learning inference. Thus, we use models that are first fine-tuned on the large MNLI dataset and have thereby acquired a basic understanding of the task. Then, we fine-tune them further on the smaller non-assertive dataset to sharpen their conceptions of entailment and contradiction so that they do not predict entailment or contradiction, but rather neutral, when the premise is non-assertive. To test our assumption, we also include a version of RoBERTa-large that is not already fine-tuned to MNLI in our fine-tuning experiments. If it performs better than the others who are already fine-tuned to MNLI, our assumption is falsified, otherwise, it is verified.

The models are DeBERTa-base (He et al., 2020), XLNET-base (Yang et al., 2019), both 110M parameters, and RoBERTa-large (Liu et al., 2019), 355M parameters. Our DeBERTa-model is fine-tuned to MNLI using the method proposed by Reimers and Gurevych (2019), the XLNET-model by the adversarial method proposed in Morris et al. (2020), and for RoBERTa, we use the original fine-tuned version by Liu et al. (2019). We obtain all of our models from Huggingface (Wolf et al., 2019).

5.2 Datasets

We run GKR over randomly chosen premises of the train split of MNLI. As compute time per sample is rather high (about 30 sec per sample in our setting), we stopped the process after receiving 1875 premises that GKR classified as either interrogative or imperative (a label also given to sentence fragments lacking a subject), and hence non-assertive. The same run also yielded 8546 premises that GKR classified as assertions. Based on this, we develop a manually corrected evaluation dataset as well as a number of systematically varied fine-tuning datasets.

Evaluation-Datasets We use a subpart of the 1875 non-assertive premises, namely 636 premises, to compile an evaluation dataset: We manually verify that these premises are indeed not expressing a determinate claim (either because they are questions, commands, or incomplete beyond understanding), resulting in 406 premises. We then select the three premise-hypothesis-pairs corresponding to each premise in the MNLI dataset (for each premise there was an entailment, a contradiction and a neutral pair created). This results in 1218 pairs whose correct relationship should be neutral due to their premise, but which were written up by crowdworkers to be evenly split among the labels of entailment, contradiction, and neutral.[6] We call this evaluation dataset "GKR-n" for "GKR-neutral". The second dataset that we use to evaluate our fine-tuned models is MNLI-Matched ("MNLI-M"), the matched evaluation dataset provided by Williams et al. (2018).

Fine-Tuning-Datasets We compile 8 different fine-tuning datasets, each consisting of a train split containing 6000 samples and a validation split containing 600 samples, evenly distributed across the three labels. In addition to a dataset that solely consists of unfiltered MNLI-train samples (mnli_u) as well as a dataset consisting solely of samples whose premises GKR classified as assertive (GKR_a), we compile six datasets combining these two sources (see Table 2). These six datasets are combinations from two different datasets for entailment and contradiction labels (entailment-contradiction 1 & 2, in short, ec1 & ec2) with three different datasets for neutral labels (neutral 1,2, 3: n1,n2,n3).

Name	Ent. & Contr.	Neutral
mnli_u	(no filtering)	(no filtering)
ec1_n1	1/3 GKR-ass.	1/3 GKR non-ass.
ec1_n2	1/3 GKR-ass.	2/3 GKR non-ass.
ec1_n3	1/3 GKR-ass.	3/3 GKR non-ass.
ec2_n1	2/3 GKR-ass.	1/3 GKR non-ass.
ec2_n2	2/3 GKR-ass.	2/3 GKR non-ass.
ec2_n3	2/3 GKR-ass.	3/3 GKR non-ass.
GKR_a	3/3 GKR-ass.	3/3 GKR-ass.

Table 2: Fine-tuning datasets used in the main experiment. They result from combining unfiltered MNLI samples with samples filtered by GKR; if nothing is specified, the quantity in question is provided by unfiltered pairs from the MNLI training split. All datasets contain 2.2k samples originally labeled entailment, 2.2k contradiction, and 2.2k neutral. For example, in ec1_n1, 1/3 of its 4.4k entailment and contradiction samples have been filtered by GKR to make sure their premises are assertive ("1/3 GKR-ass."), and 1/3 of its 2.2k neutral samples have been filtered by GKR to have non-assertive premises ("1/3 GKR non-ass").

For example, the dataset ec2_n2 in Table 2 is composed of 6600 samples in total, of which 2200 are entailment, 2200 contradiction, and 2200 neu-

[6] Note that some premises in MNLI are used in more than three pairs, leading to minimal distortions in the scaling up.

tral. Of the entailment and contradiction samples, making up 4400 samples, 2/3 are such that GKR has identified their premises as assertions (2nd column in T 2). Furthermore, 2/3 of the neutral samples are such that GKR has identified their premise as non-assertive (3rd column in Table 2).

The basic idea behind fine-tuning on these 8 different datasets is to see what factors influence performance on the evaluation dataset: ec1 differs from ec2 in containing only 1/3 as opposed to 2/3 of pairs whose premises have been confirmed by GKR to be assertive. From n1 over n2 to n3, the portion of neutral pairs with non-assertive premises increases from 1/3 over 2/3 to 3/3. Testing all combinations of these datasets allows us to determine whether assertive premises in entailment and contradictions samples are more important than non-assertive premises in neutral samples when it comes to performance on the evaluation dataset, where all of the labels should be neutral due to the non-assertive premises of all the samples used there. Including the mnli_u dataset as fine-tuning dataset allows us to test whether our fine-tuning method leads to any distortions: unless our fine-tuning method is flawed, models fine-tuned on mnli_u should perform on MNLI-M approximately as they did before fine-tuning. After all, here we just perform further fine-tuning with the same data that has been used for the original fine-tuning run.[7]

5.3 Fine-Tuning Experiment

We fine-tune the four different transformer-based LLMs on a single GPU of a DGX-2 cluster. We fine-tune each model on each dataset for two epochs, using the trainer API provided by Huggingface. The results shown are the average over three fine-tuning runs per model and dataset. We use a batch size of 8 throughout, and we begin with an initial learning rate of 2e-5.

5.4 Results & Discussion

The results of our experiment are shown in Figure 1. We give the individual models' results on the two evaluation datasets sorted by the fine-tuning dataset that was used.

With regard to our decision to use models previously fine-tuned to MNLI (see above, 4.1), the results confirm our assumptions: roberta-large performs overall 28% worse than the version of the model that was previously fine-tuned to MNLI (abbreviated by roberta-lmnli in figure 1). As a consequence, we do not consider it in our presentation and discussion of results anymore.

Figure 1 shows that the most important factor for performance on the GKR-n evaluation dataset is the portion of neutral samples that are neutral because their premise is non-assertive. The accuracy of all models is 32% on average, and hence almost exactly random, if no such samples have been specifically selected and added to the fine-tuning dataset (as is the case in mnli_u as well as GKR_a, see the first and the penultimate columns, respectively). This accuracy increases steadily if the portion of neutral samples of said kind is increased from n1, n2, to n3, where it reaches 89% for roberta-large-mnli. Performance on MNLI-matched decreases from n1 to n2 and n3, but in much smaller steps: from 86% to 82% to 77%.

These results allow for three main insights. First, without fine-tuning on our datasets, the LLMs do indeed fail to show any sensitivity for the fact that questions, orders, or incomprehensible fragments cannot entail or contradict anything. This follows from the random accuracy that the models reach after being fine-tuned on mnli_u, it confirms our first hypothesis, and it lends further support to the tension found in MNLI's concept of inference. Considering the fact that MNLI is the *de facto* standard fine-tuning dataset, this means that the standard method used currently to fine-tune LLMs to NLI tasks very likely results in models that falsely classify pairs such as (1), (2), or (3) as contradicting or entailing each other.

The second insight, confirming our second hypothesis, is that our fine-tuning approach shows much promise in getting the models to understand that nothing follows logically from non-assertive premises. In particular, this applies to the models fine-tuned to ec1_n3, i.e., to a dataset that contains 1/3 of pairs with a premise that is assertive according to GKR in entailment and contradiction and 3/3 of pairs with non-assertive premises in neutral.

The third insight is that acquiring this sensitivity does not take a heavy toll on the accuracy of MNLI-matched, with an effective accuracy difference of 3.3%. While the performance difference seems greater at first sight (10% from 87% to 77%), it must be noted that 10% of the MNLI-premises

[7] Note that it would not be useful for our purposes to convert non-assertive premises to assertions. We need to have them marked as neutrals/non-assertive as systems need to be able to differentiate between these pragmatic functions (see discussion in section 1).

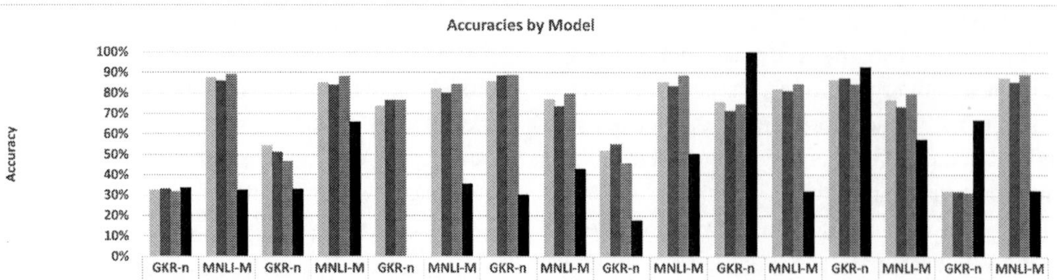

	mnli_u		ec1_n1		ec1_n2		ec1_n3		ec2_n1		ec2_n2		ec2_n3		GKR_a	
	GKR-n	MNLI-M	GKR-n	MNLI-M	GKR-n	MNLI-M	GKR-n	MNLI-M	GKR-n	MNLI-M	GKR-n	MNLI-M	GKR-n	MNLI-M	GKR-n	MNLI-M
ce-deberta-base	33%	87%	54%	85%	74%	82%	86%	77%	52%	85%	76%	82%	86%	77%	32%	87%
ta-xlnet-base-cased	33%	86%	51%	84%	76%	80%	88%	73%	55%	83%	71%	81%	87%	73%	32%	85%
roberta-lmnli	32%	89%	47%	88%	76%	84%	89%	80%	46%	88%	74%	84%	84%	80%	31%	89%
roberta-large	33%	32%	33%	66%	0%	35%	30%	43%	17%	50%	100%	32%	93%	57%	67%	32%

Figure 1: Accuracy by model and fine-tuning dataset (each fine-tuning was run three times and the average of the three runs is reported). For instance, the column on the very left gives the accuracies on our GKR-n evaluation dataset after fine-tuning on mnli_u for each of the three models. Performance of roberta-large, which was not already fine-tuned on MNLI, is on average 28% lower than roberta-large-mnli.

are anyway non-assertive (see Section 4) and thus those of them (approximately 2/3, 6.6%) that are labeled as entailments or contradictions are mislabeled, yielding an actual loss in accuracy of 3.3%. We emphasize that performing well at GKR-n requires that the LLMs predict neutral for any of the pairs in that dataset (because their premises are all non-assertive), while performing well at MNLI-M of course requires to predict all of the three labels with equal frequency. It is reassuring that the same LLMs manage to perform well at both evaluation datasets, confirming our research hypothesis 3.

6 Outlook: Exploration of ChatGPT

Following recent advances in the area we are curious to see whether ChatGPT, a general-purpose chatbot trained by OpenAI[8] a) has a better notion of entailment than other LLMs, and b) can correctly identify non-assertive statements and treat them accordingly. To address these questions, we manually explore ChatGPT: We manually prompt the Chatbot with 96 premise-hypothesis-pairs with non-assertive premises according to GKR that were originally intended as entailment pairs by the creators of MNLI. We join premise and hypothesis to obtain a question (see also Appendix C).

We find that, although ChatGPT gets the general definition of logical entailment perfectly right ("entailment is a relationship between two propositions, in which the truth of the premise guarantees the truth of the conclusion", something that it tends to assert quite often, see the Appendix, section B), it often fails to apply it to the given examples: it states that the hypothesis is logically implied (entailed) by the non-assertive premise in 54% of the cases. Interestingly, from the remaining 46% of the cases, where ChatGPT indeed answers negatively, i.e., that there is no entailment, we observe that in 27% of the samples the non-assertiveness of the premise stems from its being too fragmentary to express a specific proposition. This indicates that ChatGPT is indeed able to tell when a premise is too incomplete to express a determinate claim. Hence, this very small sample might suggest that ChatGPT has a more accurate notion of entailment than the best models tested in the main experiment, but this does not fundamentally alter the scene: ChatGPT can perform better with incomplete sentences, realizing that nothing can be logically inferred from them, but relatively poorly with questions or commands.

7 Conclusion

In sum, we take the results of our experiments to be very encouraging. While LLMs that have been fine-tuned only on MNLI show no sensibility for the fact that nothing follows logically from questions, commands, or incomprehensible fragments, fine-tuning on our datasets can address this potentially consequential shortcoming without losing too much accuracy on MNLI-matched. In the future, we plan to experiment with more sophisticated fine-tuning methods and datasets to maximize performance on non-assertive prompts. Furthermore, we hope to probe ChatGPT using larger datasets, as the preliminary results obtained here are very interesting.

[8]See this blogpost, last consulted on December 14, 2023. All interaction occurred on December 14, 2022, via OpenAI's research interface: `https://chat.openai.com/chat`.

Limitations

We see two main limitations of this work. First, it is clear that the quality of the proposed fine-tuning method (with the non-assertive datasets) heavily depends on the quality of the GKR parser, used for the detection of non-assertive statements. Since the parser has an F-score of 84.3%, as evaluated within this work, it is to be expected that some of the examples used for fine-tuning will be faulty (mistakenly classified as non-assertive and thus mistakenly classified as neutrals). This means that the models are not given entirely clean input to learn from and thus, their performance could further improve if the quality of the GKR parser (or another similar parser) could improve. Note however that this only concerns the fine-tuning datasets and not the evaluation dataset, as this was manually checked for correctness (and thus, there is no impact on the results we report). The second limitation concerns our experimentation with ChatGPT: we were only able to experiment with a small amount of samples (due to the extremely expensive manual effort required) and thus, our findings will need to be reproduced through a larger-scale study. However, our findings agree with Bang et al. (2023), who find that ChatGPT performs reasonably well on deductive and abductive inference tasks.

Ethics Statement

For fine-tuning our models, we have used parts of the existing MNLI dataset. Thus, we see no additional risk of adding personally protected information, offensive material, or biases that could discriminate against marginalized groups.

References

Kevin D Ashley. 2018. Automatically extracting meaning from legal texts: opportunities and challenges. *Ga. St. UL Rev.*, 35:1117.

John Austin. 1962. *How to do things with words.* Clarendon Press.

John Langshaw Austin. 1975. *How to do things with words.* Oxford university press.

Yejin Bang, Samuel Cahyawijaya, Nayeon Lee, Wenliang Dai, Dan Su, Bryan Wilie, Holy Lovenia, Ziwei Ji, Tiezheng Yu, Willy Chung, et al. 2023. A multitask, multilingual, multimodal evaluation of chatgpt on reasoning, hallucination, and interactivity. *arXiv preprint arXiv:2302.04023.*

Jean-Philippe Bernardy and Stergios Chatzikyriakidis. 2019. What kind of natural language inference are nlp systems learning: Is this enough? In *ICAART (2)*, pages 919–931.

Samuel R Bowman, Gabor Angeli, Christopher Potts, and Christopher D Manning. 2015. A large annotated corpus for learning natural language inference. In *Conference on Empirical Methods in Natural Language Processing, EMNLP 2015*, pages 632–642. Association for Computational Linguistics (ACL).

Tyler Burge. 2010. *Origins of Objectivity.* Oxford: Oxford University Press.

Tiffany Chien and Jugal Kumar Kalita. 2020. Adversarial analysis of natural language inference systems. *2020 IEEE 14th International Conference on Semantic Computing (ICSC)*, pages 1–8.

Ido Dagan, Oren Glickman, and Bernardo Magnini. 2005. The pascal recognising textual entailment challenge. In *Proceedings of the Machine Learning Challenges Workshop*, pages 177–190, Southampton, UK. Springer.

Wayne Davis. 2019. Implicature. In Edward N. Zalta, editor, *The Stanford Encyclopedia of Philosophy*, Fall 2019 edition. Metaphysics Research Lab, Stanford University.

Jacob Devlin, Ming-Wei Chang, Kenton Lee, and Kristina Toutanova. 2019. BERT: Pre-training of deep bidirectional transformers for language understanding. In *Proceedings of the 2019 Conference of the North American Chapter of the Association for Computational Linguistics: Human Language Technologies, Volume 1 (Long and Short Papers)*, pages 4171–4186, Minneapolis, Minnesota. Association for Computational Linguistics.

Matthew S Dryer. 1996. Focus, pragmatic presupposition, and activated propositions. *Journal of pragmatics*, 26(4):475–523.

James W Garson. 2006. *Modal logic for philosophers.* Cambridge: Cambridge University Press.

Herbert P Grice. 1975. Logic and conversation. In *Speech Acts*, pages 41–58. Brill.

Jeroen Antonius Gerardus Groenendijk and Martin Johan Bastiaan Stokhof. 1984. *Studies on the Semantics of Questions and the Pragmatics of Answers.* Ph.D. thesis, Univ. Amsterdam.

Reto Gubelmann. 2023. A Loosely Wittgensteinian Conception of the Linguistic Understanding of Artificial Neural Networks. *Forthcoming in Grazer Philosophische Studien.*

Reto Gubelmann, Christina Niklaus, and Siegfried Handschuh. 2022. A philosophically-informed contribution to the generalization problem of neural natural language inference: Shallow heuristics, bias, and the varieties of inference. In *Proceedings of the 3rd*

Natural Logic Meets Machine Learning Workshop (NALOMA III), pages 38–50.

Suchin Gururangan, Swabha Swayamdipta, Omer Levy, Roy Schwartz, Samuel Bowman, and Noah A Smith. 2018. Annotation artifacts in natural language inference data. In *Proceedings of the 2018 Conference of the North American Chapter of the Association for Computational Linguistics: Human Language Technologies, Volume 2 (Short Papers)*, pages 107–112.

Pengcheng He, Xiaodong Liu, Jianfeng Gao, and Weizhu Chen. 2020. Deberta: Decoding-enhanced bert with disentangled attention. In *International Conference on Learning Representations*.

Nan-Jiang Jiang and Marie-Catherine de Marneffe. 2022. Investigating reasons for disagreement in natural language inference. *arXiv preprint arXiv:2209.03392*.

Aikaterini-Lida Kalouli. 2021. *Hy-NLI : a Hybrid system for state-of-the-art Natural Language Inference*. Ph.D. thesis, Universität Konstanz, Konstanz.

Aikaterini-Lida Kalouli, Annebeth Buis, Livy Real, Martha Palmer, and Valeria de Paiva. 2019. Explaining simple natural language inference. In *Proceedings of the 13th Linguistic Annotation Workshop*, pages 132–143, Florence, Italy. Association for Computational Linguistics.

Aikaterini-Lida Kalouli and Richard Crouch. 2018. Gkr: the graphical knowledge representation for semantic parsing. In *Workshop on Computational Semantics beyond Events and Roles (SemBEaR 2018)*, pages 27–37.

Aikaterini-Lida Kalouli, Hai Hu, Alexander F. Webb, Lawrence S. Moss, and Valeria de Paiva. 2023. Curing the SICK and Other NLI Maladies. *Computational Linguistics*, pages 1–45.

Lauri Karttunen and Stanley Peters. 1979. Conventional Implicature. In *Presupposition*, pages 1–56. Brill.

Zhenzhong Lan, Mingda Chen, Sebastian Goodman, Kevin Gimpel, Piyush Sharma, and Radu Soricut. 2019. Albert: A lite bert for self-supervised learning of language representations. In *International Conference on Learning Representations*.

Ernie Lepore and Matthew Stone. 2010. Against metaphorical meaning. *Topoi. Orient – Occident*, 29:165–180.

Stephen C Levinson. 2017. Speech acts. In *Oxford handbook of pragmatics*, pages 199–216. Oxford: Oxford University Press.

Mike Lewis, Yinhan Liu, Naman Goyal, Marjan Ghazvininejad, Abdelrahman Mohamed, Omer Levy, Veselin Stoyanov, and Luke Zettlemoyer. 2020. Bart: Denoising sequence-to-sequence pre-training for natural language generation, translation, and comprehension. *ArXiv*, abs/1910.13461.

Yinhan Liu, Myle Ott, Naman Goyal, Jingfei Du, Mandar Joshi, Danqi Chen, Omer Levy, Mike Lewis, Luke Zettlemoyer, and Veselin Stoyanov. 2019. Roberta: A robustly optimized bert pretraining approach. *arXiv preprint arXiv:1907.11692*.

Bill MacCartney. 2009. *Natural Language Inference*. Ph.D. thesis, Stanford University, Stanford, CA, USA. AAI3364139.

John Morris, Eli Lifland, Jin Yong Yoo, Jake Grigsby, Di Jin, and Yanjun Qi. 2020. Textattack: A framework for adversarial attacks, data augmentation, and adversarial training in nlp. In *Proceedings of the 2020 Conference on Empirical Methods in Natural Language Processing: System Demonstrations*, pages 119–126.

OpenAI. ChatGPT.

Ellie Pavlick and Tom Kwiatkowski. 2019. Inherent disagreements in human textual inferences. *Transactions of the Association for Computational Linguistics*, 7:677–694.

Stanley Peters. 1979. A truth-conditional formulation of Karttunen's account of presupposition. *Synthese. An International Journal for Epistemology, Methodology and Philosophy of Science*, 40:301–316.

Alvin Plantinga. 1974. *The Nature of Necessity*. Oxford: Oxford University Press.

Adam Poliak, Jason Naradowsky, Aparajita Haldar, Rachel Rudinger, and Benjamin Van Durme. 2018. Hypothesis only baselines in natural language inference. In *Proceedings of the Seventh Joint Conference on Lexical and Computational Semantics*, pages 180–191. Association for Computational Linguistics.

Christopher Potts. 2004. *The Logic of Conventional Implicatures*, volume 7. OUP Oxford.

Christopher Potts. 2015. Presupposition and implicature. *The handbook of contemporary semantic theory*, pages 168–202.

Colin Raffel, Noam Shazeer, Adam Roberts, Katherine Lee, Sharan Narang, Michael Matena, Yanqi Zhou, Wei Li, and Peter J Liu. 2019. Exploring the limits of transfer learning with a unified text-to-text transformer. *arXiv preprint arXiv:1910.10683*.

Chrysi Rapanta, Merce Garcia-Mila, and Sandra Gilabert. 2013. What is meant by argumentative competence? an integrative review of methods of analysis and assessment in education. *Review of Educational Research*, 83(4):483–520.

Nils Reimers and Iryna Gurevych. 2019. Sentence-bert: Sentence embeddings using siamese bert-networks. *arXiv preprint arXiv:1908.10084*.

Bertrand Russell. 1905. On denoting. *Mind*, 14(56):479–493.

Victor Sanh, Lysandre Debut, Julien Chaumond, and Thomas Wolf. 2019. Distilbert, a distilled version of bert: Smaller, faster, cheaper and lighter. *arXiv preprint arXiv:1910.01108*.

John Searle. 1969. *Speech Acts: An Essay in the Philosophy of Language*. Cambridge: Cambridge University Press.

John Searle. 1985. *Expression and meaning: Studies in the theory of speech acts*. Cambridge: Cambridge University Press.

Stewart Shapiro and Teresa Kouri Kissel. 2021. Classical Logic. In Edward N. Zalta, editor, *The Stanford Encyclopedia of Philosophy*, Spring 2021 edition. Metaphysics Research Lab, Stanford University.

Raymond M. Smullyan. 1968. *First-Order Logic*. Dover.

Ashish Vaswani, Noam Shazeer, Niki Parmar, Jakob Uszkoreit, Llion Jones, Aidan N. Gomez, undefinedukasz Kaiser, and Illia Polosukhin. 2017. Attention is all you need. In *Proceedings of the 31st International Conference on Neural Information Processing Systems*, NIPS'17, page 6000–6010, Red Hook, NY, USA. Curran Associates Inc.

Adina Williams, Nikita Nangia, and Samuel Bowman. 2018. A broad-coverage challenge corpus for sentence understanding through inference. In *Proceedings of the 2018 Conference of the North American Chapter of the Association for Computational Linguistics: Human Language Technologies, Volume 1 (Long Papers)*, pages 1112–1122. Association for Computational Linguistics.

Ludwig Wittgenstein. 2006/1953. Philosophische untersuchungen. In *Werkausgabe Band 1*. Frankfurt am Main: Suhrkamp.

Thomas Wolf, Lysandre Debut, Victor Sanh, Julien Chaumond, Clement Delangue, Anthony Moi, Pierric Cistac, Tim Rault, Rémi Louf, Morgan Funtowicz, Joe Davison, Sam Shleifer, Patrick von Platen, Clara Ma, Yacine Jernite, Julien Plu, Canwen Xu, Teven Le Scao, Sylvain Gugger, Mariama Drame, Quentin Lhoest, and Alexander M. Rush. 2019. Huggingface's transformers: State-of-the-art natural language processing. *arXiv preprint arXiv:1910.03771*.

Zhilin Yang, Zihang Dai, Yiming Yang, Jaime Carbonell, Russ R Salakhutdinov, and Quoc V Le. 2019. Xlnet: Generalized autoregressive pretraining for language understanding. *Advances in Neural Information Processing Systems*, 32.

Xinliang Frederick Zhang and Marie-Catherine de Marneffe. 2021. Identifying inherent disagreement in natural language inference. In *Proceedings of the 2021 Conference of the North American Chapter of the Association for Computational Linguistics: Human Language Technologies*.

A Full Instructions Given to Crowdworkers

Williams et al. (2018, 1114) specify the following tasks for the crowdworkers:

"This task will involve reading a line from a non-fiction article and writing three sentences that relate to it. The line will describe a situation or event. Using only this description and what you know about the world:

- Write one sentence that is definitely correct about the situation or event in the line.
- Write one sentence that might be correct about the situation or event in the line.
- Write one sentence that is definitely incorrect about the situation or event in the line. "

B ChatGPT on logical relationships involving commands and hopelessly incomplete premises

All interaction occurred on December 14, 2022, via OpenAI's research interface: `https://chat.openai.com/chat`.

Human: Is there a relation of logical entailment between "What is the capital of france?" and "Paris"?

ChatGPT: Yes, there is a relation of logical entailment between the question "what is the capital of France?" and the answer "Paris". In logic, entailment is a relationship between two propositions (statements or sentences) in which the truth of one proposition (the premise) guarantees the truth of the other proposition (the conclusion). In other words, if the premise is true, then the conclusion must also be true.

In the case of the question "what is the capital of France?" and the answer "Paris", the premise is the information about the country of France, and the conclusion is the name of its capital city. Since we know that Paris is the capital of France, the truth of the premise (the information about France) logically entails the truth of the conclusion (the name of its capital city). In other words, if the premise is true (i.e. if we are asking about the capital of France), then the conclusion must also be true (i.e. the answer is "Paris").

Human: Is there a relation of logical entailment between "the kids" and "the adults"?

ChatGPT: No, there is no relation of logical entailment between the phrases "the kids" and "the adults". In logic, entailment is a relationship between two propositions (statements or sentences) in which the truth of one proposition (the premise) guarantees the truth of the other proposition (the conclusion). In other words, if the premise is true, then the conclusion must also be true. In the case of the phrases "the kids" and "the adults", there is no logical connection or relationship between the two. The phrases refer to two different groups of people, and there is no inherent logic that would guarantee that one group must be true if the other is true. For example, if we know that "the kids" are present, it does not necessarily follow that "the adults" are also present. Therefore, there is no relation of logical entailment between these two phrases.

Human: Is there a relation of logical entailment between "Close the door now!" and any other sentence?

ChatGPT: Yes, there is a potential relation of logical entailment between the order "Close the door now!" and any other sentence that provides information about the intended action or outcome of the order. In logic, entailment is a relationship between two propositions (statements or sentences) in which the truth of one proposition (the premise) guarantees the truth of the other proposition (the conclusion). In other words, if the premise is true, then the conclusion must also be true. In the case of the order "Close the door now!", the premise is the command to close the door, and the conclusion is the intended action or outcome. Therefore, any sentence that provides information about the intended action or outcome of the order can be considered the conclusion of the entailment relationship. For example, if the order "Close the door now!" is followed by the sentence "The door is now closed", this sentence can be considered the conclusion of the entailment relationship, because the truth of the premise (the command to close the door) logically entails the truth of the conclusion (the door is now closed).

In general, the relation of logical entailment between "Close the door now!" and any other sentence will depend on the specific information provided by the other sentence. If the sentence provides information that is logically entailed by the premise of [here the response from ChatGPT ended rather abruptly].

C Full Output from ChatGPT Prompting with non-assertive premises

In tables 3, 4, and 5, we can see the predictions of ChatGPT for a selection of 96 pairs with non-assertive premises from the validation split of our dataset. For each of the pairs, we prompted ChatGPT with the following template:

(5) Does "PREMISE" entail "HYPOTHESIS"?

ChatGPT always responded with a clear, albeit sometimes somewhat verbose, yes (represented with “1” in the tables) or no (represented with “0” in the tables). The tables show that ChatGPT correctly predicts neutral (“0”) in 44 of 96 prompts.

For example, here is the full turn with ChatGPT's explanation of its response for one sample with an incomplete sentence as premise.

(6) (P) : Heaven's Highway (H) Paradise's Road.

Human: Does “: Heavaen's Highway” entail “Paradise's Road?”

ChatGPT It is not clear whether the phrase ": Heaven's Highway" entails that "Paradise's Road". The phrase ": Heaven's Highway" is not a complete sentence and is difficult to interpret or understand. It appears to describe a specific location or path (Heaven's Highway), but it is not clear what this location or path entails or whether it relates to the second phrase ("Paradise's Road"). In order to determine whether the first phrase entails the second phrase, you would need to provide more information about the context in which the phrase is used and the intended meaning of the speaker.

ID	Premise	Hypothesis	True	Pred.
11906e	Would it not be a terrible shock to her?	Would it shock her?	0	0
145506e	Why did our emperor get up so early,and why is he sitting enthroned at the city's main gate,in state, wearing the crown?	The emperor has a crown on his head.	0	0
8021e	Inside both maps of the connections in the alleged right-wing conspiracy against Clinton, profiles of Al Gore (steely-eyed in this time of crisis), and still more pop-psychologizing about Clinton's personality.	The evaluations of Al Gore are part of the psychological profiling of Clinton	0	0
116777e	dirt and noise	mud and sounds	0	0
113150e	From the Place des Abbesses, take Rue Ravignan to 13 Place Emile-Goudeau.	To get to 13 Place Emile-Goudeau from the Place des Abbesses, take Rue Ravignan.	0	1
124577e	Says who?'	Who said that?	0	0
95036e	that be all right between them and	Would they both be ok with it?	0	0
144940e	Get out and explore the streets, the open markets, the cafe.	Go and see the streets, open markets, and cafe.	0	1
61713e	Come on, Jeffrey.	Jeffery should hurry up.	0	0
20169e	Are they using financial statements?	Are financial statements being used?	0	1
86509e	You have raced him, senor ?"he asked Drew with formal courtesy.	Have you raced him, sir? he asked Drew.	0	0
57980e	Closed Sabbath.	It's closed on the Sabbath.	0	1
21565e	What day was it when you searched the prisoner's room?	You searched the prisoner's room, right? On what day?	0	0
17577e	Prepared for Office of Air Quality Planning and Standards, US Environmental Protection Agency, Research Triangle Park, NC and Air Quality Management Division, National Park Service, Denver, CO.	The National Park Service is based in Denver Colorado.	0	0
90510e	Then head back to Alicante, just 28 km (17 miles) away.	Go back to Alicante, which is only 28km away.	0	1
108189e	Can't keep even with 'em.	Can't stay even.	0	0
79930e	What was happening to her?	What happened to her?	0	0
37447e	um something with the defense uh	It's related to protection	0	0
110960e	(Thank you.)	Thanks was given.	0	0
52731e	Old values versus new, old virtues and new injustices.	It was the old vs the new.	0	0
145261e	Fuck the gravy	To hell with the gravy.	0	0
27635e	Use of Program Oversight	Overseeing the program.	0	1
144659e	a professional mother a person	A professional mother and a person.	0	0
38885e	back grind tape on and off the wafers	Take the tape on and off the wafers.	0	0
91077e	Randy's Self-Reference Wrap-Up	Randy's Wrap-Up of Himself.	0	1
60546e	in cold frames or whatever the	in cold frames.	0	0
16026e	But how come Kitchell could hide out in Apache country?	How was it the Kitchell was able to stay undetected in Apache lands?	0	0
86644e	sought and respected by the organizations' business managers.	sought and respected by the organizations' business managers.	0	1
797e	Contact the Hong Kong Yacht Club at Tel. 2832 2817 for information.	the contact number for the Hong Kong Yacht Club is 2832 2817	0	1
45789e	And the second point? I asked.	What is the second point?	0	0
65272e	well really just commune with nature	We commune with nature.	0	0
109942e	But does that mean that we face a repeat of the dark years of soup kitchens and brownshirts leading up to world war?	Does that mean we're going to see something similar to the bad times before the world war?	0	0
123225e	Summary of Major Sections	Summary of important sections	0	1

Table 3: Full output from ChatGPT-Prompting 1/3.

ID	Premise	Hypothesis	True	Pred.
31686e	Interest (unless classified elsewhere), dividends, and rents (except for mineral rights) on Government property.	Mineral rights are excluded from rents on government property.	0	1
88124e	'Yes sir, Mr. Franklin?'	Can I help you Mr. Franklin?	0	0
19958e	Are they often used, may I ask?"	Are the things utilized frequently?	0	0
137712e	Personal Communication with J. Urbas, Reliant Energy, August 13, 2001.	Direct communication with J. Urbas.	0	1
34689e	A sign of failure, of a feeble economy, perhaps?	Is that a sign of a bad economy?	0	0
126927e	Department of Labor, Division of Foreign Labor Certifications, Revised June 1999 [hereinafter FY 1998 H-2A Report].	Department of Labor includes the Division ofForeign Labor Certifications.	0	1
145094e	National Saving and Investment?	Saving and Investment across the country.	0	0
110340e	A Nation of Spendthrifts?	It is a nation of spendthrifts.	0	0
48026e	Then climb (even higher!)	Then climb higher than you are.	0	0
106750e	You think he'd get after her?	The person being spoke to think he'd go after her.	0	0
134219e	U.S. airports sufficient toprotect the safety of passengers and equipment?	Is protecting passengers a task that US airports aren't capable of handling?	0	0
96401e	The verdict?	The decision?	0	1
2818e	What was it?	Do you know what it was?	0	0
56782e	How did we lose our rich tradition of porcine references?	There are fewer pig references than there were in the past.	0	0
104984e	What money?	What money do you mean?	0	0
595e	Does Hillary Clinton believe her husband's denials?	It's not sure whether Clinton believes her husband or not.	0	0
123277e	For example, in lieu of hiring a large number of seasonal	Instead of hiring a lot of seasonal	0	1
141791e	So why Clinton's aggressive defense of Helms-Burton?	Why is Clinton so defensive of helms Burton	0	0
125428e	um-hum treatment before for dismissal type thing	Treatment before dismissal thing.	0	0
71972e	Kaaterskill Falls ,by Allegra Goodman (Dial Press).	Goodman wrote a book called Kaaterskill Falls.	0	1
29030	That's th way you think it's gonna be, Croaker?	Is that the way you think it will be, Croaker?	0	1
71243e	Which tradition does John belong to?	John belongs to which institution?	0	0
40851e	Take the m??tro to Rambuteau and start at the corner of the Rue des Archives and Rue des Francs-Bourgeois, named after the poor people who were al?lowed to live here tax-free during the 14th century.	Take the metro to Rambuteau and start at the corner of the Rue des Archives.	0	1
85667e	: Heaven's Highway	Paradise's Road.	0	0
110009e	things that uh get you on the edge of your seat a little too much for her	She doesn't like things that get you on the edge of your seat.	0	0
40765e	Many thanks to readers Bill Moran, Darren Thorneycroft, and Nicholas Lemann* (author of The Big Test) for flagging this one.	There was reason to flag this.	0	1
34376e	Understand what?	Understand what?	0	1
133820e	Could they take the place of one of the 56 channels of movies?	Could they replace one of the 56 movie channels?	0	1
102665e	Jingoistic Java Juggernaut	The Java Juggernaut is Jingoistic	0	1
75235e	So who does?	Well, who is doing it?	0	1
93725e	, annual mean PM concentration) as inputs to the health and welfare C-R functions of the benefits analysis.	PM concentration is an input to the C-R functions.	0	1
124139e	(The difference between the rates divided by the number of grams in the weight interval).	The rates are divided by the number of grams.	0	1
82736e	10 See the appendix for a further explanation about electronic signatures and GAO's review of such applications.	If you want a further explanation about GAO see the appendix.	0	0
4522e	Rival explanations	explanations that disagree.	0	1
38499e	The Blue Room , by David Hare (Cort Theatre, New York City).	The Blue Room was written by David Hare.	0	1

Table 4: Full output from ChatGPT-Prompting 2/3.

ID	Premise	Hypothesis	True	Pred.
73920e	(1) How long are seasonal agricultural workers typically in the United States?	Do seasonal agricultural workers stay in the US for a while?	0	1
64748e	If I don't, how should I handle it, given that we'll see each other around?	We will end up seeing each other around.	0	1
33128e	Kinda free with a gun, leastwise at showin' it.	They are showing that they are free with a gun.	0	1
118355e	Click on the British flag for an English version of the site.	There is an English version of the website.	0	1
105826e	just to see the show just to see the show right	Only to watch the show, correct?	0	1
58056e	Participate in the graceful tea ceremony or watch the dazzling display of skill in kendo (stick fighting), with its impressively fierce battle cries.	Join in the ceremony of tea or view the kendo performance.	0	1
48341e	Disk compression and networking into Windows.	Disk compression and networking is possible in Windows.	0	1
36136e	Can you describe him at all?"	Can you provide his characteristics?	0	1
50508e	How could productivity indexes–which basically measure the ability of workers to produce a given set of goods–properly take account of such revolutionary innovations as automobiles, antibiotics, air conditioning, and long-playing records?	Productivity indexes measure the ability of workers to make goods.	0	1
39272e	Our A Low-Wage Workforce Without the Brown People.	Brown people make up the low-wage workforce.	0	0
52111e	Acute inflammation and respiratory cell damage	Respiratory cells can be damaged.	0	1
116968e	for each household in the sample.	Individual households are sampled.	0	1
122452e	Evaluation Synthesis.	Synthesis of the evaluation.	0	1
117542e	What would you really choose as a profession, if you could just consult your inclination?	What do you want to do for a living?	0	1
83373e	from front-line employees and managers, and a variety of implementation issues, such as workload demands.	One of the implementation hurdles that will be faced is workload demand.	0	1
109228e	Continue along this road to reach the pretty coastal town of Molyvos (also known by its ancient name, Mithymna), a popular spot for tourists.	Molyvos is a coastal town and a hot spot for tourism.	0	1
46914e	Section 610(e) of the Hearing Aid Compatibility Act of 1988, 47 U.S.C.	The Hearing Aid Compatibility Act was passed in the late 1980's.	0	1
69496e	Why are you coming at me with that pillow?	Why are you tossing the pillow at me?	0	0
115705e	um oh i never heard of that	I have never heard of that.	0	1
25776e	Who was this man who held in his finger these curiously variegated links of an unknown chain?	Who was this man who held these links of chain?	0	1
98779e	Au revoir, my clever and charming young lady. Tuppence sped lightly down the stairs.	Tuppence swiftly left as the watcher whispered goodbye.	0	0
109425e	Best Practices of Leading Commercial Companies	The most dominant commercial companies' best practices	0	1
86775e	Am I an idiot?	Am I an idiot?	0	1
5396e	Greetings, Dave Hanson.	I greet you Dave Hanson.	0	1
105613e	Buchanan or Bush vs. the congressional Republicans.	There are Republicans in Congress.	0	1
132469e	Far from perfect.	It is not perfect.	0	1
112205e	Look out for Robert le Lorrain's fine sculpted horses of Apollo over the old stables in the second courtyard.	Sculptures of horses can be seen in the second courtyard.	0	1
93047e	Who knows?	Who knows?	0	1

Table 5: Full output from ChatGPT-Prompting 3/3.

Analyzing Syntactic Generalization Capacity of Pre-trained Language Models on Japanese Honorific Conversion

Ryo Sekizawa and **Hitomi Yanaka**
The University of Tokyo
{ryosekizawa,hyanaka}@is.s.u-tokyo.ac.jp

Abstract

Using Japanese honorifics is challenging because it requires not only knowledge of the grammatical rules but also contextual information, such as social relationships. It remains unclear whether pre-trained large language models (LLMs) can flexibly handle Japanese honorifics like humans. To analyze this, we introduce an honorific conversion task that considers social relationships among people mentioned in a conversation. We construct a Japanese honorifics dataset from problem templates of various sentence structures to investigate the syntactic generalization capacity of GPT-3, one of the leading LLMs, on this task under two settings: fine-tuning and prompt learning. Our results showed that the fine-tuned GPT-3 performed better in a context-aware honorific conversion task than the prompt-based one. The fine-tuned model demonstrated overall syntactic generalizability towards compound honorific sentences, except when tested with the data involving direct speech.

1 Introduction

The correct use of Japanese honorifics is difficult because it requires both the knowledge of grammatical rules (i.e., verb conjugation) and contextual information (i.e., social relationships among the speaker, the hearer, and the people mentioned in a conversation) (Harada, 1976). We expect this syntactic and pragmatic ability for pre-trained large language models (LLMs), as they have shown high performance on natural language tasks (Brown et al., 2020, Ouyang et al., 2022, *inter alia*). However, it remains unclear whether LLMs can handle Japanese honorifics in a similar manner to humans, based on sentence structures and social context.

Several studies proposed datasets of Japanese honorifics for classification (Liu and Kobayashi, 2022; Someya and Oseki, 2022) and generation (Matsumoto et al., 2022). Liu and Kobayashi (2022) introduced a task in which a model takes an honorific sentence as input and classifies its honorific level or the types of honorifics used in the sentence. Someya and Oseki (2022) provided a Japanese acceptability classification dataset called JCoLA. In JCoLA, subject honorifics are categorized as sub-categories of subject-verb agreement tasks. However, these datasets aim to evaluate the syntactic performance of language models, and they do not analyze their pragmatic ability to understand honorifics by considering social relationships behind sentences. Matsumoto et al. (2022) introduced an evaluation dataset for an honorific conversion task in which the input was a non-honorific sentence, and the output was an honorific sentence. Matsumoto et al. (2022) mentioned the necessity of considering the information on social relationships among people in honorific conversion but did not clarify how such information should be processed in the task. In summary, the existing benchmark datasets of Japanese honorifics focus on either syntactic or pragmatic knowledge required for honorific understanding, not both (Appendix A). Additionally, none of these existing studies discusses the generalization capacity toward various syntactic structures of honorific sentences.

In this research, we introduce a new honorific conversion task that uses information on person's social relationships as additional input. In Matsumoto et al. (2022)'s proposed honorific conversion, the input was only a non-honorific sentence. In our task, social relationships are expressed as a sentence and concatenated into an input sentence (Section 2). This enables us to analyze whether LLMs could consider information on social relationships when executing honorific conversion. We also construct a dataset to investigate the syntactic generalizability of LLMs for this honorific task. We create hand-crafted templates and generate problems for the task by filling in the placeholders (Section 3). By focusing on the syntactic generalization

*Proceedings of the The 12th Joint Conference on Lexical and Computational Semantics (*SEM 2023)*, pages 40–47
July 13-14, 2023

Type	Target of respect and deference	Example
Subject honorifics (SH)	Agent	Sensei-ga Hanako-o **homete-irasshatta**. Teacher-NOM Hanako-ACC praised-SH
Object honorifics (OH)	Patient	(Watashi-ga) sensei-no-tokoro-ni **ukagau**. (I-NOM) teacher-POSS-place-LOC visit-OH

Table 1: Types of Japanese honorifics with conjugation rules. The underlined part is a person to whom the speaker should show respect or deference. The bolded parts are conjugated verbs. A verb *hometa* (praised) conjugates to its subject honorific form *homete-irasshatta* by attaching a suffix *irasshatta* and *tazuneru* (visit) conjugates to its object honorific form *ukagau*.

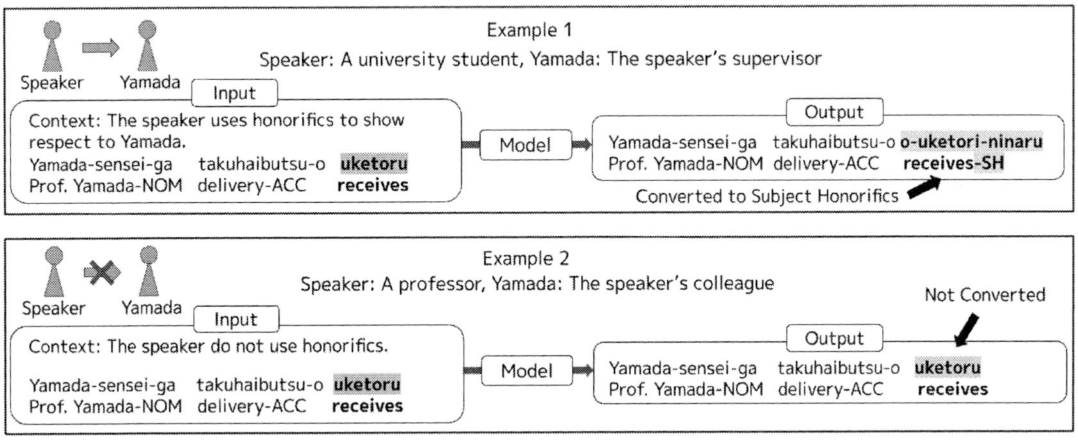

Figure 1: Examples of an honorific conversion task that considers contextual information. The bolded verbs conjugate to their honorific form if needed, considering the context.

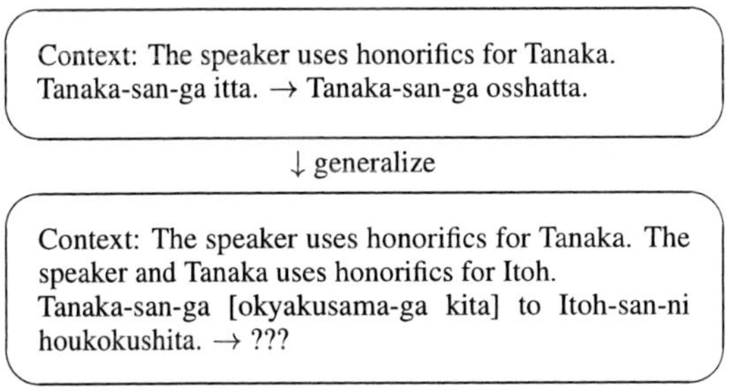

Figure 2: An example of the syntactic generalization of honorifics. The lower problem is made of a more complex sentence structure (center embedding and indirect speech) than the upper problem.

capacity, we analyze how flexibly LLMs can apply the grammatical rules of honorifics. Using our dataset, we then fine-tune and evaluate the performance of GPT-3 on the task (Section 4). Additionally, we evaluate the models using zero-shot learning to determine how well these models perform for honorific conversion using the prompt-based method. Our experiments indicate that the fine-tuned GPT-3 successfully generalizes to sentences with more complex structures, such as scrambling, but not to those involving direct speech. We also show that the model with prompt learning demonstrates much lower performance than that with fine-tuning.

Our dataset will be publicly available at `https://github.com/ynklab/japanese_honorifics`.

2 Task Overview

Japanese Honorifics Japanese honorifics are based on various linguistic phenomena (Council for Cultural Affairs, 2007; Nihongo Kijutsu-bunpou Kenkūkai, 2009); some have grammatical rules of conjugation. We target Subject Honorifics (SH) and Object Honorifics (OH). As shown in Table 1, these honorifics are applied depending on the grammatical position of *sensei* (a teacher) so that the speaker can express respect or deference towards the teacher. SH is applied to the predicate when *agent* has a higher social status than the speaker, and OH is applied when the *patient* has a higher social status than the speaker.

Honorific Conversion The existing research proposed honorific conversion (Matsumoto et al.,

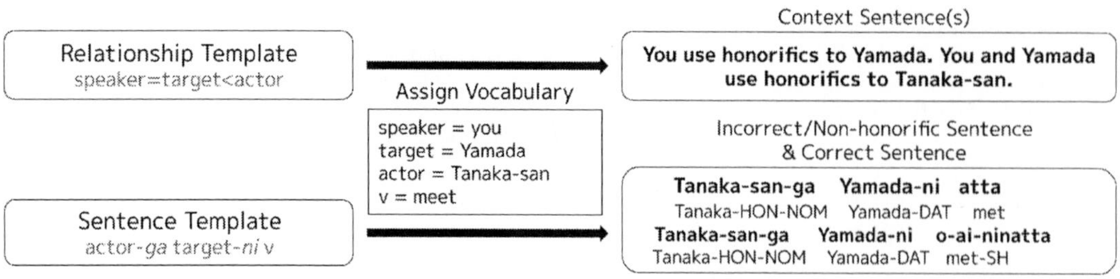

Figure 3: Overview of the process of dataset construction. The bolded sentences are used in the task. The verb *met* has to conjugate to its subject honorific form *met*-SH (*o-ai-ni-natta*) since the speaker is supposed to use honorifics for *Tanaka-san*.

2022). We extend this task to include sentences explaining social relationships as input. In the upper example of Figure 1, the speaker is talking about supervisor Yamada's actions, so the verb *uketoru* (receive) should be converted into the subject honorific form. In the lower example, the speaker and Yamada are in a casual relationship because they are colleagues; therefore, the model should output the same sentence as the input without honorific conjugation.

Syntactic Generalization We focus on the models' syntactic generalization ability to capture whether models can flexibly use honorific rules. In this paper, syntactic generalization refers to a model's ability to use honorific rules for not only simple syntactic structures but also complex syntactic structures (see Figure 2).

3 Dataset Construction

We construct a Japanese honorific dataset by manually creating problem templates and filling their placeholders with vocabulary using dictionaries to evaluate LLMs' performance on the honorific task. Our dataset construction method is shown in Figure 3. We take this approach instead of automatically collecting data from corpora for two reasons. First, it is difficult to create sentence data with complex structures, such as scrambling, from corpora in a controlled manner. This possibly makes it easier for a model to do honorific conversion than when the information is implicit. Second, we need to prepare controlled settings for social relationship information to evaluate whether LLMs utilize it in honorific conversion; however, such information does not appear explicitly in the corpora.

The second problem is related to the fact that words in argument positions are often dropped in Japanese, especially in dialogue sentences. (1) and (2) display a conversation between a junior worker and their boss.

(1) *A boss asks a question to a junior*
Okashi-tte mada nokotteru ?
snack-TOP, still remain ?
'Are there any snacks left?'

(2) *The junior answers*
ϕ_i nokori wa itadakimashita$_i$
ϕ remained TOP had-OH
'I/We had them all.'

In this conversation, two ambiguous points must be clarified to determine the honorific relationship behind the conversation. The first point is that the junior answers with object honorifics to show deference in (2), but the target of deference is ambiguous without additional context. If snacks are something the boss originally brought to their office, the boss is the target of the junior's deference. However, if the snacks are prepared by some third person with a higher rank of job position than the junior, the deference must be towards them instead of the boss. The second point is that the subject is dropped in (2) (pro-drop), but we cannot determine whether ϕ refers to the junior or to a group of workers containing the junior. Considering such language-specific phenomena, we take a template-based approach instead of a corpus-based approach for dataset construction.

3.1 Templates

We create 39 problem templates based on the literature on Japanese linguistics (Council for Cultural Affairs, 2007; Nihongo Kijutsu-bunpou Kenkūkai, 2009). A graduate student with a linguistic background created the templates by consulting a linguistics researcher. Each problem template has three elements for generating input and output data for honorific conversion: the relationship template, sentence template, and honorific type.

Relationship Templates Relationship templates represent social relationships among a speaker, a person who makes an action (agent), and one who is the target of the action (patient) in an equation-like format. For example, *speaker=actor<target* means that the speaker and actor do not use honorifics for each other and should use honorifics for the target.

Sentence Templates Sentence templates have placeholders for person's names and verbs. Based on their structural complexities, we prepare two types of sentence templates: SIMPLE and COMPLEX. SIMPLE is a template that has one clause and S(O)V structure, and COMPLEX is a template that has more complex syntactic structures: scrambling (SC), center embedding (CE), direct speech (DS), and indirect speech (IS). The first two structures change the argument positions within a sentence, potentially posing challenges for the model in capturing subject-verb agreement. The last two are related to honorific application, depending on whether the sentence has quotation marks (brackets) or not (see Appendix B). A COMPLEX template may contain multiple structures (e.g., IS & CE). See Appendix B for further details.

3.2 Problem Generation

We create problem data for training and evaluating models by filling in placeholders of the templates for verbs and person's names. From the relationship template, context sentences are generated that explain the social relationships between the speaker and the people mentioned in the input sentence. In addition, from the sentence template, we create an incorrect or non-honorific sentence and a correct honorific sentence. The verb conjugates according to the honorific type given when its placeholder is being filled. We used 23 verbs and 19 names in this experiment. We chose the verbs which are commonly used in daily conversation. We also avoid verbs such as *nusumu*(steal) because honorifics cannot usually be applied to disrespectful actions. Regarding the names of people, we used the 19 most common family names in Japan in 2022[1]. Finally, a set of the following data is generated from each problem template: context sentences, an incorrect or non-honorific sentence, and a correct sentence.

[1] `https://myoji-yurai.net/prefectureRanking.htm`

4 Experiments

4.1 Experimental Setup

We evaluate GPT-3 models on the proposed honorific conversion task under two different experimental settings: fine-tuning and prompt learning. Despite the general expectation of the superior performance of fine-tuning compared to zero-shot prompt learning, no prior research has aimed to evaluate the performance of LLM on honorific conversion in a prompt-based method. Thus, we compare the scores of these two methods to validate whether the same goes true for honorific conversion. For the two settings accordingly, we use `davinci` (Brown et al., 2020) and `text-davinci-003` (Ouyang et al., 2022), which are available in the OpenAI API (see Appendix C for details including hyperparameter settings).

Fine-tuning We fine-tune two models that differ in the training dataset's size to measure how much data are needed to generalize the problems. SIMPLE_TRAIN is used for training and SIMPLE_TEST and COMPLEX_TEST for evaluation. **3_times** is a model trained with 117 problems we prepare by generating three data from each problem template, and in the same way, **7_times** is trained with 273 problems. Although our dataset has relatively little data, we consider it enough for the experiments because the minimum dataset size for fine-tuning GPT-3 is "a few hundred."[2] As shown in Figure 1, the input is a concatenation of condition sentences and an incorrect sentence, and the output is a proper honorific sentence.

Prompt Learning GPT-3 is known for zero-shot learning, solving some tasks given only a natural language description as a prompt. In addition to the input text used for fine-tuning, we include a task description in the input prompt (see Appendix E).

Evaluation We manually calculate the percentage of correct sentences generated by a model. In this experiment, we regard the output as correct if the verb conjugates to one of the possible honorific forms. We also ignore mistakes unrelated to verb conjugation (e.g., adding a comma in a natural position). We create test datasets using the same problem templates and vocabulary as the training datasets. SIMPLE_TEST contains 108 examples, and COMPLEX_TEST has 408 examples (see Appendix D).

[2] `https://platform.openai.com/docs/guides/fine-tuning/preparing-your-dataset`

Context: The speaker uses honorifics for Kimura. The speaker and Kimura use honorifics for Takahashi-san. →Speaker<Kimura<Takahashi	
Translation	*Takahashi says "Kimura is going home."*
Source	Takahashi-san ga "Kimura ga okaerininaru (=*go-home*-SH)" to ossharu.
Target	Takahashi-san ga "Kimura ga kaeru (=*go-home*)" to ossharu.
Model's Prediction	Takahashi-san ga "Kimura ga okaerininaru (=*go-home*-SH)" to ossharu. (Not converted)

Table 2: An example of the errors regarding direct speech. The speech within brackets is made by Takahashi. The verb *kaeru* should not be in a subject honorific form *okaerininaru* because Takahashi does not use honorifics for Kimura, given their relationships.

Setting		Simple	Complex			
			CE	SC	IS	DS
FT	**3_times**	.889	.230	.297	.081	**.368**
FT	**7_times**	**.990**	**.326**	**.452**	**.231**	.293
PL	**zero-shot**	.212	.115	.174	.168	.100

Table 3: Evaluation results of the models on our test dataset through honorific conversion. FT refers to fine-tuning, and PL to prompt learning.

4.2 Results

Table 3 shows the scores under all settings of our experiments on the honorific conversion task. Overall, the fine-tuning scores surpass those of the prompt-based method.

4.2.1 Fine-tuning

The scores plummeted when the models were tested with COMPLEX_TEST compared to SIMPLE_TEST. When we increased the data size, the scores increased in most cases, except when tested for problems with direct speech sentences. In Table 2, the model failed to convert a direct speech sentence (*Takahashi-san ga "Kimura ga okaerininaru" to ossharu*). The verb *kaeru* should not be in a subject honorific form (*okaerininaru*) because Takahashi does not use honorifics for Kimura, given their relationships. However, if the brackets (quotation marks in Japanese, see Appendix B) are removed, the sentence (*Takahashi-san ga Kimura ga okaerininaru to ossharu*) becomes an indirect speech sentence and thus becomes proper honorifics. Based on this characteristic, we suppose that the model applied the same honorific knowledge as indirect speech to direct speech, ignoring the role of brackets.

4.2.2 Prompt Learning

The scores were relatively higher when tested with SIMPLE_TEST than with COMPLEX_TEST, but the scores under all of our settings were lower than 25%. We found that the models transferred non-honorific sentences to polite forms in almost all cases by simply changing the last letters of the verbs that end *-suru* into *-shimasu* instead of applying SH or OH. This conversion is possibly caused by our prompt instructing the models to "convert to the proper honorific sentence," which may include polite forms too. To validate whether the models use contextual information, we need to construct a prompt that can differentiate SH and OH from polite speech because polite forms are less restricted to social relationships.

5 Conclusions and Future Work

In this paper, we introduced an honorific conversion task that requires not only syntactic knowledge but also pragmatic knowledge, such as social relationships among people. We constructed a Japanese honorific dataset using problem templates created manually and evaluated the syntactic generalization capacity of GPT-3 models on the task using our dataset. The experiments showed that the fine-tuned models could solve problems with simple structures but failed to generalize to problems with more complex structures, particularly with direct speech. Regardless of the sentence structure, the prompt-based models did not successfully solve the problems with our current prompt setting.

In future work, we plan to expand our dataset to include more diverse Japanese honorific expressions, such as predicates other than verbs or honorific prefixes attached to nouns. For the prompt-based experiments, we evaluated the models using zero-shot learning. It would be valuable to test them using few-shot learning by including simple examples in the prompts.

We conducted experiments by explicitly providing information about social relationships. We will also continue to seek data construction methods to extract such information from the corpora, although we did not apply these corpora-based methods in this paper.

Limitations

We discuss two limitations of this research in this section. First, this research focuses on Japanese honorifics with grammatical rules of verb conjugation, which we can judge whether the honorific conversion is correct based on social relationships and sentence structures created in a controlled manner. Japanese honorifics have more expressions based on linguistic phenomena that we did not include in our templates, such as noun honorifics (e.g., *ofutagata*, a polite and formal way of saying "the two people"). Creating templates for noun honorifics requires more detailed settings because they are based on information on context other than social relationships. Second, GPT-3 is the only language model evaluated on our honorific conversion task. This research aims to analyze how capable the well-known, high-performing GPT-3 is of generalizing Japanese honorific sentences and not to explore which existing LLM can achieve the best performance in honorific conversion.

Acknowledgements

We thank three anonymous reviewers for their helpful comments and suggestions. We would also like to thank Anirudh Reddy Kondapally, Tomoki Sugimoto, Tomoya Kurosawa, and the other laboratory members for their helpful advice. This work was supported by JSPS KAKENHI Grant Number JP20K19868.

References

Tom Brown, Benjamin Mann, Nick Ryder, Melanie Subbiah, Jared D Kaplan, Prafulla Dhariwal, Arvind Neelakantan, Pranav Shyam, Girish Sastry, Amanda Askell, Sandhini Agarwal, Ariel Herbert-Voss, Gretchen Krueger, Tom Henighan, Rewon Child, Aditya Ramesh, Daniel Ziegler, Jeffrey Wu, Clemens Winter, Chris Hesse, Mark Chen, Eric Sigler, Mateusz Litwin, Scott Gray, Benjamin Chess, Jack Clark, Christopher Berner, Sam McCandlish, Alec Radford, Ilya Sutskever, and Dario Amodei. 2020. Language Models are Few-Shot Learners. In *Advances in Neural Information Processing Systems*, volume 33, pages 1877–1901. Curran Associates, Inc.

Council for Cultural Affairs. 2007. Keigo no Shishin (Guidelines of Honorifics) (in Japanese). online. `http://www.bunka.go.jp/kokugo_nihongo/bunkasingi/pdf/keigo_tousin.pdf`, accessed: 2023-03-01.

Shin-ichi Harada. 1976. Honorifics. In Masayoshi Shibatani, editor, *Syntax and Semantics: Japanese Generative Grammar*, volume 5, pages 499–561. New York: Academic Press.

Muxuan Liu and Ichiro Kobayashi. 2022. Construction and Validation of a Japanese Honorific Corpus Based on Systemic Functional Linguistics. In *Proceedings of the Workshop on Dataset Creation for Lower-Resourced Languages within the 13th Language Resources and Evaluation Conference*, pages 19–26, Marseille, France. European Language Resources Association.

Yuta Matsumoto, Yu Hayashizaki, Kotaro Kitayama, Hiroaki Funayama, Masato MIta, and Kentaro Inui. 2022. Proposal of Honorific Style Transfer Task for Supporting Japanese Language Learners (in Japanese). *In the proceedings of the 36th Annual Conference of the Japanese Society for Artificial Intelligence.*

Nihongo Kijutsu-bunpou Kenkūkai. 2009. *Danwa, Taigu Hyogen (Discourse, Attitudinal Expression) (in Japanese)*, volume 7 of *Gendai Nihongo Bunpou (Modern Japanese Grammar)*. Kuroshio Shuppan.

Long Ouyang, Jeff Wu, Xu Jiang, Diogo Almeida, Carroll L. Wainwright, Pamela Mishkin, Chong Zhang, Sandhini Agarwal, Katarina Slama, Alex Ray, John Schulman, Jacob Hilton, Fraser Kelton, Luke Miller, Maddie Simens, Amanda Askell, Peter Welinder, Paul Christiano, Jan Leike, and Ryan Lowe. 2022. Training language models to follow instructions with human feedback.

Taiga Someya and Yohei Oseki. 2022. Nihongoban CoLA no Kouchiku (Constructing Japanese CoLA Dataset) (in Japanese). *In the proceedings of the 28th Annual Conference of the Association for Natural Language Processing.*

A Existing Datasets

Table 4 shows examples of existing Japanese honorifics datasets.

B Templates

Table 5 shows examples of templates we created. Table 6 shows examples of indirect and direct speech in Japanese.

C Model Details

`davinci` is the largest model among the ones provided for fine-tuning, and `text-davinci-003` is trained by reinforcement learning on human feedback and aimed at being used with prompt learning.

Hyperparameters For fine-tuning GPT-3, `n_epochs` is set to 2. For text generation, we set `max_tokens` to 50 and `temperature` to 0.

Table 4: Examples from the existing honorific datasets.

Original	Converted	Label
朝ごはんはトーストにバターとベジマイトを薄くぬって食べました。 (I had toast for breakfast with a thin layer of butter and Vegemite.)	朝ごはんはトーストにバターとベジマイトを薄くぬっていただきました。 (I **had_OH** toast for breakfast with a thin layer of butter and Vegemite.)	変換:謙譲語 (Converted: OH)
そして10時くらいに、喫茶店でレーシャルとジョノサンとベルに会いました。 (Then, at around 10:00, I met Rachel, Jonathan, and Belle at a coffee shop.)	そして10時くらいに、喫茶店でレーシャルとジョノサンとベルに会いました。 (Then, at around 10:00, I met Rachel, Jonathan, and Belle at a coffee shop.)	無変換 (Not converted)

(Matsumoto et al., 2022)

Sentences from KeiCO corpus	Honorific level	Respectful 尊敬語	Humble 謙譲語	Polite 丁寧語	Field
本日は、かねてより相談したいことがあり、参上しました. (I have come here today to discuss something that I have been wanting to discuss for some time.)	1	0	1	0	相談 consult
今日は、折り入ってご相談したいことがあって伺ったのですが. (I came here today because I wanted to ask you about something.)	2	0	1	0	相談 consult
今日は相談したいことがあったため、来ました. (I came here today because I had something I wanted to discuss.)	3	0	0	1	相談 consult
今日はずっと相談したいことがあって来た. (I came here today to consult with you about something.)	4	0	0	0	相談 consult
⋮	⋮	⋮	⋮	⋮	⋮

(Liu and Kobayashi, 2022)

Pre-training Data of GPT-3 GPT-3 can input and output Japanese texts because some of its pre-training datasets (Common Crawl, WebText) contain Japanese texts, although the proportion of Japanese texts is not clarified.

D Test Dataset

Within the COMPLEX_TEST dataset, 156 data have center embedding, 252 for scrambling, 160 for indirect speech, and 160 for direct speech. Scrambling and center embedding can not appear in one problem data; the same goes for indirect and direct speech.

E Prompt Example

Figure 4 shows an example of our prompt used for prompt learning.

> 以下の文はあなたの発言です。人物間の敬語の条件を踏まえて、敬語が不十分かそれらを誤って使っている場合は正しい敬語に変換してください。**(The following sentence is your speech. Given the condition of usage of honorifics between people, convert the sentence to the proper honorific one if it contains wrong or insufficient honorifics.)**
> ===
> 敬語の条件:あなたは田中に敬語を使います。
> (Condition: You use honorifics for Tanaka.)
> 田中が受け取る (Tanaka receives) ->

Correct output: 田中がお受け取りになる (Tanaka receives-SH)

Figure 4: An example of the prompt used for zero-shot learning. The bold text is a task description.

Relationship template	Honorific type	Sentence template and an example of created correct sentence	Structure type
speaker=actor_1=target_1	v_ni_1 → NA	actor_1 *ga* target_1 *ni* v_ni_1。 actor_1 NOM target_1 DAT v_ni_1。 Sasaki ga Saito ni au。 (Sasaki meets Saito.)	SIMPLE
speaker=target_1<actor_1	v_ni_1 → SH	actor_1 *ga* target_1 *ni* v_ni_1。 actor_1 NOM target_1 DAT v_ni_1。 Takahashi-kyoju ga Kimura ni o-ai-ninaru。 (Prof. Takahashi meets Kimura.)	SIMPLE
speaker=target_1<actor_1	v_o_1 → SH	actor_1 *ga* target_1 *o* v_o_1。 actor_1 NOM target_1 ACC v_o_1。 Kimura-hakase ga Yamada o shokai-nasaru。 (Dr. Kimura introduces Yamada.)	SIMPLE
speaker=actor_1=target_1	v_ni_1 → NA	target_1 *ni* actor_1 *ga* v_ni_1。 target_1 DAT actor_1 NOM v_ni_1。 Kimura ni Yamamoto ga kanshasuru。 (Yamamoto thanks Kimura.)	COMPLEX (SC)
speaker=actor_1=actor_2	v_to_1 → NA v_single_2 → NA	actor_1 *ga* "actor_2 *ga* v_single_2" *to* v_to_1。 actor_1 NOM "actor_2 NOM v_single_2" CITE v_to_1。 Itoh ga "Matsumoto ga iku" to iu。 (Itoh says "Matsumoto goes.")	COMPLEX (DS, CE)
speaker<actor_2<actor_1	v_to_1 → SH v_single_2 → NA	"actor_2 *ga* v_single_2" *to* actor_1 *ga* v_to_1。 "actor_2 NOM v_single_2" CITE actor_1 NOM v_to_1。 "Kimura-sensei ga uketoru" to Kato-hakase ga o-kangae-ninaru。 (Dr. Kato considers, "Kimura-sensei will receive it.")	COMPLEX (DS, SC)
speaker<actor_2<actor_1	v_to_1 → SH v_single_2 → SH	actor_2 *ga* v_single_2 *to* actor_1 *ga* v_to_1。 actor_2 NOM v_single_2 CITE actor_1 NOM v_to_1。 Kimura-sensei ga o-uketori-ninaru to Kato-hakase ga o-kangae-ninaru。 (Dr. Kato considers that Kimura-sensei will receive it.)	COMPLEX (IS, SC)

Table 5: Examples of problem templates. NA in the honorific type section means no honorific needs to be applied to a verb. SC=scrambling, CE=center embedding, DS=direct speech, IS=indirect speech

Social relationships: Speaker<Taro=Hanako

Indirect speech	Taro-**san**-ga **irasshatta** to Hanako-san-ga itta. Taro-**HON**-NOM **came-SH** CITE Hanako-HON-NOM said.
Direct speech	「Taro-ga **kita**」 to Hanako-san-ga itta. Taro-NOM **came** CITE Hanako-HON-NOM said.

Table 6: Examples of indirect speech and direct speech in Japanese. Indirect speech is the citation of someone's speech without quotation marks (brackets), and direct speech is the one with them. In the example of indirect speech, subject honorifics are applied to Taro's name (*-san*) and his action (*irasshatta*) to express the speaker's respect for him. In contrast, the sentence within brackets is written without any honorifics in direct speech. Hanako does not use honorifics for Taro's actions according to their social relationships, so the quoted sentence is what Hanako said, and no honorifics from the speaker's view of the entire sentence are reflected.

Improving Toponym Resolution with Better Candidate Generation, Transformer-based Reranking, and Two-Stage Resolution

Zeyu Zhang and **Steven Bethard**
School of Information, The University of Arizona, Tucson, AZ, USA
{zeyuzhang, bethard}@arizona.edu

Abstract

Geocoding is the task of converting location mentions in text into structured data that encodes the geospatial semantics. We propose a new architecture for geocoding, GeoNorm. GeoNorm first uses information retrieval techniques to generate a list of candidate entries from the geospatial ontology. Then it reranks the candidate entries using a transformer-based neural network that incorporates information from the ontology such as the entry's population. This generate-and-rerank process is applied twice: first to resolve the less ambiguous countries, states, and counties, and second to resolve the remaining location mentions, using the identified countries, states, and counties as context. Our proposed toponym resolution framework achieves state-of-the-art performance on multiple datasets. Code and models are available at https://github.com/clulab/geonorm.

1 Introduction

Geospatial information extraction is a type of semantic extraction that plays a critical role in tasks such as geographical document classification and retrieval (Bhargava et al., 2017), historical event analysis based on location data (Tateosian et al., 2017), tracking the evolution and emergence of infectious diseases (Hay et al., 2013), and disaster response mechanisms (Ashktorab et al., 2014; de Bruijn et al., 2018). Such information extraction can be challenging because different geographical locations can be referred to by the same place name (e.g., *San Jose* in Costa Rica vs. *San Jose* in California, USA), and different place names can refer to the same geographical location (e.g., *Leeuwarden* and *Ljouwert* are two names for the same city in the Netherlands). It is thus critical to resolve these place names by linking them with their corresponding coordinates from a geospatial ontology or knowledge base.

Geocoding, also called toponym resolution or toponym disambiguation, is the subtask of geoparsing that disambiguates place names (known as *toponyms*) in text. Given a textual mention of a location, a geocoder chooses the corresponding geospatial coordinates, geospatial polygon, or entry in a geospatial database. Approaches to geocoding include generate-and-rank systems that first use information retrieval systems to generate candidate entries and then rerank them with hand-engineered heuristics and/or supervised classifiers (e.g., Grover et al., 2010; Speriosu and Baldridge, 2013; Wang et al., 2019), vector-space systems that use deep neural networks to encode place names and database entries as vectors and measure their similarity (e.g., Hosseini et al., 2020; Ardanuy et al., 2020), and tile-classification systems that use deep neural networks to directly predict small tiles of the map rather than ontology entries (e.g., Gritta et al., 2018a; Cardoso et al., 2019; Kulkarni et al., 2021). The deep neural network tile-classification approaches have been the most successful, but they do not naturally produce an ontology entry, which contains semantic metadata needed by users.

We propose a new architecture, GeoNorm, shown in Figure 1, which builds on all of these lines of research: it uses pre-trained deep neural networks for the improved robustness in matching place names, while leveraging a generate-then-rank architecture to produce ontology entries as output. It couples this generate-and-rank process with a two-stage approach that first resolves the less ambiguous countries, states, and counties, and then resolves the remaining location mentions, using the identified countries, states, and counties as context.

Our work makes the following contributions:

- Our proposed architecture for geocoding achieves new state-of-the-art performance, outperforming prior work by large margins on toponym resolution corpora: 19.6% improvement on Local Global Lexicon (LGL), 9.0%

*Proceedings of the The 12th Joint Conference on Lexical and Computational Semantics (*SEM 2023)*, pages 48–60
July 13-14, 2023 ©2023 Association for Computational Linguistics

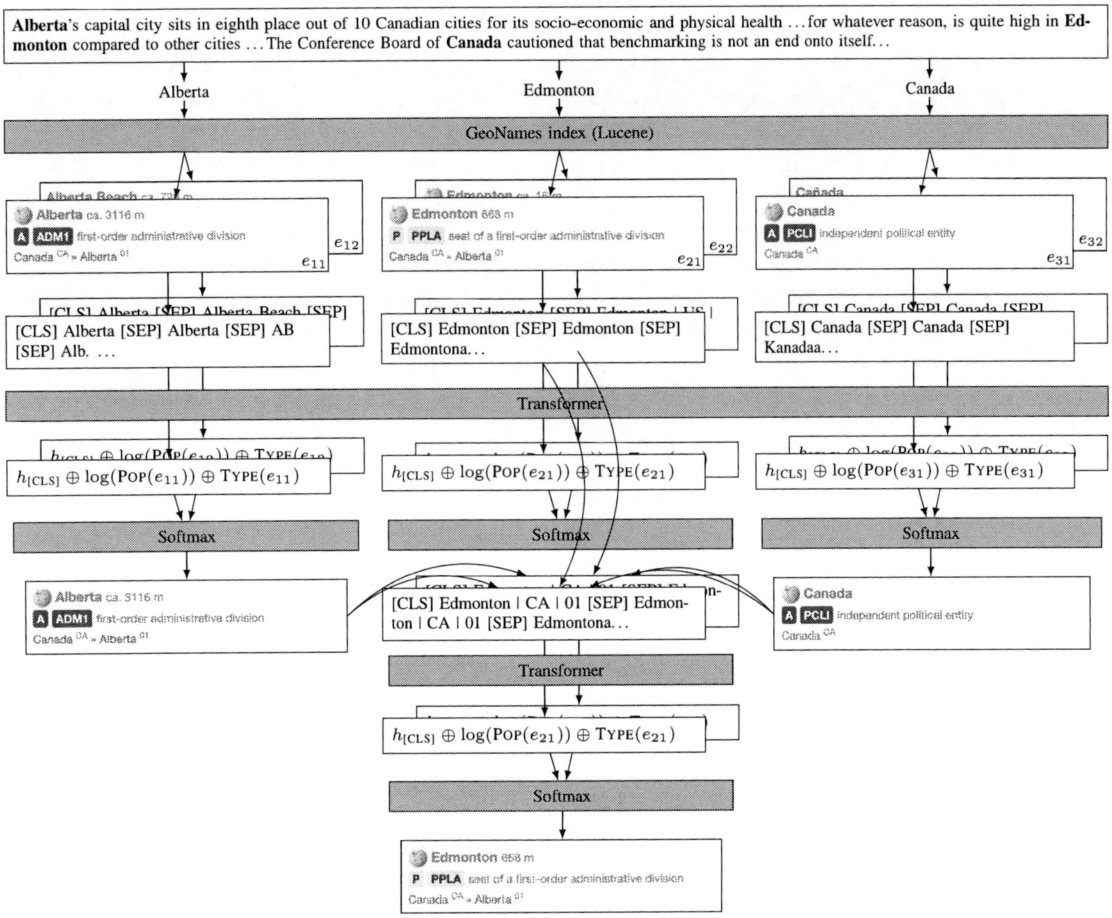

Figure 1: The architecture of our model, GeoNorm, applied to a sample text. The location mentions to be resolved are in bold.

on GeoWebNews, and 16.8% on TR-News.

- Our candidate generator alone, based on simple information retrieval techniques, outperforms more complex neural models, demonstrating the importance of establishing strong baselines for evaluation.
- Our reranker is the first application of pretrained transformers for encoding location mentions and context for toponym resolution.
- Our two-stage resolution provides a simple and effective new approach to incorporating document-level context for geocoding.

2 Related Work

The current work focuses on mention-level geocoding. Related tasks include document-level geocoding and geotagging. Document-level geocoding takes as input an entire text and produces as output a location from a geospatial ontology, as in geolocating Twitter users or microblog posts (Roller et al., 2012; Rahimi et al., 2015; Lee et al., 2015; Rahimi et al., 2017; Hoang and Mothe, 2018; Kumar and Singh, 2019; Luo et al., 2020) and geographic document retrieval and classification (Gey et al., 2005; Adams and McKenzie, 2018). Geotagging takes as input an entire text and produces as output a list of location phrases (Gritta et al., 2018b). Mention-level geocoding, the focus of the current article, takes as input location phrases from a text and produces as output their corresponding locations in a geospatial ontology. This is related to the task of linking phrases to Wikipedia, though geospatial ontologies do not have full text articles for each of their concepts, which are required for training many recent Wikipedia linking approaches (e.g., Yamada et al., 2022; Ayoola et al., 2022b).

Early systems for mention-level geocoding used hand-crafted rules and heuristics to predict geospatial labels for place names: Edinburgh geoparser (Grover et al., 2010), Tobin et al. (2010), Lieberman et al. (2010), Lieberman and Samet (2011), CLAVIN (Berico Technologies, 2012), GeoTxt (Karimzadeh et al., 2013), and Laparra and Bethard (2020). The most common features and heuristics were based on string matching, population count, and type of place (city, country, etc.).

Later geocoding systems used heuristics of rule-based systems as features in supervised machine learning models, including logistic regression (WISTR, Speriosu and Baldridge, 2013), support vector machines (Martins et al., 2010; Zhang and Gelernter, 2014), random forests (MG, Freire et al., 2011; Lieberman and Samet, 2012), stacked LightGBMs (DM_NLP, Wang et al., 2019) and other statistical learning methods (Topocluster, DeLozier et al., 2015; CBH, SHS, Kamalloo and Rafiei, 2018). These systems typically applied a generate-then-rerank framework: the mention text is used to query an information retrieval index of the geospatial ontology and produce candidate ontology entries, then a supervised machine-learning model reranks the candidates using additional features.

Some deep learning models approach geocoding as a vector-space problem. Both the mention text and ontology entries are converted into vectors, and vector similarity is used to select the most appropriate ontology entry for each mention (Hosseini et al., 2020; Ardanuy et al., 2020). Such approaches should allow more flexible matching of mentions to concepts, but we find that simple information retrieval techniques outperform these models.

Other deep learning models approach geocoding as a classification problem by dividing the Earth's surface into an $N \times N$ grid of tiles. Place names and their features are mapped to one of these tiles using convolutional (CamCoder, Gritta et al., 2018a; MLG, Kulkarni et al., 2021) or recurrent neural networks (Cardoso et al., 2019). Such approaches can flexibly match mentions to concepts and can also incorporate textual context, but do not naturally produce ontology entries, which contain semantic metadata needed by users.

Our proposed approach combines the tight ontology integration of the generate-and-rerank systems with the robust text and context encoding of the deep neural network classifiers.

3 Proposed Methods

We define the task of toponym resolution as follows. We are given an ontology or knowledge base with a set of entries $E = \{e_1, e_2, ..., e_{|E|}\}$. Each input is a text made up of sentences $T = \{t_1, t_2, \ldots, t_{|T|}\}$ and a list of location mentions $M = \{m_1, m_2, ..., m_{|M|}\}$ in the text. The goal is to find a mapping function $f(m_i) = e_j$ that maps each location mention in the text to its corresponding entry in the ontology.

We approach toponym resolution using a candidate generator followed by a candidate reranker. The candidate generator, $G(m, E) \rightarrow E_m$, takes a mention m and ontology E as input, and generates a list of candidate entries E_m, where $E_m \subseteq E$ and $|E_m| \ll |E|$. As the candidate generator must search a large ontology and produce only a short list of candidates, the goal for G will be high recall and high runtime efficiency. The candidate reranker, $R(m, E_m) \rightarrow \widehat{E_m}$, takes a mention m and the list of candidate ontology entries E_m, and sorts them by their relevance or importance to produce a new list, $\widehat{E_m}$. As the candidate ranker needs to work only with a short list of candidates, the goal for R will be high precision, especially at rank 1, with less of a focus on runtime efficiency.

3.1 Candidate Generator

Our candidate generator is inspired by prior work on geocoding in using information retrieval techniques to search for candidates in the ontology (Grover et al., 2010; Berico Technologies, 2012). Accurate candidate generation is essential, since the generator's recall is the ceiling performance for the reranker. As we will see in section 5, our proposed candidate generator alone is competitive with complex end-to-end systems from prior work.

Our sieve-based approach, detailed in alg. 1, tries searches ordered from least precise to most precise until we find ontology entries that match the location mention. Intuitively, our goal is for mentions like *Austria* to match the entry AUSTRIA [2782113] in GeoNames before it matches AUSTRALIA [2077456], but still allow a typo like *Australa* to match AUSTRALIA [2077456].

We create one document in the index for each name n_e of an entry e in the GeoNames ontology. A location mention m is matched to a name n_e by attempting a search with each of the following matching strategies, in order:

EXACT m exactly matches (ignoring whitespace) the string n_e

FUZZY m is within a 2 character Levenshtein edit distance (ignoring whitespace) of n_e

Algorithm 1: Candidate generator.

```
Input: a location mention, m
       a maximum number of candidates, k
       the GeoNames ontology, E
Output: a list of candidate entries E_m
// Index ontology
I ← ∅
for e ∈ E do
    name ← CANONICALNAME(E, e)
    synonyms ← SYNONYMS(E, e)
    for n ∈ {name} ∪ synonyms do
        I ← I ∪ {CREATEDOCUMENT(n, e)}
// Search for candidates
E_m ← ∅
for t ∈ { EXACT, FUZZY, CHARACTERNGRAM,
  TOKEN, ABBREVIATION, COUNTRYCODE } do
    E_m ← SEARCH(I, m, t)
    if E_m ≠ ∅ then
        break
// Select top entries by population
E_m ← SORT(E_m, KEY=e → POPULATION(E, e))
return top k elements of E_m
```

CHARACTERNGRAM m has at least one character 3-gram overlap with n_e

TOKEN m has at least one token (according to the Lucene StandardAnalyzer) overlap with n_e

ABBREVIATION m exactly matches the capital letters of n_e

COUNTRYCODE e is a country and m exactly matches a e's country code

Once one of the searches has retrieved a list of matching names, we recover the ontology entry for each name, sort those ontology entries by their population in the GeoNames ontology, and return the k most populous ontology entries. This list, E_m is then the input to the candidate reranker.

3.2 Candidate Reranker

Our candidate reranker is inspired by work on medical concept normalization (Xu et al., 2020; Ji et al., 2020). The reranker takes a mention, m, and the list of candidate entities from the candidate generator, E_m, encodes them with a transformer network, and uses these encoded representations to perform classification over the list to select the most probable entry. Formally, the model prediction, $\text{GEONORM}(m, E_m) = \hat{e}$, is calculated as:

$$
\begin{aligned}
s^i &= \text{TOINPUT}(m, E_m^i) \\
\mathbf{A}^i &= \text{TRANSFORMER}(s^i) \\
\mathbf{b}^i &= \mathbf{A}_0^i \oplus \log(\text{POP}(E, E_m^i)) \oplus \text{TYPE}(E, E_m^i) \\
c^i &= (\mathbf{b}^i \mathbf{W}_1^T)\mathbf{W}_2^T \\
\hat{\mathbf{y}} &= \text{softmax}(c^0 \oplus \ldots \oplus c^k)
\end{aligned}
$$

where:

- E_m^i is the ith candidate entry for mention m
- $\text{TOINPUT}(m, e)$ produces a string of the form `[CLS]` m `[SEP]` $C(E, e)$ `[SEP]` $S(E, e)_1$ `[SEP]` ... `[SEP]` $S(E, e)_{|S(E,e)|}$ `[SEP]`, where $C(E, e)$ is the canonical name of e in the ontology, and $S(E, e)$ is the list of alternate names of e in the ontology.
- $\text{TRANSFORMER}(s)$ tokenizes the string s into word-pieces and produces contextualized embeddings for each of the word-pieces.
- $\mathbf{A}_0^i$ is the contexualized representation for the `[CLS]` token of candidate entry i's input string
- $\text{POP}(E, e)$ is the population of concept e in the ontology E
- $\text{TYPE}(E, e)$ is a one-hot vector identifying which of the T types in the ontology E the concept represents[1]
- $\oplus$ denotes vector concatenation
- $W_1 \in \mathbb{R}^{150 \times (H+1+T)}$ and $W_2 \in \mathbb{R}^{1 \times 150}$ are learned weight matrices, where H is the transformer's hidden dimension
- $\hat{\mathbf{y}}$ is a probability distribution over the k entries proposed by the candidate generator

We represent the mention text + candidate entity synonyms with the contextualized representation of the `[CLS]` token, similar to applications of transformers to text classification. We include the population feature to allow the model to learn that locations in text are more likely to refer to high population than low population places (e.g., Paris, France vs. Paris, Texas, USA), and we take the logarithm of the population under the assumption that it is more important to capture the order of magnitude (e.g., thousands vs. millions) than the exact number. We include the type feature to allow the model to learn that locations in text are more likely to refer to some types of geographical features than others (e.g., San José, the capital of Costa Rica, vs. San José, the province).

The candidate reranker is trained with a standard classification loss:

$$L_R = \mathbf{y} \cdot log(\hat{\mathbf{y}})$$

where $\mathbf{y} \in \mathbb{R}^{|E_m|}$ is a one-hot vector representing the correct candidate entry.

[1]GeoNames has $T = 681$ types. For example, PPLC means *capital of a political entity*. Definitions for all types ("feature codes") are at `http://download.geonames.org/export/dump/featureCodes_en.txt`

3.3 Context Incorporation

The text around a mention may provide clues (e.g., the context *Minnesota State Patrol urges motorists to drive with caution... in Becker, Clay, and Douglas* suggests that *Clay* refers to Clay County, Minnesota, even though Clay County, Missouri is more populous). Thus, we consider two approaches to incorporating context.

context=$c$sent A simple approach is to take the c-sentence window surrounding the mention m and encode it with the the same transformer as was used to encode $m + e$. The contextualized representation of the c-sentence window's `[CLS]` token can then be concatenated into $\mathbf{b}$ alongside the other features. The 512 word-piece limit on the size of the transformer input means that this approach cannot incorporate the entire document.

context=2stage To include the full document context, we take advantage of the fact (demonstrated in appendix A.1) that toponyms at the top of the hierarchy, like countries and states, can often be resolved precisely without context as they are less ambiguous. We thus propose Algorithm 2, a two-stage approach to geocoding. Lines 3-7 are the context-free stage, where GeoNorm is first applied to all location mentions. If the feature type of a predicted entry, $\text{TYPE}(e)$, is an administrative district 1-3 (i.e., the top of the geographic hierarchy: countries, states, or counties), then the prediction is accepted. Such predictions are converted to their administrative codes (e.g., *United States* $\rightarrow$ `US`) and added to the context. Lines 8-11 are the second stage, where the geocoding system is applied to all remaining location mentions but this time incorporating the collected context. The context is formed by concatenating together the collected toponym codes, where for example, if Canada (CA) and Alberta (01) were found in the document as in fig. 1, the context string would look like "CA || 01".

Algorithm 2: Two-stage toponym resolution using document-level context.

Input: location mentions, M
GeoNames ontology, E

1 $\hat{R} \leftarrow \{\}$
2 $C \leftarrow \emptyset$
`// Resolve toponyms without context`
3 **for** $m \in M$ **do**
4     $\hat{e} \leftarrow \text{GEONORM}(m, E)$
5   **if** $\text{TYPE}(\hat{e}) \in \{\mathit{adm1}, \mathit{adm2}, \mathit{adm3}\}$ **then**
6         $\hat{R}[m] \leftarrow \hat{e}$
7         $C \leftarrow C \cup \{\text{CODE}(\hat{e})\}$
`// Resolve toponyms with context`
8 $c \leftarrow$ `"||".join(C)`
9 **for** $m \in M$ **do**
10   **if** $m \notin \hat{R}$ **then**
11         $\hat{R}[m] \leftarrow \text{GEONORM}(m + c, E)$
12 **return** $\hat{R}$

Dataset	Train		Dev.		Test	
	Topo.	Art.	Topo.	Art.	Topo.	Art.
LGL	3112	411	419	58	931	119
GeoWebNews	1641	140	281	20	477	40
TR-News	925	82	68	11	282	25

Table 1: Numbers of articles (Art.) and manually annotated toponyms (Topo.) in the train, development, and test splits of the toponym resolution corpora.

4 Experiments

4.1 Datasets

We conduct experiments on three toponym resolution datasets. Local Global Lexicon (LGL; Lieberman et al., 2010) was constructed from 588 news articles from local and small U.S. news sources. GeoWebNews (Gritta et al., 2019) was constructed from 200 articles from 200 globally distributed news sites. TR-News (Kamalloo and Rafiei, 2018) was constructed from 118 articles from various global and local news sources. As there are no standard publicly available splits for these datasets, we split each dataset into a train, development, and test set according to a 70%, 10% , and 20% ratio. To enable replicability, we will release these splits upon publication. The statistics of all datasets are shown in table 1.

4.2 Database

Our datasets use GeoNames[2], a crowdsourced database of geospatial locations, with almost 7 million entries and a variety of information such as geographic coordinates (latitude and longitude), alternative names, feature type (country, city, river, mountain, etc.), population, elevation, and positions within a political geographic hierarchy. An example entry from GeoNames is shown in fig. 2.

4.3 Evaluation Metrics

There is not yet agreement in the field of toponym resolution on a single evaluation metric. Therefore, we gather metrics from prior work and use all of them for evaluation.

[2] `https://www.geonames.org/`

Figure 2: An entry for *Tucson* in GeoNames

Accuracy is the number of location mentions where the system predicted the correct database entry ID, divided by the number of location mentions. Higher is better, and a perfect model would have accuracy of 1.0.

Accuracy@161km measures the fraction of system-predicted (latitude, longitude) points that were less than 161 km (100 miles) away from the human-annotated (latitude, longitude) points. Higher is better, and a perfect model would have Accuracy@161km of 1.0.

Mean error distance calculates the mean over all predictions of the distance between each system-predicted and human-annotated (latitude, longitude) point. Lower is better, and a perfect model would have a mean error distance of 0.0.

Area Under the Curve calculates the area under the curve of the distribution of geocoding error distances. Lower is better, and a perfect model would have an area under the curve of 0.0.

4.4 Implementation details

We implement the candidate reranker with Lucene[3] v8.4.1 under Java 1.8. When indexing GeoNames, we also index countries under their adjectival forms in Wikipedia[4]. We implement the candidate reranker with the PyTorch[5] v1.7.0 APIs in Huggingface Transformers v2.11.0 (Wolf et al., 2020), using either `bert-base-uncased` or `bert-multilingual-uncased`. We train with the Adam optimizer, a learning rate of 1e-5, a maximum sequence length of 128 tokens, and a number of epochs of 30. We explored a small number of learning rates (1e-5, 1e-6, 5e-6) and epoch numbers (10, 20, 30, 40) on the development data. When training without context, we use one Tesla V100 GPU with 32GB memory and a batch size of 8. When training with context, we use four Tesla V100 GPU with 32GB memory and a batch size of 32. The total number of parameters in our model is 168M and the training time is about 3 hours.

[3]https://lucene.apache.org/

[4]https://en.wikipedia.org/wiki/List_of_adjectival_and_demonymic_forms_for_countries_and_nations

[5]https://pytorch.org/

4.5 Systems

We compare to a variety of geocoding systems:

Edinburgh Grover et al. (2010) introduced a rule-based extraction and disambiguation system that uses heuristics such as population count, spatial minimization, type, country, and some contextual information (containment, proximity, locality, clustering) to score, rank, and choose a candidate.

Mordecai Halterman (2017) introduced a generate-and-rank approach that uses Elasticsearch to generate candidates and neural networks based on word2vec (Mikolov et al., 2013) to rerank them. Its models are trained on proprietary data.

CamCoder Gritta et al. (2018a) introduced a tile-classification approach that combines a convolutional network over the target mention and 400 tokens of context with a population vector derived from location mentions in the context and populations from GeoNames. CamCoder predicts one of 7823 tiles of the earth's surface. See appendix A.2 for further CamCoder details.

DeezyMatch Hosseini et al. (2020) introduced a vector-space approach that first pre-trains an LSTM-based classifier on GeoNames taking string pairs as input, and then fine-tunes the pair classifier on the target dataset. The trained DeezyMatch model compares mentions to database entries by generating vector representations for both and measuring their L2-norm distance or cosine similarity.

SAPBERT Liu et al. (2021) introduced a vector-space approach that pretrains a transformer network on the database using a self-alignment metric learning objective and online hard pairs mining to cluster synonyms of the same concept together and move different concepts further away. The pre-trained SAPBERT is then fine-tuned on the target dataset. SAPBERT was trained for the biomedical domain, but is easily retrained for other domains. We pretrain SAPBERT on GeoNames and finetune it on the toponym resolution datasets.

Model	LGL (test)		GeoWebNews (test)		TR-News (test)	
	R@1	R@20	R@1	R@20	R@1	R@20
DeezyMatch (Hosseini et al., 2020)	.172	.538	.262	.671	.206	.702
SAPBERT (Liu et al., 2021)	.245	.742	.428	.746	.355	.780
GeoNorm (+gen, -rank)	.606	.962	.694	.866	.716	.965

Table 2: Performance of candidate generators on the test sets. R@1 is useful for measuring the accuracy of the candidate generator when used directly as a geocoder. R@20 is useful for estimating the ceiling performance of a top-20 reranker based on that candidate generator.

Model	LGL (test)				GeoWebNews (test)				TR-News (test)			
	Acc	A161	Err	AUC	Acc	A161	Err	AUC	Acc	A161	Err	AUC
Edinburgh (Grover et al., 2010)	.611	-	-	-	.738	-	-	-	.750	-	-	-
CamCoder (Gritta et al., 2018a)	.580	.651	82	.288	.572	.665	155	.290	.660	.778	89	.196
Mordecai (Halterman, 2017)	.322	.375	926	.594	.291	.333	1072	.633	.472	.553	6558	.427
DeezyMatch (Hosseini et al., 2020)	.172	.182	654	.704	.262	.323	537	.601	.206	.220	741	.705
SAPBERT (Liu et al., 2021)	.245	.260	566	.630	.428	.499	357	.446	.355	.362	595	.568
ReFinED (Ayoola et al., 2022a)	.576	-	-	-	.658	-	-	-	.720	-	-	-
ReFinED (fine-tuned)	.786	-	-	-	.782	-	-	-	.858	-	-	-
GeoNorm (+gen -rank)	.606	.685	119	.263	.694	.774	92	.194	.716	.812	95	.169
GeoNorm (+gen +rank, -context)	.761	.785	59	.167	.788	.834	61	.131	.798	.816	89	.154
GeoNorm (+gen +rank, +context=2stage)	**.807**	**.824**	**46**	**.135**	**.828**	**.862**	**55**	**.114**	**.918**	**.933**	**34**	**.057**
GeoNorm (+gen +rank, +context=2stage, +alldata)	.799	.828	52	.136	.832	.876	54	.104	.897	.911	36	.073

Table 3: Performance on the test sets. Higher is better for accuracy (Acc) and accuracy@161km (A161). Lower is better for mean error (Err) and area under the error distances curve (AUC). We do not report distance-based metrics for Edinburgh or ReFinED as these extraction+disambiguation systems do not make predictions for all mentions. The best performance on each dataset+metric is in bold (excluding the final model that was trained on more data).

ReFinED Ayoola et al. (2022a) introduced a vector-space approach for joint extraction and disambiguation of Wikipedia entities. One transformer network generates contextualized embeddings for tokens in the text, another generates embeddings for entries in the ontology, and tokens are matched to entries by comparing dot products over embeddings. ReFinED was trained on Wikipedia, and Wikipedia entries for place names have GeoNames IDs, so ReFinED can be used as a geocoder.

ReFinED (fine-tuned) ReFinED can also be fine-tuned, so we take the released version of ReFinED and fine-tune it for geocoding on each of the toponym datasets.

5 Results

We first evaluate our context-free candidate generator, comparing it to recent context-free candidate generators. Table 2 shows that our approach outperforms approaches from prior work by large margins, both in accuracy of the top entry (R@1) and whether the correct entry is in the top 20 (R@20).

We next evaluate our complete generate-and-rank system against other geocoders. We first perform model selection on the development set as described in appendix A.3 to select four models to run on the test set: the candidate generator alone, the best generate-and-rank system with no context, and the best generate-and-rank system with context. Table 3 shows that our proposed GeoNorm model outperforms all prior work across all toponym resolution test sets on all metrics. Even without incorporating context, our generate-and-rank framework meets or exceeds the performance of almost all models from prior work. The exception is ReFinED, where our context-free model outperforms ReFinED out-of-the-box, but slightly underperforms our finetuned version of ReFinED. However, adding the novel two-stage document-level context yields large gains over the context free version of our model, and outperforms even the finetuned ReFinED. The final row the table shows the peformance of a model trained on the combined training data from all datasets, which we release for English geocoding under the Apache License v2.0, for off-the-shelf use at `https://github.com/clulab/geonorm`.

	Example	Candidate				Rank				
		Name	Pop.	Type	State	RF	G	GR	GRC3	GRCD
1	*The educational philosophy at the Washing-*	**Alexandria**	159467	PPLA2						1
	ton Latin School in Alexandria is somewhat	City of Alexandria	139966	ADM2		1				
	similar to Ahlstrom's previous endeavors.									
2		Los Angeles County	9818605	ADM2			1	2		
	It was Los Angeles police officers she at-	**Los Angeles**	3971883	PPLA2			2	1		
	tempted to blow up.	Los Angeles	125430	PPLA2			3	3		
		Los Angeles	4217	PPL			4	4		
3	*the Minnesota State Patrol urges motorists to*	Clay County	221939		Missouri			1		4
	drive with caution as flooding continues to	Clay County	190865		Florida			2		3
	affect area highways. Water over the road-	**Clay County**	58999		Minnesota			3		1
	way is currently affecting the following areas	Clay County	26890		Indiana			4		2
	in Becker, Clay, and Douglas									
4		New London County	274055	ADM2			1		3	4
	he writes, as do my efforts to insure	New London	27179	PPL			2		1	1
	New London is a safe community.	New London	7172	PPL			3		2	3
		New London	1882	PPL			4		4	2

Table 4: Examples of predictions from ReFinED (RF), our candidate generator alone (G), our generate-and-rerank system without context (GR), our system with sentence context (GRC3), and our system with 2-stage document context (GRCD). Target location mentions are underlined. Human annotated ontology entries are in bold.

6 Qualitative Analysis

Table 4 shows some qualitative analysis of errors that ReFinED and different variants of GeoNorm made. Row 1 shows an example where ReFinED fails but GeoNorm succeeds, by more effectively using geospatial metadata such as population and feature type. Row 2 shows an example where GeoNorm fails with a candidate generator alone but succeeds with a context-free reranker, by not relying on population alone and instead jointly considering the name, population, and feature type information (ADM2 represents a county, PPLA2 represents a city). Row 3 shows an example where GeoNorm fails without context but succeeds with context, by taking advantage of the *Minnesota* in the context to select the *Clay County* that would otherwise seem implausible due to its lower population. Finally, row 4 shows an example where our best GeoNorm model still fails. The candidate generator includes the correct ontology entry in its top-k list, but neither the name, population, feature code, nor nearby context suggest the correct candidate. The global context includes toponyms from the same state, allowing the model with document context to move the correct answer up from rank 4 to rank 2. But fully addressing this issue would likely require predicting countries and states of toponyms in the text before resolving them.

7 Limitations

GeoNorm's candidate generator is based on information retrieval. This is efficient but not very flexible in string matching, and when the candidate generator fails to produce the correct candidate entry, the candidate reranker also necessarily fails. For example, as table 2 shows, GeoNorm's reranker achieves only .866 recall@20 on the GeoWebNews dataset, meaning that 13.4% of the time, the correct candidate is not in the top 20 results returned by the candidate generator. One solution might be to replace the information retrieval based candidate generator with a neural network to provide more robust string matching, though the neural network candidate generators from prior work in table 2 actually perform worse than GeoNorm's candidate generator. Another solution may be to find smarter ways to filter the generated candidates, perhaps by building on the two-stage resolution approach to use document-level context to filter the candidates to those in appropriate countries and states.

GeoNorm is also limited by its training and evaluation data, which covers only thousands of English toponyms from news articles, while there are many millions of toponyms in many different languages across the world. It is likely that there are regional differences in GeoNorm's accuracy that will need to be addressed by future research.

8 Conclusion

We propose a new toponym resolution architecture, GeoNorm, that combines the tight ontology integration of generate-and-rerank systems with the robust text encoding of deep neural networks. GeoNorm consists of an information retrieval-based candidate generator, a BERT-based reranker that incorporates features important to toponym resolution such as population and type of location, and a novel two-stage resolution strategy that incorporates document-level context. We evaluate our proposed architecture against prior state-of-the-art, using multiple evaluation metrics and multiple datasets. GeoNorm achieves new state-of-the-art performance on all datasets.

References

Benjamin Adams and Grant McKenzie. 2018. Crowdsourcing the character of a place: Character-level convolutional networks for multilingual geographic text classification. *Transactions in GIS*, 22(2):394–408.

Mariona Coll Ardanuy, Kasra Hosseini, Katherine McDonough, Amrey Krause, Daniel van Strien, and Federico Nanni. 2020. A deep learning approach to geographical candidate selection through toponym matching. In *Proceedings of the 28th International Conference on Advances in Geographic Information Systems*, pages 385–388.

Zahra Ashktorab, Christopher Brown, Manojit Nandi, and Aron Culotta. 2014. Tweedr: Mining twitter to inform disaster response. In *ISCRAM*, pages 269–272.

Tom Ayoola, Joseph Fisher, and Andrea Pierleoni. 2022a. Improving entity disambiguation by reasoning over a knowledge base. In *Proceedings of the 2022 Conference of the North American Chapter of the Association for Computational Linguistics: Human Language Technologies*, pages 2899–2912, Seattle, United States. Association for Computational Linguistics.

Tom Ayoola, Shubhi Tyagi, Joseph Fisher, Christos Christodoulopoulos, and Andrea Pierleoni. 2022b. ReFinED: An efficient zero-shot-capable approach to end-to-end entity linking. In *Proceedings of the 2022 Conference of the North American Chapter of the Association for Computational Linguistics: Human Language Technologies: Industry Track*, pages 209–220, Hybrid: Seattle, Washington + Online. Association for Computational Linguistics.

Berico Technologies. 2012. Cartographic location and vicinity indexer (clavin).

Preeti Bhargava, Nemanja Spasojevic, and Guoning Hu. 2017. Lithium NLP: A system for rich information extraction from noisy user generated text on social media. In *Proceedings of the 3rd Workshop on Noisy User-generated Text*, pages 131–139, Copenhagen, Denmark. Association for Computational Linguistics.

Ana Bárbara Cardoso, Bruno Martins, and Jacinto Estima. 2019. Using recurrent neural networks for toponym resolution in text. In *EPIA Conference on Artificial Intelligence*, pages 769–780. Springer.

Jens A de Bruijn, Hans de Moel, Brenden Jongman, Jurjen Wagemaker, and Jeroen CJH Aerts. 2018. Taggs: grouping tweets to improve global geoparsing for disaster response. *Journal of Geovisualization and Spatial Analysis*, 2(1):2.

Grant DeLozier, Jason Baldridge, and Loretta London. 2015. Gazetteer-independent toponym resolution using geographic word profiles. In *Proceedings of the Twenty-Ninth AAAI Conference on Artificial Intelligence*, AAAI'15, page 2382–2388. AAAI Press.

Nuno Freire, José Borbinha, Pável Calado, and Bruno Martins. 2011. A metadata geoparsing system for place name recognition and resolution in metadata records. In *Proceedings of the 11th annual international ACM/IEEE joint conference on Digital libraries*, pages 339–348.

Fredric Gey, Ray Larson, Mark Sanderson, Hideo Joho, Paul Clough, and Vivien Petras. 2005. Geoclef: the clef 2005 cross-language geographic information retrieval track overview. In *Workshop of the cross-language evaluation forum for european languages*, pages 908–919. Springer.

Milan Gritta, Mohammad Taher Pilehvar, and Nigel Collier. 2018a. Which Melbourne? augmenting geocoding with maps. In *Proceedings of the 56th Annual Meeting of the Association for Computational Linguistics (Volume 1: Long Papers)*, pages 1285–1296, Melbourne, Australia. Association for Computational Linguistics.

Milan Gritta, Mohammad Taher Pilehvar, and Nigel Collier. 2019. A pragmatic guide to geoparsing evaluation. *Language Resources and Evaluation*, pages 1–30.

Milan Gritta, Mohammad Taher Pilehvar, Nut Limsopatham, and Nigel Collier. 2018b. What's missing in geographical parsing? *Language Resources and Evaluation*, 52(2):603–623.

Claire Grover, Richard Tobin, Kate Byrne, Matthew Woollard, James Reid, Stuart Dunn, and Julian Ball. 2010. Use of the edinburgh geoparser for georeferencing digitized historical collections. *Philosophical Transactions of the Royal Society A: Mathematical, Physical and Engineering Sciences*, 368(1925):3875–3889.

Andrew Halterman. 2017. Mordecai: Full text geoparsing and event geocoding. *The Journal of Open Source Software*, 2(9).

Simon I Hay, Katherine E Battle, David M Pigott, David L Smith, Catherine L Moyes, Samir Bhatt, John S Brownstein, Nigel Collier, Monica F Myers, Dylan B George, et al. 2013. Global mapping of infectious disease. *Philosophical Transactions of the Royal Society B: Biological Sciences*, 368(1614):20120250.

Thi Bich Ngoc Hoang and Josiane Mothe. 2018. Location extraction from tweets. *Information Processing & Management*, 54(2):129–144.

Kasra Hosseini, Federico Nanni, and Mariona Coll Ardanuy. 2020. DeezyMatch: A flexible deep learning approach to fuzzy string matching. In *Proceedings of the 2020 Conference on Empirical Methods in Natural Language Processing: System Demonstrations*, pages 62–69, Online. Association for Computational Linguistics.

Zongcheng Ji, Qiang Wei, and Hua Xu. 2020. Bert-based ranking for biomedical entity normalization. *AMIA Summits on Translational Science Proceedings*, 2020:269.

Ehsan Kamalloo and Davood Rafiei. 2018. A coherent unsupervised model for toponym resolution. In *Proceedings of the 2018 World Wide Web Conference*, pages 1287–1296.

Morteza Karimzadeh, Wenyi Huang, Siddhartha Banerjee, Jan Oliver Wallgrün, Frank Hardisty, Scott Pezanowski, Prasenjit Mitra, and Alan M MacEachren. 2013. Geotxt: a web api to leverage place references in text. In *Proceedings of the 7th workshop on geographic information retrieval*, pages 72–73.

Sayali Kulkarni, Shailee Jain, Mohammad Javad Hosseini, Jason Baldridge, Eugene Ie, and Li Zhang. 2021. Multi-level gazetteer-free geocoding. In *Proceedings of Second International Combined Workshop on Spatial Language Understanding and Grounded Communication for Robotics*, pages 79–88, Online. Association for Computational Linguistics.

Abhinav Kumar and Jyoti Prakash Singh. 2019. Location reference identification from tweets during emergencies: A deep learning approach. *International journal of disaster risk reduction*, 33:365–375.

Egoitz Laparra and Steven Bethard. 2020. A dataset and evaluation framework for complex geographical description parsing. In *Proceedings of the 28th International Conference on Computational Linguistics*, pages 936–948, Barcelona, Spain (Online). International Committee on Computational Linguistics.

Sunshin Lee, Mohamed Farag, Tarek Kanan, and Edward A Fox. 2015. Read between the lines: A machine learning approach for disambiguating the geo-location of tweets. In *Proceedings of the 15th ACM/IEEE-CS Joint Conference on Digital Libraries*, pages 273–274.

Michael D Lieberman and Hanan Samet. 2011. Multifaceted toponym recognition for streaming news. In *Proceedings of the 34th international ACM SIGIR conference on Research and development in Information Retrieval*, pages 843–852.

Michael D Lieberman and Hanan Samet. 2012. Adaptive context features for toponym resolution in streaming news. In *Proceedings of the 35th international ACM SIGIR conference on Research and development in information retrieval*, pages 731–740.

Michael D Lieberman, Hanan Samet, and Jagan Sankaranarayanan. 2010. Geotagging with local lexicons to build indexes for textually-specified spatial data. In *2010 IEEE 26th international conference on data engineering (ICDE 2010)*, pages 201–212. IEEE.

Fangyu Liu, Ehsan Shareghi, Zaiqiao Meng, Marco Basaldella, and Nigel Collier. 2021. Self-alignment pretraining for biomedical entity representations. In *Proceedings of the 2021 Conference of the North American Chapter of the Association for Computational Linguistics: Human Language Technologies*, pages 4228–4238.

Xiangyang Luo, Yaqiong Qiao, Chenliang Li, Jiangtao Ma, and Yimin Liu. 2020. An overview of microblog user geolocation methods. *Information Processing & Management*, 57(6):102375.

Bruno Martins, Ivo Anastácio, and Pável Calado. 2010. A machine learning approach for resolving place references in text. In *Geospatial thinking*, pages 221–236. Springer.

Tomás Mikolov, Kai Chen, Greg Corrado, and Jeffrey Dean. 2013. Efficient estimation of word representations in vector space. In *1st International Conference on Learning Representations, ICLR 2013, Scottsdale, Arizona, USA, May 2-4, 2013, Workshop Track Proceedings*.

Afshin Rahimi, Timothy Baldwin, and Trevor Cohn. 2017. Continuous representation of location for geolocation and lexical dialectology using mixture density networks. In *Proceedings of the 2017 Conference on Empirical Methods in Natural Language Processing*, pages 167–176, Copenhagen, Denmark. Association for Computational Linguistics.

Afshin Rahimi, Duy Vu, Trevor Cohn, and Timothy Baldwin. 2015. Exploiting text and network context for geolocation of social media users. In *Proceedings of the 2015 Conference of the North American Chapter of the Association for Computational Linguistics: Human Language Technologies*, pages 1362–1367, Denver, Colorado. Association for Computational Linguistics.

Stephen Roller, Michael Speriosu, Sarat Rallapalli, Benjamin Wing, and Jason Baldridge. 2012. Supervised text-based geolocation using language models on an adaptive grid. In *Proceedings of the 2012 Joint Conference on Empirical Methods in Natural Language Processing and Computational Natural Language Learning*, pages 1500–1510, Jeju Island, Korea. Association for Computational Linguistics.

Michael Speriosu and Jason Baldridge. 2013. Text-driven toponym resolution using indirect supervision. In *Proceedings of the 51st Annual Meeting of the Association for Computational Linguistics (Volume 1: Long Papers)*, pages 1466–1476, Sofia, Bulgaria. Association for Computational Linguistics.

Laura Tateosian, Rachael Guenter, Yi-Peng Yang, and Jean Ristaino. 2017. Tracking 19th century late blight from archival documents using text analytics and geoparsing. In *Free and open source software for geospatial (FOSS4G) conference proceedings*, volume 17, page 17.

Richard Tobin, Claire Grover, Kate Byrne, James Reid, and Jo Walsh. 2010. Evaluation of georeferencing. In *proceedings of the 6th workshop on geographic information retrieval*, pages 1–8.

Xiaobin Wang, Chunping Ma, Huafei Zheng, Chu Liu, Pengjun Xie, Linlin Li, and Luo Si. 2019. DM_NLP at SemEval-2018 task 12: A pipeline system for toponym resolution. In *Proceedings of the 13th International Workshop on Semantic Evaluation*, pages 917–923, Minneapolis, Minnesota, USA. Association for Computational Linguistics.

Thomas Wolf, Lysandre Debut, Victor Sanh, Julien Chaumond, Clement Delangue, Anthony Moi, Pierric Cistac, Tim Rault, Remi Louf, Morgan Funtowicz, Joe Davison, Sam Shleifer, Patrick von Platen, Clara Ma, Yacine Jernite, Julien Plu, Canwen Xu, Teven Le Scao, Sylvain Gugger, Mariama Drame, Quentin Lhoest, and Alexander Rush. 2020. Transformers: State-of-the-art natural language processing. In *Proceedings of the 2020 Conference on Empirical Methods in Natural Language Processing: System Demonstrations*, pages 38–45, Online. Association for Computational Linguistics.

Dongfang Xu, Zeyu Zhang, and Steven Bethard. 2020. A generate-and-rank framework with semantic type regularization for biomedical concept normalization. In *Proceedings of the 58th Annual Meeting of the Association for Computational Linguistics*, pages 8452–8464, Online. Association for Computational Linguistics.

Ikuya Yamada, Koki Washio, Hiroyuki Shindo, and Yuji Matsumoto. 2022. Global entity disambiguation with BERT. In *Proceedings of the 2022 Conference of the North American Chapter of the Association for Computational Linguistics: Human Language Technologies*, pages 3264–3271, Seattle, United States. Association for Computational Linguistics.

Wei Zhang and Judith Gelernter. 2014. Geocoding location expressions in twitter messages: A preference learning method. *Journal of Spatial Information Science*, 2014(9):37–70.

A Appendix

A.1 Performance by toponym type

Table A1 shows that without context, GeoNorm is most precise at resolving toponyms at the top of the hierarchy, like countries and states.

A.2 CamCoder details

The original CamCoder code, when querying GeoNames to construct its input population vector from location mentions in the context, assumes it has been given canonical names for those locations. Since canonical names are not known before locations have been resolved to entries in the ontology, we have CamCoder use mention strings instead of canonical names for querying GeoNames.

A.3 Model selection

We performed model selection on the development sets as shown in table A2. All GeoNorm models that included a reranker (R) outperformed the candidate generator (G) alone. We explored the population (P) and type (T) features in models without context, and found that they helped slightly on LGL and GeoWebNews but hurt slightly on TR-News. For models with context, rerankers fine-tuned from `bert-multilingual-uncased` (M) slightly outperformed models fined-tuned from `bert-base-uncased`. Adding sentence level context (C1/C3/C5) to the rerankers helped on TR-News, but did not help on LGL or GeoWebNews. Applying the two-stage algorithm for document-level context led to large gains on LGL and TR-News, but did not help on GeoWebNews.

We thus selected the following models for evaluation: GeoNorm G, GeoNorm GRPT, and GeoNorm GRPTMCD.

A.4 Artifact intended use and coverage

The intended use of `bert-base-uncased` and `bert-multilingual-uncased` is to be "fine-tuned on tasks that use the whole sentence"[6]. We have used them for that purpose when encoding the context, but also for the related task of encoding place names, which are usually short phrases. These artifacts are trained on English books and English Wikipedia and released under an Apache 2.0 license which is compatible with our use.

The intended use of our geocoding model is matching English place names in text to the GeoNames ontology. Though GeoNames covers millions of place names, our evaluation corpora cover only English news articles, and thus the performance we report is only predictive of performance in that domain.

[6] `https://huggingface.co/bert-base-uncased`

Dataset	Precision				Recall			
	Country	State	County	Other	Country	State	County	Other
LGL	0.968	0.806	0.829	0.745	0.893	0.915	0.739	0.763
GWN	1.000	0.765	0.778	0.752	0.966	0.591	1.000	0.810
TR-News	1.000	1.000	0.000	0.830	1.000	1.000	0.000	0.830

Table A1: Precision and recall of GeoNorm (without context) on three geocoding development sets.

	LGL (dev)				GeoWebNews (dev)				TR-News (dev)			
Model	Acc	A161	Err	AUC	Acc	A161	Err	AUC	Acc	A161	Err	AUC
GeoNorm G	.594	.671	201	.289	.644	.858	73	.165	.677	.735	187	.242
GeoNorm GR	.802	.819	64	.141	.865	.925	39.5	.072	**.897**	**.912**	64.0	.081
GeoNorm GRP	.792	.819	68	.141	.861	.918	34.7	.072	.868	.882	65.7	.100
GeoNorm GRT	.807	**.828**	61	.134	.865	.915	31.9	.073	**.897**	**.912**	**42.7**	**.074**
GeoNorm GRPT	.797	.821	**57**	.140	**.886**	**.940**	**29.8**	**.060**	.882	.897	63.5	.090
GeoNorm GRPTM	**.814**	**.828**	60	**.132**	.879	.922	43.2	.072	.882	.897	65.0	.092
GeoNorm GRPTC1	.807	.823	55	.132	.865	.915	39.3	.075	.882	.882	110	.109
GeoNorm GRPTC3	.807	.816	65	.142	.868	.918	40.3	.073	.882	.897	64.9	.092
GeoNorm GRPTC5	.802	.814	68	.145	.865	.911	42.8	.078	.897	.912	64.0	.081
GeoNorm GRPTMC1	.816	.831	62	.133	.872	**.940**	**23.5**	**.057**	.882	.897	64.6	.090
GeoNorm GRPTMC3	.809	.833	59	.129	.875	.922	35.4	.073	.912	.927	40.6	.063
GeoNorm GRPTMC5	.807	.823	61	.137	.872	**.940**	29.4	.060	.868	.882	72.6	.103
GeoNorm GRPTMCD	**.885**	**.897**	**29**	**.079**	**.879**	.925	31.0	.065	**.971**	**.985**	**6.8**	**.010**

Table A2: Performance on the development sets. Higher is better for accuracy (Acc) and accuracy@161km (A161). Lower is better for mean error (Err) and area under the error distances curve (AUC). The top score in each group is in bold, the second best score is underlined. Model features are indicated by the string of characters: G means the candidate generator was applied, R means a reranker was applied, P means the reranker included the population feature, T means the reranker included the type feature, M means the reranker was fine-tuned from `bert-multilingual-uncased` instead of `bert-base-uncased`, C1/C3/C5 means the reranker included 1/3/5 sentences of context, and CD means the reranker included the two-stage document-level context algorithm.

CRAPES:Cross-modal Annotation Projection for Visual Semantic Role Labeling

Abhidip Bhattacharyya and **Martha Palmer** and **Christoffer Heckman**
University of Colorado Boulder
firstname.lastname@colorado.edu

Abstract

Automatic image comprehension is an important yet challenging task that includes identifying actions in an image and corresponding action participants. Most current approaches to this task, now termed **G**rounded **S**ituation **R**ecognition (GSR), start by predicting a verb that describes the action and then predict the nouns that can participate in the action as arguments to the verb. This problem formulation limits each image to a single action even though several actions could be depicted. In contrast, text-based **S**emantic **R**ole **L**abeling (SRL) aims to label all actions in a sentence, typically resulting in at least two or three predicate argument structures per sentence. We hypothesize that expanding GSR to follow the more liberal SRL text-based approach to action and participant identification could improve image comprehension results. To test this hypothesis and to preserve generalization capabilities, we use general-purpose vision and language components as a front-end. This paper presents our results, a substantial 28.6 point jump in performance on the SWiG dataset, which confirm our hypothesis. We also discuss the benefits of loosely coupled broad-coverage off-the-shelf components which generalized well to out of domain images, and can decrease the need for manual image semantic role annotation.

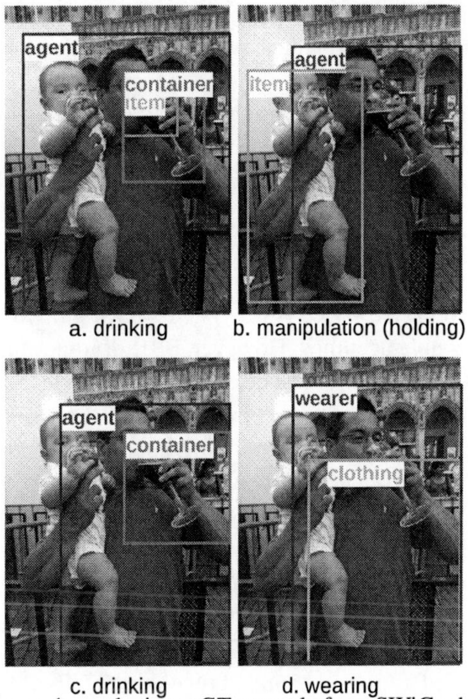

Figure 1: a. depicts a GT example from SWiG where the man is the agent of drinking. b., c., and d. show frames extracted by our method. Bounding boxes depict grounding and role annotation for each frame.

1 Introduction

Automatic image comprehension can positively contribute to many modern applications, such as description generation, cross-modal retrieval, and human-robot interaction. To comprehend an image it is important to identify the action(s) and participants in the action such asan agent (who is performing the action), a patient (who is being affected by the action), and an instrument. To address this problem (Yatskar et al., 2016b; Pratt et al., 2020) proposed the task of grounded situation recognition (GSR). Many approaches (Pratt et al., 2020; Cooray et al., 2020; Cho et al., 2021) have been proposed to perform the task of GSR. Most of these frameworks have two steps: in the first step verbs are predicted, and in the second step nouns and roles are predicted in an auto-regressive manner. Some other methods deployed include another layer to refine the quality of detection (Cho et al., 2021; Wei et al., 2021; Cheng et al., 2022).

One fundamental limitation of these models derives from the problem formulation. In the current formulation, verb frames would compete for an image, limiting the expressiveness of the image's semantic representation. In reality, various actions can co-exist in an image, even sharing participants. This limitation of one frame per image is imposed by the predominant dataset of GSR: the SWiG dataset (Pratt et al., 2020). For example, Fig-

*Proceedings of the The 12th Joint Conference on Lexical and Computational Semantics (*SEM 2023)*, pages 61–70
July 13-14, 2023 ©2023 Association for Computational Linguistics

ure 1a depicts a ground-truth (GT) annotation of an image from SWiG and has a GT annotation only with respect to a `drinking` frame. In fact, there are other frames, such as `holding, wearing`.

Semantic role labeling (SRL) of natural text, on the other hand, is a well researched problem in the domain of computational linguistics. Semantic role annotation, based on paradigms such as PropBank or Framenet (Palmer et al., 2005; Fillmore et al., 2003), is used to train semantic parsers that then convey knowledge about *who is doing what to whom, when* as predicate-argument structure labeling. In other words, given an action in a sentence, it identifies who is performing the action (the agent), who is affected by the action (the patient), what instrument is being used, etc. to comprehend the meaning of the sentence. Semantic roles of a sentence have the capability representing more than one predicate-argument structure for that sentence. Current text-based SRL systems have gained remarkable accuracy. However, SRL of images has yet to enjoy similar success.

We hypothesize that expanding GSR to follow the more liberal text-based SRL approach to action, participant identification could improve image comprehension results. Here, we propose a framework (CRAPES) with cross-modal *annotation projection* (AP) for visual semantic role labeling. AP is a well-known paradigm in text-based cross-lingual semantic role labeling (Kozhevnikov and Titov, 2013; Padó and Lapata, 2009; Akbik et al., 2015; Jindal et al., 2022) that has not been previously extended to cross-modal applications. Moreover, to preserve generalization capabilities, we focus on reusing general-purpose vision and language (V+L) components and text-based SRL components. This framework offers the following advantages over traditional GSR approaches:

- With our updated formulation of GSR, this framework can be trained to accommodate co-existing verb frames in an image. It can also be specialised to one verb frame per image.
- Additionally, image representations can be learned separately from the SRL task; in doing so, CRAPES can leverage advantages of large-scale multi-modal image representations.
- Success of text-based SRL systems trained on large, broad-coverage corpora of frames and roles, is helpful in widening its ability for detecting out-of-domain frames.
- Moreover the two modules can be trained separately, thereby decreasing the need for manual image semantic role annotation.
- As image representation and SRL are not tightly coupled, CRAPES can be extended to alternative semantic role labeling paradigms, such as FrameNet or PropBank.

2 Related Work

(Yatskar et al., 2016b) proposed the task of situation recognition (SR) together with an image situation recognition dataset (imSitu). Based on the architecture, methods for SR can be stratified into the following categories: 1) Conditional random field (*CRF*) (Yatskar et al., 2016b), 2) CRF-based model with data augmentation (*CRF+dataAug*) (Yatskar et al., 2016a), 3) RNN model with a VGG backbone for vision features (*VGG+RNN*) (Mallya and Lazebnik, 2017), 4) *graph based models* (Li et al., 2017; Suhail and Sigal, 2019), and 5) query based models such as *CAQ* (Cooray et al., 2020).

The idea of grounding nouns in the image was coined by (Pratt et al., 2020), thereby proposing the task of GSR and the SWiG dataset. A recurrent framework with ResNet-50 embedding was used to detect the verb and then the noun for each role. A RetinaNet backbone was used for object grounding. (Cooray et al., 2020; Cho et al., 2021) model visual SRL as query based vision reasoning. (Cooray et al., 2020) adopt a top-down attention model (Anderson et al., 2018) and deploy inter-dependent queries to model relations among semantic roles. (Cho et al., 2021) use a transformer encoder to classify verbs and to create image representations. Then the image representation was queried with the concatenation of roles and verbs. However, most of these aforementioned approaches use two-stage frameworks where in the first step the verb is predicted independently and then nouns and roles are predicted in an autoregressive manner depending on the verb. However, subsequent work (Cho et al., 2022; Wei et al., 2021) identified that this emphasis on the detection of the verb may confuse the prediction. Furthermore, verb miss-classification may result in miss-recognition of semantic roles.

Therefore, they adopted a three-stage framework. In the first two stages candidate verbs and nouns were detected. The third stage mostly refined the prediction. During the detection of the candidate, information flows either from verb to noun (Wei et al., 2021) or from noun to verb (Cho et al., 2022). This ignores the semantic dependency in the other

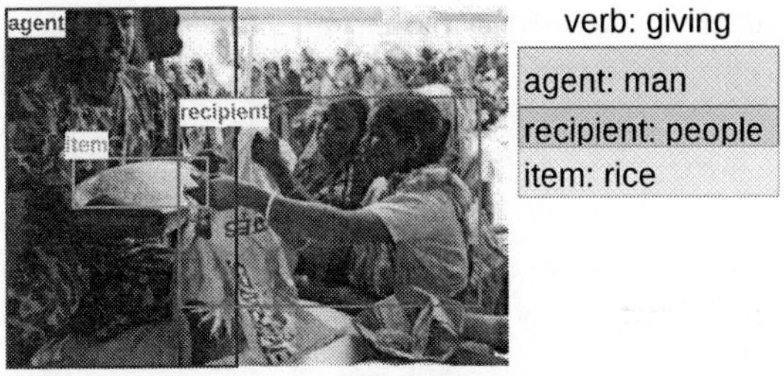

Figure 2: An example of GSR from the SWiG dataset.

direction. Moreover, this refinement can be done in only one iteration. (Cheng et al., 2022) solved these issues by designing an iterative method through message passing between verb and noun prediction modules. Recently, (Li et al., 2022) addressed the task of GSR, even though their main goal was to propose a pre-training schema using event based cross-modal alignment. All of these methods are limited to predicting one verb per image. None of these models acknowledge the existence of multiple actions and therefore multiple verb frames.

3 Approach

To detect semantic roles in images we adopted the idea of AP, as discussed above, from cross-lingual semantic role labeling in the text domain. In AP, auto-predicted semantic roles from source language is transferred to a target language using soft word alignments. Alignment is learned using large-scale parallel corpus. In the case of GSR we consider the image as our target domain.

3.1 Problem Formulation

Given an image $\mathcal{I}$ the task of GSR is to detect structured verb frame(s) $\mathcal{G} = \{v, \mathcal{R}_v\}$ where $v \in V$ is the action (verb) in the image. $\mathcal{R}_v = \{(r_v, n^r, b_v^r) | r_v \in \mathscr{R}_v, n^r \in \mathcal{N}, b_v^r \in \mathbb{R}^4\}$ where $\mathscr{R}_v = \{r_v^1, .., r_v^m\}$ set of semantic role types associated with the verb v. Therefore, each role is a triplet of a role type r_v, a noun label n^r and a bounding box (bbox), b_v^r that is grounded with respect to the v and the role of the noun n^r . For example in Figure 2 the given image is annotated with the verb "giving". The verb has role types *agent, recipient* and *item*. The nouns for these roles are `man`, `people` and `rice`, respectively.

Issues with current approaches. As discussed above in section 2, current methods (Pratt et al., 2020; Cho et al., 2021; Li et al., 2017) modeled this problem as:

$$\mathcal{P}(\mathcal{G}|\mathcal{I}) = \mathcal{P}(v|\mathcal{I})\mathcal{P}(\mathcal{R}_v|v, \mathcal{I}). \tag{1}$$

There are two complications with this kind of formulation: first, action prediction without knowledge of participants results in inaccurate verb prediction. Second, errors in verb prediction can adversely affect accuracy of noun and role prediction. To address this issue, recent methods (Wei et al., 2021; Cho et al., 2021) adopt a three stage framework. (Wei et al., 2021) formulated the problem as given in Equation 2:

$$\begin{aligned}\mathcal{P}(\mathcal{G}|\mathcal{I}) = \mathcal{P}(V_c|\mathcal{I})\mathcal{P}(\mathcal{R}_{\mathcal{V}_c}|V_C, \mathcal{I}) \\ \mathcal{P}(v, \mathcal{R}_v|V_C, \mathcal{R}_{\mathcal{V}_c}\mathcal{I}).\end{aligned} \tag{2}$$

In this formulation candidate verbs are detected first, then candidate nouns. In the final stage these candidates are used to refine the final result. (Cho et al., 2021) on the other hand, used candidate nouns to detect the verb and ultimately refined the frame predictions (Equation 3):

$$\begin{aligned}&\mathcal{P}(\mathcal{G}|\mathcal{I}) = \\ &\quad \mathcal{P}(\mathcal{N}_{\mathcal{V}_c}|\mathcal{I})\mathcal{P}(v|\mathcal{N}_{\mathcal{V}_c}, \mathcal{I})\mathcal{P}(v, \mathcal{R}_v|\mathcal{N}_{\mathcal{V}_c}, \mathcal{I}).\end{aligned} \tag{3}$$

Both the approaches used nouns to determine the verb at some point, ignoring the restrictions applied in the other direction. Moreover, even with these revised formulations, verbs compete with each other for a given image. On contrast, in a scene image more than one verb can coexist.

3.2 Methodology

To overcome the limitation imposed by the traditional formulation, we propose an alternative formulation given as:

$$\begin{aligned}\mathcal{P}(\mathcal{G}|\mathcal{I}) &= \sum_i \mathcal{P}(\mathcal{G}_i|\mathcal{I}) \\ &= \underbrace{\mathcal{P}(\mathcal{T}|\mathcal{I})}_{\text{V+L}} \underbrace{\sum_i \mathcal{P}(\mathcal{G}_i|\mathcal{T}, \mathcal{I})}_{\text{SRL}}\end{aligned}$$

To capture the complete essence of the intertwined relations of a verb and its roles, we use a V+L model which creates a text-based holistic representation $\mathcal{T}$ using self-attention. Text-based SRL then extracts all possible predicate-argument structures. The soft alignments from the V+L model is used to project the SRL back to the image (Figure 3). To

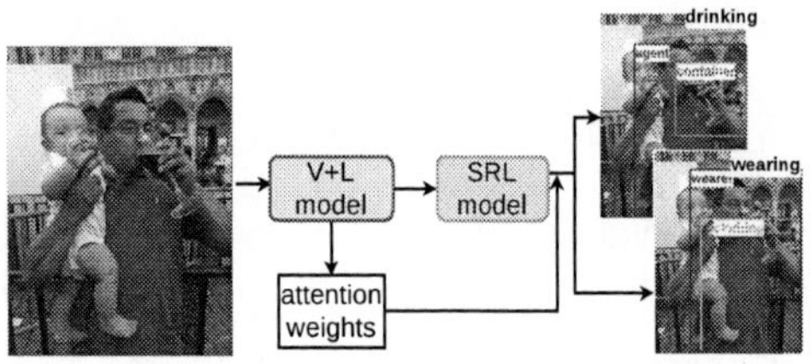

Figure 3: Our overall framework. 1. The V+L model projects the image into the text domain. The SRL annotator detects the semantic roles and the action. Attention from the V+L model is used to align semantic roles

preserve generalization capabilities, we used off-the-shelf general-purpose V+L components and a text based SRL system. Being trained on data outside the SWiG dataset, this framework has more potential to detect out-of-domain frames.

3.3 Pipeline

Our framework has two modules: 1) V+L model, and 2) text-based SRL system. (refer to Figure 3)

V+L. We chose Oscar (Li et al., 2020; Zhang et al., 2021) to this end. Oscar is a transformer based architecture that learns generic image-text representations for V+L understanding and generation tasks. Typically Oscar model would take three inputs- word tokens, object labels and object features. One of the novelties of Oscar lies in the notion of the 'view' of the data during pre-training. In a dictionary view elements from similar semantic spaces are considered together (words and object labels). On the other hand, in the modality view elements from the same modality are considered together. We trained Oscar with image region features $\mathcal{I} = \{(\varsigma_i, l_i) | \varsigma_i \in \mathbb{R}^d \; l_i \in \Sigma \; d = 2056\}$. We used (Zhang et al., 2021) to extract 2048 dimensional image region features and then concatenated with 6 positional features for the region (normalised coordinates of bounding boxes, height, width). Σ denotes the vocabulary for the language model. For the purpose of CRAPES, two separate models of Oscar are trained on the Flickr30k and the SWiG datasets, see Table 1. During inference the captions generated by Oscar are passed to the SRL module.

SRL. We experimented with two text based FrameNet SRL systems. For a given sentence T consisting of tokens $< t_1, t_2, .., t_k >$ a typical SRL system produces collections of verbs and their roles. Briefly $T_{srl} = \{(v, \mathcal{R}_v^T)\}$ where $\mathcal{R}_v^T$ is set of semantic roles given the verb v. It is a collection of tuples of the form $\{(r_v^i, (s_v^i, e_v^i))\}$ where $r_v^i \in \mathscr{R}_v$ is the semantic role and (s_v^i, e_v^i) marks the start and end indices of the phrase spanned by the role. For our experimentation we used an off the shelf annotator span-finder (Xia et al., 2021) for FrameNet annotation. We trained a second SRL consisting of BERT-base model with CRF at the top layer, on SWiG frames (see Table 1).

Cross-modal Annotation Projection. Our SRL system detects the semantic roles and the nouns from the text given by the V+L model. For grounding the roles to image bboxes we used attention weights from the V+L model. For each role span, corresponding cross-modal attention is retrieved from the V+L model. Attention is aggregated over all the tokens in the span:

$$\text{role}(\text{bbox}_j) = r_v^t, \text{ where}$$
$$j = \arg\max(\alpha_i) \text{ and } \alpha_i = \sum_{l,h} \alpha_{l,h}(i, s_v^t, e_v^t),$$

where l and h are spans over number of attention layers and head accordingly.

4 Experiments

4.1 Experimental Set up

Data Preparation. We experimented with SWiG (Pratt et al., 2020). SwiG provides FrameNet semantic role labeling of images. The SwiG dataset provides grounding for all visible semantic roles in terms of image bboxes. SWiG contains 126102 images with 504 verbs and 190 semantic role types, and each verb is accompanied by 1 to 6 semantic roles. The official splits are $75K/25K/25K$ images for training, dev, and test set, respectively. Unlike Flickr30k, this dataset does not have any textual image descriptions.

Data augmentation. Figure 4 presents an overview of data flow during training. To train CRAPES with SWiG, we created templates for each verb frame using roles. For each image, the corresponding verb frame and template are retrieved. Roles in the template were replaced with the corresponding noun values from the annotation of the image to generate the sentence. This sentence along with the image is used to train the V+L model, and the sentence with the roles is used to train the BERT+CRF SRL model.

Evaluation Metric. We used the following metric (Pratt et al., 2020) to report our results. 1)

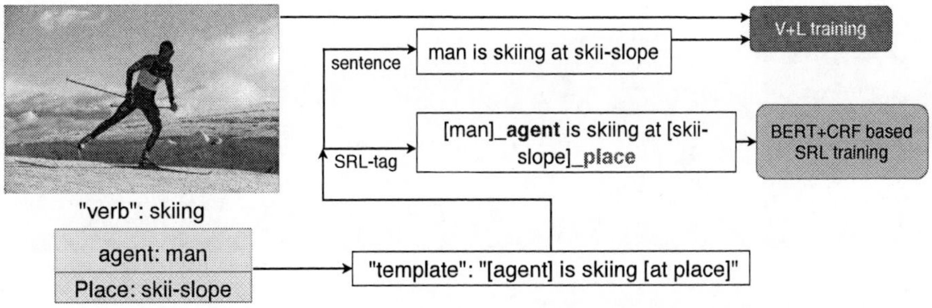

Figure 4: Training pipeline of CRAPES for the SWiG dataset. SWiG images are not accompanied by sentences. Using the ground truth (GT) frames, template sentences are created. The image and sentence pair is used to train the V+L model. Sentence and frames are used to train the BERT+CRF srl model

Model	Description	Annotation
CRAPES$_1$	Oscar with flickr, LOME framenet	FN
CRAPES$_2$	Oscar with SWiG, BERT+CRF on SWiG	FN

Table 1: Different versions of CRAPES based on training data of V+L and different SRL models. In last column FN stands for Framenet.

`verb`: the accuracy of verb prediction; 2) `value`: accuracy of noun prediction for individual roles; 3) `value-all`: accuracy of the prediction of nouns for the whole role set; 4) `grounded-value (grnd)`: accuracy of noun prediction with correct grounding (bboxes) for individual semantic roles; 5) `grounded-value-all (grnd-all)`: accuracy of noun prediction with correct grounding (bboxes) for the whole role set.

Implementation Details. We used the pre-trained Oscar base model ($H = 768$) fine-tuned for caption generation. This model was trained on the MSCOCO dataset (Lin et al., 2014). We trained two separate versions of Oscar with the Flickr30k train (Young et al., 2014) and SWiG dev datasets with an AdamW Optimizer (Loshchilov and Hutter, 2019) for 20 epochs with learning rate 3×10^{-5}. We trained the text-based BERT+CRF SRL system on the template generated sentences of the train split of the SWiG dataset.

4.2 Quantitative Results

A quantitative comparison with recent approaches on the SWiG benchmark based on both SR and GSR is presented in Table 2, using the categorization from section 2. We report our results on SWiG with the top-1 set up. CRAPES leads in the `value`, `value-all`, and `grnd` metrics. CRAPES has a dramatic absolute gain of 28.6 points and relative gain of 76% in `value` with respect to GSRFormer, the previous SOTA. Similarly, in `val-all` and `grnd` it has a relative gain of 31% and 15% accordingly. Oscar pretraining tasks (Li et al., 2020) have a major role in these improvements. As discussed in subsection 3.3 Oscar pretraining tasks were designed around two major views on how to use object labels. The first view considered object labels as members of text modality where as the second one considered them as part of the image modality. This form of training enables OSCAR to include object labels in the generated description. These object-labels contribute toward the noun prediction task in GSR. Moreover, OSCAR fine-tuned with template generated sentences is able to replicate similar structures during inference. Similarly, our BERT+CRF based SRL parser, trained on a similar domain of sentences, is able to annotate them with semantic roles. So Table 2 *firmly supports our hypotheses about the benefits of reusing general-purpose V+L components.* However, there are still certain image-verb frame combinations that confuse our system. We discuss this in our qualitative analysis.

4.3 Discussion

Table 1 lists different versions of CRAPES. Table 3 presents performance of CRAPES on FrameNet annotation. From Table 3 apparently the performance of CRAPES$_1$ is poor. However, this version of CRAPES actually gave atomic frames and parallel frames for a given image. Because of Oscar being trained on human generated sentences and the LOME parser being trained on text corpora for FrameNet, CRAPES$_1$ is able to predict out-of-domain verbs and frames. The current metrics can not reflect this capability adequately. Fig-

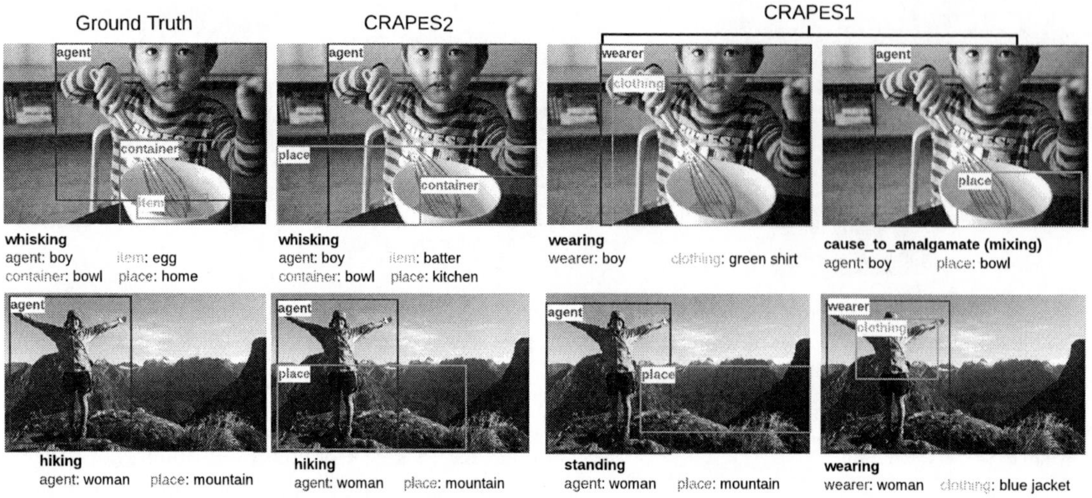

Figure 5: Examples of predictions made by CRAPES. The first column lists the GT image and frame from the SWiG test set. The second column lists the prediction from CRAPES$_2$ (V+L and SRL parser trained on SWiG). Last two columns depicts parallel frames detected by CRAPES$_1$ (V+L trained on Flickr30k and LOME parser)

Model	**value**	**val-all**	**verb**	**grnd**	**grnd-all**
situation recognition					
CRF (Yatskar et al., 2016b)	24.6	14.2	32.3	–	–
CRF+dataAug (Yatskar et al., 2016a)	26.45	15.51	34.12	–	–
VGG+RNN (Mallya and Lazebnik, 2017)	27.45	16.36	35.90	–	–
FC-Graph (Li et al., 2017)	27.52	19.25	36.72	–	–
CAQ (Cooray et al., 2020)	30.23	18.47	38.19	–	–
Kernel-Graph (Suhail and Sigal, 2019)	35.41	19.38	43.27	–	–
grounded situation recognition					
ISL (Pratt et al., 2020)	30.09	18.62	39.36	22.73	7.72
JSL (Pratt et al., 2020)	31.44	18.87	39.94	24.86	9.66
GSRTR (Cho et al., 2021)	32.52	19.63	41.06	26.04	10.44
SituFormer (Wei et al., 2021)	35.24	21.86	44.20	29.22	13.41
CoFormer (Cho et al., 2022)	35.98	22.22	44.66	29.05	12.21
CLIP Event (Li et al., 2022)	33.1	20.1	45.6	26.1	10.6
GSRFormer (Cheng et al., 2022)	37.48	23.32	46.53	31.53	14.23
CRAPES$_2$	**66.08**	**30.64**	41.86	**36.73**	6.47

Table 2: Performance (%) of state-of-the-art GSR methods on the SWiG dataset test set based on top-1 verb.

Model	**value**	**val-all**	**verb**	**grnd**	**grnd-all**
CRAPES$_1$	18.12	0.357	5.72	14.33	0.63
CRAPES$_2$	65.98	30.53	41.86	35.13	5.78
+union of BBoxes	65.98	30.53	41.86	35.13	6.1
attention from lower4 layer	66.08	30.64	41.86	36.31	6.47

Table 3: Performance (%) of SWiG test set with different combinations of V+L and Framenet parsers

Model	**grnd**	**grnd-all**
attention from top 3 layer	35.13	5.78
+ include union of boxes	35.87	6.10
attention from $5-8$ layer	36.31	6.26
attention from all layer	36.35	6.31
attention from layer $1-4$	36.73	6.47

Table 4: Affect of attention layers on bbox grounding reported on SWiG test set

ure 5 demonstrates examples of the frames predicted by CRAPES. Frames like `wearing` and `cause-to-amalgamate` (first row of Figure 5), will be considered as misclassifications by the current metrics with respect to GT.

However, CRAPES lags in terms of grounded-value-all. Note that this metric required that all bboxes be annotated correctly with nouns from

GT verb	Competing verbs in CRAPES_2
retraining	arresting, detaining, subduing, handcuffing
hunting	pouncing, shooting, chasing, attacking
teaching	lecturing, educating, helping, preaching
cooking	frying, baking, chopping, stirring, scooping
filming	videotaping, photographing, recording, carrying
raking	hoeing, shoveling, clearing, sweeping
tying	lacing, stitching, adjusting, stapling
watering	sprinkling, moistening, gardening, spraying, wetting

(a) Examples of verb confusions by CRAPES_2

GT verb	Co-existing verbs in CRAPES_1
cooking	wearing, cause-to-amalgamate, cutting, standing
baking	wearing, cause-to-amalgamate, cutting, measure_volume
teaching	wearing, standing, sitting, reading, writing, speaking
lecturing	wearing, standing, sitting, reading, talking
arresting	walking, arresting, striking, law_enforcement_agency, hostile_encounter
detaining	walking, arresting, striking, law_enforcement_agency, attacking

(b) Examples of verb co-existence detection by CRAPES_1

Table 5: Comparison between frame competitions and frame co-existance

the GT annotation. Therefore missing one bbox annotation can affect the metric for an image significantly. One possible reason for the poor performance could be the distribution shift between the V + L model and the SRL model. Another source of error is a limitation of the interpretability of the attention weights. To align bounding boxes with SRL we used attention between bboxes and words from Oscar attention layers. In our experiment we noticed that the 5th head from layers 5 and 6 mostly attended to bboxes. However, to our surprise, it did not provide much improvement. Attention from the lower 4 layers gave us the best result, meriting further investigation. Table 4 shows experimental results of using alignment from different attention layers.

4.4 Qualitative Results

One of the main advantages of CRAPES is that it can predict out-of-domain frames that are otherwise not present in the SWiG dataset. Figure 1 depicts one such example from SWiG where the GT annotation contains only the frame for '`drinking`'. CRAPES_1 detects the action '`drinking`' along with two other frames '`holding`' and '`wearing`'. These frames are not only missing in the GT image, they were not listed in the vocabulary of the SWiG dataset. The LOME FrameNet parser, trained on the FrameNet v1.7 corpus, a huge text base corpus for SRL, enables CRAPES_1 to detect those frames. Moreover, CRAPES can accommodate coexisting verb frames. This is because Oscar, being trained on Flickr30k sentences, learned to create holistic representations of the image. Similar examples can be found in the last two columns of Figure 5 where CRAPES_1 provides parallel frames, not present in the GT annotation. *This shows the efficacy of our reformulation of the GSR and the advantage of reusing general-purpose SRL systems.*

For the sake of bench-marking we trained CRAPES_2 with template generated sentences from the SWiG dataset. Predictions made by CRAPES_2 contained one frame per image as desired by the SWiG dataset. This demonstrates the flexibility of the overall framework. The second column of Figure 5 depicts some example predictions by CRAPES_2.

CRAPES does commit mistakes which can be categorized mainly into three types: 1) *the predicted verb is different than GT*. Figures`6a,b` depict two examples from the SWiG dataset where CRAPES detected a different frame. These are indeed very plausible mistakes. Table 5a shows examples of some GT verbs along with a list of verbs that CRAPES_2 confused with the GT verb. This fact is supported by CRAPES_1 as well. Table 5b lists examples of parallel verb frames detected by CRAPES_1 for GT images with a given verb. For example *cooking* is often confused with `baking`(Table 5a). From Table 5b it can be observed that both of these verbs have similar co-existing frames like `cutting`, `cause-to-amalgamate`. Similar phenomena can be noticed for *arresting* and *detaining*; 2) *predicted noun for a role is different than GT*. In the first image of column CRAPES_2 from Figure 5,the noun for role *item* is predicted as *batter*. 3) *grounded bbox for a noun is different than GT*. In Figure 6c the action `jogging` is attributed to a different bbox in the image. Mistakes made by CRAPES are reasonable, relevant and plausible. For these examples, predictions are different than the GT but still

Figure 6: Reasonable mistakes made by CRAPES. For each image left column shows GT annotations and right column depicts mistakes made by CRAPES$_2$. For a, b, c prediction of CRAPES$_2$ can not be classified as wrong. For d CRAPES$_2$ struggled to detect correct bbox.

Figure 7: Parallel frames detected by CRAPES in Flickr30k images using PropBank style role labeling.

relevant to the given image. However, sometimes CRAPES struggles to ground the roles (Figure 6d).

5 Future work

Current GSR models cannot go beyond the SWiG dataset. Moreover predicted semantic roles are restricted to follow a particular paradigm of SRL. On the contrary, having independent V+L enables CRAPES to work on other image datasets. In addition, having a separate SRL module enables extension to other SRL paradigms. We performed preliminary experiments on the Flickr30k dataset with PropBank (Palmer et al., 2005) annotation. Figure 7 depicts one such example. We would like to extend our experiments to the version of Flickr30k used in (Bhattacharyya et al., 2022). However, our preliminary experiments suggest that experiments with Flickr30k are more challenging for several reasons.

- Flickr30k does not provide semantic roles for images. Therefore, we need to follow a similar approach to (Bhattacharyya et al., 2022) in creating silver standard data.
- The silver standard data will have multiple frames for an image. Current metrics of GSR presuppose one GT frame per image.
- Flickr30k images are general scene images with many agents,objects and actions, whereas images in SWiG focus mostly on one salient action and a small number of participants.
- As pointed out by (Bhattacharyya et al., 2022), PropBank annotation of Flickr30k has abstract conceptual roles such as temporal, direction, manner, purpose, etc. denoted with `ArgM-`. It is hard to learn concrete representations for these roles, let alone ground them in an image.

Our formulation of CRAPES can accommodate PropBank SRL experiments on Flickr30k. However, a more rigorous study with human evaluation is required to correctly measure the potential of CRAPES. Therefore, this a critical future direction for us. It requires a new dataset with images annotated with more than one frame. One choice is to extend the SWiG dataset to accommodate more than one frame per image. Another choice is to enhance the current Flickr30k annotation. Ideally we would do both. However, the current proposed evaluation metrics for GSR are incompatible wih a multi-frame scenario. More robust and appropriate evaluation metrics also need to be developed.

6 Conclusion

In this paper we identified a fundamental issue in the problem formulation of the GSR task. The current formulation limits an image to a single verb frame. We propose an alternate formulation allowing for multiple actions as implemented in **Cr**oss-modal **A**nnotation **P**rojection for Visual **S**emantic Role Labeling (CRAPES). A V+L model trained on image-text parallel corpora and an SRL module trained independently on text corpora allow the model to integrate domain-specific knowledge with out-of-domain knowledge, which dramatically improves over the SOTA by 28.6 points. In addition, CRAPES can accommodate co-existing verb frames for an image (CRAPES_1) yet can also be trained to select only one verb frame for a given image (CRAPES_2). Moreover, inter module independence allows CRAPES to extend its labeling to alternative paradigms of SRL (such as FrameNet or PropBank). However one major area for improvement is `grnd-all`, that requires better semantic comprehension and guidance of attention weights produced by the V+L module. Therefore, improving on `grnd-all` along with Flickr30k and PropBank will be our next endeavour. We will also explore extending datasets to have multiple ground truth frames per image and more appropriate evaluation metrics for reporting results on those datasets.

7 Acknowledgements

We gratefully acknowledge the support of DARPA KAIROS Program No. FA8750-19-2-1004. Any opinions, findings, conclusions, or recommendations expressed in this material are those of the authors and do not necessarily reflect the views of DARPA or the U.S. government.

References

Alan Akbik, Laura Chiticariu, Marina Danilevsky, Yunyao Li, Shivakumar Vaithyanathan, and Huaiyu Zhu. 2015. Generating high quality proposition Banks for multilingual semantic role labeling. In *Proceedings of the 53rd Annual Meeting of the Association for Computational Linguistics and the 7th International Joint Conference on Natural Language Processing (Volume 1: Long Papers)*, pages 397–407, Beijing, China. Association for Computational Linguistics.

Peter Anderson, Xiaodong He, Chris Buehler, Damien Teney, Mark Johnson, Stephen Gould, and Lei Zhang. 2018. Bottom-up and top-down attention for image captioning and visual question answering.

Abhidip Bhattacharyya, Cecilia Mauceri, Martha Palmer, and Christoffer Heckman. 2022. Aligning images and text with semantic role labels for fine-grained cross-modal understanding. In *Proceedings of the Thirteenth Language Resources and Evaluation Conference*, pages 4944–4954, Marseille, France. European Language Resources Association.

Zhi-Qi Cheng, Qi Dai, Siyao Li, Teruko Mitamura, and Alexander Hauptmann. 2022. Gsrformer: Grounded situation recognition transformer with alternate semantic attention refinement. In *Proceedings of the 30th ACM International Conference on Multimedia*, MM '22, page 3272–3281, New York, NY, USA. Association for Computing Machinery.

Junhyeong Cho, Youngseok Yoon, and Suha Kwak. 2022. Collaborative transformers for grounded situation recognition. In *Proceedings of the IEEE/CVF Conference on Computer Vision and Pattern Recognition (CVPR)*.

Junhyeong Cho, Youngseok Yoon, Hyeonjun Lee, and Suha Kwak. 2021. Grounded situation recognition with transformers. In *British Machine Vision Conference (BMVC)*.

Thilini Cooray, Ngai-Man Cheung, and Wei Lu. 2020. Attention-based context aware reasoning for situation recognition. In *2020 IEEE/CVF Conference on Computer Vision and Pattern Recognition (CVPR)*, pages 4735–4744.

Charles Fillmore, Christopher Johnson, and Miriam Petruck. 2003. Background to framenet. *International Journal of Lexicography*, 16.

Ishan Jindal, Alexandre Rademaker, Michał Ulewicz, Ha Linh, Huyen Nguyen, Khoi-Nguyen Tran, Huaiyu Zhu, and Yunyao Li. 2022. Universal proposition bank 2.0. In *Proceedings of the Language Resources and Evaluation Conference*, pages 1700–1711, Marseille, France. European Language Resources Association.

Mikhail Kozhevnikov and Ivan Titov. 2013. Cross-lingual transfer of semantic role labeling models. In *Proceedings of the 51st Annual Meeting of the Association for Computational Linguistics (Volume 1: Long Papers)*, pages 1190–1200, Sofia, Bulgaria. Association for Computational Linguistics.

Manling Li, Ruochen Xu, Shuohang Wang, Luowei Zhou, Xudong Lin, Chenguang Zhu, Michael Zeng, Heng Ji, and Shih-Fu Chang. 2022. Clip-event: Connecting text and images with event structures. In *Proceedings of the IEEE/CVF Conference on Computer Vision and Pattern Recognition*, pages 16420–16429.

R. Li, M. Tapaswi, R. Liao, J. Jia, R. Urtasun, and S. Fidler. 2017. Situation recognition with graph neural networks. In *2017 IEEE International Conference on Computer Vision (ICCV)*, pages 4183–4192, Los Alamitos, CA, USA. IEEE Computer Society.

Xiujun Li, Xi Yin, Chunyuan Li, Xiaowei Hu, Pengchuan Zhang, Lei Zhang, Lijuan Wang, Houdong Hu, Li Dong, Furu Wei, Yejin Choi, and Jianfeng Gao. 2020. Oscar: Object-semantics aligned pre-training for vision-language tasks. *ECCV 2020*.

Tsung-Yi Lin, Michael Maire, Serge Belongie, James Hays, Pietro Perona, Deva Ramanan, Piotr Dollár, and C. Lawrence Zitnick. 2014. Microsoft COCO: Common objects in context.

Ilya Loshchilov and Frank Hutter. 2019. Decoupled weight decay regularization. In *International Conference on Learning Representations*.

Arun Mallya and Svetlana Lazebnik. 2017. Recurrent models for situation recognition. In *Proceedings - 2017 IEEE International Conference on Computer Vision, ICCV 2017*, Proceedings of the IEEE International Conference on Computer Vision, pages 455–463, United States. Institute of Electrical and Electronics Engineers Inc. Funding Information: This work was partially supported by the National Science Foundation under Grants CIF-1302438 and IIS-1563727, Xerox UAC, the Sloan Foundation, and a Google Research Award Publisher Copyright: © 2017 IEEE.; 16th IEEE International Conference on Computer Vision, ICCV 2017 ; Conference date: 22-10-2017 Through 29-10-2017.

Sebastian Padó and Mirella Lapata. 2009. Cross-lingual annotation projection of semantic roles. *J. Artif. Int. Res.*, 36(1):307–340.

Martha Palmer, Daniel Gildea, and Paul Kingsbury. 2005. The proposition bank: An annotated corpus of semantic roles. 31(1):71–106.

Sarah Pratt, Mark Yatskar, Luca Weihs, Ali Farhadi, and Aniruddha Kembhavi. 2020. Grounded situation recognition. *ArXiv*, abs/2003.12058.

Mohammed Suhail and Leonid Sigal. 2019. Mixture-kernel graph attention network for situation recognition. In *2019 IEEE/CVF International Conference on Computer Vision (ICCV)*, pages 10362–10371.

Meng Wei, Long Chen, Wei Ji, Xiaoyu Yue, and Tat-Seng Chua. 2021. Rethinking the two-stage framework for grounded situation recognition. *arXiv preprint arXiv:2112.05375*.

Patrick Xia, Guanghui Qin, Siddharth Vashishtha, Yunmo Chen, Tongfei Chen, Chandler May, Craig Harman, Kyle Rawlins, Aaron Steven White, and Benjamin Van Durme. 2021. LOME: Large ontology multilingual extraction. In *Proceedings of the 16th Conference of the European Chapter of the Association for Computational Linguistics: System Demonstrations*, pages 149–159.

Mark Yatskar, Vicente Ordonez, Luke Zettlemoyer, and Ali Farhadi. 2016a. Commonly uncommon: Semantic sparsity in situation recognition. *2017 IEEE Conference on Computer Vision and Pattern Recognition (CVPR)*, pages 6335–6344.

Mark Yatskar, Luke Zettlemoyer, and Ali Farhadi. 2016b. Situation recognition: Visual semantic role labeling for image understanding. In *2016 IEEE Conference on Computer Vision and Pattern Recognition (CVPR)*, pages 5534–5542.

Peter Young, Alice Lai, Micah Hodosh, and Julia Hockenmaier. 2014. From image descriptions to visual denotations: New similarity metrics for semantic inference over event descriptions. 2:67–78.

Pengchuan Zhang, Xiujun Li, Xiaowei Hu, Jianwei Yang, Lei Zhang, Lijuan Wang, Yejin Choi, and Jianfeng Gao. 2021. Vinvl: Making visual representations matter in vision-language models. *CVPR 2021*.

Not All Counterhate Tweets Elicit the Same Replies: A Fine-Grained Analysis

Abdullah Albanyan,[θ] **Ahmed Hassan,**[υ] and **Eduardo Blanco**[ϒ]
[θ]College of Computer Engineering and Sciences, Prince Sattam Bin Abdulaziz University
[υ]Department of Communication and Information Engineering, Zewail City University
[ϒ]Department of Computer Science, University of Arizona
a.albanyan@psau.edu.sa s-ahmed_hassan@zewailcity.edu.eg eduardoblanco@arizona.edu

Abstract

Counterhate arguments can effectively fight and limit the spread of hate speech. However, they can also exacerbate the hate, as some people may respond with aggression if they feel threatened or targeted by the counterhate. In this paper, we investigate replies to counterhate arguments beyond whether the reply agrees or disagrees with the counterhate argument. We present a corpus with 2,621 replies to counterhate arguments countering hateful tweets, and annotate them with fine-grained characteristics. We show that (a) half of the replies (51%) to the counterhate arguments disagree with the argument, and (b) this kind of reply often supports the hateful tweet (40%). We also analyze the language of counterhate arguments that elicit certain types of replies. Experimental results show that it is feasible to anticipate the kind of replies a counterhate argument will elicit.

1 Introduction

Hate messages and offensive language are commonplace in social media platforms. Twitter reported that more than 1.1 million accounts spread hateful content in the second half of 2020, a 77% increase with respect to the first half of the same year.[1] In a recent survey of 10,093 adults in the U.S., 41% of participants reported online harassment on a personal level, and almost two-thirds of adults under the age of 30 reported experiencing internet harassment (Vogels, 2021). These figures, alongside other surveys,[2,3] demonstrate the prevalence of hate speech on the internet. To address this problem, the European Commission partnered with popular social media platforms to announce a "Code of conduct on countering illegal hate speech online" (European Commission, 2019), which contains several commitments to prevent the spread of online hate speech across Europe.

[1]https://time.com/6080324/twitter-hate-speech-penalties/
[2]https://legalresearch.elsa.org/library/ohs/
[3]https://rm.coe.int/1680700016

The enormous amount of daily data makes these platforms rely on users who manually flag hateful content (Crawford and Gillespie, 2016). This approach requires spending millions of dollars yearly on manual hate speech verification and moderation (Seetharaman, 2018). An alternative is to automatically fight hate speech by using hate speech classifiers (Section 2). However, removing users' content—as effective as it may be—restricts free speech. According to the Pew Research Center (Duggan, 2017), "Despite this broad concern over online harassment, 45% of Americans say it is more important to let people speak their minds freely online, and 53% feel that it is more important for people to feel welcome and safe online."

A complementary strategy to address hateful content that does not interfere with free speech is to counter the hate with counterhate arguments in order to divert the discourse away from hate. Counterhate arguments can effectively fight and limit the spread of hate speech without removing or blocking any content (Gagliardone et al., 2015; Schieb and Preuss, 2016). Counterhate arguments usually are positive arguments that oppose hate speech with logic and facts. However well-intentioned, counterhate arguments may worsen the situation, as some people may respond with aggression if they feel threatened or targeted by the argument (Rains, 2013; Clayton et al., 2019).

Upon these motivations, we study the kind of replies counterhate arguments elicit. Specifically, we investigate replies to counterhate arguments beyond whether the reply agrees or disagrees with the counterhate argument. We consider Twitter threads consisting of (a) a hateful tweet, (b) a counterhate tweet countering (a), and (c) all replies to the counterhate tweet. We define a hateful tweet as any tweet that contains abusive language directed to individuals or groups of people. On the other hand, a counterhate tweet is a response tweet that explicitly or implicitly disagrees with the hateful

*Proceedings of the The 12th Joint Conference on Lexical and Computational Semantics (*SEM 2023)*, pages 71–88
July 13-14, 2023 ©2023 Association for Computational Linguistics

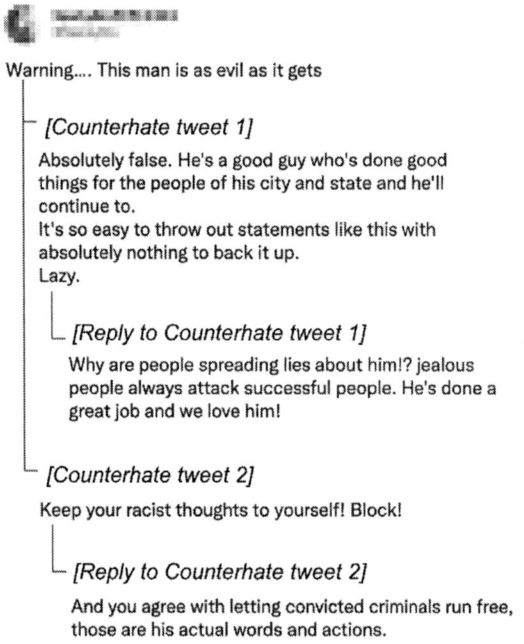

Figure 1: Twitter thread originating with a hateful tweet. This paper investigates the replies to counterhate tweets. In the first example, the reply not only agrees with the counterhate tweet, but also adds additional counterhate. On the other hand, the second reply not only disagrees with the counterhate tweet, but also shows support for the hateful tweet.

tweet. A reply is any response to the counterhate tweet. Consider the example in Figure 1. The hateful tweet contains hateful content towards a man (shown in a picture in the original tweet). The reply to the first counterhate tweet not only agrees with the counterhate tweet, but also includes additional counterhate arguments (e.g., *he's done a great job*). Conversely, the reply to the second counterhate tweet not only disagrees with the counterhate tweet, but also includes an opinion supporting the hateful tweet (i.e., *And you agree with letting convicted criminals run free*). While the author of the second counterhate tweet may have had good intentions, the tweet elicited more hate and made the discourse undesirable. This paper presents a fine-grained characterization of replies to counterhate tweets and opens the door to forecasting which counterhate tweets may elicit more hate instead of alleviating the spread of hate.

In summary, the main contributions of this paper are:[4] (a) a corpus with 2,621 (hateful tweet, counterhate tweet, reply) triples annotated with fine-grained characteristics (whether the reply agrees with the counterhate tweet, supports the hateful tweet, attacks the author of the counterhate tweet, or adds additional counterhate); (b) linguistic analysis of the counterhate tweets depending on our fine-grained characterization of the replies they elicit; (c) experimental results showing it is feasible to anticipate the kind of replies a counterhate tweet will elicit, and modest improvements using data augmentation and blending related datasets; and (d) qualitative analysis revealing when it is harder to perform any of the four classification tasks.

[4]https://github.com/albanyan/counterhate_reply

2 Previous Work

Recently, considerable literature has grown around identifying hateful content in user-generated content (Fortuna and Nunes, 2018). Existing research has created a variety of datasets to detect hate speech from several sources, including Twitter (Waseem and Hovy, 2016; Davidson et al., 2017), Reddit (Qian et al., 2019), Fox News (Gao and Huang, 2017), Yahoo! (Nobata et al., 2016; Djuric et al., 2015), and Gab (Mathew et al., 2021). Other studies have worked on identifying the target of hate, including whether the hateful content was directed toward a group, a person, or an object (Basile et al., 2019; Zampieri et al., 2019a; Ousidhoum et al., 2019). Another area of research aims to explore the role of context in hate and counterhate speech detection (Yu et al., 2022).

Previous efforts also detect and generate counterhate content. For counterhate detection, Garland et al. (2020) work with hateful and counterhate German tweets from two well-known groups. Mathew et al. (2020) collect and analyze pairs of hateful tweets and replies using the hate speech template *I hate <group>*, and detect whether a reply to a hateful tweet is a counterhate reply or not. In addition to analyzing or detecting counterhate replies, Albanyan and Blanco (2022) identify four fine-grained aspects of the relationship between a hateful tweet and a reply (e.g., whether the reply counters the hateful tweet with a justification). For counterhate generation, some studies have worked on collecting datasets with the help of crowd workers (Qian et al., 2019) or trained operators (Fanton et al., 2021; Chung et al., 2019).

There are several attempts to predict whether content will lead to additional hateful content. Zhang et al. (2018) identify whether a reply will result in a personal attack. Liu et al. (2018) predict the number of hateful comments that an instgram post would receive. On the other hand, there are few efforts on investigating the impact of counterhate content, as stated in a recent survey by Alsagheer et al. (2022). Mathew et al. (2019) analyze YouTube comments and found that counterhate comments received more likes and interactions than non-counterhate comments. Other studies found that there is a positive association between counterhate efficiency and both its author's ethnicity (Munger, 2017) and how immediate the response to the hateful content is posted (Schieb and Preuss, 2018). Finally, Garland et al. (2022) analyze hateful and counterhate German tweets and find that organized counterhate tweets elicit more counterhate replies and decrease the severity of the hate speech. Unlike these previous studies, we consider Twitter threads consisting of hateful tweets, a counterhate argument, and *all* replies to the counterhate argument. To our knowledge, we are the first to analyze the replies with fine-grained characteristics and tackle the problem of forecasting what kind of replies a counterhate arguments will elicit.

3 Dataset Collection and Annotation

We start our study by collecting triples consisting of hateful tweets, counterhate tweets, and replies to counterhate tweets. Then, we annotate the triples with our fine-grained characterization of the replies to the counterhate tweets. Unlike previous works (Section 2), our corpus enables us to (a) investigate whether counterhate tweets are successful at stopping the hate (Section 4), (b) analyze the language people use in counterhate tweets depending on the replies they elicit (Section 4), and (c) predict the kind of replies a counterhate tweet will elicit (Section 5).

Collecting Hateful Tweets, Counterhate Tweets, and Replies We use three strategies to collect a sufficient number of hateful tweets, counterhate tweets, and replies. The first strategy is to start with corpora consisting of (hateful tweet, counterhate tweet) pairs that include the tweet identifiers (Mathew et al., 2020; Albanyan and Blanco, 2022). Then, we use the Twitter API to collect all replies to the counterhate tweets. This strategy resulted in only 260 triples because some tweets are no longer available and not all counterhate tweets have replies. Note that other corpora not including identifiers cannot be used.

In the second strategy, we start collecting hateful tweets from corpora that only provide hateful tweets (Mathew et al., 2021; Chandra et al., 2021; He et al., 2021; Vidgen et al., 2020) including tweet identifiers. Then, we follow these steps:

1. Collect the replies to the hateful tweets. Let us consider them *candidate* counterhate tweets.
2. Select actual counterhate tweets from the candidates using an existing counterhate classifier (Albanyan and Blanco, 2022).
3. Collect the replies to the counterhate tweets to construct (hateful tweets, counterhate tweet, reply) triples.

This strategy resulted in 230 triples. Since the total number of triples is relatively low (490 triples), we designed a third strategy.

The third strategy is the same than the second but with an alternative approach to collect the hateful tweets. Instead of using existing corpora, we use (a) the hate pattern *I <hateful_verb> <target_group>* defined by Silva et al. (2021) to select candidate hate tweets and (b) HateXPlain (Mathew et al., 2021) to select actual hate tweets. These strategy resulted in 3,820 triples.

The total number of triples after combining the three strategies is 4,310. We finalized the collection process by validating the triples. The final size of our corpus after the validation process is 2,621 (hateful tweet, counterhate tweet, reply) triples. The total number of hateful tweets is 1,147, while the number of counterhate tweets is 1,685. The number of counterhate tweets per hateful tweet ranges between 1 and 20, while the number of replies per counterhate tweet ranges between 1 and 88.

Annotation Guidelines Along with determining whether a reply agrees with the counterhate tweet, we identify finer-grained characteristics of the replies. Accordingly, we define three steps to answer four questions in the annotation process.

The first step is determining whether the reply **agrees** with the counterhate tweet. We consider that a reply agrees if it does not oppose the counterhate tweet either explicitly or implicitly. On the other hand, we consider that a reply disagrees if it opposes the counterhate tweet, including sarcasm (e.g., you are missing something!) or casting doubt (e.g., are you kidding?).

The second step provides fine-grained characteristics when the reply disagrees with the counterhate tweet. First, we ask whether the reply **supports**

Hateful Tweet 1: I f**king hate <ethnicity> people. [...] I hope you all f**king die.

Counterhate Tweet: not all <ethnicity> part take in this. cant discriminate a whole race bc some f**k up; do sick things. White's abuse animals too

Reply: but down in <country> they are horrible f**king people

Agree? No	Support? Yes
Attacks Author? No	Addtl. Counterhate? n/a

Hateful Tweet 2: I admit it, I don't like white people

Counterhate Tweet: Appreciate the honesty. You do realize that makes you racist, right?

Reply: thats not wt racism means. f**k off w that bullshit.

Agree? No	Support? No
Attacks Author? Yes	Addtl. Counterhate? n/a

Hateful Tweet 3: If <country> had only shown the true numbers and severity of this virus then maybe some countries would have taken it more seriously much earlier.

Counterhate Tweet: <country> has shown you that 10 of 1000s people infected for about two months. Few of countries take serious action.

Reply: <country> is doing a good job[...] truthful Govt. that cares about citizens. A shining beacon on a hill for the world to emulate.

Agree? Yes	Support? n/a
Attacks Author? n/a	Addtl. Counterhate? Yes

Table 1: Three annotation examples of hateful tweets, counterhate tweets, and replies from our corpus. Annotations include four binary questions: whether the reply (a) *Agrees* with the counterhate tweet, (b) *Supports* the hate when it disagrees with the counterhate tweet, (c) *Attacks the Author* of the counterhate tweet when it disagrees with the counterhate tweet, and (d) adds *Additional Counterhate* when it agrees with the counterhate tweet.

the hateful tweet. We consider the reply to support the hateful tweet if it includes a justification for the hateful content (e.g., the news says the opposite!) or introduces additional hateful content (e.g., first example in Table 1). Second, we identify whether the reply **attacks the author** of the counterhate tweet. We include in the definition of *attack* any mockery or insults towards the author of the counterhate tweet (e.g., stupid never understand!).

	Observed (%)	Cohen's κ
Agree?	91.1	0.82
Support?	89.1	0.77
Attacks Author?	92.3	0.79
Addtl. Counterhate?	91.7	0.81

Table 2: Inter-annotator agreements in our corpus. We provide the observed agreements (percentage of times annotators agreed) and Cohen's κ. κ coefficients between 0.6 and 0.8 are considered *substantial* agreement, and above 0.8 (nearly) perfect (Artstein and Poesio, 2008).

The third step provides fine-grained characteristics when the reply agrees with the counterhate tweet. Finally, when the reply agrees with the counterhate tweet, we distinguish whether the reply includes **additional counterhate**. Namely, we identify whether the reply contains additional counterhate by providing a new opinion or factual argument to support the counterhate tweet (e.g., he is also known for his charitable work and donations). Only agreeing with the counterhate tweet (e.g., you are correct!) does not contain additional arguments.

Examples Table 1 shows examples from our corpus. In the first example, the reply not only disagrees with the counterhate tweet but also *supports* the hateful tweet with new hate content against the mentioned people. Note that replies can also show disagreement without including any support for the hateful tweet (e.g., do you have any evidence?!!).

In the second example, the reply *attacks the author* of the counterhate tweet without including any justification or support for the hateful tweet. This also indicates that the reply disagrees with the counterhate tweet. Note that replies can disagree with the counterhate tweet without attacking the author (e.g., don't be their lawyer).

Finally, the reply in the third example not only agrees with the counterhate tweet, but also includes *additional counterhate* (honest vs. successful government). Note that replies can agree with the counterhate tweet without adding additional counterhate (e.g., convincing response!).

Annotation Process and Inter-Annotator Agreements We used the Label Studio annotation tool.[5] The tool showed the hateful tweet, counterhate tweet, and reply. It displayed the screenshots of the tweets taken from the Twitter website to prevent

[5] https://github.com/heartexlabs/label-studio

	%Yes	%No
Agree?	49	51
Support?	40	60
Attacks Author?	24	76
Addtl. Counterhate?	35	65

Table 3: Percentages for Yes and No labels per question.

readability issues when displaying the tweets (e.g., special characters). Additionally, annotators are provided with instructions for each question (i.e., definitions and examples).

The 2,621 (hateful tweet, counterhate tweet, reply) triples were independently annotated by two graduate students active on social media platforms. We are interested in how regular social media users interpret hateful tweets, counterhate tweets, and replies. Table 2 presents the inter-annotator agreements. For all questions, the observed agreements are almost 90%. Cohen's k coefficients indicate (a) *substantial* agreement in two questions: whether the reply *supports* the hateful tweet and *attacks the author* of the counterhate tweets, and (b) *nearly* perfect agreements in two questions: whether the reply *agrees* with the counterhate tweet and includes *additional counterhate*. k coefficients between 0.60 and 0.80 are considered *substantial* agreement, and above 0.80 are considered *nearly* perfect (Artstein and Poesio, 2008). We note that it is easier to determine whether a reply *agrees* and adds *additional counterhate* tasks than *supports* and *attacks the author* tasks. This is due to the use of sarcasm and nuanced language when the reply supports the hateful tweet or attacks the author of the counterhate tweet. After the two annotators finished all the annotations independently, they debated the points of disagreement and decided on the final label.

4 Corpus Analysis

Label Distribution Table 3 presents the percentages of *yes* and *no* labels per question. Around half of the replies to the counterhate tweets do not agree with the counterhate tweet (51%), and it is common for them to *support* the hateful tweet when they do not agree (40%). In addition, it is somewhat rare for these replies to *attack the author* of the counterhate tweet when they disagree (24%). On the other hand, it is less likely for the replies to include *additional counterhate* arguments when they agree (35%). This shows that most replies that agree with the counterhate tweet do not include any additional arguments to support the counterhate tweet (e.g., you are correct).

Linguistic Insights We analyze the language people use in the counterhate tweets that lead to certain types of replies. We count the number of tokens, pronouns, and proper nouns using spaCy (Neumann et al., 2019). We use the lexicons of offensive words[6] and lexicons by Mohammad and Turney (2013) to count offensive, positive, negative, and sadness words. Finally, we use Profanity-check[7] to calculate the profanity score and TextBlob[8] to calculate the subjectivity score. All correlations between linguistic features are below 0.30, except for a few that involve the number of tokens (Appendix A, Figures 2–5). We check the predictive power of the selected features using t-test. We also report if a test passes the Bonferroni correction (Table 4). The p-values reveal several interesting insights:

- Counterhate tweets with more tokens or pronouns elicit replies that do *not attack the author* of the counterhate tweet or include *additional counterhate* if they agree.
- Counterhate tweets with more question marks lead to replies that (a) *agree* with the counterhate tweets and do not add *additional counterhate*, or (b) *support* the hateful tweet and do *not attack the author*.
- We find that (a) positive words elicit replies that do *not attack the author* or add *additional counterhate*, (b) negative words elicit replies that do not add *additional counterhate*, and (c) offensive words elicit replies that *agree* with the counterhate, or *attack the author*.
- Profanity in counterhate tweets elicits replies that *agree* with the counterhate tweet or do *not support* the hateful tweet.
- Comparing hateful tweets and counterhate tweets reveals that counterhate tweets with (a) less offensive content lead to replies that *agree* with the counterhate tweet or do *not support* the hateful tweet, (b) less sadness words elicit replies that *agree* with the counterhate or do *not attack the author* of the counterhate tweet, and (c) less subjectivity lead to replies that *attack the author* of the counterhate or do not add *additional counterhate*.

[6]https://github.com/zacanger/profane-words
[7]https://github.com/vzhou842/profanity-check
[8]https://github.com/sloria/TextBlob

	Agree?		Support?		Attacks Author?		Addtl. Counterhate?	
	p-value	Bonf.	p-value	Bonf.	p-value	Bonf.	p-value	Bonf.
Number of ...								
tokens					↓↓↓	✓	↑↑↑	✓
pronouns					↓↓↓	✓	↑↑↑	✓
proper nouns	↑	✗			↓	✗		
question marks	↑	✗	↑↑↑	✓	↓↓↓	✓	↑	✗
positive words					↓↓↓	✓	↑↑↑	✓
negative words					↓	✗	↓↓	✓
offensive words	↑	✗			↑	✗		
Profanity score	↑	✗	↓	✗				
With respect to the hateful tweet								
offensive words	↑↑	✓	↓↓	✗				
sadness words	↑↑	✗			↓↓	✗		
subjectivity					↑↑	✗	↓	✗

Table 4: Linguistic analysis of the counterhate tweets depending on our fine-grained characterization of the replies they elicit. Number of arrows indicate the p-value (t-test; one: $p < 0.05$, two: $p < 0.01$, and three: $p < 0.001$). Arrow direction indicates whether higher values correlate with *yes* (up) or *no* (down). We use a check mark to indicate tests that pass the Bonferroni correction. Counterhate tweets without offensive words tend to elicit replies that *agree* with the counterhate tweet and *do not support* the hate when they *disagree*.

5 Experiments and Results

We create a binary classifier for each task, namely, whether the reply: (a) agrees with the counterhate tweet, (b) supports the hateful tweet, (c) attacks the author of the counterhate tweet, or (d) includes additional counterhate arguments. We split the dataset into 70:10:20 ratios for training, validation, and testing. Each instance consists of a hateful tweet, a counterhate tweet, and a reply.

Baselines The baseline models we use in our experiments are the *majority* and *random* models. In the *majority* model, the majority label is predicted (*no* label for all tasks, Table 3). In the *random* model, a random label of *no* or *yes* is predicted.

Neural Network Architecture and Training In all experiments, we used the transformer-based BERTweet model (Nguyen et al., 2020). BERTweet is a BERT-based (Devlin et al., 2019) model but was pre-trained using the RoBERTa training strategy (Liu et al., 2019) on 850M English tweets. The neural architecture consists of the base architecture of BERTweet followed by a linear layer with 128 neurons and ReLU activation. Then, we added a final linear layer with 2 neurons and a Softmax activation to do the binary classification between labels *yes* and *no*. We perform the experiments using different textual inputs:

1. the hateful tweet alone,
2. the counterhate tweet alone,
3. the reply alone, and
4. combinations of (1–3) above.

We use the '</s>' special token to concatenate the inputs. Then, we apply three strategies to enhance the performance of neural models:

Data Augmentation We adapt Easy Data Augmentation Marivate and Sefara (2020) called. Specifically, we use *Synonym Replacement* (randomly replacing a word), *Random Insertion* (inserting a synonym of a random word), and *Random Swap* (randomly swapping the positions of two words).

Concatenating Language Features Language features have been shown to improve pre-trained models' performance in text classification tasks (Lim and Tayyar Madabushi, 2020). To this end, we experiment with complementing embeddings with manually defined language features. Inspired by the analyses in Section 4, we calculate count-based language features for the replies, such as the *number of tokens, pronouns, nouns, verbs, negative and positive words* (using the lexicons by Mohammad and Turney (2013)), *question marks, proper nouns,* and *first-person pronouns*. Examples are shown in Appendix C (Table 7). We then use the significance test (t-test) to keep the significant features (p< 0.05). The common significant features between the tasks are the *number of tokens, bad words, nouns and verbs,* and *positive words*. We concatenate these

	Agree?			Support?			Attacks Author?			Addtl. Counterhate?		
	No	Yes	Avg.	No	Yes	Avg.	No	Yes	Avg.	No	Yes	Avg.
Baselines												
Majority	0.67	0.00	0.34	0.75	0.00	0.45	0.87	0.00	0.66	0.79	0.00	0.51
Random	0.52	0.48	0.50	0.51	0.44	0.48	0.58	0.30	0.51	0.54	0.39	0.49
BERTweet trained with ...												
reply	0.71	0.70	0.70	0.82	0.64	0.75	0.89	0.62	0.83	0.89	0.78	0.85
counterhate tweet	0.64	0.60	0.62	0.70	0.38	0.57	0.86	0.13	0.69	0.73	0.51	0.66
hateful tweet	0.61	0.59	0.60	0.72	0.30	0.55	0.86	0.00	0.66	0.76	0.42	0.64
reply + counterhate tweet	0.72	0.75	0.73	0.80	0.69	0.76	0.89	0.64	0.83	0.89	0.79	0.85
reply + hateful tweet	0.67	0.75	0.71	0.82	0.73	0.78	0.88	0.59	0.81	0.87	0.76	0.83
best pair + the other tweet	0.74	0.71	0.73	0.80	0.68	0.75	0.88	0.56	0.81	0.88	0.76	0.83
best input + EDA	0.75	0.74	0.75	0.84	0.74	0.80	0.89	0.64	0.83	0.89	0.77	0.85
best input + LF	0.74	0.74	0.74	0.84	0.67	0.78	0.90	0.64	0.84	0.88	0.77	0.84
best input + Blending	0.76	0.74	0.75	0.84	0.79	0.82	0.90	0.66	0.84	0.88	0.80	0.85

Table 5: Results obtained with several systems (F1-scores; *Avg.* refers to the *weighted average*). *Best pair*: the pair input that leads to the best pair result (*reply+counterhate tweet* or *reply+hateful tweet*). *The other tweet*: either the counterhate tweet or hateful tweet. *Best input*: the textual input or combinations of inputs of (reply, counterhate tweet, and hateful tweet) that leads to the best performance (underlined). *EDA*: easy data augmentation. *LF*: language features. Tables 8–11 in Appendix D provide detailed results per label and subtask.

features with each other and with the input embeddings using the '</s>' special token.

Blending Complementary Corpora We finally investigate pretraining with complementary tasks. We adopt the method by Shnarch et al. (2018), which integrates labeled data from related tasks with various ratios in each training epoch. This is done by blending the related task instances with our dataset for training, and decrease the ratio in each epoch to reach zero in the last one. The corpora we blend with are: (a) a stance dataset (Mohammad et al., 2016) consisting of 4,163 tweets about abortion, atheism, climate change, feminism, and Hillary Clinton annotated with *in favor*, *against*, or *none*; (b) an offensive dataset (Zampieri et al., 2019b) containing over 14K tweets annotated with *offensive* or *not offensive*, and (c) a hateful tweet-reply dataset (Albanyan and Blanco, 2022), annotated with whether the reply *counters* the hateful tweet (5,652 pairs), counters the hate with *justification* (1,145), *attacks the author* of the hateful tweet (1,145), and includes *additional hate* (4,507).

5.1 Quantitative Results

Table 5 shows the results using the F1-score for *no* and *yes* labels, and the weighted average. Appendix D (Tables 8–11) contains detailed results showing the precision, recall, and F1-score. The F1-scores for the majority baseline are 0.34, 0.45, 0.66, and 0.51.

The results using the neural models with different inputs (the hateful tweet, the counterhate tweet, the reply, or a combination of different tweets) reveal several insights:

- Using only the hateful tweet or counterhate tweet as an input outperforms the baselines, showing that certain hateful tweets or counterhate tweets elicit particular kinds of replies.
- Feeding to the network only the reply yields the best results out of all single-tweet inputs.
- Combining the reply with the hateful tweet outperforms the models in *support* the hateful tweet task since, in this task, the reply is related to the hateful tweet. On the other hand, including the counterhate tweets improves the results in the other three tasks. We note that it barely affects the *attacks the author* task. We hypothesize this is because the attack can be detected from the reply alone.
- Including a third input (either the counterhate tweet or hateful tweet) to the best pairs (reply+counterhate tweet or reply+hateful tweet) worsens the results (0.73, 0.78, 0.83, and 0.85 vs. 0.73, 0.75, 0.81, and 0.83).

Additionally, the results show modest improvements when applying the three strategies we work

	Agree?	Support?	Attacks Author?	Additl. Counterhate?
Intricate text				
Sarcasm and implicit meaning	18	20	15	18
Mentions many named entities	6	5	7	6
All	24	25	22	24
General knowledge	16	19	17	12
Short text, less than 5 tokens	20	12	21	14
Misspellings and abbreviations	11	9	11	12
Rhetorical question	8	14	9	9

Table 6: Error types made by the best performing model in each task (*best input + blending*, as shown in Table 5). All the numbers are percentages.

with (Data Augmentation, Language Features, and Blending Complementary Corpora). We find that:

- Data augmentation benefits the neural network trained with the best input combination in two tasks: *agree* with the counterhate tweet and *support* the hateful tweet.
- Language features are barely beneficial.
- Blending complementary corpora always yields higher results. More details about the related datasets that lead to the best results in all tasks can be found in Appendix D.

We also tried combining the strategies and found out that doing so does not improve results.

When do the best models make errors? While our best models in each task produce strong results (best input + blending, Table 5), we manually analyzed the wrong predictions made by each model. Table 6 shows the error types we found. We started the analysis by randomly selecting 100 samples from the model produced in the *agree* task. We considered all the wrong predictions for the other three tasks since they were less than 100 samples. They were 59 samples in the *support* task, 46 in the *attacks the author* task, and 43 in the *additional counterhate* task. The error types are:

- Intricate text (24%, 25%, 22%, and 24%), which involves using sarcasm and implicit meaning, or mentioning many individuals or entities (e.g., Reply: don't block me I need you so bad. *Agree?* Gold: *No*, Predicted: *Yes*).
- General knowledge (16%, 19%, 17%, and 12%), which requires world knowledge and commonsense to understand the meaning of the tweet (e.g., Reply: it's on sky news mate!. *Supports?* Gold: *Yes*, Predicted: *No*).
- Short text (20%, 12%, 21%, and 14%), tweets with less than 5 tokens (e.g., Reply: chill out. *Attack the Author?* Gold: *No*, Predicted: *Yes*).
- Misspellings and abbreviations (11%, 9%, 11%, and 12%), (e.g., Reply: @auscoups Why r they trending these things. *Addit. counterhate?* Gold: *Yes*, Predicted: *No*).
- Rhetorical question (8%, 14%, 9%, and 9%), where a question in a tweet is asked to deliver a point (e.g., Reply: you think this is funny?. *Agree?* Gold: *Yes*, Predicted: *No*).

6 Conclusions

Countering hateful content is an effective way to fight hate speech (Gagliardone et al., 2015). Additionally, countering hate speech—unlike blocking—does not interfere with free speech. However well-intentioned, however, counterhate arguments may worsen the situation by eliciting additional hate.

In this work, we analyze the discourse following a counterhate tweet. Specifically, we analyze all replies to counterhate tweets and reveal fine-grained characteristics beyond whether the reply agrees with the counterhate argument. Namely, we determine whether the reply (a) not only disagrees with the counterhate tweet but also supports the hateful tweet or attacks the author of the counterhate arguments, or (b) not only agrees with the counterhate tweet but also adds additional counterhate arguments. To our knowledge, this work is the first to analyze the language of counterhate tweets based on the replies they elicit.

The work presented here is empirical and explores genuine counterhate arguments and the replies they elicit. We believe that it is critical to analyze genuine social media discourse and how hate spreads (and does not spread). We avoid making any causal claims; instead, we draw insights from genuine social media discourse around hateful content. Our future work includes generating counterhate arguments (a) customized to specific hateful content and (b) following the characteristics we found to be more effective at stopping hatred. We hypothesize that doing so will be more effective than generic or even expert-driven counterhate.

Limitations

In the data collection process (Section 3), we collect (hateful tweet, counterhate tweet, and reply) triples from existing hateful tweet-reply and hateful tweet corpora (the first and second strategies). However, this ends with fewer triples since some tweets are no longer available and not all counterhate tweets have replies. In addition, we use hate speech and counterhate classifiers to discard non-hateful and non-counterhate tweets. This step might (a) discard actual hateful or counterhate tweets that are detected wrongly and (b) keep hateful or counterhate tweets that should be discarded. Another limitation is that we only consider the tweet text. However, some tweets contain text accompanied by images or sometimes images only. Including the tweets' images in the analysis may add more insights.

References

Abdullah Albanyan and Eduardo Blanco. 2022. Pinpointing fine-grained relationships between hateful tweets and replies. *Proceedings of the AAAI Conference on Artificial Intelligence*, 36(10):10418–10426.

Dana Alsagheer, Hadi Mansourifar, and Weidong Shi. 2022. Counter hate speech in social media: A survey. *arXiv preprint arXiv:2203.03584*.

Ron Artstein and Massimo Poesio. 2008. Survey article: Inter-coder agreement for computational linguistics. *Computational Linguistics*, 34(4):555–596.

Valerio Basile, Cristina Bosco, Elisabetta Fersini, Debora Nozza, Viviana Patti, Francisco Manuel Rangel Pardo, Paolo Rosso, and Manuela Sanguinetti. 2019. SemEval-2019 task 5: Multilingual detection of hate speech against immigrants and women in Twitter. In *Proceedings of the 13th International Workshop on Semantic Evaluation*, pages 54–63, Minneapolis, Minnesota, USA. Association for Computational Linguistics.

Mohit Chandra, Manvith Reddy, Shradha Sehgal, Saurabh Gupta, Arun Balaji Buduru, and Ponnurangam Kumaraguru. 2021. "a virus has no religion": Analyzing islamophobia on twitter during the covid-19 outbreak. In *Proceedings of the 32nd ACM Conference on Hypertext and Social Media*, HT '21, page 67–77, New York, NY, USA. Association for Computing Machinery.

Yi-Ling Chung, Elizaveta Kuzmenko, Serra Sinem Tekiroglu, and Marco Guerini. 2019. CONAN - COunter NArratives through nichesourcing: a multilingual dataset of responses to fight online hate speech. In *Proceedings of the 57th Annual Meeting of the Association for Computational Linguistics*, pages 2819–2829, Florence, Italy. Association for Computational Linguistics.

Russell B Clayton, Annie Lang, Glenn Leshner, and Brian L Quick. 2019. Who fights, who flees? an integration of the lc4mp and psychological reactance theory. *Media Psychology*, 22(4):545–571.

Kate Crawford and Tarleton Gillespie. 2016. What is a flag for? social media reporting tools and the vocabulary of complaint. *New Media & Society*, 18(3):410–428.

Thomas Davidson, Dana Warmsley, Michael Macy, and Ingmar Weber. 2017. Automated hate speech detection and the problem of offensive language. *Proceedings of the International AAAI Conference on Web and Social Media*, 11(1).

Jacob Devlin, Ming-Wei Chang, Kenton Lee, and Kristina Toutanova. 2019. BERT: Pre-training of deep bidirectional transformers for language understanding. In *Proceedings of the 2019 Conference of the North American Chapter of the Association for Computational Linguistics: Human Language Technologies, Volume 1 (Long and Short Papers)*.

Nemanja Djuric, Jing Zhou, Robin Morris, Mihajlo Grbovic, Vladan Radosavljevic, and Narayan Bhamidipati. 2015. Hate speech detection with comment embeddings. In *Proceedings of the 24th International Conference on World Wide Web*, WWW '15 Companion, page 29–30, New York, NY, USA. Association for Computing Machinery.

Maeve Duggan. 2017. Online harassment 2017. *Pew Research Center*.

European Commission. 2019. The EU Code of Conduct on Countering Illegal Hate Speech Online. Accessed: 2021-5-12.

Margherita Fanton, Helena Bonaldi, Serra Sinem Tekiroğlu, and Marco Guerini. 2021. Human-in-the-loop for data collection: a multi-target counter narrative dataset to fight online hate speech. In *Proceedings of the 59th Annual Meeting of the Association for Computational Linguistics and the 11th International Joint Conference on Natural Language Processing (Volume 1: Long Papers)*, pages 3226–3240, Online. Association for Computational Linguistics.

Paula Fortuna and Sérgio Nunes. 2018. A survey on automatic detection of hate speech in text. *ACM Comput. Surv.*, 51(4).

Iginio Gagliardone, Danit Gal, Thiago Alves, and Gabriela Martinez. 2015. *Countering online hate speech*. Unesco Publishing.

Lei Gao and Ruihong Huang. 2017. Detecting online hate speech using context aware models. In *Proceedings of the International Conference Recent Advances in Natural Language Processing, RANLP 2017*, pages 260–266, Varna, Bulgaria. INCOMA Ltd.

Joshua Garland, Keyan Ghazi-Zahedi, Jean-Gabriel Young, Laurent Hébert-Dufresne, and Mirta Galesic. 2020. Countering hate on social media: Large scale classification of hate and counter speech. In *Proceedings of the Fourth Workshop on Online Abuse and Harms*, pages 102–112, Online. Association for Computational Linguistics.

Joshua Garland, Keyan Ghazi-Zahedi, Jean-Gabriel Young, Laurent Hébert-Dufresne, and Mirta Galesic. 2022. Impact and dynamics of hate and counter speech online. *EPJ data science*, 11(1):3.

Bing He, Caleb Ziems, Sandeep Soni, Naren Ramakrishnan, Diyi Yang, and Srijan Kumar. 2021. Racism is a virus: Anti-asian hate and counterspeech in social media during the covid-19 crisis. In *Proceedings of the 2021 IEEE/ACM International Conference on Advances in Social Networks Analysis and Mining*, pages 90–94.

Wah Meng Lim and Harish Tayyar Madabushi. 2020. UoB at SemEval-2020 task 12: Boosting BERT with corpus level information. In *Proceedings of the Fourteenth Workshop on Semantic Evaluation*, pages 2216–2221, Barcelona (online). International Committee for Computational Linguistics.

Ping Liu, Joshua Guberman, Libby Hemphill, and Aron Culotta. 2018. Forecasting the presence and intensity of hostility on instagram using linguistic and social features. In *Proceedings of the Twelfth International Conference on Web and Social Media, ICWSM 2018, Stanford, California, USA, June 25-28, 2018*, pages 181–190. AAAI Press.

Yinhan Liu, Myle Ott, Naman Goyal, Jingfei Du, Mandar Joshi, Danqi Chen, Omer Levy, Mike Lewis, Luke Zettlemoyer, and Veselin Stoyanov. 2019. Roberta: A robustly optimized bert pretraining approach. *arXiv preprint arXiv:1907.11692*.

Ilya Loshchilov and Frank Hutter. 2017. Decoupled weight decay regularization.

Vukosi Marivate and Tshephisho Sefara. 2020. Improving short text classification through global augmentation methods. In *International Cross-Domain Conference for Machine Learning and Knowledge Extraction*, pages 385–399. Springer.

Binny Mathew, Navish Kumar, Pawan Goyal, and Animesh Mukherjee. 2020. Interaction dynamics between hate and counter users on twitter. In *Proceedings of the 7th ACM IKDD CoDS and 25th COMAD*, CoDS COMAD 2020, page 116–124, New York, NY, USA. Association for Computing Machinery.

Binny Mathew, Punyajoy Saha, Hardik Tharad, Subham Rajgaria, Prajwal Singhania, Suman Kalyan Maity, Pawan Goyal, and Animesh Mukherjee. 2019. Thou shalt not hate: Countering online hate speech. *Proceedings of the International AAAI Conference on Web and Social Media*, 13(01):369–380.

Binny Mathew, Punyajoy Saha, Seid Muhie Yimam, Chris Biemann, Pawan Goyal, and Animesh Mukherjee. 2021. Hatexplain: A benchmark dataset for explainable hate speech detection. *Proceedings of the AAAI Conference on Artificial Intelligence*, 35(17):14867–14875.

Saif Mohammad, Svetlana Kiritchenko, Parinaz Sobhani, Xiaodan Zhu, and Colin Cherry. 2016. SemEval-2016 task 6: Detecting stance in tweets. In *Proceedings of the 10th International Workshop on Semantic Evaluation (SemEval-2016)*, pages 31–41, San Diego, California. Association for Computational Linguistics.

Saif M Mohammad and Peter D Turney. 2013. Crowdsourcing a word–emotion association lexicon. *Computational intelligence*, 29(3):436–465.

Kevin Munger. 2017. Tweetment effects on the tweeted: Experimentally reducing racist harassment. *Political Behavior*, 39(3):629–649.

Mark Neumann, Daniel King, Iz Beltagy, and Waleed Ammar. 2019. ScispaCy: Fast and robust models for biomedical natural language processing. In *Proceedings of the 18th BioNLP Workshop and Shared Task*.

Dat Quoc Nguyen, Thanh Vu, and Anh Tuan Nguyen. 2020. BERTweet: A pre-trained language model for English tweets. In *Proceedings of the 2020 Conference on Empirical Methods in Natural Language Processing: System Demonstrations*, pages 9–14, Online. Association for Computational Linguistics.

Chikashi Nobata, Joel Tetreault, Achint Thomas, Yashar Mehdad, and Yi Chang. 2016. Abusive language detection in online user content. In *Proceedings of the 25th International Conference on World Wide Web*, WWW '16, page 145–153, Republic and Canton of Geneva, CHE. International World Wide Web Conferences Steering Committee.

Nedjma Ousidhoum, Zizheng Lin, Hongming Zhang, Yangqiu Song, and Dit-Yan Yeung. 2019. Multilingual and multi-aspect hate speech analysis. In *Proceedings of the 2019 Conference on Empirical Methods in Natural Language Processing and the 9th International Joint Conference on Natural Language Processing (EMNLP-IJCNLP)*, pages 4675–4684, Hong Kong, China. Association for Computational Linguistics.

Jing Qian, Anna Bethke, Yinyin Liu, Elizabeth Belding, and William Yang Wang. 2019. A benchmark dataset for learning to intervene in online hate speech. In *Proceedings of the 2019 Conference on Empirical*

Methods in Natural Language Processing and the 9th International Joint Conference on Natural Language Processing (EMNLP-IJCNLP), pages 4755–4764, Hong Kong, China. Association for Computational Linguistics.

Stephen A Rains. 2013. The nature of psychological reactance revisited: A meta-analytic review. *Human Communication Research*, 39(1):47–73.

Carla Schieb and Mike Preuss. 2016. Governing hate speech by means of counterspeech on facebook. In *66th ica annual conference, at fukuoka, japan*, pages 1–23.

Carla Schieb and Mike Preuss. 2018. Considering the elaboration likelihood model for simulating hate and counter speech on facebook. *SCM Studies in Communication and Media*, 7(4):580–606.

Deepa Seetharaman. 2018. Facebook Throws More Money at Wiping Out Hate Speech and Bad Actors . *The Wall Street Journal*.

Eyal Shnarch, Carlos Alzate, Lena Dankin, Martin Gleize, Yufang Hou, Leshem Choshen, Ranit Aharonov, and Noam Slonim. 2018. Will it blend? blending weak and strong labeled data in a neural network for argumentation mining. In *Proceedings of the 56th Annual Meeting of the Association for Computational Linguistics (Volume 2: Short Papers)*, pages 599–605, Melbourne, Australia. Association for Computational Linguistics.

Leandro Silva, Mainack Mondal, Denzil Correa, Fabrício Benevenuto, and Ingmar Weber. 2021. Analyzing the targets of hate in online social media. *Proceedings of the International AAAI Conference on Web and Social Media*, 10(1):687–690.

Bertie Vidgen, Scott Hale, Ella Guest, Helen Margetts, David Broniatowski, Zeerak Waseem, Austin Botelho, Matthew Hall, and Rebekah Tromble. 2020. Detecting East Asian prejudice on social media. In *Proceedings of the Fourth Workshop on Online Abuse and Harms*, pages 162–172, Online. Association for Computational Linguistics.

Emily A Vogels. 2021. The state of online harassment. *Pew Research Center*, 13.

Zeerak Waseem and Dirk Hovy. 2016. Hateful symbols or hateful people? predictive features for hate speech detection on Twitter. In *Proceedings of the NAACL Student Research Workshop*, pages 88–93, San Diego, California. Association for Computational Linguistics.

Thomas Wolf, Lysandre Debut, Victor Sanh, Julien Chaumond, Clement Delangue, Anthony Moi, Pierric Cistac, Tim Rault, Remi Louf, Morgan Funtowicz, Joe Davison, Sam Shleifer, Patrick von Platen, Clara Ma, Yacine Jernite, Julien Plu, Canwen Xu, Teven Le Scao, Sylvain Gugger, Mariama Drame, Quentin Lhoest, and Alexander Rush. 2020. Transformers: State-of-the-art natural language processing. In *Proceedings of the 2020 Conference on Empirical Methods in Natural Language Processing: System Demonstrations*, pages 38–45, Online. Association for Computational Linguistics.

Xinchen Yu, Eduardo Blanco, and Lingzi Hong. 2022. Hate speech and counter speech detection: Conversational context does matter. In *Proceedings of the 2022 Conference of the North American Chapter of the Association for Computational Linguistics: Human Language Technologies*, pages 5918–5930, Seattle, United States. Association for Computational Linguistics.

Marcos Zampieri, Shervin Malmasi, Preslav Nakov, Sara Rosenthal, Noura Farra, and Ritesh Kumar. 2019a. Predicting the type and target of offensive posts in social media. In *Proceedings of the 2019 Conference of the North American Chapter of the Association for Computational Linguistics: Human Language Technologies, Volume 1 (Long and Short Papers)*, pages 1415–1420, Minneapolis, Minnesota. Association for Computational Linguistics.

Marcos Zampieri, Shervin Malmasi, Preslav Nakov, Sara Rosenthal, Noura Farra, and Ritesh Kumar. 2019b. SemEval-2019 task 6: Identifying and categorizing offensive language in social media (OffensEval). In *Proceedings of the 13th International Workshop on Semantic Evaluation*, pages 75–86, Minneapolis, Minnesota, USA. Association for Computational Linguistics.

Justine Zhang, Jonathan Chang, Cristian Danescu-Niculescu-Mizil, Lucas Dixon, Yiqing Hua, Dario Taraborelli, and Nithum Thain. 2018. Conversations gone awry: Detecting early signs of conversational failure. In *Proceedings of the 56th Annual Meeting of the Association for Computational Linguistics (Volume 1: Long Papers)*, pages 1350–1361, Melbourne, Australia. Association for Computational Linguistics.

A Inter-Feature Correlations

Figures 2–5 show the inter-feature correlations for the the linguistic features used in the linguistic analysis (Section 4, Table 4). Most correlation coefficients are less than 0.30 in all four tasks (whether the reply agrees with the counterhate tweet, supports the hateful tweet, attacks the author of the counterhate tweet, or includes additional counterhate). This shows that our analysis captures various kinds of counterhate tweets.

B Implementation Details

We used the transformer-based BERTweet model. The neural architecture consists of the base architecture of BERTweet followed by a linear layer with 128 neurons and a ReLU activation. Then, we added a final linear layer with 2 neurons and

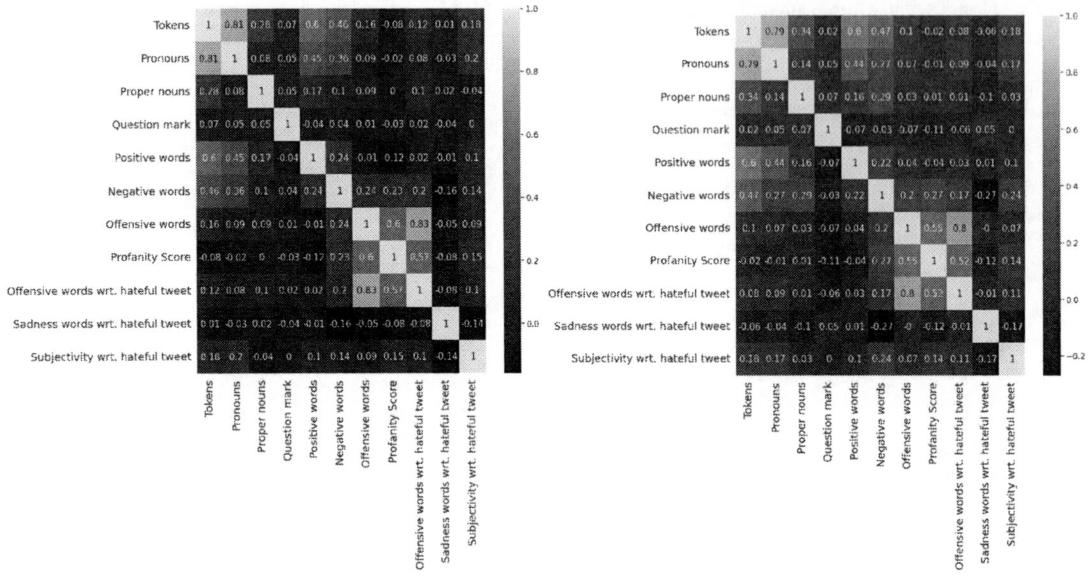

Figure 2: Correlation coefficients between features used in the linguistic analysis. The left and right heatmaps show the correlations with counterhate tweet for the replies that *agree* and do *not agree* with the counterhate tweet respectively.

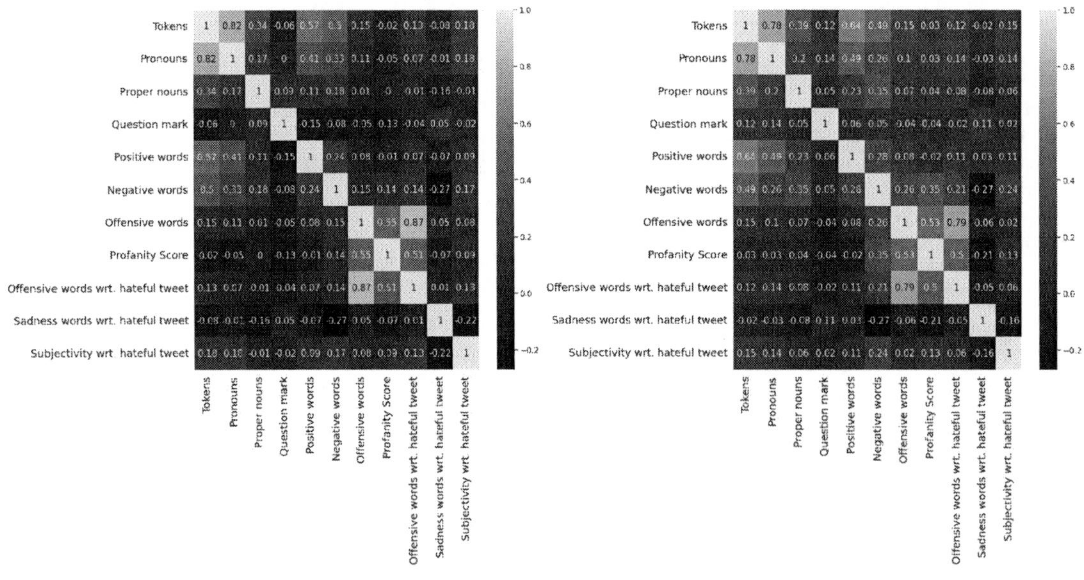

Figure 3: Correlation coefficients between features used in the linguistic analysis. The left and right heatmaps show the correlations with counterhate tweet for the replies that *support* and do *not support* the hateful tweet respectively.

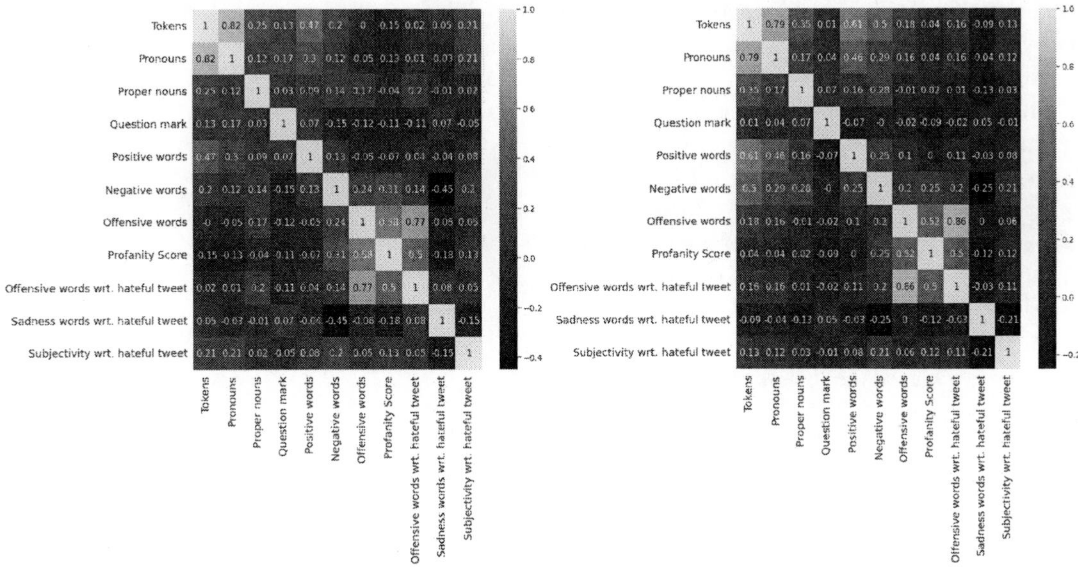

Figure 4: Correlation coefficients between features used in the linguistic analysis. The left and right heatmaps show the correlations with counterhate tweet for the replies that *attack* and do *not attack* the author of the counterhate tweet respectively.

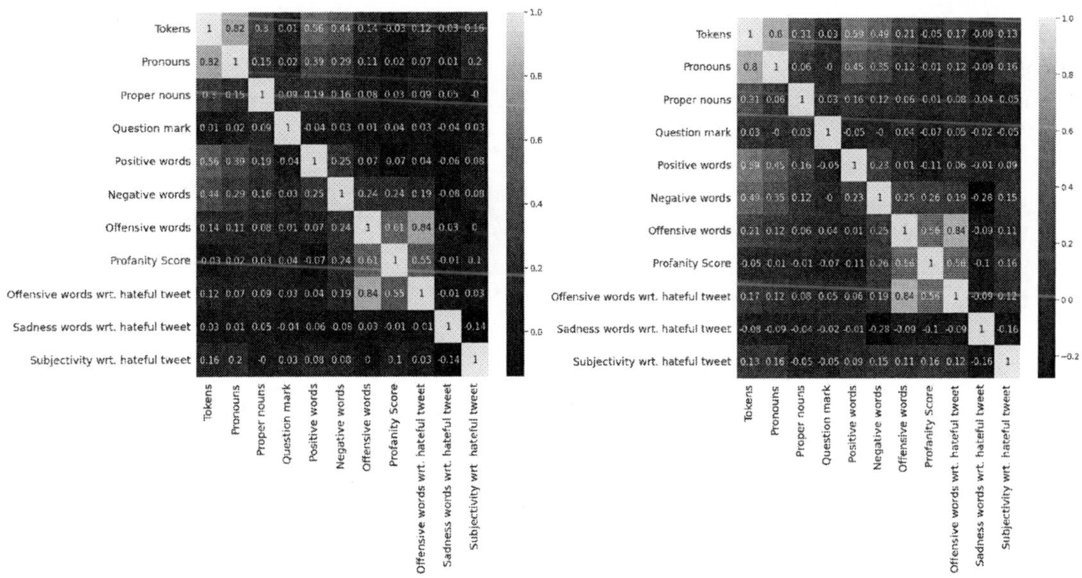

Figure 5: Correlation coefficients between features used in the linguistic analysis. The left and right heatmaps show the correlations with counterhate tweet for the replies that *include* and do *not include* additional counterhate respectively.

a Softmax activation. We prepared the dataset by removing URLs, symbols, additional spaces and then, normalized all text to lowercase. We used the pre-processed data as input to the BERTweet model architecture provided by HuggingFace (Wolf et al., 2020) with its own tokenizer. We used the AdamW optimizer (Loshchilov and Hutter, 2017) with a learning rate of 1e-5, a batch size of 16, and a sparse categorical cross-entropy loss function. The number of tokens per input was 128 with automatic padding enabled for shorter inputs using the <pad> token. Models were fine-tuned for 6 epochs and the final fine-tuned model is loaded after the epoch in which it achieved the lowest validation loss.

C Language Features

Table 7 presents examples of applying the language feature strategy on the replies (Section 5). We experiment with concatenating language features presented in the table with input embeddings. The selected language features are number of tokens, pronouns, nouns and verbs, negative and positive words, question marks, proper nouns, and first-person pronouns.

D Detailed Results

Tables 8–11 show the detailed results presented in Table 5. We provide Precision, Recall and F1-score (a) using different tweet combinations and (b) applying the three strategies to enhance the results. In addition, we show the results of each related dataset used in the *Blending with Complementary Tasks* strategy. The **related datasets** that lead to the best results in *each task* are:

- **stance dataset** to determine whether the reply *agrees* with counterhate tweet;
- **hateful tweet-reply pair dataset** regarding if a reply includes additional hate, to determine whether the reply *supports* the hateful tweet task;
- **hateful tweet-reply pair dataset** regarding if a reply attacks the author of the hateful tweet, to determine whether the reply *attacks the author* of the counterhate tweet; and
- **hateful tweet-reply pair dataset** regarding if a reply counters the hate with justification, to determine whether the reply adds *additional counterhate*.

	Language Features							
	tokens	pron.	N-and-V	pos.	neg.	QM	PR	FP-pron.
the least you can do is watch what u say, but ur too ignorant.	14	3	4	0	1	0	0	0
Also why poor Becky? She's with a great leading man. I get hating Franco but why the RoHo hate?	19	2	5	0	2	2	3	1
b**ch you lame as f**k hope you got that sh*t if you love gays	14	3	9	2	2	0	1	0
Right??? Like this dude is insane	6	0	1	0	1	3	0	0
Also, I never had the thought to bully someone because I found them weird, that's so toxic wth???	18	5	6	1	3	3	0	2
Who is this one? Are you dumb?	7	2	0	0	1	2	0	0
If there overprotective dosent mean they hate u you know??	10	3	5	0	1	2	0	0
Oh so we are doing that huh , Well Imo killing irl people is cool sounds dumb doesn't it ?	20	3	4	1	2	1	1	1

Table 7: Examples of the calculated language features for the replies. We explore pretraining with the language features as shown in Table 5. *pron.*: Pronouns. *N-and-V*: Nouns and Verbs. *pos.*: Positive words. *neg.*: Negative words. *QM*: Question Marks. *PR*: Proper Nouns. *FP-pron.*: First Person Pronouns.

	No			Yes			Weighted Avg.		
	P	R	F1	P	R	F1	P	R	F1
Baselines									
Majority	0.50	1.00	0.67	0.00	0.00	0.00	0.25	0.50	0.34
Random	0.51	0.54	0.52	0.50	0.47	0.48	0.50	0.50	0.50
BERTweet trained with ...									
reply	0.70	0.72	0.71	0.72	0.69	0.70	0.70	0.70	0.70
counterhate tweet	0.61	0.67	0.64	0.63	0.57	0.60	0.62	0.62	0.62
hateful tweet	0.60	0.62	0.61	0.58	0.59	0.59	0.60	0.60	0.60
reply + counterhate tweet	0.77	0.68	<u>0.72</u>	0.71	0.79	<u>0.75</u>	0.74	0.73	<u>0.73</u>
reply + hateful tweet	0.81	0.57	0.67	0.66	0.86	0.75	0.73	0.71	0.71
best pair + the other tweet	0.71	0.78	0.74	0.75	0.68	0.71	0.73	0.73	0.73
best input + EDA	0.75	0.74	0.75	0.74	0.75	0.74	0.74	0.74	0.74
best input + LF	0.75	0.73	0.74	0.73	0.75	0.74	0.74	0.74	0.74
best input + Blending with ...									
stance	0.73	0.78	0.76	0.77	0.71	0.74	0.74	0.75	0.75
offensive	0.65	0.83	0.76	0.87	0.49	0.62	0.76	0.71	0.69
counterhate	0.72	0.70	0.71	0.70	0.72	0.71	0.71	0.71	0.71
justification	0.71	0.78	0.74	0.75	0.68	0.71	0.73	0.73	0.73
attack	0.73	0.81	0.76	0.78	0.69	0.73	0.75	0.75	0.75
additional hate	0.69	0.71	0.70	0.70	0.68	0.69	0.70	0.70	0.70

Table 8: Detailed results (P, R, and F) predicting whether the reply *agrees* with the counterhate tweet. *Best pair*: the pair input that leads to the best pair result (reply+counterhate tweet or reply+hateful tweet). *The other tweet*: either counterhate tweet or hateful tweet. *Best input*: a textual input or a combination of (reply, counterhate tweet, and hateful tweet) that leads to the best performance (underline). *EDA*: easy data augmentation. *LF*: language features. This table complements Table 5.

	No			Yes			Weighted Avg.		
	P	R	F1	P	R	F1	P	R	F1
Baselines									
Majority	0.60	1.00	0.75	0.00	0.00	0.00	0.36	0.60	0.45
Random	0.58	0.45	0.51	0.39	0.51	0.44	0.50	0.48	0.48
BERTweet trained with …									
reply	0.74	0.91	0.82	0.79	0.53	0.64	0.76	0.65	0.74
counterhate tweet	0.63	0.80	0.70	0.51	0.30	0.38	0.58	0.60	0.57
hateful tweet	0.62	0.86	0.72	0.51	0.21	0.30	0.57	0.60	0.55
reply + counterhate tweet	0.78	0.83	0.80	0.72	0.66	0.69	0.76	0.76	0.76
reply + hateful tweet	0.81	0.83	<u>0.82</u>	0.74	0.72	<u>0.73</u>	0.78	0.78	<u>0.78</u>
best pair + the other tweet	0.77	0.83	0.80	0.71	0.64	0.68	0.75	0.75	0.75
best input + EDA	0.82	0.86	0.84	0.77	0.72	0.74	0.80	0.80	0.80
best input + LF	0.75	0.96	0.84	0.89	0.54	0.67	0.81	0.79	0.78
best input + Blending with …									
stance	0.84	0.73	0.78	0.66	0.80	0.72	0.77	0.76	0.77
offensive	0.78	0.72	0.75	0.63	0.70	0.66	0.72	0.71	0.71
counterhate	0.82	0.80	0.81	0.71	0.73	0.72	0.77	0.77	0.77
justification	0.83	0.83	0.83	0.75	0.75	0.75	0.80	0.80	0.80
attack	0.86	0.78	0.82	0.72	0.81	0.76	0.80	0.79	0.79
additional hate	0.89	0.79	0.84	0.73	0.86	0.79	0.83	0.82	0.82

Table 9: Detailed results (P, R, and F) predicting whether the reply contains *support* to the hateful tweet. *Best pair*: the pair input that leads to the best pair result (reply+counterhate tweet or reply+hateful tweet). *The other tweet*: either counterhate tweet or hateful tweet. *Best input*: a textual input or a combination of (reply, counterhate tweet, and hateful tweet) that leads to the best performance (underline). *EDA*: easy data augmentation. *LF*: language features. This table complements Table 5.

	No			Yes			Weighted Avg.		
	P	R	F1	P	R	F1	P	R	F1
Baselines									
Majority	0.76	1.00	0.87	0.00	0.00	0.00	0.58	0.76	0.66
Random	0.74	0.47	0.58	0.22	0.47	0.30	0.62	0.47	0.51
BERTweet trained with ...									
reply	0.88	0.90	0.89	0.66	0.59	0.62	0.82	0.83	0.83
counterhate tweet	0.77	0.97	0.86	0.45	0.08	0.13	0.70	0.76	0.69
hateful tweet	0.76	1.00	0.86	0.00	0.00	0.00	0.58	0.76	0.66
reply + counterhate tweet	0.88	0.91	0.89	0.67	0.61	0.64	0.83	0.84	0.83
reply + hateful tweet	0.87	0.90	0.88	0.64	0.55	0.59	0.81	0.82	0.81
best pair + the other tweet	0.85	0.91	0.88	0.64	0.50	0.56	0.80	0.81	0.81
best input + EDA	0.89	0.89	0.89	0.64	0.64	0.64	0.83	0.83	0.83
best input + LF	0.88	0.92	0.90	0.69	0.59	0.64	0.83	0.84	0.84
best input + Blending with ...									
stance	0.85	0.97	0.91	0.81	0.47	0.59	0.84	0.85	0.83
offensive	0.87	0.86	0.87	0.57	0.59	0.58	0.80	0.80	0.80
counterhate	0.91	0.85	0.88	0.61	0.73	0.67	0.84	0.83	0.83
justification	0.88	0.92	0.90	0.70	0.61	0.65	0.84	0.84	0.84
attack	0.89	0.92	0.90	0.71	0.62	0.67	0.85	0.85	0.85
additional hate	0.87	0.93	0.90	0.70	0.55	0.61	0.83	0.84	0.83

Table 10: Detailed results (P, R, and F) predicting whether the reply *attacks the author* of the counterhate tweet. *Best pair*: the pair input that leads to the best pair result (reply+counterhate tweet or reply+hateful tweet). *The other tweet*: either counterhate tweet or hateful tweet. *Best input*: a textual input or a combination of (reply, counterhate tweet, and hateful tweet) that leads to the best performance (underline). *EDA*: easy data augmentation. *LF*: language features. This table complements Table 5.

	No			Yes			Weighted Avg.		
	P	R	F1	P	R	F1	P	R	F1
Baselines									
Majority	0.65	1.00	0.79	0.00	0.00	0.00	0.42	0.65	0.51
Random	0.63	0.47	0.54	0.33	0.48	0.39	0.52	0.47	0.49
BERTweet trained with …									
reply	0.88	0.90	0.89	0.80	0.76	0.78	0.85	0.85	0.85
counterhate tweet	0.74	0.73	0.73	0.51	0.51	0.51	0.66	0.66	0.66
hateful tweet	0.70	0.82	0.76	0.52	0.36	0.42	0.64	0.66	0.64
reply + counterhate tweet	0.88	0.90	0.89	0.81	0.77	0.79	0.85	0.86	0.85
reply + hateful tweet	0.88	0.86	0.87	0.75	0.77	0.76	0.83	0.83	0.83
best pair + the other tweet	0.86	0.90	0.88	0.80	0.73	0.76	0.84	0.84	0.84
best input + EDA	0.85	0.94	0.89	0.85	0.70	0.77	0.85	0.85	0.85
best input + LF	0.87	0.89	0.88	0.78	0.75	0.77	0.84	0.84	0.84
best input + Blending with …									
stance	0.91	0.85	0.88	0.75	0.84	0.79	0.85	0.85	0.85
offensive	0.89	0.83	0.86	0.71	0.82	0.76	0.83	0.82	0.82
counterhate	0.90	0.83	0.86	0.72	0.84	0.77	0.84	0.83	0.83
justification	0.91	0.85	0.88	0.76	0.85	0.80	0.86	0.85	0.85
attack	0.88	0.84	0.86	0.72	0.78	0.75	0.82	0.82	0.82
additional hate	0.89	0.81	0.84	0.69	0.80	0.74	0.82	0.81	0.81

Table 11: Detailed results (P, R, and F) predicting whether the reply contains *additional counterhate*. *Best pair*: the pair input that leads to the best pair result (reply+counterhate tweet or reply+hateful tweet). *The other tweet*: either counterhate tweet or hateful tweet. *Best input*: a textual input or a combination of (reply, counterhate tweet, and hateful tweet) that leads to the best performance (underline). *EDA*: easy data augmentation. *LF*: language features. This table complements Table 5 .

Evaluating Factual Consistency of Texts with Semantic Role Labeling

Jing Fan* and **Dennis Aumiller*** and **Michael Gertz**
Institute of Computer Science, Heidelberg University
`j.fan@stud.uni-heidelberg.de`
`{aumiller, gertz}@informatik.uni-heidelberg.de`

Abstract

Automated evaluation of text generation systems has recently seen increasing attention, particularly checking whether generated text stays truthful to input sources. Existing methods frequently rely on an evaluation using task-specific language models, which in turn allows for little interpretability of generated scores. We introduce **SRLScore**, a reference-free evaluation metric designed with text summarization in mind. Our approach generates fact tuples constructed from Semantic Role Labels, applied to both input and summary texts. A final factuality score is computed by an adjustable scoring mechanism, which allows for easy adaption of the method across domains. Correlation with human judgments on English summarization datasets shows that **SRLScore** is competitive with state-of-the-art methods and exhibits stable generalization across datasets without requiring further training or hyperparameter tuning. We experiment with an optional co-reference resolution step, but find that the performance boost is mostly outweighed by the additional compute required. Our metric is available online at: `https://github.com/heyjing/SRLScore`

1 Introduction

One of the remaining issues that prevents productive deployments of neural text summarization systems is the low correlation of system outputs with human preferences. Among those, *factuality*, i.e., the agreement of facts in the generated summaries with those present in the input text, is not part of the general training objectives of models, which frequently leads to hallucinated facts that are detrimental to perceived system performance (ter Hoeve et al., 2020; Fabbri et al., 2021). Prior work has therefore introduced metrics for automated testing of factuality in generated text (Goodrich et al., 2019; Kryscinski et al., 2020; Yuan et al., 2021), which allows for a more nuanced verification of model capabilities. In particular, one of the first relevant works by Goodrich et al. (2019) introduces the idea of representing text as a series of "fact tuples", in their case as (`subject, predicate, object`) triplets. Their method exhibits some assumptions about the underlying data, which hampers correlation with human ratings. For example, subject or object may vary for the same sentence meaning expressed using different syntactic structures, e.g., active and passive forms. Semantic Role Labeling (SRL), however, allows for a syntactically independent meaning representation. Our metric, **SRLScore**, improves factuality evaluation, building on fact tuples similar to Goodrich et al. It distinguishes itself in several ways from existing approaches, though:

1. To account for a more nuanced fact representation, we employ SRL to produce abstract representations of sentences that are *independent of their syntactic formulations*.
2. Fact tuples in **SRLScore** are generated on the *input text* instead of gold summaries; as a consequence, our method is reference-free, and may be applied for evaluation irrespective of the availability of labeled datasets.
3. We introduce a novel weighting scheme for fact tuple comparison, where adjustable weights allow for user optimization.
4. Finally, we experiment with extensions along different parts of the pipeline, including an optional co-reference resolution step and alternative similarity scoring functions.

Notably, **SRLScore** entirely relies on publicly available software components and may be used without any further domain adaption required. While our experiments are performed on English, we argue that the transfer of our approach to other languages is possible given only the existence of a language-specific tokenizer and a sufficiently good SRL tagger. Furthermore, **SRLScore** offers the

*Both authors contributed equally to this work.

*Proceedings of the The 12th Joint Conference on Lexical and Computational Semantics (*SEM 2023)*, pages 89–100
July 13-14, 2023 ©2023 Association for Computational Linguistics

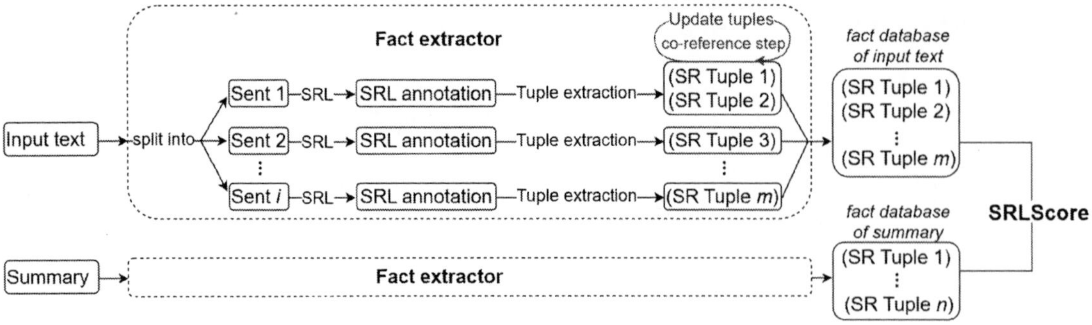

Figure 1: Visual explanation of **SRLScore**. An input text and its associated summary are transformed into a series of fact tuples (*SR Tuple*) through extraction from SRL (and optional co-reference) annotations. The final factuality score is computed based on the similarity of the summary facts with fact tuples generated from the input text.

additional benefit of being an *interpretable* metric, due to its composition on top of fact tuples. In comparison, metrics used for factuality evaluation that are based on the intermediate presentations of language models, e.g., *generation perplexity* (Zhang et al., 2020; Thompson and Post, 2020; Yuan et al., 2021), cannot present insightful reasons *why* a particular score was achieved. Furthermore, it has been empirically demonstrated that generation-based evaluators exhibit a *self-preference* of outputs generated by models similar to the factuality evaluator (Fabbri et al., 2021; Liu et al., 2023). This makes them a questionable choice over interpretable metrics. We empirically show that the correlation of **SRLScore** with human ratings is on par with existing methods, and perform several ablations to study the impact of algorithmic choices within our pipeline.

2 Related Work

Automated analysis of (abstractive) summaries became more relevant in recent years, with the influx of generic summarization systems becoming available (Nallapati et al., 2016; See et al., 2017; Lewis et al., 2020). In particular, Goodrich et al. (2019) were the first to propose a reference-based estimator for factuality of generated summaries. As mentioned, their approach is based on a tuple representation of "facts" in the generated and gold summary. Fact tuples are extracted based on a weakly supervised end-to-end tagger and subsequently compared on the basis of matching arguments. Notably, no readily available implementation of their method currently exists.

Later work has proposed alternative metrics based on textual entailment (Falke et al., 2019; Mishra et al., 2021) and Question Answering (QA) (Wang et al., 2020; Durmus et al., 2020), where agreement of answers to questions on the reference and summary are used for estimating factuality. However, QA-based metrics require additional task-specific fine-tuning on generic datasets, which makes the adoption to new domains fairly expensive.

The only other work that to our knowledge utilizes some form of SRL-based factuality estimation is presented by Fischer et al. (2022). In comparison to **SRLScore**, their method aggregates "role buckets" at the document level, instead of creating sentence-specific fact tuples. Empirically, their implementation has lower correlation with human ratings than compared approaches, which is contrary to our own findings.

Li et al. (2022) frame factuality estimation as an in-filling task, where fact statements are withheld as masked tokens in a generated summary, and a separate model is trained to predict missing facts. Notably, this relies on the assumption that the majority of factual mistakes stems from noun phrases and entity mentions (Pagnoni et al., 2021).

An alternative body of literature has explored the possibility to exploit Language Models (LMs) directly for estimating factual consistency: Some works, such as BertScore (Zhang et al., 2020), use LM-generated representations to generate alignments for scoring. In comparison, PRISM (Thompson and Post, 2020) or BARTScore (Yuan et al., 2021) directly use model perplexity as a factuality estimate. Xie et al. (2021) explore masking approaches, which fall somewhere between the works of Li et al. (2022) and BARTScore; their framing of counterfactual estimation still relies on model-based likelihood scores for computation.

The majority of prior work expresses metric perfor-

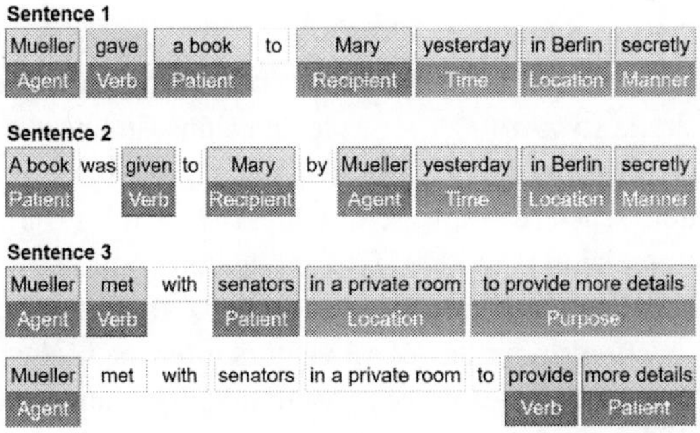

Figure 2: Examples of semantic role label annotations. Labels may remain consistent across different syntactic forms (Sentence 1 & 2). A single sentence can also include several relations at the same time (Sentence 3).

mance in terms of correlation with human factuality ratings. Notably, annotations exist for subsets of the popular CNN/DailyMail (Hermann et al., 2015; Nallapati et al., 2017) and XSUM summarization corpora (Narayan et al., 2018). Where Wang et al. (2020) collect user annotations from crowd workers, Fabbri et al. (2021) additionally sample expert judgments, and find that expert ratings tend to be more representative. Maynez et al. (2020) study several aspects of summarization evaluation beyond just factuality, but do not disclose the background of annotators for evaluation.

Generally, reliably evaluating correlation of summarization metrics with human preferences is no easy task, either: Deutsch et al. (2022) show that system-level evaluation metrics for text summarization rarely outperform simplistic metrics, such as ROUGE (Lin, 2004), to a statistically significant degree. Partially, this can be attributed to the small number of human-annotated samples available, generally less than 1000 different instances.

3 SRLScore

Our factual consistency metric, called **SRLScore**, is implemented as a two-stage process: first, extracting fact tuples using Semantic Role Labeling (SRL) on both the source texts and the summary texts, and then determining a factuality score based on tuple comparison. The measure outputs human-interpretable scores between 0 and 1, where a higher score indicates greater factual consistency of a summary text. In this section, we detail the algorithmic choices and present an adaptive weighting scheme for computing the final factuality scores.

3.1 Generating Fact Tuples with Semantic Role Labeling

As Figure 1 shows, we operate on the sentence level, primarily because existing SRL tools work well on this level of granularity (Shi and Lin, 2019; Xu et al., 2021). The goal of our fact extractor is to produce *a fact database* comprised of semantic role tuples for each input text.
The primary task of SRL is to find all role-bearing constituents in a sentence and label them with their respective roles (Màrquez et al., 2008). Typical semantic roles include *agent*, *patient/theme*, *recipient*, *goal*, *instrument*, *manner*, *time*, *location* and so on. From the many semantic labels available, we include seven roles based on availability in tagging schemes to construct a fact tuple: *agent*, *negation*, *relation*, *patient*, *recipient*, *time*, and *location*. We further note that not every sentence needs to contain *all* of these roles; absent labels are represented by *None* in this work. Importantly, roles reveal the semantic relations between a predicate (verb) and its arguments, which implies that one can generate several fact tuples from a single sentence, depending on the number of verbs in it. To illustrate an exemplary fact tuple, the extracted semantic tuple from sentence 1 in Figure 2 is `(Mueller, None, gave, a book, Mary, yesterday, in Berlin)`.

3.2 Scoring Texts by Comparing Fact Tuples

Once fact tuples for both the input and summary texts are generated, the second step in our pipeline is to compute a factual accuracy score. We implement a dynamic weighting system, which crucially improves over a naive comparison, as we empirically show in Section 4.6. Furthermore, we describe the drop-in replacements for exact matching during similarity computation.

Scoring Algorithm. Given an input text R and summary text S, let F_R and F_S be *fact databases*, representing the semantic information contained in R and S, respectively. Individual fact tuples are represented as an ordered list of fact arguments, e.g., $f = (agent,\ negation,\ relation,\ patient,\ recipient,\ time,\ location) \in F$. Particular arguments in a fact tuple are referred to by their index position, meaning *agent* $= f^0$, *negation* $= f^1$, and so on. We further assume that there exists a scoring function that expresses the *factual support of summary tuple f_s, given an input tuple f_r*, denoted as $S(f_s|f_r)$. To obtain a factuality score, we attempt to extract the best match $\hat{f}_r \in F_R$ for each summary fact $f_s \in F_s$ where $\hat{f}_r$ maximizes the support score $S(f_s|\hat{f}_r)$. Importantly, we differ from, e.g., Goodrich et al. (2019), by considering the entirety of F_R, instead of subsets that match both the agent and relation of the fact tuple. The factual accuracy is then the average across all maximized tuple scores in F_S. With that, **SRLScore** is defined as:

$$\textbf{SRLScore}(R, S) := \frac{1}{|F_S|} \sum_{f_s \in F_s} \max_{f_r \in F_R} S(f_s|f_r) \quad (1)$$

The final part of this scoring system is the computation of factual support $S(f_s|f_r)$. Tuples are scored by comparing the corresponding attributes of each tuple, formally:

$$S(f_s|f_r) := \sum_i \mathbb{1}_{f_s^i \neq None} \cdot sim(f_s^i, f_r^i) \cdot w_i, \quad (2)$$

where the summation over i addresses all attributes of the fact tuples, $\mathbb{1}_{f_s^i \neq None}$ represents an indicator function considering only non-empty arguments f_s^i (zero otherwise), and w_i assigns static weights to arguments in position i. Generally, it should be assumed that the weights allow for a maximum factuality score of 1, i.e., $\sum_i w_i = 1$. Finally, $sim(f_s^i, f_r^i)$ is the pairwise argument similarity of f_s^i and f_r^i. We consider different similarity metrics, as described in the following paragraphs.

Dynamic Weighting System. The generic weighting in Equation (2) does not necessarily apply to the particular case of evaluating factual consistency in summarization, since a summary is still factually correct even if it leaves out particular aspects (e.g., dropping the date of an event), which were present in the input text. With static weights, however, absent arguments are still contributing to the scoring of the tuple f_s, which means that leaving arguments out might potentially be considered as a penalization of factuality. To address this issue, we introduce a weight re-normalization factor, W_{norm}, that distributes the static weights w_i across only those attributes that are present in the current summary fact. In particular, this also increases penalties for actual mistakes over simple fact omission. The weight normalization is defined as follows:

$$W_{norm} := \frac{1}{\sum_i \mathbb{1}_{f_s^i \neq None} \cdot w_i} \quad (3)$$

With re-normalization enabled, we replace the existing computation of $S(f_s|f_r)$ by the product $W_{norm} \cdot S(f_s|f_r)$.

String Similarity Methods. We experiment with different methods to calculate the pairwise similarity $sim(f_s^i, f_r^i)$: exact matching (in line with prior work), but also approximate matching functions, such as word vector similarity[1] and ROUGE-1 precision (Lin, 2004). Computation of similarity with vectors and ROUGE each have their own respective strengths. Word vectors offer the highest flexibility in terms of recognizing argument similarity, enabling semantic comparison instead of purely syntactic equivalence. ROUGE-1 similarity does not offer the same level of flexibility in terms of matching, but shines with its comparatively faster computation, while still recognizing partial matches.

3.3 Improved Surface Form Invariance with Co-reference Resolution

In light of the fact that sentence-level SRL extraction misses co-references of the same entity across the texts, we integrate an optional component that takes co-reference resolution into account during the tuple generation. Concretely, we employ an off-the-shelf co-reference resolution tool (Lee et al., 2017) to identify and store all reference clusters in an external *entity dictionary*. There, all linguistic expressions that refer to the same entity will be grouped together, which allows for later disambiguation. As shown in Figure 3, if an extracted semantic role tuple contains co-references, a single fact tuple will be *expanded* into multiple tuples, representing the Cartesian product over all synonymous entity surface forms.

The key idea here is to enable a better matching of potential facts across input texts and summaries, effectively increasing the recall of matches. The disadvantage is that this directly affects the runtime of our method by a strong factor, since the additional tuples in F_S and F_R will undoubtedly increase the number of comparisons.

4 Experiments

We empirically demonstrate the performance of our method through a number of experiments on two popular datasets for factual consistency evaluation, which are covered in this section. We further share implementation details and the choices for extracting SRL tuples and extracting co-reference clusters.

[1]We use spaCy's vector similarity, see `https://SpaCy.io/usage/linguistic-features#vectors-similarity`, last accessed: 2023-03-06.

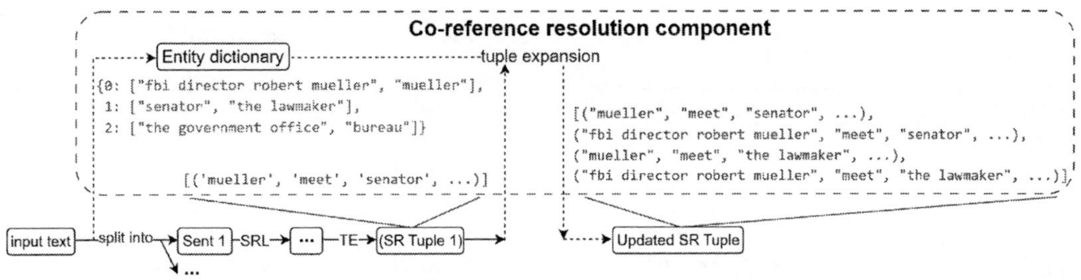

Figure 3: Example of the tuple expansion step through co-reference resolution. In addition to the original SR tuple, we add tuples with all possible permutations of the surface forms of mentioned entities.

In addition to the experimental analysis, we also study the behavior of **SRLScore** through a number of ablation experiments and a brief error analysis.

4.1 Evaluation Datasets

QAGS (Wang et al., 2020). The dataset comprises of two separate splits: the first contains 235 instances collected from the test split of CNN/DailyMail (Nallapati et al., 2016), where each instance contains a source article and a model-generated summary using the bottom-up approach by Gehrmann et al. (2018). A secondary set contains 239 further instances from the test split of XSUM (Narayan et al., 2018), with generated summaries sampled from BART (Lewis et al., 2020).

SummEval (Fabbri et al., 2021). It includes synthetic summaries from 16 different abstractive and extractive models of 100 randomly selected articles from the test split of CNN/DailyMail. Unlike QAGS, which collected annotations from MTurk[2], each SummEval sample was evaluated by five crowd-sourced annotators and three experts. For each summary, judges were asked to evaluate the coherence, consistency, fluency and relevance. For our evaluation, we use the expert ratings with regard to factual consistency as the gold score, based on the recommendation by Fabbri et al. (2021).

4.2 Evaluation Metrics and Significance

In line with prior work, we evaluate metrics by computing Pearson correlation (denoted as ρ) and Spearman correlation (denoted as s) between model predictions and human reference ratings. Given the limited size of all considered evaluation datasets, we further test results for significance using permutation tests (Riezler and Maxwell, 2005; Deutsch et al., 2021), following the recommendation of Dror et al. (2018). In all tables, † denotes a significance level of 0.05 ($p < 0.05$) and ‡ a level of 0.01 ($p < 0.01$). When testing significance against several systems, we further apply Bonferroni correction of significance levels (Dunn, 1961).

4.3 Implementation

We use AllenNLP (Gardner et al., 2018), specifically version 2.1.0, to extract semantic role labels. AllenNLP implements a BERT-based SRL tagger (Shi and Lin, 2019), with some modifications. The output of AllenNLP uses PropBank convention (Palmer et al., 2005; Bonial et al., 2012; Pradhan et al., 2022), which lists for each verb its permitted role labels using numbered arguments (*ARG0, ARG1, ...*) instead of names, due to the difficulty of providing a small, predefined list of semantic roles that is sufficient for all verbs. Since numbered arguments are meant to have a verb-specific meaning (Yi et al., 2007), this implies that our mapping between numbered arguments and semantic roles may not always be consistent. The exact mapping used in our experiments is detailed in Appendix A. For co-reference, we similarly use the model provided by AllenNLP (Lee et al., 2017), which matches the output format of the SRL tagger.

All experiments were carried out on a system with an Intel Xeon Silver 4210 CPU, two TITAN RTX GPUs (24 GB GPU VRAM each) and 64 GB of main memory. We run inference for the SRL model and co-reference component on separate GPUs.

We report scores of all system and baseline variants across a single random seed only. Since we are comparing provided "plug-and-play" metrics, it is reasonable to assume that these are the primary choice for others evaluating their own datasets. Particularly for **SRLScore**, we further note that due to the system design, no fine-tuning or training is necessary. The only parameters varied during the experiments are thus the argument weights, which we describe in the following section.

[2]https://www.mturk.com/, last accessed: 2023-03-06.

Metrics	QAGS-CNN/DM		QAGS-XSUM		SummEval		Avg.
	ρ	s	ρ	s	ρ	s	ρ
ROUGE-1 (F1)	0.34	0.32	−0.01	−0.05	0.13	0.14	0.15
BLEU	0.13	0.33	0.08	0.03	0.09	0.14	0.10
METEOR	0.33	0.36	0.06	0.01	0.12	0.14	0.17
BARTScore	0.65	0.57	0.00	0.02	0.27	0.26	0.31
$\text{BARTScore}_{\text{cnn}}$	**0.73**	**0.68**	0.19	0.18	0.35	0.32	0.42
$\text{BARTScore}_{\text{cnn+para}}$	0.69	0.62	0.07	0.07	0.42	**0.37**	0.39
$\text{CoCo}_{\text{span}}$	0.64	0.55	0.22	0.20	0.40	0.35	0.42
$\text{CoCo}_{\text{sent}}$	0.68	0.59	0.16	0.14	0.39	0.35	0.41
$\text{ClozE-R}_{\text{en\_core\_web\_trf}}{}^{*}$	0.66	-	0.32	-	0.47	-	**0.48**
$\text{ClozE-R}_{\text{confidence}}{}^{*}$	0.65	-	0.29	-	**0.48**	-	0.47
$\text{SRLScore}_{\text{base}}$	0.67	0.59	0.20	0.18	0.43	0.33	0.43
$\text{SRLScore}_{\text{coref}}$	0.65	0.58	0.27	0.26	0.43	0.32	0.45
$\text{SRLScore}_{\text{coref-optimized}}$	-	-	**0.33**	**0.33**	-	-	-

Table 1: Pearson (ρ) and Spearman (s) correlation of metrics with human ratings on the evaluated datasets. Bold scores indicate highest absolute values. For **SRLScore** variants, we report highest scores across all similarity functions. No significant differences were found between the correlation scores of factuality-specific metrics.
*: results were taken from the respective paper, as there is no existing code to reproduce their results as of now.

4.4 System Variants

We compare with a number of generic automatic evaluation metrics, including BLEU (Papineni et al., 2002), ROUGE (Lin, 2004), and METEOR (Banerjee and Lavie, 2005). Besides, we also consider several metrics specifically developed for factuality estimation, which have reported prior state-of-the-art correlation. Wherever possible, we reproduce scores with the official scripts provided by authors. Comparison is done with three variants of BARTScore (Yuan et al., 2021), two variants of CoCo (Xie et al., 2021), and two variants of ClozE (Li et al., 2022). For more details on reproducibility, see Appendix B. We chose each variant such that the highest self-reported scores of each paper on all evaluated datasets are considered.

For our own method, $\text{SRLScore}_{\text{base}}$ represents a default setting, assigning equal weights $w_i = \frac{1}{7}$ to all attributes (*agent, negation, relation, patient, recipient, time, location*); the respective similarity function (exact match, spaCy vector, or ROUGE similarity) is chosen to maximize dataset-specific performance (see results of Table 2). $\text{SRLScore}_{\text{coref}}$ uses the same weights, with co-reference enabled. We further provide model ablations to test various specifications of our models. As we could not find a implementation based on the original tuple extraction approach by Goodrich et al. (2019), we introduce $\text{SRLScore}_{\text{openie}}$ and $\text{SRLScore}_{\text{goodrich}}$ as approximations of their method. Here, fact tuples are reduced to `(agent, relation, patient)` triplets (with equal weights $w_i = \frac{1}{3}$). We note that this is not a true equivalence to the original method, although "[i]n most English sentences the subject is the agent" (Bates and Macwhinney, 1982); in reality, a broader variety of roles in the subject position may be encountered. The same applies for our mapping between *object* and the *patient* role. However, by using the same upstream labeling tool (i.e., the SRL model provided by AllenAI), we may more accurately compare the algorithmic scoring methods, independent of the annotation accuracy. We argue that our SRL-based modeling of relationship triplets allows for a better generalization beyond Wikipedia, which Goodrich et al. were using in their own experiments.

The difference of $\text{SRLScore}_{\text{openie}}$ and $\text{SRLScore}_{\text{goodrich}}$ lies in the implemented scoring function, where the OpenIE variant employs our own scoring algorithm, $\text{SRLScore}_{\text{goodrich}}$ uses the preliminary filtering step defined in Goodrich et al. (2019). We do not apply a co-reference system in either one of the two ablation settings. Finally, $\text{SRLScore}_{\text{coref-optimized}}$ illustrates the possibility of adapting our method to a particular dataset. For this variant, we optimize available hyperparameters (weights, scoring function, co-reference) in order to obtain the highest possible scores.

4.5 Main Results

The central evaluation results with recommended default settings are shown in Table 1. In almost all cases, specialized factuality metrics show higher correlation than generic summarization evaluation metrics (ROUGE-1, BLEU and METEOR). Notably, despite the high increase in absolute scores, we do not always detect a significant level of improvement between factuality-specific metrics and generic metrics, particularly on QAGS-XSUM; we will discuss further implications of this in more detail later. When testing our own method, $\text{SRLScore}_{\text{base}}$, against generic metrics, we find strongly significant improvements only for Pearson correlation of QAGS-CNN/DM and SummEval, as well as Spearman correlation on SummEval ($p < 0.01$, with Bonferroni correction).

It should be further noted that $\text{BARTScore}_{\text{cnn}}$ and CoCo results use BART models (Lewis et al., 2020) that were fine-tuned on the CNN/DailyMail corpus (respectively a variant fine-tuned on XSUM for CoCo on QAGS-XSUM); this may shift the results in favor of these methods for the particular dataset. In comparison, **SRLScore** does not make such assumptions, which may indicate a potentially stronger generalization to unseen datasets.

The results in Table 1 also show that there are no significant differences between any of the factuality-specific metrics (**SRLScore**, BARTScore, and CoCo), particularly after applying Bonferroni correction for the comparison against several methods. These insights open up discussions about the current claims of "state-of-the-art" performance, which may not be easily distinguished on the current evaluation datasets. We admit that there is likely no trivial solution to this (besides further annotations), as the main problem seems to stem from the high variance on small sample sizes.

4.6 Ablation Study

Given the limited expressiveness of the generic result evaluation, we perform a series of ablation studies on **SRLScore**, to support the individual algorithmic choices made in our method.

Extending Tuple Attributes. We investigate the assumption that semantic representations of sentences are usually far more complicated than the simplistic view of (*agent*, *relation*, *patient*) triplets, and the fact that errors may involve further roles. To this end, we compared $\text{SRLScore}_{\text{openie}}$, using a triplet representation, against $\text{SRLScore}_{\text{base}}$ with seven roles. The results in Table 2 confirm that extending tuples to cover more semantic roles is effective across datasets and metrics; $\text{SRLScore}_{\text{base}}$ scores consistently better than $\text{SRLScore}_{\text{openie}}$, with significant improvements primarily on SummEval (the largest considered dataset).

Metrics		QCNNDM		QXSUM		SummE	
		ρ	s	ρ	s	ρ	s
$\text{SRLScore}_{\text{openie}}$	Exact	0.59	0.51	0.09	0.09	0.34	0.28
	ROUGE	0.62	0.56	0.07	0.07	0.41	0.32
	SpaCy	0.59	0.53	0.13	0.10	0.37	0.32
$\text{SRLScore}_{\text{base}}$	Exact	0.61	0.54	0.14	0.15	$0.37^{\dagger}$	$0.31^{\ddagger}$
	ROUGE	**0.67**	**0.59**	$0.15^{\dagger}$	0.13	$\mathbf{0.43}^{\dagger}$	0.33
	SpaCy	0.63	0.55	**0.20**	**0.18**	$0.40^{\dagger}$	$\mathbf{0.34}^{\dagger}$

Table 2: Comparison of **SRLScore** with a simplified triplet representation ($\text{SRLScore}_{\text{openie}}$). Extending the fact tuples strictly improves correlation with human ratings across all similarity functions. Significance markers indicate improvements over the same similarity function of the $_{\text{openie}}$ variant.

Weight Setting	QCNNDM		QXSUM		SummE	
	ρ	s	ρ	s	ρ	s
Static weights	0.59	0.49	0.09	0.09	0.38	0.28
Dynamic weights	**0.67**	**0.59**	**0.20**	**0.18**	**0.43**	**0.33**

Table 3: Correlation scores of $\text{SRLScore}_{\text{base}}$ with and without weight re-normalization enabled.

Performance of Similarity Functions. Also seen in Table 2 is the difference in scores across various similarity functions. **SRLScore** achieves generally higher correlation when using vector (spaCy) or ROUGE similarity over exact matching, although not to a significant degree. These observations can be attributed to the hypothesis that abstractive entity references will not be detected by exact matching. Also note that results on QAGS-XSUM are particularly affected by this, which shows higher levels of abstraction than CNN/DM-derived resources (Wang et al., 2020; Pagnoni et al., 2021). This is also visible for the $\text{SRLScore}_{\text{coref}}$ variant, as seen in Table 1, which can further improve the matching of re-formulations.

Dynamic Weight Re-Normalization. We next analyze the contribution of our dynamic weighting scheme through removing the weight re-normalization W_{norm} and instead defaulting to a static weighting on $\text{SRLScore}_{\text{base}}$. Results in Table 3 demonstrate that re-distributing static weights dynamically to present roles is very effective, however, results show no statistical significance.

Scoring Method	QCNNDM		QXSUM		SummE	
	ρ	s	ρ	s	ρ	s
SRLScore$_{goodrich}$	0.45	0.38	0.05	0.07	0.29	0.24
SRLScore$_{openie}$	**0.62**†	**0.56**†	**0.13**	**0.10**	**0.41**‡	**0.32**†

Table 4: Results of the ablation experiment comparing the scoring method by Goodrich et al. (2019) with our proposed scheme, based on triplet representations.

SRLScore		BARTScore		
base	coref	base	cnn	cnn+para
2.35	19.32	0.22	0.23	0.23

Table 5: Average processing time (in seconds) per instance in QAGS-CNN/DM. **SRLScore** uses ROUGE similarity. BARTScore is run with a batch size of 4.

Ablation of Goodrich Scoring Method. We finally examine the performance of our scoring system against the partial matching approach of Goodrich et al. For fairness, we compare results on the reduced triplet sets. SRLScore$_{openie}$ uses the presented weighting function, SRLScore$_{goodrich}$ implements an equivalent scoring to Goodrich et al. Results in Table 4 show that the presented scoring algorithm performs better than the scores determined by Goodrich's approach on different datasets, in most instances to a significant degree.

Performance of Co-reference Resolution System. Results in Table 1 reveal that the co-reference system is not always improving scores, particularly on the CNN/DailyMail-derived datasets. However, the use of co-reference resolution will significantly increase the processing time, as shown in Table 5. This is expected, given that there are now more fact tuples due to the *tuple expansion*; since the presented scoring method requires the comparison of each fact tuple in the summary against *all* input text tuples. We further compare the runtime against BARTScore, which only requires a single forward-pass through a neural net and can be batched easily, resulting in a 10x speed-up. In contrast, **SRLScore** requires construction and comparison the fact tuples, which are the main contributors for slower inference times.

4.7 Error Analysis

To better understand the limitations of our presented methods, we examine a number of instances manually, particularly those where there are large differences between model-generated scores and human annotations on QAGS-XSUM. Table 6 shows two instances, where **SRLScore** respectively predicts a much higher and lower factuality score than human annotators. Notably, human raters tend to drastically reduce factuality scores in the presence of even a single mistake (what we refer to as *"strike-out scoring"*). In comparison, **SRLScore** and other factuality metrics tend to be more heavily influenced by the correctness of the *majority* of attributes, which can be seen as a *"bottom-up scoring"* (scores are built up from a initial factuality of zero instead of deducing from an initial score of one). On the other hand, highly abstractive samples, which retain factuality according to human raters, may pose a challenge for tuple-based **SRLScore**. In the second example of Table 6, synonymous expressions like *step down* instead of *resign* cause low predicted similarity; potential solutions could be found in verb sense disambiguation (Brown et al., 2011, 2022).

5 Conclusion and Future Directions

In this work, we presented a semantically consistent metric for estimating the factual truthfulness of two pieces of text: we applied our presented metric to the problem of text summarization evaluation, and demonstrated that it performs on par with existing approaches. In fact, we find that due to the small sample sizes of evaluation datasets, there are no significant differences between any of the considered state-of-the-art factuality estimation metrics. Our approach strikes with its relative simplicity and interpretability due to the intermediate representation of "fact tuples", which makes it possible for human annotators to review how or why system decisions were made. Furthermore, we have demonstrated the suitability of our approach over more naive tuple-based scoring methods through a series of ablation experiments, which also show the adaptability of our method to particular unseen settings by simply adjusting a series of parameters.

In our opinion, there are two key challenges concerning the effective deployment of **SRLScore**. The current implementation still suffers from impractically long runtimes for longer input texts. Notably, however, both the tuple generation and comparison stages can be parallelized and we are currently working on improving the compute effi-

	Sample Text	Extracted Fact Tuples	Human	SRLScore
Input	Former England fast bowler Chris Tremlett has announced his retirement ...	(Former England fast bowler chris tremlett, announce, his retirement, ...)	0	0.87
Summary	Former England seamer James Tremlett has announced his retirement ...	(Former England seamer james tremlett, announce, his retirement, ...)		
Input	The head of Japanese advertising group Dentsu is to step down following the suicide of an employee ...	(The head of japanese advertising group dentsu, step, ..., following the suicide of an employee, ...)	1	0.10
Summary	The chief executive of Japanese advertising firm Dentsu will resign after a worker killed herself ...	(The chief executive of japanese advertising firm dentsu, resign, ..., after a worker killed herself, ...), (a worker, killed, herself, ...)		

Table 6: Examples from the QAGS-XSUM dataset where the majority vote of human ratings differs strongly from **SRLScore**'s predicted factuality. Colored text segments highlight the position of relevant facts, where red text indicates a factual discrepancy between input and summary segments.

ciency of our method. Secondly, we have seen a general trend that factuality estimation metrics are scoring differently from human annotators, who are putting heavy emphasis on a *completely* factual summary instead. We suspect that adopting a similar *strike-out scoring* for estimation may better correlate with human ratings, although it will require sufficiently accurate taggers to ensure correct recognition of all entities.

Limitations

While the presented method exhibits stable correlation with human judgments on some of the evaluated datasets, it still exhibits instances under which it will predict opposing factuality scores. It should therefore be considered an *addition* to human evaluation, but at this point not fully replace it.

We also want to point out that the underlying summarization datasets that were used to compare human ratings on are known for their own set of limitations, particularly being fairly extractive in nature. This plays well with **SRLScore**'s estimation of matching between individual tuples extracted from single sentences; on the other hand, if summary texts contain facts derived from multiple source sentences (or undergo otherwise complex structural changes), fact tuples may be insufficient in their current form.

Another limitation is the expressiveness of results on the fairly small human-annotated datasets. Here, statistically significant differences can rarely be obtained. However, we are to our knowledge the first to demonstrate this insight about (significant) differences between existing methods, which we consider a particularly useful insight for future work.

We further want to point out that our method was only evaluated on English datasets; we argue that it can be applied to other languages, given a similarly performing SRL labeling model. In practice, however, the existence of available models is currently limited for non-English languages.

Ethics Statement

The paper considers the automated analysis of factuality in generated text. While we see no imminent risk in the development of our presented method, we want to point to the explicitly spelled out limitations of the current method (see the previous section). The blind application of factuality metrics could be considered harmful in instances where the predicted scores are differing strongly from human ratings. We therefore recommend that factuality metrics should be employed purely as a *complementary* evaluation, and never directly replace analysis with humans in the loop.

Acknowledgments

We thank the anonymous reviewers for their helpful comments and suggestions. The work of Jing Fan is supported by a scholarship of the China Scholarship Council (CSC).

References

Satanjeev Banerjee and Alon Lavie. 2005. METEOR: An automatic metric for MT evaluation with improved correlation with human judgments. In *Proceedings of the ACL Workshop on Intrinsic and Extrinsic Evaluation Measures for Machine Translation and/or Summarization*, pages 65–72, Ann Arbor, Michigan. Association for Computational Linguistics.

Elizabeth Bates and Brian Macwhinney. 1982. Functionalist approaches to grammar. *Child Language: The State of the Art*.

Claire Bonial, Jena Hwang, Julia Bonn, Kathryn Conger, Olga Babko-Malaya, and Martha Palmer. 2012. English propbank annotation guidelines. *Center for Computational Language and Education Research Institute of Cognitive Science University of Colorado at Boulder*, 48.

Susan Windisch Brown, Julia Bonn, Ghazaleh Kazeminejad, Annie Zaenen, James Pustejovsky, and Martha Palmer. 2022. Semantic representations for NLP using verbnet and the generative lexicon. *Frontiers Artif. Intell.*, 5:821697.

Susan Windisch Brown, Dmitriy Dligach, and Martha Palmer. 2011. VerbNet class assignment as a WSD task. In *Proceedings of the Ninth International Conference on Computational Semantics (IWCS 2011)*.

Daniel Deutsch, Rotem Dror, and Dan Roth. 2021. A statistical analysis of summarization evaluation metrics using resampling methods. *Transactions of the Association for Computational Linguistics*, 9:1132–1146.

Daniel Deutsch, Rotem Dror, and Dan Roth. 2022. Re-examining system-level correlations of automatic summarization evaluation metrics. In *Proceedings of the 2022 Conference of the North American Chapter of the Association for Computational Linguistics: Human Language Technologies*, pages 6038–6052, Seattle, United States. Association for Computational Linguistics.

Rotem Dror, Gili Baumer, Segev Shlomov, and Roi Reichart. 2018. The hitchhiker's guide to testing statistical significance in natural language processing. In *Proceedings of the 56th Annual Meeting of the Association for Computational Linguistics (Volume 1: Long Papers)*, pages 1383–1392, Melbourne, Australia. Association for Computational Linguistics.

Olive Jean Dunn. 1961. Multiple comparisons among means. *Journal of the American statistical association*, 56(293):52–64.

Esin Durmus, He He, and Mona Diab. 2020. FEQA: A question answering evaluation framework for faithfulness assessment in abstractive summarization. In *Proceedings of the 58th Annual Meeting of the Association for Computational Linguistics*, pages 5055–5070, Online. Association for Computational Linguistics.

Alexander R. Fabbri, Wojciech Kryściński, Bryan McCann, Caiming Xiong, Richard Socher, and Dragomir Radev. 2021. SummEval: Re-evaluating summarization evaluation. *Transactions of the Association for Computational Linguistics*, 9:391–409.

Tobias Falke, Leonardo F. R. Ribeiro, Prasetya Ajie Utama, Ido Dagan, and Iryna Gurevych. 2019. Ranking generated summaries by correctness: An interesting but challenging application for natural language inference. In *Proceedings of the 57th Annual Meeting of the Association for Computational Linguistics*, pages 2214–2220, Florence, Italy. Association for Computational Linguistics.

Tim Fischer, Steffen Remus, and Chris Biemann. 2022. Measuring faithfulness of abstractive summaries. In *Proceedings of the 18th Conference on Natural Language Processing (KONVENS 2022)*, pages 63–73, Potsdam, Germany. KONVENS 2022 Organizers.

Matt Gardner, Joel Grus, Mark Neumann, Oyvind Tafjord, Pradeep Dasigi, Nelson F. Liu, Matthew Peters, Michael Schmitz, and Luke Zettlemoyer. 2018. AllenNLP: A deep semantic natural language processing platform. In *Proceedings of Workshop for NLP Open Source Software (NLP-OSS)*, pages 1–6, Melbourne, Australia. Association for Computational Linguistics.

Sebastian Gehrmann, Yuntian Deng, and Alexander Rush. 2018. Bottom-up abstractive summarization. In *Proceedings of the 2018 Conference on Empirical Methods in Natural Language Processing*, pages 4098–4109, Brussels, Belgium. Association for Computational Linguistics.

Ben Goodrich, Vinay Rao, Peter J. Liu, and Mohammad Saleh. 2019. Assessing the factual accuracy of generated text. In *Proceedings of the 25th ACM SIGKDD International Conference on Knowledge Discovery & Data Mining, KDD 2019, Anchorage, AK, USA, August 4-8, 2019*, pages 166–175. ACM.

Karl Moritz Hermann, Tomás Kociský, Edward Grefenstette, Lasse Espeholt, Will Kay, Mustafa Suleyman, and Phil Blunsom. 2015. Teaching machines to read and comprehend. In *Advances in Neural Information Processing Systems 28: Annual Conference on Neural Information Processing Systems 2015, December 7-12, 2015, Montreal, Quebec, Canada*, pages 1693–1701.

Dan Jurafsky and James H. Martin. 2009. *Speech and language processing: an introduction to natural language processing, computational linguistics, and speech recognition, 2nd Edition*. Prentice Hall series in artificial intelligence. Prentice Hall, Pearson Education International.

Wojciech Kryscinski, Bryan McCann, Caiming Xiong, and Richard Socher. 2020. Evaluating the factual consistency of abstractive text summarization. In *Proceedings of the 2020 Conference on Empirical Methods in Natural Language Processing (EMNLP)*, pages 9332–9346, Online. Association for Computational Linguistics.

Kenton Lee, Luheng He, Mike Lewis, and Luke Zettlemoyer. 2017. End-to-end neural coreference resolution. In *Proceedings of the 2017 Conference on Empirical Methods in Natural Language Processing*, pages 188–197, Copenhagen, Denmark. Association for Computational Linguistics.

Mike Lewis, Yinhan Liu, Naman Goyal, Marjan Ghazvininejad, Abdelrahman Mohamed, Omer Levy, Veselin Stoyanov, and Luke Zettlemoyer. 2020. BART: Denoising sequence-to-sequence pre-training for natural language generation, translation, and comprehension. In *Proceedings of the 58th Annual Meeting of the Association for Computational Linguistics*, pages

7871–7880, Online. Association for Computational Linguistics.

Yiyang Li, Lei Li, Qing Yang, Marina Litvak, Natalia Vanetik, Dingxin Hu, Yuze Li, Yanquan Zhou, Dongliang Xu, and Xuanyu Zhang. 2022. Just cloze! A fast and simple method for evaluating the factual consistency in abstractive summarization. *CoRR*, abs/2210.02804.

Chin-Yew Lin. 2004. ROUGE: A package for automatic evaluation of summaries. In *Text Summarization Branches Out*, pages 74–81, Barcelona, Spain. Association for Computational Linguistics.

Yang Liu, Dan Iter, Yichong Xu, Shuohang Wang, Ruochen Xu, and Chenguang Zhu. 2023. G-eval: NLG evaluation using GPT-4 with better human alignment. *CoRR*, abs/2303.16634.

Lluís Màrquez, Xavier Carreras, Kenneth C. Litkowski, and Suzanne Stevenson. 2008. Semantic role labeling: An introduction to the special issue. *Comput. Linguistics*, 34(2):145–159.

Joshua Maynez, Shashi Narayan, Bernd Bohnet, and Ryan McDonald. 2020. On faithfulness and factuality in abstractive summarization. In *Proceedings of the 58th Annual Meeting of the Association for Computational Linguistics*, pages 1906–1919, Online. Association for Computational Linguistics.

Anshuman Mishra, Dhruvesh Patel, Aparna Vijayakumar, Xiang Lorraine Li, Pavan Kapanipathi, and Kartik Talamadupula. 2021. Looking beyond sentence-level natural language inference for question answering and text summarization. In *Proceedings of the 2021 Conference of the North American Chapter of the Association for Computational Linguistics: Human Language Technologies*, pages 1322–1336, Online. Association for Computational Linguistics.

Ramesh Nallapati, Feifei Zhai, and Bowen Zhou. 2017. Summarunner: A recurrent neural network based sequence model for extractive summarization of documents. In *Proceedings of the AAAI Conference on Artificial Intelligence*, volume 31.

Ramesh Nallapati, Bowen Zhou, Cícero Nogueira dos Santos, Çaglar Gülçehre, and Bing Xiang. 2016. Abstractive text summarization using sequence-to-sequence rnns and beyond. In *Proceedings of the 20th SIGNLL Conference on Computational Natural Language Learning, CoNLL 2016*, pages 280–290. Association for Computational Linguistics.

Shashi Narayan, Shay B. Cohen, and Mirella Lapata. 2018. Don't give me the details, just the summary! topic-aware convolutional neural networks for extreme summarization. In *Proceedings of the 2018 Conference on Empirical Methods in Natural Language Processing*, pages 1797–1807, Brussels, Belgium. Association for Computational Linguistics.

Artidoro Pagnoni, Vidhisha Balachandran, and Yulia Tsvetkov. 2021. Understanding factuality in abstractive summarization with FRANK: A benchmark for factuality metrics. In *Proceedings of the 2021 Conference of the North American Chapter of the Association for Computational Linguistics: Human Language Technologies*, pages 4812–4829, Online. Association for Computational Linguistics.

Martha Palmer, Daniel Gildea, and Paul Kingsbury. 2005. The Proposition Bank: An annotated corpus of semantic roles. *Computational Linguistics*, 31(1):71–106.

Kishore Papineni, Salim Roukos, Todd Ward, and Wei-Jing Zhu. 2002. Bleu: a method for automatic evaluation of machine translation. In *Proceedings of the 40th Annual Meeting of the Association for Computational Linguistics*, pages 311–318, Philadelphia, Pennsylvania, USA. Association for Computational Linguistics.

Sameer Pradhan, Julia Bonn, Skatje Myers, Kathryn Conger, Tim O'gorman, James Gung, Kristin Wright-bettner, and Martha Palmer. 2022. PropBank comes of Age—Larger, smarter, and more diverse. In *Proceedings of the 11th Joint Conference on Lexical and Computational Semantics*, pages 278–288, Seattle, Washington. Association for Computational Linguistics.

Stefan Riezler and John T. Maxwell. 2005. On some pitfalls in automatic evaluation and significance testing for MT. In *Proceedings of the ACL Workshop on Intrinsic and Extrinsic Evaluation Measures for Machine Translation and/or Summarization*, pages 57–64, Ann Arbor, Michigan. Association for Computational Linguistics.

Abigail See, Peter J. Liu, and Christopher D. Manning. 2017. Get to the point: Summarization with pointer-generator networks. In *Proceedings of the 55th Annual Meeting of the Association for Computational Linguistics (Volume 1: Long Papers)*, pages 1073–1083, Vancouver, Canada. Association for Computational Linguistics.

Peng Shi and Jimmy Lin. 2019. Simple BERT models for relation extraction and semantic role labeling. *CoRR*, abs/1904.05255.

Maartje ter Hoeve, Julia Kiseleva, and Maarten de Rijke. 2020. What makes a good summary? reconsidering the focus of automatic summarization. *CoRR*, abs/2012.07619.

Brian Thompson and Matt Post. 2020. Automatic machine translation evaluation in many languages via zero-shot paraphrasing. In *Proceedings of the 2020 Conference on Empirical Methods in Natural Language Processing (EMNLP)*, pages 90–121, Online. Association for Computational Linguistics.

Alex Wang, Kyunghyun Cho, and Mike Lewis. 2020. Asking and answering questions to evaluate the factual consistency of summaries. In *Proceedings of the 58th Annual Meeting of the Association for Computational*

Linguistics, pages 5008–5020, Online. Association for Computational Linguistics.

Yuexiang Xie, Fei Sun, Yang Deng, Yaliang Li, and Bolin Ding. 2021. Factual consistency evaluation for text summarization via counterfactual estimation. In *Findings of the Association for Computational Linguistics: EMNLP 2021*, pages 100–110, Punta Cana, Dominican Republic. Association for Computational Linguistics.

Kun Xu, Han Wu, Linfeng Song, Haisong Zhang, Linqi Song, and Dong Yu. 2021. Conversational semantic role labeling. *IEEE/ACM Transactions on Audio, Speech, and Language Processing*, 29:2465–2475.

Szu-ting Yi, Edward Loper, and Martha Palmer. 2007. Can semantic roles generalize across genres? In *Human Language Technology Conference of the North American Chapter of the Association of Computational Linguistics*, pages 548–555. Association for Computational Linguistics.

Weizhe Yuan, Graham Neubig, and Pengfei Liu. 2021. Bartscore: Evaluating generated text as text generation. In *Advances in Neural Information Processing Systems 34: Annual Conference on Neural Information Processing Systems 2021, NeurIPS 2021, December 6-14, 2021, virtual*, pages 27263–27277.

Tianyi Zhang, Varsha Kishore, Felix Wu, Kilian Q. Weinberger, and Yoav Artzi. 2020. Bertscore: Evaluating text generation with BERT. In *8th International Conference on Learning Representations, ICLR 2020, Addis Ababa, Ethiopia, April 26-30, 2020*. OpenReview.net.

A Mapping of PropBank Arguments to Semantic Role Tuple Attributes

In our implementation, we extract sentence spans with label ARG0 as *agent* and spans with label ARG1 as *patient*. The extraction of *time* and *location* also does not pose any difficulties, because ARGM-TMP and ARGM-LOC are both given as modifiers that remain relatively stable across predicates (Jurafsky and Martin, 2009). However, as shown in Table 7, there is no one-to-one relationship between numbered arguments and the *recipient* role. For the sake of simplicity, we extracted elements with label ARG2 as *recipient*, because the probability that ARG2 correlates to *recipient* is the highest among all other possible roles (Yi et al., 2007).

ARG0	agent	**ARG1**	patient
ARG2	instrument, recipient, attribute	**ARG3**	starting point, recipient, attribute
ARG4	ending point	**ARGM**	modifier

Table 7: Mapping between numbered arguments in PropBank and semantic roles (Bonial et al., 2012). Particularly the mapping of argument 2 makes simplifying assumptions about different verb forms.

B Reproducing Scores of Related Work

We use the official scripts provided by the authors of BARTScore[3] and CoCo[4]. Unfortunately, no public implementation exists at the time of writing for the work of Li et al. (2022), which prevents significance testing against ClozE models. For the work by (Goodrich et al., 2019), we similarly found no publicly available implementation; however, we note their wikipedia-based training data for generating fact extractors is available online[5].

When attempting to reproduce the scores of Xie et al. (2021), based on their own implementation, we encountered wildly differing scores compared to the values reported by the authors. Some results show drastic improvements from a reported Pearson correlation 0.58 to a reproduced score of 0.68, while other values dropped (e.g., on QAGS-XSUM, we see a reduction of scores from 0.24 to 0.16 in terms of Pearson correlation). For the sake of reproducibility, we have included the exact commands that were used to run the CoCo models in our repository.

On the other hand, all of our reproduced scores for BARTScore (Yuan et al., 2021) match the available self-reported results by the authors.

For significance testing, we use our own implementation of a permutation-based significance test, again included in the code repository. We fix the initial `NumPy` random seed to 256, and compute results over 10,000 iterations for each test.

[3] `https://github.com/neulab/BARTScore`, last accessed: 2023-02-01.

[4] `https://github.com/xieyxclack/factual_coco`, last accessed: 2023-03-16.

[5] `https://github.com/google-research-datasets/wikifact`, last accessed: 2023-05-17

Language models are not naysayers: An analysis of language models on negation benchmarks

Thinh Hung Truong[1] **Timothy Baldwin**[1,3] **Karin Verspoor**[2,1] **Trevor Cohn**[1,*]
[1]University of Melbourne [2]RMIT University [3]MBZUAI
hungthinht@student.unimelb.edu.au tb@ldwin.net
karin.verspoor@rmit.edu.au trevor.cohn@unimelb.edu.au

Abstract

Negation has been shown to be a major bottleneck for masked language models, such as BERT. However, whether this finding still holds for larger-sized auto-regressive language models ("LLMs") has not been studied comprehensively. With the ever-increasing volume of research and applications of LLMs, we take a step back to evaluate the ability of current-generation LLMs to handle negation, a fundamental linguistic phenomenon that is central to language understanding. We evaluate different LLMs — including the open-source GPT-neo, GPT-3, and InstructGPT — against a wide range of negation benchmarks. Through systematic experimentation with varying model sizes and prompts, we show that LLMs have several limitations including insensitivity to the presence of negation, an inability to capture the lexical semantics of negation, and a failure to reason under negation.

1 Introduction

Despite being a core linguistic phenomenon, negation remains a major stumbling block for modern NLP architectures (Kassner and Schütze, 2020; Hossain et al., 2022). A reason for this could be that texts containing negation are underrepresented in training data of language models, as humans tend to express themselves using affirmative rather than negative expressions (Ettinger, 2020). Regardless, negation has been shown to be challenging even for humans to correctly interpret due to the diversity of forms across domains (Truong et al., 2022a). For instance, in clinical documents, many acronyms are used to denote negation such as *NAD (no abnormality detected)*, and implicit negation abounds, such as *normal chest x-ray scan*, which implies the absence of an abnormality. Even more complex is the use of negation in combination with other linguistic phenomena such as quantifiers, gradable adjectives (*not unattractive* does not imply *attractive*) (Truong et al., 2022b); licensing context (negative polarity items, e.g. *any, either, yet*, normally appear in certain negative grammatical contexts Warstadt et al. (2019)); downward entailment (*A man owns a dog* entails *A man owns an animal* but *A man does not own a dog* does not entail *A man does not own an animal*) (Geiger et al., 2020).

Traditionally, negation has been treated as a standalone problem, e.g. as negation detection (Chapman et al., 2001). The investigation of the impact of negation in various downstream tasks (Hossain et al., 2022; Hossain and Blanco, 2022a), or through probing (Ettinger, 2020) has revealed several limitations of modern large language models ("LLMs") in handling negation. Given that LLMs are being adopted in an ever-growing range of tasks and have been shown to display emergent abilities for high-level tasks that require complex reasoning (Wei et al., 2022a), we are interested in exploring how the handling of negation has progressed.

In this work, we investigate the performance of auto-regressive language models on different negation-focused benchmarks. Instead of just looking at samples containing negation in common NLP datasets, we consider datasets in which negation plays an important role in making the correct judgement. In particular, we classify the benchmarks into three categories corresponding to the requisite negation reasoning abilities: (1) sensitivity to negation through cloze completion (fill-in-the-blank) queries of factual statements; (2) lexical semantics of negation through classification of antonym/synonym relationships; and (3) ability to reason with negation through language inference tasks.

We conduct extensive experiments using prompt-based learning to facilitate zero- and few-shot evaluation of LLMs, and find the following:

- larger LMs are more insensitive to negation compared to smaller ones (Section 3);

*Now at Google DeepMind.

*Proceedings of the The 12th Joint Conference on Lexical and Computational Semantics (*SEM 2023)*, pages 101–114
July 13-14, 2023

Benchmark	Task	# Samples	Example
MKR-NQ	Completion	3360	Query: *Iburofen isn't a kind of [MASK].* Wrong completions: *NSAID, painkiller, drug, medicine.*
MWR	Completion	27546	Query: *Demand is an antonym of [MASK].* Wrong completions: *necessitate, demands, request, requirement, imposition, need, demand.*
SAR	NLI	2000	Word 1: *Superiority* / Word 2: *Inferiority* / Label: Antonym
NegNLI	NLI	4500	P: *They watched me constantly for weeks.* / H: *They did not leave me on my own for weeks.* / Label: Entailment
NaN-NLI	NLI	258	P: *Not all people have had the opportunities you have had.* / H: *Some people have not had the opportunities you have had.* / Label: Entailment
MoNLI	NLI	200	P: *The man does not own a dog.* / H: *The man does not own a mammal.* / Label: Not Entailment

Table 1: Summary of the negation-related benchmark datasets used in this paper.

- LLMs lack lexical semantic knowledge about negation, yielding almost random performance for synonym/antonym classification (Section 3);
- LLMs have limited ability to reason under negation, performing worse than random across most NLI datasets (Section 3). Only with the latest instruction fine-tuned model (Ouyang et al., 2022; Chung et al., 2022) do we observe above-chance performance (Section 3);
- For each dataset, we also experiment with prompt variations and find that in most cases, providing more information (context, instruction, simple wording) leads to a degradation in performance.

2 Experimental settings

In this section, we outline the settings that , including benchmark datasets, models to evaluate, and the prompts that were used. Our code is available at `https://github.com/joey234/llm-neg-bench`.

2.1 Benchmarks

We use a range of benchmark datasets that exhibit the effects of negation across a wide range of tasks, in the form of either cloze completion or classification tasks. An overview of the datasets is presented in Table 1, categorized according to purpose and the type of negation they contain. Specifically, we focus on: (1) investigating whether LLMs are sensitive to the presence of negation in factual statements; (2) testing whether LLMs capture negation in lexical semantics relations (synonym/antonym relations); and (3) investigating whether LLMs are able to reason under negation through multiple natural language inference benchmarks. We discuss the datasets in greater detail in Section 3.

2.2 Models

For the LLMs, we primarily focus on open-source auto-regressive LLMs with up to 6.7B parameters, including GPT-Neo (Black et al., 2021), and OPT (Zhang et al., 2022), which are claimed to be comparable in performance to similar-sized GPT-3 class models. Architecture-wise, they are both decoder-only PLMs pre-trained with a causal LM objective, with the main difference being in their pre-training corpora: GPT-neo was trained solely on the Pile dataset (Gao et al., 2020) consisting of 22 sub-datasets spanning different sources, whereas OPT was trained on the combination of datasets used in RoBERTa (Liu et al., 2019), Pile, and PushShift Reddit (Baumgartner et al., 2020). We use the official model checkpoints from HuggingFace hub,[1] as detailed in Appendix A. We experiment with smaller-sized variants of these two classes of models to observe the effect of scaling on their performance over different benchmarks.

We also consider base GPT-3 (175B) (Brown et al., 2020), and its instruction fine-tuned variant InstructGPT (Ouyang et al., 2022), as well as a strong open-source instruction-tuned model FLAN-T5-XXL (11B) (Chung et al., 2022), to examine how recent commercial LLMs perform on negation.

[1] `https://huggingface.co/models`

Task	Prompt name	Example
MKR-NQ	Default	An expectorant isn't a type of ___
	Contrasting	**An expectorant is a type of medicine.** An expectorant isn't a type of ___
	Discourse	**An expectorant is a type of medicine. Therefore,** an expectorant isn't a type of ___
	Mask	An **[MASK]** is a type of medicine. An **[MASK]** isn't a type of ___
MWR	Default	Greed is an antonym of ___
	Quote	**The word** "greed" is an antonym of **the word "** ___
SAR	Default	Choose the correct answer: bad and good are antonyms or synonyms? Answer: ___
	Simple	**Choose the correct answer:** bad and good are **opposite** or **similar**? **Answer:** ___
	Negation	**Antonyms are words with opposite meaning. Synonyms are words with similar meaning. Choose the correct answer:** bad and good are antonyms or synonyms? **Answer:** ___
NLI	Default	Not all people have had the opportunities you have had. **Question:** Some people have not had the opportunities you have had. True, False, or Neither? **Answer:** ___
	Negation	**The question requires reasoning about negation.** Not all people have had the opportunities you have had. **Question:** Some people have not had the opportunities you have had. True, False, or Neither? **Answer:** ___

Table 2: Prompts used for each task

2.3 Prompts

We adopt prompt-based learning to enable zero- and few-shot evaluation of LLMs (Radford et al., 2019). Given that LLMs have been found to be sensitive to prompt variation (Wei et al., 2021), and that more natural-sounding prompts correlate with model performance (Gonen et al., 2022), we also experiment with different types of prompts (see Table 2).

We use GPT-3 style prompts (Brown et al., 2020) as the *Default* setting. As handling negation plays an important role in all tasks, we also design prompts to prime the LLMs to focus more on the negation context, by introducing modifications specific to each task. In detail, for the cloze completion task MKR-NQ, we investigate whether a given model can detect the difference between two contrasting sentences (with/without negation). To achieve this, we prepend the prompt with the corresponding sentence without negation (*Contrasting* prompt). In addition, we also evaluate alternative prompts where we connect the two sentences with a discourse marker (*Discourse* prompt), or mask the main subject to encourage the model to attend more to negation cues (*Mask* prompt).

For antonym/synonym-related tasks (MWR, SAR), we also experiment with simplifying the prompt and use descriptive terms rather than the formal names of the relations (e.g. *antonyms, synonyms* $\rightarrow$ *opposite of, similar to*), based on the intuition that these terms will appear more frequently in the pre-training data.

Finally, for classification tasks, we propose negation-aware prompting (*Negation* prompt) by modifying the prompts to explicitly state that the task involves reasoning about negation. Note that we explicitly include class options in the prompts to help reduce the effect of the surface form competition causing LLMs to assign lower probabilities to the correct answers (Holtzman et al., 2021).

For datasets with an accompanying training set (SAR, MoNLI), we also experiment with few-shot evaluation formulated as *in-context learning* by prepending the input prompts with 10 random samples from the training set.

2.4 Metrics

To evaluate cloze completion tasks, we employ *Weighted Hit Rate (WHR)* (Jang et al., 2022b), which measures the number of matches between the top-k predicted words and a given set of target wrong predictions, taking into account the prediction probabilities:

$$WHR_k(x, W) = \frac{\sum_{i=1}^{k} c_i \times \mathbb{1}(w_i \in W_x)}{\sum_{i=1}^{k} c_i} \quad (1)$$

where W_x is the wrong prediction set of the input query x, and w_i is the top i-th prediction with confidence score c_i, obtained by taking the softmax of log probabilities $p(w_i|x)$ from the LM. Note that the model performance is better if there are fewer matches between models' predictions and wrong completions, *WHR* is an error metric (lower is better). One problem with the *WHR* metric is that we can only evaluate using a fixed set of wrong predictions. Regardless, we believe the relative performance numbers are indicative of model performance.

For classification tasks, we evaluate using *Accuracy*, noting that all datasets are reasonably balanced.

3 Main findings

We summarize the main findings in this section. In general, the performance of GPT-neo and OPT follows a similar trend across all benchmarks (we present GPT-neo results; results of OPT models are in Appendix B).

Finding 1: Larger LMs are more insensitive to negation

MKR-NQ (Jang et al., 2022b) Masked Knowledge Retrieval – Negated Query (MKR-NQ) is a negated version of the LAMA dataset (Petroni et al., 2019), which contains lexicalized statements of triples in ConceptNet (Speer et al., 2017). This dataset contains factual statements with verbal negations (i.e. negators *not, don't* are associated with the main verb of the sentence), e.g. *Iburofen is a type of medicine. → Iburofen isn't a type of medicine*.

Each sample contains the query along with a set of wrong word completions, supporting the evaluation of the sensitivity of the model to negation by measuring how likely a model will generate incorrect completions. Note that MKR-NQ only considers sample sentences that contain a single verb, making it trivial to negate the original sentences.

Findings From Figure 1, which is based on LLMs with a negated factual statement (*Default* prompt), we observe relatively low hit rates ($<$ 0.15) across all model sizes, and a clear inverse scaling trend between model sizes and their performance. The smallest variant (`GPT-neo-125M`) has the best performance, which is comparable to that of masked language model of a similar size (`BERT-base`, 110M parameters) (Jang et al., 2022b). This phenomenon reflects the finding that larger models tend to memorize the training data more (McKenzie et al., 2022; Jang et al., 2022a). Moreover, higher hit rates for top-1 predictions suggest that models predict wrongly with high confidence.

For *Contrasting* prompts, in which we prepend the negated statement with its non-negated version, we notice a drastic increase in *WHR*, showing that models are prone to repeating what is presented in the prior context, confirming the finding of Kassner and Schütze (2020). When a discourse term is added to connect the two sentences (*Discourse* prompt), we do not observe any improvement, and the performance of the largest model is even worse. To investigate whether this phenomenon is attributable to models not being able to detect the presence/absence of negation, we experiment with masking out the main noun/verb of the queries (*Mask* prompt). We observed even higher *WHR*, especially for the top-1 prediction in this setting. The results suggest that repetitions are caused more by LLMs being easily primed by repeating what is present in the previous context, than by generating words that are closely associated with the main subject of interest. This again shows that the models cannot differentiate between identical contexts, differing only on whether negation is present or absent (i.e., outputs tend to be similar with or without negation).

To further analyze the outputs, we calculate the perplexity (PPL) of the generated predictions to determine their plausibility (Wilcox et al., 2020). Here, we choose the model with the best WHR_5 score on the MKR-NQ benchmark, and calculate the mean perplexity over all queries for each prompt type (5 completions for each query). PPL is calculated as the exponentiated average negative log-likelihood of a sequence, with exponent base e. As a point of reference, we calculated the average perplexity of the provided completion of the original non-negated dataset (denoted *Corpus*). From the reported perplexities (Table 3), we can see that *Default* output are the most plausible (with PPL markedly lower than *Corpus*), while *Contrast-*

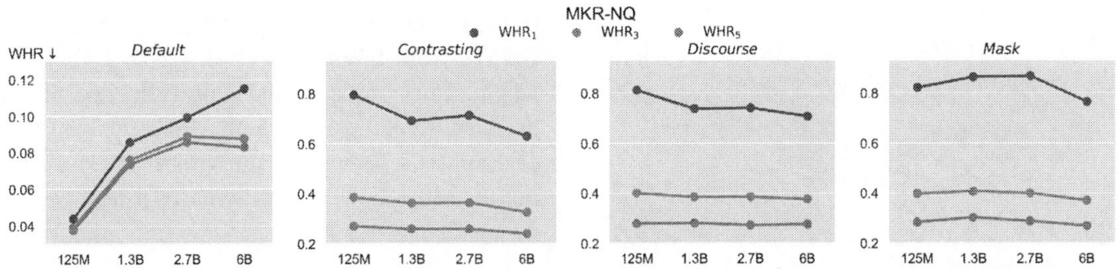

Figure 1: Zero-shot performance of GPT-neo on MKR-NQ using different prompts under the Weighted Hit Rate (WHR) metrics (lower scores are better). Note the different scale for the left-most plot.

Setting	Example	Mean PPL↓
Corpus	[Baseball is a type of sport.]	434.42
Default	[Baseball isn't a type of sport.]	288.94
Contrasting	Baseball is a type of sport. [Baseball isn't a type of sport.]	533.56
Discourse	Baseball is a type of sport. Therefore, [baseball isn't a type of sport.]	477.44
Mask	MASK is a type of sport. [MASK isn't a type of sport.]	448.23

Table 3: Mean perplexity (PPL) calculated using the `GPT-J-6B` model. Only the strings enclosed in square brackets are considered during calculation in order to provide a fair comparison with similar token length. For Corpus, PPL is calculated using the provided gold completion.

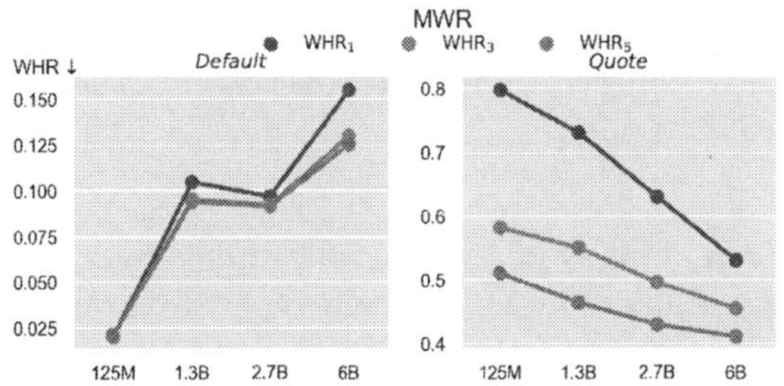

Figure 2: Zero-shot performance of GPT-neo on MWR using different prompts (WHR metrics; lower is better)

Query	Wrong completions	Top-5 predictions
Greed is an antonym of	*greed, avarice, desire, greeds, gluttony*	*altruism, self-sacrifice, self-denial, self-abnegation,* ***gods***
Finale is an antonym of	*conclusion, finish, finales, finale*	*last,* ***epiphany,*** *finality,* ***anti-climax, anti-climactic***

Table 4: Example output of `GPT-J-6B` on MWR. **bolded** words are related to target words, but are neither synonyms nor antonyms. underlined are wrong antonyms but are not in the given set of wrong completions.

ing is the least natural. The remaining prompts types (*Discourse, Mask*) are comparable to *Corpus*. These results show that LLMs can indeed generate plausible and human-like output for this task.

Finding 2: LMs fail to capture synonym/antonym lexical relations

MWR (Jang et al., 2022b) To test the ability of LMs to capture negative lexical semantics, we use MWR dataset, where models are asked to predict the antonym/synonym of a target word. The dataset was constructed by using the most frequent nouns, adjectives, and adverbs that appear in SNLI (Bowman et al., 2015), then choosing their corresponding synonyms and antonyms from ConceptNet (Speer et al., 2017). The dataset also contains different wordings for antonym-asking and synonym-asking queries (e.g. *is the opposite of, is different from* and *is similar to, is a rephrasing of*) to test model sensitivity to prompt variations.

Findings From Figure 2, we can observe the same inverse scaling trend as for MKR-NQ using the *Default* prompt, where the hit rate of the smallest model is around 0.02, better than previously-reported SOTA results (Jang et al., 2022b). With a more natural query with more focus on the target words via quotation marks (*Quote* prompt), surprisingly, we noticed a drastic jump in hit rates. However, MWR may not be a good indicator of model performance due to how the task is framed. One problem is that models can generate words that are not in the given wrong prediction set, but are also irrelevant, and are also neither antonyms nor synonyms of the given target words, as demonstrated in Table 4.

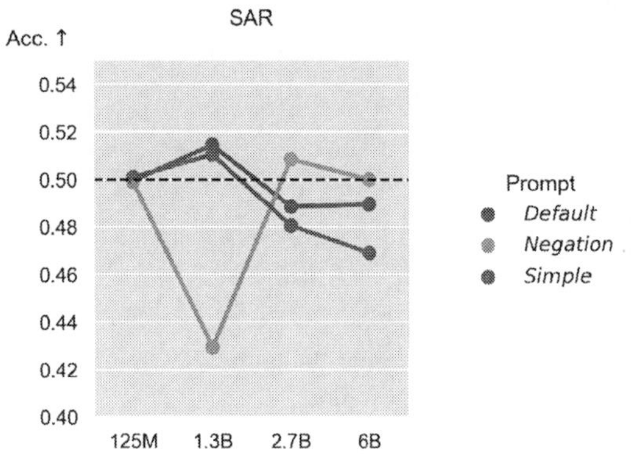

Figure 3: Zero-shot performance of GPT-neo on SAR dataset using different prompts (accuracy metric; higher is better)

SAR (Jang et al., 2022b) To further investigate the ability of LLMs to capture negative lexical semantics, we consider the antonym/synonym relation classification task (SAR). Different from the MWR cloze-style synonym/antonym prediction task, this benchmark is framed as a binary classification task of predicting the correct antonym or synonym relationship between two given words. Data is once again taken from ConceptNet, where triplets with synonym and antonym relations are extracted in equal numbers (1000 samples for each relation).

Findings In contrast to the high results for MWR, we find that for this task, model performance is equivalent to random, with accuracy fluctuating around 0.5 (Figure 3). For prompt variants, we do not observe any meaningful improvement, in that *Simple* follows a similar trend to *Default* and *Negation* performs better for larger models (2.7B and 6B). This is a huge degradation from previous fully fine-tuned results over encoder models. For instance, Jang et al. (2022b) reported that $\text{BERT}_{\text{large}}$ achieves 92.5% accuracy on SAR. We argue that this is a specific task that is not captured in the next token prediction training objective of LLMs and thus, requires explicit supervision.

Finding 3: LLMs are unable to reason under negation

NegNLI (Hossain et al., 2020) NegNLI contains 4500 premise–hypothesis pairs with *important* negation, where negation is essential in making the correct judgement about the relationship between the premise–hypothesis pairs. Samples are extracted from the commonly-used NLI datasets (RTE Dagan et al. (2005), SNLI Bowman et al. (2015), MNLI Williams et al. (2018)), then the negator *not* is added to the main verb either in the premise, hypothesis, or both. Here, we consider each subset separately, as the number of classes are not the same, and denote them SNLI-neg, MNLI-neg, RTE-neg.

MoNLI (Geiger et al., 2020) MoNLI is an NLI dataset focused on lexical entailment and negation. Specifically, the dataset investigates the downward monotonicity property where negation reverses entailment relations (e.g. *dance* entails *move*, but *not move* entails *not dance*). MoNLI was created by extending samples from SNLI by substituting the nouns by their hypernyms/hyponyms from WordNet (Miller, 1998).

NaN-NLI (Truong et al., 2022b) NaN-NLI is a test suite which focuses on sub-clausal negation, in which only part of the sentence's meaning is negated, thus making it harder to correctly determine the correct negation scope (e.g. in *Not the first time that they pulled that off* the negation scope is only *Not the first time* and the main clause of the sentence *they pulled that off* is not negated). Each premise–hypothesis pair is constructed so that the corresponding hypotheses are constructed to reflect different interpretations that the negated instance in the premise are likely to be misunderstood for.

Findings Similar to the antonym/synonym classification task, the performance for most negation-focused NLI benchmarks is low. In particular, for all NLI datasets, the performance is generally lower than baseline. As shown in Figure 4, scaling up model size has almost no effect, and the largest model performs worse in many cases, even when the prompt explicitly states that the task requires reasoning about negation (*Negation* prompt). For datasets which include a training set (SAR, MoNLI), we also experimented with few-shot learning but did not observe any noticable improvement (Figure 5). One exception is that the 2.7B model seems to pick up some signal from the provided MoNLI training samples, but falls back again when we increase the model size to 6B.

Even with general NLI datasets, zero-shot applications of LLMs were previously shown to be roughly equivalent to a random baseline (Wei et al., 2021). When negation is involved, the task becomes even more complex. As pointed out in Brown et al. (2020), one possible reason that LLMs

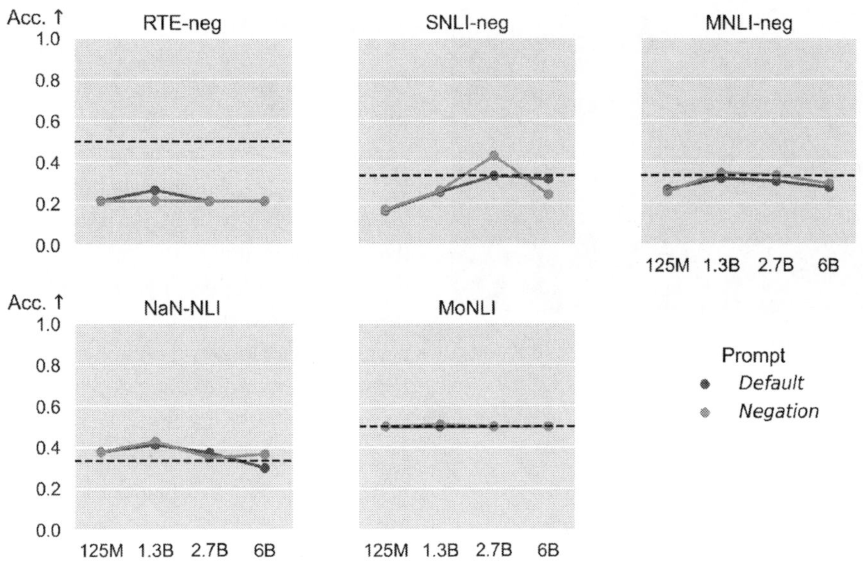

Figure 4: Zero-shot performance of GPT-neo on NLI datsets using different prompts (higher is better). The dashed line denotes a random baseline. Note that RTE-neg and MoNLI are 2-way classification tasks while the rest are 3-way.

Benchmark		GPT-J-6B	GPT-3	InstructGPT	InstructGPT w/ *Neg.* prompt	FLAN-T5-XXL w/ *Neg.* prompt
MKR-NQ	*WHR*↓	**0.083**	0.172	0.195	NA	NA
MWR		**0.125**	0.488	0.504	NA	NA
SAR	*Accuracy*↑	0.490	0.501	0.687	**0.780**	0.507
SNLI-neg		0.316	0.267	0.640	**0.673**	0.477
MNLI-neg		0.275	0.359	0.548	**0.625**	0.354
RTE-neg		0.211	0.525	0.767	**0.807**	0.770
NaN-NLI		0.298	0.469	0.647	**0.682**	0.376
MoNLI		0.500	**0.540**	0.470	0.400	0.500

Table 5: Zero-shot results on the different benchmarks. "NA" denotes that *Negation* prompts are not applicable to MKR-NQ and MWR. The best results are bolded for each task (row).

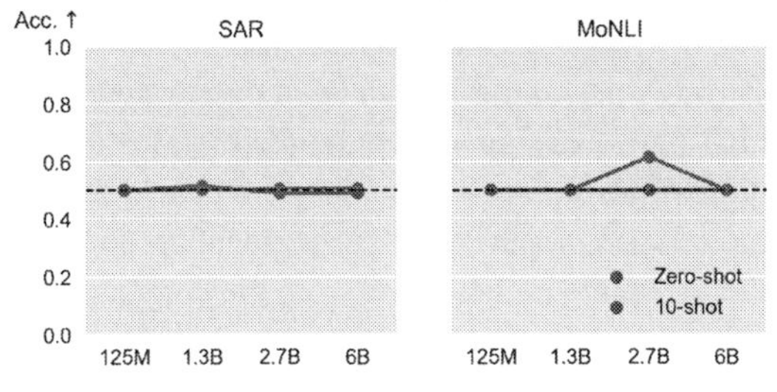

Figure 5: 10-shot performance of GPT-neo on SAR and MoNLI using *Default* prompt (higher is better)

struggle with NLI is that the samples consist of two disjoint sentences, which are unlikely to appear naturally in standard training corpora. We hypothesise that NLI is a generally hard task that requires substantially more supervision in order for models to detect meaningful patterns.

Finding 4: Instruction fine-tuning improves reasoning under negation

We further evaluate with GPT-3 class models of significantly larger scale (175B), which have been shown to achieve strong results in zero- and few-shot settings across a wide range of tasks (Brown et al., 2020). In detail, we benchmark the largest GPT-3 model (`text-davinci-001`: Brown et al. (2020)) and its variant InstructGPT, which is trained to follow human instructions using reinforcement learning (`text-davinci-003`: Ouyang et al. (2022)). The results can be found in Table 5.

For the base GPT-3 model, the results over most benchmarks are no better than much smaller language models (`GPT-neo-125M`). For cloze-completion tasks, consistent with the earlier-

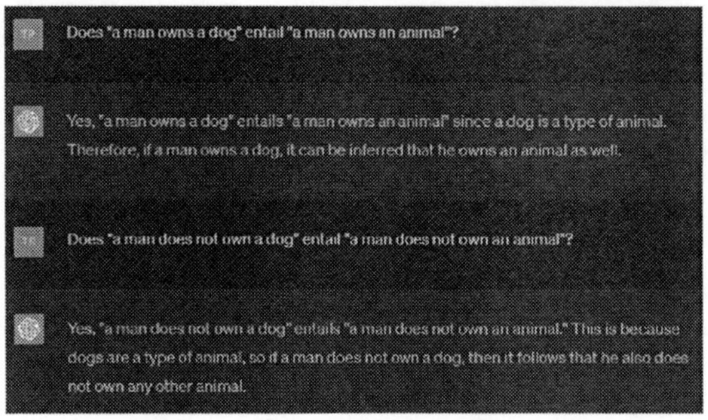

Figure 6: A ChatGPT-generated output of a failed negative monotonicity reasoning sample. The output was generated using ChatGPT Feb 13 Version

observed trend of larger models performing worse, we observe higher (worse) *WHR* scores compared to that of smaller language models, confirming our finding that larger models are more *in*sensitive to the presence of negation. Results get even worse with using the instruction fine-tuned model.

On the other hand, for most classification tasks, InstructGPT achieves better zero-shot results than other models. In addition, using this model in combination with explicit instruction about negation (*Negation* prompt) further improves performance, which we did not observe for other LLMs. It is, however, unclear what data the instruction-tuning process was performed on. Thus, the huge gain in performance could be attributed to the existence of similar patterns in the training set (i.e. explicit supervision over similar tasks). Interestingly, InstructGPT performance on MoNLI did not increase (it underperfomed other models). We hypothesize that this is due to an inductive bias from model's ability to reason with hypernymy. For instance, the model can understand that "*dog* is an *animal*" (and therefore *own an animal* entails *own a dog*), but incorrectly generalizes this logic to a similar sample containing negation (*not own a dog* entails *not own an animal*). This is indeed true when we look at the explanation generated by ChatGPT, the subsequent model to InstructGPT (Figure 6).

We also experiment with the instruction-tuned FLAN-T5-XXL model (Chung et al., 2022) and find that the results are better than GPT-3 for most NLI tasks, despite being $\sim$16x smaller. These results suggest that instruction fine-tuning has much greater impact than model scaling in terms of models developing the ability to perform reasoning tasks under negation.

4 Related work

Our work builds upon previous research on negation. In particular, we were inspired by the pioneering works of Kassner and Schütze (2020) and Ettinger (2020), which reveal that pre-trained language models have a major issue in being insensitive to the presence of negation, based on evaluation over a set of cloze-style queries. Following this line of research, Jang et al. (2022b) also explored negation in a cloze completion context by negating factual statements extracted from ConceptNet and come to a similar finding.

In a broader context, Hossain et al. (2020, 2022) investigated the performance of BERT-based methods on samples containing negation in the GLUE (Wang et al., 2018) and SuperGLUE (Wang et al., 2019) datasets. Their main finding is that the results for the subsets containing only negation are lower than those without, as well as the whole test set, showing that models struggle with negation, even when fine-tuned on relevant training data. Ravichander et al. (2022) proposed the challenging CONDAQA dataset to test the ability of models to reason about the implications of negation. The authors conducted comprehensive analysis of different types of LLMs under different settings, and found that the best-performing models were still well below human performance. Negation has also been investigated as part of psycholinguistic probing datasets (Lialin et al., 2022; Jumelet et al., 2021; Staliūnaitė and Iacobacci, 2020). Contrasting previous finding, Gubelmann and Handschuh (2022) found that the ability to understand negation of LMs is underestimated in previous studied. Through designing a controlled dataset with minimal pairs varying in syntactic structure, gender, profession, and first name, they concluded that the models are indeed sensitive to negation and thus, their struggle comes more from the contextualization of the tasks.

As part of the analysis on emergent abilities of LMs, negation has been shown to be one of the tasks that displays a flat scaling curve (Wei et al., 2022a) or even inverse-scaling (McKenzie et al., 2022). This behaviour was later shown to be alleviated by instruction fine-tuning (Wei et al., 2022b). The effectiveness of instruction fine-tuning is further supported in Jang and Lukasiewicz (2023). The authors investigated the logical consistency of ChatGPT and found that ChatGPT understands negation and antonyms much better than previous models.

Beside probing and evaluation, there have also been works on making language models more robust to negation, including unlikelihood training (Hosseini et al., 2021), adaptive pre-training on relevant data (Truong et al., 2022a), leveraging affirmative interpretations from negation (Hossain and Blanco, 2022b), and learning better representation of negation through contrastive learning (Jiang et al., 2022; Wang et al., 2022).

5 Conclusion

We have shown that LLMs still struggle with different negation benchmarks through zero- and few-shot evaluations, implying that negation is not properly captured through the current pre-training objectives. With the promising results from instruction-tuning, we can see that rather than just scaling up model size, new training paradigms are essential to achieve better linguistic competency. Through this investigation, we also encourage the research community to focus more on investigating other fundamental language phenomena, such as quantification, hedging, lexical relations, and downward entailment.

6 Limitations

First, regarding the experimental settings, the *WHR* metrics used to evaluate cloze completion tasks are imperfect, as we discussed. Framing cloze completion tasks in the style of multiple-choice question answering to limit the options that models are evaluated on would be a good direction to follow (Robinson et al., 2022). In addition, the prompt engineering in this work is in no way exhaustive, and could be extended using different prompt engineering strategies such as soft prompt tuning (Lester et al., 2021), or mining- and paraphrasing-based methods to generate high quality prompts (Jiang et al., 2020).

Second, due to computational constraints, we could not perform an extensive set of experiments for larger models like PaLM (with up to 540B parameters) (Chowdhery et al., 2022). Recent work by Wei et al. (2022b) has shown that the inverse scaling trend on several benchmarks can be alleviated using the large instruction fine-tuned models such as FLAN-PaLM-540B, which is largely in line with our findings regarding InstructGPT and FLAN-T5. With a small-scale experiment, we found that ChatGPT displayed strong performance on challenging samples in the investigated benchmark, so the main findings of the paper may not hold true for newer LLMs.

Finally, this work only considers negation in the English language. There is every reason to believe that negation is an equally challenging problem in other languages. As this is a linguistically-intensive task, and requires native speakers to conduct thorough analysis of the results, we leave this for future work.

Acknowledgement

The authors would like to thank the anonymous reviewers for their detailed, kind, and constructive reviews. This research was conducted by the Australian Research Council Training Centre in Cognitive Computing for Medical Technologies (project number ICI70200030) and funded by the Australian Government. This research was undertaken using the LIEF HPC-GPGPU Facility hosted at the University of Melbourne. This Facility was established with the assistance of LIEF Grant LE170100200.

References

Jason Baumgartner, Savvas Zannettou, Brian Keegan, Megan Squire, and Jeremy Blackburn. 2020. The PushShift Reddit dataset. In *Proceedings of the International AAAI Conference on Web and Social Media*, volume 14, pages 830–839.

Sid Black, Leo Gao, Phil Wang, Connor Leahy, and Stella Biderman. 2021. GPT-Neo: Large Scale Autoregressive Language Modeling with Mesh-Tensorflow.

Samuel R. Bowman, Gabor Angeli, Christopher Potts, and Christopher D. Manning. 2015. A large annotated corpus for learning natural language inference. In *Proceedings of the 2015 Conference on Empirical Methods in Natural Language Processing*, pages 632–642, Lisbon, Portugal. Association for Computational Linguistics.

Tom Brown, Benjamin Mann, Nick Ryder, Melanie Subbiah, Jared D Kaplan, Prafulla Dhariwal, Arvind Neelakantan, Pranav Shyam, Girish Sastry, Amanda Askell, et al. 2020. Language models are few-shot learners. *Advances in neural information processing systems*, 33:1877–1901.

Wendy W Chapman, Will Bridewell, Paul Hanbury, Gregory F Cooper, and Bruce G Buchanan. 2001. A simple algorithm for identifying negated findings and diseases in discharge summaries. *Journal of Biomedical Informatics*, 34(5):301–310.

Aakanksha Chowdhery, Sharan Narang, Jacob Devlin, Maarten Bosma, Gaurav Mishra, Adam Roberts, Paul Barham, Hyung Won Chung, Charles Sutton, Sebastian Gehrmann, et al. 2022. Palm: Scaling language modeling with pathways. *arXiv preprint arXiv:2204.02311*.

Hyung Won Chung, Le Hou, Shayne Longpre, Barret Zoph, Yi Tay, William Fedus, Eric Li, Xuezhi Wang, Mostafa Dehghani, Siddhartha Brahma, et al. 2022. Scaling instruction-finetuned language models. *arXiv preprint arXiv:2210.11416*.

Ido Dagan, Oren Glickman, and Bernardo Magnini. 2005. The Pascal Recognising Textual Entailment challenge. In *Machine learning challenges workshop*, pages 177–190. Springer.

Allyson Ettinger. 2020. What BERT is not: Lessons from a new suite of psycholinguistic diagnostics for language models. *Transactions of the Association for Computational Linguistics*, 8:34–48.

Leo Gao, Stella Biderman, Sid Black, Laurence Golding, Travis Hoppe, Charles Foster, Jason Phang, Horace He, Anish Thite, Noa Nabeshima, et al. 2020. The Pile: An 800gb dataset of diverse text for language modeling. *arXiv preprint arXiv:2101.00027*.

Atticus Geiger, Kyle Richardson, and Christopher Potts. 2020. Neural natural language inference models partially embed theories of lexical entailment and negation. In *Proceedings of the Third BlackboxNLP Workshop on Analyzing and Interpreting Neural Networks for NLP*, pages 163–173, Online. Association for Computational Linguistics.

Hila Gonen, Srini Iyer, Terra Blevins, Noah A Smith, and Luke Zettlemoyer. 2022. Demystifying prompts in language models via perplexity estimation. *arXiv preprint arXiv:2212.04037*.

Reto Gubelmann and Siegfried Handschuh. 2022. Context matters: A pragmatic study of PLMs' negation understanding. In *Proceedings of the 60th Annual Meeting of the Association for Computational Linguistics (Volume 1: Long Papers)*, pages 4602–4621, Dublin, Ireland. Association for Computational Linguistics.

Ari Holtzman, Peter West, Vered Shwartz, Yejin Choi, and Luke Zettlemoyer. 2021. Surface form competition: Why the highest probability answer isn't always right. In *Proceedings of the 2021 Conference on Empirical Methods in Natural Language Processing*, pages 7038–7051, Online and Punta Cana, Dominican Republic. Association for Computational Linguistics.

Md Mosharaf Hossain and Eduardo Blanco. 2022a. Leveraging affirmative interpretations from negation improves natural language understanding. *arXiv preprint arXiv:2210.14486*.

Md Mosharaf Hossain and Eduardo Blanco. 2022b. Leveraging affirmative interpretations from negation improves natural language understanding. In *Proceedings of the 2022 Conference on Empirical Methods in Natural Language Processing*, pages 5833–5847, Abu Dhabi, United Arab Emirates. Association for Computational Linguistics.

Md Mosharaf Hossain, Dhivya Chinnappa, and Eduardo Blanco. 2022. An analysis of negation in natural language understanding corpora. In *Proceedings of the 60th Annual Meeting of the Association for Computational Linguistics (Volume 2: Short Papers)*, pages 716–723, Dublin, Ireland. Association for Computational Linguistics.

Md Mosharaf Hossain, Venelin Kovatchev, Pranoy Dutta, Tiffany Kao, Elizabeth Wei, and Eduardo Blanco. 2020. An analysis of natural language inference benchmarks through the lens of negation. In *Proceedings of the 2020 Conference on Empirical Methods in Natural Language Processing (EMNLP)*, pages 9106–9118, Online. Association for Computational Linguistics.

Arian Hosseini, Siva Reddy, Dzmitry Bahdanau, R Devon Hjelm, Alessandro Sordoni, and Aaron Courville. 2021. Understanding by understanding not: Modeling negation in language models. In *Proceedings of the 2021 Conference of the North American Chapter of the Association for Computational Linguistics: Human Language Technologies*, pages 1301–1312, Online. Association for Computational Linguistics.

Joel Jang, Seonghyeon Ye, and Minjoon Seo. 2022a. Can large language models truly understand prompts? a case study with negated prompts. *arXiv preprint arXiv:2209.12711*.

Myeongjun Jang and Thomas Lukasiewicz. 2023. Consistency analysis of chatgpt. *arXiv preprint arXiv:2303.06273*.

Myeongjun Jang, Frank Mtumbuka, and Thomas Lukasiewicz. 2022b. Beyond distributional hypothesis: Let language models learn meaning-text correspondence. In *Findings of the Association for Computational Linguistics: NAACL 2022*, pages 2030–2042, Seattle, United States. Association for Computational Linguistics.

Ting Jiang, Jian Jiao, Shaohan Huang, Zihan Zhang, Deqing Wang, Fuzhen Zhuang, Furu Wei, Haizhen Huang, Denvy Deng, and Qi Zhang. 2022. PromptBERT: Improving BERT sentence embeddings with prompts. In *Proceedings of the 2022 Conference on Empirical Methods in Natural Language Processing*, pages 8826–8837, Abu Dhabi, United Arab Emirates. Association for Computational Linguistics.

Zhengbao Jiang, Frank F. Xu, Jun Araki, and Graham Neubig. 2020. How can we know what language models know? *Transactions of the Association for Computational Linguistics*, 8:423–438.

Jaap Jumelet, Milica Denic, Jakub Szymanik, Dieuwke Hupkes, and Shane Steinert-Threlkeld. 2021. Language models use monotonicity to assess NPI licensing. In *Findings of the Association for Computational Linguistics: ACL-IJCNLP 2021*, pages 4958–4969, Online. Association for Computational Linguistics.

Nora Kassner and Hinrich Schütze. 2020. Negated and misprimed probes for pretrained language models: Birds can talk, but cannot fly. In *Proceedings of the 58th Annual Meeting of the Association for Computational Linguistics*, pages 7811–7818, Online. Association for Computational Linguistics.

Brian Lester, Rami Al-Rfou, and Noah Constant. 2021. The power of scale for parameter-efficient prompt tuning. In *Proceedings of the 2021 Conference on Empirical Methods in Natural Language Processing*, pages 3045–3059, Online and Punta Cana, Dominican Republic. Association for Computational Linguistics.

Vladislav Lialin, Kevin Zhao, Namrata Shivagunde, and Anna Rumshisky. 2022. Life after BERT: What do other muppets understand about language? In *Proceedings of the 60th Annual Meeting of the Association for Computational Linguistics (Volume 1: Long Papers)*, pages 3180–3193, Dublin, Ireland. Association for Computational Linguistics.

Yinhan Liu, Myle Ott, Naman Goyal, Jingfei Du, Mandar Joshi, Danqi Chen, Omer Levy, Mike Lewis, Luke Zettlemoyer, and Veselin Stoyanov. 2019. RoBERTa: A robustly optimized bert pretraining approach. *arXiv preprint arXiv:1907.11692*.

Ian McKenzie, Alexander Lyzhov, Alicia Parrish, Ameya Prabhu, Aaron Mueller, Najoung Kim, Sam Bowman, and Ethan Perez. 2022. Inverse scaling prize: Round 1 winners.

George A Miller. 1998. *WordNet: An electronic lexical database*. MIT press.

Long Ouyang, Jeffrey Wu, Xu Jiang, Diogo Almeida, Carroll Wainwright, Pamela Mishkin, Chong Zhang, Sandhini Agarwal, Katarina Slama, Alex Gray, John Schulman, Jacob Hilton, Fraser Kelton, Luke Miller, Maddie Simens, Amanda Askell, Peter Welinder, Paul Christiano, Jan Leike, and Ryan Lowe. 2022. Training language models to follow instructions with human feedback. In *Advances in Neural Information Processing Systems*.

Fabio Petroni, Tim Rocktäschel, Sebastian Riedel, Patrick Lewis, Anton Bakhtin, Yuxiang Wu, and Alexander Miller. 2019. Language models as knowledge bases? In *Proceedings of the 2019 Conference on Empirical Methods in Natural Language Processing and the 9th International Joint Conference on Natural Language Processing (EMNLP-IJCNLP)*, pages 2463–2473, Hong Kong, China. Association for Computational Linguistics.

Alec Radford, Jeff Wu, Rewon Child, David Luan, Dario Amodei, and Ilya Sutskever. 2019. Language models are unsupervised multitask learners. *OpenAI blog*.

Abhilasha Ravichander, Matt Gardner, and Ana Marasović. 2022. CONDAQA: A contrastive reading comprehension dataset for reasoning about negation. *arXiv preprint arXiv:2211.00295*.

Joshua Robinson, Christopher Michael Rytting, and David Wingate. 2022. Leveraging large language models for multiple choice question answering. *arXiv preprint arXiv:2210.12353*.

Robyn Speer, Joshua Chin, and Catherine Havasi. 2017. ConceptNet 5.5: An open multilingual graph of general knowledge. In *Thirty-first AAAI conference on artificial intelligence*.

Ieva Staliūnaitė and Ignacio Iacobacci. 2020. Compositional and lexical semantics in RoBERTa, BERT and DistilBERT: A case study on CoQA. In *Proceedings of the 2020 Conference on Empirical Methods in Natural Language Processing (EMNLP)*, pages 7046–7056, Online. Association for Computational Linguistics.

Thinh Truong, Timothy Baldwin, Trevor Cohn, and Karin Verspoor. 2022a. Improving negation detection with negation-focused pre-training. In *Proceedings of the 2022 Conference of the North American Chapter of the Association for Computational Linguistics: Human Language Technologies*, pages 4188–4193, Seattle, United States. Association for Computational Linguistics.

Thinh Hung Truong, Yulia Otmakhova, Timothy Baldwin, Trevor Cohn, Jey Han Lau, and Karin Verspoor. 2022b. Not another negation benchmark: The NaN-NLI test suite for sub-clausal negation. In *Proceedings of the 2nd Conference of the Asia-Pacific Chapter of the Association for Computational Linguistics and the 12th International Joint Conference on Natural Language Processing (Volume 1: Long Papers)*, pages 883–894, Online only. Association for Computational Linguistics.

Alex Wang, Yada Pruksachatkun, Nikita Nangia, Amanpreet Singh, Julian Michael, Felix Hill, Omer Levy, and Samuel R. Bowman. 2019. SuperGLUE: A stickier benchmark for general-purpose language understanding systems. *CoRR*, abs/1905.00537.

Alex Wang, Amanpreet Singh, Julian Michael, Felix Hill, Omer Levy, and Samuel Bowman. 2018. GLUE: A multi-task benchmark and analysis platform for natural language understanding. In *Proceedings of the 2018 EMNLP Workshop BlackboxNLP: Analyzing and Interpreting Neural Networks for NLP*, pages 353–355, Brussels, Belgium. Association for Computational Linguistics.

Hao Wang, Yangguang Li, Zhen Huang, Yong Dou, Lingpeng Kong, and Jing Shao. 2022. Sncse: Contrastive learning for unsupervised sentence embedding with soft negative samples.

Alex Warstadt, Yu Cao, Ioana Grosu, Wei Peng, Hagen Blix, Yining Nie, Anna Alsop, Shikha Bordia, Haokun Liu, Alicia Parrish, Sheng-Fu Wang, Jason Phang, Anhad Mohananey, Phu Mon Htut, Paloma Jeretic, and Samuel R. Bowman. 2019. Investigating BERT's knowledge of language: Five analysis methods with NPIs. In *Proceedings of the 2019 Conference on Empirical Methods in Natural Language Processing and the 9th International Joint Conference on Natural Language Processing (EMNLP-IJCNLP)*, pages 2877–2887, Hong Kong, China. Association for Computational Linguistics.

Jason Wei, Maarten Bosma, Vincent Zhao, Kelvin Guu, Adams Wei Yu, Brian Lester, Nan Du, Andrew M Dai, and Quoc V Le. 2021. Finetuned language models are zero-shot learners. In *International Conference on Learning Representations*.

Jason Wei, Yi Tay, Rishi Bommasani, Colin Raffel, Barret Zoph, Sebastian Borgeaud, Dani Yogatama, Maarten Bosma, Denny Zhou, Donald Metzler, et al. 2022a. Emergent abilities of large language models. *Transactions on Machine Learning Research*.

Jason Wei, Yi Tay, and Quoc V Le. 2022b. Inverse scaling can become U-shaped. *arXiv preprint arXiv:2211.02011*.

Ethan Gotlieb Wilcox, Jon Gauthier, Jennifer Hu, Peng Qian, and Roger P. Levy. 2020. On the predictive power of neural language models for human real-time comprehension behavior. In *Proceedings of the 42nd Annual Meeting of the Cognitive Science Society*, page 1707–1713.

Adina Williams, Nikita Nangia, and Samuel Bowman. 2018. A broad-coverage challenge corpus for sentence understanding through inference. In *Proceedings of the 2018 Conference of the North American Chapter of the Association for Computational Linguistics: Human Language Technologies, Volume 1 (Long Papers)*, pages 1112–1122, New Orleans, Louisiana. Association for Computational Linguistics.

Susan Zhang, Stephen Roller, Naman Goyal, Mikel Artetxe, Moya Chen, Shuohui Chen, Christopher Dewan, Mona Diab, Xian Li, Xi Victoria Lin, et al. 2022. OPT: Open pre-trained transformer language models. *arXiv preprint arXiv:2205.01068*.

A Model checkpoints

For open-sourced LMs, we consider the official released checkpoints on the HuggingFace hub at:

- `https://huggingface.co/EleutherAI/x`
- `https://huggingface.co/facebook/y`

where x in {*gpt-neo-125M,gpt-neo-1.3B,gpt-neo-2.7B,gpt-j-6B*}, and y in {*opt-125m,opt-350m,opt-1.3b,opt-2.7b,opt-6.7b*}.

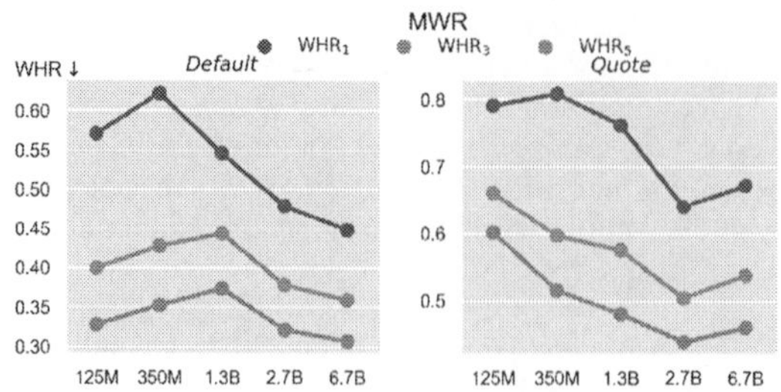

Figure 7: Zero-shot performance of OPT on MWR using different prompts

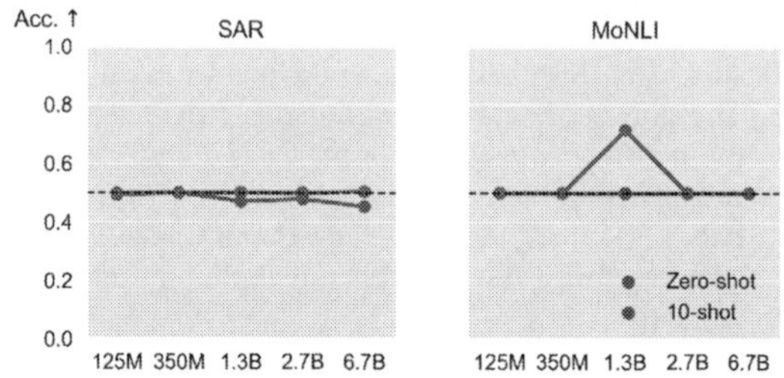

Figure 8: Zero-shot performance of OPT on SAR using different prompts

For GPT-3 models, we access them through the official API at `https://openai.com/api/`, using the *Text completion* endpoint. The considered model identifiers along with their sizes are:

- `text-ada-001`: 350M
- `text-babbage-001`: 1.3B
- `text-curie-001`: 6.7B
- `text-davinci-001`: 175B
- `text-davinci-003`: 175B

B OPT results

For MWR, although we observe improvements with increasing model sizes, the WHR scores are much higher than those of GPT-neo, showing that OPT is worse at predicting antonyms and synonyms of words. The gap in performance may lie in differences in training data between the two types of models.

C Model outputs

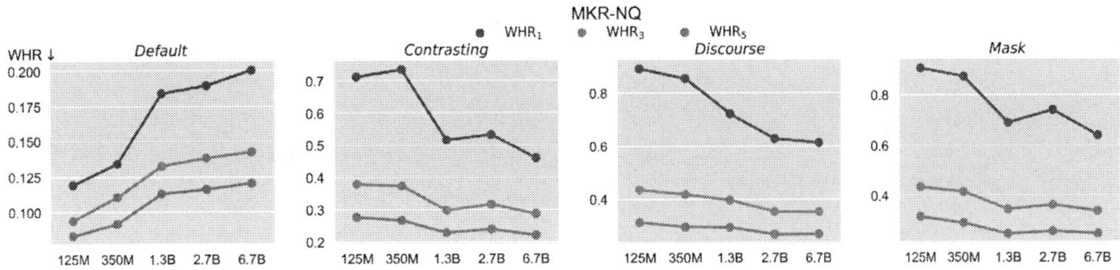

Figure 9: Zero-shot performance of OPT on MKR using different prompts

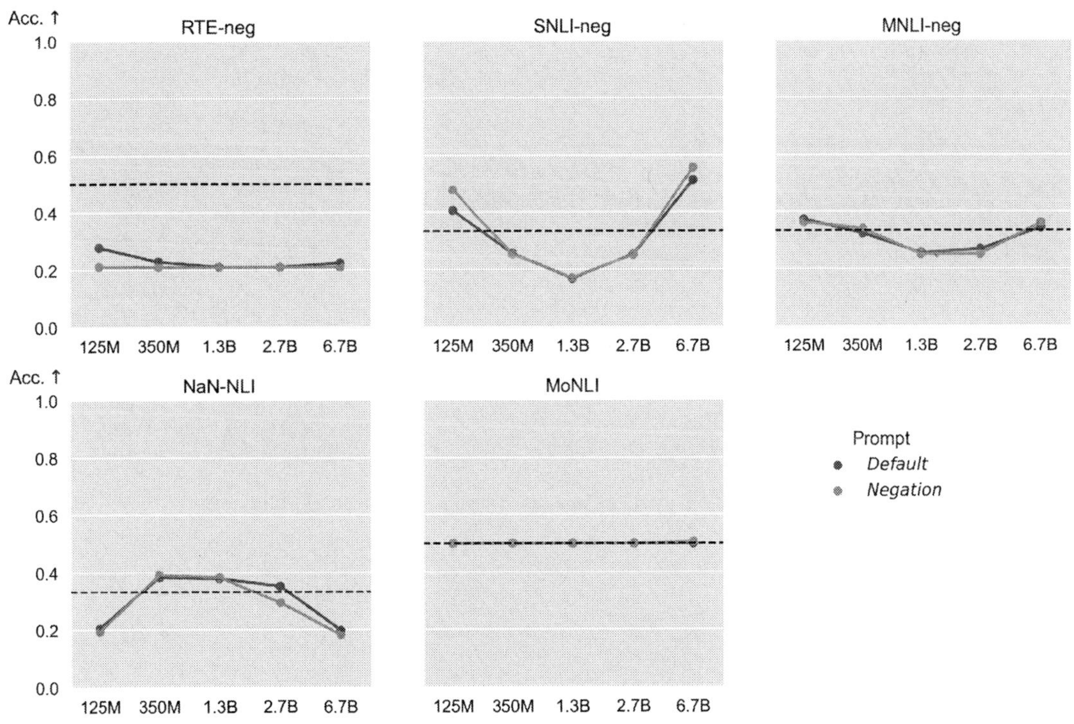

Figure 10: Zero-shot performance of OPT on NLI tasks using different prompts

Prompt	Model	Output
Paracetamol isn't a kind of	GPT-neo-125M	*muscle*
	GPT-J-6B	painkiller
	OPT-125M	pain
	OPT-6.7B	medicine
	GPT-3	medication
	InstructGPT	NSAID
Entrance is an antonym of	GPT-neo-125M	*interest*
	GPT-J-6B	entrance
	OPT-125M	entrance
	OPT-6.7B	exit
	GPT-3	departure
	InstructGPT	entrance
Choose the correct answer: flimsy and sturdy are synonyms or antonyms?	GPT-neo-125M	Synonyms
	GPT-J-6B	Synonyms
	OPT-125M	Antonyms
	OPT-6.7B	Synonyms
	GPT-3	Antonyms
	InstructGPT	Antonyms
I can not think of a few reasons for the allergy to substance. Question: There are not reasons why there's an allergy. True, False, or Neither? Answer:	GPT-neo-125M	True
	GPT-J-6B	True
	OPT-125M	True
	OPT-6.7B	Neither
	GPT-3	False
	InstructGPT	Neither
The man does not own a dog. Question: the man does not own a mammal. True or Not true? Answer:	GPT-neo-125M	True
	GPT-J-6B	True
	OPT-125M	True
	OPT-6.7B	True
	GPT-3	True
	InstructGPT	Not True

Table 6: Example outputs of models. Wrong answers are highlighted

JSEEGraph: Joint Structured Event Extraction as Graph Parsing

Huiling You[1], **Samia Touileb**[2] and **Lilja Øvrelid**[1]
[1]University of Oslo
[2]University of Bergen
{huiliny, liljao}@ifi.uio.no
samia.touileb@uib.no

Abstract

We propose a graph-based event extraction framework JSEEGraph that approaches the task of event extraction as general graph parsing in the tradition of Meaning Representation Parsing. It explicitly encodes entities and events in a single semantic graph, and further has the flexibility to encode a wider range of additional IE relations and jointly infer individual tasks. JSEEGraph performs in an end-to-end manner via general graph parsing: (1) instead of flat sequence labelling, nested structures between entities/triggers are efficiently encoded as separate nodes in the graph, allowing for nested and overlapping entities and triggers; (2) both entities, relations, and events can be encoded in the same graph, where entities and event triggers are represented as nodes and entity relations and event arguments are constructed via edges; (3) joint inference avoids error propagation and enhances the interpolation of different IE tasks. We experiment on two benchmark datasets of varying structural complexities; ACE05 and Rich ERE, covering three languages: English, Chinese, and Spanish. Experimental results show that JSEEGraph can handle nested event structures, that it is beneficial to solve different IE tasks jointly, and that event argument extraction in particular benefits from entity extraction. Our code and models are released as open-source[1].

1 Introduction

Event extraction (EE) deals with the extraction of complex, structured representations of events from text, including overlapping and nested structures (Sheng et al., 2021; Cao et al., 2022). While there are existing datasets annotated with such rich representations (Doddington et al., 2004; Song et al., 2015), a majority of current approaches model this task using simplified versions of these datasets or sequence-labeling-based encodings which are not capable of capturing the full complexity of the events. Figure 1 shows an example from the Rich ERE dataset (Song et al., 2015) of a sentence containing both nested and overlapping events: *"buy"* serves as trigger for two overlapping events, `transfermoney` and `transferownership` with their respective argument roles, and similarly *"made"* for two `artifact` events triggered by the coordination of two GPE entities *Canada* and *USA*; at the same time, the event trigger *"made"* is nested inside the entity span *"things made in Canada or USA"*. For this example, models based on token tagging (such as the commonly used BIO-encoding) would fail completely when a token contributes to multiple information extraction elements. In this case, the version of the ACE05 dataset widely employed for EE would not fully capture the double-tagged event triggers, by simply disregarding one of the two events, and the nested entity *"things made in Canada or USA"* would be *"things"*.

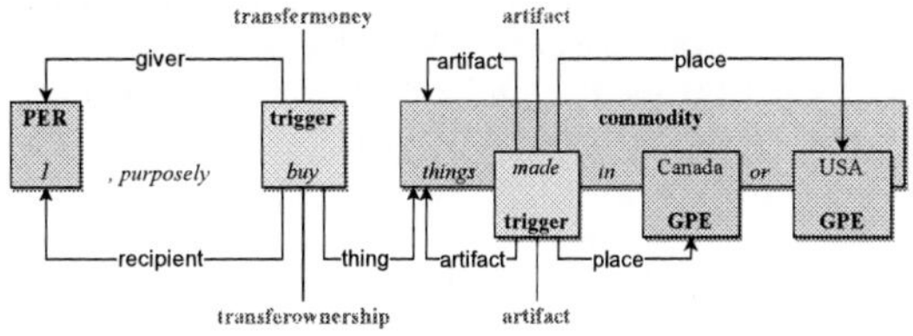

Figure 1: Example of nested and overlapping events in the sentence *"I, purposely buy things made in Canada or USA."*, *taken from Rich ERE (Song et al., 2015).*

Event extraction is a subtask of a wider set of Information Extraction (IE) tasks, jointly dealing with extracting various types of structured information from unstructured texts, from named entities, relations, to events. There have been continued efforts in creating benchmark datasets that can be used for evaluating a wide range of IE tasks. Both ACE05 (Doddington et al., 2004)[2] and Rich

[1]https://github.com/huiling-y/JSEEGraph

[2]https://catalog.ldc.upenn.edu/LDC2006T06

*Proceedings of the The 12th Joint Conference on Lexical and Computational Semantics (*SEM 2023)*, pages 115–127
July 13-14, 2023 ©2023 Association for Computational Linguistics

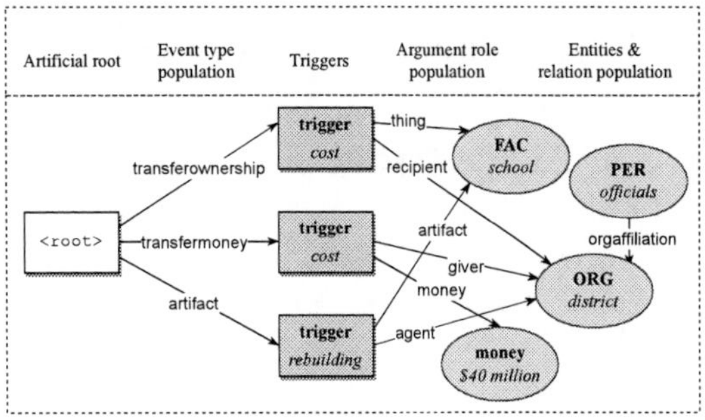

Figure 2: Example of graph representation for entities, relations, and events from the sentence *"School district officials have estimated the cost of rebuilding an intermediate school at $40 million."*, from Rich ERE (Song et al., 2015).

ERE (Song et al., 2015)[3] provide consistent annotations of entities, relations, and events. While there are clear inter-relations between these different elements, and despite the availability of rich annotations, existing works often deal with individual tasks, such as named entity recognition (NER) (Chiu and Nichols, 2016; Bekoulis et al., 2018) or event extraction (EE) (Yang and Mitchell, 2016; Du and Cardie, 2020; Li et al., 2020). Recently there have been some efforts in jointly modelling multiple IE tasks (Wadden et al., 2019; Lin et al., 2020; Nguyen et al., 2022), but these methods explicitly avoid nested instances.

We here propose to represent events, along with entities and relations, as general graphs and approach the task of event extraction as Meaning Representation Parsing (Oepen et al., 2020; Samuel and Straka, 2020). As shown in Figure 2, in such an information graph, event triggers and entities are represented as nodes; event types, argument roles, and relations are constrained edges; and nested/overlapped structures are straightforwardly represented, since a surface string can be abstracted into an unlimited number of nodes, as illustrated by the two separate nodes for the event triggers for *"cost"*. Our approach does not rely on ontology- or language-specific features or any external syntactic/semantic parsers, but directly parses raw text into an information graph. We experiment on the benchmark datasets ACE05 (Doddington et al., 2004) and Rich ERE (Song et al., 2015), zooming in on nested structures. Our results show JSEE-Graph to be versatile in solving entity, relation, and event extraction jointly, even for heavily nested instances and across three different languages. Ablation studies consistently show that event extraction especially benefits from entity extraction.

The paper is structured as follows: section 2 provides the relevant background for our work, and section 3 further describes the tasks addressed and the datasets we employ, focusing in particular on their complexity, as measured by level of nesting. Section 4 presents the JSEE graph parsing framework and section 5 the experimental setup for evaluating the JSEE parser. Section 6 presents the results of our evaluations and provides a study of the performance for nested structures, as well as an ablation study assessing the effect of joint IE modeling and an error analysis. Finally we provide conclusions (Section 7) and discuss limitations of our work.

2 Related work

Event extraction is commonly approached as supervised classification, even though other approaches relying *e.g.* on generation (Paolini et al., 2021; Lu et al., 2021; Li et al., 2021; Hsu et al., 2022) or prompt tuning inspired by natural language understanding tasks (Shin et al., 2020; Gao et al., 2021; Li and Liang, 2021; Liu et al., 2022) also are gaining ground. Classification-based methods break event extraction into several subtasks (trigger detection/classification, argument detection/-classification), and either solve them separately in a pipeline-based manner (Ji and Grishman, 2008; Li et al., 2013; Liu et al., 2020; Du and Cardie, 2020; Li et al., 2020) or jointly infer them as multiple subtasks (Yang and Mitchell, 2016; Nguyen et al., 2016; Liu et al., 2018; Wadden et al., 2019; Lin et al., 2020). Classification-based joint methods typically apply sequence-labeling-based encoding and extract all event components in one pass, whereas pipeline methods break the problem into separate stages which are performed sequentially. Whereas sequence-labeling approaches cannot distinguish overlapping events/arguments by the nature of the BIO-encoding, pipeline methods may in principle detect these. However, they typically suffer from error propagation and are not equipped to model the interactions between the different event elements (triggers, arguments).

Nested events Some previous work addresses the problem of overlapping or nested arguments in EE. Xu et al. (2020) address overlapping arguments in the Chinese part of the ACE05 dataset and jointly perform predictions for event triggers and argu-

[3]https://catalog.ldc.upenn.edu/LDC2020T18

ments based on common feature representations derived from a pre-trained language model. Sheng et al. (2021) propose a joint framework with cascaded decoding to tackle overlapping events, and sequentially perform type detection, event and argument extraction in a Chinese financial event dataset. They deal with cases of both "overlapping events" and "overlapping arguments", however, their approach may suffer from error propagation due to the cascading approach. Cao et al. (2022) distinguish between overlapped and nested events and propose the OneEE tagging scheme which formulates EE as a word-to-word relation recognition, distinguishing separate span and role relations. OneEE is evaluated on the FewFC Chinese financial event dataset and the biomedical event datasets Genia11 and Genia13. While specifically focusing on nested events, these previous works are limited by focusing only on one language or on specialized (financial/biomedical) domains. In this work we aim to provide a more comprehensive evaluation over two datasets in several versions with increasing levels of structural complexity (see below) and across three different languages.

Joint IE approaches Wadden et al. (2019) propose the DyGIE++ model which approaches joint modeling of IE entities and relations via span-based prediction of entities and event triggers, and subsequent dynamic graph propagation based on relations. They evaluate on ACE05 and Genia datasets and limit their experiments to English only. Their approach is restricted to a certain span width, limiting the length of possible entities. OneIE (Lin et al., 2020) is a joint system for IE using global features to model cross-subtask or cross-instance interactions between the subtasks and predict an information graph. They propose the E+ extension of ACE05 which includes multi-token events (E^+) as we do. As in our work, they also present results on Spanish and Chinese as well and develop a multilingual model, but their experiments avoid nested structures, by using only the head of entity mentions and specifically removing overlapped entities. Nguyen et al. (2022) model joint IE in a two-stage procedure which first identifies entities and event triggers and subsequently classify relations between these starting from a fully connected dependency graph; a GCN is employed to encode the resulting dependency graphs for computation of the joint distribution. While the approach is shown to be effective, it is still a pipeline approach which can suffer from error propagation. Since it relies on sequence labeling for entity/event detection, it cannot identify overlapping entities/event triggers. Furthermore, the approach relies on syntactic information from an external parser and focuses only on English and Spanish in the Light ERE dataset (Song et al., 2015).

Meaning Representation Parsing Meaning Representation Parsing (MRP) (Oepen et al., 2014, 2015, 2020) is a framework covering several types of dependency-based semantic graph frameworks. Unlike syntactic dependency representations, these semantic representations are not trees, but rather general graphs, characterised by potentially having multiple top nodes (*roots*) and not necessarily being connected, since not every token is necessarily a node in the graph. The semantic frameworks include representations with varying levels of "anchoring" to the input string (Oepen et al., 2020), ranging from the so-called "bi-lexical" representations where every node in the graph corresponds to a token in the input string to a framework like AMR (Banarescu et al., 2013) which constitutes the most abstract and unanchored type of framework, such that the correspondence between the nodes in a graph and tokens in the string is completely flexible. This allows for straightforward representation of nesting and overlapping structures, where multiple nodes may be anchored to overlapping sub-strings. There have been considerable progress in developing variants of both transition-based and graph-based dependency parsers capable of producing such semantic graphs (Hershcovich et al., 2017; Dozat and Manning, 2018; Samuel and Straka, 2020). Previous research has further made use of AMR-based input representations to constrain the tasks of event extraction (Huang et al., 2018) and more recently joint information extraction (Zhang and Ji, 2021), where an off-the-shelf AMR parser is used to derive candidate enitity and event trigger nodes before classifying pairwise relations guided by the AMR hierarchical structure. While there are clear parallels between the MRP semantic frameworks and the tasks proposed in IE, little work has focused on the direct application of MRP parsing techniques to these tasks. You et al. (2022) is a notable exception in this respect, who presents an adaptation of the PERIN semantic parser (Samuel and Straka, 2020) to the event extraction task. While their work is promising it is limited to only one dataset (ACE05), which does

Lang	Split	#Sents	#Events	#Roles	#Entities	#Relations
			Dataset: ACE05			
en	Train	19 371	4 419	6 609	47 546	7 172
	Dev	896	468	759	3 421	729
	Test	777	461	735	3 828	822
zh	Train	6 706	2 928	5 576	29 674	8 003
	Dev	511	217	406	2 246	601
	Test	521	190	336	2 389	686
			Dataset: Rich ERE			
en	Train	12 421	8 368	15 197	34 611	7 498
	Dev	692	459	797	1 998	366
	Test	745	566	1 195	2 286	544
zh	Train	9 253	5 325	9 066	26 128	6 044
	Dev	541	366	522	1 609	379
	Test	483	439	776	2 022	502
es	Train	8 292	5 013	8 575	20 347	4 140
	Dev	383	254	447	1 068	199
	Test	598	334	609	1 438	287

Table 1: Statistics of the preprocessed datasets.

not contain a lot of nested structures and is further limited to English event extraction only. In this work we extend their approach to the task of joint information extraction, covering both entities, events and relations taken from two different datasets in several versions and for three languages, and further demonstrates the effectiveness of approaching general information extraction from text via graph-parsing and the interpolation of different IE tasks.

3 Task and Data

While the main focus of this work is on event extraction, we hypothesize that our graph-based approach lends itself to dealing with two challenging aspects of current research on this task: the processing of nested and overlapping event structures, and the joint modeling of inter-related IE structures. In the following we quantify the level of nesting in two widely used datasets which contain rich annotations for both entities, events, and relations. We further propose two versions of each dataset with varying potential for nesting, which allows us to focus on this aspect during evaluation.

Event Extraction is the task of extracting events into structured forms, namely event triggers and their arguments. An event trigger is the word(s) that most clearly describes an event, such as *"buy"*, which evokes a `transferownership` and an `transfermoney` event in Figure 1. Event arguments are the participants and attributes of an event, and can be tagged as entities at the same time, as demonstrated in Figure 2.

We use the benchmark datasets ACE05 (Doddington et al., 2004) and Rich ERE (Song et al., 2015), both containing consistent annotations for entities, relations, and events, for joint evaluation of multiple IE tasks and in multiple languages (ACE05 in English and Chinese, and ERE in English, Chinese, and Spanish). Table 1 summarizes the relevant statistics of the datasets. The inventory of event types, argument roles, entity types and relation types are listed in Table 2. Despite targeting the same IE tasks, from ACE05 to Rich ERE, the annotation guidelines have shifted towards more sophisticated representations, resulting in more complex structures in Rich ERE (Song et al., 2015). Prominent differences between ACE05 and Rich ERE are:

Dataset	#Event-types	#Argument-roles	#Entity types	#Relation type
ACE05	33	22	7	6
Rich ERE	38	20	15	6

Table 2: Inventory of event types, argument roles, entity types and relation types in ACE05 and Rich ERE.

- **Entities**, and hence event arguments, are more fine-grained in Rich ERE, with 15 entity types, as compared to 7 types in ACE05. In terms of entity spans, ACE05 explicitly marks the head of the entity versus the entire mention, providing the possibility of solving a simpler task for entity extraction and recognizing only the head token as opposed to the full span of the entity in question. This is commonly done for this task in previous work of EE. However, in Rich ERE, the entire string of text is annotated for entity mentions, and heads are only marked explicitly for nominal mentions that are not named entities or pronominal entities.
- **Event triggers** can be double-tagged in Rich ERE, namely one trigger can serve multiple event mentions, giving rise to overlapping events, as shown in Figure 1, while in ACE05, an event trigger only evokes one event. This means that Rich ERE presents a more complex task of event extraction.

We measure the nested instances in ACE05 and Rich ERE as a way to showcase different levels of complexity for extracting entities, relations, and events. More specifically, we quantify nested instances in two versions of each dataset, one using only the head of an entity mention (when it is annotated), and the other with the entire mention text. Following Lin et al. (2020) we dub the version which only marks the head of entities ACE-E^+ and

Dataset	Lang	Nesting			#Sents	
		Trg-Trg	Ent-Ent	Trg-Ent	Nested	All
ACE05-E$^+$	en	0	0	4	4	21044
	zh	0	4	9	12	7738
ACE05-E^{++}	en	0	13387	716	5315	21044
	zh	0	10797	252	3748	7738
Rich ERE-E$^+$	en	1066	1329	244	1529	13858
	zh	301	1383	284	1266	10277
	es	485	523	97	712	9273
Rich ERE-E^{++}	en	1063	9453	1517	4277	13858
	zh	301	7303	622	2993	10277
	es	485	5526	854	2614	9273

Table 3: Nesting instances in ACE05 and Rich ERE. Nesting between a pair of event triggers is referred to as `Trg-Trg`; between a pair of entity mentions as `Ent-Ent`, and between an event trigger and an entity as `Trg-Ent`. For both datasets, in the E$^+$ version, entity mentions include only heads, while in the E^{++} version, entity mentions include the full text spans.

Rich ERE-E$^+$, and introduce two additional versions of the datasets, dubbed, ACE-E^{++} and Rich ERE-E^{++} which retain the full annotated mention text span. Nesting is measured between any pair of triggers and entities. Note that our notion of nesting subsumes both *overlapping* and *nested* target/entities (Cao et al., 2022), *i.e.* both full and partial overlap of text spans. As shown in Table 3, Rich ERE features many cases of nested triggers, while these are not found in ACE05, due to the aforementioned double-tagging in Rich ERE (see Figure 1); when only considering the head of an entity, ACE05 exhibits very little nesting, but Rich ERE exhibits a considerable amount of nesting within entities, as well as between entity-trigger. The reason for this is that in Rich ERE, only certain nominal mentions are marked with explicit heads; when the full entity mentions are considered, both datasets are heavily nested.

As mentioned above, this work deals with three IE tasks, as exemplified by Figure 2: entities, relations, and events. Given a sentence, our JSEEGraph framework extracts its entity mentions, relations, and event mentions. In addition to event extraction, we thus target two additional IE tasks in our graph-based model:

Entity Extraction is to identify entity mentions from text and classify them into types according to a pre-defined ontology. For example, in Figure 2, *"district"* is an organization (`ORG`) entity.

Relation Extraction aims to assign a relation type to an ordered pair of entity mentions, based on a pre-defined relation ontology. For example, in Figure 2, the relation between `PER` *"officials"* and `ORG` *"district"* is `orgaffiliation`.

4 Graph parsing framework

Our JSEEGraph framework is a text-to-graph parser tailored for EE tasks, additionally with different IE components explicitly encoded in a single graph, as shown in Figure 2. Our framework builds on Samuel and Straka (2020) who developed the PERIN parser in the context of Meaning Representation Parsing (Oepen et al., 2020), as well as (You et al., 2022) who applied PERIN to the task of event extraction. We here extend this parser to the IE graphs shown in Figure 2 in a multilingual setting.

Given a sentence, as the example shown in Figure 3, JSEEGraph encodes the input tokens with the pre-trained language model XLM-R (Conneau et al., 2020) to obtain the contextualized embeddings and further maps the embeddings onto queries; nodes (triggers and entities) are predicted by classifying the queries and anchored to surface tokens via a deep biaffine classifier (Dozat and Manning, 2017); edges are constructed between nodes with two biaffine classifiers, assigning arguments to predicted events and relations to entity pairs. We describe each module in detail in what follows.

4.1 Sentence encoding

We use XLM-R (Conneau et al., 2020) to obtain the contextualized embeddings of the input sequence. To be specific, a trainable weight w_l is used to get a weighted sum of representations of different layers, so the final contextual embedding $\mathbf{e} = \sum_{l=1}^{L} \mathrm{softmax}(w_l)\mathbf{e}_l$ with $\mathbf{e}_l$ as the intermediate output from the lth layer. If an input token consists of multiple subwords, the final contextual embedding will be the weighted sum over all subword embeddings with a learned subword attention.

Each contextual embedding is mapped into $\mathbf{q} = \{\mathbf{q}_1, \cdots, \mathbf{q}_n\}$ queries via a linear layer, and further transformed into hidden features $\mathbf{h} = \{\mathbf{h}_1, \cdots, \mathbf{h}_n\}$ with a stack of transformer encoder layers, which models inter-query dependency with multi-head self-attention.

4.2 Node prediction

The node prediction module consists of a node label classifier and an anchor biaffine attention classifier.

The node label classifier is a linear classifier classifying each query into a node in the graph, and the node label is predicted by a single-layer feedforward network (FNN). If a query is classified

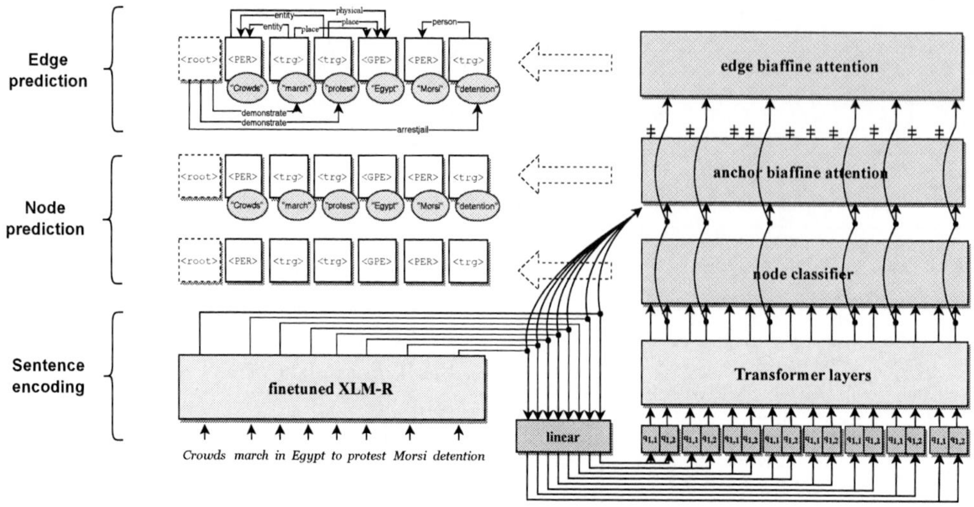

Figure 3: An illustration of our JSEEGraph parsing the sentence *"Crowds march in Egypt to protest Morsi detention."*, example from Rich ERE.

into "null", no node is created from this query.

Node anchoring, as shown in Equation (1), is performed by biaffine attention (Dozat and Manning, 2018) between the contextual embeddings **e** and hidden feature of queries **h**, to map each query (a candidate node) to surface tokens, as shown in Equation (3). For each query, every input token is binary classified into anchor or non-anchor.

$$\mathrm{Bilinear}(\mathrm{X}_1, \mathrm{X}_2) = \mathrm{X}_1^T \mathrm{U} \mathrm{X}_2 \quad (1)$$

$$\mathrm{Biaffine}(\mathrm{X}_1, \mathrm{X}_2) = \mathrm{X}_1^T \mathrm{U} \mathrm{X}_2 + \mathrm{W}(\mathrm{X}_1 \oplus \mathrm{X}_2) + b \quad (2)$$

$$\mathrm{node}^{(\mathrm{anchor})} = \mathrm{Biaffine}^{(\mathrm{anchor})}(\mathbf{h}, \mathbf{e}) \quad (3)$$

Node prediction is complete with queries that are classified into nodes and anchored to corresponding surface tokens. Predicted nodes are either event triggers or entities, labeled as "trigger" or entity type. A dummy node is randomly generated to add to predicted nodes to play the role of `<root>` node, and always holds the first position.

4.3 Edge prediction

Edge prediction between nodes is performed with two deep biaffine classifiers, as in Equation (6), one to predict edge presence between a pair of nodes and the other to predict the corresponding edge label. To construct edges between nodes, only queries from which nodes have been constructed will be used, and the new hidden features is $\mathbf{h}'$, which are further split into two parts with a single-layer FNN, as show in Equation (4) and (5).

$$\mathbf{h}_1^{\prime(\mathrm{edge})} = \mathrm{FNN}_1^{(\mathrm{edge})}(\mathbf{h}') \quad (4)$$

$$\mathbf{h}_2^{\prime(\mathrm{edge})} = \mathrm{FNN}_2^{(\mathrm{edge})}(\mathbf{h}') \quad (5)$$

$$\mathrm{edge} = \mathrm{Biaffine}^{(\mathrm{edge})}(\mathbf{h}_1^{\prime(\mathrm{edge})}, \mathbf{h}_2^{\prime(\mathrm{edge})}) \quad (6)$$

The edge presence biaffine classifier performs binary classification, deciding whether or not an edge should be constructed between a pair of nodes. The edge label biaffine classifier performs multi-class classification, and the edge label set is the union of argument roles and relation types.

4.4 Constrained decoding

During inference, we apply a set of constraints specifically developed for the correct treatment of event arguments and entity relations based on the graph encoding we define for the information graph (Figure 2): 1) directed edges from the `<root>` node can only connect to a trigger node, and the corresponding edge label is an event type; 2) directed edges from a trigger node to an entity indicates an event argument, with the argument role placed as edge label; 3) directed edges between a pair of entities indicate an entity relation, and the corresponding relation type is assigned to the edge label.

5 Experimental setup

5.1 Data

As mentioned above, we evaluate our system on the benchmark datasets ACE05[4] (LDC2006T06) and Rich ERE[5] (LDC2020T18). As mentioned above, Table 1 summarizes the statistics of the preprocessed datasets.

Following Lin et al. (2020), we keep 33 event types, 22 argument roles, 7 entity types, and 6 relation types for both the English and Chinese parts of ACE05. We follow You et al. (2022) in employing the ACE-E^{++} version of this data, which uses the full text span of entity mentions instead of only the head, as described in section 3 above.

For Rich ERE, we keep 18 out of 38 event types defined in the Rich ERE event ontology [6], 18 out of 21 argument roles [7], 15 entity types, and 6 relation types for English, Chinese, and Spanish. Given no existing data splits, we randomly sample similar proportions of documents for train, development, and testing as the split proportions in ACE05.

5.2 Evaluation metrics

Following previous work (Lin et al., 2020; Nguyen et al., 2021), precision (P), recall (R), F1 scores are reported for the following information elements.

- **Entity** An entity mention is correctly extracted if its offsets and entity type match a reference entity.
- **Relation** A relation is correctly extracted if its relation type, and offsets of both entity mentions match those of reference entities.
- **Event trigger** An event trigger is correctly identified (Trg-I) if its offsets match a reference trigger, and correctly classified (Trg-C) if its event type also matches a reference trigger.
- **Event argument** The evaluation of an argument is conditioned on correct event type prediction; if a predicted argument plays a role in an event that does not match any reference event types, the argument is automatically considered a wrong prediction. An argument is correctly identified (Arg-I) if its offsets match a reference argument, and correctly classified (Arg-C) if its argument role also matches the reference argument.

5.3 Implementation detail

We adopt multi-lingual training for each dataset for the reported results. Results of monolingual models are listed in Appendix B. Detailed hyperparameter settings and runtimes are included in Appendix A.

5.4 System comparison

We compare our JSEEGraph to the following systems: 1) ONEIE (Lin et al., 2020); 2) GraphIE (Nguyen et al., 2022); 3) FourIE (Nguyen et al., 2021); 4) JMCEE (Xu et al., 2020); 5) EventGraph (You et al., 2022) on the ACE05 dataset. For Rich ERE there is little previous work to compare to; the only previously reported results (Li et al., 2022) for EE only solve the task of argument extraction, using gold entity and trigger information, hence their work is not included in our system comparison.

6 Results and discussion

We here present the results for our JSEEGraph model for the EE task, as well as its performance for the additional IE components: entities and relations, evaluated as described above. We further zoom in on the nested structures identified in Section 3 and assess the performance of our system on these rich structures which have largely been overlooked in previous work on event extraction. We go on to assess the influence of inter-related IE components in an ablation study. Finally we provide an error analysis of our model's predictions.

6.1 Overall performance

As shown in Table 4, on ACE-E^{+}, our overall results align with other systems. Our JSEEGraph results are especially strong for event argument extraction, with an improvement of around 10 percentage points from the best results of the previous best performing systems in our comparison.

On the newly introduced ACE-E^{++}, despite having more complex structures, with a higher degree of nested structures, the results of JSEEGraph on trigger extraction remain stable. We further note that our results on argument, entity, and relation extraction suffers some loss from highly nested entities, which is not surprising.

[4] https://catalog.ldc.upenn.edu/LDC2006T06

[5] https://catalog.ldc.upenn.edu/LDC2020T18

[6] The Rich ERE event ontology defines 38 event types, but for Chinese and Spanish data, only 18 event types are annotated. For consistency, we also use the same 18 event types for the English part.

[7] 3 argument roles for the reduced event types are thus excluded.

Model	Trg-I	Trg-C	Arg-I	Arg-C	Entity	Relation
			Dataset: ACE05-E$^+$ English			
EventGraph	——	70.0	——	65.4	——	——
GraphIE	——	**74.8**	——	59.9	91.0	**65.4**
ONEIE	75.6	72.8	57.3	54.8	89.6	58.6
FourIE	**76.7**	73.3	59.5	57.5	**91.1**	63.6
JSEEGraph	74.2	71.3	**70.7**	**68.4**	90.7	62.6
JSEEGraph w/o ent&rel	74.8	71.7	67.5	64.6	——	——
			Dataset: ACE05-E$^+$ Chinese			
JMCEE	**82.3**	**74.0**	53.7	50	——	——
ONEIE	——	67.7	——	53.2	**89.9**	62.9
FourIE	——	70.3	——	56.1	89.1	**65.9**
JSEEGraph	71.9	69.6	**74.3**	**70.1**	87.4	63.3
JSEEGraph w/o ent&rel	70.5	67.8	69.2	65.5	——	——
			Dataset: ACE05-E^{++} English			
EventGraph	——	**74.0**	——	58.6	——	——
JSEEGraph	73.5	70.0	**62.3**	**59.6**	**85.6**	**56.6**
JSEEGraph w/o ent&rel	**75.0**	71.3	60.3	57.7	——	——
			Dataset: ACE05-E^{++} Chinese			
JSEEGraph	**69.9**	**67.8**	**71.1**	**66.9**	**85.2**	**58.4**
JSEEGraph w/o ent&rel	69.5	67.4	66.5	63.3	——	——

Table 4: Experimental results on ACE05 (F1-score, %). We bold the highest score of each sub-task.

Model	Lang	Trg-I	Trg-C	Arg-I	Arg-C	Entity	Relation
			Dataset: Rich ERE-E$^+$				
JSEEGraph	en	68.6	62.3	59.6	56.2	80.3	53.7
	zh	62.7	59.0	53.1	50.1	78.1	53.2
	es	59.1	51.9	59.9	54.0	74.1	51.8
JSEEGraph w/o ent&rel	en	67.7	62.9	57.9	54.7	——	——
	zh	63.7	60.0	50.7	48.2	——	——
	es	62.3	54.3	57.3	52.5	——	——
			Dataset: Rich ERE-E^{++}				
JSEEGraph	en	67.3	62.7	55.6	52.8	77.9	46.1
	zh	65.2	61.7	51.0	48.7	77.5	54.3
	es	59.7	54.1	59.1	55.4	70.2	49.4
JSEEGraph w/o ent&rel	en	66.4	61.9	52.9	50.7	——	——
	zh	63.2	58.7	49.2	47.2	——	——
	es	57.2	48.9	50.8	46.4	——	——

Table 5: Experimental results on Rich ERE (F1-score).

From Table 5, we find that the scores on Rich ERE are consistently lower compared to those of ACE05. The double-tagging of event triggers described in Section 3 clearly pose a certain level of difficulty for the model to disambiguate events with a shared trigger. Argument and entity extraction also suffers from more fined-grained entity types.

6.2 Nesting

In order to directly evaluate our model's performance on nested instances, we split each test set into nested and non-nested parts and report the corresponding scores, as shown in Table 6[8].

We observe that JSEEGraph is quite robust in tackling nested instances across different IE tasks and languages. On ACE05-E^{++}, more than half of the test data are nested for both English and Chinese, and the results on the nested parts are lower, however consistently comparable with the non-nested parts of the datasets. On Rich ERE-E$^+$, nested instances make up only a small part of the test data, but the results are still comparable to the non-nested part. On Rich ERE-E^{++}, about one third of the test data are nested, results of the nested parts are in fact consistently better for trigger, entity, and relation extraction, but inferior for argument extraction.

To conclude, JSEEGraph does not suffer considerable performance loss from nesting among different IE elements, and in many cases actually gains in performance from more complex structures, notably for trigger, entity, and relation extraction. It is clear that the system can make use of inter-relations between the different IE elements of the information graph in order to resolve these structures.

[8]ACE05-E$^+$ is not included as it lacks sufficient nested instances.

Lang	Nested	#sents	Trg-I	Trg-C	Arg-I	Arg-C	Entity	Relation
				Dataset: ACE05-E^{++}				
en	✓	418	72.1	68.5	59.2	57.0	85.1	57.0
	✗	359	77.0	74.0	73.2	69.0	87.4	47.5
zh	✓	277	72.2	69.7	68.9	65.5	85.4	60.8
	✗	244	57.6	57.6	87.9	77.3	84.5	33.6
				Dataset: Rich ERE-E$^+$				
en	✓	93	81.3	71.6	54.8	51.4	81.3	49.8
	✗	652	61.4	56.9	64.0	60.5	79.8	56.3
zh	✓	101	72.0	66.6	47.5	45.1	79.7	56.0
	✗	382	54.2	52.2	59.5	55.9	77.1	49.9
es	✓	51	78.1	64.7	55.5	52.3	78.4	51.8
	✗	547	49.9	45.5	63.8	55.6	73.1	51.8
				Dataset: Rich ERE-E^{++}				
en	✓	251	75.4	69.2	53.0	50.5	81.0	45.7
	✗	494	46.0	45.3	75.0	70.6	71.0	49.4
zh	✓	197	70.4	67.0	49.0	46.8	80.4	57.2
	✗	286	45.9	41.8	63.9	61.1	69.7	23.3
es	✓	163	66.0	59.3	57.2	53.7	75.2	53.5
	✗	435	47.0	43.0	65.3	61.7	61.4	30.0

Table 6: Experimental results on test data with nesting as compared to without nesting (F1-score, %).

6.3 Ablation study

In order to gauge the effect of the joint modeling of entities, events, and relations, we perform an ablation study where we remove the entity and relation information from our information graph, hence only performing the task of event extraction directly from text. In the reduced information graph, node labels for entity types are removed, and relation edges between entities are also removed. We find that event extraction clearly benefits from entity and relation extraction, especially for event argument extraction. As shown in Table 4 and Table 5, when we train our model only for event extraction, the performance on argument extraction drops consistently across different datasets and languages, but the performance on trigger extraction remains quite stable.

6.4 Error analysis

The experimental results show that JSEEGraph has an advantage when it comes to the task of argument extraction. In a manual error analysis we therefore focus on the errors of event trigger extraction. After a manual inspection of our model's predictions on the test data, we find that the errors fall into the following main categories.

Over-predict non-event sentences. Our system tends to be more greedy in extracting event mentions, and wrongly classifies some tokens as event triggers even though the sentence does not contain event annotation. For instance, the sentence *"Anne-Marie will get the couple's 19-room home in New York state"* (from ACE05) does not have annotated events, but our system extracts *"get"* as trigger for a `Transfer-Ownership` event; in this case, however, one could argue that the `Transfer-Ownership` should be annotated.

Under-predict multi-event sentences When a sentence contains multiple event mentions, JSEEGraph sometimes fails to extract all of the event triggers. For example, this sentence *"Kelly , the US assistant secretary for East Asia and Pacific Affairs , arrived in Seoul from Beijing Friday to brief Yoon, the foreign minister"* from ACE05 contains a `Transport` event triggered by *"arrived"* and a `Meet` event triggered by *"brief"*, but our system fails to extract the trigger for the `Meet` event; in this example, it requires a certain level of knowledge to be able to identify *"brief"* as an event trigger, which is beyond the capacity of our model.

Wrong event types In some cases, even though our model successfully identifies an event trigger, it assigns a wrong event type. Some event types can easily be confused with each other. In this sentence from Rich ERE, *"The University of Arkansas campus was buzzing Friday after a student hurt himself when a gun went off in his backpack in the KUAF building"*, an `Injure` event is evoked by *"hurt"*, but our model assigns an event type of `Attack`. Clearly, `Injure` and `Attack` events are one typical case of event types that can be easily confused.

Context beyond sentence This error applies specifically to Rich ERE: even though the annotation of events is on a sentence level, annotators were instructed to take into account the context of the whole article. Our model fails completely when a trigger requires context beyond the sentence. For instance, this sentence *"If Mickey can do it , so can we!"* is taken from an article describing an on-going demonstration in Disney Land, and *"it"* is the trigger for a `demonstrate` event; without the context, our model fails to identify the trigger. These are cases which would require information about event coreference.

7 Conclusion

In this paper, we have proposed JSEEG, a graph-based approach for joint structured event extraction, alongside entity, and relation extraction. We experiment on two benchmark datasets ACE05 and Rich ERE, covering the three languages English, Chinese, and Spanish. We find that our proposed JSEEGraph is robust in solving nested event structures, and is especially strong in event argument extraction. We further demonstrate that it is beneficial to jointly perform EE with other IE tasks, and event argument extraction especially gains from entity extraction.

Limitations

Our work has two main limitations. Firstly, we do not compare our system to previous works on the Rich ERE dataset. This is mainly due to the fact that most work use the light ERE (Song et al., 2015) dataset. We were unfortunately not able to got access to this version of the data[9], which is why no experiments were carried out on it.

Secondly, we only experiment with one language model, the multilingual model XLM-R. As our model is language agnostic, and we aimed to test its performance on datasets in different languages, the choice of a multilingual model was obvious. XLM-R has been chosen based on its good performance in other tasks, and to make our work comparable to previous work (You et al., 2022). However, another approach would be to test our model with a selection of language-specific language models.

Acknowledgements

This work was supported by industry partners and the Research Council of Norway with funding to *MediaFutures: Research Centre for Responsible*

[9]Here we refer to the datasets with LDC codes: *LDC2015E29*, *LDC2015E68*, and *LDC2015E78* for English ERE, and *LDC2015E107* for the Spanish ERE.

Media Technology and Innovation, through the centers for Research-based Innovation scheme, project number 309339.

References

Laura Banarescu, Claire Bonial, Shu Cai, Madalina Georgescu, Kira Griffitt, Ulf Hermjakob, Kevin Knight, Philipp Koehn, Martha Palmer, and Nathan Schneider. 2013. Abstract meaning representation for sembanking. In *Proceedings of the 7th linguistic annotation workshop and interoperability with discourse*, pages 178–186.

Giannis Bekoulis, Johannes Deleu, Thomas Demeester, and Chris Develder. 2018. Adversarial training for multi-context joint entity and relation extraction. In *Proceedings of the 2018 Conference on Empirical Methods in Natural Language Processing*, pages 2830–2836, Brussels, Belgium. Association for Computational Linguistics.

Hu Cao, Jingye Li, Fangfang Su, Fei Li, Hao Fei, Shengqiong Wu, Bobo Li, Liang Zhao, and Donghong Ji. 2022. OneEE: A one-stage framework for fast overlapping and nested event extraction. In *Proceedings of the 29th International Conference on Computational Linguistics*, pages 1953–1964, Gyeongju, Republic of Korea. International Committee on Computational Linguistics.

Jason P.C. Chiu and Eric Nichols. 2016. Named entity recognition with bidirectional LSTM-CNNs. *Transactions of the Association for Computational Linguistics*, 4:357–370.

Alexis Conneau, Kartikay Khandelwal, Naman Goyal, Vishrav Chaudhary, Guillaume Wenzek, Francisco Guzmán, Edouard Grave, Myle Ott, Luke Zettlemoyer, and Veselin Stoyanov. 2020. Unsupervised cross-lingual representation learning at scale. In *Proceedings of the 58th Annual Meeting of the Association for Computational Linguistics*, pages 8440–8451, Online. Association for Computational Linguistics.

George Doddington, Alexis Mitchell, Mark Przybocki, Lance Ramshaw, Stephanie Strassel, and Ralph Weischedel. 2004. The automatic content extraction (ACE) program – tasks, data, and evaluation. In *Proceedings of the Fourth International Conference on Language Resources and Evaluation (LREC'04)*, Lisbon, Portugal. European Language Resources Association (ELRA).

Timothy Dozat and Christopher D. Manning. 2017. Deep biaffine attention for neural dependency parsing. In *International Conference on Learning Representations*.

Timothy Dozat and Christopher D. Manning. 2018. Simpler but more accurate semantic dependency parsing. In *Proceedings of the 56th Annual Meeting of the Association for Computational Linguistics (Volume 2: Short Papers)*, pages 484–490, Melbourne, Australia. Association for Computational Linguistics.

Xinya Du and Claire Cardie. 2020. Event extraction by answering (almost) natural questions. In *Proceedings of the 2020 Conference on Empirical Methods in Natural Language Processing (EMNLP)*, pages 671–683, Online. Association for Computational Linguistics.

Tianyu Gao, Adam Fisch, and Danqi Chen. 2021. Making pre-trained language models better few-shot learners. In *Proceedings of the 59th Annual Meeting of the Association for Computational Linguistics and the 11th International Joint Conference on Natural Language Processing (Volume 1: Long Papers)*, pages 3816–3830, Online. Association for Computational Linguistics.

Daniel Hershcovich, Omri Abend, and Ari Rappoport. 2017. A transition-based directed acyclic graph parser for UCCA. In *Proceedings of the 55th Annual Meeting of the Association for Computational Linguistics (Volume 1: Long Papers)*, pages 1127–1138, Vancouver, Canada. Association for Computational Linguistics.

I-Hung Hsu, Kuan-Hao Huang, Elizabeth Boschee, Scott Miller, Prem Natarajan, Kai-Wei Chang, and Nanyun Peng. 2022. Degree: A data-efficient generative event extraction model. In *Proceedings of the 2022 Conference of the North American Chapter of the Association for Computational Linguistics (NAACL)*.

Lifu Huang, Heng Ji, Kyunghyun Cho, Ido Dagan, Sebastian Riedel, and Clare Voss. 2018. Zero-shot transfer learning for event extraction. In *Proceedings of the 56th Annual Meeting of the Association for Computational Linguistics (Volume 1: Long Papers)*, pages 2160–2170, Melbourne, Australia. Association for Computational Linguistics.

Heng Ji and Ralph Grishman. 2008. Refining event extraction through cross-document inference. In *Proceedings of ACL-08: HLT*, pages 254–262, Columbus, Ohio. Association for Computational Linguistics.

Fayuan Li, Weihua Peng, Yuguang Chen, Quan Wang, Lu Pan, Yajuan Lyu, and Yong Zhu. 2020. Event extraction as multi-turn question answering. In *Findings of the Association for Computational Linguistics: EMNLP 2020*, pages 829–838, Online. Association for Computational Linguistics.

Qi Li, Heng Ji, and Liang Huang. 2013. Joint event extraction via structured prediction with global features. In *Proceedings of the 51st Annual Meeting of the Association for Computational Linguistics (Volume 1: Long Papers)*, pages 73–82, Sofia, Bulgaria. Association for Computational Linguistics.

Rui Li, Wenlin Zhao, Cheng Yang, and Sen Su. 2022. A dual-expert framework for event argument extraction. In *Proceedings of the 45th International ACM*

SIGIR Conference on Research and Development in Information Retrieval, pages 1110–1121.

Sha Li, Heng Ji, and Jiawei Han. 2021. Document-level event argument extraction by conditional generation. In *Proceedings of the 2021 Conference of the North American Chapter of the Association for Computational Linguistics: Human Language Technologies*, pages 894–908, Online. Association for Computational Linguistics.

Xiang Lisa Li and Percy Liang. 2021. Prefix-tuning: Optimizing continuous prompts for generation. In *Proceedings of the 59th Annual Meeting of the Association for Computational Linguistics and the 11th International Joint Conference on Natural Language Processing (Volume 1: Long Papers)*, pages 4582–4597, Online. Association for Computational Linguistics.

Ying Lin, Heng Ji, Fei Huang, and Lingfei Wu. 2020. A joint neural model for information extraction with global features. In *Proceedings of the 58th Annual Meeting of the Association for Computational Linguistics*, pages 7999–8009, Online. Association for Computational Linguistics.

Jian Liu, Yubo Chen, Kang Liu, Wei Bi, and Xiaojiang Liu. 2020. Event extraction as machine reading comprehension. In *Proceedings of the 2020 Conference on Empirical Methods in Natural Language Processing (EMNLP)*, pages 1641–1651, Online. Association for Computational Linguistics.

Xiao Liu, Heyan Huang, Ge Shi, and Bo Wang. 2022. Dynamic prefix-tuning for generative template-based event extraction. In *Proceedings of the 60th Annual Meeting of the Association for Computational Linguistics (Volume 1: Long Papers)*, pages 5216–5228, Dublin, Ireland. Association for Computational Linguistics.

Xiao Liu, Zhunchen Luo, and Heyan Huang. 2018. Jointly multiple events extraction via attention-based graph information aggregation. In *Proceedings of the 2018 Conference on Empirical Methods in Natural Language Processing*, pages 1247–1256, Brussels, Belgium. Association for Computational Linguistics.

Ilya Loshchilov and Frank Hutter. 2019. Decoupled weight decay regularization. In *7th International Conference on Learning Representations, ICLR 2019, New Orleans, LA, USA, May 6-9, 2019*. OpenReview.net.

Yaojie Lu, Hongyu Lin, Jin Xu, Xianpei Han, Jialong Tang, Annan Li, Le Sun, Meng Liao, and Shaoyi Chen. 2021. Text2Event: Controllable sequence-to-structure generation for end-to-end event extraction. In *Proceedings of the 59th Annual Meeting of the Association for Computational Linguistics and the 11th International Joint Conference on Natural Language Processing (Volume 1: Long Papers)*, pages 2795–2806, Online. Association for Computational Linguistics.

Minh Van Nguyen, Viet Dac Lai, and Thien Huu Nguyen. 2021. Cross-task instance representation interactions and label dependencies for joint information extraction with graph convolutional networks. In *Proceedings of the 2021 Conference of the North American Chapter of the Association for Computational Linguistics: Human Language Technologies*, pages 27–38, Online. Association for Computational Linguistics.

Minh Van Nguyen, Bonan Min, Franck Dernoncourt, and Thien Nguyen. 2022. Joint extraction of entities, relations, and events via modeling inter-instance and inter-label dependencies. In *Proceedings of the 2022 Conference of the North American Chapter of the Association for Computational Linguistics: Human Language Technologies*, pages 4363–4374, Seattle, United States. Association for Computational Linguistics.

Thien Huu Nguyen, Kyunghyun Cho, and Ralph Grishman. 2016. Joint event extraction via recurrent neural networks. In *Proceedings of the 2016 Conference of the North American Chapter of the Association for Computational Linguistics: Human Language Technologies*, pages 300–309, San Diego, California. Association for Computational Linguistics.

Stephan Oepen, Omri Abend, Lasha Abzianidze, Johan Bos, Jan Hajic, Daniel Hershcovich, Bin Li, Tim O'Gorman, Nianwen Xue, and Daniel Zeman. 2020. MRP 2020: The second shared task on cross-framework and cross-lingual meaning representation parsing. In *Proceedings of the CoNLL 2020 Shared Task: Cross-Framework Meaning Representation Parsing*, pages 1–22, Online. Association for Computational Linguistics.

Stephan Oepen, Marco Kuhlmann, Yusuke Miyao, Daniel Zeman, Silvie Cinkova, Dan Flickinger, Jan Hajic, and Zdenka Uresova. 2015. SemEval 2015 Task 18: Broad-Coverage Semantic Dependency Parsing. *Proceedings of the 9th International Workshop on Semantic Evaluation (SemEval 2015)*, pages 915–926.

Stephan Oepen, Marco Kuhlmann, Yusuke Miyao, Daniel Zeman, Dan Flickinger, Jan Hajic, Angelina Ivanova, and Yi Zhang. 2014. SemEval 2014 Task 8: Broad-Coverage Semantic Dependency Parsing. *Proceedings of the 8th International Workshop on Semantic Evaluation (SemEval 2014)*, pages 63–72.

Giovanni Paolini, Ben Athiwaratkun, Jason Krone, Jie Ma, Alessandro Achille, RISHITA ANUBHAI, Cicero Nogueira dos Santos, Bing Xiang, and Stefano Soatto. 2021. Structured prediction as translation between augmented natural languages. In *International Conference on Learning Representations*.

David Samuel and Milan Straka. 2020. ÚFAL at MRP 2020: Permutation-invariant semantic parsing in PERIN. In *Proceedings of the CoNLL 2020 Shared Task: Cross-Framework Meaning Representation Parsing*, pages 53–64, Online. Association for Computational Linguistics.

Jiawei Sheng, Shu Guo, Bowen Yu, Qian Li, Yiming Hei, Lihong Wang, Tingwen Liu, and Hongbo Xu. 2021. CasEE: A joint learning framework with cascade decoding for overlapping event extraction. In *Findings of the Association for Computational Linguistics: ACL-IJCNLP 2021*, pages 164–174, Online. Association for Computational Linguistics.

Taylor Shin, Yasaman Razeghi, Robert L. Logan IV, Eric Wallace, and Sameer Singh. 2020. AutoPrompt: Eliciting Knowledge from Language Models with Automatically Generated Prompts. In *Proceedings of the 2020 Conference on Empirical Methods in Natural Language Processing (EMNLP)*, pages 4222–4235, Online. Association for Computational Linguistics.

Zhiyi Song, Ann Bies, Stephanie Strassel, Tom Riese, Justin Mott, Joe Ellis, Jonathan Wright, Seth Kulick, Neville Ryant, and Xiaoyi Ma. 2015. From light to rich ERE: Annotation of entities, relations, and events. In *Proceedings of the The 3rd Workshop on EVENTS: Definition, Detection, Coreference, and Representation*, pages 89–98, Denver, Colorado. Association for Computational Linguistics.

David Wadden, Ulme Wennberg, Yi Luan, and Hannaneh Hajishirzi. 2019. Entity, relation, and event extraction with contextualized span representations. In *Proceedings of the 2019 Conference on Empirical Methods in Natural Language Processing and the 9th International Joint Conference on Natural Language Processing (EMNLP-IJCNLP)*, pages 5784–5789, Hong Kong, China. Association for Computational Linguistics.

Nuo Xu, Haihua Xie, and Dongyan Zhao. 2020. A novel joint framework for multiple Chinese events extraction. In *Proceedings of the 19th Chinese National Conference on Computational Linguistics*, pages 950–961, Haikou, China. Chinese Information Processing Society of China.

Bishan Yang and Tom M. Mitchell. 2016. Joint extraction of events and entities within a document context. In *Proceedings of the 2016 Conference of the North American Chapter of the Association for Computational Linguistics: Human Language Technologies*, pages 289–299, San Diego, California. Association for Computational Linguistics.

Huiling You, David Samuel, Samia Touileb, and Lilja Øvrelid. 2022. Eventgraph: Event extraction as semantic graph parsing. In *Proceedings of CASE: The 5th Workshop on Challenges and Applications of Automated Extraction of Socio-political Events from Text*.

Zixuan Zhang and Heng Ji. 2021. Abstract Meaning Representation guided graph encoding and decoding for joint information extraction. In *Proceedings of the 2021 Conference of the North American Chapter of the Association for Computational Linguistics: Human Language Technologies*, pages 39–49, Online. Association for Computational Linguistics.

A Training detail

We use the large version of XLM-R available on HuggingFace `transformers`[10] for obtaining contextual embeddings of the input sequence. We use the same hyperparameter configuration for all our models, as shown in Table 7, and weights are optimized with AdamW (Loshchilov and Hutter, 2019) following a warmed-up cosine learning rate schedule.

Hyperparameter	**JSEEGraph**
batch_size	16
beta_2	0.98
decoder_learning_rate	1.0e-4
decoder_weight_decay	1.2e-6
dropout_transformer	0.25
dropout_transformer_attention	0.1
encoder	*"xlm-roberta-large"*
encoder_learning_rate	4.0e-6
encoder_weight_decay	0.1
epochs	110
hidden_size_anchor	256
hidden_size_edge_label	256
hidden_size_edge_presence	256
n_transformer_layers	3
query_length	2
warmup_steps	1 000

Table 7: Hyperparameter setting for our system, and we use the same configuration for all models.

The training was done on a single node of Nvidia RTX3090 GPU. The runtimes and sizes (including the pretrained XLM-R) of the multilingual models for each dataset are listed in Table 8,

Dataset	**Runtime**	**Model size**
ACE05-E^+	27:52 h	343.8 M
ACE05-E^{++}	27:25 h	343.8 M
Rich ERE-E^+	33:13 h	344.6 M
Rich ERE-E^{++}	32:16 h	344.6 M

Table 8: The training times and model sizes (number of trainable weights) of all our experiments.

[10]`https://huggingface.co/docs/transformers/index`

Lang	**Trg-I**	**Trg-C**	**Arg-I**	**Arg-C**	**Entity**	**Relation**
			Dataset: ACE05-E^+			
en	73.1	70.0	68.5	65.4	90.4	61.4
	73.2	69.8	66.7	64.2	—	—
zh	69.2	67.0	71.4	67.8	85.6	60.2
	64.8	62.6	62.5	59.3	—	—
			Dataset: ACE05-E^{++}			
en	73.8	70.3	63.7	60.6	85.3	55.4
	72.7	69.9	58.9	56.3	—	—
zh	66.7	64.5	66.0	63.1	82.1	53.7
	66.0	64.3	62.2	58.4	—	—
			Dataset: Rich ERE-E^+			
en	65.3	60.5	59.8	56.1	80.6	53.6
	68.7	62.4	56.0	52.8	—	—
zh	62.3	57.7	53.9	50.2	78.3	54.5
	62.4	59.0	48.2	46.3	—	—
es	54.2	47.9	52.5	46.7	72.9	44.7
	56.7	49.7	51.3	47.3	—	—
			Dataset: Rich ERE-E^{++}			
en	66.9	60.4	54.6	52.1	76.3	42.1
	66.2	59.2	49.5	46.8	—	—
zh	63.6	60.2	47.1	44.8	76.2	51.5
	60.5	57.2	41.5	38.8	—	—
es	54.4	48.9	47.2	43.2	68.2	43.0
	54.5	48.4	35.7	32.1	—	—

Table 9: Experimental results of monolingual models (F1-score, %)

B Monolingual training results

Apart from multilingual training, we also train two monolingual models for each language, one for joint event extraction with entity and relation and the for event extraction only. Results of monolingual models are summerized in Table 9.

Generative Data Augmentation for Aspect Sentiment Quad Prediction

An Wang[†] Junfeng Jiang[‡] Youmi Ma[†] Ao Liu[†] Naoaki Okazaki[†]
[†]Tokyo Institute of Technology [‡]The University of Tokyo
an.wang@nlp.c.titech.ac.jp
jiangjf@is.s.u-tokyo.ac.jp
{youmi.ma@nlp., ao.liu@nlp., okazaki@}c.titech.ac.jp

Abstract

Aspect sentiment quad prediction (ASQP) analyzes the aspect terms, opinion terms, sentiment polarity, and aspect categories in a text. One challenge in this task is the scarcity of data owing to the high annotation cost. Data augmentation techniques are commonly used to address this issue. However, existing approaches simply rewrite texts in the training data, restricting the semantic diversity of the generated data and impairing the quality due to the inconsistency between text and quads. To address these limitations, we augment quads and train a quads-to-text model to generate corresponding texts. Furthermore, we designed novel strategies to filter out low-quality data and balance the sample difficulty distribution of the augmented dataset. Empirical studies on two ASQP datasets demonstrate that our method outperforms other data augmentation methods and achieves state-of-the-art performance on the benchmarks.[1]

Source Text:
It is one the nicest outdoor restaurants I have ever seen in NY.
Label: [ambience general, outdoor restaurants, nicest, positive]

Augmented Text (Previous Methods):
Back Translation:
It is one of the most beautiful outdoor restaurants I have ever seen in NY.
Random Deletion:
It is one the nicest restaurants I have ever seen in NY.
Synonym Replacement:
It is one the best outdoor restaurants I have ever seen in NY.

Our Method:
Augmented Label:
[ambience general, space, Great, positive],
[ambience general, outdoor restaurants, nothing special, positive]
Augmented Text:
Great space for meetings, but the outdoor restaurants is nothing special.

Figure 1: Examples of text data augmentation methods. We observe that the augmented texts from previous methods fail to include all spans in the label and the augmented texts are semantically very similar to the source text. Our method addresses these problems by generating texts from augmented labels.

1 Introduction

Aspect-based sentiment analysis (ABSA) aims to mine opinions expressed regarding specific aspects of a given text. Recently, Zhang et al. (2021a) proposed a challenging compound subtask of ABSA called aspect sentiment quad prediction (ASQP), which predicts four kinds of elements (aspect category, aspect term, opinion term, sentiment polarity) as quadruplets (quads). A single text may contain multiple quads. For example, the text "*The pizza is delicious but expensive.*" mentions one aspect term (*pizza*) and two opinion terms (*delicious* and *expensive*). Because these two opinions are related to the same aspect, the text includes two quads: (taste, pizza, delicious, positive) and (price, pizza, expensive, negative).

Traditional methods (Cai et al., 2020; Wan et al., 2020; Cai et al., 2021) address such compound subtasks of ABSA in a discriminative manner. Recent studies (Zhang et al., 2021b; Hu et al., 2022) have primarily concentrated on sequence-to-sequence frameworks for ASQP because of their superior performance. Specifically, These frameworks transform the input text into a sequence of linearized quads.

Despite the success of the field of ASQP, the scarcity of annotated data is still a remaining challenge. For instance, Rest15 and Rest16 ASQP datasets only consist of 834 and 1,264 training samples respectively. However, manual annotation is costly and time consuming. One solution for expanding the number of training samples is data augmentation. EDA (Wei and Zou, 2019) adopted some typical data augmentation techniques such as random swapping, inserting, deleting words, and synonym replacement to improve text classification. Back-translation (Yu et al., 2018) obtained augmented data by translating the original text in English into another language and then translating

[1]The source code is available at https://github.com/AnWang-AI/AugABSA

*Proceedings of the The 12th Joint Conference on Lexical and Computational Semantics (*SEM 2023)*, pages 128–140
July 13-14, 2023 ©2023 Association for Computational Linguistics

it back into English. However, applying these operations to ASQP datasets usually disrupts crucial spans, such as aspect or opinion terms, resulting in label mismatches with the original input text. Additionally, traditional data augmentation methods only focus on augmenting texts that preserve semantic information similar to the original text in the training dataset. Therefore, the ability of these methods to help models generalize to unseen data is limited.

In this study, we propose a novel **Gen**erative **D**ata **A**ugmentation method (GenDA) by proposing a quads-to-text (Q2T) generation task—the reverse task of ASQP, which aims to generate a text based on the input quads. We synthesize a large number of quads by mixing the labels from the ASQP training dataset. Then, we feed these labels to the trained Q2T model which uses a sequence-to-sequence model to generate new parallel data with high diversity. Figure 1 shows some examples of the traditional text augmentation methods and our method. In addition, we propose a data filtering strategy concerning the unalignment of the aspect and opinion terms between text and quads to remove low-quality augmented data. Furthermore, we propose a new measurement, Average Context Inverse Document Frequency (AC-IDF), to evaluate the difficulty of augmented samples and a strategy to balance the difficulty distribution. Finally, we can augment sufficient training data with good diversity and high quality.

To evaluate our method, we conducted empirical studies using two ASQP datasets. We applied the proposed data augmentation with the previous ASQP model. These studies demonstrate that our method outperforms other data augmentation methods and achieves state-of-the-art performance on the benchmark. In addition, the experimental analysis also verifies that our method successfully generates data with stronger diversity. Additionally, we conducted a detailed ablation study to confirm the effectiveness of each component of our method and provide insights into how they contribute to the performance of our method.

The contributions of this study are summarized as follows: (1) We propose the synthesis of diverse parallel data using a Q2T model for ASQP. To the best of our knowledge, this is the first study to achieve data augmentation by text generation for ABSA. (2) We propose a data filtering strategy to remove low-quality augmented data and a measurement to evaluate the difficulty of the augmented samples, which is used to balance the augmented dataset. (3) Our experiments demonstrate that the proposed method achieves state-of-the-art performance on the two ASQP datasets.

2 Preliminaries

2.1 Task Definition of ASQP

Aspect sentiment quad prediction aims to predict all sentiment-related quadruplets (ac, at, ot, sp) from a given text x. The elements of each quadruplet are aspect category (ac), aspect term (at), opinion term (ot), and sentiment polarity (sp). In particular, the aspect category belongs to a specific category set AC and the sentiment polarity falls into sentiment classes $\{\texttt{POS}, \texttt{NEU}, \texttt{NEG}\}$ denoting positive, neutral, and negative sentiments toward the aspect. Note that if the aspect and opinion terms are not explicitly mentioned in the given text, they are set as NULL.

2.2 Generative ASQP Methods

Although early work handled ABSA in a discriminative manner, recent studies (Zhang et al., 2021a,b; Hu et al., 2022) have mainly focused on generative ASQP methods because of their better performances.

PARAPHRASE (Zhang et al., 2021a) formulated ASQP into a paraphrasing problem. They transformed sentiment-related quadruplets into a natural language. Specifically, given a quad (ac, at, ot, sp), they designed the following template: "ac is sp because at is ot.", where ac and sp are projected onto the natural language format. When the input text contains multiple quads, the quads are transformed into different templated sentences separately and then concatenated with a special marker [SSEP]. Hu et al. (2022) explored the effect of the order of each quad element in the template. In addition, they proposed a more effective target template: "[AT] at [OT] ot [AC] ac [SP] sp", where [AT], [OT], [AC], and [SP] are special tokens.

Inspired by previous generative ASQP methods, we consider the reverse process of text-to-quads and further propose a generative data augmentation method based on it.

3 Methodology

To alleviate the problem of annotated data scarcity and to generate augmented data with strong diver-

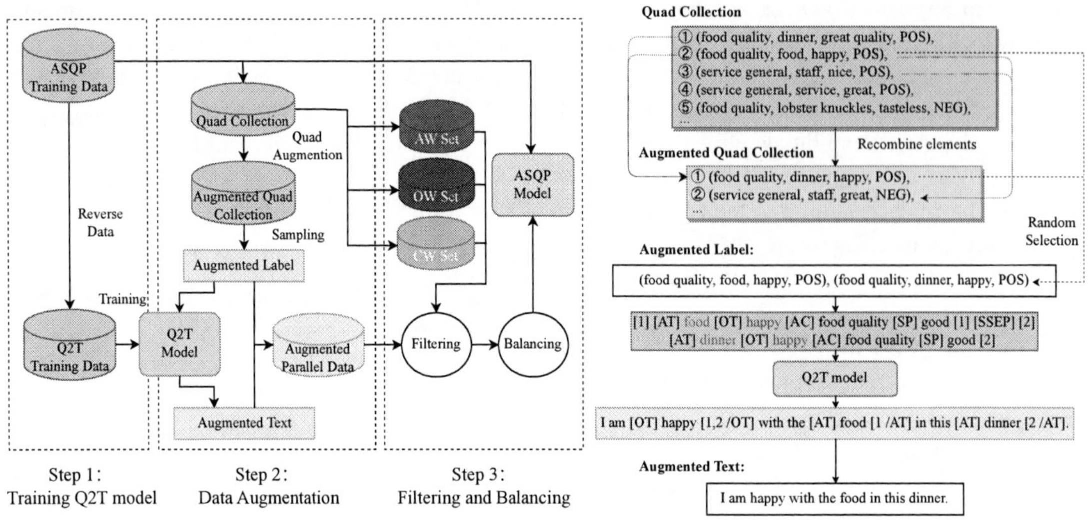

(a) Pipeline of our method.

(b) Example of generating augmented text.

Figure 2: Overview of our proposed method. In Step 3 of Figure (a), AW Set, OW Set, and CW Set represent aspect word set, opinion word set, and context word set, respectively. They are utilized to aid the filtering process. Figure (b) shows an example of synthesizing augmented parallel data consisting of a text, "I am happy with the food in this dinner," and an associated label, "(food quality, food, happy, POS), (food quality, dinner, happy, POS)". The dotted line indicates the source of the quad or label.

sity and high quality for the ASQP task, we propose a novel generative data augmentation method. Figure 2 presents an overview of the proposed method. The proposed method consists of three main steps. (1) We reverse the data in the ASQP dataset to create a new training set, which we then use to train a quads-to-text model. (2) We aim to generate data that are semantically different from the training data. Hence, we collect all labels from the training set and propose mixing them to create an augmented quad set. We then randomly sample several mixed quads and feed them into the quads-to-text model to generate the corresponding source text. (3) To further improve the performance of our data augmentation, we propose two strategies to filter out generated texts that do not match the given quads and balance the sample difficulty distribution of the augmented data. Finally, we combine the augmented data with the original training set to train an ASQP model.

3.1 Quads-to-Text Task

Before introducing our generative data augmentation method, we first define a new text generation task, the quads-to-text (Q2T) task, and then design a Q2T model based on a pre-trained sequence-to-sequence model.

3.1.1 Task Definition of Quads-to-Text Task

To obtain parallel augmented data for our generative ASQP data augmentation, we first propose a quads-to-text task. Q2T aims to generate text describing the given quads. Given n quads $\{q_1, q_2, ..., q_n\}$, where $q_i = (ac_i, at_i, ot_i, sp_i)$, the task requires generating a text x that includes and only includes the input quads.

3.1.2 Quads-to-Text Model

To handle the Q2T problem, we utilize the pre-trained sequence-to-sequence model following other works on controllable text generation (Zhang et al., 2022). Unlike conventional text generation methods, our designed Q2T model not only generates texts but also provides a mechanism to conveniently judge whether the generated statement meets the task requirements of Q2T. In our method, we mainly focus on the input and output designs of the model.

For the input sequence of the model, we formulate the given quads as template sentences similarly to Hu et al. (2022). The difference is that we insert special indexing markers before and after each sentence to distinguish multiple quads. Specifically, the i-th quad (ac_i, at_i, ot_i, sp_i) is transformed into a templated text:

$$\text{[i][AT] } at_i \text{ [OT] } ot_i \text{ [AC] } ac_i \text{ [SP] } sp_i \text{ [i]}$$

The final transformed texts are linked with a special marker [SSEP] following previous work (Zhang et al., 2021b; Hu et al., 2022).

For the output sequence of the model, instead of only generating the source text, the Q2T model can generate text with annotations. The annotations identify aspect terms and opinion terms in the text. In addition, the annotation also includes the relation information between aspects and opinions. The model annotates aspect and opinion terms of i-th quad in the text using special markers "[AT]", "[i /AT]", "[OT]", and "[i /OT]". Special tokens [AT] and [OT] denote the beginning of an aspect and opinion term while [i /AT] and [i /OT] denote the ending position. When there are multiple aspects in a text that are described by the same opinion or there are multiple opinions describing the same aspect, they can be grouped together using a comma-separated list of numbers within square brackets, such as [1,2 AT] to indicate that the first and second opinion describe the same aspect. We will explain the function of these annotations in detail in Section 3.2.2.

3.1.3 Training

To make the Q2T model generate text that meets our requirements, we first build Q2T datasets based on ASQP datasets. ASQP aims to predict quads from the given text, thus, we obtain Q2T datasets by simply inverting the input and label of the ASQP dataset. To enhance the ability to understand the meaning of the special index markers, we augment Q2T data by permuting the order of quads in the templated input of Q2T model. After training the Q2T model, the model can be used to obtain more abundant augmented data for the ASQP task.

3.2 Augmention Strategy

In this section, we first propose a novel method for obtaining a diverse augmented dataset based on the Q2T model. We then propose a filtering strategy and a difficulty balancing strategy to further improve the performance of data augmentation.

3.2.1 Synthesizing Augmented Quads

To obtain diverse data that are meaningfully different from the data in the original ASQP training dataset, we propose to diversify the input of the Q2T as shown in figure 2.

First, we collect all quads from the ASQP training dataset as a quad collection, denoted as $\mathcal{S}_{origin} = \{(ac_i, at_i, ot_i, sp_i)\}$. Subsequently, for those quads that **share the same aspect category** ac_i, we randomly exchange their aspect term at and opinion term ot with sentiment polarity sp to create new quads. The opinion term and sentiment polarity from the same original quad will be bound together to avoid getting new quads where elements conflict with each other. For example, given two quads: (price, pizza, cheap, `POS`) and (price, steak, expensive, `NEG`), we can synthesize new quads (price, steak, cheap, `POS`) and (price, pizza, expensive, `NEG`). Finally, we balance the number of synthesized quads for each aspect category to obtain the augmented quad collection, denoted as $\mathcal{S}_{augment}$. Subsequently, each time we randomly select $1 \sim 3$ quads from $\mathcal{S}_{origin} \cup \mathcal{S}_{augment}$, and feed them to the Q2T model for data augmentation. During the training of the ASQP model, we remove the annotations such as [AT] in the augmented text.

3.2.2 Data Filtering

For ASQP data augmentation, a common problem is that the augmented texts may not be faithful to the given quads. Specifically, the generated texts from the Q2T model may contain fewer or more quads compared to input quads. Using unfaithful text as ground truth for given quads to train the ASQP model will introduce noise that decreases the performance. Thus we propose a two-step filtering strategy to remove these low-quality data.

The first step of filtering involves checking the consistency between the output text of the Q2T model and the input quads. As introduced in Section 3.1.2, our Q2T model annotates aspect terms and opinion spans using special markers when generating texts. This allows us to collect aspect-opinion pairs from the output text and then check the consistency between the detected pairs and input quads. We filter out the examples with inconsistent aspect and opinion terms.

However, the generated texts that pass the first filtering step may contain additional aspect or opinion terms that are not annotated with special markers. Training the ASQP model with such data may lead to a lower recall. To address this issue, we propose the second step of data filtering. The process involves building two keyword sets (an aspect word set and an opinion word set) and a context word set. Specifically, we begin by collecting all the texts from the training data. Because the aspect and opinion terms are annotated, we categorize the words in the text based on labels into three groups:

aspect words, opinion words, and context words. After that, we gather all the aspect words to create the aspect word set. Similarly, we collect all the opinion words to form the opinion word set and all the context words to construct the context word set. If the unmarked part (i.e., the context) of a generated text contains any word that belongs to the keyword sets but does not exist in the context word set, we consider this example as containing additional aspect/opinion terms and remove it from the augmented dataset.

3.2.3 Difficulty Balancing

In addition to the existence of low-quality data, another problem we observe is that more than half of the generated texts are simple expressions. These generated texts are far simpler than most texts in the ASTE dataset. A text can be divided into three different parts, aspect terms, opinion terms, and context. Even if being given different quads as inputs, the Q2T model usually generates text with relatively similar context, such as 'The *at* is *ot*'. When most augmented training data are too simple, the model may not learn the complex patterns required to make accurate predictions on unseen data. Therefore, it is necessary to balance the distribution of the sample difficulty of the augmented dataset.

To assess the sample difficulty, we propose a new measurement factor, called the Average Context Inverse Document Frequency (AC-IDF). The difficulty of a text can be defined as the level of language proficiency required to understand the text (Fulcher, 1997). A text that uses many uncommon words is considered more difficult than one that uses simple and common language. Therefore, one way to measure the difficulty of a text is to calculate the average IDF score of the words in the text. Furthermore, because aspects and opinions are directly copied from the input of the model, it is critical to evaluate the difficulty of the context part of the text. Therefore, we propose using the context difficulty to measure the learning difficulty of the sample for our model.

Specifically, given a text collection X from the dataset, we remove all aspects and opinions terms to obtain only the context words. We denote the preprocessed text collection by $\bar{X}$. Then, for each text $\bar{x}_i$ after preprocessing, we calculate the AC-IDF$_i$ of the text as follows:

$$\text{AC-IDF}_i = \frac{1}{n_i} \sum_{j=1}^{n_i} \text{IDF}(t_{ij}), \quad (1)$$

$$\text{IDF}(t_{ij}) = \ln \frac{|\bar{X}|}{1 + |\{\bar{x} \in \bar{X} : t_{ij} \in \bar{x}\}|}, \quad (2)$$

where t_{ij} is the j-th word in $\bar{x}_i$, n_i is the number of words in $\bar{x}_i$, $|\bar{X}|$ denotes the size of $\bar{X}$, and $|\{\bar{x} \in \bar{X} : t_{ij} \in \bar{x}\}|$ represents the total number of texts where t_{ij} appears.

We build a subset according to the AC-IDF of the generated texts so that the difficulty of the selected data follows a uniform distribution. Specifically, we set several intervals according to the sample difficulty and randomly sample similar amounts of data from the entire augmented dataset for each interval. Finally, we create a subset whose data obey an approximate uniform distribution with respect to the sample difficulty. Thus, the model learns to predict quads from diverse and balanced data to improve performance.

4 Experiment

4.1 Datasets

We evaluate our method on two ASQP datasets: `Rest15` and `Rest16` (Zhang et al., 2021b), which originates from the SemEval Challenges (Pontiki et al., 2015, 2016). Their domain is of restaurant reviews. Detailed statistics are shown in Appendix A. We also evaluate our method on four Aspect Sentiment Triplet Extraction (ASTE) datasets (Peng et al., 2020) in Appendix 5.

4.2 Experiment Setting

In accordance with previous studies (Zhang et al., 2021a; Hu et al., 2022), our method also employs T5-base (Raffel et al., 2020) as the pre-trained backbone for both Q2T and ASQP tasks. The parameter count is twice the size of the backbone model (one for the Q2T model and one for the ASQP model), which is equivalent to 2×220 million parameters. We set the batch size to 8 and the learning rate to 1e-4. During the inference stage, greedy decoding is used to generate the output sequence. The amount of augmented data is four times that of training data. The experiments are run for a maximum of 20 epochs. All reported results are the average of five runs initialized with different random seeds. We use precision, recall, and micro F1 scores as the evaluation metric. A sentiment quad prediction is considered accurate only when all of its predicted elements match the ground truth exactly. We also report the standard errors of our base model and proposed data augmentation method.

4.3 Main Results

4.3.1 Compared Methods

Previous ASQP methods can be categorized into two types: BERT (Devlin et al., 2019) based methods and T5 (Raffel et al., 2020) based methods. The BERT based methods include **HGCN** (Cai et al., 2020), **TASO** (Wan et al., 2020), and **Extract-Classify-ACOS** (Cai et al., 2021). T5 based methods include **GAS** (Zhang et al., 2021b), **PARAPHRASE** (Zhang et al., 2021a), **DLO** and **ILO** (Hu et al., 2022). We report the performance of these methods directly copied from their paper. **PARAPHRASE + Marked Template** is a variant of the PARAPHRASE method. It uses a different target template with special markers which are proposed by Hu et al. (2022). We implement it by ourselves and adopt it as our base model to apply our data augmentation method.

4.3.2 Analysis

Table 1 shows the evaluation results on the ASQP task. We observe that our proposed data augmentation method, **GenDA**, clearly improves the performance of the base model by +2.22 and +2.18 F1 score on `Rest15` an `Rest16`. GenDA achieves state-of-the-art performance on the ASQP benchmark. Note that GenDA has a higher precision score while maintaining a good recall compared with other methods. This observation indicates that our proposed data augmentation method helps to improve the robustness of our model, and therefore, predicts the sentiment quadruplets more precisely.

Our base model **PARAPHRASE + Marked Template** achieves better performance than the original PARAPHRASE method but does not outperform DLO and ILO. The reason why we do not choose DLO or ILO as our base model is that these two methods are relatively complex and not suitable for integrating our data augmentation methods.

4.4 Effects of Augmentation Methods

To demonstrate the effectiveness of the data augmentation method we proposed, we also compare it with several representative data augmentation methods on the ASQP benchmark. For all data augmentation methods, the amount of augmented data is four times that of training data.

EDA (Wei and Zou, 2019) adopts four operations including synonym replacement, random insertion, random swap, and random deletion to the input texts. We additionally design two ASQP-specific variants of EDA: **CEDA** applies EDA only in the context of input text whereas **AOEDA** applies EDA on the aspect terms and opinion terms of the input text. Note that the terms in quads will also be revised correspondingly. **AEDA** (Karimi et al., 2021) is an simpler data augmentation method that randomly inserts punctuation into the input texts. **Back Translation** (Yu et al., 2018) augments data by translating text from English to another language and then back to English. We used the machine translation models proposed by Ng et al. (2019) in our experiment.

Comparison results are reported in Table 2. Compared with existing data augmentation methods, we observe that applying EDA and Back Translation on the base model brings no noticeable improvement and can even reduce performance. We attribute it to the fact that sometimes these methods disrupt the matching of input text and labels because they may revise some important spans including aspects or opinion terms. To explore whether directly modifying traditional data augmentation methods to adapt the ASQP task can improve model performance, we evaluate AOEDA and CEDA, two simple variants of EDA which avoid mismatches between text and labels of augmented data. The results show that both two variants could improve the performance slightly, but the improvement is limited, likely because the existing data augmentation methods cannot provide training samples with high diversity. Finally, our method GenDA significantly outperforms all traditional data augmentation methods under all evaluation metrics. Compared with the best F1 scores of previous data augmentation methods, the improvement of our method reaches 1.26 and 1.04. These results demonstrate the effectiveness of our data augmentation method.

4.5 Analysis of the Text Diversity

We analyze the text diversity of different data augmentation methods. In Figure 3, we visualize the text representations of the entire `Rest 16` training dataset and 4000 augmented data generated by different data augmentation methods. Specifically, we first adopt a BERT-based encoder to transform each text into a representative vector and then use t-

PLM	Method	Rest 15			Rest 16		
		P	R	F1	P	R	F1
BERT	HGCN-Linear (Cai et al., 2020)	24.43	20.25	22.15	25.36	24.03	24.68
	HGCN-TFM (Cai et al., 2020)	25.55	22.01	23.65	27.40	26.41	26.90
	TASO-Linear (Wan et al., 2020)	41.86	26.50	32.46	49.73	40.70	44.77
	TASO-CRF (Wan et al., 2020)	44.24	28.66	34.78	48.65	39.68	43.71
	Extract-Classify-ACOS (Cai et al., 2021)	35.64	37.25	36.42	38.40	50.93	43.77
T5	GAS (Zhang et al., 2021b)	45.31	46.70	45.98	54.54	57.62	56.04
	PARAPHRASE (Zhang et al., 2021a)	46.16	47.72	46.93	56.63	59.30	57.93
	DLO (Hu et al., 2022)	47.08	49.33	48.18	<u>57.92</u>	**61.80**	<u>59.79</u>
	ILO (Hu et al., 2022)	<u>47.78</u>	**50.38**	<u>49.05</u>	57.58	61.17	59.32
	PARAPHRASE + Marked Template	47.40 $\pm$0.20	48.18 $\pm$0.44	47.79 $\pm$0.30	57.85 $\pm$0.30	59.58 $\pm$0.42	58.70 $\pm$0.35
	+ GenDA	**49.74** $\pm$0.28	<u>50.29</u> $\pm$0.35	**50.01** $\pm$0.31	**60.08** $\pm$0.34	<u>61.70</u> $\pm$0.12	**60.88** $\pm$0.13

Table 1: Evaluation results (%) on `Rest 16` and `Rest 15` datasets of ASQP for comparing with previous state-of-the-art methods. The best and second-best performances are highlighted in bold and underlined, respectively.

Type	Method	Rest 15			Rest 16		
		P	R	F1	P	R	F1
Baseline	PARAPHRASE + Marked Template	47.40	48.18	47.79	57.85	59.58	58.70
Previous Data Augmentation	+ EDA	47.77	48.27	47.85	57.70	58.85	58.27
	+ CEDA	47.44	48.63	48.19	58.47	60.43	59.43
	+ AOEDA	47.78	48.40	48.09	58.22	60.30	59.24
	+ AEDA	48.17	48.65	48.40	58.40	59.70	59.04
	+ Back Translation	47.08	47.30	47.19	58.58	59.86	59.21
Ablation	+ GenDA	**49.74**	**50.29**	**50.01**	**60.08**	**61.70**	**60.88**
	+ GenDA (original label)	48.88	49.48	49.18	59.23	61.08	60.14
	+ GenDA w/o Filtering & Balancing	47.95	48.55	48.25	58.33	60.45	59.37
	+ GenDA w/o Balancing	48.34	49.21	48.77	58.84	60.61	59.71
	+ GenDA w/o Filtering	48.63	49.18	48.91	59.39	61.05	60.21

Table 2: Evaluation results (%) on `Rest 16` and `Rest 15` datasets of ASQP for comparing different data augmentation methods and ablations. All involved data augmentation methods use PARAPHRASE + Marked Template as the base model for a fair comparison. GenDA (original label) denotes only using original labels from the training dataset instead of augmented quads for Q2T.

SNE (Van der Maaten and Hinton, 2008) to reduce dimension for visualizing the distributions.

To quantify the difference between the training dataset and the augmented dataset, we calculate the average Euclidean distance between each point in the augmented dataset and its nearest neighbor in the training dataset. We also provide the Self-BLEU scores (Zhu et al., 2018) to evaluate the diversity of each augmented dataset. Lower Self-BLEU means better diversity.

From Figure 3, we observe that the semantic representations of most EDA-augmented texts are coincident with original texts, showing the smallest average distance. The high Self-BLEU score of EDA further indicates the low diversity of EDA-augmented texts. Back Translation achieves a much lower Self-BLEU score than EDA, but the visualization shows a high semantic similarity between the original and augmented data. By contrast, our proposed method GenDA achieves the largest distance score and lowest Self-BLEU, demonstrating that it can generate texts that are more diverse and less likely to semantically overlap with the original texts.

4.6 Ablation Studies

To investigate the effectiveness of each component of our proposed method, we conduct an ablation study on two ASQP datasets as shown in Table 2. Even without adopting our filtering or balancing strategies, our model can outperform the base model. After applying our filtering strategy, we observe an improvement because it filters out noisy and irrelevant data. The balancing strategy also brings a performance gain, which indicates that addressing the sample difficulty imbalance issue in the augmented datasets is beneficial for models to learn. Note that compared to the filtering strategy, the balancing strategy contributes more to performance gains, which means that sample difficulty imbalance has a worse impact on performance than the low-quality problem. Furthermore, when the filtering and balancing strategies are applied jointly, our model achieves a further performance

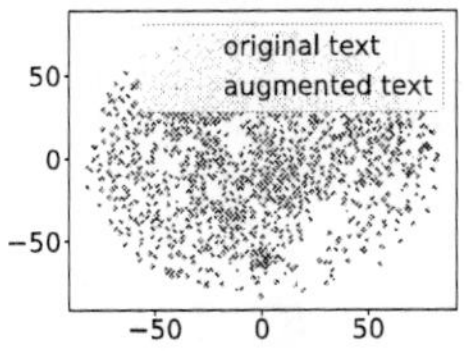

EDA
(a) Distance=3.72
Self-BLEU=85.00

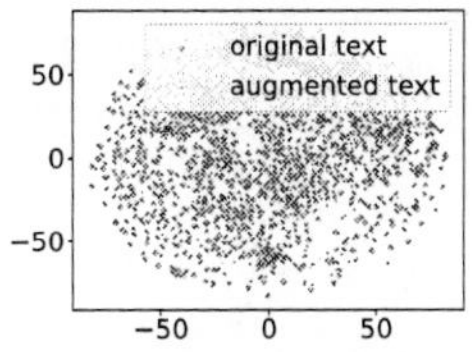

Back Translation
(b) Distance=4.97
Self-BLEU=62.02

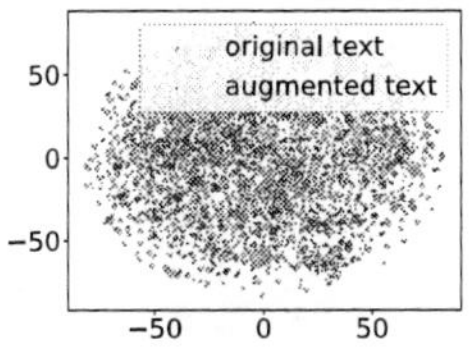

GenDA
(c) Distance=10.03
Self-BLEU=55.89

Figure 3: Visualization of text semantic representation. Each subfigure shows the distribution of original texts (in salmon color) from the Rest16 training dataset and corresponding augmented texts (in blue color) obtained using different methods. In each subcaption, we report the distance between two datasets and the Self-BLEU score (%) computed on each augmented dataset.

gain. In addition, when only the original labels are input, the model's f1 scores noticeably decline by 0.83 and 0.74 compared to when augmented labels are input.

5 Effects on ASTE task

We conduct experiments on the ASTE task to verify that our method is also effective on other ABSA subtasks. We compare our method with strong previous work.

ASTE methods Previous ASTE methods can be categorized into three types: pipeline-based methods, end-to-end discrimination methods, and text-generation methods. The pipeline-based methods include CMLA (Wang et al., 2017), RINATE+ (Dai and Song, 2019), Li-unified-R (Li et al., 2019), P-pipeline (Peng et al., 2020), and Two-Stage (Huang et al., 2021). End-to-end discrimination methods include BMRC (Chen et al., 2021), SPAN-ASTE (Xu et al., 2021), EMC-GCN (Chen et al., 2022), and COM-MRC (Zhai et al., 2022). Text-generation methods for ASTE include GAS (Zhang et al., 2021b) and PARAPHRASE (Zhang et al., 2021a).

We select three types of ASTE methods for comparison: 1) Pipeline based methods including CMLA (Wang et al., 2017), RINATE+ (Dai and Song, 2019), Li-unified-R (Li et al., 2019), P-pipeline (Peng et al., 2020) and Two-Stage (Huang et al., 2021); 2) End-to-end discrimination methods: BMRC (Chen et al., 2021), SPAN-ASTE (Xu et al., 2021), EMC-GCN (Chen et al., 2022) and COM-MRC (Zhai et al., 2022); and 3)Text-generation methods: GAS (Zhang et al., 2021b) and PARAPHRASE (Zhang et al., 2021a).

Analysis Table 3 shows the evaluation results of baselines and our methods on four datasets of ASTE task, including `Lap14`, `Rest14`, `Rest15`, and `Rest16`. Compared to ASQP, ASTE only needs to predict three kinds of elements. In our method, the target template of ASTE is changed to

$$\text{[i] [AT] } at_i \text{ [OT] } ot_i \text{ [SP] } sp_i \text{ [i]},$$

for the i-th triplet (at_i, ot_i, sp_i). Other designs for the ASTE task are the same as the ASQP task. We find that with this slight revision, our methods outperform the best results by 1.53, 1.73, 1.27, and 2.53 f1 score on these four datasets respectively, achieving new state-of-the-art performance.

6 Related Work

6.1 Aspect-based Sentiment Analysis

ABSA aims to analyze fine-grained sentiment elements including not only the sentiment polarity but also the aspect term, opinion term, and aspect category. Intuitively, these elements are related. Therefore, recent studies tried to model them jointly, such as constructing aspect-sentiment pairs (Cai et al., 2020) or triples (Peng et al., 2020). Furthermore, there is a growing interest in modeling these four elements simultaneously, with two promising directions being proposed. Cai et al. (2021) proposed a two-stage method that first extracts aspect and opinion terms, and then uses them to classify aspect category and sentiment polarity. Another framework is based on a generation model (Zhang et al., 2021a,b), which predicts the quadruplet in an end-to-end manner by paraphrasing the input text to a target template. Since they additionally exploit the information from label semantics, the generation-based method achieves dominantly better performance in the field of ABSA.

6.2 Data Augmentation

Data augmentation is a common technique in language and vision domains to improve model performance. Previous data augmentation methods

Backbone	Method	L14	R14	R15	R16
BERT	CMLA (Wang et al., 2017)	33.16	42.79	37.01	41.72
	RINATE+ (Dai and Song, 2019)	34.95	20.07	29.97	23.87
	Li-unified-R (Li et al., 2019)	42.34	51.00	47.82	44.31
	P-pipeline (Peng et al., 2020)	42.87	51.46	52.32	54.21
	Jet (Xu et al., 2018)	51.04	62.40	57.53	63.83
	GTS (Wu et al., 2020)	55.21	64.81	54.88	66.08
	Two-Stage (Huang et al., 2021)	58.58	68.16	58.59	67.52
	BMRC (Chen et al., 2021)	57.82	67.99	60.02	65.75
	SPAN-ASTE (Xu et al., 2021)	59.38	71.85	63.27	70.26
	EMC-GCN (Chen et al., 2022)	58.81	71.78	61.93	68.33
	COM-MRC (Zhai et al., 2022)	60.17	72.01	<u>64.53</u>	71.57
T5	GAS (Zhang et al., 2021b)	58.19	70.52	60.23	69.05
	PARAPHRASE (Zhang et al., 2021a)	<u>61.13</u>	<u>72.03</u>	62.56	<u>71.70</u>
	GenDA	**62.66**	**73.76**	**65.80**	**74.23**

Table 3: Evaluation results (%) on four datasets of ASTE for comparing with previous state-of-the-art methods. The best and second-best performances are highlighted in bold and underlined, respectively.

can be categorized into three types. The first type only augments the input, such as image flipping, rotation, and scaling (Bjerrum, 2017) for images, and text modification (Wei and Zou, 2019) as well as back translation (Yu et al., 2018) for natural language. The second type only augments the output, such as generating target-side soft pseudo sequences (Xie et al., 2022). These approaches are particularly relevant for generation tasks where the order of words is important. The third type augments both the input and the output, such as the mixup approach (Zhang et al., 2018) which generates virtual training examples through linear combinations of feature vectors and their associated targets. To the best of our knowledge, our work is the first to propose a data augmentation method of the third type specifically for subtasks of ABSA. Unlike previous methods in this realm that augment only the input (Li et al., 2020) or output (Hu et al., 2022), our method augments both input and output, leading to augmenting more diverse samples. Our method reduces the model's reliance on a limited set of examples and enables it to better generalize to unseen data, thereby mitigating the problem of overfitting and achieving better performance on test data.

7 Conclusion

In this paper, we have proposed a new approach to tackle the problem of data scarcity in the ASQP task. To address this challenge, we present a generative data augmentation method based on a pre-trained quads-to-text model. Our method generates new parallel data by synthesizing a large number of quads from the training dataset and generating corresponding pseudo texts. Moreover, we propose a data filtering strategy to remove low-quality generated data and a measurement to balance the difficulty of augmented samples. Our empirical studies on two ASQP datasets have demonstrated the superiority of our method compared to other data augmentation methods and the effectiveness of each component in our method. Our approach not only is an innovative solution to the problem of data scarcity in ASQP, but also provides a potential direction for future work in other related fields, such as relation extraction and event extraction.

Limitation

Firstly, because our data augmentation method relies on the quality of the quads-to-text (Q2T) model's generation, the performance of our method may be limited by the quality of the generated text. Besides, the quads-to-text (Q2T) model is trained by the original ASQP dataset, thus it may fail to generate expressions that do not appear in the dataset. Additionally, training an extra Q2T model brings additional computational costs. Furthermore, as the model inputs are randomly sampled from the augmented quad collection, some quad combinations may not be suitable for text generation, which could affect the effectiveness of data augmentation.

Ethics Statement

There are no ethical problems in this paper. All of the datasets are publicly available.

Acknowledgements

This work was supported by JSPS KAKENHI Grant Number 19H01118. We sincerely appreciate Sakae Mizuki and Marco Cognetta for their generous assistance and valuable discussions. We also express our gratitude to all reviewers for their insightful comments and constructive feedback.

References

Esben Jannik Bjerrum. 2017. Smiles enumeration as data augmentation for neural network modeling of molecules. *arXiv preprint arXiv:1703.07076*.

Hongjie Cai, Yaofeng Tu, Xiangsheng Zhou, Jianfei Yu, and Rui Xia. 2020. Aspect-category based sentiment analysis with hierarchical graph convolutional network. In *Proceedings of the 28th international conference on computational linguistics*, pages 833–843.

Hongjie Cai, Rui Xia, and Jianfei Yu. 2021. Aspect-category-opinion-sentiment quadruple extraction with implicit aspects and opinions. In *Proceedings of the 59th Annual Meeting of the Association for Computational Linguistics and the 11th International Joint Conference on Natural Language Processing (Volume 1: Long Papers)*, pages 340–350.

Hao Chen, Zepeng Zhai, Fangxiang Feng, Ruifan Li, and Xiaojie Wang. 2022. Enhanced multi-channel graph convolutional network for aspect sentiment triplet extraction. In *Proceedings of the 60th Annual Meeting of the Association for Computational Linguistics (Volume 1: Long Papers)*, pages 2974–2985.

Shaowei Chen, Yu Wang, Jie Liu, and Yuelin Wang. 2021. Bidirectional machine reading comprehension for aspect sentiment triplet extraction. In *Proceedings of the AAAI conference on artificial intelligence*, volume 35, pages 12666–12674.

Hongliang Dai and Yangqiu Song. 2019. Neural aspect and opinion term extraction with mined rules as weak supervision. *arXiv preprint arXiv:1907.03750*.

Jacob Devlin, Ming-Wei Chang, Kenton Lee, and Kristina Toutanova. 2019. BERT: Pre-training of deep bidirectional transformers for language understanding. In *Proceedings of the 2019 Conference of the North American Chapter of the Association for Computational Linguistics: Human Language Technologies, Volume 1 (Long and Short Papers)*, pages 4171–4186, Minneapolis, Minnesota. Association for Computational Linguistics.

Glenn Fulcher. 1997. Text difficulty and accessibility: Reading formulae and expert judgement. *System*, 25(4):497–513.

Mengting Hu, Yike Wu, Hang Gao, Yinhao Bai, and Shiwan Zhao. 2022. Improving aspect sentiment quad prediction via template-order data augmentation. *arXiv preprint arXiv:2210.10291*.

Lianzhe Huang, Peiyi Wang, Sujian Li, Tianyu Liu, Xiaodong Zhang, Zhicong Cheng, Dawei Yin, and Houfeng Wang. 2021. First target and opinion then polarity: Enhancing target-opinion correlation for aspect sentiment triplet extraction. *arXiv preprint arXiv:2102.08549*.

Akbar Karimi, Leonardo Rossi, and Andrea Prati. 2021. AEDA: An easier data augmentation technique for text classification. In *Findings of the Association for Computational Linguistics: EMNLP 2021*, pages 2748–2754, Punta Cana, Dominican Republic. Association for Computational Linguistics.

Kun Li, Chengbo Chen, Xiaojun Quan, Qing Ling, and Yan Song. 2020. Conditional augmentation for aspect term extraction via masked sequence-to-sequence generation. In *Proceedings of the 58th Annual Meeting of the Association for Computational Linguistics*, pages 7056–7066.

Xin Li, Lidong Bing, Piji Li, and Wai Lam. 2019. A unified model for opinion target extraction and target sentiment prediction. In *Proceedings of the AAAI conference on artificial intelligence*, volume 33, pages 6714–6721.

Nathan Ng, Kyra Yee, Alexei Baevski, Myle Ott, Michael Auli, and Sergey Edunov. 2019. Facebook FAIR's WMT19 news translation task submission. In *Proceedings of the Fourth Conference on Machine Translation (Volume 2: Shared Task Papers, Day 1)*, pages 314–319, Florence, Italy. Association for Computational Linguistics.

Haiyun Peng, Lu Xu, Lidong Bing, Fei Huang, Wei Lu, and Luo Si. 2020. Knowing what, how and why: A near complete solution for aspect-based sentiment analysis. In *Proceedings of the AAAI Conference on Artificial Intelligence*, volume 34, pages 8600–8607.

Maria Pontiki, Dimitrios Galanis, Haris Papageorgiou, Ion Androutsopoulos, Suresh Manandhar, Mohammad Al-Smadi, Mahmoud Al-Ayyoub, Yanyan Zhao, Bing Qin, Orphée De Clercq, et al. 2016. Semeval-2016 task 5: Aspect based sentiment analysis. In *International workshop on semantic evaluation*, pages 19–30.

Maria Pontiki, Dimitrios Galanis, Harris Papageorgiou, Suresh Manandhar, and Ion Androutsopoulos. 2015. Semeval-2015 task 12: Aspect based sentiment analysis. In *Proceedings of the 9th international workshop on semantic evaluation (SemEval 2015)*, pages 486–495.

Colin Raffel, Noam Shazeer, Adam Roberts, Katherine Lee, Sharan Narang, Michael Matena, Yanqi Zhou, Wei Li, and Peter J Liu. 2020. Exploring the limits of transfer learning with a unified text-to-text transformer. *The Journal of Machine Learning Research*, 21(1):5485–5551.

Laurens Van der Maaten and Geoffrey Hinton. 2008. Visualizing data using t-sne. *Journal of machine learning research*, 9(11).

Hai Wan, Yufei Yang, Jianfeng Du, Yanan Liu, Kunxun Qi, and Jeff Z Pan. 2020. Target-aspect-sentiment joint detection for aspect-based sentiment analysis. In *Proceedings of the AAAI conference on artificial intelligence*, volume 34, pages 9122–9129.

Wenya Wang, Sinno Jialin Pan, Daniel Dahlmeier, and Xiaokui Xiao. 2017. Coupled multi-layer attentions for co-extraction of aspect and opinion terms. In *Proceedings of the AAAI conference on artificial intelligence*, volume 31.

Jason Wei and Kai Zou. 2019. EDA: Easy data augmentation techniques for boosting performance on text classification tasks. In *Proceedings of the 2019 Conference on Empirical Methods in Natural Language Processing and the 9th International Joint Conference on Natural Language Processing (EMNLP-IJCNLP)*, pages 6382–6388, Hong Kong, China. Association for Computational Linguistics.

Thomas Wolf, Lysandre Debut, Victor Sanh, Julien Chaumond, Clement Delangue, Anthony Moi, Pierric Cistac, Tim Rault, Rémi Louf, Morgan Funtowicz, et al. 2019. Huggingface's transformers: State-of-the-art natural language processing. *arXiv preprint arXiv:1910.03771*.

Zhen Wu, Chengcan Ying, Fei Zhao, Zhifang Fan, Xinyu Dai, and Rui Xia. 2020. Grid tagging scheme for aspect-oriented fine-grained opinion extraction. *arXiv preprint arXiv:2010.04640*.

Shufang Xie, Ang Lv, Yingce Xia, Lijun Wu, Tao Qin, Tie-Yan Liu, and Rui Yan. 2022. Target-side input augmentation for sequence to sequence generation. In *International Conference on Learning Representations*.

Hu Xu, Bing Liu, Lei Shu, and Philip S Yu. 2018. Double embeddings and cnn-based sequence labeling for aspect extraction. *arXiv preprint arXiv:1805.04601*.

Lu Xu, Yew Ken Chia, and Lidong Bing. 2021. Learning span-level interactions for aspect sentiment triplet extraction. *arXiv preprint arXiv:2107.12214*.

Adams Wei Yu, David Dohan, Minh-Thang Luong, Rui Zhao, Kai Chen, Mohammad Norouzi, and Quoc V Le. 2018. Qanet: Combining local convolution with global self-attention for reading comprehension. *arXiv preprint arXiv:1804.09541*.

Zepeng Zhai, Hao Chen, Fangxiang Feng, Ruifan Li, and Xiaojie Wang. 2022. COM-MRC: A COntext-masked machine reading comprehension framework for aspect sentiment triplet extraction. In *Proceedings of the 2022 Conference on Empirical Methods in Natural Language Processing*, pages 3230–3241, Abu Dhabi, United Arab Emirates. Association for Computational Linguistics.

Hongyi Zhang, Moustapha Cisse, Yann N. Dauphin, and David Lopez-Paz. 2018. mixup: Beyond empirical risk minimization. In *International Conference on Learning Representations*.

Wenxuan Zhang, Yang Deng, Xin Li, Yifei Yuan, Lidong Bing, and Wai Lam. 2021a. Aspect sentiment quad prediction as paraphrase generation. In *Proceedings of the 2021 Conference on Empirical Methods in Natural Language Processing*, pages 9209–9219, Online and Punta Cana, Dominican Republic. Association for Computational Linguistics.

Wenxuan Zhang, Xin Li, Yang Deng, Lidong Bing, and Wai Lam. 2021b. Towards generative aspect-based sentiment analysis. In *Proceedings of the 59th Annual Meeting of the Association for Computational Linguistics and the 11th International Joint Conference on Natural Language Processing (Volume 2: Short Papers)*, pages 504–510.

Wenxuan Zhang, Xin Li, Yang Deng, Lidong Bing, and Wai Lam. 2022. A survey on aspect-based sentiment analysis: tasks, methods, and challenges. *IEEE Transactions on Knowledge and Data Engineering*.

Yaoming Zhu, Sidi Lu, Lei Zheng, Jiaxian Guo, Weinan Zhang, Jun Wang, and Yong Yu. 2018. Texygen: A benchmarking platform for text generation models. In *The 41st international ACM SIGIR conference on research & development in information retrieval*, pages 1097–1100.

Dataset	#Text	
	Rest15	Rest16
Train	834	1264
Validation	209	316
Test	537	544

Table 4: Statistics of datasets of ASQP task.

Dataset	#Text			
	Laptop14	Rest14	Rest15	Rest16
Train	1300	920	593	842
Validation	323	228	148	210
Test	496	339	318	320

Table 5: Statistics of datasets of ASTE task.

A Dataset Statistic

We conduct experiments on two publicly available ASQP datasets, namely Rest15 and Rest16 (Zhang et al., 2021a). In these datasets, each sample includes a text as input, with sentiment quads as ground truth. Datasets are split to train, validation, and test sets officially. Table 4 presents the relevant statistics. We also conduct experiments for Aspect Sentiment Triplet Extraction (ASTE) task, which aims to predict (aspect, opinion, sentiment polarity) triplets from the given text. Table 5 presents statistics of four ASTE datasets.

B Experimental Environment and Runtime

All our experiments are conducted with a single NVIDIA Tesla V100 GPU. Our method was implemented using the Hugging Face transformers library (Wolf et al., 2019). The training process of our method on GPU for one run took approximately 50 minutes including 20 minutes for training the Q2T model and 30 minutes for the ASQP model.

C Distribution of Context Difficulty

We present the frequency distribution histogram of the AC-IDF values of texts in the training dataset and augmented datasets in Figure 4. The AC-IDF frequency distribution of the training dataset follows a Gaussian distribution, with most data points falling between AC-IDF values of 4 and 6. However, for the augmented dataset generated without the balancing strategy, most of the data points fall

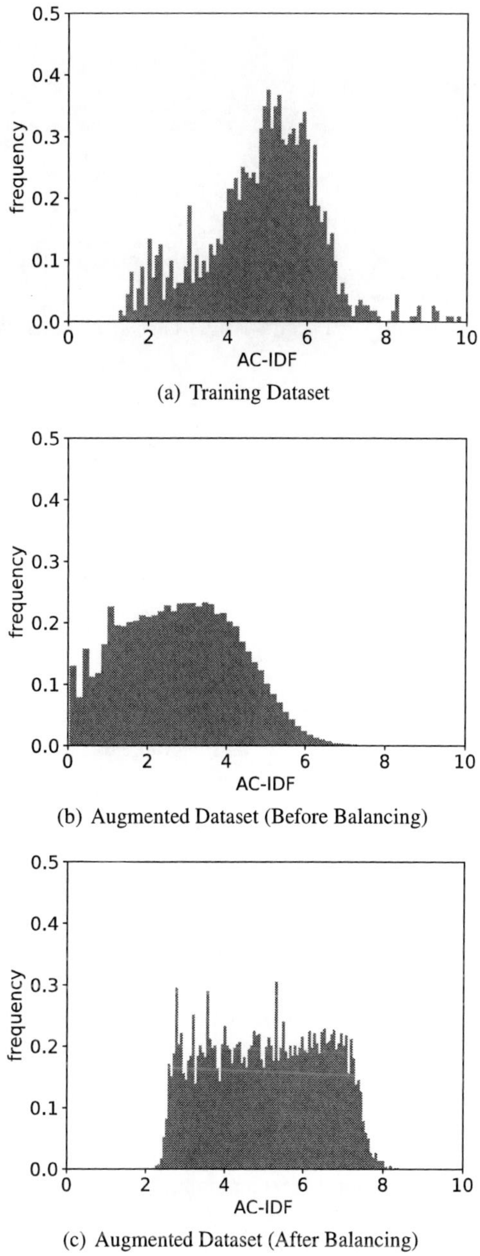

(a) Training Dataset

(b) Augmented Dataset (Before Balancing)

(c) Augmented Dataset (After Balancing)

Figure 4: Frequency distribution histogram for AC-IDF of texts in the training dataset and augmented datasets.

between AC-IDF values of 0 and 4. This indicates that most of the generated texts are relatively simple and differ significantly from the distribution of the training dataset. After applying the balancing strategy, the augmented dataset shows a more uniform distribution of data points between AC-IDF values of 3 and 7. This indicates that the balancing strategy has effectively created a more balanced distribution of sample difficulty.

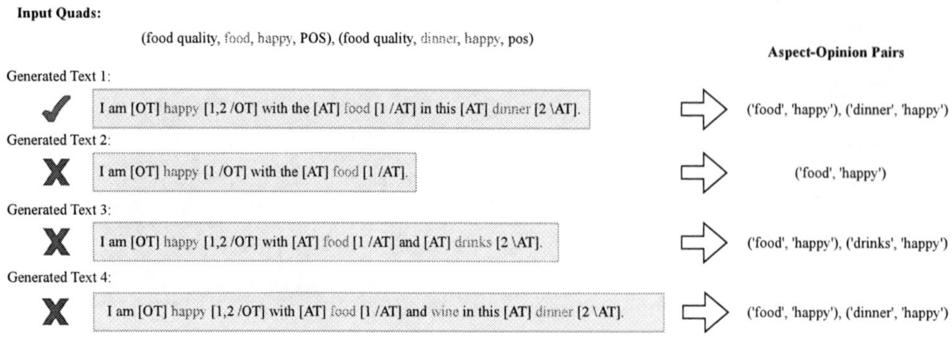

Figure 5: Examples of generative data.

Case 1
Sentence: If there is a line every day of the week for the entire time a place is open, you know it is great. **Predicted Quadruplet:** (restaurant miscellaneous, place, great, positive) **Gold Quadruplet:** (restaurant general, place, great, positive)
Case 2
Sentence: To be honest, I've had better frozen pizza. **Predicted Quadruplet:** (food quality, frozen pizza, better, negative) **Gold Quadruplet:** (food quality, pizza, better, negative)

Table 6: Two error examples of our methods.

D Examples of Generative Text

We present four examples of generative text: one correct example and three low-quality examples. The provided examples illustrate the issues of low-quality generated text and the motivation of our data filtering strategies. The first example is a high-quality one, faithful to the input quads. The second and third examples are low-quality ones that can be filtered out by the first step of the proposed two-step filtering strategy, which checks consistency between the output text and input quads. The fourth example is another low-quality one, which contains an additional aspect that is not present in the input but not annotated by the special markers. Such noisy texts would escape the first-step filtering but can be identified by the second-step filtering.

E Error Analysis

After conducting a comprehensive analysis of the error cases, we present two specific examples to shed light on the challenges encountered by our approach, as illustrated in Figure 6. In the first case, our model incorrectly identifies the predicted aspect category as "restaurant miscellaneous" instead of the correct label "restaurant general." This error highlights a limitation of our model in accurately categorizing certain aspects where the classification boundaries become ambiguous. In the second case, we observe a flaw in aspect extraction. The predicted aspect is "frozen pizza," whereas the correct aspect should have been "pizza." This error reveals that our model sometimes faces difficulties in extracting the precise aspect when there are subtle variations or distinctions within the aspect terms. Consequently, our data augmentation approach may not effectively assist the model when it encounters such challenging instances.

Are Language Models Sensitive to Semantic Attraction? A Study on Surprisal

Yan Cong
Purdue University; Feinstein Institutes
yancong222@gmail.com

Emmanuele Chersoni
The Hong Kong Polytechnic University
emmanuele.chersoni@polyu.edu.hk

Yu-Yin Hsu
The Hong Kong Polytechnic University
yu-yin.hsu@polyu.edu.hk

Alessandro Lenci
University of Pisa
alessandro.lenci@unipi.it

Abstract

In psycholinguistics, *semantic attraction* is a sentence processing phenomenon in which a given argument violates the selectional requirements of a verb, but this violation is not perceived by comprehenders due to its attraction to another noun in the same sentence, which is syntactically unrelated but semantically sound.

In our study, we use autoregressive language models to compute the sentence-level and the target phrase-level Surprisal scores of a psycholinguistic dataset on semantic attraction.

Our results show that the models are sensitive to semantic attraction, leading to reduced Surprisal scores, although none of them perfectly matches the human behavioral patterns.

1 Introduction

Cases of similarity-based interference have always been at the center of interest for sentence processing studies, as they offer strong evidence for cue-based models of memory retrieval during language comprehension (Cunnings and Sturt, 2018). According to such accounts, interference emerges because an item with some cues has to be retrieved from memory, and because those cues are simultaneously matched by multiple items (Van Dyke, 2007; Lewis and Vasishth, 2013).

Consider the examples in (1) (Wagers et al., 2009):

(1) a. The key to the **cells** unsurprisingly were rusty.
b. The key to the **cell** unsurprisingly were rusty.

Compared to fully grammatical sentences, both elicit longer reading times in humans, but the effect is attenuated in 1a., where there is an **attractor** (*cells*) matching the number of the verb, causing an **illusion of grammaticality**. This phenomenon is known as **morphological attraction**.

Attraction has also been observed at the semantic level, as in the following example from the eye-tracking study by Cunnings and Sturt (2018):

(2) a. Julia saw the beer that the lady with the **meal** quite happily ate during an expensive night out.
b. Julia saw the beer that the lady with the **wine** quite happily ate during an expensive night out.

Again, both sentences are implausible, because *beer* violates the selectional restrictions of the verb *ate*, but the authors of the study observed that (2a) was processed faster than (2b), due to the presence of a semantically fitting noun (*meal*) that generates a **semantic illusion**. Both types of illusion are *facilitatory* interferences, as they attenuate the effects of anomalies leading to higher costs for the human language processing system. This is a case of **semantic attraction**.

The recent literature in Natural Language Processing (NLP), on the other hand, has shown an increasing interest in using the **Surprisal** scores (Hale, 2001; Levy, 2008) computed with Neural Language Models (NLMs) to account for sentence processing phenomena (Futrell et al., 2018; Van Schijndel and Linzen, 2018; Wilcox et al., 2018; Michaelov and Bergen, 2020, 2022a; Michaelov et al., 2023). This also includes investigations on interferences at the morphosyntactic level (Ryu and Lewis, 2021). To our knowledge, there have been no attempts to model semantic attraction with NLMs yet.

We aim at filling this gap by presenting a Surprisal-based analysis of a psycholinguistic dataset on semantic attraction with three autoregressive NLMs of different sizes. We found that NLMs are sensitive to both the plausibility of the sentences and semantic attraction effects. However, NLM Surprisal for a target phrase seems to be affected by attraction regardless of general sentence

*Proceedings of the The 12th Joint Conference on Lexical and Computational Semantics (*SEM 2023)*, pages 141–148
July 13-14, 2023 ©2023 Association for Computational Linguistics

plausibility, differently from human reading behavior. On the other hand, sentence-level Surprisal is not affected by semantic attraction.

2 Related Work

2.1 Semantic Attraction in Implausible Sentences

The work by Cunnings and Sturt (2018) has recently brought evidence of the existence of semantic attraction in semantically implausible sentences. They collected eye-tracking fixations for sentences in four conditions, by crossing the factors of the plausibility of the sentence (the plausible or implausible arguments are in italic) and the plausibility of an attractor noun (in bold):

(3) a. Julia saw the *cake* that the lady with the **meal** quite happily ate during an expensive night out. (*plausible sentence, plausible attractor*)

b. Julia saw the *cake* that the lady with the **wine** quite happily ate during an expensive night out. (*plausible sentence, implausible attractor*)

c. Julia saw the *beer* that the lady with the **meal** quite happily ate during an expensive night out. (*implausible sentence, plausible attractor*)

d. Julia saw the *beer* that the lady with the **wine** quite happily ate during an expensive night out. (*implausible sentence, implausible attractor*)

The results showed that fixations were significantly longer in implausible sentences, but the effect was attenuated in presence of a plausible attractor (condition (3c)), while in plausible sentences the attractor did not have any significant effect. The authors explained the finding in terms of "verb-specific cues that may guide retrieval to grammatically illicit, but plausible, constituents during the resolution of filler-gap dependencies".

The follow-up study by Laurinavichyute and von der Malsburg (2022) instead used a forced choice completion judgement task to compare semantic and morphosyntactic attraction. First, they presented a target verb to the participants, and then they presented them with a sentence fragment, asking participants whether the verb could have been a fitting continuation for the sentence. In such a scenario, it is expected that violations will elicit negative answers, with attraction phenomena possibly increasing the error rates of the participants. Their stimuli contained violations either at the morphosyntactic or at the semantic level, and have either a morphosyntactic or a semantic attractor. The authors reported considerably higher error rates for the conditions with a violation and an attractor of the same type, supporting the idea that morphosyntactic and semantic attraction work similarly.

Our study on NLMs uses the stimuli from the datasets by Cunnings and Sturt (2018) to test whether they are sensitive to semantic attraction in sentence processing, which may be reflected by the Surprisal scores of the stimuli words. We also want to test whether semantic plausibility and attraction in NLMs interact like in humans, to what extent (cf. the claim in Cunnings and Sturt (2018) that semantic attraction has a facilitatory effect only when the sentence is not plausible) and if the effects are the same in NLMs of different sizes.

2.2 NLM Estimation of Word Surprisal

Transformer-based NLMs (Vaswani et al., 2017; Devlin et al., 2019; Radford et al., 2019) have become increasingly popular in NLP in recent years, and a number of studies designed tests to investigate their actual linguistic abilities (Tenney et al., 2019a; Jawahar et al., 2019; Tenney et al., 2019b). Some of these studies specifically analyzed the **Surprisal** scores computed by the models, to understand to what extent they are sensitive to linguistic phenomena that have been showed to affect human sentence processing. For example, Misra et al. (2020) investigated the predictions of BERT in a setting aimed at reproducing human semantic priming; they reported that BERT was indeed sensitive to "priming" and predicted a word with lower Surprisal values when the context included a related word as opposed to an unrelated one.Using a similar methodology, Cho et al. (2021) modeled the priming effect of verb aspect on the prediction of typical event locations, finding that BERT outputs lower surprisal scores for typical locations, but differently from humans, it does so regardless of verb aspect manipulations.

Michaelov and Bergen (2022a) investigated the issue of collateral facilitation, that is, when anomalous words in a sentence are processed more easily by humans because of the presence of semantically-related words in the context. They compared the Surprisal scores obtained with several Transformer NLMs and showed that most of them reproduce the same significant differences between conditions observed in humans. In Michaelov et al. (2023) the same authors used NLM Surprisal to replicate the effect of discourse context in reducing the N400 amplitude for anomalous words, using the Dutch stimuli of the experiments by Nieuwland and Van Berkum (2006).

Probably the closest relative to the topic of our study, Ryu and Lewis (2021) proved that the Surprisal values extracted with the GPT-2 language model predict the facilitatory effects of interference in ungrammatical sentences in which an attractor noun is matching in number with the verb or with a reflexive pronouns. However, they focused on morphosyntactic attraction, while we aim at modeling the facilitatory effects of semantic attraction.

3 Experimental Settings

3.1 Dataset

We derived our dataset from the Experiment 1 of the eye-tracking study by Cunnings and Sturt (2018). The authors employed a total of 32 items, each of them coming in four conditions, for a total of 128 stimuli. The stimuli were stories composed of an introduction sentence, a critical sentence and a wrap-up sentence. In our experiment, we just fed the NLMs with the critical sentence:

(4) Julia saw the *cake/beer* (plausible/implausible) that the lady with the **meal/wine** (plausible/implausible) quite happily ate during an expensive night out.

The sentences in the four conditions, as shown in Example (4), were differing for i) a fitting or a selectional preference-violating direct object (in *italic*) for the verb in the subordinate clause (underlined), which would determine the plausibility of the sentence; ii) a plausible or an implausible attractor noun (in **bold**), not syntactically related with the verb but with a high degree of thematic fit with it.[1] The authors reported main effects of both sentence plausibility (implausible sentences induce longer fixations) and attractor plausibility (a plausible attractor has a facilitatory effect) in the total viewing times.[2] They also reported a significant interaction between the two: total viewing times for implausible sentences were shorter when the attractor was plausible compared to implausible, while no significant difference was observed in plausible sentences as a result of attractor plausibility.

3.2 Language Models

For the models in this paper, we use the implementation of Minicons (Misra, 2022)[3], an open source library that provides a standard API for behavioral and representational analyses of NLMs. We make the code and the test data available for additional testing.[4] We experiment with three variants of autoregressive LMs of different sizes: the original GPT-2 Base, with 124 million parameters (Radford et al., 2019); DistilGPT-2 with 82 million parameters (Sanh et al., 2019), trained as a student network with the supervision of GPT-2; and GPT-Neo that, with 1.3 billion parameters (Gao et al., 2020; Black et al., 2021), is close to the size of the smallest models of the GPT-3 family.

Using autoregressive NLMs, we computed the Surprisal scores at the target in the stimuli (the verb in the subordinate clause), and also at the level of the entire sentence. When the NLMs tokenizer splits the target in more than one token, we take the average of the Surprisal scores of its subtokens.

More formally, the Surprisal of the target T in the context C (**Surp**) was computed as:

$$Surp(T|C) = \frac{\sum_{t \in T} -logP(t|C)}{count(t)} \quad (1)$$

where $P(t|C)$ is the probability of each subtoken $t \in T$ given the previous context C, while $count(t)$ is the number of subtokens in the target phrase T.

The Surprisal of the sentence S (**SentSurp**) instead is simply the sum of the Surprisals of each token T normalized by the length of the sentence:

$$SentSurp(S) = \frac{\sum_{T \in S} Surp(T)}{count(T)} \quad (2)$$

where $count(T)$ is the total number of tokens in the sentence S.[5]

[1] We refer to the notion of *thematic fit* as the degree of compatibility between a predicate and a noun filling one of its semantic roles (McRae and Matsuki, 2009; Sayeed et al., 2016; Santus et al., 2017).

[2] To address a remark by Reviewer 1, we checked the logarithmic frequencies of the attractor nouns (the target nouns were the same in all conditions), which were not mentioned in the original study (see the materials in the Appendix). We have not found any significant difference between noun frequencies across conditions.

[3] `https://github.com/kanishkamisra/minicons-experiments`

[4] `https://github.com/yancong222/transformers-semantic-attraction-surprisal`

[5] Notice that the sentences may differ in the number of tokens, in the cases when the object and/or the attractor nouns are splitted by the tokenizer. This is why we did not use the

	GPT-2			DistilGPT-2			GPTNeo		
	B	SE	*p*	*B*	SE	*p*	*B*	SE	*p*
Intercept	9.72	0.54	<.001	9.62	0.54	<0.001	9.92	0.49	<0.001
SentPlaus	3.40	0.28	<0.001	2.17	0.28	<0.001	4.39	0.31	<0.001
AttrPlaus	0.84	0.28	0.003	1.01	0.28	<0.001	0.84	0.31	.008
Length	0.13	0.20	0.08	0.22	0.19	0.09	0.05	0.18	0.78
SentPlaus:AttrPlaus			0.29			0.19			0.11
S1-A0 : S0-A0	-3.69	0.39	< 0.001	-2.45	0.31	< 0.001	-4.87	0.43	< 0.001
S0-A1 : S0-A0	-1.12	0.39	0.021	-1.38	0.31	< 0.001	-1.32	0.43	0.013
S1-A1 : S0-A0	-4.24	0.39	< 0.001	-3.26	0.31	< 0.001	-5.22	0.43	< 0.001
S0-A1 : S1-A0	2.56	0.39	< 0.001	1.07	0.31	0.003	3.55	0.43	< 0.001
S1-A1 : S1-A0	-0.56	0.39	0.48	-0.82	0.31	0.039	-0.36	0.43	0.84
S1-A1 : S0-A1	-3.12	0.39	< .001	-1.89	0.31	< 0.001	-3.91	0.43	< 0.001

Table 1: Summary for the results of predictors of **Surp**, and of the interaction between *SentPlaus* and *AttrPlaus*. In the pairwise comparisons *cond1:cond2*, the reference level is *cond2* (meaning, if the estimate *B* is negative, the Surprisal of *cond1* is lower than *Cond2*, otherwise it is higher).

	GPT-2			DistilGPT-2			GPTNeo		
	B	SE	*p*	*B*	SE	*p*	*B*	SE	*p*
Intercept	7.20	0.53	<0.001	7.84	0.56	<0.001	7.94	0.51	<0.001
SentPlaus	0.10	0.02	<0.001	0.06	0.02	0.011	0.16	0.02	<0.001
AttrPlaus	0.02	0.02	0.382	0.03	0.02	0.06	0.01	0.02	0.829
Length	-0.07	0.01	<.001	-0.08	0.02	<0.001	-0.10	0.01	<0.001
SentPlaus:AttrPlaus			0.33			0.038			0.84
S1-A0 : S0-A0	-0.10	0.03	< 0.001	-0.06	0.03	0.078	-0.172	0.03	< 0.001
S0-A1 : S0-A0	-0.01	0.03	0.96	-0.01	0.03	0.967	-0.02	0.03	0.89
S1-A1 : S0-A0	-0.12	0.03	< 0.001	-0.11	0.03	< 0.001	-0.17	0.03	< 0.001
S0-A1 : S1-A0	0.09	0.03	0.003	0.05	0.03	0.214	0.15	0.03	< 0.001
S1-A1 : S1-A0	-0.02	0.03	0.77	-0.05	0.03	0.249	0.01	0.03	0.992
S1-A1 : S0-A1	-0.11	0.03	< 0.001	-0.10	0.03	< 0.001	-0.15	0.03	< 0.001

Table 2: Summary for the results of predictors of **SentSurp**, and of the interaction between *SentPlaus* and *AttrPlaus*. In the pairwise comparisons *cond1:cond2*, the reference level is *cond2* (meaning, if the estimate *B* is negative, the Surprisal of *cond1* is lower than *Cond2*, otherwise it is higher).

For each NLM, we fitted a linear mixed-effects model using **Surp** or **SentSurp** as the dependent variable, which was estimated for each of the experimental stimuli. The independent variables were: the plausibility of the sentence *SentPlaus* (plausible vs. implausible; plausible as the base of comparison), the plausibility of the attractor *AttrPlaus* (plausible vs. implausible; plausible as the base of comparison), their interactions, and the token length of the stimulus *length*. We included items as a random intercept in our models. We use the LME4 package (Bates et al., 2014) for model fitting and results; the pairwise comparisons with Tukey adjustment were carried out by the EMMEANS package (Lenth, 2019) in R.

4 Results

The findings of the experiments are summarized in Tables 1 and 2.

Considering the main effects, we found that all models were able to distinguish plausible from implausible items at the sentence level (see SentPlaus in Tables 1 and 2), with significantly higher Surprisal scores for the latter.

As shown in Table 1, the models based on **Surp** were also sensitive to the attractor plausibility, and marginally to the token length of the stimuli. No significant main effect of interaction between sentence and attractor plausibility was found. The models based on **SentSurp** (Table 2) were sensitive to token length, but not to the attractor plausibility, with the only exception of a marginal significance for DistilGPT2. The SentSurp model based on DistilGPT2 is the only one showing (at least marginally) significant effects for the plausibility of both sentence ($p = 0.011$) and attractor ($p = 0.06$) and for their interaction ($p = 0.038$) (see Table 2 and Figure 1), while no interaction was found in any of the other models. The fact that this behavior was found in the smallest model may represent another case of what has been called "inverse scaling" in the NLM literature, that is, the performance decreases at the increase of model size (Wei et al., 2022; Jang et al., 2023), or in the

sum of the Surprisal scores, as per Reviewer 3's comment.

case of psycholinguistic modeling, the behavior becomes less human-like (Michaelov and Bergen, 2022b; Oh and Schuler, 2022).

The post hoc analyses of the pairwise comparison showed some interesting contrasts. We noticed that significant differences were found between the plausible sentences with plausible attractors and the two implausible conditions (i.e. in Figure 1, a vs. c and a vs. d, with $ps < 0.001$). Differently from human total viewing times, no significant differences and no consistent facilitatory effects are observed between c and d in the **SentSurp** models (notice also in Figure 1 that the median of condition d. is actually slightly lower than c., and the medians for c. and d. tend to be close in all the **SentSurp** models, cf. the boxplots in the Appendix, right column), while facilitation is found for all the **Surp** models.

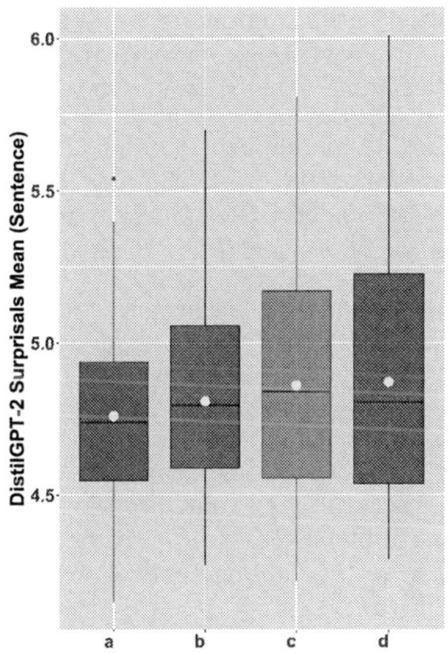

Figure 1: Sentence Surprisal scores from DistilGPT-2 (means in yellow). Conditions are the same of Ex. 3.

It is also noticeable that all models show no sensitivity to plausible attractors with the sentence-level Surprisal metrics, but the Surprisal at the target word with implausible attractors is always significantly higher. However, since no significant main effect of interactions was found for **Surp** models, we conclude that semantic attraction seems to to have a general facilitation effect on its own, regardless of sentence plausibility.

It would be interesting, in the future, to analyze how the attractors concretely affect the predictions, for example using techniques like contrastive explanations (Yin and Neubig, 2022) that can shed light on which tokens contribute to the prediction of the target verb rather than a plausible alternative word (in our case, this could be a verb in a thematic fit relation with the implausible attractor noun, e.g. *drank* for *wine* in examples 2. *b-d*).

5 Conclusions

In this work, we presented a study on Surprisal to investigate whether NLMs predictions are sensitive to semantic attraction. Our results on the data of the eye-tracking experiment by Cunnings and Sturt (2018) reveal that all models are sensitive to the general plausibility of the sentence, and that semantically-plausible attractors decrease the Surprisal at the target phrase, although this effect generally does not interact with sentence plausibility as in humans.

At the sentence level, no effects of attractor plausibility were observed, with the only, partial exception of a marginal significance with DistilGPT2. Interestingly, the most human-like pattern -including the interaction- has been observed with this model, the smallest one, although the specific contrasts between conditions pattern differently from human total viewing times.

Acknowledgments

We would like to thank the three anonymous reviewers for their insightful feedback.

This research was made possible by the start-up research fund (1-BD8S) at the Hong Kong Polytechnic University.

References

Douglas Bates, Martin Mächler, Ben Bolker, and Steve Walker. 2014. Fitting Linear Mixed-effects Models Using lme4. *arXiv preprint arXiv:1406.5823*.

Sid Black, Gao Leo, Phil Wang, Connor Leahy, and Stella Biderman. 2021. GPT-Neo: Large Scale Autoregressive Language Modeling with Mesh-Tensorflow. *zenodo.org*.

Won Ik Cho, Emmanuele Chersoni, Yu-Yin Hsu, and Chu-Ren Huang. 2021. Modeling the Influence of Verb Aspect on the Activation of Typical Event Locations with BERT. In *Findings of ACL-IJCNLP*.

Ian Cunnings and Patrick Sturt. 2018. Retrieval Interference and Semantic Interpretation. *Journal of Memory and Language*, 102:16–27.

Jacob Devlin, Ming-Wei Chang, Kenton Lee, and Kristina Toutanova. 2019. BERT: Pre-training of Deep Bidirectional Transformers for Language Understanding. In *Proceedings of NAACL*.

Richard Futrell, Ethan Wilcox, Takashi Morita, and Roger Levy. 2018. RNNs as Psycholinguistic Subjects: Syntactic State and Grammatical Dependency. *arXiv preprint arXiv:1809.01329*.

Leo Gao, Stella Biderman, Sid Black, Laurence Golding, Travis Hoppe, Charles Foster, Jason Phang, Horace He, Anish Thite, Noa Nabeshima, et al. 2020. The Pile: An 800GB Dataset of Diverse Text for Language Modeling. *arXiv preprint arXiv:2101.00027*.

John Hale. 2001. A Probabilistic Earley Parser as a Psycholinguistic Model. In *Proceedings of NAACL*.

Joel Jang, Seonghyeon Ye, and Minjoon Seo. 2023. Can Large Language Models Truly Understand Prompts? A Case Study with Negated Prompts. In *Transfer Learning for Natural Language Processing Workshop*.

Ganesh Jawahar, Benoît Sagot, and Djamé Seddah. 2019. What Does BERT Learn about the Structure of Language? In *Proceedings of ACL*.

Anna Laurinavichyute and Titus von der Malsburg. 2022. Semantic Attraction in Sentence Comprehension. *Cognitive Science*, 46(2):e13086.

Russell Lenth. 2019. *emmeans: Estimated Marginal Means, aka Least-Squares Means*. R Package Version 1.4.2.

Roger Levy. 2008. Expectation-based Syntactic Comprehension. *Cognition*, 106(3):1126–1177.

Richard L Lewis and Shravan Vasishth. 2013. An Activation-based Model of Sentence Processing as Skilled Memory Retrieval. In *Cognitive Science*, pages 375–419. Routledge.

Ken McRae and Kazunaga Matsuki. 2009. People Use their Knowledge of Common Events to Understand Language, and Do So as Quickly as Possible. *Language and Linguistics Compass*, 3(6):1417–1429.

James A Michaelov and Benjamin K Bergen. 2020. How Well Does Surprisal Explain N400 Amplitude under Different Experimental Conditions? In *Proceedings of CONLL*.

James A Michaelov and Benjamin K Bergen. 2022a. Collateral Facilitation in Humans and Language Models. In *Proceedings of CONLL*.

James A Michaelov and Benjamin K Bergen. 2022b. 'Rarely'a Problem? Language Models Exhibit Inverse Scaling in their Predictions Following 'Few'-type Quantifiers. *arXiv preprint arXiv:2212.08700*.

James A Michaelov, Seana Coulson, and Benjamin K Bergen. 2023. Can Peanuts Fall in Love with Distributional Semantics? *arXiv preprint arXiv:2301.08731*.

Kanishka Misra. 2022. minicons: Enabling Flexible Behavioral and Representational Analyses of Transformer Language Models. *arXiv preprint arXiv:2203.13112*.

Kanishka Misra, Allyson Ettinger, and Julia Taylor Rayz. 2020. Exploring BERT's Sensitivity to Lexical Cues using Tests from Semantic Priming. In *Findings of EMNLP*.

Mante S Nieuwland and Jos JA Van Berkum. 2006. When Peanuts Fall in Love: N400 Evidence for the Power of Discourse. *Journal of Cognitive Neuroscience*, 18(7):1098–1111.

Byung-Doh Oh and William Schuler. 2022. Why Does Surprisal From Larger Transformer-Based Language Models Provide a Poorer Fit to Human Reading Times? In *Transactions of the Association for Computational Linguistics*.

Alec Radford, Jeffrey Wu, Rewon Child, David Luan, Dario Amodei, and Ilya Sutskever. 2019. Language Models are Unsupervised Multitask Learners. In *Open-AI Blog*.

Soo Hyun Ryu and Richard L Lewis. 2021. Accounting for Agreement Phenomena in Sentence Comprehension with Transformer Language Models: Effects of Similarity-based Interference on Surprisal and Attention. In *Proceedings of the NAACL Workshop on Cognitive Modeling and Computational Linguistics*.

Victor Sanh, Lysandre Debut, Julien Chaumond, and Thomas Wolf. 2019. DistilBERT, a Distilled Version of BERT: Smaller, Faster, Cheaper and Lighter. In *Proceeding of the NeurIPS* $EMC^2 Workshop$.

Enrico Santus, Emmanuele Chersoni, Alessandro Lenci, and Philippe Blache. 2017. Measuring Thematic Fit with Distributional Feature Overlap. In *Proceedings of EMNLP*.

Asad Sayeed, Clayton Greenberg, and Vera Demberg. 2016. Thematic Fit Evaluation: An Aspect of Selectional Preferences. In *Proceedings of the ACL Workshop on Evaluating Vector Space Representations for NLP*.

Robyn Speer. 2022. rspeer/wordfreq: v3.0.

Ian Tenney, Dipanjan Das, and Ellie Pavlick. 2019a. BERT Rediscovers the Classical NLP Pipeline. In *Proceedings of ACL*.

Ian Tenney, Patrick Xia, Berlin Chen, Alex Wang, Adam Poliak, R Thomas McCoy, Najoung Kim, Benjamin Van Durme, Samuel R Bowman, Dipanjan Das, et al. 2019b. What Do You Learn from Context? Probing for Sentence Structure in Contextualized Word Representations. *arXiv preprint arXiv:1905.06316*.

Julie A Van Dyke. 2007. Interference Effects from Grammatically Unavailable Constituents During Sentence Processing. *Journal of Experimental Psychology: Learning, Memory, and Cognition*, 33(2):407.

Walter JB Van Heuven, Pawel Mandera, Emmanuel Keuleers, and Marc Brysbaert. 2014. SUBTLEX-UK: A New and Improved Word Frequency Database for British English. *Quarterly Journal of Experimental Psychology*, 67(6):1176–1190.

Marten Van Schijndel and Tal Linzen. 2018. Modeling Garden Path Effects without Explicit Hierarchical Syntax. In *Proceedings of CogSci*.

Ashish Vaswani, Noam Shazeer, Niki Parmar, Jakob Uszkoreit, Llion Jones, Aidan N Gomez, Łukasz Kaiser, and Illia Polosukhin. 2017. Attention Is All You Need. *Advances in Neural Information Processing Systems*, 30.

Matthew W Wagers, Ellen F Lau, and Colin Phillips. 2009. Agreement Attraction in Comprehension: Representations and Processes. *Journal of Memory and Language*, 61(2):206–237.

Jason Wei, Yi Tay, and Quoc V Le. 2022. Inverse Scaling Can Become U-shaped. *arXiv preprint arXiv:2211.02011*.

Ethan Wilcox, Roger Levy, Takashi Morita, and Richard Futrell. 2018. What Do RNN Language Models Learn about Filler-gap Dependencies? *arXiv preprint arXiv:1809.00042*.

Kayo Yin and Graham Neubig. 2022. Interpreting Language Models with Contrastive Explanations. In *Proceedings of EMNLP*.

Appendix

Descriptive statistics

The statistics for the Surprisal scores can be seen in Table 3 and 4, while the logarithmic frequencies of attractor and target nouns are in Table 5 and 6 (notice that the target nouns were the same in all the experimental conditions).

Boxplots

The boxplots for the Surprisal scores for all the metrics and models are shown in Figure 2.

Models	Sentence Min	Max	Mean	Std
GPT-2	3.88	5.76	4.525	0.319
DistilGPT-2	4.150	6.010	4.824	0.399
GPT-Neo	3.400	5.460	4.268	0.391

Table 3: Cunnings dataset Surprisal mean descriptive statistics (sentence).

Models	Target Min	Max	Mean	Std
GPT-2	0.74	17.35	7.597	3.759
DistilGPT-2	0.67	19.66	7.984	3.039
GPT-Neo	1.40	18.09	7.308	3.819

Table 4: Cunnings dataset Surprisal mean descriptive statistics (target phrase).

Cond.	Min	Max	Mean	Std
a,c	0.000002	0.000513	0.000085	0.000123
b,d	0.000001	0.000513	0.000077	0.000122

Table 5: Log-transformed frequency statistics for the attractor nouns across conditions in the Cunnings dataset. The frequencies were extracted with the Wordfreq library (Speer, 2022), which relies on the SUBTLEX database (Van Heuven et al., 2014).

Cond.	Min	Max	Mean	Std
a,b,c,d	0.000001	0.000525	0.000053	0.000109

Table 6: Log-transformed frequency frequency statistics for the target nouns in the Cunnings dataset. The frequencies were extracted with the Wordfreq library (Speer, 2022), which relies on the SUBTLEX database (Van Heuven et al., 2014).

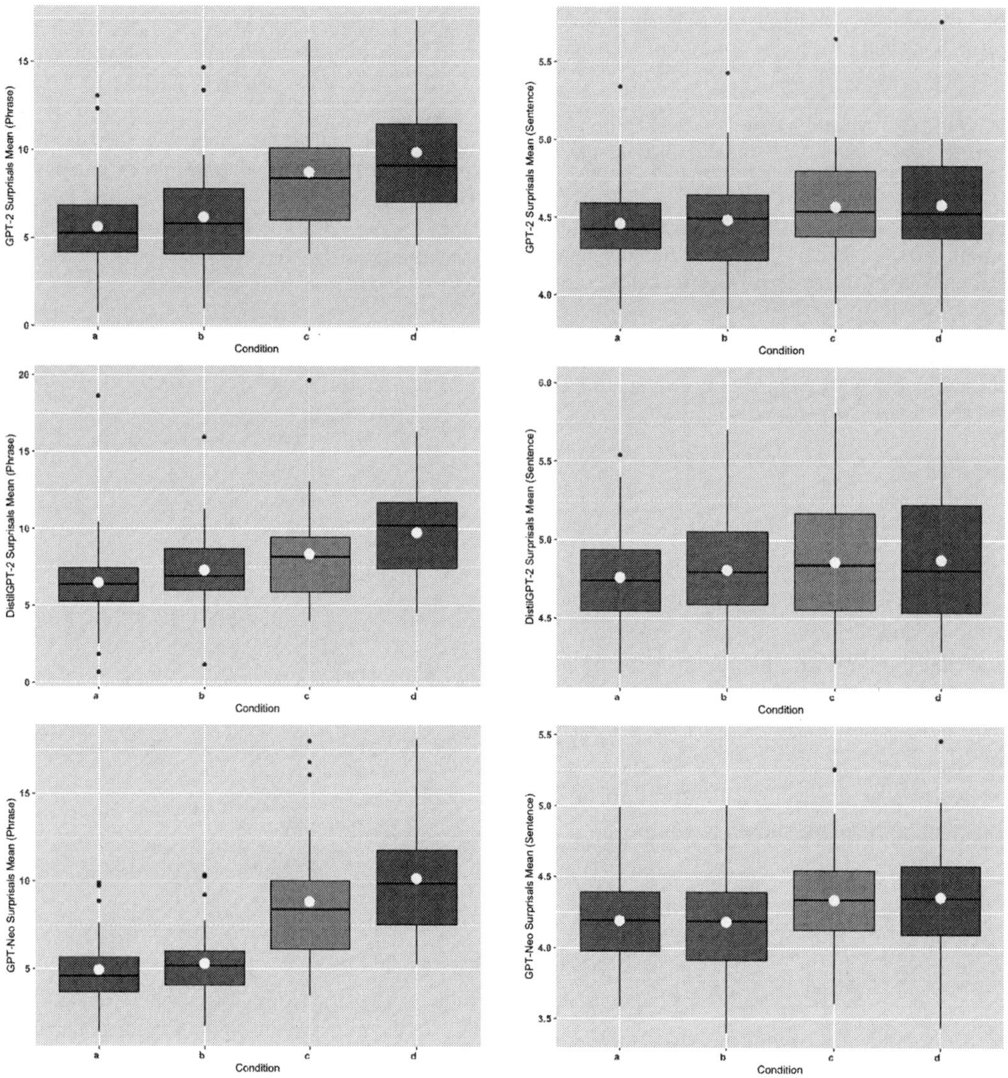

Figure 2: Boxplots of the Surprisal for all the metrics-model combinations: target Surprisal scores on the left, sentence Surprisal on the right; GPT-2 in the top row, DistilGPT-2 in the middle row, GPTNeo at the bottom.

Syntax and Semantics Meet in the "Middle": Probing the Syntax-Semantics Interface of LMs Through Agentivity

Lindia Tjuatja, Emmy Liu, Lori Levin, Graham Neubig
Language Technologies Institute
Carnegie Mellon University
`{ltjuatja, mengyan3, lsl, gneubig}@cs.cmu.edu`

Abstract

Recent advances in large language models have prompted researchers to examine their abilities across a variety of linguistic tasks, but little has been done to investigate how models handle the interactions in meaning across words and larger syntactic forms—i.e. phenomena at the intersection of syntax and semantics. We present the semantic notion of *agentivity* as a case study for probing such interactions. We created a novel evaluation dataset by utilitizing the unique linguistic properties of a subset of optionally transitive English verbs. This dataset was used to prompt varying sizes of three model classes to see if they are sensitive to agentivity at the lexical level, and if they can appropriately employ these word-level priors given a specific syntactic context. Overall, GPT-3 `text-davinci-003` performs extremely well across all experiments, outperforming all other models tested by far. In fact, the results are even better correlated with human judgements than both syntactic and semantic corpus statistics. This suggests that LMs may potentially serve as more useful tools for linguistic annotation, theory testing, and discovery than select corpora for certain tasks.

1 Introduction

Consider the English sentences in (1) below:

(1) a. This author writes easily.

b. This passage writes easily.

These sentences display an interesting property of certain optionally transitive verbs in English. Although they share an identical surface syntactic structure—a noun phrase in subject position followed by the intransitive form of the verb and an adverb phrase modifying the verb—they entail very different things about the roles of their subjects.

The subject of (1a) is someone that does the action of writing; in other words, *this author* is an **agent** in the writing event. On the other hand, the subject of (1b), *this passage*, doesn't do any writing—it is what is created in the event of writing. In contrast to *this author*, *this passage* is a **patient**. The agent and patient roles are not discrete categories, but rather prototypes on opposite ends of a continuum. These "protoroles" have a number of contributing properties such as causing an event for agents and undergoing change of state for patients (Dowty, 1991).

The contrast between the minimal pair in (1) suggests that there are lexical semantic properties of the subjects that give rise to these two distinct readings: one that describes how the subject generally *does* an action as in (1a), and another that describes how an event generally unfolds when the subject *undergoes* an action as in (1b). Intuitively, a speaker may know from the meaning of *author* that authors are animate, have some degree of volition, and typically write things, whereas passages (of text) are inanimate, have no volition, and are typically written. The knowledge of these aspects of meaning must somehow interact with the syntactic form of the sentences in (1) to disambiguate between the two possible readings, and an agent or patient role for the subject follows from the meaning of the statement as a whole.

Now consider the (somewhat unusual) sentences in (2) which use the transitive form of *write*:

(2) a. Something writes this author easily.

b. This passage writes something easily.

At first glance, the above sentences (with the same sense of *write* as in 1) are infelicitous unless we imagine some obscure context where *this author* is something like a character in a text and *this passage* is somehow anthropomorphized and capable of writing; these contexts go against our natural intuitions of the semantics of "passage" and "author".[1] Unlike the syntactic form of the sentences

[1]There is another reading of (2a) that uses a different sense of *write*, where *this author* is a recipient (*Something writes*

*Proceedings of the The 12th Joint Conference on Lexical and Computational Semantics (*SEM 2023)*, pages 149–164
July 13-14, 2023

in (1), the explicit inclusion of both arguments (subject and direct object) now forces whatever is in subject position to be the agent and whatever is in object position to be more like a patient, regardless of the typical semantic properties of the arguments.

Taken together, the examples in (1) and (2) illustrate a compelling interaction at the *syntax-semantics interface*. More specifically, we see a two-way interaction: first, near-identical surface forms acquire completely different entailments about their subjects *solely* depending on the choice of subject, while conversely certain syntactic forms can influence the semantic role of an argument *regardless* of the usual behavior of said argument. We aim to investigate the linguistic capabilities of language models with regards to this interaction.

Prior work in studying LMs as psycholinguistic subjects has largely focused on syntax and grammatical well-formedness (Futrell et al. 2019; Linzen and Baroni 2021, inter alia). However, as illustrated in the above examples, there are instances of near-identical syntactic structures that can give rise to different meanings depending on the individual lexical items as well as surrounding context. Thus evaluating LMs on syntax, while a necessary starting point, does not give us a sufficient measure of LM linguistic capabilities. While other work such as Ettinger (2020), Kim and Linzen (2020), and Misra et al. (2022) (among others) evaluate LMs on a variety of tests involving semantics and pragmatics, they do not investigate the interaction between the meanings associated with syntactic forms and those of individual lexical items.

Thus, we not only need to evaluate syntax and utilization of semantic knowledge, but we also need to understand how interactions of meaning at different linguistic levels—i.e. morphological, lexical, phrasal—may alter model behavior. Exploring phenomena within the syntax-semantics interface is a compelling approach as it gives us access to specific aspects of semantics while allowing precise control over syntactic form between levels.

In this work, we probe the syntax-semantics interface of several language models, focusing on the semantic notion of agentivity. We do this by prompting models to label nouns in isolation or in context as either agents or patients from a curated test set of noun-verb-adverb combinations that display the alternation shown in example (1). We then compare the performance of LMs to both human judgements and corpus statistics.

Probing for LMs for their knowledge of agentivity in syntactic constructions as in (1) and (2) is a particularly insightful case study as it allows us to explore three interconnected questions in a highly controlled syntactic setting:

I. Do models display sensitivity to aspects of word-level semantics independent of syntactic context, and is such sensitivity aligned with human judgements? (§3.1)

II. Can models employ lexical semantics to determine the appropriate semantics of a sentence where the syntax is ambiguous between readings (as in 1)? (§3.2)

III. Can models determine the semantics of a sentence from syntax, disregarding lexical semantics when necessary (as in 2)? (§3.3)

Additionally, the relatively infrequent pairings of semantic function and syntactic form of sentences such as (1b) are also interesting from a learnability and acquisition perspective for both LMs and humans. How both come to process and acquire exceptions to a general "rule" has been a topic of debate since early connectionist models (Rumelhart and McClelland, 1986). Hence, knowledge of LM capabilities in acquiring and processing these linguistic anomalies may serve as valuable insight to linguists, cognitive scientists, and NLP practitioners alike.

2 Methodology

We constructed three experiments, each targeting one of the above questions through the lens of agentivity. We will first give a broad overview of each, and then go into detail about the general approach.

Experiment 1 (§3.1) tests whether language models are sensitive to the word-level semantics of nouns with regards to agentivity, such as whether nouns like *author* and *passage* are more likely to be agents or patients without any surrounding context. This is analogous to the idea that speakers have intuition for how entities prototypically act in events, e.g. that *authors* write and *passages* are written, and that this extends to how we categorize their roles in events (Rissman and Majid, 2019).

Experiment 2 (§3.2) tests whether language models can disambiguate between the possible readings of sentences of the form in (1)—i.e. if

(to) this author easily). Regardless, given that the agent and patient roles as defined by Dowty (1991) are prototypes on a scale, *this author* in the recipient reading is closer to the patient role.

Exp 1: noun (lexical level)	Exp 2: intransitive (ambiguous mapping)	Exp 3: transitive (deterministic mapping)
noun: John agent/patient: agent	Sentence: John walks quickly. Is John an agent or a patient?: agent	Sentence: Jack throws something easily. Is Jack an agent or a patient?: agent
noun: vase agent/patient: patient	Sentence: This vase breaks easily. Is vase an agent or a patient?: patient	Sentence: Something hires the nurse swiftly. Is nurse an agent or a patient?: patient
noun: nurse agent/patient: agent	Sentence: This nurse works swiftly. Is nurse an agent or a patient?: agent	Sentence: The hammer breaks something quickly. Is hammer an agent or a patient?: agent
noun: mango agent/patient: patient	Sentence: This mango blends well. Is mango an agent or a patient?: patient	Sentence: Something blends the mango well. Is mango an agent or a patient?: patient
noun: <noun> agent/patient:	Sentence: <intr-agent/intr-patient> Is <noun> an agent or a patient?:	Sentence: <trans-agent>/<trans-patient> Is <noun> an agent or a patient?:

Figure 1: Prompt setup for each experiment. Note that the examples given for Exp 1 are not meant to be hard labels, rather they are "tendencies" for these nouns. In Exp 2, the noun itself determines whether the sentence is considered **intr-agent** or **intr-patient**; in Exp 3, we force the noun to take the agent or patient role by placing it in subject (**trans-agent**) or object (**trans-patient**) position.

they can identify whether the syntactic subject is an agent or a patient when the verb can allow for either. Sentences with the intransitive form of the verb that describe how the subject (an agent) does an action demonstrate *object drop* (as the direct object of the normally transitive verb is "dropped"), while sentences that describe how an event unfolds when the subject (a patient) undergoes an action are called *middles*, short for the linguistic term *dispositional middle* (van Oosten 1977; Jaeggli 1986; Condoravdi 1989; Fagan 1992, inter alia).[2] In our experimental setup, we will refer to these as **intr-agent** and **intr-patient**, respectively. If a model can do this task successfully by employing semantic information about the noun, we would expect not only to see that nouns in subject position are classified correctly as agents or patients, but also that these predictions for the most part correlate to the predictions in the first experiment.

Finally, **Experiment 3** (§3.3) tests whether language models can disregard word-specific priors to identify whether the noun of interest in a sentence with a transitive verb (such as those in 2) is an agent or patient. Since the semantic role of the noun maps directly to its syntactic position in these sentences, all subjects should be agents and all objects should be patients. For our test set, we create sentences where the position of the noun is the subject (**trans-agent**) and sentences where it is the object (**trans-patient**) for every noun.

[2]Note that in English, dispositional middles also allow for what are considered non-patient promoted objects (such as paths, e.g. *The desert crosses easily*) (Tenny 1994, 1992), but for convenience we will treat them as being in the same category as patients.

2.1 General approach and data curation

In all of these experiments, we rely on the prompting paradigm to elicit LM probabilities of an "agent" or "patient" label for a given noun in isolation or within a sentence. Our prompting method consists of four examples with gold labels, followed by the unlabeled test example in the same format, as shown in Figure 1. As this task has not been explored in prior literature, we had to construct our own examples to test on.

The highly controlled syntactic setting that allows us to explore the alternation in agentivity as displayed in (1) and (2) is a double-edged sword—while this setting provides us with a minimal pair, it also restricts the types of verbs that work in this experimental setup. The second (**intr-agent** vs. **intr-patient**) and third (**trans-agent** and **trans-patient**) experiments require verbs that are optionally transitive and have no preference for whether an agent or a patient is the subject of the intransitive form, as in (1). These requirements together highly constrain the class of verbs that work in this experimental setup, and as far we can tell there exists no definitive list in the linguistics literature of English verbs that display both properties.

As a starting point to curate a list of verbs, we consulted literature on verbs that display object drop (Gillon 2012; Fillmore 1986, as well as Levin 1993 for an overview of English verb classes). We compiled a list of 23 verbs (see Appendix A), though this list is certainly non-exhaustive. For each verb, we list nouns and adverbs that can work in combination with each other in all of the templates in Table 1. Criteria for adding nouns and adverbs are listed in the Appendix B.

In total, we have 233 unique nouns and a total of 820 noun-verb-adverb combinations. Out of these combinations, 343 form **intr-agent** sentences and 477 form **intr-patient** sentences. Since we can put any noun into syntactic subject or object position for the transitive sentences, we have 820 sentences each for **trans-agent** and **trans-patient**.

Sentence	Template
	This **<noun> <verb> <adverb>**.
intr-agent	This author writes easily.
intr-patient	This paper writes easily.
	This **<noun> <verb>** something **<adv>**.
trans-agent	This author writes something easily.
	This paper writes something easily.
	Something **<verb>** this **<noun> <adv>**.
trans-patient	Something writes this author easily.
	Something writes this paper easily.

Table 1: Templates for experiments 2 and 3. Sentences highlighted in pink contain a **<noun>** with an "agent" label, while those in blue with "patient".

2.2 Approximating "ground truth" agentivity labels for nouns out of context

Getting a gold "agent" or "patient" label is straightforward in the experiments with nouns in context: for sentences with the intransitive this was done ad hoc during data curation, and for sentences with the transitive this is a one-to-one mapping to syntax. However, using a hard label for nouns in isolation is problematic as a semantic role label is meaningless without context of the event; in principle, given an appropriate context, anything can act upon something else or have something done to it (literally or figuratively).

To get around this, we have two methods for finding an approximate label for the "typical" agentivity of a noun. The first was to collect human judgements. 19 annotators (native/fluent bilingual English proficiency) were given nouns without any context and were tasked to judge how likely each noun is to be an agent in any arbitrary event where both an agent and patient are involved. Their judgements were collected via ratings on a scale from 1 (very unlikely to be an agent) to 5 (very likely to be an agent). For nouns that have multiple common word senses (e.g. "model" can refer to both a fashion model or machine learning model, among other things) we include a disambiguating description. This description does not contain any verbs or other explicit indications of what events the noun may occur in (e.g. for "model", we give human annotators "model (person)").[3] We then average the ratings across all annotators and normalize so that the values fall between 0 and 1. To calculate inter-annotator agreement, we randomly divide the annotators into two groups (of 9 and 10), average their ratings for each noun, and calculate the correlation between the two; doing this seven times yields an average inter-group correlation of 0.968.

The second method uses statistics from linguistically annotated corpora as a proxy for the "typical" agentivity of a noun. We do this by calculating the frequency of "agenthood" for a noun (**agent ratio**), i.e. dividing the number of times the noun appears as an agent by the number of times it is either an agent or patient. The ideal annotated corpus for this would be one with semantic role labels such as Propbank (Kingsbury and Palmer, 2002), where the "ARG0" label corresponds to agent and "ARG1" to patient. However, many of the nouns in our data appeared only a few times in Propbank or not at all—out of all 233 nouns, only 166 of them occurred within an ARG0 or ARG1 span.[4]

Thus, we also tried utilizing syntax as a proxy using Google Syntactic Ngrams biarcs (Goldberg and Orwant, 2013), as it is significantly larger. The biarcs portion of the corpus covers dependency relations between three connected content words, which includes transitive predicates. To calculate a similar ratio, we divide the number of times a noun occurs as a subject by the total number of subject and direct object occurrences (we call this the **subject ratio**). A value closer to 1 should correlate with a tendency to occur more often as an agent, as agents are generally coded as subjects of English transitive verbs and patients as direct objects. All but one of our nouns contained at least one instance of occurring with a "nsubj" or "dobj" label.

3 Experimental Results

We evaluate BLOOM (Scao et al., 2022), GPT-2 (Radford et al., 2019), and GPT-3 (Brown et al., 2020) models of varying sizes for all experiments. Since previous work has shown that models are highly sensitive to the ordering of examples (Lu et al., 2021), we run each experiment twice: once with the order shown in Figure 1 where an agent

[3]Additional details on collecting human ratings can be found in Appendix C.

[4]We used Propbank annotations for BOLT, EWT, and Ontonotes 5.0 from `https://github.com/propbank/propbank-release`.

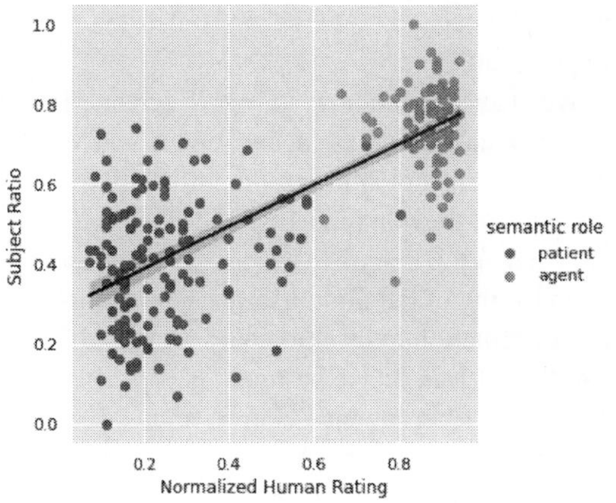

Figure 2: Correlation between subject ratio (from Google Syntactic Ngrams) and human ratings for each noun ($r = 0.762$). The semantic role label is the role the noun takes as the subject of the intransitive verb within our test set.

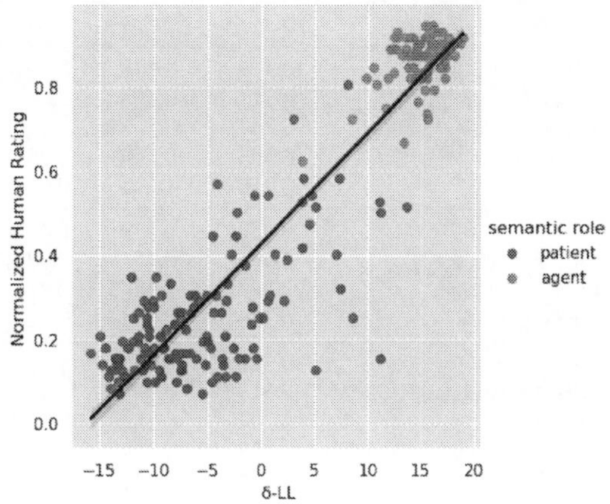

Figure 3: Correlation between δ-LL in Experiment 1 for GPT-3 `davinci-003` and the normalized human rating in the APAP experiment. Note that a negative δ-LL means the "patient" label is more likely.

is first (APAP ordering) and again with the first example moved to the bottom (PAPA ordering). We compare models based on their average performance across both orderings. Note, however, that some models are more sensitive to orderings than others; some models (like `text-davinci-003`) are largely invariant to example ordering. In Appendix D, we report results from both experiments.

3.1 Exp 1: Agentivity at the lexical level

In order to see if models are sensitive to the notion of how "typically" agentive a noun is, we compare the difference in log-likelihood between predicting "agent" or "patient" for that noun (δ-LL) with the normalized human ratings as well as corpus statistics from Google Syntactic Ngrams and Propbank.

Before we compare models with Ngrams and Propbank, we first ask how well-correlated both are with human ratings. We find that the subject ratio calculated from occurrence counts in Google Syntactic Ngrams is positively correlated with the average human rating with Pearson's r of 0.762, though the human rating has a stronger divide between agents and patients. This can be seen in Figure 2. When comparing with humans, using Syntactic Ngrams for this task actually turns out to be better than using Propbank: for the 166 nouns that occur with ARG0/1 labels, there is a correlation of 0.555 with human ratings (see Appendix E for details).

Overall, as seen in Table 2, we find that most models have a weak correlation with human ratings, with the exception of GPT-3 `text-davinci-003` (henceforth `davinci-003`), shown in Figure 3. We also see that `davinci-003` is not only both better correlated with human judgements than with corpus statistics, but surprisingly there is also a stronger correlation between its δ-LL and human ratings than between these proxies (syntactic and semantic) and human ratings. In fact, `davinci-003` is extremely close to the average inter-annotator group correlation, and furthermore this correlation is largely invariant to the ordering of prompts.

The observation that `davinci-003` is better correlated with human judgement than both syntactic (Ngrams) and semantic (Propbank) corpus statistics is intriguing as both types of corpora have been used in modeling prediction of *thematic fit*, or how well a noun fulfills a certain thematic role with a verb (Sayeed et al., 2016). Thus, we may naturally expect this to also work well with "general tendencies" or typicality judgements for nouns by themselves. However, it seems that such corpora may be too small or genre-biased to fully capture the nuances of human judgements, and such judgements may be better captured by LMs that have seen vast quantities of data across a wide variety of domains, even without explicit human annotation.

3.2 Exp 2: Disambiguating agentivity with the intransitive

In this experiment, we evaluate models along two metrics: how accurate the model is in predicting the

Model	Human	Ngrams	PB
BLOOM 560m	0.549	0.519	0.377
BLOOM 1b1	0.374	0.358	0.291
BLOOM 1b7	0.340	0.288	0.278
BLOOM 3b	0.305	0.348	0.231
BLOOM 7b1	0.016	-0.129	0.011
GPT-2 small	0.650	0.569	0.463
GPT-2 medium	0.394	0.451	0.333
GPT-2 large	0.499	0.544	0.412
GPT-2 xl	0.358	0.349	0.227
GPT-3 ada-001	0.594	0.575	0.490
GPT-3 babbage-001	0.311	0.337	0.158
GPT-3 curie-001	0.107	0.181	0.128
GPT-3 davinci-001	0.467	0.461	0.330
GPT-3 davinci-003	**0.939**	**0.730**	**0.574**
Inter-annotator	0.968	–	–
Google Syntactic Ngrams	0.762	–	–
Propbank	0.555	–	–

Table 2: Correlation between the difference in log-likelihood of predicting "agent" or "patient" with human ratings, subject ratio calculated from Google Syntactic Ngrams (232/233 nouns), and agent ratio calculated from Propbank (166/233 nouns), averaged across APAP and PAPA experiments.

correct label in context and how strongly correlated the δ-LL in this experiment is with the δ-LL from Experiment 1.

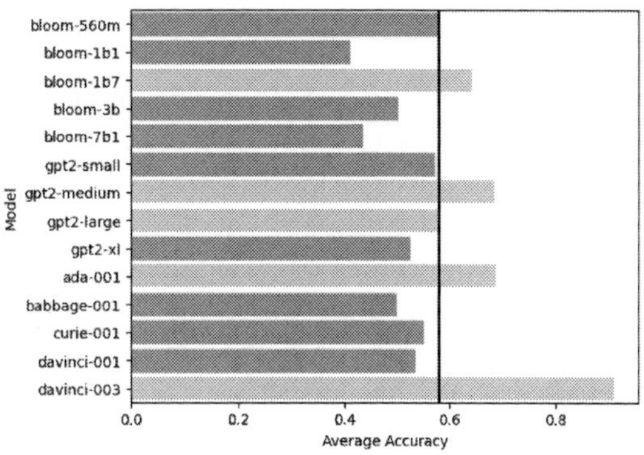

Figure 4: Average accuracy for predicting the label of nouns in **intr-agent/intr-patient** sentences. The black line indicates majority class performance; blue bars indicate above majority class performance.

Figure 4 shows the accuracy of each model in predicting (giving a higher probability to) the correct semantic label. Over half of the models do not achieve chance performance (predicting the majority class $\approx$ 0.582). Interestingly, we find that there is no monotonic increase in performance for this task with respect to model size (Kaplan et al., 2020)—for example, performance drops drastically between text-ada-001 and text-babbage-001. This is also the case in Experiment 1.

We also evaluate how strongly correlated the δ-LL between predicting "agent" or "patient" for the noun in subject position of the intransitive is with the δ-LL of the noun in isolation. Since the role of the noun in the intransitive is heavily dependent on the meaning of the noun itself, if a model is using this information to disambiguate we would expect that the δ-LL in this experiment is correlated with δ-LL from Experiment 1. Furthermore, we would also want it to be strongly correlated with our approximate "ground truth" measures for agentivity, especially human ratings.

These correlations are shown in Table 3. As expected, davinci-003 displays a strong relationship between the δ-LL from intransitive sentences with the δ-LL from Experiment 1, and furthermore also has a strong correlation with human ratings. Like in Experiment 1, davinci-003's performance is invariant to changes in example orders.

Model	Noun δ-LL	Human	Ngrams	PB
BLOOM 560m	0.605	0.217	0.147	0.100
BLOOM 1b1	0.702	-0.0344	0.0200	0.0511
BLOOM 1b7	0.540	0.706	0.562	0.441
BLOOM 3b	0.258	0.280	0.190	0.0871
BLOOM 7b1	0.385	0.161	0.124	0.0689
GPT-2 small	0.655	0.424	0.309	0.290
GPT-2 medium	0.611	0.523	0.516	0.505
GPT-2 large	0.551	0.609	0.489	0.447
GPT-2 xl	0.548	0.507	0.445	0.363
GPT-3 ada-001	0.541	0.496	0.358	0.307
GPT-3 babbage-001	0.127	-0.176	-0.170	-0.125
GPT-3 curie-001	0.130	0.156	0.189	0.0953
GPT-3 davinci-001	0.487	0.647	0.515	0.376
GPT-3 davinci-003	**0.914**	**0.919**	**0.715**	**0.567**

Table 3: Correlation between the δ-LL from **intr-agent/intr-patient** sentences with the δ-LL from the noun in isolation, human ratings, subject (Google Syntactic Ngrams), and agent ratios (Propbank).

3.3 Exp 3: Agentivity with the transitive

As previously discussed, the syntactic position of the noun in the transitive sentences (subject or object) directly map to their semantic roles (agent and patient, respectively). Figure 5 shows accuracy split by **trans-agent** and **trans-patient**.

As in the previous experiments, GPT-3 davinci-003 outperforms all other models (0.994 for **trans-agent** and 0.991 for **trans-patient**—it is actually the *only* model which performs significantly above chance for both Experiments 2 and 3, and is also consistent across both example orderings.

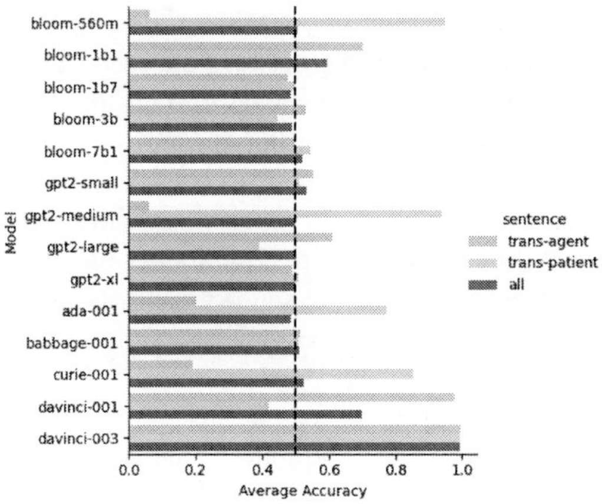

Figure 5: Average accuracy across **trans-agent**, **trans-patient**, and all transitive sentences. The dashed line indicates chance performance.

4 A Closer Look at davinci-003

Given that GPT-3 `davinci-003` does extremely well, a natural question to ask is whether `davinci-003` "fails" in similar ways to humans—i.e. we can see whether the nouns that are misclassified in the intransitive sentence setting (§3.2) are more ambiguous to humans as well.

In both APAP and PAPA orderings, all or nearly all of what `davinci-003` gets incorrect are patient subjects; all 78 incorrectly classified subjects of sentences in the APAP ordering are patients, and 69 of the 70 incorrect subjects in the PAPA ordering are patients. From this, one way to answer the above question is to compare this subset of nouns with the subset of nouns with a "patient" label (in the intransitive construction) that humans tend to rate as more agentive.

4.1 Animacy and thematic fit

Table 4 lists the latter subset of nouns, i.e. the most "agent-like" nouns with a "patient" label in the intransitive construction. Recall that human annotators were asked to rate each noun in isolation from a scale from 1 (very unlikely to be an agent) to 5 (very likely to be an agent) which is then normalized to a scale from 0 to 1, whereas the gold labels for nouns are determined by role it takes in the constructed (in this case, intransitive) sentences.

Animate nouns, such as "model (person)", "animal", and "fish" are unsurprisingly in this list, as many linguists have noted that the notion of agentivity is closely related to animacy (Silverstein 1976; Comrie 1989, inter alia). However, across both orderings, the only noun that was misclassified was "model" in the sentence *This model photographs beautifully/nicely*. Nevertheless, it could be argued that an agent interpretation in this context is plausible.

It appears that there are two interactions that are occurring in the above example. First, we must consider the *selectional restrictions* and of the verb, i.e. what arguments are allowable in the event described by the verb (Chomsky 1965; Katz and Fodor 1963). While selectional restrictions are traditionally viewed as binary features, a weaker, gradient version of this is *selectional preferences*, or the degree to which an argument fulfills the restrictions of the event (Resnik, 1996). A closely related notion to this is *thematic fit*, which is how much a word fulfills these preferences.

Secondly, the *Animacy Hierarchy*—of which humans are at the top—plays a role in such selectional restrictions and preferences, and thus in thematic fit (Trueswell et al., 1994). Since *photograph* requires a human-like entity as an agent, it could be argued that the interpretation of "model" being an agent in this sentence is not invalid (though likely a less salient interpretation by English speakers), as nothing in the "photographing" event rules out a subtype of a human "model" being the agent. This contrasts with the example with "animal" in our test set (*This animal photographs beautifully/nicely*), which would be far less acceptable with an animal agent interpretation, and falls below "human model" in the Animacy Hierarchy.

4.2 Verbs with vehicle objects

The other class of nouns present in Table 4, which also happen to be the remaining nouns, are vehicles. With regards to the relationship between animacy and agentivity, prior work such as Zaenen et al. (2004) has noted that "intelligent machinery" (such as computers and robots) and vehicles also often act as animates (below humans and above inanimates). Interestingly, nearly half of the examples that `davinci-003` gets wrong are sentences containing verbs with vehicle objects (*This car/vehicle/SUV/tractor/etc. drives nicely, This jet/plane/aircraft/etc. flies smoothly*). In fact, the examples that `davinci-003` gets the "most wrong" (higher $LL_{incorrect} - LL_{correct}$) are sentences with these verb-noun combinations.

Like the above examples with "model", some of

Noun	Human	Ngrams	Noun δ-LL
model (person)	0.806	0.523	8.06
animal	0.722	0.699	2.97
jet	0.583	0.562	7.27
aircraft	0.583	0.551	3.92
fish	0.569	0.467	-4.08
vehicle	0.542	0.468	4.66
bus	0.542	0.394	0.537
tank	0.542	0.564	-0.639
plane	0.528	0.565	11.1
car	0.528	0.565	3.83
motorcycle	0.514	0.184	5.11
truck	0.514	0.437	13.6
SUV	0.480	0.500	-2.27
tractor	0.401	0.500	11.2

Table 4: Nouns in **intr-patient** sentences with normalized human ratings ≥ 0.5, along with their subject ratio from Google Syntactic Ngrams and the average δ-LL from nouns in isolation (3.1). The average δ-LL for "patient" nouns ranges from -15.7 to 13.6. Note that *model* was presented to annotators with a disambiguating word sense (*person*).

these sentences have a possible alternative reading and are more ambiguous compared to sentences with verbs like *sell* (as in, *This car sells well.*). More specifically, they have a possible (though also less salient) unergative reading: e.g. in *This jet flies smoothly*, it could be a statement about how the jet flies on its own as opposed to about how the jet flies when someone flies it. Out of all the sentences in the test set, these are the only ones (along with some sentences with "turn") where the **intr-agent** has this possible unergative reading.

5 Related Works

There has been extensive work in the psycholinguistics literature investigating how humans make use of the relationship between events described by verbs and nouns that may participate in these events, which is especially relevant to the analysis described in §4.1. Works such as Tanenhaus et al. (1989) and Trueswell et al. (1994) have shown that humans utilize information about thematic fit to resolve ambiguity in sentence processing, mainly focusing on garden-path sentences.

Along this line of work, McRae et al. (1998) and Padó (2007) created human judgement datasets for thematic fit by asking humans to rate nouns associated with events (e.g. a crook arresting/being arrested by someone) on a scale from 1 (very uncommon/implausible) to 7 (very common/plausible). As stimuli, humans are given the noun, the verb describing the event, and the role of the noun. While this setup is similar to our dataset, they focus on the explicit relationship between the event and the noun, while our data is meant to focus on the relationship between the prototypical role of a noun (out of context) and its role in a controlled syntactic environment. Furthermore, as we would like the agent/patient distinction to be a minimal pair resulting changing the noun in an identical surface form, the sets of nouns and verbs between their studies and ours only partially overlap.

This study also follows a well-established line of work on LMs as psycholinguistic subjects (Futrell et al. 2019; Ettinger 2020; Linzen and Baroni 2021, inter alia). A large portion of this work focuses on probing LMs for sensitivity to the well-formedness of sentences containing various syntactic structures such as subject-verb agreement (Linzen et al., 2016), relative clauses (Gulordava et al. 2018; Ravfogel et al. 2021), and filler-gap dependencies (Wilcox et al., 2018), among others. A closely-related work by Papadimitriou et al. (2022) investigates how BERT classifies grammatical role of entities in non-prototypical syntactic positions, similar to our setup in Experiment 3.

There have also been works on evaluating and probing LMs for semantic/pragmatic knowledge. Ettinger (2020) created a suite of tests drawn from human language experiments to evaluate commonsense reasoning, event knowledge, and negation. The COGS challenge (Kim and Linzen, 2020), which contains related tests to ours with regards to argument alternation, tests for whether LMs can learn to generalize about passivization and unnacusative-transitive alternations in English. Misra et al. (2022) test LMs for their ability to attribute properties to concepts and further test property inheritance. With regards to lexical semantics, Vulić et al. (2020) investigate how type-level lexical information from words in context is stored in models across six typologically diverse languages.

However, our work is distinct from both previous syntax- and semantics-focused probing and evaluation in its focus on the interactions between the aspects of meaning in individual lexical items with larger syntactic structures or constructions. Nevertheless, methodologies from these research areas have informed the construction of our experiments. Our use of minimal pairs to form sentences with contrasting semantic roles is similar to the construction of the BLiMP dataset (Warstadt et al., 2020) and other test suites. Furthermore, we treat the "agent"/"patient" labelling task as classification based on the generation probabilities of the labels, following Linzen et al. (2016)'s method of using generation probabilities for grammaticality judgements.

Another relevant recent line of work within NLP is inspired by Construction Grammar (CxG), a branch of theories within cognitive linguistics that posits that *constructions*—defined as form-meaning pairings—are the basic building blocks of language (Goldberg 1995; Croft 2001, inter alia). Mahowald (2023) conducted a similar prompting experiment on the English Article-Adjective-Numeral-Noun construction, though this was focused on grammaticality judgements as opposed to aspects of semantics. Weissweiler et al. (2022) probe for both syntactic and semantic understanding of the English comparative correlative. Our study differs in that we analyze the impact of individual lexical items in what otherwise appears to be an identical syntactic construction, as opposed to analyzing competence of the construction as a whole. Finally, Li et al. (2022) find that sentences sharing the same argument structure constructions (ASCs) are closer in the embedding space than those sharing the main verb; in light of our results, an interesting direction would be to see if sentences of the same surface construction may cluster based on finer-grained semantic distinctions.

One consequence of our work—specifically with regards to `davinci-003`'s extremely high correlation with human judgements—is the potential for LMs as a tool for discovery in theoretical linguistics. This also has been argued recently by Petersen and Potts (2022), who demonstrate this in the realm of lexical semantics through a case study of the English verb *break*.

6 Conclusion

In order to gain insight into the behavior of LMs with respect to the syntax-semantics interface, we created a suite of prompting experiments focusing on agentivity. We prompt varying sizes of BLOOM, GPT-2, and GPT-3 to see if they are sensitive to aspects of agentivity at the lexical level, and then to see if they can either utilize or discard these word-level priors given the appropriate syntactic context. GPT-3 `davinci-003` performs exceptionally well in all three of our experiments—outperforming all other models tested by far—and is even better correlated with human judgements than some proxy corpus statistics. We find it surprising that `davinci-003` is able to capture an abstract notion of agentivity extremely well, but this ability does not appear to come from the size of the model alone as performance does not increase monotonically across any of the model families tested. What aspects of model training/data contribute to `davinci-003`'s (or other models') performance on linguistic tasks may be an interesting area for future work.

Furthermore, a qualitative analysis of what `davinci-003` gets incorrect reveals examples involving a number of linguistic confounders that make them more ambiguous to humans as well. The model's ability to "pick out" these linguistically interesting examples, combined with the high correlation with human ratings in Experiment 1, showcases the potential of LMs as tools for linguistic discovery for new phenomena, such as finding new classes of words or syntactic constructions that behave in unexpected ways. We hope these results encourage a more lively discussion between NLP researchers and linguists to unlock the potential of LMs as tools for theoretical linguistics research.

7 Limitations

While the use of a particular subset of English transitive verbs allows us to have precise control over the surface forms we are evaluating LMs on, this restricts our scope to a specific alternation in one language as well as a relatively small evaluation set. Nevertheless, we hope the methodology presented in this work can be extended to other phenomena across languages.

Additionally, while we explored a variety of ways to prompt these models, it may be the case that the prompt is non-optimal and therefore does not elicit the best possible output with respect to the task. Furthermore, the "prompt" to elicit human judgements is not the same as the prompt given to models, nor are the output formats (humans are asked to respond on a discrete scale from 1-5, while models are evaluated by their label log likelihoods). Evaluating whether the methodology in this line of work is a fair comparison between models and humans may be an interesting direction for future work.

8 Acknowledgements

This work was supported by NSF CISE RI grant number 2211951. For helpful comments and suggestions, we thank Kyle Mahowald and John Beavers, as well as the three anonymous reviewers and meta-reviewer. Finally, we would like to thank Thomas Lu, Saujas Vaduguru, Leilani Zhang, Russell Emerine, Vijay Viswanathan, Jeremiah Milbauer, Qianli Ma, Alex Wilf, Amanda Bertsch, Sireesh Gururaja, Yingshan Chang, Clara Na, Zhiruo Wang, Cathy Jiao, Simran Khanuja, Atharva Kulkarni, Anubha Kabra, Leena Mathur, and Shuyan Zhou for their help in annotating nouns in our dataset.

References

Tom Brown, Benjamin Mann, Nick Ryder, Melanie Subbiah, Jared D Kaplan, Prafulla Dhariwal, Arvind Neelakantan, Pranav Shyam, Girish Sastry, Amanda Askell, et al. 2020. Language models are few-shot learners. *Advances in neural information processing systems*, 33:1877–1901.

Noam Chomsky. 1965. *Aspects of the Theory of Syntax*. MIT press.

Bernard Comrie. 1989. *Language universals and linguistic typology: Syntax and morphology*. University of Chicago press.

Cleo Condoravdi. 1989. The middle: Where semantics and morphology meet. In *MIT Working Papers in Linguistics 11*, pages 16–31. MIT Press.

William Croft. 2001. *Radical construction grammar: Syntactic theory in typological perspective*. Oxford University Press on Demand.

David Dowty. 1991. Thematic proto-roles and argument selection. *Language*, 67(3):547–619.

Thomas Ernst. 2001. *The syntax of adjuncts*, volume 96. Cambridge University Press.

Allyson Ettinger. 2020. What BERT is not: Lessons from a new suite of psycholinguistic diagnostics for language models. *Transactions of the Association for Computational Linguistics*, 8:34–48.

Sarah M. B. Fagan. 1992. *The Syntax and Semantics of Middle Constructions*. Cambridge University Press, Cambridge.

Charles J Fillmore. 1986. Pragmatically controlled zero anaphora. In *Annual Meeting of the Berkeley Linguistics Society*, volume 12, pages 95–107.

Richard Futrell, Ethan Wilcox, Takashi Morita, Peng Qian, Miguel Ballesteros, and Roger Levy. 2019. Neural language models as psycholinguistic subjects: Representations of syntactic state. In *Proceedings of the 2019 Conference of the North American Chapter of the Association for Computational Linguistics: Human Language Technologies, Volume 1 (Long and Short Papers)*, pages 32–42, Minneapolis, Minnesota. Association for Computational Linguistics.

Brendan S Gillon. 2012. Implicit complements: a dilemma for model theoretic semantics. *Linguistics and Philosophy*, 35:313–359.

Adele E.. Goldberg. 1995. *Constructions: A construction grammar approach to argument structure*. University of Chicago Press.

Yoav Goldberg and Jon Orwant. 2013. A dataset of syntactic-ngrams over time from a very large corpus of English books. In *Second Joint Conference on Lexical and Computational Semantics (*SEM), Volume 1: Proceedings of the Main Conference and the Shared Task: Semantic Textual Similarity*, pages 241–247, Atlanta, Georgia, USA. Association for Computational Linguistics.

Kristina Gulordava, Piotr Bojanowski, Edouard Grave, Tal Linzen, and Marco Baroni. 2018. Colorless green recurrent networks dream hierarchically. In *Proceedings of the 2018 Conference of the North American Chapter of the Association for Computational Linguistics: Human Language Technologies, Volume 1 (Long Papers)*, pages 1195–1205, New Orleans, Louisiana. Association for Computational Linguistics.

Ray S Jackendoff. 1972. Semantic interpretation in generative grammar.

Osvaldo A. Jaeggli. 1986. Passive. *Linguistic Inquiry*, 17:587–622.

Jared Kaplan, Sam McCandlish, Tom Henighan, Tom B Brown, Benjamin Chess, Rewon Child, Scott Gray, Alec Radford, Jeffrey Wu, and Dario Amodei. 2020. Scaling laws for neural language models. *arXiv preprint arXiv:2001.08361*.

Jerrold J Katz and Jerry A Fodor. 1963. The structure of a semantic theory. *Language*, 39(2):170–210.

Najoung Kim and Tal Linzen. 2020. COGS: A compositional generalization challenge based on semantic interpretation. In *Proceedings of the 2020 Conference on Empirical Methods in Natural Language Processing (EMNLP)*, pages 9087–9105, Online. Association for Computational Linguistics.

Paul R Kingsbury and Martha Palmer. 2002. From treebank to propbank. In *LREC*, pages 1989–1993.

Beth Levin. 1993. *English verb classes and alternations: A preliminary investigation*. University of Chicago press.

Bai Li, Zining Zhu, Guillaume Thomas, Frank Rudzicz, and Yang Xu. 2022. Neural reality of argument structure constructions. In *Proceedings of the 60th Annual Meeting of the Association for Computational Linguistics (Volume 1: Long Papers)*, pages 7410–7423, Dublin, Ireland. Association for Computational Linguistics.

Tal Linzen and Marco Baroni. 2021. Syntactic structure from deep learning. *Annual Review of Linguistics*, 7(1):195–212.

Tal Linzen, Emmanuel Dupoux, and Yoav Goldberg. 2016. Assessing the ability of LSTMs to learn syntax-sensitive dependencies. *Transactions of the Association for Computational Linguistics*, 4:521–535.

Yao Lu, Max Bartolo, Alastair Moore, Sebastian Riedel, and Pontus Stenetorp. 2021. Fantastically ordered prompts and where to find them: Overcoming few-shot prompt order sensitivity. *CoRR*, abs/2104.08786.

Kyle Mahowald. 2023. A discerning several thousand judgments: GPT-3 rates the Article + Adjective + Numeral + Noun construction. *arXiv preprint arXiv:2301.12564*.

Ken McRae, Michael J. Spivey-Knowlton, and Michael K. Tanenhaus. 1998. Modeling the influence of thematic fit (and other constraints) in on-line sentence comprehension. *Journal of Memory and Language*, 38(3):283–312.

Kanishka Misra, Julia Taylor Rayz, and Allyson Ettinger. 2022. COMPS: Conceptual minimal pair sentences for testing property knowledge and inheritance in pre-trained language models. *arXiv preprint arXiv:2210.01963*.

Ulrike Padó. 2007. The integration of syntax and semantic plausibility in a wide-coverage model of human sentence processing.

Isabel Papadimitriou, Richard Futrell, and Kyle Mahowald. 2022. When classifying arguments, BERT doesn't care about word order...except when it matters. In *Proceedings of the Society for Computation in Linguistics 2022*, pages 203–205, online. Association for Computational Linguistics.

Erika Petersen and Christopher Potts. 2022. Lexical semantics with large language models: A case study of English *break*. Ms., Stanford University.

Alec Radford, Jeffrey Wu, Rewon Child, David Luan, Dario Amodei, Ilya Sutskever, et al. 2019. Language models are unsupervised multitask learners. *OpenAI blog*, 1(8):9.

Shauli Ravfogel, Grusha Prasad, Tal Linzen, and Yoav Goldberg. 2021. Counterfactual interventions reveal the causal effect of relative clause representations on agreement prediction. In *Proceedings of the 25th Conference on Computational Natural Language Learning*, pages 194–209, Online. Association for Computational Linguistics.

Philip Resnik. 1996. Selectional constraints: An information-theoretic model and its computational realization. *Cognition*, 61(1-2):127–159.

Lilia Rissman and Asifa Majid. 2019. Thematic roles: Core knowledge or linguistic construct? *Psychonomic bulletin & review*, 26(6):1850–1869.

David E Rumelhart and James L McClelland. 1986. On learning the past tenses of English verbs.

Asad Sayeed, Clayton Greenberg, and Vera Demberg. 2016. Thematic fit evaluation: an aspect of selectional preferences. In *Proceedings of the 1st Workshop on Evaluating Vector-Space Representations for NLP*, pages 99–105, Berlin, Germany. Association for Computational Linguistics.

Teven Le Scao, Angela Fan, Christopher Akiki, Ellie Pavlick, Suzana Ilić, Daniel Hesslow, Roman Castagné, Alexandra Sasha Luccioni, François Yvon, Matthias Gallé, et al. 2022. BLOOM: A 176b-parameter open-access multilingual language model. *arXiv preprint arXiv:2211.05100*.

Michael Silverstein. 1976. Shifters, linguistic categories, and cultural description. *Meaning in anthropology*.

Michael K. Tanenhaus, Greg Carlson, and John C. Trueswell. 1989. The role of thematic structures in interpretation and parsing. *Language and Cognitive Processes*, 4(3-4):SI211–SI234.

Carol Tenny. 1992. The aspectual interface hypothesis. pages 490–508. CSLI Publications, Stanford.

Carol Tenny. 1994. *Aspectual Roles and the Syntax-Semantic Interface*. Kluwer, Dordrecht.

J.C. Trueswell, M.K. Tanenhaus, and S.M. Garnsey. 1994. Semantic influences on parsing: Use of thematic role information in syntactic ambiguity resolution. *Journal of Memory and Language*, 33(3):285–318.

Jeanne van Oosten. 1977. Subjects and agenthood in English. In *CLS 13*, pages 451–471.

Ivan Vulić, Edoardo Maria Ponti, Robert Litschko, Goran Glavaš, and Anna Korhonen. 2020. Probing pretrained language models for lexical semantics. In *Proceedings of the 2020 Conference on Empirical Methods in Natural Language Processing (EMNLP)*, pages 7222–7240, Online. Association for Computational Linguistics.

Alex Warstadt, Alicia Parrish, Haokun Liu, Anhad Mohananey, Wei Peng, Sheng-Fu Wang, and Samuel R. Bowman. 2020. BLiMP: The benchmark of linguistic minimal pairs for English. *Transactions of the Association for Computational Linguistics*, 8:377–392.

Leonie Weissweiler, Valentin Hofmann, Abdullatif Köksal, and Hinrich Schütze. 2022. The better your syntax, the better your semantics? Probing pretrained language models for the English comparative correlative. *arXiv preprint arXiv:2210.13181*.

Ethan Wilcox, Roger Levy, Takashi Morita, and Richard Futrell. 2018. What do RNN language models learn about filler-gap dependencies? *arXiv preprint arXiv:1809.00042*.

Annie Zaenen, Jean Carletta, Gregory Garretson, Joan Bresnan, Andrew Koontz-Garboden, Tatiana Nikitina, M Catherine O'Connor, and Thomas Wasow. 2004. Animacy encoding in English: Why and how. In *Proceedings of the workshop on discourse annotation*, pages 118–125.

A Noun-Verb-Adverb Combinations

verb	***sells***
nouns	patients: *toy, book, novel, magazine, hat, lotion, album, car, SUV, product, make, item, CD, drug, snack* agents: *salesman, saleswoman, businessman, businesswoman, trader, peddler, telemarketer, dealer, shopkeeper*
adverbs	*easily, well, quickly*

verb	***drives***
nouns	patients: *car, SUV, truck, convertible, vehicle, tank, bus, tractor, van* agents: *driver, person, chauffeur*
adverbs	*nicely, smoothly, well*

verb	***flies***
nouns	patients: *plane, kite, jet, aircraft* agents: *pilot, person, aviator, captain*
adverbs	*nicely, smoothly, well*

verb	***cooks***
nouns	patients: *mushroom, pepper, fish, salmon, tuna, fillet, vegetable, herb, meat, ingredient, steak* agents: *chef, cook, baker, caterer*
adverbs	*nicely, well, terribly*

verb	***bakes***
nouns	patients: *pizza, potato, bread, cake, pastry, dough, pie, clay* agents: *patissier, chef, cook, baker, person, confectioner*
adverbs	*nicely, well, terribly*

verb	***reads***
nouns	patients: *passage, poem, verse, line, passage, script, abstract, essay, letter, report* agents: *student, orator, person, narrator, announcer, broadcaster, teacher*
adverbs	*nicely, well*

verb	***paints***
nouns	patients: *wall, fabric, glass, canvas, wood, surface, panel* agents: *painter, artist, person, illustrator, portraitist*
adverbs	*easily, terribly, well, beautifully*

verb	***writes***
nouns	patients: *section, passage, proposal, code, essay* agents: *student, person, notetaker, journalist, scribe, doctor, professor, essayist, blogger, poet, novelist, author*
adverbs	*quickly, easily*

verb	***performs***
nouns	patients: *routine, song, choreography, sonata, concerto, scene* agents: *musician, person, actor, comedian, dancer, singer, soloist*
adverbs	*easily*

verb	***photographs***
nouns	patients: *building, animal, landscape, lake, mountain, model, view* agents: *photographer, cameraman*
adverbs	*nicely, beautifully*

verb	***plays***
nouns	patients: *cello, piano, violin, instrument, flute, clarinet* agents: *musician, violinist, cellist, pianist, drummer, flutist, clarinetist*
adverbs	*nicely, beautifully*

verb	***cuts***
nouns	patients: *meat, cardboard, packaging, board, paper, fabric* agents: *hairdresser, barber, butcher, chef*
adverbs	*nicely, roughly, cleanly, effortlessly*

verb	***cleans***
nouns	patients: *jewelry, window, countertop, floor, surface, carpet, windshield, mirror, pot, silverware, bedding* agents: *janitor, maid, cleaner, housekeeper, busboy, waiter, waitress*
adverbs	*easily, quickly, effortlessly*

verb	***washes***
nouns	patients: *bottle, tub, shirt, car, windshield, dish, bedding, blanket, bowl* agents: *worker, maid, cleaner, busboy*
adverbs	*easily, quickly*

verb	***shaves***
nouns	patients: *beard, stubble, sideburn* agents: *barber, hairdresser*
adverbs	*neatly, nicely, smoothly*

verb	***packs***
nouns	patients: *crate, lunchbox, basket, container, coat, jacket, bag, duffle, food, suitcase, tent, backpack* agents: *mover, traveller, clerk, worker, backpacker, roadtripper, hiker, camper*
adverbs	*well, easily*
verb	***stitches***
nouns	patients: *silk, quilt, cotton, cut, cloth, fabric, wound* agents: *surgeon, tailor, machine, upholsterer, dressmaker*
adverbs	*easily, smoothly, nicely, poorly*
verb	***embroiders***
nouns	patients: *cushion, thread, cloth, fabric* agents: *tailor, seamster, seamstress*
adverbs	*well, nicely, beautifully, poorly*
verb	***knits***
nouns	patients: *yarn, wool, pattern* agents: *person, lady, man, woman*
adverbs	*well, nicely, beautifully, poorly, easily*
verb	***sews***
nouns	patients: *fabric, material* agents: *tailor, seamster, machine*
adverbs	*well, nicely, beautifully, poorly*
verb	***turns***
nouns	patients: *screw, knob, car, bike, motorcycle, valve, handle* agents: *driver, racer, motorist, pilot*
adverbs	*smoothly, easily, nicely, roughly*
verb	***carves***
nouns	patients: *pumpkin, wood, stone, gem, ice, steak, turkey* agents: *sculptor, person, jeweler, artisan, carver*
adverbs	*beautifully, nicely, cleanly, flawlessly*
verb	***sculpts***
nouns	patients: *wood, stone, marble, ice, clay* agents: *sculptor, person, potter, mason, carver*
adverbs	*beautifully, nicely, cleanly*

B Data Curation Criteria

After collecting a list of optionally transitive verbs that appear as intransitive via object drop (agent subject) or object promotion in the form of the middle construction (patient subject), we then had to curate adverbs and nouns that work in the templates as described in Table 1.

Adverbs must be manner adverbs, but they should not be *agent-oriented* adverbs (Jackendoff 1972; Ernst 2001) that express the mental state of the agent. Examples of such adverbs include *furiously, happily, angrily*, etc.

Then for each verb and a list of adverbs for each verb, we come up with a list of patient and agent nouns. All of the nouns must work in intransitive and transitive templates using the same sense of the verb. For nouns added as patients in the intransitive, the noun must not be an entity that causes the event described by the verb. Furthermore, it should not be necessarily oblique in the transitive form. In the example below, *needle* cannot be the direct object of the transitive and can only appear in the *with* prepositional phrase, so we do not include it in the list of nouns:

(4) a. This needle sews easily.

b. The tailor sews easily with this needle.

c. *The tailor sews this needle easily.

For nouns added as agents, in the intransitive it must be clear that the noun is the one doing the action. For human agents, we try to add agents that are most closely associated to the action described for the event, especially with those that tend to take human direct objects in the transitive form, such as *shave*.

C Human Annotation Details

We had 19 human annotators rate all 233 unique nouns on Google Forms. Each annotator saw a different random order of the nouns and were presented with 10 nouns on each page of the form, though they could go back to alter previous responses. All annotators are fluent in English. Annotators were also asked to self-identify as native or non-native speakers; 14 of 19 consider themselves native speakers.

For nouns that have multiple common and highly distinct word senses, we gave annotators a short disambiguating description. This description does not contain any verbs or any other indicator for what types of events the entity may occur in. A list of these nouns with their disambiguating description is given in Table 5.

Noun	Description
make	product of a particular company, such as of a car
plane	airplane
kite	a light frame covered with paper, cloth, or plastic, often with a stabilizing tail
jet	aircraft
line	of a text/a poem/etc.
passage	of a text/an essay/etc.
panel	of wood/a hard surface/etc.
model	person
routine	a part of an entertainment act
board	a long, thin, flat piece of wood or other hard material
letter	a sheet of paper with words on it in an envelope
proposal	a formal plan or suggestion
turkey	meat

Table 5: Nouns and disambiguating descriptions given to annotators.

C.1 Instructions provided to annotators

An **agent** is something that initiates an action, possibly with some degree of volition. In other words, nouns that tend to be agents have a tendency to do things.

A **patient** is something that undergoes an action and often experiences a change. In other words, nouns that tend to be patients have a tendency to have things done to it.

In this form, you are tasked to annotate how "agentive" you think a noun typically is—in other words, how likely it is to be an agent or a patient when an action involving both an agent and a patient occur.

Ex: The plant was watered by John.
The plant = patient
John = agent

Ex: The sun burns John.
The sun = agent
John = patient

A more formal definition is given by Dowty (1991), who outlines contributing properties of agents and patients:

(1) Contributing properties for the Agent Proto-Role:

- volitional involvement in the event or state — sentience (and/or perception)
- causing an event or change of state in another participant
- movement (relative to the position of another participant)
- (exists independently of the event named by the verb)

(2) Contributing properties for the Patient Proto-Role:

- undergoes change of state
- incremental theme (something that changes incrementally over the course of an event)
- causally affected by another participant
- stationary relative to movement of another participant
- (does not exist independently of the event, or not at all)

For the sake of simplicity, disregard events described by reflexives (such as John shaved himself). For each of the following nouns, rate it on the following scale:

1 = very unlikely to be an agent
2 = somewhat unlikely to be an agent
3 = no preference between agent and patient
4 = somewhat likely to be an agent
5 = very likely to be an agent

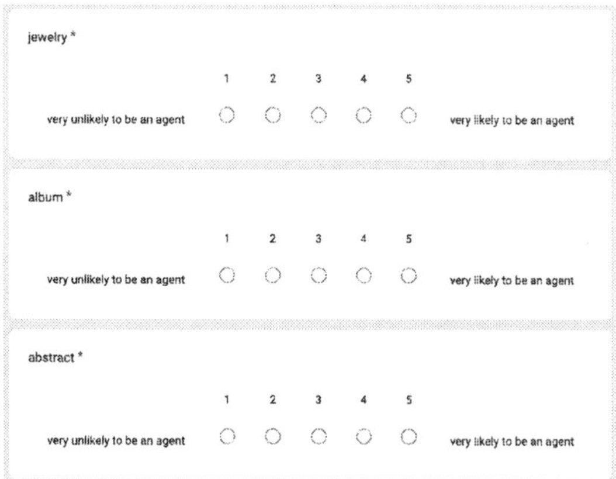

Figure 6: Example of Google Form question format given to annotators.

Model	APAP	PAPA	δ
BLOOM 560m	0.566	0.531	0.036
BLOOM 1b1	0.384	0.365	0.019
BLOOM 1b7	0.308	0.371	0.062
BLOOM 3b	0.476	0.133	0.343
BLOOM 7b1	-0.118	0.150	0.268
GPT-2 small	0.648	0.652	0.004
GPT-2 medium	0.420	0.367	0.053
GPT-2 large	0.501	0.496	0.005
GPT-2 xl	0.486	0.231	0.255
GPT-3 ada-001	0.589	0.598	0.009
GPT-3 babbage-001	0.394	0.228	0.166
GPT-3 curie-001	0.418	-0.204	0.622
GPT-3 davinci-001	0.579	0.356	0.223
GPT-3 davinci-003	**0.934**	**0.943**	0.010

Table 6: **Experiment 1**: Correlation between the difference in log-likelihood of predicting "agent" or "patient" with human ratings for nouns in isolation in both example orderings.

Model	APAP	PAPA	δ
BLOOM 560m	0.214	0.219	0.005
BLOOM 1b1	-0.096	0.027	0.124
BLOOM 1b7	0.618	0.795	0.177
BLOOM 3b	0.049	0.512	0.463
BLOOM 7b1	0.050	0.272	0.223
GPT-2 small	0.658	0.190	0.468
GPT-2 medium	0.546	0.500	0.047
GPT-2 large	0.632	0.586	0.045
GPT-2 xl	0.484	0.531	0.047
GPT-3 ada-001	0.574	0.417	0.157
GPT-3 babbage-001	-0.030	-0.322	0.292
GPT-3 curie-001	0.045	0.266	0.221
GPT-3 davinci-001	0.673	0.622	0.051
GPT-3 davinci-003	**0.927**	**0.911**	0.017

Table 7: **Experiment 2**: Correlation between the difference in log-likelihood of predicting "agent" or "patient" with human ratings for nouns in intransitive sentences in both example orderings.

D Results by Example Order

Tables 6, 7, and 8 show performance in both APAP and PAPA orderings in Experiments 1 (nouns in isolation), 2 (nouns in intransitive sentences), and 3 (nouns in transitive sentences) respectively. For simplicity, we only report correlations with human judgements.

Both GPT-3 davinci-001 and davinci-003 are very robust to changes in example ordering for all three experiments, as are BLOOM 560m and 1b1. The three largest BLOOM models are remarkably sensitive to ordering, especially in Experiment 3, as are GPT-2 xl and GPT-3 curie-001 and babbage-001.

E Propbank Statistics

When calculating model correlations with Propbank, we use all nouns with at least one occurrence of appearing within an ARG0/1 span in the parse tree to maximize the number of nouns we can compare with. However, we recognize that this may mess with correlation values since nouns with only one occurrence will have values at either 0 or 1. Furthermore, depending on the role the noun has in that particular sentence, it may push its agent rating to the opposite end of the spectrum compared to its "typical" behavior. Thus, we also tried calculating the correlation only for nouns that occur some greater number of times (within an ARG0/1 span) in Propbank. We call the minimum number of times the noun must appear the **count threshold**.

Figure 7 plots the Propbank agent ratio correlation with human ratings against the count threshold (in green). We also plot the number of nouns that meet this count threshold (in blue). The minimum count threshold to have a greater correlation than Google Syntactic Ngrams (pink line) is 27, however only 33 nouns meet this threshold. To meet meet the average human inter-annotator group correlation, the threshold is 268; only two nouns meet this.

F Adjusting Threshold for Exp 2

We also considered the possibility that the models may have a bias towards either the "agent" or "patient" label and may actually be correctly classifying nouns given an appropriate non-zero threshold for δ-LL. To account for this, we recalculate accuracies with thresholds that provide the best performance for each model as an "upper bound" for performance, as seen in Figure 8. After this adjustment, all models do at least as well as predicting the majority class, with GPT-2 xl experiencing the largest gain in accuracy. Nevertheless, GPT-3 davinci-003 still outperforms all other models by far.

Model	trans-agent APAP	trans-agent PAPA	trans-agent δ	trans-patient APAP	trans-patient PAPA	trans-patient δ
BLOOM 560m	0.034	0.090	0.056	0.962	0.932	0.031
BLOOM 1b1	0.620	0.781	0.161	0.516	0.457	0.059
BLOOM 1b7	0.940	0.013	0.927	0.007	0.989	0.982
BLOOM 3b	1.000	0.059	0.941	0.000	0.895	0.895
BLOOM 7b1	0.974	0.017	0.957	0.088	1.000	0.912
GPT-2 small	0.313	0.796	0.483	0.811	0.210	0.600
GPT-2 medium	0.121	0.000	0.121	0.877	1.000	0.123
GPT-2 large	0.829	0.389	0.440	0.163	0.623	0.461
GPT-2 xl	0.978	0.001	0.977	0.018	1.000	0.982
GPT-3 ada-001	0.313	0.089	0.224	0.611	0.933	0.322
GPT-3 babbage-001	0.987	0.044	0.943	0.023	0.994	0.971
GPT-3 curie-001	0.353	0.034	0.319	0.740	0.963	0.224
GPT-3 davinci-001	0.987	0.968	0.018	0.413	0.427	0.013
GPT-3 davinci-003	0.996	0.993	0.004	0.999	0.984	0.015

Table 8: **Experiment 3**: Accuracy in both example orderings for predicting the role of the noun in transitive sentences, where **trans-agent** corresponds to the noun in subject position and **trans-patient** to object position.

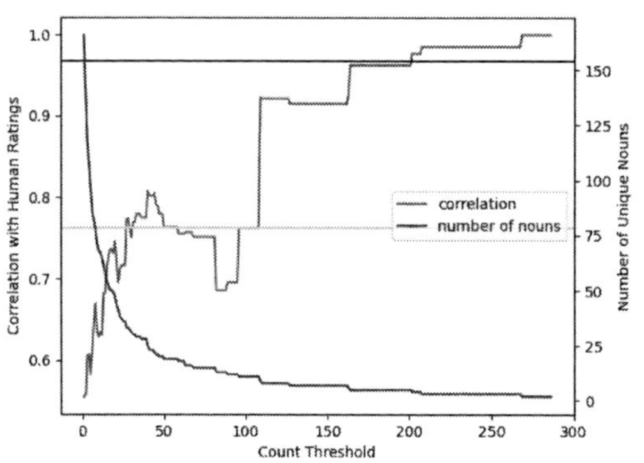

Figure 7: Count threshold versus the correlation between noun agent ratios and human ratings and the number of unique nouns that surpass the threshold. The pink horizontal line shows the correlation of Google Syntactic Ngrams with human ratings; the black line shows the average inter-annotator group correlation.

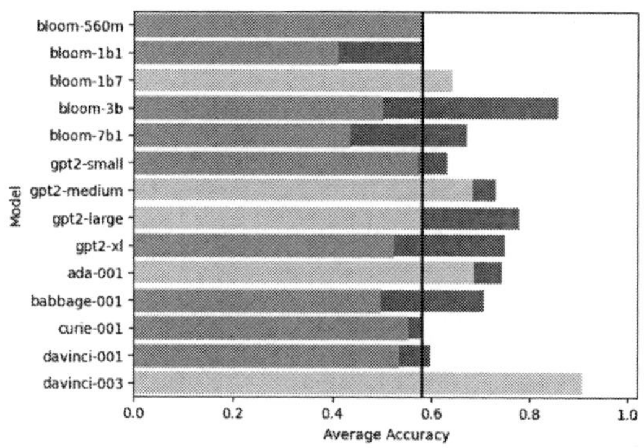

Figure 8: Average accuracy for predicting the label in **intr-agent/intr-patient** sentences with adjusted thresholds. After this adjustment, all models are at or above majority class accuracy. Magenta segments show increase in performance.

Can Pretrained Language Models Derive Correct Semantics from Corrupt Subwords under Noise?

Xinzhe Li, Ming Liu, Shang Gao

School of IT, Deakin University, Australia
{lixinzhe, m.liu,shang.gao}@deakin.edu.au

Abstract

For Pretrained Language Models (PLMs), their susceptibility to noise has recently been linked to subword segmentation. However, it is unclear which aspects of segmentation affect their understanding. This study assesses the robustness of PLMs against various disrupted segmentation caused by noise. An evaluation framework for subword segmentation, named Contrastive Lexical Semantic (CoLeS) probe, is proposed. It provides a systematic categorization of segmentation corruption under noise and evaluation protocols by generating contrastive datasets with canonical-noisy word pairs. Experimental results indicate that PLMs are unable to accurately compute word meanings if the noise introduces completely different subwords, small subword fragments, or a large number of additional subwords, particularly when they are inserted within other subwords.

1 Introduction

The capability to understand the meaning of noisy words through character arrangements is a crucial aspect of human cognitive abilities (Rawlinson, 2007). This capability is highly sought after in practical applications such as machine translation and sentiment analysis (Belinkov and Bisk, 2018). However, despite their success in in-distribution test data with standardized word forms, Pretrained Language Models (PLMs), which serve as the backbone models, tend to perform poorly on rare or noisy words (Kumar et al., 2020; Baron, 2015). These noisy words may be caused by accidental typos (Belinkov and Bisk, 2018) or spelling variants on social media (Ritter et al., 2010).

Prior studies show that most subword-based PLMs perform poorly under noise largely due to subword segmentation (Zhuang and Zuccon, 2022), while character-based PLMs show more robustness (El Boukkouri et al., 2020). Examining the impact of subword segmentation factors on PLMs is also crucial for defending against the adversarial attacks that leverage the sensitivity of subword segmentation to noise (Liu et al., 2022). However, rare work has investigated how the subword segmentation from noisy words affects the word meaning.

To help address this question, we design and develop a contrastive framework (CoLes) to assess the robustness of PLMs in the face of various forms of segmentation corruption. As subword segmentation can be influenced by noise in various ways, such as adding extra subwords or losing original subwords, we systematically categorize the ways into four main categories and two additional subcategories based on three subword sets, as exemplified in Table 1. Two types of noise models are proposed to effectively generate all the types of corruption except missing corruption, and a contrastive dataset consisting of noisy and standard word pairs is created. This framework enables us to evaluate the significance of preserved subwords and the impact of subwords added by noise.

The experimental results provide the following insights: 1) complete corruption: the PLMs struggle to infer meaning accurately if no subwords from the original segmentation are retained. The worst performance is observed when the meaning of original words is stored in the embedding; 2) partial corruption: preserving larger subword chunks can aid the understanding of PLMs, whereas retaining smaller subword pieces tend to be ineffective; and 3) additive corruption: even with all original subwords, however, the addition of subwords can harm the meaning of words, particularly when they are placed within other subwords. The more additive subwords, the greater the deviation in word semantics. All the results are consistent on the three PLMs with different vocabularies and segmentation algorithms.

2 Contrastive Lexical-Semantic Probe

The CoLeS probe framework has segmentation corruption and noise models that produce noisy

*Proceedings of the The 12th Joint Conference on Lexical and Computational Semantics (*SEM 2023)*, pages 165–173
July 13-14, 2023

Corruption Types	Examples	Segmentation Sets		
		Missing	Overlap	Additive
Complete (intact)	tasty → taaasty	tasty		ta, aa, sty
Complete	stun → stunn	s, tun		stu, nn
Partial	effectiveness → efeectiveness	effect	iveness	efe, ect
Additive (infix)	insubstantial → insuubstantial		ins, ub, stan, tial	u
Additive (affix)	hilarious → hilariousss		hil, ario, us	s, s
Missing	insubstantial → insstantial	ub	ins, stan, tial	

Table 1: Examples of different types of segmentation corruption. Complete/partial: completely/partially disrupting the original segmentation; additive: creating unnecessary subwords; missing: ignoring a token. A distinct form of complete corruption, referred to as "intact corruption", arises when a clean word is tokenized into a single subword that does not appear in the segmentation of its noisy counterpart. In the given example of intact corruption, the term "tasty" serves as an intact token.

words leading to different types of segmentation corruption. These noisy words, along with their corresponding canonical forms, are organized in a contrastive lexical dataset $\mathbb{D}_{\text{contrastive}}$ [1]. An evaluation protocol is designed to examine the effect of various corruption types.

2.1 Segmentation Corruption under Noise

A PLM consists of a tokenizer $\text{Seg}(\cdot)$, which segments a given word w into a sequence of subwords, i.e., $\text{Seg}(w) = (\tilde{w}_1, ..., \tilde{w}_K)$, and a PLM encoder $\text{Enc}(\cdot)$, which takes $\text{Seg}(w)$ and outputs a word representation. Formally, the segmentation of a canonical word $\text{Seg}(w)$ can be represented as a set $\mathbb{S}$, while the segmentation of a noisy word $\text{Seg}(\tilde{w})$ can be represented as set $\tilde{\mathbb{S}} = \{\tilde{w}_1, ..., \tilde{w}_K\}$. We can then utilize set operations to define the overlap set (consisting of retained subwords), the missing set, and the additive set (comprising additional tokens that are not present in $\mathbb{S}$) as $\mathbb{O} = \mathbb{S} \cap \tilde{\mathbb{S}}$, $\mathbb{M} = \mathbb{S} - \mathbb{O}$ and $\mathbb{A} = \tilde{\mathbb{S}} - \mathbb{O}$, respectively.

The set data structure cannot count duplicated tokens, which frequently occur in additive corruption scenarios, such as the additive (affix) corruption example presented in Table 1. Hence, we utilize a multiset implementation of $\mathbb{S}$ and $\tilde{\mathbb{S}}$ since such a data structure also stores the frequencies of elements, helping us assess the impact of duplicated tokens. Since the multiset implementation only includes unique elements without considering their order of appearance, we further differentiate the two types of additive corruption by iteratively comparing elements from two queue implementations of $\text{Seg}(w)$ and $\text{Seg}(\tilde{w})$.

In this study, we distinguish a unique category of corruption referred to as "intact corruption" from complete corruption, as the canonical words in this category (with whole-word vectors) remain unchanged. In total, there are six different types of corruption, as outlined in Table 1.

Identification of corruption types. During the evaluation, we need to filter each word pair according to its corruption type. First, we segment each word pair in $\mathbb{D}_{\text{contrastive}}$ by a model-specific tokenizer $\text{Seg}(\cdot)$ into subwords $(\mathbb{S}, \tilde{\mathbb{S}})$. We then identify the corruption type according to the following conditions: 1) Complete corruption: $\mathbb{S}$ and $\tilde{\mathbb{S}}$ are disjoint, i.e., $\mathbb{O} = \emptyset$. If the length of the missing set $\mathbb{M}$ is 1, this noise leads to intact corruption; 2) Partial corruption: the corruption only occurs to one of the subwords (i.e., the one in $\mathbb{M}$), and the other subwords (i.e., those in $\mathbb{O}$) are not affected. The prerequisite is that there exist more than one subwords in the original segmentation set $\mathbb{S}$. We can find such word pairs satisfy $\mathbb{M}, \mathbb{O}, \mathbb{A} \neq \emptyset$; 3) The conditions for additive corruption and missing corruption are $\mathbb{S} \in \tilde{\mathbb{S}}$ (or $\mathbb{M} = \emptyset$) and $\tilde{\mathbb{S}} \in \mathbb{S}$ (or $\mathbb{A} = \emptyset$), respectively. [2]

2.2 Creation of Contrastive Dataset

Most prior noisy datasets added noise to sentences, not individual words (Belinkov and Bisk, 2018; Kumar et al., 2020; Warstadt et al., 2019; Hagiwara and Mita, 2020). Besides, as contrastive datasets containing both the original and noisy form of a word are not readily available, we create our own lexical dataset which includes both forms. Examples of the generated dataset can be found in Table 2.

[1] Sentiment lexicon used is from `https://www.cs.uic.edu/~liub/FBS/sentiment-analysis.html#lexicon`.

[2] See `https://github.com/xinzhel/word_corruption/blob/main/word_corruption.py` for concrete implementation.

Canonical Words	Keyboard	Swap	Letter-reduplication
bad	NA	NA	baddddddd, baaaadddd, bbbbaaaaddddd
crazy	craxy	carzy	crazzyyyyyyyyy, crazzzzzy
amazing	amazijg	amzaing	amazing, amazinnng, amazinggg, amaaazzziiingggg

Table 2: Examples of contrastive datasets with canonical-noisy word pairs. Three types of noise models are applied: Swap-typos, Keyboard typos and letter reduplication. NA: we discard generated noisy words since typos on these words generate noisy words that are even unrecognizable to humans.

Noise models. Two sources of noise models are used to generate the lexical dataset. Findings given in Appendix E indicate that both types of noise models have comparable effects on model performance.

1) **Naturally and frequently occurring typos.** Users often type neighboring keys due to mobile penetration across the globe and fat finger problem (Kumar et al., 2020), while typing quickly may result in swapping two letters Belinkov and Bisk (2018). We refer to them as *Keyboard* and *Swap* typos, respectively. Our implementation of these typos is based on Wang et al. (2021). Specifically, for *Keyboard*, we only use letters in the English alphabet within one keyboard distance as the substitute symbols. Further, we avoid unrecognizable word forms (e.g., "bad→bqd" or "top → tpp") by selecting words with more than four characters.

According to the psycholinguistic study (Davis, 2003), to make noisy words recognizable for humans, we only apply noise to the middle characters and keep characters at the beginning and the end. Besides such a constraint, *Swap* typo also requires at least two distinct characters in the middle for swapping. However, words like "aggressive" can still be transformed into the same word by swapping "ss", so we transform them until we get a distinct word. Finally, we set a one-edit constraint for typos.

2) **Non-standard orthography.** We gather words with letter reduplication from 1.6 million tweets (Go et al., 2009). To create the canonical and noisy word pairs, we match specific noisy word forms (e.g. words with repeated letters for emphasis) to their corresponding canonical forms (a sequence of definite characters). We use simple regular expression patterns to search for words with repeated letters [3]. Examples in Table 3 show how effective these types of noise are in triggering different types of segmentation corruption.

[3]For example, pattern "\bb+a+d+" for "bad" matches "baddddddd".

Data-generating process. We create a contrastive dataset, $\mathbb{D}_{\text{contrastive}}$, by applying the noise models to the lexical dataset $\mathbb{D}_{\text{canonical}}$, which contains words in their canonical form. The noise models are applied to each word in $\mathbb{D}_{\text{canonical}}$ to create two misspelled words. Additionally, a random number of noisy words is extracted from the collection of 1.6 million tweets. As for the lexical dataset, $\mathbb{D}_{\text{canonical}}$, we choose adjectives from a sentiment lexicon that, by definition, provides positive or negative sentiment labels for use with downstream classifiers.

Evaluation. To assess the extent to which the meanings of noisy words diverge from the standard word forms, we calculate the cosine similarity between $\text{Enc}(\mathbb{S})$ and $\text{Enc}(\tilde{\mathbb{S}})$. For words that consist of multiple subwords, we aggregate their vectors into a single representation by averaging the token embeddings obtained from the PLMs. It is important to note that the output embedding spaces of PLMs exhibit varying levels of anisotropy (Ethayarajh, 2019; Yan et al., 2021; Gao et al., 2019). Thus, the similarity scores cannot be directly compared across different models. It is necessary to set a baseline by computing the similarity between $\text{Enc}(\mathbb{S})$ and a random embedding (we use the embedding of token "the", i.e., Enc(the)).

Additionally, we fine-tune downstream classifiers denoted as $y = \text{Cls}(x)$, where y represents an arbitrary semantic dimension and x corresponds to the encoded representation obtained from the PLMs $\text{Enc}(\text{Seg}(\cdot))$. We focus on sentiment classification as individuals frequently use sentiment words creatively on social media to express their emotions. To conduct our experiments, the sentiment of each word and its noisy variations is derived from the sentiment lexicon.

To gauge the semantic deviation caused by noise, we measure the accuracy of the noisy counterparts of words that are accurately classified in their original form.

Tokenizers	Intact	Complete	Partial
BERT	0.36	0.14	0.49
RoBERTa	0.46	0.12	0.42
ALBERT	0.38	0.13	0.49

(a) Typos.

Intact	Complete	Partial	Additive affix	Additive infix
0.70	0.02	0.06	0.22	0
0.61	0	0.06	0.30	0.01
0.61	0.02	0.06	0.29	0.02

(b) Letter Reduplication.

Table 3: Frequency of each segmentation corruption.

3 Experimental Results

Experiments are performed on three widely used PLMs: **BERT$_{\text{BASE}}$**, **RoBERTa$_{\text{BASE}}$** and **ALBERT$_{\text{BASE}}$** (See Appendix A for details). **BERT** (Devlin et al., 2019) accepts inputs from a Wordpiece tokenizer (Schuster and Nakajima, 2012), while **RoBERTa** (Liu et al., 2019), another popular frequent-based segmentation scheme, uses BPE (Sennrich et al., 2016). For comparison, we include **ALBERT** (Lan et al., 2020) with a probabilistic tokenizer called Sentencepiece (Kudo and Richardson, 2018).

Subwords retention is important for maintaining the correct semantics. Table 4 shows the severity of semantic deviation for each type of corruption. Generally, the more subwords the segmentation retains, the better the semantics are maintained (additive corruption > partial corruption > complete and intact corruption). Under additive corruption, the PLMs can always maintain more semantics from noisy words than random words (the baseline), while only RoBERTa has similarity score higher than the baseline under partial corruption. All the PLMs cannot infer word meaning from complete corruption.

What subwords, if retained, would enhance the comprehension of PLMs? We find that partial corruption can preserve word meaning if it retains a significant portion of the words, such as "upset" for "upsetting" or "phenomena" for "phenomenal" (See Appendix B). This is backed up by the finding that PLMs have the capability of learning morphological information, where stems contain more semantic meaning in a word compared to smaller components such as inflectional morphemes (Hofmann et al., 2021).

Are words more impacted by noise under complete corruption if their meaning is stored in the embeddings? According to Hofmann et al. (2021), if a word is represented as a single vector, PLMs can access its meaning directly from the embedding (referred to as the "storage route") instead of deducing it from the combination of subwords (known as the "computation route"). We presume that PLMs struggle to maintain the original meaning of these words when exposed to noise. We classify this type of corruption as "intact corruption", which is a particular variation to complete corruption. To validate our assumption, we evaluate the performance of PLMs on words under intact corruption. Results show that words with intact corruption consistently perform worse than those with complete corruption, despite both having completely distinct subwords. Although intact corruption consistently yields the lowest similarity score, the PLMs may still be able to better infer some semantic dimensions, such as sentiment, under intact corruption compared to complete corruption. (Appendix C).

Presence of additive subwords can damage the meaning of words, particularly when they are inserted in the middle of other subwords. In some cases, words under additive corruption (keeping all subwords) can perform worse than those under partial corruption (keeping only some subwords), as seen in the letter reduplication experiment (Appendix C). The finding suggests that the retention of subwords is not the only factor impacting the performance of PLMs. To uncover other factors affecting the word meaning, we analyzed 10 worst and best instances for each corruption type based on similarity scores (Appendix B). All the poorly performing cases have incorrect predictions, further highlighting the damaging impact on semantic meaning. The results show that the number of additive tokens (i.e., the cardinality of $\mathbb{A}$) is a distinct feature between good and bad instances. All the good cases have only 1 additive token, while the bad cases have at least 2 additive tokens (3.8 for partial corruption and 8.7 for additive corruption on average).

Thus, our hypothesis is that as the number of additive subwords increases, PLMs will have dif-

Models	Intact	Complete	Partial	Additive	Baseline
BERT	0.29	0.41	0.58	0.69	0.69
RoBERTa	0.54	0.66	0.76	0.85	0.72
ALBERT	0.41	0.47	0.62	0.74	0.68

(a) Similarity.

Intact	Complete	Partial	Additive
0.56	0.65	0.8	0.91
0.66	0.60	0.75	0.95
0.61	0.63	0.76	0.93

(b) Accuracy.

Table 4: Performance of PLMs under various types of corruption. Similarity scores of pretrained representations and accuracy of downstream classifiers are evaluated. The best result per row is highlighted in gray, and the second-best is in light gray. As a baseline, we compare the similarity scores between canonical and random words ("the" used). The unaffected accuracy is 1 since the canonical forms selected for evaluation are always correctly predicted.

Models	Infix	Suffix
BERT	0.59	0.70
RoBERTa	0.85	0.95
ALBERT	0.66	0.74

(a) Similarity.

Infix	Suffix
0.74	0.91
0.95	1
0.82	0.94

(b) Accuracy.

Table 5: Comparison of two types of additive corruption.

ficulty determining the correct meaning of words. We test the hypothesis by examining the performance of PLMs on both additive and intact corruption, where the missing and overlap sets remain constant. For additive corruption, we limit our experiments to only one unique additive subword and vary its frequency. We find 23 words with at least 3 noisy versions, each creating an additive set with the same element but different multiplicities. Take "amazing" as an example: one of its noisy instances ("amazinggggggg") has the multiplicity of 3 according to its additive set $\mathbb{A} = \{\text{"gg"}, \text{"gg"}, \text{"gg"}\}$ while "gg" only appears twice in another instance ("amazinggggg"). We sort every collection of noisy words in either of two ways, depending on the similarity scores or the multiplicities of additive tokens. In 17 out of 23 collections, these two sorting criteria produce identical results. This discovery also holds true for intact corruption, where the subwords within an additive set are typically diverse. Figure 1 illustrates a strong negative correlation between the number of additive tokens and the average similarity of noisy words for all the three models under intact corruption, where the sizes of missing sets and overlap sets are fixed to 1 and 0.

Besides, as shown in Table 5, additive subwords placed within subwords cause more harm than those that act as suffixes.

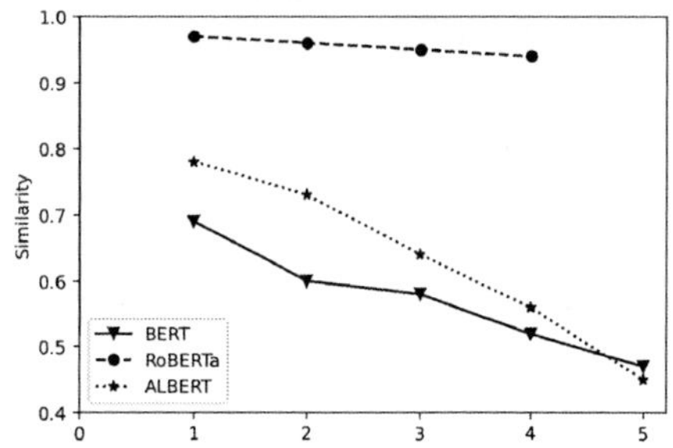

Figure 1: Correlation between the number of additive subwords and the cosine similarity of noisy words with their canonical forms. The range of quantity of additive subwords is subject to change depending on the tokenizer used.

4 Conclusion

We proposed the CoLeS framework which can evaluate how corrupt segmentation under noise affects PLMs' understanding. The experimental results show that three challenges can impair the PLMs' understanding of noisy words: insertion of additive subwords (especially within existing subwords), loss of original subwords, and incapacity of computing the word meanings through the aggregation of smaller subword units.

Reproducibility. Data and source code for noisy data generation, corruption types identification and PLMs' performance evaluation are released on Github [4].

Limitations

The omission of missing corruption from the evaluation process is justified due to its infrequent occurrence in real-world scenarios (refer to Appendix D for elaboration). Nevertheless, further investigation into rare instances of missing corruption may be warranted for research purposes. Our evaluation of language models was limited to auto-encoders based on the BERT architecture. Future studies are anticipated to expand the scope of PLMs under

[4] https://github.com/xinzhel/word_corruption

consideration [5].

References

Naomi S Baron. 2015. *Words onscreen: The fate of reading in a digital world*. Oxford University Press, USA.

Yonatan Belinkov and Yonatan Bisk. 2018. Synthetic and natural noise both break neural machine translation. In *ICLR*.

Matt Davis. 2003. Psycholinguistic evidence on scrambled letters in reading.

Jacob Devlin, Ming-Wei Chang, Kenton Lee, and Kristina Toutanova. 2019. BERT: Pre-training of deep bidirectional transformers for language understanding. In *NAACL*.

Hicham El Boukkouri, Olivier Ferret, Thomas Lavergne, Hiroshi Noji, Pierre Zweigenbaum, and Jun'ichi Tsujii. 2020. CharacterBERT: Reconciling ELMo and BERT for word-level open-vocabulary representations from characters. In *CoLing*, pages 6903–6915.

Kawin Ethayarajh. 2019. How contextual are contextualized word representations? Comparing the geometry of BERT, ELMo, and GPT-2 embeddings. In *EMNLP-IJCNLP*, pages 55–65, Hong Kong, China.

Jun Gao, Di He, Xu Tan, Tao Qin, Liwei Wang, and Tieyan Liu. 2019. Representation degeneration problem in training natural language generation models. In *ICLR*.

Alec Go, Richa Bhayani, and Lei Huang. 2009. Twitter sentiment classification using distant supervision. *CS224N project report, Stanford*.

Masato Hagiwara and Masato Mita. 2020. GitHub typo corpus: A large-scale multilingual dataset of misspellings and grammatical errors. In *Language Resources and Evaluation Conference (LREC)*.

Maria Heath. 2018. Orthography in social media: Pragmatic and prosodic interpretations of caps lock. *Proceedings of the Linguistic Society of America*.

Valentin Hofmann, Janet Pierrehumbert, and Hinrich Schütze. 2021. Superbizarre is not superb: Derivational morphology improves BERT's interpretation of complex words. In *ACL-IJCNLP*.

Taku Kudo and John Richardson. 2018. SentencePiece: A simple and language independent subword tokenizer and detokenizer for neural text processing. In *EMNLP: System Demonstrations*, pages 66–71.

Ankit Kumar, Piyush Makhija, and Anuj Gupta. 2020. Noisy text data: Achilles' heel of BERT. In *Proceedings of the Sixth Workshop on Noisy User-generated Text (W-NUT 2020)*.

[5]Instructions within our codebase facilitate the evaluation of various types of pre-trained language models accessible via Huggingface`https://huggingface.co/models`.

Zhenzhong Lan, Mingda Chen, Sebastian Goodman, Kevin Gimpel, Piyush Sharma, and Radu Soricut. 2020. ALBERT: A lite BERT for self-supervised learning of language representations. In *ICLR*.

Aiwei Liu, Honghai Yu, Xuming Hu, Shu'ang Li, Li Lin, Fukun Ma, Yawen Yang, and Lijie Wen. 2022. Character-level white-box adversarial attacks against transformers via attachable subwords substitution. In *EMNLP*.

Yinhan Liu, Myle Ott, Naman Goyal, Jingfei Du, Mandar Joshi, Danqi Chen, Omer Levy, Mike Lewis, Luke Zettlemoyer, and Veselin Stoyanov. 2019. Roberta: A robustly optimized bert pretraining approach. *arXiv preprint arXiv:1907.11692*.

Graham Rawlinson. 2007. The significance of letter position in word recognition. *IEEE Aerospace and Electronic Systems Magazine*.

Alan Ritter, Colin Cherry, and Bill Dolan. 2010. Unsupervised modeling of Twitter conversations. In *NAACL-HLT*, pages 172–180.

Mike Schuster and Kaisuke Nakajima. 2012. Japanese and korean voice search. In *2012 IEEE International Conference on Acoustics, Speech and Signal Processing (ICASSP)*, pages 5149–5152.

Rico Sennrich, Barry Haddow, and Alexandra Birch. 2016. Neural machine translation of rare words with subword units. In *ACL*.

Ashish Vaswani, Noam Shazeer, Niki Parmar, Jakob Uszkoreit, Llion Jones, Aidan N Gomez, Ł ukasz Kaiser, and Illia Polosukhin. 2017. Attention is all you need. In *Advances in Neural Information Processing Systems*.

Xiao Wang, Qin Liu, Tao Gui, Qi Zhang, et al. 2021. Textflint: Unified multilingual robustness evaluation toolkit for natural language processing. In *ACL-IJCNLP: System Demonstrations*, Online.

Alex Warstadt, Amanpreet Singh, and Samuel R. Bowman. 2019. Neural network acceptability judgments. *TACL*.

Thomas Wolf, Lysandre Debut, Victor Sanh, Julien Chaumond, Clement Delangue, Anthony Moi, Pierric Cistac, Tim Rault, Remi Louf, Morgan Funtowicz, Joe Davison, Sam Shleifer, Patrick von Platen, Clara Ma, Yacine Jernite, Julien Plu, Canwen Xu, Teven Le Scao, Sylvain Gugger, Mariama Drame, Quentin Lhoest, and Alexander Rush. 2020. Transformers: State-of-the-art natural language processing. In *EMNLP: System Demonstrations*.

Yuanmeng Yan, Rumei Li, Sirui Wang, Fuzheng Zhang, Wei Wu, and Weiran Xu. 2021. ConSERT: A contrastive framework for self-supervised sentence representation transfer. In *ACL-IJCNLP*.

Shengyao Zhuang and Guido Zuccon. 2022. Characterbert and self-teaching for improving the robustness of dense retrievers on queries with typos. SIGIR.

A Fine-tuning Pretrained Language Models

All the PLMs use BERT-based architecture, i.e., the encoding part of the transformer (Vaswani et al., 2017). **BERT$_{\text{BASE}}$** (110M parameters) and **RoBERTa$_{\text{BASE}}$** (125M parameters) are pretrained on BookCorpus and Wikipedia as masked language models. Only the pretraining of **ALBERT$_{\text{BASE}}$** (11M parameters) includes extra news and web data (Wolf et al., 2020). They are then fine-tuned for sentiment classification on the SST-2 dataset. All the models are publicly available on the Huggingface Hub website `https://huggingface.co/textattack`. Some configurations are shown as below. The BERT and RoBERTa models are fine-tuned using a learning rate of $2e^{-5}$ with no scheduling employed. The batch size is set to 32, and the training process spans 3 epochs, maintaining a gradient norm of 1. ALBERT is fined-tuned with a learning rate of $3e^{-5}$, a batch size of 32, and a total of 5 training epochs.

B Good and Bad Cases

Figure 2 shows the good and bad cases of partial and additive corruption under letter reduplication.

Partial — *Bad*

clean_word	noisy_word	overlap_set	missing_set	additive_set
enrich	enricch	{'en': 1}	{'rich': 1}	{'ric': 1, 'ch': 1}
nifty	niffty	{'ni': 1}	{'ft': 1, 'y': 1}	{'ff': 1, 'ty': 1}
genial	geniaaaaaaaal	{'gen': 1}	{'ial': 1}	{'ia': 1, 'aa': 3, 'al': 1}
redeem	redeeem	{'red': 1}	{'eem': 1}	{'ee': 1, 'em': 1}
relish	rellish	{'re': 1}	{'lish': 1}	{'llis': 1, 'h': 1}
loot	looooooooooooottttttt	{'lo': 1}	{'ot': 1}	{'oo': 5, 'ott': 1, 'tt': 2, 't': 1}
loot	loooooooooooot	{'lo': 1}	{'ot': 1}	{'oo': 5, 'oot': 1}
loot	looooooooooot	{'lo': 1}	{'ot': 1}	{'oo': 4, 'oot': 1}
chic	chiccccc	{'chi': 1}	{'c': 1}	{'cc': 3}
stun	sttun	{'n': 1}	{'stu': 1}	{'st': 1, 'tu': 1}

Additive — *Bad*

clean_word	noisy_word	overlap_set	additive_set
good	ggoodd	{'good': 1}	{'g': 1, 'd': 1}
decent	decenttttt	{'decent': 1}	{'tt': 2}
warm	warmmmmmmmmmmmmmmmmmmmmmmmmmmmmmmmmmmmmmmmmm	{'warm': 1}	{'mm': 19, 'm': 1}
hot	hottttttttttttttttttttttttttttttttttttt	{'hot': 1}	{'tt': 18}
super	superrrrrr	{'super': 1}	{'rr': 2, 'r': 1}
super	superrrrrrrr	{'super': 1}	{'rr': 3, 'r': 1}
super	superrrrrrrrrrr	{'super': 1}	{'rr': 5}
hot	hotttttttttt	{'hot': 1}	{'tt': 4, 't': 1}
free	freeeeeeeeeeeeeeeeeeeeeeeeeeeeeeeeeee	{'free': 1}	{'ee': 16, 'e': 1}
free	freeeeeeeeeeeeeeeeeeeeeeeeeeeeeeeeeee	{'free': 1}	{'ee': 16}

Good (Partial)

clean_word	noisy_word	overlap_set	missing_set	additive_set
uneventful	uneventfull	{'uneven': 1, 'tf': 1}	{'ul': 1}	{'ull': 1}
snobish	snobbish	{'s': 1, 'nob': 1}	{'ish': 1}	{'bis': 1, 'h': 1}
disown	dissown	{'di': 1, 'wn': 1}	{'so': 1}	{'sso': 1}
phenomenal	phenomenall	{'phenomena': 1}	{'l': 1}	{'ll': 1}
stupendous	stupendouss	{'stu': 1, 'pen': 1, 'dou': 1}	{'s': 1}	{'ss': 1}
sucky	suckky	{'suck': 1}	{'y': 1}	{'ky': 1}
crappy	crapppy	{'crap': 1}	{'py': 1}	{'ppy': 1}
upseting	upsetting	{'upset': 1}	{'ing': 1}	{'ting': 1}
dismal	dismall	{'di': 1, 'sma': 1}	{'l': 1}	{'ll': 1}
nicer	niceer	{'nice': 1}	{'r': 1}	{'er': 1}

Good (Additive)

clean_word	noisy_word	overlap_set	additive_set
abysmal	abysmall	{'ab': 1, 'ys': 1, 'mal': 1}	{'l': 1}
ungrateful	ungratefull	{'un': 1, 'grate': 1, 'ful': 1}	{'l': 1}
vengeful	vengefull	{'ve': 1, 'nge': 1, 'ful': 1}	{'l': 1}
sceptical	scepticall	{'sc': 1, 'ept': 1, 'ical': 1}	{'l': 1}
gloomy	gloomyy	{'gloom': 1, 'y': 1}	{'y': 1}
awkwardness	awkwardnesss	{'awkward': 1, 'ness': 1}	{'s': 1}
shameful	shamefull	{'shame': 1, 'ful': 1}	{'l': 1}
awesomeness	awesomenesss	{'awesome': 1, 'ness': 1}	{'s': 1}
caustic	causticc	{'ca': 1, 'ust': 1, 'ic': 1}	{'c': 1}
craziness	crazinesss	{'cr': 1, 'azi': 1, 'ness': 1}	{'s': 1}

Figure 2: Good and bad cases of partial and additive corruption under letter reduplication.

C PLM Robustness to Segmentation Corruption under Different Types of Noise

Table 6 displays the robustness of PLMs to segmentation corruption under various forms of noise. The results are largely consistent with those seen in Table 4. However, we notice that for letter reduplication, PLMs may perform worse with additive corruption than with partial corruption. Additionally, the accuracy of intact corruption can be better than that of complete corruption, despite they consistently having the lowest similarity score.

D Noisy words for Missing Corruption

As per the findings of Heath et al. (Heath, 2018), English word recognition by humans is predominantly influenced by consonants. Consequently, our investigation aims to identify abbreviations that disregard vowels and certain consonants when examining tweets. To be precise, an abbreviation is considered acceptable if its first letter and arbitrary consonants appear in a sequence that adheres to canonical words. For instance, the pattern of regular expression for term "sorry" can be "\bsr?r?y?" in such cases. However, we find that even humans have difficulties in recognizing all these abbreviations. While the inclusion of all consonants may enhance human recognition, we contend that assessing this form of corruption is

Models	Intact	Complete	Partial	Additive
BERT	0.24	0.34	0.62	0.69
RoBERTa	0.54	0.73	0.8	0.85
ALBERT	0.42	0.53	0.77	0.74

(a) Similarity.

Intact	Complete	Partial	Additive
0.54	0.47	0.92	0.91
0.54	0.73	0.87	0.95
0.63	0.79	0.91	0.93

(b) Accuracy.

Letter Reduplication

Models	Intact	Complete	Partial	Additive
BERT	0.34	0.41	0.58	/
RoBERTa	0.55	0.65	0.75	/
ALBERT	0.4	0.47	0.61	/

(c) Similarity.

Intact	Complete	Partial	Additive
0.59	0.66	0.79	/
0.6	0.57	0.74	/
0.59	0.61	0.75	/

(d) Accuracy.

Typos

Table 6: Performance of PLMs under different types of corruption. *Similarity scores of pretrained representations* and *accuracy of downstream classifiers* are measured. The best result per row is highlighted in gray, the second-best is in light gray. There is no result for additive corruption under typos because intra-word noise (modifying characters except for the first and last characters) (i.e., typos) never results in additive corruption. Baseline similarity scores are calculated between canonical words and the word "the".

superfluous. This assertion stems from our demonstration in Table 7 that such aggressive search criteria are improbable to produce missing corruption.

Models	Intra
BERT	0.50%
RoBERTa	0.52%
ALBERT	0.43%

Table 7: Proportion of abbreviations causing missing corruption.

Provided below is a comprehensive inventory of the canonical words and their corresponding noisy counterparts responsible for inducing missing corruption. It is worth noting that these noisy words are completely imperceptible to human cognition.

- 24 word pairs under RoBERTa: enthral-enth, upgradable-upgr, abysmal-abys, chintzy-chzy, emphatic-emph, enslave-ensl, extraneous-extr, implacable-impl, implausible-impl, implicate-impl, imprudent-impr, inflame-infl, instable-inst, intransigent-intr, irksomeness-irks, obscenity-obsc, obtrusive-obtr, ungrateful-ungr, unscrupulous-unsc, unsteadily-unst, unsteadiness-unst, unsteady-unst, unsteady-unsty, untruthful-untr;
- 23 word pairs under BERT: enthral-enth, exemplar-expl, exemplar-empl, idyllic-idyl, stylish-styl, abysmal-abys, brutish-brsh, crummy-crmy, enslave-ensl, hysteric-hyst, impenitent-impt, incognizant-inct, inconstant-inct, inexplainable-inpl, infamy-inmy, inflame-infl, irksomeness-irks, obscenity-obsc, obtrusive-obtr, unscrupulous-unsc, unspeakable-unsp, untrue-untr, untruthful-untr;
- 2 word pairs under ALBERT: enthral-enth, exemplar-exmp.

E Performance of PLMs under Different Noise

We compare the effect of two noise models "Naturally and frequently occurring typos" and "Non-standard orthography" with both the lexicon dataset and two sentential datasets. For a fair comparison, we constrain the length of *letter-reduplication* to 1. The accuracy of the noisy data and their standard deviation are reported in Table 8 and Table 9, respectively. It can be seen that the types of noise models in our experiments have no much distinction on model performance, except for the *Swap*.

Data	Noise Type	BERT	RoBERTa	ALBERT
Accuracy				
SST-2	Clean	0.93	0.85	0.92
	Keyboard	0.66	0.66	0.67
	Swap	0.71	0.72	0.72
	Letter-repetition	0.63	0.7	0.65
AG-News	Clean	0.95	0.8	0.92
	Keyboard	0.88	0.62	0.86
	Swap	0.89	0.62	0.86
	Letter-repetition	0.88	0.61	0.86
Similarity				
Setiment Lexicon	Keyboard	0.39	1	0.47
	Swap	0.45	1	0.5
	Letter-repetition	0.36	1	0.49
SST-2	Keyboard	0.5	0.52	0.61
	Swap	0.61	0.56	0.66
	Letter-repetition	0.46	0.55	0.58
AG-News	Keyboard	0.85	0.47	0.72
	Swap	0.87	0.5	0.75
	Letter-repetition	0.85	0.48	0.74

Table 8: Performance of PLMs under Different Noise

Data	BERT	RoBERTa	ALBERT
Similarity			
Lexicon	0.037	0	0.016
SST-2	0.061	0.016	0.035
AG-News	0.009	0.013	0.013
Accuracy			
SST-2	0.035	0.022	0.033
AG-News	0.004	0.004	0.004

Table 9: Standard deviations of PLMs' performance under different types of noise.

How Are Idioms Processed Inside Transformer Language Models?

Anonymous ACL submission

Abstract

Idioms such as "call it a day" and "piece of cake", are ubiquitous in natural language. How do Transformer language models process idioms? This study examines this question by analysing three models - BERT, Multilingual BERT, and DistilBERT. We compare the embeddings of idiomatic and literal expressions across all layers of the networks at both the sentence and word levels. Additionally, we investigate the attention directed from other sentence tokens towards a word within an idiom as opposed to in a literal context. Results indicate that while the three models exhibit slightly different internal mechanisms, they all represent idioms distinctively compared to literal language, with attention playing a critical role. These findings suggest that idioms are semantically and syntactically idiosyncratic, not only for humans but also for language models.

1 Introduction

"Why would you put all your eggs in one basket? I can't wrap my head around it". Idioms such as "put all one's eggs in one basket" and "wrap one's head around" are used frequently in natural conversations. Despite their abundance, much remains to be explored regarding their syntactic, semantic, and pragmatic characteristics, and how they are processed by the human brain as well as NLP models. Recent Transformer-based large language models have demonstrated strong capabilities in a sweep of tasks involving natural language understanding (e.g. Brown et al. (2020)). However, few attempts have been made to understand the inner workings of these language models in terms of idiom processing. In this study, we conduct three experiments to explore the inner workings of transformer language models in idiom processing. Specifically, we investigate the processing of BERT, Multilingual BERT and DistilBERT by comparing the embeddings on the sentence level and on the word level. We also explore the attention mechanism on idioms compared to literal contexts. We ask three questions:

- How do Transformer language models (LMs) represent idiomatic sentences as opposed to their literal spelt-out counterparts across different layers in the network? For example, "Birds of a feather flock together" versus "People with similar interests stick together".
- How do LMs represent a word inside an idiom compared to the same word in a literal context? For example, the word "feather" in "Birds of a feather flock together" versus "My parakeet dropped a green feather."
- How do LMs pay attention to a word inside an idiom compared to a literal context?

1.1 Related Work

The current study is related to linguistic research on idioms, research on the inner workings of BERT, often coined "BERTology", and more specifically BERT's processing of idiomatic expressions.

Linguistic theories of idioms: Idioms seem easy to spot but difficult to define. They are conventionalised, affective, and often figurative multi-word expressions used primarily in informal speech (Baldwin and Kim, 2010). Idioms are non-compositional - their meanings often cannot be predicted based on the words they is composed of (Nunberg et al., 1994). Sinclair and Sinclair (1991) postulate that humans process idioms by treating them as a "single independent token".

BERT and BERTology: BERT (Devlin et al., 2018) is a large Transformer network pre-trained on 3.3 billion tokens of written corpora including the BookCorpus and the English Wikipedia (Vaswani et al., 2017). Each layer contains multiple self-attention heads that compute attention weights between all pairs of tokens. Attention weights can

*Proceedings of the The 12th Joint Conference on Lexical and Computational Semantics (*SEM 2023)*, pages 174–179
July 13-14, 2023 ©2023 Association for Computational Linguistics

be seen as deciding how relevant every token is in relation to every other token for producing the representation on the following layer (Clark et al., 2019).

Many studies have explored how different linguistic information is represented in BERT (Mickus et al., 2020; Jawahar et al., 2019; Tenney et al., 2019). Jawahar et al. (2019) observed that different layers encode different linguistic information. Lower layers capture phrase-level information (i.e. surface features), middle layers capture syntactic information and higher layers capture semantic features. Studies disagree on where and how much semantic information is encoded. For example, Tenney et al. (2019) suggests that semantics is spread across the entire model. Lenci et al. (2021) found that the uppermost layer in BERT was the worst-performing in downstream tasks. So far, there has been less research on the inner workings of DistilBERT (Sanh et al., 2019) and Multilingual BERT (Pires et al., 2019). Most studies focus on comparing performance cross-lingually or in downstream tasks between these models (Ulčar and Robnik-Sikonja, 2021; Wu and Dredze, 2020; Sajjad et al., 2021; Lenci et al., 2021).

Idiom processing in Language Models: Studies are becoming increasingly engaged with the challenge of idiom representation in language models (Socolof et al., 2021; Garcia et al., 2021b; Dankers et al., 2022). Nedumpozhimana and Kelleher (2021) investigated how BERT recognises idioms, suggesting that the indicator is found both within the expression and in the surrounding context. Madabushi et al. (2021) explored how various input features (e.g. the effect of different problem setups - zero-shot, one-shot, and few-shot) affect LMs' ability to represent idioms. Both studies analyse the aggregated embeddings in the final layer, and do not investigate how representations vary across different layers. Garcia et al. (2021a) probed the representation of noun compounds in LMs, varying in compositionality, in order to assess the retention of idiomatic meaning. Our paper follows a similar paradigm but includes an attention analysis. Finally, Dankers et al. (2022) analysed idiom processing for pre-trained neural machine translation Transformer models from English to seven European languages and found that when the model produces a non-literal (intended) translation of the idiom, the encoder processes idioms more as single lexical units compared to literal expressions.

2 Experiments

To look into the black box of how LMs process idiomatic language, we conducted three experiments to assess sentence embeddings, word embeddings and attention across all layers of the networks.

2.1 Dataset

We utilised the idioms from the EPIE dataset (Saxena and Paul, 2020) to obtain a list of 838 English idioms that occur frequently in language. We then created sentences for the following conditions: for each idiom, we created (1) a sentence containing that idiom, (2) a spelt-out sentence expressing the same idiom in literal language, and (3) two unrelated literal sentences containing a key-word from the idiom (for experiment 2). An example of a datapoint[1]:

- **Idiom :** under the weather
- **Idiom sentence :** I'm feeling under the weather today.
- **Spelt-out meaning:** I'm feeling unwell today.
- **Unrelated literal sentence 1:** Today's weather is nice.
- **Unrelated literal sentence 2:** The weather is meant to change at 10am today.

2.2 Experiment 1: Idiom versus Spelt-out sentence embedding analysis

Experiment 1 investigates how sentence embeddings of idiomatic sentences evolve across layers.

2.2.1 Methods and Results

To embed the sentences, we used the Python library Transformers from Hugging Face (Wolf et al., 2020). We used the medium-sized BERT model (`BERT-base-uncased`), Multilingual BERT (`BERT-base-multilingual-uncased`), and DistilBERT (`distilBERT-base-uncased`). The first two models contain 12 layers and 12 attention heads, while DistilBERT contains 6 layers and 12 attention heads. Let S denote the dataset of all (idiom, and spelt-out) sentence tuples (in the notations below we represent idiom sentences with s_i, and spelt-out sentences with s_s).

We determine whether an LM's representation of an idiom sentence is similar to its spelt-out counterpart using two metrics:

[1]The entire dataset is released with the paper.

- Metric 1: the *raw cosine similarity* $\phi(s_i, s_s) = \frac{s_i \cdot s_s}{\max(||s_i||_2 \cdot ||s_s||_2, \epsilon)}$ computed for all $(s_i, s_s) \in \mathcal{S}$.

- Metric 2: the *cosine similarity ranking* computed for all (s_i, s_s) with $(s_i, s_s) \in \mathcal{S} \times \mathcal{S}$.

The raw cosine similarity in Metric 1 indicates how close an idiom and spelt-out pair is in the embedding space, while the similarity *ranking* in Metric 2 determines the quality of an embedding in capturing semantic nuances compared to controls (all other non-counterpart spelt-out sentences). A close idiom and spelt-out pair relative to controls should converge to a rank close to 0. The reasoning is that when an idiomatic sentence s_i is compared against all spelt-out sentences s_s in the dataset, its spelt-out counterpart should be the most similar in semantic content.

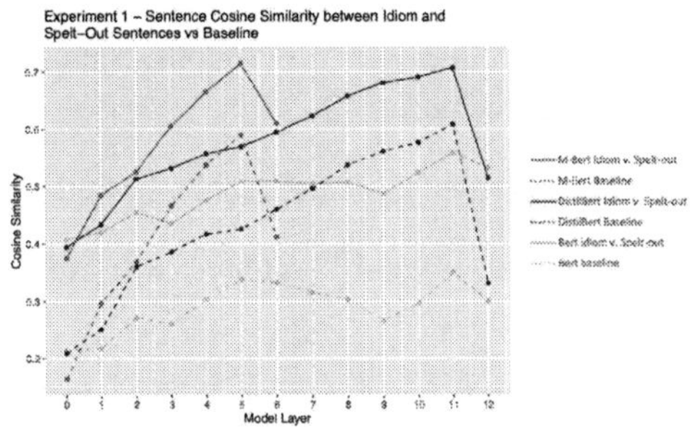

Figure 1: Experiment 1 - Sentence Cosine similarity of Idiom and Spelt-out sentence pairs

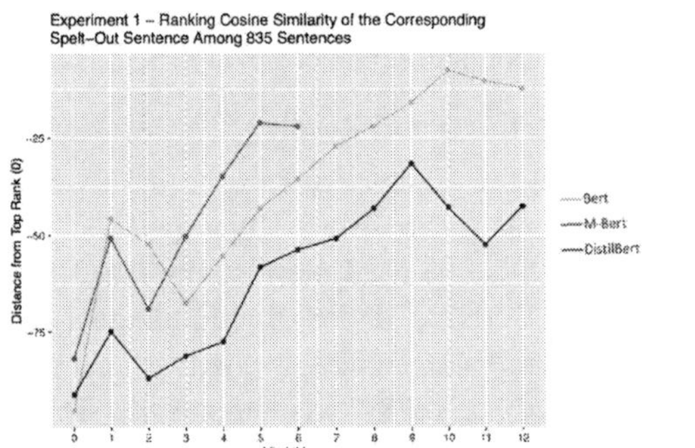

Figure 2: Experiment 1 - Similarity ranking, where we plot the similarity *ranking* of the spelt-out counterpart - the closer to zero, the more similar the spelt-out counterpart is to the idiom sentence compared to controls.

The results are shown in Figure 1 and Figure 2. Overall, the cosine similarity[2] between idiom sentence and its spelt-out counterpart is higher than the random baseline for all three models. For all three models and for every layer in each model, there was a significant difference (all p-values < 0.001) in sentence cosine similarity. Moreover, the t-values increased in deeper layers, which shows that these layers better processed semantic similarities between idioms and their spelt-out counterparts, supporting our hypothesis that the semantic meaning of idioms is captured in deeper layers of BERT.

Among the three LMs, the patterns of DistilBERT and Multilingual BERT most resemble each other, with similarity rising steadily, peaking on the penultimate layer, and dropping on the last layer. In order to evaluate if the LMs represent a literal spelt-out sentence to be *more* similar to random controls, we evaluated a similarity *ranking* metric.

The pair ranking results (Figure 2) show that similarity ranking reaches the highest point in mid to late layers for all 3 LMs, peaking at layer 10 for BERT, at layer 9 for Multilingual BERT and at layer 5 (penultimate layer) for DistilBERT.

2.3 Experiment 2: How does the embedding of a word within an idiom change compared to the same word in a literal context

Experiment 2 investigates how *word* embeddings change for words in idiomatic versus literal contexts. To do this, we see how the the cosine similarity of the embedding of a word inside an idiom versus in a literal context changes across layers, and compare that with a baseline cosine similarity where the word appears in two literal contexts.

Dataset: For each idiom sentence we manually created two unrelated literal sentences which contain a word from the associated idiom. For example, idiom sentence: *Don't beat around the [bush].* Unrelated literal sentences: (1) *There's a small [bush] in the garden*, and (2) *The dog jumped over the [bush].* Target word: "*bush*".

Methods and Results: We identified the index of the target word after the sentences were tokenised, and retrieved the embedding for this word across

[2] We concatenated the activations of all sentence tokens into a single flattened vector. In order to calculate the cosine similarity between two sentences of different lengths, we pad the shorter sentence in each pair with [PAD] so that the two have the same number of tokens. We calculate the cosine similarity between each idiom sentence and its spelt-out counterpart. As a baseline, we calculate the cosine similarity between an idiom sentence and a random spelt-out sentence. In all cases, we report the mean cosine similarity.

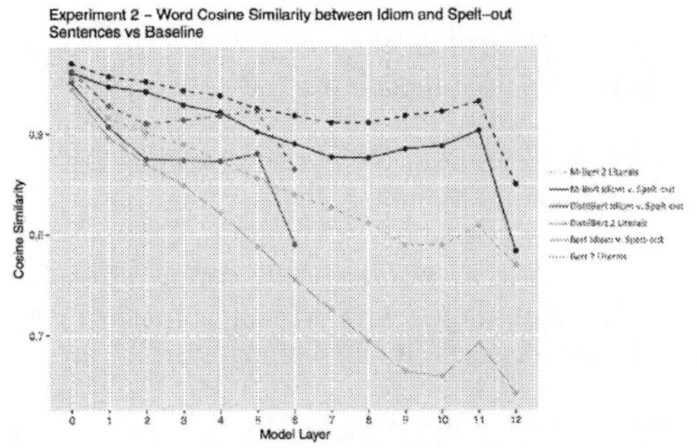

Figure 3: Experiment 2 - Cosine similarities of word embeddings between idiomatic and literal uses of the word

all layers for the idiom sentence and the two unrelated literal sentences. We calculated the cosine similarity for the word embedding (1) between idiom and literal contexts and (2) between the two literal contexts as a baseline.

Figure 3 shows that for all three language models, the similarity of word in two literal contexts (dotted line) is higher than that between idiom and literal contexts (solid line). Like in experiment 1, DistilBERT and Multilingual BERT resemble each other in their patterns. For BERT, the similarity of word embedding between literal and idiom contexts drops significantly more than between two literal contexts. T-test results showed the same pattern observed in experiment 1 as well; there was a significant difference (all p-values < 0.001) in cosine similarity in every layer for all three models, and the absolute value of t-value increased in deeper layers. This confirms our hypothesis that the semantic meaning of idioms is captured in deeper layers of BERT, where words inside idiom drift further from their literal meaning. We see a similar but reduced pattern in Multilingual BERT and DistilBERT.

2.4 Experiment 3: Does BERT pay different attentions to words inside idioms versus literal context

Experiment 1 and 2 show that LMs treat idioms differently to literal expressions. What is the mechanism that allows the networks to process this difference? As self-attention is central to the power of Transformer models, we hypothesise that the network integrates idioms by paying different attention when a word is in an idiom versus a literal context. Specifically, we hypothesise that words inside idioms are less connected to the rest of the sentence, following the linguistic theory that idiomatic expressions function as a single unit (Sinclair and Sinclair, 1991).

2.4.1 Methods and Results

For each idiom sentence, we selected a word inside the idiom and the indices of the target word (e.g. "bush") in both the idiom and the literal sentence. Then for each sentence and for each layer, we calculated the average attention from all other sentence tokens to the target word.

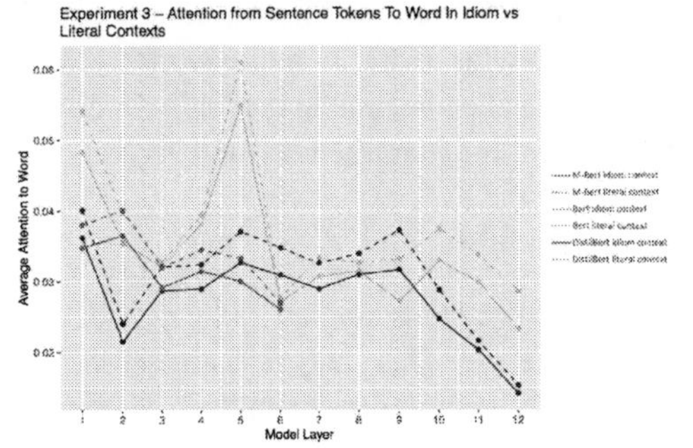

Figure 4: Experiment 3 - Attention from other sentence tokens to word inside an idiom sentence versus a literal sentence

Figure 4 plots the attention in each layer of LMs from all other sentence tokens to the target word. For all three language models, sentence tokens pay *less* attention to a word inside an idiom (solid lines) than they do to the same word in a literal context (dotted lines), meaning that words inside idioms interact less with the rest of the sentence compared to words in literal contexts. Like in experiment 1 and experiment 2, there was a significant difference between attention to a word inside an idiom and that inside a literal context in each layer in all three models (p-values < 0.01). This supports the idea that LMs see idioms as more idiosyncratic units. However, while DistilBERT and Multilingual BERT showed a similar trend in t-values that decreased in degree in the last 2 layers, BERT did not show any particular pattern in t-statistics. Once again we observe that DistilBERT and Multilingual BERT share a similar pattern, whereas BERT displays more variations across its layers.

3 Results Summary

We investigated how Transformer LMs process idioms across their layers on a sentence level and a word level. Experiment 1 shows that on a sentence level, LMs represent an idiom sentence to be similar to its literal spelt-out counterpart. Experiment 2 shows that on a word level, LMs represent a word inside an idiom versus a literal context differently across layers. Experiment 3 shows that words in an idiom receive *less* attention from the rest of the sentence, and thus have a weaker link to words outside of the idiom, echoing the findings of Dankers et al. (2022). All of these results hold across BERT, Multilingual BERT and DistilBERT. We also observe slight differences between the three LMs, with DistilBERT and Multilingual BERT resembling each other in their internal workings more closely than they each do with BERT. In future work we will investigate this phenomenon in models with different architectures, for example GPT and XLNet.

4 Conclusion

Idiomatic expressions are part and parcel of everyday language use. This study investigates the inner workings of idiom processing in three Transformer language models. Results show that LMs represent idioms differently to literal language. Words inside idioms receive less attention compared to words in literal contexts, supporting the linguistic theory that idioms are idiosyncratic even for language models.

A Limitations

While this work sheds light on how language models process idioms, we recognise that experimentation at present has been constrained to BERT. As mentioned in section 3, we aim to probe our findings further by repeating these experiments on a wider range of model architectures, such as GPT, Flan-T5, and LLaMA. Additionally, we recognise that our current dataset only contains English idioms; it would be interesting to extend this to include other languages for future studies.

References

Timothy Baldwin and Su Nam Kim. 2010. Multiword expressions. *Handbook of natural language processing*, 2:267–292.

Tom B. Brown, Benjamin Mann, Nick Ryder, Melanie Subbiah, Jared Kaplan, Prafulla Dhariwal, Arvind Neelakantan, Pranav Shyam, Girish Sastry, Amanda Askell, Sandhini Agarwal, Ariel Herbert-Voss, Gretchen Krueger, Tom Henighan, Rewon Child, Aditya Ramesh, Daniel M. Ziegler, Jeffrey Wu, Clemens Winter, Christopher Hesse, Mark Chen, Eric Sigler, Mateusz Litwin, Scott Gray, Benjamin Chess, Jack Clark, Christopher Berner, Sam McCandlish, Alec Radford, Ilya Sutskever, and Dario Amodei. 2020. Language models are few-shot learners. *?*

Kevin Clark, Urvashi Khandelwal, Omer Levy, and Christopher D Manning. 2019. What does bert look at? an analysis of bert's attention. In *Proceedings of the Second BlackboxNLP Workshop on Analyzing and Interpreting Neural Networks for NLP*, pages 276–286. Association for Computational Linguistics.

Verna Dankers, Christopher G Lucas, and Ivan Titov. 2022. Can transformer be too compositional? analysing idiom processing in neural machine translation. *arXiv preprint arXiv:2205.15301*.

Jacob Devlin, Ming-Wei Chang, Kenton Lee, and Kristina Toutanova. 2018. Bert: Pre-training of deep bidirectional transformers for language understanding. *Proceedings of the 2019 Conference of the North American Chapter of the Association for Computational Linguistics: Human Language Technologies, Volume 1 (Long and Short Papers)*.

Marcos Garcia, Tiago Kramer Vieira, Carolina Scarton, Marco Idiart, and Aline Villavicencio. 2021a. Assessing the representations of idiomaticity in vector models with a noun compound dataset labeled at type and token levels. In *Proceedings of the 59th Annual Meeting of the Association for Computational Linguistics and the 11th International Joint Conference on Natural Language Processing (Volume 1: Long Papers)*, pages 2730–2741, Online. Association for Computational Linguistics.

Marcos Garcia, Tiago Kramer Vieira, Carolina Scarton, Marco Idiart, and Aline Villavicencio. 2021b. Probing for idiomaticity in vector space models. In *Proceedings of the 16th Conference of the European Chapter of the Association for Computational Linguistics: Main Volume*, pages 3551–3564, Online. Association for Computational Linguistics.

Ganesh Jawahar, Benoît Sagot, and Djamé Seddah. 2019. What does bert learn about the structure of language? In *Proceedings of the 57th Annual Meeting of the Association for Computational Linguistics*.

Alessandro Lenci, Magnus Sahlgren, Patrick Jeuniaux, Amaru Cuba Gyllensten, and Martina Miliani. 2021. A comprehensive comparative evaluation and analysis of distributional semantic models. *arXiv preprint arXiv:2105.09825v1*.

Harish Tayyar Madabushi, Edward Gow-Smith, Carolina Scarton, and Aline Villavicencio. 2021. Astitchinlanguagemodels: Dataset and methods for the exploration of idiomaticity in pre-trained language models. *CoRR*, abs/2109.04413.

Timothee Mickus, Denis Paperno, Mathieu Constant, and Kees van Deemter. 2020. What do you mean, bert? assessing bert as a distributional semantics model. *Proceedings of the Society for Computation in Linguistics*, 3(34).

Vasudevan Nedumpozhimana and John Kelleher. 2021. Finding BERT's idiomatic key. In *Proceedings of the 17th Workshop on Multiword Expressions (MWE 2021)*, pages 57–62, Online. Association for Computational Linguistics.

Geoffrey Nunberg, Ivan A Sag, and Thomas Wasow. 1994. Idioms. *Language*, 70(3):491–538.

Telmo Pires, Eva Schlinger, and Dan Garrette. 2019. How multilingual is multilingual bert? *arXiv preprint arXiv:1906.01502*.

Hassan Sajjad, Fahim Dalvi, Nadir Durrani, and Preslav Nakov. 2021. On the effect of dropping layers of pre-trained transformer models. *Journal of Computer Speech and Language*.

Victor Sanh, Lysandre Debut, Julien Chaumond, and Thomas Wolf. 2019. Distilbert, a distilled version of bert: smaller, faster, cheaper and lighter. *arXiv preprint arXiv:1910.01108*.

Prateek Saxena and Soma Paul. 2020. Epie dataset: A corpus for possible idiomatic expressions.

John Sinclair and Les Sinclair. 1991. *Corpus, concordance, collocation*. Oxford University Press, USA.

Michaela Socolof, Jackie Chi Kit Cheung, Michael Wagner, and Timothy J O'Donnell. 2021. Characterizing idioms: Conventionality and contingency. *arXiv preprint arXiv:2104.08664*.

Ian Tenney, Dipanjan Das, and Ellie Pavlick. 2019. Bert rediscovers the classical nlp pipeline. *arXiv preprint arXiv:1905.05950*.

Matej Ulčar and Marko Robnik-Sikonja. 2021. Training dataset and dictionary sizes matter in bert models: the case of baltic languages.

Ashish Vaswani, Noam Shazeer, Niki Parmar, Jakob Uszkoreit, Llion Jones, Aidan N Gomez, Lukasz Kaiser, and Illia Polosukhin. 2017. Attention is all you need. *arXiv preprint arXiv:1706.03762*.

Thomas Wolf, Julien Chaumond, Lysandre Debut, Victor Sanh, Clement Delangue, Anthony Moi, Pierric Cistac, Morgan Funtowicz, Joe Davison, Sam Shleifer, et al. 2020. Transformers: State-of-the-art natural language processing. In *Proceedings of the 2020 Conference on Empirical Methods in Natural Language Processing: System Demonstrations*, pages 38–45.

Shijie Wu and Mark Dredze. 2020. Are all languages created equal in multilingual bert? pages 120–130.

Is Shortest Always Best?
The Role of Brevity in Logic-to-Text Generation

Eduardo Calò[α] **Jordi Levy**[ω] **Albert Gatt**[α] **Kees van Deemter**[α]
[α]Utrecht University [ω]IIIA, CSIC
{e.calo,a.gatt,c.j.vandeemter}@uu.nl levy@iiia.csic.es

Abstract

Some applications of artificial intelligence make it desirable that logical formulae be converted computationally to comprehensible natural language sentences. As there are many logical equivalents to a given formula, finding the most suitable equivalent to be used as input for such a "logic-to-text" generation system is a difficult challenge. In this paper, we focus on the role of brevity: Are the shortest formulae the most suitable? We focus on propositional logic (PL), framing formula minimization (i.e., the problem of finding the shortest equivalent of a given formula) as a Quantified Boolean Formulae (QBFs) satisfiability problem. We experiment with several generators and selection strategies to prune the resulting candidates. We conduct exhaustive automatic and human evaluations of the comprehensibility and fluency of the generated texts. The results suggest that while, in many cases, minimization has a positive impact on the quality of the sentences generated, formula minimization may ultimately not be the best strategy.

https://gitlab.nl4xai.eu/eduardo.calo/brevity-PL

1 Introduction

Logical formulae (LFs) are essential for scholars in many scientific fields, such as artificial intelligence and linguistics (e.g., formal semantics). For instance, some explainable artificial intelligence (XAI) methods (e.g., Guidotti et al., 2018) use LFs to provide interpretable and faithful explanations to black-box models. However, one of the drawbacks of these XAI methods is that their output formulae might be complex, hindering their understandability. Grasping the meaning of formulae is also hard for students of logic, especially when they are exposed to formalisms they are not yet accustomed to (Rector et al., 2004). Natural language generation (NLG) methods can be employed to simplify and translate LFs into understandable text in natural languages (NLs), effectively providing explanations for them.

Recently, NLG has made remarkable progress. In particular, in the context of data-to-text generation, good results have been achieved in different domains and datasets, such as sport (e.g., the ROTOWIRE dataset (Wiseman et al., 2017; Thomson et al., 2020)), restaurant (e.g., the E2E Challenge (Smiley et al., 2018; Dušek et al., 2020)), or WebNLG (Gardent et al., 2017). However, the texts produced in these contexts are often relatively poor in logical and rhetorical structure. Moreover, neural language models still fail to encode the semantics of logical formulae (Traylor et al., 2021b) and acquire analytical and deductive logical reasoning capabilities (Ryb et al., 2022). In particular, they struggle with logical connectives, where they fail to differentiate between conjunction and disjunction (Traylor et al., 2021a). Logic-to-text generation thus addresses an area of natural language processing where further progress is much needed.

One way in which the task of generating NL from complex LFs could be facilitated is by simplifying the input. We are interested in understanding the factors that make a formula more or less suitable as an input for a generator. In our work, we focus on brevity. The concept of brevity has long been a topic of linguistic discussion, dating back to at least Grice (1975), where Grice's submaxim of brevity states that shorter utterances should be favored over longer ones, avoiding unnecessary verbosity. Brevity has loomed large in computational accounts of language use as well, especially in the modeling of the human production of referring expressions (see §6 for discussion), a research area known as referring expressions generation (REG). Brevity could also be useful in our situation, in which case a shorter formula, instead of a lengthier logical equivalent, once verbalized using an NLG

*Proceedings of the The 12th Joint Conference on Lexical and Computational Semantics (*SEM 2023)*, pages 180–192
July 13-14, 2023 ©2023 Association for Computational Linguistics

algorithm, might lead to NL sentences that are more fluent and easier to understand.

In this paper, we study the role of brevity in logic-to-text generation, focusing on propositional logic (PL), a formalism for which logical equivalence is decidable. We formulate propositional logic formula minimization (i.e., finding the shortest logical equivalent of a given formula) as a Quantified Boolean Formulae (QBFs) satisfiability problem and employ the algorithm introduced in Calò and Levy (2023) that consistently identifies the shortest equivalents for a given formula.

It is not a foregone conclusion that the shortest formula must always lead to the best verbalization in English. To see this, suppose the input to the generator is of the form $\neg p \vee \neg q$. If the Sheffer stroke, $|$, (i.e., the NAND operator) is a permitted symbol, then the same information can be written more briefly as $p|q$, yet a "direct" verbalization of the former formula (e.g., *Not p or not q*) could well be more comprehensible and fluent than a direct verbalization of the latter (e.g., *It is not the case that p and q*), because the Sheffer stroke does not have a convenient shorthand in English.

Following this line of thought, several questions arise: When verbalizing an input logical formula into English, is it useful to start by finding the shortest formula that is equivalent to the input? Is the resulting text comprehensible to humans? How do we choose among the pool of potential shortest equivalent candidates?

The last question specifically opens up the issue of selecting the optimal translation, given that all potential shortest candidates are exactly of the same length. In our work, we experiment with several deterministic rule-based generators (thus controlling for faithfulness) and a number of selection strategies based on linguistic criteria, ranging from heuristics to neural metrics, to prune the resulting NL candidates. Finally, we conduct comprehensive automatic and human evaluations to assess comprehensibility and fluency of the generated texts.

2 Background

Logical Optimization Extensive research has been conducted on optimizing complex Boolean expressions, particularly in the field of electronic circuits, where practical considerations (i.e., a more complicated circuit with more logic gates takes up more physical space and produces more heat) make it paramount to find the smallest possible circuit, and hence the shortest possible (i.e., "minimal") formula representing its content. Popular methods for minimization include the Quine-McCluskey algorithm (Quine, 1952, 1955; McCluskey, 1956), Karnaugh maps (Karnaugh, 1953), the Petrick's method (Petrick, 1956), and the Espresso heuristic logic minimizer (Brayton et al., 1982). However, most work has focused on a limited set of canonical forms, such as conjunctive normal form (CNF) or disjunctive normal form (DNF). For our purposes (i.e., studying the interactions between logic and language), we need a general approach where a larger set of connectives and a wider variety of logical structures can be taken into account.

Quantified Boolean Formulae Quantified Boolean Formulae (QBFs) are an extension of propositional logic, where universal and existential quantifications over Boolean variables are allowed (Kleine Büning and Bubeck, 2009). Any QBF ϕ can be rewritten in a canonical prenex conjunctive normal form (PCNF) without any loss in expressivity, as follows. Let $\mathcal{B}$ be a finite set of Boolean variables, and $\mathcal{Q} = \{\forall, \exists\}$. A QBF ϕ over $\mathcal{B}$ in PCNF is given by $\phi := Q_1B_1.Q_2B_2 \dots Q_nB_n.\psi$, where $Q_i \in \mathcal{Q}$, $B_i \subseteq \mathcal{B}$, and ψ is a Boolean formula over $\mathcal{B}$ in CNF. The part including only quantifiers and bound variables $Q_1B_1.Q_2B_2 \dots Q_nB_n$ is called the *prefix*, and ψ is called the *matrix*.

The QBF satisfiability problem (Giunchiglia et al., 2009) involves determining the truth of a given QBF ϕ. For example, given the QBF $\phi := \exists x_1, \dots, x_n.\forall y_1, \dots, y_m.\exists z_1, \dots, z_t.\psi$, ϕ is true iff, there exists a truth assignment to $x_1, \dots, x_n$, such that, for all truth assignments to $y_1, \dots, y_m$, there exists a truth assignment to $z_1, \dots, z_t$ such that ψ is true. To solve this problem, several QBF solvers have been developed.[1] Practical applications of QBFs include AI, logic, planning, and games (Cashmore and Fox, 2010; Diptarama and Shinohara, 2016; Shukla et al., 2019). In our study, we utilize QBFs to encode and solve PL formula minimization.

Logic-to-Text Generation Logic-to-text generation is the task of generating NL text, starting from a logical formalism (e.g., propositional logic, description logic, or first-order logic). Although the bulk of recent work on NLG (see e.g., Gatt and Krahmer (2018) for a survey) has focused on other areas, generating text from logic nonetheless

[1] http://www.qbflib.org

has a long tradition, with approaches ranging from rule-based methodologies (Wang, 1980; De Roeck and Lowden, 1986; Calder et al., 1989; Shieber et al., 1989; Shemtov, 1996; Carroll and Oepen, 2005; Mpagouli and Hatzilygeroudis, 2009; Coppock and Baxter, 2010; Butler, 2016; Flickinger, 2016; Kasenberg et al., 2019) to statistical (Wong and Mooney, 2007; Lu and Ng, 2011; Basile, 2015) and neural models (Manome et al., 2018; Hajdik et al., 2019; Chen et al., 2020; Liu et al., 2021; Wang et al., 2021; Lu et al., 2022).

One of the complicating factors for this task is the problem of *logical-form equivalence* (Appelt, 1987; Shieber, 1988, 1993), which implies that every logical formula is equivalent to infinitely many other formulae, where the question of whether two formulae are logically equivalent is, in many formalisms (e.g., first-order logic), undecidable. In the present paper, we circumvent this problem by focusing on a decidable fragment of logic, as did, e.g., van Deemter and Halldórsson (2001) and Minock (2014) before us in different ways.

In a closely related work, Calò et al. (2022) manipulate a given first-order formula to obtain logically equivalent simplified versions via logical equivalence laws, yet their algorithm is not guaranteed to return the shortest formula.

3 Algorithm

To solve our PL minimization problem, we leverage the QBF-based algorithm presented in Calò and Levy (2023). We define formula length as the number of symbols (i.e., predicates and connectives, parentheses excluded) contained in a formula.

In outline, given (i) a PL formula ψ and (ii) a functionally complete set C of PL connectives, the algorithm produces the set $\mathcal{P} = \{\psi'_1, \ldots, \psi'_n\}$ of all those PL formulae such that (a) ψ and ψ'_i are logically equivalent, (b) ψ'_i does not contain any connectives that are not members of C, and (c) there does not exist any strictly shorter sentence χ satisfying (a) and (b).

The strength of the QBF-based algorithm is that it computes a *scheme* T_n of all candidates ψ'_i of length n, instead of checking each one of ψ'_i for equivalence with ψ. Tseitin transformation (Tseitin, 1983) is used to encode the equivalence of T_n and ψ as a QBF formula, which is checked for satisfiability (see Section 2) by a QBF solver (Tentrup, 2019). The algorithm can find all $\psi'_i \in \mathcal{P}$ of a certain length n. By making several calls to the QBF solver, increasing n, we make sure that the first found solution is a minimal solution.

The fact that the algorithm computes a unique *scheme* for all candidates of length n makes it very efficient, compared with other straightforward approaches. We refer the reader to Calò and Levy (2023) for details on the implementation.

4 Experiments

Our experimentation strategy can be summarized as follows: (i) we simplify the input formulae using the algorithm described in §3, (ii) we realize all the outputs using different generators, and (iii) we prune the resulting candidate realizations using a number of selection strategies.

We use three rule-based generators: (i) a BASELINE, (ii) the system presented in Ranta (2011), and (iii) LoLA (Calò et al., 2022). BASELINE is a system that generates near-literal translations of the formulae. Ranta performs some syntactic optimization (e.g., flattening, aggregation, etc.) to improve fluency. LoLA is an extension of Ranta that performs heuristic logical optimization based on standard equivalence laws to the input formula before verbalizing it. The generators were evaluated for faithfulness (i.e., whether the generated text conveys all and only the information of the input formula) in Calò et al. (2022) and shown to guarantee faithful translations. We refer the reader to Ranta (2011) and Calò et al. (2022) for more details on the systems.

For pruning, we experiment with the following five selection strategies: (i) length in number of words, (ii) pseudo-perplexity using BERT (Devlin et al., 2019), (iii) pseudo-SLOR using BERT, (iv) perplexity (PPL) using GPT-2 (Radford et al., 2019), (v) SLOR using GPT-2.[2] SLOR (Syntactic Log-Odds Ratio; Pauls and Klein, 2012; Kann et al., 2018) is a metric based on negative log-likelihood that penalizes highly probable unigrams. In detail, the score given by SLOR consists of the log probability of a sentence under a given language model, normalized by unigram log probability and sentence length. The intuition behind the normalizations is that a rare token should not bring down the sentence's score and shorter sentences should not be preferred over equally fluent longer ones. In our case, this should help us make fairer comparisons, as the length of the sentences generated by the re-

[2]We use `bert-large-cased` and `gpt-2-large`, respectively.

alizers varies considerably, and logical variables and constants (e.g., x, y, etc., which a language model treats as unigrams), which appear regularly in our sentences, have a unigram probability much higher than the other tokens in the lexicon. We compute PPL and SLOR with BERT, following the methodologies described in Salazar et al. (2020) and Lau et al. (2020) for masked language models.

For the experiments, we consider the Grade Grinder Corpus (GGC; Barker-Plummer et al., 2011), a parallel corpus where each NL sentence is paired with multiple logically equivalent formulae. We retrieve all PL formulae that are parsable by the generators we use. We first simplify the formulae using the algorithm described in §3 and obtain, for each formula, a set of logical equivalents, maximally reduced in terms of length. Out of 1092 PL formulae, 680 got simplified; the others were already in their shortest form. Table 1 shows some descriptive statistics. As a concrete example, starting from the following GGC formula containing 10 symbols:

$$(Tet(a) \wedge Tet(c)) \rightarrow \neg(\neg Large(a) \wedge \neg Large(c))$$

we end up with these shortest equivalents, with the number of symbols reduced to 7:[3]

$$Large(a) \vee ((Tet(c) \wedge Tet(a)) \rightarrow Large(c))$$
$$(Tet(c) \rightarrow Large(c)) \vee (Tet(a) \rightarrow Large(a))$$
$$(Tet(c) \wedge Tet(a)) \rightarrow (Large(c) \vee Large(a))$$
$$\ldots$$

	μ	σ	Min.	Max.
Original	7.12	2.62	1	18
Minimized	5.52	1.97	1	11

Table 1: Statistics on the length of the GGC formulae before and after minimization.

We proceed with translating the resulting formulae into English using the three rule-based generators. Additionally, we also translate the original GGC formula with the three generators.

At the logic level, all potential candidates are exactly of the same length. Therefore, once NL sentences are generated, we prune the candidates by (i) scoring them using the five selection strategies mentioned above, (ii) selecting the one with the lowest score for each strategy. After this process, for each GGC input formula, we end up with 18 realizations: 15 after the pruning process (3 realizers $\times$ 5 selection strategies), plus 3 from translating the original GGC formula with the three realizers. Table 2 presents some examples.

5 Evaluation

5.1 Automatic Evaluation

We set up an automatic evaluation comparing the translations by the 18 systems presented in §4 vs. the ground truth NL references associated with the original input formulae in the GGC. We use six automatic metrics, three of which are based on $n-$gram overlap, namely, BLEU (Papineni et al., 2002),[4] METEOR (Banerjee and Lavie, 2005), and ROUGE-L (Lin, 2004), and three on BERT, namely, BERTScore (Zhang et al., 2020),[5] BLEURT (Sellam et al., 2020), a learned metric based on human ratings,[6] and SBERT (Reimers and Gurevych, 2019).[7] For all the metrics except SBERT, we use the implementations provided by HuggingFace (Wolf et al., 2020).[8] Table 3 summarizes the results obtained.

Several trends emerge from analyzing the table. The results hint that formula minimization generally improves the translations, as the scores (particularly $n-$gram-based metrics) for the systems that get the minimized versions of the formulae as input are generally higher than the others. Different selection strategies score very similarly, sometimes with negligible differences. The difference in behavior between semantics-based and $n-$gram-based metrics corroborates the findings in Calò et al. (2022). Excluding BLEURT, whose low results are probably due to the nature of the data on which it was pre-trained and the lack of fine-tuning on our side, the results of semantics-based metrics are comparable across the systems, especially when it comes to BERTScore. This can be seen as a confirmation that the generated texts are paraphrases of the GGC ground truth references. However, BERTScore's results need to be taken with a grain of salt, since BERT-like models are known for missing semantic

[3]We list just some of the equivalents, as the algorithm returns many more formulae of length 7 in the actual output.

[4]We adopt the SacreBLEU (Post, 2018) implementation for improved reproducibility.

[5]We use the model `roberta-large_L17_no-idf`.

[6]We use the model `bleurt-base-128` without fine-tuning.

[7]We compute cosine similarity after obtaining sentence embeddings with the model `all-distilroberta-v1`.

[8]`https://huggingface.co/evaluate-metric`

System + Selection Strategy	Translation
Orig. BASELINE	*Iff f is large, then f is a cube or iff f is large, then f is a dodecahedron.*
Orig. Ranta	*At least one of these holds: - iff f is large, then f is a cube* *- iff f is large, then f is a dodecahedron.*
Orig. LOLA	*f is not large, f is a cube, f is not large or f is a dodecahedron.*
Minim. BASELINE BERT SLOR	*f is a dodecahedron or iff f is large, then f is a cube.*
Minim. Ranta GPT PPL	*Iff f is large, then f is a cube or f is a dodecahedron.*
Minim. LOLA Length	*f is not large, f is a cube or f is a dodecahedron.*

Table 2: Some translations from the original formula $(Large(f) \rightarrow Cube(f)) \vee (Large(f) \rightarrow Dodec(f))$.

System + Selection Strategy	$n-$gram-based Metrics			Semantics-based Metrics		
	METEOR	ROUGE-L	SacreBLEU	BERTScore	BLEURT	SBERT
Orig. BASELINE	0.5514	0.4386	10.8638	0.9051	−0.0916	0.7819
Orig. Ranta	0.5654	0.4697	12.1577	0.9082	−0.1099	0.7464
Orig. LOLA	0.5655	0.5012	14.0046	0.9115	−0.0492	0.7672
Minim. BASELINE Length	0.5639	0.4955	14.7115	0.9129	−0.0131	**0.7935**
Minim. BASELINE BERT PPL	0.5677	0.4977	14.8686	0.9123	0.0028	0.7928
Minim. BASELINE BERT SLOR	0.5652	0.4980	14.8386	0.9129	−0.0151	0.7926
Minim. BASELINE GPT PPL	0.5752	0.4999	14.9506	0.9122	−0.0017	0.7916
Minim. BASELINE GPT SLOR	0.5717	0.5077	14.5815	**0.9136**	0.0008	**0.7935**
Minim. Ranta Length	0.5802	0.5037	15.5895	0.9130	0.0126	0.7794
Minim. Ranta BERT PPL	0.5807	**0.5143**	15.1632	0.9123	0.0077	0.7720
Minim. Ranta BERT SLOR	**0.5865**	0.5099	**15.6208**	0.9132	0.0117	0.7797
Minim. Ranta GPT PPL	0.5759	0.5020	15.3613	0.9120	0.0092	0.7720
Minim. Ranta GPT SLOR	0.5780	0.5005	15.3833	0.9132	**0.0141**	0.7792
Minim. LOLA Length	0.5722	0.5050	15.5769	0.9133	−0.0005	0.7805
Minim. LOLA BERT PPL	0.5771	0.5137	15.2999	0.9134	−0.0028	0.7769
Minim. LOLA BERT SLOR	0.5811	0.5131	15.3199	0.9133	−0.0006	0.7800
Minim. LOLA GPT PPL	0.5689	0.4995	15.0712	0.9132	0.0048	0.7756
Minim. LOLA GPT SLOR	0.5709	0.4967	15.3573	0.9132	−0.0107	0.7799

Table 3: Performance of the 18 systems against the GGC ground truth references according to the automatic metrics.

nuances, such as negation (Ettinger, 2020), which is crucial for evaluating our task.

5.2 Human Evaluation

We conduct a human evaluation to understand the impact of formulae minimization on the translations. We recruit a group of 42 human evaluators and ask them to give feedback on (i) **comprehensibility** (i.e., whether the message conveyed by the sentence is understandable and not open to multiple interpretations), and (ii) **fluency** (i.e., whether the sentence sounds like a natural English sentence and is grammatically correct). These are central requirements to look for, as text generated from logic can be extremely disfluent and incomprehensible (e.g., a literal translation from a formula), while still being faithful to the input.

Evaluators are asked to rate the comprehensibility and fluency of each translation on a 7−point Likert scale (Likert, 1932). If comprehensibility receives a score < 4, participants are asked to give the motivations for which the sentence is hard to understand (i.e., ambiguity, complexity, or length of the sentence, or other). See Appendix A for more information on how we conduct the evaluation and the instructions given to the evaluators.

We sample 48 references from the GGC and select translations of the corresponding formula by 6 systems. The systems we choose are Orig. BASELINE, Orig. Ranta, and Orig. LOLA and Minim. BASELINE BERT SLOR, Minim. Ranta BERT SLOR, and Minim. LOLA BERT SLOR (henceforth, Minim. BBS, Minim. RBS, and Minim. LBS, respectively; see §4). Among the minimized variants, we choose BERT SLOR for two reasons: (i) BERT-based scoring seems to perform slightly better than the other selection strategies (see §5.1), and (ii) given that SLOR and PPL scores are nearly identical across systems, we opt for SLOR for theoretical reasons (see §4). After the selection, we end up with a total of 48 (references) $\times$ 6 (systems) $=$ 288 experimental items.

Participants and experimental items are randomly assigned to one of six groups and rotated through a 6 (systems) $\times$ 6 (participant groups) Latin square (Fisher, 1925). This guarantees that every item is shown to approximately the same number of participants, that every participant is shown the same number of items (48), and that participants only see one system translation per original formula.

5.3 Results

The overall comprehensibility and overall fluency of each translation are computed as the means of the ratings given by the evaluators on the two dimensions. The inter-annotator agreements for both dimensions are low (comprehensibility: Krippendorff's $\alpha = 0.329$; fluency: Krippendorff's $\alpha = 0.282$). We find a very strong positive correlation between the two dimensions (Pearson's $r = 0.89; p \ll 0.001$), indicating that more fluent translations are also more comprehensible.

Figure 1 shows the boxplot with the distribution of the ratings on comprehensibility and fluency for all the systems. The translations from Minim. RBS receive the highest mean on both comprehensibility ($\mu = 5.19$) and fluency ($\mu = 4.89$). One-way ANOVA analyses reveal that for both comprehensibility and fluency, the differences between systems are statistically significant (comprehensibility: $F(5, 282) = 21.72; p \ll 0.001$; fluency: $F(5, 282) = 13.39; p \ll 0.001$).

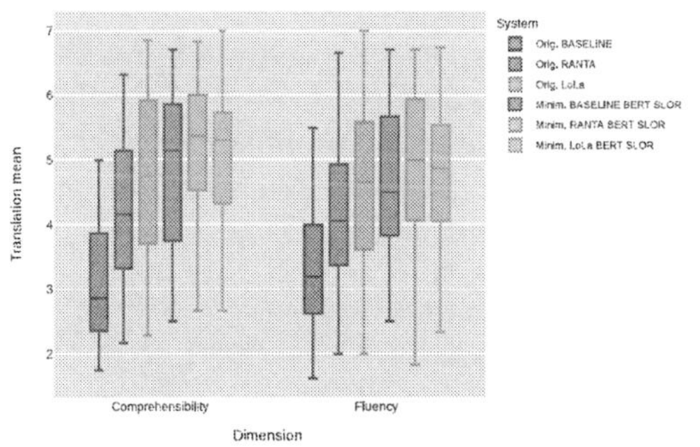

Figure 1: Boxplot with the distribution of translations' mean ratings across systems, for both comprehensibility and fluency.

Tukey's HSD tests for multiple comparisons show comparable results on the two dimensions. In general, Orig. LoLA is not significantly different from all the minimized variants. This suggests that human evaluators did not perceive a difference between settings where the input was manipulated using equivalence laws (*à la* LoLA) and settings where QBF minimization was used. Moreover, the tests show that all the minimized variants do not significantly differ from each other. This may be an indication that formula minimization plays an important role beforehand and the choice of the realizer used for translation does not matter much. Lastly, we notice less variance when BERT SLOR variants are involved, especially in comprehensibility with Ranta and LoLA.

We compute correlations between the human ratings and the score assigned by BERTScore, ROUGE-L, and SBERT to the questions rated by the evaluators, for both comprehensibility and fluency. Figure 2 shows the scatterplots and Table 4 the numerical results. The results are comparable across the two dimensions and we find low, but statistically significant positive correlations with human judgments on both comprehensibility and fluency.

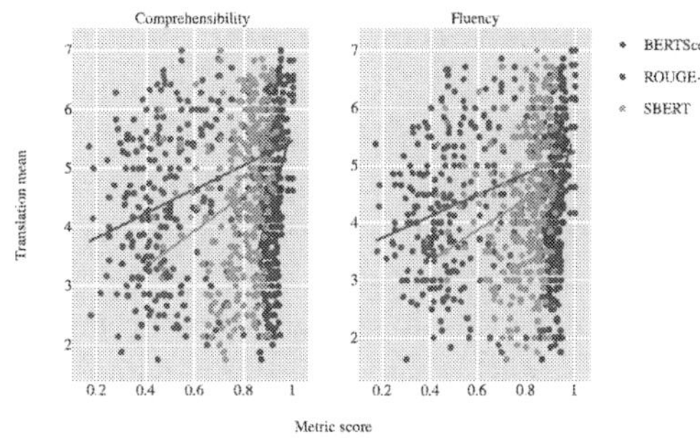

Figure 2: Scatterplots with the correlations between translations' mean ratings on comprehensibility and fluency and scores assigned by the automatic metrics.

	BERTScore	ROUGE-L	SBERT
Comprehensibility	0.331	0.315	0.223
Fluency	0.342	0.302	0.205

Table 4: Correlations between human ratings and automatic metrics on comprehensibility and fluency. All results are computed using Pearson's r and are statistically significant ($p < 0.001$).

We shed some light on the reasons why certain translations achieve low comprehensibility by inspecting the responses to the follow-up questions that were presented when comprehensibility is rated poorly (see §5.2). In most cases, low intelligibility corresponds to ambiguities detected in the translation (selected 330 times). Next comes the complexity of the linguistic structure (306), and finally the length of the translation (110). Other reasons are also chosen (118). We break down in Table 5 the detailed figures per system. We clearly

	Orig. BASELINE	Orig. Ranta	Orig. LoLA	Minim. BBS	Minim. RBS	Minim. LBS
Ambiguity	119	56	48	39	33	35
Complexity	110	58	46	38	28	26
Length	46	13	11	14	7	9
Other	33	26	14	15	12	18

Table 5: Figures for the reasons of translations' low comprehensibility per system.

Sentence	*If b is a tetrahedron, then b is a tetrahedron and it is not the case that c is a tetrahedron.*
Interpretation 1	*(If b is a tetrahedron, then b is a tetrahedron) and (it is not the case that c is a tetrahedron).*
Interpretation 2	*If (b is a tetrahedron), then (b is a tetrahedron and it is not the case that c is a tetrahedron).*
Original Formula	$Tet(b) \rightarrow (Tet(b) \wedge \neg Tet(c))$

Table 6: An ambiguous translation and its possible interpretations.

notice that manipulating the input formula helps improve the comprehensibility of the sentences, as the number of problematic cases decreases with LoLA and the minimized variants. We proceed with a manual check of the translations and report some interesting cases.

A noteworthy example of ambiguity is presented in Table 6. The sentence can have (at least) two interpretations. We need to resort to the original formula in the GGC to disambiguate the sentence and retrieve the intended meaning, which corresponds to the second interpretation. The sentence is generated by Orig. BASELINE. Other systems greatly improve the translation's comprehensibility, e.g., the corresponding translation by Minim. LBS *b is not a tetrahedron or c is not a tetrahedron* is rated much higher by the evaluators ($\mu = 4.43$ vs. $\mu = 2.86$).

Problematic cases pertaining to the complexity and length of the sentence include those presenting bulleted lists. Evaluators are ambivalent about their use: Some systematically give high scores to sentences containing bulleted lists, while others severely criticize them. One example that particularly baffled the evaluators is the following, as it contains nested levels of indentation:

At least one of these holds:
- *d is a dodecahedron and d is small*
- *all these hold:*
  - *d is not a dodecahedron or d is not small*
  - *a is small*

Further, we inspect in which circumstances formula minimization leads to better translations. We consider the scores on comprehensibility[9] of the translations by Orig. BASELINE vs. Minim. BBS, and Orig. Ranta vs. Minim. RBS. We select the top 10 instances where the score difference is the highest. We do not consider LoLA to keep the analysis controlled, as LoLA performs further logical manipulation before verbalization. We manually inspect the original and minimized formulae, and find out, unsurprisingly, that the outputs are improved mostly thanks to redundancy removal (e.g., repeated predicates and double negation) from the input. As an example, the GGC formula $\neg(BackOf(c, a) \rightarrow \neg FrontOf(c, e)) \wedge FrontOf(c, e)$ gets translated by Orig. Ranta as *It is not the case that if c is in back of a, then c is not in front of e and c is in front of e.* After minimization, the resulting formula $FrontOf(c, e) \wedge BackOf(c, a)$ gets translated by Minim. RBS as *c is in front of e and in back of a*, gaining 2.71 points in comprehensibility.

6 Conclusion

We have studied the role of brevity in logic-to-text generation. We employed a state-of-the-art (in terms of speed) QBF-based algorithm (Calò and Levy, 2023) that always finds the shortest equivalents to an input PL formula. We verbalized the outputs experimenting with several realizers and selection strategies to study whether the translations from shorter formulae are more comprehensible and fluent than those from their longer logically equivalent counterparts.

The results of our evaluations suggest that manipulating the original input formula (using logical equivalence laws as in LoLA or via minimization) improves the sentences generated. Our study taught us some other lessons as well. For example, the free text comments that our evaluators provided suggest

[9]We get similar results when we look at fluency.

that there is a need to (i) take measures to mitigate ambiguity in the generated sentences (see also Table 5 and Table 6), and (ii) further improve fluency, despite the fact that both Ranta and LoLA already take some measures to do it (the former performing syntactic optimizations and the latter performing both syntactic and logical optimizations).

In conclusion, is brevity valid as a principle that guides logic-to-text generation? A comparison with referring expressions generation (REG) might be helpful here. Researchers in REG build computational models of the choices that human speakers make when referring. Early REG algorithms (Dale, 1992) always generated the shortest expression that singles out the intended referent. However, such brevity-oriented REG algorithms have been found both computationally infeasible (Dale and Reiter, 1995) and dissimilar to the approaches followed by human speakers. Recent REG models all strike a compromise between brevity and a number of other factors (Van Deemter, 2016); they can be seen as approximating brevity to different degrees. It is conceivable, likewise, that future work on logic-to-text generation ends up following a similar pattern. For example, although the results reported in this paper suggest that brevity has a role to play, future logic-to-text algorithms might achieve even better performance by deviating from brevity to some extent. Perhaps brevity in logic-to-text generation should be weighed less heavily in some communicative situations, just as speakers are known to generate more elaborate referring expressions when referential situations are complex (Koolen et al., 2011; Paraboni and van Deemter, 2014).

We hope that future research, in which logical formulae and their natural language "translations" are embedded in well-understood practical tasks, for example in logic teaching or XAI, may shed further light on these questions.

Limitations

In the present paper, we have concentrated on PL. The first natural extension of this work would be to see if the QBF-based algorithm (or similar methods) could scale up to other (more expressive) formalisms, e.g., first-order logic. This would open up a range of interesting research questions, as in first-order logic, equivalence is in general undecidable. As a first step, an approach based on the use of a first-order theorem prover (e.g., VAMPIRE (Riazanov and Voronkov, 2002)) to check logical equivalence could be explored. This would not guarantee total coverage but might handle the vast majority of cases.

Our work has focused on four common logical operators, i.e., negation, conjunction, disjunction, and implication. When including other operators, such as the biconditional or the Sheffer stroke, the results could differ. For example, given that the Sheffer stroke is functionally complete on its own, we could have very short formulae but that may result in incomprehensible or disfluent texts.

Our conclusions are drawn from a limited number of realizers sharing similar properties (i.e., all of them are rule-based and derived from the system originally presented in Ranta (2011)). On the other hand, because of this, we were able to perform controlled generation and zoom in on the impact of minimization, which would not be straightforward in other settings, e.g., neural.

Moreover, we have only tackled English as NL. Brevity is drastically language-dependent and experimenting with other (especially typologically diverse) languages could bring different results.

Finally, the evaluation process could be further refined, as hinted by some comments we received in the human evaluation. For instance, some suggest that working within practical domains, especially with the help of pictures, would have eased the work of the evaluators.

Acknowledgments

We thank the anonymous reviewers for their careful reading of our manuscript and their insightful comments and suggestions.

This project has received funding from the European Union's Horizon 2020 research and innovation program under the Marie Skłodowska-Curie grant agreement № 860621.

References

Douglas E. Appelt. 1987. Bidirectional grammars and the design of natural language generation systems. In *Theoretical Issues in Natural Language Processing 3*.

Satanjeev Banerjee and Alon Lavie. 2005. METEOR: An automatic metric for MT evaluation with improved correlation with human judgments. In *Proceedings of the ACL Workshop on Intrinsic and Extrinsic Evaluation Measures for Machine Transla-*

tion and/or Summarization, pages 65–72, Ann Arbor, Michigan. Association for Computational Linguistics.

Dave Barker-Plummer, Richard Cox, and Robert Dale. 2011. Student translations of natural language into logic: the Grade Grinder Corpus release 1.0. In *Proceedings of the 4th International Conference on Educational Data Mining*, pages 51–60.

Valerio Basile. 2015. *From logic to language: Natural language generation from logical forms*. Ph.D. thesis, University of Groningen.

Robert K. Brayton, Gary D. Hachtel, Lane A. Hemachandra, A. Richard Newton, and Alberto Luigi M. Sangiovanni-Vincentelli. 1982. A comparison of logic minimization strategies using espresso: An apl program package for partitioned logic minimization. In *Proceedings of the International Symposium on Circuits and Systems*, pages 42–48.

Alastair Butler. 2016. Deterministic natural language generation from meaning representations for machine translation. In *Proceedings of the 2nd Workshop on Semantics-Driven Machine Translation (SedMT 2016)*, pages 1–9, San Diego, California. Association for Computational Linguistics.

Jonathan Calder, Mike Reape, and Henk Zeevat. 1989. An algorithm for generation in unification categorial grammar. In *Fourth Conference of the European Chapter of the Association for Computational Linguistics*, Manchester, England. Association for Computational Linguistics.

Eduardo Calò, Elze van der Werf, Albert Gatt, and Kees van Deemter. 2022. Enhancing and evaluating the grammatical framework approach to logic-to-text generation. In *Proceedings of the 2nd Workshop on Natural Language Generation, Evaluation, and Metrics (GEM)*, pages 148–171, Abu Dhabi, United Arab Emirates (Hybrid). Association for Computational Linguistics.

Eduardo Calò and Jordi Levy. 2023. General boolean formula minimization with QBF solvers.

John Carroll and Stephan Oepen. 2005. High efficiency realization for a wide-coverage unification grammar. In *Second International Joint Conference on Natural Language Processing: Full Papers*.

Michael Cashmore and Maria Fox. 2010. Planning as qbf. In *International Conference on Automated Planning and Scheduling Doctoral Consortium (ICAPS 2010)*.

Zhiyu Chen, Wenhu Chen, Hanwen Zha, Xiyou Zhou, Yunkai Zhang, Sairam Sundaresan, and William Yang Wang. 2020. Logic2Text: High-fidelity natural language generation from logical forms. In *Findings of the Association for Computational Linguistics: EMNLP 2020*, pages 2096–2111, Online. Association for Computational Linguistics.

Elizabeth Coppock and David Baxter. 2010. A translation from logic to english with dynamic semantics. In *New Frontiers in Artificial Intelligence*, pages 197–216, Berlin, Heidelberg. Springer Berlin Heidelberg.

Robert Dale. 1992. *Generating referring expressions: Constructing descriptions in a domain of objects and processes*. The MIT Press.

Robert Dale and Ehud Reiter. 1995. Computational interpretations of the gricean maxims in the generation of referring expressions. *Cognitive science*, 19(2):233–263.

A.N. De Roeck and B.G.T. Lowden. 1986. Generating English paraphrases from formal relational calculus expressions. In *Coling 1986 Volume 1: The 11th International Conference on Computational Linguistics*.

Jacob Devlin, Ming-Wei Chang, Kenton Lee, and Kristina Toutanova. 2019. BERT: Pre-training of deep bidirectional transformers for language understanding. In *Proceedings of the 2019 Conference of the North American Chapter of the Association for Computational Linguistics: Human Language Technologies, Volume 1 (Long and Short Papers)*, pages 4171–4186, Minneapolis, Minnesota. Association for Computational Linguistics.

Ryo Yoshinaka Diptarama and Ayumi Shinohara. 2016. Qbf encoding of generalized tic-tac-toe. In *4th International Workshop on Quantified Boolean Formulas (QBF) Co-located with 19th International Conference on Theory and Applications of Satisfiability Testing (SAT), Bordeaux, France*, pages 14–26.

Ondřej Dušek, Jekaterina Novikova, and Verena Rieser. 2020. Evaluating the state-of-the-art of end-to-end natural language generation: The e2e nlg challenge. *Computer Speech & Language*, 59:123–156.

Allyson Ettinger. 2020. What BERT Is Not: Lessons from a New Suite of Psycholinguistic Diagnostics for Language Models. *Transactions of the Association for Computational Linguistics*, 8:34–48.

Ronald Aylmer Fisher. 1925. *Statistical methods for research workers*. Edinburgh, Scotland: Oliver and Loyd.

Dan Flickinger. 2016. Generating English paraphrases from logic. *From Semantics to Dialectometry*.

Claire Gardent, Anastasia Shimorina, Shashi Narayan, and Laura Perez-Beltrachini. 2017. The WebNLG challenge: Generating text from RDF data. In *Proceedings of the 10th International Conference on Natural Language Generation*, pages 124–133, Santiago de Compostela, Spain. Association for Computational Linguistics.

Albert Gatt and Emiel Krahmer. 2018. Survey of the state of the art in natural language generation: Core tasks, applications and evaluation. *Journal of Artificial Intelligence Research*, 61:65–170.

Enrico Giunchiglia, Paolo Marin, and Massimo Narizzano. 2009. Reasoning with quantified boolean formulas. In *Handbook of satisfiability*, pages 761–780. IOS Press.

Herbert P Grice. 1975. Logic and conversation. In *Speech acts*, pages 41–58. Brill.

Riccardo Guidotti, Anna Monreale, Salvatore Ruggieri, Dino Pedreschi, Franco Turini, and Fosca Giannotti. 2018. Local rule-based explanations of black box decision systems.

Valerie Hajdik, Jan Buys, Michael Wayne Goodman, and Emily M. Bender. 2019. Neural text generation from rich semantic representations. In *Proceedings of the 2019 Conference of the North American Chapter of the Association for Computational Linguistics: Human Language Technologies, Volume 1 (Long and Short Papers)*, pages 2259–2266, Minneapolis, Minnesota. Association for Computational Linguistics.

Katharina Kann, Sascha Rothe, and Katja Filippova. 2018. Sentence-level fluency evaluation: References help, but can be spared! In *Proceedings of the 22nd Conference on Computational Natural Language Learning*, pages 313–323, Brussels, Belgium. Association for Computational Linguistics.

Maurice Karnaugh. 1953. The map method for synthesis of combinational logic circuits. *Transactions of the American Institute of Electrical Engineers, Part I: Communication and Electronics*, 72(5):593–599.

Daniel Kasenberg, Antonio Roque, Ravenna Thielstrom, Meia Chita-Tegmark, and Matthias Scheutz. 2019. Generating justifications for norm-related agent decisions. In *Proceedings of the 12th International Conference on Natural Language Generation*, pages 484–493, Tokyo, Japan. Association for Computational Linguistics.

Hans Kleine Büning and Uwe Bubeck. 2009. Theory of quantified boolean formulas. In *Handbook of satisfiability*, pages 735–760. IOS Press.

Ruud Koolen, Albert Gatt, Martijn Goudbeek, and Emiel Krahmer. 2011. Factors causing referential overspecification in definite descriptions. *Journal of Pragmatics*, 43(13):3231–3250. Factors causing referential overspecification in definite descriptions Pagination: 20.

Jey Han Lau, Carlos Armendariz, Shalom Lappin, Matthew Purver, and Chang Shu. 2020. How furiously can colorless green ideas sleep? sentence acceptability in context. *Transactions of the Association for Computational Linguistics*, 8:296–310.

Rensis Likert. 1932. A technique for the measurement of attitudes. *Archives of psychology*.

Chin-Yew Lin. 2004. ROUGE: A package for automatic evaluation of summaries. In *Text Summarization Branches Out*, pages 74–81, Barcelona, Spain. Association for Computational Linguistics.

Jiangming Liu, Shay B. Cohen, and Mirella Lapata. 2021. Text generation from discourse representation structures. In *Proceedings of the 2021 Conference of the North American Chapter of the Association for Computational Linguistics: Human Language Technologies*, pages 397–415, Online. Association for Computational Linguistics.

Wei Lu and Hwee Tou Ng. 2011. A probabilistic forest-to-string model for language generation from typed lambda calculus expressions. In *Proceedings of the 2011 Conference on Empirical Methods in Natural Language Processing*, pages 1611–1622, Edinburgh, Scotland, UK. Association for Computational Linguistics.

Xuantao Lu, Jingping Liu, Zhouhong Gu, Hanwen Tong, Chenhao Xie, Junyang Huang, Yanghua Xiao, and Wenguang Wang. 2022. Parsing natural language into propositional and first-order logic with dual reinforcement learning. In *Proceedings of the 29th International Conference on Computational Linguistics*, pages 5419–5431, Gyeongju, Republic of Korea. International Committee on Computational Linguistics.

Kana Manome, Masashi Yoshikawa, Hitomi Yanaka, Pascual Martínez-Gómez, Koji Mineshima, and Daisuke Bekki. 2018. Neural sentence generation from formal semantics. In *Proceedings of the 11th International Conference on Natural Language Generation*, pages 408–414, Tilburg University, The Netherlands. Association for Computational Linguistics.

Edward Joseph McCluskey. 1956. Minimization of boolean functions. *The Bell System Technical Journal*, 35(6):1417–1444.

Michael Minock. 2014. In pursuit of decidable'logical form'. In *The Fifth Swedish Language Technology Conference, 13-14 November 2014, Uppsala*.

Aikaterini Mpagouli and Ioannis Hatzilygeroudis. 2009. A Knowledge-based System for Translating FOL Formulas into NL Sentences. In Iliadis, Maglogiann, Tsoumakasis, Vlahavas, and Bramer, editors, *Artificial Intelligence Applications and Innovations III*, volume 296, pages 157–163. Springer US, Boston, MA. Series Title: IFIP Advances in Information and Communication Technology.

Kishore Papineni, Salim Roukos, Todd Ward, and Wei-Jing Zhu. 2002. Bleu: a method for automatic evaluation of machine translation. In *Proceedings of the 40th Annual Meeting of the Association for Computational Linguistics*, pages 311–318, Philadelphia, Pennsylvania, USA. Association for Computational Linguistics.

Ivandré Paraboni and Kees van Deemter. 2014. Reference and the facilitation of search in spatial domains. *Language, Cognition and Neuroscience*, 29(8):1002–1017.

Adam Pauls and Dan Klein. 2012. Large-scale syntactic language modeling with treelets. In *Proceedings of the 50th Annual Meeting of the Association for Computational Linguistics (Volume 1: Long Papers)*, pages 959–968, Jeju Island, Korea. Association for Computational Linguistics.

Stanley R. Petrick. 1956. A direct determination of the irredundant forms of a boolean function from the set of prime implicants. *Air Force Cambridge Res. Center Tech. Report*, pages 56–110.

Matt Post. 2018. A call for clarity in reporting BLEU scores. In *Proceedings of the Third Conference on Machine Translation: Research Papers*, pages 186–191, Brussels, Belgium. Association for Computational Linguistics.

Willard V. Quine. 1952. The problem of simplifying truth functions. *The American Mathematical Monthly*, 59(8):521–531.

Willard V. Quine. 1955. A way to simplify truth functions. *The American Mathematical Monthly*, 62(9):627–631.

Alec Radford, Jeffrey Wu, Rewon Child, David Luan, Dario Amodei, Ilya Sutskever, et al. 2019. Language models are unsupervised multitask learners. Technical report, OpenAI.

Aarne Ranta. 2011. Translating between language and logic: what is easy and what is difficult. In *Proceedings of the International Conference on Automated Deduction*, pages 5–25. Springer.

Alan Rector, Nick Drummond, Matthew Horridge, Jeremy Rogers, Holger Knublauch, Robert Stevens, Hai Wang, and Chris Wroe. 2004. Owl pizzas: Practical experience of teaching owl-dl: Common errors & common patterns. In *Engineering Knowledge in the Age of the Semantic Web: 14th International Conference, EKAW 2004, Whittlebury Hall, UK, October 5-8, 2004. Proceedings 14*, pages 63–81. Springer.

Nils Reimers and Iryna Gurevych. 2019. Sentence-BERT: Sentence embeddings using Siamese BERT-networks. In *Proceedings of the 2019 Conference on Empirical Methods in Natural Language Processing and the 9th International Joint Conference on Natural Language Processing (EMNLP-IJCNLP)*, pages 3982–3992, Hong Kong, China. Association for Computational Linguistics.

Alexandre Riazanov and Andrei Voronkov. 2002. The design and implementation of vampire. *AI communications*, 15(2-3):91–110.

Samuel Ryb, Mario Giulianelli, Arabella Sinclair, and Raquel Fernández. 2022. AnaLog: Testing analytical and deductive logic learnability in language models. In *Proceedings of the 11th Joint Conference on Lexical and Computational Semantics*, pages 55–68, Seattle, Washington. Association for Computational Linguistics.

Julian Salazar, Davis Liang, Toan Q. Nguyen, and Katrin Kirchhoff. 2020. Masked language model scoring. In *Proceedings of the 58th Annual Meeting of the Association for Computational Linguistics*, pages 2699–2712, Online. Association for Computational Linguistics.

Thibault Sellam, Dipanjan Das, and Ankur Parikh. 2020. BLEURT: Learning robust metrics for text generation. In *Proceedings of the 58th Annual Meeting of the Association for Computational Linguistics*, pages 7881–7892, Online. Association for Computational Linguistics.

Hadar Shemtov. 1996. Generation of paraphrases from ambiguous logical forms. In *COLING 1996 Volume 2: The 16th International Conference on Computational Linguistics*.

Stuart M. Shieber. 1988. A uniform architecture for parsing and generation. In *Coling Budapest 1988 Volume 2: International Conference on Computational Linguistics*.

Stuart M. Shieber. 1993. The problem of logical form equivalence. *Computational Linguistics*, 19(1):179–190.

Stuart M. Shieber, Gertjan van Noord, Robert C. Moore, and Fernando C. N. Pereira. 1989. A semantic-head-driven generation algorithm for unification-based formalisms. In *27th Annual Meeting of the Association for Computational Linguistics*, pages 7–17, Vancouver, British Columbia, Canada. Association for Computational Linguistics.

Ankit Shukla, Armin Biere, Luca Pulina, and Martina Seidl. 2019. A Survey on Applications of Quantified Boolean Formulas. In *2019 IEEE 31st International Conference on Tools with Artificial Intelligence (ICTAI)*, pages 78–84, Portland, OR, USA. IEEE.

Charese Smiley, Elnaz Davoodi, Dezhao Song, and Frank Schilder. 2018. The E2E NLG challenge: A tale of two systems. In *Proceedings of the 11th International Conference on Natural Language Generation*, pages 472–477, Tilburg University, The Netherlands. Association for Computational Linguistics.

Leander Tentrup. 2019. CAQE and QuAbS: Abstraction Based QBF Solvers. *Journal on Satisfiability, Boolean Modeling and Computation*, 11:155–210.

Craig Thomson, Ehud Reiter, and Somayajulu Sripada. 2020. SportSett:basketball - a robust and maintainable data-set for natural language generation. In *Proceedings of the Workshop on Intelligent Information Processing and Natural Language Generation*, pages 32–40, Santiago de Compostela, Spain. Association for Computational Lingustics.

Aaron Traylor, Roman Feiman, and Ellie Pavlick. 2021a. AND does not mean OR: Using formal languages to study language models' representations. In *Proceedings of the 59th Annual Meeting of the Association for Computational Linguistics and the 11th International*

Joint Conference on Natural Language Processing (Volume 2: Short Papers), pages 158–167, Online. Association for Computational Linguistics.

Aaron Traylor, Ellie Pavlick, and Roman Feiman. 2021b. Transferring representations of logical connectives. In *Proceedings of the 1st and 2nd Workshops on Natural Logic Meets Machine Learning (NALOMA)*, pages 22–25, Groningen, the Netherlands (online). Association for Computational Linguistics.

Grigori Samuilovitsch Tseitin. 1983. On the Complexity of Derivation in Propositional Calculus. In Jörg H. Siekmann and Graham Wrightson, editors, *Automation of Reasoning: 2: Classical Papers on Computational Logic 1967–1970*, pages 466–483. Springer Berlin Heidelberg, Berlin, Heidelberg.

Kees Van Deemter. 2016. *Computational models of referring: a study in cognitive science*. MIT Press.

Kees van Deemter and Magnús M. Halldórsson. 2001. Logical form equivalence: the case of referring expressions generation. In *Proceedings of the ACL 2001 Eighth European Workshop on Natural Language Generation (EWNLG)*, Toulouse, France. Association for Computational Linguistics.

Chunliu Wang, Rik van Noord, Arianna Bisazza, and Johan Bos. 2021. Evaluating text generation from discourse representation structures. In *Proceedings of the 1st Workshop on Natural Language Generation, Evaluation, and Metrics (GEM 2021)*, pages 73–83, Online. Association for Computational Linguistics.

Juen-tin Wang. 1980. On computational sentence generation from logical form. In *COLING 1980 Volume 1: The 8th International Conference on Computational Linguistics*.

Sam Wiseman, Stuart Shieber, and Alexander Rush. 2017. Challenges in data-to-document generation. In *Proceedings of the 2017 Conference on Empirical Methods in Natural Language Processing*, pages 2253–2263, Copenhagen, Denmark. Association for Computational Linguistics.

Thomas Wolf, Lysandre Debut, Victor Sanh, Julien Chaumond, Clement Delangue, Anthony Moi, Pierric Cistac, Tim Rault, Remi Louf, Morgan Funtowicz, Joe Davison, Sam Shleifer, Patrick von Platen, Clara Ma, Yacine Jernite, Julien Plu, Canwen Xu, Teven Le Scao, Sylvain Gugger, Mariama Drame, Quentin Lhoest, and Alexander Rush. 2020. Transformers: State-of-the-art natural language processing. In *Proceedings of the 2020 Conference on Empirical Methods in Natural Language Processing: System Demonstrations*, pages 38–45, Online. Association for Computational Linguistics.

Yuk Wah Wong and Raymond Mooney. 2007. Generation by inverting a semantic parser that uses statistical machine translation. In *Human Language Technologies 2007: The Conference of the North American Chapter of the Association for Computational Linguistics; Proceedings of the Main Conference*, pages 172–179, Rochester, New York. Association for Computational Linguistics.

Tianyi Zhang, Varsha Kishore, Felix Wu, Kilian Q Weinberger, and Yoav Artzi. 2020. Bertscore: Evaluating text generation with bert. In *International Conference on Learning Representations*.

A Details on Human Evaluation

We conduct the human evaluation via Prolific.[10] The 42 evaluators we recruit are all native speakers of English and completed at least high school. They are paid £3 for an estimated workload of 20 minutes. Figure 3 presents the instructions provided to the evaluators and an example sentence.

[10] `https://www.prolific.co/`

Thank you very much for participating in this experiment!

It will take approximately 20 minutes to fill in this survey. If you do wish to participate, your response will be handled anonymously: The information in this study will only be used in ways that will not reveal who you are. You will not be identified in any publication from this study or in any data files shared with other researchers. Your participation in this study is confidential. If at any point you would like to stop, you can close this form and your response will be deleted.

I have read the above information and understand the purpose of the research and that data will be collected from me. I agree that data gathered for the study may be published or made available, provided my name or other identifying information is not used.

○ I confirm this.
○ I do not confirm this and I want to withdraw from participation.

The purpose of the experiment is to assess the quality of some automatically generated English sentences concerning geometrical shapes and their properties. We are interested in receiving feedback on (i) comprehensibility (i.e., do you understand precisely the message conveyed by the sentence?), and (ii) fluency (i.e., does the sentence sound natural to you?).

We will present to you 48 sentences, and for each, we would like to know your feedback on the aforementioned aspects. In detail, you will have to answer the following questions:

1. How **comprehensible** is the sentence? By a comprehensible sentence, we mean that it is understandable and does not have multiple interpretations.
2. How **fluent** is the sentence? By a fluent sentence, we mean that it sounds like a natural English sentence and is grammatically correct.

Please, note down the definitions of comprehensibility and fluency, in case you want to refer to them later.

Here's an example:

Sentence:
If it is not the case that c is a cube, then a is a tetrahedron, and if it is not the case that d is a cube, then b is a cube.

Comprehensibility
①②③④⑤⑥⑦
Fluency
①②③④⑤⑥⑦

Why do you think that the sentence is hard to understand?
(In the real questionnaire, this appears only if comprehensibility < 4)
Note: with 'the sentence is ambiguous', we mean 'the sentence has multiple meanings'.

○ The sentence is ambiguous
○ The sentence is too long
○ The language structure is too complex
○ Other: [ ]

Now it is your turn!

Figure 3: The instructions provided to the evaluators during our human evaluation.

Seeking Clozure: Robust Hypernym Extraction from BERT with Anchored Prompts

Chunhua Liu **Trevor Cohn*** **Lea Frermann**
School of Computing and Information Systems
The University of Melbourne
chunhua@student.unimelb.edu.au
{tcohn,lfrermann}@unimelb.edu.au

Abstract

The automatic extraction of hypernym knowledge from large language models like BERT is an open problem, and it is unclear whether methods fail due to a lack of knowledge in the model or shortcomings of the extraction methods. In particular, methods fail on challenging cases which include rare or abstract concepts, and perform inconsistently under paraphrased prompts. In this study, we revisit the long line of work on pattern-based hypernym extraction, and use it as a diagnostic tool to thoroughly examine the hypernomy knowledge encoded in BERT and the limitations of hypernym extraction methods. We propose to construct prompts from established pattern structures: definitional (*X is a Y*); lexico-syntactic (*Y such as X*); and their anchored versions (*Y such as X or Z*). We devise an automatic method for anchor prediction, and compare different patterns in: (i) their effectiveness for hypernym retrieval from BERT across six English data sets; (ii) on challenge sets of rare and abstract concepts; and (iii) on consistency under paraphrasing. We show that anchoring is particularly useful for abstract concepts and in enhancing consistency across paraphrases, demonstrating how established methods in the field can inform prompt engineering.[1]

1 Introduction

Semantic relations play a central role in knowledge representation (Miller, 1995) and taxonomy construction (Snow et al., 2006; Navigli et al., 2011). As the backbone of semantic relations, hyponymy/hypernymy relations express a hierarchical relation between a specific concept (the hyponym; e.g., dog) and a general one (the hypernym; e.g., mammal), and form the foundation of human concept understanding (Yu et al., 2015) and relation reasoning (Lyons, 1977; Green et al.,

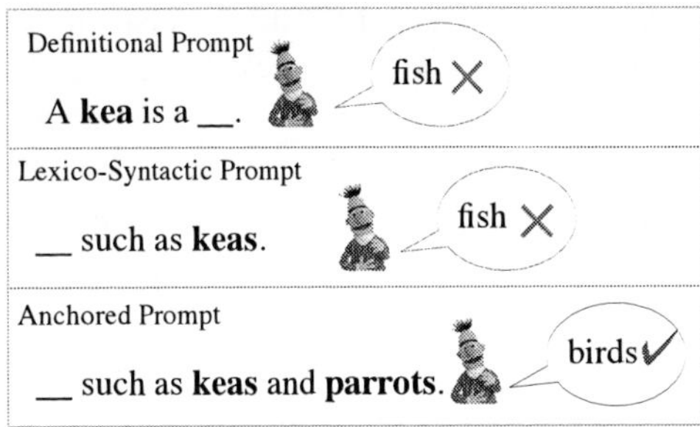

Figure 1: Example prompts for hypernym prediction, derived from established pattern structures.

2002). Given its fundamental role, the automatic extraction of hypernym knowledge from large texts (Hearst, 1992; Roller et al., 2018) or pre-trained language models (PLMs) (Takeoka et al., 2021; Jain and Espinosa Anke, 2022), and its injection into NLP methods are active areas of research (Peters et al., 2019).

The unsupervised extraction of hypernyms from PLMs by prompting has attracted recent attention, e.g., using patterns like *A dog is a type of [MASK]* and retrieving the most likely filler words from the model (Ettinger, 2020; Weir et al., 2020; Jain and Espinosa Anke, 2022). Results were mixed: while PLMs can reliably predict hypernyms of concrete and frequent hyponyms (Ettinger, 2020; Weir et al., 2020), experiments on more challenging data sets show a quick deterioration in the face of rare concepts (Schick and Schütze, 2019), and a lack of response consistency across paraphrased prompts (Ravichander et al., 2020; Elazar et al., 2021). How to alleviate these issues and extract more reliable hypernyms from PLMs remain open questions.

In this paper, we draw connections between prompting for hypernyms and pattern-based hypernym extraction (Hearst, 1992; Snow et al., 2004) (see Figure 1 and Table 1). We systematically investigate the utility of different styles of patterns as BERT prompts, and use them as diagnostic tools

*Now at Google DeepMind.

[1]Code and test sets are available at https://github.com/ChunhuaLiu596/AnchoredPrompts

*Proceedings of the The 12th Joint Conference on Lexical and Computational Semantics (*SEM 2023)*, pages 193–206
July 13-14, 2023 ©2023 Association for Computational Linguistics

to better understand the conditions under which probing for hypernyms is effective and consistent.

Pattern-based hypernym extraction from raw text has a long history, starting from Hearst (1992)'s seminal work which promotes lexico-syntactic patterns (*Y such as X*)[2] as more effective than definitional patterns (*X is a type of Y*). Follow-up work (Hovy et al., 2009) incorporated a co-hyponym, a concept that shares a hypernym with X, into the pattern (*Y such as X and Z*) to provide additional context signals. Figure 1 illustrates this, where the anchor *parrot* provides additional information to facilitate the prediction of the correct hypernym of *kea*. This method of 'anchoring' has been shown to improve the quality of automatically extracted hypernym knowledge. We apply these established patterns from the hypernym extraction literature in the context of language model prompting, and systematically study the existence and gaps of hyponym/hypernym knowledge in BERT. We conduct experiments on six English data sets and address three questions:

How to effectively construct anchored prompts? We devise a scalable method to automatically retrieve high-quality anchors (co-hyponyms) to construct anchored prompts. Anchors are mined from PLMs with established co-hyponym patterns (e.g., *such as X and ___*) and evaluated with WordNet (Miller, 1995).

How do different pattern structures compare as prompts under different data conditions? We ground our prompts in hypernym patterns from which have been successfully used to mine hypernyms from raw corpora, and investigate their effectiveness for zero-shot PLM hypernym retrieval. We find strong, consistent benefits of anchored prompts, particularly for rare or abstract concepts.

Robust extraction of hypernym knowledge. Much recent work has shown that PLM prompting results are brittle under prompt paraphrases, calling into question whether prompting surfaces robust knowledge encoded in the PLMs or rather superficial associations. We compare the robustness of different patterns under paraphrasing, and find, again, a benefit of anchored prompts for retrieving more consistently correct hypernyms.

In summary, we contribute to the on-going research on hypernym extraction by unifying the long-standing work of pattern-based and prompt-based approaches, demonstrating that anchoring prompts can unlock a wealth of hidden knowledge within BERT, and providing a framework of automatic construction of anchoring prompts.

`DFP`	A(n) X is a Y. A(n) X is a type of Y. A(n) X is a kind Y.	`DFP`$^{+A}$	A(n) X or Z is a Y. A(n) X or Z is a type of Y. A(n) X or Z is a kind Y.
`LSP`	Y such as X. Y, including X. Y, especially X. X or other Y. X and other Y. such Y as X.	`LSP`$^{+A}$	Y such as X and Z. Y, including X and Z. Y, especially X and Z. X, Z or other Y. X, Z and other Y. such Y as X and Z.

Table 1: Four types of pattern structures: definitional patterns (`DFP`; top) and lexico-syntactic patterns (`LSP`; bottom); and their anchored versions: `DFP`$^{+A}$ and `LSP`$^{+A}$ (right).

2 Background

We introduce the two approaches for hypernym extraction on which we build in this paper: pattern-based (§ 2.1) and prompting PLMs (§ 2.2).

2.1 Pattern-based Hypernym Extraction

The pattern-based approach applies hyponym-hypernym patterns to large corpora to extract hypernyms. Two widely-used pattern structures have been identified: lexico-syntactic and definitional.

2.1.1 Lexico-Syntactic Patterns (`LSP`)

Lexico-syntactic patterns (`LSP`; Table 1 bottom left) were first introduced by Hearst (1992) and have since been used to mine hyponym-hypernym pairs or build ontologies from large corpora (Pasca, 2004; Pantel and Pennacchiotti, 2006; Etzioni et al., 2005; Roller et al., 2018). The six `LSP` (1) all indicate the hyponym-hypernym relation with explicit signals (e.g., *such as, especially*), (2) frequently occur in text, and (3) are applicable to nouns or noun-phrases.

Anchored `LSP` (`LSP`$^{+A}$) Hovy et al. (2009) proposed an 'anchored' version of `LSP` to mine hypernyms (`LSP`$^{+A}$)[3] which uses patterns like *Y such as X and Z*, where Z is an anchor which reduces ambiguity and assists the extraction of Y (Table 1, bottom right). A similar idea of using anchors to improve hypernym classifiers is used in Snow et al. (2004) and Bernier-Colborne and Barrière (2018). `LSP`$^{+A}$ has been shown to be effective at extracting reliable hypernyms from text corpora, however,

[2]We use Y to denote hypernyms, X for hyponyms and Z for the co-hyponym of X.

[3]`LSP`$^{+A}$ is referred to as `DAP`$^{-1}$ in the original paper.

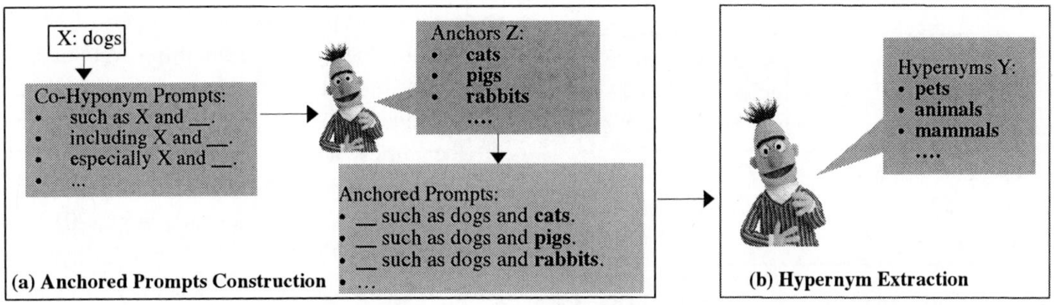

Figure 2: The workflow of constructing anchored prompts (a) and extracting hypernyms from PLMs (b).

like all pattern-based approaches, it suffers from low recall because it needs X, Y and Z to co-occur. The sparsity issue can be potentially remedied by using embeddings from PLMs to represent X and Z when used as prompts. However, this hasn't been studied in the context of extracting knowledge from PLMs. Inspired by this line of work and PLM prompting, we use $\texttt{LSP}^{+A}$ to mine hypernyms from PLMs and examine the benefit of anchors.

2.1.2 Definitional Patterns (DFP)

In contrast to LSP that conveys the hypernym relation implicitly, definitional Patterns (DFP; Table 1 top left) explicitly define an *Is-A* relation between X and Y (Lyons, 1977). A common use of DFP is to mine sentences for definition extraction (Borg et al., 2009; Navigli et al., 2010) or ontology/dictionary building (Muresan and Klavans, 2002). Recently, DFP has been widely used in prompting studies (Schick and Schütze, 2020; Ettinger, 2020; Ravichander et al., 2020; Hanna and Mareček, 2021) to probe hypernym knowledge in PLMs.

Anchored DFP ($\texttt{DFP}^{+A}$) Analogous to $\texttt{LSP}^{+A}$, we augment DFP with anchors for disambiguation (Table 1 top right). To the best of our knowledge, Hanna and Mareček (2021) is the only work which uses anchored definitional patterns to prompt PLMs for hypernyms, described in more detail below.

2.2 Prompting-based Hypernym Extraction

With recent advances in PLMs, increasingly rich knowledge is captured language models. A stream of research aims at automatically extracting this knowledge, e.g., by probing PLMs for hypernym knowledge (Ettinger, 2020; Weir et al., 2020; Peng et al., 2022). Hanna and Mareček (2021) examined the effects of single hypernym patterns (e.g., *'X is a Y'*, *'A Y such as X'*) on prompting PLMs and showed that performance varies with patterns. Similarly, Ravichander et al. (2020) found that PLMs fail to retrieve consistent knowledge over prompts paraphrased with singular vs plural hyponyms.

Most previous work on prompting was conducted under relatively simple conditions with one pattern structure and a single data set. We systematically investigate the effects of well-established patterns (LSP/$\texttt{LSP}^{+A}$ and DFP/$\texttt{DFP}^{+A}$) on extracting hypernyms across six widely-used datasets and paint a more nuanced picture of hypernym knowledge in BERT by explicitly studying the challenging cases of rare or abstract concepts.

3 Anchored Prompts

We now introduce our framework of extracting hypernyms from a PLM by constructing sets of prompts given a hyponym X and a pattern type $\in \{\texttt{DFP}, \texttt{DFP}^{+A}, \texttt{LSP}, \texttt{LSP}^{+A}\}$. We illustrate the workflow in Figure 2, with $\texttt{LSP}^{+A}$ as an example.

Prompt Construction For each pattern type, we construct a set of prompts by instantiating each of its assigned patterns (cells in Table 1) with a concept in positions X and Z, and a [MASK] token in position Y. For DFP and LSP we can construct prompt sets directly given a hyponym X of interest. To construct prompts for $\texttt{LSP}^{+A}$ and $\texttt{DFP}^{+A}$ we need to additionally provide meaningful anchors Z. We next describe a way to effectively mine such anchors from language models (see Figure 2 (a)).

Anchor Extraction Given X, we use BERT to automatically extract a set of anchors, i.e., concepts Z that share a hypernym with X. To acquire such anchors, we again adopt a set of established lexico-syntactic patterns that indicate the fact that X and Z share a common hypernym (Hearst, 1992; Snow et al., 2004; Etzioni et al., 2005). Table 2 presents the full list of patterns we used to mine

such as X and Z.	including X and Z.
such as X or Z.	including X or Z.
such as X, Z,	including X, Z,
especially X and Z.	X, Z or other
especially X or Z.	X, Z and other
especially X, Z,	

Table 2: Co-hyponym patterns for anchor extraction, adapted from Hearst (1992).

anchors. Each pattern is converted into a prompt by filling in X and replacing Z with a [MASK] token, resulting in a set of co-hyponyms prompts $\mathcal{C}$. We retrieve the 10 most likely filler words according to language model probability for each pattern $\mathcal{C}_i \in \mathcal{C}$. We score candidates z by their average probability across the patterns that contained z among the top 10 fillers:

$$s_{LM}(z|x, \mathcal{C}) = \frac{1}{|\mathcal{C}_z|} \sum_{i=1}^{|\mathcal{C}|} P_{LM}(z|x, \mathcal{C}_i), \quad (1)$$

where $P_{LM}(z|x, \mathcal{C})$ is the probability of z in the ith pattern instantiated with x and $|\mathcal{C}_z|$ is the number of patterns that predicted z. We finally keep the M highest scoring concepts as anchors, and instantiate M copies of $\texttt{LSP}^{+A}$ and $\texttt{DFP}^{+A}$ with the different anchors, respectively.

Hypernym Extraction Being able to construct sets of prompts for vanilla ($\mathcal{P}_{\texttt{DFP}}, \mathcal{P}_{\texttt{LSP}}$) and anchored prompts ($\mathcal{P}_{\texttt{DFP}^{+A}}, \mathcal{P}_{\texttt{LSP}^{+A}}$), we are now in a position to prompt PLMs for hypernyms. Separately for each prompt set $\mathcal{P}$,[4] we score hypernym candidates y by their average probability across patterns $\mathcal{P}_i \in \mathcal{P}$:

$$s_{LM}(y|x, \mathcal{P}) = \frac{1}{|\mathcal{P}|} \sum_{i=1}^{|\mathcal{P}|} \log P_{LM}(y|x, \mathcal{P}_i), \quad (2)$$

where $\mathcal{P} = \{\mathcal{P}_{\texttt{LSP}}, \mathcal{P}_{\texttt{DFP}}, \mathcal{P}_{\texttt{LSP}^{+A}}, \mathcal{P}_{\texttt{DFP}^{+A}}\}$. The hypernyms ranked by $s_{LM}(y|x, \mathcal{P})$ and the top K are retained as hypernym candidates.

4 Experimental Setup

Datasets We conduct experiments on six English datasets. CLSB (Devereux et al., 2014) and DIAG (Ravichander et al., 2020) have been recently used to probe for hypernym knowledge in PLMs (Devlin et al., 2019). The remaining four data sets are widely-used test sets for hypernym extraction more generally (Shwartz et al., 2017; Roller et al., 2018), namely BLESS (Baroni and Lenci, 2011), EVAL (Santus et al., 2015), LEDS (Baroni et al., 2012), and SHWARTZ (Shwartz et al., 2017). We only consider NOUN-NOUN hyponym-hypernym pairs from the datasets. Dataset statistics are reported in Table 9 in the Appendix. Data sets vary widely in terms of their corpus size, the ratio of abstractness and concreteness, concept frequency and their construction methods, and hence underlying knowledge sources. While most data sets are based on WordNet, SHWARTZ builds on a wider set of resources, including ConceptNet and Wikipedia and hence includes more obscure concepts. EVAL stands out with a relatively high proportion of abstract concepts, unlike the other data sets which are predominantly concrete. Section 6 explores performance using these data conditions.

Model All our experiments are based on BERT-large-uncased (Devlin et al., 2019) from Huggingface[5] and use a zero-shot approach to probe the model. To allow for comparability of results across data sets, we adopt an *open vocabulary* approach throughout, considering the whole BERT vocabulary as hypernym candidates.[6] We remove test instances where the hypernym is not in the BERT vocabulary.[7] We set the number of anchors in anchored prompts to $M = 5$.[8]

Evaluation Metrics Following previous work (Petroni et al., 2019; Qin and Eisner, 2021), we retain the K=10 hypernym candidates and report Precision at 10 (P@10) as the extent to which correct hypernyms are included in the top 10 model predictions ranked by Equation 2. We also report mean reciprocal rank (MRR) of the true label. We evaluate model predictions at the *concept level*, normalizing predictions into their canonical form, i.e., accepting any inflection of the correct hypernym,[9] and exclude punctuation, stop words, numbers and the hyponym x from the predictions.

[4] We drop subscripts to avoid clutter.

[5] `https://huggingface.co/bert-large-uncased`

[6] Prior work (Ravichander et al., 2020) adopted a *closed-vocabulary* approach, limiting the set of candidate y to hypernyms in a particular data set.

[7] Note that there is no such restriction on hyponyms so that results in § 6.2 are not biased.

[8] This number was optimized on BLESS.

[9] We used pyinflect 0.5.1.

Dataset	MRR	P@1	P@5	P@10
BLESS	73.9	66.0	86.6	89.6
DIAG	34.9	28.6	43.8	48.8
CLSB	60.3	51.2	73.2	77.7
SHWARTZ	23.7	16.8	33.1	39.8
EVAL	33.6	26.1	44.1	49.4
LEDS	45.8	35.7	59.7	66.3

Table 3: Anchor evaluation results, where predicted anchors z for a concept x are validated by checking whether x and z share a hypernym in WordNet.

x	Top 5 predicted anchors ($\mathcal{Z}$)
car	**truck**, **motorcycle**, **boat**, yes, **bike**
apple	**grape**, **pear**, nuts, vegetable, **date**
train	**bus**, plane, **car**, **tram**, **truck**
corn	bean, potato, **barley**, **wheat**, pea
panzer	**tank**, infantry, gun, artillery, panther
motel	hotel, yes, sure, restaurant, actually
daisy	rose, yes, lavender, rush, fern
murre	dog, bird, fox, crow, rabbit
trireme	warship, frigate, ship, ferry, battleship

Table 4: Examples of mined anchors ($\mathcal{Z}$) for hyponyms that share ≥ 1 (top) or zero (bottom) co-hyponyms with WordNet. Anchors confirmed in WordNet in bold.

We measure the significance of differences with paired t-tests at $p<0.05$ after Holm-Bonferroni correction for multiple comparisons to adjust for comparisons across six data sets (Dror et al., 2017).

Analyses In addition to the main results, we aim to understand underlying factors that might affect the performance of hypernym extraction. We analyse the performance of pattern types on different types of concepts. We distinguish sets of hyponyms and hypernyms in terms of their frequency and abstractness and test consistency of predictions across prompt paraphrases.

5 Anchor Validation

How accurate are the automatically mined anchors? We qualitatively and quantitatively inspect retrieved anchor concepts. We use WordNet for this purpose, and follow Schick and Schütze (2020) to consider a candidate z to be a valid anchor of x if they share a common ancestor, within two levels above x and four levels above z. We exclude hyponyms that are not in WordNet in this analysis.

Table 3 reports the results across six datasets. For three of the data sets (BLESS, CLSB, LEDS), a correct anchor is predicted as top 1 result more than 33% of the time, and contained among the top 10 predictions we consider close to 70% of the time. The other data sets are overall challenging due to diversity and/or low frequency of concepts.

Qualitative inspection reveals that retrieved anchors that are not WordNet siblings according to our definition above are often reasonable, see Table 4. As we shall see in Section 6 the utility of anchors does not seem to hinge on them being actual co-hyponyms, and that the topically related anchors as produced by our method effectively improve hypernym extraction.

6 Hypernym Evaluation

We first examine the effectiveness of `LSP` vs `DFP` and the added value of anchoring on our six data sets overall (§ 6.1). Afterwards, we inspect specifically rare (§ 6.2) and abstract (§ 6.3) concepts as well as the well-known issue of inconsistency of responses in the face of prompt paraphrases (§ 6.4), explore different patterns in these contexts and end with an error analysis (§ 6.5).

6.1 Main Results

Table 5 presents the main results. Performance over datasets varies widely, with SCHWARTZ standing out with particularly low performance. SHWARTZ is dominated by proper noun hyponyms (e.g., city/person names), and includes a very broad range of hypernyms (1.1K). Performance on the other data sets are more comparable.

Do `LSP` *and* `DFP` *differ?* Comparing row one (`DFP`) and three (`LSP`) in Table 5, we see no consistent trend. While performance is often comparable, on BLESS `LSP` outperforms `DFP`. The reverse is true for EVAL. BLESS contains frequent and largely unambiguous hyponyms which are presumably more frequently discussed in natural patterns as comprised by `LSP`. EVAL is dominated by ambiguous and abstract concepts, which are perhaps more commonly described by formal, definition-style language.

Do anchors help retrieve more accurate hypernym knowledge? Table 5 reveals a consistent improvement of adding anchors for `DFP` (row 1 vs. 2) but not for `LSP` (row 3 vs. 4): definitional patterns benefit from anchoring via co-hyponyms

	BLESS		DIAG		CLSB		SHWARTZ		EVAL		LEDS	
	MRR	P@10	MRR	P@10	MRR	P@10	MRR	P@10	MRR	P@10	MRR	P@10
DFP	23.6	42.4	42.6	66.8	39.8	67.5	6.3	12.8	**24.0**	**46.7**	32.6	60.1
DFP^{+A}	25.7^{+}	47.2^{+}	**45.5^{+}**	**67.2^{+}**	**42.3^{+}**	**70.5^{+}**	5.9^{+}	13.6^{+}	22.1^{+}	43.3^{+}	**35.7^{+}**	**64.3^{+}**
LSP	**27.1^{*}**	**53.9^{*}**	**45.5**	66.1	40.8	68.2	6.4	**15.2^{*}**	17.3^{*}	39.5^{*}	33.4	60.5
LSP^{+A}	26.5	53.2	42.8^{+}	62.7	40.4	67.7	**6.5**	14.9	17.0	38.1	34.0	61.6

Table 5: Main results on six hypernym extraction datasets. Bold number indicates the highest score per data set and metric. * indicates significant difference of LSP vs. DFP; + indicates significant difference wrt. the non-anchored counterpart (i.e., LSP vs LSP^{+A} and DFP vs. DFP^{+A}).

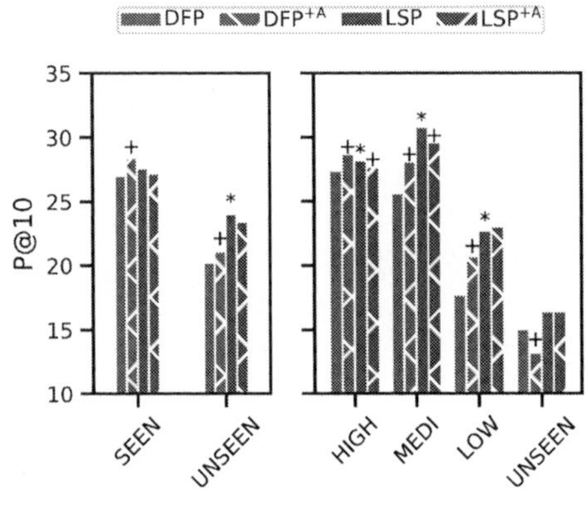

Figure 3: Performance of different pattern structures rare vs common hyponyms. Left: hyponyms seen in BERT vocabulary and not. Right: hyponyms frequency of different frequency bands estimated from large corpora. + and * as in Table 5.

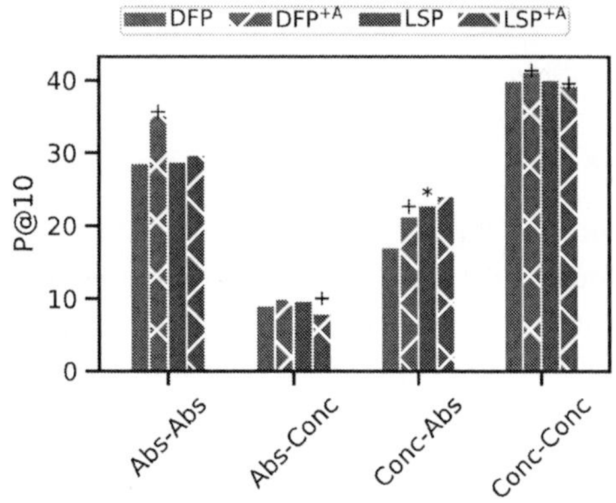

Figure 4: Performance of different pattern structures on: abstract hypo- and hypernym (Abs-Abs); abstract hypo- concrete hypernym (Abs-Conc); concrete hypo- abstract hypernym (Conc-Abs); and concrete hypo- and hypernym (Conc-Conc). + and * as in Table 5.

while lexico-syntactic patterns don't.[10]

Next, in §6.2-§6.4 we disentangle the main results, considering a range of conditions which have been identified as challenging in prior work, and examine whether different patterns and/or anchoring can improve hypernym retrieval from BERT in these contexts.

6.2 The Impact of Frequency

Previous work (Ravichander et al., 2020; Hanna and Mareček, 2021; Schick and Schütze, 2020) found that *BERT often fails to predict hypernyms for uncommon hyponyms.* Here, we examine whether incorporating anchors can alleviate this issue. This is driven by the intuition that humans often draw on surrounding context signals to help understand the relationship between concepts. For example, even if we are unfamiliar with the concept of *kea*, knowing an anchor like *parrot* can help us infer that *bird* is one of the hypernyms. We expect that anchors can provide more linking context to the hypernym and improve the hypernym extraction performance when the hyponyms are rare. To verify this, we look into two aspects that reflect frequency: (a) existence in the BERT vocabulary - hyponyms that are included as single-tokens are frequent; (b) frequency in large corpora. We obtain term frequency from WorldLex (Gimenes and New, 2016) and categorize frequency into four levels based on absolute count: High (> 100), Medium (10-100), Low (1-10), and Unseen (0). For this analysis, we aggregate instances from all datasets to increase statistical power.

Figure 3 presents experimental results. We find that rare hyponyms have lower performance in general, aligning with previous work (Ravichander et al., 2020; Hanna and Mareček, 2021). More in-

[10]We estimate the upper-bound of anchoring prompts with oracle anchors from WordNet, finding that better anchors can bring more benefits (see Table 10 in the Appendix).

x	DFP Predictions	DFP^{+A} Predictions	Top 5 predicted anchors ($\mathcal{Z}$)
terebinth	stone, sculpture, rock	**tree**, plant, sculpture	fern, shell, plant, shrub, tree
dray	boat, machine, tool	**vehicle**, cart, wagon	wagon, tractor, cart, horse, yes
gannet	computer, net, network	**bird**, fish, dolphin	seal, dolphin, herr, whale, penguin
happiness	joy, life, pleasure	joy, feeling, **emotion**	love, joy, good, personal, maybe
principle	rule, law, concept	rule, law, **value**	practice, rule, procedure, guideline, value
snoopy	toy, pigeon, mouse	toy, puppet, **character**	peanut, snoop, batman, garfield, cartoon

Table 6: Examples of rare (top) and abstract (bottom) hyponyms x, along with their predicted hypernyms from DFP and DFP^{+A}, and predicted anchors. Correct hypernyms are in **bold**.

	Singular Probes	Plural Probes	BLESS	DIAG	CLSB	SHWARTZ	EVAL	LEDS
DFP	A(n) X is a(n) Y.	X are Y.	2.7	4.5	3.5	0.4	1.7	4.8
DFP^{+A}	A(n) X or Z is a(n) Y.	X or Z are Y.	0.2	2.3	0.3	0.0^{+}	0.1	0.6
LSP	Y such as a(n) X.	Y such as X.	**51.2**	46.0	60.9	4.4	26.2	40.6
LSP^{+A}	Y such as a(n) X or Z.	Y such as X or Z.	**51.2**	**51.6**$^{+}$	**65.0**$^{+}$	**10.4**$^{+}$	**32.5**$^{+}$	**52.5**$^{+}$

Table 7: Experimental results (P@10) on pairwise number consistency. X/Z in singular probes are instantiated as singular (e.g., car), and in plural probes as plural (e.g., cars). $^{+}$ as in Table 5.

	BLESS	DIAG	CLSB	SHWARTZ	EVAL	LEDS
DFP	21.9	42.5	44.7	4.6	23.7	34.3
DFP^{+A}	**31.7**$^{+}$	**49.0**	**53.8**$^{+}$	**8.3**$^{+}$	**28.3**$^{+}$	**42.2**$^{+}$
LSP	26.8	32.8	45.8	2.6	10.2	29.0
LSP^{+A}	**31.7**$^{+}$	**39.9**$^{+}$	**52.5**$^{+}$	**4.7**$^{+}$	**13.3**$^{+}$	**36.1**$^{+}$

Table 8: Experimental results (P@10) on group consistency. $^{+}$ as in Table 5.

terestingly, unlike in the main results, LSP exhibits a significant advantage over DFP on unseen and low frequency hyponyms (solid bars in UNSEEN and LOW blocks in Figure 3). Moreover, on the same blocks, we see that incorporating anchors into DFP significantly improves the performance on low frequent hyponyms (solid gray vs dashed gray). This confirms our hypothesis that anchors are beneficial for uncommon hyponyms by guiding BERT to predict hypernyms (see examples in Table 6). This is of practical relevance as it demonstrates that anchored prompts help for uncommon hyponyms, which can inform hypernym extraction in domain-specific or low-resources situations.

6.3 The Impact of Concreteness

Previous work on distributional semantics has shown that abstract words have higher contextual variability and are more difficult to predict than concrete concepts (Naumann et al., 2018). Here, we examine specifically whether the degree of concept abstractness affects hypernym extraction accuracy, as well as the impact of different patterns and anchoring in this context. To obtain the concept concreteness level, we use the Brysbaert dataset (Brysbaert et al., 2014),[11] which covers abstractness ratings for 40K common English concepts. Each concept was scored by at least 25 human annotators on a scale from 1 (most abstract) to 5 (most concrete). We use the median score to represent the abstractness of each word and bin them into Abstract (<3) and Concrete (≥ 3). We inspect all four possible combinations of {concrete, abstract} $\times$ {hypernym, hyponym}, and again aggregate instances across data sets.

Figure 4 shows that hypernyms of hyponyms at same abstraction levels (e.g., Conc–Conc) are predicted with higher accuracy than those under different levels (e.g., Abs-Conc). This result is intuitive as words in same abstraction level tend to co-occur more (Bhaskar et al., 2017; Frassinelli et al., 2017). Overall, concrete hyponym-hypernym pairs are predicted with higher accuracy than pairs involving an abstract concept, indicating that abstract knowledge is more difficult to retrieve from BERT. More interestingly, we find that DFP^{+A} brings remarkable improvements on abstract hypernyms, effectively reducing the gap between abstract and concrete hypernyms. A closer look at abstract hypernyms that failed with DFP but succeed on anchored prompts reveals failure on abstract hypernyms such as {*emotion, organization, language, event*}. For example, for the prompt *excitement is a* ___ BERT predicts {*thrill, fear, rush*}. However, by incorporating anchors like *surprise* or *anxiety*, BERT predicts the

[11]We exclude hyponyms and hypernyms that are not in the Brysbaert dataset.

correct hypernym *emotion*. This finding is encouraging because it points to the weakness of using hyponyms alone to prompt PLMs for abstract hypernyms and can potentially inform future work on prompt design for retrieving specific types of knowledge (e.g., concrete or abstract) and building ontologies.

6.4 Consistency

Despite the success of prompting, a persistent challenge is an inconsistency of responses under slight rephrasing of the prompt (Elazar et al., 2021). In the context of hypernomy prediction, Ravichander et al. (2020) showed that compared to singular prompts (*a car is a* ___.), plural versions (*cars are* ___.) returned different and worse results. We study consistency more systematically by including different paraphrases, and exploring the utility of anchoring on the robustness of results. We investigate: (a) consistency across prompts paraphrased with singular and plural hyponyms; and (b) consistency over prompts paraphrased with pattern type instantiations (cells in Table 1). We only score the prediction for a test instance as correct, if it was correctly predicted by *all* prompt paraphrases.

Pairwise Number Consistency Following Ravichander et al. (2020), we construct pairwise probes for singular and plural hyponyms, obtaining one representative pair for each of our four pattern types as listed in Table 7 (left). The results in Table 7 show that consistency strongly correlates with the choice of patterns: `DFP` prompts (row 1) produce inconsistent results, while `LSP` (row 3) shows strong potential for retrieving consistent knowledge. One reason is ambiguity in the plural `DFP`: the prompt *Xs are [MASK]* tends to return verbs and adjectives as candidates (e.g., *carrots are {grown, eaten, orange}.*), as plausible completions. In contrast, `LSP` contexts are more specific. Moreover, the consistency improves significantly for all but one data set when incorporating the anchors into `LSP`.[12] This finding is important as it identifies a promising means of retrieving consistent knowledge from PLMs.

Group Consistency Our sets of pattern-type specific prompts suggest a natural, stricter consistency evaluation, namely to test whether BERT reliably predicts the same, true hypernym for all prompts associated with a pattern type (i.e, each of the cells of Table 1). Table 8 presents the results. What stands out in the table is that anchored prompts significantly improve group consistency, which aligns with our observation in the pairwise number consistency tests above. In summary, our results show that anchors, in particular $\texttt{LSP}^{+A}$, can help retrieve more robust and consistent hypernyms from PLMs. This is not only important for downstream tasks which rely on (automatic) high-quality hypernym knowledge, such as taxonomy creation, but could also inform strategies to probe BERT for genuine, systematic knowledge, rather than superficial associations.

6.5 Error Analysis

When does anchoring hurt? Beyond benefits from anchors, we also observed that incorporating anchors at times degrades performance. Closer inspection identified **sense ambiguity** as a prevalent reason, especially for polysemous hyponyms, which have multiple hypernyms of different senses (e.g., fan is a person or an appliance.) With anchors, BERT predictions are skewed to a specific sense as selected by the anchor, which can be different from the true hypernym. Another situation is noisy anchors, including generic and irrelevant anchors (e.g., actually), or topically related anchors that are not co-hyponyms (e.g., wood and lake).

How do anchors improve consistency? We analyse hypernyms that are not consistently predicted correctly without anchors but are correct with anchors. There are three reasons for the inconsistency: (a) overly generic predictions from non-anchored patterns, e.g., *Y, especially X* often produces hypernyms like *things* or *items*; (b) predictions of co-hyponyms instead of hypernyms without anchors (*e.g., a dog is a cat.*), which is especially common with pattern *A X is a Y*, for which 30% of its predictions contain co-hyponyms from WordNet; (c) hypernyms in the intermediate levels of the WordNet taxonomy (e.g., garment, jewelry, sweet) are less consistent for patterns without anchors, e.g., anchors improve consistency by 11% for hypernyms whose minimum taxonomy depth is 7.[13] This suggests that anchors can improve the consistency of mining new intermediate hypernyms from PLMs, aligning with prior work of using anchors to mine intermediate hypernyms from corpora (Hovy

[12]Indeed, when comparing against the less strict evaluation in Table 5, $\texttt{LSP}^{+A}$ incurs the smallest performance drop.

[13]Table 12 in the Appendix lists the consistency of all depths.

et al., 2009).

7 Conclusion

In this work, we bridge two powerful techniques in hypernym extraction: the pattern-based and prompt-based approach and use them as a diagnose tool to probe knowledge in BERT. We provide a thorough study of how patterns from the corpus-mining literature can be used to probe neural models. We find that `LSP` and `DFP` exhibit similar capacities, while anchored patterns bring consistent and significant benefits, suggesting a way to overcome challenging scenarios. In particular, we demonstrated clear benefits for rare hyponyms and abstract hypernyms, and an increase in the reliability of retrieved hypernyms under paraphrased prompts. This finding can direct future work on prompt design to extract robust and consistent hypernyms knowledge. The idea of anchoring prompts can be extended to other semantic relations such as part-of and synonyms to advance taxonomy induction and knowledge graph construction.

8 Limitations

Effectiveness beyond noun-noun concepts: we apply our method to hyponym-hypernym pairs over nouns in the general domain. This idea of anchored prompts can also be extended mine hypernyms for other parts-of-speech using patterns developed for text corpora (Chklovski and Pantel, 2004; Kozareva, 2014), as well as semantic relations beyond hyponyms-hyponyms, e.g., Part-Whole (Girju et al., 2003). We leave this exploration for future work.

Time efficiency vs performance boost: incorporating anchors boost the performance for hypernym extraction, however, we also need to consider that the performance improvements comes with additional time cost. Querying with anchored prompts require more computation when multiple anchors are used, although runtimes for the experiments in the paper are all very low.

Hypernym diversity: current work on extracting hypernyms with BERT predominantly considers single-word hypernyms and does not consider multi-word hypernyms or hypernyms that are not in the BERT vocabulary. Our work is no exception.

Language diversity: Most work in both hypernymy retrieval as well as language model prompting focuses on English, and as a consequence there is a lack of data sets in other languages. The extension of technologies to less well-resourced languages is a pressing direction for future research.

Scale of Language Models We focus on comparing different pattern structures with a single model, BERT-large. The behaviours of patterns under larger language models such as GPT3 (Brown et al., 2020) remains to be examined (Wei et al., 2022).

References

Marco Baroni, Raffaella Bernardi, Ngoc-Quynh Do, and Chung-chieh Shan. 2012. Entailment above the word level in distributional semantics. In *Proceedings of the 13th Conference of the European Chapter of the Association for Computational Linguistics*, pages 23–32, Avignon, France. Association for Computational Linguistics.

Marco Baroni and Alessandro Lenci. 2011. How we blessed distributional semantic evaluation. In *Proceedings of the GEMS 2011 Workshop on GEometrical Models of Natural Language Semantics*, page 1–10. Association for Computational Linguistics.

Gabriel Bernier-Colborne and Caroline Barrière. 2018. CRIM at SemEval-2018 task 9: A hybrid approach to hypernym discovery. In *Proceedings of the 12th International Workshop on Semantic Evaluation*, pages 725–731, New Orleans, Louisiana. Association for Computational Linguistics.

Sai Abishek Bhaskar, Maximilian Köper, Sabine Schulte Im Walde, and Diego Frassinelli. 2017. Exploring multi-modal Text+Image models to distinguish between abstract and concrete nouns. In *Proceedings of the IWCS workshop on Foundations of Situated and Multimodal Communication*.

Claudia Borg, Mike Rosner, and Gordon Pace. 2009. Evolutionary algorithms for definition extraction. In *Proceedings of the 1st Workshop on Definition Extraction*, pages 26–32, Borovets, Bulgaria. Association for Computational Linguistics.

Tom Brown, Benjamin Mann, Nick Ryder, Melanie Subbiah, Jared D Kaplan, Prafulla Dhariwal, Arvind Neelakantan, Pranav Shyam, Girish Sastry, Amanda Askell, Sandhini Agarwal, Ariel Herbert-Voss, Gretchen Krueger, Tom Henighan, Rewon Child, Aditya Ramesh, Daniel Ziegler, Jeffrey Wu, Clemens Winter, Chris Hesse, Mark Chen, Eric Sigler, Mateusz Litwin, Scott Gray, Benjamin Chess, Jack Clark, Christopher Berner, Sam McCandlish, Alec Radford, Ilya Sutskever, and Dario Amodei. 2020. Language models are few-shot learners. In *Advances in Neural Information Processing Systems*, volume 33, pages 1877–1901. Curran Associates, Inc.

Marc Brysbaert, Amy Beth Warriner, and Victor Kuperman. 2014. Concreteness ratings for 40 thousand generally known english word lemmas. *Behavior Research Methods*, 46:904–911.

Timothy Chklovski and Patrick Pantel. 2004. VerbOcean: Mining the web for fine-grained semantic verb relations. In *Proceedings of the 2004 Conference on Empirical Methods in Natural Language Processing*, pages 33–40, Barcelona, Spain. Association for Computational Linguistics.

Barry Devereux, Lorraine K. Tyler, Jeroen Geertzen, and Billi Randall. 2014. The centre for speech, language and the brain (cslb) concept property norms. *Behavior Research Methods*, 46:1119 – 1127.

Jacob Devlin, Ming-Wei Chang, Kenton Lee, and Kristina Toutanova. 2019. BERT: Pre-training of deep bidirectional transformers for language understanding. In *Proceedings of the 2019 Conference of the North American Chapter of the Association for Computational Linguistics: Human Language Technologies, Volume 1 (Long and Short Papers)*, pages 4171–4186, Minneapolis, Minnesota. Association for Computational Linguistics.

Rotem Dror, Gili Baumer, Marina Bogomolov, and Roi Reichart. 2017. Replicability analysis for natural language processing: Testing significance with multiple datasets. *Transactions of the Association for Computational Linguistics*, 5:471–486.

Yanai Elazar, Nora Kassner, Shauli Ravfogel, Abhilasha Ravichander, Eduard Hovy, Hinrich Schütze, and Yoav Goldberg. 2021. Measuring and improving consistency in pretrained language models. *Transactions of the Association for Computational Linguistics*, 9:1012–1031.

Allyson Ettinger. 2020. What BERT is not: Lessons from a new suite of psycholinguistic diagnostics for language models. *Transactions of the Association for Computational Linguistics*, 8:34–48.

Oren Etzioni, Michael Cafarella, Doug Downey, Ana-Maria Popescu, Tal Shaked, Stephen Soderland, Daniel S. Weld, and Alexander Yates. 2005. Unsupervised named-entity extraction from the web: An experimental study. *Artificial Intelligence*, 165(1):91–134.

Diego Frassinelli, Daniela Naumann, Jason Utt, and Sabine Schulte m Walde. 2017. Contextual characteristics of concrete and abstract words. In *IWCS 2017 — 12th International Conference on Computational Semantics — Short papers*.

Manuel Gimenes and Boris New. 2016. Worldlex: Twitter and blog word frequencies for 66 languages. *Behavior Research Methods*, 48:963–972.

Roxana Girju, Adriana Badulescu, and Dan Moldovan. 2003. Learning semantic constraints for the automatic discovery of part-whole relations. In *Proceedings of the 2003 Human Language Technology Conference of the North American Chapter of the Association for Computational Linguistics*, pages 80–87.

Rebecca Green, Carol A. Bean, and Sung Hyon Myaeng. 2002. *The Semantics of Relationships: An Interdisciplinary Perspective*. Kluwer Academic Publishers, USA.

Michael Hanna and David Mareček. 2021. Analyzing BERT's knowledge of hypernymy via prompting. In *Proceedings of the Fourth BlackboxNLP Workshop on Analyzing and Interpreting Neural Networks for NLP*, pages 275–282, Punta Cana, Dominican Republic. Association for Computational Linguistics.

Marti A. Hearst. 1992. Automatic acquisition of hyponyms from large text corpora. In *COLING*.

Eduard Hovy, Zornitsa Kozareva, and Ellen Riloff. 2009. Toward completeness in concept extraction and classification. In *Proceedings of the 2009 Conference on Empirical Methods in Natural Language Processing*, pages 948–957, Singapore. Association for Computational Linguistics.

Devansh Jain and Luis Espinosa Anke. 2022. Distilling hypernymy relations from language models: On the effectiveness of zero-shot taxonomy induction. In *Proceedings of the 11th Joint Conference on Lexical and Computational Semantics*, pages 151–156, Seattle, Washington. Association for Computational Linguistics.

Zornitsa Kozareva. 2014. Simple, fast and accurate taxonomy learning. In *Text Mining: From Ontology Learning to Automated Text Processing Applications*, pages 41–62, Cham. Springer International Publishing.

J. Lyons. 1977. *Semantics: Volume 2*. ACLS Humanities E-Book. Cambridge University Press.

George A. Miller. 1995. Wordnet: A lexical database for english. *Commun. ACM*, 38(11):39–41.

Smaranda Muresan and Judith Klavans. 2002. A method for automatically building and evaluating dictionary resources. In *Proceedings of the Third International Conference on Language Resources and Evaluation (LREC'02)*, Las Palmas, Canary Islands - Spain. European Language Resources Association (ELRA).

Daniela Naumann, Diego Frassinelli, and Sabine Schulte im Walde. 2018. Quantitative semantic variation in the contexts of concrete and abstract words. In *Proceedings of the Seventh Joint Conference on Lexical and Computational Semantics*, pages 76–85, New Orleans, Louisiana. Association for Computational Linguistics.

Roberto Navigli, Paola Velardi, and Stefano Faralli. 2011. A graph-based algorithm for inducing lexical taxonomies from scratch. In *Proceedings of the Twenty-Second International Joint Conference on Artificial Intelligence - Volume Volume Three*, IJCAI'11, page 1872–1877. AAAI Press.

Roberto Navigli, Paola Velardi, and Juana Maria Ruiz-Martínez. 2010. An annotated dataset for extracting definitions and hypernyms from the web. In *Proceedings of the Seventh International Conference on Language Resources and Evaluation (LREC'10)*, Valletta, Malta. European Language Resources Association (ELRA).

Patrick Pantel and Marco Pennacchiotti. 2006. Espresso: Leveraging generic patterns for automatically harvesting semantic relations. In *Proceedings of the 21st International Conference on Computational Linguistics and 44th Annual Meeting of the Association for Computational Linguistics*, pages 113–120, Sydney, Australia. Association for Computational Linguistics.

Marius Pasca. 2004. Acquisition of categorized named entities for web search. In *Proceedings of the Thirteenth ACM conference on Information and knowledge management - CIKM '04*, page 137, Washington, D.C., USA. ACM Press.

Bo Peng, Emmanuele Chersoni, Yu-Yin Hsu, and Chu-Ren Huang. 2022. Discovering financial hypernyms by prompting masked language models. In *Proceedings of the 4th Financial Narrative Processing Workshop @LREC2022*, pages 10–16, Marseille, France. European Language Resources Association.

Matthew E. Peters, Mark Neumann, Robert Logan, Roy Schwartz, Vidur Joshi, Sameer Singh, and Noah A. Smith. 2019. Knowledge enhanced contextual word representations. In *Proceedings of the 2019 Conference on Empirical Methods in Natural Language Processing and the 9th International Joint Conference on Natural Language Processing (EMNLP-IJCNLP)*, pages 43–54, Hong Kong, China. Association for Computational Linguistics.

Fabio Petroni, Tim Rocktäschel, Sebastian Riedel, Patrick Lewis, Anton Bakhtin, Yuxiang Wu, and Alexander Miller. 2019. Language models as knowledge bases? In *Proceedings of the 2019 Conference on Empirical Methods in Natural Language Processing and the 9th International Joint Conference on Natural Language Processing (EMNLP-IJCNLP)*, pages 2463–2473, Hong Kong, China. Association for Computational Linguistics.

Guanghui Qin and Jason Eisner. 2021. Learning how to ask: Querying LMs with mixtures of soft prompts. In *Proceedings of the 2021 Conference of the North American Chapter of the Association for Computational Linguistics: Human Language Technologies*, pages 5203–5212, Online. Association for Computational Linguistics.

Abhilasha Ravichander, Eduard Hovy, Kaheer Suleman, Adam Trischler, and Jackie Chi Kit Cheung. 2020. On the systematicity of probing contextualized word representations: The case of hypernymy in BERT. In *Proceedings of the Ninth Joint Conference on Lexical and Computational Semantics*, pages 88–102, Barcelona, Spain (Online). Association for Computational Linguistics.

Stephen Roller, Douwe Kiela, and Maximilian Nickel. 2018. Hearst patterns revisited: Automatic hypernym detection from large text corpora. In *Proceedings of the 56th Annual Meeting of the Association for Computational Linguistics (Volume 2: Short Papers)*, pages 358–363, Melbourne, Australia. Association for Computational Linguistics.

Enrico Santus, Frances Yung, Alessandro Lenci, and Chu-Ren Huang. 2015. EVALution 1.0: an evolving semantic dataset for training and evaluation of distributional semantic models. In *Proceedings of the 4th Workshop on Linked Data in Linguistics: Resources and Applications*, pages 64–69, Beijing, China. Association for Computational Linguistics.

Timo Schick and Hinrich Schütze. 2019. Rare words: A major problem for contextualized embeddings and how to fix it by attentive mimicking. In *AAAI Conference on Artificial Intelligence*.

Timo Schick and Hinrich Schütze. 2020. Rare words: A major problem for contextualized representation and how to fix it by attentive mimicking. In *Proceedings of the Thirty-Fourth AAAI Conference on Artificial Intelligence*.

Vered Shwartz, Enrico Santus, and Dominik Schlechtweg. 2017. Hypernyms under siege: Linguistically-motivated artillery for hypernymy detection. In *Proceedings of the 15th Conference of the European Chapter of the Association for Computational Linguistics: Volume 1, Long Papers*, pages 65–75, Valencia, Spain. Association for Computational Linguistics.

Rion Snow, Daniel Jurafsky, and Andrew Ng. 2004. Learning syntactic patterns for automatic hypernym discovery. In *Advances in Neural Information Processing Systems*, volume 17. MIT Press.

Rion Snow, Daniel Jurafsky, and Andrew Y. Ng. 2006. Semantic taxonomy induction from heterogenous evidence. In *Proceedings of the 21st International Conference on Computational Linguistics and 44th Annual Meeting of the Association for Computational Linguistics*, pages 801–808, Sydney, Australia. Association for Computational Linguistics.

Kunihiro Takeoka, Kosuke Akimoto, and Masafumi Oyamada. 2021. Low-resource taxonomy enrichment with pretrained language models. In *Proceedings of the 2021 Conference on Empirical Methods in Natural Language Processing*, pages 2747–2758, Online and Punta Cana, Dominican Republic. Association for Computational Linguistics.

Jason Wei, Yi Tay, Rishi Bommasani, Colin Raffel, Barret Zoph, Sebastian Borgeaud, Dani Yogatama, Maarten Bosma, Denny Zhou, Donald Metzler, Ed H. Chi, Tatsunori Hashimoto, Oriol Vinyals, Percy Liang, Jeff Dean, and William Fedus. 2022. Emergent abilities of large language models. *Transactions on Machine Learning Research*. Survey Certification.

Nathaniel Weir, Adam Poliak, and Benjamin Van Durme. 2020. Probing neural language models for human tacit assumptions.

Zheng Yu, Haixun Wang, Xuemin Lin, and Min Wang. 2015. Learning term embeddings for hypernymy identification. In *Proceedings of the 24th International Conference on Artificial Intelligence*, IJCAI'15, page 1390–1397. AAAI Press.

A Hypernym Evaluation

Dataset Statistics Table 9 presents the statistics on all datasets we used for experiments. We exclude hypernyms that are not included as single tokens in BERT vocabulary. The ratio of discarded (x, y) pairs is lower than 1% for most datasets, except for BLESS (30% is discarded) and CLSB (17% is discarded).

Comparison with oracle anchors To estimate the upper bound of anchored prompts, we treat siblings from WordNet (Miller, 1995) as oracle anchors and evaluate their effects on hypernym extraction. We select top five siblings with the highest rank of their path similarities calculated from WordNet, i.e., $\frac{1}{p(x,z)+1}$, where p is the length of the shortest path between the x and z among their top two synsets. We use random sampling among siblings with the same score to select up to five anchors. The experimental results are presented in Table 10. We observe that using WordNet anchors can indeed lead to significant improvements in performance on datasets directly built from WordNet. For example, we observed large improvements for DIAG and LEDS when using WordNet anchors in combination with DFPA patterns. However, for other datasets, BERT anchors produce similar results as WorNet anchors. This highlights that with the improvement of anchor quality, anchoring prompts can unlock more hidden knowledge within BERT.

Computational Resources All experiments are conducted on single NVIDIA V100 GPU. A single run on each data set takes less than 2 hours, except for the large-scale dataset SHWARTZ, which takes nearly 24 hours on anchored prompts.

B Consistency

B.1 Pairwise consistency on close vocab

To compare our work with Ravichander et al. (2020) on pairwise probes using close vocab (nine hypernyms), we conduct the same experiments on DIAG dataset. Table 11 presents the results. The conclusion aligns with the open vocab set up: anchored patterns improve the consistency largely.

B.2 Group consistency over different depths of hypernyms

Table 12 reports the group consistency across different depths of hypernyms.

Dataset	#Hypon	#Hyper	#Pairs	WordNet Coverage (%)	Concreteness
BLESS (Baroni and Lenci, 2011)	200	85	935	99.8	100 / 91.4
DIAG (Ravichander et al., 2020)	576	9	576	100	97.9/ 100
CLSB (Devereux et al., 2014)	508	232	1079	98.1	100/ 98.2
SHWARTZ (Shwartz et al., 2017)	11061	1101	12724	44.1	66.4/ 92.3
LEDS (Baroni et al., 2012)	1073	364	1262	100	83.7/ 79.2
EVAL (Santus et al., 2015)	621	348	953	99.8	88.1/ 83.4

Table 9: The statistics of datasets. WordNet Coverage is the coverage of hyponym-hypernym that are connected in WordNet on hypernyms hierarchy. Concreteness is the percentage of concrete hyponyms/hypernyms, measured by the concreteness rating from Brysbaert et al. (2014) for the shared vocab.

	BLESS		DIAG		CLSB		SHWARTZ		EVAL		LEDS	
	MRR	P@10	MRR	P@10	MRR	P@10	MRR	P@10	MRR	P@10	MRR	P@10
DFP	23.6	42.4	42.6	66.8	39.8	67.5	6.3	12.8	**24.0**	**46.7**	32.6	60.1
DFP^{+A}	25.7^{+}	47.2^{+}	**45.5**$^{+}$	**67.2**$^{+}$	**42.3**$^{+}$	**70.5**$^{+}$	5.9^{+}	13.6^{+}	22.1^{+}	43.3^{+}	**35.7**$^{+}$	**64.3**$^{+}$
DFP$^{+A}_{oracle}$ ♯	23.9	41.9	65.4	84.6	41.2	68.2	8.9	15.6	23.3	45.1	37.7	66.2
LSP	**27.1***	**53.9***	**45.5***	66.1	40.8	68.2	6.4	**15.2***	17.3*	39.5*	33.4	60.5
LSP^{+A}	26.5	53.2	42.8^{+}	62.7^{+}	40.4	67.7	**6.5**	14.9	17.0	38.1	34.0	61.6
LSP$^{+A}_{oracle}$ ♯	26.2	49.6	65.6	85.8	41.9	68.3	9.1	18.8	18.7	40.5	37.1	66.3

Table 10: Main results on six hypernym extraction datasets with oracle anchors from WordNet. Bold number indicates the highest score per data set and metric. * indicates significant difference of LSP vs. DFP; $^{+}$ indicates significant difference wrt. the non-anchored counterpart (i.e., LSP vs LSP^{+A} and DFP vs. DFP^{+A}). The ♯ symbol denotes that we report the average over 3 runs on sampled anchors from WordNet.

Model	Patterns		Accuracy		
	Singular	Plural	Singular	Plural	Singular&Plural
Majority	-	-	22.9	22.9	22.9
BERT (Ravichander et al., 2020) [14]	A(n) X is a(n) Y	X are Y	67.5	44.1	36.6
DFP	A(n) X is a(n) Y.	X are Y.	70.8	52.3	43.6
DFP^{+A}	A(n) X or Z is a(n) Y.	X or Z are Y.	73.8	61.6	**57.1**
LSP	Y such as a(n) X.	Y such as X.	47.6	64.6	42.7
LSP^{+A}	Y such as a(n) X or Z.	Y such as X or Z.	59.2	73.3	55.6

Table 11: Experimental results on pairwise singular-plural probes. X in singular patterns are singular format (e.g., car), while X in plural patterns are plural format (e.g., cars).

Depth	#Instances	LSP	LSP^{+A}	Δ	Hypernym Examples
1	5	20.0	20.0	0.0	transaction, conflict
2	104	1.0	7.7	6.7	object, group, relation, proceeding, battle
3	352	2.8	3.7	0.9	person, language, event, collection, trait
4	1335	8.5	12.2	3.7	band, organization, island, food, lake
5	1572	6.7	11.1	4.4	place, river, mountain, organisation, settlement
6	4829	8.4	11.5	3.1	film, village, company, animal, work
7	1017	29.7	41.5	11.8	vehicle, tool, country, plant, sport
8	1773	9.4	14.8	5.4	city, town, fruit, weapon, illness
9	1110	32.0	36.2	4.2	book, bird, magazine, mammal, tree
10	348	28.2	32.5	4.3	fish, ship, flower, airline, word
11	15	6.7	6.7	0.0	airplane, hawk, plane, vulture, murder
12	12	16.7	25.0	8.3	cancer, lizard, falcon, pine
13	55	5.5	9.1	3.6	human, pest, cat
14	54	7.4	7.4	0.0	horse
16	2	50.0	100.0	50.0	cattle
17	2	0.0	0.0	0.0	cow

Table 12: Analysis on depth of hypernyms in WordNet. Column LSP and LSP^{+A} are the group consistency (as in § 6.4) across depth. Δ is the gains from anchors (i.e., LSP^{+A}- LSP).

LEXPLAIN: Improving Model Explanations via Lexicon Supervision

Orevaoghene Ahia[◇] **Hila Gonen**[◇] **Vidhisha Balachandran**[♠]
Yulia Tsvetkov[◇] **Noah A. Smith**[◇♡]
[◇]Paul G. Allen School of Computer Science & Engineering, University of Washington
[♠]Language Technologies Institute, Carnegie Mellon University
[♡]Allen Institute for Artificial Intelligence
oahia@cs.washington.edu

Abstract

Model explanations that shed light on the model's predictions are becoming a desired additional output of NLP models, alongside their predictions. Challenges in creating these explanations include making them trustworthy and faithful to the model's predictions. In this work, we propose a novel framework for guiding model explanations by supervising them explicitly. To this end, our method, LEXPLAIN, uses task-related lexicons to directly supervise model explanations. This approach consistently improves the plausibility of model's explanations without sacrificing performance on the task, as we demonstrate on sentiment analysis and toxicity detection. Our analyses show that our method also demotes spurious correlations (i.e., with respect to African American English dialect) on toxicity detection, improving fairness.

1 Introduction

Extensive recent work has sought to advance NLP models so that they offer explanations for their predictions (Rajani et al., 2019; Lundberg and Lee, 2017; Camburu et al., 2018). Here we focus on methods that extract features from the input text to explain a classifier's prediction, known variously as "feature attribution" or "rationales" (Lundberg and Lee, 2017; Li et al., 2016).

Beyond high accuracy on unseen data, classifiers that offer explanations are expected to provide explanations that are faithful to the workings of the model and also intuitive to human users, goals that might be contradicting. We begin with an approach designed for faithfulness (SELFEXPLAIN, §2 and Rajagopal et al., 2021a) and introduce supervision that guides its explanations toward lexical clues already established to be associated with the classification task. Ancillary goals are to *improve* model accuracy through the construction of explanations, and to *remove reliance on spurious features* that can bias a classifier's output in unwanted ways.

Our method, LEXPLAIN (§3), encourages the model to be "confused" in the absence of words from a task-specific lexicon, i.e., to assign a uniform probability distribution across labels, and promotes model explanations that contain task-specific lexemes. We apply LEXPLAIN to sentiment analysis and toxicity detection tasks, and our controlled experiments (§5, §6) comparing LEXPLAIN to SELFEXPLAIN (which does not use supervision for explanations) show that:

(a) LEXPLAIN does not show an accuracy drop relative to the baseline. (b) LEXPLAIN not only promotes lexicon entries as explanations, but also generalizes to additional terms that are related to them but excluded from the lexicon. (c) LEXPLAIN's explanations are usually more sufficient than the baseline's explanations (i.e., the model makes the same prediction on the explanation as on the full input). (d) In toxicity detection, spurious correlations between the toxicity label and African American English (Sap et al., 2019) are reduced in the predictions of LEXPLAIN, relative to the baseline. We view this result as a positive side effect of guiding the model to use task-relevant lexemes. (e) Most importantly, LEXPLAIN's explanations are preferred by human judges 3–4× more often than the baseline's explanations.

We believe these results are encouraging, as they suggest that type-level (lexicon) supervision is a viable alternative to methods that require costly annotation of explanations (Zaidan and Eisner, 2008; Huang et al., 2021).[1]

2 Background: SELFEXPLAIN

Our goal is to improve model explanations in supervised text classification tasks. By supervising explanations, we incorporate inductive biases into models, making them robust to spurious artifacts. Our base model is SELFEXPLAIN (Rajagopal et al.,

[1]Code available at https://github.com/orevaahia/supex

*Proceedings of the The 12th Joint Conference on Lexical and Computational Semantics (*SEM 2023)*, pages 207–216

2021a), a framework that explains a text classifier's predictions with phrase attribution. We describe SELFEXPLAIN (omitting the global interpretable layer, as we focus on local explanations) and in Section 3 present our proposed method, LEXPLAIN.

Starting with a neural classifier, let $\mathbf{u}_s$ be the masked LM's (Yang et al., 2019) final layer representation of the "[CLS]" token for one instance. $\mathbf{u}_s$ is passed through ReLU, affine, and softmax layers to yield a probability distribution over outputs; the loss is the negative log probability, summed over training instances i:

$$\boldsymbol{\ell} = \text{softmax}(\text{affine}(\text{ReLU}(\mathbf{u}_s))) \quad (1)$$

$$L_{task} = -\sum_i \log \boldsymbol{\ell}[y_i^*] \quad (2)$$

y_i^* is the correct label for instance i. Parameters of the affine layer are suppressed here for simplicity.

A set of phrases is extracted from the data with a phrase-structure parser (Kitaev and Klein, 2018). Let $\mathbf{u}_j$ be the average of the MLM representations of tokens in phrase j. The output distribution *without* phrase j is modeled by transforming the difference (Shrikumar et al., 2017; Montavon et al., 2017) between $\mathbf{u}_s$ and $\mathbf{u}_j$.

$$\mathbf{s}_j = \text{softmax}(\text{affine}(\text{ReLU}(\mathbf{u}_s) - \text{ReLU}(\mathbf{u}_j))) \quad (3)$$

Vector $\mathbf{s}_j$ is a probability distribution over labels, with phrase j absent: the closer $\mathbf{s}_j$ is to $\boldsymbol{\ell}$ (Eq. 1), the less important phrase j is. A secondary log loss L_{LIL} is formed from the probability assigned to the correct label without phrase j, taking a learned weighted sum over all of instance i's phrases, and interpolating with the original log loss (Eq. 2) with a hyperparameter α_1 to weight the secondary loss:

$$\text{loss} = L_{task} + \alpha_1 L_{LIL} \quad (4)$$

The relevance of each phrase j can be defined as the change in probability of the correct label when j is included vs. excluded:

$$r_j = [\boldsymbol{\ell}]_{y_i^*} - [\mathbf{s}_j]_{y_i^*} \quad (5)$$

where higher r_j signify more relevant phrases to the prediction, and as such serve as better explanations.

3 Supervising Explanations

On inspecting explanations retrieved from SELFEXPLAIN, in many cases they do not align intuitively with the predictions. Table 1 illustrates the problem: the explanation of SELFEXPLAIN sentence (1) is the phrase ***on this planet*** which is not a good explanation for the predicted toxic label, unlike ***the biggest idiot***, which can better explain the model's prediction, having the toxic word ***idiot***.

Our modeling innovation is to supervise the explanations encoded in the LIL, rather than letting them emerge from the secondary loss function (L_{LIL} in Equation 4). We incorporate a task lexicon as a source of supervision during training via a third loss component to encourage the model to prefer phrases that contain words in our lexicon as explanations. Table 1 lists examples in the datasets, showing the advantage of our method with more intuitive explanations that better reflect the predicted label.

Our proposed method, named LEXPLAIN, assumes that good explanations within the input are crucial for predictions, thus we encourage the model to be "confused" in the *absence* of lexicon entries, which we expect to be good explanations.

Formally, we minimize the KL divergence between the predicted label distribution $\mathbf{s}_j$, which stands for the distribution in the absence of phrase j (as described in Section 2) and the uniform distribution $\mathbf{s}_{unif}$, for every phrase j:

$$L_{\text{LEXPLAIN}} = D_{KL}(\mathbf{s}_j, \mathbf{s}_{unif}) \quad (6)$$

This objective is used for only lexicon phrases. LEXPLAIN interpolates the third loss, weighted by hyperparameter α_2, with the other two:

$$\text{loss} = L_{task} + \alpha_1 L_{LIL} + \alpha_2 L_{\text{LEXPLAIN}} \quad (7)$$

4 Experimental Setup

Datasets We experiment on three datasets and evaluate explanations based on alignment with model predictions and plausibility with humans. We focus on sentiment analysis and toxicity detection, as judging explanations is easy, intuitive and high-quality lexicons are available. Toxicity detection also allows us to analyze the efficacy of our method in demoting spurious racial correlations, as detailed in §6.

For sentiment analysis, we use the SST-2 dataset (Socher et al., 2013), where the task is to predict the sentiment of movie reviews. For toxicity detection we use **DWMW17** (Davidson et al., 2017) and **FDCL18** (Founta et al., 2018); both Twitter datasets annotated for toxicity and dialect: African

Input	SELFEXPLAIN	LEXPLAIN
she is the biggest idiot on the planet.	on this planet	the biggest idiot
Haha , says the little bitch who let someone take his phone . a real man would n't have let that happen . a little bitch would.	someone take his phone	a little bitch would
All you hoes wanna be like me so bad.	bad	you hoe s
I 'm so ugly & april fools bitch you thought.	you thought	so ugly
He draw (for " big bad love ") is a solid performance by arliss howard.	big bad love	a solid performance
A lackluster , unessential sequel to the classic disney adaptation of j.m. barrie 's peter pan	the classic dis ney adaptation	the classic disney adaptation

Table 1: Explanations from SELFEXPLAIN and LEXPLAIN for DWMW17, FDCL18 and SST2 (2 examples each). Predicted labels are toxic for DWMW17 and FDCL18. First and second SST2 examples are positive and negative, respectively. Explanations of LEXPLAIN align better with the model prediction and contain more task-related terms.

American English (AAE) and White American English. The AAE annotations are obtained from a demographically aligned ensemble model that learns a posterior distribution of topics corresponding to African American tweets (Blodgett et al., 2016). Our task lexicons and full experiment details are described in appendix section A.

Training We use SELFEXPLAIN as our baseline. When training both the baseline and LEXPLAIN, we keep the same hyperparameters and weights from the pretraining of the XLNet encoder and finetune the model for 5 epochs. In LEXPLAIN we do not use the GIL, since initial experiments showed no difference between adding and removing the GIL.

For LEXPLAIN, we perform hyperparameter tuning for $\alpha_1 \in \{0.01, 0.05, 0.1\}$ and $\alpha_2 \in \{0.8, 1.5.2.0\}$ on the development set. We report results on the best configuration on the test sets.

We extract phrases from sentences, by parsing each sentence with a constituency parser (Kitaev and Klein, 2018) and extracting all non-terminals with a token length of up to 5 words in the parse tree.

5 Evaluating Explanations

The goal of LEXPLAIN is to train models to produce plausible explanations that align with their predictions. We start with an intrinsic evaluation, verifying that LEXPLAIN indeed promotes *lexicon entries* as explanations. We then analyze the sufficiency of the explanations and conduct human evaluation to show that explanations from LEXPLAIN are more *plausible* and preferred by humans.

Intrinsic evaluation: are lexicon entries ranked higher as explanations of the model? The LIL outputs explanations as a rank of all input phrases. Following lexicon supervision, we expect to see that phrases ranked higher contain more lexicon entries, indicating that supervision was effective. To quantify this, we compute in Table 2 the mean reciprocal rank (MRR) of the lexicon entries within the ranked phrases of LEXPLAIN vs. the baseline.

Across all datasets, LEXPLAIN ranks lexicon entries higher than the baseline on average, showing the effectiveness of our supervision in providing explanations included in the task lexicon. We note that high-rank phrases should be the focus, thus in Appendix 2 we plot the raw counts of lexicon entries that appear in each rank, across sentences in each dataset. Clearly, LEXPLAIN puts more lexicon entries higher in the rank, this is especially noticeable in the highest ranked explanations (rank 1).

Dataset	Model	MRR(Full lexicon)	MRR(50% lexicon)
FDCL18	Baseline	0.29	0.31
	LEXPLAIN	**0.33**	**0.35**
DWMW17	Baseline	0.32	0.20
	LEXPLAIN	**0.35**	**0.24**
SST2	Baseline	0.23	0.18
	LEXPLAIN	**0.25**	**0.22**

Table 2: Mean reciprocal rank (MRR) of lexicon phrases across the full ranking of explanations on the test set.

Do explanations sufficiently reflect model predictions? *Sufficiency* measures how indicative explanations alone are of the model's predicted label (Jacovi et al., 2018; Yu et al., 2019). Sufficient explanations are expected to reflect the prediction of the predicted label on their own. To measure that, we use the FRESH pipeline (Jain et al., 2020): we train a BERT-based classifier to perform the task with only the explanations as input, and with the originally predicted labels as output. Higher accuracy on this task indicates that the explanations are more reflective of the model predictions. We train the sufficiency models with the top ranking explanations of each sentence as input.

Following Jain et al. (2020), we measure this with a BERT classifier trained with top ranked phrases as input and predicted label as output. Higher accuracy indicates more sufficient explanations. Table 3 shows that LEXPLAIN explanations have higher predictive performance and are more sufficient on average compared to the baseline.

Dataset	Model	Top 1	Top 2
SST-2	Baseline	64.99	68.90
	LEXPLAIN	**68.00**	**70.00**
FDCL18	Baseline	82.25	87.37
	LEXPLAIN	**83.79**	**87.79**
DWMW17	Baseline	**88.16**	89.00
	LEXPLAIN	85.12	**91.10**

Table 3: Test set accuracy of sufficiency models trained on the top-1 and top-2 explanation as input.

Do humans prefer LEXPLAIN explanations? To evaluate how plausible our model's explanations are (Singh et al., 2019; Jin et al., 2020) we ask annotators to select their preferred explanations, comparing explanations from both the baseline and LEXPLAIN. We provide 3 annotators with 50 samples from the test set of each of our three datasets (9 annotators in total). All annotators are computer science graduate students and were already familiar with the tasks. Annotators were given a pair of explanations about the same input (one from the baseline, one from LEXPLAIN), in random order, and asked to select the one they prefer. They could also judge "both unsatisfactory" or "both satisfactory." The exact phrasing of the instructions can be found in Section B in the Appendix.

We analyse the human evaluations and take the max-vote preference of all three annotations per task. In Figure 1, we present the results of the human judgments. The differences between LEXPLAIN and the baseline are striking with LEXPLAIN being preferred about 3-4× more often than the baseline.

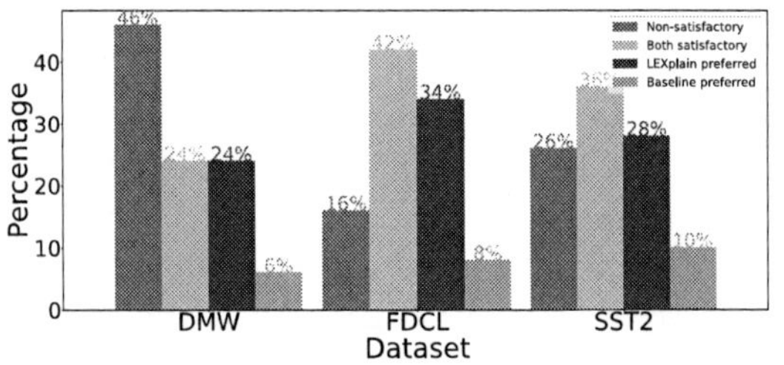

Figure 1: Results of human evaluation of explanation preference. LEXPLAIN is preferred by annotators 3-4× more often than the baseline.

6 Downstream Performance Analysis

To test our hypothesis that supervising explanations not only leads to plausible explanations, but robust models overfitting less to spurious confounds, we evaluate downstream classification performance.

Sentiment Analysis We obtain an accuracy of 93.92% and 93.35% for LEXPLAIN and SELF-EXPLAIN respectively. This slight improvement shows that the added supervision for explanations maintains the utility of the model.

Toxicity Detection We report the results on toxicity detection in Table 4. The accuracy results of LEXPLAIN are competitive with the baseline, also showing that additionally supervising explanations does not hurt the results of the classification task.

Dataset	Dialect	Model	Accuracy	FPR	FNR
FDCL18	All dialects	Baseline	93.94	**3.94**	10.05
		LEXPLAIN	94.10	4.24	**9.03**
	AAE	Baseline	93.60	**12.43**	4.21
		LEXPLAIN	93.60	13.87	**3.36**
DWMW17	All dialects	Baseline	96.06	10.98	**2.48**
		LEXPLAIN	96.30	**5.99**	3.24
	AAE	Baseline	98.00	21.69	**1.10**
		LEXPLAIN	97.95	**12.05**	1.59

Table 4: Toxicity accuracy, FPR, FNR on the test sets.

Demoting Spurious Correlations with Race Neural classifiers have been shown to rely on spurious artifacts in the training data (Kumar et al., 2019; Gururangan et al., 2018; McCoy et al., 2019), sometimes causing unfair predictions, when they relate to attributes like gender or race (Sap et al., 2019; Xia et al., 2020). We ask if guiding models to influential input phrases using lexicon reduces reliance on these artifacts and promote fairness.

Our toxicity data have dialect labels: African American English (AAE) and White American English. We inspect if our model demotes racial correlations. When a model relies on correlations harmfully, we expect higher false negatives rate (FNR), as more non-toxic instances are falsely labelled toxic because of reliance on dialectal features. In Table 4 we report the FPR (false positive rate) and FNR on DWMW17 and FDCL18. We get a much lower FPR on the full DWMW17, and more significant reduction on AAE samples. On the FDCL18 data, we see a slightly higher FPR than the baseline.

Lexicon Generalization We inspect the generalization abilities of LEXPLAIN: does it generalize and promote task related terms in explanations but not present in the lexicon? We randomly select 50% of lexicon words and use them only to supervise while training. We compute MRR with respect to the other half not used for supervision on the same test set. If the phrases are ranked higher on average, even without being seen during training, it indicates that LEXPLAIN generalizes over lexicon phrases.

Table 2 shows the MRR of lexicon entries (not used as supervision). We show that our method generalizes consistently across all tasks: even lexicon entries absent during supervision are ranked higher with LEXPLAIN when compared to the baseline.

7 Related Work

Different works have approached interpreting models trained for various downstream tasks using post hoc (Simonyan et al., 2014; Jin et al., 2020; Smilkov et al., 2017) and intrinsic (Rajagopal et al., 2021b; Alvarez Melis and Jaakkola, 2018) methods. In this work we focus on intrinsic methods that highlight rationales (Denil et al., 2014; Rajani et al., 2019; Luo et al., 2021) – where parts of the input influential for prediction are extracted.

Some works leveraged interpretability methods to improve model performance (Han and Tsvetkov, 2021; Hase and Bansal, 2022). Wei et al. (2022) teach models to do commonsense tasks by providing step-by-step instructions. For classification tasks, Madaan et al. (2021) use free-form explanation generation and Hayati et al. (2022); Zaidan and Eisner (2008); Huang et al. (2021) use human rationales as model feedback. These methods require expensive annotation to elicit good explanations. We instead aim to supervise rationales using task lexicons, and show it yields improved explanations.

8 Conclusion

We propose LEXPLAIN, a method to improve model explanations by directly supervising them using task lexicons as the source of supervision. We show that our method is indeed able to promote dictionary entries as explanations, resulting in explanations that align well with the model's predicted label without sacrificing accuracy, and that the explanations are more plausible according to human evaluation. We also show that LEXPLAIN is able to generalize well to features that are not present in the supervising lexicon. Finally, we show that by promoting task related lexicon entries, we are able to demote spurious correlations with AAE annotations on toxicity datasets.

Limitations and Future Work

One limitation of LEXPLAIN stems from the reliance on task lexicons. First, a reliable task lexicon is required in order to adequately supervise explanations, and this might be non-trivial to create for an arbitrary task. We do show, however, that LEXPLAIN is able to generalize beyond lexicon entries, which suggests that even partial lexicon for the task at hand can provide a significant improvement in explanations. Second, the chosen lexicon might include certain biases itself, that might in turn be incorporated in the model and its explanations.

Another limitation, shared with the majority of existing interpretability methods, is that the faithfulness of interpretations is not guaranteed. In other words, there is no theoretical guarantee that the retrieved explanations reflect the actual mechanisms of the model in making predictions. We partially mitigate this by choosing SELFEXPLAIN as our base model. It is more faithful by design: it is trained to enforce the alignment between model outputs in the task classification and the LIL.

Finally, LEXPLAIN requires fine-tuning the model for the task and incorporating the LIL on top of a pretrained language model, and we established its success only with one model (XLNet). Future work should explore adaptations of other language models, and extensions to language generation, to facilitate model interpretability in new settings.

Ethics Statement

Our work aims at developing interpretable models that do not overfit to artifacts in the training data. However, there is no guarantee that we fully mitigate model reliance on all spurious correlations. Further, by incorporating new lexicons that might contain annotation biases (Sap et al., 2022), there is an additional risk to incorporate and amplify social biases. We mitigate these risks through manual analyses and fairness evaluations presented in §6.

We conduct fairness evaluations on the commonly used toxicity datasets (Davidson et al., 2017; Founta et al., 2018) annotated for AAE (Blodgett et al., 2016). These AAE annotations for the toxicity datasets are a useful but imperfect proxy for information about race. For example, these datasets are not annotated by in-group members and annotators had insufficient social context (Sap et al., 2019). Future work should focus on a more careful dataset curation that would enable a more reliable fairness evaluation.

Acknowledgments

This research is supported in part by by the National Science Foundation (NSF) under grants IIS2203097 and IIS2125201. This research is supported in part by the Office of the Director of National Intelligence (ODNI), Intelligence Advanced Research Projects Activity (IARPA), via the HIATUS Program contract #2022-22072200004. The views and conclusions contained herein are those of the authors and should not be interpreted as necessarily representing the official policies, either expressed or implied, of ODNI, IARPA, or the U.S. Government. The U.S. Government is authorized to reproduce and distribute reprints for governmental purposes notwithstanding any copyright annotation therein.

References

David Alvarez Melis and Tommi Jaakkola. 2018. Towards robust interpretability with self-explaining neural networks. In *Advances in Neural Information Processing Systems*, volume 31. Curran Associates, Inc.

Su Lin Blodgett, Lisa Green, and Brendan O'Connor. 2016. Demographic dialectal variation in social media: A case study of African-American English. In *Proceedings of the 2016 Conference on Empirical Methods in Natural Language Processing*, pages 1119–1130, Austin, Texas. Association for Computational Linguistics.

Oana-Maria Camburu, Tim Rocktäschel, Thomas Lukasiewicz, and Phil Blunsom. 2018. e-snli: Natural language inference with natural language explanations. In *NeurIPS*.

Thomas Davidson, Dana Warmsley, Michael W. Macy, and Ingmar Weber. 2017. Automated hate speech detection and the problem of offensive language. In *ICWSM*.

Misha Denil, Alban Demiraj, and Nando de Freitas. 2014. Extraction of salient sentences from labelled documents. *ArXiv*, abs/1412.6815.

Antigoni-Maria Founta, Constantinos Djouvas, Despoina Chatzakou, Ilias Leontiadis, Jeremy Blackburn, Gianluca Stringhini, Athena Vakali, Michael Sirivianos, and Nicolas Kourtellis. 2018. Large scale crowdsourcing and characterization of twitter abusive behavior. *ArXiv*, abs/1802.00393.

Suchin Gururangan, Swabha Swayamdipta, Omer Levy, Roy Schwartz, Samuel Bowman, and Noah A. Smith. 2018. Annotation artifacts in natural language inference data. In *Proceedings of the 2018 Conference of the North American Chapter of the Association for Computational Linguistics: Human Language Technologies, Volume 2 (Short Papers)*, pages 107–112, New Orleans, Louisiana. Association for Computational Linguistics.

Xiaochuang Han and Yulia Tsvetkov. 2021. Influence tuning: Demoting spurious correlations via instance attribution and instance-driven updates. In *Findings of the Association for Computational Linguistics: EMNLP 2021*, pages 4398–4409.

Peter Hase and Mohit Bansal. 2022. When can models learn from explanations? a formal framework for understanding the roles of explanation data. In *Proceedings of the First Workshop on Learning with Natural Language Supervision*, pages 29–39, Dublin, Ireland. Association for Computational Linguistics.

Shirley Anugrah Hayati, Kyumin Park, Dheeraj Rajagopal, Lyle Ungar, and Dongyeop Kang. 2022. Stylex: Explaining styles with lexicon-based human perception. *arXiv preprint arXiv:2210.07469*.

Minqing Hu and Bing Liu. 2004. Mining and summarizing customer reviews. *Proceedings of the tenth ACM SIGKDD international conference on Knowledge discovery and data mining*.

Quzhe Huang, Shengqi Zhu, Yansong Feng, and Dongyan Zhao. 2021. Exploring distantly-labeled rationales in neural network models. *ArXiv*, abs/2106.01809.

Clayton J. Hutto and Eric Gilbert. 2014. Vader: A parsimonious rule-based model for sentiment analysis of social media text. In *ICWSM*.

Alon Jacovi, Oren Sar Shalom, and Yoav Goldberg. 2018. Understanding convolutional neural networks for text classification. In *Proceedings of the 2018 EMNLP Workshop BlackboxNLP: Analyzing and Interpreting Neural Networks for NLP*, pages 56–65, Brussels, Belgium. Association for Computational Linguistics.

Sarthak Jain, Sarah Wiegreffe, Yuval Pinter, and Byron Wallace. 2020. Learning to faithfully rationalize by construction. pages 4459–4473.

Xisen Jin, Junyi Du, Zhongyu Wei, X. Xue, and Xiang Ren. 2020. Towards hierarchical importance attribution: Explaining compositional semantics for neural sequence models. *ArXiv*, abs/1911.06194.

Nikita Kitaev and Dan Klein. 2018. Constituency parsing with a self-attentive encoder. In *Proceedings of the 56th Annual Meeting of the Association for Computational Linguistics (Volume 1: Long Papers)*, pages 2676–2686, Melbourne, Australia. Association for Computational Linguistics.

Sachin Kumar, Shuly Wintner, Noah A. Smith, and Yulia Tsvetkov. 2019. Topics to avoid: Demoting latent confounds in text classification. In *Proceedings of the 2019 Conference on Empirical Methods in Natural Language Processing and the 9th International Joint Conference on Natural Language Processing (EMNLP-IJCNLP)*, pages 4153–4163, Hong Kong, China. Association for Computational Linguistics.

Jiwei Li, Will Monroe, and Dan Jurafsky. 2016. Understanding neural networks through representation erasure. *ArXiv*, abs/1612.08220.

Scott M. Lundberg and Su-In Lee. 2017. A unified approach to interpreting model predictions. In *Proceedings of the 31st International Conference on Neural Information Processing Systems*, NIPS'17, page 4768–4777, Red Hook, NY, USA. Curran Associates Inc.

Siwen Luo, Hamish Ivison, Soyeon Caren Han, and Josiah Poon. 2021. Local interpretations for explainable natural language processing: A survey. *ArXiv*, abs/2103.11072.

Aman Madaan, Niket Tandon, Dheeraj Rajagopal, Yiming Yang, Peter Clark, Keisuke Sakaguchi, and Eduard H. Hovy. 2021. Improving neural model performance through natural language feedback on their explanations. *ArXiv*, abs/2104.08765.

Tom McCoy, Ellie Pavlick, and Tal Linzen. 2019. Right for the wrong reasons: Diagnosing syntactic heuristics in natural language inference. In *Proceedings of the 57th Annual Meeting of the Association for Computational Linguistics*, pages 3428–3448, Florence, Italy. Association for Computational Linguistics.

Grégoire Montavon, Sebastian Lapuschkin, Alexander Binder, Wojciech Samek, and Klaus-Robert Müller. 2017. Explaining nonlinear classification decisions with deep taylor decomposition. *Pattern Recognition*, 65:211–222.

Dheeraj Rajagopal, Vidhisha Balachandran, Eduard H. Hovy, and Yulia Tsvetkov. 2021a. Selfexplain: A self-explaining architecture for neural text classifiers. *CoRR*, abs/2103.12279.

Dheeraj Rajagopal, Vidhisha Balachandran, Eduard H Hovy, and Yulia Tsvetkov. 2021b. SELFEXPLAIN: A self-explaining architecture for neural text classifiers. In *Proceedings of the 2021 Conference on Empirical Methods in Natural Language Processing*, pages 836–850, Online and Punta Cana, Dominican Republic. Association for Computational Linguistics.

Nazneen Fatema Rajani, Bryan McCann, Caiming Xiong, and Richard Socher. 2019. Explain yourself! leveraging language models for commonsense reasoning. In *Proceedings of the 57th Annual Meeting of the Association for Computational Linguistics*, pages 4932–4942, Florence, Italy. Association for Computational Linguistics.

Maarten Sap, Dallas Card, Saadia Gabriel, Yejin Choi, and Noah A. Smith. 2019. The risk of racial bias in hate speech detection. In *Proceedings of the 57th Annual Meeting of the Association for Computational Linguistics*, pages 1668–1678, Florence, Italy. Association for Computational Linguistics.

Maarten Sap, Swabha Swayamdipta, Laura Vianna, Xuhui Zhou, Yejin Choi, and Noah A. Smith. 2022. Annotators with attitudes: How annotator beliefs and identities bias toxic language detection. In *Proceedings of the 2022 Conference of the North American Chapter of the Association for Computational Linguistics: Human Language Technologies*, pages 5884–5906, Seattle, United States. Association for Computational Linguistics.

Avanti Shrikumar, Peyton Greenside, and Anshul Kundaje. 2017. Learning important features through propagating activation differences. In *ICML*.

Karen Simonyan, Andrea Vedaldi, and Andrew Zisserman. 2014. Deep inside convolutional networks: Visualising image classification models and saliency maps. *CoRR*, abs/1312.6034.

Chandan Singh, W. James Murdoch, and Bin Yu. 2019. Hierarchical interpretations for neural network predictions. In *International Conference on Learning Representations*.

Daniel Smilkov, Nikhil Thorat, Been Kim, Fernanda B. Viégas, and Martin Wattenberg. 2017. Smoothgrad: removing noise by adding noise. *CoRR*, abs/1706.03825.

Richard Socher, Alex Perelygin, Jean Wu, Jason Chuang, Christopher D. Manning, Andrew Ng, and Christopher Potts. 2013. Recursive deep models for semantic compositionality over a sentiment treebank. In *Proceedings of the 2013 Conference on Empirical Methods in Natural Language Processing*, pages 1631–1642, Seattle, Washington, USA. Association for Computational Linguistics.

Jason Wei, Xuezhi Wang, Dale Schuurmans, Maarten Bosma, Ed Chi, Quoc Le, and Denny Zhou. 2022. Chain of thought prompting elicits reasoning in large language models. *arXiv preprint arXiv:2201.11903*.

Michael Wiegand, Josef Ruppenhofer, Anna Schmidt, and Clayton Greenberg. 2018. Inducing a lexicon of abusive words – a feature-based approach. In *Proceedings of the 2018 Conference of the North American Chapter of the Association for Computational Linguistics: Human Language Technologies, Volume 1 (Long Papers)*, pages 1046–1056, New Orleans, Louisiana. Association for Computational Linguistics.

Mengzhou Xia, Anjalie Field, and Yulia Tsvetkov. 2020. Demoting racial bias in hate speech detection. In *Proceedings of the Eighth International Workshop on Natural Language Processing for Social Media*, pages 7–14, Online. Association for Computational Linguistics.

Zhilin Yang, Zihang Dai, Yiming Yang, Jaime G. Carbonell, Ruslan Salakhutdinov, and Quoc V. Le. 2019. Xlnet: Generalized autoregressive pretraining for language understanding. In *Neural Information Processing Systems*.

Mo Yu, Shiyu Chang, Yang Zhang, and Tommi S Jaakkola. 2019. Rethinking cooperative rationalization: Introspective extraction and complement control. *arXiv preprint arXiv:1910.13294*.

Omar Zaidan and Jason Eisner. 2008. Modeling annotators: A generative approach to learning from annotator rationales. In *EMNLP*.

A Experimental Details

Training We use SELFEXPLAIN as our baseline. When training both the baseline and LEXPLAIN, we keep the same hyperparameters and weights from the pretraining of the XLNet encoder and finetune the model for 5 epochs. In LEXPLAIN we do not use the GIL, since initial experiments showed no difference between adding and removing the GIL.

For LEXPLAIN, we perform hyperparameter tuning for $\alpha_1 \in \{0.01, 0.05, 0.1\}$ and $\alpha_2 \in \{0.8, 1.5.2.0\}$ on the development set. We report results on the best configuration on the test sets.

Toxicity Dataset DWMW17 is a Twitter dataset with 25,000 tweets that have been annotated for hate speech, offensive, or none alongside dialect labels: African American English (AAE) and White American English. We merge the hatespeech and offensive examples and regard all of them as toxic. FDCL18 is also a Twitter dataset with 100,000 tweets annotated for hate, abuse, spam, and none. We select all instances, except for the ones labeled as spam. Again, we merge the hate and abuse examples and regard all of them as toxic. For all datasets we use the provided splits to train/dev./test.[2]

Task Lexicons Our sentiment lexicon of 2,470 words is derived by combining two existing lexicons: Hutto and Gilbert (2014) and Hu and Liu (2004). For toxicity detection, we use the lexicon from Wiegand et al. (2018), from which we extract 350 toxic words that appear in our datasets. We were only able to obtain a toxic lexicon. Our attempts to create a lexicon of non-toxic words by extracting the most salient words present in the non-toxic instances did not yield improved explanations. We opt to only supervise toxic instances in the training data.

B Human Evaluation

We ask annotators to select preferred explanations between the baseline and LEXPLAIN. They are presented with the model input, the original label and the predicted label and also All annotators are familiar with the tasks and are computer science graduate students.

Instructions given to human evaluators The task here is sentiment analysis. The labels are 0 for negative instances and 1 for positive instances. Please enter **X** or **Y** in the last column for the algorithm that provides the best explanation for the predicted label. If the explanations are the same for both algorithms, please enter **XY**. If the explanations for both algorithms are not satisfactory, please enter **NXY**. If explanations are not same, but both are satisfactory, please enter **SXY**.

[2]Train/dev./test: FDCL18: 54120/10145/11825, DWMW17: 17849/3001/3501, SST2: 66976/872/1821.

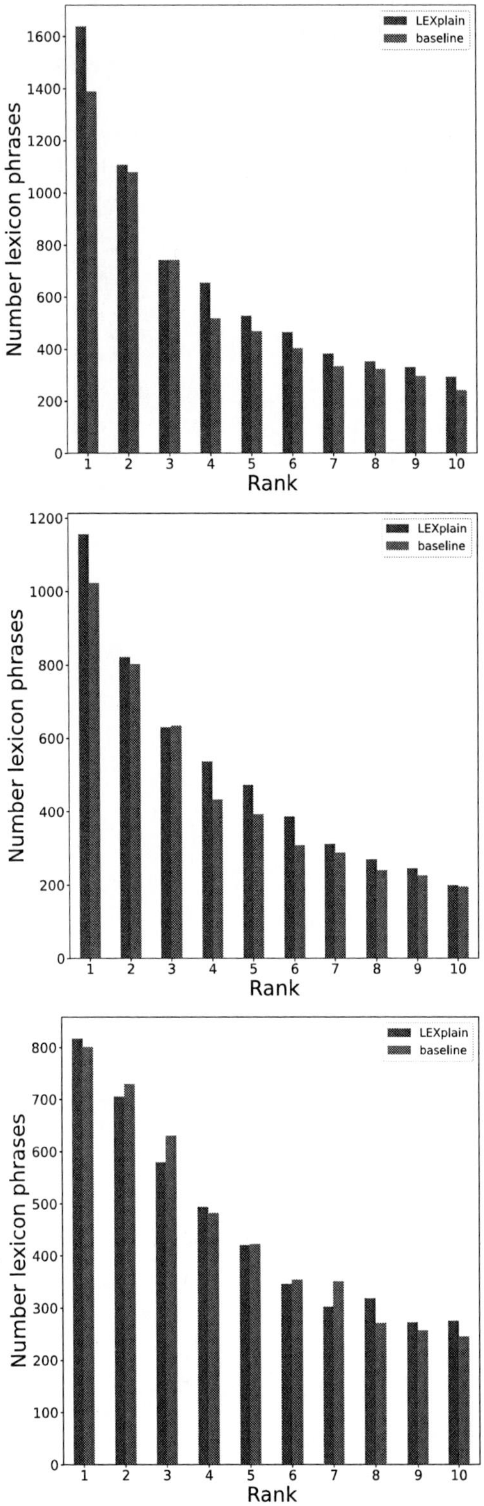

Figure 2: Number of lexicon entries in each rank across all sentences in each test set in the order of [FDCL18, DWMW17 and SST2].

KGLM: Integrating Knowledge Graph Structure in Language Models for Link Prediction

Jason Youn[1,2,3] and **Ilias Tagkopoulos** [1,2,3]
[1] Department of Computer Science, University of California, Davis, CA 95616, USA.
[2] Genome Center, University of California, Davis, CA 95616, USA.
[3] USDA/NSF AI Institute for Next Generation Food Systems (AIFS), University of California, Davis, CA 95616, USA.
{jyoun, itagkopoulos}@ucdavis.edu

Abstract

The ability of knowledge graphs to represent complex relationships at scale has led to their adoption for various needs including knowledge representation, question-answering, and recommendation systems. Knowledge graphs are often incomplete in the information they represent, necessitating the need for knowledge graph completion tasks. Pre-trained and fine-tuned language models have shown promise in these tasks although these models ignore the intrinsic information encoded in the knowledge graph, namely the entity and relation types. In this work, we propose the Knowledge Graph Language Model (KGLM) architecture, where we introduce a new entity/relation embedding layer that learns to differentiate distinctive entity and relation types, therefore allowing the model to learn the structure of the knowledge graph. In this work, we show that further pre-training the language models with this additional embedding layer using the triples extracted from the knowledge graph, followed by the standard fine-tuning phase sets a new state-of-the-art performance for the link prediction task on the benchmark datasets.

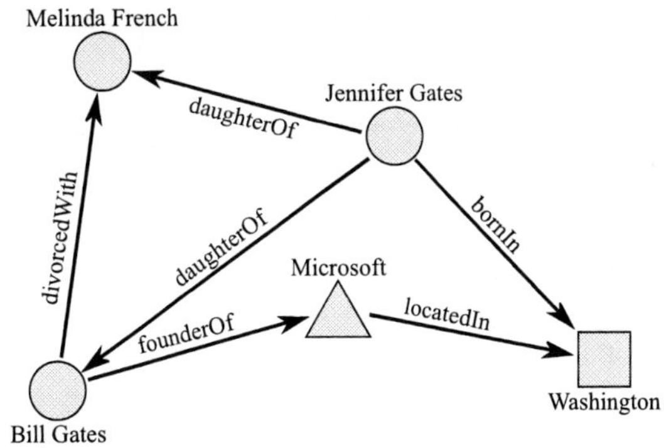

Figure 1: Sample knowledge graph with 6 triples. The graph contains three unique entity types (circle for person, triangle for company, and square for location) and 5 unique relation types or 10 if considering both the forward and inverse relations. The task of the knowledge graph completion is to complete the missing links in the graph, e.g., (*Bill Gates*, *bornIn?*, *Washington*) using the existing knowledge graph.

1 Introduction

Knowledge graph (KG) is defined as a directed, multi-relational graph where entities (nodes) are connected with one or more relations (edges) (Wang et al., 2017). It is represented with a set of triples, where a triple consists of (*head entity*, *relation*, *tail entity*) or (h, r, t) for short, for example (*Bill Gates*, *founderOf*, *Microsoft*) as shown in Figure 1. Due to their effectiveness in identifying patterns among data and gaining insights into the mechanisms of action, associations, and testable hypotheses (Li and Chen, 2014; Silvescu et al., 2012), both manually curated KGs like DBpedia (Auer et al., 2007), WordNet (Miller, 1998), KIDS (Youn et al., 2022), and CARD (Alcock et al., 2020), and automatically curated ones like FreeBase (Bollacker et al., 2008), Knowledge Vault (Dong et al., 2014), and NELL (Carlson et al., 2010) exist. However, these KGs often suffer from incompleteness. For example, 71% of the people in FreeBase have no known place of birth (West et al., 2014). To address this issue, knowledge graph completion (KGC) methods aim at connecting the missing links in the KG.

Graph feature models like path ranking algorithm (PRA) (Lao and Cohen, 2010; Lao et al., 2011) attempt to solve the KGC tasks by extracting the features from the observed edges over the KG to predict the existence of a new edge (Nickel et al., 2015). For example, the existence of the path *Jennifer Gates* $\xrightarrow{daughterOf}$ *Melinda French* $\xleftarrow{divorcedWith}$ *Bill Gates* in Figure 1 can be used as a clue to infer the triple (*Jennifer Gates*, *daughterOf*, *Bill Gates*). Other popular types of models are latent feature models such as TransE (Bordes et al., 2013), TransH (Wang et al., 2014), and RotatE (Sun et al., 2019) where entities and relations are converted into a latent space using embeddings.

*Proceedings of the The 12th Joint Conference on Lexical and Computational Semantics (*SEM 2023)*, pages 217–224
July 13-14, 2023 ©2023 Association for Computational Linguistics

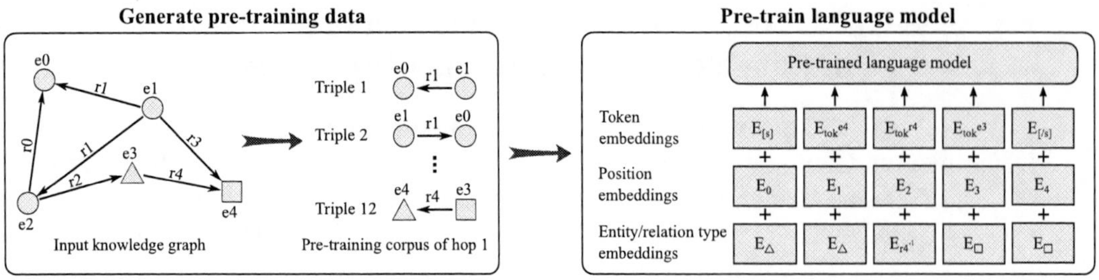

Figure 2: Proposed pre-training approach of the KGLM. First, both the forward and inverse triples are extracted from the knowledge graph to serve as the pre-training corpus. We then continue pre-training the language model, RoBERTa in our case, using the masked language model training objective, with an additional entity/relation-type embedding layer. The entity/relation-type embedding scheme shown here corresponds to the KGLM_{GER}, the most fine-grained version where both the entity and relation types are considered unique. Note that the inverse relation denoted by $^{-1}$ is different from its forward counterpart. For demonstration purposes, we assume all entities and relations to have a single token.

TransE, a representative latent feature model, models the relationship between the entities by interpreting them as a translational operation. That is, the model optimizes the embeddings by enforcing the vector operation of head entity embedding $\boldsymbol{h}$ plus the relation embedding $\boldsymbol{r}$ to be close to the tail entity embedding $\boldsymbol{t}$ for a given fact in the KG, or simply $\boldsymbol{h} + \boldsymbol{r} \approx \boldsymbol{t}$.

Recently, pre-trained language models like BERT (Devlin et al., 2018) and RoBERTa (Liu et al., 2019) have shown state-of-the-art performance in all of the natural language processing (NLP) tasks. As a natural extension, models like KG-BERT (Yao et al., 2019) and BERTRL (Zha et al., 2021) that utilize these pre-trained language models by treating a triple in the KG as a textual sequence, e.g., (*Bill Gates*, *founderOf*, *Microsoft*) as '*Bill Gates founder of Microsoft*', have also shown state-of-the-art results on the downstream KGC tasks. Although such *textual encoding* (Wang et al., 2021) models are generalizable to unseen entities or relations (Zha et al., 2021), they still fail to learn the intrinsic structure of the KG as the models are only trained on the textual sequence. To solve this issue, a hybrid approach like StAR (Wang et al., 2021) has recently been proposed to take advantage of both latent feature models and textual encoding models by enforcing a translation-based graph embedding approach to train the textual encoders. Yet, current textual encoding models still suffer from entity ambiguation problems (Cucerzan, 2007) where an entity *Apple*, for example, can refer to either the company Apple Inc. or the fruit. Moreover, there are no ways to distinguish forward relation (*Jennifer Gates*, *daughterOf*, *Melinda French*) from inverse relation (*Melinda French*, *daughterOf*$^{-1}$, *Jennifer Gates*).

In this paper, we propose the Knowledge Graph Language Model (KGLM) (Figure 2), a simple yet effective language model pre-training approach that learns from both the textual and structural information of the knowledge graph. We continue pre-training the language model that has already been pre-trained on other large natural language corpora using the corpus generated by converting the triples in the knowledge graphs as textual sequences, while enforcing the model to better understand the underlying graph structure and by adding an additional entity/relation-type embedding layer. Testing our model on the WN18RR dataset for the link prediction task shows that our model improved the mean rank by 21.2% compared to the previous state-of-the-art method (51 vs. 40.18, respectively). All code and instructions on how to reproduce the results are available online.[1]

2 Background

Link Prediction. The link prediction (LP) task, one of the commonly researched knowledge graph completion tasks, attempts to predict the missing head entity (h) or tail entity (t) of a triple (h, r, t) given a KG $G = (E, R)$, where $\{h, t\} \in E$ is the set of all entities and $r \in R$ is the set of all relations. Specifically, given a single test positive triple (h, r, t), its corresponding link prediction test dataset can be constructed by corrupting either the head or the tail entity in the filtered setting (Bordes et al., 2013) as

[1] https://github.com/ibpa/KGLM

$$\mathcal{D}_{LP}^{(h,r,t)} = \{(h,r,t') \mid t' \in (E - \{h,t\}) \wedge (h,r,t') \notin \mathcal{D}\} \cup\{(h',r,t) \mid h' \in (E - \{h,t\}) \wedge (h',r,t) \notin \mathcal{D}\} \cup\{(h,r,t)\}, \tag{1}$$

where $\mathcal{D} = \mathcal{D}_{train} \cup \mathcal{D}_{val} \cup \mathcal{D}_{test}$ is the complete dataset. Evaluation of the link prediction task is measured with mean rank (MR), mean reciprocal rank (MRR), and hits@N (Rossi et al., 2021). MR is defined as

$$MR = \frac{\sum\limits_{(h,r,t)\in\mathcal{D}_{test}} rank((h,r,t) \mid \mathcal{D}_{LP}^{(h,r,t)})}{|\mathcal{D}_{test}|}, \tag{2}$$

where $rank(\cdot|\cdot)$ is the rank of the positive triple among its corrupted versions and $|\mathcal{D}_{test}|$ is the number of positive test triples. MRR is the same as MR except that the reciprocal rank $1/rank(\cdot|\cdot)$ is used. Hits@N is defined as

$$hits@N = \frac{\sum\limits_{(h,r,t)\in\mathcal{D}_{test}} \begin{cases} 1, \text{ if } rank((h,r,t) \mid \mathcal{D}_{LP}^{(h,r,t)}) < N \\ 0, \ otherwise \end{cases}}{|\mathcal{D}_{test}|}, \tag{3}$$

where $N \in \{1, 3, 10\}$ is commonly reported. Higher MRR and hits@N values are better, whereas, for MR, lower values denote higher performance.

3 Proposed Approach

In this work, we propose to continue pre-training, instead of pre-training from scratch, the language model RoBERTa$_{\text{LARGE}}$ (Liu et al., 2019) that has already been trained on English-language corpora of varying sizes and domains, using both the forward and inverse knowledge graph textual sequences (Figure 2). Following the convention used in the KG-BERT and StAR (see Appendix A), we use a textual representation of a given triple, e.g., (*Bill Gates, founderOf, Microsoft*) as '*Bill Gates founder of Microsoft*', to generate the pre-training corpus. However, instead of extracting only the forward triple as done in the previous work, we extract both the forward and inverse versions of the triple, e.g., (*Jennifer Gates, daughterOf, Bill Gates*) and (*Bill Gates, daughterOf*$^{-1}$*, Jennifer Gates*), where the $^{-1}$ notation denotes the inverse direction of the corresponding relation.

Table 1: Statistics of the benchmark knowledge graphs used for link prediction.

Dataset	# ent	# rel	# train	# val	# test
WN18RR	40,943	11	86,835	3,034	3,134
FB15k-237	14,951	237	272,115	17,535	20,466
UMLS	135	46	5,216	652	661

To enforce the model to learn the knowledge graph structure, we introduce a new embedding layer *entity/relation-type embedding* (ER-type embedding) in addition to the pre-existing token and position embeddings of RoBERTa as shown in Figure 2. This additional layer aims to embed the tokens in the input sequence with its corresponding entity/relation-type, where the set of entities E in the knowledge graph can have t_E different entity types depending on the schema of the knowledge graph, (e.g., $t_E = 3$ for person, company, and location in Figure 1). Note that many knowledge graphs do not specify the entity types, in which case $t_E = 1$. For the set of relations R, there exist $t_R = 2n_R$, where n_R is the number of unique relations in the knowledge graph and the multiplier of 2 comes from forward and inverse directions (e.g., $t_R = 10$ for the sample knowledge graph in Figure 1).

In this work, we propose three different variations of ER-type embeddings. KGLM$_{\text{Base}}$ is the simplified version where all entities are assigned a single entity type and relations are assigned either forward or inverse relation type regardless of their unique relation types, resulting in a total of 3 ER-type embeddings. The KGLM$_{\text{GR}}$ is a version with granular relation types with $t_R + 1$ ER-type embeddings. The KGLM$_{\text{GER}}$ is the most granular version where we utilize all $t_E + t_R$ ER-type embeddings. In other words, all entity types as well as all relation types including both directions are considered.

To be specific, we convert a triple (h, r, t) to a sequence of tokens $w^{(h,r,t)} = \langle \texttt{[s]} w_a^h w_b^r w_c^t \texttt{[/s]} : a \in \{1..|h|\} \,\&\, b \in \{1..|r|\} \,\&\, c \in \{1..|t|\}\rangle \in \mathbb{R}^{(|h|+|r|+|t|+2)}$, where `[s]` and `[/s]` are special tokens denoting beginning and end of the sequence, respectively. The input to the RoBERTa model is then constructed by adding the ER-type embedding $\mathbf{t}^{(h,r,t)}$ and the $\mathbf{p}^{(h,r,t)}$ position embeddings to the

Table 2: Link prediction results on the benchmark datasets WN18RR, FB15k-237, and UMLS. Bold numbers denote the best performance for a given metric and class of models. Underlined numbers denote the best performance for a given metric regardless of the model type. Note that we do not report KGLM_{GER} performance since the tested datasets do not specify entity types in their schema.

	WN18RR					FB15k-237					UMLS	
Method	Hits @1	Hits @3	Hits @10	MR	MRR	Hits @1	Hits @3	Hits @10	MR	MRR	Hits@10	MR
Model type: Not based on language models												
TransE	.043	.441	.532	2300	.243	.198	.376	.441	323	.279	.989	1.84
TransH	.053	.463	.540	2126	.279	.306	.450	.613	219	.320	-	-
DistMult	.412	.470	.504	7000	.444	.199	.301	.446	512	.281	.846	5.52
ComplEx	.409	.469	.530	7882	.449	.194	.297	.450	546	.278	.967	2.59
ConvE	.390	.430	.480	5277	.46	.239	.350	.491	246	.316	**.990**	**1.51**
RotatE	.428	.492	.571	3340	.476	.241	.375	.533	177	.338	-	-
GAAT	.424	**.525**	**.604**	**1270**	.467	**.512**	**.572**	**.650**	187	**.547**	-	-
LineaRE	**.453**	.509	.578	1644	**.495**	.264	.391	.545	155	.357	-	-
QuatDE	.438	.509	.586	1977	.489	.268	.400	.563	**90**	.365	-	-
Model type: Based on language models												
KG-BERT	.041	.302	.524	97	.216	-	-	.420	153	-	.990	1.47
StAR	.243	.491	.709	51	.401	**.205**	**.322**	**.482**	**117**	**.296**	.991	1.49
$\text{KGLM}_{\text{Base}}$	.305	.518	.730	47.97	.445	-	-	-	-	-	-	-
KGLM_{GR}	**.330**	**.538**	**.741**	**40.18**	**.467**	.200	.314	.468	125.9	.289	**.995**	**1.19**

$\mathbf{w}^{(h,r,t)}$ token embeddings, as

$$\mathbf{X}^{(h,r,t)} = \mathbf{w}^{(h,r,t)} + \mathbf{p}^{(h,r,t)} + \mathbf{t}^{(h,r,t)}. \quad (4)$$

Unlike the segment embeddings in the KG-BERT and StAR that were used to mark the input tokens with either the entity ($\mathbf{s}_e$) or relation ($\mathbf{s}_r$), the ER-type embedding now replaces its functionality. Finally, we pre-train the model using the masked language model (MLM) training objective (Liu et al., 2019).

For fine-tuning, we extend the idea of how the KG-BERT scores a triple (see Equation 6 in Appendix A) to take advantage of the ER-type embeddings learned in our pre-training stage. For a given target triple, we calculate the weighted average score of both directions as

$$\begin{aligned} score_{KGLM}(h, r, t) = \alpha\text{SeqCls}(\mathbf{X}^{(h,r,t)}) + \\ (1 - \alpha)\text{SeqCls}(\mathbf{X}^{(t,r^{-1},h)}), \end{aligned} \quad (5)$$

where SeqCls(·) is a RoBERTa model transformer with a sequence classification head on top of the pooled output (last layer hidden-state of the [CLS] token followed by dense layer and tanh activation function), (t, r^{-1}, h) denotes the inverse version of (h, r, t), and $0 \leq \alpha \leq 1$ denotes the weight used for balancing the scores from forward and inverse scores. For example, $\alpha = 1.0$ considers only the forward direction score.

4 Experiments and Results

4.1 Datasets

We tested our proposed method on three benchmark datasets WN18RR, FB15k-237, and UMLS as shown in Table 1. WN18RR (Dettmers et al., 2018) is derived from WordNet (Miller, 1998), a large English lexical database of semantic relationships between words, FB15k-237 (Toutanova and Chen, 2015) is extracted from Freebase (Bollacker et al., 2008), a large community-drive KG of general facts about the world, and UMLS contains biomedical relationships. WN18RR and FB15k-237 are subsets of WN18 (Bordes et al., 2013) and FB15k (Bordes et al., 2013), respectively, where the *inverse relation test leakage* problem, i.e. the problem of inverted test triples appearing in the training set, has been corrected.

4.2 Settings

We used $\text{RoBERTa}_{\text{LARGE}}$ (Liu et al., 2019), a $\text{BERT}_{\text{LARGE}}$-based architecture with 24 layers, 1024 hidden size, 16 self-attention heads, and 355M parameters, for the pre-trained language model as it has been shown in a previous study to perform better than BERT (hits@1 0.243 vs. 0.222 and MR 51 vs. 99, link prediction on WN18RR) (Wang et al., 2021). For pre-training, we used learning rate = 5e-05, batch size = 32, epoch = 20 (WN18RR), 10 (FB15k-237), and 1,000 (UMLS),

Table 3: Breakdown of the original hypothesis and their results on WN18RR. For claim 1, we continued to pre-train RoBERTa$_{\text{LARGE}}$ using the knowledge graph without the ER-type embeddings. Note that we did not also use the ER-type embeddings layer in the fine-tuning stage. For claim 2, we learned the ER-type embeddings in the fine-tuning stage only without any further pre-training.

		ER-type embeddings						
Model	Continue pre-training	Pre-train	Fine-tune	Hits @1	Hits @3	Hits @10	MR	MRR
Claim 1	o	x	x	**0.331**	0.529	0.728	53.5	0.462
Claim 2	x	-	o	0.322	0.489	0.672	66.4	0.439
KGLM$_{\text{GR}}$	o	o	o	0.330	**0.538**	**0.741**	**40.18**	**0.467**

and AdamW optimizer (Loshchilov and Hutter, 2017). For fine-tuning training data, we sampled 10 negative triples for a positive triple by corrupting both the head and tail entity 5 times each. We used the validation set to find the optimal learning rates = $\{1e-06, 5e-07\}$, batch size = $\{16, 32\}$, epochs = $\{1, 2, 3, 4, 5\}$ for WN18RR and FB15k-237 and 25, 50, 75, 100 for UMLS, and α from 0.0 to 1.0 with an increment of 0.1. For all experiments, we set $\alpha = 0.5$ based on the WN18RR validation set performance. Both pre-training and fine-tuning were performed on 3 $\times$ Nvidia Quadro RTX 6000 GPUs in a distributed manner using the 16-bit mixed precision and DeepSpeed (Rasley et al., 2020; Rajbhandari et al., 2020) library in the stage-2 setting. We used the Transformers library (Wolf et al., 2019).

4.3 Link Prediction Results

The hypothesis behind the KGLM was that learning the ER-type embedding layers in the pre-training stage using the corpus generated by the knowledge graph, followed by fine-tuning has the best performance. To test our hypothesis, we broke down the hypothesis into two separate claims. For the first claim, we only continued pre-training RoBERTa$_{\text{LARGE}}$ followed by fine-tuning without the ER-type embeddings. This test removes the contribution from the ER-type embeddings and solely tests the performance gained by further pre-training the model with the knowledge graph as input. Table 3 shows that claim 1 falls behind the KGLM$_{\text{GR}}$ in all metrics except for hits @1 (0.331 vs. 0.330, respectively). For the second claim, we did not continue pre-training and instead used the RoBERTa$_{\text{LARGE}}$ pre-trained weights as-is. We then learned the ER-type embeddings in the fine-tuning stage. This test shows if the ER-type embeddings can be learned only during the fine-tuning stage. Table 3 shows that KGLM$_{\text{GR}}$ outperforms all of the metrics obtained using the second claim. This result shows that the combination of these two claims works in a non-linear fashion to maximize performance.

The results of performing link prediction on the benchmark datasets are shown in Table 2. Compared to StAR, which had the best performance on MR and hits@10 on WN18RR, KGLM$_{\text{GR}}$ outperformed all the metrics with 21.2% improved MR (40.18 vs. 51, respectively) and 4.5% increased hits@10 (0.709 vs. 0.741, respectively). Although still inferior compared to the graph embedding approaches, KGLM$_{\text{GR}}$ has 35.8% improved hits@1 compared to the best language model-based approach StAR (0.243 vs. 0.330, respectively). Across all model types, KGLM$_{\text{GR}}$ has the best performance on all metrics for WN18RR except for hits@1. Although we did not observe any improvement compared to StAR for the FB15k-237 dataset, we had the best performance on all metrics for UMLS with 21.2% improved MR than ComplEx (1.19 vs. 1.51, respectively). KGLM$_{\text{GR}}$ outperformed KGLM$_{\text{Base}}$ in all metrics.

5 Conclusion

In this work, we presented KGLM, which introduces a new entity/relation (ER)-type embedding layer for learning the structure of the knowledge graph. Compared to the previous language model-based methods that only fine-tune for a given task, we found that learning the ER-type embeddings in the pre-training stage followed by fine-tuning resulted in better performance. In future work, we plan to further test the version of KGLM that takes into account entity types, KGLM$_{\text{GER}}$, on domain-specific knowledge graphs like KIDS (Youn et al., 2022) with entity types in their schema.

Limitations

Although KGLM outperforms state-of-the-art models when the training set includes full sentences (e.g., UMLS and WN18RR), the model performed similarly to the state-of-the-art in cases where the training dataset had only ontological relationships, such as the /music/artist/origin relation present in the FB15k-237 dataset. One major limitation of the proposed method is the long training and inference time, which we plan to alleviate by adopting Siamese-style textual encoders (Wang et al., 2021; Li et al., 2022) in future work.

Ethics Statement

The authors declare no competing interests.

Acknowledgements

We would like to thank the members of the Tagkopoulos lab for their suggestions. This work was supported by the USDA-NIFA AI Institute for Next Generation Food Systems (AIFS), USDA-NIFA award number 2020-67021-32855 and the NIEHS grant P42ES004699 to I.T. J.Y. conceived the project and performed all experiments. Both J.Y. and I.T. wrote the manuscript. I.T. supervised all aspects of the project.

References

Brian P Alcock, Amogelang R Raphenya, Tammy TY Lau, Kara K Tsang, Mégane Bouchard, Arman Edalatmand, William Huynh, Anna-Lisa V Nguyen, Annie A Cheng, Sihan Liu, et al. 2020. Card 2020: antibiotic resistome surveillance with the comprehensive antibiotic resistance database. *Nucleic acids research*, 48(D1):D517–D525.

Sören Auer, Christian Bizer, Georgi Kobilarov, Jens Lehmann, Richard Cyganiak, and Zachary Ives. 2007. Dbpedia: A nucleus for a web of open data. In *The semantic web*, pages 722–735. Springer.

Kurt Bollacker, Colin Evans, Praveen Paritosh, Tim Sturge, and Jamie Taylor. 2008. Freebase: a collaboratively created graph database for structuring human knowledge. In *Proceedings of the 2008 ACM SIGMOD international conference on Management of data*, pages 1247–1250.

Antoine Bordes, Nicolas Usunier, Alberto Garcia-Duran, Jason Weston, and Oksana Yakhnenko. 2013. Translating embeddings for modeling multi-relational data. *Advances in neural information processing systems*, 26.

Andrew Carlson, Justin Betteridge, Bryan Kisiel, Burr Settles, Estevam R Hruschka, and Tom M Mitchell. 2010. Toward an architecture for never-ending language learning. In *Twenty-Fourth AAAI conference on artificial intelligence*.

Silviu Cucerzan. 2007. Large-scale named entity disambiguation based on wikipedia data. In *Proceedings of the 2007 joint conference on empirical methods in natural language processing and computational natural language learning (EMNLP-CoNLL)*, pages 708–716.

Tim Dettmers, Pasquale Minervini, Pontus Stenetorp, and Sebastian Riedel. 2018. Convolutional 2d knowledge graph embeddings. In *Thirty-second AAAI conference on artificial intelligence*.

Jacob Devlin, Ming-Wei Chang, Kenton Lee, and Kristina Toutanova. 2018. Bert: Pre-training of deep bidirectional transformers for language understanding. *arXiv preprint arXiv:1810.04805*.

Xin Dong, Evgeniy Gabrilovich, Geremy Heitz, Wilko Horn, Ni Lao, Kevin Murphy, Thomas Strohmann, Shaohua Sun, and Wei Zhang. 2014. Knowledge vault: A web-scale approach to probabilistic knowledge fusion. In *Proceedings of the 20th ACM SIGKDD international conference on Knowledge discovery and data mining*, pages 601–610.

Ni Lao and William W Cohen. 2010. Relational retrieval using a combination of path-constrained random walks. *Machine learning*, 81(1):53–67.

Ni Lao, Tom Mitchell, and William Cohen. 2011. Random walk inference and learning in a large scale knowledge base. In *Proceedings of the 2011 conference on empirical methods in natural language processing*, pages 529–539.

Da Li, Ming Yi, and Yukai He. 2022. Lp-bert: Multi-task pre-training knowledge graph bert for link prediction. *arXiv preprint arXiv:2201.04843*.

Yixue Li and Luonan Chen. 2014. Big biological data: challenges and opportunities. *Genomics, proteomics & bioinformatics*, 12(5):187.

Yinhan Liu, Myle Ott, Naman Goyal, Jingfei Du, Mandar Joshi, Danqi Chen, Omer Levy, Mike Lewis, Luke Zettlemoyer, and Veselin Stoyanov. 2019. Roberta: A robustly optimized bert pretraining approach. *arXiv preprint arXiv:1907.11692*.

Ilya Loshchilov and Frank Hutter. 2017. Decoupled weight decay regularization. *arXiv preprint arXiv:1711.05101*.

George A Miller. 1998. *WordNet: An electronic lexical database*. MIT press.

Maximilian Nickel, Kevin Murphy, Volker Tresp, and Evgeniy Gabrilovich. 2015. A review of relational machine learning for knowledge graphs. *Proceedings of the IEEE*, 104(1):11–33.

Samyam Rajbhandari, Jeff Rasley, Olatunji Ruwase, and Yuxiong He. 2020. Zero: Memory optimizations toward training trillion parameter models. In *SC20: International Conference for High Performance Computing, Networking, Storage and Analysis*, pages 1–16. IEEE.

Jeff Rasley, Samyam Rajbhandari, Olatunji Ruwase, and Yuxiong He. 2020. Deepspeed: System optimizations enable training deep learning models with over 100 billion parameters. In *Proceedings of the 26th ACM SIGKDD International Conference on Knowledge Discovery & Data Mining*, pages 3505–3506.

Andrea Rossi, Denilson Barbosa, Donatella Firmani, Antonio Matinata, and Paolo Merialdo. 2021. Knowledge graph embedding for link prediction: A comparative analysis. *ACM Transactions on Knowledge Discovery from Data (TKDD)*, 15(2):1–49.

Adrian Silvescu, Doina Caragea, and Anna Atramentov. 2012. Graph databases. *Artificial Intelligence Research Laboratory Department of Computer Science, Iowa State University.*

Zhiqing Sun, Zhi-Hong Deng, Jian-Yun Nie, and Jian Tang. 2019. Rotate: Knowledge graph embedding by relational rotation in complex space. *arXiv preprint arXiv:1902.10197.*

Kristina Toutanova and Danqi Chen. 2015. Observed versus latent features for knowledge base and text inference. In *Proceedings of the 3rd workshop on continuous vector space models and their compositionality*, pages 57–66.

Thanh Vu, Tu Dinh Nguyen, Dat Quoc Nguyen, Dinh Phung, et al. 2019. A capsule network-based embedding model for knowledge graph completion and search personalization. In *Proceedings of the 2019 Conference of the North American Chapter of the Association for Computational Linguistics: Human Language Technologies, Volume 1 (Long and Short Papers)*, pages 2180–2189.

Bo Wang, Tao Shen, Guodong Long, Tianyi Zhou, Ying Wang, and Yi Chang. 2021. Structure-augmented text representation learning for efficient knowledge graph completion. In *Proceedings of the Web Conference 2021*, pages 1737–1748.

Quan Wang, Zhendong Mao, Bin Wang, and Li Guo. 2017. Knowledge graph embedding: A survey of approaches and applications. *IEEE Transactions on Knowledge and Data Engineering*, 29(12):2724–2743.

Zhen Wang, Jianwen Zhang, Jianlin Feng, and Zheng Chen. 2014. Knowledge graph embedding by translating on hyperplanes. In *Proceedings of the AAAI Conference on Artificial Intelligence*, volume 28.

Robert West, Evgeniy Gabrilovich, Kevin Murphy, Shaohua Sun, Rahul Gupta, and Dekang Lin. 2014. Knowledge base completion via search-based question answering. In *Proceedings of the 23rd international conference on World wide web*, pages 515–526.

Thomas Wolf, Lysandre Debut, Victor Sanh, Julien Chaumond, Clement Delangue, Anthony Moi, Pierric Cistac, Tim Rault, Rémi Louf, Morgan Funtowicz, et al. 2019. Huggingface's transformers: State-of-the-art natural language processing. *arXiv preprint arXiv:1910.03771.*

Liang Yao, Chengsheng Mao, and Yuan Luo. 2019. Kg-bert: Bert for knowledge graph completion. *arXiv preprint arXiv:1909.03193.*

Jason Youn, Navneet Rai, and Ilias Tagkopoulos. 2022. Knowledge integration and decision support for accelerated discovery of antibiotic resistance genes. *Nature Communications*, 13(1):1–11.

Hanwen Zha, Zhiyu Chen, and Xifeng Yan. 2021. Inductive relation prediction by bert. *arXiv preprint arXiv:2103.07102.*

A Previous Work

A.1 KG-BERT

KG-BERT (Yao et al., 2019) is a fine-tuning method that utilizes the base version of the pre-trained language model BERT ($\text{BERT}_{\text{BASE}}$) (Devlin et al., 2018) as an encoder for entities and relations of the knowledge graph. Specifically, KG-BERT first converts a triple (h, r, t) to a sequence of tokens $w^{(h,r,t)} = \langle \texttt{[CLS]} w_a^h \texttt{[SEP]} w_b^r \texttt{[SEP]} w_c^t \texttt{[SEP]} : a \in \{1..|h|\} \,\&\, b \in \{1..|r|\} \,\&\, c \in \{1..|t|\}\rangle$, where w_n denotes the nth token of either entity or relation, `[CLS]` and `[SEP]` are the special tokens, while $|h|$, $|r|$, and $|t|$ denote the number of tokens in the head entity, relation, and tail entity, respectively. This textual token sequence is then converted to a sequence of token embeddings $\mathbf{w}^{(h,r,t)} \in \mathbb{R}^{d\times(|h|+|r|+|t|+4)}$, where d is the dimension of the embeddings and 4 is from the special tokens. Then the segment embeddings $\mathbf{s}^{(h,r,t)} = \langle(\mathbf{s}_e)_{\times(|h|+2)}(\mathbf{s}_r)_{\times(|r|+1)}(\mathbf{s}_e)_{\times(|t|+1)}\rangle$, where $\mathbf{s}_e$ and $\mathbf{s}_r$ are used to differentiate entities from relations, respectively, as well as the position embeddings $\mathbf{p}^{(h,r,t)} = \langle \mathbf{p}_i : i \in \{1..(|h|+|r|+|t|+4)\}\rangle$ are added to the token embeddings $\mathbf{w}^{(h,r,t)}$ to form a final input representation $\mathbf{X}^{(h,r,t)} \in \mathbb{R}^{d\times(|h|+|r|+|t|+4)}$ that is fed to BERT as input. Then, the score of how likely a given triple (h, r, t) is to be true is computed by

$$score_{\text{KG-BERT}}(h, r, t) = \text{SeqCls}(\mathbf{X}^{(h,r,t)}). \quad (6)$$

KG-BERT significantly improved the MR of the link prediction task compared to the previous state-of-the-art approach CapsE (Vu et al., 2019) (97 compared to 719, an 86.5% decrease), but suffered from poor hits@1 of 0.041 due to the entity ambiguation problem and lack of structural learning (Wang et al., 2021; Cucerzan, 2007).

A.2 StAR

StAR (Wang et al., 2021) is a hybrid model that learns both the contextual and structural information of the knowledge graph by augmenting the structured knowledge in the encoder. It divides a triple into two parts, (*h*, *r*) and (*t*), and applies a Siamese-style transformer with a sequence classification head to generate $\boldsymbol{u} = \text{Pool}(\mathbf{X}^{(h,r)}) \in \mathbb{R}^{d\times(|h|+|r|+3)}$ and $\boldsymbol{v} = \text{Pool}(\mathbf{X}^{(t)}) \in \mathbb{R}^{d\times(|t|+2)}$, respectively, where Pool(·) is the output of the RoBERTa's pooling layer. The first scoring module focuses on classifying the triple by applying a

$$score^{c}_{\text{StAR}}(h, r, t) = \text{Cls}([\boldsymbol{u}; \boldsymbol{u} \times \boldsymbol{v}; \boldsymbol{u} - \boldsymbol{u}; \boldsymbol{v}]), \tag{7}$$

where Cls(·) is a neural binary classifier with a dense layer followed by a softmax activation function. The second scoring module then adopts the idea of how translation-based graph embedding methods like TransE learns the graph structure by minimizing the distance between $\boldsymbol{u}$ and $\boldsymbol{v}$ as

$$score^{d}_{\text{StAR}}(h, r, t) = -||\boldsymbol{u} - \boldsymbol{v}||, \tag{8}$$

where $|| \cdot ||$ is the *L2*-normalization. During the training, StAR uses a weighted average of the binary cross entropy loss computed using $score^{c}_{\text{StAR}}(h, r, t)$ and the margin-based hinge loss computed using $score^{d}_{\text{StAR}}(h, r, t)$, whereas only the $score^{c}_{\text{StAR}}(h, r, t)$ is used for inference. This approach shows a new state-of-the performance over the metrics MR (51) and hits@10 (0.709), as well as significantly improving the hits@1 compared to the KG-BERT (0.041 to 0.243, a 492.7% increase).

Probing Out-of-Distribution Robustness of Language Models with Parameter-Efficient Transfer Learning

Hyunsoo Cho[†], **Choonghyun Park**[†], **Junyeop Kim**[†], **Hyuhng Joon Kim**[†], **Kang Min Yoo**[†‡], **Sang-goo Lee**[†]
[†] Seoul National University, [‡] NAVER
{johyunsoo,pch330,juny116,heyjoonkim,sglee}@europa.snu.ac.kr
{kangmin.yoo}@navercorp.com

Abstract

As the size of the pre-trained language model (PLM) continues to increase, numerous parameter-efficient transfer learning methods have been proposed recently to compensate for the tremendous cost of fine-tuning. Despite the impressive results achieved by large pre-trained language models (PLMs) and various parameter-efficient transfer learning (PETL) methods on sundry benchmarks, it remains unclear if they can handle inputs that have been distributionally shifted effectively. In this study, we systematically explore how the ability to detect out-of-distribution (OOD) changes as the size of the PLM grows or the transfer methods are altered. Specifically, we evaluated various PETL techniques, including fine-tuning, Adapter, LoRA, and prefix-tuning, on three different intention classification tasks, each utilizing various language models with different scales.

1 Introduction

Pre-trained language models (PLM), which are pre-trained on large-scale corpora using transformer-based architectures (Vaswani et al., 2017), have achieved groundbreaking success on sundry benchmarks (Wang et al., 2019b; Rajpurkar et al., 2016; Wang et al., 2019a), establishing themselves as the standard neural model in countless applications. Moreover, language models pre-trained with larger parameters on a rich volume of corpora tend to exhibit more intriguing potentials, such as the ability to capture world knowledge (Petroni et al., 2019), generate codes (Poesia et al., 2022), and even solve mathematical problems (Henighan et al., 2020), on top of understanding linguistic knowledge (e.g., semantic or syntactic). To explore the apex of pre-trained language models (PLMs), the size of PLMs is growing exponentially and has reached billions to a trillion (Brown et al., 2020; Chowdhery et al., 2022; Fedus et al., 2022; Hoffmann et al., 2022).

Under these circumstances, the conventional method for transferring PLMs to a target task (i.e., fine-tuning) is now infeasible as it entails prohibitive costs to train and store the entire parameters of large PLMs for every desired task. To mitigate this issue, several recent parameter-efficient transfer learning (PETL) methods have been proposed to improve task scalability. For instance, adapter-based (Houlsby et al., 2019; Hu et al., 2022) approaches insert small neural modules into each layer of the PLM and update those lightweight modules in the training phase. Inspired by the recent success of textual prompts (Brown et al., 2020), prompt-based methods (Li and Liang, 2021; Lester et al., 2021; Shin et al., 2020) concatenate extra tunable tokens to the front of the input or hidden layers and update prepended soft prompts in the training phase.

Despite these breakthroughs in NLP, even very recent anomaly detection studies (Cho et al., 2022; Shen et al., 2021) are still limited to relatively small bi-directional PLMs (e.g., BERT, RoBERTa). Thus, *how large-scale PLMs or auto-regressive PLMs cope with outliers* is uncharted territory, naturally begging the following questions:

- **Q1**: Does increasing model size improve OOD detection performance without model parameters?
- **Q2**: If so, does scaling the size of PLM makes the model robust enough to utilize them without any additional process?
- **Q3**: Do fine-tuning and various PETL methodologies display differences in OOD detection performance according to the size of PLMs?
- **Q4**: Can the OOD detection methods from previous works (usually for the bi-directional PLMs) be transferred to auto-regressive PLMs (GPT)?

To resolve these questions, this paper investigates the capability of large PLMs as outlier detectors from various perspectives. Specifically, we compare the robustness to outliers with various transfer learning techniques on several OOD bench-

*Proceedings of the The 12th Joint Conference on Lexical and Computational Semantics (*SEM 2023)*, pages 225–235
July 13-14, 2023 ©2023 Association for Computational Linguistics

marks: Full fine-tuning, LoRA (Hu et al., 2022), Adapter (Houlsby et al., 2019), and prefix-tuning (Li and Liang, 2021) on various auto-regressive PLMs with different sizes, i.e., GPT2-S, M, L, XL (Radford et al., 2019), GPT-Neo (Black et al., 2021) and GPT-J (Wang and Komatsuzaki, 2021). From in-depth investigations, we share several intriguing observations: (1) As the size of the PLM increases, the performance improves without any update of model parameters. However, it is still challenging to use it without supervision since their performances still lag far behind compared to the fine-tuned small PLM (i.e., BERT-base). (2) PETLs outperform fine-tuning with sufficiently large PLMs in both IND and OOD metrics. (3) Lastly, leveraging the information of the last hidden representation, which is the most prevailing method for bi-directional PLM in recent OOD detection, does not transfer well in auto-regressive PLM, requiring a novel representation extracting technique. We believe that these findings will help future anomaly detection studies.

2 Probing OOD Robustness

2.1 Backbones and Models

To investigate the trend of OOD performance under varying scales of PLM, we consider three factors during backbone selection. They should be (1) publicly available, (2) reasonably large, and (3) share identical structures to eliminate factors other than size. Since recent large PLMs utilize auto-regressive objectives due to their computational complexity, we adopt six auto-regressive PLMs as the backbone of our experiments accordingly: **GPT2 (S,M,L,XL)**, **GPT-Neo**, and **GPT-J**.

For the parameter-efficient transfer methods, we selected two methods: two adapter-based and one prompt engineering-based. Namely, **Adapter** (Houlsby et al., 2019), **LoRA** (Hu et al., 2022), and **Prefix-tuning** (Li and Liang, 2021) are selected for the adapter approach, which is compatible with classification tasks, for the prompt approach. We also report the performance of linear evaluation, i.e., single layer perceptron (SLP) on top of PLMs, and fine-tuning, which act like a lower-bound and upper-bound, respectively.

2.2 Dataset and Metrics

Dataset. We evaluate our model on two datasets, CLINC150 and Banking77, widely used in OOD detection. CLINC150 dataset (Larson et al., 2019) contains 150 class labels (15 intents for 10 domains), while Banking77 dataset (Casanueva et al., 2020) consists of fine-grained 77 bank-related intents. Following the experimental settings from previous works (Cho et al., 2022; Zhang et al., 2022; Shu et al., 2017; Fei and Liu, 2016; Lin and Xu, 2019), we validate our models in two different scenarios: far-OOD setting and close-OOD setting. For CLINC dataset, we train our model with the whole training dataset and test with an independent OOD test split from CLINC dataset, which does not overlap with 150 classes in the training dataset. Outliers in CLINC OOD split are distributionally far from the training distribution (Zhang et al., 2022), so it is relatively easy to discern. For Banking77, we partition the dataset into 2 disjoint datasets (i.e., IND / OOD dataset) based on the class label. Since both IND and OOD datasets originated from the equivalent dataset, they share similar distributions and properties, making the task more demanding. Thus, we refer to a CLINC OOD setting as far-OOD and split settings in Banking as close-OOD settings, respectively.

Metrics. To evaluate IND performance, we measured the classification accuracy. And for OOD performance, we adopt two metrics commonly used in recent OOD detection literature:

- **FPR@95.** The false-positive rate at the true-positive rate of 95% (FPR@95) measures the probability of classifying OOD input as IND input when the true-positive rate is 95%.
- **AUROC.** The area under the receiver operating characteristic curve (AUROC) is a threshold-free metric that indicates the ability of the model to discriminate outliers from IND samples.

2.3 OOD Evaluation Methods

Evaluation in OOD detection is done via a scoring function, which outputs the appropriateness of the input into a single scalar value (p). Then we compare p with the pre-set threshold δ to determine whether the input is an outlier or not:

$$I_\delta(\boldsymbol{x}) = \begin{cases} \text{IND} & p(\boldsymbol{x}) \geq \delta \\ \text{OOD} & p(\boldsymbol{x}) < \delta, \end{cases} \tag{1}$$

In this paper, we evaluate the performance of our method in 4 different evaluation methods, which can be categorized into 2 higher branches: representation-based and logit-based.

Logit-based approaches exploit the PLM's prediction result extracted from the classification layer as

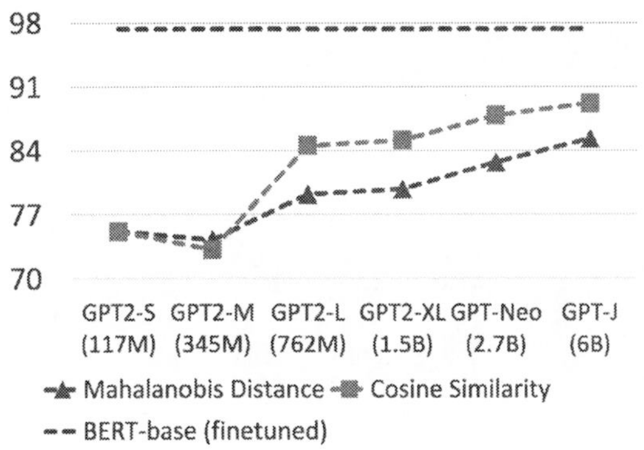

(a) Performance on far-OOD setting.

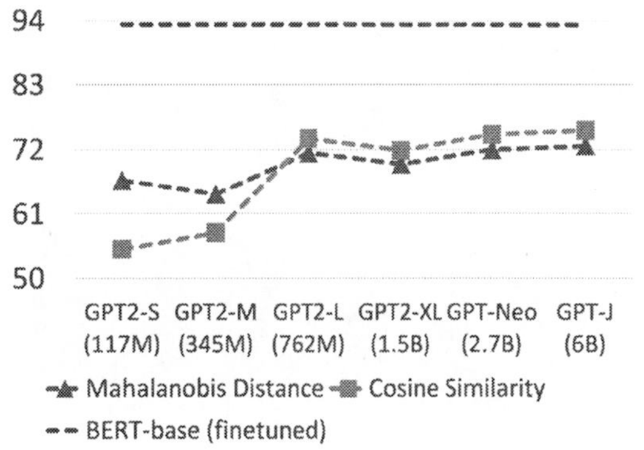

(b) Performance on close-OOD setting.

Figure 1: OOD detection performance of PLMs without updating the model parameters.

their primary information to discern outliers. Logit-based approaches are simple and have their own dominance in computational cost since it pursues OOD detection and general classification nigh simultaneously.

• **MSP** is a baseline method in this branch that employs the maximum softmax probability to score the appropriateness of the given input, based on the idea that the model will output more certain output (higher probability) to a normal sample (Hendrycks and Gimpel, 2017):

$$p(\boldsymbol{x}) = \frac{e^{f_i(\boldsymbol{x})}}{\Sigma_{j=1}^{N} e^{f_j(\boldsymbol{x})}}, \tag{2}$$

where $f_i(\boldsymbol{x})$ refer to as max value from the classification layer (max logit value).

• **Energy** is a variant of MSP, which calibrates logit value based on energy function (Liu et al., 2020):

$$p(\boldsymbol{x}) = -E(\boldsymbol{x}; f) = T \cdot \log \Sigma_i^N e^{f(\boldsymbol{x})/T}. \tag{3}$$

Representation-based approaches, on the other hand, employ the hidden representation from PLM as their primary source. Since the size of the hidden representation is larger and inheres more copious information, they generally yield a more precise decision than logit-based approaches. However, they require more inference time to derive a final score. We employed Mahalanobis distance-based and cosine similarity-based methods in this branch.

• **Mahalanobis distance** refers to the distance between the specific distribution and the input. In OOD detection, we estimate the gaussian distribution of the training dataset and utilize the minimum Mahalanobis distance to score the input suitability (Lee et al., 2018):

$$p(\boldsymbol{x}) = (\boldsymbol{h} - \boldsymbol{\mu}_k)^\top \Sigma^{-1} (\boldsymbol{h} - \boldsymbol{\mu}_k), \tag{4}$$

where training distribution is $(\mathcal{N}(\boldsymbol{\mu}_i, \Sigma)$ for $i \in i = \{1, 2, \cdots, |C|\})$, and k refers to a index of minimum mahalanobis distance.

• **Cosine Similarity** method utilizes the cosine distance between the representation of the given input ($z(x)$) and the nearest neighbor $z(x_{nn})$ (Tack et al., 2020):

$$p(\boldsymbol{x}) = \text{sim}(\boldsymbol{z}(\boldsymbol{x}), \boldsymbol{z}(\boldsymbol{x}_{nn})) \tag{5}$$

3 Analysis

In this section, we share several intriguing findings and insights from various settings.

3.1 OOD Robustness of PLMs without Supervision.

In this experiment, we investigate the OOD detection capability of PLMs without parameter tuning. Precisely, we extract the final layer representation from each frozen PLM and evaluate their performance via representation-based evaluation methods. (Logit-based evaluation methods are not used as they require additional training of the classification layer.) Figure 1 summarizes the results in two scenarios (i.e., far-OOD and close-OOD). We verified the correlation between the size of PLMs and their OOD detection ability, but utilizing them without parameter supervision is roughly impossible since they still lag far behind the small supervised methods (i.e., BERT-base with Mahalanobis evaluation) in a barebone setting. Moreover, performance improvement from the scaling saturates in a more harsh setting (i.e., close-OOD), displaying an unbridgeable gap with the fine-tuned model.

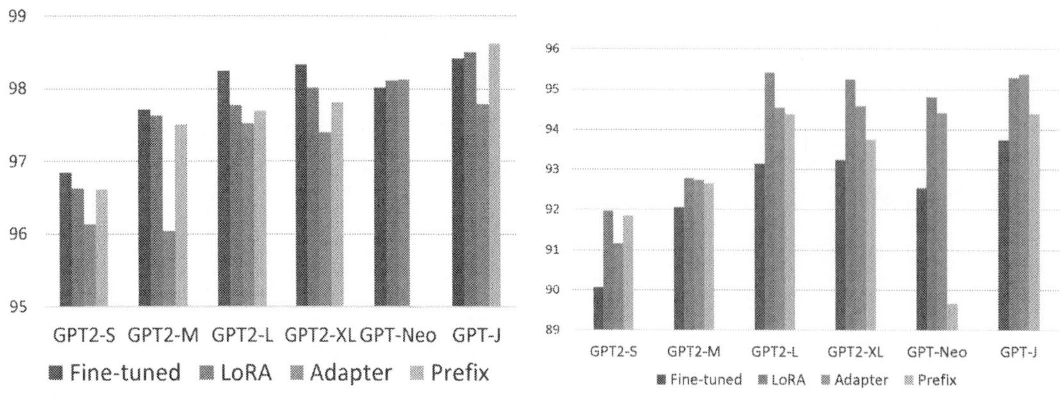

(a) Performance on far-OOD setting.

(b) Performance on close-OOD setting.

Figure 2: OOD detection performance of PLMs without updating the model parameters.

Setting	Backbone	Evaluation Method			
		MSP	Energy	Mahal.	Cosine
CLINC Setting	GPT2-S	93.22	**95.79**	77.63	76.34
	GPT2-M	95.41	**97.63**	82.42	79.82
	GPT2-L	96.21	**97.77**	96.93	97.57
	GPT2-XL	96.48	**97.99**	97.28	97.66
	GPT-Neo	96.04	**97.72**	96.59	97.64
	GPT-J	97.34	**98.50**	97.91	98.20
Banking Split 25%	GPT2-S	90.12	**91.32**	75.32	73.11
	GPT2-M	91.74	**92.78**	78.03	76.56
	GPT2-L	93.02	**93.45**	92.44	93.41
	GPT2-XL	94.29	**94.95**	93.24	94.10
	GPT-Neo	93.83	**94.85**	92.79	93.88
	GPT-J	94.11	**95.10**	93.66	94.80

Table 1: AUROC of each PLMs trained with LoRA. Energey function consistently outperforms other methods .

3.2 Evaluation methods for auto-regressive PLMs.

Many recent OOD works (Zhou et al., 2021; Shen et al., 2021) leverage hidden representation-based evaluation, as they generally surpass logit-based evaluations (Podolskiy et al., 2021). The reasonable conjecture behind their success is that hidden representations have more copious information than the logit value. However, in auto-regressive PLMs, logit-based evaluations (i.e., MSP and Energy) outperform representation-based methods (i.e., Mahalanobis distance and cosine similarity), as shown in Table 1. The reasonable conjecture for this phenomenon is due to the characteristic of the language model. Unlike bi-directional models (e.g., BERT, RoBERTa, DeBERTa), decoder models (e.g., GPT and its variants) do not have [CLS] embedding, which assembles the token embeddings to capture holistic information (Devlin et al., 2019; Kim et al., 2021). Therefore, auto-regressive PLMs generally utilize the last token embedding as a final feature embedding replacing [CLS] embedding of encoder-based models. While the last token of GPT is befitted for predicting the next token, however, it cannot extract the holistic semantics of the sentence suitably, unlike [CLS] embedding. We believe extracting a better representation through various pooling (Wang and Kuo, 2020) methods might be a possible avenue for auto-regressive models to improve the OOD robustness further.

3.3 PETLs VS. Fine-tuning

In this experiment, we investigate the performance gap between various PETL methods (i.e., Adapter, LoRA, prefix-tuning) and model fine-tuning. To compare the performance of each method under similar circumstances, we set every PETL method to utilize a similar number of parameters sufficient enough to reach maximum accuracy. Moreover, we utilized the energy function to evaluate each method as they displayed the best performance among other evaluation methods, i.e., cosine, Mahalanobis, and MSP, in the previous experiments. Table 2 summarizes the results.

From this experiment, we observed that PETL methods are more robust than fine-tuning with reasonably large PLMs (i.e., GPT-J). Specifically, most PELT methods on GPT-J outperform fine-tuning with proper tunable parameters. Nevertheless, size is not the ultimate answer. While it is clear that the scale of a model is an essential factor in OOD robustness, larger models are still vulnerable to close-OOD inputs. The capability to detect

Setting	Method	# Params.	Backbone					
			GPT2 (S)	GPT2 (M)	GPT2 (L)	GPT2 (XL)	GPT Neo	GPT-J
CLINC (far-ood)	Linear (SLP)	0%	83.03	87.39	88.47	89.55	89.44	91.94
	Fine-tuning	100%	96.84	97.71	98.24	98.33	98.01	98.41
	LoRA	0.1%	95.00	96.54	97.66	97.72	98.14	97.79
		0.5%	96.41	96.04	97.52	97.45	98.12	97.89
		1%	96.13	95.89	97.61	97.40	98.11	98.50
	Adapter	0.1%	96.62	97.52	97.74	97.71	97.81	96.80
		0.5%	95.64	97.07	97.86	96.94	97.98	98.37
		1%	95.79	97.63	97.77	97.99	98.12	98.50
	Prefix	0.1%	95.53	96.93	96.38	97.88	90.25	98.55
		0.5%	96.91	96.96	97.78	97.88	89.81	97.92
		1%	96.97	97.50	97.69	97.81	88.98	98.62
Banking split 25% (close-ood)	Linear (SLP)	0%	72.97	75.17	80.46	77.59	86.55	89.12
	Fine-tuning	100%	90.06	92.06	93.14	93.23	92.54	93.73
	LoRA	0.1%	91.18	91.74	94.65	94.58	94.29	95.82
		0.5%	91.16	92.98	94.54	94.04	94.55	94.65
		1%	91.39	92.39	93.45	93.59	94.81	95.29
	Adapter	0.1%	91.97	93.24	94.90	94.69	93.26	95.59
		0.5%	92.90	92.63	95.18	95.24	93.61	95.83
		1%	91.32	92.78	95.41	94.95	94.41	95.37
	Prefix	0.1%	91.22	91.92	93.96	93.48	81.9	94.93
		0.5%	91.85	92.55	93.84	93.34	80.82	93.99
		1%	92.09	92.65	94.38	93.74	89.66	94.39

Table 2: AUROC of various PETL methods with various number of parameters evaluated by the energy function.

far-OOD inputs (far from the training distribution) improves proportionally as the size grows, while the ability to identify close-OOD input improves rather trivially. PLM's vulnerability to close-OOD has already been reported in other studies (Zhang et al., 2022), and this may be related to shortcut learning (Geirhos et al., 2020) that predicts with high probability by looking at specific words. Generating OOD data with particular keywords or utilizing another pretext task, such as (Moon et al., 2021), can be worthy approaches to alleviate such phenomena. A suitable OOD approach is necessary to alleviate the aforementioned issue, as it can further boost the robustness. We conduct additional experiments with PETLs on three different numbers of tunable parameters: 0.1%, 0.5%, and 1% of the PLM parameters. Figure 2 summarizes the results. With sufficient parameters to reach maximum performance, there is no meaningful difference or improvement within each methodology. Also, empirically, we confirmed that LoRA is the most stable during learning and that prefix-tuning fluctuates severely according to learning.

4 Conclusion and Future Work

In this study, we showed that the scale of the language model is an important factor in OOD robustness. Moreover, we also showed that various methodologies outperform fine-tuning when applied to sufficiently large PLM. Our follow-up work seeks to create a methodology that allows large PLMs to be more robust to OOD input. The performance improvement that can be achieved by the size of PLM and OOD technique is orthogonal. In line with the growing size of PLM, the OOD technique needs to be developed in a more parameter-efficient way. As such, developing a proper OOD technique compatible with the parameter-efficient transfer methods is our proper goal.

References

Jimmy Lei Ba, Jamie Ryan Kiros, and Geoffrey E Hinton. 2016. Layer normalization. *arXiv preprint arXiv:1607.06450*.

Sid Black, Leo Gao, Phil Wang, Connor Leahy, and Stella Biderman. 2021. GPT-Neo: Large

Scale Autoregressive Language Modeling with Mesh-Tensorflow.

Tom Brown, Benjamin Mann, Nick Ryder, Melanie Subbiah, Jared D Kaplan, Prafulla Dhariwal, Arvind Neelakantan, Pranav Shyam, Girish Sastry, Amanda Askell, et al. 2020. Language models are few-shot learners. *Advances in neural information processing systems*, 33:1877–1901.

Iñigo Casanueva, Tadas Temčinas, Daniela Gerz, Matthew Henderson, and Ivan Vulić. 2020. Efficient intent detection with dual sentence encoders. In *Proceedings of the 2nd Workshop on Natural Language Processing for Conversational AI*.

Hyunsoo Cho, Choonghyun Park, Jaewook Kang, Kang Min Yoo, Tae-uk Kim, and Sang-goo Lee. 2022. Enhancing out-of-distribution detection in natural language understanding via implicit layer ensemble. In *Findings of the Association for Computational Linguistics: EMNLP*.

Aakanksha Chowdhery, Sharan Narang, Jacob Devlin, Maarten Bosma, Gaurav Mishra, Adam Roberts, Paul Barham, Hyung Won Chung, Charles Sutton, Sebastian Gehrmann, et al. 2022. Palm: Scaling language modeling with pathways. *arXiv preprint arXiv:2204.02311*.

Jacob Devlin, Ming-Wei Chang, Kenton Lee, and Kristina Toutanova. 2019. BERT: pre-training of deep bidirectional transformers for language understanding. In *Proceedings of the 2019 Conference of the North American Chapter of the Association for Computational Linguistics, NAACL*.

William Fedus, Barret Zoph, and Noam Shazeer. 2022. Switch transformers: Scaling to trillion parameter models with simple and efficient sparsity. *Journal of Machine Learning Research*, 23(120):1–39.

Geli Fei and Bing Liu. 2016. Breaking the closed world assumption in text classification. In *Proceedings of the 2016 Conference of the North American Chapter of the Association for Computational Linguistics, NAACL*.

Tianyu Gao, Adam Fisch, and Danqi Chen. 2021. Making pre-trained language models better few-shot learners. In *Proceedings of the 59th Annual Meeting of the Association for Computational Linguistics, ACL*.

Robert Geirhos, Jörn-Henrik Jacobsen, Claudio Michaelis, Richard Zemel, Wieland Brendel, Matthias Bethge, and Felix A Wichmann. 2020. Shortcut learning in deep neural networks. *Nature Machine Intelligence*, 2(11):665–673.

Dan Hendrycks and Kevin Gimpel. 2017. A baseline for detecting misclassified and out-of-distribution examples in neural networks. In *5th International Conference on Learning Representations, ICLR*.

Tom Henighan, Jared Kaplan, Mor Katz, Mark Chen, Christopher Hesse, Jacob Jackson, Heewoo Jun, Tom B Brown, Prafulla Dhariwal, Scott Gray, et al. 2020. Scaling laws for autoregressive generative modeling. *arXiv preprint arXiv:2010.14701*.

Jordan Hoffmann, Sebastian Borgeaud, Arthur Mensch, Elena Buchatskaya, Trevor Cai, Eliza Rutherford, Diego de Las Casas, Lisa Anne Hendricks, Johannes Welbl, Aidan Clark, et al. 2022. Training compute-optimal large language models. *arXiv preprint arXiv:2203.15556*.

Neil Houlsby, Andrei Giurgiu, Stanislaw Jastrzebski, Bruna Morrone, Quentin De Laroussilhe, Andrea Gesmundo, Mona Attariyan, and Sylvain Gelly. 2019. Parameter-efficient transfer learning for nlp. In *International Conference on Machine Learning*.

Edward J. Hu, Yelong Shen, Phillip Wallis, Zeyuan Allen-Zhu, Yuanzhi Li, Shean Wang, Lu Wang, and Weizhu Chen. 2022. Lora: Low-rank adaptation of large language models. In *The Tenth International Conference on Learning Representations, ICLR*.

Zhengbao Jiang, Frank F. Xu, Jun Araki, and Graham Neubig. 2020. How can we know what language models know. *Transactions of the Association for Computational Linguistics*.

Taeuk Kim, Kang Min Yoo, and Sang-goo Lee. 2021. Self-guided contrastive learning for BERT sentence representations. In *Proceedings of the 59th Annual Meeting of the Association for Computational Linguistics ACL*.

Stefan Larson, Anish Mahendran, Joseph J. Peper, Christopher Clarke, Andrew Lee, Parker Hill, Jonathan K. Kummerfeld, Kevin Leach, Michael A. Laurenzano, Lingjia Tang, and Jason Mars. 2019. An evaluation dataset for intent classification and out-of-scope prediction. In *Proceedings of the 2019 Conference on Empirical Methods in Natural Language Processing EMNLP*.

Kimin Lee, Kibok Lee, Honglak Lee, and Jinwoo Shin. 2018. A simple unified framework for detecting out-of-distribution samples and adversarial attacks. In *Advances in Neural Information Processing Systems*, pages 7167–7177.

Brian Lester, Rami Al-Rfou, and Noah Constant. 2021. The power of scale for parameter-efficient prompt tuning. In *Proceedings of the 2021 Conference on Empirical Methods in Natural Language Processing, EMNLP*.

Tian Li, Xiang Chen, Shanghang Zhang, Zhen Dong, and Kurt Keutzer. 2021. Cross-domain sentiment classification with contrastive learning and mutual information maximization. In *ICASSP 2021-2021 IEEE International Conference on Acoustics, Speech and Signal Processing (ICASSP)*, pages 8203–8207. IEEE.

Xiang Lisa Li and Percy Liang. 2021. Prefix-tuning: Optimizing continuous prompts for generation. In *Proceedings of the 59th Annual Meeting of the Association for Computational Linguistics, ACL.*

Ting-En Lin and Hua Xu. 2019. Deep unknown intent detection with margin loss. In *Proceedings of the 57th Conference of the Association for Computational Linguistics, ACL.*

Weitang Liu, Xiaoyun Wang, John Owens, and Yixuan Li. 2020. Energy-based out-of-distribution detection. *Advances in Neural Information Processing Systems*, 33:21464–21475.

Xiao Liu, Yanan Zheng, Zhengxiao Du, Ming Ding, Yujie Qian, Zhilin Yang, and Jie Tang. 2021. Gpt understands, too. *arXiv preprint arXiv:2103.10385.*

Ilya Loshchilov and Frank Hutter. 2019. Decoupled weight decay regularization. In *7th International Conference on Learning Representations, ICLR.*

Seung Jun Moon, Sangwoo Mo, Kimin Lee, Jaeho Lee, and Jinwoo Shin. 2021. MASKER: masked keyword regularization for reliable text classification. In *Thirty-Fifth AAAI Conference on Artificial Intelligence, AAAI 2021.*

Fabio Petroni, Tim Rocktäschel, Sebastian Riedel, Patrick S. H. Lewis, Anton Bakhtin, Yuxiang Wu, and Alexander H. Miller. 2019. Language models as knowledge bases? In *Proceedings of the 2019 Conference on Empirical Methods in Natural Language Processing, EMNLP.*

Jonas Pfeiffer, Aishwarya Kamath, Andreas Rücklé, Kyunghyun Cho, and Iryna Gurevych. 2021. Adapterfusion: Non-destructive task composition for transfer learning. In *Proceedings of the 16th Conference of the European Chapter of the Association for Computational Linguistics, EACL.*

Alexander Podolskiy, Dmitry Lipin, Andrey Bout, Ekaterina Artemova, and Irina Piontkovskaya. 2021. Revisiting mahalanobis distance for transformer-based out-of-domain detection. In *Thirty-Fifth AAAI Conference on Artificial Intelligence, AAAI 2021.*

Gabriel Poesia, Alex Polozov, Vu Le, Ashish Tiwari, Gustavo Soares, Christopher Meek, and Sumit Gulwani. 2022. Synchromesh: Reliable code generation from pre-trained language models. In *The Tenth International Conference on Learning Representations, ICLR.*

Alec Radford, Jeffrey Wu, Rewon Child, David Luan, Dario Amodei, Ilya Sutskever, et al. 2019. Language models are unsupervised multitask learners. *OpenAI blog*, 1(8):9.

Colin Raffel, Noam Shazeer, Adam Roberts, Katherine Lee, Sharan Narang, Michael Matena, Yanqi Zhou, Wei Li, and Peter J. Liu. 2020. Exploring the limits of transfer learning with a unified text-to-text transformer. *Journal of Machine Learning Research.*

Samyam Rajbhandari, Jeff Rasley, Olatunji Ruwase, and Yuxiong He. 2020. Zero: Memory optimizations toward training trillion parameter models. In *SC20: International Conference for High Performance Computing, Networking, Storage and Analysis*, pages 1–16.

Pranav Rajpurkar, Jian Zhang, Konstantin Lopyrev, and Percy Liang. 2016. Squad: 100, 000+ questions for machine comprehension of text. In *Proceedings of the 2016 Conference on Empirical Methods in Natural Language Processing, EMNLP.*

Timo Schick and Hinrich Schütze. 2021. Exploiting cloze-questions for few-shot text classification and natural language inference. In *Proceedings of the 16th Conference of the European Chapter of the Association for Computational Linguistics, EACL.*

Yilin Shen, Yen-Chang Hsu, Avik Ray, and Hongxia Jin. 2021. Enhancing the generalization for intent classification and out-of-domain detection in SLU. In *Proceedings of the 59th Annual Meeting of the Association for Computational Linguistics ACL.*

Taylor Shin, Yasaman Razeghi, Robert L. Logan IV, Eric Wallace, and Sameer Singh. 2020. Autoprompt: Eliciting knowledge from language models with automatically generated prompts. In *Proceedings of the 2020 Conference on Empirical Methods in Natural Language Processing, EMNLP.*

Lei Shu, Hu Xu, and Bing Liu. 2017. DOC: deep open classification of text documents. In *Proceedings of the 2017 Conference on Empirical Methods in Natural Language Processing, EMNLP.*

Jihoon Tack, Sangwoo Mo, Jongheon Jeong, and Jinwoo Shin. 2020. CSI: novelty detection via contrastive learning on distributionally shifted instances. In *Advances in Neural Information Processing Systems 33, NeurIPS 2020.*

Ashish Vaswani, Noam Shazeer, Niki Parmar, Jakob Uszkoreit, Llion Jones, Aidan N Gomez, Łukasz Kaiser, and Illia Polosukhin. 2017. Attention is all you need. In *Advances in neural information processing systems.*

Alex Wang, Yada Pruksachatkun, Nikita Nangia, Amanpreet Singh, Julian Michael, Felix Hill, Omer Levy, and Samuel Bowman. 2019a. Superglue: A stickier benchmark for general-purpose language understanding systems. *Advances in neural information processing systems.*

Alex Wang, Amanpreet Singh, Julian Michael, Felix Hill, Omer Levy, and Samuel R. Bowman. 2019b. GLUE: A multi-task benchmark and analysis platform for natural language understanding. In *7th International Conference on Learning Representations, ICLR.*

Ben Wang and Aran Komatsuzaki. 2021. GPT-J-6B: A 6 Billion Parameter Autoregressive Language Model. `https://github.com/kingoflolz/mesh-transformer-jax`.

Bin Wang and C-C Jay Kuo. 2020. Sbert-wk: A sentence embedding method by dissecting bert-based word models. *IEEE/ACM Transactions on Audio, Speech, and Language Processing*, 28:2146–2157.

Thomas Wolf, Lysandre Debut, Victor Sanh, Julien Chaumond, Clement Delangue, Anthony Moi, Pierric Cistac, Tim Rault, Remi Louf, Morgan Funtowicz, Joe Davison, Sam Shleifer, Patrick von Platen, Clara Ma, Yacine Jernite, Julien Plu, Canwen Xu, Teven Le Scao, Sylvain Gugger, Mariama Drame, Quentin Lhoest, and Alexander Rush. 2020. Transformers: State-of-the-art natural language processing. In *Proceedings of the 2020 Conference on Empirical Methods in Natural Language Processing: System Demonstrations*, pages 38–45, Online. Association for Computational Linguistics.

Zhiyuan Zeng, Keqing He, Yuanmeng Yan, Zijun Liu, Yanan Wu, Hong Xu, Huixing Jiang, and Weiran Xu. 2021. Modeling discriminative representations for out-of-domain detection with supervised contrastive learning. In *Proceedings of the 59th Annual Meeting of the Association for Computational Linguistics, ACL.*

Jianguo Zhang, Kazuma Hashimoto, Yao Wan, Zhiwei Liu, Ye Liu, Caiming Xiong, and Philip Yu. 2022. Are pre-trained transformers robust in intent classification? a missing ingredient in evaluation of out-of-scope intent detection. In *Proceedings of the 4th Workshop on NLP for Conversational AI.*

Zihao Zhao, Eric Wallace, Shi Feng, Dan Klein, and Sameer Singh. 2021. Calibrate before use: Improving few-shot performance of language models. In *Proceedings of the 38th International Conference on Machine Learning, ICβML.*

Wenxuan Zhou, Fangyu Liu, and Muhao Chen. 2021. Contrastive out-of-distribution detection for pretrained transformers. In *Proceedings of the 2021 Conference on Empirical Methods in Natural Language Processing, EMNLP.*

Appendix

A Related Work

Parameter-Efficient Transfer Learning is drawing considerable attention lately, emerging as an alternative strategy to fine-tuning. Compared to fine-tuning, parameter-efficient transfer methods show superiority in the number of trainable parameter usage while achieving performance analogous to fine-tuning. Depending on the characteristics of the methods, parameter-efficient transfer methods can be categorized into *Adapter-based* and *Prompt-Engineering* approaches.

Adapter (Houlsby et al., 2019; Pfeiffer et al., 2021) refers to a lightweight neural module injected within each layer of PLM. The structure of the adapter generally consists of a bottleneck layer (down-projection and up-projection), a nonlinear function, a normalization layer, and a residual connection. The adapter has many different variants due to numerous design choices, such as the order or specifics of each component (e.g., which normalization technique will be used) and where the adapter will be attached. For example, LoRA (Hu et al., 2022) inserts low-rank decomposition matrices in each weight in self-attention (Vaswani et al., 2017) (i.e., query, key, and value).

Another line of work, *prompt engineering*, casts the existing task as a text generation problem to fully leverage the capability of PLMs to predict the appropriate word in the given sentence. This approach requires an empirical endeavor of optimizing the prompt to maximize a PLM's performance. Earlier works exploit handcrafted manual prompts (Schick and Schütze, 2021; Jiang et al., 2020) or by providing demonstrations to PLM [1] (Brown et al., 2020; Raffel et al., 2020; Gao et al., 2021; Zhao et al., 2021). More recent work replaces the manual prompt with a soft prompt (Li and Liang, 2021; Lester et al., 2021; Shin et al., 2020; Liu et al., 2021), a machine trainable continuous vector. The soft prompt is a more modular and versatile method that evades additional latency in the inference phase because it detaches the additionally trained parameters and solely employs the final output of the trained parameters as the prompt.

While former parameter-efficient transfer methods showed noticeable achievements, their evaluations generally assume the train and test distributions are identical (i.e., i.i.d. assumption); however, this condition is rarely satisfied in real-world scenarios due to the diversity and volatility of user input. Consequently, if the model can not correctly handle distribution-shifted malicious input and misconceives it as an in-distribution (IND) example, it may lead to fatal accidents.

Despite its practical importance, how large PLMs or parameter-efficient transfer learning cope with unknown input is poorly understood. This work aims to understand language models' capabilities to detect outliers through parameter-efficient transfer learning methods.

[1] also termed as in-context learning.

B Parameter-Efficient Transfer Learning

Adapter The adapter approach inserts small trainable adapter modules between transformer layers while the parameters of the original network remain fixed. The adapter module uses a bottleneck architecture which projects the input dimension h to a lower-dimensional space specified by bottleneck dimension r, followed by a nonlinear activation function, and a up-projection to initial dimension h. In this work, we attach adapter modules in two places, i.e., after the projection following multi-head attention and after the two feed-forward layers, following original implementation in (Houlsby et al., 2019). Also, we use relu as a nonlinear function and layer normalization (Ba et al., 2016).

LoRA LoRA injects trainable low-rank matrices into transformer layers to approximate the weight updates. For a pre-trained weight matrix $W \in \mathbb{R}^{h \times k}$, LoRA decompose $\Delta W = W_{down}W_{up}$ where $W_{down} \in \mathbb{R}^{h \times r}, W_{up} \in \mathbb{R}^{r \times k}$ are trainable parameters. Specifically we attach LoRA in weight matrices in the self attention module. Specifically we attached LoRA to query and key vector following the original implementation.

Prefix-Tuning Prefix tuning prepends l tunable prefix vectors to the keys and values of the multi-head attention at every layer. Following the original implementation, we reparametrize the prefix matrix of dimension h by a smaller matrix of dimension r composed with a large feedforward neural network with tanh as a nonlinear function.

C Expanded Configuration Details

C.1 Common Environment

For the experiments, 4 Tesla V100 SXM2 32GB GPUs are used. The batch size is 8 per GPU. When the GPU is too small for the batch size, we set

dataset	#domain	#intent	#data (train/val/test/ood)
CLINC	10	15	15000/3000/4500/1000
Banking	1	77	7812 / 1520 / 3040

Table 3: Dataset statistics.

BERT-base	CLINC150 Full		
	ACC ↑	FPR-95 ↓	AUROC ↑
Shu et al. (2017)	94.51±0.45	23.33±1.27	95.92±0.05
Li et al. (2021)	96.1±0.37	10.6±0.26	97.72±0.03
Zeng et al. (2021)	94.19±0.28	23.4±1.97	95.75±0.2
Zhou et al. (2021)	95.79±0.13	10.7±0.95	97.6±0.11
Shen et al. (2021)	96.66	10.88	97.43
Cho et al. (2022)	**96.96**±0.39	**6.67** ±0.51	**98.27** ±0.16

Table 4: Results of each model trained on the CLINC150 dataset. The best performance in each metric is indicated in **bold**.

batch size to 4 and the number of gradient accumulation steps to 2. We implemented our model based on Transformers (Wolf et al., 2020) library by Huggingface. Additionally, we used deepspeed (Rajbhandari et al., 2020) to train models. Specifically, we used ZeRO2 with cpu offload on a 240GB RAM CPU. In this setting, fine-tuning GPT-J on CLINC150 full dataset takes about 7.1 GPU hours per epoch. We used AdamW (Loshchilov and Hutter, 2019) optimizer with epsilon 1e-6 and weight decay 0.1. Furthermore, we apply the cosine annealing scheduler. For GPT-neo, the minimum learning rate is 0. For GPT-J, the minimum learning rate is the one fifth of maximum learning rate.

C.2 Number of Trainable-Parameter

For each method, a feed-forward layer is added at the end of the model. In this section, we will calculate the number of additional trainable parameters of each training methods discussed in this paper. Biases are omitted for better readability.

Adapter Adapter method adds four feed-forward layers per transformer layer in the model. Two of them are down-projection layers, and the others are up-projection layers. When the original embedding size of the model is h, the bottleneck dimension is r, and the number of transformer layers is L, the number of the trainable parameters of these layers is calculated as $4Lhr$, excluding the bias of the added layers.

LoRA Similar to adapter, LoRA also adds feed-forward layers per transformer layer. Therefore, the number of the trainable parameters of $4Lhr$. However, the number of parameters are less than adapter if h and r is the same, since LoRA does not use bias of the feed-forward layers.

Prefix-Tuning There are two trainable elements in prefix tuning. The first one is the prefix embeddings. When the number of prefixes is l, and the embedding size is h, lh parameters are used by the prefixes. Second, the reparametrization matrix is also trained. The down-projection matrix has hr parameters, when the reduced dimension for reparametrization is r. The up-projection matrix has $2Lhr$ parameters. As a result, there are $h(2Lr + l)$ trainable parameters on prefix tuning approach.

C.3 Hyper-parameter Search

Tab 5 summarizes hyper parameters for each model.

D Selecting SOTA OOD Method.

The Tab.4 summarizes the results with recently proposed OOD approaches on BERT-base with CLINC dataset. The best performing model (Cho et al., 2022) is selected as the baseline.

Method	Parameters	Values
LoRA	Learning rate	2e-4 (GPT-Neo), 5e-5 (GPT-J)
	Bottleneck dim	8 (GPT-Neo / 0.1%), 80 (GPT-Neo / 1%), 12 (GPT-J /0.1%), 128 (GPT-J / 1%)
	Location	query, value
Adapter	Learning rate	8e-5 (GPT-Neo / 0.1%), 1e-4 (GPT-Neo / 1%), 5e-5 (GPT-J), 5e-4 (GPT-J / 0.1%), 1e-4 (GPT-J / 1%)
	Bottleneck dim	6 (GPT-Neo / 0.1%), 80 (GPT-Neo / 1%), 11 (GPT-J /0.1%), 128 (GPT-J / 1%)
	Location	after Multi-head, after Feed-forward,
Prefix-tuning	Learning rate	2E-4 (GPT-Neo), 5E-5 (GPT-J)
	Bottleneck dim	12 (GPT-Neo / 0.1%), 160 (GPT-Neo / 1%), 20 (GPT-J /0.1%), 256 (GPT-J / 1%)
	Prefix length	5, 10, 20

Table 5: Hyper-parameter search for each model.

Limits for learning with Language Models

Nicholas Asher
CNRS, IRIT
asher@irit.fr

Swarnadeep Bhar
Université de Toulouse 3
IRIT
swarnadeep.bhar@irit.fr

Akshay Chaturvedi
Université de Toulouse 3
IRIT
akshay91.isi@gmail.com

Julie Hunter
LINAGORA
jhunter@linagora.com

Soumya Paul
TELINDUS
soumya.paul@gmail.com

Abstract

With the advent of large language models (LLMs), the trend in NLP has been to train LLMs on vast amounts of data to solve diverse language understanding and generation tasks. The list of LLM successes is long and varied. Nevertheless, several recent papers provide empirical evidence that LLMs fail to capture important aspects of linguistic meaning. Focusing on universal quantification, we provide a theoretical foundation for these empirical findings by proving that LLMs cannot learn certain fundamental semantic properties including semantic entailment and consistency as they are defined in formal semantics. More generally, we show that LLMs are unable to learn concepts beyond the first level of the Borel Hierarchy, which imposes severe limits on the ability of LMs, both large and small, to capture many aspects of linguistic meaning. This means that LLMs will continue to operate without formal guarantees on tasks that require entailments and deep linguistic understanding.

1 Introduction

The success of large language models (LLMs) has led researchers in NLP to harness LLMs trained on vast amounts of data to solve a variety of language understanding and generation tasks, and some have claimed that LLMs can solve any task that can be specified via prompting (Brown et al., 2020). While the list of LLM successes is long, there have been several recent papers that provide empirical evidence that LLMs at least sometimes fail to capture important aspects of linguistic meaning (Kuhnle and Copestake, 2019; Sinha et al., 2020; Yuksekgonul et al., 2022; Chaturvedi et al., 2022; Kalouli et al., 2022). Those who have dabbled in "BERTology" with respect to linguistic meaning often have the feeling that fixing one LLM deficiency just leads to the discovery of new ones.

This paper provides a theoretical explanation of certain of these observed failings of LLMs. In particular, we prove that LLMs cannot learn the notions of semantic entailment or consistency as defined in formal semantics (Dowty et al., 1981) because they are incapable of mastering universal quantification. Our work builds on Siegelmann and Sontag (1992); Siegelmann (2012); Weiss et al. (2018), concerning the expressive power of neural networks, but we focus on the learnability of semantic concepts and use novel tools.

Our argument has widespread implications: not only does a general capacity to recognize semantic entailment and consistency underlie everyday conversational interactions, but the meanings of a great many common linguistic expressions depend on universal quantification. This set includes—but is certainly not limited to—a long list of quantifiers (*every, some, many, most,... every other*, ...), temporal adverbs (*always, never, eventually*) that are essential to planning (Lamport, 1980), modal operators (*possibly*, *necessarily*,...), and certain discourse connectives and adverbs (*therefore*, *if / then*, *except*, *because*, ...).

We begin in Section 2 by contextualizing our claims in terms of expectations about the linguistic capacities and applications of LLMs. In Section 3, we introduce the framework of continuation semantics, which will allow us to adapt certain notions central to truth-conditional semantics to the case of LLMs. Section 4 lays out the core of our theoretical argument, focusing first on what is needed to learn universal quantification and then generalizing our argument to a wide range of linguistic expressions. Our theoretical argument suggests that we should expect certain empirical failures from LLMs, and in Section 5, we provide evidence that our predictions are borne out. Section 6 concludes.

2 Context

Our results are particularly relevant to downstream tasks that require an agent to not only create fluent, creative and contextually relevant speech but also

*Proceedings of the The 12th Joint Conference on Lexical and Computational Semantics (*SEM 2023)*, pages 236–248
July 13-14, 2023 ©2023 Association for Computational Linguistics

to act precisely based on the meaning of linguistic expressions and reliably recognize semantic inconsistency. For a robot that has been instructed (via conversation) to tighten *every* screw of a door, to *never* walk on an airplane wing, or to *stop* drilling *immediately if* certain conditions hold, acting appropriately requires being able to infer what do to based on the *linguistic meaning* of the words *every, never, stop, immediately* and *if*—and in these cases, getting things *mostly* right won't do, especially if lives or substantial economic loss are at risk.

An important corollary of our argument is that while it might be tempting to separate reasoning and linguistic competence (Mahowald et al., 2023), the former is in fact inextricably tied to our ability to draw inferences based on *linguistic* content—not just on, say, mathematical or real-world facts. This in turn suggests that approaches which attempt to patch up knowledge deficiencies for LLMs by giving them access to external models (Mialon et al., 2023) will fall short in developing reliable models of linguistic understanding because LLMs fail to grasp the notions that underlie the very way that sentences (and actions) are woven together in conversation.

Empirical studies like Chaturvedi et al. (2022) show that LLM failures to respect semantic entailment in question answering tasks follow from fundamental features of LLM training; thus while extensive training and large data sets may improve LLM results, performance will inevitably remain unstable and we should continue to expect hallucinations and reasoning errors in NLP tasks like question-answering and natural language inference.

3 Language models and formal semantics with continuations

3.1 LLMs and strings

We consider LLMs trained on transformer architectures over very large corpora using classic language modeling tasks, namely masked language modeling or next sentence prediction. The former involves masking certain words in a given corpus and training the model to guess the missing words, while in the latter, a context (a sentence typically) is provided to the model, which is trained to predict the sentence that follows. This unsupervised training allows language models to build rich internal representations that have been shown through probing to contain at least implicitly a large amount of linguistic information (Devlin et al., 2019; Liu et al., 2019; Tenney et al., 2018).

Formally, LLMs learn a function $f : C \times X \rightarrow [0, 1]$ that assigns a probability to a word (or string or discourse move) $x \in X$ given a context (or finite string) C. More abstractly, let V be a countable set called the vocabulary. For $i > 0$, let V^i denote the set of all length i strings in the vocabulary V and $V^{\leq i}$ denote the set of all strings V whose length is at most i. V^* denotes the set of all finite strings and V^ω the set of countably infinite strings in V. We can then rewrite f as $f\colon V^{\leq n} \rightarrow \mu$, where μ is a probability measure (which is often called its *prediction*) over V^{n+m} for $m \geq 1$. Typically, the prediction function is used on strings of length m where m is smaller than n.

By exploiting f, an LLM can extend μ to a distribution on the set of strings V^*. The most straightforward way is to follow autoregressive models that calculate the probability of strings via conditionalization. For a new sentence $s' = (w_1, w_2, ..., w_{m+1})$, and an input string s of length n provided as context, we have:

$$\mu^{n+m+1}(s'|s) = \mu^{n+1}(w_1|s) \times \mu^{n+2}(w_2\,|s, w_1) \times \\ ... \times \mu^{n+m}(w_n\,|s, w_{m-1}, ..., w_1) \tag{1}$$

For any $s' \in V^*$, $\mu(s')$ represents the confidence with which an LLM predicts s', after training on strings in $V^{\leq n}$.

3.2 Linguistic meaning

In what follows, we are in interested strings that have a well formed meaning and are evaluable as true or false. Linguists use truth conditional semantics to define the meanings of strings or well formed sentences in terms of the conditions under which they are true. Thanks to the work of Tarski (1944, 1956), we can formalize the notion of truth conditions using the set-theoretic notion of a model that defines denotations or truth conditions for sentences recursively from denotations for sentential constituents (Dowty et al., 1981).

The notion of a model not only serves to define truth conditions; it also captures entailments. We define the notion of *semantic consequence* using the notion of a model or structure $\mathfrak{A}$ as follows (Chang and Keisler, 1973):

Definition 1. ϕ is a semantic consequence of Γ (in symbols, $\Gamma \models \phi$) if and only if in every structure $\mathfrak{A}$ in which Γ is satisfied ($\mathfrak{A} \models \Gamma$), $\mathfrak{A}$ also makes true or satisfies ϕ ($\mathfrak{A} \models \phi$). That is: $\forall \mathfrak{A}$, $\mathfrak{A} \models \Gamma \Rightarrow \mathfrak{A} \models \phi$

The notion of semantic consequence integrates entailment with truth conditional meaning; two strings have exactly the same entailments just in case they are true in the same models. Accordingly we can capture the truth conditional meaning of a string in terms of the strings that it entails. *Socrates is a man*, for example, entails *Socrates is human*, *Socrates is mortal*, *Socrates is an adult* but also that *someone* is a man, human, mortal and so on. What it means for Socrates to be a man (and, indirectly, the meaning of *man*) can be captured by the full set of these entailments.

Our idea is to apply truth conditional semantics to LLMs by representing models themselves as strings. Semanticists have used strings and *continuation semantics* (Reynolds, 1974) —in which the meaning of a string s is defined in terms of its possible *continuations*, the set of longer strings S that contain s—to investigate the meaning and strategic consequences of conversational moves (Asher et al., 2017), temporal expressions (Fernando, 2004), generalized quantifiers (Graf, 2019), and the "dynamic" formal semantics of (Kamp and Reyle, 1993; Asher, 1993)(De Groote, 2006; Asher and Pogodalla, 2011). In our case, we will use strings to define models $\mathfrak{A}_s$. We will use this trick to reformulate semantic consequence: where $||\phi||$ is the set of strings describing models that satisfy a truth evaluable string ϕ:$\Gamma \models \phi$ iff $||\Gamma|| \subseteq ||\phi||$.

LLMs naturally find their place in such a framework (Fernando, 2022): given their training regime, the meaning of any natural language expression for an LLM is a function from input contexts to sets of larger strings or continuations. LLMs provide a probability distribution over possible continuations and can predict possible continuations of a given text or discourse.

4 Learning limits for semantic concepts

Semantic consequence defines linguistic entailments and importantly provides the fundamental connection between meaning and inference that ensures linguistic understanding (Montague, 1974). Crucial to $\models$ is the use of universal quantification over all possible structures—an infinite space of possible circumstances of evaluation or set of possibilities. A true grasp of semantic consequence thus requires an understanding of universal quantification at least over countably infinite domains. In Section 4.1, we show that an LLM's training regime makes it fundamentally unable to learn the concept of universal quantification. In Section 4.2, we generalize our argument to show that LLMs are incapable of learning a wide variety of everyday semantic concepts.

4.1 Learning the full meaning of *every*

To see if the set of strings that define the concept *every* is learnable for an LLM, consider (1).

(1) Every object is blue.

We will use strings of atomic formulas and their negations to define models (or more precisely their atomic diagrams) that we will use to test whether an LLM M can learn the concept of universal quantification through inductive reasoning from a series of individual trials over finite subsequences of strings representing countably infinite domains. In particular, we will ask whether it is possible to train an LLM M to judge, for a string s of arbitrary length n, whether s is consistent with (1), or equivalently, given that s defines a model $\mathfrak{A}_s$, whether given $\mathfrak{A}_s$, (1) is true. If M can reliably judge in which models $\mathfrak{A}_s$ (1) is true, we can conclude it has learned the meaning of *every*.

To this end, consider a language $\mathcal{L}$ containing negation, the predicate *is blue* and a countably infinite number of constants a_i enumerating objects of a countably infinite domain. $\mathcal{L}$ formulas are of the form a_i *is blue* and a_i *is not blue*. We use the formulas of $\mathcal{L}$ as "words" to define the set of finite strings, $V_{\mathcal{L}}^*$ and the set of countably infinite strings $V_{\mathcal{L}}^{\omega}$. Each such string corresponds to a finite or countably infinite model in which (1) is true or not.

In the course of training, M will be presented with finite sequences that define structures of increasing size. For each n and set of models of size n, M will form a set of hypotheses $\mathcal{H}^n$, where for $h \in \mathcal{H}^n, h : V_{\mathcal{L}}^n \rightarrow \{0, 1\}$. $\mathcal{H}^n$ corresponds to the hypothesis space of the problem; each h^n says whether a presented sequence of length n is consistent with (1). As each $h^n \in \mathcal{H}^n$ is a characteristic function of a subset of $V_{\mathcal{L}}^n$, we can identify hypotheses with sets of strings. So for instance, $h_{\forall}^n$ is the set of strings in $V_{\mathcal{L}}^n$ that are consistent with (1) and that define models in which (1) is true. We will additionally assume that $h_{\forall}^n$ picks out a suitable set for each V^n, and similarly for each h_k^n.

However simply learning $h_{\forall}^n$ for some n will not be sufficient for M to learn the meaning of *every*. Universal quantification is a concept that applies to arbitrarily large domains. So the question, *Can M*

inductively learn the meaning of every*?* becomes *Can* M *inductively learn hypothesis* $h^{\omega}_{\forall} \in \mathcal{H}^{\omega}$*?*

To answer this question, we first have to specify what we mean by inductive learning. Recall that an LLM M has learned from unsupervised training a function $f\colon V^{\leq n} \to \mu(V^{\leq n+m})$ with $\mu(V^{\leq n+m})$ a probability distribution over completions of length m of contexts of length n. An LLM can use this distribution to compute probability values for arbitrarily long strings or continuations using Equation 1.

In the case at hand, M needs to use this distribution over $\mathcal{L}$ strings to compute the probability that a string s is in $h_{\forall}$ or the probability of s given $h_{\forall}$. To learn inductively M must use its training data $D^{\leq n}$ to update its prior for the distribution μ^n using a rationally justifiable form of *inductive inference*; e.g., for $h \in \mathcal{H}^n$, $\mu^n(s|h) = \frac{\mu^n(h|s) \times \mu^n(s)}{\mu^n(h)}$.

Additionally, we consider two constraints on distributions to define learning in terms of an inductively inferred change in the distribution from the priors. The first constraint, *Max Ent*, says that the distribution μ prior to training should assign all hypotheses a weight based on maximum entropy or a least informative distribution. This is usual with auto-regressive models and a common assumption in other models.

The second constraint is that distributions for inductive learning should be *non-degenerate*. We have assumed that our LLM M has been trained over sequences of length n. Through Equation 1, M can extend the distribution it has learned for V^n to one over V^{n+m} for any string of finite length $n + m$. Recall that we are looking at strings of $\mathcal{L}$ that define structures; the structures defined by strings of length $n + m$ are independent of those defined in V^n and none is intuitively more likely than another. So the prior distribution over V^{n+m} should consider as equally likely all continuations $s.a \in V^{n+m}$, where $s \in V^n$, $a \in V^m$ and . is concatenation. There are also correspondingly more hypotheses in $\mathcal{H}^{n+m}$ than in $\mathcal{H}^n$, since there are $V^{|m|}$ more strings in V^{n+m} than in V^n. Thus $\mu^{n+m}(s.a|h_k) < \mu^n(s.a|h_k)$ for $s.a \in V^{n+m}, s \in V^n$ for each h_k. Non-degenerate distributions will reflect this and should make the model converge to the least general hypothesis supported by the evidence (Muggleton et al., 1992; Plotkin, 1972).

Definition 2. M's distributions over sets of hypotheses $\mathcal{H}^n$, $\mu^n(\mathcal{H}^n)$, after training over V^n are *non-degenerate* if $\forall h\ \forall \delta\ (0 < \delta \leq 1), \exists m > 0$ such that $\forall a \in V^m\ \forall s \in V^n :\ \mu^n(s.a|h) = \max\{0, \mu^n(s|h) - \delta\}$, where $s.a \in V^{n+m}$.

Proposition 1. Models that calculate distributions over strings using Equation 1 have non-degenerate distributions.

As continuations get longer the probability of the continuation will decrease monotonically.□

Because quantifiers like *every* and *some* are eliminable in terms of Boolean functions when we consider finite structures definable with strings in V^*, we must consider strings in V^{ω} to define countably infinite models that capture the full truth conditions of *every*. To extend a distribution over V^n for finite n to a distribution over V^{ω}, we lift the probability of a string to the set of its continuations. In V^{ω}, the set of strings A characterizes the set $A.V^{\omega}$, where $A.V^{\omega}$ is the set of all strings formed by concatenating a string from A with a string from V^{ω}. Using this correspondence, the probabilities of sets of finite strings in V^n can lifted to probabilities of sets of the form $V^n.V^{\omega}$. The laws of probability extend the distribution to complements, intersections and unions of such sets.

We now propose a simple but general notion of inductive learning.

Definition 3. Suppose μ_0 is M's Max Ent prior distribution and let $h \in \mathcal{H}^{\beta}$ for some countable β. M *effectively learns* h iff after some finite amount of training using inductive inference, there is an α, such that: for any $s \in V^{\beta}$, $\mu^{\beta}(s|h) > \alpha > \mu_0(s|h)$ iff $s \in h$.

Proposition 2. If M can effectively learn $h^n_{\forall}$ from sequences of $V^n_{\mathcal{L}}$ for arbitrarily large $n \in \omega$, then M can effectively learn $h^{\omega}_{\forall}$

Assume that M cannot effectively learn $h^{\omega}_{\forall}$ but it can effectively learn $h^n_{\forall}$ for arbitrarily large $n \in \omega$. Then it must admit some string $s \in V^{\omega}_{\mathcal{L}}$, such that $s \notin h^{\omega}_{\forall}$. But then at some finite stage i, s_i must have $\neg blue(a_i)$. By hypothesis M has learned $h^i_{\forall}$. So it has ruled out s_i and *a fortiori* s. □

We now negatively answer our question, *Can* M *inductively learn hypothesis* $h^{\omega}_{\forall}$*?*, under either of two conditions: (i) M has non-degenerate distributions; (ii) M obeys Max Ent and inductive inference.

Proposition 3. Suppose M's distributions are non-degenerate. Then $h^{\omega}_{\forall}$ is not effectively learnable by M over $\mathcal{H}^{\omega}$.

Suppose M trained on $V^{\leq n}$ has effectively learned $h^n_\forall$. So $\forall s \in h^n_\forall$, $\mu^n(s|h_\forall) > \alpha$ where α is as in Definition 3. Since M's distributions are non-degenerate, $\exists m$, such that for all $s \in V^m$, $\exists \delta$: $0 < \delta \leq 1$ where $\mu^m(s|h_\forall) - \delta < \alpha$ and a continuation of s, $s.a$, such that $s.a \in h^{m+n}_\forall$ but $\mu^{m+n}(s.a|h_\forall) = \mu^m(s|h_\forall) - \delta < \alpha$. $\square$

By Propositions 1 and 3, a basic auto-regressive model cannot learn $h_\forall$. We can generalize Proposition 3 to other :

Proposition 4. Suppose M's priors only obey Max Ent and M uses inductive inference. Then $h^\omega_\forall$ is not effectively learnable by M over $\mathcal{H}^\omega$.

Suppose M's training data $D^{\leq n} \subseteq V^{\leq n}$ and M has learned $h^n_\forall$. To learn $h^{n+m}_\forall$, M must project its distribution of $\mathcal{H}^n$ onto $\mathcal{H}^{n+m}$. But the distributions in $\mathcal{H}^n$ and $\mathcal{H}^{n+m}$ are *independent*; for one thing the cardinality of $\mathcal{H}^n$, $|\mathcal{H}^n|$, is such that $|\mathcal{H}^n| < |\mathcal{H}^{n+m}| = |\mathcal{H}^n| \times 2^m$. Our assumptions about inductive inference on $D^{\leq n}$ make it no more likely that *every* will be associated with $h_\forall$ than it is with any of the 2^m $h \in \mathcal{H}^{n+m}$, where strings in h contain the same n prefix as an $s \in h^n_\forall$ but $h \cap h^{n+m}_\forall = \varnothing$. In $\mathcal{H}^{n+m}$ these hypotheses h can be distinguished from $h_\forall$. Max Ent priors over $\mathcal{H}^{n+m}$ imply that for any $s \in V^{n+m}$, $\mu^{n+m}(s|h_\forall) = \frac{1}{2^m}\mu^n(s|h_\forall)$. $\square$

Corollary 1. M cannot effectively learn $h^n_\forall$ from sequences in $V^n_\mathcal{L}$ for arbitrarily large $n \in \mathbb{N}$. There is some n such that $h^n_\forall$ is not effectively learnable.

While LLMs can represent any Borel function to an arbitrary degree of precision (Hornik et al., 1989), Propositions 3 and 4 shows they cannot always learn such functions, given either the constraints of inductive epistemology or the way LLMs generate probabilities for strings. In particular, given our assumptions, no LLM can effectively learn $h^\omega_\forall$. In addition, each LLM is bounded by some number n in the size of sequences for which it can learn $h^n_\forall$. LLMs do not have the capacity to learn the meaning of 'every' even over all finite domains.[1]

Even supposing that an LLM can effectively learn $h^n_\forall$ for some n, this does not amount to understanding *every*. $h^n_\forall$ can be effectively represented with quantifier free conjunctions of formulae, and these do *not* correctly approximate reasoning with a sentence like (2) that applies to arbitrarily large domains. Identifying $\forall$ with a finite conjunction of length n will make $\forall x Fx$ consistent with $\neg\forall x Fx$ in larger structures. In ω structures, for example, $\neg\forall x Fx$ is consistent with every finite subset of the Π^0_1 string $blue(0)$, $blue(1)$, $blue(2)$, ..., in $h^\omega_\forall$, making it inevitable that LLMs will reason incorrectly with *every* in large enough structures.

The situation worsens with sampling: suppose that when we present our model M a long string, M only samples some of the elements in the string; the threat of inconsistency in such a situation can become high and we have no guarantees that such inconsistencies will not arise.[2] But this reasoning is not *independent* of the meaning of *every*; as the semantics and rules of first order logic show, this reasoning is *an integral part* of the meaning of *every*. As a result, LLMs unable to grasp semantic consequence defined in terms of universal quantification; and we thus cannot provide them guarantees that they follow semantic entailments when asked to do semantic tasks. This predicts phenomena like LLM hallucinations and observed elementary reasoning errors.

4.2 Generalizing our answer to Q2

Using tools from statistical learning and the Borel Hierarchy, we now generalize Propositions 3 and 4 to other concepts beyond *every*.

Statistical learning examines the application of a learned function over a test domain and the expected loss over novel applications. The ability to bring the error over test to that over the training set is typically taken to indicate an ability to generalize (Neyshabur et al., 2017). Villa et al. (2013) define learnability in statistical learning theory via the notion of *uniform consistency*. Let μ be a distribution over $\mathcal{H}$ and μ_n the update of μ after n training samples $z_i = (x_i, y_i)$. Let A_{z_n} be an algorithm for picking out a hypothesis from $\mathcal{H}$ based on n training samples. $inf_\mathcal{H}$ is the hypothesis in $\mathcal{H}$ with the lowest possible error (Shalev-Shwartz et al., 2010; Kawaguchi et al., 2017).

Definition 4. An algorithm A on a hypothesis space $\mathcal{H}$ is uniformly consistent if and only if

$$\forall \epsilon > 0 \; lim_{n\to\infty} sup_\mu \; \mu_n(\{z_n : \mathbb{E}_\mu(\{A_{z_n} - inf_\mathcal{H}\mathbb{E}_\mu > \epsilon\}) = 0$$

[1]Unlike Hume's problem of induction (Popper, 1963) and (Wolpert et al., 1995), we exploit particularities of LLMs and the structure of a classification problem. The finite bound on learning of hypotheses goes beyond standard Humean conclusions

[2]Approximation and approximation error can also affect learnability of mathematical functions (Colbrook et al., 2022).

In our case, the best hypothesis, $inf_{\mathcal{H}}$, for instance $h_{\forall}$, will yield 0 error. Our question is whether there is an algorithm that converges to that hypothesis given a certain $\mathcal{H}$ and certain assumptions.

Definition 5. A class of hypotheses $\mathcal{H}$ is *uniformally learnable* just in case there exists a uniformly consistent algorithm for $\mathcal{H}$.

This enables us to link learnability with a number of other features:

Theorem 1. (Anthony et al., 1999) Let $Y = \{0, 1\}$. Then the following conditions are equivalent: (i) $\mathcal{H}$ is uniformly learnable; (ii) Empirical risk minimization on $\mathcal{H}$ is uniformly consistent; (iii) $\mathcal{H}$ is a uGC-class; (iv) the VC-dimension of $\mathcal{H}$ is finite.

The Borel Hierarchy We now turn to generalize the hypotheses we are investigating. V^{ω} has a natural topology, the Cantor topology, which allows us to characterize linguistic concepts precisely. To define the topology, we first define the basic open sets to be sets of the form $A.V^{\omega}$, denoted as $\mathcal{O}(A)$, where $A \subseteq V^*$ is a set of finite strings. Importantly, $\mathcal{O}(A)$ sets are both open and closed or *clopen*, because if $A \subset V^*$ is a countable set, then the complement of $A.V^{\omega}$, $(V^* \setminus A).V^{\omega}$, is also open. And thus, $A.V^{\omega}$ is also closed. The Δ^0_1 class is at the intersection of the Σ^0_1 and Π^0_1 classes and consists of the clopen sets. Σ^0_1 sets include countable unions of Δ^0_1 sets, while Π^0_1 are complements of Σ^0_1 sets and so include countable intersections of Δ^0_1 sets.

These sets form the basis of the *Borel hierarchy* of sets that includes the Δ^0_1, Σ^0_1, and Π^0_1 sets, and more generally includes $\Sigma^0_{\alpha+1}$ as the countable union of all Π^0_{α} and Δ^0_{α} sets, and $\Pi^0_{\alpha+1}$ as the complement of $\Sigma^0_{\alpha+1}$ sets, with $\Delta^0_{\alpha} = \Sigma^0_{\alpha} \cap \Pi^0_{\alpha}$. The hierarchy is strict and does not collapse (Kechris, 1995). We will use this hierarchy to characterize linguistic concepts. Below is a picture of some simple Borel sets and their $\subseteq$ relations.

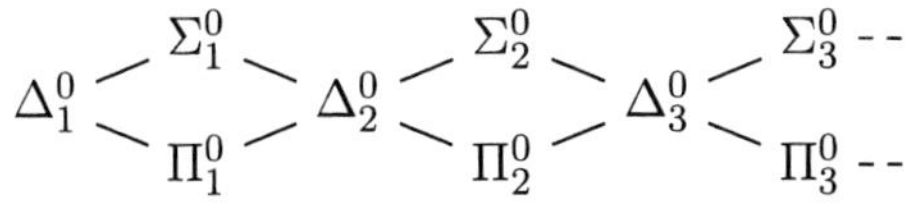

As an example, $h^{\omega}_{\forall} \subseteq V^{\omega}_{\mathcal{L}}$ of the previous section is a Π^0_1 Borel set; i.e., $h^{\omega}_{\forall} = \bigcap_{i \in \omega} B_i$ where the B_i are Δ^0_1.

We are interested in the learnability of Borel sets B with respect to a hypothesis space. The hypothesis space $\mathcal{H}^n$ for $V^{\leq n}$ and algorithem $\mathcal{A}^n$ that an LLM can consider is typically fixed by the maximal length strings it has been trained on. But we will be looking at how an LLM extends its training generalizing to longer and longer strings. More generally, we consider a countable collection of hypotheses—in the case of *every* and $V_{\mathcal{L}}$, the set consists of $h_{\forall}, h_{the first\ 2^n}$ etc. We will assume a countable hypothesis space $\mathcal{H}^{\omega}$ for the Borel sets in V^{ω}, with $|V| > 2$ we want to learn in what follows.

Definition 6. An LLM M can effectively learn a Borel set $S \subset V^{\omega}$ out of a countable set of hypotheses $\mathcal{H}$ iff M has a uniformly consistent algorithm such that $h_S = inf\mathcal{H}$, as in Definition 4, and where $h_S : V^{\omega} \to \{0, 1\}$ defines S.

Clearly if h is $inf\mathcal{H}$, and $\mathcal{A}$ is uniformly consistent, then Definition 3 is satisfied; i.e., there is some $\alpha > \epsilon$ such that $\mu(s|h) > \alpha$ iff $s \in h$.

Theorem 2. An LLM with either (a) non degenerate distribution or (b) Max Ent priors and trained on $V^{<n}$ for some finite n to learn $h \subset V^{\omega}$ via inductive inference (i) can effectively learn a Δ^0_1 set $\mathcal{O}(S) \subset V^{\omega}_{\mathcal{L}}$, where S is a finite subset of $V^{\leq n}$, given $\mathcal{H}_{\mathcal{O}(V^{<n})}$, a hypothesis space restricted to Δ^0_1 sets; but (ii) it cannot effectively learn any Π^0_1 Borel set $B \subset V^{\omega}_{\mathcal{L}}$.

We first show (i). Let $\mathcal{H} = \{\mathcal{O}(A) : A \subseteq V^{<n}\}$. Any $h \in \mathcal{H}$ is determined by a finite set of prefixes P in $V^{<n}$. There are only finitely many such sets in $V^{\leq n}$, and so M has an algorithm A that eliminates at each finite stage of training some Δ^0_1 $\mathcal{O}(P)$ sets. This enables it to converge uniformly toward 0 expected error for the set of finite prefixes that determines $\mathcal{O}(S)$ and so eventually M will have effectively learned $\mathcal{O}(S)$.

Now for (ii). We first consider the case (ii.a) where our learned model has non-degenerate distributions. Consider an arbitrary Π^0_1 complete set B. So $B = \bigcap_{n \in \omega} \mathcal{O}(B_n)$, with $\mathcal{O}(B_{n+1}) \subset \mathcal{O}(B_n)$, where the $B_i \subset V^*$. To compute B, M needs a uniformly consistent algorithm $\mathcal{A}$ over our countable hypothesis space $\mathcal{H}$ that converges on h_B, the hypothesis defining B. Now suppose M has been trained on strings in $V^{<n}$; its algorithms $\mathcal{A}$ are thus restricted to $\mathcal{H}^{<n}$.

Suppose M trained on $V^{\leq n}$ has effectively learned $h^n_{B_n}$. Let $s \in h^n_{B_n}$. Since M's distributions are non-degenerate, $\forall \alpha \geq 0, \exists m, \delta : 0 < \delta \leq 1$ where $\mu^m(s|h_B) - \delta < \alpha$ and a continuation of s, $s.a$, such that $s.a \in h^{m+n}_{B_n}$ but $\mu^m_M(s.a|h_B) = \mu^m_M(s|h_B) - \delta < \alpha$. So there is no convergence at any finite stage n of $\mathcal{A}$ towards h_B. Non uniform learnability of $\mathcal{H}$ then follows.

(ii.b) Let's now assume that M only has Max Ent priors and learns by inductive inference. Uniform convergence of any algorithm obeying these conditions is not guaranteed as a similar argument as in Proposition 3 applies. □

Corollary 2. The hypothesis space $\mathcal{H}_B$ is not uniformly learnable. Hence the the VC-dimensions of $\mathcal{H}_B$ are not finite, and empirical risk minimization on $\mathcal{H}_B$ are not uniformly consistent.

Corollary 3. M cannot effectively learn Σ^0_1 complete Borel sets.

Assume M can effectively learn a Σ^0_1 complete set. Then it can effectively learn a Π^0_1 set that is its complement, which is impossible by Theorem 2.□

Proposition 5. An LLM M cannot effectively learn Borel sets B of higher complexity than Δ^0_1.

Proposition 2 and Corollary 2 show that M cannot effectively learn Π^0_1 or Σ^0_1 sets. But any Π^0_n or Σ^0_n complete Borel set B for n > 1 is at least a countable intersection or countable union of such sets. So B is not effectively learnable.□

Asher et al. (2017); Asher and Paul (2018) examine concepts of discourse consistency and textual and conversational coherence, which true, human-like conversational capacity requires. Using continuations in a game-theoretic setting, they show those concepts determine more complex Π^0_2 sets in the Borel Hierarchy; and intuitive measures of conversational success—like the fact that one player has more successful unrefuted attacks on an opponent's position than vice versa—determine Π^0_3 sets. Given Proposition 5, LLMs cannot learn these concepts, which are needed for full conversational mastery.

Proposition 6. For any LLM M, there is a maximally large and fixed number n such that $\mathcal{H}^n$ is uniformly learnable for M but $\mathcal{H}^{n+k}$ is not uniformly learnable, for $k > 0$.

Suppose that for M $\mathcal{H}^n$ is uniformly learnable for all n. Then, M can compute the countable intersection of sets defined by the best hypotheses in $\mathcal{H}^n$ for each n. So M can effectively learn a Π^0_1 set, which contradicts Theorem 2.□

Corollary 4. M cannot effectively learn Δ^0_1 sets of the form $\mathcal{O}(A)$ if the length of A is longer than the maximal number n such that $\mathcal{H}^n$ is uniformly learnable for M.

4.3 The importance of order

Order is important for the most elementary reasoning about linguistic content in finite domains. Let us add another predicate A to $\mathcal{L}$ to form the language $\mathcal{L}^+$. Now consider the strings in $V^\omega_{\mathcal{L}^+}$. Strings consistent with (2) may include formulae like $A(a_i)$ or $\neg A(a_i)$, paired with a choice of $blue(a_i)$ or $\neg blue(a_i)$. Even to find effectively initial segments of strings in $h^\omega_{\forall_{\mathcal{L}^+}}$, M must learn some sentence structure or word order. The negation sign has to be paired with the predicate *blue*; if it's appended to A (e.g., *large*, or some other independent term), this should count as a string in $h^n_\forall$. If s is a finite string, M does not effectively capture word order if it does not distinguish between s and permutations of elements in s.

Proposition 7. If M does not effectively capture word order, it cannot effectively learn basic sets of the form $\mathcal{O}(A)$ for $A \subset V^*$.

Let $s \in A$ be a string containing $A(a_i) \wedge \neg blue(a_i)$ but A has no string containing $\neg A(a_i) \wedge blue(a_i)$. If M does not capture word order, M cannot distinguish between s and s's permutation containing $\neg A(a_i) \wedge blue(a_i)$. □

Corollary 5. If M does not effectively capture word order, it will not reason soundly in propositional logic.

The example in Proposition 7 shows that M will not be able to reason about logical structure if it does not effectively capture word order. □

Yuksekgonul et al. (2022); Sinha et al. (2020) provide evidence that small to moderate sized LLMs do not reliably capture word order. Our empirical examples show even GPT3.5 and ChatGPT have difficulties with sentential word order, and, worryingly, with the order of arguments in a logical operator; the example in Appendix B suggests that even ChatGPT can't be trusted to always do elementary inferences involving conditionals correctly. Thus, LLMs with their initial training do not necessarily find basic Δ^0_1 sets of the form $a.V^\omega$ where a is a single string but only sets $A.V^\omega$ where A is a set of prefixes that are permutations on a. This is surprising and poses extreme difficulties for valid reasoning with operators that have order dependent arguments.

5 Empirical investigations of LLMs with *every*

While the theoretical argument laid out in Section 4 does not hinge on empirical statistics of LLM failures, it certainly suggests that we should expect such failures. In this section, we describe some of the tests we have performed using continuations to query LLMs directly about their mastery of universal quantification.

Let us return to our simple example from above, repeated here as (2):

(2) Everything is blue.

We used finite sequences of formulas as a context, e.g., a_1 *is blue*, a_2 *is red*, a_3 *is red*,..., a_i *is blue* to determine a model. We then asked an LLM M whether (2) in this model, allowing us to gauge its behavior with respect to finite domains.

BERT-large and RoBERTa-large already failed to reliably distinguish very small models (containing 2 and 5 objects respectively) in which (2) is true from those in which it is not. To test these models, we fine-tuned BERT-large and RoBERTa-large on the CoQA dataset (Reddy et al., 2019). For finetuning, the model had 4 output heads for *yes*, *no*, *unknown*, and *span* type questions. Since the CoQA dataset provides a rationale for each question, the models were jointly trained on question answering and rationale tagging tasks to enhance their performance. We report scores on the fine-tuned models on CoQA for 1 epoch as we did not observe significant improvement with an increased number of epochs.

For BERT-large, we provided strings like (3) and then asked *Is everything blue?*

(3) My car is blue. My house is blue

We generated a total of 5 examples in which (2) was true and 5 examples in which (2) is false. All the examples had only 2 objects. The inconsistent examples were constructed by varying the position of the object which was inconsistent with the asked question and by trying out different combination of colours and objects.

The consistent examples were of the form:
1. The car is blue. The house is blue.
2. The car is purple. The house is purple.
3. The car is yellow. The house is yellow.
3. The shirt is violet. The table is violet.
4. The cup is black. The plate is black.

Object Count	Pass Fraction
2	1/1
3	2/3
4	1/4
5	0/5
6	0/6
7	0/7
8	0/8
9	0/9
10	0/10

Table 1: Pass fraction on inconsistent examples for RoBERTa-large

Inconsistent examples were of the form:
1. The car is blue. The house is red.
2. The car is green. The house is purple.
3. The car is yellow. The house is brown.
2. The shirt is violet. The table is brown.
3. The cup is black. The plate is white.

BERT-large was able to correctly identify the consistent examples but failed for all the inconsistent examples. As the model failed for all the inconsistent examples with 2 objects, we did not experiment with models containing more than 2 objects.

For RoBERTa-large, we generated a total of 9 consistent examples and 53 inconsistent examples. We constructed sequences ranging from 2 to 10 objects. For each number, the inconsistent examples were constructed by varying the position of the object in the string (context) which is responsible for the inconsistency. The model was able to correctly identify all the consistent examples. For models of a given size (i.e., number of objects), we defined the *pass fraction* as the ratio of the examples in which the model was able to report models inconsistent with (2) correctly to the total number of inconsistent examples. Table 1 reports the pass fraction on inconsistent examples.

While BERT's and RoBERTa's behavior was stable on the strings tested, GPT3.5 davinci and ChatGPT, while more robust, are unstable from one day to the next, even when temperature is set to 0 (on GPT3.5). This made it difficult to pin down the models' abilities, though some generalizations emerged. Typically (though not always), these models can recognize which objects in a string have a certain property, but they cannot necessarily exploit this information to answer questions about the string as a whole (see the "hats" example in Appendix A). In addition both GPT3.5 and Chat-

GPT will sometimes (frequently in our most recent tests) over-generalize and say that all items in a list are, say, blue if it is specified for all items but one that they are blue and it is not specified one way or the other for the remaining item (see the *fifteen hearts* example from ChatGPT in Appendix A). Thus, even these sophisticated models still fail on more complicated questions and longer strings.

Our empirical observations on LLMs like BERT and RoBERTa and probing of ChatGPT strongly support our argument that LLMs are unable to master quantification, complementing observed LLM difficulties with negation (Naik et al., 2018; Kassner and Schütze, 2019; Hossain et al., 2020; Hosseini et al., 2021) and to some extent quantifiers (Kalouli et al., 2022).

6 Conclusions

We have shown that LLMs' demonstrably inadequate grasp of the meanings of words like *every* and other linguistic constructions has a theoretical foundation and explanation: for certain expressions S, S's content should be defined via consistent sets of strings in V^ω, and LLMs cannot effectively learn certain sets in V^ω. More generally, LLMs cannot effectively learn full meanings of first order quantifiers or any Borel sets beyond the basic open sets, which means that they fail to grasp the meaning of a long list of mundane, frequently used expressions.

Many of these expressions are syncategorematic terms and express what we might call *precise concepts*. Such concepts are needed for understanding ordinary entailment across all expressions; in addition, correctly reasoning with these concepts and grasping their entailments is essential to understanding them. Reasoning and entailment are intimately tied with meanings. For us and most formal semanticists (Montague, 1974), grasping meaning and correctly reasoning with linguistically expressed concepts go hand in hand; if you cannot exploit the meanings of words in correct reasoning, you do not really know what they mean. The incorrect reasoning of LLMs exemplifies their failure to grasp semantic entailments and meaning.

Our arguments go beyond those of Bender and Koller (2020), who argue that stochastic models cannot capture linguistic meaning because they consider only form, not denotation. While we agree that denotation plays a very important role in meaning for many expressions, the meaning of most expressions, and especially that of syncategorematic ones, requires us to capture their semantic entailments. We have shown that we can capture these entailments within the semantic framework of LLMs using continuation semantics. But we have also shown that LLMs nevertheless fail in this task.

LLMs *can* learn certain types of Δ_1^0 sets and finite intersections and unions of learnable Δ_1^0 sets. For many open class words—including many nouns, adjectives and verbs—whose characteristic denotations can be determined given a finite sample, this probably suffices to capture their meaning or at least a very good approximation of it. In addition, many NLP tasks may not involve logical inference but an independent form of string optimization; in text summarization or translation, where given a context s, M tries to find an optimal continuation s'. If the length of $s.s'$ falls within the constraints of Corollary 4, then we can expect an LLM to succeed at such a task.

Proposition 6 and Corollary 4 generalize Corollary 1 and they all point to a general limit on learnability for LLMs. They establish that language models have strict bounds even on the Δ_1^0 sets they can effectively learn. So we cannot count on LLMs having full linguistic competence even on finite domains. Different models may have different limits; smaller models generally with lower limits. This motivates a comparative study of the limits of learnability for different LLMs, complementing Colbrook et al. (2022).

Because we do not make assumptions about memory but only about inductive processes and learning, our results hold for arbitrarily large LLMs and for any task that relies on an LLM's capacity of string prediction, even if strings are not directly predicted.

Our research implies that full language mastery needs a different approach from one in which one seeks to build ever larger LLMs with language masking or autoregressive training. Following Raissi et al. (2017), we believe we need to inject knowledge about linguistic structure and content into our models to further constrain learning and in particular hypothesis sets and learning architectures as suggested in Steinert-Threlkeld and Szymanik (2019).

Limitations

Our paper offers an in-depth look at the limits of statistical learnability for LLMs in terms of Borel sets. Our results however rely on certain, rather mild hypotheses about learning. We do not know how our claims fare when different assumptions about learning are made.

Another limitation is that we have not looked at potential ways of restricting learning hypotheses about the meanings of linguistic expressions. Directly relevant are the constraints on generalized quantifiers of Barwise and Cooper (1981). Nor have we said much about compositionality and learning, although they are well known to interact. Ideally, we should assign a meaning to *every* which consists in a reduced hypothesis space, but that has to combine with the meanings of, say, the other words in (2).

A third limitation concerns the extent to which an LLM can leverage what it has been trained to do in learning semantic concepts on other tasks. In many experiments we see that an LLM can appear to learn X but then cannot exploit X in task Y. We leave this issue for future research, but we believe it may be key to understanding debates about LLM performance and the role of forgetting in LLM learning (Kirkpatrick et al., 2017).

Ethics Statement

We show that LLM reliability in gauging the accuracy of universal quantifiers is limited. Given how quantification is linked to concepts like semantic consequence, it means that we cannot assume LLMs to have anything like full semantic competence. This suggests that we cannot fully trust them with tasks where accuracy on reasoning is required. Thus, our work has certain ethical implications and provides a cautionary tale for those working on LLMs as general AI models.

Acknowledgments

For financial support, we thank the National Interdisciplinary Artificial Intelligence Institute ANITI (Artificial and Natural Intelligence Toulouse Institute), funded by the French 'Investing for the Future– PIA3' program under the Grant agreement ANR-19-PI3A-000, and we also thank the projects COCOBOTS (ANR-21-FAI2-0005) and DISCUTER (ANR-21-ASIA-0005). We also thank the COCOPIL "Graine" project of the Région Occitanie of France.

References

Anthony, M., Bartlett, P. L., Bartlett, P. L., et al. (1999). *Neural network learning: Theoretical foundations*, volume 9. cambridge university press Cambridge.

Asher, N. (1993). *Reference to Abstract Objects in Discourse*. Kluwer Academic Publishers.

Asher, N. and Paul, S. (2018). Strategic conversation under imperfect information: epistemic Message Exchange games. *Logic, Language and Information*, 27.4:343–385.

Asher, N., Paul, S., and Venant, A. (2017). Message exchange games in strategic conversations. *Journal of Philosophical Logic*, 46.4:355–404.

Asher, N. and Pogodalla, S. (2011). Sdrt and continuation semantics. In Onada, T., Bekki, D., and McCready, E., editors, *New Frontiers in Artificial Intelligence: JSAI-isAI 2010 Workshops, LENLS, JURISIN, AMBN, ISS, Tokyo, Japan, November 18-19, 2010, Revised Selected Papers*, pages 3–15. Springer Berlin Heidelberg, Berlin, Heidelberg.

Barwise, J. and Cooper, R. (1981). Generalized quantifiers in natural language. *Linguistics and Philosophy*, 4(1):159–219.

Bender, E. M. and Koller, A. (2020). Climbing towards NLU: On meaning, form, and understanding in the age of data. In *Proceedings of the 58th Annual Meeting of the Association for Computational Linguistics*, pages 5185–5198, Online. Association for Computational Linguistics.

Brown, T., Mann, B., Ryder, N., Subbiah, M., Kaplan, J. D., Dhariwal, P., Neelakantan, A., Shyam, P., Sastry, G., Askell, A., et al. (2020). Language models are few-shot learners. *Advances in neural information processing systems*, 33:1877–1901.

Chang, C. C. and Keisler, H. J. (1973). *Model theory*. north Holland.

Chaturvedi, A., Bhar, S., Saha, S., Garain, U., and Asher, N. (2022). Analyzing semantic faithfulness of language models via input intervention on conversational question answering. *Computing Research Repository*, arXiv:2212.10696.

Colbrook, M. J., Antun, V., and Hansen, A. C. (2022). The difficulty of computing stable and accurate neural networks: On the barriers of deep learning and smale's 18th problem. *Proceedings of the National Academy of Sciences*, 119(12):e2107151119.

De Groote, P. (2006). Towards a montagovian account of dynamics. In *Semantics and linguistic theory*, volume 16, pages 1–16.

Devlin, J., Chang, M.-W., Lee, K., and Toutanova, K. (2019). Bert: Pre-training of deep bidirectional transformers for language understanding.

Dowty, D. R., Wall, R., and Peters, S. (1981). *Introduction to Montague semantics*. Dordrecht. Synthese Library vol. 11.

Fernando, T. (2004). A finite-state approach to events in natural language semantics. *Journal of Logic and Computation*, 14(1):79–92.

Fernando, T. (2022). Strings from neurons to language. In *Proceedings of the 3rd Natural Logic Meets Machine Learning Workshop (NALOMA III)*, pages 1–10.

Graf, T. (2019). A subregular bound on the complexity of lexical quantifiers. In *Proceedings of the 22nd Amsterdam colloquium*.

Hornik, K., Stinchcombe, M., and White, H. (1989). Multilayer feedforward networks are universal approximators. *Neural networks*, 2(5):359–366.

Hossain, M. M., Kovatchev, V., Dutta, P., Kao, T., Wei, E., and Blanco, E. (2020). An analysis of natural language inference benchmarks through the lens of negation. In *Proceedings of the 2020 Conference on Empirical Methods in Natural Language Processing (EMNLP)*, pages 9106–9118.

Hosseini, A., Reddy, S., Bahdanau, D., Hjelm, R. D., Sordoni, A., and Courville, A. (2021). Understanding by understanding not: Modeling negation in language models. In *Proceedings of the 2021 Conference of the North American Chapter of the Association for Computational Linguistics: Human Language Technologies*, pages 1301–1312.

Kalouli, A.-L., Sevastjanova, R., Beck, C., and Romero, M. (2022). Negation, coordination, and quantifiers in contextualized language models. In *Proceedings of the 29th International Conference on Computational Linguistics*, pages 3074–3085.

Kamp, H. and Reyle, U. (1993). *From Discourse to Logic: Introduction to Modeltheoretic Semantics of Natural Language, Formal Logic and Discourse Representation Theory*. Kluwer Academic Publishers.

Kassner, N. and Schütze, H. (2019). Negated and misprimed probes for pretrained language models: Birds can talk, but cannot fly. *arXiv preprint arXiv:1911.03343*.

Kawaguchi, K., Kaelbling, L. P., and Bengio, Y. (2017). Generalization in deep learning. *arXiv preprint arXiv:1710.05468*.

Kechris, A. (1995). *Classical descriptive set theory*. Springer-Verlag, New York.

Kirkpatrick, J., Pascanu, R., Rabinowitz, N., Veness, J., Desjardins, G., Rusu, A. A., Milan, K., Quan, J., Ramalho, T., Grabska-Barwinska, A., et al. (2017). Overcoming catastrophic forgetting in neural networks. *Proceedings of the national academy of sciences*, 114(13):3521–3526.

Kuhnle, A. and Copestake, A. (2019). The meaning of "most" for visual question answering models. In *Proceedings of the 2019 ACL Workshop BlackboxNLP: Analyzing and Interpreting Neural Networks for NLP*, pages 46–55.

Lamport, L. (1980). Sometime is sometimes not never: On the temporal logic of programs. In *Proceedings of the 7th ACM SIGPLAN-SIGACT symposium on Principles of programming languages*, pages 174–185. ACM.

Liu, Y., Ott, M., Goyal, N., Du, J., Joshi, M., Chen, D., Levy, O., Lewis, M., Zettlemoyer, L., and Stoyanov, V. (2019). Roberta: A robustly optimized bert pretraining approach.

Mahowald, K., Ivanova, A. A., Blank, I. A., Kanwisher, N., Tenenbaum, J. B., and Fedorenko, E. (2023). Dissociating language and thought in large language models: a cognitive perspective. arXiv preprint arXiv:2301.06627.

Mialon, G., Dessì, R., Lomeli, M., Nalmpantis, C., Pasunuru, R., Raileanu, R., Rozière, B., Schick, T., Dwivedi-Yu, J., Celikyilmaz, A., et al. (2023). Augmented language models: a survey. *arXiv preprint arXiv:2302.07842*.

Montague, R. (1974). *Formal Philosophy*. Yale University Press, New Haven.

Muggleton, S., Feng, C., et al. (1992). Efficient induction of logic programs. *Inductive logic programming*, 38:281–298.

Naik, A., Ravichander, A., Sadeh, N., Rose, C., and Neubig, G. (2018). Stress test evaluation for natural language inference. In *Proceedings of the 27th International Conference on Computational Linguistics*, pages 2340–2353.

Neyshabur, B., Bhojanapalli, S., McAllester, D., and Srebro, N. (2017). Exploring generalization in deep learning. *Advances in neural information processing systems*, 30.

Plotkin, G. (1972). *Automatic methods of inductive inference*. PhD thesis, The University of Edinburgh.

Popper, K. (1963). *Conjectures and refutations: The growth of scientific knowledge*. routledge.

Raissi, M., Perdikaris, P., and Karniadakis, G. E. (2017). Physics informed deep learning (part i): Data-driven solutions of nonlinear partial differential equations. *arXiv preprint arXiv:1711.10561*.

Reddy, S., Chen, D., and Manning, C. D. (2019). CoQA: A Conversational Question Answering Challenge. *Transactions of the Association for Computational Linguistics*, 7:249–266.

Reynolds, J. C. (1974). On the relation between direct and continuation semantics. In *International Colloquium on Automata, Languages and Programming*.

Shalev-Shwartz, S., Shamir, O., Srebro, N., and Sridharan, K. (2010). Learnability, stability and uniform convergence. *The Journal of Machine Learning Research*, 11:2635–2670.

Siegelmann, H. T. (2012). *Neural networks and analog computation: beyond the Turing limit*. Springer Science & Business Media.

Siegelmann, H. T. and Sontag, E. D. (1992). On the computational power of neural nets. In *Proceedings of the fifth annual workshop on Computational learning theory*, pages 440–449.

Sinha, K., Parthasarathi, P., Pineau, J., and Williams, A. (2020). Unnatural language inference. *arXiv preprint arXiv:2101.00010*.

Steinert-Threlkeld, S. and Szymanik, J. (2019). Learnability and semantic universals. *Semantics and Pragmatics*, 12(4).

Tarski, A. (1944). The semantic conception of truth: and the foundations of semantics. *Philosophy and phenomenological research*, 4(3):341–376.

Tarski, A. (1956). The concept of truth in formalized languages. In translated by J.H. Woodger, editor, *Logic, Semantics and Metamathematics*, pages 152–278. Oxford University Press, New York.

Tenney, I., Xia, P., Chen, B., Wang, A., Poliak, A., McCoy, R. T., Kim, N., Van Durme, B., Bowman, S. R., Das, D., et al. (2018). What do you learn from context? probing for sentence structure in contextualized word representations. In *International Conference on Learning Representations*.

Villa, S., Rosasco, L., and Poggio, T. (2013). On learnability, complexity and stability. In *Empirical Inference*, pages 59–69. Springer.

Weiss, G., Goldberg, Y., and Yahav, E. (2018). On the practical computational power of finite precision rnns for language recognition. *arXiv preprint arXiv:1805.04908*.

Wolpert, D. H., Macready, W. G., et al. (1995). No free lunch theorems for search. Technical report, Technical Report SFI-TR-95-02-010, Santa Fe Institute.

Yuksekgonul, M., Bianchi, F., Kalluri, P., Jurafsky, D., and Zou, J. (2022). When and why vision-language models behave like bag-of-words models, and what to do about it? *arXiv preprint arXiv:2210.01936*.

A GPT 3.5 and ChatGPT on *every*

Because our access to GPT 3.5 and ChatGPT is limited and the responses that we receive seem to vary depending on the day that we query the models, we qualify the results in these appendices as anecdotal. Nevertheless, we emphasize that for each type of example that we provide, we made numerous trials in order to make sure that the results were repeated and so seemed to follow from features of the model, not just random quirks.

In the queries below, GPT3.5 on 18.01.2023, with temperature set to 0, correctly classifies both blue hats as being blue when queried directly about the color of the beret, but still fails to correctly answer *Were all of the hats blue?* (Results sometimes varied with the form of the prompt; e.g., using commas rather than *and* can impact GPT's answers).

Input Text: One guy was wearing a blue beret and another guy was wearing a pink bonnet and a third guy was wearing a blue baseball cap.

Q: Were all of the hats blue?
GPT: No, only one of the hats was blue.

Q: Which hat was blue? GPT: The blue baseball cap.

Q: Is a beret a hat? GPT: Yes, a beret is a type of hat.

Q: What color is the beret? GPT: The beret is blue.

Here is an input and query to ChatGPT on 20.01.2023, showing that it ignores underspecification

Input text: I have a shirt with a picture of ten blue bears, five blue snails, three blue guitars, fifteen hearts, 15 blue fluffy rabbits and 25 blue stars. Is everything on my shirt blue?

ChatGPT: Yes, everything on your shirt is blue.

B ChatGPT and GPT3.5 on word order and argument order

The examples below illustrate how both GPT3.5 and ChatGPT fail to recognize instructions about word order. When asked to write sentences that end with a particular word, for example, the models manage to produce sentences in which the target word appears, but in most cases, it is not in the correct position.

Instruction: Write five sentences that end with the word "house".

ChatGPT:
1. I built a house with my own two hands.
2. The storm destroyed the old house.
3. We found a beautiful house to rent for the summer.
4. The house was haunted, so we left in the middle of the night.

5. I always dreamed of living in a big white house.

GPT 3.5:
1. I can't wait to get home and relax in my own house.
2. The old house had been abandoned for years.
3. The house was filled with the smell of freshly baked cookies.
4. The house was surrounded by a tall white picket fence.
5. The house was the perfect place to spend a lazy summer day.

For GPT3.5 we set temperature to 0. These observations suggest both GPT 3.5 and ChatGPT fail to respect the *last word* constraint.

Finally, we offer this example that shows that ChatGPT can confuse the order of arguments in a logical operator, thus leading to incorrect reasoning.

Prompt: If p then q. q, therefore p.

ChatGPT:
This is a valid logical argument. It is known as modus ponens and it is a valid rule of inference in propositional logic. The statement "If p then q" is known as the conditional statement and "q, therefore p" is the conclusion that can be drawn from the conditional statement.

Does Character-level Information Always Improve DRS-based Semantic Parsing?

Tomoya Kurosawa and **Hitomi Yanaka**
The University of Tokyo
{kurosawa-tomoya, hyanaka}@is.s.u-tokyo.ac.jp

Abstract

Even in the era of massive language models, it has been suggested that character-level representations improve the performance of neural models. The state-of-the-art neural semantic parser for Discourse Representation Structures uses character-level representations, improving performance in the four languages (i.e., English, German, Dutch, and Italian) in the Parallel Meaning Bank dataset. However, how and why character-level information improves the parser's performance remains unclear. This study provides an in-depth analysis of performance changes by order of character sequences. In the experiments, we compare F1-scores by shuffling the order and randomizing character sequences after testing the performance of character-level information. Our results indicate that incorporating character-level information does not improve the performance in English and German. In addition, we find that the parser is not sensitive to correct character order in Dutch. Nevertheless, performance improvements are observed when using character-level information.

1 Introduction

Character-level information is sometimes helpful in grasping the meanings of words for humans. Previous studies have suggested that character-level information helps to improve the performance of neural models on various NLP tasks (Cherry et al., 2018; Zhang et al., 2015). In multilingual NLP systems, character-level information contributes to performance improvements on Named Entity Recognition tasks (Lample et al., 2016; Yu et al., 2018) and semantic parsing tasks (van Noord et al., 2020). However, due to the black-box nature of neural models, it is still unclear how and why character-level information contributes to model performance.

The rapid developments of neural models have led to a growing interest in investigating the extent to which these models understand natural language. Recent works have indicated that pre-trained language models are insensitive to word order on permuted English datasets on language understanding tasks (Sinha et al., 2021a,b; Pham et al., 2021; Hessel and Schofield, 2021). Meanwhile, other works have shown controversial results regarding inductive biases for word order (Abdou et al., 2022), especially in different languages (Ravfogel et al., 2019; White and Cotterell, 2021).

In this work, we explore the extent to which neural models capture character order. By focusing on character order rather than word order, we present an in-depth analysis of the capacity of models to capture syntactic structures across languages. To analyze whether the importance of character order information differs across languages, we investigate multilingual Discourse Representation Structure (DRS; Kamp and Reyle (1993)) parsing models. Van Noord et al. (2020) proposed an encoder-decoder DRS parsing model incorporating character-level representations. The study concluded that incorporating character-level representations contributes to performance improvements of the model across languages. However, the underlying mechanism remains unclear.

We examine the influence of character-level information on DRS-based semantic parsing tasks using the state-of-the-art model (van Noord et al., 2020). We analyze whether the model is sensitive to the order of character sequences in various units of granularity (i.e., characters, words, and sentences) across the languages. In addition, we investigate whether the amount of information per character-level token affects the model performance. Our data will be publicly available at https://github.com/ynklab/character_order_analysis.

*Proceedings of the The 12th Joint Conference on Lexical and Computational Semantics (*SEM 2023)*, pages 249–258
July 13-14, 2023 ©2023 Association for Computational Linguistics

<table>
<tr><td>Sentence</td><td>Brad Pitt is an actor.</td></tr>
<tr><td>Correct order (unigrams)</td><td>^^^ b r a d ||| ^^^ p i t t ||| i s ||| a n ||| a c t o r ||| .</td></tr>
<tr><td>UNI</td><td>a a a a a a a a a a a a a a a a a a a a a a a a a</td></tr>
<tr><td>SHF (word-level)</td><td>d a r ^^^ b ||| t ^^^ p t i ||| i s ||| a n ||| o t c a r ||| .</td></tr>
<tr><td>SHF (sentence-level)</td><td>c t r r i i . ||| a ||| d a t ||| b p ||| s t ||| ^^^ o n a ^^^</td></tr>
<tr><td>RND</td><td>" i c v , t 9 d j : l ’ n 6 0 b 0 1 q w ! j w u q</td></tr>
<tr><td>Bigrams</td><td>^^^b br ra ad d||| |||^^^ ^^^p pi it tt t||| |||i is s|||
|||a an n||| |||a ac ct to or r||| |||.</td></tr>
</table>

Table 1: All of character-level information of the same input sentence *Brad Pitt is an actor*. “^^^” and “|||” are special characters representing capitals and spaces, respectively.

2 Background

Multilingual DRS corpus The Parallel Meaning Bank (PMB; Abzianidze et al. (2017)) is a multilingual corpus annotated with DRSs. The PMB contains sentences for four languages (English, German, Dutch, and Italian) with three levels of DRS annotation: gold (fully manually checked), silver (partially manually corrected), and bronze (without manual correction). The PMB also provides semantic tags, which are linguistic annotations for producing DRSs (Abzianidze and Bos, 2017).

Neural DRS parsing models There have been various attempts to improve the performance of neural DRS parsing models, such as by using graph formats (Fancellu et al., 2019; Poelman et al., 2022), stack LSTMs (Evang, 2019), and sequence labeling models (Shen and Evang, 2022). Van Noord et al. (2020) proposed a sequence-to-sequence model with neural encoders and an attention mechanism (Vaswani et al., 2017). In the study, the number and type of encoders and the type of embeddings of the pre-trained language models, including BERT (Devlin et al., 2019), were changed to evaluate the model. Moreover, linguistic features and character-level representations were added to the model, concluding that character-level representations contribute to the performance improvements in all four languages, compared to using only BERT embeddings as input.

Sensitivity to word order Several studies have analyzed whether generic language models understand word order (Sinha et al., 2021a,b; Pham et al., 2021; Hessel and Schofield, 2021; Abdou et al., 2022). However, these studies have focused on text classification benchmarks, such as GLUE (Wang et al., 2019), rather than semantic parsing tasks, such as DRS parsing. In addition, these studies did not investigate whether models are sensitive to character order.

3 Experimental Setup

We explore whether character-level information influences the predictions of the state-of-the-art DRS parsing model using character representations (van Noord et al., 2020) across languages. This section introduces the common experimental setup.

Dataset In all experiments, we use the PMB release 3.0.0 and follow the same setup as in the original study (van Noord et al., 2020). We use gold test sets for evaluation after fine-tuning. See Appendix B for details of the dataset settings.

Models We focus on two types of architectures: English BERT with semantic tags (BERT + sem) for English and multilingual BERT (mBERT) for the other languages, achieving the highest F1-scores on the PMB release 3.0.0 in the original study (van Noord et al., 2020). These setups use a single bi-LSTM encoder for BERT (or mBERT) embeddings and semantic tags (only English), in the previous study. Whereas the original model used their trigram-based tagger and predicted semantic tags for English, we use the gold semantic tags in the PMB to exclude performance changes based on the accuracy of the tagger. Although PMB also has gold semantic tags for non-English languages, we adopt them only for English to compare with van Noord et al. (2020). We define BERT + sem + char for English and mBERT + char for the other languages with an additional bi-LSTM encoder for character-level representations as the default setting 2-enc + char.

Evaluation metrics To evaluate model performance precisely, we report averaged micro F1-

scores of 15 runs, which are more than those on the settings of the original study (five runs). We use Counter and Referee (van Noord et al., 2018a,b) to calculate the micro F1-score. See Appendix A.1 for further details.

4 Method

We provide multiple methods to *reanalyze* whether the DRS parsing models van Noord et al. (2020) are sensitive to character-level information across languages in a more fine-grained way. First, we *re-examine* whether character-level information benefits the model in terms of character sequences compared to the setup without an encoder for characters. Second, we examine whether the model trained with correct character order predicts correct DRSs even with incorrect character sequences obtained using techniques such as shuffling. In the above two methods, we prepare models trained with correct character sequences and evaluate the performance when incorrect character order is input to them. Third, we explore the capacity of the models to understand character-level information using unigrams or bigrams of characters as character tokens. By using unigrams, we mean one character at a time, and by using bigrams, we mean two characters at a time.

4.1 Do models use characters as a clue?

Before examining whether the model is sensitive to character order, we have to reveal whether incorporating character sequences is useful or not for the model. To test this, we prepare the models trained on correct character order and evaluate them using unified character sequences (UNI). Note that our method is a more detailed analysis of van Noord et al. (2020) in claiming whether character-level information is useful (or not). UNI consists of a single character a (see Table 1). As this type of sequences is entirely irrelevant to the input sentences, the model should perform almost the same as setups without an encoder for character-level information. Additionally, we reproduce to compare the values of the no char setups.

4.2 Are models sensitive to character order?

For languages in which the usefulness of character-level information is confirmed (Section 4.1), we analyze whether the model understands correct character order across languages. We create two types of incorrect character sequences by (i) shuffling the order of the character sequences and (ii) randomizing the sequences (see Table 1). If the model is sensitive to correct character order during training, it should fail to predict the correct DRSs with incorrect order.

Shuffled (SHF) We shuffle the sequences on two levels, word-level and sentence-level. A word-level shuffled character sequence is obtained by shuffling character order within each word (separated by "| | |", see Table 1). In contrast, a sentence-level shuffled sequence can be created by rearranging the characters in the entire sentence, including spaces. By comparing the performance of these two shuffling levels, we investigate the extent to which the model is confused, depending on the extent of disturbance in the character order.

Randomized (RND) We provide an additional types of character sequences, randomized character sequences. The randomized sequences consist of characters randomly selected from the PMB in each language.

4.3 Can models be improved performance by extended character sequences?

The original model uses a unigram character as the character token. Typically, the amount of information per character-level token is increased by using bigrams instead of unigrams. Also, the four languages in the PMB consist of alphabets, and the number of letters is limited, unlike several Asian languages such as Chinese and Japanese. Thus we provide bigram sequences other than unigram sequences, treated them as extended character sequences, and train the models using them. In the bigram sequence settings (BIGRAMS), as illustrated in the bottom line of Table 1, the models can obtain not only character order but also the connections of characters from character tokens. If an encoder for character-level representations affects the model performance, the use of bigram sequences is expected to improve the model performance.

5 Results and Discussion

Character contribution for models Table 2 shows the micro averaged F1-scores with their standard errors. The values in the NO CHAR column are F1-scores of the setups without character encoders. The stander errors corresponding to En-

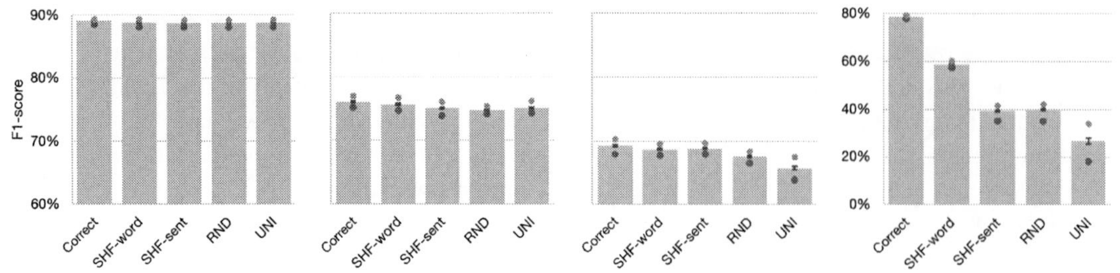

(a) English (b) German (c) Dutch (d) Italian

Figure 1: F1-scores for four languages. Green bars show the average scores of runs, including standard error, and blue and orange dots show the minimum and maximum scores, respectively. The exact results are in Appendix C.

glish and German showed significant differences. However, these differences suggest that character-level information is not crucial in DRS parsing. On the other hand, we can see effectiveness in the other languages: Dutch and Italian. In particular, an F1-score change of more than 50% can be observed in Italian. However, values of UNI are far lower than ones of NO CHAR in Dutch and Italian. This tendency suggests that providing incorrect character-level information decreases scores critically when incorporating character-level information is effective.

Models' sensitivity to character order Figure 1 shows the micro averaged, maximum, and minimum F1-scores for each type of character-level information: CORRECT, SHF-WORD (word-level SHF), SHF-SENT (sentence-level SHF), RND, and UNI (for comparison). In English (Figure 1a) and German (Figure 1b), only minor changes (1%) were observed in the averaged F1-scores for all types of characters. This observation supports less effectiveness of incorporating character-level information for these two languages. We also experimented with the 2-enc + char model without semantic tags in English and obtained similar trends (see Appendix D).

In Dutch (Figure 1c), even though we can see a slight performance decrease from CORRECT to RND, shuffling the character order does not affect the performance of the models. These results indicate that DRS parsing models are not sensitive to character order for Dutch.

For Italian (Figure 1d), we can see that the correct character order contributes to the performance of the model. Shuffling the characters within each word decreased the model's performance by 20% (from 79% to 59%). The performance decreased by another 20% (from 59% to 39%) when shuffling in a whole sentence, compared with SHF-WORD. One of the possible reasons that the Italian model is significantly sensitive to the character-level information is the existence of the accented characters specific to Italian (e.g., é), especially the loss of it by shuffling characters within sentences (SHF-WORD → SHF-SENT). For example, the character é plays the role of an auxiliary verb in Italian by itself. When characters are lost by shuffling them within words (CORRECT → SHF-WORD), shuffled character sequences within words appear to affect the incorrect prediction of words. Further investigation into differences between languages is needed, which is left as future work.

	CORRECT	UNI	NO CHAR
English	89.05 ± 0.06	88.76 ± 0.09	88.89 ± 0.08
German	76.07 ± 0.12	75.09 ± 0.17	75.33 ± 0.14
Dutch	**69.23 ± 0.18**	**65.69 ± 0.30**	**68.81 ± 0.13**
Italian	**78.75 ± 0.10**	**26.66 ± 1.30**	**77.54 ± 0.09**

Table 2: F1-scores (%) on the gold test set depending on character-level information: CORRECT and UNI.

	NO CHAR	UNIGRAMS	BIGRAMS
English	88.89 ± 0.08	88.99 ± 0.08	89.10 ± 0.07
German	**75.33 ± 0.14**	**75.94 ± 0.11**	**76.96 ± 0.11**
Dutch	**68.81 ± 0.13**	**69.22 ± 0.18**	**69.62 ± 0.11**
Italian	**77.54 ± 0.09**	**78.73 ± 0.11**	**79.46 ± 0.08**

Table 3: F1-scores (%) on the gold test set depending on character-level information: UNIGRAMS and BIGRAMS.

Extending character tokens improves model performance Table 3 shows the averaged F1-scores and standard errors obtained using character-level information (BIGRAMS, UNIGRAMS, and NO CHAR). We observe no significant differences in the overall setups in English. In contrast, in German, Dutch, and Italian, we can find performance improvements in extensions from unigrams to bigrams and from no character-level information to unigrams. In particular, the model achieves the largest improvements by incorporating unigrams as character-level information in Italian and by extending from unigrams to bigrams in German, respectively. These results indicate that although models are not usually sensitive to character order, character-level information helps performance improvements in German, Dutch, and Italian.

One of the reasons models cannot achieve any improvements in English, while improvements are observed in non-English languages, is the quantity and quality of data in the PMB. As noted in the statistics of PMB 3.0.0 (Appendix B and Table 4), we can use over 6.6k English gold training data. In addition, nearly 100k sliver cases are available. In contrast, the German dataset only contains 1.2k gold and 5.3k silver cases, and there is no gold case in both Dutch and Italian.

6 Conclusion and Future Work

In this study, we carried out a further exploration of the extent to which character-level representations contribute to the performance improvements of multilingual DRS parsing models. We found that character-level information provided little performance improvement in English and German but improved performance in Dutch and Italian. However, we find that the model is sensitive to character order in Italian but not in Dutch. The take-away message from our investigation is that the importance of character-level information in DRS-based semantic parsing depends on the language and syntactic structures of the sentences.

In future work, we will analyze in more detail the significant differences between the four languages, especially Italian, and other languages. Another direction of our future work is to investigate the relationship between the neural models and humans in reading performance for incorrect character order. It would be interesting to analyze whether the results on DRS parsing tasks are consistent with those of these studies (Ferreira et al., 2002; Gibson et al., 2013; Traxler, 2014).

Limitations

In this study, we focus on DRS parsing tasks, and do not consider other representation formats for semantic parsing tasks.

Acknowledgements

We thank the three anonymous reviewers for their helpful comments and suggestions, which improved this paper. We also thank our colleagues, Aman Jain and Anirudh Reddy Kondapally, for proofreading and providing many comments on our paper. This work was supported by JST, PRESTO grant number JPMJPR21C8, Japan.

References

Mostafa Abdou, Vinit Ravishankar, Artur Kulmizev, and Anders Søgaard. 2022. Word order does matter and shuffled language models know it. In *Proceedings of the 60th Annual Meeting of the Association for Computational Linguistics (Volume 1: Long Papers)*, pages 6907–6919, Dublin, Ireland. Association for Computational Linguistics.

Lasha Abzianidze, Johannes Bjerva, Kilian Evang, Hessel Haagsma, Rik van Noord, Pierre Ludmann, Duc-Duy Nguyen, and Johan Bos. 2017. The Parallel Meaning Bank: Towards a multilingual corpus of translations annotated with compositional meaning representations. In *Proceedings of the 15th Conference of the European Chapter of the Association for Computational Linguistics: Volume 2, Short Papers*, pages 242–247, Valencia, Spain. Association for Computational Linguistics.

Lasha Abzianidze and Johan Bos. 2017. Towards universal semantic tagging. In *Proceedings of the 12th International Conference on Computational Semantics (IWCS)*, Montpellier, France. Association for Computational Linguistics.

Colin Cherry, George Foster, Ankur Bapna, Orhan Firat, and Wolfgang Macherey. 2018. Revisiting character-based neural machine translation with capacity and compression. In *Proceedings of the 2018 Conference on Empirical Methods in Natural Language Processing*, pages 4295–4305, Brussels, Belgium. Association for Computational Linguistics.

Jacob Devlin, Ming-Wei Chang, Kenton Lee, and Kristina Toutanova. 2019. BERT: Pre-training of deep bidirectional transformers for language understanding. In *Proceedings of the 2019 Conference of the North American Chapter of the Association for Computational Linguistics: Human Language Technologies, Volume 1 (Long and Short Papers)*, pages 4171–4186, Minneapolis, Minnesota. Association for Computational Linguistics.

Kilian Evang. 2019. Transition-based DRS parsing using stack-LSTMs. In *Proceedings of the IWCS Shared Task on Semantic Parsing*, pages 16–23, Gothenburg, Sweden. Association for Computational Linguistics.

Federico Fancellu, Sorcha Gilroy, Adam Lopez, and Mirella Lapata. 2019. Semantic graph parsing with recurrent neural network DAG grammars. In *Proceedings of the 2019 Conference on Empirical Methods in Natural Language Processing and the 9th International Joint Conference on Natural Language Processing (EMNLP-IJCNLP)*, pages 2769–2778, Hong Kong, China. Association for Computational Linguistics.

Fernanda Ferreira, Karl G. D. Bailey, and Vittoria Ferraro. 2002. Good-enough representations in language comprehension. *Current Directions in Psychological Science*, 11(1):11–15.

Edward Gibson, Leon Bergen, and Steven T. Piantadosi. 2013. Rational integration of noisy evidence and prior semantic expectations in sentence interpretation. *Proceedings of the National Academy of Sciences*, 110(20):8051–8056.

Jack Hessel and Alexandra Schofield. 2021. How effective is BERT without word ordering? implications for language understanding and data privacy. In *Proceedings of the 59th Annual Meeting of the Association for Computational Linguistics and the 11th International Joint Conference on Natural Language Processing (Volume 2: Short Papers)*, pages 204–211, Online. Association for Computational Linguistics.

Hans Kamp and Uwe Reyle. 1993. *From Discourse to Logic*. Springer, Dordrecht.

Guillaume Lample, Miguel Ballesteros, Sandeep Subramanian, Kazuya Kawakami, and Chris Dyer. 2016. Neural architectures for named entity recognition. In *Proceedings of the 2016 Conference of the North American Chapter of the Association for Computational Linguistics: Human Language Technologies*, pages 260–270, San Diego, California. Association for Computational Linguistics.

Thang Pham, Trung Bui, Long Mai, and Anh Nguyen. 2021. Out of order: How important is the sequential order of words in a sentence in natural language understanding tasks? In *Findings of the Association for Computational Linguistics: ACL-IJCNLP 2021*, pages 1145–1160, Online. Association for Computational Linguistics.

Wessel Poelman, Rik van Noord, and Johan Bos. 2022. Transparent semantic parsing with Universal Dependencies using graph transformations. In *Proceedings of the 29th International Conference on Computational Linguistics*, pages 4186–4192, Gyeongju, Republic of Korea. International Committee on Computational Linguistics.

Shauli Ravfogel, Yoav Goldberg, and Tal Linzen. 2019. Studying the inductive biases of RNNs with synthetic variations of natural languages. In *Proceedings of the 2019 Conference of the North American Chapter of the Association for Computational Linguistics: Human Language Technologies, Volume 1 (Long and Short Papers)*, pages 3532–3542, Minneapolis, Minnesota. Association for Computational Linguistics.

Minxing Shen and Kilian Evang. 2022. DRS parsing as sequence labeling. In *Proceedings of the 11th Joint Conference on Lexical and Computational Semantics*, pages 213–225, Seattle, Washington. Association for Computational Linguistics.

Koustuv Sinha, Robin Jia, Dieuwke Hupkes, Joelle Pineau, Adina Williams, and Douwe Kiela. 2021a. Masked language modeling and the distributional hypothesis: Order word matters pre-training for little. In *Proceedings of the 2021 Conference on Empirical Methods in Natural Language Processing*, pages 2888–2913, Online and Punta Cana, Dominican Republic. Association for Computational Linguistics.

Koustuv Sinha, Prasanna Parthasarathi, Joelle Pineau, and Adina Williams. 2021b. UnNatural Language Inference. In *Proceedings of the 59th Annual Meeting of the Association for Computational Linguistics and the 11th International Joint Conference on Natural Language Processing (Volume 1: Long Papers)*, pages 7329–7346, Online. Association for Computational Linguistics.

Matthew J. Traxler. 2014. Trends in syntactic parsing: anticipation, bayesian estimation, and good-enough parsing. *Trends in Cognitive Sciences*, 18(11):605–611.

Rik van Noord, Lasha Abzianidze, Hessel Haagsma, and Johan Bos. 2018a. Evaluating scoped meaning representations. In *Proceedings of the Eleventh International Conference on Language Resources and Evaluation (LREC 2018)*, Miyazaki, Japan. European Language Resources Association (ELRA).

Rik van Noord, Lasha Abzianidze, Antonio Toral, and Johan Bos. 2018b. Exploring neural methods for parsing discourse representation structures. *Transactions of the Association for Computational Linguistics*, 6:619–633.

Rik van Noord, Antonio Toral, and Johan Bos. 2020. Character-level representations improve DRS-based semantic parsing even in the age of BERT. In *Proceedings of the 2020 Conference on Empirical Methods in Natural Language Processing (EMNLP)*, pages 4587–4603, Online. Association for Computational Linguistics.

Ashish Vaswani, Noam Shazeer, Niki Parmar, Jakob Uszkoreit, Llion Jones, Aidan N Gomez, Łukasz Kaiser, and Illia Polosukhin. 2017. Attention is all you need. In *Advances in Neural Information Processing Systems*, volume 30. Curran Associates, Inc.

Alex Wang, Amanpreet Singh, Julian Michael, Felix Hill, Omer Levy, and Samuel R. Bowman. 2019. GLUE: A multi-task benchmark and analysis platform for natural language understanding. In *Proceedings of the Seventh International Conference on Learning Representations*, New Orleans, Louisiana. International Conference on Learning Representations.

Jennifer C. White and Ryan Cotterell. 2021. Examining the inductive bias of neural language models with artificial languages. In *Proceedings of the 59th Annual Meeting of the Association for Computational Linguistics and the 11th International Joint Conference on Natural Language Processing (Volume 1: Long Papers)*, pages 454–463, Online. Association for Computational Linguistics.

Xiaodong Yu, Stephen Mayhew, Mark Sammons, and Dan Roth. 2018. On the strength of character language models for multilingual named entity recognition. In *Proceedings of the 2018 Conference on Empirical Methods in Natural Language Processing*, pages 3073–3077, Brussels, Belgium. Association for Computational Linguistics.

Xiang Zhang, Junbo Zhao, and Yann LeCun. 2015. Character-level convolutional networks for text classification. In *Advances in Neural Information Processing Systems*, volume 28. Curran Associates, Inc.

	Gold			Silver	Bronze
	Train	Dev	Test	Train	Train
English	6,620	885	898	97,598	146,371
German	1,159	417	403	5,250	121,111
Dutch	0	529	483	1,301	21,550
Italian	0	515	547	2,772	64,305

Table 4: The data statistics of PMB release 3.0.0.

A DRS Parsing Task

DRS parsing is a task to convert natural language sentences into DRS-based meaning representations. In van Noord et al. (2020) and this study, the outputs of the models are clausal forms with relative naming for the variables. See van Noord et al. (2018b) for the further details.

A.1 Evaluation

This study follows micro F1-scores based on matching clauses between predicted and gold DRSs adopted by van Noord et al. (2020). The tool for calculating the values is Counter (van Noord et al., 2018a), which searches for the best mapping of variables between two DRSs and calculates the values based on the number of clauses. Referee (van Noord et al., 2018b) verifies whether an output DRS is well-formed. An output DRS is ill-formed (i.e., not well-formed) when it has illegal clauses or the tool fails to solve variable references.

B Dataset Settings

We use PMB release 3.0.0 and the same setup as that in the previous study (van Noord et al., 2020). As pre-training datasets, we use a merged set of the gold and the silver training sets for English, a merged set of all training sets (gold, silver, and bronze) for German[1], and combined sets of silver and bronze training sets for Dutch and Italian. As datasets for fine-tuning, we use the gold training set for English, a combined set of the gold and silver training sets for German, and the silver training sets for Dutch and Italian. Table 4 shows data statistics of the PMB release 3.0.0.

C Numerical Results

Table 5 shows numerical values reported in Figure 1.

[1]We also experiment on the setup described in van Noord et al. (2020). See Appendix E.2

D Results in English without Semantic Tags

Figure 2 and Table 6 show the results of the 2-enc + char model without semantic tags in English. Compared with 2-enc + char (Figure 1a), we can observe slightly larger but minor changes in the averaged F1-scores. Thus, regardless of the existence of semantic tags, our experimental results indicate that the model is not sensitive to the order of character sequences in English.

E Additional Analysis

E.1 Score change by character-level information per case

We look at the performance changes in individual cases. Figure 3 shows scatter diagrams of the four languages. In these diagrams, we plot the averaged F1-score changes of 15 runs by adding (i.e., from NO CHAR to UNIGRAMS) and extending (i.e., from UNIGRAMS to BIGRAMS) character-level information. We observe many cases whose averaged F1-score increases with the addition and extension of character-level information (plotted in the first quadrant). However, these numbers are lower than those in the second and fourth quadrants, indicating that the improvement works only by either adding or extending the information. Moreover, we observed cases whose scores decrease in both aspects, plotted in the third quadrant. These trends are observed for all languages, even though the overall scores improved for all languages except English.

E.2 Why do our values deviate from van Noord et al. (2020)?

The values reported in this study are lower than those from the previous study van Noord et al. (2020), especially in German. We follow nearly all the setups reported in van Noord et al. (2020), but the values are still low.

Van Noord et al. (2020) reports that they only used the gold and silver data if gold (train) data is available in a certain language. The German data in PMB release 3.0.0 has the gold train data comprising 1,159 documents. Therefore, we experiment with the model pre-trained on the merged set of the gold and silver data and fine-tuned on the gold data only. We reported an averaged value of five runs in Table 7 with one from van Noord et al. (2020). A large deviation between the two F1-scores can be observed.

	Avg	SE	Min	Max	Avg values per pre-train
CORRECT	89.05	0.06	88.47	89.39	89.04, 88.95, 89.17
SHF-WORD	88.80	0.09	88.03	89.34	88.80, 88.75, 88.87
SHF-SENT	88.75	0.09	88.04	89.20	88.79, 88.53, 88.93
RND	88.65	0.09	88.01	89.19	88.74, 88.48, 88.74
UNI	88.76	0.09	88.04	89.25	88.62, 88.61, 89.05

(a) English

	Avg	SE	Min	Max	Avg values per pre-train
CORRECT	76.07	0.12	75.21	77.02	76.24, 76.24, 75.74
SHF-WORD	75.68	0.13	74.76	76.75	75.69, 75.88, 75.46
SHF-SENT	75.07	0.13	73.90	76.09	74.89, 75.28, 75.03
RND	74.81	0.11	74.22	75.46	74.72, 74.83, 74.88
UNI	75.09	0.17	74.34	76.26	75.02, 75.25, 74.99

(b) German

	Avg	SE	Min	Max	Avg values per pre-train
CORRECT	69.23	0.18	67.89	70.26	69.41, 69.33, 68.95
SHF-WORD	68.69	0.13	67.70	69.60	68.94, 68.68, 68.46
SHF-SENT	68.82	0.13	67.95	69.68	69.31, 68.59, 68.55
RND	67.47	0.14	66.52	68.34	67.65, 67.50, 67.26
UNI	65.69	0.30	63.90	67.47	65.68, 65.76, 65.64

(c) Dutch

	Avg	SE	Min	Max	Avg values per pre-train
CORRECT	78.75	0.10	77.99	79.29	78.97, 78.53, 78.75
SHF-WORD	58.84	0.20	57.59	60.30	58.74, 58.34, 59.43
SHF-SENT	39.37	0.42	35.22	41.78	39.37, 38.08, 40.66
RND	39.95	0.46	35.08	42.26	39.83, 40.30, 39.73
UNI	26.66	1.30	18.23	34.16	28.06, 30.14, 21.77

(d) Italian

Table 5: The numerical values (%) reported in Figure 1. SE is the abbreviation of standard error.

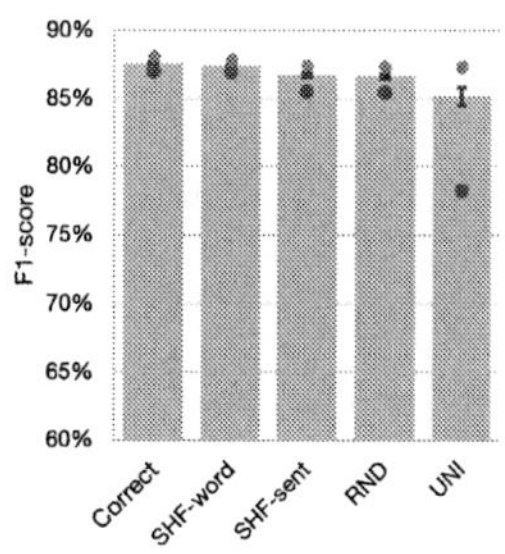

Figure 2: F1-scores of the gold test set predicted by the 2-enc + char model without semantic tags in English.

	Avg	SE	Min	Max
CORRECT	87.58	0.10	87.01	88.14
SHF-WORD	87.39	0.08	86.97	87.84
SHF-SENT	86.73	0.16	85.54	87.40
RND	86.61	0.17	85.48	87.34
UNI	85.15	0.70	78.25	87.34

Table 6: The numerical values (%) reported in Figure 2, the 2-enc + char model without semantic tags in English. SE is the abbreviation of standard error.

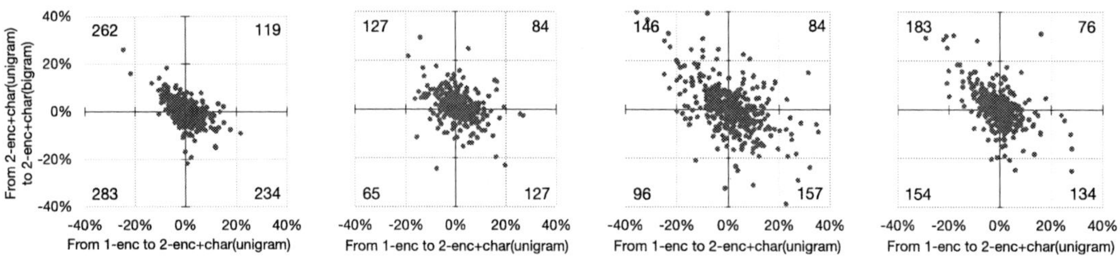

(a) English (898 cases) (b) German (403 cases) (c) Dutch (583 cases) (d) Italian (547 cases)

Figure 3: Distribution of F1-score changes from NO CHAR to UNIGRAMS (x-axis) and from UNIGRAMS to BIGRAMS (y-axis) per case on the gold test set of the four languages. The numbers on the corners are the numbers of cases in each quadrant. 1, 5, and 2 cases are out of bounds (>40%) in German, Dutch, and Italian, respectively.

	Average	All values
Van Noord et al. (2020)	82.0	N/A
Our replication	68.52	68.54, 67.95, 69.38, 68.61, 68.10

Table 7: F1-scores (%) from van Noord et al. (2020) and our replication experiment in German. The models is pre-trained on the unified set of the gold and silver train data and fine-tuned on the gold train data.

Testing Paraphrase Models on Recognising Sentence Pairs at Different Degrees of Semantic Overlap

Qiwei Peng David Weir Julie Weeds
University of Sussex
Brighton, UK
{qiwei.peng, d.j.weir, j.e.weeds}@sussex.ac.uk

Abstract

Paraphrase detection is useful in many natural language understanding applications. Current works typically formulate this problem as a sentence pair binary classification task. However, this setup is not a good fit for many of the intended applications of paraphrase models. In particular, such applications often involve finding the closest paraphrases of the target sentence from a group of candidate sentences where they exhibit different degrees of semantic overlap with the target sentence. To apply models to this paraphrase retrieval scenario, the model must be sensitive to the degree to which two sentences are paraphrases of one another. However, many existing datasets ignore and fail to test models in this setup. In response, we propose adversarial paradigms to create evaluation datasets, which could examine the sensitivity to different degrees of semantic overlap. Empirical results show that, while paraphrase models and different sentence encoders appear successful on standard evaluations, measuring the degree of semantic overlap still remains a big challenge for them.

1 Introduction

Detecting paraphrases is useful in many natural language understanding applications, such as question answering (Yin et al., 2015; Gan and Ng, 2019), fact checking (Jiang et al., 2020), and text summarisation (Kryściński et al., 2018, 2019). Researchers have constructed paraphrase identification benchmarks, typically formulating the problem as a sentence pair classification task (Dolan and Brockett, 2005; Lan et al., 2017; Iyer et al., 2017; Zhang et al., 2019b).

Sentence pairs that have the same or largely equivalent semantics are considered as paraphrases of each other (Androutsopoulos and Malakasiotis, 2010; Bhagat and Hovy, 2013). For example:

a) More than half of the songs were purchased as albums, Apple said.

b) Apple noted that half the songs were purchased as part of albums.

Not only is it unclear what the criteria is for determining when a sentence pair has sufficiently similar semantics to be considered paraphrases, but as Chen et al. (2020) point out, the standard paraphrase classification task is not a good fit for many of the intended applications of paraphrase models. In particular, such applications are often retrieval tasks that involve finding the closest paraphrases of some target sentences within a set of documents, where candidate sentences exhibit different degrees of semantic overlap with the target sentence. To apply models to a paraphrase retrieval scenario, a paraphrase model must be sensitive to the degree to which two sentences are paraphrases of one another.

We use the term partial paraphrase to refer to situations where a sentence pair has **some** overlap in meaning, but this can range from nearly exact paraphrases to pairs that share very little meaning. An example of an intermediate case is given below:

a) More than half of the songs were purchased as albums, Apple said yesterday in a meeting with Sony.

b) Apple noted that half the songs were purchased as part of albums.

The setup used for standard paraphrase classification can be adapted to the partial paraphrase task, where the softmax confidence score is used as an estimate of the degree to which two sentences are paraphrases of one another. Indeed, this has been used in ranking tasks across different domains (MacAvaney et al., 2019; Ji et al., 2020; Sun and Duh, 2020). However, while pre-trained language models have shown good performance on the standard classification task (Devlin et al., 2019; Liu et al., 2019), as we will show, these models are often fooled by partial paraphrases where there is significant, but far from complete, semantic over-

*Proceedings of the The 12th Joint Conference on Lexical and Computational Semantics (*SEM 2023)*, pages 259–269
July 13-14, 2023 ©2023 Association for Computational Linguistics

lap.

Current paraphrase identification datasets do not test models in a partial paraphrase ranking setup. Though the semantic textual similarity (STS) tasks (Agirre et al., 2012; Cer et al., 2017) exhibit similarities to this setup as they also try to measure gradations of meaning overlap, there are some significant differences. Firstly, the ranking setup in STS concerns comparing completely different sentence pairs (e.g., $(a, b) > (c, d)$), while most paraphrase applications aim to compare different sentences with the same pivot sentence (e.g., $(a, b) > (a, c)$). Secondly, as Wang et al. (2022) point out that the definition of similarity in STS is rather vague and various complicated relations between sentence pairs all contribute to the similarity score. The difference in the similarity score cannot guarantee the different degree of semantic overlap.

Our aim, in this paper, is to rectify this deficiency. We draw inspiration from previous adversarial testing works utilising word swapping and number replacement (Zhang et al., 2019b; Wang et al., 2021) to produce negative examples. In this work, we propose adversarial paradigms (multiple word swap) to create evaluation datasets that consist of high-quality partial paraphrase pairs with graded semantic overlap. We aim to test whether the paraphrase score produced by existing paraphrase models and sentence encoders is a good reflection of the degree of semantic overlap. In contrast to their strong performance on standard paraphrase classification tasks, our analysis reveals that measuring the degree of semantic overlap still remains a challenge.

Our main contributions are as follow. First, in Section 3, we follow the standard fine-tuning strategy to produce two paraphrase models and then demonstrate their good performance on standard evaluation tasks and insensitivity to partial paraphrases. We then present (in Section 4) evaluation datasets which consist of high-quality partial paraphrase pairs with graded semantic overlap, constructed by multiple word swapping. We further show (in Section 5) that the distinction between partial paraphrase and exact paraphrase is a challenge for paraphrase models, and that their paraphrase scores are not a good reflection of the degree of semantic overlap. Finally, our work demonstrates that similarity scores produced by sentence encoders, though being widely used as a measure of similarity in meaning, are dominated by the degree of lexical overlap, and are poor estimators of the degree to which sentences are partial paraphrases.

2 Related Work

The definition of paraphrase has been long debated, as have the characteristics of paraphrase pairs (Androutsopoulos and Malakasiotis, 2010; Bhagat and Hovy, 2013; Rus et al., 2014; Liu et al., 2022). A widely accepted definition is that two sentences should exhibit the same or largely equivalent semantics, which suggests a bi-directional entailment relation. As Madnani and Dorr (2010) pointed out, paraphrases may occur at different levels, such as word-level, phrase-level, and sentence-level. Although there has been some work that concerned the identification of lexical and phrasal paraphrases (Ganitkevitch et al., 2013; Pavlick et al., 2015), most recent work on paraphrase identification has been performed at the sentence level, and has involved determining whether a given sentence pair is a paraphrase or not in a classification setup (Dolan and Brockett, 2005; Fernando and Stevenson, 2008; Xu et al., 2014; Zhang et al., 2019b; Liu et al., 2022).

However, paraphrase detection has been utilised in other NLP tasks. In question answering, Dong et al. (2017) utilised paraphrase detection to discover most probable paraphrases of a given question from a group of potential paraphrases by comparing their paraphrase scores. Similarly, Wang et al. (2020) integrated paraphrase detection in a information retrieval system to select the best paraphrased queries which are used to expand the original query list. Accordingly, Chen et al. (2020) argued that the standard binary classification setup of paraphrase identification is ill-suited to many real-world applications which involve paraphrase retrieval. To apply paraphrase models to such a retrieval scenario, the model must be sensitive to the degree to which two sentences share semantic content.

Though pre-trained language models show good performance when fine-tuned on paraphrase identification datasets (Devlin et al., 2019; Liu et al., 2019; Arase and Tsujii, 2021), a performance drop is often observed when being tested for robustness under different adversarial scenarios. Zhang et al. (2019b) utilised word swapping and back-translation to produce adversarial examples. Yang et al. (2019) adopted the same approach to produce adversarial pairs in a multilingual scenario. Shi and Huang (2020) modified shared words to produce both positive and negative pairs. Wang et al. (2021) additionally proposed a robustness evaluation platform which can perform different transformations to sentence pairs, including word swapping, template-based generation and number replacement. Nighojkar and Licato (2021) employed paraphrase generators to produce sentence pairs that are both lexically and syntactically disparate. Such transformations can create partial paraphrases in different types. However, these partial paraphrases do not exhibit decreasing semantic overlap. To measure the sensitivity of models to different degrees of semantic overlap, we draw inspiration from them and create a list of partial paraphrases with decreasing semantic overlap for each paraphrase pair.

3 Background and Preliminaries

The classification setup for the evaluation of paraphrase identification involves identifying whether the given sentence pair is a paraphrase or not. In this section, we follow previous work and first fine-tune BERT (Devlin et al., 2019) and RoBERTa (Liu et al., 2019) on widely used paraphrase datasets to produce standard paraphrase models and check whether their success on standard evaluation benchmarks could transfer to the recognition of partial paraphrases with different degrees of semantic overlap.

3.1 Datasets

In this paper, we mainly consider two commonly used paraphrase datasets, $\text{PAWS}_{\text{Wiki}}$ and PAWS_{QQP} (Zhang et al., 2019b). The Paraphrase Adversaries from Word Scrambling (PAWS) datasets utilise word scrambling (swapping words that have same part-of-speech or name entity tags) and back translation to produce both positive and negative examples for given sentences while maintaining high lexical overlap. Though less often used than datasets like Microsoft Research Paraphrase Corpus (MRPC) (Dolan and Brockett, 2005) where a large percentage of positive sentence pairs just have partial overlap in meaning, PAWS datasets contain high quality sentence pairs that are mostly exact paraphrases. PAWS datasets do not have a specific license and can be used freely for any purpose[1]. In the following sections, we propose adversarial evaluation datasets that are derived from the test sets of these two datasets.

Datasets	Train	Dev	Test
PAWS_{QQP}	11,986	-	677
$\text{PAWS}_{\text{Wiki}}$	49,401	8,000	8,000

Table 1: Statistics of two PAWS datasets.

The statistics of these datasets are listed in Table 1. Below we give some brief descriptions:

- **PAWS_{QQP}**: With the aim of assessing sensitivity to word order and syntactic structure, Zhang et al. (2019b) proposed a paraphrase identification dataset that contains sentence pairs of high lexical overlap. They are created by applying back translation and word scrambling to sentences taken from the Quora Question Pairs (Wang et al., 2017).
- **$\text{PAWS}_{\text{Wiki}}$**: The same process is applied to sentences obtained from Wikipedia articles to construct paraphrase and non-paraphrase pairs.

The construction process ensures positive sentence pairs in PAWS datasets are mostly exact paraphrases.

Model	$\text{PAWS}_{\text{Wiki}}$		PAWS_{QQP}	
	ACC	F1	ACC	F1
BERT	92.31	91.59	89.07	81.95
RoBERTa	94.10	93.44	92.91	87.76

Table 2: Classification results on PAWS datasets; we report the F1 score of the positive class and the overall accuracy.

3.2 Models

We evaluate two pre-trained language models, BERT and RoBERTa[2]. They are widely used, and have achieved good performance on paraphrase identification tasks. Following previous work, we first fine-tune them on the paraphrase datasets to produce standard paraphrase models. As shown in Zhang et al. (2019b), the best performance is achieved by training on the combination of the original QQP dataset (which has 384,348 training sentence pairs), PAWS_{QQP} and $\text{PAWS}_{\text{Wiki}}$. We follow the same strategy, fine-tuning both BERT-base

[1]https://github.com/google-research-datasets/paws/blob/master/LICENSE

[2]We use their huggingface implementations: https://huggingface.co/bert-base-uncased (110 million parameters) and https://huggingface.co/roberta-base (123 million parameters)

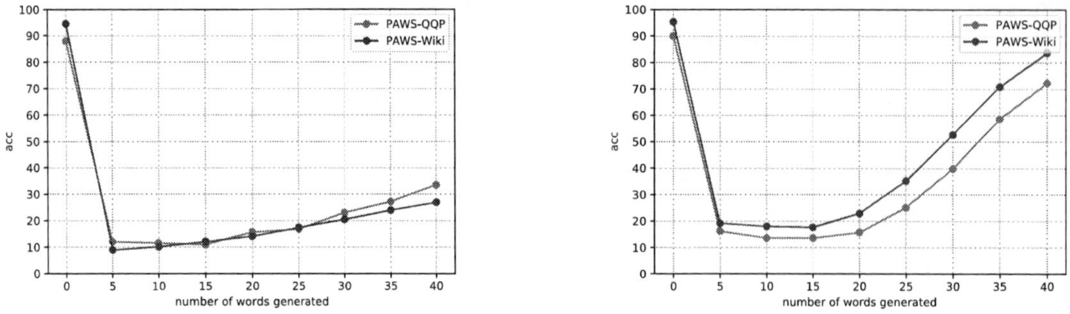

(a) BERT (b) RoBERTa

Figure 1: Performance of BERT and RoBERTa on generation-based adversarial evaluation datasets in the classification setup. X-axis: The number of generated words added to sentence A. Y-axis: The accuracy.

and RoBERTa-base on this combined training set[3]. Also following Zhang et al. (2019b), we use the QQP development set as our development set for early stopping. Each model is fine-tuned for 3 epochs with batch size of 16. We use the Adam optimiser with learning rate of 2e-5 and a linear learning rate warm-up over 10% of the training data. We fine-tune each model five times and choose the best for later experiments according to their performance on the development set. All of our experiments are conducted on one RTX 3090 GPU and each epoch takes around one hour.

We include the results on the standard evaluation benchmarks in Table 2. We can see that both BERT and RoBERTa have achieved high accuracy and F1 scores, which appears to demonstrate their ability to identify paraphrases.

3.3 Partial Paraphrases

A typical example of partial paraphrase is where one sentence contains all of the semantics of another but also contains additional information (see the example in the Introduction). We therefore adopt a straightforward approach to produce an initial adversarial test of partial paraphrase identification.

Given a positive sentence pair (a, b) in PAWS test sets, we take a as context and utilise the GPT2[4] generation model (Radford et al., 2019) to generate additional tokens, giving a new sentence that we denote $\hat{a}$. To avoid disrupting the meaning of the existing content, we further add ", and" to the end of a. Compared to the original pair (a, b), the new pair $(\hat{a}, b)$ has lower semantic overlap given the additional information in $\hat{a}$.

Here, we give an example of generated partial paraphrase pairs:

a) He was born in New York City in East Broadway on October 23, 1806**, and was raised in Baltimore]], Maryland, where the family moved]] to live in 1900 with]] two sons and two daughters.]]**

b) He was born on 23 October 1806 in New York, East Broadway.

The bold part is the generated text, and the coloured "]]" symbols indicate places where we truncate the added content (every five generated tokens). The idea is that the dataset contains a range of examples that systematically vary in terms of the degree of semantic overlap. We evaluate previously fine-tuned paraphrase models on this generation-based evaluation set (no further training) and investigate at what point they detect that the given pair is no longer an exact paraphrase.

Experimental results are summarised in Figure 1, where we report the overall accuracy. We observe that when no extra words are added, these two models show near-perfect performance on recognising the given positive pair as paraphrase of each other. However, when we add 5 words to produce a partial paraphrase pair as a negative example of a paraphrase, performance drops dramatically, demonstrating the lack of sensitivity of these models to the distinction between an exact paraphrase and a partial paraphrases. The accuracy gradually increases as we generate more words to sentence

[3]We also tried training on individual datasets rather than the combined one. The results show worse performance on the standard classification evaluation and no different trend on following ranking tasks.

[4]We choose GPT2 because it generates satisfactory results and is free to access.

a) Tagging [Bhagat Beni] [has] [also] [said] [that] [Guru] [Arjan Dev] [attained] [enlightenment] [only] [through] [the] [Holy] [Word]
PERSON VBZ RB VBN IN NNP PERSON VBD NN RB IN DT NNP NNP

b) Groupping [Bhagat Beni, Arjan Dev] [has, said, attained] [also, only] [that, through] [Guru, enlightenment, Holy, Word] [the]
PERSON VERBS RB IN NOUNS DT

c) Sampling [Bhagat Beni, Arjan Dev] [also, only] [Guru, enlightenment, Holy, Word]

d) Swapping (1-swap) Arjan Dev has also said that Guru Bhagat Beni attained enlightenment only through the Holy Word
(2-swap) Arjan Dev has only said that Guru Bhagat Beni attained enlightenment also through the Holy Word
(3-swap) Arjan Dev has only said that Guru Bhagat Beni attained Word also through the Holy enlightenment

Figure 2: Illustration of the multi-swap method in four steps. a) Tag words and phrases with part-of-speech (POS) and named entities. b) produce candidate sets by grouping words and phrases with the same tag. c) Sample three groups from the candidate sets that have two or more words/phrases. d) Swap position.

A. However, the increase only becomes substantial when we append at least than 20 words. We can see that good performance on the original test sets is not translating to the task of distinguishing partial paraphrases from exact paraphrases.

Though paraphrase models are can be fooled by partial paraphrases, they do exhibit increased ability to recognise them as the difference in semantics grows. The poor performance on close partial paraphrases might be explained by the paraphrase score decreasing as the degree of semantic overlap reduces, but the decrease not being large enough to bring the score down below the binary classification threshold, resulting in the wrong prediction. To explore whether this is the case and whether the paraphrase score could act as a reliable indicator to the degree of semantic overlap, we now turn to the evaluation of paraphrase models in a ranking scenario, requiring candidates to be ranked based on the amount of semantic overlap.

Problematically, however, sentences produced by the generation-based method exhibit significant differences in sentence length as well as the degree of lexical overlap. These differences would be an obvious clues in a ranking task[5]. In this regard, we adopted a different approach to produce ranking-based evaluation datasets which was to utilise word swapping.

4 Partial Paraphrase Construction

To create partial paraphrases at decreasing degrees of semantic overlap, while maintaining lexical overlap and sentence length, we draw inspiration from Zhang et al. (2019b) and Wang et al. (2021) who create negative examples by swapping words and entities. We take positive sentence pairs from PAWS test sets and create corresponding partial paraphrases with graded semantic overlap by making multiple word swaps. Since the semantics are equivalent for positive sentence pairs, we always make modifications to sentence B to produce partial paraphrase variants and compare them with the original sentence A. This can increase the task difficulty as the lexical overlap will be high for negative pairs. Models that produce high scores based on high lexical overlap are likely to fail in this scenario.

	# original	# after 3 swaps
$\text{PAWS}_{\text{Wiki}}$	3536	1382
PAWS_{QQP}	191	63

Table 3: The number of examples before and after performing 3 swaps. We take only positive examples (3536/191) from original datasets and filter out sentence pairs that do not meet our criteria as described in the construction process. We end up with 1382/63 positive examples and each now has 3 swap-based negative variants.

Figure 2 illustrates the multi-swap procedure. Given a paraphrase pair (a, b), we first perform part-of-speech tagging[6] (POS) on b to obtain tags for each word. We further detect named entities like locations, person names, organisations, and dates using a named entity tagger, and replace POS tags with entity tags when there is overlap. Words and phrases that have the same tag[7] are then grouped together. We deduplicate each group to avoid swapping the position between two identical words/phrases. Given that a swap requires at least

[5]Our initial experiments show that sentence encoders can achieve extremely high performance on ranking these sentence pairs by capturing such clues.

[6]We use Spacy large web-based model pipeline (en_core_web_lg) for both POS and NER tagging.

[7]We do not distinguish different POS tags for verbs (e.g., VBZ, VBN, VBD) and nouns (e.g., NNP, NNPS, NN, NNS). We also exclude "to be" verbs, as swapping them does not guarantee changes in semantics.

Source	Sentence A	Sentence B	Paraphrase Degree
PAWS$_{Wiki}$	**(no-swap)** Bhagat Beni also said that the guru Arjan Dev has obtained enlightenment only through the Holy Word.	Bhagat Beni has also said that Guru Arjan Dev attained enlightenment only through the Holy Word.	4
	(1-swap) Arjan Dev has also said that Guru Bhagat Beni attained enlightenment only through the Holy Word.		3
	(2-swap) Arjan Dev has only said that Guru Bhagat Beni attained enlightenment also through the Holy Word.		2
	(3-swap) Arjan Dev has only said that Guru Bhagat Beni attained Word also through the Holy enlightenment.		1
PAWS$_{QQP}$	**(no-swap)** Was increasing funding to protect Benghazi before the attack denied by Congress. If so, who voted against it?	Was increased funding to protect Benghazi before the attack denied by Congress. If so, who voted against it?	4
	(1-swap) Was increased attack to protect Benghazi before the funding denied by Congress. If so, who voted against it?		3
	(2-swap) Was increased attack to protect Congress before the funding denied by Benghazi. If so, who voted against it?		2
	(3-swap) Was denied attack to protect Congress before the funding increased by Benghazi. If so, who voted against it?		1

Table 4: Examples of swapped sentences taken from two PAWS datasets (We swap sentence B to produce swap-based partial paraphrases). Different colours denote different swaps and each swap is performed based on previous swaps to ensure the degrading semantic overlap. Sentence pair with paraphrase degree of 4 is **exact paraphrase** and 3, 2, 1 are **partial paraphrases** with decreasing semantic overlap.

two words/phrases, we discard tag groups that have less than two words/phrases. In order to produce enough candidates for ranking, we filter out sentences that have less than 3 tag groups. For each sentence with at least three tag groups, we randomly sample three groups, and from each group we randomly sample two words/phrases. In the end, we swap the position of sampled words/phrases to produce swapped sentences. We perform each swap based on previous swaps, with a maximum of three swaps. In summary, given a positive sentence pair (a, b), we apply our multi-swap strategy on b, and produce a group of sentence pairs $[(a, b), (\hat{b}_{1swap}, b), (\hat{b}_{2swap}, b), (\hat{b}_{3swap}, b)]$, where they exhibit decreasing semantic overlap.

The statistics of the resulting evaluation datasets are given in Table 3. Examples taken from the swap-based partial paraphrase datasets are shown in Table 4. In the same group, sentences with higher paraphrase degree are more likely to be exact paraphrases. Our evaluation setup is as follow: given a paraphrase scoring function f, and a set of sentence pairs $\{(a, b), (\hat{b}_{1swap}, b), (\hat{b}_{2swap}, b), (\hat{b}_{3swap}, b)\}$. We expect $f(a, b) > f(\hat{b}_{1swap}, b) > f(\hat{b}_{2swap}, b) > f(\hat{b}_{3swap}, b)$.

5 Experiments

We compare previous fine-tuned paraphrase models (BERT and RoBERTa in Section 3) with sentence encoders. Sentence encoders, such as SBERT(Reimers and Gurevych, 2019) and SimCSE (Gao et al., 2021), are widely used in various ranking scenarios which aim to measure the similarity in meaning between two sentences. They use a contrastive learning objective, intended to derive high-quality sentence representations by pulling sentences with similar semantics closer together and pushing dissimilar ones apart. Although they have achieved relatively good performance on STS tasks, it is unclear whether the similarity score they produce can be used to measure the extent to which sentence pairs are paraphrases.

In this experiment, we evaluate SimCSE[8], two variants of SimCSE, namely, SimCSE+PAS (Peng et al., 2022) and SimCSE+BERTScore[9] (Zhang et al., 2019a), and two SBERT models[10] (Reimers and Gurevych, 2020) which are specifically trained on paraphrase datasets. We denote

[8]https://github.com/princeton-nlp/SimCSE

[9]https://github.com/Tiiiger/bert_score

[10]https://github.com/UKPLab/sentence-transformers

one as $SBERT_{v1}$[11] and the other as $SBERT_{v2}$[12].

For paraphrase models, we use its softmax confidence of being positive as the **paraphrase score** to rank sentence pairs. For sentence encoders, we rank sentence pairs using their default strategy to produce a paraphrase score. Specifically, SBERT and SimCSE utilise the cosine similarity between two sentences; SimCSE+PAS increases the interaction between two sentences by considering the aggregated score over predicate-argument alignments; and SimCSE+BERTScore considers the IDF-weighted F1 measure in terms of word matching.

5.1 Evaluation

The ranking results are summarised in Table 5. We report both the average R-Precision and the average Spearman rank correlation between the predicted ranking and the true ranking across all groups. R-Precision measures the ability to retrieve best paraphrases and Spearman rank correlation measures the overall sensitivity to different degrees of semantic overlap as it concerns relative position shifts in the group. Similarly, we can turn this ranking task into a classification problem by regarding sentence pairs with paraphrase degree of 4 as positive and sentence pairs that have lower degree as negative. In this setup, we only evaluate paraphrase models. The classification results are shown in Figure 3.

From Figure 3, we observe similar patterns as in previous generation-based classification experiments. Both BERT and RoBERTa show good performance on recognising the given pair as paraphrases when no-swap is applied. However, after we perform one swap, the performance drops significantly, showing that these models fail to recognise the distinction. Both models begin to recover from this situation after two swaps[13]. This, again, indicates that paraphrase models are often confused by small semantic differences in the classification setup.

In terms of the ranking results presented in Table 5, we can see that sentence encoders show limited ability to distinguish the exact paraphrase from partial paraphrases on $PAWS_{Wiki}$, which is evidenced by the low R-Precision score. Although their overall performance is higher on $PAWS_{QQP}$, we suspect this is due to the high lexical overlap, which we investigate in detail in Section 5.2. Compared to sentence encoders, paraphrase models show generally better performance in terms of R-Precision on both datasets. It is worth noting that, under the classification setup, paraphrase models achieve good accuracy on recognising non-swap positive pairs (see the high accuracy of 0-swap in Figure 3). However, when we mix the non-swap pair together with other swapped partial paraphrases, both BERT and RoBERTa are unable to achieve equivalent R-Precision scores. This shows that paraphrase scores produced for partial paraphrases are often higher than those for exact paraphrases, demonstrating that they are not a reliable indicator as to how close two sentences are to being paraphrases. Since the number of candidates to rank (only four sentence pairs in each group) is small, the Spearman rank correlation obtained by both models is insufficient to demonstrate a strong positive correlation and implies many position shifts in the predicted ranking. Although the two versions of the SBERT model are specifically trained on paraphrase datasets, they do not exhibit better performance than SimCSE.

Model	$PAWS_{Wiki}$ (swap)		$PAWS_{QQP}$ (swap)	
	RPrec	Spearman	RPrec	Spearman
BERT	77.57	73.42	69.84	78.10
SimCSE	41.97	57.68	71.43	83.81
SimCSE+PAS	48.99	69.71	63.93	81.64
SimCSE+BERTScore	42.33	71.43	66.67	88.89
RoBERTa	85.31	69.90	76.19	69.21
SimCSE	43.20	56.98	66.67	79.05
SimCSE+PAS	42.19	62.13	62.30	83.61
SimCSE+BERTScore	44.21	69.90	71.43	87.62
$SBERT_{v1}$	35.60	47.97	74.60	81.90
$SBERT_{v2}$	28.44	37.77	66.67	77.46

Table 5: The results on the swap-based ranking evaluation. The backbone of sentence encoders in the first block is BERT-base and RoBERTa-base in the second block. We report the R-Precision and Spearman correlation.

5.2 The Impact of Lexical Overlap

One observation we have from Table 5 is that all sentence encoders have higher R-Precision and Spearman correlation on $PAWS_{QQP}$ compared to the performance on $PAWS_{Wiki}$. As shown in Table 6, we can see that positive sentence pairs in $PAWS_{QQP}$ have significantly higher lexical overlap. Thus, we suspect that the higher lexical overlap

[11] sentence-transformers/paraphrase-MiniLM-L12-v2

[12] sentence-transformers/paraphrase-distilroberta-base-v2

[13] As we increase the number of swaps, models become more confident in distinguishing whether the sentence pair is a paraphrase or not. This trend also reflects the quality of swap-based examples we create.

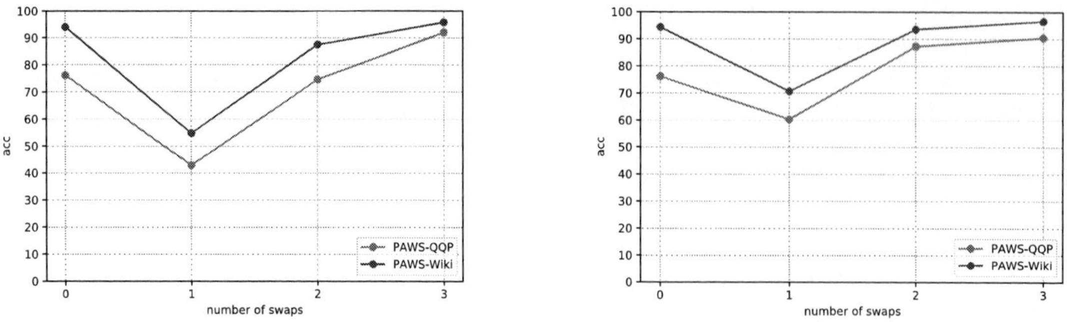

(a) BERT

(b) RoBERTa

Figure 3: Performance of BERT and RoBERTa on swap-based evaluation datasets in the classification setup. X-axis: Number of swaps performed. Y-axis: The accuracy. For Swap-0, all sentence pairs are positive and the accuracy is the percentage of sentence pairs classified as paraphrases. For Swap 1 to 3, sentence pairs are now all turned into negatives and the accuracy is the percentage of sentence pairs correctly classified as non-paraphrases by the model after we perform different word swaps.

	Lexical Overlap
$\text{PAWS}_{\text{Wiki}}$ (swap)*	83.46%
- after back-translation	75.79%
PAWS_{QQP} (swap)	95.03%
- after back-translation	59.56%

Table 6: The lexical overlap of the positive sentence pair (pair of paraphrase degree of 4). * denotes the randomly sampled dataset. We calculate the lexical overlap in terms of Jaccard Similarity with ngram=1.

Model	$\text{PAWS}_{\text{Wiki}}$ (swap) (100sample-bt)		PAWS_{QQP} (swap) (bt)	
	RPrec	Spearman	RPrec	Spearman
BERT	67.00	71.00	65.08	75.56
SimCSE	31.00	48.40	31.75	54.60
SimCSE+PAS	41.00	61.20	33.33	59.68
SimCSE+BERTScore	31.00	61.60	30.16	58.73
RoBERTa	74.00	69.20	73.02	68.57
SimCSE	33.00	47.80	33.33	55.56
SimCSE+PAS	32.00	51.20	36.51	57.14
SimCSE+BERTScore	30.00	56.00	26.98	53.02
SBERT_{v1}	26.00	38.20	28.57	53.97
SBERT_{v2}	15.00	17.20	4.76	7.30

Table 7: The results on the swap-based ranking evaluation (back-translated). We report the R-Precision and Spearman correlation.

makes sentence encoders produce higher scores which enable them to "guess" the correct answer.

To verify the impact of lexical overlap, we apply back-translation[14] to the positive sentence A so that the positive pair now has much lower lexical overlap. Given the PAWS_{QQP} (swapped) is of small size (63 groups), we manually check the results of back-translation and correct them if the translated sentence A is no longer an exact paraphrase of sentence B. $\text{PAWS}_{\text{Wiki}}$ (swapped) has more then 1,300 groups of sentence pairs, so we randomly sample 100 groups from it and apply the same process. As shown in Table 6, the lexical overlap has been significantly reduced after we apply back translation.

We evaluate all models on the back-translated datasets and the results are presented in Table 7. After reducing lexical overlap for positive pairs, we observe performance drops for all models. In particular, both R-Precision and Spearman rank correlation have decreased significantly across all sentence encoders. This indicates that sentence encoders are largely affected by lexical overlap while BERT and RoBERTa seem more robust to different degrees of lexical overlap between two sentences. Furthermore, we see that the performance of both predicate-argument alignment (PAS) and word matching (BERTScore) is only slightly better than that of SimCSE in terms of the sensitivity to semantic overlap. This demonstrates that the changes in similarity scores they produce are not good measurements as to how close two sentences are to being paraphrases. Given the unsatisfactory performance of paraphrase models and sentence encoders, we stress that more efforts are necessary to improve models' sensitivity to different degrees of semantic overlap, and it is important to consider specific ranking objectives and the proximity be-

[14]We utilise the Marian machine translation model (Junczys-Dowmunt et al., 2018) and use German as the pivot language.

tween different sentence pairs.

6 Conclusion

In this paper, we explore whether paraphrase scores produced by paraphrase models and sentence encoders are reliable indicators of the degree to which two sentences share semantic content. Accordingly, we propose an adversarial paradigms (multiple word swap) to create evaluation datasets that consist of high-quality partial paraphrases with graded semantic overlap in a ranking setup. Our experimental results show that the similarity score produced by sentence encoders is not a good indicator of how close two sentences are to being exact paraphrases, and is heavily affected by lexical overlap. Whilst paraphrase models show generally better performance, the confidence scores they produce are still far from acting as a reliable indicator to different degrees of semantic overlap. Measuring the degree of semantic overlap between two sentences remains a significant challenge. Our future work includes producing larger ranking datasets and extending this paradigm to other relevant datasets.

Limitations

The remaining limitations in our work are two-fold. First, for specific paraphrase models, our experiments are limited to consideration of BERT-base and RoBERTa-base models. This choice is made following their generality and good performance on various NLP tasks, but larger language models could also be considered. The second limitation of this paper is that, under the swap-based strategy, the sentence after three swaps sometimes are semantically problematic though grammatically correct. Despite having shown that paraphrase models have improved ability to distinguish partial paraphrases after two swaps, it would be better to use naturally occurring sentences and reduce the clue of irregular word or phrase usages.

Acknowledgement

We thank all anonymous reviewers for their insightful comments. We would like to further thank Bowen Wang for helpful discussions and proofreading.

References

Eneko Agirre, Daniel Cer, Mona Diab, and Aitor Gonzalez-Agirre. 2012. Semeval-2012 task 6: A pilot on semantic textual similarity. In ** SEM 2012: The First Joint Conference on Lexical and Computational Semantics–Volume 1: Proceedings of the main conference and the shared task, and Volume 2: Proceedings of the Sixth International Workshop on Semantic Evaluation (SemEval 2012)*, pages 385–393.

Ion Androutsopoulos and Prodromos Malakasiotis. 2010. A survey of paraphrasing and textual entailment methods. *Journal of Artificial Intelligence Research*, 38:135–187.

Yuki Arase and Junichi Tsujii. 2021. Transfer fine-tuning of bert with phrasal paraphrases. *Computer Speech & Language*, 66:101164.

Rahul Bhagat and Eduard Hovy. 2013. What is a paraphrase? *Computational Linguistics*, 39(3):463–472.

Daniel Cer, Mona Diab, Eneko Agirre, Iñigo Lopez-Gazpio, and Lucia Specia. 2017. Semeval-2017 task 1: Semantic textual similarity multilingual and crosslingual focused evaluation. In *Proceedings of the 11th International Workshop on Semantic Evaluation (SemEval-2017)*, pages 1–14.

Hannah Chen, Yangfeng Ji, and David K Evans. 2020. Pointwise paraphrase appraisal is potentially problematic. In *Proceedings of the 58th Annual Meeting of the Association for Computational Linguistics: Student Research Workshop*, pages 150–155.

Jacob Devlin, Ming-Wei Chang, Kenton Lee, and Kristina Toutanova. 2019. Bert: Pre-training of deep bidirectional transformers for language understanding. In *Proceedings of the 2019 Conference of the North American Chapter of the Association for Computational Linguistics: Human Language Technologies, Volume 1 (Long and Short Papers)*, pages 4171–4186.

William B. Dolan and Chris Brockett. 2005. Automatically constructing a corpus of sentential paraphrases. In *Proceedings of the Third International Workshop on Paraphrasing (IWP2005)*.

Li Dong, Jonathan Mallinson, Siva Reddy, and Mirella Lapata. 2017. Learning to paraphrase for question answering. In *Proceedings of the 2017 Conference on Empirical Methods in Natural Language Processing*, pages 875–886.

Samuel Fernando and Mark Stevenson. 2008. A semantic similarity approach to paraphrase detection. In *Proceedings of the 11th annual research colloquium of the UK special interest group for computational linguistics*, pages 45–52. Citeseer.

Wee Chung Gan and Hwee Tou Ng. 2019. Improving the robustness of question answering systems to question paraphrasing. In *Proceedings of the 57th Annual Meeting of the Association for Computational Linguistics*, pages 6065–6075.

Juri Ganitkevitch, Benjamin Van Durme, and Chris Callison-Burch. 2013. Ppdb: The paraphrase database. In *Proceedings of the 2013 Conference of the North American Chapter of the Association for Computational Linguistics: Human Language Technologies*, pages 758–764.

Tianyu Gao, Xingcheng Yao, and Danqi Chen. 2021. Simcse: Simple contrastive learning of sentence embeddings. In *Proceedings of the 2021 Conference on Empirical Methods in Natural Language Processing*, pages 6894–6910.

Shankar Iyer, Nikhil Dandekar, Kornél Csernai, et al. 2017. First quora dataset release: Question pairs. *data. quora. com.*

Zongcheng Ji, Qiang Wei, and Hua Xu. 2020. Bert-based ranking for biomedical entity normalization. *AMIA Summits on Translational Science Proceedings*, 2020:269.

Shan Jiang, Simon Baumgartner, Abe Ittycheriah, and Cong Yu. 2020. Factoring fact-checks: Structured information extraction from fact-checking articles. In *Proceedings of The Web Conference 2020*, pages 1592–1603.

Marcin Junczys-Dowmunt, Roman Grundkiewicz, Tomasz Dwojak, Hieu Hoang, Kenneth Heafield, Tom Neckermann, Frank Seide, Ulrich Germann, Alham Fikri Aji, Nikolay Bogoychev, André F. T. Martins, and Alexandra Birch. 2018. Marian: Fast neural machine translation in C++. In *Proceedings of ACL 2018, System Demonstrations*, pages 116–121, Melbourne, Australia. Association for Computational Linguistics.

Wojciech Kryściński, Nitish Shirish Keskar, Bryan McCann, Caiming Xiong, and Richard Socher. 2019. Neural text summarization: A critical evaluation. In *Proceedings of the 2019 Conference on Empirical Methods in Natural Language Processing and the 9th International Joint Conference on Natural Language Processing (EMNLP-IJCNLP)*, pages 540–551.

Wojciech Kryściński, Romain Paulus, Caiming Xiong, and Richard Socher. 2018. Improving abstraction in text summarization. In *Proceedings of the 2018 Conference on Empirical Methods in Natural Language Processing*, pages 1808–1817.

Wuwei Lan, Siyu Qiu, Hua He, and Wei Xu. 2017. A continuously growing dataset of sentential paraphrases. In *Proceedings of the 2017 Conference on Empirical Methods in Natural Language Processing*, pages 1224–1234.

Timothy Liu et al. 2022. Towards better characterization of paraphrases. In *Proceedings of the 60th Annual Meeting of the Association for Computational Linguistics (Volume 1: Long Papers)*, pages 8592–8601.

Yinhan Liu, Myle Ott, Naman Goyal, Jingfei Du, Mandar Joshi, Danqi Chen, Omer Levy, Mike Lewis, Luke Zettlemoyer, and Veselin Stoyanov. 2019. Roberta: A robustly optimized bert pretraining approach. *arXiv preprint arXiv:1907.11692*.

Sean MacAvaney, Andrew Yates, Arman Cohan, and Nazli Goharian. 2019. Cedr: Contextualized embeddings for document ranking. In *Proceedings of the 42nd international ACM SIGIR conference on research and development in information retrieval*, pages 1101–1104.

Nitin Madnani and Bonnie J Dorr. 2010. Generating phrasal and sentential paraphrases: A survey of data-driven methods. *Computational Linguistics*, 36(3):341–387.

Animesh Nighojkar and John Licato. 2021. Improving paraphrase detection with the adversarial paraphrasing task. In *Proceedings of the 59th Annual Meeting of the Association for Computational Linguistics and the 11th International Joint Conference on Natural Language Processing (Volume 1: Long Papers)*, pages 7106–7116.

Ellie Pavlick, Pushpendre Rastogi, Juri Ganitkevitch, Benjamin Van Durme, and Chris Callison-Burch. 2015. Ppdb 2.0: Better paraphrase ranking, fine-grained entailment relations, word embeddings, and style classification. In *Proceedings of the 53rd Annual Meeting of the Association for Computational Linguistics and the 7th International Joint Conference on Natural Language Processing (Volume 2: Short Papers)*, pages 425–430.

Qiwei Peng, David Weir, and Julie Weeds. 2022. Towards structure-aware paraphrase identification with phrase alignment using sentence encoders. In *Proceedings of the 29th International Conference on Computational Linguistics*, pages 4113–4123.

Alec Radford, Jeffrey Wu, Rewon Child, David Luan, Dario Amodei, Ilya Sutskever, et al. 2019. Language models are unsupervised multitask learners.

Nils Reimers and Iryna Gurevych. 2019. Sentence-bert: Sentence embeddings using siamese bert-networks. In *Proceedings of the 2019 Conference on Empirical Methods in Natural Language Processing and the 9th International Joint Conference on Natural Language Processing (EMNLP-IJCNLP)*, pages 3982–3992.

Nils Reimers and Iryna Gurevych. 2020. Making monolingual sentence embeddings multilingual using knowledge distillation. In *Proceedings of the 2020 Conference on Empirical Methods in Natural Language Processing*. Association for Computational Linguistics.

Vasile Rus, Rajendra Banjade, and Mihai Lintean. 2014. On paraphrase identification corpora. In *Proceedings of the Ninth International Conference on Language Resources and Evaluation (LREC'14)*, pages 2422–2429.

Zhouxing Shi and Minlie Huang. 2020. Robustness to modification with shared words in paraphrase identification. In *Findings of the Association for Computational Linguistics: EMNLP 2020*, pages 164–171.

Shuo Sun and Kevin Duh. 2020. Clirmatrix: A massively large collection of bilingual and multilingual datasets for cross-lingual information retrieval. In *Proceedings of the 2020 Conference on Empirical Methods in Natural Language Processing (EMNLP)*, pages 4160–4170.

Bin Wang, C-c Kuo, and Haizhou Li. 2022. Just rank: Rethinking evaluation with word and sentence similarities. In *Proceedings of the 60th Annual Meeting of the Association for Computational Linguistics (Volume 1: Long Papers)*, pages 6060–6077.

Xiao Wang, Qin Liu, Tao Gui, Qi Zhang, Yicheng Zou, Xin Zhou, Jiacheng Ye, Yongxin Zhang, Rui Zheng, Zexiong Pang, et al. 2021. Textflint: Unified multilingual robustness evaluation toolkit for natural language processing. In *Proceedings of the 59th Annual Meeting of the Association for Computational Linguistics and the 11th International Joint Conference on Natural Language Processing: System Demonstrations*, pages 347–355.

Xiao Wang, Craig Macdonald, and Iadh Ounis. 2020. Deep reinforced query reformulation for information retrieval. *arXiv preprint arXiv:2007.07987*.

Zhiguo Wang, Wael Hamza, and Radu Florian. 2017. Bilateral multi-perspective matching for natural language sentences. In *Proceedings of the 26th International Joint Conference on Artificial Intelligence*, pages 4144–4150.

Wei Xu, Alan Ritter, Chris Callison-Burch, William B Dolan, and Yangfeng Ji. 2014. Extracting lexically divergent paraphrases from twitter. *Transactions of the Association for Computational Linguistics*, 2:435–448.

Yinfei Yang, Yuan Zhang, Chris Tar, and Jason Baldridge. 2019. Paws-x: A cross-lingual adversarial dataset for paraphrase identification. In *Proceedings of the 2019 Conference on Empirical Methods in Natural Language Processing and the 9th International Joint Conference on Natural Language Processing (EMNLP-IJCNLP)*, pages 3687–3692.

Pengcheng Yin, Nan Duan, Ben Kao, Junwei Bao, and Ming Zhou. 2015. Answering questions with complex semantic constraints on open knowledge bases. In *Proceedings of the 24th ACM International on Conference on Information and Knowledge Management*, pages 1301–1310.

Tianyi Zhang, Varsha Kishore, Felix Wu, Kilian Q Weinberger, and Yoav Artzi. 2019a. Bertscore: Evaluating text generation with bert. In *International Conference on Learning Representations*.

Yuan Zhang, Jason Baldridge, and Luheng He. 2019b. Paws: Paraphrase adversaries from word scrambling. In *Proceedings of the 2019 Conference of the North American Chapter of the Association for Computational Linguistics: Human Language Technologies, Volume 1 (Long and Short Papers)*, pages 1298–1308.

„Mann“ is to “Donna” as 「国王」 is to « Reine » Adapting the Analogy Task for Multilingual and Contextual Embeddings

Timothee Mickus[♠] **Eduardo Calò**[♡] **Léo Jacqmin**[◇]
Denis Paperno[♡] **Mathieu Constant**[♣]

[♠]University of Helsinki, timothee.mickus@helsinki.fi
[♡]Utrecht University, {e.calo,d.paperno}@uu.nl
[◇]Orange Labs, leo.jacqmin@orange.com
[♣]ATILF, CNRS/Université de Lorraine, mconstant@atilf.fr

Abstract

How does the word analogy task fit in the modern NLP landscape? Given the rarity of comparable multilingual benchmarks and the lack of a consensual evaluation protocol for contextual models, this remains an open question. In this paper, we introduce MATS: a multilingual analogy dataset, covering forty analogical relations in six languages, and evaluate human as well as static and contextual embedding performances on the task. We find that not all analogical relations are equally straightforward for humans, static models remain competitive with contextual embeddings, and optimal settings vary across languages and analogical relations. Several key challenges remain, including creating benchmarks that align with human reasoning and understanding what drives differences across methodologies.

https://github.com/ATILF-UMR7118/MATS

1 Introduction

Ever since the work of Mikolov et al. (2013b), analogy solving has been a staple of public outreach in NLP: It has been featured both in science communication[1] and in the classroom.[2] This task consists in finding a target word b_2, given a cue word b_1 it is related to, and another pair of words a_1 and b_2 that express the same relation. For example, we can ask what is the word that relates to “*king*” in the same manner that “*woman*” relates to “*man*”: This target ought to be “*queen*”.

The introduction of pre-trained contextualized embeddings (Peters et al., 2018) opened up a new research area where to expand prior knowledge about static models. This includes the analogy task. Suggestions have been put forward as to how to best adapt it: Ushio et al. (2021) propose to use a prompt-based method, whereas Vulić et al. (2020) and Lenci et al. (2022) try to derive static embeddings from BERT to fall back on the algorithm of Mikolov et al. (2013b). However, much work remains to be done to properly contrast and compare the performance of contextual and static embedding models on the analogy task. Another observation to be made is that reliable comparisons across languages are rare. On the one hand, datasets for English—such as the GATS (Google Analogy Test Set, Mikolov et al., 2013a) and BATS (Balanced Analogy Test Set, Gladkova et al., 2016) benchmarks—have been adapted or translated to a wide variety of languages. On the other hand, approaches specifically focusing on establishing multilingual comparisons are, to our knowledge, limited to Grave et al. (2018), Ulčar et al. (2020), and Peng et al. (2022)—none of which considers contextual embeddings.

How do embeddings—and in particular contextual models—perform on the analogy task beyond English? In the present paper, we argue that a principled approach to comparing embeddings on the analogy task across languages consists in creating resources designed to be directly comparable. The most natural way of achieving this is by relying on manual translations, so as to retain a certain degree of control on the output quality and to produce resources that are maximally comparable. Given the weaknesses of GATS outlined by Gladkova et al. (2016), the more reasonable starting point for these translations would be the BATS dataset. These considerations effectively rule out the only similar dataset that we know of, by Ulčar et al. (2020), where analogies accept only one valid answer, as in GATS.

To that end, we introduce MATS, a Multilingual Analogy Test Set for six languages: Dutch, French, German, Italian, Mandarin, and Spanish, derived from the original BATS dataset of Glad-

[1]E.g., it is discussed by the Computerphile YouTube channel, cf. https://youtu.be/gQddtTdmG_8?t=662.

[2]To take an example, see the Winter 2017 NLP lectures at Stanford, https://youtu.be/ASn7ExxLZws?t=3257.

*Proceedings of the The 12th Joint Conference on Lexical and Computational Semantics (*SEM 2023)*, pages 270–283
July 13-14, 2023 ©2023 Association for Computational Linguistics

kova et al., spanning across 40 analogical relations equally partitioned between inflectional, derivational, lexicographic and encyclopedic. Using this new benchmark, we observe that different adaptations of the analogy task to mBERT contextual embeddings need not yield comparable results: Not only do we observe different performances when deriving static embeddings from contextual models and when using prompts, we also see that the exact wording of the prompt significantly impacts the model's behavior. We also share some anecdotal evidence questioning the validity of approaches to this task that assume there is a single gold answer—trained linguists attempting to solve this task often provide answers that do not match any of the expected targets, which further validates that single-target analogy benchmarks are ill-suited.

2 Related Works

Analogy, and specifically the offset approach of Mikolov et al. (2013b), has inspired the field at large (e.g., Roller et al., 2014; Bonami and Paperno, 2018; Ethayarajh, 2019; Chen et al., 2022). However, this approach has been criticized for methodological and ethical reasons (Bolukbasi et al., 2016; Linzen, 2016; Rogers et al., 2017; Schluter, 2018; Garg et al., 2018; Adewumi et al., 2022).

Two groups of related analogy datasets are often cited: those adapted from GATS (Google Analogy Test Set, Mikolov et al., 2013a) and those derived from BATS (Balanced Analogy Test Set, Gladkova et al., 2016). The latter distinguishes itself from the former on two major characteristics: First, it is designed for a balanced assessment of performances on the analogies and covers a larger collection of analogical relations; second, it admits multiple valid answers whenever relevant. These differences aim to mitigate some of the flaws Gladkova et al. (2016) perceived in GATS: The emphasis of this dataset on balance is intended to provide a more accurate picture of a model's capabilities when it comes to word analogy solving, and the inclusion of multiple answers aims to mitigate the impact of spelling variation and dataset limitations.

Datasets similar to BATS exist in Japanese and Icelandic (Karpinska et al., 2018; Friðriksdóttir et al., 2022), whereas GATS has been translated in Portuguese, Hindi, French, Polish, and Spanish (Hartmann et al., 2017; Grave et al., 2018; Cardellino, 2019). Other independently constructed datasets do exist (e.g., Venekoski and Vankka, 2017; Svoboda and Brychcín, 2018)—crucially, covering all languages of interest to this study: in Chinese (Jin and Wu, 2012; Chen et al., 2015; Li et al., 2018), Dutch (Garneau et al., 2021), English (Turney 2008; Mikolov et al. 2013b, a.o.), French (Grave et al., 2018), German (Köper et al., 2015), Italian (Berardi et al., 2015), and Spanish (Cardellino, 2019). On the other hand, these resources were created by different research groups and may contain items that are not easily comparable or of lesser quality.[3]

Similar to our approach, Grave et al. (2018) and Ulčar et al. (2020) both conduct multilingual comparisons of word embeddings on the analogy task, whereas Peng et al. (2022) study how analogies behave under cross-lingual mappings. All three works rely on GATS-style benchmarks (where only one valid target is admissible for each analogy relation); all are more limited in the scope of analogies they cover than BATS-style datasets; none study how contextual embeddings fit in this picture. This last point is partly due to the initial conception of the task for static models: Plenty of works discuss why static models develop linear analogies (Arora et al., 2016; Ethayarajh et al., 2019; Allen and Hospedales, 2019; Fournier and Dunbar, 2021)—similar evidence has yet to emerge for contextual models. As such, some studies delineate its relevance to static embeddings (e.g., Apidianaki, 2022), but it has been adapted to contextual models (Vulić et al., 2020; Ushio et al., 2021; Lenci et al., 2022).

3 The Multilingual Analogy Test Set

To study how analogy fares in a multilingual context, we introduce a Multilingual Analogy Test Set (MATS), adapted from BATS (Gladkova et al., 2016) for Dutch, French, German, Italian, Mandarin, and Spanish. This analogy benchmark is structured in two tiers: Individual sub-categories instantiating specific analogical relations (e.g., *country—capital*) are grouped into four general categories, namely **I**nflection, **D**erivation, **E**ncyclopedia, and **L**exicography. The former two correspond to morphological relations, such as the relation between two inflected forms of a word or the relation between a verb and the corresponding agent noun. The latter two are more closely aligned to commonsense reasoning and include relations such as synonymy or the relation between the name of a coun-

[3] E.g., the French dataset of Grave et al. (2018) mixes grammatical and social gender in masculine–feminine analogies.

try and that of its capital city. The original resource by Gladkova et al. (2016) emphasizes balance by ensuring that each of the four super-sections contains exactly 10 sub-sections, and that each of the 10 sub-sections contains exactly 50 instances of the same analogical relation; analogy quadruples are created by exhaustively iterating across pairs of instances. This totals to 98,000 distinct analogy quadruplets to test models on, around five times as many items as what is mentioned in Ulčar et al. (2020), and mitigates concerns of class imbalance.

Direct translations from the original BATS were taken as starting points before performing language-specific adaptations (cf. infra); we refer the reader to Gladkova et al. (2016) for supplementary details. In all languages, unidiomatic direct translations and analogically invalid pairs were removed. Multi-word expressions (MWE) were also removed,[4] before padding all categories except E03 to 50 pairs following the relation of each category. An overview of the outcome with examples and figures can be found in Table 1. We break down the choices per language in the following paragraphs.

Dutch The encyclopedic section E03 was localized using Dutch *provincies* and their capital cities.

French The inflectional section I03 was replaced with gender inflection of adjectives since comparatives are periphrastic constructions (e.g., *jolie* 'cute', *plus jolie* 'cuter'). The derivational section D01 was replaced with denominal adjectives using the suffix *-el*, as the formation of privatives using suffixes is not a productive morphological operation. The encyclopedic section E03 was localized using a random selection of 50 French *départements* and their capital cities, barring those that would be tokenized as MWE.

German The encyclopedic section E03 was localized with German *Länder* and their capital cities.

Italian The inflectional section I03 was replaced with gender inflection of adjectives, since Italian comparatives are periphrastic constructions (e.g., *bella* 'cute', *più bella* 'cuter'). The derivational section D01 was replaced with noun diminutives using the suffixes *-ino*, *-ina*, for the same reason as in French. The encyclopedic section E03 was localized using Italian *regioni* and their capital cities.

Mandarin Given the typological differences with English, we removed the whole section concerning inflectional morphology and completely reshaped the one on derivational morphology. In particular, given that derivation by means of affixes is a very productive process (Packard, 2000), we selected eight affixes, namely -度 '-ness/-ity', -化 '-ize', -性 '-ness/-ity', -学 '-ology', -主义 '-ism', -儿 'prosodic suffix', -机 'instrument', 小- 'diminutive prefix/small/young', and created corresponding categories. We set the focus of D09 on agent formation from verbs, much like D08 in all other languages, whereas for D10 we took inspiration from Li et al. (2018) focusing on reduplication of monosyllabic verbs having 'a bit' as semantic nuance. In the lexicographic category, we exploited elastic words (Guo, 1938; Duanmu, 2007) to build L08. We filled it using the list of elastic words in the Appendix of Dong (2015), focusing only on free monomorphemic adjectives and their corresponding long forms. The encyclopedic section E03 was localized using Chinese 省 and their capital cities. We incorporated the original E06 in D08 and replaced it with a category on nouns and their respective classifiers, disregarding the general classifier 个 that is not semantically informative.

Spanish The inflectional section I03 was replaced with gender inflection of adjectives since Spanish comparatives are periphrastic constructions (e.g., *linda* 'cute', *más linda* 'cuter'). The derivational section D01 was replaced with noun diminutives using the suffixes *-ito*, *-ita*, for the same reasons as in French and Italian. The encyclopedic section E03 was localized using Spanish *comunidades autónomas* and their capital cities.

4 Setting Baseline Expectations

We first focus on establishing the difficulty of our analogy benchmark, and how it compares to the English BATS. We provide a human baseline and static embedding scores on MATS.

Human Performance One aspect rarely addressed in analogy benchmarks is that of how consensual and accurate they are. Yet, some analogy relations are fundamentally debatable: For instance, whether "*tonne*" is to "*kilogram*" as "*flower*" is to "*petal*" depends on one's exact definition of a meronymic relation.[5] As such, the assumptions or intuitions of a given resource's designer may or

[4]Note this is a departure from BATS. This is for practical purposes, as we are also testing on static embeddings.

[5]These pairs are both in the L06 subcategory of BATS.

	de	es	fr	it	nl	zh
I01	Tag : Tage	día : dias	jour : jours	dio : dèi	rol : rollen	✗
I02	Rat : Räte	voz : voces	bail : baux	base : basi	vlo : vlooien	✗
I03	süß : süßer	barato : barata	chanceux : chanceuse	colto : colta	oud : ouder	✗
I04	rein : reinste	feo : feísimo	drôle : drôlissime (33)	duro : durissimo	rijk : rijkst	✗
I05	hören : hört	crear : crea	dire : dit	godere : gode	vraagen : vraagt	✗
I06	teilnehmen : teilnehmend	creer : creyendo	gérer : gérant	gestire : gestendo	leren : lerend	✗
I07	sehen : gesehen	decir : dicho	croire : cru	perdere : perso	hoor : gehoord	✗
I08	glaubend : glaubt	girando : gira	lisant : lit	succedendo : succede	gaand : gaat	✗
I09	fragend : gefragt	uniendo : unido	ratant : raté	capendo : capito	vragend : gevraagd	✗
I10	wird : geworden	ejecuta : ejecutado	suit : suivi	sente : sentito	volgt : gevolgd	✗
D01	Arm : armlos	cabeza : cabecita	culture : culturel	stella : stellina	ego : egoloos	强: 强度
D02	fähig : unfähig	edito : inédito	pair : impair	certo : incerto	zeker : onzeker	国际: 国际化
D03	Kind : kindlich	real : realmente	fort : fortement	ampio : ampiamente	feest : feestelijk	重要: 重要性
D04	mäßig : übermäßig	poblado : sobrepoblado	aigu : suraigu	umano : sovrumano	vol : overvol	语言: 语言学
D05	fest : Festigkeit	fijo : fijeza	fou : folie	raro : rarità	vast : vastheid	自由: 自由主义
D06	geben : wiedergeben	mandar : remandar	lire : relire	spedire : rispedire	bouwen : herbouwen	虫: 虫儿
D07	haften : haftbar	evitar : evitable	jeter : jetable	vivere : vivibile	eeten : eetbaar	打火: 打火机
D08	tun : Täter	diseñar : diseñador	tuer : tueur	gestire : gestore	boksen : bokser	孩子: 小孩子
D09	reduzieren : Reduktion	acusar : acusación	priver : privation	mutare : mutazione	inspireren : inspiratie	开发: 开发员
D10	erklären : Erklärung	elevar : elevamiento	licencier : licenciement	pagare : pagamento	verklaren : verklaring	想: 想想
L01	Kuh : Wirbeltier/...	ganso : pájaro/...	caille : vertébré/...	ape : insetto/...	coyote : carnivoor/...	猫头鹰: 鸟/...
L02	Foto : Bild/...	sofá : mueble/...	bureau : objet/...	pompelmo : frutto/...	jas : eenheid/...	架: 家具/...
L03	Boot : Post/...	color : blanco/...	mois : décembre/...	canzone : inno/...	tasse : gral/...	甜点: 蛋糕/...
L04	Bart : Haar	agua : oxígeno/...	océan : eau	neve : acqua/...	staal : ijzer/...	旗: 纸/...
L05	Kalb : Vieh/...	cantante : coro/...	juré : jury	pecora : gregge	kal : vee/...	鹅: 群
L06	Byte : Bit	guitarra : cuerda/...	film : épisode/...	corpo : petto/...	euro : cent	门: 铰链/...
L07	ängstlich : entsetzt/...	amar : adorar/...	poney : cheval	triste : depresso/...	aap : gorilla	湿: 浸泡/...
L08	Fahrrad : Rad	madre : mamá	marché : bazar	roccia : sasso	vader : papa	勇: 勇敢
L09	heiß : frostig/...	claro : oscuro	sec : humide/...	sano : pazzo/...	jong : gaga/...	甜: 酸/...
L10	tot : lebendig	sucio : limpio	chute : montée	dopo : prima	west : oost	内: 外
E01	Lima : Peru	Bagdad : Irak	Damas : Syrie	Kiev : Ucraina	Zagreb : Kroatië	安曼: 约旦
E02	Iran : Persisch	Camboya : jemer	Égypte : arabe	Marocco : berbero/...	Cuba : Spaans	伯利兹: 英语
E03	München : Bayern (13)	Barcelona : Cataluña (11)	Nîmes : Gard (50)	Roma : Lazio (17)	Maastricht : Limburg (10)	西安: 陕西 (27)
E04	Marx : Deutsch	Homero : griego	Tolstoi : russe	Pascal : francese	Hegel : Duits	孟子: 中国
E05	Dante : Dichter	Depp : actor/...	Lincoln : président	Hawking : fisico/...	Locke : filosoof	孔子: 哲学家
E06	Ente : Küken	cigüeña : cigoñino	daim : faon	ape : larva	eend : eendje/...	筷子: 双/...
E07	Kuh : muhen	lobo : aúlla	hyène : rire	cane : abbaiare	ezel : balken/...	猫: 喵/...
E08	Wal : Meer/...	castor : río	bovin : étable	corvo : nido/...	beer : kooi/...	狐狸: 洞穴
E09	Kirsch : rot/...	peonía : roja/...	sel : blanc	tè : nero/...	bloed : rood	蚂蚁: 黑色/...
E10	Stier : Kuh	niño : niña	roi : reine	leone : leonessa	opa : oma	老公: 老婆
Tot	1,963	1,961	1,983	1,967	1,960	1,477

Table 1: MATS: examples per subcategory. All subcategories contain 50 pairs, except if specified in (parentheses).

may not match with that of the community in general. Rare words may also factor in performances and dialectal variation can entail differences in spelling or vocabulary. Lastly, translation-based resources like ours may contain ambiguous cues and unknown cultural references.

So as to derive a human-level performance point of reference, for each language, we ask two trained linguists to manually solve 3 analogy items per subcategory, as well as two non-linguists for English[6] (cf. Appendix A). Annotators need not speak the same dialect, nor the dialect of the translators. While this may impact the reliability of the annotations, we choose to do so for two reasons. Firstly, the multiplicity of valid targets in the original BATS dataset was intended as a means to mitigate existing variations in the language at hand. Secondly, embeddings trained on large crawled corpora of internet texts will often span multiple dialects, and therefore factoring in linguistic variation provides a more principled point of comparison.

Annotators are provided with three of the four terms and ask them to propose a valid fourth term. We then measure (i) their **accuracy** on the task (i.e., the proportion of analogy items that were solved by the annotators with a valid fourth term in MATS) and (ii) their **agreement** rate (i.e., the proportion of analogy items where the two annotators produced the same answer).

Results in Table 2 show three global trends: (i) mistakes are made on almost all categories, (ii) linguistic training does help, and (iii) annotators' responses do not match 24%–46% of the time. Though these agreement scores may seem low, one ought to expect some variation across speakers in their ability to solve analogies—in part due to their familiarity with lexical semantics, in part due to dialectal variations between annotators, and in

[6]Results on English throughout this paper correspond to scores on Gladkova et al.'s BATS.

		Avg. accuracy					Agreement				
		I	**D**	**E**	**L**	**all**	**I**	**D**	**E**	**L**	**all**
en	ℓ	1.00	0.97	0.72	0.63	0.83	1.00	0.87	0.57	0.23	0.67
	$\neg\ell$	0.93	0.77	0.55	0.43	0.68	0.87	0.60	0.55	0.21	0.56
de		0.93	0.78	0.62	0.50	0.71	0.85	0.58	0.43	0.28	0.54
es		0.83	0.83	0.77	0.56	0.75	0.77	0.77	0.54	0.32	0.60
fr		0.88	0.97	0.70	0.48	0.76	0.83	0.93	0.52	0.30	0.65
it		0.97	0.93	0.75	0.57	0.80	0.93	0.86	0.81	0.42	0.76
nl		0.93	0.78	0.67	0.37	0.69	0.98	0.80	0.61	0.18	0.64
zh		—	0.85	0.62	0.35	0.61	—	0.83	0.57	0.43	0.61
all		0.92	0.86	0.67	0.49	—	0.89	0.78	0.51	0.30	—

Table 2: Manual annotations of MATS/BATS samples. $\ell/\neg\ell$: higher education in/not in linguistics.

part due to actual cases of linguistic ambiguity. In particular, we remark that both E and L include analogies that are less straightforward to solve for a human as compared with I and D, and some subcategories leave room for different interpretations due to their open-ended nature as described earlier. This is reflected in the overall lower accuracy and agreement scores for these two categories. In fact, annotators that indicate having looked up some of the analogy terms only report so for E and L. Crucially, performances on L are systematically the lowest, suggesting that this category is less in line with human reasoning.[7]

Static Embeddings Performance We now turn to static embeddings, which have been traditionally the target of analogy benchmarks. We consider two sets of available pre-trained static embeddings: the fastText models of Grave et al. (2018),[8] and the CoNLL-2017 Shared Task word2vec models (Zeman et al., 2017);[9] we set aside the CoNLL-2017 Chinese embeddings, as they correspond to traditional characters, whereas our resource is written in simplified characters.

We compute results on MATS, using the offset method of Mikolov et al. (2013b), a.k.a. 3CosAdd:

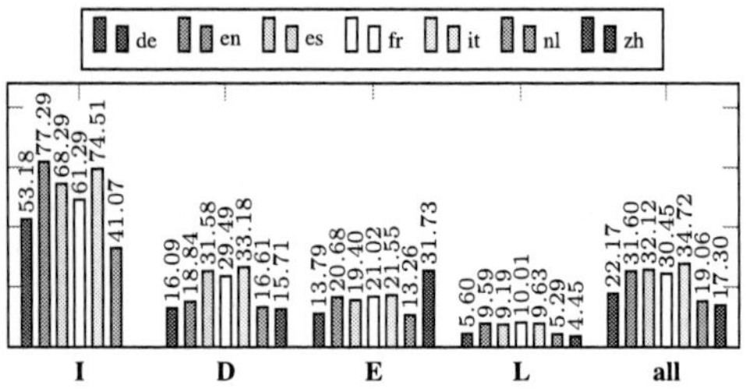

(a) fastText models from Grave et al. (2018).

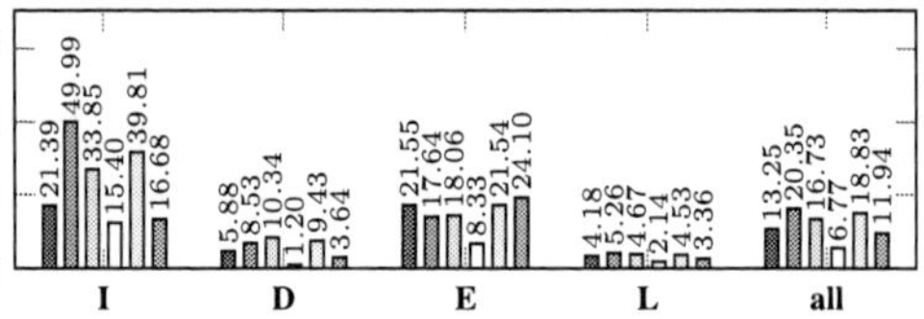

(b) word2vec models from Zeman et al. (2017).

Figure 1: Static models performance (3CosAdd, Equation (1)).

$$\mathbf{b}_2^* = \underset{\mathbf{w}}{\operatorname{argmax}} \cos\left(\mathbf{w}, \mathbf{b}_1 + \mathbf{a}_2 + -\mathbf{a}_1\right) \quad (1)$$

This method consists in predicting as a target $\mathbf{b}_2^*$ the word w whose embedding $\mathbf{w}$ is the most codirectional to the offset-based approximation $\mathbf{b}_1 + \mathbf{a}_2 - \mathbf{a}_1$. The starting point of this approach is the assumption that for any two pairs of words instantiating the same semantic relation a_1, a_2 and b_1, b_2, their corresponding embeddings should be related by means of a stable offset. In other words, we assume that there exists a vector $\mathbf{x}$ such that

[7] It is also worth discussing the gap between English linguists and other languages: Beyond the variance that one expects given the very small sample size that was manually annotated, our English linguist annotators both use similar orthographic conventions as the original BATS resource; both also report a more extensive use of online search tools in case of doubts than annotators of other languages. Similar favorable conditions were never met for other languages. In short, the lower performances we observe for our resources should not be entirely imputed to them being translations.

[8] These cover 157 languages, including the seven of the present study. Note that their Chinese model corresponds to a mixture of traditional and simplified characters.

[9] Available at `http://vectors.nlpl.eu/repository/`.

$\mathbf{a}_1 + \mathbf{x} = \mathbf{a}_2$ and $\mathbf{b}_1 + \mathbf{x} = \mathbf{b}_2$, or equivalently $\mathbf{a}_2 - \mathbf{a}_1 = \mathbf{b}_2 - \mathbf{b}_1$, which we can reformulate to solve for $\mathbf{b}_2$ as $\mathbf{b}_2 = \mathbf{b}_1 + \mathbf{a}_2 - \mathbf{a}_1$. This method can therefore be seen as a direct assessment of whether analogical relations are encoded as stable offsets in the embedding space. In this work, we specifically rely on the `vecto` library implementation of `3CosAdd`.[10]

Results in Figure 1 show that fastText models perform better than CoNLL-2017 word2vec models, confirming the known trend (e.g., Bojanowski et al., 2017; Lenci et al., 2022). The noteworthy low performances on the L category across the board can be imputed to its lesser quality. In particular, fastText models score much higher for I and D, the two categories with morphological relations, likely thanks to their learning of character n-gram representations rather than word type representations—which makes fastText models overall more in line with manual annotations.

Beyond these general observations, language also impacts the scores we observe. For instance, the high scores observed for English word2vec on the I category are never attested for word2vec models in other languages—which can be pinned on the rather simplistic inflectional system in English. Both Dutch models along with the CoNLL-2017 French model perform surprisingly poorly. In the case of Dutch, this is likely due to training data limitations: Zeman et al. (2017) report training Dutch models on fewer than 3B words, whereas all other languages were trained on over 5B words.

Discussion The experiments conducted in Section 4 have helped us establish baseline expectations. Much of what we observe echoes previous findings: The improvement of fastText models on I and D analogy items was already documented in Bojanowski et al. (2017), and Levy and Goldberg (2014) or Gladkova et al. (2016) already highlighted lower performances on E and L analogies.

What is novel beyond these replicated findings is the observation that humans also struggle with E and L analogies. This can account in part for the lower performances observed for these categories. This also suggests that more lenient benchmarks like BATS, which allow multiple valid answers, are preferable to stricter ones, such as GATS.

[10] `https://vecto.space/`

	Sents	Tokens	Bytes	Types
de	300M	4.472B	28.448B	1.042M
en	300M	6.698B	35.396B	0.502M
es	300M	8.294B	46.133B	0.702M
fr	300M	6.058B	33.114B	0.581M
it	300M	7.266B	41.666B	0.631M
nl	300M	4.269B	24.320B	0.678M
zh	300M	15.594B	92.836B	1.531M

Table 3: Oscar corpora statistics. The last column tallies unique word types occurring at least 50 times.

5 Analogies and Contextual Embeddings

We now turn to benchmarking a contextual architecture, viz. uncased mBERT (Devlin et al., 2019). By definition, such architecture computes contextual representations of words: Unlike static embeddings, contextual embeddings vary depending on the entire input sequence. The default use-case intended for these models pertains to token-level semantics—whereas analogy benchmarks evaluate word-type-level semantics. One word may have different meanings depending on context—depending on which context we use, results on the task may vary drastically. This complicates the use of these representations for the analogy task, by introducing the need of deriving some form of type-level judgment from token-level representations.

Static Representations from mBERT One possible approach to testing a contextual model on the analogy task consists in deriving word type representations from mBERT, and proceeding as one would with static embeddings. To determine which word types we need vectors for, we construct reference corpora of 300M sentences per language sampled from Oscar (Ortiz Suárez et al., 2019), and retrieve all word types with at least 50 occurrences.[11] All corpora were case-folded and tokenized using `spaCy`.[12] For Mandarin, we normalized all characters to their simplified form using `OpenCC`.[13] Corpora statistics are shown in Table 3.

We experiment with layer pooling and two different means of deriving static word-type vectors. **Singleton** embeddings are derived by embedding

[11] This would correspond to a reasonable frequency filtering with word2vec embeddings, and matches what we used in supplementary experiments in Appendix C.

[12] `https://spacy.io/`

[13] `https://pypi.org/project/OpenCC/`

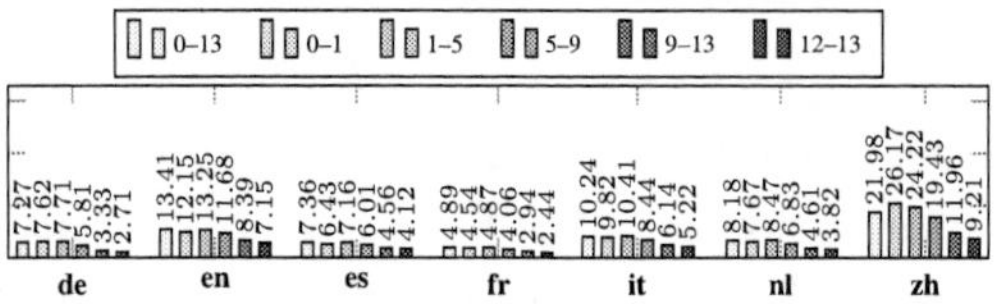

(a) Singleton embeddings.

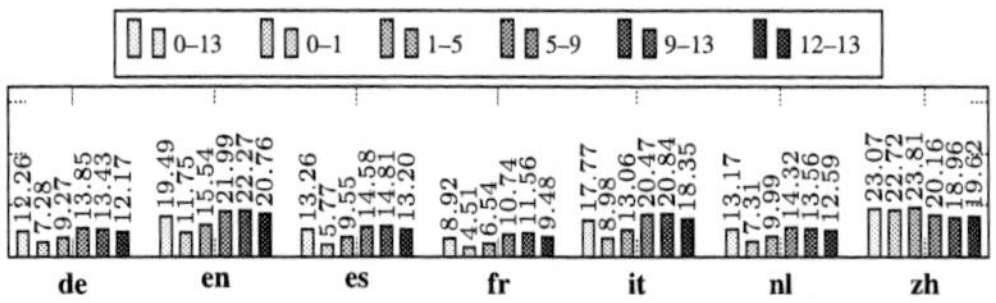

(b) Context-sample embeddings.

Figure 2: Static mBERT: overall results (3CosAdd).

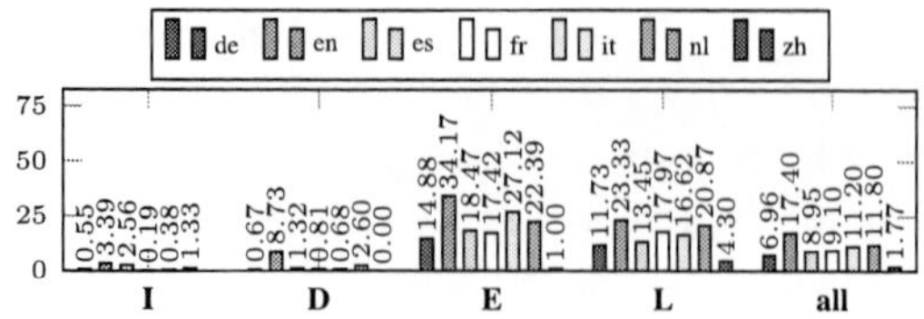

(a) Unquoted templates.

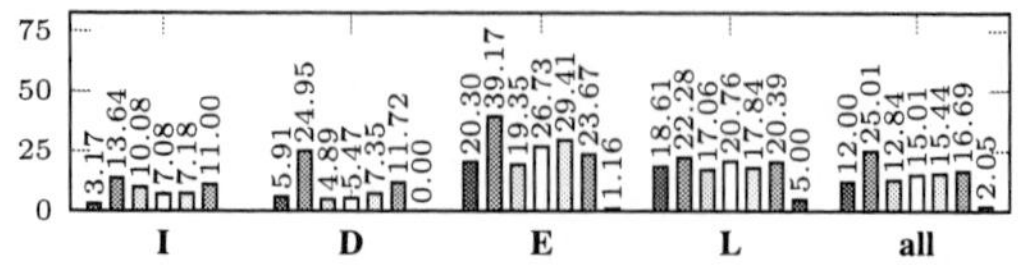

(b) Quoted templates.

Figure 3: mBERT prompt-based performance.

word types as if they were simple sentences comprised of a single word and control tokens (`[CLS]` and `[SEP]`); we then sum across the whole sequence, and average over the layer representations of interest. For **context-sample** embeddings, we retrieve the first 10 contexts of occurrence of every word type[14] to compute the average embedding of that word type. In both cases, we draw representations from layers 0–1 (input embeddings), 12–13 (output vectors), 0–13 (all layers), 1–5, 5–9, and 9–13.

Overall accuracy results are displayed in Figure 2; results per category are available in Appendix B, Figure 7. Context-sample embeddings almost systematically outperform or equal the singleton approach for all layer groups and languages. Mandarin performs surprisingly well, and scores for all languages on the L category are extremely poor. With singleton embeddings, lower layers tend to perform better, which matches with previous studies (Vulić et al., 2020; Lenci et al., 2022), but performances for Mandarin are better when considering the embedding layer, whereas all other languages benefit most from pooling across the first four Transformer layers. On the other hand, European-language context-sample embeddings yield their highest performances with middle or top layers. We suspect that Mandarin has a very regular segmentation for D items, whereas Latin-alphabet languages may have different segmentations for otherwise regular suffixal construction, and therefore require some computation in order to properly reconstruct formal regularities. Scores per category provided in Figure 7, Appendix B confirm that much (almost all) of the performance attested for Mandarin is indeed driven by the D category.

Prompt-based Approaches Contextualized embeddings can also be tested by converting the task to a prompt format. We draw inspiration from the methodology of Ushio et al. (2021), but frame our analogies as an unmasking task. We fill a three-slot template $\mathcal{T}$ that contains a mask with three given analogy cues a_1, b_1, and a_2, and perform unmasking given the resulting sequence $\mathcal{T}(a_1, b_1, a_2)$. We measure a model's zero-shot accuracy by considering whether the unmasked word-pieces match with any of the listed valid targets' word-pieces.

All relevant templates are listed in Table 4. All templates were formulated by native speakers. In the case of targets split across multiple word-pieces, we include one mask token per word-piece; as such prompt scores are *stricto sensu* upper bounds.

Given the relative novelty of prompt-based approaches, we explore whether results are reliable across small changes of the prompts, such as the presence of quotation marks around analogy terms. Results in Figure 3 show that, besides English, performances are often lower than what we observed previously, and especially low on the I category. Prompts only outperform static vectors on the L category, which we established to be less reliable. Using quotes alleviates this trend, with a more pronounced effect on I and D. The higher English BATS scores are likely due to the large proportion of English training samples in mBERT.

We also test how behavior changes across semantically equivalent templates, using four alternative German templates, along with the effects of enquoting analogy terms. These templates are listed in Table 5. Results are displayed in Figure 4; the alternative template $\mathcal{T}_4$ corresponds to the default

[14]We choose 10 contexts in order to strike a reasonable balance between diversity of contexts and computational costs.

	Unquoted	Quoted
de	a_1 verhält sich zu b_1 wie a_2 zu [MASK].	"a_1" verhält sich zu "b_1" wie "a_2" zu "[MASK]".
es	a_1 es a b_1 como a_2 es a [MASK].	"a_1" es a "b_1" como "a_2" es a "[MASK]".
fr	a_1 est à b_1 ce que a_2 est à [MASK].	"a_1" est à "b_1" ce que "a_2" est à "[MASK]".
it	a_1 sta a b_1 come a_2 sta a [MASK].	"a_1" sta a "b_1" come "a_2" sta a "[MASK]".
nl	a_1 staat tot b_1 zoals a_2 staat tot [MASK].	"a_1" staat tot "b_1" zoals "a_2" staat tot "[MASK]".
zh	a_1与b_1的关系就像a_2与[MASK]的关系。	「a_1」与「b_1」的关系就像「a_2」与「[MASK]」的关系。

Table 4: Templates for prompt-based approach.

	Unquoted	Quoted
$\mathcal{T}_1$	de a_1 ist für b_1 was a_2 für [MASK] ist.	"a_1" ist für "b_1" was "a_2" für "[MASK]" ist.
$\mathcal{T}_2$	a_1 ist so zu b_1 wie a_2 zu [MASK] ist.	"a_1" ist so zu "b_1" wie "a_2" zu "[MASK]" ist.
$\mathcal{T}_3$	a_1 steht in Relation zu b_1 so wie a_2 zu [MASK].	"a_1" steht in Relation zu "b_1" so wie "a_2" zu "[MASK]".
$\mathcal{T}_4$	a_1 verhält sich zu b_1 wie a_2 zu [MASK].	"a_1" verhält sich zu "b_1" wie "a_2" zu "[MASK]".

Table 5: Alternative German templates.

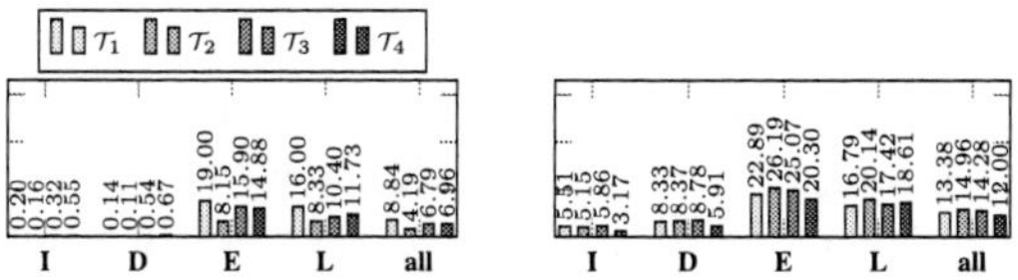

(a) Unquoted templates. (b) Quoted templates.

Figure 4: Prompt-based performance of mBERT, using alternative German templates.

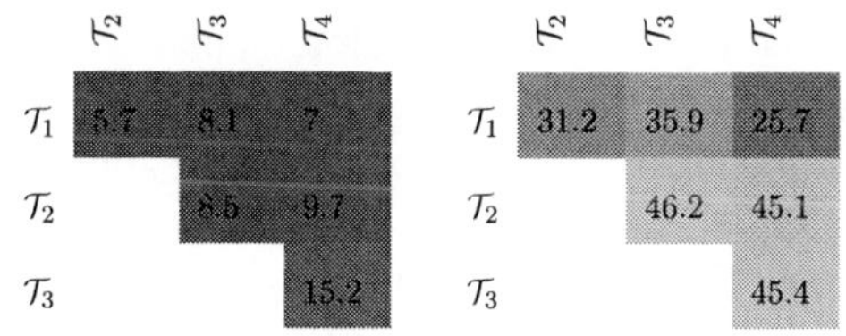

(a) Unquoted templates. (b) Quoted templates.

Figure 5: Prediction agreement (in %).

template for German in Figure 3. Quoted variants always outperform their unquoted counterparts; the model struggles most with the I and D categories. Yet, templates contrast starkly: E.g., by using the unquoted template $\mathcal{T}_1$ instead of $\mathcal{T}_2$, performance on E more than doubles, but this does not carry on with their quoted counterparts. In Figure 5, we tabulate how often predictions for the same analogy quadruple match across templates: Predictions of the mBERT uncased model tend to differ more often than they match, and this is much more pronounced with unquoted templates. In all, this model is sensitive to the exact wording of the prompt (cf. also Webson and Pavlick, 2022).

Discussion To sum up some key observations, we find mBERT ranks in between existing fastText and word2vec pre-trained embeddings. Results on the L category tend to be very low (except in the prompt-based approach). Scores for mBERT are highly dependent on methodology: Whether to include quotation marks in a prompt, or which layers static representations are derived from produce different effects across languages and categories.

All of this suggests that how to test contextual models like mBERT with analogies remains an open question. We observed different patterns across different languages and different methodologies. Some trends do emerge: For instance, static embeddings derived from mBERT do not appear to encode lexicographic and encyclopedic relations in any meaningful way, and Mandarin static mBERT embeddings are extremely apt at capturing derivational relationships, owing to their regular spelling. Likewise, recall that mBERT is not trained uniformly on all languages: This is most likely the reason why performance on English is higher. Prompt-based approaches, on the other hand, appear to capture E and L categories best, whereas I and D analogies are often poorly handled. This is the opposite of what we observed with human annotators in Section 4, which are more accurate on I and D rather than E and L items. Also worrying is the high volatility of the behavior: Prompt wording, or minor differences such as the presence or absence of quotes, can account for stark differences in the response patterns of mBERT.

For every methodological choice we explored—

which language and type of analogy to study, whether to use embeddings or prompts, how to derive the embeddings, or how to phrase the prompts—we observe distinct and often conflicting results. This is a direct consequence of the more complex architecture used in mBERT: The more varied means of probing and interacting with this model at our disposal also entail that we get a more diverse set of observations. As such, one can expect similar remarks to hold for other tasks. Establishing reasonable means of deciding which observations to select is both a captivating area for further inquiry and beyond the scope of this paper.

6 Conclusions

In this paper, we have presented a Multilingual Analogy Test Set, a resource five times larger than prior comparable datasets, with which we have looked at the analogy task in a multilingual context and studied how it fits in the modern NLP landscape. The dataset allows for a comparable multilingual evaluation of embedding models across a wide range of semantic analogy relations. Manual evaluation showed that the quality of MATS data in specific languages is comparable to the original English BATS. We saw that not all analogy types are equally straightforward not only to computational models but also to humans, and that behavior on the task depends on the language, the embedding model, and the methodology involved. This also entails that static model behavior is not a reliable indicator of what contextual models might yield.

We have been able to establish some trends across most of the methodological approaches we adopted here. In particular, from this work, we can outline three major conclusions. First, that not all categories are equally straightforward for humans (Section 4); this also explains why lower performances are attested on semantic analogies across most of our experiments. Second, that static models remain competitive with multilingual embedding models such as mBERT (Sections 4 and 5)—which replicates the conclusions of Lenci et al. (2022). Third, that equally valid prompts can yield vastly differing results (Section 5)—or more broadly, that different methodologies for adapting the analogy task to contextual embeddings can yield conflicting results. These conclusions also entail some practical guidelines for future work. In particular, there is a need to factor in human uncertainty as to what the correct target is; moreover, when adopting a prompt-based approach, testing a diverse array of prompts is necessary to properly establish how volatile a model's behavior is and how much variance in performance we should expect.

As such, a number of key challenges remain in the field of analogy solving, such as devising benchmarks that more closely match human intuitions or providing an explanatory framework for the discrepancies observed across prompts and methodologies. There are other aspects we have left open, such as whether the analogy task is suitable for lexical semantic evaluation (cf. Appendix C). We look forward to conducting future work in these directions, as well as expanding our observations to other architectures and methodologies.

Acknowledgment

We thank Alex Boulton, Guanyi Chen, Maria Copot, Yupei Du, Hermes Martínez, Giada Palmieri, Hugo Quené, Alisa Rieger, Vincent Segonne, William Soto, Joost Zwarts, and others for their help with the present work.

This work is part of the FoTran project, funded by the European Research Council (ERC) under the EU's Horizon 2020 research and innovation program (agreement № 771113). We also thank the CSC-IT Center for Science Ltd., for computational resources. This work was also supported by a public grant overseen by the French National Research Agency (ANR) as part of the "Investissements d'Avenir" program: Idex *Lorraine Université d'Excellence* (reference: ANR-15-IDEX-0004). This project has also received funding from the European Union's Horizon 2020 research and innovation program under the Marie Skłodowska-Curie grant agreement № 860621. This work was also supported by the ROCKY project, funded by the European Research Council (ERC) under the European Union's Horizon 2020 research and innovation programme (grant agreement № 742204).

References

Tosin Adewumi, Foteini Liwicki, and Marcus Liwicki. 2022. Word2vec: Optimal hyperparameters and their impact on natural language processing downstream tasks. *Open Computer Science*, 12(1):134–141.

Carl Allen and Timothy Hospedales. 2019. Analogies explained: Towards understanding word embeddings. In *Proceedings of the 36th International Conference on Machine Learning*, volume 97 of *Proceedings of Machine Learning Research*, pages 223–231. PMLR.

Marianna Apidianaki. 2022. From Word Types to Tokens and Back: A Survey of Approaches to Word Meaning Representation and Interpretation. *Computational Linguistics*, pages 1–60.

Sanjeev Arora, Yuanzhi Li, Yingyu Liang, Tengyu Ma, and Andrej Risteski. 2016. A latent variable model approach to PMI-based word embeddings. *Transactions of the Association for Computational Linguistics*, 4:385–399.

Siamak Barzegar, Brian Davis, Manel Zarrouk, Siegfried Handschuh, and Andre Freitas. 2018. SemR-11: A multi-lingual gold-standard for semantic similarity and relatedness for eleven languages. In *Proceedings of the Eleventh International Conference on Language Resources and Evaluation (LREC 2018)*, Miyazaki, Japan. European Language Resources Association (ELRA).

Giacomo Berardi, Andrea Esuli, and Diego Marcheggiani. 2015. Word embeddings go to italy: A comparison of models and training datasets. In *IIR*.

Piotr Bojanowski, Edouard Grave, Armand Joulin, and Tomas Mikolov. 2017. Enriching word vectors with subword information. *Transactions of the Association for Computational Linguistics*, 5:135–146.

Tolga Bolukbasi, Kai-Wei Chang, James Y Zou, Venkatesh Saligrama, and Adam T Kalai. 2016. Man is to computer programmer as woman is to homemaker? debiasing word embeddings. In *Advances in Neural Information Processing Systems*, volume 29. Curran Associates, Inc.

Olivier Bonami and Denis Paperno. 2018. Inflection vs. derivation in a distributional vector space. *Lingue e linguaggio, Rivista semestrale*, 2/2018:173–196.

Cristian Cardellino. 2019. Spanish Billion Words Corpus and Embeddings.

Jiangjie Chen, Rui Xu, Ziquan Fu, Wei Shi, Zhongqiao Li, Xinbo Zhang, Changzhi Sun, Lei Li, Yanghua Xiao, and Hao Zhou. 2022. E-KAR: A benchmark for rationalizing natural language analogical reasoning. In *Findings of the Association for Computational Linguistics: ACL 2022*, pages 3941–3955, Dublin, Ireland. Association for Computational Linguistics.

Xinxiong Chen, Lei Xu, Zhiyuan Liu, Maosong Sun, and Huanbo Luan. 2015. Joint learning of character and word embeddings. In *Proceedings of the 24th International Conference on Artificial Intelligence*, IJCAI'15, page 1236–1242. AAAI Press.

Jacob Devlin, Ming-Wei Chang, Kenton Lee, and Kristina Toutanova. 2019. BERT: Pre-training of deep bidirectional transformers for language understanding. In *Proceedings of the 2019 Conference of the North American Chapter of the Association for Computational Linguistics: Human Language Technologies, Volume 1 (Long and Short Papers)*, pages 4171–4186, Minneapolis, Minnesota. Association for Computational Linguistics.

Yan Dong. 2015. *The prosody and morphology of elastic words in Chinese: annotations and analyses*. Ph.D. thesis, University of Michigan.

San Duanmu. 2007. *The phonology of standard Chinese*. OUP Oxford.

Kawin Ethayarajh. 2019. Rotate king to get queen: Word relationships as orthogonal transformations in embedding space. In *Proceedings of the 2019 Conference on Empirical Methods in Natural Language Processing and the 9th International Joint Conference on Natural Language Processing (EMNLP-IJCNLP)*, pages 3503–3508, Hong Kong, China. Association for Computational Linguistics.

Kawin Ethayarajh, David Duvenaud, and Graeme Hirst. 2019. Towards understanding linear word analogies. In *Proceedings of the 57th Annual Meeting of the Association for Computational Linguistics*, pages 3253–3262, Florence, Italy. Association for Computational Linguistics.

Louis Fournier and Ewan Dunbar. 2021. Paraphrases do not explain word analogies. In *Proceedings of the 16th Conference of the European Chapter of the Association for Computational Linguistics: Main Volume*, pages 2129–2134, Online. Association for Computational Linguistics.

Steinunn Rut Friðriksdóttir, Hjalti Daníelsson, Steinþór Steingrímsson, and Einar Sigurdsson. 2022. IceBATS: An Icelandic adaptation of the bigger analogy test set. In *Proceedings of the Thirteenth Language Resources and Evaluation Conference*, pages 4227–4234, Marseille, France. European Language Resources Association.

Nikhil Garg, Londa Schiebinger, Dan Jurafsky, and James Zou. 2018. Word embeddings quantify 100 years of gender and ethnic stereotypes. *Proceedings of the National Academy of Sciences*, 115(16):E3635–E3644.

Nicolas Garneau, Mareike Hartmann, Anders Sandholm, Sebastian Ruder, Ivan Vulić, and Anders Søgaard. 2021. Analogy training multilingual encoders. *Proceedings of the AAAI Conference on Artificial Intelligence*, 35(14):12884–12892.

Anna Gladkova, Aleksandr Drozd, and Satoshi Matsuoka. 2016. Analogy-based detection of morphological and semantic relations with word embeddings: what works and what doesn't. In *Proceedings of the NAACL Student Research Workshop*, pages 8–15, San Diego, California. Association for Computational Linguistics.

Edouard Grave, Piotr Bojanowski, Prakhar Gupta, Armand Joulin, and Tomas Mikolov. 2018. Learning word vectors for 157 languages. In *Proceedings of the Eleventh International Conference on Language Resources and Evaluation (LREC 2018)*, Miyazaki, Japan. European Language Resources Association (ELRA).

Shaoyu Guo. 1938. 中国语词之弹性作用(The function of elastic word length in Chinese). *Yen Ching Hsueh Pao*, 24:1–34.

Nathan Hartmann, Erick Fonseca, Christopher Shulby, Marcos Treviso, Jéssica Silva, and Sandra Aluísio. 2017. Portuguese word embeddings: Evaluating on word analogies and natural language tasks. In *Proceedings of the 11th Brazilian Symposium in Information and Human Language Technology*, pages 122–131, Uberlândia, Brazil. Sociedade Brasileira de Computação.

Peng Jin and Yunfang Wu. 2012. SemEval-2012 task 4: Evaluating Chinese word similarity. In **SEM 2012: The First Joint Conference on Lexical and Computational Semantics – Volume 1: Proceedings of the main conference and the shared task, and Volume 2: Proceedings of the Sixth International Workshop on Semantic Evaluation (SemEval 2012)*, pages 374–377, Montréal, Canada. Association for Computational Linguistics.

Marzena Karpinska, Bofang Li, Anna Rogers, and Aleksandr Drozd. 2018. Subcharacter information in Japanese embeddings: When is it worth it? In *Proceedings of the Workshop on the Relevance of Linguistic Structure in Neural Architectures for NLP*, pages 28–37, Melbourne, Australia. Association for Computational Linguistics.

Maximilian Köper, Christian Scheible, and Sabine Schulte im Walde. 2015. Multilingual reliability and "semantic" structure of continuous word spaces. In *Proceedings of the 11th International Conference on Computational Semantics*, pages 40–45, London, UK. Association for Computational Linguistics.

Alessandro Lenci, Magnus Sahlgren, Patrick Jeuniaux, Amaru Cuba Gyllensten, and Martina Miliani. 2022. A comparative evaluation and analysis of three generations of distributional semantic models. *Lang. Resour. Eval.*, 56(4):1269–1313.

Omer Levy and Yoav Goldberg. 2014. Linguistic regularities in sparse and explicit word representations. In *Proceedings of the Eighteenth Conference on Computational Natural Language Learning*, pages 171–180, Ann Arbor, Michigan. Association for Computational Linguistics.

Shen Li, Zhe Zhao, Renfen Hu, Wensi Li, Tao Liu, and Xiaoyong Du. 2018. Analogical reasoning on Chinese morphological and semantic relations. In *Proceedings of the 56th Annual Meeting of the Association for Computational Linguistics (Volume 2: Short Papers)*, pages 138–143, Melbourne, Australia. Association for Computational Linguistics.

Tal Linzen. 2016. Issues in evaluating semantic spaces using word analogies. In *Proceedings of the 1st Workshop on Evaluating Vector-Space Representations for NLP*, pages 13–18, Berlin, Germany. Association for Computational Linguistics.

Tomás Mikolov, Kai Chen, Greg Corrado, and Jeffrey Dean. 2013a. Efficient estimation of word representations in vector space. In *1st International Conference on Learning Representations, ICLR 2013, Scottsdale, Arizona, USA, May 2-4, 2013, Workshop Track Proceedings*.

Tomas Mikolov, Wen-tau Yih, and Geoffrey Zweig. 2013b. Linguistic regularities in continuous space word representations. In *Proceedings of the 2013 Conference of the North American Chapter of the Association for Computational Linguistics: Human Language Technologies*, pages 746–751, Atlanta, Georgia. Association for Computational Linguistics.

Pedro Javier Ortiz Suárez, Benoît Sagot, and Laurent Romary. 2019. Asynchronous pipelines for processing huge corpora on medium to low resource infrastructures. In *Proceedings of the Workshop on Challenges in the Management of Large Corpora (CMLC-7) 2019. Cardiff, 22nd July 2019*, pages 9 – 16, Mannheim. Leibniz-Institut für Deutsche Sprache.

Jerome L Packard. 2000. *The morphology of Chinese: A linguistic and cognitive approach*. Cambridge University Press.

Xutan Peng, Mark Stevenson, Chenghua Lin, and Chen Li. 2022. Understanding linearity of cross-lingual word embedding mappings. *Transactions on Machine Learning Research*.

Matthew E. Peters, Mark Neumann, Mohit Iyyer, Matt Gardner, Christopher Clark, Kenton Lee, and Luke Zettlemoyer. 2018. Deep contextualized word representations. In *Proceedings of the 2018 Conference of the North American Chapter of the Association for Computational Linguistics: Human Language Technologies, Volume 1 (Long Papers)*, pages 2227–2237, New Orleans, Louisiana. Association for Computational Linguistics.

Radim Řehůřek and Petr Sojka. 2010. Software Framework for Topic Modelling with Large Corpora. In *Proceedings of the LREC 2010 Workshop on New Challenges for NLP Frameworks*, pages 45–50, Valletta, Malta. ELRA. `http://is.muni.cz/publication/884893/en`.

Anna Rogers, Aleksandr Drozd, and Bofang Li. 2017. The (too many) problems of analogical reasoning with word vectors. In *Proceedings of the 6th Joint Conference on Lexical and Computational Semantics (*SEM 2017)*, pages 135–148, Vancouver, Canada. Association for Computational Linguistics.

Stephen Roller, Katrin Erk, and Gemma Boleda. 2014. Inclusive yet selective: Supervised distributional hypernymy detection. In *Proceedings of COLING 2014, the 25th International Conference on Computational Linguistics: Technical Papers*, pages 1025–1036, Dublin, Ireland. Dublin City University and Association for Computational Linguistics.

Natalie Schluter. 2018. The word analogy testing caveat. In *Proceedings of the 2018 Conference of the North American Chapter of the Association for Computational Linguistics: Human Language Technologies, Volume 2 (Short Papers)*, pages 242–246, New Orleans, Louisiana. Association for Computational Linguistics.

Lukáš Svoboda and Tomáš Brychcín. 2018. New word analogy corpus for exploring embeddings of czech words. In *Computational Linguistics and Intelligent Text Processing*, pages 103–114, Cham. Springer International Publishing.

Peter D. Turney. 2008. The latent relation mapping engine: Algorithm and experiments. *J. Artif. Int. Res.*, 33(1):615–655.

Matej Ulčar, Kristiina Vaik, Jessica Lindström, Milda Dailidėnaitė, and Marko Robnik-Šikonja. 2020. Multilingual culture-independent word analogy datasets. In *Proceedings of the Twelfth Language Resources and Evaluation Conference*, pages 4074–4080, Marseille, France. European Language Resources Association.

Asahi Ushio, Luis Espinosa Anke, Steven Schockaert, and Jose Camacho-Collados. 2021. BERT is to NLP what AlexNet is to CV: Can pre-trained language models identify analogies? In *Proceedings of the 59th Annual Meeting of the Association for Computational Linguistics and the 11th International Joint Conference on Natural Language Processing (Volume 1: Long Papers)*, pages 3609–3624, Online. Association for Computational Linguistics.

Viljami Venekoski and Jouko Vankka. 2017. Finnish resources for evaluating language model semantics. In *Proceedings of the 21st Nordic Conference on Computational Linguistics*, pages 231–236, Gothenburg, Sweden. Association for Computational Linguistics.

Ivan Vulić, Edoardo Maria Ponti, Robert Litschko, Goran Glavaš, and Anna Korhonen. 2020. Probing pretrained language models for lexical semantics. In *Proceedings of the 2020 Conference on Empirical Methods in Natural Language Processing (EMNLP)*, pages 7222–7240, Online. Association for Computational Linguistics.

Albert Webson and Ellie Pavlick. 2022. Do prompt-based models really understand the meaning of their prompts? In *Proceedings of the 2022 Conference of the North American Chapter of the Association for Computational Linguistics: Human Language Technologies*, pages 2300–2344, Seattle, United States. Association for Computational Linguistics.

Daniel Zeman, Martin Popel, Milan Straka, Jan Hajič, Joakim Nivre, Filip Ginter, Juhani Luotolahti, Sampo Pyysalo, Slav Petrov, Martin Potthast, Francis Tyers, Elena Badmaeva, Memduh Gokirmak, Anna Nedoluzhko, Silvie Cinková, Jan Hajič jr., Jaroslava Hlaváčová, Václava Kettnerová, Zdeňka Urešová, Jenna Kanerva, Stina Ojala, Anna Missilä, Christopher D. Manning, Sebastian Schuster, Siva Reddy, Dima Taji, Nizar Habash, Herman Leung, Marie-Catherine de Marneffe, Manuela Sanguinetti, Maria Simi, Hiroshi Kanayama, Valeria de Paiva, Kira Droganova, Héctor Martínez Alonso, Çağrı Çöltekin, Umut Sulubacak, Hans Uszkoreit, Vivien Macketanz, Aljoscha Burchardt, Kim Harris, Katrin Marheinecke, Georg Rehm, Tolga Kayadelen, Mohammed Attia, Ali Elkahky, Zhuoran Yu, Emily Pitler, Saran Lertpradit, Michael Mandl, Jesse Kirchner, Hector Fernandez Alcalde, Jana Strnadová, Esha Banerjee, Ruli Manurung, Antonio Stella, Atsuko Shimada, Sookyoung Kwak, Gustavo Mendonça, Tatiana Lando, Rattima Nitisaroj, and Josie Li. 2017. CoNLL 2017 shared task: Multilingual parsing from raw text to Universal Dependencies. In *Proceedings of the CoNLL 2017 Shared Task: Multilingual Parsing from Raw Text to Universal Dependencies*, pages 1–19, Vancouver, Canada. Association for Computational Linguistics.

A Manual Annotation Details

All annotators in Section 4 are volunteers and colleagues of the authors (or acquaintances, in the case of the two non-linguist English annotators), and are native speakers of the languages at hand. Provided instructions are shown in Figure 6.

> Each row is an incomplete analogy, please add your guess for the missing fourth term in a new column.
> For instance, given the three cues "king", "queen", "man", the fourth term ought to be "woman", since king is to queen as man is to woman.
>
> You can do multiple guesses, please put the one you're most confident about in first.
> For instance if you have a row where the three first columns are:
> `squirrel, squirrels, platypus`
> then fill the fourth column with
> *platypuses/platypi/platypodes*
> if you think "platypuses" is the most likely fourth term, but that "platypi" and "platypodes" are likely to be valid answers.
> All of your guesses should be single words.
>
> You are allowed to google things up if it helps: we are testing whether you can recover the relation, rather than whether you'd win at Jeopardy!.

Figure 6: Instruction provided to annotators.

B Detailed Results for Static mBERT

We provide per-category results for singleton and context-sample vectors on MATS in Figure 7. Key insights from Section 5 also hold for individual categories: Context-sample embeddings outperform

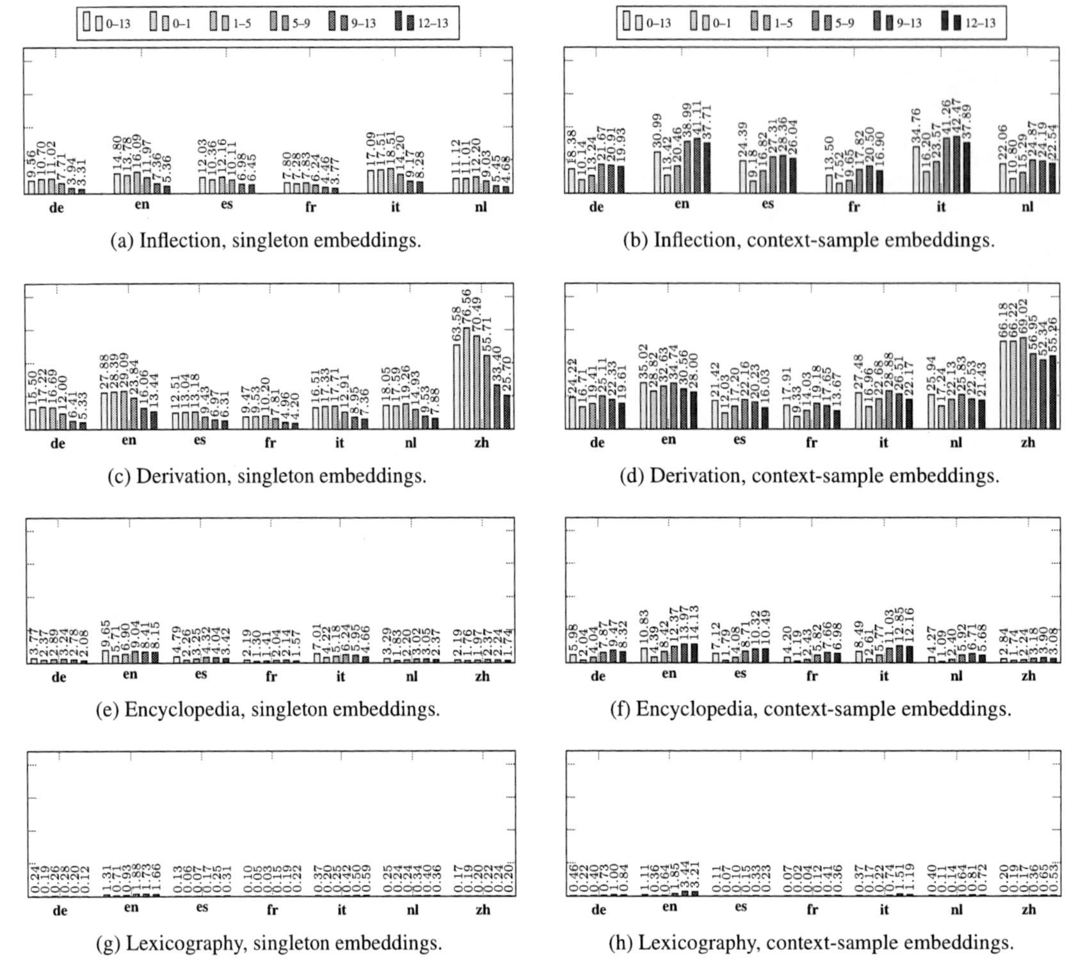

(a) Inflection, singleton embeddings. (b) Inflection, context-sample embeddings.

(c) Derivation, singleton embeddings. (d) Derivation, context-sample embeddings.

(e) Encyclopedia, singleton embeddings. (f) Encyclopedia, context-sample embeddings.

(g) Lexicography, singleton embeddings. (h) Lexicography, context-sample embeddings.

Figure 7: Static representations from mBERT: detailed results. All subplots share the same scale.

Param.	Values	Optimum on MATS					
		de	es	fr	it	nl	zh
window	$\{5, 10, 20\}$	20	20	20	5	20	20
neg. examples	$\{5, 10, 20\}$	10	20	5	20	20	20
shrink	$\{\top, \bot\}$	$\bot$	$\bot$	$\bot$	$\top$	$\bot$	$\top$
min freq.	$\{5, 50\}$	5	50	50	50	50	50
epochs	$\{1, 5\}$	5	5	5	5	5	5

Table 6: Hyperparameter search space.

singleton embeddings, and optimal layer groups vary across languages and categories.

C Supplementary Experiment: Analogy vs. Semantic Similarity

An aspect we have not broached in the main body of this article is to what extent the analogy task is suitable to assess the semantic quality of the representations.

To answer this, we train 72 word2vec models per language with varying hyperparameters (cf. Table 6), on top of the static vectors derived from mBERT in Section 4 as well as similar static embeddings from the cased variant of mBERT, for a total of 24 mBERT-based static models per language.[15] Models were trained with `gensim` (Řehůřek and Sojka, 2010), using the reference corpus from Section 5. We then compare MATS overall accuracy scores to paired word cosine vs. human ratings correlation scores on the WS353 translations from Barzegar et al. (2018).

Results are displayed in Figure 8, and suggest that our static and contextual models behave differently. In the case of the former, the two benchmarks are not necessarily correlated (Table 7): While one can argue a trend exists for Italian and German, such a position is not supported for other languages.

[15] We ignore English to compare among translated benchmarks only.

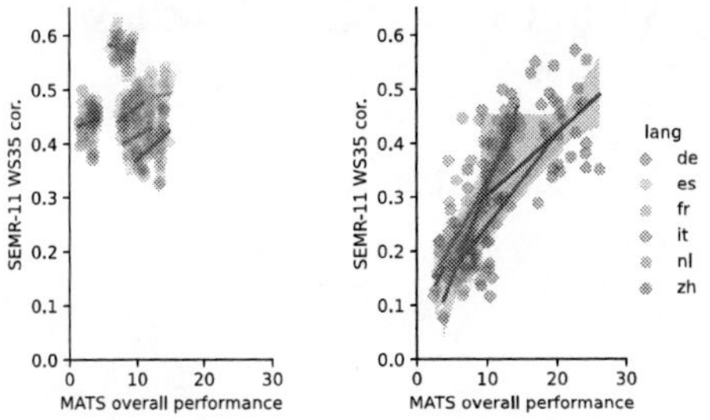

(a) word2vec. (b) mBERT.

Figure 8: Behavior on MATS vs. on WS353.

		de	es	fr	it	nl	zh
w2v	cor.	0.42598	0.26613	0.29494	0.45498	-0.08502	0.15261
	p-val.	0.00019	0.02385	0.01190	0.00006	0.47765	0.20061
BERT	cor.	0.75217	0.78522	0.59913	0.64957	0.76174	0.29913
	p-val.	0.00002	0.00001	0.00198	0.00059	0.00002	0.15562

Table 7: Spearman correlation, WS353 vs. MATS.

As for mBERT, correlations appear to be reliable for all languages but Mandarin; note however that we have fewer observations than for word2vec. Furthermore, we notice little variation with word2vec, as highlighted by the clusters we get in Figure 8a.

In all, the behavior of earlier static models on lexical tasks such as similarity and analogy need not match with that of modern contextual embeddings. This also transpired in our earlier experiments: When comparing performances by category, the patterns we observe across categories seem quite specific to the architectures we test.

D Computational Costs

Throughout this paper, experiments involving mBERT have been performed using a single V100 GPU. This includes computing static embeddings and prompt-based scores. For the former, we observed variation across languages—e.g., Mandarin context-sample embeddings required over a day, but Dutch only took 4 hours. For the latter, processing one template took under 2 hours.

All other computations were run on clusters of 40 CPU cores. This includes training the word2vec models used in Appendix C, as well as running MATS and BATS evaluations for all static embeddings. Word2vec training scripts generally finished in under 4 hours. Evaluation runtimes on MATS and BATS depend on language, category, and vocabulary size, and range from under an hour to under a day per category (I, D, E, or L) and per model.

E Limitations

One limitation of our study is the inherent noisiness of the translations. Despite the language-specific adaptions, MATS is based on direct translations of BATS which was designed for English, and as such may not be entirely equivalent to a resource that has been specifically designed for the target languages. Gladkova et al. (2016) furthermore implemented datapoint selection criteria (such as a frequency-based filtering of target words) that we have not replicated in this work. Another element of quality control to address concerns the manual annotations in Section 4: Due to material limitations, annotations cover a very limited portion of the dataset and were conducted remotely.

Additionally, we only tested a few models in our study—word2vec and fastText for static embeddings and mBERT for contextual embeddings. This may not be representative of the full range of pre-trained language models, especially contextual ones. A similar point holds for the grid-search evaluation conducted in Appendix C. There are some word2vec hyperparameters we have not looked at and that could impact performances on both tasks: chief of which the dimension of the embeddings and the training corpus. More generally, expanding the number of models tested in future work could provide a more comprehensive understanding of the analogy task.

Another limitation is the lack of language diversity in our study. With the exception of Mandarin, all the languages we translated BATS into are Indo-European languages belonging to two sub-families (West Germanic or Romance languages).

Finally, the high computational power required to train the numerous word2vec models with varying hyperparameters in Section C (cf. Appendix D) both contributes to carbon emissions and limits the replicability of this work.

Scalable Performance Analysis for Vision-Language Models

Santiago Castro* **Oana Ignat*** **Rada Mihalcea**
University of Michigan – Ann Arbor, USA
{sacastro,oignat,mihalcea}@umich.edu

Abstract

Joint vision-language models have shown great performance over a diverse set of tasks. However, little is known about their limitations, as the high dimensional space learned by these models makes it difficult to identify semantic errors. Recent work has addressed this problem by designing highly controlled probing task benchmarks. Our paper introduces a more scalable solution that relies on already annotated benchmarks. Our method consists of extracting a large set of diverse features from a vision-language benchmark and measuring their correlation with the output of the target model. We confirm previous findings that CLIP behaves like a bag of words model and performs better with nouns and verbs; we also uncover novel insights such as CLIP getting confused by concrete words. Our framework is available at https://github.com/MichiganNLP/Scalable-VLM-Probing and can be used with other multimodal models and benchmarks.

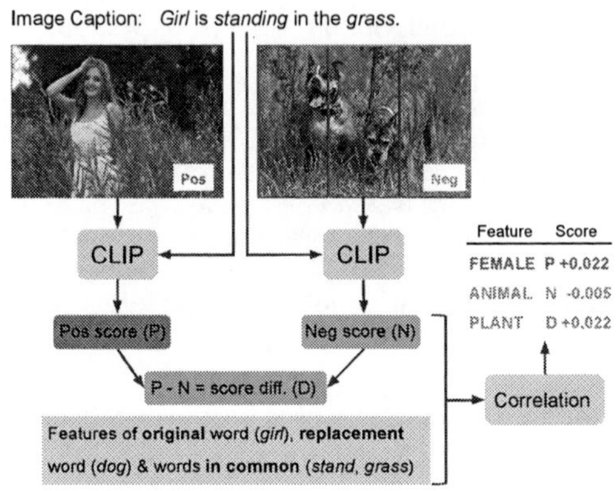

Figure 1: We propose a simple framework to analyze CLIP performance on SVO-Probes data. We test CLIP on the benchmark, extract a diverse set of semantic features from the data, and measure the correlation between each feature and the CLIP score (P, N, or D). Features with positive correlation (e.g., *Female, Plant*) impact positively the model performance, while features with negative correlation (e.g., *Animal*) impact negatively the model performance.

1 Introduction

Recent years have witnessed an explosion of vision-language models (Lu et al., 2019; Li et al., 2019; Zhang et al., 2021; Radford et al., 2021; Singh et al., 2022). These models have shown great performance in a variety of tasks, such as image/video classification and text-image/video retrieval (Radford et al., 2021; Luo et al., 2022), even without leveraging task-specific or in-domain training. In addition, these models have shown to be practical when leveraged as underlying models for text-to-image generation such as DALL-E 2 (Ramesh et al., 2022) and image captioning such as ClipCap (Mokady et al., 2021).

Little is however known about the limitations of these models. Recent work, such as Winoground (Thrush et al., 2022), SVO-Probes (Hendricks and Nematzadeh, 2021), or VALSE (Parcalabescu et al., 2022), have designed benchmark probing tasks by annotating data to follow specific properties (i.e., object color, location, size, swapping word order, replacing words). This line of research led to valuable insights into the limitations of current state-of-the-art multi-modal models such as CLIP (Radford et al., 2021) and ViLBERT (Lu et al., 2019).

An important limitation of current work is the reliance on time-consuming data annotation procedures, making it unscalable and limited in scope. As a complementary solution, we propose a method to probe vision-language models by relying on existing data, without requiring extra annotations. The method consists of extracting a large set of candidate features from a vision-language benchmark and testing their correlation with respect to

*Equal contribution.

*Proceedings of the The 12th Joint Conference on Lexical and Computational Semantics (*SEM 2023)*, pages 284–294
July 13-14, 2023 ©2023 Association for Computational Linguistics

the output of the target models on the given benchmark.

By applying our method on CLIP (Radford et al., 2021), a widely used state-of-the-art multi-modal model, using the SVO-Probes (Hendricks and Nematzadeh, 2021) benchmark, we confirm the findings of Thrush et al. (2022) of CLIP behaving like a bag of words model and that of Parcalabescu et al. (2022) of CLIP performing better with nouns and verbs. We also find that CLIP gets confused by concrete words and that it surprisingly improves in performance for more ambiguous words while noting little change from the word frequencies. To the best of our knowledge, we are the first to conduct an in-depth analysis of how language semantic properties influence CLIP's performance.

We summarize our contributions as follows. First, we propose a scalable way of measuring the limitations of vision-language models. Second, we test our method using a state-of-the-art vision-language model (CLIP) and a popular benchmark (SVO-Probes), validate known challenges, and uncover new ones. Third, our work opens up avenues for future models to focus on solving the newly discovered challenges.

2 Related Work

Recently, an increasing number of benchmarks have been created for the evaluation of vision-language model abilities to perform various multi-modal tasks.

Hendricks and Nematzadeh (2021) evaluate state-of-the-art vision-language models by building SVO-Probes, a probing benchmark focused on verb understanding. They show that image–language transformers fail to distinguish fine-grained differences between images and find that they are worse at verb understanding compared to subjects or objects. In our work, we continue their proposed future work direction by analyzing model performance on fine-grained verb categories.

Other work focuses on testing more precise capabilities of vision-language models using other probing techniques. In VALSE, Parcalabescu et al. (2022) demonstrate that vision-language models have difficulty in counting objects and in correctly classifying spatial relations between objects. Salin et al. (2022); Zhao et al. (2022) show that, although state-of-the-art vision-language models can grasp color, they do not fully understand more difficult concepts such as object size and position in the image.

In Winoground, Thrush et al. (2022) designed adversarial examples that require differentiating between a similar image and text, where the text pairs only differ in their word order. Their results show that state-of-the-art vision-language models lack compositional reasoning abilities. Several other works build benchmarks on probing vision-language on compositional reasoning (Akula et al., 2020; Ma et al., 2023; Liu et al., 2023; Park et al., 2022; Yuksekgonul et al., 2023) find that they behave like a bag-of-words model – i.e., have poor relational understanding and a severe lack of word order sensitivity.

In contrast, our work focuses not on creating new probing tasks for vision-language models, but on using current benchmarks to learn additional, more fine-grained features that can be discovered using simple correlation methods. To the best of our knowledge, we are the first to analyze the performance of CLIP on a diverse set of semantic features and use correlation methods to draw insights about what concepts are challenging for the model.

3 Methodology to Probe CLIP

Given a benchmark, we measure how a vision-language model performs on a variety of semantic concepts. Our aim is to quantify which concepts are the most and the least challenging for the model. Our setting is illustrated in Figure 1, and can be described in three main steps.

First, we use CLIP (Radford et al., 2021) to compute scores for instances from the SVO-Probes (Hendricks and Nematzadeh, 2021) dataset and obtain two corresponding alignment scores for each sentence and its corresponding *positive* and *negative* image. Next, we extract and process a diverse set of semantic features from SVO-Probes. Finally, we compute the correlation coefficients between each feature and the CLIP score. The features with the highest coefficients will represent concepts that CLIP performs well on, while features with the lowest coefficients will represent challenging concepts for CLIP.

3.1 Dataset

We choose the SVO-Probes (Hendricks and Nematzadeh, 2021) dataset due to its design and large scale size (421 verbs and over 48,000 image-sentence pairs). SVO-Probes was designed for probing image-text models for their understanding of **s**ubject, **v**erb, **o**bject triplets. Each instance from the dataset consists of a text caption, a *positive* image that matches the caption, and a controlled (adversarial) *negative* image that shares two out of three aspects (subject, verb, and object) from the sentence but does not match the other one, as shown in Figure 1. These controlled examples enable one to probe models for their understanding of verbs as well as subjects and objects. The instances also include information about the negative image, such as a (hidden) associated negative caption which we leverage in this paper.

We propose to use this dataset to evaluate the CLIP (Radford et al., 2021) model. We choose to test CLIP, as opposed to other language-vision models, due to its widely-spread use and impressive zero-shot performance on a variety of vision-language tasks (e.g., text-to-image retrieval, image question answering, human action segmentation, image-sentence alignment – Cafagna et al. 2021). Furthermore, Hendricks and Nematzadeh (2021) test only ViLBERT-based (Lu et al., 2019) models, which are known to perform worse than CLIP (Cafagna et al., 2021).

3.2 Model Output

As depicted in Figure 1, we obtain three CLIP scores for each pair of *positive* and *negative* images: a *positive* score (P), computed between the caption and the *positive* image; a *negative* score (N), computed between the caption and the *negative* image; and the *difference* between these scores ($D = P - N$).

Because the text and the positive image are aligned, P represents an absolute alignment score. In the case of the text and the negative image, even though the negative image is similar in some ways to the text (because of how SVO-Probes was designed), they do not correspond to each other. Thus, N represents an absolute misalignment score. D represents a relative alignment score. Ideally, CLIP should have a high P score and a low N score, and a high difference between them (a high D). We propose to pay special attention to D given that CLIP is generally used in relative comparisons, such as when using it for classification (choosing the class text that maximizes the alignment score, given an image) or when using it for retrieval (finding the text/image that maximizes the alignment score given an image/text).

3.3 Feature Extraction

For each given sentence and corresponding image in the benchmark, we extract features from the words marked in the SVO-Probes benchmark (i.e., subject, verb, and object).

If the corresponding image is *positive*, all the extracted features are from words *in common*, i.e., that appear both in the image and the text. Otherwise, if the corresponding image is *negative*, in addition to words *in common*, we also extract features from words present in the sentence and not in the image (*original* word) and words present in the image but not in the text (*replacement* word). As an example, in Figure 1 the words *in common* are "sit" and "grass", the *original* word is "girl" and the *replacement* word is "dogs". The *original* and *replacement* words represent what is different between the image and the text, while the words *in common*, as the name suggests, represent what is common between the image and the text.

We extract the following **semantic** textual features: Levin (1993) verb classes, LIWC psycholinguistic markers (Pennebaker et al., 2007, 2015), General Inquirer (Stone et al., 1967) semantic classes, WordNet hypernyms (Miller, 1995), word presence, semantic similarity, ambiguity, frequency, sentence length, and concreteness (Brysbaert et al., 2014).

Levin verb classes. Levin (1993) groups verbs according to their semantic content and also according to their participation in argument alternations.

Levin's semantic content-based taxonomy provides a classification of 3,024 verbs into 48 broad classes and 192 fine-grained classes.[1] A verb can belong to one or more classes. Some examples of verb classes are: (1) broad *change of state* (e.g., clean, divide, soak), *manner of motion* (e.g., climb, drop, run) or *social interaction* (e.g., marry, meet, hug); (2) fine-grained: *"roll" verbs* (e.g., bounce, coil, drift), *"run" verbs* (e.g., amble, bolt, race) or *"hug" verbs* (e.g., cover, encircle, touch)

LIWC psycholinguistic markers. Linguistic Inquiry and Word Count (LIWC) (Pennebaker et al., 2007, 2015) is a widely used word-counting software that includes dictionaries of English words related to human cognitive processes. Specifically, we use the LIWC2015 dictionary, which contains 6,400 words and word stems. Each word or word

[1] `https://websites.umich.edu/~jlawler/levin.verbs`

stem defines one or more categories: e.g., the word "mother" is assigned the categories: *female, family, social*.

General Inquirer classes. General Inquirer (Stone et al., 1967) is a resource for automatic content analysis. More specifically, it categorizes words into emotional and cognitive states, as well as into diverse semantic categories outlined in the Lasswell dictionary (Namenwirth and Weber, 1987, pg. 46–53).

WordNet classes. WordNet (Miller, 1995) is a large lexical database of English words that are grouped into sets of cognitive synonyms, known as synsets. The synsets are interlinked by semantic and lexical relations. The most frequent relation among synsets is the super-subordinate relation, also called *hyperonymy*. It links more general synsets to specific ones: e.g., "building" is a *hypernym* of "house" and "school". For each given word, we collect all the hypernyms of the most common word synset.

Word presence. For each given word, we use a marker to indicate if the word is present or not in the sentence. Note that studying the effect of specific words does not imply that they have no dependencies with other words. Their role may change depending on the context; however, we study them in aggregate.

Sentence length. We measure the length of each sentence as the number of words in the sentence.

Semantic similarity. In the case of *negative* images, we compute the cosine similarity score between the *original* words and the corresponding *replacement* words. The word representations are computed using Sentence-Transformers (Reimers and Gurevych, 2019), with the model `all-MiniLM-L6-v2`, which is based on MiniLM (Wang et al., 2020).

Concreteness score. For measuring the concreteness of words, we use a dataset of words with associated concreteness scores from Brysbaert et al. (2014). Each word is labeled by a human annotator with a value between 1 (very abstract) and 5 (very concrete). Abstract words (e.g., "beauty", "sadness") denote ideas, feelings, or other intangible concepts while concrete words (e.g., "table", "write") refer to objects and actions.

Ambiguity. We measure the ambiguity of a given word by counting the number of synsets in WordNet (Miller, 1995).

Frequency. We measure the word frequency in a subset ($\sim$13M image captions) of LAION (Schuhmann et al., 2021), a dataset representative of CLIP's training data.

3.4 Feature Representation

The **binary** features, i.e., Levin, LIWC, General Inquirer, WordNet classes, and word presence, are represented as binary vectors, while the **numerical** features i.e., sentence length, concreteness, similarity, ambiguity, and frequency are standardized. All the features are then concatenated together.

3.5 Feature Selection

We measure the degree of correlation between each feature and the model performance. For each of the **binary** features, we compute a two-sample two-tailed t-test (Student, 1908) along with the model output score. This test evaluates if the means of the populations coming from each feature value (true or false) are significantly different. If so, we compute the difference of means as a reference value. In the case of **numerical** features, we compute the Pearson's correlation coefficient (Benesty et al., 2009) between each feature and the model performance score.

Next, we employ a one-sample, two-tailed t-test to determine if the coefficient is significantly different from zero, i.e., if there is any correlation according to this metric. We chose a p-value threshold of 0.05 (a confidence level of 95%) to filter out the features.[2]

3.6 Experimental Details

We use an OpenAI pre-trained CLIP (Radford et al., 2021) ViT-L/14 (Dosovitskiy et al., 2021) model.

4 Results

Our main observations and takeaways from this evaluation are the following:

(1) CLIP behaves like a bag-of-words model. As shown in Figure 2, the distributions of P and N highly overlap. This is explained partly by the negative image being adversarial; it contains elements

[2]See the obtained scores and p-values in the web page from this paper: `https://github.com/MichiganNLP/Scalable-VLM-Probing`.

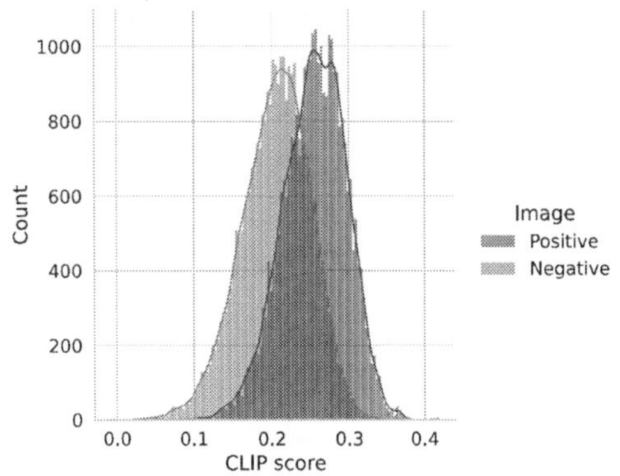

Figure 2: Histogram plot of the distribution of CLIP scores between the text with the positive image, and the text with the negative image. A kernel density estimation curve is included to aid this visualization.

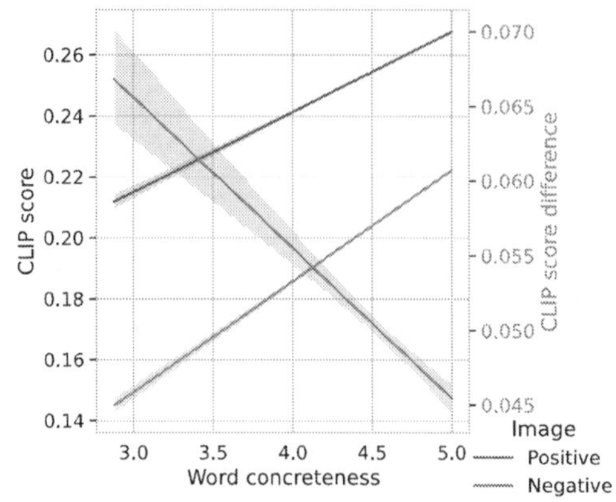

Figure 3: Linear regression plot of the average concreteness for the words in the sentence that are common to both images vs. the CLIP score. The shadowed areas are 95%-confidence intervals for the expected value.

in common with the text. This finding is coherent with that of Thrush et al. (2022), that CLIP performs like a bag-of-words model.

This finding is also supported by the fact that many features from words *in common* contribute to increasing both the positive (P) and the negative scores (N): e.g., hypernym_food.n.02 increases P by 0.042 and N by 0.050; LIWC "money" increases P by 0.036, and N by 0.032. As described in Section 3.5, we measure the importance of each feature as the difference of means between the CLIP scores when the feature is present and when is not. We observed that many of the features for the words *in common* appeared to influence similarly both P and N, confirming this hypothesis.

(2) CLIP performs better with nouns than with verbs. When computing the number of times CLIP assigns a higher score to the similarity between the text and the *positive* image as compared to the similarity between the text and the *negative* image, the verbs obtain 81.45% accuracy while the subjects get 86.87% and the objects 88.78%. The number obtained for verbs is relatively close to that of a similar setting experimented by the VALSE benchmark (Parcalabescu et al., 2022), in which they reported 75.6% accuracy (also considering that we could not determine which pretrained CLIP variant the authors evaluated). At the same time, the noun (objects and subjects) replacement numbers are consistent with those reported by the same authors (88.8%), obtained from FOIL it! (Shekhar et al., 2017).

(3) CLIP gets confused by concrete words. Figure 3 shows both the *positive* and *negative* CLIP scores improve the more concrete a word is (words from the caption represented in both the positive and the negative images). As seen in this figure, however, the *negative* score increases faster. This implies that, in an image classification or image-to-text retrieval setting, CLIP will more likely consider an incorrect text as correct if it has more concrete words than the actual correct text.

(4) CLIP prefers average-length sentences. We present in Figure 4 how the score is affected by the caption sentence word length. CLIP presents a low performance when the sentences are very short (around 3 words long), improving when the sentences are longer since the difference between the *positive* and *negative* scores (D) gets larger with the sentence length.

Figure 5 shows how the CLIP scores are distributed for the different number of words, showing for example that there is a great overlap between the similarity scores between texts of length 6 and a *negative* image, and the similarity scores between texts of length 3 and a *positive* image. This implies CLIP is more likely to select the wrong text when comparing an image with a short correct text and one with long incorrect text.

(5) CLIP is affected by word frequency. Figure 6 studies the frequency effect on the score for the words that represent concepts that appear in both the *positive* and *negative* images. The more frequent a word is, the higher the CLIP score. Still, the difference in scores is barely affected.

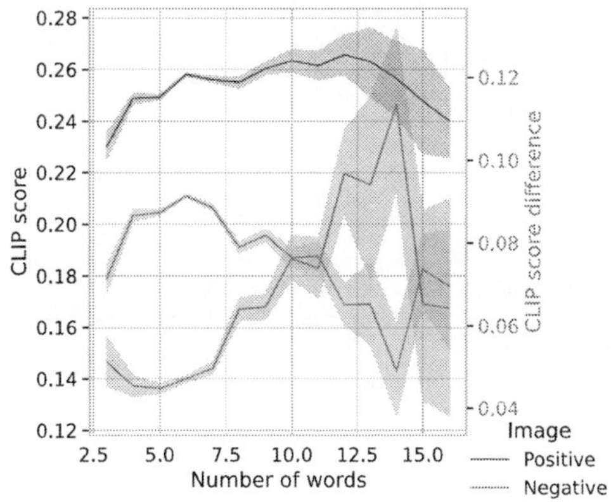

Figure 4: Line plot of the number of words in the caption sentence vs. the CLIP score. The shadowed areas are 95%-confidence intervals for the expected value.

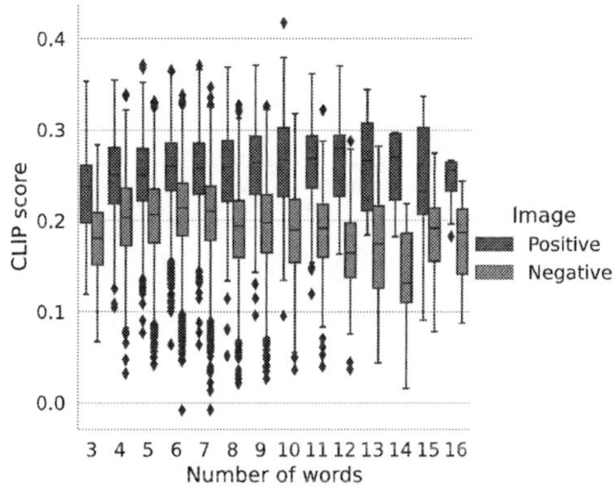

Figure 5: Box plot for the number of words in the caption sentence vs. the CLIP score. Unlike Figure 4 that shows the expected values, this plot shows the distributions.

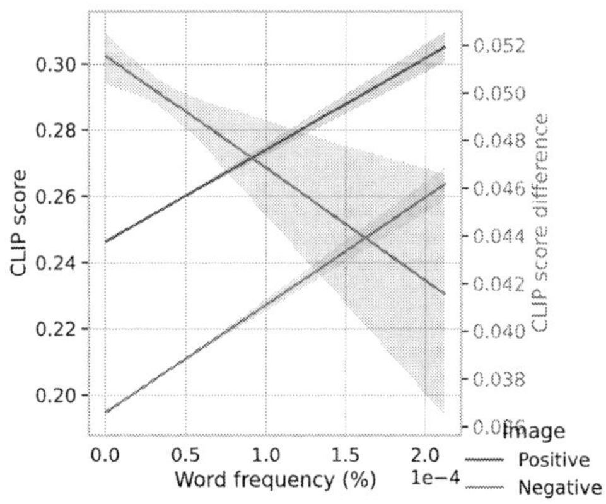

Figure 6: Linear regression plot of the average frequency for the words in the sentence that are common to both images vs. the CLIP score. The shadowed areas are 95%-confidence intervals for the expected value.

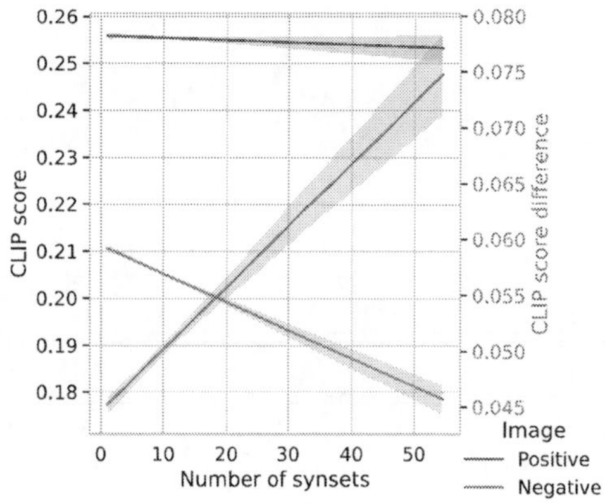

Figure 7: Linear regression plot of the average synset count for the words in the sentence that are common to both images vs. the CLIP score. The shadowed areas are 95%-confidence intervals for the expected value.

(6) The score improves for more ambiguous words. Surprisingly, there is a larger gap in the score difference (D) when the words have more meanings associated with them (for the words that represent concepts in both the *positive* and *negative images)*, as shown in Figure 7. The positive score seems to remain almost constant while the negative score drops, widening the difference. The word frequency seems not to be a confounding factor based on (5).

(7) Similar situations confuse CLIP. Unsurprisingly, the higher the similarity between the caption and the negative image caption, the higher the *negative* CLIP score, as depicted by Figure 8.

We also studied the influence of the similarity between the *original* word (from the caption) and the *replacement* word (from the text associated with the negative image) in Figure 9. The effect of the word change seems to be smaller than that of the whole sentence change.

(8) CLIP performs relatively better on *nature-related* and *personal care* concepts and relatively worse on *furniture, transportation, herbivores, sports, academia.* As mentioned in Section 3.2, score D measures the relative CLIP performance, which is more relevant for retrieval models like CLIP. Therefore, we measure the importance of each feature with respect to D. Specifically, we compute the mean differences of the D scores when the binary feature is present and when is not. We show the CLIP performance analysis on **binary** features in Table 1. Following the example of

Topic	Feature	Mean diff.	Example Words
	CLIP PERFORMS BETTER ON		
Natural Phenomenon	Hypernym physical_phenomenon.n.01 (original)	0.038	snow, fog, rain, mist
	Hypernym physical_phenomenon.n.01 (replacement)	0.022	snow, rain, cloud, fog, mist
Waterfront Infrastructure	Hypernym platform.n.01 (original)	0.038	pier, deck, podium
	Hypernym horizontal_surface.n.01 (original)	0.032	pier, pavement, quay
Landscapes	Hypernym community.n.06 (original)	0.038	meadow, desert, grassland
	Hypernym natural_elevation.n.01 (original)	0.035	dune, sandbar, reef
	Hypernym geological_formation.n.01 (original)	0.027	beach, shore, cliff
	Hypernym plant.n.02 (original)	0.025	grass, tree, flower
	Hypernym natural_elevation.n.01 (replacement)	0.020	mountain, hill
Grooming	Presence of word "wash" (original)	0.035	wash
	Levin "floss verbs" (original)	0.030	wash, brush, shave
	Levin "wipe verbs"(original)	0.022	wear, sweep, trim, rub
	Levin "dress verbs" (original)	0.027	exercise, bathe, dress
Domestic Animals	Hypernym young.n.01 (original)	0.033	puppy, kitten, foal
	Hypernym domestic_animal.n.01 (original)	0.032	puppy, retriever, pug
	General Inquirer "animal" (replacement)	0.023	dog, animal, cat, goat
	Hypernym canine.n.02 (replacement)	0.021	puppy, retriever, pug
	CLIP PERFORMS WORSE ON		
Furniture	Presence of word "sofa" (in common)	-0.032	sofa
	Hypernym bedroom_furniture.n.01 (in common)	-0.026	bed, sofa
	Hypernym furniture.n.01 (in common)	-0.017	couch, bed, sofa, chair, bench
	LIWC "home" (in common)	-0.015	bed, window, sofa, room
Transportation	Presence of word "ride" (original)	-0.027	ride
	Hypernym vessel.n.02 (in common)	-0.019	boat, ship, yacht
	Levin "pedal" verbs (original)	-0.018	ride, drive, fly, sail, cruise
	Hypernym craft.n.02 (in common)	-0.018	boat, balloon, ship, scooter, kayak
Herbivores	Hypernym ungulate.n.01 (in common)	-0.021	horse, cow, camel, goat, deer
	Presence of word "horse" (in common)	-0.019	horse
Sports	Hypernym happening.n.01 (in common)	-0.021	wave, win, tap, slam
	Hypernym contestant.n.01 (in common)	-0.020	footballer, golfer, goalkeeper, cricketer, tackle
	Levin "admire" verbs (original)	-0.017	stand, enjoy, admire, support
Academia	General Inquirer "academia" (in common)	-0.020	student, classroom, library, teacher, book, computer, conference
	Presence of word "student" (in common)	-0.020	student

Table 1: CLIP relative performance analysis on a subset of binary features: the top-5 **easier** topics are *Natural Phenomenon*, *Waterfront Infrastructure*, *Landscapes*, *Grooming* and *Domestic Animals*, while the top-5 **harder** topics are *Furniture*, *Transportation*, *Herbivores*, *Sports* and *Academia*.

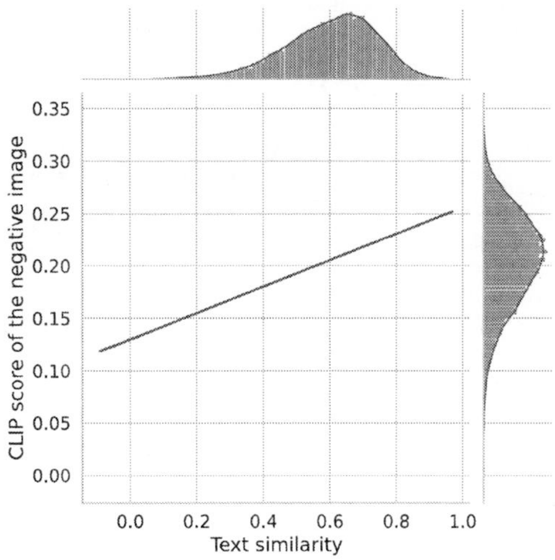

Figure 8: Linear regression plot of the similarity between the text caption and the negative image text caption vs. the CLIP score for the negative image. The shadowed areas are 95%-confidence intervals for the expected value. The unimodal distributions are also shown.

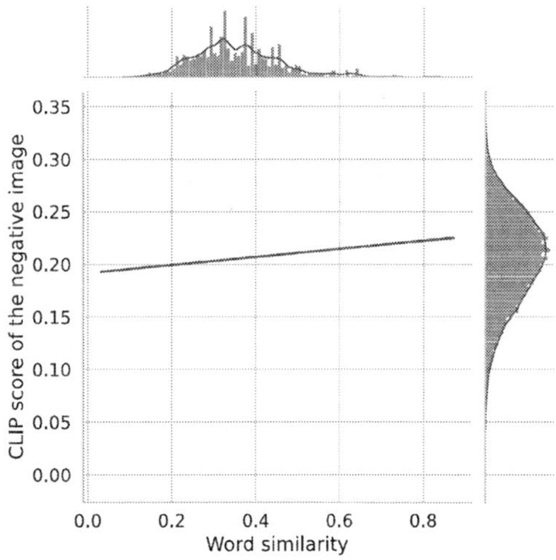

Figure 9: Linear regression plot of the similarity between the originally replaced word from the text caption and new word from the negative image text caption vs. the CLIP score for the negative image. The shadowed areas are 95%-confidence intervals for the expected value. The unimodal distributions are also shown.

SEAL (Rajani et al., 2022), we use ChatGPT to cluster the features under a broad topic automatically.[3]

We find that CLIP performs relatively **better** on topics related to nature: *Natural Phenomenon*, *Waterfront Infrastructure*, *Landscapes*, *Domestic Animals*, and personal care: *Grooming*, and **worse** on topics like *Furniture*, *Transportation*, *Herbivores*, *Sports* and *Academia*.

5 Conclusion

In this work, we proposed a simple and effective method to probe vision-language models. Our method is scalable, as it does not require data annotation and makes use of existing datasets. With our method, we analyzed the performance of CLIP, a popular state-of-the-art multi-modal model, on the SVO-Probes benchmark. We confirmed the recent findings of Thrush et al. (2022) of CLIP behaving like a bag of words model and that of Parcalabescu et al. (2022) of CLIP performing better with nouns and verbs. We also uncovered novel findings, for instance, that CLIP gets confused by concrete words, surprisingly improves performance for more ambiguous terms, or that the frequency of words does not significantly change the behavior of CLIP.

We hope our work contributes to ongoing efforts to discover the limitations of multi-modal models and help build more robust and reliable systems. Our framework can be easily used to analyze other benchmarks, features, and multi-modal models, and it is publicly available at `https://github.com/MichiganNLP/Scalable-VLM-Probing`.

Limitations

SVO-Probes dataset is not balanced. For example, "person", "man", and "woman" are considerably more frequent than other words. Future work can address this limitation by aggregating data from multiple datasets and balancing it out. At the same time, the target dataset should reflect the phenomenon one wants to study. For example, LAION (Schuhmann et al., 2021) could be employed to study how VLMs perform with everyday human actions. Still, it may be too centered around objects (as opposed to actions) and overly noisy – future work can consider using subsets instead. A

[3]We use the following prompt: "Name a topic for the following words: . . . "

smaller yet cleaner alternative is Conceptual Captions (Sharma et al., 2018).

Another limitation is not considering the polysemy when using LIWC or Levin dictionaries. This may lead to incorrect word categorization and influence the error analysis. Future work can mediate this limitation by linking semantic dictionaries such as Levin or LIWC with their WordNet synsets.

Acknowledgements

We want to thank the anonymous reviewers for their helpful comments. We also thank Artem Abzaliev, Fabian Caba, Mohamed El Banani, and Karan Desai for the productive discussions. This material is partly based on work supported by the Automotive Research Center ("ARC"). Any opinions, findings, conclusions, or recommendations expressed in this material are those of the authors and do not necessarily reflect the views of ARC or any other related entity.

References

Arjun Akula, Spandana Gella, Yaser Al-Onaizan, Song-Chun Zhu, and Siva Reddy. 2020. Words aren't enough, their order matters: On the robustness of grounding visual referring expressions. In *Proceedings of the 58th Annual Meeting of the Association for Computational Linguistics*, pages 6555–6565, Online. Association for Computational Linguistics.

Jacob Benesty, Jingdong Chen, Yiteng Huang, and Israel Cohen. 2009. Pearson correlation coefficient. In *Noise reduction in speech processing*, pages 37–40. Springer.

Steven Bird, Ewan Klein, and Edward Loper. 2009. *Natural Language Processing with Python: Analyzing Text with the Natural Language Toolkit*. O'Reilly Media, Inc.

Marc Brysbaert, Amy Beth Warriner, and Victor Kuperman. 2014. Concreteness ratings for 40 thousand generally known english word lemmas. *Behavior research methods*, 46(3):904–911.

Michele Cafagna, Kees van Deemter, and Albert Gatt. 2021. What vision-language models 'see' when they see scenes. *ArXiv*, abs/2109.07301.

Casper da Costa-Luis, Stephen Karl Larroque, Kyle Altendorf, Hadrien Mary, richardsheridan, Mikhail Korobov, Noam Raphael, Ivan Ivanov, Marcel Bargull, Nishant Rodrigues, Guangshuo Chen, Antony Lee, Charles Newey, CrazyPython, JC, Martin Zugnoni, Matthew D. Pagel, mjstevens777, Mikhail Dektyarev, Alex Rothberg, Alexander Plavin, Daniel Panteleit, Fabian Dill, FichteFoll, Gregor Sturm, HeoHeo, Hugo van Kemenade, Jack McCracken, MapleCCC, and Max Nordlund. 2023. tqdm: A fast, Extensible Progress Bar for Python and CLI.

Alexey Dosovitskiy, Lucas Beyer, Alexander Kolesnikov, Dirk Weissenborn, Xiaohua Zhai, Thomas Unterthiner, Mostafa Dehghani, Matthias Minderer, Georg Heigold, Sylvain Gelly, Jakob Uszkoreit, and Neil Houlsby. 2021. An image is worth 16x16 words: Transformers for image recognition at scale. In *International Conference on Learning Representations*.

Charles R Harris, K Jarrod Millman, Stéfan J Van Der Walt, Ralf Gommers, Pauli Virtanen, David Cournapeau, Eric Wieser, Julian Taylor, Sebastian Berg, Nathaniel J Smith, et al. 2020. Array programming with NumPy. *Nature*, 585(7825):357–362.

Lisa Anne Hendricks and Aida Nematzadeh. 2021. Probing image-language transformers for verb understanding. In *Findings of the Association for Computational Linguistics: ACL-IJCNLP 2021*, pages 3635–3644, Online. Association for Computational Linguistics.

Matthew Honnibal, Ines Montani, Sofie Van Landeghem, and Adriane Boyd. 2020. spaCy: Industrial-strength Natural Language Processing in Python.

John D Hunter. 2007. Matplotlib: A 2D graphics environment. *Computing in science & engineering*, 9(03):90–95.

Beth Levin. 1993. *English verb classes and alternations: A preliminary investigation*. University of Chicago press.

Quentin Lhoest, Albert Villanova del Moral, Patrick von Platen, Thomas Wolf, Mario Šaško, Yacine Jernite, Abhishek Thakur, Lewis Tunstall, Suraj Patil, Mariama Drame, Julien Chaumond, Julien Plu, Joe Davison, Simon Brandeis, Victor Sanh, Teven Le Scao, Kevin Canwen Xu, Nicolas Patry, Steven Liu, Angelina McMillan-Major, Philipp Schmid, Sylvain Gugger, Nathan Raw, Sylvain Lesage, Anton Lozhkov, Matthew Carrigan, Théo Matussière, Leandro von Werra, Lysandre Debut, Stas Bekman, and Clément Delangue. 2021. Datasets: A Community Library for Natural Language Processing. In *Proceedings of the 2021 Conference on Empirical Methods in Natural Language Processing: System Demonstrations*, pages 175–184. Association for Computational Linguistics.

Liunian Harold Li, Mark Yatskar, Da Yin, Cho-Jui Hsieh, and Kai-Wei Chang. 2019. VisualBERT: A simple and performant baseline for vision and language. *ArXiv*, abs/1908.03557.

Fangyu Liu, Guy Edward Toh Emerson, and Nigel Collier. 2023. Visual spatial reasoning. *Transactions of the Association for Computational Linguistics*.

Jiasen Lu, Dhruv Batra, Devi Parikh, and Stefan Lee. 2019. ViLBERT: Pretraining task-agnostic visiolinguistic representations for vision-and-language tasks.

In *Advances in Neural Information Processing Systems*, volume 32. Curran Associates, Inc.

Huaishao Luo, Lei Ji, Ming Zhong, Yang Chen, Wen Lei, Nan Duan, and Tianrui Li. 2022. CLIP4Clip: An empirical study of CLIP for end to end video clip retrieval and captioning. *Neurocomputing*, 508:293–304.

Zixian Ma, Jerry Hong, Mustafa Omer Gul, Mona Gandhi, Irena Gao, and Ranjay Krishna. 2023. CREPE: Can vision-language foundation models reason compositionally? In *Proceedings of the IEEE/CVF Conference on Computer Vision and Pattern Recognition (CVPR)*, pages 10910–10921.

George A. Miller. 1995. WordNet: A lexical database for English. *Commun. ACM*, 38(11):39–41.

Ron Mokady, Amir Hertz, and Amit H Bermano. 2021. ClipCap: CLIP prefix for image captioning. *arXiv preprint arXiv:2111.09734*.

J. Zvi Namenwirth and Robert Philip Weber. 1987. *Dynamics of culture*. Allen & Unwin – Boston, Mass., USA.

Letitia Parcalabescu, Michele Cafagna, Lilitta Muradjan, Anette Frank, Iacer Calixto, and Albert Gatt. 2022. VALSE: A task-independent benchmark for vision and language models centered on linguistic phenomena. In *Proceedings of the 60th Annual Meeting of the Association for Computational Linguistics (Volume 1: Long Papers)*, pages 8253–8280, Dublin, Ireland. Association for Computational Linguistics.

Jae Sung Park, Sheng Shen, Ali Farhadi, Trevor Darrell, Yejin Choi, and Anna Rohrbach. 2022. Exposing the limits of video-text models through contrast sets. In *Proceedings of the 2022 Conference of the North American Chapter of the Association for Computational Linguistics: Human Language Technologies*, pages 3574–3586, Seattle, United States. Association for Computational Linguistics.

Adam Paszke, Sam Gross, Francisco Massa, Adam Lerer, James Bradbury, Gregory Chanan, Trevor Killeen, Zeming Lin, Natalia Gimelshein, Luca Antiga, Alban Desmaison, Andreas Kopf, Edward Yang, Zachary DeVito, Martin Raison, Alykhan Tejani, Sasank Chilamkurthy, Benoit Steiner, Lu Fang, Junjie Bai, and Soumith Chintala. 2019. PyTorch: An Imperative Style, High-Performance Deep Learning Library. In *Advances in Neural Information Processing Systems 32*, pages 8024–8035. Curran Associates, Inc.

F. Pedregosa, G. Varoquaux, A. Gramfort, V. Michel, B. Thirion, O. Grisel, M. Blondel, P. Prettenhofer, R. Weiss, V. Dubourg, J. Vanderplas, A. Passos, D. Cournapeau, M. Brucher, M. Perrot, and E. Duchesnay. 2011. Scikit-learn: Machine learning in Python. *Journal of Machine Learning Research*, 12:2825–2830.

James W. Pennebaker, Roger John Booth, and Martha E. Francis. 2007. Linguistic inquiry and word count (LIWC2007).

James W. Pennebaker, Ryan L. Boyd, Kayla Jordan, and Kate G. Blackburn. 2015. The development and psychometric properties of LIWC2015.

Alec Radford, Jong Wook Kim, Chris Hallacy, Aditya Ramesh, Gabriel Goh, Sandhini Agarwal, Girish Sastry, Amanda Askell, Pamela Mishkin, Jack Clark, Gretchen Krueger, and Ilya Sutskever. 2021. Learning transferable visual models from natural language supervision. In *Proceedings of the 38th International Conference on Machine Learning*, volume 139 of *Proceedings of Machine Learning Research*, pages 8748–8763. PMLR.

Nazneen Rajani, Weixin Liang, Lingjiao Chen, Margaret Mitchell, and James Zou. 2022. SEAL: Interactive tool for systematic error analysis and labeling. In *Proceedings of the 2022 Conference on Empirical Methods in Natural Language Processing: System Demonstrations*, pages 359–370, Abu Dhabi, UAE. Association for Computational Linguistics.

Aditya Ramesh, Prafulla Dhariwal, Alex Nichol, Casey Chu, and Mark Chen. 2022. Hierarchical text-conditional image generation with CLIP latents. *arXiv preprint arXiv:2204.06125*.

Nils Reimers and Iryna Gurevych. 2019. Sentence-BERT: Sentence embeddings using Siamese BERT-networks. In *Proceedings of the 2019 Conference on Empirical Methods in Natural Language Processing and the 9th International Joint Conference on Natural Language Processing (EMNLP-IJCNLP)*, pages 3982–3992, Hong Kong, China. Association for Computational Linguistics.

Emmanuelle Salin, Badreddine Farah, S. Ayache, and Benoit Favre. 2022. Are vision-language transformers learning multimodal representations? a probing perspective. In *AAAI Conference on Artificial Intelligence*, pages 11248–11257.

Christoph Schuhmann, Richard Vencu, Romain Beaumont, Robert Kaczmarczyk, Clayton Mullis, Aarush Katta, Theo Coombes, Jenia Jitsev, and Aran Komatsuzaki. 2021. LAION-400M: Open dataset of CLIP-filtered 400 million image-text pairs. In *Proceedings of the NeurIPS Data Centric AI Workshop*.

Skipper Seabold and Josef Perktold. 2010. statsmodels: Econometric and statistical modeling with python. In *9th Python in Science Conference*.

Piyush Sharma, Nan Ding, Sebastian Goodman, and Radu Soricut. 2018. Conceptual Captions: A cleaned, hypernymed, image alt-text dataset for automatic image captioning. In *Proceedings of the 56th Annual Meeting of the Association for Computational Linguistics (Volume 1: Long Papers)*, pages 2556–2565, Melbourne, Australia. Association for Computational Linguistics.

Ravi Shekhar, Sandro Pezzelle, Yauhen Klimovich, Aurélie Herbelot, Moin Nabi, Enver Sangineto, and Raffaella Bernardi. 2017. FOIL it! find one mismatch between image and language caption. In *Proceedings of the 55th Annual Meeting of the Association for Computational Linguistics (Volume 1: Long Papers)*, pages 255–265, Vancouver, Canada. Association for Computational Linguistics.

Amanpreet Singh, Ronghang Hu, Vedanuj Goswami, Guillaume Couairon, Wojciech Galuba, Marcus Rohrbach, and Douwe Kiela. 2022. FLAVA: A foundational language and vision alignment model. In *Proceedings of the IEEE/CVF Conference on Computer Vision and Pattern Recognition (CVPR)*, pages 15638–15650.

Philip J. Stone, Dexter C. Dunphy, and Marshall S. Smith. 1967. The general inquirer: A computer approach to content analysis. *American Educational Research Journal*, 4:397.

Student. 1908. The probable error of a mean. *Biometrika*, pages 1–25.

The pandas development team. 2023. pandas-dev/pandas: Pandas.

Tristan Thrush, Ryan Jiang, Max Bartolo, Amanpreet Singh, Adina Williams, Douwe Kiela, and Candace Ross. 2022. Winoground: Probing vision and language models for visio-linguistic compositionality. In *Proceedings of the IEEE/CVF Conference on Computer Vision and Pattern Recognition (CVPR)*, pages 5238–5248.

Pauli Virtanen, Ralf Gommers, Travis E Oliphant, Matt Haberland, Tyler Reddy, David Cournapeau, Evgeni Burovski, Pearu Peterson, Warren Weckesser, Jonathan Bright, et al. 2020. SciPy 1.0: fundamental algorithms for scientific computing in python. *Nature methods*, 17(3):261–272.

Wenhui Wang, Furu Wei, Li Dong, Hangbo Bao, Nan Yang, and Ming Zhou. 2020. MiniLM: Deep self-attention distillation for task-agnostic compression of pre-trained transformers. In *Advances in Neural Information Processing Systems*, volume 33, pages 5776–5788. Curran Associates, Inc.

Michael L. Waskom. 2021. seaborn: statistical data visualization. *Journal of Open Source Software*, 6(60):3021.

Thomas Wolf, Lysandre Debut, Victor Sanh, Julien Chaumond, Clement Delangue, Anthony Moi, Pierric Cistac, Tim Rault, Remi Louf, Morgan Funtowicz, Joe Davison, Sam Shleifer, Patrick von Platen, Clara Ma, Yacine Jernite, Julien Plu, Canwen Xu, Teven Le Scao, Sylvain Gugger, Mariama Drame, Quentin Lhoest, and Alexander Rush. 2020. Transformers: State-of-the-art natural language processing. In *Proceedings of the 2020 Conference on Empirical Methods in Natural Language Processing: System Demonstrations*, pages 38–45, Online. Association for Computational Linguistics.

Mert Yuksekgonul, Federico Bianchi, Pratyusha Kalluri, Dan Jurafsky, and James Zou. 2023. When and why vision-language models behave like bags-of-words, and what to do about it? In *The Eleventh International Conference on Learning Representations*.

Pengchuan Zhang, Xiujun Li, Xiaowei Hu, Jianwei Yang, Lei Zhang, Lijuan Wang, Yejin Choi, and Jianfeng Gao. 2021. VinVL: Revisiting visual representations in vision-language models. In *Proceedings of the IEEE/CVF Conference on Computer Vision and Pattern Recognition (CVPR)*, pages 5579–5588.

Tiancheng Zhao, Tianqi Zhang, Mingwei Zhu, Haozhan Shen, Kyusong Lee, XiaoPeng Lu, and Jianwei Yin. 2022. VL-CheckList: Evaluating pre-trained vision-language models with objects, attributes and relations. *ArXiv*, abs/2207.00221.

PCFG-Based Natural Language Interface Improves Generalization for Controlled Text Generation

Jingyu Zhang
Johns Hopkins University
jzhan237@jhu.edu

James Glass
MIT
glass@mit.edu

Tianxing He
University of Washington
goosehe@cs.washington.edu

Abstract

Existing work on controlled text generation (CTG) assumes a control interface of categorical attributes. In this work, we propose a natural language (NL) interface, where we craft a PCFG to embed the control attributes into natural language commands, and propose variants of existing CTG models that take commands as input. In our experiments, we design tailored setups to test the model's generalization abilities. We find our PCFG-based command generation approach is effective for handling unseen commands compared to fix-set templates. Further, our proposed NL models can effectively generalize to unseen attributes (a new ability enabled by the NL interface), as well as unseen attribute combinations. Interestingly, in model comparisons, the simple conditional generation approach, enhanced with our proposed NL interface, is shown to be a strong baseline in those challenging settings.

1 Introduction

With the advancement of large-scale pretraining, language models (LM) are now able to generate increasingly more realistic text (Radford et al., 2019; Brown et al., 2020; Rae et al., 2021; Hoffmann et al., 2022; Smith et al., 2022; Thoppilan et al., 2022). Therefore, how to control the generation of LMs has become an important research topic. In *controlled text generation* (CTG), a series of works (Keskar et al., 2019; Dathathri et al., 2020; Krause et al., 2021; Yang and Klein, 2021; Liu et al., 2021; Yu et al., 2021; Li et al., 2022, *inter alia*) propose model frameworks to generate text conditioned on some desired (user-specified) attribute a. These attributes, which depend on the datasets of interest, could be topic, formality, sentiment, etc.

An important assumption behind this controlled generation setting is that the attributes are chosen from **a fixed set** (i.e., they are treated as categorical random variables). Although this setting is convenient, it seriously limits the applications of the CTG system: (1) Since the attribute set is fixed during training, it would be impossible for the model to generalize to unseen options if used as-is. (2) This interface is not very human-friendly, because it could be difficult for users to navigate through the (possibly long) lists of options. Motivated by these limitations, in this work we propose a *natural language interface* for CTG, illustrated in Figure 1. With this change of interface, the input to the CTG model changes from one-hot vectors to natural language commands (for short, *commands*). To efficiently train this system and enable it to generalize, we design a probabilistic context-free grammar (PCFG) to embed categorical attributes into a diverse set of natural language commands.

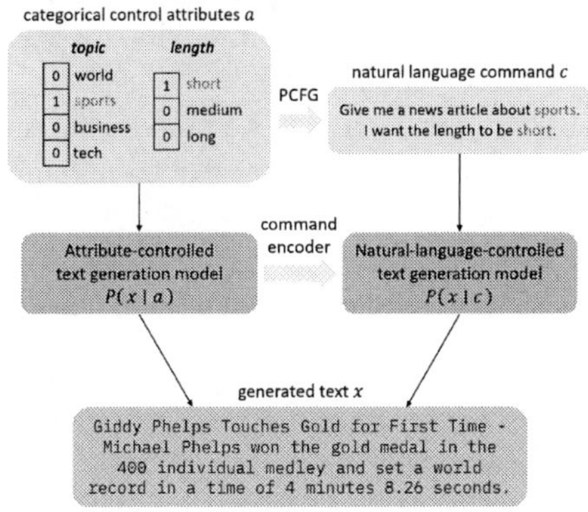

Figure 1: We explore generation models that take natural language commands as input. For training, we use PCFG to embed categorical control attributes into natural language commands.

Using natural language instruction has been explored in recent work (Sanh et al., 2021; Wei et al., 2022; Mishra et al., 2022; Reif et al., 2022; Schick and Schütze, 2021). Our work differs from theirs in (1) We focus on the task of CTG as opposed to the performance on cross-task generalization, and design tailored scenarios for evaluation. (2) We introduce PCFG for command generation, which has

*Proceedings of the The 12th Joint Conference on Lexical and Computational Semantics (*SEM 2023)*, pages 295–313
July 13-14, 2023 ©2023 Association for Computational Linguistics

not been explored by previous work. We discuss this relationship in more detail in Section 2.

The change of interface brings several immediate benefits: (1) Natural language inputs enable the system to generalize to unseen attribute options (as long as they can be expressed in natural language). (2) Unlike fixed-set template sentences in previous works, the PCFG can generate diverse natural language variation during training, which we will show is crucial for generalization. (3) The input process becomes more natural and interactive to a human user, and it can be linked with, for example, a speech recognition module.

With this new interface, we propose variants of several existing CTG systems that take commands as input, and design experiments to compare different CTG models under tailored scenarios. We briefly summarize our main contributions below:

- We propose a PCFG-based natural language interface for controlled text generation. The natural language interface enables zero-shot generalization on control attributes unseen during training, a capability previously impossible due to the fixed-set assumption.
- We show that training with commands generated by a PCFG is an effective method for increasing natural language variation over using fixed-set templates, allowing natural language CTG models to better generalize to commands unseen during training.
- We test the proposed natural language CTG models on settings where the models need to generalize to unseen attributes and attribute combinations. Surprisingly, the simple conditional generation approach is shown to be a strong baseline in these challenging setups.

2 Related Work

Controlled Text Generation In open-ended text generation, a series of approaches have been proposed to control the generation to satisfy certain attributes (e.g. topic) (Keskar et al., 2019; Dathathri et al., 2020; Krause et al., 2021; Yang and Klein, 2021; Liu et al., 2021, *inter alia*). Some of these studies utilize a trained classifier to guide the generative model towards the desired attribute, while others use a smaller LM to reweight LM logits. Very recently, Li et al. (2022) focus on controlling more complex attributes such as syntactic structure with a non-autoregressive LM. Another line of work conducts CTG via prompt learning (Clive et al., 2022; Yang et al., 2022). These work assume a fixed set of control attributes.

Our NL interface is more related to Yu et al. (2021), which uses an attribute alignment function to embed attribute words into a hidden representation that guides LM generation. The attribute alignment function does not assume attribute tokens are from a fixed set, so it is possible to do inference on an attribute token not seen in training. Keyword2Text (Pascual et al., 2021) shift the distribution over vocabulary toward words that are semantically similar to control keywords in a discriminator-free manner, thus does not assume a fixed set of keywords. Besides attribute control, lexically constrained decoding (Post and Vilar, 2018) has also been used to enforce certain key phrases to be included in the generation (Mao et al., 2020). Different from these work which uses keywords, we utilize PCFG to construct fully-natural-language sentences as commands.

Instruction Following A recent series of work proposes to describe NLP tasks in natural language, and use the task description as an instruction to promote zero-shot generalization for LMs (Sanh et al., 2021; Wei et al., 2022, *inter alia*). Such task descriptions are manually created, detailed definitions of NLP tasks, which contain explanations about input, output, emphasis, and possibly a small number of demonstrative examples. InstructGPT (Ouyang et al., 2022) uses an RL policy to improve LM's capability to follow user instructions.

Although our work resembles these works in the form of natural language instructions, we note several important differences. First, existing works focus on general instruction following that is applicable to a very broad range of tasks and evaluate on generalization capabilities across tasks. We specifically consider the use of NL commands in the CTG setting and compare variants of CTG models in tailored test scenarios. Moreover, previous works in natural language instruction employ a fixed number of templates for each task, whereas we craft a PCFG that can generate a diverse set of command sentences to serve as templates. We show the effectiveness of our PCFG over fixed-set templates in subsequent experiments in Section 5.1. Finally, prompting models with NL instructions fails for moderately sized LMs without any modifications Li and Liang (2021). Thus, it is non-trivial to adapt NL instruction to smaller models.

3 Framework

The goal of controlled text generation is to model the conditional distribution $P(x|a)$ so that the generated text x satisfies the desired attributes a. a could include multiple attributes (e.g., topic and length), and we will use a_i to denote the ith attribute. In the standard categorical setting, the attribute a_i are from a fixed set of pre-defined options. We assume there are m attributes of interest ($m \leqslant 2$ in our experiments). In the next few sections, we describe the PCFG that we craft to embed the categorical attributes, and our proposed NL variants of several existing CTG systems.

3.1 Embedding Attributes into Commands

We embed categorical attributes into natural language commands with a PCFG.[1] We favor PCFG due to its ability to generate diverse NL variations expressing the same control semantics. For simplicity, most of the probability weights are set to uniform. In this section, we will describe it at the high-level, and more details and the full set of rules are provided in Appendix C. Table 1 is a concrete example of how a command describing an AG news article with a sports topic could be generated by our PCFG. We clarify that while the PCFG is used for training and testing in our work, the end user will not need to use it, as the model can generalize to unseen commands (Section 5.1).

Our command generation has three steps. First, a template with m attribute slots is generated by the PCFG. We design the PCFG to generate templates that "ask" the system to generate text with some attributes and domains. We first sample a top-level seed template from `ROOT` that determines high-level sentence structure (e.g., `[PLS]` `[HEAD-FORM]` a `[TEXT-FORM]` `[LABEL-SEG]`), then fill in sentence segments with PCFG rules (e.g., `[HEAD-FORM]` will be substituted by "generate"). These sentence segments are neither domain nor attribute specific and thus can be used regardless of the attributes. In contrast to writing a set of fixed templates, our PCFG has multiple levels of rule and can greatly improve NL variation.

Next, we verbalize the domain media D, attribute a, and attribute name A into natural language by crafting PCFG rules that transform them into words or phrases. Considering the fact that different words could have similar meanings in natural language, these mappings could be one-to-many to further improve NL variation. For instance, news about "business" can also be described as "commerce", and "very negative" is similar to "terrible".

Finally, we conduct a postprocessing step to correct simple grammar errors, e.g., "a AG news article" would be corrected as "an AG news article".

In our preliminary attempts, we attempted to train a conditional neural LM for command generation, instead of using a PCFG. Although the neural model has better diversity, the stochastic nature of sampling makes the attribute embedding inaccurate. Besides, training such a neural LM would require a large amount of (attribute, command) paired data. Therefore we turn to a PCFG approach as it has guaranteed accuracy, with decent diversity.

1. PCFG-based template generation
(1) Generate top-level seed template from `ROOT`: ⇒ `[PLS]` `[HEAD-FORM]` a `[TEXT-FORM]` `[LABEL-SEG]`. (2) Select PCFG rules to generate template: `[PLS]` → ... → please, `[HEAD-FORM]` → ... → generate, `[TEXT-FORM]` → ... → D `[LABEL-SEG]` → ... → with a a A ⇒ please generate a D with a a A.
2. Verbalize
⇒ please generate a AG news report with a sports topic.
3. Postprocess
⇒ Please generate an AG news report with a sports topic.

Table 1: Examples of PCFG command generation. `ROOT` is the PCFG start symbol. Newly replaced segments are highlighted in red. In step 1.(2), we omit intermediate PCFG expansions to "→ ... →".

3.2 Models

In this section, we first review some existing CTG models. For the new NL interface, we propose natural variants of the models which take commands as input. All models are based on a pretrained autoregressive LM, denoted by P_b.

3.2.1 PrefixLM

A direct method to model the conditional distribution $P(x|a)$ is to encode the attribute as a prefix and finetune the base model to generate x conditioned on the prefix. In the standard categorical attribute setting, we randomly initialize an embedding vector for each attribute and feed the corresponding embeddings as the prefix. Multiple attributes are arranged in a pre-defined order.

PrefixLM-NL The NL variant of PrefixLM is straightforward. We just use the command as the prefix. No extra parameters need to be added.

[1]Note that our command generation process is not strictly a PCFG, but it is very close.

3.2.2 Future Discriminator Controlled Generation (FUDGE)

FUDGE (Yang and Klein, 2021) decomposes the conditional distribution using Bayes' rule according to Equation 1:

$$P_{\text{fudge}}(x_i|x_{1:i-1}, a) \propto P_{\text{b}}(x_i|x_{1:i-1})P_{\text{cls}}(a|x_{1:i}). \tag{1}$$

It involves training a future discriminator to predict whether the generated prefix $x_{1:i}$ will lead to a full generation that satisfies the attribute a. Following FUDGE's original formulation, we assume different attributes are conditionally independent and train a discriminator $P(a_k|x_{1:i})$ for each attribute a_k. We then use their product as the probability that all attributes are satisfied, i.e., $P(a_1, \ldots, a_m|x_{1:i}) = \prod_k P(a_k|x_{1:i})$.

As we consider attributes with multiple options (e.g., 4 topics or 5 sentiments), the FUDGE discriminator for a single attribute is a multiclass classification model that predicts the conditional distribution $P(a|x_{1:i})$ over all possible options of attribute a.

FUDGE-NL In order to enable FUDGE to handle natural-language commands, we utilize a binary alignment discriminator to judge whether the generated text aligns with the command. Given a command c, let $y_c \in \{0, 1\}$ be a binary variable that denotes whether the prefix $x_{1:i}$ aligns with the command. Control is achieved by generating from the conditional distribution $P(x_i|x_{1:i-1}, y_c = 1)$ that the alignment property is satisfied. We modify FUDGE's decomposition as Equation 2:

$$\begin{aligned} P_{\text{fudge-nl}}&(x_i|x_{1:i-1}, y_c = 1) \\ &\propto P_{\text{b}}(x_i|x_{1:i-1})P_{\text{cls}}(y_c = 1|x_{1:i}). \end{aligned} \tag{2}$$

$P_{\text{cls}}(y_c = 1|x_{1:i})$ is modeled by a binary classifier trained on a dataset of command and generation prefix pairs $\{(c, x_{1:i})\}$. To create this data, for a given example text x with attributes a, we first apply our PCFG to generate a true command c^{pos}. We then randomly flip one (or both) of the attribute in a, and generate a false command c^{neg}. By pairing c^{pos} and c^{neg} with x, we obtain the positive/negative training data for the discriminator. In practice, we concatenate the command and generation prefix (separated by a special `[SEP]` token) and feed it as input to the alignment discriminator.

FUDGE-Binary One major difference between FUDGE and its NL variant is that the discriminator is always binary for FUDGE-NL due to the alignment objective. This inspires us to propose a binary variant of the FUDGE model, FUDGE-Binary, which operates with the categorical interface. Similar to FUDGE-NL, we use a binary variable y_a to denote whether $x_{1:i}$ aligns with attribute a, and modify the decomposition as:

$$\begin{aligned} P_{\text{fudge-bin}}&(x_i|x_{1:i-1}, y_a = 1) \\ &\propto P_{\text{b}}(x_i|x_{1:i-1})P_{\text{cls}}(y_a = 1|x_{1:i}). \end{aligned} \tag{3}$$

FUDGE-Binary's discriminator will always make a binary prediction even if there are more than two options for a single attribute. Since attributes are still from a fixed set, we use a single classification model but attach a separate classifier head for each option. During training, the classification head W_{a*} that matches the correct attribute a^* receives a correct label $y = 1$, and all other classification heads $\{W_a\}_{a \neq a^*}$ receive label $y = 0$. At test time, we select the classification head W_a base on the desired attribute a to predict the alignment probability $P(y_a = 1|x_{1:i})$. Although this variant is a simple modification from the original FUDGE, empirically we find it to achieve stronger performance in the categorical interface.

4 Experimental Setup

4.1 Datasets

We utilize two popular text classification datasets for our experiments: AG News and Yelp Review.[2] For each dataset, we consider two control attributes: label and length. The label attribute is extracted from the classification label, i.e., topic labels for AG News and sentiment labels for Yelp Review. There are 4 topics {world, sports, business, science/tech} in AG News and 5 sentiment classes ranging from most positive to most negative in Yelp Review. The length attribute is created by dividing the dataset to n_{len} length ranges so that number of training examples in each length range is balanced. We use $n_{\text{len}} = 3$ for AG News and $n_{\text{len}} = 5$ for Yelp Review. We refer readers to Appendix A for details about dataset preprocessing.

4.2 Evaluation Metrics

We measure the generation performance in three aspects: control accuracy, quality, and diversity. In our experiments, we find that different variants of models mostly perform comparably on quality or

[2] Obtained from Hugging Face Datasets.

diversity aspects. Therefore, we will mainly focus our discussion on control accuracy.

Control Accuracy To evaluate the effectiveness of the control, we consider three types of control accuracy: LABEL ACCURACY refers to the accuracy that the generation satisfies the classification label, i.e., topic classification accuracy on AG News and sentiment classification accuracy on Yelp. This metric is computed by a RoBERTa classifier finetuned on the corresponding classification dataset. LENGTH ACCURACY refers to the accuracy that the generation's tokenized length lies within the predefined length range. COMPOSITIONAL ACCURACY is the accuracy that both label and length attributes are satisfied.

Text Quality We consider two metrics to measure the quality of the generated text. GPT-NEO PERPLEXITY (G-PPL): we finetune the GPT-Neo-1.3B model[3] on the corresponding datasets (without the labels), and report the perplexity of the generated text given by it. BLEU score: we randomly sample 100 examples from the AG News or Yelp test set as the reference, and compute the 4-gram BLEU score.

Diversity We measure diversity of the generated text using 4-gram TEXT ENTROPY (Zhang et al., 2018). That is, treat the generated token frequency as a discrete distribution, and compute its entropy.

4.3 Model Instantiation

Here we describe the implementation of models mentioned in Section 3.2. We use the Hugging Face transformers library (Wolf et al., 2020) and adapt from FUDGE's released code.[4]

For all models, we produce generation by top-k sampling with $k = 20$ unless otherwise stated.

PrefixLM variants We finetune a GPT-2 (Radford et al., 2019) small model without any modification (except for adding necessary special tokens) for both PrefixLM and PrefixLM-NL. At test time, we feed the desired attributes or command sentences as the prefix and evaluate on the continuation produced by the model.

FUDGE variants The backbone language model P_b for FUDGE models is a GPT-2 small model finetuned on the corresponding dataset, using the same data available at discriminator training. That is, under the zero-shot setting, we use the same data configuration to finetune the backbone LM.

For FUDGE and FUDGE-Binary, we train two discriminator for each of the label (topic or sentiment) and length attribute; FUDGE-NL use a single alignment discriminator to handle commands.

Each discriminator for FUDGE and FUDGE-NL is a GPT-2 small model followed by a single linear classification layer (with different numbers of output classes). The discriminator for FUDGE-Binary is a GPT-2 small model followed by multiple linear classification layers, with each one corresponding to an option for the label or length attribute. Each classification layer makes a binary prediction about whether the generation prefix satisfies the particular option of the attribute.

5 Experiments

We design experiments to test natural language CTG models' generalization capabilities, where the models need to generalize to (1) unseen commands (2) unseen attribute options (3) unseen combinations of attribute options. Additionally, we compare natural language CTG models with their categorical counterparts under the standard full-data setting to test whether the NL interface would degrade the model's performance.

5.1 Generalization to Unseen Commands

A key challenge introduced by the new interface is the diversity of natural language: commands with different surface forms can have the same underlying semantic. Thus we design a set of experiments to test natural language CTG models' ability to generalize to commands unseen during training. Specifically, we compare the effectiveness of our proposed PCFG with commands generated by fix-set templates, as adopted in previous works (Sanh et al., 2021; Wei et al., 2022; Mishra et al., 2022).

To create a setup similar to previous work, we hand-crafted 20 diverse templates for each dataset. This is already twice the number of templates used in Wei et al. (2022) and comparable to the number of seed templates in our PCFG. We denote models trained on this set of templates by "-T20" suffix. We also explore a stronger version of fix-set templates by doubling the number of templates, totaling 40 templates for each dataset, denoted by "-T40" suffix. We test the above models on 20 hand-crafted unseen templates that are different

[3] A publicly-available replication of GPT-3 obtained from https://huggingface.co/EleutherAI/gpt-neo-1.3B.

[4] Our code and data will be released in the public version of this manuscript.

DATASET	METHOD	*Control Accuracy* LABEL ↑	LENGTH ↑	COMP. ↑	*Text Quality* G-PPL ↓	BLEU ↑	*Diversity* ENT. ↑
AG News	PrefixLM-NL-T20	.922	.522	.458	12.345	.865	11.412
	PrefixLM-NL-T40	.923	.496	.424	11.981	.863	11.405
	PrefixLM-NL-PCFG	**.933**	**.567**	**.505**	12.350	.868	11.381
	FUDGE-NL-T20	.936	.717	.603	11.677	.864	11.368
	FUDGE-NL-T40	.938	.759	.664	11.678	.864	11.355
	FUDGE-NL-PCFG	**.955**	**.936**	**.826**	12.174	.863	11.369
Yelp Review	PrefixLM-NL-T20	.389	.612	.177	10.523	.943	11.916
	PrefixLM-NL-T40	.398	.603	.216	10.309	.943	11.935
	PrefixLM-NL-PCFG	**.443**	**.721**	**.250**	10.251	.945	11.869
	FUDGE-NL-T20	.364	.531	.148	9.567	.936	12.155
	FUDGE-NL-T40	.538	.619	.249	9.986	.944	11.918
	FUDGE-NL-PCFG	**.687**	**.864**	**.462**	10.341	.941	11.836

Table 2: Results for experiment on PCFG effectiveness. Training NL CTG models with PCFG-generated commands greatly improves controllability on unseen commands, compared to models trained on fixed-set templates.

from both the PCFG and fixed-set templates, and compare results with our proposed PCFG-based models, denoted by "-PCFG" suffix.

The results in Table 2, show that when conditioning on unseen commands, both the PrefixLM-NL and FUDGE-NL models with PCFG have notably better controllability compared to fixed-set template models. The above experiments provide empirical evidence that **our PCFG can effectively improve the model's generalization ability on natural language variation within commands**.

5.2 Generalization to Unseen Attributes

CTG models with categorical attributes can only control a fixed set of attribute options. It is impossible for these models to control unseen attribute options without re-training due to architecture constraints (e.g., FUDGE trains a classifier with a fixed number of labels). In contrast, our proposed NL interface naturally allows CTG models to generalize to unseen options by embedding novel attributes into an NL command using a verbalizer phrase unseen during training, as long as the novel attributes could be described in natural language. In this section, we conduct experiments to test our PCFG-based natural language CTG models' capabilities to generalize control to unseen attribute options.

Experimental setup In this section, we control a single attribute (topic) for ease of presentation. Although it is possible to also experiment on the length attribute, they are similar in nature. For an attribute with n classes (e.g., 4 different topics), we create n zero-shot data splits and delete examples from one of the n classes (i.e. the zero-shot class) completely during training. We test on both the zero-shot and other seen classes separately and report the average result over all n splits. We conduct zero-shot experiments on the AG News dataset.

Adding extra data Since natural-language CTG models do not assume the attribute is from a fixed set of options, it is possible to train the model to control attributes by using extra data with different attribute options. This is another capability enabled by our NL interface, previously unavailable due to the fix-set assumption. We experiment training the models on the zero-shot AG News split along with similar datasets in the news domain, aiming to test whether the model can learn from extra data and generalize to a wider range of attribute options. We utilize three extra news topic classification datasets: News Popularity, News Category (Misra, 2022; Misra and Grover, 2021), and the Inshorts News dataset.[5] Topics that overlap with AG News are removed. We refer readers to Appendix A for more details. For these datasets, we use the same PCFG as AG News. When mixing multiple datasets during training, we follow Raffel et al. (2020) and use examples-proportional mixing to control the relative frequency of examples from each dataset. We set the artificial limit of each extra dataset to the size of the original AG News dataset.

The zero-shot results are shown in Table 3. Since the categorical interface does not allow unseen categories, we introduce a no-control baseline by fine-tuning the base LM with the same zero-shot data and producing generations from it directly without control. Both FUDGE-NL and PrefixLM-NL beat

[5]Obtained from Hugging Face Datasets and Kaggle.

		Control		*Text Quality*				*Diversity*	
		Acc. ↑		G-PPL ↓		BLEU ↑		Ent. ↑	
Setup	Method	Z.S.	Reg.	Z.S.	Reg.	Z.S.	Reg.	Z.S.	Reg.
No Control Baseline	GPT-2-finetuned	.009	.343	11.050	11.062	.866	.867	9.745	9.735
Zero-shot data	PrefixLM-NL	**.222**	**.967**	14.797	11.556	.867	.860	9.736	9.726
	FUDGE-NL	.038	.927	21.604	11.497	.601	.863	9.359	9.748
	PrefixLM-NL-unb	**.204**	**.913**	12.980	11.387	.871	.862	9.738	9.737
	FUDGE-NL-unb	.203	.773	21.547	11.795	.623	.862	9.537	9.762
+Extra data	PrefixLM-NL	**.448**	**.960**	17.559	12.521	.868	.860	9.772	9.759
	FUDGE-NL	.071	.935	22.727	11.430	.782	.863	9.536	9.741
	PrefixLM-NL-unb	**.455**	**.928**	14.611	11.716	.867	.861	9.734	9.752
	FUDGE-NL-unb	.416	.784	24.898	11.933	.769	.864	9.587	9.748

Table 3: Results for zero-shot setting. Z.S. (zero-shot) denote metrics computed with the zero-shot class, Reg. (regular) denote metrics computed with seen classes during training. The simple PrefixLM-NL approach outperforms FUDGE-NL. Adding extra data doubles the zero-shot accuracy.

		Compositional Accuracy			*Text Quality*		*Diversity*
Dataset	Method	Test ↑	Orig. ↑	Diff. ↓	G-PPL ↓	BLEU ↑	Ent. ↑
AG News	PrefixLM-NL	**.593**	.612	**.019**	11.793	.861	10.293
	FUDGE-NL	.548	.914	.366	57.295	.677	10.140
Yelp Review	PrefixLM-NL	**.537**	.547	**.010**	13.831	.944	10.892
	FUDGE-NL	.046	.640	.551	19.335	.779	9.725

Table 4: Results for compositional setting. Test denote accuracy for unseen attribute combinations, Orig. denote accuracy in full-data setting, and Diff. shows the difference. PrefixLM-NL suffers little performance loss when generalizing to unseen attribute combinations, but FUDGE-NL's performance substantially degrades.

this baseline.

We observe that the simple PrefixLM-NL approach outperforms FUDGE-NL by a large margin in both zero-shot data and zero-shot + extra data setting. Moreover, as measured by both perplexity and BLEU, PrefixLM has higher generation quality as well. While there is still a large gap between the zero-shot and non-zero-shot label accuracy, **the extra data approach managed to *double* the zero-shot accuracy in both NL models, showing the generalization potential of the natural language interface**. Qualitatively (shown in Table 8 to Table 11), we found that in cases where the output has the wrong topic, there are still signs that the generation is guided by the command. For example, when we zero-shot on the *world* topic, we obtain text about sports with multiple country names.

Backbone unblock experiment Due to the nature of the zero-shot experiment, we also block examples of the zero-shot class from the finetuning data of the backbone language model P_b. As a comparison, we try finetuning P_b with full data, while still blocking the zero-shot class from prefix or classifier training, which mimics the setting where only unlabeled data is available.

Results are shown in Table 3 as the "-unb" models. We observe a large performance boost for the FUDGE-NL model. This shows that extra unsupervised data is also helpful for control generalization.

5.3 Generalization to Unseen Attribute Combinations

In this section, we design experiments to test whether the models can generalize to unseen *combinations* of attributes to test their compositional generalization abilities. We describe our setup for AGNews below, which is similar to Yelp.

Following Lake and Baroni (2018), for each split, we select one of the topic classes (e.g., sports) as the non-compositional class, and for all training samples with this class, we do not include length in attributes or commands (i.e., the model never see combinations of `sports` and any length attribute in training). Note that the combinations of length attributes and other topics classes are kept (e.g., the model still sees combinations of `business` and `short length`). At test time, we set the topic to be the non-compositional class and randomly sample

Dataset	Method	*Control Accuracy* Label ↑	Length ↑	Comp. ↑	*Text Quality* G-PPL ↓	BLEU ↑	*Diversity* Ent. ↑
AG News	PrefixLM	.907	.559	.574	11.369	.862	11.325
	PrefixLM-NL	**.933**	**.677**	**.612**	12.126	.866	11.371
	FUDGE	.963	.962	.880	12.055	.862	11.286
	FUDGE-Binary	**.980**	.958	**.918**	12.617	.864	11.276
	FUDGE-NL	.965	**.972**	.914	12.197	.865	11.368
Yelp Review	PrefixLM	**.644**	**.949**	**.590**	10.406	.942	11.800
	PrefixLM-NL	.637	.919	.547	10.361	.943	11.828
	FUDGE	.620	.794	.564	10.628	.940	11.217
	FUDGE-Binary	**.871**	.942	**.805**	10.402	.943	11.727
	FUDGE-NL	.775	**.972**	.640	10.410	.941	11.802

Table 5: Results for full-data setting. NL model performance is on par with their categorical counterparts.

the length attribute to control. We run experiments across all n possible compositionality splits and report the averaged result.

Results are shown in Table 4, with qualitative examples available in Table 12 to Table 15. We focus on the accuracy gap between this compositionality setting and the full-data setting. PrefixLM-NL has little trouble generalizing to unseen attribute combinations as indicated by the small gap. However, FUDGE-NL performed poorly on generalizing to unseen attribute combinations. Not only did FUDGE-NL's compositional accuracy drop by a large margin, but it also produced low-quality text.

5.4 Full-data Setting

In the full-data setting, we train the models on all data of the AG News or Yelp review dataset, with the purpose to test whether the new NL interface would degrade the model's performance. This is the regular setup for existing works on CTG except that we aim to control two attributes simultaneously instead of one. The results for the full-data setting are shown in Table 5, with qualitative examples available in Table 6 and Table 7 in the appendix.

Performance comparison between the NL and categorical interface We notice that the generated text quality and diversity between different models are similar in the full-data setting. While PrefixLM-NL and its categorical variant PrefixLM have similar control accuracy on both datasets, FUDGE-NL consistently outperforms the original FUDGE setup. In either case, the performance of the NL variant is on par with its original model, suggesting our NL interface does not degrade CTG performance in the full-data setting. Somewhat surprisingly, FUDGE-Binary outperforms FUDGE-NL and the original FUDGE model, especially on the Yelp dataset where the classification is more difficult. The reason could be that the task of the binary classification is less noisy than the multiclass classification, which leads to stronger control.

Performance across model families Across two datasets, FUDGE-based models outperform PrefixLM models, with the exception that FUDGE does not beat (but is comparable to) PrefixLM on Yelp. This is largely consistent with previous results that discriminator-based CTG approaches can achieve higher controllability than conditional LMs (Yang and Klein, 2021, *inter alia*). However, as we show in the previous sections, its performance is inferior in the settings requiring NL generalization.

6 Conclusion

In this work, we propose a natural language interface for CTG, where we craft a PCFG to embed categorical attributes into natural language commands. We propose variants of existing CTG models that take commands as input. We design tailored experiments to test the natural language CTG model's generalization capabilities. We show that our PCFG-based command generation approach is effective for handling unseen commands compared to fix-set templates. Additionally, our proposed NL models can effectively generalize to unseen attributes, an ability newly enabled by the NL interface. Finally, we find the simple PrefixLM approach shows robust generalization ability with the NL interface and outperforms FUDGE-based models, demonstrating significant modeling challenges and potentials with this new interface. We hope our work could motivate further research into this challenging interface for CTG.

Limitations

In this section, we point out several limitations restricted by the scope of our work. While the PCFG we create has decent diversity and is guaranteed to be accurate in embedding attributes, they are still rule-based and could not cover all the variations in natural language.

The natural language interface brings modelling challenges. The CTG model is now required to first extract salient information from the command sentence, while in the original categorical interface they are provided directly.

In this work, we have focused our experiments on PrefixLM and FUDGE. While these approaches are representative, there are still other relevant models we did not test. For instance, guiding the generation of an LM with a smaller LM (Liu et al., 2021), or prompt-based CTG approaches such as Yang et al. (2022). It would also be interesting to test how other models perform under the NL interface.

Finally, while we experiment with controlling more than a single attribute in a single CTG model, in principle a NL command could be more complex and fine-grained. For example, it is possible to describe detailed semantic or syntactic constraints in a command sentence, and we leave those to future work.

Ethics Statement

We acknowledge controlled text generation is potentially capable of generating harmful outputs such as producing offensive languages or hate speech. However, it is also shown in previous work that controlled text generation techniques can achieve text detoxification if used properly (Dathathri et al., 2020; Krause et al., 2021). When changing the control interface from a categorical setting to natural language commands, we are giving the user a larger freedom of input. Thus, extra care should be taken when deploying natural-language controlled text generation models to the general public to avoid malicious user inputs.

References

Tom Brown, Benjamin Mann, Nick Ryder, Melanie Subbiah, Jared D Kaplan, Prafulla Dhariwal, Arvind Neelakantan, Pranav Shyam, Girish Sastry, Amanda Askell, Sandhini Agarwal, Ariel Herbert-Voss, Gretchen Krueger, Tom Henighan, Rewon Child, Aditya Ramesh, Daniel Ziegler, Jeffrey Wu, Clemens Winter, Chris Hesse, Mark Chen, Eric Sigler, Mateusz Litwin, Scott Gray, Benjamin Chess, Jack Clark, Christopher Berner, Sam McCandlish, Alec Radford, Ilya Sutskever, and Dario Amodei. 2020. Language models are few-shot learners. In *Advances in Neural Information Processing Systems*, volume 33, pages 1877–1901. Curran Associates, Inc.

Jordan Clive, Kris Cao, and Marek Rei. 2022. Control prefixes for parameter-efficient text generation. In *Proceedings of the 2nd Workshop on Natural Language Generation, Evaluation, and Metrics (GEM)*, pages 363–382, Abu Dhabi, United Arab Emirates (Hybrid). Association for Computational Linguistics.

Sumanth Dathathri, Andrea Madotto, Janice Lan, Jane Hung, Eric Frank, Piero Molino, Jason Yosinski, and Rosanne Liu. 2020. Plug and play language models: A simple approach to controlled text generation. In *International Conference on Learning Representations*.

Jordan Hoffmann, Sebastian Borgeaud, Arthur Mensch, Elena Buchatskaya, Trevor Cai, Eliza Rutherford, Diego de Las Casas, Lisa Anne Hendricks, Johannes Welbl, Aidan Clark, Tom Hennigan, Eric Noland, Katie Millican, George van den Driessche, Bogdan Damoc, Aurelia Guy, Simon Osindero, Karen Simonyan, Erich Elsen, Jack W. Rae, Oriol Vinyals, and L. Sifre. 2022. Training compute-optimal large language models. *ArXiv*, abs/2203.15556.

Nitish Shirish Keskar, Bryan McCann, Lav R. Varshney, Caiming Xiong, and Richard Socher. 2019. CTRL: A conditional transformer language model for controllable generation. *CoRR*, abs/1909.05858.

Ben Krause, Akhilesh Deepak Gotmare, Bryan McCann, Nitish Shirish Keskar, Shafiq Joty, Richard Socher, and Nazneen Fatema Rajani. 2021. GeDi: Generative discriminator guided sequence generation. In *Findings of the Association for Computational Linguistics: EMNLP 2021*, pages 4929–4952, Punta Cana, Dominican Republic. Association for Computational Linguistics.

Brenden M. Lake and Marco Baroni. 2018. Generalization without systematicity: On the compositional skills of sequence-to-sequence recurrent networks. In *ICML*.

Xiang Lisa Li and Percy Liang. 2021. Prefix-tuning: Optimizing continuous prompts for generation. In *Proceedings of the 59th Annual Meeting of the Association for Computational Linguistics and the 11th International Joint Conference on Natural Language Processing (Volume 1: Long Papers)*, pages 4582–4597, Online. Association for Computational Linguistics.

Xiang Lisa Li, John Thickstun, Ishaan Gulrajani, Percy Liang, and Tatsunori Hashimoto. 2022. Diffusion-lm improves controllable text generation. *ArXiv*, abs/2205.14217.

Alisa Liu, Maarten Sap, Ximing Lu, Swabha Swayamdipta, Chandra Bhagavatula, Noah A. Smith, and Yejin Choi. 2021. DExperts: Decoding-time controlled text generation with experts and anti-experts. In *Proceedings of the 59th Annual Meeting of the Association for Computational Linguistics and the 11th International Joint Conference on Natural Language Processing (Volume 1: Long Papers)*, pages 6691–6706, Online. Association for Computational Linguistics.

Yuning Mao, Xiang Ren, Heng Ji, and Jiawei Han. 2020. Constrained abstractive summarization: Preserving factual consistency with constrained generation. *CoRR*, abs/2010.12723.

Swaroop Mishra, Daniel Khashabi, Chitta Baral, and Hannaneh Hajishirzi. 2022. Cross-task generalization via natural language crowdsourcing instructions. In *ACL*.

Rishabh Misra. 2022. News category dataset. *arXiv preprint arXiv:2209.11429*.

Rishabh Misra and Jigyasa Grover. 2021. *Sculpting Data for ML: The first act of Machine Learning*.

Long Ouyang, Jeff Wu, Xu Jiang, Diogo Almeida, Carroll L. Wainwright, Pamela Mishkin, Chong Zhang, Sandhini Agarwal, Katarina Slama, Alex Ray, John Schulman, Jacob Hilton, Fraser Kelton, Luke E. Miller, Maddie Simens, Amanda Askell, Peter Welinder, Paul Francis Christiano, Jan Leike, and Ryan J. Lowe. 2022. Training language models to follow instructions with human feedback. *ArXiv*, abs/2203.02155.

Damian Pascual, Beni Egressy, Clara Meister, Ryan Cotterell, and Roger Wattenhofer. 2021. A plug-and-play method for controlled text generation. In *Findings of the Association for Computational Linguistics: EMNLP 2021*, pages 3973–3997, Punta Cana, Dominican Republic. Association for Computational Linguistics.

Matt Post and David Vilar. 2018. Fast lexically constrained decoding with dynamic beam allocation for neural machine translation. In *Proceedings of the 2018 Conference of the North American Chapter of the Association for Computational Linguistics: Human Language Technologies, Volume 1 (Long Papers)*, pages 1314–1324, New Orleans, Louisiana. Association for Computational Linguistics.

Alec Radford, Jeff Wu, Rewon Child, David Luan, Dario Amodei, and Ilya Sutskever. 2019. Language models are unsupervised multitask learners.

Jack W. Rae, Sebastian Borgeaud, Trevor Cai, Katie Millican, Jordan Hoffmann, H. Francis Song, John Aslanides, Sarah Henderson, Roman Ring, Susannah Young, Eliza Rutherford, Tom Hennigan, Jacob Menick, Albin Cassirer, Richard Powell, George van den Driessche, Lisa Anne Hendricks, Maribeth Rauh, Po-Sen Huang, Amelia Glaese, Johannes Welbl, Sumanth Dathathri, Saffron Huang, Jonathan Uesato, John Mellor, Irina Higgins, Antonia Creswell, Nat McAleese, Amy Wu, Erich Elsen, Siddhant M. Jayakumar, Elena Buchatskaya, David Budden, Esme Sutherland, Karen Simonyan, Michela Paganini, Laurent Sifre, Lena Martens, Xiang Lorraine Li, Adhiguna Kuncoro, Aida Nematzadeh, Elena Gribovskaya, Domenic Donato, Angeliki Lazaridou, Arthur Mensch, Jean-Baptiste Lespiau, Maria Tsimpoukelli, Nikolai Grigorev, Doug Fritz, Thibault Sottiaux, Mantas Pajarskas, Toby Pohlen, Zhitao Gong, Daniel Toyama, Cyprien de Masson d'Autume, Yujia Li, Tayfun Terzi, Vladimir Mikulik, Igor Babuschkin, Aidan Clark, Diego de Las Casas, Aurelia Guy, Chris Jones, James Bradbury, Matthew Johnson, Blake A. Hechtman, Laura Weidinger, Iason Gabriel, William S. Isaac, Edward Lockhart, Simon Osindero, Laura Rimell, Chris Dyer, Oriol Vinyals, Kareem Ayoub, Jeff Stanway, Lorrayne Bennett, Demis Hassabis, Koray Kavukcuoglu, and Geoffrey Irving. 2021. Scaling language models: Methods, analysis & insights from training gopher. *CoRR*, abs/2112.11446.

Colin Raffel, Noam Shazeer, Adam Roberts, Katherine Lee, Sharan Narang, Michael Matena, Yanqi Zhou, Wei Li, and Peter J. Liu. 2020. Exploring the limits of transfer learning with a unified text-to-text transformer. *Journal of Machine Learning Research*, 21(140):1–67.

Emily Reif, Daphne Ippolito, Ann Yuan, Andy Coenen, Chris Callison-Burch, and Jason Wei. 2022. A recipe for arbitrary text style transfer with large language models. In *Proceedings of the 60th Annual Meeting of the Association for Computational Linguistics (Volume 2: Short Papers)*, pages 837–848, Dublin, Ireland. Association for Computational Linguistics.

Victor Sanh, Albert Webson, Colin Raffel, Stephen H. Bach, Lintang A. Sutawika, Zaid Alyafeai, Antoine Chaffin, Arnaud Stiegler, Teven Le Scao, Arun Raja, Manan Dey, M SAIFUL BARI, Canwen Xu, Urmish Thakker, Shanya Sharma, Eliza Szczechla, Taewoon Kim, Gunjan Chhablani, Nihal V. Nayak, Debajyoti Datta, Jonathan Chang, Mike Tian-Jian Jiang, Han Wang, Matteo Manica, Sheng Shen, Zheng Xin Yong, Harshit Pandey, Rachel Bawden, Thomas Wang, Trishala Neeraj, Jos Rozen, Abheesht Sharma, Andrea Santilli, Thibault Févry, Jason Alan Fries, Ryan Teehan, Stella Rose Biderman, Leo Gao, T. G. Owe Bers, Thomas Wolf, and Alexander M. Rush. 2021. Multitask prompted training enables zero-shot task generalization. *ArXiv*, abs/2110.08207.

Timo Schick and Hinrich Schütze. 2021. Few-shot text generation with natural language instructions. In *Proceedings of the 2021 Conference on Empirical Methods in Natural Language Processing*, pages 390–402, Online and Punta Cana, Dominican Republic. Association for Computational Linguistics.

Shaden Smith, Mostofa Ali Patwary, Brandon Norick, Patrick LeGresley, Samyam Rajbhandari, Jared Casper, Zhun Liu, Shrimai Prabhumoye, George Zerveas, Vijay Anand Korthikanti, Elton Zhang, Rewon Child, Reza Yazdani Aminabadi, Julie

Bernauer, Xia Song, Mohammad Shoeybi, Yuxiong He, Michael Houston, Saurabh Tiwary, and Bryan Catanzaro. 2022. Using deepspeed and megatron to train megatron-turing nlg 530b, a large-scale generative language model. *ArXiv*, abs/2201.11990.

Romal Thoppilan, Daniel De Freitas, Jamie Hall, Noam M. Shazeer, Apoorv Kulshreshtha, Heng-Tze Cheng, Alicia Jin, Taylor Bos, Leslie Baker, Yu Du, Yaguang Li, Hongrae Lee, Huaixiu Zheng, Amin Ghafouri, Marcelo Menegali, Yanping Huang, Maxim Krikun, Dmitry Lepikhin, James Qin, Dehao Chen, Yuanzhong Xu, Zhifeng Chen, Adam Roberts, Maarten Bosma, Yanqi Zhou, Chung-Ching Chang, I. A. Krivokon, Willard James Rusch, Marc Pickett, Kathleen S. Meier-Hellstern, Meredith Ringel Morris, Tulsee Doshi, Renelito Delos Santos, Toju Duke, Johnny Hartz Søraker, Ben Zevenbergen, Vinodkumar Prabhakaran, Mark Díaz, Ben Hutchinson, Kristen Olson, Alejandra Molina, Erin Hoffman-John, Josh Lee, Lora Aroyo, Ravindran Rajakumar, Alena Butryna, Matthew Lamm, V. O. Kuzmina, Joseph Fenton, Aaron Cohen, Rachel Bernstein, Ray Kurzweil, Blaise Aguera-Arcas, Claire Cui, Marian Croak, Ed Chi, and Quoc Le. 2022. Lamda: Language models for dialog applications. *ArXiv*, abs/2201.08239.

Jason Wei, Maarten Bosma, Vincent Zhao, Kelvin Guu, Adams Wei Yu, Brian Lester, Nan Du, Andrew M. Dai, and Quoc V Le. 2022. Finetuned language models are zero-shot learners. In *International Conference on Learning Representations*.

Thomas Wolf, Lysandre Debut, Victor Sanh, Julien Chaumond, Clement Delangue, Anthony Moi, Pierric Cistac, Tim Rault, Remi Louf, Morgan Funtowicz, Joe Davison, Sam Shleifer, Patrick von Platen, Clara Ma, Yacine Jernite, Julien Plu, Canwen Xu, Teven Le Scao, Sylvain Gugger, Mariama Drame, Quentin Lhoest, and Alexander Rush. 2020. Transformers: State-of-the-art natural language processing. In *Proceedings of the 2020 Conference on Empirical Methods in Natural Language Processing: System Demonstrations*, pages 38–45, Online. Association for Computational Linguistics.

Kevin Yang and Dan Klein. 2021. FUDGE: Controlled text generation with future discriminators. In *Proceedings of the 2021 Conference of the North American Chapter of the Association for Computational Linguistics: Human Language Technologies*, pages 3511–3535, Online. Association for Computational Linguistics.

Kexin Yang, Dayiheng Liu, Wenqiang Lei, Baosong Yang, Mingfeng Xue, Boxing Chen, and Jun Xie. 2022. Tailor: A prompt-based approach to attribute-based controlled text generation. *ArXiv*, abs/2204.13362.

Dian Yu, Zhou Yu, and Kenji Sagae. 2021. Attribute alignment: Controlling text generation from pre-trained language models. In *Findings of the Association for Computational Linguistics: EMNLP 2021*, pages 2251–2268, Punta Cana, Dominican Republic. Association for Computational Linguistics.

Yizhe Zhang, Michel Galley, Jianfeng Gao, Zhe Gan, Xiujun Li, Chris Brockett, and William B. Dolan. 2018. Generating informative and diverse conversational responses via adversarial information maximization. In *NeurIPS*.

A Dataset Details

A.1 Main datasets

Yelp Review This is a dataset of user-written reviews for Yelp. It is a text classification dataset where the 5-sentiment labels are inferred from 1 to 5 stars given to the review. For each star, there are 130,000 training examples and 10,000 testing examples. In total, there are 650,000 training examples and 50,000 testing examples. We limit text length to 200 after tokenization. After this preprocessing step, there are 450,773 training and 34,620 testing examples, for a total of 485,393 examples. We sample a validation set from the train set with about the same size as the test set, and create a final dataset with 415,901/34,872/34,620 train/val/test examples.

The label attribute for Yelp Review is constructed from the 5 sentiment labels, which we verbalize as {very negative, negative, neutral, positive, very positive}. For the length attribute, we create 5 length classes {very short, short, medium-length, long, very long} with cut-offs 43,72,104,144 so that number of training examples in each length class is balanced. The dataset is obtained from `https://huggingface.co/datasets/yelp_review_full`.

AG News This is a news topic classification dataset with 4 topics {world, sports, business, science/tech}. The news text used is the title and description. For each topic, there are 30,000 training examples and 1,900 testing examples, for a total of 120,000 training and 7,600 testing examples. We limit text length to 256 after tokenization. After this pre-processing step, there are 119,955 training and 7,599 testing examples, for a total of 127,554 examples. We sample a validation set from the train set with about 10% of the original train set size, and create a final dataset with 107,959/11,996/7,599 train/val/test examples.

We use the topic labels as the label attribute, while adding alternative names for the labels. For the length attribute, we limit text length to 256. Because the text length in AG News is concentrated in a narrow range, we create 3 length classes {short, medium, long} with cut-offs 43 and 56 to make the number of training examples in each class balanced. The dataset is obtained from `https://huggingface.co/datasets/ag_news`.

A.2 Extra data

News Category The News Category dataset contains about 200K news headlines and short descriptions between 2012 and 2018 obtained from HuffPost. The advantage of this dataset is that it has a wide variety of topics, thus making the corresponding template very diverse. The list of topics and corresponding article counts is shown in Listing 1. We remove topics that has overlap with AG News: `THE WORLDPOST`, `WORLDPOST`, `WORLD NEWS`, `SPORTS`, `BUSINESS`, `SCIENCE`, `TECH`. The dataset is obtained from `https://huggingface.co/datasets/Fraser/news-category-dataset`.

News Popularity The News Popularity in Multiple Social Media Platforms dataset is a dataset of social media sharing data of news articles about `economy`, `microsoft`, `obama`, and `palestine`. We use the concatenation of the `headline` and `short_description` fields as the news text. The size of this dataset is around 93K. The dataset is obtained from `https://huggingface.co/datasets/newspop`.

Inshort News The Inshort News dataset is a dataset of news with topics `sports`, `politics`, `entertainment`, `world`, `automobile`, and `science`. We remove the topics that has overlap with AG News: `sports`, `world`, `science`. The filtered dataset contains about 5K examples. The dataset is obtained from `https://www.kaggle.com/datasets/kishanyadav/inshort-news`.

B Experiment Details

B.1 Training

On AG News, we use an Adam optimizer with a learning rate 0.00005 and train 10 epochs to train the PrefixLM models as well as FUDGE discriminators. On Yelp Review, we use an Adam optimizer with a learning rate of 0.0001 and train 5 epochs. We conduct all experiments on a single NVIDIA Tesla V100 GPU with 32GB memory. The training time of each model depends on the particular setup, but is within 24 hours for all models. The number of trainable parameters for the PrefixLM, PrefixLM-NL, and FUDGE-NL model is approximately 120M.

The number of trainable parameters for FUDGE and FUDGE-Binary is approximately 120M for each of label or length attribute model, and approximately 240M in total.

Listing 1: News Category dataset topics with corresponding number of examples.

```
POLITICS: 32739
WELLNESS: 17827
ENTERTAINMENT: 16058
TRAVEL: 9887
STYLE & BEAUTY: 9649
PARENTING: 8677
HEALTHY LIVING: 6694
QUEER VOICES: 6314
FOOD & DRINK: 6226
BUSINESS: 5937
COMEDY: 5175
SPORTS: 4884
BLACK VOICES: 4528
HOME & LIVING: 4195
PARENTS: 3955
THE WORLDPOST: 3664
WEDDINGS: 3651
WOMEN: 3490
IMPACT: 3459
DIVORCE: 3426
CRIME: 3405
MEDIA: 2815
WEIRD NEWS: 2670
GREEN: 2622
WORLDPOST: 2579
RELIGION: 2556
STYLE: 2254
SCIENCE: 2178
WORLD NEWS: 2177
TASTE: 2096
TECH: 2082
MONEY: 1707
ARTS: 1509
FIFTY: 1401
GOOD NEWS: 1398
ARTS & CULTURE: 1339
ENVIRONMENT: 1323
COLLEGE: 1144
LATINO VOICES: 1129
CULTURE & ARTS: 1030
EDUCATION: 1004
```

The FUDGE models have an extra backbone language model that is kept frozen during discriminator training. The size of this backbone language model is approximately 120M. Backbones are first fine-tuned on corresponding classification datasets with a learning rate of 0.0001 for 5 epochs.

B.2 Hyperparameter choice under different settings

We find that the experimental results are not particularly sensitive to training hyperparameters such as learning rate and batch size. At testing, the FUDGE conditioning strength hyperparameter λ does have a notable effect on control accuracy. We report results with λ that gives the highest control accuracy while maintaining text quality. For the FUDGE model family (FUDGE, FUDGE-Binary, FUDGE-NL), we set $\lambda = 14$ on the full-data and low-resource experiments, and $\lambda = 6$ on zero-shot experiments. On compositionality experiments, we set $\lambda = 6$ for AG News and $\lambda = 4$ for Yelp Review. We set a smaller λ for zero-shot and compositionality settings because a larger λ in these cases leads to a significant increase in repetition. Following FUDGE's original setup, we consider only the top 200 possible output tokens when modifying the LM logits for computational efficiency.

C Command PCFG Details

The full template for the AG News and Yelp Review datasets are available in Listing 2 and Listing 3. We briefly explain important elements of the custom PCFG syntax below:

- We first randomly sample a template in the `<templates>` section. These are templates with attribute slots which will be filled later. Besides attribute slots, there are other non-terminals in the template that corresponds to sentence segments. Rules for these elements are written in the `<variables>` sections.
- Rules in the `<variables>` sections are compressed PCFG where rules with the same LHS are grouped together in a single line. They constitute the verbalization of domain names, attribute names, as well as a variety of sentence segments to increase the diversity of the PCFG.
- To verbalize the label attribute, the `<label>` section contains the mapping from categorical class indices to verbalized class names. Since the mapping could be one-to-many, different verbalizations of the same attribute class is separated by a comma.
- To verbalize the length attribute, the `<length>` section contains length cut-off values with the corresponding verbalized length level names, having similar syntax with the `<label>` section. An example with tokenized length l will be treated as the longest length level such that the corresponding cut-off does not exceed l.

D Qualitative Examples

We show qualitative examples for different experimental settings in Table 6 to Table 15.

Listing 2: PCFG template for AG News

```
<variables>
[TEXT-CLASS]   AG news, AG news
[TEXT-FORM]    [TEXT-CLASS], [TEXT-CLASS], [TEXT-CLASS] article, piece of [TEXT-CLASS], [TEXT-CLASS]
    report, [TEXT-CLASS] item, AG newspaper article
[HEAD-FORM]    give me, generate, tell me about, show, show me, fetch me, output, I need, I want,
    need, I request, write
[TOPIC-NOUN]   topic, topic, theme, focus
[TOPIC-NOUNED] topic, topic, themed, focused, related
[TOPIC-PREP]   about, related to, concerning, regarding, pertinent to
[TOPIC-UPDATEWORD]    updated, informed
[TOPIC-SEG]    [TOPIC-PREP] [TOPIC], [TOPIC-PREP] [TOPIC], that is [TOPIC-PREP] [TOPIC], that is [
    TOPIC-PREP] [TOPIC], that can keep me [TOPIC-UPDATEWORD] with [TOPIC]
[TOPIC-BESEG]  [TOPIC-PREP] [TOPIC], [TOPIC-PREP] [TOPIC], [TOPIC-PREP] [TOPIC], can keep me [TOPIC-
    UPDATEWORD] with [TOPIC]
[PLS]  please, ,
[COMMA-PLS]    / please, , # use '/' as comma (escaped)
[BEFORE-BE]    let it, make sure to, I want it to

<length>
43      short, concise, very short, pretty short, extremely short, extra short
56      medium-length, normal-length
256     long, lengthy, very long, pretty long, extremely long, extra long

<label> [TOPIC]
0       the world, the world, the globe, international matters
1       sports, sports, sporting events
2       business, business, commerce
3       science, science, technology, technology, tech

<templates>
# label and length
[HEAD-FORM] a [LENGTH] [TEXT-FORM] [TOPIC-SEG] [COMMA-PLS] .
[PLS] [HEAD-FORM] a [TEXT-FORM] . [BEFORE-BE] be [LENGTH] and [TOPIC-BESEG] .
[PLS] [HEAD-FORM] a [TEXT-FORM] [TOPIC-SEG], and I need it to be [LENGTH] .
[HEAD-FORM] a [TEXT-FORM] [TOPIC-SEG] , and [BEFORE-BE] be [LENGTH] [COMMA-PLS] .
[HEAD-FORM] a [TEXT-FORM] . I want the [TOPIC-NOUN] to be [TOPIC], and length to be [LENGTH] .
[HEAD-FORM] a [TEXT-FORM] . I want the length to be [LENGTH], and [TOPIC-NOUN] to be [TOPIC] .
[HEAD-FORM] a [TEXT-FORM] . [BEFORE-BE] be not only [LENGTH] but also have a [TOPIC-NOUN] on [TOPIC]
    .
# label only
[HEAD-FORM] a [TOPIC] [TOPIC-NOUNED] [TEXT-FORM] [COMMA-PLS] .
[PLS] [HEAD-FORM] a [TOPIC] [TOPIC-NOUNED] [TEXT-FORM] .
[HEAD-FORM] a [TEXT-FORM] [TOPIC-SEG] [COMMA-PLS] .
[PLS] [HEAD-FORM] a [TEXT-FORM] [TOPIC-SEG] .
[PLS] [HEAD-FORM] a [TEXT-FORM] . Let it have a [TOPIC] [TOPIC-NOUN] .
[HEAD-FORM] a [TEXT-FORM] . Let it have a [TOPIC] [TOPIC-NOUN] [COMMA-PLS] .
[HEAD-FORM] a [TEXT-FORM] . I want the [TOPIC-NOUN] to be [TOPIC] .
# length only
[HEAD-FORM] a [LENGTH] [TEXT-FORM] [COMMA-PLS] .
[PLS] [HEAD-FORM] a [TEXT-FORM] . [BEFORE-BE] be [LENGTH] .
[PLS] [HEAD-FORM] a [TEXT-FORM] , and I need it to be [LENGTH] .
[HEAD-FORM] a [TEXT-FORM] , and [BEFORE-BE] be [LENGTH] [COMMA-PLS] .
[PLS] [HEAD-FORM] a [TEXT-FORM] , and [BEFORE-BE] be [LENGTH] .
[HEAD-FORM] a [TEXT-FORM]. I want the length to be [LENGTH] .
[HEAD-FORM] a [TEXT-FORM]. I want the length to be [LENGTH] [COMMA-PLS] .
```

Listing 3: PCFG template for Yelp Review

```
<variables>
[TEXT-CLASS]   yelp review, yelp review, yelp comment
[TEXT-FORM]    [TEXT-CLASS], [TEXT-CLASS], [TEXT-CLASS] article, [TEXT-CLASS] passage, [TEXT-CLASS]
    paragraph, [TEXT-CLASS] piece, piece of [TEXT-CLASS], yelp review chapter, [TEXT-CLASS] item
[HEAD-FORM]    give me, generate, tell me about, show, show me, fetch me, output, I need, I want,
    need, I request, write
[SENT-NOUN]    tone, sentiment, attitude, mood
[SENT-PREP]    with, with, with, that has, / which has, of
[SENT-SEG]     [SENT-PREP] a [SENT] [SENT-NOUN]
[PLS]  please, ,
[COMMA-PLS]    / please, , # use '/' as comma (escaped)
[BEFORE-BE]    let it, make sure to, I want it to

<length>
43      very short, pretty short, extremely short, extra short
72      short, concise
104     medium-length, normal-length
144     long, lengthy
200     very long, pretty long, extremely long, extra long

<label> [SENT]
0       very negative, terrible, very bad, extremely negative
1       negative, bad
2       neutral, unopinionated
3       positive, good, promising
4       very positive, very good, excellent, splendid, extremely positive

<templates>
# label and length
[HEAD-FORM] a [LENGTH] [TEXT-FORM] [SENT-SEG] [COMMA-PLS] .
[PLS] [HEAD-FORM] a [TEXT-FORM] . [BEFORE-BE] be [LENGTH] and having a [SENT] [SENT-NOUN] .
[PLS] [HEAD-FORM] a [TEXT-FORM] [SENT-SEG], and I need it to be [LENGTH] .
[HEAD-FORM] a [TEXT-FORM] [SENT-SEG] , and [BEFORE-BE] be [LENGTH] [COMMA-PLS] .
[HEAD-FORM] a [TEXT-FORM] . I want the [SENT-NOUN] to be [SENT], and length to be [LENGTH] .
[HEAD-FORM] a [TEXT-FORM] . I want the length to be [LENGTH], and [SENT-NOUN] to be [SENT] .
[HEAD-FORM] a [TEXT-FORM] . [BEFORE-BE] be not only [LENGTH] but also have a [SENT] [SENT-NOUN] .
# label only
[HEAD-FORM] a [SENT] [SENT-NOUN] [TEXT-FORM] [COMMA-PLS] .
[PLS] [HEAD-FORM] a [SENT] [SENT-NOUN] [TEXT-FORM] .
[HEAD-FORM] a [TEXT-FORM] [SENT-SEG] [COMMA-PLS] .
[PLS] [HEAD-FORM] a [TEXT-FORM] [SENT-SEG] .
[PLS] [HEAD-FORM] a [TEXT-FORM] . Let it have a [SENT] [SENT-NOUN] .
[HEAD-FORM] a [TEXT-FORM] . Let it have a [SENT] [SENT-NOUN] [COMMA-PLS] .
[HEAD-FORM] a [TEXT-FORM] . I want the [SENT-NOUN] to be [SENT] .
# length only
[HEAD-FORM] a [LENGTH] [TEXT-FORM] [COMMA-PLS] .
[PLS] [HEAD-FORM] a [TEXT-FORM] . [BEFORE-BE] be [LENGTH] .
[PLS] [HEAD-FORM] a [TEXT-FORM] , and I need it to be [LENGTH] .
[HEAD-FORM] a [TEXT-FORM] , and [BEFORE-BE] be [LENGTH] [COMMA-PLS] .
[PLS] [HEAD-FORM] a [TEXT-FORM] , and [BEFORE-BE] be [LENGTH] .
[HEAD-FORM] a [TEXT-FORM]. I want the length to be [LENGTH] .
[HEAD-FORM] a [TEXT-FORM]. I want the length to be [LENGTH] [COMMA-PLS] .
```

PrefixLM-NL: Show me an AG news. I want the length to be concise, and topic to be the world. Two Indonesian women hostages released The two Indonesian women hostages have been released, two days before their scheduled arrival in the US under the terms of a new US policy in Southeast Asia.
FUDGE-NL: Generate an AG news article. Make sure to be not only pretty long but also have a focus on sporting events. No. 18 Utah Defeats Oregon, 71-60 (AP) AP - Cedric Benson scored 29 points, Jeri Dean added 15 and 18 points, and No. 18 Utah defeated Oregon 71-60 on Saturday night in an exhibition game that featured a balanced offense and a balanced defense.
PrefixLM: [WORLD][SHORT] Two Indonesian women hostages released Indonesia #39;s Foreign Ministry said Wednesday two female Indonesian women hostages were released Tuesday at dawn from an Al-Arabiya TV station, a day after it broadcast a videotape of their captivity.
FUDGE: [TECH][LONG] Macromedia #39;s #39;Blog #39; to Make New Web Sites Macromedia is setting out to make Web site-hosting Web sites, starting with blog, a key part of its strategy for making new sites more relevant and useful.
FUDGE-Binary: [BUSINESS][MEDIUM-LEN] Update 2: Oil Prices Drop Below \$52 a Barrel Despite Hurricane Oil futures prices dropped below \$52 on Friday, even though Hurricane Ivan, which was projected to hit the Gulf Coast late last week, was nonetheless expected to remain a drag on global oil supplies

Table 6: AG News generation in full-data setting. All models can provide sensible generations with descent quality.

PrefixLM-NL: Show me a yelp review passage. I want the length to be pretty short, and tone to be very negative. This place is a total joke. I called to place an order for delivery tonight and received a message with no answer.
FUDGE-NL: Generate a yelp review passage. Let it be long and having an extremely positive attitude. OMG I don't know where i got my hair cut. We started with the salon manager. I have to say I am a little disappointed on this. The place is nice, staff nice and the haircut was good. My stylist was very knowledgable. She did an excellent job with the color and cut. I was so impressed. I am going back here for my next cut. The staff is nice and very helpful. I will give it one more try before I leave. The price was very reasonable for it being in such a nice shopping center. I was surprised at the quality.
PrefixLM: [NEUTRAL][MEDIUM-LEN] Great for a quick meal but not really great. They do have a very good salad bar and the pizza is pretty good as well. If they had more seating and less of those annoying flies, I might have given them 4 stars. I am looking forward to trying more of their pizzas but they need more seating. I think I'll still go back, but not on a regular basis.
FUDGE: [NEGATIVE][SHORT] Disorganized and unorganized. No water in the shower and no soap dispenser in the bathroom. Very noisy when you come in during lunch hour. Very disappointed and will not go back.
FUDGE-Binary: [POSITIVE][SHORT] Great location! The pizza's are huge and the crust was thin. We had the sausage, pepperoni and sausage pizza and sausage was delicious. If you're looking for a good pie to eat late night, this is definitely the spot.

Table 7: Yelp Review generation in full-data setting.

Show me an AG news that is about business. China Stocks Set to Open Lower (AP) AP - China's consumer and investment markets are set to open relatively slackened this week due in part to lower oil prices, but stocks were slightly higher Monday #151; despite falling in recent weeks on the strength of the dollar and other key economic indicators.
Give me an AG news item that can keep me updated with international matters, please. China #39;s economy booming, but challenges persist China #39;s economy is booming and it is struggling to meet growing economic challenges, but it faces tough foreign competition quot;from within its own ranks quot;, China #39;s top official said Sunday.
Show a sports related AG news report. Update 1: Tennis: Masters Cup Semi Draws Three Aussies Aussies were forced to face three Australian players they will face in next month #39;s semi-finals, a spokesman said Tuesday.
Show an AG newspaper article. I want the topic to be technology. Google #39;s initial public offering The initial public offering of the Internet search engine is expected to be much higher than Google Inc #39;s initial public offering.

Table 8: Zero-shot generation of the PrefixLM-NL model. Zero-shot class generation is shown. Interestingly, the model seems to be generating overlapping topics between zero-shot and non-zero-shot classes, e.g., the generated business news talks about China's stock market, which the model probably learned from the world topic that is not blocked.

Give me a technology topic AG news. Microsoft to launch Xbox One console in India Microsoft is set to announce an Xbox One console in India on December 1. According to ET Now, the company will announce the launch on December 10. Microsoft announced the console on December 8. Its rival PlayStation 4 is also coming soon.
Show me an AG news item. Let it have a world topic, please. India plans to launch second space station A second crew to the International Space Station will start service next year as India completes a five-year mission to the moon and comes within one day of meeting the International Space Station crew.
Give me a sporting events themed AG news, please. Tennis: Oleg Tsunoda, Serena Williams Open in London (Reuters) Reuters - Two days before the third consecutive U.S. Open, tennis's biggest event, Nov. 8, will be staged on a hilltop overlooking London's
I request a commerce related AG news, please. U.S. Pounds Oil, Prices Surge in Asia (AP) AP - The United States pounds oil as the world's largest petroleum consumer enters a pivotal year in growth, pushing prices for gasoline and heating oil to new lows in Asia and boosting the U.S. energy industry.

Table 9: Zero-shot generation of the PrefixLM-NL model trained with extra data. Zero-shot class generation is shown. In the tech generation, the Microsoft topic is from one of the extra datasets.

Write an AG news item. I want the topic to be the globe. Sports industry executives to be legal firms CEO's offices on businesses, companies, companies not business clients, companies executives, business travelers.
Give me a sporting events related AG news. Fierce Fighting Roars Past a Home on the Wild Atlantic OAST LONDON - A series of strong Atlantic storms ripped through a British home on Tuesday, unleashing heavy rains, fierce winds and ferocious waves that washed away scores
Please generate a piece of AG news that is regarding commerce. Oracle Wins Contingency Bid For PeopleSoft (AP) AP - Oracle Corp.'s Oracle Corp. has won its contract for PeopleSoft Inc.'s business software division, Oracle Corp. said Friday.
Show an AG newspaper article. Let it have a technology theme, please. UN envoy urges Sudan resolution Sudanese authorities in Africa's top government urged Sudan to adopt a UN resolution on humanitarian crises in Africa in an effort to end fighting in the war-torn country.

Table 10: Zero-shot generation of the FUDGE-NL model. Zero-shot class generation is shown. In many cases the model ignores the command, and goes on to generate text related to seen topics.

Please generate a piece of AG news that is regarding the world. Paisley, Sharman hold India to 4 wickets for second innings (AFP) AFP - Shane Warne's unbeaten 141 against South Africa at the WACA was bowled out in the second and final innings as Australia held India to four wickets for a total of 141.
Generate an AG news. Let it have a sports theme. Beltre Leads Red Sox Past Yankees 7-4 (AP) AP - Mark Buehrle pitched seven shutout innings of two-hit ball, and Boston clinched its eighth straight AL East crown, 7-4 over the New York Yankees on Saturday.
Give me a commerce related AG news. Yahoo! Earnings Fall in First Quarter Yahoo! Inc.'s (YHOO.O: Quote, Profile, Research) quarterly earnings fell sharply, as the world #39;s largest Internet advertising and search company reported narrower
Please show me an AG news. Let it have a technology focus. Tech giants IBM profits rise tech giants IBM and Hewlett-Packard reported big gains yesterday as their technology businesses grew more profitable in August. Shares of Hewlett-Packard jumped as much as 2.

Table 11: Zero-shot generation of the FUDGE-NL model trained with extra data. Zero-shot class generation is shown. Signs of the model being influenced by the command is evident from time to time, e.g., the world topic generation, although is actually sports-topic, contains many country names.

Example
Generate an AG news. Make sure to be long and about international matters. US Forces Storm School in Mosul, 40 Dead MOSUL, Iraq (Reuters) - U.S. tanks, aircraft and artillery rumbled through a Mosul rebel-held school on Saturday, 40 days after a suicide car bomb blast killed at least 39 people outside a police academy in a town near Baghdad.
Need an AG news. I want it to be extra short and can keep me updated with sports. Soccer: England win draw at Moldova England won their opening game against Moldova after defeating Poland 1-0 in a friendly draw at Frno, the Football Association said Thursday.
I want an AG news report. I want it to be extremely short and can keep me informed with business. Oil Prices Surge to Record Highs on Ivan Crushing $52 Oil prices jumped to multi-week highs yesterday on fears that Hurricane Ivan would hit the Southeast US Gulf Coast early next week.
Give me an extra long AG news article related to science. Microsoft to Release Longhorn as Open Beta Microsoft announced it would release Longhorn in 2006, with features such as a new file system, new system management, and support for 64-bit extensions in addition to standard 64-bit capabilities.

Table 12: Compositional generation of the PrefixLM-NL model on AG News. Non-compositional class generation is shown. The model generate fluent, on topic text without much performance degradation from full-data setup.

Example
Generate an AG news article. I want the focus to be international matters, and length to be pretty short. Italy arrests Italian businessman Italy yesterday arrested a businessman and a German national working for a major French and British industrial group and two others for connections to a major European political party scandal in Italy two years ago.
Give me a piece of AG news. I want the focus to be sporting events, and length to be long. NFL Wrap: Brees, Brees Lead the Giants to the Playoffs Jamal Lewis ran for 147 yards and two touchdowns Saturday night to lead the Giants to playoff berth games Sunday at Philadelphia and Sunday at Atlanta and clinch Sunday #39;s NFC title <b>;...</b>
Need an AG news article. Make sure to be not only medium-length but also have a focus on commerce. Oil prices rebound sharply from record highs <b&gt...</b&gt VIYUYYashko men took no charge as they trawl past what lookto evidence indicate Since arriving earlier earlier early today many children wandered past makeshift shelters and makeshift stalls. At least two dozen workers - many of them women - entered the battered warehouse, but as...
Generate an AG news article. I want the focus to be technology, and length to be pretty short. Computer security chief steps down Computer security chief William Donaldson steps down today, the government said today. Mr Donaldson was leaving his department in his final days of the career.

Table 13: Compositional generation of the FUDGE-NL model on AG News. Non-compositional class generation is shown. The text quality is notably lower than both PrefixLM's compositional generations (Table 12) as well as FUDGE-NL's generation in full-data setting (Table 6).

Write an extremely short yelp review passage of a very negative tone. This place is a joke!!!!!! I called to place an order for delivery tonight and they quoted me $50! And the food wasn't even good at all!!!
Write an extremely short yelp review passage of a negative tone. This place is a total joke. I wish I had just gone to another place before coming here. The food was ok (but not really worth wasting $40 on a meal) The service suck!!!
Generate a yelp review. Let it be concise and having an unopinionated attitude. Not bad, not great (except for the wait for service and for the food being cold). However, the place is really small and is always crowded. The food is good (although a bit pricey) and the ambiance is relaxing. But again not great.\nThe servers are nice and accommodating.
I need a yelp review item. I want the length to be extra short, and tone to be promising Very happy with this hotel! Good deals, clean room and great service. The staff was very helpful. Will stay here again.
I need a yelp review passage. I want the mood to be very good, and length to be very long I am a HUGE fan of this place! This is the type of place that I go to when I'm in the area! The food is fantastic! I have always had great service here. I usually go at dinner time on weekends but have yet to be disappointed. I love their wings! They are not your average wings. They come covered with a wonderful sauce and just a hint of garlic! They are always hot. I am a big guy though, so I tend to eat wings on the go. \n\nTheir pizza is amazing as well. I love that you can order a large size with no toppings, which is very convenient for me. I also love their ranch dressing, which is amazing as well. \n\nI always look forward to coming back to this place for some wings!

Table 14: Compositional generation of the PrefixLM-NL model on Yelp Review. Non-compositional class generation is shown. Similar to scenario in AG News (Table 12), the model can generalize to unseen attributes combinations without much performance degradations.

Show a yelp review. Let it be not only lengthy but also have an extremely negative tone. Love this place. Great coffee and delicious sandwiches, wraps, and salads. The service is wonderful and everyone is helpful and friendly.
Write a yelp comment that has a bad sentiment, and make sure to be short. I really wanted to love this place. I love the concept. The food. Unfortunately, I was not impressed.
I need a yelp review paragraph. Make sure to be not only short but also have a neutral attitude. It was ok. Great tasting bread with your sandwiches and cookies on your cookie crust to make it look like a fancy bakery with your cookies.... No wow... Really!?!?!?..... Never ever ever ever ever when ever I have been. Kind it kinda of defeats thinking about this at all. Service goes off without any notice.
I request a yelp review piece. I want the length to be extra long, and tone to be positive. So much for the good reviews. My sister-in-law was going to give this place a try, but it seems a little overrated.\n\nI came for lunch with her, and ordered a half salad, soup, and sandwich combo. My salad came with the soup, but only half of it was actually soup! The soup was alright, but it came with a small piece of lettuce on top. The sandwich was decent.\n\nThe sandwich was nothing spectacular. I've had better for half the price!
I want a piece of yelp comment that has a very good mood, and make sure to be pretty long. Always a great place. Food & service always great & prices are reasonable especially for the quality & quantity they give you. Food comes out hot. My kids eat there every time & are always happy with their meals. Prices have always been very reasonable for the quality & quantity they give you. Owner is the man, & he is the reason I come back to this place, & I hope he is getting his act together soon! Give it a try & please try them out for yourself!! You will leave happy & full!! :) Thanks Chef! Keep hustling for quality & quality food! Happy eating! Thanks Chef :) :)) :) Enjoy! :-) :) See ya! :) ;) :) :) :) :) :) :) ;) ;)

Table 15: Compositional generation of the FUDGE-NL model on Yelp Review. Non-compositional class generation is shown. Text quality is notably low, with the model generates repetitive phrases or emoji from time to time.

True Detective: A Deep Abductive Reasoning Benchmark Undoable for GPT-3 and Challenging for GPT-4

Maksym Del and **Mark Fishel**
Institute of Computer Science
University of Tartu, Estonia
{maksym,mark}@tartunlp.ai

Abstract

Large language models (LLMs) have demonstrated solid zero-shot reasoning capabilities, which is reflected in their performance on the current test tasks. This calls for a more challenging benchmark requiring highly advanced reasoning ability to be solved. In this paper, we introduce such a benchmark, consisting of 191 long-form (1200 words on average) mystery narratives constructed as detective puzzles. Puzzles are sourced from the "5 Minute Mystery" platform and include a multiple-choice question for evaluation. Only 47% of humans solve a puzzle successfully on average, while the best human solvers achieve over 80% success rate. We show that GPT-3 models barely outperform random on this benchmark (with 28% accuracy) while state-of-the-art GPT-4 solves only 38% of puzzles. This indicates that there is still a significant gap in the deep reasoning abilities of LLMs and humans and highlights the need for further research in this area. Our work introduces a challenging benchmark for future studies on reasoning in language models and contributes to a better understanding of the limits of LLMs' abilities.[1]

1 Introduction

Large language models (LLMs) have gained significant attention in recent years due to their impressive performance on a wide range of natural language processing tasks, including reasoning tasks (Srivastava et al., 2022; Wei et al., 2022). This calls for new, genuinely challenging benchmarks requiring LLMs to possess truly advanced reasoning capabilities to be solved.

Abductive reasoning is a type of inference aiming at finding the minimal and most justified explanation for the set of phenomena or observations. Previous benchmarks on this topic, such as Mostafazadeh et al. (2016), consisted of short and straightforward common-sense observations and were solved by GPT models (Radford and Narasimhan, 2018). However, the canonical example of abductive reasoning, a demanding process of a detective finding the best solution to a complex crime based on the clues and observations, was not explored as a foundation for the LLM benchmark in the literature.

Motivated by the need for a new reasoning benchmark and inspired by the complexities and particularities of a detective enterprise, we present a novel abductive reasoning benchmark consisting of 191 detective puzzles/mysteries. Mysteries are sourced from the "5 Minute Mystery" platform, where professional and aspiring authors wrote them. A puzzle is structured as a >1000 words story with 4-5 answer options. Over the last 15 years, puzzles were attempted by humans around 2000 times each with an average solve rate of 47% (only the first try for each human for each puzzle counts). However, top human solvers (top 10) achieve a success rate of over 80% solving more than 154 of 192 puzzles correctly.

Moreover, additional modifications such as chain-of-thought (CoT) prompting Wei et al. (2022); Kojima et al. (2022) that are meant to invoke emergent reasoning abilities in LLMs do not help for GPT-3.

In this study, we also assess the performance of the current state-of-the-art GPT-3 and GPT-4 models on our newly proposed dataset. We show that these models, even equipped with the Chain of Thought prompts (Wei et al., 2022; Kojima et al., 2022), are getting an accuracy rate of only 28%, barely better than random guessing (GPT-3.5), or scoring 38% (GPT-4), which is halfway between random guessing and average human baseline, and far behind top human solvers with their 80% solve rate. These results reveal a significant gap in the reasoning abilities of GPT models and humans.

In our ablation study, we also supply models

[1] https://github.com/TartuNLP/true-detective

*Proceedings of the The 12th Joint Conference on Lexical and Computational Semantics (*SEM 2023)*, pages 314–322
July 13-14, 2023 ©2023 Association for Computational Linguistics

with golden CoTs. Golden CoTs are narratives that represent the reasoning behind the correct answer for each story (written by the mystery authors). When we attach golden CoTs to the input prompt, the best-performing GPT-3.5 model only achieves a solve rate of 63%. This indicates LLMs' difficulty making even trivial inferences from the complex long-form story. GPT-4 models, however, get as good as the best human solvers when presented with our chain of thoughts (even though humans do not have access to the golden CoTs).

Our contributions in this paper are twofold: (1) a new challenging benchmark for evaluating LLMs for advanced abductive reasoning; (2) a showcase of GPT-3.5 and GPT-4 models failing to perform reasonably.

2 Related Work

Mostafazadeh et al. (2016) introduced the ROCStories benchmark: narrative cloze test, which requires choosing the correct ending of the four-sentence story. Bhagavatula et al. (2020) expand on this dataset, requiring finding plausible explanations for narrative gaps instead of focusing on the sequence of events. Our benchmark contains stories of around 70 sentences that require solving the detective mystery (as opposed to simply figuring out commonsense story continuation), which is a much harder inference.

Natural language inference (NLI) is another related domain, but NLI tasks usually include much simpler and smaller inferences (Bowman et al., 2015; Williams et al., 2018). Zellers et al. (2018) introduced the SWAG dataset that offers a large-scale natural language inference challenge where grounded knowledge is required to make an inference. This shares some commonality with our dataset, as some mysteries might require a share of grounded knowledge about the real world. Unlike Zellers et al. (2018), we only offer a test set, but our stories are broader and more involved. On the other hand, Grimm and Cimiano (2021) introduced a question-answering benchmark that requires deeper text understanding based on the football match commentaries. Their questions range from counting the number of goals to identifying the game-winner. While answers to many of these questions are not explicitly provided in the football commentary, our mysteries require solving the whole case specifically designed to be challenging even for humans.

Lastly, Wei et al. (2022) find that while eliciting "Chain of Thought" reasoning helps with stronger models, it can hurt when solving harder tasks with smaller models. We observe this behavior when comparing GPT-3.5 and GPT-4 on our benchmark.

3 Benchmark

3.1 5 Minute Mystery Platform

The data for this AI research was obtained from the "5 Minute Mystery"[2] online platform. This website is an online platform that has functioned for over ten years and allows users to submit and solve mysteries of varying difficulty (see Appendix A for an example mystery).

Based on the website author guidelines, the mysteries on the website collection are intended for readers at the sixth to eighth-grade reading level and have a recommended length of around 1200 words. To facilitate comprehension and challenge the reader, each mystery includes around four suspects and one guilty suspect. Of the 191 mysteries, the overwhelming majority ask the reader to identify the guilty suspect, with only occasional ones asking for the geographic location or the missing person. The aim is for the reader to demonstrate their abductive reasoning abilities by solving the mystery and identifying the correct solution (e.g., the murderer). Typically, one character in the story is faced with the key puzzle, and at the end of the mystery, they exclaim something like: "I figured out who is guilty!" At this point, the reader must choose the correct answer from a list of options.

In addition, mystery writers provided an explanation for the answer: a full solution (golden CoT) that elicits reasoning that leads to the correct answer. The reasoning is presented on behalf of one of the story characters (the one who says, "I know who did it" at the end of the story).

The website also has a unique scoring system that rewards users for correctly solving mysteries, encouraging participation and engagement. In addition to providing entertainment, the website can also be used in an educational setting to help students develop their comprehension and critical thinking skills.

3.2 Benchmark Dataset

The mysteries in this study were obtained from the "5 Minute Mystery" (5MM) platform. We have included links to the original mysteries and to the

[2]https://www.5minutemystery.com/

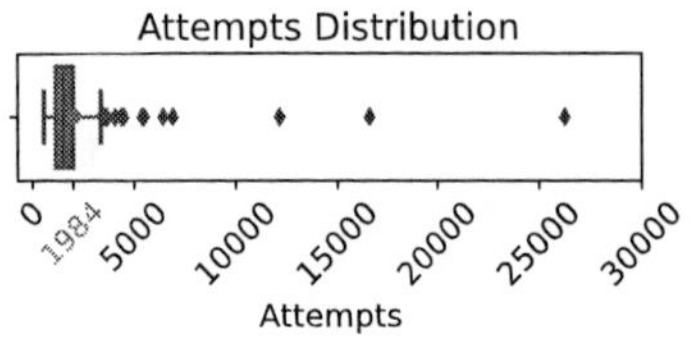

Figure 1: Distribution of the number of attempts for each mystery. The red dot indicates that almost 2000 people attempted mysteries on average. This suggests that our dataset provides a robust estimate of human performance and is representative of human performance on the mysteries.

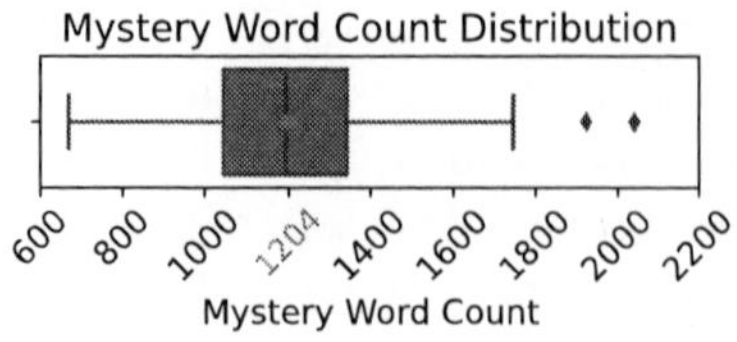

Figure 3: Number of words in each mystery in the dataset. Mysteries range from 600 to around 2000 words with most of them being around 1204 words (red dot). This suggests that not only does the task require drawing highly nontrivial conclusions from the text but also doing so over relatively large texts.

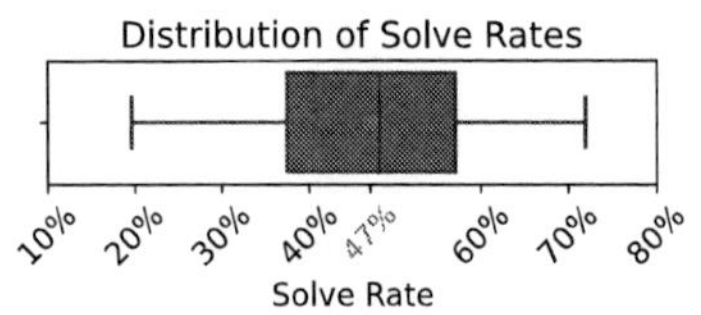

Figure 2: Average human solve rate for each mystery in the dataset. The performance for most puzzles is around 40-60%. The red dot indicates the average solve rate. This figure reveals that the majority of puzzles are challenging for human solvers, providing a good benchmark for evaluating the performance of AI models on these types of tasks.

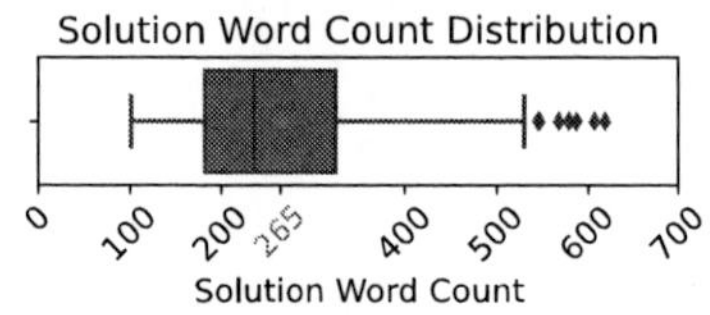

Figure 4: Number of words in the solution explanations for each mystery. The red dot indicates the average number of words per explanation. This figure reveals that the average solution length is 265 words, and the longest solutions are around 600 words. Solutions (golden CoTs) are useful for a setup testing the ability of LLMs to do a trivial final answer inference over the given CoT.

author pages in the study, and we want to emphasize that all copyrights remain with the original authors and the 5MM team. See the authors list in the Appendix B section.

Dataset size and the number of answers. The dataset used in this study consists of 191 puzzles, including 160 puzzles with four answer options, 30 puzzles with five answer options, and one puzzle with three answer options.

Attempts. The "5 Minute Mystery" platform has been in operation for approximately 14 years and has attracted thousands of users, with over 20,000 registered by 2013. These users have made numerous attempts at each mystery, but only their first attempt is counted towards the platform's statistics. As shown in Figure 1, the average number of attempts per mystery is 1984, with only a few puzzles being significantly more or less popular.

With such a large sample size, the resulting human performance estimate is highly robust and reliable as a benchmark.

Human Solve Rate. In the 5MM platform, human solvers have achieved moderate success. The average solve rate is 47%, significantly higher than random guessing (around 24%), indicating that the tasks are challenging even for humans. The top ten human solvers have an average solve rate of 80-90%, per platform statistics. Figure 2 shows that most mysteries are solved between 40% and 60% of the time, with some being solved up to 70% of the time and others close to random guessing. While the mysteries were designed to vary in difficulty, it is possible that the best explanation provided by humans may not always align with the author's intended solution for the hardest ones. However, we continue to include these mysteries in our dataset to investigate whether language models can better infer the author's intent in these cases.

Mystery word count. Figure 3 shows the distribution of the number of words in each mystery in the dataset. On average, mysteries have 1204 words, with some being as long as 2000 words. This suggests that the puzzles used in the study not only require advanced reasoning skills to solve but also require finding relevant clues from a relatively long body of text that can incriminate or exonerate suspects. This further complicates the task.

Golden CoTs. Each mystery in the dataset includes a full-text solution that provides an explanation of how one of the story characters came up with the correct answers. The average length of these solutions is 265 words, as shown in Figure 4. The solution lengths do not vary significantly, with the longest solution being around 600 words.

These solutions can be considered as ground-truth Chains-of-Thought (cite paper here), which provide insight into the author's reasoning for each puzzle. This information is valuable for a few reasons. First, it can be used as part of few-shot learning examples (again, cite). Second, as we demonstrate in Section 4, we can use these Chains-of-Thought to simplify the abductive reasoning task and evaluate whether language models can perform inference when the solution is strongly hinted at.

4 Evaluation

4.1 Models

The models used in this study are the InstructGPT-3.5 models *GPT-3.5 (FeedME)*, *GPT-3.5 (PPO)* (OpenAI, 2022), and *GPT-4* (OpenAI, 2023). They are causal language models based on the Transformer architecture (Vaswani et al., 2017) featuring supposedly around 175B parameters for GPT-3.5s.

GPT-3.5 (FeedME): a model was trained using the FeedME method, a supervised fine-tuning method based on human-written instructions and model samples (Ouyang et al., 2022; OpenAI, 2022).

GPT-3.5 (PPO): is a more performant update over *GPT-3.5 (FeedME)* model. Apart from instruction tuning, it was also calibrated with RLHF, a reinforcement learning method that uses reward models trained from human comparisons (Stiennon et al., 2020; OpenAI, 2022).

GPT-4: state-of-the-art commercial model from OpenAI. Achieves human parity on multiple extremely challenging tasks (OpenAI, 2023).

4.2 Methods

In this study, we tested GPTs in a zero-shot manner in three scenarios. This subsection outlines them.

Vanilla: This method involves the task description, mystery body, and an immediate request for the final answer (Brown et al., 2020).

CoT: This method asks LLMs to generate a Chain-of-Thought first (Wei et al., 2022; Kojima et al., 2022) and only then requests the final answer. Chain-of-thought, if reasonable, allows the model to approach complex problems gradually and unlocks strong reasoning abilities at a particular model scale (Wei et al., 2022).

Golden CoT: This method involves generating answers to instruction-based questions by using a set of ground-truth Chain-of-Though solutions included as part of the prompt. This significantly simplifies the task for the model as it does not need to come up with CoT, so we can test how much of the performance depends on the CoT and how much on the final abductive reasoning step.

4.3 Prompt Templates

Figure 5 shows the task instruction that we give to the InstructGPT models at the beginning of the prompt.

Instruction

```
"""Your task is to solve a given mystery.
The mystery is a detective puzzle presented as a
short story.
You will be given a list of answer options apart
from the mystery content.
Please give your final answer as
(x) Your Answer
where x is the number of the answer option.
Only one answer from the list is correct, and your
task is to identify which one.\n\n\n"""
```

Figure 5: Task instruction that we use as a prompt prefix.

Then we always add the mystery name, list of suspects, and mystery content (body) to the prompt.

When we want to invoke Chain-of-Though reasoning, we also append the following:

```
Full answer:
Let's think step by step.
```

When we want to provide a golden Chain-of-thought, we append the following prompt:

```
Solution:
{solution}
```

Finally, we always ask for the final answer with

```
Final answer:
```

4.4 Results and Discussion

The evaluation results shown in Table 1 indicate that the performance of both *davinci* models under both *Vanilla* and *CoT* prompting scenarios is close to random. In our analysis, we also found that there is no correlation between the length of the mystery or human solve rate and the GPT's correctness.

Our Golden CoT ablation study (Table 1) demonstrates that even with relevant explanatory CoT, GPT-3.5s can only solve 63% of puzzles correctly, suggesting that difficulty lies not only in generating

Method	Solve rate
Random guess	0.24
Human average	0.47
Human top	0.8-0.9
Vanilla	
GPT-3.5 (FeedME)	0.28
GPT-3.5 (PPO)	0.26
GPT-4	0.27
CoT	
GPT-3.5 (FeedME)	0.26
GPT-3.5 (PPO)	0.29
GPT-4	**0.38**
Golden CoT*	
GPT-3.5 (FeedME)	0.46
GPT-3.5 (PPO)	0.63
GPT-4	0.83

Table 1: Performance of GPT-3.5 (FeedME), GPT-3.5 (PPO), and GPT-4 under different prompting scenarios against the human baseline. Both vanilla task formation (Instruction and immediate answer request) and "step-by-step" chain-of-thought approaches perform almost equivalent to random guess. Even in unfair comparison, GPTs cannot match/outperform top human solvers when provided with golden chains of thought.

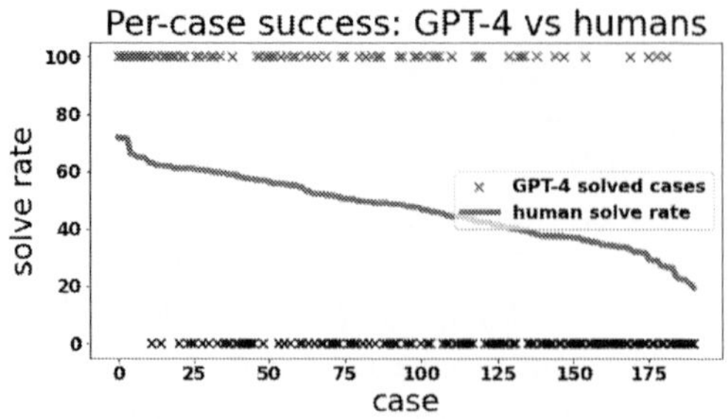

Figure 6: Red line indicates case difficulty for humans, green points indicate cases where GPT-4 (CoT) solved the case successfully, and black points are for cases where GPT-4 failed. Black points are crowded on the right and green points are crowded on the left which correlates with hard and easy cases (as per humans) respectively. Therefore, GPT-4 and humans find similar cases easy/difficult.

the correct theory for the crime but also in making final inferences when all information is available. On the other hand, GPT-4 does not help such a problem with 83%.

CoT performance of GPT-3.5 models show small to no gains in performance compared to Vanilla. As indicated in Wei et al. (2022), a similar decrement (between GPT-3 and smaller models) was observed in models that weren't sufficiently powerful for the task suggesting that the GPT-3.5 models might also not be strong enough to generate CoT chains that would benefit the task. On the other hand, CoT GPT-4 performs better, although still underachieving compared to the average human solve rate.

The complexity of the long-form multi-character narrative and the level of reasoning required to solve the detective puzzle makes our benchmark especially difficult and sets it apart.

Finally, we explore the complexity of the cases that GPT-4 (CoT) found easier or harder to manage. In our study, we did not observe a direct correlation between the length of a mystery and the level of difficulty it presented. However, when considering the level of concurrence between human decisions and those made by GPT-4, Figure 6 demonstrates a considerable degree of agreement. Specifically, the cases perceived as challenging or straightforward by the GPT-4 were often viewed similarly by human subjects.

5 Conclusion

We presented a new benchmark in the form of detective puzzles to evaluate the abductive reasoning capabilities of Large Language Models. Results from state-of-the-art GPT-3.5 models across three prompting strategies showed poor performance close to random. GPT-4 managed to show comparably solid performance (when prompted with CoT), but even this model is behind the average human solve rate on our benchmark. When provided with golden CoTs, which significantly simplifies the task, GPT-4 shows good performance, while GPT-3 is still unable to do a final inference well enough. Overall, our benchmark offers insights into LLMs' limitations and provides a difficult challenge for future research on abductive reasoning in large LMs.

6 Limitations

Our evaluation focused solely on the performance of leading-edge GPT models details and weights of which are not publicly available. However, there is potential value in extending this study to incorporate other models like PaLM (Chowdhery et al.) or LLaMA (Touvron et al.), which we have earmarked for future research.

Also, as the performance for average humans is only 47% it is possible that some mysteries are ill-defined or unreasonably complicated. Among the top 10 human solvers, the solve rate is also only around 80-90%, and GPT-4 only solves 83% of tasks when provided with ground truth CoTs which drastically simplifies the task.

References

Chandra Bhagavatula, Ronan Le Bras, Chaitanya Malaviya, Keisuke Sakaguchi, Ari Holtzman, Hannah Rashkin, Doug Downey, Wen tau Yih, and Yejin Choi. 2020. Abductive commonsense reasoning. In *International Conference on Learning Representations*.

Samuel R. Bowman, Gabor Angeli, Christopher Potts, and Christopher D. Manning. 2015. A large annotated corpus for learning natural language inference. In *Proceedings of the 2015 Conference on Empirical Methods in Natural Language Processing*, pages 632–642, Lisbon, Portugal. Association for Computational Linguistics.

Tom Brown, Benjamin Mann, Nick Ryder, Melanie Subbiah, Jared D Kaplan, Prafulla Dhariwal, Arvind Neelakantan, Pranav Shyam, Girish Sastry, Amanda Askell, Sandhini Agarwal, Ariel Herbert-Voss, Gretchen Krueger, Tom Henighan, Rewon Child, Aditya Ramesh, Daniel Ziegler, Jeffrey Wu, Clemens Winter, Chris Hesse, Mark Chen, Eric Sigler, Mateusz Litwin, Scott Gray, Benjamin Chess, Jack Clark, Christopher Berner, Sam McCandlish, Alec Radford, Ilya Sutskever, and Dario Amodei. 2020. Language models are few-shot learners. In *Advances in Neural Information Processing Systems*, volume 33, pages 1877–1901. Curran Associates, Inc.

Aakanksha Chowdhery, Sharan Narang, Jacob Devlin, Maarten Bosma, Gaurav Mishra, Adam Roberts, Paul Barham, Hyung Won Chung, Charles Sutton, Sebastian Gehrmann, Parker Schuh, Kensen Shi, Sasha Tsvyashchenko, Joshua Maynez, Abhishek Rao, Parker Barnes, Yi Tay, Noam Shazeer, Vinodkumar Prabhakaran, Emily Reif, Nan Du, Ben Hutchinson, Reiner Pope, James Bradbury, Jacob Austin, Michael Isard, Guy Gur-Ari, Pengcheng Yin, Toju Duke, Anselm Levskaya, Sanjay Ghemawat, Sunipa Dev, Henryk Michalewski, Xavier Garcia, Vedant Misra, Kevin Robinson, Liam Fedus, Denny Zhou, Daphne Ippolito, David Luan, Hyeontaek Lim, Barret Zoph, Alexander Spiridonov, Ryan Sepassi, David Dohan, Shivani Agrawal, Mark Omernick, Andrew M. Dai, Thanumalayan Sankaranarayana Pillai, Marie Pellat, Aitor Lewkowycz, Erica Moreira, Rewon Child, Oleksandr Polozov, Katherine Lee, Zongwei Zhou, Xuezhi Wang, Brennan Saeta, Mark Diaz, Orhan Firat, Michele Catasta, Jason Wei, Kathy Meier-Hellstern, Douglas Eck, Jeff Dean, Slav Petrov, and Noah Fiedel. 2022. Palm: Scaling language modeling with pathways.

Frank Grimm and Philipp Cimiano. 2021. BiQuAD: Towards QA based on deeper text understanding. In *Proceedings of *SEM 2021: The Tenth Joint Conference on Lexical and Computational Semantics*, pages 105–115, Online. Association for Computational Linguistics.

Takeshi Kojima, Shixiang Shane Gu, Machel Reid, Yutaka Matsuo, and Yusuke Iwasawa. 2022. Large language models are zero-shot reasoners.

Nasrin Mostafazadeh, Nathanael Chambers, Xiaodong He, Devi Parikh, Dhruv Batra, Lucy Vanderwende, Pushmeet Kohli, and James Allen. 2016. A corpus and cloze evaluation for deeper understanding of commonsense stories. In *Proceedings of the 2016 Conference of the North American Chapter of the Association for Computational Linguistics: Human Language Technologies*, pages 839–849, San Diego, California. Association for Computational Linguistics.

OpenAI. 2022. Model index for researchers. `https://beta.openai.com/docs/model-index-for-researchers`.

OpenAI. 2023. Gpt-4 technical report.

Long Ouyang, Jeff Wu, Xu Jiang, Diogo Almeida, Carroll L. Wainwright, Pamela Mishkin, Chong Zhang, Sandhini Agarwal, Katarina Slama, Alex Ray, John Schulman, Jacob Hilton, Fraser Kelton, Luke E. Miller, Maddie Simens, Amanda Askell, Peter Welinder, Paul Francis Christiano, Jan Leike, and Ryan J. Lowe. 2022. Training language models to follow instructions with human feedback. *ArXiv*, abs/2203.02155.

Alec Radford and Karthik Narasimhan. 2018. Improving language understanding by generative pretraining.

Aarohi Srivastava, Abhinav Rastogi, Abhishek Rao, Abu Awal Md Shoeb, Abubakar Abid, Adam Fisch, Adam R. Brown, Adam Santoro, Aditya Gupta, Adrià Garriga-Alonso, Agnieszka Kluska, Aitor Lewkowycz, Akshat Agarwal, Alethea Power, Alex Ray, Alex Warstadt, Alexander W. Kocurek, Ali Safaya, Ali Tazarv, Alice Xiang, Alicia Parrish, Allen Nie, Aman Hussain, Amanda Askell, Amanda Dsouza, Ambrose Slone, Ameet Rahane, Anantharaman S. Iyer, Anders Andreassen, Andrea Madotto, Andrea Santilli, Andreas Stuhlmüller, Andrew Dai, Andrew La, Andrew Lampinen, Andy Zou, Angela Jiang, Angelica Chen, Anh Vuong, Animesh Gupta, Anna Gottardi, Antonio Norelli, Anu Venkatesh, Arash Gholamidavoodi, Arfa Tabassum, Arul Menezes, Arun Kirubarajan, Asher Mullokandov, Ashish Sabharwal, Austin Herrick, Avia Efrat, Aykut Erdem, Ayla Karakaş, B. Ryan Roberts, Bao Sheng Loe, Barret Zoph, Bartłomiej Bojanowski, Batuhan Özyurt, Behnam Hedayatnia, Behnam Neyshabur, Benjamin Inden, Benno Stein, Berk Ekmekci, Bill Yuchen Lin, Blake Howald, Cameron Diao, Cameron Dour, Catherine Stinson, Cedrick Argueta, César Ferri Ramírez, Chandan Singh, Charles Rathkopf, Chenlin Meng, Chitta Baral, Chiyu Wu, Chris Callison-Burch, Chris Waites, Christian Voigt, Christopher D. Manning, Christopher Potts, Cindy Ramirez, Clara E. Rivera, Clemencia Siro, Colin Raffel, Courtney Ashcraft, Cristina Garbacea, Damien Sileo, Dan Garrette, Dan Hendrycks, Dan Kilman, Dan Roth, Daniel Freeman, Daniel Khashabi, Daniel Levy, Daniel Moseguí González, Danielle Perszyk, Danny Hernandez, Danqi Chen, Daphne Ippolito,

Dar Gilboa, David Dohan, David Drakard, David Jurgens, Debajyoti Datta, Deep Ganguli, Denis Emelin, Denis Kleyko, Deniz Yuret, Derek Chen, Derek Tam, Dieuwke Hupkes, Diganta Misra, Dilyar Buzan, Dimitri Coelho Mollo, Diyi Yang, Dong-Ho Lee, Ekaterina Shutova, Ekin Dogus Cubuk, Elad Segal, Eleanor Hagerman, Elizabeth Barnes, Elizabeth Donoway, Ellie Pavlick, Emanuele Rodola, Emma Lam, Eric Chu, Eric Tang, Erkut Erdem, Ernie Chang, Ethan A. Chi, Ethan Dyer, Ethan Jerzak, Ethan Kim, Eunice Engefu Manyasi, Evgenii Zheltonozhskii, Fanyue Xia, Fatemeh Siar, Fernando Martínez-Plumed, Francesca Happé, Francois Chollet, Frieda Rong, Gaurav Mishra, Genta Indra Winata, Gerard de Melo, Germán Kruszewski, Giambattista Parascandolo, Giorgio Mariani, Gloria Wang, Gonzalo Jaimovitch-López, Gregor Betz, Guy Gur-Ari, Hana Galijasevic, Hannah Kim, Hannah Rashkin, Hannaneh Hajishirzi, Harsh Mehta, Hayden Bogar, Henry Shevlin, Hinrich Schütze, Hiromu Yakura, Hongming Zhang, Hugh Mee Wong, Ian Ng, Isaac Noble, Jaap Jumelet, Jack Geissinger, Jackson Kernion, Jacob Hilton, Jaehoon Lee, Jaime Fernández Fisac, James B. Simon, James Koppel, James Zheng, James Zou, Jan Kocoń, Jana Thompson, Jared Kaplan, Jarema Radom, Jascha Sohl-Dickstein, Jason Phang, Jason Wei, Jason Yosinski, Jekaterina Novikova, Jelle Bosscher, Jennifer Marsh, Jeremy Kim, Jeroen Taal, Jesse Engel, Jesujoba Alabi, Jiacheng Xu, Jiaming Song, Jillian Tang, Joan Waweru, John Burden, John Miller, John U. Balis, Jonathan Berant, Jörg Frohberg, Jos Rozen, Jose Hernandez-Orallo, Joseph Boudeman, Joseph Jones, Joshua B. Tenenbaum, Joshua S. Rule, Joyce Chua, Kamil Kanclerz, Karen Livescu, Karl Krauth, Karthik Gopalakrishnan, Katerina Ignatyeva, Katja Markert, Kaustubh D. Dhole, Kevin Gimpel, Kevin Omondi, Kory Mathewson, Kristen Chiafullo, Ksenia Shkaruta, Kumar Shridhar, Kyle McDonell, Kyle Richardson, Laria Reynolds, Leo Gao, Li Zhang, Liam Dugan, Lianhui Qin, Lidia Contreras-Ochando, Louis-Philippe Morency, Luca Moschella, Lucas Lam, Lucy Noble, Ludwig Schmidt, Luheng He, Luis Oliveros Colón, Luke Metz, Lütfi Kerem Şenel, Maarten Bosma, Maarten Sap, Maartje ter Hoeve, Maheen Farooqi, Manaal Faruqui, Mantas Mazeika, Marco Baturan, Marco Marelli, Marco Maru, Maria Jose Ramírez Quintana, Marie Tolkiehn, Mario Giulianelli, Martha Lewis, Martin Potthast, Matthew L. Leavitt, Matthias Hagen, Mátyás Schubert, Medina Orduna Baitemirova, Melody Arnaud, Melvin McElrath, Michael A. Yee, Michael Cohen, Michael Gu, Michael Ivanitskiy, Michael Starritt, Michael Strube, Michał Swędrowski, Michele Bevilacqua, Michihiro Yasunaga, Mihir Kale, Mike Cain, Mimee Xu, Mirac Suzgun, Mo Tiwari, Mohit Bansal, Moin Aminnaseri, Mor Geva, Mozhdeh Gheini, Mukund Varma T, Nanyun Peng, Nathan Chi, Nayeon Lee, Neta Gur-Ari Krakover, Nicholas Cameron, Nicholas Roberts, Nick Doiron, Nikita Nangia, Niklas Deckers, Niklas Muennighoff, Nitish Shirish Keskar, Niveditha S. Iyer, Noah Constant, Noah Fiedel, Nuan Wen, Oliver Zhang, Omar Agha, Omar Elbaghdadi, Omer Levy, Owain Evans, Pablo Antonio Moreno Casares, Parth Doshi, Pascale Fung, Paul Pu Liang, Paul Vicol, Pegah Alipoormolabashi, Peiyuan Liao, Percy Liang, Peter Chang, Peter Eckersley, Phu Mon Htut, Pinyu Hwang, Piotr Miłkowski, Piyush Patil, Pouya Pezeshkpour, Priti Oli, Qiaozhu Mei, Qing Lyu, Qinlang Chen, Rabin Banjade, Rachel Etta Rudolph, Raefer Gabriel, Rahel Habacker, Ramón Risco Delgado, Raphaël Millière, Rhythm Garg, Richard Barnes, Rif A. Saurous, Riku Arakawa, Robbe Raymaekers, Robert Frank, Rohan Sikand, Roman Novak, Roman Sitelew, Ronan LeBras, Rosanne Liu, Rowan Jacobs, Rui Zhang, Ruslan Salakhutdinov, Ryan Chi, Ryan Lee, Ryan Stovall, Ryan Teehan, Rylan Yang, Sahib Singh, Saif M. Mohammad, Sajant Anand, Sam Dillavou, Sam Shleifer, Sam Wiseman, Samuel Gruetter, Samuel R. Bowman, Samuel S. Schoenholz, Sanghyun Han, Sanjeev Kwatra, Sarah A. Rous, Sarik Ghazarian, Sayan Ghosh, Sean Casey, Sebastian Bischoff, Sebastian Gehrmann, Sebastian Schuster, Sepideh Sadeghi, Shadi Hamdan, Sharon Zhou, Shashank Srivastava, Sherry Shi, Shikhar Singh, Shima Asaadi, Shixiang Shane Gu, Shubh Pachchigar, Shubham Toshniwal, Shyam Upadhyay, Shyamolima, Debnath, Siamak Shakeri, Simon Thormeyer, Simone Melzi, Siva Reddy, Sneha Priscilla Makini, Soo-Hwan Lee, Spencer Torene, Sriharsha Hatwar, Stanislas Dehaene, Stefan Divic, Stefano Ermon, Stella Biderman, Stephanie Lin, Stephen Prasad, Steven T. Piantadosi, Stuart M. Shieber, Summer Misherghi, Svetlana Kiritchenko, Swaroop Mishra, Tal Linzen, Tal Schuster, Tao Li, Tao Yu, Tariq Ali, Tatsu Hashimoto, Te-Lin Wu, Théo Desbordes, Theodore Rothschild, Thomas Phan, Tianle Wang, Tiberius Nkinyili, Timo Schick, Timofei Kornev, Timothy Telleen-Lawton, Titus Tunduny, Tobias Gerstenberg, Trenton Chang, Trishala Neeraj, Tushar Khot, Tyler Shultz, Uri Shaham, Vedant Misra, Vera Demberg, Victoria Nyamai, Vikas Raunak, Vinay Ramasesh, Vinay Uday Prabhu, Vishakh Padmakumar, Vivek Srikumar, William Fedus, William Saunders, William Zhang, Wout Vossen, Xiang Ren, Xiaoyu Tong, Xinran Zhao, Xinyi Wu, Xudong Shen, Yadollah Yaghoobzadeh, Yair Lakretz, Yangqiu Song, Yasaman Bahri, Yejin Choi, Yichi Yang, Yiding Hao, Yifu Chen, Yonatan Belinkov, Yu Hou, Yufang Hou, Yuntao Bai, Zachary Seid, Zhuoye Zhao, Zijian Wang, Zijie J. Wang, Zirui Wang, and Ziyi Wu. 2022. Beyond the imitation game: Quantifying and extrapolating the capabilities of language models.

Nisan Stiennon, Long Ouyang, Jeffrey Wu, Daniel Ziegler, Ryan Lowe, Chelsea Voss, Alec Radford, Dario Amodei, and Paul F Christiano. 2020. Learning to summarize with human feedback. In *Advances in Neural Information Processing Systems*, volume 33, pages 3008–3021. Curran Associates, Inc.

Hugo Touvron, Thibaut Lavril, Gautier Izacard, Xavier Martinet, Marie-Anne Lachaux, Timothée Lacroix, Baptiste Rozière, Naman Goyal, Eric Hambro, Faisal Azhar, Aurelien Rodriguez, Armand Joulin, Edouard

Grave, and Guillaume Lample. 2023. Llama: Open and efficient foundation language models.

Ashish Vaswani, Noam Shazeer, Niki Parmar, Jakob Uszkoreit, Llion Jones, Aidan N Gomez, Ł ukasz Kaiser, and Illia Polosukhin. 2017. Attention is all you need. In *Advances in Neural Information Processing Systems*, volume 30. Curran Associates, Inc.

Jason Wei, Xuezhi Wang, Dale Schuurmans, Maarten Bosma, Brian Ichter, Fei Xia, Ed Chi, Quoc Le, and Denny Zhou. 2022. Chain of thought prompting elicits reasoning in large language models.

Adina Williams, Nikita Nangia, and Samuel Bowman. 2018. A broad-coverage challenge corpus for sentence understanding through inference. In *Proceedings of the 2018 Conference of the North American Chapter of the Association for Computational Linguistics: Human Language Technologies, Volume 1 (Long Papers)*, pages 1112–1122, New Orleans, Louisiana. Association for Computational Linguistics.

Rowan Zellers, Yonatan Bisk, Roy Schwartz, and Yejin Choi. 2018. SWAG: A large-scale adversarial dataset for grounded commonsense inference. In *Proceedings of the 2018 Conference on Empirical Methods in Natural Language Processing*, pages 93–104, Brussels, Belgium. Association for Computational Linguistics.

A Example: The Easter Egg Mystery

This appendix provides the most attempted mystery under 700 words as an example. Copyright belongs to the mystery author.

Metadata

- Mystery Name: The Easter Egg Mystery
- Author: Tom Fowler[3]
- Solve Rate: 60.8%
- Attempts: 1871
- Answer options: (a) Anna; (b) Cole; (c) Justin; (d) Lizzie; (e) Rachel.

Mystery Body Karen Sheldon had loved Easter egg hunts ever since she was a little girl. That is why she eagerly volunteered to assist with this year's Hunt for the children at her church.

This year, the Children's Day Out mothers decided to do something different. Because there were so many children of all ages in the congregation, they split the hunt up into age groups. Karen's job was to oversee several of the 6-10 year olds.

Within her group were five children she knew well. They were Rachel Smithson, whose mother Karla had volunteered to help a very grateful Karen, Justin Bates, a classmate of Rachel's, Karen's daughter Lizzie, Lizzie's best friend Anna Laughlin and Cole Bryant, who was also the Sheldon's next door neighbor.

The Easter egg hunt was on Saturday morning, the day before Easter Sunday. It was held in the large field in back of the church. Karen and Karla were grateful that today was sunny and warm although it was a bit windy. Karen was excited as the children prepared for the hunt, which was to begin at 10:00 am and last for one hour. Just before the start whistle blew, Karen told the children, "I have placed a golden Easter egg in our hunting area. There is an extra bag of candy for the child who finds it." Only Karla and she knew that the golden egg was placed in back of the largest tree in the field, an old oak in the far corner to the left of where she and the children now stood and an area dedicated to the 6-10 year old age group.

During the hunt, Karen and Karla visited while they watched the egg hunt. During the hunt, Karen noticed that Cole stayed focused on the evergreen shrubbery in the middle of the field, finding several eggs there, much to his delight.

Karen was amused when Rachel ran to her mother and told her, "I have found a lot of eggs. I'm heading back to the rock pile. I bet I will find the golden egg there!" The rock pile was to the right of the evergreen shrubbery.

In the middle of the hunt, Karen excused herself to go inside the church to get a drink of water and sit for a few minutes. When she returned, Karla told her, "I had to run over and warn Lizzie to be careful of the dead branches on the big oak tree. One of them fell last week, hitting one of the older kids."

As the hunt began to wind down, Karla walked out to speak with a very agitated Anna. After returning to Karen, she told her, "Anna is upset because she has found only a few eggs. I told her to keep looking; there are still a few minutes to go." Karen noticed that Anna stayed close to Karla for the remainder of the hunt.

As the whistle blew to end the hunt, Karen walked to the center of the field to wave Justin back in. He was in the far right corner of the field, where he had been for the entire hunt. There was a sand pit in that area and Justin found several eggs

[3]https://www.5minutemystery.com/author/tfowler

there.

As the kids headed back to the start area, Karen once again excused herself to go inside. The wind had blown a speck of dust in her eye when waving Justin down and it was very painful. When she returned from rinsing her eyes, Karla and the five children were smiling at her. She asked, "What's up?"

Karla answered, "One of our kids found the golden egg. We want you to guess which one."

Karen smiled in return, saying, "So that's it!" Thinking for a moment, she said, "I only have one question. When I was inside the first time, did any of the children move from one side of the field to another?"

Karla answered, "No."

Karen tousled Justin's hair and said, "Good. Then I know who has the golden egg!"

A.1 Golden CoT and Answer

Golden CoT. "Good naturedly, Karla exclaimed, "How do you know?" Smiling at Anna, she answered, "It's not too hard to figure out. Let me explain." The eyes of all of the children and Karla were upon her as she continued, "I placed the golden egg behind the big oak tree." Smiling next at Cole, she said, "Cole spent the entire hour in the shrubbery, in the middle of the field, far away from the oak tree." She patted Rachel's shoulder and said; "Rachel did all of her hunting in the rock pile, even farther away from the oak tree." Looking back at Anna, Karen said, "I know you don't have the golden egg, sweetie. You were upset that you had so few eggs with only a few minutes left in the hunt and stayed close to Karla until the whistle blew." Patting her hand, she added, "I'm sure you will do better next year." Turning to Justin, Karen said, "You were farther away from the oak than anyone. You spent the whole hour far out in the sand pit. I even had to come get you because you could not hear the whistle." All eyes turned toward Lizzie. Her mother said, "So, you must have the egg. Karla told me she had to warn you of the dead branches on the oak. You were the only one near it." Pausing, she added, "I hope everyone believes that I did not tell you where I put that egg! Karla jumped in, "Of course we do not think that!" All of the kids echoed their support. Lizzie broke the silence. She said, "I didn't know about the egg until Mother told everyone else before the hunt." Walking over to her side, Lizzie looked at Anna and offered her the golden egg, saying, "I would like for you to have this." Tearfully, Anna thanked her friend, saying, "This is the best Easter egg hunt ever!" Karen was so proud of Lizzie that she heartily agreed with Anna."

Answer: (d) Lizzie

B Mystery Authors Acknowledgment

We thank all the 5MM mystery writers: Moe Zilla, Tom Fowler, William Shepard, Laird Long, Robbie Cutler, Barney Parmington, Stefanina Hill, Steve Shrott, Nick Andreychuk, Nicholas LeVack, Ernest Capraro, Andrea Hein, Doug Fellin, Tammy-Lee Miller, Meghan Ford, Brad Marsh, Susanne Shaphren, Randy Godwin, Ryan Hogan, Matthew Lieff, Perry McCarney, Nicholas Lovell, Mike Wever, Meg A. Write, Elsa Darcy, PIP Writer, Julie Hockenberry.

Guiding Zero-Shot Paraphrase Generation with Fine-Grained Control Tokens

Teemu Vahtola and **Mathias Creutz** and **Jörg Tiedemann**
Department of Digital Humanities
Faculty of Arts
University of Helsinki
Finland

Abstract

Sequence-to-sequence paraphrase generation models often struggle with the generation of diverse paraphrases. This deficiency constrains the viability of leveraging paraphrase generation in different Natural Language Processing tasks. We propose a translation-based guided paraphrase generation model that learns useful features for promoting surface form variation in generated paraphrases from cross-lingual parallel data. Our proposed method leverages multilingual neural machine translation pretraining to learn zero-shot paraphrasing. Furthermore, we incorporate dedicated prefix tokens into the training of the machine translation models to promote variation. The prefix tokens are designed to affect various linguistic features related to surface form realizations, and can be applied during inference to guide the decoding process towards a desired solution. We assess the proposed guided model on paraphrase generation in three languages, English, Finnish, and Swedish, and provide analysis on the feasibility of the prefix tokens to guided paraphrasing. Our analysis suggests that the attributes represented by the prefix tokens are useful in promoting variation, by pushing the paraphrases generated by the guided model to diverge from the input sentence while preserving semantics conveyed by the sentence well.

1 Introduction

Paraphrasing is a way of conveying some given meaning using different wording. Automatic paraphrase generation aims to produce sequences that carry similar semantics to some arbitrary input sentence but are realized in different surface forms. Table 1 presents examples of paraphrases. Approaches for natural language generation incorporating diverse paraphrasing can be highly influential for many natural language processing (NLP) tasks where it is important to recognize sequences that share contextual meaning regardless of their surface form realizations. Such tasks include, but are not limited to, question answering (Dong et al., 2017), machine translation (Callison-Burch et al., 2006; Mehdizadeh Seraj et al., 2015), summarization (Nema et al., 2017), and simplification (Nisioi et al., 2017). Models that reliably represent similar meanings regardless of their surface forms can also be highly useful for instance in style transfer (Krishna et al., 2020), conversational applications (Dopierre et al., 2021), and tracking how information changes across multiple domains (Wright et al., 2022). However, for generated paraphrases to be useful in various NLP tasks, their realizations must deviate enough from the original sequences while preserving the semantics of the original sequence well. Sequence-to-sequence-based paraphrasing is prone to generating sequences whose surface forms highly resemble the original sentence by producing trivial rewrites of the input sentence (Kumar et al., 2019). This impediment constrains their practical viability to the aforementioned tasks.

To increase variation, we propose the training of a guided multilingual neural machine translation (NMT) system that can be applied to diverse zero-shot paraphrase generation by leveraging dedicated prefix tokens designed to enhance variation. We train our multilingual translation system in English, Finnish, and Swedish, and apply it to guided zero-shot paraphrasing in the three languages. The model does not see parallel monolingual sentence pairs during training, but we guide it to produce monolingual paraphrases during inference.

During training, our proposed model learns the semantics of a set of dedicated prefix tokens that are designed to capture certain attributes of language, and can be used for promoting diversity in generated text during inference. The attributes we consider are length, lexical variation, word order, and negation. When generating paraphrases, we can thus guide the model to produce sentences that vary in the given attributes by assigning corresponding values to the prefix tokens. Apart from a

*Proceedings of the The 12th Joint Conference on Lexical and Computational Semantics (*SEM 2023)*, pages 323–337
July 13-14, 2023 ©2023 Association for Computational Linguistics

Original	Paraphrase
They are excellent dancers.	They dance extremely well.
The dinner will be served in the dining area.	The dining area is where the dinner will be served.
He enjoys playing the guitar.	Playing the guitar brings him joy.

Table 1: Examples illustrating paraphrasing.

few language-specific rules for recognizing explicit negation, our control tokens are language-agnostic.

By evaluating the applicability of multilingual NMT pretraining with prefix tokens to paraphrasing, we analyze whether the dedicated prefix tokens increase variation in sequence-to-sequence-based paraphrasing. We asses the generated sequences with respect to the references using BLEU (Papineni et al., 2002), and analyze the ranking of generated correct references using Mean Reciprocal Rank. Additionally, we analyze how faithful the model is to the given instructions during decoding by comparing the accuracy of the guided model outputs to the prefix tokens. We also apply the models to a novel test suite (Vahtola et al., 2022), designed for analyzing how language models represent negation. Our analysis suggests that the paraphrases generated by the proposed model are more diverse compared to the baseline model, especially when selecting hypotheses from n-best lists with smaller n-sizes, and preserve semantics of the original sentence well.

The main advantage of our approach is that we train our system on parallel cross-lingual translation pairs rather than monolingual paraphrase data. Translation examples are available for a far larger number of languages and in larger quantities than monolingual paraphrases. As a result, our approach can be extended to a considerably larger number of languages than models that depend on existing paraphrase data. Furthermore, our model is not tied to diversity in the monolingual paraphrase examples in obtaining variation in the generated sequences. As we use cross-lingual training examples, the model can learn characteristics that might not be prominent in the existing paraphrase data sets. For instance, large language models do not reliably represent negation (Ettinger, 2020), which can be a result of not having a sufficient number of such examples in the training data. We show that the proposed model can learn the semantics of a set of dedicated guiding tokens, for instance a token for negation from sentence pairs where an explicit negation occurs, and that these tokens can then be used to guide the decoder to produce sentences with desired characteristics.

Finally, we show that, especially when selecting hypotheses from smaller n-best lists, the guided paraphrase generation model goes beyond variation that can be achieved by filtering beam search (Kumar et al., 2019), as the prefix tokens provide more control for variation.

2 Previous Research

Previous research has studied paraphrase generation inspired by NMT systems. Prakash et al. (2016) use a deep LSTM network for paraphrase generation using monolingual parallel training data. Sjöblom et al. (2020) train encoder-decoder-based paraphrase generation systems for six languages, likewise using paraphrastic sentence pairs.

As an alternative to paraphrase data, cross-lingual parallel data has been used for finding paraphrases (Bannard and Callison-Burch, 2005; Callison-Burch, 2008; Ganitkevitch et al., 2013; *inter alia*). Mallinson et al. (2017) generate paraphrases via bilingual pivoting using a NMT system. Similarly, models based on NMT have been used in generating synthetic paraphrase pairs for learning paraphrastic sentence embeddings (Wieting et al., 2017; Wieting and Gimpel, 2018).

Additionally, multilingual NMT systems have been applied for paraphrase generation leveraging both parallel and monolingual data (Tiedemann and Scherrer, 2019), and assessing generalization to zero-shot paraphrasing while also promoting variation in the generated sequences by penalizing matching tokens in the source and output sentences (Thompson and Post, 2020). Zero-shot paraphrasing using large multilingual language models has also been explored (Guo et al., 2019).

Exploiting various linguistic features to control the decoding process of sequence-to-sequence models has been studied in different NLP tasks and granularities. Auxiliary control tokens have been used for controlling the language of the output in multilingual NMT (Johnson et al., 2017). Schioppa et al. (2021) use various features for controlling output translations from a NMT system. In addition to prefix-based control tokens, they use vector-based interventions that guide the decoding process to certain directions. The complexity of the generated translations have been controlled by utilizing reading level tags, and by partitioning data based on reading or grade levels (Marchisio et al., 2019; Agrawal and Carpuat, 2019). Takeno et al. (2017) and Lakew et al. (2019) control length of the translated sequences with control tokens. Additionally, control tokens have been used with NMT systems for instance in domain adaptation (Kobus et al., 2017; Takeno et al., 2017), formality transfer (Sennrich et al., 2016; Niu et al., 2018), and voice control (Yamagishi et al., 2016).

Outside of machine translation, control tokens have been used successfully for instance in sentence simplification (Martin et al., 2020). Additionally, control tokens have been applied to sentences mined from the internet to obtain synthetic simplification data (Martin et al., 2022). In paraphrase generation, additional linguistic information obtained from the training data has been used for example in syntactic guiding (Iyyer et al., 2018; Huang and Chang, 2021; Sun et al., 2021).

Our approach to promoting variation is inspired by Schioppa et al. (2021) and Martin et al. (2022). We leverage existing translation corpora to learn controlled zero-shot paraphrasing using dedicated prefix tokens whose semantics the model learns directly from the training data. Our control tokens are designed to affect various properties of natural language. However, unlike Schioppa et al. (2021), we do not assess our model on machine translation, but take one step further, and evaluate it in zero-shot paraphrasing. We do not only attempt at increasing variation in lexical choices or divergence in syntactic realizations, for instance, but aim to affect both concurrently.

3 Guiding Attributes

To guide the decoding process, we need a method for signaling which decisions the decoder should take. Here, we use a prefix token-based approach, where we extract certain features from the source-target pairs in the training data, and concatenate the extracted information to the source side in the form of prefix tokens. We let the model learn to represent the semantics of each prefix token from the information incorporated in the translation pairs. Consequently, we can guide the decoding process of the proposed paraphrase model by applying these prefix tokens in monolingual transformation triggered by a target language token.

To promote variation in the generated paraphrases, we use the following attributes to control for various properties of natural language: length, lexical variation, word order, and negation.

3.1 Length

Inspired by automatic text simplification, we include a length-controlling token into our experiments. We represent the length attribute as a ratio between the lengths of source and target sentences after SentencePiece tokenization (Kudo and Richardson, 2018). We use pretrained SentencePiece models with a vocabulary size of 32 000 from the Opus-MT project (Tiedemann and Thottingal, 2020). If the sentences in a translation pair have exactly the same length after segmentation, the length ratio between the sentences is 100% (indicating that the target sequence should consist of 100% of the segments of the source sequence). Similarly, if the number of tokens in the target sentence is half of the number of tokens in the source, the length ratio is 50%. We round the length values to the nearest 10 to limit the number of features the model has to learn for controlling length.

3.2 Lexical Variation

Lexical variation could easily be measured in the monolingual case. However, we base our paraphrase generation model on multilingual machine translation and, therefore, need to apply a different mechanism to promote variation in lexical choices. We choose to base this prefix token on tf-idf. In previous research, tf-idf values have been used to measure lexical complexity of a sentence (Huang et al., 2021), but in our approach we apply them to promote lexical variation.

When calculating the tf-idf values, we treat each target sentence as a document, and calculate tf-idf over all the sentences in a given language pair. We consider the highest value in the resulting vector as a rough proxy of the lexical complexity of the sentence.

We automatically assign the obtained values into quartiles. Intuitively, sentences assigned into the first quartile should consist of simpler and more frequent tokens, whereas sentences in the subsequent quartiles should include less frequent, and increasingly difficult tokens. We hypothesize that controlling for tf-idf quartiles will promote divergence in terms of lexical variation in sentence-to-sentence paraphrasing. Additionally, it could provide a simplifying effect if applied to simplification tasks.

3.3 Word Order

As an attribute of word order, we use the monotonicity of word alignments as proposed by Schioppa et al. (2021). Here, monotonicity refers to the degree of preservation of word order in the source compared to the target sentence. First, we apply `fast_align` (Dyer et al., 2013) to encode sentence pair alignment in the "Pharaoh" format, where the *i*th token of the input sentence is paired with the *j*th token of the output sentence, and the alignments are indicated by the corresponding word indices (e.g., 0-0 1-1 2-2 for a bijective alignment of two sentences with three tokens, or 0-2 1-1 2-0 for reversed word order). Next, we apply the following calculation from Schioppa et al. (2021):

$$\delta(s) = \frac{1}{\#\{(i,j)\}} \sum_{(i,j)} \left| \frac{i}{n} - \frac{j}{m} \right| + 0.1 \quad (1)$$

where $\#\{(i,j)\}$ stands for the cardinality of the alignments.

We assign the obtained monotonicity values $\delta(s)$ for each sentence pair automatically into quartiles, similarly as with the lexical variation tokens. We hypothesize that during inference, keeping other prefix token features constant, controlling for monotonicity promotes variation in word order in relation to the input sentence by guiding the model for either more monotone or more varied choices of word order.

3.4 Negation

Previous research has suggested that language models do not reliably represent negation (Ettinger, 2020; Hartmann et al., 2021). Therefore, we include a prefix token for controlling polarity of a generated sentence. By applying polarity change, we focus on one specific case of paraphrase formulation, namely, antonym substitution (Bhagat and Hovy, 2013). In this paradigm, some word in a sentence is substituted to a word that carries the opposite meaning to the original word, that is, its antonym. Concurrently, to maintain the original meaning, a negation is either inserted to or deleted from a corresponding position in the sequence. As an example, the sentence *My brother is asleep* could be paraphrased as *My brother is not awake*, by using antonym substitution as defined in Bhagat and Hovy (2013).

As a control token for polarity change, we use Boolean values to indicate whether an explicit negation occurs in the target sentence. We use handwritten rules to automatically recognize negation in each target sentence. These rules are designed to only grasp explicit negation (e.g., *not*) as opposed to alternative ways of conveying opposite meanings, such as negative prefixes (e.g., *un-*, *im-*, *dis-*, *il-*, *ir-*, and *in-* in English). Our hypothesis is that by explicitly expressing the presence of a negation token in a target sentence, the prefix token can be used for controlling polarity of a paraphrase.

4 Experiments

We train two multilingual NMT models for English, Finnish and Swedish from scratch: a baseline model without prefix tokens apart from the target language token, and our proposed model with prefix tokens. Both models are based on the Transformer architecture (Vaswani et al., 2017), and trained using OpenNMT (Klein et al., 2017) with standard hyperparameters for training a Transformer. We gather training data from OpenSubtitles (Lison and Tiedemann, 2016) using OpusTools (Aulamo et al., 2020), by filtering for one-to-one aligned sentences with a time stamp overlap threshold of 0.85.[1] The obtained training set consists of approximately 17 million sentence pairs in three language pairs (en-fi, en-sv, fi-sv). We extract 10 000 sentence pairs from each direction to serve as validation data for tuning the translation models. We train the models for all cross-lingual directions on two GPUs for one million steps or until early stopping criteria is met.

We evaluate the models on true paraphrase pairs extracted from the Opusparcus test sets (Creutz, 2018). The sizes of the filtered English, Finnish and Swedish test sets are 723, 669, and 732 sentence pairs, respectively. Opusparcus is a sentential paraphrase corpus that consists of paraphrastic bi-texts in six languages, English, Finnish, and Swedish included. The data is collected from the OpenSubtitles corpus, and therefore matches the domain of the training data. Consequently, the translation models may have seen some of the sentences included in the test sets during training, either on the encoder or the decoder side, but not as parallel

[1]Time-overlap ratio based on the time information given for each pair of aligned subtitle lines in the corpus.

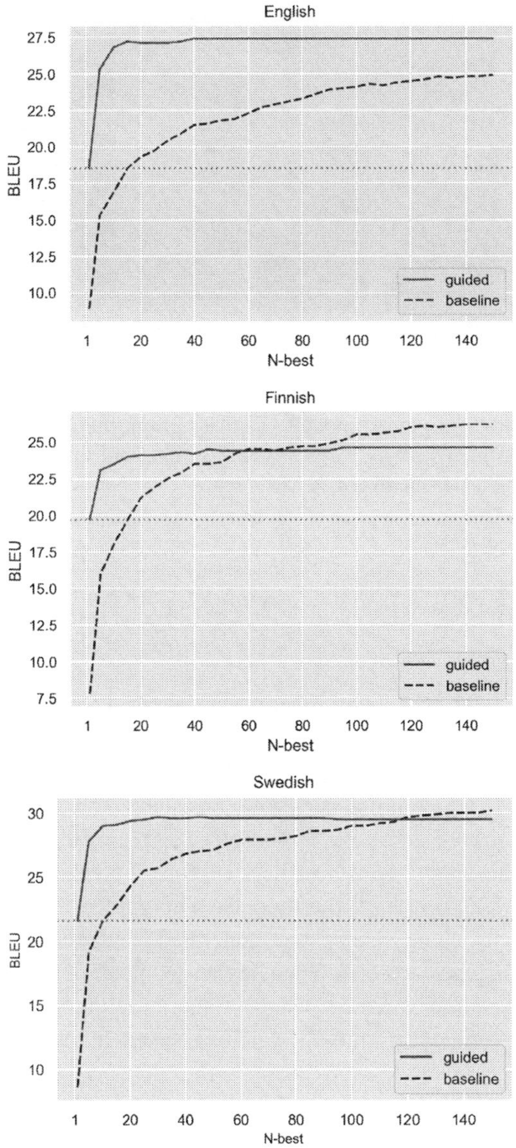

Figure 1: Obtained BLEU scores calculated on the Opusparcus test sets for the guided and the baseline models for sentences selected from different n-best lists. The x-axis denotes the size of the n-best list where the best hypothesis is selected from. The y-axis denotes the obtained BLEU scores. The horizontal line indicates the obtained accuracy of the 1-best translation from the guided model.

monolingual pairs.

5 Results

5.1 Automatic Evaluation

We assess the alignment of the generated paraphrases to their reference sentence based on BLEU, and further analyze the quality of the systems in terms of Mean Reciprocal Rank.

5.1.1 BLEU

We evaluate our model by testing how well it can generate a paraphrase of a source sentence that closely aligns to the desired target sentence. To quantify this, we use BLEU, which is an established metric in machine translation, for comparing a produced translation to a given reference. As the test examples are designed to exhibit surface form variation (Creutz, 2018), increase in BLEU implies increased variation in sentences generated by the models.

During inference, the guided model requires prefix tokens to perform guided paraphrase generation. We calculate the true guiding values for the prefix tokens from the test set examples, and input them together with the source sentence to the guided model. For calculating the test set prefix tokens, we first train `fast_align` parameters for each language using the first 500 000 paraphrase pairs from the corresponding Opusparcus training sets, and use these alignment parameters for calculating the word order features. For the lexical variation attribute, we use the tf-idf weights learnt from the training data to assign the lexical variation values of each target sentence. Consequently, the guided model can leverage this information about the ground truth reference during decoding. The baseline model, however, has no information about the reference sentence during decoding. As such, this evaluation setup would result in an unfair comparison of the models. Therefore, we use beam search with a beam size of 250 to generate n-best hypotheses from both models. From the n-best lists, we choose the hypothesis that most accurately matches the desired prefix tokens. Now, also the baseline model has a fair chance of producing a sentence the matches the desired guiding values, if such a hypothesis is available in the n-best list.[2]

Figure 1 presents BLEU scores of the models for n-best lists ranging in size from 1 to 150. The results indicate that our proposed guided paraphrase

[2]When determining which hypothesis is the best match for the desired guiding values, we treat the prefix token values as vectors. The negation tokens are mapped from Boolean values into their binary feature representation $\{0, 1\}$ and the other prefix tokens are normalized in the range $[0, 1]$ using min-max normalization. We calculate the cosine similarity of the ground truth prefix token values and all the hypotheses' prefix token values, and choose the one that maximizes cosine similarity. If multiple hypotheses maximize the similarity (e.g., multiple hypotheses have cosine similarity of 1.0), we choose the hypothesis with the highest translation score.

generation model greatly benefits from the information provided by the prefix tokens. Considering only the 1-best hypotheses for each language, the guided paraphrase generation model obtains significantly higher BLEU scores than the baseline model (18.6 vs. 8.9, 19.7 vs. 7.8, and 21.6 vs. 8.6 for English, Finnish and Swedish, respectively). Increasing the pool of hypotheses to 5-best increases BLEU scores of both models.

The steep increase of BLEU scores between 1-best and 5-best, which is obtained by the guided model, may seem surprising at first. Why does the 1-best translation not match the guidance values the best? We hypothesize that this is caused by the model balancing between what it considers the best translation and the decisions it is supposed to be making based on the prefix tokens. In practice, the model might find a solution that it considers a better translation, even if it means partly ignoring the guiding tokens. Consequently, increasing n-best size results in the model selecting a sentence that better matches the guiding tokens, which in turn increases the obtained BLEU score. However, on average, the guided model does not benefit from n-best sizes larger than 15. At this point, the model has found a solution that maximizes the similarity to the ground truth prefix tokens for each input sentence.

The baseline models benefit greatly from filtering from a larger collection of hypotheses. Albeit beginning from a very low BLEU score in all languages, the results for Finnish and Swedish surpass the ones obtained by the guided model when selecting from a sufficiently large set of hypotheses (approximately 60-best hypotheses for Finnish, and 110-best hypotheses for Swedish). In terms of the guided model, the prefix tokens constrain the options where the model can choose from during decoding, since it also needs to consider the given instructions. As a result, the output sequences are close to the desired outputs in terms of the prefix tokens to begin with. In case of multiple hypotheses that maximize the similarity to the reference prefix tokens, we choose the first such occurrence in the n-best list. This is not always the one that maximizes alignment to the reference translation.

5.1.2 Mean Reciprocal Rank

Mean Reciprocal Rank (MRR) calculates the average of the reciprocals of the first generated sequence that exactly matches the reference:

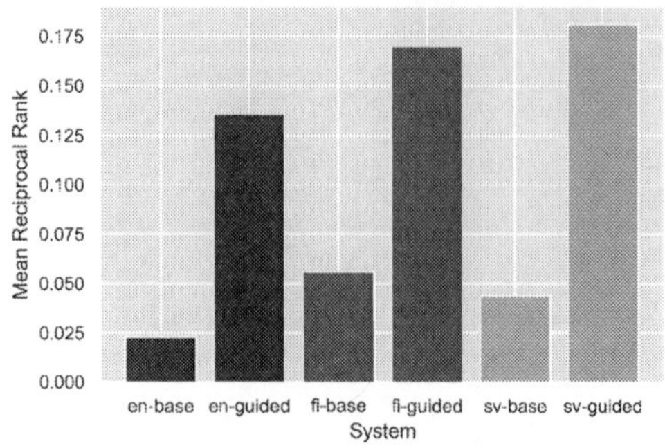

Figure 2: Obtained Mean Reciprocal Rank of the baseline and guided models calculated from the 250-best lists. The x-axis denotes the system, and the y-axis indicates the obtained MRR score.

$$MRR = \frac{1}{N} \sum_{i=1}^{N} \frac{1}{rank_i}, \quad (2)$$

where N is the number of paraphrased sentences, and $rank_i$ refers to the position in the n-best list of the first sentence that matches the reference.[3]

The score indicates how consistently the models retrieve and rank the correct references high in the generated n-best lists. Figure 2 presents the MRR scores of the models. The guided models consistently rank the generated sentence that matches the reference higher compared to the baseline models, whereas the baseline model struggles in ranking matching sentences high in the n-best list. We believe that the low ranking performance of the baseline model is mainly caused by the decoding algorithm. Beam search is known to produce bland outputs (Holtzman et al., 2020), and when applied in paraphrasing, this realizes in copies or trivial rewrites of the input sentence. In fact, the 1-best outputs of the baseline model exactly match the source sentence in 71% of the cases in English, whereas the guided model ranks a copy of the source as the best paraphrase only in 12% of the cases (46% vs. 10%, and 60% vs. 10% in Finnish and Swedish, respectively). If the reference sentence is produced by the baseline model, it is ranked lower in the n-best list, since the model prefers repetitions of the input. When decoding is restricted with the guiding tokens, the decoder works with a notion of assumed diversity, resulting in outputs that may be closer to the

[3]The rank is defined as 0 if none of the proposed target sentences in the n-best list match the desired reference.

Input	I haven't been contacted by anybody.
Baseline	Guided
I haven't been contacted by anyone.	Nobody has contacted me yet.
I haven't been contacted by anybody.	I have not been contacted.
I have not been contacted by anyone.	No one has contacted me.
I haven't been approached by anyone.	I was contacted by nobody.
I've never been contacted by anyone.	*Nobody's contacted me.*

Table 2: Top-5 generated sequences from the baseline and the guided model for the input sentence: I haven't been contacted by anybody. The gold reference is highlighted in cursive.

Language	Negation	Length	Lexical Variation	Word Order
English	99.72	99.31	87.00	55.46
Finnish	100.0	98.51	79.07	63.86
Swedish	100.0	98.09	88.93	58.20

Table 3: Prefix token accuracy [%] calculated from the observed realizations of the guided models' 1-best hypotheses with respect to the ground truth reference prefix tokens.

reference to begin with. An example illustrating this phenomenon is provided in Table 2. Finally, even when the baseline model generates sentences that better match the reference, as indicated by increase in BLEU with large n-best sizes, it does not generate exact matches of the references, or fails to rank them high in the n-best list.

To conclude, we observe two opposite factors working in favor of the models: On the one hand, the use of explicit prefix tokens in the guided models produces high BLEU values instantly, even for very small-sized n-best lists. This makes it possible to use smaller beam sizes, which leads to faster inference. On the other hand, the absence of explicit guiding tokens in the baseline models seems to constrain the decoding process less, which may eventually result in translations that match the references better, if we can afford large n-best lists. However, that requires larger beam sizes and heavier computation. Additionally, the favorable trend for the baseline model is observed only for Finnish and Swedish.

5.2 Faithfulness to the Control Tokens

Automatic evaluation suggests that the guided paraphrase generation model obtains more variation and increases the quality of the generated paraphrases compared to the baseline model, especially when paraphrase hypotheses are selected from smaller n-best lists. To analyze how faithful the model is to the given prefix tokens, we calculate the accuracy of each prefix token of the generated sequences with respect to the ground truth prefix tokens. Table 3 presents the results.

The model seems to learn the semantics of two tokens, negation and length, especially well, but somewhat struggles with the features designed for promoting variation in lexical choices and in word order. The word order attribute seems particularly difficult to the model. This weakness can be a consequence of two aspects. First, when assigning the feature values for the word order feature, we binned the sentences into four (nearly) equally sized buckets automatically. Hence, sentences appointed in adjacent buckets may only have minor differences. This, in turn, makes recognizing differences between the adjacent quantiles unnecessarily difficult for the model, and the model can not generalize to this information. Secondly, the sentences in the Opusparcus test sets are rather short, which restricts the possibilities for finding solutions that incorporate variation in word order.

In addition to analyzing how accurately the model learns to follow the given prefix tokens, we assess whether the prefix tokens affect the output as expected by focusing on each prefix token separately. We generate hypotheses from the guided model using a beam size of 5 and only consider the top-1 hypothesis. Now, we do not rely on the prefix token values calculated from the reference sentences. Instead, we manually tune the values of the prefix tokens to obtain diverse paraphrases with the desired surface form variation. Controlling for different attributes demonstrates how changing the prefix token values affect the generated sequences. We present examples of English paraphrases with the given prefix token values in Tables 4–7. Examples for Finnish and Swedish paraphrasing are provided in the Appendix A.

Negation	Length	Lexical Variation	Word Order	Input	Output
True	100	1	4	Time's short.	Not much time left.
True	100	1	2	He must remain here.	He cannot leave here.
True	100	1	2	Has this ever happened to you?	This has never happened to you?
False	100	3	4	Don't be silly.	Stop fooling around here.
False	100	1	4	I didn't have much choice.	I had little choice, though.
False	100	3	4	I'm not feeling very well.	I'm feeling a little poorly.

Table 4: Generated sentences from the guided model using different prefix token values for controlling negation in the output. The prefix token for negation indicates whether there should be an explicit negation in the output sequence or not.

Input				Can I ask a simple question?
Negation	Length	Lexical Variation	Word Order	Output
False	50	1	3	A question?
False	80	1	3	Can I ask you?
False	100	1	3	Can I ask you a question?
False	120	1	3	Can I ask you a very easy question?
False	150	1	3	Do you mind if I ask you a simple question?

Table 5: Generated sentences from the guided model using different prefix token values for guiding for the length of the output. The prefix token value denotes the ratio between the tokenized input and output sequences.

Negation Table 4 provides examples of how the negation token affects the generated outputs. To further analyze the prefix token that controls negation, we use a recent test suite for analyzing vector-based representations of antonymy and negation (Vahtola et al., 2022). The data consists of approximately 3000 test examples where an input sentence, for instance *I'm guilty*, is paired with three hypothetical paraphrases: *I'm innocent, I'm not guilty*, and *I'm not innocent*. The first two hypotheses semantically oppose the input sentence, whereas the last hypothesis carries the closest meaning to the input sentence. Using this test suite, we analyze how our proposed model learns the semantics of the negation token.

In practice, we use the translation probabilities to find which of the three hypotheses each model would translate the input sentence to, and calculate the accuracy of the model over the test set based on the preferred output. The baseline model obtains an accuracy of 30%, which is lower than acquired by random choice (33%). The guided model obtains a higher accuracy, 41%, suggesting that explicit information about negation assists the model in generating better representations of negation. However, the model does not seem to reliably learn the interplay of negation and antonymy in sentence semantics. Regardless, examples given in Table 4 show that the guided model learns, at least to some extent, to reformulate sentences with polarity change while maintaining meaning close to the original.

Length Table 5 provides examples of how the length guiding feature effects the generated output. Keeping other prefix tokens constant, but guiding for five different values for length (50, 80, 100, 120, and 150), the model does follow the given instructions faithfully, further validating the results obtained with accuracy on the different guiding tokens.

Lexical Variation Table 6 provides examples of the effect of changing the lexical variation value while keeping other prefix tokens constant. Increasing the value for lexical variation does not only promote for varied lexical choices, but can also push for potentially less frequent word types (e.g., *'bout* and *wanna*) for sequences guided with larger values (3 and 4).

Word Order Learning the semantics related to the attribute guiding for variation in word order is difficult for the model, as indicated by the obtained accuracies on the prefix token (Table 3). Similarly, the examples in Table 7 demonstrate that the prefix token does not work exactly as expected, as sentences with word order values 1 and 2 are identical. However, when pushing for more variation in word order with larger values, the model generates sequences with syntactic alteration. The results suggest that as such the prefix token may not be

Input				Would you like a drink?
Negation	Length	Lexical Variation	Word Order	Output
False	120	1	4	Can I get you a drink?
False	120	2	4	May I offer you a drink?
False	120	3	4	How 'bout a drink?
False	120	4	4	Wanna have a drink '?

Table 6: Generated sentences from the guided model using different prefix token values for promoting lexical variation in the output sequences. Sentences in bucket 1 should only include frequent tokens, and subsequent buckets should contain sentences where also less frequent and potentially difficult tokens are present.

Input				There's really nothing you can do.
Negation	Length	Lexical Variation	Word Order	Output
True	80	1	1	There is nothing you can do.
True	80	1	2	There is nothing you can do.
True	80	1	3	There really is nothing to do.
True	80	1	4	You really can't do anything.

Table 7: Generated sentences from the guided model using different prefix token values for guiding output sequence's word order in relation to the input sentence. The sentences with lower values should preserve the word order of the input well, whereas sentences with larger values should deviate more from the input sentence in terms of word order.

optimized perfectly, but with careful redesigning of the attribute, it could provide a method of promoting variation in word order.

6 Conclusions

We propose a paraphrase generation model that is based on multilingual NMT, leveraging cross-lingual parallel examples as diverse paraphrase data. We apply dedicated diversity-promoting prefix tokens to the training of the model in order to obtain a paraphrase model designed for guided zero-shot paraphrasing, and compare the model to a baseline paraphrase generation model based on multilingual NMT without prefix guiding. Compared to the baseline model, the results suggest that the proposed guided paraphrase generation model benefits significantly from the guiding information, and produces paraphrases that deviate more from the original sentence but maintain the meaning of the original sentence well, especially with lower n-sizes of n-best decoding. The analysis also suggests that there is still room for improvement, and especially the prefix tokens promoting lexical and word order variation are not perfectly optimized.

In future work, we would like to further improve the aforementioned prefix tokens by either optimizing the bucketing based on the observed values better, or by modeling the variation promoting attributes directly within a paraphrase generation model. We would also like to evaluate the applicability of dedicated guiding attributes with different data sets or transfer tasks, such as simplification. The method could also be expanded to a larger number of languages by fine-tuning existing multilingual NMT models for guided paraphrasing. Finally, we plan to explore modular architectures for diverse paraphrasing.

Acknowledgments

This work was supported by the Behind the Words project, funded by the Academy of Finland. We wish to acknowledge *CSC - The Finnish IT Center for Science* for the generous computational resources they have provided. We thank the anonymous reviewers for their insightful comments.

References

Sweta Agrawal and Marine Carpuat. 2019. Controlling text complexity in neural machine translation. In *Proceedings of the 2019 Conference on Empirical Methods in Natural Language Processing and the 9th International Joint Conference on Natural Language Processing (EMNLP-IJCNLP)*, pages 1549–1564, Hong Kong, China. Association for Computational Linguistics.

Mikko Aulamo, Umut Sulubacak, Sami Virpioja, and Jörg Tiedemann. 2020. OpusTools and parallel corpus diagnostics. In *Proceedings of the Twelfth Language Resources and Evaluation Conference*, pages 3782–3789, Marseille, France. European Language Resources Association.

Colin Bannard and Chris Callison-Burch. 2005. Paraphrasing with bilingual parallel corpora. In *Proceedings of the 43rd Annual Meeting of the Association for Computational Linguistics (ACL'05)*, pages 597–604, Ann Arbor, Michigan. Association for Computational Linguistics.

Rahul Bhagat and Eduard Hovy. 2013. Squibs: What is a paraphrase? *Computational Linguistics*, 39(3):463–472.

Chris Callison-Burch. 2008. Syntactic constraints on paraphrases extracted from parallel corpora. In *Proceedings of the 2008 Conference on Empirical Methods in Natural Language Processing*, pages 196–205, Honolulu, Hawaii. Association for Computational Linguistics.

Chris Callison-Burch, Philipp Koehn, and Miles Osborne. 2006. Improved statistical machine translation using paraphrases. In *Proceedings of the Human Language Technology Conference of the NAACL, Main Conference*, pages 17–24, New York City, USA. Association for Computational Linguistics.

Mathias Creutz. 2018. Open subtitles paraphrase corpus for six languages. In *Proceedings of the Eleventh International Conference on Language Resources and Evaluation (LREC 2018)*, Miyazaki, Japan. European Language Resources Association (ELRA).

Li Dong, Jonathan Mallinson, Siva Reddy, and Mirella Lapata. 2017. Learning to paraphrase for question answering. In *Proceedings of the 2017 Conference on Empirical Methods in Natural Language Processing*, pages 875–886, Copenhagen, Denmark. Association for Computational Linguistics.

Thomas Dopierre, Christophe Gravier, and Wilfried Logerais. 2021. PROTAUGMENT: Unsupervised diverse short-texts paraphrasing for intent detection meta-learning. In *Proceedings of the 59th Annual Meeting of the Association for Computational Linguistics and the 11th International Joint Conference on Natural Language Processing (Volume 1: Long Papers)*, pages 2454–2466, Online. Association for Computational Linguistics.

Chris Dyer, Victor Chahuneau, and Noah A. Smith. 2013. A simple, fast, and effective reparameterization of IBM model 2. In *Proceedings of the 2013 Conference of the North American Chapter of the Association for Computational Linguistics: Human Language Technologies*, pages 644–648, Atlanta, Georgia. Association for Computational Linguistics.

Allyson Ettinger. 2020. What BERT is not: Lessons from a new suite of psycholinguistic diagnostics for language models. *Transactions of the Association for Computational Linguistics*, 8:34–48.

Juri Ganitkevitch, Benjamin Van Durme, and Chris Callison-Burch. 2013. PPDB: The paraphrase database. In *Proceedings of the 2013 Conference of the North American Chapter of the Association for Computational Linguistics: Human Language Technologies*, pages 758–764, Atlanta, Georgia. Association for Computational Linguistics.

Yinpeng Guo, Yi Liao, Xin Jiang, Qing Zhang, Yibo Zhang, and Qun Liu. 2019. Zero-shot paraphrase generation with multilingual language models. *CoRR*, abs/1911.03597.

Mareike Hartmann, Miryam de Lhoneux, Daniel Hershcovich, Yova Kementchedjhieva, Lukas Nielsen, Chen Qiu, and Anders Søgaard. 2021. A multilingual benchmark for probing negation-awareness with minimal pairs. In *Proceedings of the 25th Conference on Computational Natural Language Learning*, pages 244–257, Online. Association for Computational Linguistics.

Ari Holtzman, Jan Buys, Li Du, Maxwell Forbes, and Yejin Choi. 2020. The curious case of neural text degeneration. In *International Conference on Learning Representations*.

Bo Huang, Yang Bai, and Xiaobing Zhou. 2021. hub at SemEval-2021 task 1: Fusion of sentence and word frequency to predict lexical complexity. In *Proceedings of the 15th International Workshop on Semantic Evaluation (SemEval-2021)*, pages 598–602, Online. Association for Computational Linguistics.

Kuan-Hao Huang and Kai-Wei Chang. 2021. Generating syntactically controlled paraphrases without using annotated parallel pairs. In *Proceedings of the 16th Conference of the European Chapter of the Association for Computational Linguistics: Main Volume*, pages 1022–1033, Online. Association for Computational Linguistics.

Mohit Iyyer, John Wieting, Kevin Gimpel, and Luke Zettlemoyer. 2018. Adversarial example generation with syntactically controlled paraphrase networks. In *Proceedings of the 2018 Conference of the North American Chapter of the Association for Computational Linguistics: Human Language Technologies, Volume 1 (Long Papers)*, pages 1875–1885, New Orleans, Louisiana. Association for Computational Linguistics.

Melvin Johnson, Mike Schuster, Quoc V. Le, Maxim Krikun, Yonghui Wu, Zhifeng Chen, Nikhil Thorat, Fernanda Viégas, Martin Wattenberg, Greg Corrado, Macduff Hughes, and Jeffrey Dean. 2017. Google's multilingual neural machine translation system: Enabling zero-shot translation. *Transactions of the Association for Computational Linguistics*, 5:339–351.

Guillaume Klein, Yoon Kim, Yuntian Deng, Jean Senellart, and Alexander Rush. 2017. OpenNMT: Open-source toolkit for neural machine translation. In *Proceedings of ACL 2017, System Demonstrations*, pages 67–72, Vancouver, Canada. Association for Computational Linguistics.

Catherine Kobus, Josep Crego, and Jean Senellart. 2017. Domain control for neural machine translation. In

Proceedings of the International Conference Recent Advances in Natural Language Processing, RANLP 2017, pages 372–378, Varna, Bulgaria. INCOMA Ltd.

Kalpesh Krishna, John Wieting, and Mohit Iyyer. 2020. Reformulating unsupervised style transfer as paraphrase generation. In *Proceedings of the 2020 Conference on Empirical Methods in Natural Language Processing (EMNLP)*, pages 737–762, Online. Association for Computational Linguistics.

Taku Kudo and John Richardson. 2018. SentencePiece: A simple and language independent subword tokenizer and detokenizer for neural text processing. In *Proceedings of the 2018 Conference on Empirical Methods in Natural Language Processing: System Demonstrations*, pages 66–71, Brussels, Belgium. Association for Computational Linguistics.

Ashutosh Kumar, Satwik Bhattamishra, Manik Bhandari, and Partha Talukdar. 2019. Submodular optimization-based diverse paraphrasing and its effectiveness in data augmentation. In *Proceedings of the 2019 Conference of the North American Chapter of the Association for Computational Linguistics: Human Language Technologies, Volume 1 (Long and Short Papers)*, pages 3609–3619, Minneapolis, Minnesota. Association for Computational Linguistics.

Surafel Melaku Lakew, Mattia Di Gangi, and Marcello Federico. 2019. Controlling the output length of neural machine translation. In *Proceedings of the 16th International Conference on Spoken Language Translation*, Hong Kong. Association for Computational Linguistics.

Pierre Lison and Jörg Tiedemann. 2016. OpenSubtitles2016: Extracting large parallel corpora from movie and TV subtitles. In *Proceedings of the Tenth International Conference on Language Resources and Evaluation (LREC'16)*, pages 923–929, Portorož, Slovenia. European Language Resources Association (ELRA).

Jonathan Mallinson, Rico Sennrich, and Mirella Lapata. 2017. Paraphrasing revisited with neural machine translation. In *Proceedings of the 15th Conference of the European Chapter of the Association for Computational Linguistics: Volume 1, Long Papers*, pages 881–893, Valencia, Spain. Association for Computational Linguistics.

Kelly Marchisio, Jialiang Guo, Cheng-I Lai, and Philipp Koehn. 2019. Controlling the reading level of machine translation output. In *Proceedings of Machine Translation Summit XVII: Research Track*, pages 193–203, Dublin, Ireland. European Association for Machine Translation.

Louis Martin, Éric de la Clergerie, Benoît Sagot, and Antoine Bordes. 2020. Controllable sentence simplification. In *Proceedings of the Twelfth Language Resources and Evaluation Conference*, pages 4689–4698, Marseille, France. European Language Resources Association.

Louis Martin, Angela Fan, Éric de la Clergerie, Antoine Bordes, and Benoît Sagot. 2022. MUSS: Multilingual unsupervised sentence simplification by mining paraphrases. In *Proceedings of the Thirteenth Language Resources and Evaluation Conference*, pages 1651–1664, Marseille, France. European Language Resources Association.

Ramtin Mehdizadeh Seraj, Maryam Siahbani, and Anoop Sarkar. 2015. Improving statistical machine translation with a multilingual paraphrase database. In *Proceedings of the 2015 Conference on Empirical Methods in Natural Language Processing*, pages 1379–1390, Lisbon, Portugal. Association for Computational Linguistics.

Preksha Nema, Mitesh M. Khapra, Anirban Laha, and Balaraman Ravindran. 2017. Diversity driven attention model for query-based abstractive summarization. In *Proceedings of the 55th Annual Meeting of the Association for Computational Linguistics (Volume 1: Long Papers)*, pages 1063–1072, Vancouver, Canada. Association for Computational Linguistics.

Sergiu Nisioi, Sanja Štajner, Simone Paolo Ponzetto, and Liviu P. Dinu. 2017. Exploring neural text simplification models. In *Proceedings of the 55th Annual Meeting of the Association for Computational Linguistics (Volume 2: Short Papers)*, pages 85–91, Vancouver, Canada. Association for Computational Linguistics.

Xing Niu, Sudha Rao, and Marine Carpuat. 2018. Multi-task neural models for translating between styles within and across languages. In *Proceedings of the 27th International Conference on Computational Linguistics*, pages 1008–1021, Santa Fe, New Mexico, USA. Association for Computational Linguistics.

Kishore Papineni, Salim Roukos, Todd Ward, and Wei-Jing Zhu. 2002. Bleu: a method for automatic evaluation of machine translation. In *Proceedings of the 40th Annual Meeting of the Association for Computational Linguistics*, pages 311–318, Philadelphia, Pennsylvania, USA. Association for Computational Linguistics.

Aaditya Prakash, Sadid A. Hasan, Kathy Lee, Vivek Datla, Ashequl Qadir, Joey Liu, and Oladimeji Farri. 2016. Neural paraphrase generation with stacked residual LSTM networks. In *Proceedings of COLING 2016, the 26th International Conference on Computational Linguistics: Technical Papers*, pages 2923–2934, Osaka, Japan. The COLING 2016 Organizing Committee.

Andrea Schioppa, David Vilar, Artem Sokolov, and Katja Filippova. 2021. Controlling machine translation for multiple attributes with additive interventions. In *Proceedings of the 2021 Conference on Empirical Methods in Natural Language Processing*, pages 6676–6696, Online and Punta Cana, Dominican Republic. Association for Computational Linguistics.

Rico Sennrich, Barry Haddow, and Alexandra Birch. 2016. Controlling politeness in neural machine translation via side constraints. In *Proceedings of the 2016 Conference of the North American Chapter of the Association for Computational Linguistics: Human Language Technologies*, pages 35–40, San Diego, California. Association for Computational Linguistics.

Eetu Sjöblom, Mathias Creutz, and Yves Scherrer. 2020. Paraphrase generation and evaluation on colloquial-style sentences. In *Proceedings of the Twelfth Language Resources and Evaluation Conference*, pages 1814–1822, Marseille, France. European Language Resources Association.

Jiao Sun, Xuezhe Ma, and Nanyun Peng. 2021. AESOP: Paraphrase generation with adaptive syntactic control. In *Proceedings of the 2021 Conference on Empirical Methods in Natural Language Processing*, pages 5176–5189, Online and Punta Cana, Dominican Republic. Association for Computational Linguistics.

Shunsuke Takeno, Masaaki Nagata, and Kazuhide Yamamoto. 2017. Controlling target features in neural machine translation via prefix constraints. In *Proceedings of the 4th Workshop on Asian Translation (WAT2017)*, pages 55–63, Taipei, Taiwan. Asian Federation of Natural Language Processing.

Brian Thompson and Matt Post. 2020. Paraphrase generation as zero-shot multilingual translation: Disentangling semantic similarity from lexical and syntactic diversity. In *Proceedings of the Fifth Conference on Machine Translation*, pages 561–570, Online. Association for Computational Linguistics.

Jörg Tiedemann and Yves Scherrer. 2019. Measuring semantic abstraction of multilingual NMT with paraphrase recognition and generation tasks. In *Proceedings of the 3rd Workshop on Evaluating Vector Space Representations for NLP*, pages 35–42, Minneapolis, USA. Association for Computational Linguistics.

Jörg Tiedemann and Santhosh Thottingal. 2020. OPUS-MT – building open translation services for the world. In *Proceedings of the 22nd Annual Conference of the European Association for Machine Translation*, pages 479–480, Lisboa, Portugal. European Association for Machine Translation.

Teemu Vahtola, Mathias Creutz, and Jörg Tiedemann. 2022. It is not easy to detect paraphrases: Analysing semantic similarity with antonyms and negation using the new SemAntoNeg benchmark. In *Proceedings of the Fifth BlackboxNLP Workshop on Analyzing and Interpreting Neural Networks for NLP*, pages 249–262, Abu Dhabi, United Arab Emirates (Hybrid). Association for Computational Linguistics.

Ashish Vaswani, Noam Shazeer, Niki Parmar, Jakob Uszkoreit, Llion Jones, Aidan N. Gomez, Łukasz Kaiser, and Illia Polosukhin. 2017. Attention is all you need. In *Proceedings of the 31st International Conference on Neural Information Processing Systems*, NIPS'17, page 6000–6010, Red Hook, NY, USA. Curran Associates Inc.

John Wieting and Kevin Gimpel. 2018. ParaNMT-50M: Pushing the limits of paraphrastic sentence embeddings with millions of machine translations. In *Proceedings of the 56th Annual Meeting of the Association for Computational Linguistics (Volume 1: Long Papers)*, pages 451–462, Melbourne, Australia. Association for Computational Linguistics.

John Wieting, Jonathan Mallinson, and Kevin Gimpel. 2017. Learning paraphrastic sentence embeddings from back-translated bitext. In *Proceedings of the 2017 Conference on Empirical Methods in Natural Language Processing*, pages 274–285, Copenhagen, Denmark. Association for Computational Linguistics.

Dustin Wright, Jiaxin Pei, David Jurgens, and Isabelle Augenstein. 2022. Modeling information change in science communication with semantically matched paraphrases. In *Proceedings of the 2022 Conference on Empirical Methods in Natural Language Processing*, pages 1783–1807, Abu Dhabi, United Arab Emirates. Association for Computational Linguistics.

Hayahide Yamagishi, Shin Kanouchi, Takayuki Sato, and Mamoru Komachi. 2016. Controlling the voice of a sentence in Japanese-to-English neural machine translation. In *Proceedings of the 3rd Workshop on Asian Translation (WAT2016)*, pages 203–210, Osaka, Japan. The COLING 2016 Organizing Committee.

A Appendix. Finnish and Swedish Examples

Tables 8–11 present examples of paraphrasing in Finnish, and tables 12–15 in Swedish. Similarly as for English, we use the guided model with a beam size of 5 and only select the top-1 hypothesis.

Negation	Length	Lexical Variation	Word Order	Input	Output
True	190	4	4	Huono idea.	Ei kuulosta hyvältä idealta.
True	130	2	3	Taidan viihtyä täällä.	Eiköhän tämä ole mukava paikka.
False	120	1	4	En ole turvassa täällä.	Tämä paikka on minulle vaarallinen.
False	60	1	1	Ei hän ole vainaa.	Hän on elossa.

Table 8: Generated sentences from the guided model for Finnish paraphrasing using different prefix token values for controlling negation in the output. The prefix token for negation indicates whether there should be an explicit negation in the output sequence or not.

Input				Minusta se näyttää hienolta.
Negation	Length	Lexical Variation	Word Order	Output
False	50	3	4	Upealta.
False	80	3	4	Näyttääpä hienolta.
False	100	3	4	Se näyttää minusta hienolta.
False	120	3	4	Näyttääpä se hienolta minusta.
False	150	3	4	Se näyttää hienolta, jos minulta kysytään.

Table 9: Generated sentences from the guided model using different prefix token values for guiding for the length of the output. The prefix token value denotes the ratio between the tokenized input and output sequences.

Input				Taidan viihtyä täällä.
Negation	Length	Lexical Variation	Word Order	Output
False	130	1	4	Minusta tuntuu, että pidän tästä.
False	130	2	4	Luulen, että viihdyn täällä.
False	130	3	4	Viihdyn täällä mainiosti.
False	130	4	4	Viihdyn täällä mainiosti.

Table 10: Generated sentences from the guided model using different prefix token values for promoting lexical variation in the output sequences. Sentences in bucket 1 should only include frequent tokens, and subsequent buckets should contain sentences where also less frequent and potentially difficult tokens are present.

Input				Uskoakseni olet kuullut hänestä.
Negation	Length	Lexical Variation	Word Order	Output
False	100	1	1	Uskon, että olet kuullut hänestä.
False	100	1	2	Uskon, että olet kuullut hänestä.
False	100	1	3	Uskon, että olet kuullut hänestä.
False	100	1	4	Olet tainnut kuulla hänestä jo.

Table 11: Generated sentences from the guided model for Finnish paraphrasing using different prefix token values for guiding output sequence's word order in relation to the input sentence. The sentences with lower values should preserve the word order of the input well, whereas sentences with larger values should deviate more from the input sentence in terms of word order.

Negation	Length	Lexical Variation	Word Order	Input	Output
False	70	2	2	Det är inte över än.	Det pågår fortfarande.
False	80	2	3	Faktiskt inte så bra.	Faktiskt ganska dåligt.
True	120	3	4	Det här är allt vi kan göra.	Vi kan inte göra nåt annat än det här.
True	100	1	2	Det är nåt helt annat.	Det är inte samma sak.

Table 12: Generated sentences from the guided model for Swedish paraphrasing using different prefix token values for controlling negation in the output. The prefix token for negation indicates whether there should be an explicit negation in the output sequence or not.

Input				Det är min bröllopsdag.
Negation	Length	Lexical Variation	Word Order	Output
False	50	2	4	Mitt bröllop
False	80	2	4	Jag gifter mig.
False	100	2	4	Det är mitt bröllop.
False	120	2	4	Det är mitt bröllop idag.
False	150	2	4	Det är mitt bröllop i dag.

Table 13: Generated sentences from the guided model using different prefix token values for guiding for the length of the output. The prefix token value denotes the ratio between the tokenized input and output sequences.

Input				Det kommer att gå jättebra.
Negation	Length	Lexical Variation	Word Order	Output
False	80	1	1	Det kommer gå bra.
False	80	2	1	Det kommer gå jättebra.
False	80	3	1	Det kommer gå smidigt.
False	80	4	1	Det blir skit bra.

Table 14: Generated sentences from the guided model using different prefix token values for promoting lexical variation in the output sequences. Sentences in bucket 1 should only include frequent tokens, and subsequent buckets should contain sentences where also less frequent and potentially difficult tokens are present.

Input				Det har jag redan sagt.
Negation	Length	Lexical Variation	Word Order	Output
False	110	2	1	Det har jag redan talat om.
False	110	2	2	Det har jag redan talat om.
False	110	2	3	Det har jag ju redan berättat.
False	110	2	4	Jag har redan talat om det.

Table 15: Generated sentences from the guided model for Swedish paraphrasing using different prefix token values for guiding output sequence's word order in relation to the input sentence. The sentences with lower values should preserve the word order of the input well, whereas sentences with larger values should deviate more from the input sentence in terms of word order.

A Tale of Two Laws of Semantic Change: Predicting Synonym Changes with Distributional Semantic Models

Bastien Liétard and **Mikaela Keller** and **Pascal Denis**
Univ. Lille, Inria, CNRS, Centrale Lille, UMR 9189 - CRIStAL, F-59000 Lille, France
first_name.last_name@inria.fr

Abstract

Lexical Semantic Change is the study of how the meaning of words evolves through time. Another related question is whether and how lexical relations over pairs of words, such as synonymy, change over time. There are currently two competing, apparently opposite hypotheses in the historical linguistic literature regarding how synonymous words evolve: the Law of Differentiation (LD) argues that synonyms tend to take on different meanings over time, whereas the Law of Parallel Change (LPC) claims that synonyms tend to undergo the same semantic change and therefore remain synonyms. So far, there has been little research using distributional models to assess to what extent these laws apply on historical corpora. In this work, we take a first step toward detecting whether LD or LPC operates for given word pairs. After recasting the problem into a more tractable task, we combine two linguistic resources to propose the first complete evaluation framework on this problem and provide empirical evidence in favor of a dominance of LD. We then propose various computational approaches to the problem using Distributional Semantic Models and grounded in recent literature on Lexical Semantic Change detection. Our best approaches achieve a balanced accuracy above 0.6 on our dataset. We discuss challenges still faced by these approaches, such as polysemy or the potential confusion between synonymy and hypernymy.

1 Introduction

Recent years have seen a surge to model lexical semantic change (LSC) with computational approaches based on Distributional Semantic Models (DSMs) (Tahmasebi et al., 2021). While most research in this area has concentrated on developing approaches for automatically *detecting* LSC for individual words, as in the dedicated SemEval 2020 shared task (Schlechtweg et al., 2020), there has also been some work on validating or even proposing laws of semantic changes through new DSM-based approaches (Dubossarsky et al., 2015; Hamilton et al., 2016; Dubossarsky et al., 2017). Ultimately, this line of work is very promising as it can provide direct contributions to the field of historical linguistics.

In this paper, we consider two laws of semantic change that are very prominent in historical linguistics, but that have to date given rise to very little computational modeling studies. Specifically, the Law of Differentiation (LD), originally due to Bréal (1897, chapter 2), posits that synonymous words tend to take on different meanings over time; or one of them will simply disappear.[1] The same idea is also discussed in more recent work, such as Clark (1993). As an example, the verbs *spread* and *broadcast* used to be synonyms (especially in farming), but now the latter is only used in the sense of *transmit*, by means of radio, television or internet. The verbs *plead* and *beseech* are synonyms, but *beseech* is no longer used nowadays compared to *plead*. By contrast, the Law of Parallel Change (LPC),[2] inspired from the work of Stern (1921), claims that two synonyms tend to undergo the same semantic change and therefore remain synonyms. As an illustration, Stern (1921, chapter 3 and 4) describes the change of *swiftly* and its synonyms from the sense of *rapidly* to the stronger sense of *immediately*. Lehrer (1985) also observes a parallel change affecting animal terms which acquire a metaphorical sense.

These two laws are interesting under several aspects. Firstly, these laws go beyond the problem of detecting semantic change in individual words, as they concern the question of whether a lexical relationship between words, in this case synonymy, is preserved or not through time. Secondly, these laws make very strong, seemingly opposite, predictions

[1] To cite Bréal (1897): *"[S]ynonyms do not exist for long: either they differ, or one of the two terms disappears."*

[2] Name coined by Xu and Kemp (2015).

*Proceedings of the The 12th Joint Conference on Lexical and Computational Semantics (*SEM 2023)*, pages 338–352
July 13-14, 2023 ©2023 Association for Computational Linguistics

on how synonyms evolve: either their meanings diverge (under LD) or they remain close (under LPC). It is likely that both of these laws might be at work, but they possibly apply to different word classes, correspond to different linguistic or extra-linguistic factors, or operate at different time scales. A large-scale study, fueled by computational methods over large quantities of texts, would be amenable to statistical analyses addressing these questions. In this work, we focus on predicting the persistence (or disappearance) of synonymy through time, as a first step toward more complete analyses.

Prima facie, DSMs appear to provide a natural resource for constructing a computational approach for assessing the importance of these laws, as they inherently –through the distributional hypothesis– capture a notion of semantic proximity, which can be used as a proxy for synonymy. Following this idea, Xu and Kemp (2015) propose the first DSM-based method for predicting how synonymous word pairs of English evolve over time (specifically, from 1890 to 1990). This research decisively concludes that there is "evidence against the Law of Differentiation and in favor of the Law of Parallel Change" for adjectives, nouns and verbs alike (i.e., the three considered POS). However, this pioneering work suffers from some limitations that cast some doubts on this conclusion. First off, the predictions made by their approach are not checked against a ground truth, thus lacks a proper evaluation. Second, the approach is strongly biased against LD, as only pairs in which *both* words have changed are considered, excluding pairs in which differentiation may occur (e.g. in *spread/broadcast*, only the latter word changed in meaning).

This paper addresses these shortcomings by introducing a more rigorous evaluation framework for testing these two laws and evaluating computational approaches. We build a dataset of English synonyms that was obtained by combining lexical resources for two time stamps (1890 and 1990) that records, for a given list of synonym pairs at time 1890, whether these pairs are still synonymous or not in 1990. The analysis of this dataset reveals that, contra Xu and Kemp (2015) and though using the same initial synonym set, synonymous words show a strong tendency to differentiate in meaning over time. With some variation across POS, we found that between 55 and 80% of synonyms in 1890 are no longer synonyms in 1990.

Moreover, we propose several new computational approaches[3], grounded in more recent DSMs, for automatically predicting whether synonymous words diverge or remain close in meaning over time, which we recast as a binary classification problem. Inspired by Xu & Kemp (2015), our first approach is unsupervised and tracks pairwise synchronic distances over time, computed over SGNS-based vector representations. Our second approach is supervised and integrates additional variables into a logistic regression model. This latter model achieves a balanced accuracy above 0.6 over the proposed dataset.

2 Related Work

Data-driven methods to detect LSC have gained popularity in the recent years (Tahmasebi et al., 2021), using increasingly powerful and expressive word representations, ranging from the simple co-occurrence word vectors (Sagi et al., 2012) to static word embeddings (Schlechtweg et al., 2019) and transformer-based contextualized word representations (Kutuzov et al., 2022; Fourrier and Montariol, 2022). This line of research lead to the development of shared tasks (Zamora-Reina et al., 2022; Schlechtweg et al., 2020; Rodina and Kutuzov, 2020). Most often, these tasks concern the evolution of individual words, in effect focusing on *absolute* semantic change (of words individually). In this paper, we take a different stand, considering the problem of *relative* change in meaning among pairs of words, specifically focusing on synonym pairs.

Previous work on word pairs are rare in the current LSC research landscape. A first exception is (Turney and Mohammad, 2019), who also study the evolution of synonyms. They propose a dataset to track how usage frequency of words evolve over time within a sets of synonyms, as well as a new task: namely, to predict whether the dominant (most frequent) word of a synonyms set will change or not. This task is actually complementary to the one we address in this work. While Turney and Mohammad (2019) assume the stability of most synonym pairs between 1800 and 2000, and rather investigate the dynamic inside sets of synonymous words across time, we question this alleged stability and attempt to track whether these words remain synonymous at all in this time period.

[3] The code used to run experiments in this paper can be found at `https://github.com/blietard/synonyms-semchange`

Another distinctive motivation of our work is in the empirical, large-scale evaluation of two proposed laws of semantic change, originating from historical linguistics. Previous work investigating laws of semantic change with DSMs include Dubossarsky et al. (2015) and Hamilton et al. (2016), who measured semantic change of words between 1800 and 2000 and attempted to draw statistical laws of semantic change from their observations. Later, Dubossarsky et al. (2017) contrasted these observations and showed that even if these effects may be real, it may be to a lesser extent.

The closest work to the current research is the study of Xu and Kemp (2015), as they already focus on the two laws of Differentiation (LD) and Parallel Change (LPC). Their main motivation was to automatically measure, using DSMs, which of the two laws was predominant between 1890 and 1999. To study which of the two laws actually operates, they focus on word pairs that (i) are synonyms in the 1890s and (ii) where both words changed significantly in meaning between 1890 and the 1990s. First, they represent words as probability distributions of direct contexts, using normalized co-occurrence count vectors. Then, they measure the (synchronic) semantic proximity of words by computing the Jensen-Shannon Divergence between the corresponding distributions. Semantic change in a word is quantified by comparing its semantic space neighborhoods in the 1890s and in the 1990s. Finally, for every selected synonymous pair, they pick a control word pair that has a smaller divergence in the 1890s than the associated synonyms. At a later time in the 1990s, if the divergence for the synonyms is larger than that for the control pair, they decide these synonyms have undergone LD, otherwise they predict LPC. Ultimately, they found that most pairs (around 60%) have undergone LPC, which would be the dominant law.

The pioneering work of Xu and Kemp (2015) faces a number of shortcomings. First, their restriction to synonymous pairs in which both words changed mechanically excludes certain cases of LD (i.e., where one one word has changed), thus introducing an artificial bias against LD. Moreover, they often select near-synonyms as controls (e.g. *instructive* and *interesting*) because they constrain control pairs to be *closer* in divergence in the 1890s than the associated synonym pairs. Furthermore, and more importantly, Xu and Kemp (2015) did not compare their predictions to any ground-truth and there is no evaluation of the reliability of their method. Finally, their choice of word representations is not among the State-of-the-Art for static methods.

In this paper, we consider all synonymous pairs, thus avoiding the bias against LD. We propose different approaches that we compare to Xu and Kemp (2015)'s control pairs, and we provide results obtained with more recent distributional semantic models. Most importantly, we propose a complete evaluation framework to benchmark the different methods, something missing in this prior work.

3 Problem Statement

Our overarching goal is to develop new computational approaches that are able to automatically predict which pairs of synonymous words underwent LD or LPC. These predictions could be used as a first step towards providing a more refined and statistically meaningful analysis of the two laws. An important milestone towards developing such an approach is to compare it to some ground truth. Otherwise, there is no way to assess whether statistics obtained for LD or LPC are indeed reliable, a problem faced by Xu and Kemp (2015).

Unfortunately, there is no existing large-scale resource that records instances of LD/LPC, beyond a handful of examples found in research papers and textbooks in historical linguistics. What exists however are historical lists of synonyms, which we can compare to obtain some form of ground truth. This forces us to consider a slightly different methodological framework, focusing on a more constrained prediction task, namely to detect pairs of synonyms at time $T1$ that have remained synonymous or that are no longer synonymous at time $T2 (> T1)$.

3.1 Formalization

Let us denote $W^{(T)}$ the set of words (or vocabulary) for a given language (say English) at time T. As language evolves through time, vocabularies at two times $T1$ and $T2$ need not have the exact same extensions: e.g., a word w in $W^{(T1)}$ might not be in $W^{(T2)}$ (i.e., w has disappeared). Making a simplistic, idealized assumption, let $\mathcal{C}$ be a mostly atemporal and exhaustive discrete set of concepts, and denote $M_w^{(T)} \subset \mathcal{C}$ the meaning of word w at time T. The definition of $M_w^{(T)}$ as a set allows homonymy and/or polysemy to be accounted for.

Given these notations, we have that $u \in W^{(T)}$

and $v \in W^{(T)}$ are synonyms at a time T if $M_u^{(T)} \cap M_v^{(T)} \neq \emptyset$. We understand that the study of LD / LPC implies to track (i) the change of $M_u^{(T)}$ and $M_v^{(T)}$ over time, (ii) the evolution of $M_u^{(T)} \cap M_v^{(T)}$ and (iii) the very persistence of both words in vocabularies $W^{(T)}$ between $T1$ and $T2$. Discussion about formalizing LD and LPC under those conditions can be found in appendix A.1.

3.2 Task Formulation: Tracking Synonyms Change

The presented formulation, though very idealized, should make it clear that the development of a computational system that attempts to directly predict LD and LPC, and even the construction of an evaluation benchmark for evaluating such a system, are very challenging tasks. First, the initial synonym set selection presupposes, not only that one has access to a list of synonyms at $T1$ and $T2$, but also that one can reliably predict LSC in one of the two words from $T1$ to $T2$; unfortunately, LSC is still an open problem for current NLP models. Second, one typically does not have meaning inventories or automatic systems (e.g. WSD systems) for mapping words to their meanings at different time stamps. Finally, even tracking the disappearance of words through time is not trivial, as it ideally requires full dictionaries at different time stamps.

Given these limitations, we suggest to narrow down our target problem to the task of predicting, for a given pair of synonymous words (u, v) at $T1$, whether (u, v) are still synonymous or not at $T2$. Stated a little more formally, we are concerned with the following binary classification problem:

$$f : \mathcal{S}^{(T1)} \rightarrow \{\text{"Syn"}, \text{"Diff"}\}$$

$$(u, v) \mapsto f((u, v)) = \begin{cases} \text{"Syn" if } (u, v) \in \mathcal{S}^{(T2)} \\ \text{"Diff" otherwise} \end{cases}$$

where $\mathcal{S}^{(T)}$ is a set of synonymous word pairs at time T, "Syn" indicates that words (u, v) that were synonymous at $T1$ remain synonymous at $T2$, while "Diff" signals that they are no longer synonymous at $T2$. This simpler problem leads to a more operational evaluation procedure, which does not require access to $M_u^{(T^*)}$ and $M_v^{(T^*)}$, but only to lists of synonyms $\mathcal{S}^{(T1)}$ and $\mathcal{S}^{(T2)}$. See Section 4 for presentation of such procedure. It should be clear that predicting which synonym pairs remain ("Syn") or cease to be synymoms ("Diff"), will provide some information about LPC and LD, although the mapping between the two problems is not one-to-one. Even if "Diff" covers pretty well LD, a pair that is still synonymous at $T2$ could either be a case of LPC (their shared meaning changed the same way for both words) or a pair of words that simply have not changed in meaning at all (or at least that their shared meaning is unchanged).

Now turning to designing a computational system that detects "Syn" vs. "Diff", a natural question that emerges is whether current DSMs, commonly used for detecting LSC in individual words, are able to capture synonym changes. More specifically, our main hypothesis will be that one can reliably track the evolution of synonymous pairs through their word vector representations at $T1$ and $T2$. This approach will be instantiated into different unsupervised and supervised models in Section 5.

4 Evaluation Dataset

This section presents a dataset designed to track the evolution of English synonymous word pairs between two time stamps $T1$ and $T2$, with $T2 > T1$. Specifically, the two time periods considered are the 1890's decade ($T1$) and the 1990's decade ($T2$). For extracting synonymous pairs in the 1890's (noted $\mathcal{S}^{(T1)}$), we use Fernald's *English Synonyms and Antonyms* (Fernald, 1896) as Xu and Kemp (2015) did. Pairs were selected based on a set of specific target words (see appendix A.7). As shown in Table 1, we obtain $1,507$ adjective pairs, $2,689$ noun pairs and $1,489$ verb pairs. To assess whether these word pairs are still synonyms in the 1990's, we use WordNet (Fellbaum and Princeton, 2010), as this lexical database was originally constructed in 1990's. Thus, WordNet provides us with $\mathcal{S}^{(T2)}$. Specifically, we considered that a pair of words/lemmas $(u, v) \in \mathcal{S}^{(T1)}$ are still synonymous if they point to at least one common *synset* in WordNet.

The construction of this dataset relies on two crucial hypotheses, which seem reasonable to make. First, both lexical resources rely on the same definition of synonymy. Second, $\mathcal{S}^{(T2)}$ meets some exhaustivity criterion, in the sense that $(u, v) \in \mathcal{S}^{(T1)}$ not appearing in $\mathcal{S}^{(T2)}$ should indicate that u and v are no longer synonymous at $T2$, and not be due to a lack of coverage of the resource (i.e., a false negative). WordNet is assumed to be exhaustive enough, as we checked that every word involved in at least one synonymous pair has its own entry in

Synonyms pairs	ADJ	NN	VERB	All
Synonyms at $T1$	1507	2689	1489	5685
& synonyms at $T2$	202	347	311	860
& synonyms at $T2$(%)	13.4	12.9	20.9	15.1
& hypernyms at $T2$	0	858	398	1256
& hypernyms at $T2$(%)	0.0	31.9	26.7	22.1
& hyp. at $T2$ (1) (%)	0.0	23.2	22.5	16.9
& hyp. at $T2$ (2) (%)	0.0	6.9	3.5	4.1
& hyp. at $T2$ (3) (%)	0.0	1.4	0.5	0.8

Table 1: Numbers of synonymous pairs extracted from Fernald (1896) ($T1$) displayed by POS, and numbers of those that are also considered as synonyms or hypernyms/hyponyms in WordNet ($T2$) For hypernyms, we detail the proportions of hypernym/hyponym pairs that are separated by 1, 2 or 3 nodes in the WordNet graph.

WordNet's database.

Table 1 provides some detailed statistics on the evolution of synonomous pairs between decades 1890's and 1990's, overall and for different parts of speech. A first observation on these datasets is that the proportion of pairs that are still synonyms at $T2$ ("*Syn*") is globally 15.1%. This implies that most synonymous pairs underwent differentiation. While it does not provide information about how change happened between $T1$ and $T2$ for the remaining 84.9%, it's a clue that the Law of Differentiation should be a dominant phenomenon among synonyms.

We exploit the structure of the WordNet database to analyze the different cases of "*Diff*". WordNet includes lexical relations of hyper-/hypo-nymy (e.g., *seat/bench*) as well as holo-/mero-nymy (e.g., *bike/wheel*) and antonymy (e.g., *small/large*) defined over synsets[4]. Note that the hyper-/hyponymy relation does not exist in WordNet among adjectives. Among nouns and verbs, we observe that around 30% of pairs that were synonyms at $T1$ are in an hyper-/hypo-nymy relation at $T2$ and two third of them are direct hypernyms in WordNet (their synsets are direct parent/child) indicating the preservation of a very close semantic link. For a further depiction of the dataset in terms of distance in WordNet's graph, see Figure 3 in appendix A.4.

One cannot entirely exclude that $\mathcal{S}^{(T1)}$ includes some hyper-/hypo-nyms as synonyms. However, even if we extend the notion of synonymy at $T2$ to include these cases, we would have only around 45% of all pairs still considered synonyms among nouns and verbs. This indicates that "Diff" largely remains the most common phenomenon with an estimated proportion between 55% and 80%. This finding contradicts the experimental results reported by Xu and Kemp (2015) with their computational approach (only 40% of differentiation).

In lack of additional indication that some of these hyper-/hypo-nym cases at $T2$ are indeed synonyms, or that they may also have been hyper-/hypo-nym at $T1$, we decided to still consider them as instances of "Diff". Another argument for this decision is precisely that there are well-known reported cases of lexical semantic changes in which the meaning of a particular word in effect "widens" to denote a larger subset (i.e., becomes an hypernym): this is the case of *dog* in English that used to denote a specific breed of dogs (Traugott and Dasher, 2001).

5 Approaches

This section presents two classes of computational approaches, unsupervised and supervised, for predicting whether pairs of synonyms at $T1$ remain synonyms ("Syn") or cease to be so ("Diff") at a later time $T2$. Common to all of these approaches is that they are based on two time-aware DSMs, one for each time stamp.

5.1 Time-aware DSMs

Inspired by work on LSC, we rely on separate DSMs for each time stamp $T1$ and $T2$, respectively yielding vector spaces $V^{(T1)}$ and $V^{(T2)}$ encoding the (possibly changing) word meanings at $T1$ and $T2$. Thus, for each synonym pair (u, v), we have two pairs of vectors : $(\mathbf{u}^{(T1)}, \mathbf{v}^{(T1)}) \in V^{(T1)} \times V^{(T1)}$ and $(\mathbf{u}^{(T2)}, \mathbf{v}^{(T2)}) \in V^{(T2)} \times V^{(T2)}$.

Specifically, we use pre-computed SGNS (Mikolov et al., 2013) from Hamilton et al. (2016) trained on the *English* part of the GoogleBooks Ngrams dataset[5] for every decade between 1800 and 2000 and extract $V^{(T1)}$ (1890) and $V^{(T2)}$ (1990). For any word $w \in W$ and any time period T, $\mathbf{w}^{(T)} \in V^{(T)}$ is a single 300 dimensional vector. We ensure synonymy is accurately reflected by checking that synonym pairs have a smaller cosine distance than non-synonymous pairs for both time periods, as in Figure 4 of appendix A.5.

Traditional DSM-based approaches for detecting LSC are based on self-similarities over time for a given word. For instance, for a given time

[4]As we did for synonyms, we assume that two words w_1 and w_2 are instances of one of these relations R if R holds for one of their corresponding synset pair.

[5]https://storage.googleapis.com/books/ngrams/books/datasetsv3.html

interval $(T1, T2)$, they compute for each word w an individual *Diachronic Distance*, noted here $DD^{(T1,T2)}(w)$. Cosine distance is often used (recall in appendix A.2).

There is no obvious distance for comparing *pairs* of word vectors, but one can instead rely on comparing the pairwise word vector distance at each time stamp T; we call this *Synchronic Distance* (denoted SD). The two types of distances for two time stamps $T1$ and $T2$ are described in Figure 1. Our unsupervised method, proposed in Sec. 5.2 directly exploit the idea of tracking different types of SD through time, while Sec. 5.3 presents a supervised approach that combines both SD and DD.

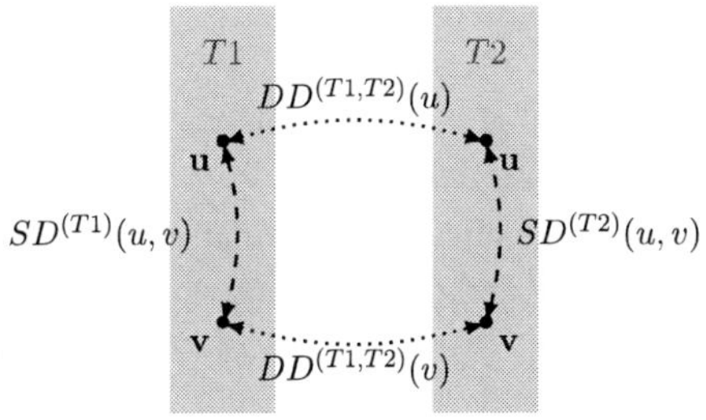

Figure 1: Pairs of word embeddings at 2 time periods and associated diachronic and synchronic distances.

5.2 Unsupervised Methods

While we don't have access to $M_u^{(T)}$ and $M_v^{(T)}$, we can represent the meaning of u and v using DSM and compare them at a given time to estimate how close they are in meaning. Indeed, if $M_u^{(T)} \cap M_v^{(T)}$ changes, this should be reflected in difference of the use contexts of u and those of v, and so reflected in the distance between $\mathbf{u}^{(T)}$ and $\mathbf{v}^{(T)}$. Let

$$SD^{(T)} : W^{(T)} \times W^{(T)} \to \mathbb{R}^+$$

be a measure of **synchronic distance** between vectors representing two words. By construction of $V^{(T)}$, $SD^{(T)}(u, v)$ is smaller for words (u, v) that appear in similar contexts than for unrelated words. We assume that there exists a value δ_T such that

$$\forall (u, v) \in \mathcal{S}^{(T)},\ SD^{(T)}(u, v) \leq \delta_T.$$

This entails that for a given pair (u, v):

$$SD^{(T)}(u, v) > \delta_T \Rightarrow (u, v) \text{ are not synonyms.}$$

In this setting, one can compare the synchronic distances within $V^{(T1)}$ and with $V^{(T2)}$ and decide if the pair differentiated or stayed synonymous.

Let (u, v) be a pair of synonyms at $T1$, as such we have that $SD^{(T1)}(u, v) \leq \delta_{T1}$. If (u, v) are not synonyms at time $T2$ then $SD^{(T2)}(u, v) > \delta_{T2}$.

Combining these two inequalities, we would say that a pair of synonyms at $T1$ has differentiated at $T2$ if:

$$\underbrace{SD^{(T2)}(u, v) - SD^{(T1)}(u, v)}_{= \Delta(u,v)} > \delta_{T2} - \delta_{T1}.$$

Ideally one could imagine that the distance threshold δ_T at which, words cease to be synonyms should be independent of the time period T. Empirically however, because word embeddings are not necessarily build with an enforced scale, there might be a dilation or shrinking in the overall synchronic distances between $T1$ and $T2$. Let us assume that

$$\delta_{T2} = \delta_{T1} + \tau,\ \tau \in \mathbb{R}.$$

Our decision rule could then be rewritten as:

$$f(u, v) = \begin{cases} \text{"Diff" if } \Delta(u, v) \geq \tau \\ \text{"Syns" otherwise.} \end{cases} \quad (1)$$

This approach is shortly denoted "Δ" in section 6. It diverges from the prior work of Xu and Kemp (2015) that chooses to rely on control pairs instead of a threshold. For the sake of comparison, we implemented their method presented as *"XK controls"*. It is not the full protocol presented by Xu and Kemp (2015), as (i) the experimental setting is not identical, they filtered out some synonym pairs and we didn't (ii) we use SGNS word representations and cosine distance instead of normalized co-occurrence counts and Jensen-Shannon Divergence. Schlechtweg et al. (2019) provided a longer comparison between word representations.

We propose a statistically-grounded criterion to set the value for the threshold τ. Since the meaning of most words is expected to remain stable[6], we argue that most pairwise distances should remain stable as well. We can then estimate the dilation between the representations in the two time periods by the average gap between the synchronic distances of words.

$$\tau = \frac{1}{|W|^2} \sum_{(w_1, w_2) \in W \times W} \Delta(w_1, w_2) \quad (2)$$

[6]Intuitively, someone in 2023 can still understand writings published in the 1890s in their original text, like books from Charles Dickens or Arthur Conan Doyle.

In practice, we experiment with two different types of synchronic distances between words. The first is the cosine distance (see A.2). That is:

$$SD^{(T)}(u,v) = \text{cos-dist}(\mathbf{u}^{(T)}, \mathbf{v}^{(T)}).$$

We shortly denote it "SD(cd)". Another measure of semantic proximity is based on the shared word neighborhood between the two vectors u and v:

$$SD^{(T)}(u,v) = \text{jaccard-dist}(\mathcal{N}_k^{(T)}(u), \mathcal{N}_k^{(T)}(v)),$$

with $\mathcal{N}_k^{(T)}(w)$ being the set of the k-nearest neighbors of the point representing w in the vector space at time T, and *jaccard-dist* being the Jaccard distance (see appendix A.2). This measure is ranged between 0 and 1, and we denote it "SD(nk)".

5.3 Supervised Methods

Approaches described so far use the labels in the dataset ("Syn" and "Diff") only for evaluation purposes. But one can also use part of the available data to learn a *supervised* classifier to predicts these labels. Concretely, for most of these models, we trained Logistic Regression (LR) models[7]

Synchronic Distances Combination In our unsupervised approach, we compute $SD^{(T1)}$ and $SD^{(T2)}$ and their difference, denoted Δ. This quantity is then compared to a fixed threshold τ. We propose to investigate two supervised approaches stemming from this: (i) simply tune τ and (ii) use a LR model to learn the optimal weighting in the linear combination of the two distances. This latter model is called "LR SD".

Accounting for Individual Change Most works about computational approaches to LSC focus on detecting the change of a single word (Tahmasebi et al., 2021), using a diachronic distance, which we noted $DD^{(T1,T2)}(w)$, across time periods $T1$ and $T2$ for individual words w.

In addition to synchronic distances, we input diachronic distances as features for a LR model. The resulting classifier (LR SD+DD) uses the 4 distances represented in Figure 1 as variables: self-similarities across time periods (*DD*s), and a distance measure within pairs for each of both time stamps (*SD*s). Similarly to synchronic distances defined in Sec. 5.2, we try two definitions of DD. First, we compare sets of neighbors at $T1$ and $T2$:

$$\text{DD}(w) = \text{jaccard-dist}(\mathcal{N}_k^{(T1)}(w), \mathcal{N}_k^{(T2)}(w)).$$

We also compute the cosine distance between $\mathbf{w}^{(T1)}$ and $\mathbf{w}^{(T2)}$ after aligning the vector space $V^{(T2)}$ to $V^{(T1)}$ using Orthogonal Procrustes (Hamilton et al., 2016; Schlechtweg et al., 2019, 2020). Denoting $\mathbf{w}_{align}^{(T2)}$ the vector $\mathbf{w}^{(T2)}$ after alignement with Orthogonal Procrustes, we have:

$$\text{DD}(w) = \text{cos-dist}(\mathbf{w}^{(T1)}, \mathbf{w}_{align}^{(T2)}).$$

Using Distances and Frequencies A final step of this process is to add word frequencies for both words at both time periods, as there exist links between usage frequency and semantic change Zipf (1945). We could observe whether adding explicit frequency information helps retrieving discriminatory clues that could be missed by using only distributional representations.

Word frequencies were estimated from the Corpus of Historical American English (COHA) list,[9] which has the advantage to be genre-balanced. As variables for both words and both periods to feed our model, we try to add either raw occurrences counts (indicated by "+FR"), either grouped frequency counts ("+FG"). The procedure to create such groups is described in appendix A.6.

All Features For the sake of comparison to previous models, we evaluate LR models that take as input an implementation of each of these features (SD + DD + frequency); and an even larger model (called "LR multi.") that reunites *all* described implementations of *SD*, *DD* and frequencies.

Non-linear Models As a further step increasing the model's complexity, we try to combine this full set of available variables in a non-linear fashion. We compare previous models to polynomial features (degree 2) preprocessing[10] and a SVM classifier with a Gaussian kernel.

6 Experiments

6.1 Experimental Settings

Target Words Selection We use a unique vocabulary W composed of $6,453$ adjectives, $16,135$ nouns and $10,073$ verbs. The process to select words is described in appendix A.7.

[7]Implemented with the *scikit-learn* library for Python[8].

[9]`https://www.ngrams.info/download_coha.asp`

[10]We also try degrees higher than 2, finding no consistent improvement.

Dataset Evaluation metric	ADJ	NN	VERB	ALL	ALL F_1*(Syn)*	 F_1*(Diff)*	 %(D)
	Balanced Accuracy						
All *(Syn)*	.50	.50	.50	.50	.48	0	0
All *(Diff)*	.50	.50	.50	.50	0	.81	100
LR F	.51	.56	.59	.55	.35	.74	75
XK controls	.52	.49	.51	.50	.33	.67	65
Δ (cd)	.50	.49	.51	.50	.27	.73	75
Δ (nk)	.48	.49	.49	.50	.32	.67	66
Δ (tuned τ)	.51	.52	.52	.51	.27	.74	79
LR SD	.60	.62	.59	.60	.48	.69	56
LR SD + DD	.61	.62	.60	.60	.48	.69	56
LR SD + F	.61	**.64**	.63	**.62**	.51	.71	57
LR SD + DD + F	**.62**	**.64**	.63	**.62**	.50	.70	57
LR multi	**.62**	**.64**	**.65**	**.62**	.51	.71	57
LR multi. poly. degree (2)	.56	.63	.62	**.62**	.50	.70	60
SVM (gaussian)	.60	**.64**	**.65**	**.62**	.50	.74	63

Table 2: Performances of the different approaches. Results are averaged over 20 random splits.

Dataset Splits For every POS tag, we have a set of word pairs that are synonymous at $T1$. We call *ALL* the dataset that comprises all pairs indistinctly of their POS. These datasets (ADJ,NN,VERB or ALL) are individually shuffled and 33% of their samples (pairs) are set aside for testing. For each dataset, a model is trained on the 66% remaining pairs and evaluated on the test part. Presented results are averaged over 20 random train/test splits.

Hyperparameters We train models with combinations of the different definitions of distances and frequency variables. Choice of synchronic distances was between SD(cd) and SD(nk) with k in $\{5, 10, 15, 20, 40, 100\}$. For DD, we tried neighborhoods with fixed size 100, like Xu and Kemp (2015), and Orthogonal Procrustes with cosine distances. For frequency, the choice is between raw counts and groups. The selected models are detailed in Appendix A.9. The ideal value for the SVM's regularization parameter is found using 5-fold cross-validation over the training set.

Evaluation Metrics We use two standard evaluation metrics: F_1 score and *Balanced Accuracy (BA)*. F_1 scores were computed for both classes, denoting it "$\mathbf{F_1}$*(Syn)*" for *Syns* and "$\mathbf{F_1}$*(Diff)*" for *Diff*. BA is defined as the average of recalls for both classes, and provide a notion of accuracy robust to class imbalance. We also display the percentage of predicted *Diff* ("%D").

Baselines The first two baselines are constant output classifiers, always predicting "*Syn*" or "*Diff*" respectively. They are expected to have a balanced accuracy of 50%, as they would be fully accurate for one class and always wrong for the other. The third baseline (*LR Frequency*) is a Logistic Regression model trained *only* with frequency variables, without any knowledge on the semantic aspect of the pair (neither *SD* or *DD*).

6.2 Results

Performances over the test parts of the different datasets are displayed Table 2.

The first observation is that, in line with the dataset's proportions, all models predict a majority of "Diff", even unsupervised ones (including our reimplementation of Xu & Kemp's control pair selection method). While our task does not directly address the question of the opposition between LD and LPC, this is an empirical clue in favor of LD, contradicting Xu and Kemp (2015). However, predicting the right amount of "Diff" does not guarantee the quality of predictions. Indeed, obtained balanced accuracies range between 0.49 and 0.65.

Considering our unsupervised methods and the Δ (tuned τ), we find no real improvement over baselines. In particular, they fail to outperform the frequency-based baseline model which performs surprisingly well. On the other hand, Logistic Regression and SVM models substantially improve

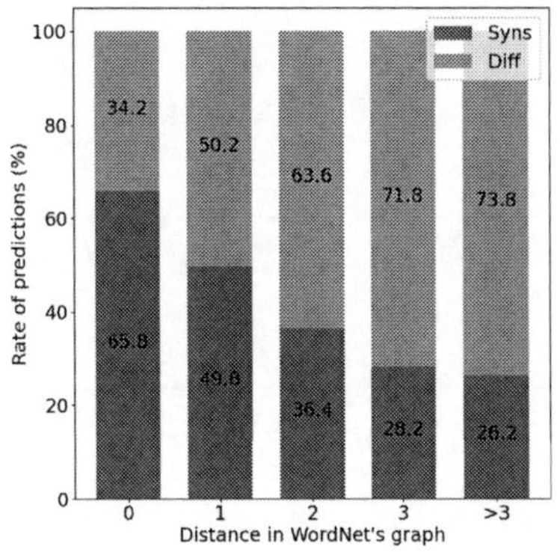

Figure 2: Proportions of predictions of the models w.r.t. the actual distance d in WordNet of *noun* pairs. Pairs with $d = 0$ are synonymous pairs in WordNet.

over the baselines, Xu & Kemp's control pairs and all Δ-based methods. Interestingly, LR SD outperforms Δ-based methods despite the fact that they rely on the same components.

The gap between baselines and models is larger for nouns and lesser for verbs. Despite these POS-specific differences, best models are consistently the ones using both SD and frequencies, while DD brings little to no improvement. This can be expected as individual changes of words seem less important on the problem of *Syn/Diff*. However, this factor could be used in future work to distinguish pairs of synonyms (among the *Syn* class) that did not change and pairs that went under LPC.

We observe that there is a substantial difference in F_1 scores between the two classes, $\mathbf{F_1}$*(Syn)* being lower than $\mathbf{F_1}$*(Diff)* across all models. Moreover, models with higher $\mathbf{F_1}$*(Syn)* are often found to be the ones with higher balanced accuracy, even when $\mathbf{F_1}$*(Diff)* is lower. This is likely linked to the fact that the datasets are highly imbalanced as presented in Table 1: the ground truth proportion of *Syn* never exceeds 21%. We also remark that Xu and Kemp (2015) decision rule based on control pairs also predicts a majority of *Diff*, contrarily to the results they showed. It may be because the protocol is not fully identical.

6.3 Confounding Factors

Using WordNet, we discuss two aspects that may be sources of errors when detecting a change in synonymy: polysemy and hypernymy. We study predictions of our best performing LR model on the noun dataset.

Polysemy WordNet provides us with different set of synonyms for every entry, corresponding to different senses or usages, and therefore we can measure the polysemy of a word at $T2$. We found that pairs misclassified as "Syn" tend to be those whose second term has fewer senses (6 senses on average as compared with well classified "Diff" which have 8 senses on average). Indeed, as we use static embeddings and no Word Sense Disambiguation (WSD) method, our model is subject to the complexity brought by polysemy. In a recent shared task about Lexical Semantic Change measures, best performing models are the one using WSD methods (Zamora-Reina et al., 2022). This finding highlights the importance of handling polysemy as a potential confounding factor.

Distances in WordNet In Figure 2 we display the percentage of prediction with respect to shortest distance between the two words of *noun* pairs in WordNet's graph. The distance d is the minimum number of nodes separating the two words.

We remark that, as expected, the model predicts more and more *Diff* as d increases. What is more interesting is that for $d = 1$ (direct hypernymy), there is still an important proportions of predicted *Syn*. This highlights that our model has difficulties to handle hypernymy and confuses it with synonymy.

7 Conclusion

In this work, we considered two contradicting laws about the semantic change of synonyms. We discussed the necessary adaptations of the problem statement for this particular type of LSC and elaborated a framework to evaluate models for this new classification problem. The use of linguistic resources from two different time periods allowed us to improve model analysis with respect to prior work on the matter. Then we proposed unsupervised and supervised approaches relying on measures of semantic change extracted or inspired by existing literature on LSC, and also leveraged the usefulness of explicit word usage frequency information. We compared these approaches in our evaluation framework, finding that distances in vector spaces from different time periods should not be considered equally. We also observed that explicit frequency information actually help distributional methods to capture the change of synonymy. Finally we discussed challenges that DSM approaches still face and opened a discussion about the interplay between hypernymy and synonymy.

Limitations

As mentioned already, the problem *Syn/Diff* does not reflect the initial question of LD/LPC. In particular, the *Syn* class of pairs that remained synonyms contains pairs that underwent LPC and pairs which shared meaning remained unchanged. The latter does not play a role in the LD/LPC dichotomy and should be discarded for deeper study of the two apparently opposite laws. Also, we restrain the study to some target words that are chosen to occur at both time periods, thus preventing us to fully measure the importance of LD. Indeed, recall that Bréal's Law of Differentiation predicts that some synonyms may disappear in the process. Thus, our *Diff* class could be considered incomplete. However, including such disappeared words would prevent the use of time-aware DSMs.

Section 3 presented synonymy as a symmetrical relation between words. However, a thesaurus like Fernald (1896) displays asymmetrical synonymy: for an entry u we have a set of synonyms $v_1, v_2, ...$ from which we extract pairs (u, v). We observe that v itself is rarely an entry of the thesaurus, and when it does, u may not appear in the list of synonyms of v. This is contradictory to WordNet's definition of synonymy that consider this relationship to be symmetrical. However, up to our knowledge, there is no lexical database (like WordNet) being also historical and that could help us ensure the notion of synonymy at both time periods is strictly the same. In the absence of such a resource, we leave potential disagreements in definition between the two linguistic resources to future investigations.

In section 4, we discussed that hyper/hypo-nymy could be misleading. We made the assumption that Fernald (1896) and Wordnet (Fellbaum and Princeton, 2010) used similar-enough notions of synonymy such that our labels *Syn/Diff* are relevant. However, thesaurus like Fernald (1896) are created as a tool for writers and authors to avoid redundancy, thus including wide lists of synonyms that include hypernyms (instead of repeating *the bench*, you could say *the seat*). In section 6.3 we showed that direct hypernymy is misleading for our model. Yet, we still miss guidelines/insights about the possibility to include some cases of hypernymy among synonyms at $T2$. Another approach would be to remove hypernyms from the source material at $T1$, which implies to automatically detect them or manually review thousands of pairs.

There are remaining factors that presented approaches do not take in account and that one could think relevant. In particular, further work could investigate the influence of pressure of words on a concept, for instance many words sharing (at least partially) a similar meaning. However, this would require access to list of senses for each word at time $T1$, which we do not have in Fernald (1896). To this extent, contextualized language models fine-tuned for the different time periods could be helpful.

Finally, because we used pre-computed SGNS embeddings on historical data binned in decade, we have no guarantee that this is the optimal setting for studying Lexical Semantic Change. Maybe different kind of changes could be observed using larger or smaller time periods, and conducting the study over a larger or a smaller time span instead of just a century.

Acknowledgements

We would like to thank the three anonymous reviewers for their helpful comments on this paper. We would also thank Anne Carlier for the thoughtful discussion about this work. This research was funded by Inria Exploratory Action COMANCHE.

References

Michel Bréal. 1897. *Essai de Sémantique*. Paris: Hachette.

Eve V. Clark. 1993. *Conventionality and contrast*, Cambridge Studies in Linguistics, page 67–83. Cambridge University Press.

Haim Dubossarsky, Y. Tsvetkov, C. Dyer, and Eitan Grossman. 2015. A bottom up approach to category mapping and meaning change. *CEUR Workshop Proceedings*, 1347:66–70.

Haim Dubossarsky, Daphna Weinshall, and Eitan Grossman. 2017. Outta control: Laws of semantic change and inherent biases in word representation models. In *Proceedings of the 2017 Conference on Empirical Methods in Natural Language Processing*, pages 1136–1145, Copenhagen, Denmark. Association for Computational Linguistics.

Christiane Fellbaum and University of Princeton. 2010. Wordnet. In *About WordNet*. Princeton University.

James Champlin Fernald. 1896. ... *English Synonyms and Antonyms*. Funk & Wagnalls Company.

Clémentine Fourrier and Syrielle Montariol. 2022. Caveats of measuring semantic change of cognates and borrowings using multilingual word embeddings.

In *Proceedings of the 3rd Workshop on Computational Approaches to Historical Language Change*, pages 97–112, Dublin, Ireland. Association for Computational Linguistics.

William L. Hamilton, Jure Leskovec, and Dan Jurafsky. 2016. Diachronic word embeddings reveal statistical laws of semantic change. In *Proceedings of the 54th Annual Meeting of the Association for Computational Linguistics (Volume 1: Long Papers)*, pages 1489–1501, Berlin, Germany. Association for Computational Linguistics.

Andrey Kutuzov, Erik Velldal, and Lilja Øvrelid. 2022. Contextualized embeddings for semantic change detection: Lessons learned. *ArXiv*, abs/2209.00154.

Adrienne Lehrer. 1985. *The influence of semantic fields on semantic change*, pages 283–296. De Gruyter Mouton, Berlin, New York.

Tomas Mikolov, Ilya Sutskever, Kai Chen, Greg S Corrado, and Jeff Dean. 2013. Distributed representations of words and phrases and their compositionality. In *Advances in Neural Information Processing Systems*, volume 26. Curran Associates, Inc.

Julia Rodina and Andrey Kutuzov. 2020. RuSemShift: a dataset of historical lexical semantic change in Russian. In *Proceedings of the 28th International Conference on Computational Linguistics*, pages 1037–1047, Barcelona, Spain (Online). International Committee on Computational Linguistics.

Eyal Sagi, Stefan Kaufmann, and Brady Clark. 2012. *Tracing semantic change with Latent Semantic Analysis*, pages 161–183. De Gruyter Mouton, Berlin, Boston.

Dominik Schlechtweg, Anna Hätty, Marco Del Tredici, and Sabine Schulte im Walde. 2019. A wind of change: Detecting and evaluating lexical semantic change across times and domains. In *Proceedings of the 57th Annual Meeting of the Association for Computational Linguistics*, pages 732–746, Florence, Italy. Association for Computational Linguistics.

Dominik Schlechtweg, Barbara McGillivray, Simon Hengchen, Haim Dubossarsky, and Nina Tahmasebi. 2020. SemEval-2020 task 1: Unsupervised lexical semantic change detection. In *Proceedings of the Fourteenth Workshop on Semantic Evaluation*, pages 1–23, Barcelona (online). International Committee for Computational Linguistics.

Gustaf Stern. 1921. *Swift, swiftly, and their synonyms: A contribution to semantic analysis and theory*. Wettergren & Kerber.

Nina Tahmasebi, Lars Borina, and Adam Jatowtb. 2021. Survey of computational approaches to lexical semantic change detection. *Computational approaches to semantic change*, 6.

Elizabeth Closs Traugott and Richard B. Dasher. 2001. *Prior and current work on semantic change*, Cambridge Studies in Linguistics, page 51–104. Cambridge University Press.

Peter D. Turney and Saif M. Mohammad. 2019. The natural selection of words: Finding the features of fitness. *PLoS ONE*, 14.

Yang Xu and Charles Kemp. 2015. A computational evaluation of two laws of semantic change. In *Proceedings of the 37th Annual Meeting of the Cognitive Science Society, CogSci 2015, Pasadena, California, USA, July 22-25, 2015*. Cognitive Science Society.

Frank D. Zamora-Reina, Felipe Bravo-Marquez, and Dominik Schlechtweg. 2022. LSCDiscovery: A shared task on semantic change discovery and detection in Spanish. In *Proceedings of the 3rd Workshop on Computational Approaches to Historical Language Change*, pages 149–164, Dublin, Ireland. Association for Computational Linguistics.

George Kingsley Zipf. 1945. The repetition of words, time-perspective, and semantic balance. *The Journal of General Psychology*, 32(1):127–148.

A Appendix

A.1 Formalizing LD and LPC

In this work, we reduced the problem from finding pairs in which LD or LPC operates to a binary classification problem between pairs that remained synonymous and those who did not. To understand the need for a reduction, let us introduce some notation and definitions.

First, let us denote by $W^{(T)}$ the set of words (or vocabulary) for a given language (say English) at time T. As language evolves through time, vocabularies at two times $T1$ and $T2$ (with $T2 > T1$) need not have the exact same extensions: e.g., a word w in $W^{(T1)}$ might not be in $W^{(T2)}$ (i.e., w has disappeared) or vice versa (i.e., w is a new word). Assuming a simple, idealized denotational semantics, we will further define $\mathcal{C}^{(T)}$ as the set of discrete concepts available at time T,[11] and $M_w^{(T)} \subset \mathcal{C}$ the meaning of word w at time T. It is defined as a set to model cases of homonymy and/or polysemy. From these definitions, we can now define *synonymy* at time T between words $u \in W^{(T)}$ and $v \in W^{(T)}$ as $M_u^{(T)} \cap M_v^{(T)} \neq \emptyset$; that is, u and v do share a common meaning. Furthermore, we can define the *semantic change* from $T1$ to $T2$ in a word w as follows: $M_w^{(T1)} \neq M_w^{(T2)}$; that is, w has different sets of meanings at $T1$ and $T2$.

[11]We take $\mathcal{C}^{(T)}$ to be mostly stable over time, but new concepts might of course appear or disappear (e.g., due to techonological or cultural evolution).

Equipped with these definitions, we are now ready to formalize the two laws LD and LPC, starting with what their common scope.

First, both laws concern synonyms: they are restricted to a set of synonyms at some initial time $T1$, defined by $\mathcal{S}^{(T1)} = \{(u,v) : M_u^{(T1)} \cap M_v^{(T1)} \neq \emptyset\}$.

Second, both LD and LPC assume some individual semantic change, from $T1$ to $T2$ (with $T2 > T1$), in at least one of two synonymous words: that is, $M_u^{(T1)} \neq M_u^{(T2)}$ or (logical) $M_v^{(T1)} \neq M_v^{(T2)}$.

Given these preconditions, the application of LD implies that either:

- one of the two words has disappeared: $u \in W^{(T1)} \wedge u \notin W^{(T2)}$ or (exclusive) $v \in W^{(T1)} \wedge v \notin W^{(T2)}$,
- u and v are no longer synonymous at $T2$: $M_u^{(T1)} \cap M_v^{(T1)} = \emptyset$.

By contrast, LPC implies that words u and v remain synonymous from $T1$ to $T2$. While this could be simply stated as: $M_u^{(T2)} \cap M_v^{(T2)} \neq \emptyset$, we feel that this misses an important aspect of the law, namely that $M_u^{(T1)}$ and $M_v^{(T1)}$ should evolve in the same way:

- either by acquiring (a) new shared sense(s): $(M_u^{(T2)} - M_u^{(T1)}) \cap (M_v^{(T2)} - M_v^{(T1)}) \neq \emptyset$,
- or inversely by losing the same sense(s): $(M_u^{(T1)} - M_u^{(T2)}) \cap (M_v^{(T1)} - M_v^{(T2)}) \neq \emptyset$.

A.2 Useful definitions

Recall the definition of *cosine distance* between two vectors $\mathbf{x}$ and $\mathbf{y}$:

$$\text{cos-dist}(\mathbf{x}, \mathbf{y}) = 1 - \frac{\langle \mathbf{x}, \mathbf{y} \rangle}{\|\mathbf{x}\| \|\mathbf{y}\|}. \tag{3}$$

We also recall the definition of *Jaccard distance* between two sets A and B:

$$\text{jaccard-dist}(A, B) = 1 - \frac{|A \cap B|}{|A \cup B|}. \tag{4}$$

A.3 Xu & Kemp's control pairs

In Table 3 we display samples of word pairs selected as control pairs following Xu and Kemp (2015)'s procedure. As we can observe, for every Part-Of-Speech, a significant number of these pairs are themselves synonymous. After manually reviewing a hundred pairs for each POS tag, we estimate that the proportion of synonyms in the selected control pairs is between 20 and 40%. Synonym pairs shouldn't be used to control other synonym pairs, which may explain why our reproduction of Xu and Kemp (2015) decision rule does not perform well according to Table 2.

A.4 Distances in WordNet

In Figure 3 are displayed the distributions of distances in WordNet. The distance in WordNet between two words (u, v) is the number of nodes of the shortest path between a synset of u and a synset of v.

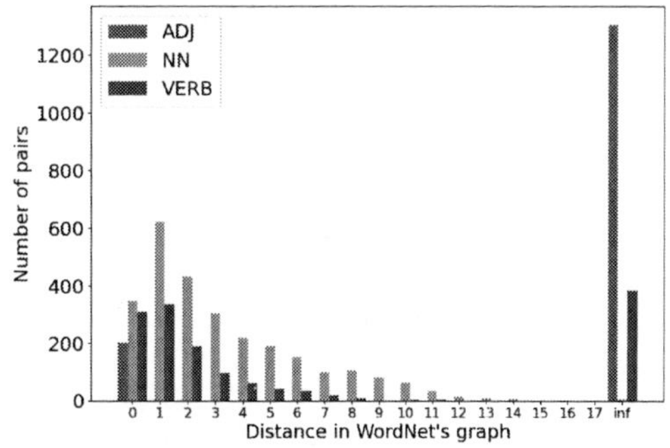

Figure 3: Distribution of shortest distances in WordNet between pairs of words that were synonymous at $T = O$. *inf* means that there is no path between the two words in WN. A distance of 0 means that they are actually synonyms, while a distance of 1 implies there is direct hypernymy.

A.5 Synonymy in our DSMs

In Figure 4 are displayed the distributions of cosine distance between word pairs at both periods. In blue are synonyms at this time (from Fernald (1896) at $T1$, and from WordNet at $T2$). In black are all possible word pairs. We observe that synonymy is indeed captured by our DSM as synonyms are significantly closer in cosine distance than other word pairs.

A.6 Frequency groups

The procedure to create a fixed number M of frequency group is the following. At a time T, the list of target words is sorted by increasing frequency, we label as group '0' the first 50% of the list. In the remaining 50%, The first half is labeled as group '1', and so on until group $M - 2$ is created. The still unlabeled words are labeled group $M - 1$, for a total of M groups. Group labels are therefore positively correlated with occurrences counts.

POS	Control pairs
ADJ	brownish/red, kindly/mild, teeming/agricultural, likeliest/meaningless, *various/heterogeneous*, *barbarous/cruel*, *abandoned/unsuccessful*, trojan/escaping, *subjective/relative*, reliable/readable.
NN	diphtheria/typhus, *muskets/pistol*, surgery/appendicitis, beech/apples, accountants/prints, commodity/substances, *cups/pots*, wife/grandmother, fool/fisherman, obstacles/multiplication.
VERB	*moan/groan*, divide/span, needed/secured, *flowed/flooded*, stall/owned, *told/asked*, *mentioned/described*, cooperate/accord, copy/filed, increased/diminished.

Table 3: Random samples of size 10 among selected control pairs. In italic are control pairs which are considered synonyms according to the definition in Section 3.1.

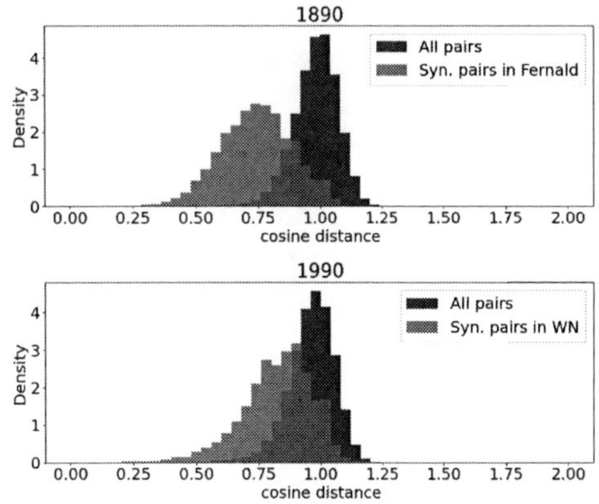

Figure 4: Distribution (as density histograms) of cosine distances between word pairs at time period $T1$ (decade 1890s) and $T2$ (decade 1990s). In blue are represented pairs of synonyms, and in black are represented all pairs of target words, without any particular constraint.

A.7 Target words selection

Among words represented in the embeddings provided by Hamilton et al. (2016), we keep only words following these three requirements. The first is to be POS-tagged as an *adjective*, a *noun* and/or as a *verb* in the COHA. For a given POS-tag among these three, the second requirement is to appear at least 3 times in every decade between 1890 and 1999. Lastly, we require words to be composed of 3 letters or more. If a word appears with multiple POS-tags in the COHA and fulfills the minimum frequency requirement with each of these tags, the same embedding is used as its representation, as Hamilton et al. (2016)'s training data aggregated POS-tags.

A.8 Unsupervised models

In Figure 5, we observe that the quantity Δ does not reflect a clear separation between *Syn* pairs and *Diff* pairs. This explains why the unsupervised methods proposed in Sec. 5.2 fail to significantly outperform baselines.

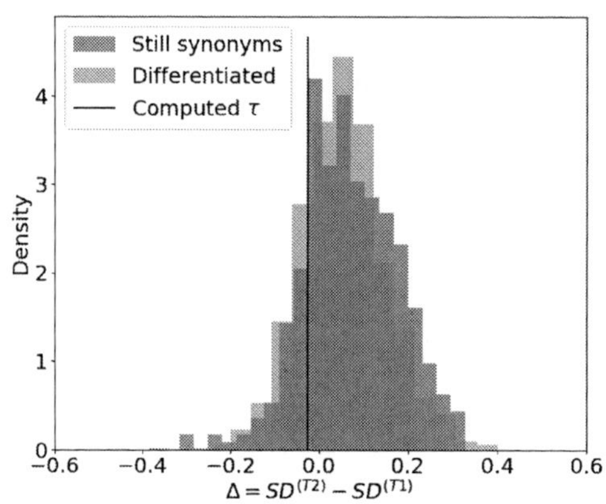

Figure 5: Histograms of the value of divergence Δ of synonymous pairs, depending whether they differentiated (orange) or stayed synonyms (blue).

In Figure 6 we show the influence of k in SD (neighbors) for the unsupervised Δ method. We see that while there is close to no change in balance accuracy, F_1 scores for both classes are more and more unbalanced as k increases, indicating a more unfair model for high values of k. This is explained by the fact that the unsupervised model predicts more *Diff* (dominant class) with higher k.

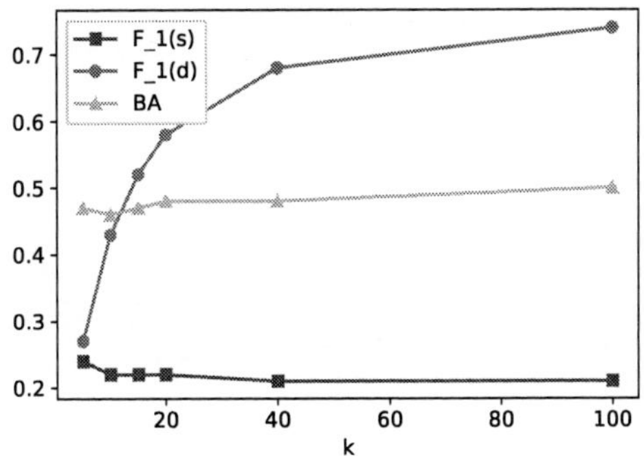

Figure 6: Unsupervised method, neighborhood-based SD, for ALL (mixed POS).

A.9 Components of selected models

Depending on the POS tag, the implementation strategies of *SD*, *DD* and frequency variables were different. Recall that these strategies were chosen given the average performances over 20 random train/test splits.

On adjectives, neighborhood based *DD* as well as raw frequency counts was found to be better than alternatives. For *SD*, cosine distance provides slightly higher performances than neighborhood-based measures, except when tuning the threshold for Δ: in this case, SD(nk) with $k = 15$ was best. Generally, for every method implying a neighbordhood based SD (Δ(nk), LR multi., as well as the two non-linear models), a small/mid ranged k was preferable (between 10 and 20).

For nouns, SD(cosine distance) was also the best choice except for Δ with tuned threshold: here, SD(nk) was preferred. Overall, the best range for the value of k for neighbors-based SD was smaller (5 to 15). Frequency groups worked better than raw frequencies, while there was no difference in performance between the two definitions of DD.

Yet, for verbs, SD(nk) with $k = 40$ actually outperforms cosine distance (except for unsupervised Δ), and DD using Orthogonal Procrustes alignment and cosine distance (Hamilton et al., 2016) was actually better than the definition relying on comparisons local neighborhoods. Both types of frequency variables (raw counts and groups) worked equally well.

Finally, on the ALL dataset reuniting pairs accross POS tags, raw frequencies provide better results than groups. Cosine distance is better than neighborhoods for synchronic distances, and both techniques of diachronic distances performed similarly. For models forced to use SD(nk) in addition to SD(cd), the choice of k did not really change the results.

A.10 Predictive variables in our model

In this supplementary section, we conduct a study about the role of some predictive variables in our best-performing Logistic Regression model, as potential sources of errors. The studied model uses SD with cosine-distance, both implementations of DD and raw frequency counts.

	Pred.		$y =$ Syn		$y =$ Diff	
	Syn	Diff	TS	FD	TD	FS
$SD^{(TT1)}$	**.64**	**.83**	**.62**	**.84**	**.83**	**.64**
$DD(u)$	.46	.46	.45	.47	.46	.47
$DD(v)$	**.50**	**.54**	**.48**	**.54**	**.54**	**.50**
$FG_u^{(T2)}$	2.3	2.2	2.4	2.1	2.2	2.2
$FG_v^{(T2)}$	**1.9**	**1.4**	**2.1**	**1.5**	**1.4**	**1.8**

Table 4: Average values of some variables for data subset based on the prediction of our best-performing LR model. TS,FS,TD,FD stand for True/False Syn/Diff. $FG_w^{(T)}$ stands for Frequency Groups of word w at time T. Significant difference within a pair of columns are in bold.

For a selected number of variables, we look for significant differences between well-classified pairs and pairs with wrong prediction, in both classes separately. For a given variable, we estimate if a difference is significant between the well-classified and the misclassified samples of this class using a t-test for Gaussian distributed variables, or a Mann-Whitney U test for other variables. A difference is significant if the p-value of the test is below 5%. Results are reported in table 4.

We observe significant differences of SD in pairs that are predicted as *Syn* and those predicted as *Diff* by our model, the first having a smaller SD at $T1$ than the latter. Because our model relies mostly on these SD to separate both classes, we wrongly classify *Syn* pairs whose $SD^{(TT1)}$ is close to that of *Diff*, and conversely *Diff* pairs whose $SD^{(TT1)}$ is close to that of *Syn* are misclassified. This indicates that our model still misses some subtleties that are now reflected by SD.

A similar non-separability of the distribution of "Syns" and "Diff" appears on DD and Frequency variable for the second word pair of the pair. While it seems logical for our model to behave so regarding to the definition of LD, it is a clue that our input variables reflect noisy information that is confusing to the model. In the same idea, Kutuzov et al. (2022) remarked that recent LSC detection models tend to raise False Positive, drawing attention to the limit of current models for LSC.

Semantically-informed Hierarchical Event Modeling

Shubhashis Roy Dipta, Mehdi Rezaee, Francis Ferraro
Department of Computer Science and Electrical Engineering
University of Maryland Baltimore County
Baltimore, MD 21250 USA
{sroydip1,rezaee1,ferraro}@umbc.edu

Abstract

Prior work has shown that coupling sequential latent variable models with semantic ontological knowledge can improve the representational capabilities of event modeling approaches. In this work, we present a novel, doubly hierarchical, semi-supervised event modeling framework that provides structural hierarchy while also accounting for ontological hierarchy. Our approach consists of multiple layers of structured latent variables, where each successive layer compresses and abstracts the previous layers. We guide this compression through the injection of structured ontological knowledge that is defined at the type level of events: importantly, our model allows for partial injection of semantic knowledge and it does not depend on observing instances at any particular level of the semantic ontology. Across two different datasets and four different evaluation metrics, we demonstrate that our approach is able to out-perform the previous state-of-the-art approaches by up to 8.5%, demonstrating the benefits of structured and semantic hierarchical knowledge for event modeling.

1 Introduction

Intuitively, there is a hierarchical nature to complex events: e.g., on Fig. 1, there are two events, one involves going to the hospital and another one is getting treatment. Even if important portions may differ, but these two situations have one abstract concept in common: **Cure** (of a disease). Clearly, there is a connection among the events reported in a situation and they all contribute to a bigger goal ("Cure" in this case). The main purpose of our work is to exploit this nature of connection to improve event modeling. However, much like linguistic structure, this event structure is generally not directly observed, making it difficult to learn event models that reflect this hierarchical nature.

For high-level inspiration, we look to past approaches in syntactic modeling (Collins, 1997; Klein and Manning, 2003; Petrov et al., 2006): we can approach hierarchical event modeling through structured learning, or through richer (semantic) data. A structural approach accounts for the hierarchy as part of the model itself, such as with hierarchical random variables (Cheung et al., 2013; Ferraro and Van Durme, 2016; Weber et al., 2018; Huang and Ji, 2020; Gao et al., 2022). Richer semantic data provides hierarchical knowledge, such as event inheritance or composition, as part of the data made available to the model and learning algorithm (Botschen et al., 2017; Edwards and Ji, 2022; Zhang et al., 2020).

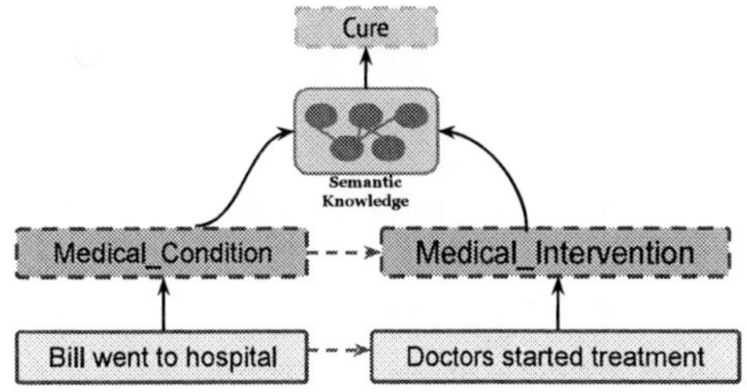

Figure 1: Complex events can be hierarchical. The purple boxes represent the events themselves (as would be reported in a news story). Blue dashed boxes are annotated semantic frames & the orange dashed box is the more abstract, general frame connecting the "Medical_Condition" and "Medical_Intervention" events. Events and frames are sequentially connected.

In this work, we provide an approach that addresses both of these notions of hierarchical event modeling jointly. Fundamentally, our model is an encoder-decoder based hierarchical model comprised of two layers of semi-supervised latent variable sequence. The first layer encodes the events to semantic frames and the next layer compresses down the semantic frames to a more abstract concept. We call these the base and compression layers, respectively. The base layer operates over the event sequence (the gray boxes in Fig. 1); when available, our base layer also considers auxiliary semantic in-

*Proceedings of the The 12th Joint Conference on Lexical and Computational Semantics (*SEM 2023)*, pages 353–369
July 13-14, 2023 ©2023 Association for Computational Linguistics

formation, such as automatically extracted semantic frames (the blue dashed boxes in Fig. 1). Meanwhile, the compression layer compresses down the semantic frames to a more abstract concept (orange dashed box in Fig. 1) using an existing structued semantic resource (in our paper, FrameNet). Our work can be thought of as extending previous work in semi-supervised event modeling (Rezaee and Ferraro, 2021) to account for both structural and semantic hierarchy.

Joining both the structural and semantic approaches together poses a number of challenges. First, getting reliable, wide-coverage semantic event annotations can be a challenge. Development of semantic annotation resources is time consuming and expensive (Baker et al., 1998; O'Gorman et al., 2016).[1] Part of our solution should leverage existing semantic annotation resources.

Second, although event extraction capabilities have steadily improved, enabling automatically produced annotations to be used directly (Padia et al., 2018; Huang and Huang, 2021), these tools still produce error-laden annotation, especially on out-of-domain text. While rich latent variable methods have been previously developed, adapting them to make use of noisy event extractions can be a challenge. Our learning approach must still be able to handle imperfect extractions. Recent work has shown how neural sequence approaches can do so (Rezaee and Ferraro, 2021), but there remains a question of how to generalize this. Part of our solution should allow for hierarchical semi-supervision.

We present a hierarchical latent variable encoder-decoder approach to address these challenges. We ground our work in the FrameNet semantic frame ontology (Baker et al., 1998), from which we extract possible abstract frames from sequences of inferred (latent) frames. This lets us leverage existing semantic resources. We develop a semi-supervised, hierarchical method capable of handling noisy event extractions. Our approach enables learning how to represent more abstract frame representations. Our contributions are:

- We provide a novel, hierarchical, semi-supervised event learning model.
- We show how to use an existing rich semantic frame resource (FrameNet) to provide both observable event frames and less observable abstract frames in a neural latent variable model.
- Our model can use FrameNet to give a more informed signal by leveraging compression of events when predicting what event comes next, what sequence of events follows an initial event, and missing/unreported events.
- With pre-training only, our model can generate event embeddings that better reflect semantic relatedness than previous works, evincing a zero-shot capability.
- We perform comprehensive ablations to show the importance of different factors of our model.

Our code is available at `https://github.com/dipta007/SHEM`.

2 Related Works

Our work draws on event modeling, latent generative modeling, lexical and semantic knowledge ontologies, and hierarchical modeling.

2.1 Event Modeling

There have been several efforts to understand events and their relationships with broader semantic notions. Previous research has explored the use of hierarchical models based on autoencoders for script generation, such as the work of Weber et al. (2018). In contrast to their work, instead of a chain-like hierarchy, we have used a multi-layer hierarchy to compress the events to abstract processes. Additionally, our approach allows for semi-supervised training, if such labels are available. Our work has shown that using semi-supervision helps the model to generalize better on both layers. In a related study, Rezaee and Ferraro (2021) used the Gumbel-Softmax technique and partially observed frames to model event sequences and generate contextualized event frames. While their approach is capable of generalizing each event in a sequence, the number of predicted frames in the sequence is equivalent to the number of events. Thus, unlike our approach, it was not designed to compress or generalize the overall event sequence.

Bisk et al. (2019) demonstrated the effectiveness of event modeling for generating a concrete concept from an abstract one, using the example of cooking. Several studies in recent years have utilized event modeling to predict event types (Chen et al., 2020; Pepe et al., 2022; Huang and Ji, 2020). These studies focus on identifying the action and

[1]While prompt-based label semantics (Hsu et al., 2022; Huang et al., 2022) are recent successful ways of enabling lower resource learning, these generally are tied to specific tasks and may be limited by what exemplars are given.

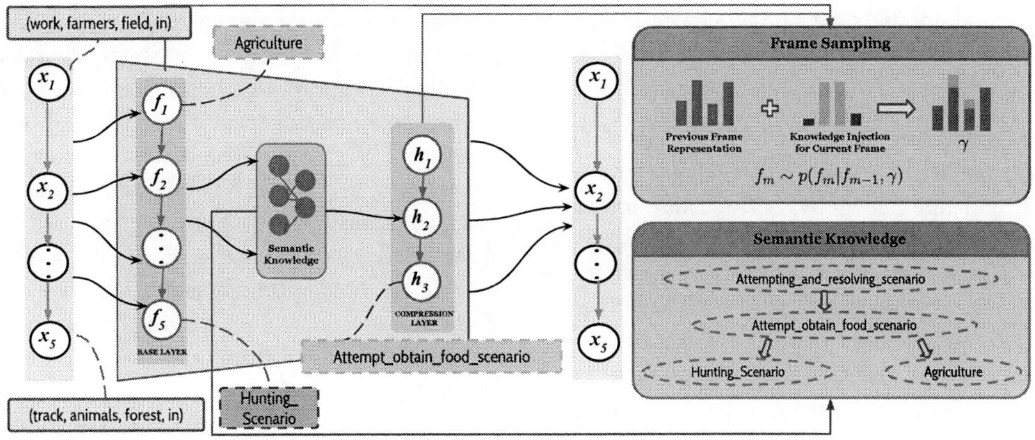

Figure 2: An overview of **S**emantically-informed **H**ierarchical **E**vent **M**odeling (SHEM). The orange dashed boxes are observed frames & the blue dashed boxed are masked frames. Top right: a frame is sampled with the injection of observed frames. Bottom right: semantic knowledge graph is shown for 4 nodes with only "Inheritance" relations.

object involved in an event, where the action represents the activity being performed and the object is the entity affected by the action.

2.2 Latent Generative Modeling

Latent generative modeling is a widely-used method for representing data x through the use of high-level, hidden representations f. Specifically, we express the joint probability $p(x, f)$ as $p(x, f) = p(x|f)p(f)$. Especially when f is not fully observed, this factorization can productively be thought as a soft grouping or clustering of the data in x. This equation will serve as the foundation for our approach.

Maximizing log-likelihood is known to be computationally challenging in this context. Kingma et al. (2014) later used a variational autoencoder (Kingma and Welling, 2013, VAE) in a semi-supervised manner to learn latent variables, dividing the dataset into observed and unobserved labels. In our case, instances are partially observed (rather than fully observed or not). Huang and Ji (2020) used a VAE both to prevent overfitting on seen event types and to enable prediction of novel types.

2.3 Lexical and Semantic Resources

Multiple resources, such as PropBank (Gildea and Jurafsky, 2002), OntoNotes (Hovy et al., 2006), AMR (Banarescu et al., 2013), VerbNet (Schuler, 2005), and FrameNet (Baker et al., 1998), provide annotations related to event semantics. Many consider predicate-argument semantics, such as defining who is performing (or experiencing) an event, and various ways that event may occur. FrameNet provides detailed predicate-argument characterizations and multi-faceted relations linking different frames together, such as frame subtyping (e.g., *inheritance*), temporal/causal (e.g., *precedes*, *causative*), and compositionality (e.g., *uses*, *subframe*). Consider the AGRICULTURE frame from Fig. 2: FrameNet defines an *inheritance* relation between it and a ATTEMPT_OBTAIN_FOOD_SCENARIO, which can be thought of as a container grouping together frames all related to a broader scenario of attempting to obtain food, such as HUNTING_SCENARIO. A scenario container frame provides a notion of compositionality, defining potential correlations or alternatives among frames. Due to these rich semantics, we focus on FrameNet in this paper as an exemplar.

Prior research has shown the utility of FrameNet in predicting the relationship between predicates (Aharon et al., 2010; Ferraro et al., 2017); frame-directed claim verification (Padia et al., 2018); and text summarization (Guan et al., 2021; Han et al., 2016; Chowanda et al., 2017). Unfortunately, while document-level frames have been of long-standing interest within targeted domains (Sundheim, 1992, 1996; Ebner et al., 2020; Du et al., 2021), development of task agnostic document-level frames has been limited. E.g., while FrameNet defines these compositional-like scenario frames, annotation coverage is limited: In the FrameNet 1.7 data used to train frame parsers, out of nearly 29,000 fulltext annotations, there are only 28 **annotated** "scenario" frames.

3 Method

Our core aim is to provide a hierarchical event model that incorporates both structural and semantic hierarchy. We call our model SHEM (**S**emantically-informed **H**ierarchical **E**vent **M**odeling). An overview is in Fig. 2, where an observed event sequence (green x_i) is latently modeled as multiple sequences of semantic frames (f_i and h_j), augmented by a semantic resource.

We examine the strengths and limitations of structural and semantic hierarchy. Our experiments explore the effect of compressing the number of frames on ability to predict what happens next in an event sequence, and, given an initial seed event, how an event sequence is likely to unfold. We also extend our work to show how our model can produce better intrinsic event representations.

3.1 Model Setup

Our model is a sequence-to-sequence hierarchical model (§3.3). It is comprised of two layers (a base and a compression layer) of an encoder & decoder (§3.2). During training (§3.4), we provide the model partially observed semantic frames in the base layer in order to guide it in encoding event sequences into latent variables. In the compression layer, we use ontologically-defined frame relations to extract semantically similar frames from the predicted frame of the first layer. These semantically similar frames guide the compression layer of the model to infer appropriate abstract frames.

3.2 Input and Output

The input to our model is event sequences. Each sequence is defined by M event tuples $(x_1, x_2, ...x_M)$. For comparability (Weber et al., 2018; Rezaee and Ferraro, 2021), we represented each event as a tuple x_m of four lexical words: a predicate, a subject, an object, and an optional event modifier. We assume an event tuple can be associated with a more general semantic frame. For example, in Fig. 2, the first event ("work farmers in field") can be linked to the FrameNet AGRICULTURE frame. We assume that each event *can* be linked but do not require this. Some frames might be masked, subject to a fixable observation probability. This allows us to test how our model behaves when semantic data may be missing or incorrect (due to, e.g., an extraction error); in Fig. 2, this can be seen for the event "track animals in forest" event, where a potential corresponding frame—"Hunting_Scenario"—is masked. This results in a corresponding sequence of (partially) observed frames $(f_1^*, f_2^*, ...f_M^*)$. The base layer uses these event tuples (x_i) to softly predict the frames (f_i) and then reconstruct the input sequence based upon those inferences. To capture additional semantic knowledge, both in traning and testing, we query FrameNet to extract more abstract frames (h_i) for the predicted frames from the base layer, such as "Attempt_obtain_food_scenario." The compression layer uses that abstract frame h_i with the original event frames f_i to softly group the events; for additional training signal, the compression layer is also trained to reconstruct the original event sequence.

Encoder The base layer embeds each token in the input event sequence, while, by default, the compression layer embeds each predicted frame from the base layer. An attention module is used to find the important parts of event sequences during prediction of frames. As our experiments validate, the encoder can be flexible, e.g., a bi-GRU or a Transformer-based large language model.

Decoder This is a standard auto-regressive model that generates tokens of an event sequence from left to right. Unless otherwise specified, the predicted frame embeddings are given as input to the decoder. See App. A.1 for additional details.

3.3 Hierarchical Model

We use two layers of an encoder-decoder: (i) a base layer (f_is in Fig. 2) and (ii) a compression layer (h_js in Fig. 2). The base layer is responsible for encoding the input event sequence into a sequence of semantic frames, while the compression layer is responsible for re-encoding the base layer's semantic frames into more abstract representations. In Fig. 2, the base layer must infer "Agriculture" & "Hunting_Scenario" from the input and observed frames; the compression layer must associate those frames with "Attempt_obtain_food_scenario." Our model is extendable to an arbitrary number of compression layers. Experiments with multiple compression layers showed that a single compression layer was sufficient for strong performance.

Given our encoder-decoder setup, inferring frame values means sampling a discrete random variable within a neural network. This must be done at both the base and compression layers. To do so, we sample frames from an ancestral Gumbel-

Softmax distribution (Jang et al., 2016; Rezaee and Ferraro, 2021): each sampled frame f_i depends on the previously sampled frame f_{i-1} and an attention weighted embedding of that layer's encoder representation. Due to space, we refer the reader to Rezaee and Ferraro (2021).

Base Layer The base layer encodes the event sequences in the same number of latent variables with the guidance of the observed frames. On the base layer, partially observed frames are fed to the model. These frames depend on the observation probability; e.g., 40% observed frames mean that 60% of the event frames will be masked, and the remaining 40% would be observable by the model as guidance. This masking, which we formalize as part of our experiments, reflects the fact that we may not always have access to sufficient semantic knowledge. To guide the base layer, a one-hot encoding of the observed frames is "injected" (added to the Gumbel-Softmax parameters), as done by Rezaee and Ferraro (2021). The number of frames is the same as the number of event sequences, so one frame for each node is passed.

Compression Layer Rezaee and Ferraro (2021) showed that providing some frame injection guidance helps learning. The compression layer aims to provide guidance to the modeling through fewer, more abstract semantic frames. However, while this is possible for the base layer, where we assume every event tuple *could* have a frame, we do not assume this for the compression layer. This in part is reflective of the lack of annotated training samples for some of these more abstract frames (see §2.3), limited beyond-sentence frame extraction tools, and our own motivation to not require beyond-sentence annotation or extraction tools.

To provide guidance, but prevent reliance on potentially missing auxiliary semantic knowledge, we extract the *inferred* frames from the base layer with the external frame ontology (rather than whatever frames may have been provided to the model). For each inferred frame f_i, we extract possible abstract frames using the FrameNet relations defined for it. E.g., since there is a frame relation between AGRICULTURE and ATTEMPT_OBTAIN_FOOD_SCENARIO, if f_i is AGRICULTURE, ATTEMPT_OBTAIN_FOOD_SCENARIO may be an abstract frame. In the case of multiple abstract frames, one single frame is chosen randomly. A special frame token (not in FrameNet) is passed if no related frames can be extracted. Each compression node h_j has an attention module, attending over the base layer's inferred frames $f_1, \ldots, f_M$, helping capture ontological hierarchy.

While the compression layer can serve as an event model in its own right (due its own decoder), its primary purposes are to help **capture the ontological hierarchy and provide feedback to the base layer**. It does this directly (predict the extracted abstract frames, given the base layer's inferred frames as input), and via its decoder.

Guidance for Abstract Frames To guide the compression layer to learn more abstract frames and help the base layer generalize, we injected the FrameNet-defined parents of the frames predicted from the base layer. E.g., if the base layer prediction is "Temporary_Stay" and a related frame is "Visiting," we inject both to the compression layer. In contrast to existing work relying on single samples, early experiments showed that averaging two Gumbel-Softmax samples yielded better results.

3.4 Training

During training, input is passed to the base layer with partially observed frames depending on the observation probability. The first layer encoder encodes the input sequence with the guidance of the partially observed frames to generate a latent variable representation (f_i). This predicted latent variable (f_i) is then passed through the decoder to regenerate text. The predicted frames from the first layer and their parent frames are passed to the second layer encoder; it then encodes it to fewer numbers of latent variables, (h_j) which is used in the decoder. Loss is computed at both layers.

We employ a linear combination of three different loss functions: the reconstruction loss, the KL divergence loss, and a frame classification loss. The reconstruction loss is used to generate the input event sequence based on the inferred latent variables from each layer. The KL divergence loss calculates the KL divergence between the prior and variational distributions for each layer. Finally, the frame classification loss guides the base layer to accurately classify the observed frames. See App. A.3 for a full formulation of our loss.

4 Experimental Setup

We describe the dataset, then baselines (§4.1), we used for our core experiments. We explored the effectiveness of latent parent frames (§5.1) and frame relations (§5.2). We show how our model accounts for missing events (§5.3). To further show the effectiveness of our model, we show how to extend our approach to provide effective representations for event similarity tasks (§5.4). We provide supplementary results and experiments in the appendix.

Dataset We used a part of the Concretely Annotated Wikipedia dataset (Ferraro et al., 2014), which is a version of English Wikipedia that provides automatically produced FrameNet semantic frame parses to enable easier subsequent examination of semantic frames. This has existing splits of training (457k), validation (16k), and test (21k) event sequences, where each training sequence has at least one extracted frame. For comparability with past approaches, we truncated documents to the first 5 events. We used a vocabulary size of 40k for event sequences (predicates and arguments) and the 500 most common semantic frames, which is consistent with prior work and has more than 99% coverage of automatically extracted frame types.

4.1 Implementation and Baselines

We use five latent variables in the base layer and three in the compression layer; these values were determined in early dev experiments. We represent the probability of observing an event's frame on the base layer with an observation probability ϵ. With ϵ likelihood, an event's frame will be observed, and with $(1-\epsilon)$ probability, an event's frame will be masked. This is meant to emulate how sufficiently accurate, extractable semantic knowledge may not always be available. This ϵ was fixed prior to training each model. Frames are **only observed during training, and never during evaluation**. More implementation details, including specific hyperparameter values and architectural decisions, are in App. A.2. We present extensive ablation experiments in App. C. These experiments provide further insight into our modeling decisions.

Baselines Most of our experiments (§ 5.1 to 5.3) compare our model with the existing methods: First, **HAQAE** (Weber et al., 2018), which employs a single layer, chain-based method for hierarchical modeling. It is designed purely as an unsupervised approach, and so we cannot provide frame guidance to it. We retrained this model on our event sequences. Second, **SSDVAE** (Rezaee and Ferraro, 2021): this is most similar to ours and effectively just the base layer. For fairness, we use the same hidden state size and pre-trained embeddings across our models and baselines.

Model	ϵ	Perplexity (↓)	INC Score (↑)
HAQAE	-	21.38 ± 0.25	24.88 ± 1.35
SSDVAE		19.84 ± 0.52	35.56 ± 1.70
ours: inf. frame	0.9	**19.39 ± 0.3**	41.35 ± 4.25
SSDVAE		21.19 ± 0.76	*39.08 ± 1.55*
ours: inf. frame	0.7	*20.26 ± 1.36*	35.86 ± 3.43
SSDVAE		31.11 ± 0.85	*40.18 ± 0.90*
ours: inf. frame	0.5	*22.16 ± 1.62*	37.3 ± 3.33
SSDVAE		33.12 ± 0.54	*47.88 ± 3.59*
ours: inf. frame	0.4	*24.02 ± 1.28*	43.25 ± 4.97
SSDVAE		33.31 ± 0.63	44.38 ± 2.10
ours: inf. frame	0.2	*30.15 ± 2.73*	**49.53 ± 1.56**

Table 1: Perplexity (lower is better) and Wikipedia Inverse Narrative Cloze Score (higher is better) for test data. Per observation probability (ϵ), the best is in *italic* form. The best overall is **bold** form. See §5.1.

5 Result and Discussion

We compute standard event modeling metrics: perplexity, to measure how well the model can predict the *next* event, and inverse narrative cloze (INC) score (Weber et al., 2018). In INC, a single seed event is given, and the model must select what the next five events are to follow it. The model is given six choices (giving random performance accuracy of 16.7%). Both have been used by our baselines and allow us to assess the effectiveness of our model. We average results over four runs with different seeds, unless otherwise specified.

5.1 Is Frame Inheritance Sufficient?

We first investigate whether frame inheritance is sufficient for learning our hierarchical model. We report the inferred frame variant previously described: the base layer first infers the latent frames; then we extract the parents of those inferred frames; and we then inject both these parent frames and base layer predicted frames in the compression layer. The compression layer is dependent on the inferred frames, rather than lexical signal. Results are in Table 1 (supplemental results in Tables 6 and 7 in the appendix). We also experimented with a lexical variant, where the input to the compression layer is an embedding of the original input event tuple rather than the inferred frames. Due to space constraints, these detailed comparisons are in App. B.1. The compression layer alone has suboptimal performance on both lexical and inferred frame models, but the signal from compression layer helped the base layer to achieve better performance. Both SSDVAE and HAQAE (no compression layer) did worse for all observation probabilities. This shows the inferred frames and semantic relations from the base layer are important for hierarchical modeling.[2]

Our model's base layer perplexity consistently outperformed the other models. Additionally, we see that our approach is better able to handle lower supervision than SSDVAE: as the observation probability decreases (fewer observed semantic frames), perplexity increases drastically for SSDVAE. In contrast, if we look at the "ours: inf. frames" perplexity, we see that any performance degradation in our model is less severe, and that in all cases our approach still outperforms the previous SOTA results. This shows the effectiveness of the compression layer in guiding the base layer reconstruction, even with limited semantic observation.

Looking at INC, with either a lot ($\epsilon = 0.9$) or a little ($\epsilon = 0.2$) of semantic observations, our approach outperforms the existing approaches, demonstrating the ability to model longer event sequences. The best overall INC performance occurs with our hierarchical model with a low amount of supervision. This is a good result, as it suggests our model can make use of limited semantic extractions and still provide effective long-range modeling. When some, but not necessarily most, of the frames may be observed, the non-hierarchical SSDVAE approach provides strong performance. This suggests that while frame inheritance (e.g., *IS-A* type relations) can be helpful for certain elements of hierarchical event modeling, it is not sufficient. However, as we will see in the next section, more considered use of semantic relations defined in FrameNet can drastically boost our model's performance, surpassing SSDVAE.

5.2 Relations Beyond Inheritance

We have shown that inheritance relations are helpful but not sufficient. As FrameNet reflects other relations, like causation, (temporal) ordering, and multiple forms of containment/composition, we explore whether six different frame relations significantly affect the predictive abilities of our model.

We also consider two special cases: first, whether different types of relations are complementary by grouping these select relations.[3] We refer to this as *grouping* in Table 2. Second, whether the compositional "scenario" frames in

Model	Frame Relation	ϵ	Next Event Pred. (Perplexity)	Event Sequence Pred. (Wiki INC Accuracy)
HAQAE	-	-	21.38 ± 0.25	24.88 ± 1.35
SSDVAE	-	0.9	19.84 ± 0.52	35.56 ± 1.70
ours	Inheritance	0.9	19.39 ± 0.53	41.35 ± 4.25
	Using		19.39 ± 0.51	*43.23 ± 2.51*
	Precedes		19.57 ± 0.58	41.43 ± 3.02
	Causative_of		19.42 ± 0.57	41.38 ± 2.23
	Inchoative_of		19.28 ± 0.32	41.35 ± 3.47
	Perspective_on		19.76 ± 0.97	40.53 ± 2.04
	Subframe		18.91 ± 0.15	40.35 ± 2.91
	grouping		19.44 ± 0.5	40.76 ± 2.86
	scenario-only		***18.81 ± 0.5***	42.29 ± 2.86
SSDVAE	-	0.2	33.31 ± 0.63	44.38 ± 2.10
ours	Inheritance	0.2	*30.15 ± 2.73*	49.53 ± 1.56
	Using		31.37 ± 2.08	49.72 ± 1.73
	Precedes		32.62 ± 1.65	47.92 ± 2.25
	Causative_of		31.82 ± 3	***49.85 ± 0.84***
	Inchoative_of		32.65 ± 1.4	48.03 ± 3.35
	Perspective_on		33.2 ± 1.47	47.85 ± 3.53
	Subframe		32.78 ± 2.09	47.88 ± 3.31
	grouping		28.17 ± 2.26	48.88 ± 1.37
	scenario-only		32.01 ± 0.7	48.1 ± 2.22

Table 2: Using frame relations beyond inheritance for the compression layer can lead to drastic improvements in both perplexity (lower is better) and Wikipedia Inverse Narrative Cloze Score (higher is better). See §5.2. For detailed result with all the layers, please refer to appendix (Apps. B.2 to B.4).

FrameNet provide a strong signal (*scenario-only* in Table 2). In FrameNet, frames that introduce a broader, abstract concept rather than an isolated one can be labeled as a "scenario" frame: e.g., *COMMERCE_SCENARIO* consists of buying, selling, business, having an agreement, and so on. For this, we only extracted an abstract frame for the compression layer if it was labeled as a "scenario."

We trained separate models (with three random seeds) for each frame relation to explore the effect of individual frame relations on the result. We focus on higher ($\epsilon = 0.9$) and lower ($\epsilon = 0.2$) frame observation cases. Table 2 shows our main results, with detailed results in the appendix (Apps. B.2 to B.4). Lower observation ($\epsilon = 0.2$) is consistently better than the previous state-of-the-art on the base and overall versions. For $\epsilon = 0.9$, base layer performance is generally improved. This reaffirms our previous results that even with limited semantic guidance, the compression layer provides valuable feedback to the base layer.

The results for the two special relations in Table 2 (*grouping* and *scenario-only*) are consistent with our previous results—our approach outperforms the state-of-the-art result. Neither grouping nor the scenario-only variant provides large additional benefit beyond the individual frames in that group. Given this and the small variation in base layer performance depending on what frame relations we use, these results suggest that the ex-

[2] In particular, Fig. 4 in the appendix shows how the compression layer can demonstrate its own generative capabilities, in addition to providing supervisory signal to the base layer.

[3] We aggregate frames connected via the Inheritance, Using, Precedes, Causative_of, Inchoative_of, and Subframe relations. We selected these given their direct connections to well-studied relationships across event semantics.

Model	ϵ	Perplexity (Masked Test Data)		
		Base Alone	Compression Alone	Base+Compr.
SSDVAE	0.9	152.44 ± 3.45	-	-
grp		*61.1 ± 1.83*	94.76 ± 1.96	76.08 ± 0.76
scn		63.48 ± 4.43	80.94 ± 7.44	71.6 ± 4.12
SSDVAE	0.7	163.08 ± 4.52	-	-
grp		63.5 ± 3.49	86.23 ± 0.7	73.98 ± 2.04
scn		***60.06 ± 1.68***	78.36 ± 4.52	68.58 ± 2.3
SSDVAE	0.5	182.63 ± 6.11	-	-
grp		79.74 ± 1.79	83.81 ± 0.96	81.75 ± 1.13
scn		*76.01 ± 5.56*	78.7 ± 1.63	77.33 ± 3.65
SSDVAE	0.4	201.55 ± 4.1	-	-
grp		84.17 ± 4.45	81.49 ± 0.14	82.8 ± 2.13
scn		*73.77 ± 7.87*	80 ± 1.89	76.77 ± 4.89
SSDVAE	0.2	212.93 ± 2.54	-	-
grp		89.73 ± 4.67	77.32 ± 0.72	83.28 ± 2.38
scn		83.86 ± 2.74	81.2 ± 1.17	*82.52 ± 1.93*

Table 3: Perplexity (lower is better) for the grouped and scenario-based models in the scenario-masked evaluation. For each ϵ, the best score is *italicized.* Best overall is **bold**. These results indicate how our approach can make use of related frames to better model sequences involving missing events. See §5.3.

istence of broader assocations that these relations enable are very helpful. This would suggest that semantically-aware event modeling could benefit from broader semantic resource coverage, with future work examining how best to encode the semantics of *any particular* relation.

5.3 Predicting Missing Events

Previously, we have looked at how using the observation probability can help us mask frames and semi-supervised learning. In this experiment, we examine the robustness of our model with respect to missing events in an input sequence along with the frame masking depending on observation probability. We first identify sequences (in our training, dev, and test data) where two events have different frames f_i and f_j that are contained within the same scenario frame. We train normally, but to evaluate, we remove an event e_j associated with a scenario-connected frame f_j from the input. Given this impoverished input, we require the model to generate the full, unmodified sequence. By construction, the missing event is not a randomly missing event: it is, according to the semantic ontology, *semantically related to another event in that sequence.* To compare our model with SSDVAE, we have trained SSDVAE with the same data and evaluated with the same masked input and full event regeneration.

Given their strong performance, we examine the grouped and scenario-based models. Results, averaged across three seeds, are in Table 3: *grp* is the model with a group of FrameNet relations, *scn*

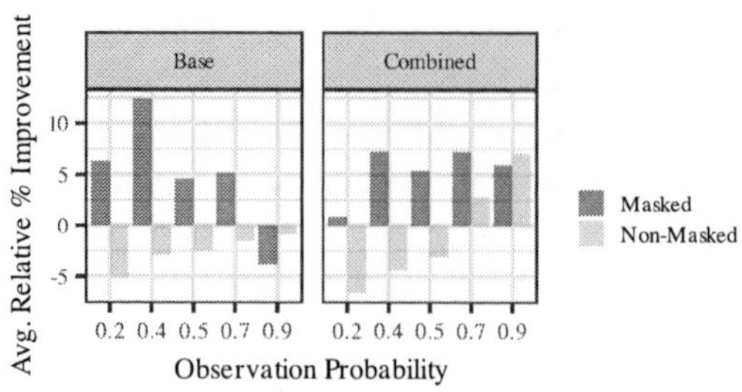

Figure 3: Relative perplexity *improvement* of the scenario-based model vs. the grouped model; higher is better. The scenario model improves across observation levels when important events are missing.

is the model with scenario sub-frames and *SSDVAE* is the SSDVAE model with different evaluation. To show the consistent benefits of our approach, we report results computed just from the base decoder, just from the compression decoder, and from a score combined from both the base and compression decoders. When an important event is masked, the scenario-based model nearly always outperforms the grouped model across observation levels. Our model can leverage training time scenario-related frame associations to better predict a missing event. Also, for all observation probabilities, both of our model's (*grp* & *scn*) individual and combined layer outperform SSDVAE. We suspect this is because SSDVAE does not have a hierarchical abstraction mechanism, so when one event is not present, the related frame is also missing. This shows the capability of the hierarchical structure of our model to understand and encapsulate the abstract meaning of an event sequence.

It is not surprising that the base layer, with more feedback during training and greater representational capacity, is a better language model than the compression layer on its own. Still, the compression layer provides active benefits: we summarize the relative improvement of the scenario-based model over the grouped model in Fig. 3. We compute this from just the base layer, or from both the base and compression layers. A positive number means that the scenario-based model was better able to (re)generate a full event sequence compared to the grouped model. Except for very high observation probability on the base layer, the **scenario-based model consistently outperformed the grouped one when semantically-relevant events were missing**. The grouped model, which covers multiple frame relations, can better model sequences when events are not missing. While this may seem intuitive, notice how using the compression layer is able to reverse this pattern and let the scenario-based model outperform the grouped one, highlighting the benefit that the compression layer can bring.

5.4 Improved Event Similarity

We have shown that both structural and semantic hierarchy can be beneficial when predicting the next event in a sequence, "rolling out" a longer sequence from an initial seed, and accounting for semantically missing events. In our final experiment, we use the latent frame representation to improve the overall event representation. We evaluate on three similarity datasets, comparing to the state-of-the-art (Gao et al., 2022). In two of the datasets, there are two event pairs and the task is to determine which pair is more similar (measured by accuracy); the third involves scalar human assessment scores for how related two events are (Spearman correlation). Data are only for evaluation, and all training is done as "pre-training." As such, our experiments demonstrate the ability to capture semantic information in our latent variable representation, and to perform in an evaluation-only (zero-shot) prediction of semantically-related events.

Gao et al. (2022) presents SWCC, a **s**imultaneous, **w**eakly supervised, **c**ontrastive learning and **c**lustering framework for event representation learning. They combine a clustering loss with the popular contrastive learning approach of InfoNCE (Oord et al., 2018). Every "query" point x (an event tuple) has positive (similar) instances $z_1, ..., z_R$, and negative (dissimilar) instances $z_{R+1}, ..., z_S$. Using a temperature-annealed similarity function on model-computed embeddings, e.g., cosine similarity on embeddings from a LLM, a probability distribution is computed over the positive and negatives (conditioned on the query). Average cross-entropy is optimized to predict the positive vs. negative instances.

This contrastive loss nicely augments our model's existing training objective from §3.4. We pre-train our hierarchical model on the same partially observable frame-annotated data from §4, using that model to extract a representation for an event, and computing the cosine similarity between two representations. We form a representation by concatenating the decoder's final token embedding and the latent frames from the compression layer. To prevent frame representations overfitting to the

Model	Hard Similarity (Accuracy %) Original	Hard Similarity (Accuracy %) Extended	Transitive Score Similarity
SWCC (16)	78.91 ± 1.31	69.2 ± 0.93	0.82 ± 0
SWCC (256)	81.09 ± 0.43	72.55 ± 1.53	$\mathbf{0.82 \pm 0}$
Ours	$\mathbf{83.26 \pm 2.29}$	$\mathbf{78.63 \pm 2.95}$	0.77 ± 0.04

Table 4: Evaluation on Similarity Tasks. SWCC (256) are Gao et al.'s reported results, using a batch size of 256. Given the importance that batch size can have with contrastive learning, we ran Gao et al.'s model with a batch size 16 (the same batch size of our model). We report this as SWCC (16). See §5.4.

	Training Variant	Hard Similarity (Accuracy %) Original	Hard Similarity (Accuracy %) Extended	Transitive Score Similarity
Ours (16)	Contrastive + LM	83.26 ± 2.29	78.63 ± 2.95	0.77 ± 0.04
	Contrastive only	67.18 ± 1.79	72.75 ± 2.06	0.72 ± 0.02
	LM only	67.83 ± 14.39	62.15 ± 16.52	0.56 ± 0.04
SWCC (16)	Contrastive + MLM	78.91 ± 1.31	69.2 ± 0.93	0.82 ± 0
	Contrastive only	78.48 ± 0.83	67.33 ± 0.19	0.78 ± 0.05
	MLM only	25.87 ± 1.31	16.78 ± 0.7	0.55 ± 0.04

Table 5: Ablation study of our model and SWCC.

predicates, rather than arguments, we applied a predicate-specific dropout of 70% on the encoder. Our hierarchical model provides a straightforward way to adopt contrastive loss; this hierarchical nature is not explicit in SSDVAE or HAQUE. Adapting these approaches to the contrastive learning setup is beyond the scope of our work.

Our results are in Table 4. We have run SWCC with a batch size of 16, which is the same as ours. Our model surpasses SWCC on two of the tasks, showing it is not only capable of event language modeling but also capable of generating better event representations. We have also run an ablation study on SWCC and our model; the results are on Table 5. The results show that neither contrastive nor LM/MLM loss are as strong as both together. We see that the LM component in our approach is important to overall performance.

6 Conclusion

We have presented a hierarchical event model that accounts for both structural and ontological hierarchy across an event sequence. We use automatically extracted semantic frames to guide the first level of concept, and then use FrameNet relations to guide abstraction and generalization. We showed improvements across multiple tasks and evaluation measures within event modeling. We showed improvements in next event prediction, longer range event prediction, missing event regeneration, and event similarity. We believe that future work can use this abstraction concept for summarization, topic modeling, or other downstream tasks.

7 Limitations

Our approach enables modeling observed event sequences through the lens of a structured semantic ontology. Though our models have shown superior performance to leverage event frames, they still suffer from the bottleneck of the information passed to the compression layer. Additionally, while these resources do exist, their coverage is not universal, and have historically been developed for English. Our experiments reflect this.

While the observance of frames is not, strictly speaking, a requirement of our model, our experiments focused on those cases when such an ontology is available during training.

Throughout our experiments, we use pretrained models/embeddings. We do not attempt to control or mitigate any biases these may exhibit or propagate.

Our work does not involve human subjects research, data annotation, or representation/analysis of potentially sensitive characteristics. As such, while we believe the direct *potential risks* of our approach are minimal we acknowledge that the joint use of pretrained models and structured semantic ontologies could result in undesired or biased semantic associations.

Acknowledgments

We would like to thank the anonymous reviewers for their comments, questions, and suggestions. This material is based in part upon work supported by the National Science Foundation under Grant No. IIS-2024878. Some experiments were conducted on the UMBC HPCF, supported by the National Science Foundation under Grant No. CNS-1920079. This material is also based on research that is in part supported by the Army Research Laboratory, Grant No. W911NF2120076, and by the Air Force Research Laboratory (AFRL), DARPA, for the KAIROS program under agreement number FA8750-19-2-1003. The U.S. Government is authorized to reproduce and distribute reprints for Governmental purposes notwithstanding any copyright notation thereon. The views and conclusions contained herein are those of the authors and should not be interpreted as necessarily representing the official policies or endorsements, either express or implied, of the Air Force Research Laboratory (AFRL), DARPA, or the U.S. Government.

References

Roni Ben Aharon, Idan Szpektor, and Ido Dagan. 2010. Generating entailment rules from framenet. In *Proceedings of the ACL 2010 Conference Short Papers*, pages 241–246.

Collin F Baker, Charles J Fillmore, and John B Lowe. 1998. The berkeley framenet project. In *COLING 1998 Volume 1: The 17th International Conference on Computational Linguistics*.

Laura Banarescu, Claire Bonial, Shu Cai, Madalina Georgescu, Kira Griffitt, Ulf Hermjakob, Kevin Knight, Martha Palmer, and Nathan Schneider. 2013. Abstract meaning representation for sembanking. In *In Proceedings of the 7th Linguistic Annotation Workshop and Interoperability with Discourse*. Citeseer.

Yonatan Bisk, Jan Buys, Karl Pichotta, and Yejin Choi. 2019. Benchmarking hierarchical script knowledge. In *Proceedings of the 2019 Conference of the North American Chapter of the Association for Computational Linguistics: Human Language Technologies, Volume 1 (Long and Short Papers)*, pages 4077–4085.

Teresa Botschen, Hatem Mousselly-Sergieh, and Iryna Gurevych. 2017. Prediction of frame-to-frame relations in the FrameNet hierarchy with frame embeddings. In *Proceedings of the 2nd Workshop on Representation Learning for NLP*.

Muhao Chen, Hongming Zhang, Haoyu Wang, and Dan Roth. 2020. What are you trying to do? semantic typing of event processes. In *Proceedings of the 24th Conference on Computational Natural Language Learning*, pages 531–542.

Jackie Chi Kit Cheung, Hoifung Poon, and Lucy Vanderwende. 2013. Probabilistic frame induction. In *NAACL*.

Alan Darmasaputra Chowanda, Albert Richard Sanyoto, Derwin Suhartono, and Criscentia Jessica Setiadi. 2017. Automatic debate text summarization in online debate forum. *Procedia computer science*, 116:11–19.

Michael Collins. 1997. Three generative, lexicalised models for statistical parsing. In *35th Annual Meeting of the Association for Computational Linguistics and 8th Conference of the European Chapter of the Association for Computational Linguistics*, pages 16–23, Madrid, Spain. Association for Computational Linguistics.

Dipanjan Das, Desai Chen, André FT Martins, Nathan Schneider, and Noah A Smith. 2014. Frame-semantic parsing. *Computational Linguistics*, 40(1):9–56.

Xinya Du, Alexander Rush, and Claire Cardie. 2021. GRIT: Generative role-filler transformers for document-level event entity extraction. In *Proceedings of the 16th Conference of the European Chapter of the Association for Computational Linguistics: Main Volume*, Online. Association for Computational Linguistics.

Seth Ebner, Patrick Xia, Ryan Culkin, Kyle Rawlins, and Benjamin Van Durme. 2020. Multi-sentence argument linking. In *Proceedings of the 58th Annual Meeting of the Association for Computational Linguistics*.

Carl Edwards and Heng Ji. 2022. Semi-supervised new event type induction and description via contrastive loss-enforced batch attention. *arXiv preprint arXiv:2202.05943*.

Francis Ferraro, Adam Poliak, Ryan Cotterell, and Benjamin Van Durme. 2017. Frame-based continuous lexical semantics through exponential family tensor factorization and semantic proto-roles. In *Proceedings of the 6th Joint Conference on Lexical and Computational Semantics (*SEM 2017)*, pages 97–103, Vancouver, Canada. Association for Computational Linguistics.

Francis Ferraro, Max Thomas, Matthew R Gormley, Travis Wolfe, Craig Harman, and Benjamin Van Durme. 2014. Concretely annotated corpora. In *4th Workshop on Automated Knowledge Base Construction (AKBC)*.

Francis Ferraro and Benjamin Van Durme. 2016. A Unified Bayesian Model of Scripts, Frames and Language. In *Proceedings of the 30th Conference on Artificial Intelligence (AAAI)*, pages 2601–2607, Phoenix, Arizona. Association for the Advancement of Artificial Intelligence.

Jun Gao, Wei Wang, Changlong Yu, Huan Zhao, Wilfred Ng, and Ruifeng Xu. 2022. Improving event representation via simultaneous weakly supervised contrastive learning and clustering. In *Proceedings of the 60th Annual Meeting of the Association for Computational Linguistics (Volume 1: Long Papers)*, pages 3036–3049, Dublin, Ireland. Association for Computational Linguistics.

Daniel Gildea and Daniel Jurafsky. 2002. Automatic labeling of semantic roles. *Computational Linguistics*, 28(3):245–288.

Yong Guan, Shaoru Guo, Ru Li, Xiaoli Li, and Hu Zhang. 2021. Frame semantics guided network for abstractive sentence summarization. *Knowledge-Based Systems*, 221:106973.

Xu Han, Tao Lv, Zhirui Hu, Xinyan Wang, and Cong Wang. 2016. Text summarization using framenet-based semantic graph model. *Scientific Programming*, 2016:5.

Eduard Hovy, Mitchell Marcus, Martha Palmer, Lance Ramshaw, and Ralph Weischedel. 2006. Ontonotes: the 90% solution. In *Proceedings of the human language technology conference of the NAACL, Companion Volume: Short Papers*, pages 57–60. Association for Computational Linguistics.

I-Hung Hsu, Kuan-Hao Huang, Elizabeth Boschee, Scott Miller, Prem Natarajan, Kai-Wei Chang, and Nanyun Peng. 2022. DEGREE: A data-efficient generation-based event extraction model. In *Proceedings of the 2022 Conference of the North American Chapter of the Association for Computational Linguistics: Human Language Technologies*.

Chieh-Yang Huang and Ting-Hao Huang. 2021. Semantic frame forecast. In *Proceedings of the 2021 Conference of the North American Chapter of the Association for Computational Linguistics: Human Language Technologies*.

James Y. Huang, Bangzheng Li, Jiashu Xu, and Muhao Chen. 2022. Unified semantic typing with meaningful label inference. In *Proceedings of the 2022 Conference of the North American Chapter of the Association for Computational Linguistics: Human Language Technologies*.

Lifu Huang and Heng Ji. 2020. Semi-supervised new event type induction and event detection. In *Proceedings of the 2020 Conference on Empirical Methods in Natural Language Processing (EMNLP)*, pages 718–724.

Eric Jang, Shixiang Gu, and Ben Poole. 2016. Categorical reparameterization with gumbel-softmax. *arXiv preprint arXiv:1611.01144*.

Diederik P Kingma and Jimmy Ba. 2014. Adam: A method for stochastic optimization. *arXiv preprint arXiv:1412.6980*.

Diederik P Kingma, Shakir Mohamed, Danilo Jimenez Rezende, and Max Welling. 2014. Semi-supervised learning with deep generative models. In *Advances in neural information processing systems*, pages 3581–3589.

Diederik P Kingma and Max Welling. 2013. Auto-encoding variational bayes. *arXiv preprint arXiv:1312.6114*.

Dan Klein and Christopher D. Manning. 2003. Accurate unlexicalized parsing. In *Proceedings of the 41st Annual Meeting of the Association for Computational Linguistics*, pages 423–430, Sapporo, Japan. Association for Computational Linguistics.

Mike Lewis, Yinhan Liu, Naman Goyal, Marjan Ghazvininejad, Abdelrahman Mohamed, Omer Levy, Ves Stoyanov, and Luke Zettlemoyer. 2019. Bart: Denoising sequence-to-sequence pre-training for natural language generation, translation, and comprehension. *arXiv preprint arXiv:1910.13461*.

Aaron van den Oord, Yazhe Li, and Oriol Vinyals. 2018. Representation learning with contrastive predictive coding. *arXiv preprint arXiv:1807.03748*.

Tim O'Gorman, Kristin Wright-Bettner, and Martha Palmer. 2016. Richer event description: Integrating event coreference with temporal, causal and bridging annotation. In *Proceedings of the 2nd Workshop on Computing News Storylines (CNS 2016)*, pages 47–56.

Ankur Padia, Francis Ferraro, and Tim Finin. 2018. Surface: semantically rich fact validation with explanations. *arXiv preprint arXiv:1810.13223*.

Sveva Pepe, Edoardo Barba, Rexhina Blloshmi, and Roberto Navigli. 2022. Steps: Semantic typing of event processes with a sequence-to-sequence approach.

Slav Petrov, Leon Barrett, Romain Thibaux, and Dan Klein. 2006. Learning accurate, compact, and interpretable tree annotation. In *Proceedings of the 21st International Conference on Computational Linguistics and 44th Annual Meeting of the Association for Computational Linguistics*, pages 433–440, Sydney, Australia. Association for Computational Linguistics.

Mehdi Rezaee and Francis Ferraro. 2021. Event representation with sequential, semi-supervised discrete variables. In *Proceedings of the 2021 Conference of the North American Chapter of the Association for Computational Linguistics: Human Language Technologies*, pages 4701–4716, Online. Association for Computational Linguistics.

Karin Kipper Schuler. 2005. *VerbNet: A broad-coverage, comprehensive verb lexicon*. Ph.D. thesis, University of Pennsylvania.

Beth Sundheim. 1992. Proceedings of the fourth message understanding conference (MUC-4).

Beth Sundheim. 1996. Overview of results of the MUC-6 evaluation. In *Proceedings of a Workshop held at Vienna, Virginia: May 6-8, 1996*.

Noah Weber, Leena Shekhar, Niranjan Balasubramanian, and Nathanael Chambers. 2018. Hierarchical quantized representations for script generation. In *Proceedings of the 2018 Conference on Empirical Methods in Natural Language Processing*, pages 3783–3792.

Li Zhang, Qing Lyu, and Chris Callison-Burch. 2020. Reasoning about goals, steps, and temporal ordering with WikiHow. In *Proceedings of the 2020 Conference on Empirical Methods in Natural Language Processing (EMNLP)*.

A Additional Model and Implementation Details

A.1 Model Details

For our input data, events are separated by a *<TUP>* token, and in case of missing values in an event frame, is replaced with a special *<NOFRAME>* token.

As mentioned in the main paper, like any auto-regressive model, previously generated decoder output and previous input texts are given as input to the decoder. An attention module is used to find the important words from the given latent embeddings predicted by encoder. Each layer tries to reconstruct the input text, and loss was generated individually for each layer, which then accumulated and back-propagated through the whole model, updating the model parameters.

A.2 Implementation Details

The values of γ_1 and γ_2 are set to 0.1 by experimenting on the validation set. 2 Gumbel-softmax samples are used to average the encoder. We use the Adam (Kingma and Ba, 2014) optimizer with a learning rate of 0.001. A batch size of 64 has been used with a gradient accumulation of 8. Early stopping has been used with patience of 10 on the validation perplexity score.

For comparability, our core event modeling results use recurrent encoders and decoders. We use pretrained Glove-300 embeddings to represent each lexical item in an event tuple. An embedding size of 500 has been used for frame embeddings. Two layers of bidirectional GRU have been used for the encoder, and two layers of uni-directional GRU have been used for the decoder. Both are used with 512 hidden sizes. Gradient clipping of 5.0 has been used to prevent gradient exploding. 0.5 has been used as the Gumbel-softmax temperature.

Similarly, our experiments involving event similarity (§5.4) use BART (Lewis et al., 2019) as our encoder and decoder module.

Across our experiments, we have used NVIDIA RTX 2080Ti or NVIDIA RTX 6000 for training. It takes around 16 hours to train with our current batch size on our dataset.

A.3 Loss Formulation

In constructing our training loss function, we take inspiration from the methodology outlined in the study conducted by (Rezaee and Ferraro, 2021). However, our model differs in that it incorporates two hidden layers, as opposed to the single latent layer utilized in the aforementioned study. Each layer we calculate the loss for both layers individually. This is done by allowing each layer j, to reconstruct the input text using its own latent variables, L_{r_j}. To prevent overfitting, we incorporate KL terms in our loss function denoted as $\mathcal{L}_{\mathrm{KL}_j}$. Additionally, for the base layer we include a classification term, designated as $\mathcal{L}_c$.

$$\begin{aligned}\mathcal{L} = & \underbrace{\alpha_1 * \mathcal{L}_{r_1} + \alpha_2 * \mathcal{L}_{r_2}}_{\text{Text Reconstruction}} \\ & + \underbrace{\beta_1 * \mathcal{L}_{\mathrm{KL}_1} + \beta_2 * \mathcal{L}_{\mathrm{KL}_2}}_{\text{Regularization}} \\ & + \underbrace{\gamma * \mathcal{L}_c.}_{\text{Observed Frame Classification}}\end{aligned} \quad (1)$$

The reconstruction and KL losses depend on the random variables inferred at each level: for the base level ($j = 1$), the losses depends on the frames sampled at the base level $f_1, \ldots, f_n$, while the compression losses ($j = 2$) depend on $h_1, \ldots, h_M$). Our latent variable model learns a variational distribution q, from which it can infer appropriate values for f_i and h_j. With this, we compute

$$\mathcal{L}_{r_1} = \mathbb{E}_{q(f_1,\ldots,f_N)}[\log p(x|f_1, \ldots, f_N)] \quad (2)$$

$$\mathcal{L}_{r_2} = \mathbb{E}_{q(h_1,\ldots,h_M)}[\log p(x|h_1, \ldots, h_M)] \quad (3)$$

$$\mathcal{L}_{\mathrm{KL}_1} = \mathbb{E}_{q(f_1,\ldots,f_N)}[\log p(f_1, \ldots, f_N)] \quad (4)$$

$$\mathcal{L}_{\mathrm{KL}_2} = \mathbb{E}_{q(h_1,\ldots,h_M)}[\log p(h_1, \ldots, h_M)] \quad (5)$$

$$\mathcal{L}_c = - \sum_{i=1: f_i^* \text{ is obs.}}^{N} \log q(f_i^* | f_{i-1}). \quad (6)$$

In $\mathcal{L}_c$, note that f_i^* represents the correct value of the ith frame. The reconstruction and frame classification losses can be computed via a cross-entropy loss (per output token for the reconstruction losses, and per predicted frame in the frame classification loss).

B Additional Results

B.1 Is Frame Inheritance Sufficient?

The detailed results for the experiment described in §5.1 are reported in Table 6 (Perplexity Score) and Table 7 (INC).

Detailed per-layer perplexity is reported in Table 6, augmenting the results in Table 1. Our model's base layer perplexity consistently outperformed the other models. However, the perplexity of the compression layer was higher. This suggests that while incorporating hierarchical layers or knowledge may not be sufficient for generating the event sequence, it provides useful, less-than-full supervised feedback to the base layer.

Model	ϵ	Perplexity (Test Data) Base	Compression	Total
HAQAE	-	-	-	21.38 ± 0.25
SSDVAE		-	-	19.84 ± 0.52
ours: inf. frame	0.9	*19.39 ± 0.3*	26.52 ± 0.55	22.68 ± 0.41
ours: lexical		***19.12 ± 0.53***	31.43 ± 1.1	24.51 ± 0.39
SSDVAE		-	-	21.19 ± 0.76
ours: inf. frame	0.7	*20.26 ± 1.36*	27.45 ± 0.5	23.57 ± 0.84
ours: lexical		*21.52 ± 1.48*	35.19 ± 0.95	27.5 ± 0.93
SSDVAE		-	-	31.11 ± 0.85
ours: inf. frame	0.5	*22.16 ± 1.62*	32.59 ± 2.86	26.62 ± 2.13
ours: lexical		*25.02 ± 1.31*	39.44 ± 0.44	31.41 ± 0.77
SSDVAE		-	-	33.12 ± 0.54
ours: inf. frame	0.4	*24.02 ± 1.28*	32.82 ± 1.44	28.07 ± 1.24
ours: lexical		*27.06 ± 0.94*	40.46 ± 2.74	33.05 ± 0.56
SSDVAE		-	-	33.31 ± 0.63
ours: inf. frame	0.2	*30.15 ± 2.73*	34.81 ± 2.81	32.84 ± 1.84
ours: lexical		*33.6 ± 1.84*	44.64 ± 1.44	38.72 ± 1.59

Table 6: Per-word perplexity for test data (lower is better). For each observation probability (ϵ), the best perplexity is in *italic* form. The best of all of them is **bold** form. See App. B.1

For INC, we look to the lexical variant, where our model's base layer outperforms the previous result with having the best of all the observation probabilities. However, the results for the compression layer underperformed the inferred variant, indicating that incorporating lexical signals may have a negative impact on the performance of the generation model. Overall, this suggests that the **inferred frames and ontological relations from the base layer are important for hierarchical modeling**.

We have reported an average change in the INC score of the base layer over the combined layer on Fig. 4. The gray and orange bars represent the two variants: inferred frames and lexical signal, respectively. Each bar is the average of the score change from the combined layer to the base layer (combined layer score – base layer score). Here, a negative score means that the base layer is better than the combined one. This figure shows if the use of compression layer has a positive impact on the INC score or not. First, for the inferred frames, the addition of a compression layer has improved the INC score by an effective margin on the base layer. This shows that the semantic frames have helped the model's base layer to understand the process better. On the other hand, for the lexical signal, the combined layer has a better INC score. This shows that having the lexical signal on the compression layer has a better and equal effect on both layers. In conclusion, the addition of a compression layer improves the model's capability of understanding event sequences and generalizing.

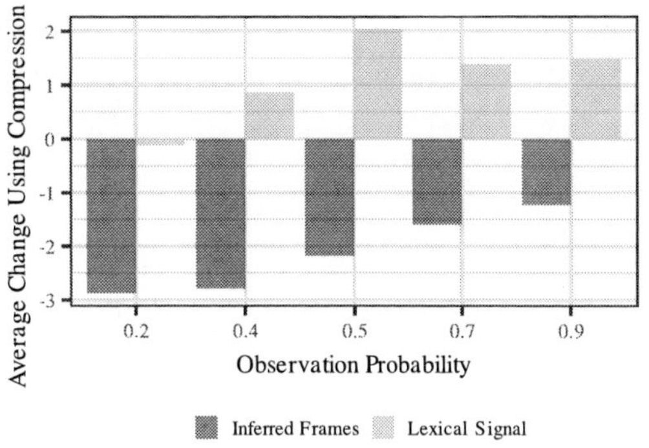

Figure 4: Average Change in INC score from combined layer to base layer, where a negative score means the base layer was better than the combined one and vice versa. The gray and orange bars indicate whether the input to the compression layer is inferred frames or lexical signal, respectively. In all cases, inferred frames has a better effect on base layer and lexical signal has improved combined layer's performance.

B.2 The Effect of Individual Frame Relations

The detailed results for the experiment described in §5.2 are reported on Table 8 (Perplexity Score) and Table 9 (Wikipedia Inverse Narrative Score).

B.3 Are scenario subframes better than other frame properties?

The detailed results for the experiment reported in Table 2 are shown in Table 10 (Perplexity Score) and Table 11 (INC).

B.4 The Effect of Grouping Frame Properties

The previous section showed that performance of our model can be further improved by using targeted frame relations. Here, we investigate whether grouping of different frame relations could have a more significant impact on generalization.

Using §5.2, we identified six frame-relations as the most important ones: Inheritance, Using, Precedes, Causative_of, Inchoative_of, and Subframe. We used this group of frame relations to extract the parent frames from the predicted frames of the base layer. With their parent frames, these frames were passed to the compression layer to learn to associate the semantically similar frames.

Looking at the perplexity results (Table 12) of this experiment, we can see that the base layer outperforms both baselines across observation lavels. Additionally, while we see the intuitive result that higher levels of frame observation during training improves perplexity, we see the largest relative improvments for $\epsilon = 0.5$ and $\epsilon = 0.4$. This suggests that our hierarchical model is able to effectively leverage the semantic ontology, even when 40% of events do not have observed frames.

We see broadly similar patterns for inverse narrative cloze, with our approach outperforming both baselines. First, our performance is highest with the lowest observation level. Second, aside from when 90% of the events have observed frames, as ϵ decreases, so does our model's variance, while the previous state-of-the-art's increases. Taken together, these results suggest that our model is better able to use the provided semantic ontology and make better longer range predictions, even with lim-

Model	ϵ	Wikipedia INC (Test Data)		
		Base	Compression	Total
HAQAE	-	-	-	24.88 ± 1.35
SSDVAE	0.9	-	-	35.56 ± 1.70
ours: inf. frame		41.35 ± 4.25	27.25 ± 1.02	40.11 ± 1.88
ours: lexical		41.35 ± 3.19	35.41 ± 2.56	*42.83 ± 1.47*
SSDVAE	0.7	-	-	*39.08 ± 1.55*
ours: inf. frame		35.86 ± 3.43	26.31 ± 2.92	34.26 ± 3.43
ours: lexical		35.61 ± 4.72	32.68 ± 6.12	37.01 ± 6.59
SSDVAE	0.5	-	-	*40.18 ± 0.90*
ours: inf. frame		37.3 ± 3.33	23.61 ± 1.34	35.13 ± 3.01
ours: lexical		37.8 ± 3	37.11 ± 3.14	39.85 ± 3.01
SSDVAE	0.4	-	-	*47.88 ± 3.59*
ours: inf. frame		43.25 ± 4.97	23.65 ± 1.34	40.46 ± 4.71
ours: lexical		39.2 ± 1.23	34.79 ± 4.75	40.06 ± 2
SSDVAE	0.2	-	-	44.38 ± 2.10
ours: inf. frame		***49.53 ± 1.56***	25.15 ± 4.34	46.65 ± 1.55
ours: lexical		46.53 ± 2.84	37.55 ± 2.8	46.41 ± 3.71

Table 7: Wikipedia Inverse Narrative Cloze Score for test data (higher is better). For each observation probability (ϵ), the best score is in *italic* form. The best of all of them is **bold** form. See App. B.1

Model	Frame Relation	ϵ	Perplexity (Test Data)		
			Base	Compression	Total
HAQAE	-	-	-	-	21.38 ± 0.25
SSDVAE	-	0.9	-	-	19.84 ± 0.52
ours	Using		19.39 ± 0.51	25.34 ± 0.22	22.16 ± 0.37
	Precedes		19.57 ± 0.58	25.83 ± 0.25	22.48 ± 0.25
	Metaphor		19.62 ± 0.75	25.21 ± 0.49	22.24 ± 0.63
	See_also		19.55 ± 0.72	25.71 ± 0.39	22.42 ± 0.54
	Causative_of		19.42 ± 0.57	25.75 ± 0.46	22.36 ± 0.53
	Inchoative_of		19.28 ± 0.32	26.01 ± 0.85	22.39 ± 0.52
	Perspective_on		19.76 ± 0.97	25.64 ± 0.57	22.5 ± 0.75
	Subframe		***18.91 ± 0.15***	26.03 ± 0.42	22.19 ± 0.27
	ReFraming_Mapping		19.56 ± 0.94	26.63 ± 1.81	22.81 ± 0.62
SSDVAE	-	0.2	-	-	33.31 ± 0.63
ours	Using		31.37 ± 2.08	38.55 ± 5.72	34.72 ± 3.23
	Precedes		32.62 ± 1.65	45.33 ± 0.74	38.45 ± 1.25
	Metaphor		32.92 ± 2.08	42.07 ± 5.83	37.18 ± 3.5
	See_also		31.83 ± 2.78	41.78 ± 5.55	36.44 ± 3.79
	Causative_of		31.82 ± 3	40.01 ± 6.23	35.67 ± 4.41
	Inchoative_of		32.65 ± 1.4	42.42 ± 3.55	37.21 ± 2.21
	Perspective_on		33.2 ± 1.47	44.18 ± 1.26	38.28 ± 0.34
	Subframe		32.78 ± 2.09	45.25 ± 0.7	38.51 ± 1.52
	ReFraming_Mapping		*31.34 ± 2.76*	36.57 ± 2.9	34.06 ± 3.15

Table 8: Per-word perplexity for test data (lower is better). For each observation probability (ϵ), the best perplexity is in *italic* form. The best of all of them is **bold** form. See App. B.2

Model	Frame Relation	ϵ	Wikipedia INC (Test Data)		
	-		Base	Compression	Total
HAQAE	-	-	-	-	24.88 ± 1.35
SSDVAE	-	0.9	-	-	35.56 ± 1.70
ours	Using	0.9	43.23 ± 2.51	26.68 ± 0.63	40.92 ± 1.85
	Precedes		41.43 ± 3.02	26.38 ± 1.51	40.03 ± 1.66
	Metaphor		41.92 ± 3.93	24.22 ± 1.53	38.8 ± 2.17
	See_also		42.67 ± 1.49	27.08 ± 0.24	41.13 ± 0.81
	Causative_of		41.38 ± 2.23	26.3 ± 1.05	40.47 ± 1.79
	Inchoative_of		41.35 ± 3.47	26.67 ± 1.33	40 ± 2.34
	Perspective_on		40.53 ± 2.04	26.38 ± 0.67	39.55 ± 1.75
	Subframe		40.35 ± 2.91	25.7 ± 0.48	38.42 ± 2.32
	ReFraming_Mapping		*43.8 ± 4.02*	26.7 ± 1.21	42.15 ± 3.19
SSDVAE	-	0.2	-	-	44.38 ± 2.10
ours	Using	0.2	***49.72*** ± ***1.73***	21.77 ± 1.1	45.93 ± 1.62
	Precedes		47.92 ± 2.25	20.67 ± 0.29	42.72 ± 1.58
	Metaphor		47.25 ± 3.81	21.12 ± 0.95	42.77 ± 3.27
	See_also		47.77 ± 3.61	21.2 ± 1.15	43.72 ± 2.78
	Causative_of		49.85 ± 0.84	21.5 ± 2.41	45.45 ± 2.03
	Inchoative_of		48.03 ± 3.35	21 ± 0.74	43.95 ± 2.61
	Perspective_on		47.85 ± 3.53	20.42 ± 0.3	43.08 ± 3.12
	Subframe		47.88 ± 3.31	20.33 ± 0.52	42.38 ± 1.86
	ReFraming_Mapping		49.05 ± 1.54	22.23 ± 0.58	45.45 ± 0.44

Table 9: Wikipedia Inverse Narrative Cloze Score for test data (higher is better). For each observation probability (ϵ), the best score is in *italic* form. The best of all of them is **bold** form. See App. B.2

Model	ϵ	Perplexity (Test Data)		
		Base	Compression	Total
HAQAE	-	-	-	21.38 ± 0.25
SSDVAE	0.9	-	-	19.84 ± 0.52
scenario-only		*18.81 ± 0.36*	25.61 ± 1.23	21.94 ± 0.5
SSDVAE	0.7	-	-	21.19 ± 0.76
scenario-only		***18.75*** ± ***0.3***	26.82 ± 0.47	22.42 ± 0.21
SSDVAE	0.5	-	-	31.11 ± 0.85
scenario-only		*23.79 ± 1.29*	31.43 ± 7.44	28.7 ± 2.04
SSDVAE	0.4	-	-	33.12 ± 0.54
scenario-only		*25.54 ± 2.34*	36.87 ± 6.01	30.63 ± 3.52
SSDVAE	0.2	-	-	33.31 ± 0.63
scenario-only		*32.01 ± 0.7*	45.28 ± 0.7	38.07 ± 0.55

Table 10: Per-word perplexity for test data (lower is better). For each observation probability (ϵ), the best perplexity is in *italic* form. The best of all of them is **bold** form. See App. B.3

ited observations. Together with the perplexity improvements, these results reaffirm our assumption that the compression layer gives a subtle but strong signal that improves generative performance.

C Ablation Study

C.1 Impact of parameter sharing of encoder and decoder

To find out the importance of multiple encoders and decoders on two layers, we have used shared parameters on both of them and see the effect on the result. The result for this experiment ($ours_{encdec}$) is reported on Table 14. We can see a substantial drop in the result, especially on the INC score for low perplexity scores (0.5, 0.4, 0.2).

Model	ϵ	Wikipedia INC (Test Data)		
		Base	Compression	Total
HAQAE	-	-	-	24.88 ± 1.35
SSDVAE	0.9	-	-	35.56 ± 1.70
scenario-only		*42.29 ± 1.79*	25.38 ± 1.84	39.86 ± 1.82
SSDVAE	0.7	-	-	*39.08 ± 1.55*
scenario-only		38.79 ± 4.11	26.83 ± 7.32	32.91 ± 7.29
SSDVAE	0.5	-	-	*40.18 ± 0.90*
scenario-only		37.59 ± 5.61	22.06 ± 1.01	35.59 ± 4.71
SSDVAE	0.4	-	-	*47.88 ± 3.59*
scenario-only		40.91 ± 2.19	22.15 ± 1.37	37.99 ± 1.86
SSDVAE	0.2	-	-	44.38 ± 2.10
scenario-only		***48.1*** ± ***2.22***	20.54 ± 0.1	43.3 ± 2.33

Table 11: Wikipedia Inverse Narrative Cloze Score for test data (higher is better). For each observation probability (ϵ), the best score is in *italic* form. The best of all of them is **bold** form. See App. B.3

Model	ϵ	Perplexity (Test Data)		
		Base	Compression	Total
HAQAE	-	-	-	21.38 ± 0.25
SSDVAE	0.9	-	-	19.84 ± 0.52
grouping		***19.44*** ± ***0.5***	31.36 ± 0.85	24.69 ± 0.64
SSDVAE	0.7	-	-	21.19 ± 0.76
grouping		*20.13 ± 1.45*	29.7 ± 0.51	24.43 ± 0.84
SSDVAE	0.5	-	-	31.11 ± 0.85
grouping		*21.52 ± 0.72*	31.62 ± 0.51	26.08 ± 0.39
SSDVAE	0.4	-	-	33.12 ± 0.54
grouping		*23.42 ± 0.59*	30.16 ± 4.2	27.45 ± 0.66
SSDVAE	0.2	-	-	33.31 ± 0.63
grouping		*28.17 ± 2.26*	34.17 ± 0.98	31 ± 1.31

Table 12: Per-word perplexity for test data (lower is better). For each observation probability (ϵ), the best perplexity is in *italic* form. The best of all of them is **bold** form. See App. B.4

C.2 Impact of parameter sharing of frame embedding

To determine the importance of multiple frame embedding weights for each layer, we have used one shared frame embedding layer across both layers. We compute results across three seeds. The result for this experiment ($ours_{frame}$) is reported on Table 14. Similar to the encoder-decoder, we can see a substantial decrease in the INC score.

C.3 Impact of summation or concatenation of both layer encoding

To illustrate if both layer encodings altogether can improve the result, we have done two experiments, one with the summation of both layers encodings ($ours_{sum}$) and another with only concatenation of both layer encodings ($ours_{cat}$). Both experiments' results are reported on Table 14. Both of the models have a large drop on INC, which demonstrates the importance of the performance of the individual encoding.

Model	ϵ	Wikipedia INC (Test Data)		
		Base	Compression	Total
HAQAE	-	-	-	24.88 ± 1.35
SSDVAE	0.9	-	-	35.56 ± 1.70
grouping		*40.76 ± 2.86*	28.23 ± 1.04	39.4 ± 1.59
SSDVAE	0.7	-	-	*39.08 ± 1.55*
grouping		38.09 ± 5.6	26.55 ± 0.51	37.83 ± 5.08
SSDVAE	0.5	-	-	*40.18 ± 0.90*
grouping		39.5 ± 3.45	25.61 ± 0.96	37.86 ± 2.56
SSDVAE	0.4	-	-	*47.88 ± 3.59*
grouping		43.83 ± 1.75	24.79 ± 0.43	42.16 ± 1.43
SSDVAE	0.2	-	-	44.38 ± 2.10
grouping		***48.88 ± 1.37***	26.64 ± 0.98	46.81 ± 1.67

Table 13: Wikipedia Inverse Narrative Cloze Score for test data (higher is better). For each observation probability (ϵ), the best score is in *italic* form. The best of all of them is **bold** form. See App. B.4

Model	ϵ	Perplexity (Test Data)			Wikipedia INC (Test Data)		
		Base	Compression	Total	Base	Compression	Total
HAQAE	-	-	-	21.39 ± 0.25	-	-	24.88 ± 1.35
SSDVAE	0.9	-	-	19.84 ± 0.52	-	-	35.56 ± 1.70
$ours_{encdec}$		26.25 ± 0.12	26.59 ± 0.13	26.42 ± 0.12	38.35 ± 1.66	38.42 ± 1.53	38.28 ± 1.65
$ours_{frame}$		20.94 ± 0.86	37.01 ± 1.55	27.83 ± 0.85	41.82 ± 2.44	28.37 ± 4.09	39.97 ± 1.16
$ours_{sum}$		*18.63 ± 0.24*	32.02 ± 4.46	24.38 ± 1.59	40.88 ± 0.25	36.15 ± 11.71	42.65 ± 5.02
$ours_{cat}$		19.34 ± 1.04	31.25 ± 2.07	24.54 ± 0.23	*44.05 ± 0.61*	25.43 ± 4.73	37.53 ± 4.54
SSDVAE	0.7	-	-	21.19 ± 0.76	-	-	39.08 ± 1.55
$ours_{encdec}$		27.15 ± 0.64	27.61 ± 0.64	27.38 ± 0.64	40.68 ± 1.78	40.37 ± 1.27	40.52 ± 1.43
$ours_{frame}$		20.77 ± 0.2	38.75 ± 1.18	28.37 ± 0.33	41.38 ± 3.48	33.22 ± 4.4	41.71 ± 2.75
$ours_{sum}$		*19.51 ± 0.5*	30.37 ± 3.29	24.33 ± 1.61	41.68 ± 1.25	31.77 ± 10.34	40.92 ± 5.04
$ours_{cat}$		20.17 ± 0.42	30.04 ± 2.89	24.59 ± 1.09	*43.42 ± 1.53*	28.15 ± 5.53	39.63 ± 3.45
SSDVAE	0.5	-	-	31.11 ± 0.85	-	-	40.18 ± 0.90
$ours_{encdec}$		26.54 ± 1.68	28.79 ± 1.55	27.65 ± 1.61	37.02 ± 5.75	37.03 ± 5.7	36.9 ± 5.9
$ours_{frame}$		19.55 ± 0.89	37.84 ± 1.72	27.19 ± 0.98	*45.48 ± 3.63*	27.9 ± 1.68	40.7 ± 3.55
$ours_{sum}$		*19.15 ± 0.38*	30.58 ± 1.28	24.19 ± 0.57	41.03 ± 1.32	43.37 ± 2.03	*46.83 ± 1.55*
$ours_{cat}$		19.59 ± 0.22	30.39 ± 1.49	24.4 ± 0.6	41.45 ± 2.05	26.12 ± 4	38.57 ± 5.59
SSDVAE	0.4	-	-	33.12 ± 0.54	-	-	***47.88 ± 3.59***
$ours_{encdec}$		25.56 ± 0.53	28.03 ± 0.47	26.77 ± 0.5	36.52 ± 3.06	36.23 ± 2.85	36.57 ± 2.97
$ours_{frame}$		19.6 ± 1.16	38.03 ± 0.74	27.29 ± 0.58	38.13 ± 2.55	26.78 ± 3.21	37.18 ± 0.73
$ours_{sum}$		18.79 ± 0.98	32.09 ± 1.27	24.56 ± 1.04	43.33 ± 0.88	37.47 ± 14.06	45.82 ± 4.8
$ours_{cat}$		*18.74 ± 0.83*	32.1 ± 2.14	24.52 ± 1.14	42.28 ± 3.73	32.37 ± 9.64	43.2 ± 2.66
SSDVAE	0.2	-	-	33.31 ± 0.63	-	-	*44.38 ± 2.10*
$ours_{encdec}$		25.62 ± 0.31	30.85 ± 0.17	28.12 ± 0.1	38.1 ± 3.1	38.32 ± 3.37	38.27 ± 3.22
$ours_{frame}$		18.63 ± 0.75	38.68 ± 0.36	26.84 ± 0.65	41.45 ± 2.33	29.62 ± 0.98	40.43 ± 2.95
$ours_{sum}$		***17.1 ± 0.21***	29.19 ± 3.06	22.33 ± 1.31	39.25 ± 4.42	31.65 ± 11.88	40.45 ± 7.24
$ours_{cat}$		17.21 ± 0.65	29.6 ± 2.78	22.56 ± 1.18	38.55 ± 0.41	20.45 ± 9.19	29.77 ± 9.34

Table 14: Wikipedia Inverse Narrative Cloze Score for test data (higher is better). For each observation probability (ϵ), the best score is in *italic* form. The best of all of them is **bold** form. See App. C.1, App. C.2, App. C.3

Representation of Lexical Stylistic Features in Language Models' Embedding Space

Qing Lyu **Marianna Apidianaki** **Chris Callison-Burch**
University of Pennsylvania
{lyuqing, marapi, ccb}@seas.upenn.edu

Abstract

The representation space of pretrained Language Models (LMs) encodes rich information about words and their relationships (e.g., similarity, hypernymy, polysemy) as well as abstract semantic notions (e.g., intensity). In this paper, we demonstrate that lexical stylistic notions such as complexity, formality, and figurativeness, can also be identified in this space. We show that it is possible to derive a vector representation for each of these stylistic notions from only a small number of seed pairs. Using these vectors, we can characterize new texts in terms of these dimensions by performing simple calculations in the corresponding embedding space. We conduct experiments on five datasets and find that static embeddings encode these features more accurately at the level of words and phrases, whereas contextualized LMs perform better on sentences. The lower performance of contextualized representations at the word level is partially attributable to the anisotropy of their vector space, which can be corrected to some extent using techniques like standardization.[1]

1 Introduction

The style of a text is often reflected in its grammatical and discourse properties, but also in local word choices made by the author. The choice of one from a set of synonyms or paraphrases with different connotations can define the style of a text in terms of complexity (e.g., *help* vs. *assist*), formality (e.g., *dad* vs. *father*), figurativeness (e.g., *fall* vs. *plummet*), and so on (Edmonds and Hirst, 2002). These *lexical stylistic features* can be useful in various scenarios, such as analyzing the style of authors or texts of different genres, and determining the appropriate word usage in language learning applications.

COMPLEXITY	doctor → medical practitioner
	laws → legislative texts
	high blood pressure → hypertension
	very common → prevalent
	a lot → significant quantity
	be bad → impact negatively
	help → assist
FORMALITY	my gosh → jesus
	breathing → respiratory
	yeah → yes
	ten years → decade
	first of all → foremost
	a whole bunch → full
	my dad → father
FIGURATIVENESS	bright → radiant
	heavy → burdened
	unsympathetic → cold-hearted
	fall → plummet
	a lot of → a sea of
	quick → lightning
	hard → ironclad

Table 1: Seed pairs for constructing vector representations of complexity (simple → complex), formality (casual → formal), and figurativeness (literal → figurative).

Previous approaches to formality detection relied on word length, frequency, as well as on the presence of specific prefixes and suffixes (e.g., *intra-*, *-ation*) (Brooke et al., 2010). Such features have also been used for complexity detection, often combined with information regarding the number of word senses and synonyms (Shardlow, 2013; Kriz et al., 2018). Recent studies have shown that the representation space of pretrained LMs encodes a wealth of lexical semantic information, including similarity, polysemy, and hypernymy (Garí Soler and Apidianaki, 2021a; Pimentel et al., 2020; Ettinger, 2020; Ravichander et al., 2020; Vulić et al., 2020, i.a.). In particular, abstract semantic notions such as intensity (e.g., *pretty* → *beautiful* → *gorgeous*) can be extracted using a lightweight approach based on simple calculations in the vector space (Garí Soler and Apidianaki, 2020, 2021b).

In this paper, we explore whether lexical stylistic

[1]Our code and data are publicly available at `https://github.com/veronica320/Lexical-Stylistic-Features`.

*Proceedings of the The 12th Joint Conference on Lexical and Computational Semantics (*SEM 2023)*, pages 370–387
July 13-14, 2023

features can also be identified in the vector space built by pretrained LMs. To do this, we extend the method of Garí Soler and Apidianaki (2020) to address complexity, formality, and figurativeness. We first construct a vector representation for each of these features using a small number of seed pairs shown in Table 1. We then use these vectors to characterize new texts according to these stylistic dimensions, by applying simple calculations in the vector space. We evaluate our method using a binary classification task: given a pair of texts that are semantically similar but stylistically different in terms of some target feature (e.g., formality), the task is to determine which text exhibits the feature more strongly (e.g., is more formal). Note that the goal of our study is not to achieve high performance on the task itself, but rather to probe for how well these stylistic features are encoded in different types of pretrained representations.

We experiment with various static and contextualized embeddings on five datasets, containing words and phrases (*doctor* vs. *medical practitioner*), or sentences (*Those recommendations were unsolicited and undesirable.* vs. *that's the stupidest suggestion EVER.*). Our results show that both types of representations can capture these stylistic features reasonably well, although static embeddings perform better at the word and phrase level, and contextualized LMs at the sentence level. We hypothesize that the sub-optimal performance of contextualized LMs on short texts might be partially due to the high *anisotropy* of their embedding space. Anisotropic word representations occupy a narrow cone instead of being uniformly distributed in the vector space, resulting in highly positive correlations even for unrelated words, thus negatively impacting the quality of the similarity estimates that can be drawn from the space (Ethayarajh, 2019; Gao et al., 2019; Cai et al., 2021; Rajaee and Pilehvar, 2021). We verify this hypothesis by implementing different anisotropy correction strategies (Timkey and van Schijndel, 2021) and discuss the observed improvements in contextualized representations' performance on short texts.

Overall, our findings contribute to the big picture of probing literature, showing that stylistic features like complexity, formality, and figurativeness can be decoded from the embedding space of pretrained representations using simple calculations, without any supervision. Our lightweight method can be easily integrated into downstream applications like authorship attribution and style transfer.

2 Related work

There has been an extensive body of literature on probing techniques aimed at identifying the linguistic and world knowledge encoded in LM representations. For example, given a Machine Translation model, does it implicitly capture the syntax structure of the source text? Existing work addresses such questions with methods like auxiliary classifiers (a.k.a. probing/diagnostic classifiers) (Veldhoen et al., 2016; Adi et al., 2017; Conneau et al., 2018), information-theoretic probing (Voita and Titov, 2020; Lovering et al., 2020), behavioral tests (Ebrahimi et al., 2018; Wallace et al., 2019; Petroni et al., 2019), geometric probing (Chang et al., 2022; Wartena, 2022; Kozlowski et al., 2019), visualization of model-internal structures (Raganato and Tiedemann, 2018), and so on. Using these methods, researchers have found that pretrained LMs do encode various types of knowledge, including syntactic (Linzen et al., 2016; Hewitt and Manning, 2019), semantic (Ettinger et al., 2016; Adi et al., 2017; Yanaka et al., 2020), pragmatic (Jeretic et al., 2020; Schuster et al., 2020), as well as factual and commonsense knowledge (Petroni et al., 2019; Thukral et al., 2021).

Our work is along the line of probing for lexical semantics with simple geometry-based methods (Vulić et al., 2020; Garí Soler and Apidianaki, 2021a), which uncovers the target knowledge encoded in the semantic space of LM representations with simple geometric computations (Vulić et al., 2020; Garí Soler and Apidianaki, 2021a). Compared to the most widely used auxiliary classifier method, geometric probing does not rely on any external model. Thus, it requires no annotated training data and avoids the potential issue of the external model itself learning the target knowledge (Hewitt and Liang, 2019).

Directly related to our work, Garí Soler and Apidianaki (2020) proposed a method to detect the intensity of scalar adjectives, where an "intensity" dimension is identified in the vector space built by the BERT model. The method draws inspiration from word analogies in gender bias work, where a gender subspace is identified in the embedding space by calculating the main direction spanned by the differences between vectors of gendered word pairs (e.g., $\overrightarrow{he}$ - $\overrightarrow{she}$, $\overrightarrow{man}$ - $\overrightarrow{woman}$) (Bolukbasi et al., 2016; Dev and Phillips, 2019). Similarly,

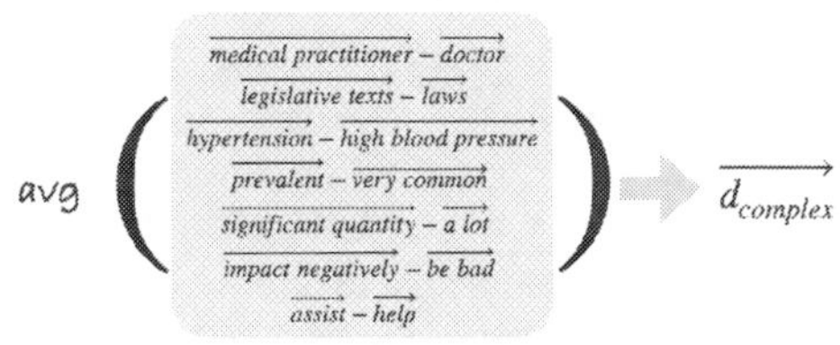

Figure 1: Complexity vector generation.

Garí Soler and Apidianaki (2020) view intensity as a direction in the embedding space which is calculated by subtracting the vector of a low-intensity adjective from that of a high-intensity adjective on the same scale (e.g., $\overrightarrow{awesome}$ - $\overrightarrow{good}$, $\overrightarrow{horrible}$ - $\overrightarrow{bad}$). Intuitively, this subtraction cancels out the adjectives' common denotation and retains their variance in intensity, which is represented by the resulting difference vector ($\overrightarrow{dVec}$). This vector can then be used to determine the intensity of new adjectives by simply taking the cosine similarity of their vector to $\overrightarrow{dVec}$. We extend this method to other lexical stylistic notions, and address words of different part-of-speech (POS) and longer texts.

3 Method

We adopt the definitions for the three stylistic features of interest (complexity, formality, and figurativeness) proposed by previous work. Simple language is "used to talk to children or non-native English speakers", whereas more complex language is "used by academics or domain experts" (Pavlick and Nenkova, 2015). Formal language is defined as "the way one talks to a superior", whereas casual language is "used with friends" (Pavlick and Nenkova, 2015). Figurative language is defined by Stowe et al. (2022) as utterances "in which the intended meaning differs from the literal compositional meaning", while literal language exhibits no such difference. Unlike the previous two features, figurativeness is often a contextual instead of lexical feature (e.g., the word *adhere* is used in a metaphorical sense in the expression "*adhere* to the rules" and in its literal sense in "*adhere* to the wall").[2] We explore the usability of our method for studying figurativeness by using a small seed set of synonyms and paraphrases that have literal and figurative connotations (e.g., *unsympathetic* → *cold-hearted*) independent of their context. These pairs are only used for constructing our figurativeness vector representation, while our evaluation is performed on a dataset containing full sentences (see Section 4 for details).

Our method involves two steps: (a) **feature vector generation**, where we construct a vector representation for each feature; and (b) **feature value prediction**, where we predict how strongly a new piece of text exhibits some target feature using the constructed feature vector. We illustrate the two steps below.

Feature vector generation. We collect a small number of seed pairs to illustrate each notion, shown in Table 1.[3] The seed pairs consist of rough paraphrases that differ in the stylistic aspect of interest. Consider complexity as an example. Given a pair of "simple → complex" texts, we subtract the vector of the simple from that of the complex one (e.g., $\overrightarrow{medical\ practitioner}$ - $\overrightarrow{doctor}$). After performing this subtraction for each pair in the seed set, we then average the resulting difference vectors to obtain a vector representing complexity which we call $\overrightarrow{d_{complex}}$. This procedure is illustrated in Figure 1. Similarly, for formality, we subtract the vector of the informal paraphrase from that of its formal counterpart (e.g., $\overrightarrow{respiratory}$ - $\overrightarrow{breathing}$), and for figurativeness, we subtract the vector of the literal expression from that with figurative meaning (e.g., $\overrightarrow{bright}$ - $\overrightarrow{radiant}$). By averaging the difference vectors for all pairs in the corresponding seed set, we obtain vectors representing formality ($\overrightarrow{d_{formal}}$) and figurativeness ($\overrightarrow{d_{fig}}$). We extend the method of Garí Soler and Apidianaki (2020), which was only applied to scalar adjectives, to words of other POS and to longer text (phrases and sentences). Finally, we compare the vectors that are built using representations from different monolingual and multilingual models.

Feature value prediction. Given a new piece of text (word, phrase, or sentence), we compute the cosine similarity between its vector representation and $\overrightarrow{d_{complex}}$, $\overrightarrow{d_{formal}}$ and $\overrightarrow{d_{fig}}$. The more similar the vector of the new text is to one of these feature

[2]In the literature, figurativeness is generally studied at the level of utterances (Stowe et al., 2022; Piccirilli and Schulte Im Walde, 2022; Chakrabarty et al., 2022). Some studies also look at the semantic properties of words and phrases as indicators for metaphor identification (Birke and Sarkar, 2006; Tsvetkov et al., 2013; Gutiérrez et al., 2016).

[3]This is based on the finding from Garí Soler and Apidianaki (2020) that using only a few or even a single pair(s) is almost as competitive as using an entire corpus in the case of intensity ranking.

Feature	Short-text (word/phrase)	Long-text (sentence)
Complexity	SimplePPDB	SimpleWikipedia
Formality	StylePPDB	GYAFC
Figurativeness	–	IMPLI

Table 2: Datasets used for each feature.

vectors, the more complex, formal, or figurative the text is considered to be.

4 Experimental Setup

Evaluation task and metrics. We evaluate the representation of the target features in a binary classification task: given a pair of texts (words, phrases, or sentences) t_0 and t_1 that are **semantically similar** but **stylistically different** in terms of some feature F (e.g., figurativeness), the task is to decide which text exhibits the feature more strongly (e.g., is more figurative). For example, given two sentences "You must adhere to the rules." (t_0) and "You must obey the rules." (t_1), the ground truth is that t_0 is more figurative. We use accuracy as our evaluation metric.

Seed pairs. For each feature, we use seven seed pairs for vector generation, as shown in Table 1. The seeds for complexity are examples from the paper describing SimplePPDB (Pavlick and Callison-Burch, 2016), and the seeds for formality are from the paper on lexical style properties of paraphrases (Pavlick and Nenkova, 2015). For figurativeness, we manually compile a set of seven seed pairs.

Datasets. The datasets used in our feature value prediction experiments (described in Table 2) contain pairs of words or phrases (short text), and pairs of sentences (long text). Note that this distinction is not based on the number of tokens, but on whether the text is a complete sentence. For complexity, we use SimplePPDB (Pavlick and Callison-Burch, 2016) and SimpleWikipedia (Kauchak, 2013); for formality, Style-annotated PPDB (StylePPDB for short) (Pavlick and Nenkova, 2015) and GYAFC (Rao and Tetreault, 2018). For figurativeness, since there is no dataset of word and/or phrase pairs, we only use the IMPLI (Idiomatic and Metaphoric Paired Language Inference) dataset (Stowe et al., 2022) that contains sentences.

For each dataset, we select the optimal configuration (see the Configuration paragraph below) using the validation set, and report its performance on the test set. To make the label distribution balanced,

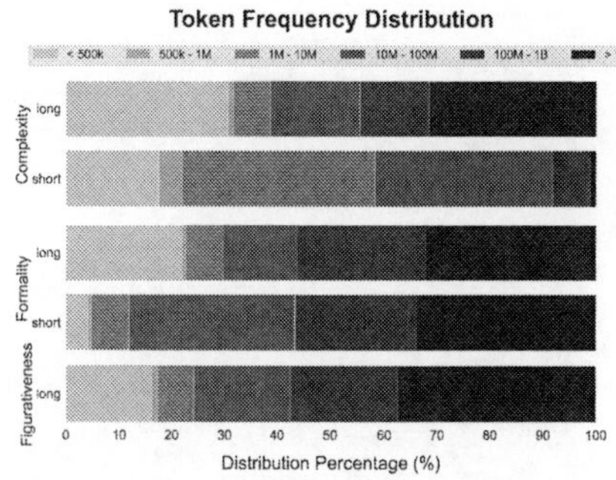

Figure 2: Distribution of token frequency in the evaluation datasets.

we randomly shuffle the order of the two pieces of text in each pair and re-assign the gold label accordingly. This ensures that a majority baseline only performs around chance. Figure 2 shows the distribution of token frequency in each dataset.[4]

Baselines. We compare our method to two simple baselines. The **majority baseline** always predicts the majority label in the dataset. The **frequency baseline** consults the frequency counts of each token in the Google N-gram corpus (Brants, 2006) and considers more frequent tokens to be simpler, more casual, and more literal. Frequency has been a strong baseline for complexity and formality in previous work, given that rare words tend to be more complex than frequently used words (Brooke et al., 2010).

Configuration. We experiment with two parameters in the configuration: LM and layer. Note that the purpose of experimenting with different configurations is not to solve the task, but rather to obtain a comprehensive picture of which embeddings best represent the target features.

- **Language Models**: We experiment with both static and contextualized representations. For static embeddings, we consider GloVe (Pennington et al., 2014) and fastText (Bojanowski et al., 2017). For contextualized LMs, we consider encoder-only monolingual and multilingual Transformer models of different sizes (base and large), including BERT (Devlin et al., 2019), mBERT (multilingual BERT) (Devlin et al., 2019), RoBERTa (Liu et al., 2019), and XLM-RoBERTa (Conneau et al., 2020).[5]

[4]See Appendix A for more details including dataset statistics, pre-processing method, dataset splits, and examples.

[5]See Appendix B for implementation details.

Pooling	Model	Complexity		Formality		Figurativeness
		short	long	short	long	long
	majority	55.1	50.6	51.2	51.8	51.4
Mean	frequency	83.2	51.0	61.0	41.4	49.7
	static	84.8 glove	60.0 glove	**76.8** glove	82.8 glove	54.3 glove
	contextualized (single layer)	**86.2** roberta-large (4)	**76.5** mbert-base (1)	68.7 bert-base (1)	82.4 roberta-large (12)	**72.9** bert-large (14)
	contextualized (layer agg)	84.4 mbert-base (10)	76.0 mbert-base (11)	67.6 bert-large (1)	**86.7** roberta-large (23)	67.2 bert-large (19)
Max	frequency	80.7	46.4	57.2	42.5	47.9
	static	**89.4** glove	58.0 glove	**76.0** glove	63.4 glove	56.0 fasttext
	contextualized (single layer)	87.7 roberta-large (4)	**69.4** roberta-base (12)	71.7 mbert-base (0)	**73.6** mbert-base (1)	**64.8** bert-large (11)
	contextualized (layeragg)	86.2 roberta-large (19)	67.6 roberta-large (4)	71.7 mbert-base (0)	71.7 roberta-large (24)	63.9 bert-large (14)

Table 3: Accuracy scores obtained on each test set using different types of embeddings and pooling methods. We report the performance of the models and layers (in parentheses) that best predicted the feature on the corresponding validation set. For contextualized representations, we report results using a single layer or layer aggregation ("layer agg"). The highest performance obtained with each pooling method (Mean/Max) is in boldface.

Pooling	Stats	Complexity		Formality		Figurativeness
		short	long	short	long	long
Mean	2 beats 1 (%)	63.0	78.0	92.9	72.4	54.3
	acc gain	2.6	4.1	4.3	5.3	0.1
Max	2 beats 1 (%)	66.1	72.4	95.3	64.6	44.9
	acc gain	3.0	3.0	4.4	3.2	-0.5
Average	2 beats 1 (%)	64.6	75.2	94.1	68.5	49.6
	acc gain	2.8	3.5	4.3	4.3	-0.2

Table 4: Comparison between single layer and layer aggregation settings. "2 beats 1 (%)" refers to the percentage of cases where layer aggregation performance is at least as high as the single layer performance, under the same configuration (LM & layer). "Acc gain" stands for the average accuracy gain of layer aggregation over single layer across all configurations. Positive accuracy gains are highlighted in green, negative ones in pink.

- **Layer** (l): For contextualized LMs, another configuration choice is which layer to obtain the representation from. We explore the knowledge encoded in different layers in the range of 0-12 for base models and 0-24 for large ones, including the embedding layer.

Pooling strategies. In order to obtain a score for a feature of interest (complexity, formality, or figurativeness) for text segments that contain more than one token (i.e., phrases and sentences), we consider two pooling strategies over the scores calculated for individual tokens:[6]

- **mean**: We compute the cosine similarity between $\overrightarrow{d_{feature}}$ and each word vector, and take the average of the similarity scores as the feature value for the text.
- **max**: We compute the cosine similarity between $\overrightarrow{d_{feature}}$ and each word vector, and take the maximum of the similarity scores as the feature value for the text.

The intuition behind max pooling is that the majority of words in a phrase or sentence would not be too extreme (i.e., too complex or too formal). By looking at the most complex or formal word in the text, we can get an idea of how extreme it might be in that dimension. Naturally, we expect this approach to perform less well than mean pooling for figurativeness, where idiomaticity is most often inferred by looking at the context of use and the word combinations within a sentence.

5 Results and Discussion

Table 3 presents the results of our evaluation. Due to space constraints, each row in the table only shows the optimal performance obtained across all configurations (LM and layers) for static and contextualized models.[7] For contextualized LMs in particular, following Vulić et al. (2020), we separately show the optimal performance under two settings: **single layer**, where only the representation from a single layer l is used; and **layer aggregation** ("layeragg" for short), where we average the representations from all layers from the 0th to a specific layer l (included).

We observe that our method outperforms the majority and frequency baselines with both static and contextualized LMs. Furthermore, mean

[6] See Appendix B for details on tokenization and multiword expression handling.

[7] See Appendix C.1 for detailed accuracy scores for each model.

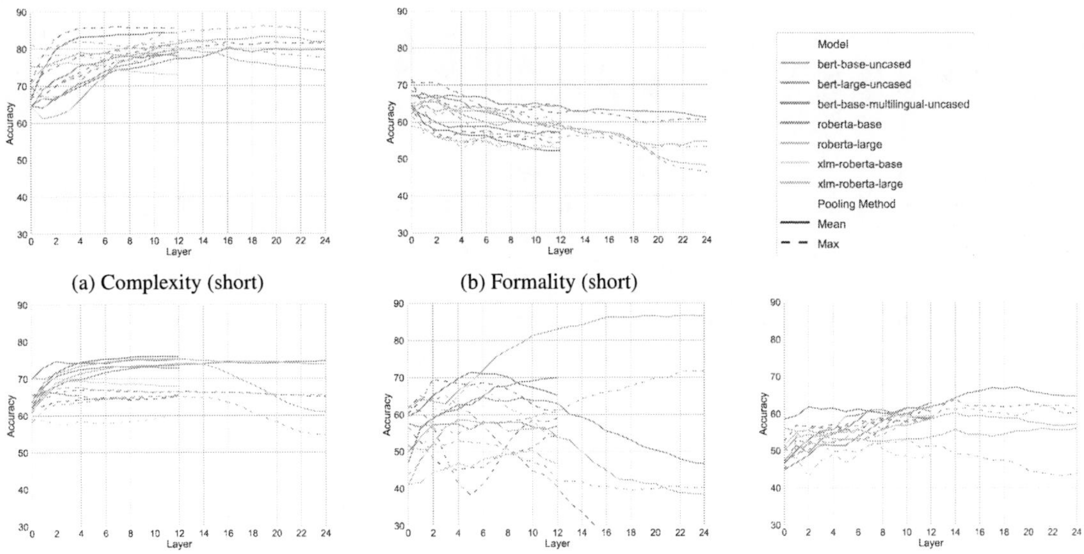

(a) Complexity (short) (b) Formality (short) (c) Complexity (long) (d) Formality (long) (e) Figurativeness (long)

Figure 3: Performance change across layers of different LMs (under the layer aggregation setting).

pooling generally works better than max pooling, although there is still room for improvement. Taking a closer look at the optimal configuration for each feature, for **complexity**, `roberta-large` and `mbert-base` are the dominant best-performing models, yet there are no consistently dominant layers; for **formality**, `bert-base` and `mbert-base` perform the best on short texts and surprisingly with the initial layers (0 or 1), while `roberta-large` is the best model for long texts with middle or final layers; for **figurativeness**, `bert-large` is consistently the best model across all settings.

Interestingly, contextualized LMs far outperform static embeddings on long text sin almost all cases, yet on short texts, static embeddings perform on par or sometimes even better than contextualized LMs. This is the case, for example, with formality "short" (with both pooling strategies) and with complexity "short" (with max pooling). This finding sounds counter-intuitive, given the generally higher performance of contextualized models in various NLP tasks. In our probing setting, we suspect that this might be due to two factors. First, the input in short-text datasets consists of isolated, rather than contextualized, instances of words. This is not natural input for a contextualized LM. Second, previous work has demonstrated that the word-level similarity estimates obtained from the vector space of contextualized LMs might be distorted due to the anisotropy of the space (Ethayarajh, 2019; Rajaee and Pilehvar, 2021). Concretely, anisotropic word representations occupy a narrow cone instead of being uniformly distributed in the vector space, resulting in excessively positive correlations even for unrelated word instances. This has a negative impact on the informativeness of measures such as the cosine and the Euclidean distance, often used for estimating representation similarity (Apidianaki, 2023). These measures are dominated by a small subset of "rogue dimensions" which drive anisotropy and the drop in representational quality in later layers of the models (Timkey and van Schijndel, 2021). In Section 6, we investigate more closely the impact of anisotropy on our results through a series of experiments involving different anisotropy reduction methods.

Finally, comparing the single layer and layer aggregation settings, their respective **optimal** configurations result in mostly similar performance across datasets, as shown in Table 3. In order to better understand their difference across all possible LM and layer configurations, we present in Table 4 two types of averaged statistics: the percentage of configurations where the layer aggregation performance is equal or higher than the single layer performance, as well as the average gain in terms of accuracy. We observe that layer aggregation improves the performance for complexity and formality (across 64.6% to 94.1% of the configurations and by an accuracy gain of 2.8 to 4.3), but makes almost no difference for figurativeness.

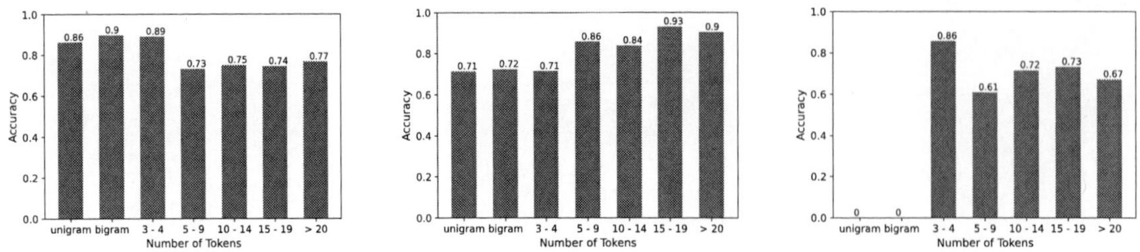

(a) Complexity (b) Formality (c) Figurativeness

Figure 4: Optimal performance over different bins of text length (under the layer aggregation setting).

Together with the results from Table 3, this suggests that although layer aggregation does not help with the best configuration, it is beneficial to most configurations on average.

In the next two subsections, we analyze the influence of two more factors on our method: layer depth and text length. For conciseness, we only report the results for the layer aggregation setting. Results for the single layer setting are given in Appendix C.

5.1 How well do different layers represent the target features?

We explore the representation of the three stylistic features inside contextualized LMs by specifically monitoring the change in accuracy observed across layers. The results are shown in Figure 3. The solid curves show results obtained using mean pooling, while the dashed ones correspond to max pooling.

We observe that information about **complexity** (3a and 3c) is more clearly and consistently encoded after layer 4 of the models, independent of their size (base or large). Across all layers, mean and max pooling exhibit mostly similar behavior for short texts, while mean pooling is clearly better for longer texts. The pattern for **figurativeness** is similar (3e), though with slightly more fluctuations. For **formality**, we see a different trend. As shown in Figure 3b, this feature is encoded more clearly in the early layers of the models for short texts. For longer texts, we see diverging patterns across layers of different models (3d). In particular, `roberta-large` encodes formality better than other tested models while its multilingual versions (`xlm-roberta-base` and `xlm-roberta-large`) give much lower results.

5.2 How does text length influence our method?

We analyze the performance change with regard to text length, represented by the average number of tokens in the two texts in a pair. For each feature, we merge examples from the short-text and long-text datasets (if available) and take the predictions from the best-performing contextualized configuration from Table 3. Based on the number of tokens, we group all examples into several bins (unigram, bigram, 3-4, 5-9, 10-14, 15-19, >20) and compute the average accuracy in each bin. Figure 4 shows the results.

Interestingly, we observe different patterns for the three features. For **complexity**, accuracy scores for shorter texts (0.86 to 0.9) are generally higher than those for long texts (0.73 to 0.77). The drop from 3-4 tokens to 5-9 tokens is particularly clear. For **formality**, on the contrary, longer texts (0.84 to 0.93) tend to be easier than short ones (0.71 to 0.72). For **figurativeness**, we do not have results for short texts since no such datasets are available. Within full sentences, we observe that our method works better for shorter sentences (with <5 tokens) than for longer ones (with >=5 tokens) by an accuracy difference of 0.13 to 0.25. One caveat is that these differences are not only influenced by text length, but also by the intrinsic data distribution in different datasets. For example, the domain of the source texts in SimplePPDB (news, legal documents, and movie subtitles) is different from that in SimpleWikipedia (encyclopedia articles). Thus, the accuracy differences could be a result of both factors — text length and text domain.

6 Anisotropy Reduction Experiments

As explained in the previous section, the anisotropy of contextualized LMs' representation space degrades the quality of the similarity estimates that can be drawn from it (Ethayarajh, 2019). To see if

Pooling	Model	Complexity		Formality		Figurativeness
		short	long	short	long	long
Mean	static	84.8	60.0	**76.8**	82.8	54.3
	contextualized (singlelayer)	86.2	**76.5**	68.7	82.4	**72.9**
	contextualized (singlelayer+**abtt**)	80.3	69.3	76.6	76.7	70.9
	contextualized (singlelayer+**standardization**)	**90.4**	73.9	74.1	80.6	68.3
	contextualized (singlelayer+**rank**)	85.6	76.0	70.8	81.7	71.8
	contextualized (layeragg)	84.4	76.0	67.6	**86.7**	67.2
	contextualized (layeragg+**abtt**)	81.7	68.5	76.6	63.0	72.6
	contextualized (layeragg+**standardization**)	**90.4**	73.6	75.2	79.9	67.6
	contextualized (layeragg+**rank**)	83.7	75.7	68.1	82.1	67.0
Max	static	89.4	58.0	76.0	63.4	56.0
	contextualized (singlelayer)	87.7	69.4	71.7	73.6	64.8
	contextualized (singlelayer+**abtt**)	80.6	64.9	78.2	80.8	66.7
	contextualized (singlelayer+**standardization**)	**90.5**	63.8	**80.9**	**81.7**	60.4
	contextualized (singlelayer+**rank**)	87.1	**69.6**	70.3	76.0	66.5
	contextualized (layeragg)	86.2	67.6	71.7	71.7	63.9
	contextualized (layeragg+**abtt**)	81.9	63.9	78.2	72.5	**71.1**
	contextualized (layeragg+**standardization**)	**90.5**	63.7	**80.9**	80.6	61.9
	contextualized (layeragg+**rank**)	86.1	69.3	71.7	71.5	67.4

Table 5: Performance of three anisotropy reduction methods (all-but-the-top/standardization/rank-based). The highest performance within each pooling method (Mean/Max) is in boldface.

this has an impact on our method, we apply three post-processing anisotropy reduction methods discussed by Timkey and van Schijndel (2021), which can be used to correct for rogue dimensions and reveal underlying representational quality.

We apply each of these methods to our feature vector construction and feature value prediction processes. Given that our stylistic characterization of new text relies on similarity measurement, we expect that a space that allows us to draw higher-quality similarity estimates would better represent these stylistic features and would also improve feature value prediction. The three methods used in our experiments are:

All-but-the-top (abtt). The method was initially proposed for static embeddings by Mu and Viswanath (2018). The main idea is to subtract the common mean vector and eliminate the top few principal components (PCs) (we use the top $\frac{d}{100}$, where d represents the dimensionality of the vector space, following their suggestion). These subtracted vectors should capture the variance of the rogue dimensions in the model and make the space more isotropic. In Timkey and van Schijndel (2021), the mean vector and PCs are computed from vector representations for an entire corpus. Since our method is unsupervised, we do not assume access to any large corpus and instead compute them based only on the seed pairs (i.e., 14 words and phrases for each feature). Thus, our method still remains lightweight and computationally efficient. It is, however, important to note that this is a **local correction** (rather than a global one) since we are just using a small number of words and phrases, as in Rajaee and Pilehvar (2021).

Formally, given a set of seed texts of size $|S|$ (here $|S| = 14$) containing token representations $x \in \mathbb{R}^d$, we compute the mean vector $\mu \in \mathbb{R}^d$

$$\mu = \frac{1}{|S|} \cdot \sum_{x \in S} x \tag{1}$$

as well as the PCs

$$u_1, ..., u_d = \text{PCA}(\{x - \mu, x \in S\}). \tag{2}$$

Then, the new representation x_{abtt} for an unseen word vector x is the result of eliminating the mean vector and the top k PCs (here $k = \frac{d}{100}$):

$$x_{abtt} = x - \mu - \sum_{i=1}^{k} \left(u_i^\top x\right) u_i. \tag{3}$$

Standardization. Based on a similar observation as **abtt** (a non-zero common mean vector and a few dominant directions), another way for adjustment is to subtract the mean vector and divide each dimension by its standard deviation (std), such that each dimension has $\mu_i = 0$ and $\sigma_i = 1$. Similarly to **abtt**, we compute the mean vector and standard deviation using only the seed pairs for each feature.

Formally, we compute the same mean vector μ as in Equation 1, as well as the standard deviation in each dimension $\sigma \in \mathbb{R}^d$

$$\sigma = \sqrt{\frac{1}{|S|} \cdot \sum_{x \in S} (x - \mu)^2} \tag{4}$$

The new representation $x_{standard}$ for an unseen word vector x becomes

$$x_{standard} = \frac{x - \mu}{\sigma}. \quad (5)$$

Rank-based. This method treats a word vector as d observations from an $|S|$-variate distribution and uses correlation metrics as a measure of similarity, instead of cosine similarity (Zhelezniak et al., 2019). Specifically, Spearman's ρ, a non-parametric correlation measure, only considers the ranks of embeddings rather than their values. Thus, it will not be dominated by the rogue dimensions of contextualized LMs. Unlike the previous two methods, this method does not require any computation over the seed pair texts. Formally, given a word vector x, the new representation x_{rank} is simply

$$x_{rank} = rank(x). \quad (6)$$

Table 5 shows the effect of applying the three anisotropy reduction strategies under the single layer and layer aggregation settings. Overall, after anisotropy reduction, contextualized LMs outperform static embeddings in all cases except formality "short", confirming our initial hypothesis. Nevertheless, there is no universally optimal strategy, although standardization works best most of the time. Comparing the two pooling strategies, we find that anisotropy correction helps more often with max pooling than with mean pooling.

It is important to reemphasize that our anisotropy correction approach is local, since it only considers a small set of words and phrases for calculating the mean vector, standard deviation, and PCs. This might be the reason for the relatively small observed effect of these correction procedures in our experiments. In future work, we plan to experiment with a larger corpus, and consequently use a larger part of the vector space for calculating the mean/std/PC vectors, in order to investigate the impact of the quantity of data on the induced similarity estimates.

7 Conclusion

We have shown that the embedding space of pretrained LMs encodes abstract stylistic notions such as formality, complexity, and figurativeness. Using a geometry-based method, we construct a vector representation for each of these features, which can be used to characterize new texts. We find that these notions are present in the space of both static and contextualized representations, and that static embeddings are better at capturing the style of short texts (words and phrases) whereas contextual embeddings at longer texts (sentences). By correcting the anisotropy of contextualized LMs' representation space, we show that it is possible to close the performance gap from static embeddings on short texts.

Our unsupervised and lightweight method is expected to be applicable for stylistic analysis in other languages and for other stylistic notions, such as concreteness, sentiment, and political stance, which we plan to address in future work. Furthermore, we plan to experiment with anisotropy correction methods on a larger corpus, and to adapt the method for style prediction on longer text (e.g., whole documents). The stylistic measurements obtained using this method can be useful in the creation of lexical style lexicons as well as in downstream applications, for authorship attribution and style transfer.

Limitations

We acknowledge the following limitations of our work: (a) The scope of our experiments is limited to the English language currently. Our method is only evaluated on the level of words, phrases, and sentences, but not at the document level. (b) The effect of anisotropy reduction strategies is shown to be rather mixed. Further investigation is required to determine under what conditions these strategies can prove beneficial in the specific context of stylistic feature extraction. (c) Our work addresses only lexical-level stylistic features and not more global aspects of writing style, such as the diversity of word choice and the utilization of unique syntactic structures. Whether this method can be extended to capture the comprehensive nuances of writing style is an interesting direction for future work.

Ethical Considerations

In this paper, our method is only tested in intrinsic evaluation settings where existing publicly available datasets have been used. It is not integrated into any downstream application, although this type of stylistic analysis could be potentially useful in different settings.

Acknowledgments

This research is based upon work supported in part by the DARPA KAIROS Program (contract FA8750-19-2-1004), the DARPA LwLL Program (contract FA8750-19-2-0201), the IARPA HIATUS Program (contract 2022-22072200005), and the NSF (Award 1928631). Approved for Public Release, Distribution Unlimited. The views and conclusions contained herein are those of the authors and should not be interpreted as necessarily representing the official policies, either expressed or implied, of DARPA, IARPA, NSF, or the U.S. Government.

References

Yossi Adi, Einat Kermany, Yonatan Belinkov, Ofer Lavi, and Yoav Goldberg. 2017. Fine-grained Analysis of Sentence Embeddings Using Auxiliary Prediction Tasks. *arXiv:1608.04207 [cs]*. ArXiv: 1608.04207.

Marianna Apidianaki. 2023. From Word Types to Tokens and Back: A Survey of Approaches to Word Meaning Representation and Interpretation. *Computational Linguistics*, pages 1–58.

Julia Birke and Anoop Sarkar. 2006. A clustering approach for nearly unsupervised recognition of nonliteral language. In *11th Conference of the European Chapter of the Association for Computational Linguistics*, pages 329–336, Trento, Italy. Association for Computational Linguistics.

Piotr Bojanowski, Edouard Grave, Armand Joulin, and Tomas Mikolov. 2017. Enriching Word Vectors with Subword Information. *Transactions of the Association for Computational Linguistics*, 5:135–146.

Tolga Bolukbasi, Kai-Wei Chang, James Y Zou, Venkatesh Saligrama, and Adam T Kalai. 2016. Man is to Computer Programmer as Woman is to Homemaker? Debiasing Word Embeddings. In *Advances in Neural Information Processing Systems 29*, pages 4349–4357. Barcelona, Spain.

Thorsten Brants. 2006. Web 1t 5-gram version 1. *http://www. ldc. upenn. edu/Catalog/CatalogEntry. jsp? catalogId= LDC2006T13*.

Julian Brooke, Tong Wang, and Graeme Hirst. 2010. Automatic acquisition of lexical formality. In *Coling 2010: Posters*, pages 90–98, Beijing, China. Coling 2010 Organizing Committee.

Xingyu Cai, Jiaji Huang, Yuchen Bian, and Kenneth Church. 2021. Isotropy in the Contextual Embedding Space: Clusters and Manifolds. In *Proceedings of the International Conference on Learning Representations (ICLR)*, Online.

Tuhin Chakrabarty, Arkadiy Saakyan, Debanjan Ghosh, and Smaranda Muresan. 2022. FLUTE: Figurative language understanding through textual explanations. In *Proceedings of the 2022 Conference on Empirical Methods in Natural Language Processing*, pages 7139–7159, Abu Dhabi, United Arab Emirates. Association for Computational Linguistics.

Tyler Chang, Zhuowen Tu, and Benjamin Bergen. 2022. The geometry of multilingual language model representations. In *Proceedings of the 2022 Conference on Empirical Methods in Natural Language Processing*, pages 119–136, Abu Dhabi, United Arab Emirates. Association for Computational Linguistics.

Alexis Conneau, Kartikay Khandelwal, Naman Goyal, Vishrav Chaudhary, Guillaume Wenzek, Francisco Guzmán, Edouard Grave, Myle Ott, Luke Zettlemoyer, and Veselin Stoyanov. 2020. Unsupervised cross-lingual representation learning at scale. In *Proceedings of the 58th Annual Meeting of the Association for Computational Linguistics*, pages 8440–8451, Online. Association for Computational Linguistics.

Alexis Conneau, German Kruszewski, Guillaume Lample, Loïc Barrault, and Marco Baroni. 2018. What you can cram into a single $&!#* vector: Probing sentence embeddings for linguistic properties. In *Proceedings of the 56th Annual Meeting of the Association for Computational Linguistics (Volume 1: Long Papers)*, pages 2126–2136, Melbourne, Australia. Association for Computational Linguistics.

Sunipa Dev and Jeff M Phillips. 2019. Attenuating Bias in Word Vectors. In *Proceedings of the 22nd International Conference on Artificial Intelligence and Statistics (AISTATS)*, Naha, Okinawa, Japan.

Jacob Devlin, Ming-Wei Chang, Kenton Lee, and Kristina Toutanova. 2019. BERT: Pre-training of deep bidirectional transformers for language understanding. In *Proceedings of the 2019 Conference of the North American Chapter of the Association for Computational Linguistics: Human Language Technologies, Volume 1 (Long and Short Papers)*, pages 4171–4186, Minneapolis, Minnesota. Association for Computational Linguistics.

Javid Ebrahimi, Anyi Rao, Daniel Lowd, and Dejing Dou. 2018. HotFlip: White-Box Adversarial Examples for Text Classification. In *Proceedings of the 56th Annual Meeting of the Association for Computational Linguistics (Volume 2: Short Papers)*, pages 31–36, Melbourne, Australia. Association for Computational Linguistics.

Philip Edmonds and Graeme Hirst. 2002. Near-Synonymy and Lexical Choice. *Computational Linguistics*, 28(2):105–144.

Kawin Ethayarajh. 2019. How Contextual are Contextualized Word Representations? Comparing the Geometry of BERT, ELMo, and GPT-2 Embeddings. In *Proceedings of the 2019 Conference on Empirical*

Methods in Natural Language Processing and the 9th International Joint Conference on Natural Language Processing (EMNLP-IJCNLP), pages 55–65, Hong Kong, China. Association for Computational Linguistics.

Allyson Ettinger. 2020. What BERT Is Not: Lessons from a New Suite of Psycholinguistic Diagnostics for Language Models. *Transactions of the Association for Computational Linguistics*, 8:34–48.

Allyson Ettinger, Ahmed Elgohary, and Philip Resnik. 2016. Probing for semantic evidence of composition by means of simple classification tasks. In *Proceedings of the 1st Workshop on Evaluating Vector-Space Representations for NLP*, pages 134–139, Berlin, Germany. Association for Computational Linguistics.

Juri Ganitkevitch, Benjamin Van Durme, and Chris Callison-Burch. 2013. PPDB: The paraphrase database. In *Proceedings of the 2013 Conference of the North American Chapter of the Association for Computational Linguistics: Human Language Technologies*, pages 758–764, Atlanta, Georgia. Association for Computational Linguistics.

Jun Gao, Di He, Xu Tan, Tao Qin, Liwei Wang, and Tieyan Liu. 2019. Representation Degeneration Problem in Training Natural Language Generation Models. In *International Conference on Learning Representations (ICLR)*, New Orleans, LA, USA.

Aina Garí Soler and Marianna Apidianaki. 2020. BERT Knows Punta Cana is not just beautiful, it's gorgeous: Ranking Scalar Adjectives with Contextualised Representations. In *Proceedings of the 2020 Conference on Empirical Methods in Natural Language Processing (EMNLP)*, pages 7371–7385, Online. Association for Computational Linguistics.

Aina Garí Soler and Marianna Apidianaki. 2021a. Let's Play Mono-Poly: BERT Can Reveal Words' Polysemy Level and Partitionability into Senses. *Transactions of the Association for Computational Linguistics*, 9:825–844.

Aina Garí Soler and Marianna Apidianaki. 2021b. Scalar Adjective Identification and Multilingual Ranking. In *Proceedings of the 2021 Conference of the North American Chapter of the Association for Computational Linguistics: Human Language Technologies*, pages 4653–4660, Online. Association for Computational Linguistics.

E. Dario Gutiérrez, Ekaterina Shutova, Tyler Marghetis, and Benjamin Bergen. 2016. Literal and metaphorical senses in compositional distributional semantic models. In *Proceedings of the 54th Annual Meeting of the Association for Computational Linguistics (Volume 1: Long Papers)*, pages 183–193, Berlin, Germany. Association for Computational Linguistics.

John Hewitt and Percy Liang. 2019. Designing and interpreting probes with control tasks. In *Proceedings of the 2019 Conference on Empirical Methods in Natural Language Processing and the 9th International Joint Conference on Natural Language Processing (EMNLP-IJCNLP)*, pages 2733–2743, Hong Kong, China. Association for Computational Linguistics.

John Hewitt and Christopher D. Manning. 2019. A Structural Probe for Finding Syntax in Word Representations. In *Proceedings of the 2019 Conference of the North American Chapter of the Association for Computational Linguistics: Human Language Technologies, Volume 1 (Long and Short Papers)*, pages 4129–4138, Minneapolis, Minnesota. Association for Computational Linguistics.

Paloma Jeretic, Alex Warstadt, Suvrat Bhooshan, and Adina Williams. 2020. Are Natural Language Inference Models IMPPRESsive? Learning IMPlicature and PRESupposition. In *Proceedings of the 58th Annual Meeting of the Association for Computational Linguistics*.

David Kauchak. 2013. Improving text simplification language modeling using unsimplified text data. In *Proceedings of the 51st Annual Meeting of the Association for Computational Linguistics (Volume 1: Long Papers)*, pages 1537–1546, Sofia, Bulgaria. Association for Computational Linguistics.

Austin C. Kozlowski, Matt Taddy, and James A. Evans. 2019. The geometry of culture: Analyzing the meanings of class through word embeddings. *American Sociological Review*, 84(5):905–949.

Reno Kriz, Eleni Miltsakaki, Marianna Apidianaki, and Chris Callison-Burch. 2018. Simplification Using Paraphrases and Context-Based Lexical Substitution. In *Proceedings of the 2018 Conference of the North American Chapter of the Association for Computational Linguistics: Human Language Technologies, Volume 1 (Long Papers)*, pages 207–217, New Orleans, Louisiana. Association for Computational Linguistics.

Tal Linzen, Emmanuel Dupoux, and Yoav Goldberg. 2016. Assessing the Ability of LSTMs to Learn Syntax-Sensitive Dependencies. *Transactions of the Association for Computational Linguistics*, 4:521–535.

Yinhan Liu, Myle Ott, Naman Goyal, Jingfei Du, Mandar Joshi, Danqi Chen, Omer Levy, Mike Lewis, Luke Zettlemoyer, and Veselin Stoyanov. 2019. RoBERTa: A Robustly Optimized BERT Pretraining Approach. *arXiv:1907.11692*.

Charles Lovering, Rohan Jha, Tal Linzen, and Ellie Pavlick. 2020. Information-theoretic Probing Explains Reliance on Spurious Features.

Jiaqi Mu and Pramod Viswanath. 2018. All-but-the-Top: Simple and Effective Postprocessing for Word Representations. In *International Conference on Learning Representations (ICLR)*, Vancouver, Canada.

Ellie Pavlick and Chris Callison-Burch. 2016. Simple PPDB: A Paraphrase Database for Simplification. In *Proceedings of the 54th Annual Meeting of the Association for Computational Linguistics (Volume 2: Short Papers)*, pages 143–148, Berlin, Germany. Association for Computational Linguistics.

Ellie Pavlick and Ani Nenkova. 2015. Inducing lexical style properties for paraphrase and genre differentiation. In *Proceedings of the 2015 Conference of the North American Chapter of the Association for Computational Linguistics: Human Language Technologies*, pages 218–224, Denver, Colorado. Association for Computational Linguistics.

Jeffrey Pennington, Richard Socher, and Christopher Manning. 2014. GloVe: Global vectors for word representation. In *Proceedings of the 2014 Conference on Empirical Methods in Natural Language Processing (EMNLP)*, pages 1532–1543, Doha, Qatar. Association for Computational Linguistics.

Fabio Petroni, Tim Rocktäschel, Sebastian Riedel, Patrick Lewis, Anton Bakhtin, Yuxiang Wu, and Alexander Miller. 2019. Language Models as Knowledge Bases? In *Proceedings of the 2019 Conference on Empirical Methods in Natural Language Processing and the 9th International Joint Conference on Natural Language Processing (EMNLP-IJCNLP)*, pages 2463–2473, Hong Kong, China. Association for Computational Linguistics.

Prisca Piccirilli and Sabine Schulte Im Walde. 2022. What drives the use of metaphorical language? negative insights from abstractness, affect, discourse coherence and contextualized word representations. In *Proceedings of the 11th Joint Conference on Lexical and Computational Semantics*, pages 299–310, Seattle, Washington. Association for Computational Linguistics.

Tiago Pimentel, Rowan Hall Maudslay, Damian Blasi, and Ryan Cotterell. 2020. Speakers Fill Lexical Semantic Gaps with Context. In *Proceedings of the 2020 Conference on Empirical Methods in Natural Language Processing (EMNLP)*, pages 4004–4015, Online. Association for Computational Linguistics.

Alessandro Raganato and Jörg Tiedemann. 2018. An analysis of encoder representations in transformer-based machine translation. In *Proceedings of the 2018 EMNLP Workshop BlackboxNLP: Analyzing and Interpreting Neural Networks for NLP*, pages 287–297, Brussels, Belgium. Association for Computational Linguistics.

Sara Rajaee and Mohammad Taher Pilehvar. 2021. A Cluster-based Approach for Improving Isotropy in Contextual Embedding Space. In *Proceedings of the 59th Annual Meeting of the Association for Computational Linguistics and the 11th International Joint Conference on Natural Language Processing (Volume 2: Short Papers)*, pages 575–584, Online. Association for Computational Linguistics.

Sudha Rao and Joel Tetreault. 2018. Dear sir or madam, may I introduce the GYAFC dataset: Corpus, benchmarks and metrics for formality style transfer. In *Proceedings of the 2018 Conference of the North American Chapter of the Association for Computational Linguistics: Human Language Technologies, Volume 1 (Long Papers)*, pages 129–140, New Orleans, Louisiana. Association for Computational Linguistics.

Abhilasha Ravichander, Eduard Hovy, Kaheer Suleman, Adam Trischler, and Jackie Chi Kit Cheung. 2020. On the systematicity of probing contextualized word representations: The case of hypernymy in BERT. In *Proceedings of the Ninth Joint Conference on Lexical and Computational Semantics*, pages 88–102, Barcelona, Spain (Online). Association for Computational Linguistics.

Sebastian Schuster, Yuxing Chen, and Judith Degen. 2020. Harnessing the linguistic signal to predict scalar inferences. In *Proceedings of the 58th Annual Meeting of the Association for Computational Linguistics*.

Matthew Shardlow. 2013. A Comparison of Techniques to Automatically Identify Complex Words. In *51st Annual Meeting of the Association for Computational Linguistics Proceedings of the Student Research Workshop*, pages 103–109, Sofia, Bulgaria. Association for Computational Linguistics.

Kevin Stowe, Prasetya Utama, and Iryna Gurevych. 2022. IMPLI: Investigating NLI models' performance on figurative language. In *Proceedings of the 60th Annual Meeting of the Association for Computational Linguistics (Volume 1: Long Papers)*, pages 5375–5388, Dublin, Ireland. Association for Computational Linguistics.

Shivin Thukral, Kunal Kukreja, and Christian Kavouras. 2021. Probing Language Models for Understanding of Temporal Expressions. In *Proceedings of the Fourth BlackboxNLP Workshop on Analyzing and Interpreting Neural Networks for NLP*, pages 396–406, Punta Cana, Dominican Republic. Association for Computational Linguistics.

William Timkey and Marten van Schijndel. 2021. All Bark and No Bite: Rogue Dimensions in Transformer Language Models Obscure Representational Quality. In *Proceedings of the 2021 Conference on Empirical Methods in Natural Language Processing*, pages 4527–4546, Online and Punta Cana, Dominican Republic. Association for Computational Linguistics.

Yulia Tsvetkov, Elena Mukomel, and Anatole Gershman. 2013. Cross-lingual metaphor detection using common semantic features. In *Proceedings of the First Workshop on Metaphor in NLP*, pages 45–51, Atlanta, Georgia. Association for Computational Linguistics.

Sara Veldhoen, Dieuwke Hupkes, Willem H Zuidema, et al. 2016. Diagnostic classifiers revealing how neural networks process hierarchical structure. In *CoCo@ NIPS*, pages 69–77. Barcelona.

Elena Voita and Ivan Titov. 2020. Information-Theoretic Probing with Minimum Description Length. *arXiv:2003.12298 [cs]*. ArXiv: 2003.12298.

Ivan Vulić, Edoardo Maria Ponti, Robert Litschko, Goran Glavaš, and Anna Korhonen. 2020. Probing pretrained language models for lexical semantics. In *Proceedings of the 2020 Conference on Empirical Methods in Natural Language Processing (EMNLP)*, pages 7222–7240, Online. Association for Computational Linguistics.

Eric Wallace, Shi Feng, Nikhil Kandpal, Matt Gardner, and Sameer Singh. 2019. Universal Adversarial Triggers for Attacking and Analyzing NLP. In *Proceedings of the 2019 Conference on Empirical Methods in Natural Language Processing and the 9th International Joint Conference on Natural Language Processing (EMNLP-IJCNLP)*, pages 2153–2162, Hong Kong, China. Association for Computational Linguistics.

Christian Wartena. 2022. On the geometry of concreteness. In *Proceedings of the 7th Workshop on Representation Learning for NLP*, pages 204–212, Dublin, Ireland. Association for Computational Linguistics.

Hitomi Yanaka, Koji Mineshima, Daisuke Bekki, and Kentaro Inui. 2020. Do Neural Models Learn Systematicity of Monotonicity Inference in Natural Language? In *Proceedings of the 58th Annual Meeting of the Association for Computational Linguistics*.

Vitalii Zhelezniak, Aleksandar Savkov, April Shen, and Nils Hammerla. 2019. Correlation coefficients and semantic textual similarity. In *Proceedings of the 2019 Conference of the North American Chapter of the Association for Computational Linguistics: Human Language Technologies, Volume 1 (Long and Short Papers)*, pages 951–962, Minneapolis, Minnesota. Association for Computational Linguistics.

A Dataset Details

All evaluation datasets we use contain semantically similar but stylistically different words, phrases, or sentences.

A.1 Data Description and Source

Complexity

- SimplePPDB (Pavlick and Callison-Burch, 2016): It contains 4.5M pairs of words and short phrases, where one is simpler and the other is more complex. It is constructed based on a subset of the Paraphrase Database (PPDB) (Ganitkevitch et al., 2013). There are both automatically generated and manually annotated pairs.[8] URL: `http://www.seas.upenn.edu/~nlp/resources/simple-ppdb.tgz`.

- SimpleWikipedia (Kauchak, 2013): It contains 167K pairs of simple/complex sentences generated by aligning Simple English Wikipedia and English Wikipedia. We are using Version 2.0 of the dataset (updated from Wikipedia pages downloaded in May 2011), the "Sentence-aligned" subset. URL: `https://cs.pomona.edu/~dkauchak/simplification/data.v2/sentence-aligned.v2.tar.gz`.

Formality

- StylePPDB (Pavlick and Nenkova, 2015): It contains 4.9K pairs of casual/formal words or short phrases from PPDB, both automatically generated and manually annotated. URL: `https://cs.brown.edu/people/epavlick/data.html#style-pp-bibtex`.

- GYAFC (Rao and Tetreault, 2018): It contains a total of 110K informal/formal sentence pairs, created using the Yahoo Answers corpus. [9]. URL: `https://github.com/raosudha89/GYAFC-corpus`.

Figurativeness

- IMPLI (Stowe et al., 2022): It consists of 25.8K literal/figurative sentence pairs,

[8] For all datasets, we only use a subset of all pairs based on quality filtering, which is described in Appendix A.2.

[9] `https://webscope.sandbox.yahoo.com/catalog.php?datatype=l&did=11`

spanning idioms and metaphors, both semi-supervised and human-annotated. URL: https://github.com/UKPLab/acl2022-impli.

A.2 Preprocessing Method

To reduce noise and construct splits, we preprocess the datasets as follows:

- SimplePPDB: There are both automatically and manually labeled subsets. We only take the manually labeled examples with $\geq 80\%$ of annotators agreeing with the final label. There are only training and validation sets in the original dataset. Since our method requires no training, we take the original training set as our validation set, and the original validation set as our test set.

- SimpleWikipedia: Since our method focuses on complexity in terms of lexical choice but not grammatical structure, we filter out pairs where the two sentences share the exact same set of tokens, or all tokens in a sentence appear in the other sentence. As there are no official splits, we randomly split the filtered dataset into train/validation/test sets of ratio 8:1:1 (since the dataset is huge).

- StylePPDB: The filtering method is the same as that used for SimplePPDB. There are no official splits either, so we randomly split the filtered dataset into a validation set and a test set of the same size (since the dataset is small).

- GYAFC: We take the Entertainment & Music subset, using pairs from the files `formal` and `informal.ref0`. Since the official splits only have training and test sets, we take only the test set and re-split it into a new validation set and test set of the same size.

- IMPLI: We take the `manual_e` subsets (manually created, entailing) for both idioms and metaphors, combine them and re-split the examples into a validation set and test set of the same size.

Finally, we randomly re-assign the label of every example for class balance.

A.3 Statistics and Examples

Table 6 shows the dataset statistics and example inputs and outputs after our preprocessing. Table 5 shows the POS distribution statistics.

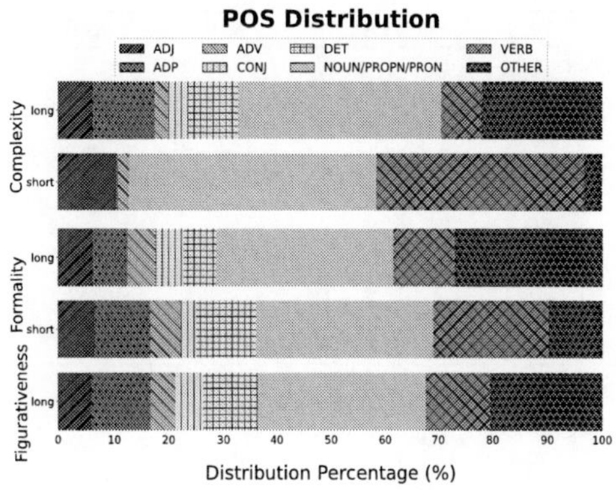

Figure 5: Distribution of token POS in evaluation datasets.

B Implementation Details

B.1 Tokenization

Given a piece of text, we tokenize it with the SpaCy tokenzier[10] into words. Then, using the method described in 3, we obtain a score for the feature of interest for each word token (if using static embeddings) or subword tokens (if using contextualized embeddings with WordPiece tokenization). In the latter case, we additionally obtain an aggregated feature score for each word from the scores of its subword tokens using a pooling strategy described in Section 4. Finally, we obtain an overall feature score for the entire piece of text from the scores of all its words using the same pooling strategy.

B.2 Representations

We use the following static embeddings: for GloVe, we use `GloVe.6B.300d`[11], consisting of 400K word vectors trained on Wikipedia 2014 and Gigaword 5; and for fastText, we use `wiki-news-300d-1M-subword`[12], consisting of 1 million word vectors trained with subword infomation on Wikipedia 2017, UMBC webbase corpus and statmt.org news dataset. Out-of-Vocabulary (OOV) tokens are represented with the all-zero vector.

For contexutalized LMs, we use the following pretrained model checkpoints from HuggingFace Transformers[13]: `bert-base-uncased` (110M parameters),

[10] https://spacy.io/api/tokenizer

[11] https://nlp.stanford.edu/projects/glove/

[12] https://fasttext.cc/docs/en/english-vectors.html

[13] https://github.com/huggingface/transformers

Feature	Dataset	# Val	# Test	Example
Complexity	SimplePPDB (short)	814	1,108	Text 0: toys Text 1: playthings Answer: 1 (more complex)
	SimpleWikipedia (long)	9,978	9,978	Text 0: Endemic types or species are especially likely to develop on biologically isolated areas such as islands because of their geographical isolation. Text 1: Endemic types are most likely to develop on islands because they are isolated. Answer: 0 (more complex)
Formality	StylePPDB (short)	367	367	Text 0: are allowed to Text 1: can Answer: 0 (more formal)
	GYAFC (long)	541	541	Text 0: I am impatiently waiting to ask my husband. Text 1: Can't wait to ask my husband!! Answer: 0 (more formal)
Figurativeness	IMPLI (long)	243	243	Text 0: You must adhere to the rules. Text 1: You must obey the rules. Answer: 0 (more figurative)

Table 6: Datasets used for evaluation. "# Val" and "# Test" stand for the number of examples in the validation set and the test set respectively. Differences between pairs are underlined.

`bert-large-uncased` (336M parameters), `bert-base-multilingual-uncased` (110M parameters), `roberta-base` (125M parameters), `roberta-large` (335M parameters), `xlm-roberta-base` (125M parameters), `xlm-roberta-large` (335M parameters).

B.3 Experiments

We perform grid search on hyperparameters including the LM and the layer (0-12 for base models, and 0-24 for large models) using the validation set and report the performance of the optimal configuration on the test set. The optimal hyperparameters can be found in Appendix C.1.

All evaluation experiments are run on a single NVIDIA GeForce RTX 2080 Ti GPU node. Each experiment takes approximately 2-20 minutes depending on the size of the dataset.

C Extended Results

In this section, we present additional results that cannot fit into Section 3 due to space limit.

C.1 Performance of Different LMs

Table 7 and Table 8 show the detailed performance of specific LMs under the single-layer and the layer aggregation settings, respectively. From the results, we find that there is no consistent winner among all LMs. In terms of layers, on StylePPDB (formality short), the initial layers (0, 1, 2) are dominantly the best-performing ones across all settings. On the other datasets, there is no clear pattern in terms of which layers perform the best.

C.2 Performance Across Layers Under Single-layer Setting

Regarding the performance change across layers, in addition to the plots shown in Section 5.1 under the layer aggregation setting, here we present the results under the single-layer setting in Figure 6. Compared to layer aggregation, the results here are noticeably more chaotic, exhibiting no clear general trends.

C.3 Performance by Text Length Under Single-layer Setting

Similarly, we also present the performance change by text length under the single-layer setting in Figure 7, complementing the results under the layer aggregation setting in Section 5.2. The trends are mostly similar between the two settings.

C.4 Effect of Anisotropy Reduction

Table 9 shows the effect of using the 3 different anisotropy reduction strategies, across all LM and layer configurations. All-but-the-top only works for figurativeness; rank-based only works for formality (long); and standardization works slightly more generally, for complexity (short), formality (short), and formality (long). Nevertheless, overall there is no strategy that works universally under every condition.

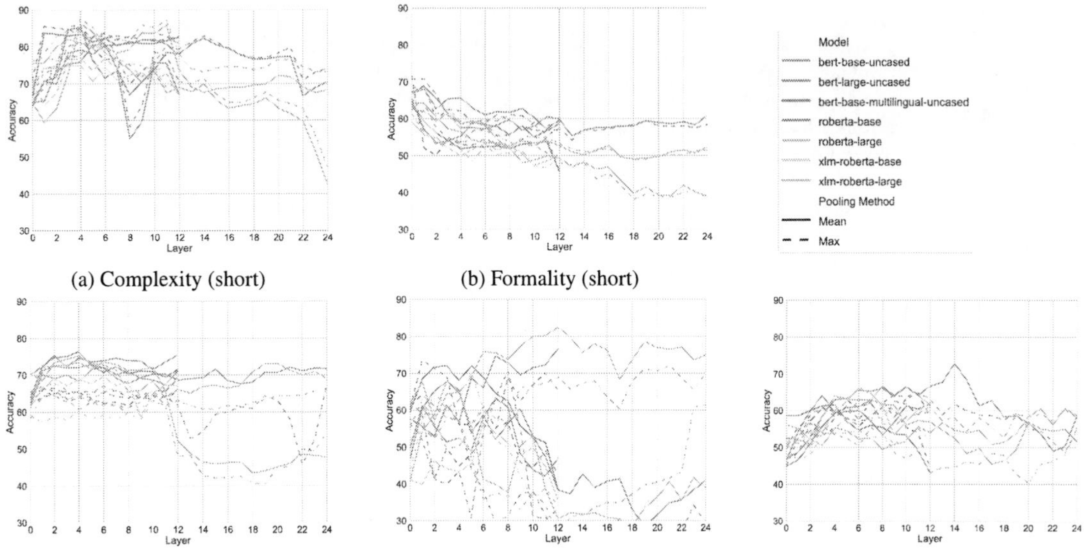

(a) Complexity (short)

(b) Formality (short)

(c) Complexity (long)

(d) Formality (long)

(e) Figurativeness (long)

Figure 6: Performance change across layers of different LMs (under the **single-layer** setting).

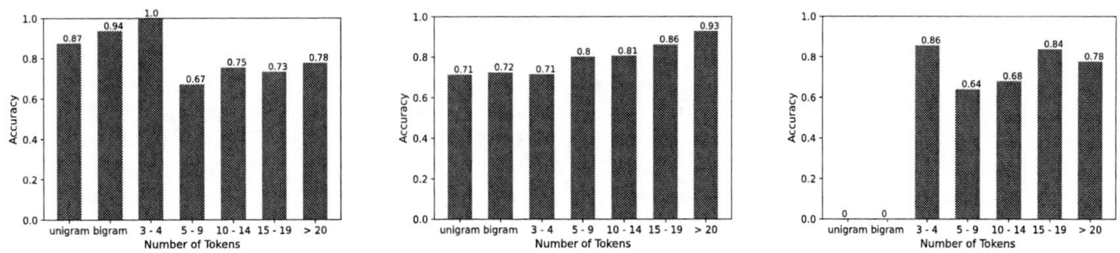

(a) Complexity

(b) Formality

(c) Figurativeness

Figure 7: Optimal performance over different bins of text length (under the **single-layer** setting).

Pooling	Model	Complexity		Formality		Figurativeness
		short	long	short	long	long
	majority	55.1	50.6	51.2	51.8	51.4
Mean	frequency	83.2	51.0	61.0	41.4	49.7
	fasttext.wiki	73.1	58.4	61.6	45.1	52.7
	glove.6B.300d	84.8	60.0	**76.8**	**82.8**	54.3
	bert-base-uncased	82.0 (10)	72.2 (6)	68.7 (1)	63.2 (7)	66.5 (10)
	bert-large-uncased	82.3 (14)	73.0 (5)	68.1 (1)	67.7 (3)	**72.9 (14)**
	bert-base-multilingual-uncased	83.8 (1)	**76.5** (4)	65.1 (0)	72.1 (5)	61.5 (4)
	roberta-base	85.2 (4)	75.5 (12)	63.5 (0)	76.7 (12)	64.1 (3)
	roberta-large	**86.2** (4)	75.3 (4)	64.3 (1)	82.4 (12)	63.9 (4)
	xlm-roberta-base	74.8 (4)	69.6 (6)	58.9 (0)	56.4 (6)	66.3 (6)
	xlm-roberta-large	85.8 (11)	73.7 (6)	62.4 (0)	67.7 (3)	60.6 (23)
Max	frequency	80.7	46.4	57.2	42.5	47.9
	fasttext.wiki	82.0	54.3	74.9	47.7	56.0
	glove.6B.300d	**89.4**	58.0	**76.0**	63.4	55.8
	bert-base-uncased	83.7 (10)	69.1 (12)	70.8 (1)	70.8 (8)	64.6 (11)
	bert-large-uncased	83.0 (6)	67.6 (24)	68.9 (1)	64.1 (1)	**64.8** (11)
	bert-base-multilingual-uncased	85.6 (1)	65.7 (3)	71.7 (0)	**73.6** (1)	60.8 (8)
	roberta-base	85.9 (4)	**69.4** (12)	64.6 (0)	70.1 (11)	62.8 (5)
	roberta-large	87.7 (4)	68.9 (24)	65.1 (0)	72.1 (21)	63.2 (6)
	xlm-roberta-base	77.3 (1)	64.3 (11)	61.6 (0)	70.2 (5)	55.1 (11)
	xlm-roberta-large	87.0 (11)	67.1 (6)	63.8 (0)	61.4 (24)	55.8 (3)

Table 7: Accuracy of different models under the **single-layer** setting. The optimal layer number for each contextualized LM is in brackets. The highest performance within each pooling method is in boldface.

Pooling	Model	Complexity		Formality		Figurativeness
		short	long	short	long	long
	majority	55.1	50.6	51.2	51.8	51.4
Mean	frequency	83.2	51.0	61.0	41.4	49.7
	fasttext.wiki	73.1	58.4	61.6	45.1	52.7
	glove.6B.300d	**84.8**	60.0	**76.8**	**82.8**	54.3
	bert-base-uncased	79.0 (12)	73.1 (10)	67.3 (2)	58.0 (9)	61.5 (11)
	bert-large-uncased	80.1 (16)	74.8 (24)	67.6 (1)	64.7 (6)	**67.2** (19)
	bert-base-multilingual-uncased	84.4 (10)	**76.0** (11)	65.1 (0)	71.5 (5)	61.9 (2)
	roberta-base	78.4 (11)	75.2 (12)	63.5 (0)	69.9 (12)	63.0 (12)
	roberta-large	83.3 (19)	75.3 (11)	65.4 (2)	**86.7** (23)	60.2 (14)
	xlm-roberta-base	76.2 (3)	69.5 (4)	58.9 (0)	50.3 (10)	59.7 (9)
	xlm-roberta-large	79.6 (13)	74.1 (13)	64.6 (1)	58.6 (4)	56.2 (0)
Max	frequency	80.7	46.4	57.2	42.5	47.9
	fasttext.wiki	82.0	54.3	74.9	47.7	56.0
	glove.6B.300d	**89.4**	58.0	**76.0**	63.4	55.8
	bert-base-uncased	81.3 (12)	66.3 (2)	70.8 (2)	62.3 (0)	58.9 (12)
	bert-large-uncased	81.8 (16)	66.9 (6)	68.4 (0)	65.4 (3)	**63.9** (14)
	bert-base-multilingual-uncased	86.0 (7)	65.3 (12)	71.7 (0)	69.5 (2)	59.1 (12)
	roberta-base	80.8 (11)	66.6 (1)	64.6 (0)	56.6 (0)	60.0 (10)
	roberta-large	86.2 (19)	**67.6** (4)	66.2 (2)	**71.7** (24)	62.4 (23)
	xlm-roberta-base	78.4 (2)	59.9 (12)	61.6 (0)	68.2 (5)	52.3 (7)
	xlm-roberta-large	82.4 (13)	65.3 (11)	65.4 (1)	52.9 (4)	53.2 (10)

Table 8: Accuracy of different models under the **layer aggregation** setting. The optimal layer number for each contextualized LM is in brackets. The highest performance within each pooling method is in boldface.

Pooling	Stats	Complexity		Formality		Figurativeness
		short	long	short	long	long
Mean	2 beats 1 (%)	25.2	21.3	44.9	40.2	74.0
	acc gain	-5.9	-5.0	-0.2	-8.2	4.3
Max	2 beats 1 (%)	18.9	28.3	48.0	44.1	59.1
	acc gain	-7.4	-2.2	0.0	-0.3	1.7
Average	2 beats 1 (%)	22.0	24.8	46.5	42.1	66.5
	acc gain	-6.7	-3.6	-0.1	-4.2	3.0

(a) All-but-the-top (single-layer)

Pooling	Stats	Complexity		Formality		Figurativeness
		short	long	short	long	long
Mean	2 beats 1 (%)	27.6	6.3	46.5	26.8	75.6
	acc gain	-4.6	-8.1	-0.2	-14.7	5.6
Max	2 beats 1 (%)	16.5	15.0	47.2	38.6	65.4
	acc gain	-6.8	-5.3	-0.1	-4.0	3.1
Average	2 beats 1 (%)	22.0	10.6	46.9	32.7	70.5
	acc gain	-5.7	-6.7	-0.1	-9.4	4.3

(b) All-but-the-top (layer aggregation)

Pooling	Stats	Complexity		Formality		Figurativeness
		short	long	short	long	long
Mean	2 beats 1 (%)	66.9	18.1	79.5	69.3	50.4
	acc gain	3.9	-3.6	5.5	9.3	-0.7
Max	2 beats 1 (%)	50.4	17.3	80.3	67.7	38.6
	acc gain	1.6	-4.8	5.1	12.1	-2.1
Average	2 beats 1 (%)	58.7	17.7	79.9	68.5	44.5
	acc gain	2.7	-4.2	5.3	10.7	-1.4

(c) Standardization (single-layer)

Pooling	Stats	Complexity		Formality		Figurativeness
		short	long	short	long	long
Mean	2 beats 1 (%)	86.6	15.0	93.7	60.6	72.4
	acc gain	6.8	-3.2	7.2	2.5	2.5
Max	2 beats 1 (%)	69.3	9.4	84.3	63.8	40.9
	acc gain	4.0	-6.1	5.7	7.6	-0.8
Average	2 beats 1 (%)	78.0	12.2	89.0	62.2	56.7
	acc gain	5.4	-4.7	6.5	5.0	0.8

(d) Standardization (layer aggregation)

Pooling	Stats	Complexity		Formality		Figurativeness
		short	long	short	long	long
Mean	2 beats 1 (%)	48.8	29.1	46.5	46.5	48.8
	acc gain	0.1	-1.1	-0.4	1.0	-0.3
Max	2 beats 1 (%)	47.2	38.6	46.5	63.8	52.0
	acc gain	-0.3	-0.8	-0.3	3.3	0.4
Average	2 beats 1 (%)	48.0	33.9	46.5	55.1	50.4
	acc gain	-0.1	-1.0	-0.4	2.1	0.1

(e) Rank-based (single-layer)

Pooling	Stats	Complexity		Formality		Figurativeness
		short	long	short	long	long
Mean	2 beats 1 (%)	54.3	32.3	33.1	36.2	54.3
	acc gain	-0.2	-1.8	-0.9	0.5	-0.2
Max	2 beats 1 (%)	54.3	48.0	43.3	71.7	62.2
	acc gain	-0.4	0.3	-0.5	3.2	0.8
Average	2 beats 1 (%)	54.3	40.2	38.2	53.9	58.3
	acc gain	-0.3	-0.8	-0.7	1.9	0.3

(f) Rank-based (layer aggregation)

Table 9: Effect of three different anisotropy reduction strategies: all-but-the-top, standardization, and rank-based (3 rows). Each strategy is evaluated under single-layer and layer aggregation settings (2 columns). In each table, "2 beats 1 (%)" refers to the percentage of cases where the performance **with** the anisotropy reduction strategy is at least as high as the performance **without** it, under the same configuration (LM & layer). "Acc gain" stands for the average accuracy gain of applying the anisotropy reduction strategy across all configurations. Positive accuracy gains are highlighted in green, negative ones in pink.

Event Semantic Knowledge in Procedural Text Understanding

Ghazaleh Kazeminejad
University of Colorado Boulder
ghazaleh.kazeminejad@colorado.edu

Martha Palmer
University of Colorado Boulder
martha.palmer@colorado.edu

Abstract

The task of entity state tracking aims to automatically analyze procedural texts – texts that describe a step-by-step process (e.g. a baking recipe). Specifically, the goal is to track various states of the entities participating in a given process. Some of the challenges for this NLP task include annotated data scarcity and annotators' reliance on commonsense knowledge to annotate implicit state information. Zhang et al. (2021) successfully incorporated commonsense entity-centric knowledge from ConceptNet into their BERT-based neurosymbolic architecture. Since English mostly encodes state change information in verbs, we attempted to test whether injecting semantic knowledge of events (retrieved from the state-of-the-art VerbNet parser) into a neural model can also improve the performance on this task. To achieve this, we adapt the methodology introduced by Zhang et al. (2021) for incorporating symbolic entity information from ConceptNet to the incorporation of VerbNet event semantics. We evaluate the performance of our model on the ProPara dataset (Mishra et al., 2018). In addition, we introduce LEXIS, our purely symbolic model for entity state tracking that uses a simple set of case statements, and is informed mostly by linguistic knowledge retrieved from various computational lexical resources. Our approach is inherently domain-agnostic, and our model is explainable and achieves state-of-the-art results on the Recipes dataset (Bosselut et al., 2017).

1 Introduction

Language understanding in humans requires at least the knowledge of the semantics of events and entities. One needs to know the sequences of subevents that together make up a 'throwing' event, as well as the causal and temporal relationships between the subevents that distinguish a 'throwing' event from a 'pouring' event, or a 'running' event. Furthermore, reasoning about entities that are participating in these events requires a deep understanding of the properties of an entity. It is the distinction between such entity properties that enables us, for example, to distinguish between 'throwing a ball' vs. 'throwing a Molotov cocktail'. In contrast to humans, many high-performing NLP models do not depend on explicit knowledge of events and entities to process natural language; rather, they rely on the surface forms and patterns of word co-occurances in colossal amounts of language data to learn the mechanics of language as well as the interpretation of linguistic forms. Since human knowledge and reasoning capabilities benefit from knowledge of events and entities, we suggest that a neural model may also benefit from such explicit symbolic knowledge. This requires successful incorporation of such symbolic knowledge into a subsymbolic system.

Explicit semantic knowledge, such as entity knowledge extracted from ontologies, has often been used in the field of natural language grounding, where the connection between natural language and the physical world is sought (Bisk et al., 2020). There are yet other NLP tasks that are likely to benefit from explicit semantic knowledge as well, such as tasks focusing on machine comprehension of how things work (e.g. how plants make food), or how a certain physical result is achieved (e.g. how to make pizza using some ingredients). The NLP task that focuses on the machine reading comprehension of texts describing processes is called *Procedural Text Understanding* (Huang et al., 2021; Tandon et al., 2019; Mishra et al., 2019). One of the subtasks in this field is *Entity State Tracking* (Mishra et al., 2018; Bosselut et al., 2017; Faghihi and Kordjamshidi, 2021; Amini et al., 2020; Gupta and Durrett, 2019), formally defined as: Given a paragraph P that describes a process, and an entity e that is one of the participants in that process, did the state of e change during the process? If so, what was the type of change that occurred to e

*Proceedings of the The 12th Joint Conference on Lexical and Computational Semantics (*SEM 2023)*, pages 388–398
July 13-14, 2023 ©2023 Association for Computational Linguistics

(usually to be chosen among a desired set of types of state change)? When did the change happen (i.e. at which time step during the process)? And finally, what was the locus of change (i.e. the location of e before and after the change) (Mishra et al., 2018)?

There are two main challenges in solving this problem. First, the size of annotated data for this task is usually small since achieving reasonable inter-annotator agreement for the task is hard, making it expensive and time-consuming. Second, when facing implicit information, annotators frequently resort to commonsense knowledge – knowledge that state-of-the-art NLP models are not explicitly aware of. Existing models for this challenging problem use some flavor of learning-based approaches to NLP (see Section 2). One of the existing approaches that is closest in theory to ours is KOALA (Zhang et al., 2021) – a neurosymbolic model encoding entity-centric knowledge into a neural network that is used to track entity states and locations during a process. We re-implemented this model and adopted it as our baseline. One of our contributions in this work is offering a method for encoding symbolic event semantic knowledge into a neural model. In practice, we are proposing an approach to expose a neural model to sequences of latent universal concepts composing an event, allowing the network to learn from the spelled out event semantics as well as the surface forms of the events realized mostly as verbs.

In addition to our neurosymbolic model (SKIP: **S**emantic **K**nowledge **I**n **P**rocedural text understanding), we have also developed a purely symbolic model[1] called LEXIS. Error analysis and ablation tests on this model demonstrate other sources of external knowledge that show promise for inclusion in a neural model in future work. In addition, we show that our theory and approach are dataset- and domain-independent, and can be used in any NLP task where knowledge of event semantics plays a major role for humans to achieve the goal of the task. We will also briefly illustrate our explanation module for LEXIS.

We evaluated SKIP on the ProPara dataset (Mishra et al., 2018), and LEXIS on both the ProPara and Recipes (Bosselut et al., 2017) datasets[2]. LEXIS achieved a new state-of-the-art performance on the Recipes dataset (70.1% F1, improving over the existing state-of-the-art model by 11.7%), and SKIP performed better than our adopted neurosymbolic baseline model, (71.8% F1, improving over the re-implemented baseline model by 4.1%)[3].

Our contributions are two-fold: (1) We adapt the methodology introduced by Zhang et al. (2021) for incorporating symbolic entity-centric knowledge to the incorporation of VerbNet event semantics. We extract and encode event semantic knowledge for injection into a neural network, and present SKIP, an end-to-end neurosymbolic model developed using this method, in conjunction with data augmentation and transfer learning techniques. (2) We present a general knowledge-based approach to text understanding using existing NLP resources, and present LEXIS, a purely symbolic model we developed for entity state tracking that achieves a new state-of-the-art on the Recipes dataset, with an architecture that is adaptable to different genres of natural language text, and is explainable[4].

2 Related Work

This work is inspired by the concept of event semantics and event structure offered by the Generative Lexicon theory, in efforts such as Pustejovsky and Moszkowicz (2011), Mani and Pustejovsky (2012), and Brown et al. (2022), where event structure is enriched to encode and dynamically track object attributes that are modified during an event. The idea is that a complex event can be decomposed into simpler ordered subevents that explicitly label the transitions between entity states.

With regard to Entity State Tracking, most recent existing models mainly rely on large language models (Amini et al., 2020; Faghihi and Kordjamshidi, 2021; Zhang et al., 2021), while earlier models (prior to 2020) rely on neural (Gupta and Durrett, 2019; Das et al., 2018; Du et al., 2019) or learning-based approaches (Ribeiro et al., 2019). The only existing neurosymbolic model (to our knowledge) is KOALA (Zhang et al., 2021), which retrieves

[1]Here, purely symbolic is used as opposed to sub-symbolic models that learn by example. (Garcez et al., 2019; Hamilton et al., 2022)

[2]The reason we did not evaluate SKIP on the Recipes dataset was that we only exposed SKIP to the knowledge extracted directly from the VerbNet parser, which does not shed light on the types of state change the model is expected to predict in the Recipes dataset. We have access to such knowledge and will perform this evaluation in future work.

[3]Our code is publicly available at https://github.com/ghamzak/SKIP (for SKIP) and https://github.com/ghamzak/Lexis (for LEXIS).

[4]Disclaimer: the models developed and introduced in this work are for research purposes only and are not to be trusted in real-world applications.

informative knowledge triples from ConceptNet (Speer et al., 2017) and performs knowledge-aware reasoning while tracking the entities. To compensate for data scarcity, they perform (raw) data augmentation by automatically retrieving the top 50 Wikipedia articles closest in content and writing style to the raw paragraphs in the ProPara dataset (using tf-idf). This augmented corpus of raw procedural texts is then used to perform transfer learning, fine-tuning a BERT encoder in two stages, first on raw procedural texts collected from Wikipedia, and then further fine-tuning it on the raw text from the dataset. The whole model follows a multi-stage training schema (more details in section 3.1).

The main difference between KOALA and SKIP is the type of external symbolic knowledge introduced to the model. Whereas KOALA only leverages entity-centric knowledge, we introduce event semantic knowledge based on the Generative Lexicon theory and its implementation in the VerbNet lexical resource (Schuler, 2005; Brown et al., 2018, 2019). This allows the model to have access to direct and explicit knowledge about entity state transitions for all the participants in an event, the roles of each participant in the event, as well as causal relationships and temporal links between subevents (Brown et al., 2022).

On the Recipes dataset, Zhang et al. (2021) evaluate only for location prediction, because location change is one of the state change types needed by ProPara as well. To enable prediction for the rest of the state change types required by the Recipes dataset , a previously lacking knowledge resource has recently become available (Kazeminejad et al., 2022) which explicitly provides the lexical semantic components indicating state changes such as changes in temperature or form, giving our symbolic model (LEXIS) an edge over other competing models[5].

3 Methodology

Following Zhang et al. (2021), we develop SKIP by neural encoding of symbolic knowledge and allowing the model to selectively pay more attention to knowledge that is conducive to more accurate predictions. As mentioned in section 1, our main contribution is proposing a way to make a neural model utilize event semantic knowledge in its predictions, and use the obtained neurosymbolic model for downstream NLP tasks where knowledge of event semantics tends to be beneficial according to linguistic theory.

In order to obtain logical representations of subevent semantics as well as temporal and causal relations between the subevents for encoding into our neural model, we rely on VerbNet – a large English verb lexicon which expands event semantics into sequences of subevents. To automate this process, we use the state-of-the-art VerbNet semantic parser (Gung, 2020; Gung and Palmer, 2021) and obtain the symbolic logical representations for individual sentences corresponding to the steps in each process. These logical representations, illustrated in Table 1, are the horsepower of our approach.

¬Degradation_Material_Integrity(e_1, The sediment)
¬Has_Physical_Form(e_1, The sediment, V_Final_State)
Degradation_Material_Integrity(e_2, The sediment)
Has_Physical_Form(e_2, The sediment, V_Final_State)

Table 1: Logical representations generated by the VerbNet parser for the sentence "The sediment breaks down." The span 'breaks down' is identified as the verb, and verb sense disambiguation classifies it as belonging to the VerbNet class `break-45.1`.

In VerbNet, verbs are classified into different classes based on similarities in their syntactic and semantic behavior. For example, all verbs belonging to the `break-45.1` class (Table 1) indicate some sort of physical change of state that leads to the breaking into parts of a `Patient` argument. Different syntactic frames may incorporate more information such as the causal agent of the event, or the instrument used by the causal agent to achieve the result. The set of semantic predicates adopted by the VerbNet lexicon (such as Degradation_Material_Integrity or Has_Physical_Form in Table 1) are universal eventive concepts that lead human cognitive contsrual of events, and are based on cognitive linguistic theories such as Force Dynamics (Talmy, 1988; Croft, 2015, 2017; De Mulder, 2021). More details on event semantic knowledge extraction will follow in 3.2.

The VerbNet-extracted event semantic knowledge is then translated into natural language so that it is neurally encodable. We choose this method of encoding over direct encoding of the logical representations, because LLMs such as BERT are already familiar with the structure of natural language, and we want to hone this existing power instead of introducing a whole new representation

[5]Again, we have not yet exposed SKIP to this knowledge resource, but this will be done in future work.

system which might be harder to learn, especially given the small size of the dataset. In order to acquaint a vanilla text encoder with the language translated from the event semantic logical representations, we fine-tune a BERT encoder (Kenton and Toutanova, 2019) on the translated knowledge extracted for the training data. This will be explained in more detail in 3.3.

3.1 Neurosymbolic Framework

The base architecture of SKIP (shown in Figure 1) is developed on top of KOALA (Zhang et al., 2021), which we adopted as our baseline model. As explained in Section 2, our major point of departure is the introduction of event semantics to the model, and, for that matter, a method to obtain such representations for free. Before attending to our differences, however, we present a brief overview of our similarities with the KOALA framework.

Following KOALA, we perform multi-stage training to obtain our text and knowledge encoders. To get contextualized embeddings for raw input paragraphs, we train a text encoder specialized in understanding procedural texts by fine-tuning a vanilla BERT encoder on a tf-idf-retrieved corpus of raw procedural texts from Wikipedia, and then on the raw paragraphs from the ProPara dataset. SKIP duplication of KOALA ends here. To obtain a knowledge encoder, since our sources of external knowledge are different, our knowledge extraction methods are different as well (see 3.2). Naturally, our post-knowledge-extraction translation rules are also different, with the event semantic translation rules being arguably more complex, the first reason being that the entities are always represented in triples, while events could be intransitive, transitive, or ditransitive, each requiring a different type of translation.

After knowledge translation, a knowledge encoder is obtained by training a vanilla BERT encoder on the knowledge translations (more details to follow in 3.3), learning to make sense of VerbNet-style event semantics, as well as ConceptNet-style entity semantics (see Figure 2). In the final training stage, SKIP (like KOALA) leverages an encoder-decoder architecture, and performs *state tracking* and *location prediction* in two separate yet parallel subtasks (as shown in Figure 1). The training objective of the model is to jointly optimize state and location prediction, as well as knowledge selection, which is attending to and selecting the best knowledge pieces that are instrumental in state and location prediction.

As shown in Figure 1, the state tracking module is endowed with a knowledge injector (see 3.4 for more details), a bi-LSTM state decoder, and a conditional random field (CRF) layer since we are performing multi-class classification for multiple target state change types. For location prediction, we use the same architecture except for the CRF layer which is changed to a linear classifier, because the model is learning to predict only one location for a given entity at a given time step in a given paragraph. Of course the learned weights and the knowledge triples selected by the attention module will be different from those in the state decoder, because the attention will need to attend to different predictor variables for state tracking and location prediction.

In the location prediction module, given that there are M location candidates for paragraph P (all nominal phrases and words extracted from P using a POS-tagger), the location decoder is executed M times, and the linear classification layer outputs a score for each location candidate at each time step t based on the decoder's hidden states. Using a Softmax function, the probability distribution for each location candidate for entity e at time-step t in paragraph P is obtained, and a loss function is used to train the optimal model for location prediction.

3.2 Event Semantic Knowledge Extraction

This paper describes the extraction and incorporation of event semantic knowledge into our neural architecture. For entity-centric knowledge extraction from ConceptNet, we simply follow Zhang et al. (2021): for each target entity, we find ConceptNet nodes representing the concept using exact string matching and fuzzy matching, finding the most similar nodes based on embedding distance. The extracted knowledge triples, which are two entities and the relation between them, are then translated into natural language using handcrafted rules that translate the relations, enabling fine-tuning for developing the knowledge encoder.

For SKIP, we selected a subset of VerbNet semantic predicates that are indicative of the types of state changes of interest for the ProPara dataset: `Move`, `Create`, and `Destroy`. It is imperative to note that selected subsets can change to match the requirements of the task at hand. For each sentence X_t in paragraph P and for entity e, the

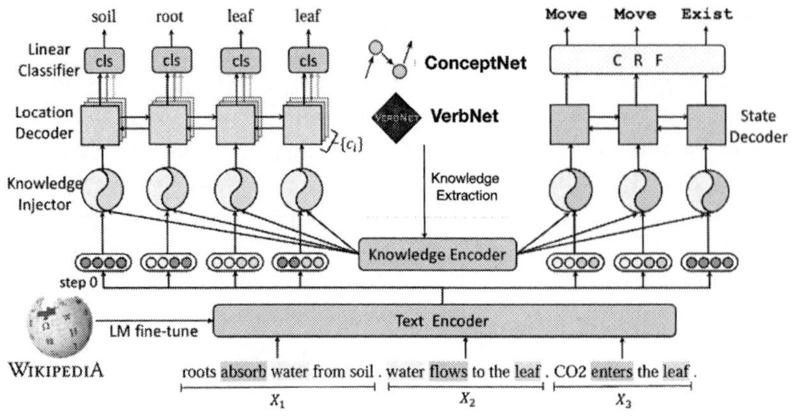

Figure 1: An overview of our model, adopted from Zhang et al. (2021). Compared to the baseline model, the sources of symbolic knowledge have been updated to include event semantics from VerbNet. Note that in the location prediction module (on the left), the whole module is applied to each entity separately and in parallel at each time step. While the text encoder is obtained by fine-tuning a BERT encoder on raw procedural texts from Wikipedia and the ProPara dataset, the knowledge encoder (see Figure 2) is obtained by fine-tuning a BERT encoder on various combinations of knowledge: knowledge from VerbNet only, from ConceptNet only, and from both.

subevents	translation
$\neg has\_location(A, B)$ $has\_location(A, B)$	A moves towards destination B
$be(A)$ $\neg be(A)$	A is destroyed
$\neg be(A)$ $be(A)$	A is created

Table 2: Sample translation rules for extracted informative subevents from VerbNet.

model reads all the generated subevents in order, and keeps those that satisfy the following two conditions: (1) the VerbNet semantic predicate is a member of the hand-selected subset of VerbNet predicates[6]; and (2) one of the arguments in the subevent has an overlap in surface form with the entity e. Finally, the retained subevents are translated into natural language using a set of handcrafted translation rules, such that the translation exposes the type of state change undergone by entity e at time step t. Table 2 has one example for each of the state change types.[7]

3.3 Event Semantic Knowledge Encoding

As shown in Figure 2, after extracting symbolic event semantic knowledge from VerbNet, we fine-tune a BERT encoder on the extracted knowledge with the aim of familiarizing the BERT encoder with the vocabulary and style of translations of knowledge statements. Subevents have important structural information which we preserve in our fine-tuning stage by separating the argument spans and the translation of the chosen semantic predicates. We use BERT special tokens for token-level separation [SEP], and begin the translated sentence by the BERT [CLS] special token to mark sentence-level detachment. For example, for the sentence 'The sound waves hit an object', the first argument is a `Theme` corresponding with the span 'The sound waves', and the second one is a `Goal` corresponding with the span 'an object'. Since the subevents in the first row in Table 2 apply to this sentence , the translated sentence with preserved structure will be *[CLS] The sound waves [SEP] moves towards destination [SEP] an object [SEP].* For fine-tuning, we modify the conventional masked language modeling (MLM) objective to fit the structural features of the extracted event semantic knowledge from VerbNet (Figure 3).

Since BERT has a bi-directional architecture, we iteratively mask out tokens and ask the encoder to predict the masked tokens given the unmasked tokens (see Figure 3). This allows the BERT encoder to better understand the relationships between different entities (realized as arguments) and between entities and events (translated into a sequence of

[6]For a complete list of these selected VerbNet predicates, see Appendix A in Kazeminejad (2023)

[7]For the complete list of translation rules see Appendix E in Kazeminejad (2023).

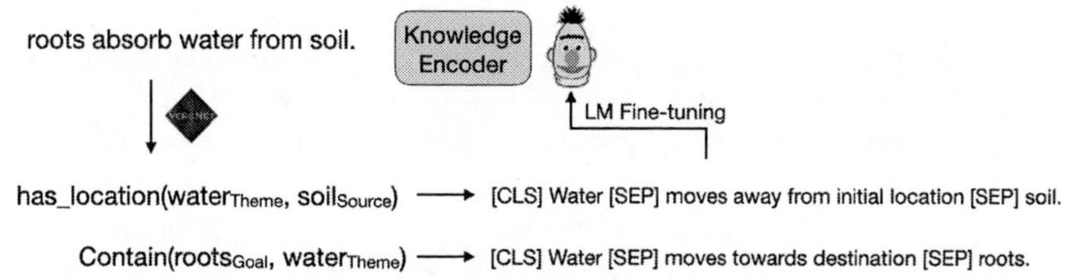

Figure 2: Developing a knowledge encoder model by fine-tuning a BERT encoder on event semantic knowledge extracted from VerbNet subevents

tokens with explicit state change information). Following the empirical results obtained by Zhang et al. (2021), if the arguments are multi-word, we mask 50% of the argument tokens at a time to make sure the model is trainable. For the translation of the semantic predicate, we mask out all the tokens at once, because the set of semantic predicates in VerbNet is a closed one, and we want the model to learn the meaning of the predicate at once and as a whole. Such fine-tuning enables the encoder to learn to model the structural information conveyed in the retained subevents.

3.4 Attentive Knowledge Infusion

Having obtained the knowledge encoder, in the final training stage, the contextualized representations of the extracted (and translated) symbolic knowledge from both VerbNet and ConceptNet are calculated by mean pooling over the knowledge encoder outputs for all tokens.

Even though we have tried to keep only the informative subevents, not all of them may end up being useful in guiding the model to predict correct labels. To enable the model to select the most relevant knowledge, the knowledge injector module injects encoded knowledge into the model before each decoder as a query to attend to the encoded knowledge, helping the model attend to knowledge relevant to the context paragraph. Each decoder is equipped with an input gate to select information from the original input and the injected knowledge. Zhang et al. (2021) empirically found out that such gate integration performs better than simply concatenating the encoded text and knowledge. The training objective is to maximize the attention weights of all "relevant" triples. By the end of training and during inference, the model is expected to better identify the relevance between knowledge and prediction targets. Finally, the overall loss function is computed as the weighted sum of the loss functions for the three sub-tasks: state tracking, location prediction, and relevant knowledge selection.

4 Experiments

We evaluate SKIP on the ProPara dataset (Mishra et al., 2018), which is an entity state tracking dataset developed by AI2, containing 488 human-authored paragraphs describing scientific processes, with an 80/10/10 data split. While state change types (`Move`, `Create`, and `Destroy`) were expertly annotated, entity location annotation was crowed-sourced, resulting in lower quality and consistency. We perform document-level evaluation on ProPara, using the official evaluation code [8].

In re-implementing the baseline model (KOALA), we only changed the batch size, downsizing from 32 to 16 due to hardware limitations[9]. KOALA's reported results along with our re-implementation results are demonstrated in the first two rows of Table 3.

The whole model contains 235M parameters including 2 BERT encoders. In LM fine-tuning, we used the uncased $BERT_{BASE}$ model, and manually tuned hyper-parameters, setting the batch size to 16 and learning rate to 5×10^{-5}. While we used the same text encoder developed by Zhang et al. (2021), our knowledge encoder was different. It was trained for 2 epochs on external knowledge. In the final training stage, we used a batch size of 10 and a learning rate of 3×10^{-5} on the Adam optimizer. The hidden size of the LSTMs was set to 256 and the dropout rate to 0.4. We performed early stopping with an impatience of 20 epochs, by evaluating changes in model accuracy over the dev set ($\sim$1.5 GPU hours). We selected the best checkpoint in prediction accuracy on the dev set.

As shown in Table 3, our three main experimental settings included changes to the source

[8] `https://github.com/allenai/aristo-leaderboard/tree/master/propara/evaluator`

[9] TITAN Xp GPU with 12 GB Memory

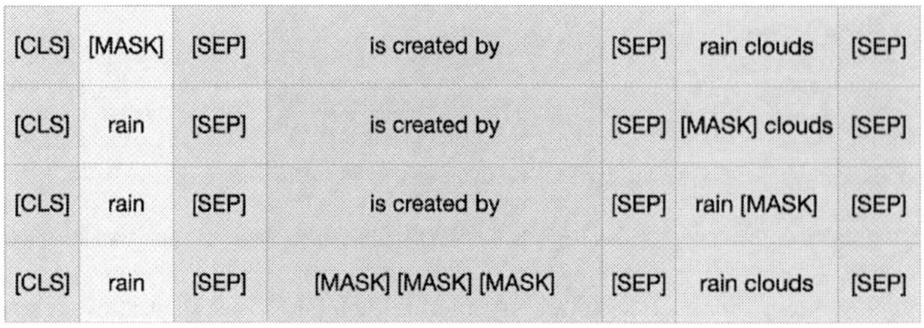

Figure 3: Translation and masking of one VerbNet-extracted subevent for the entity 'rain', indicating that "rain is created by rain clouds".

Model	Precision	Recall	F1
KOALA reported results	**77.7%**	64.4%	70.4%
KOALA reimplementation (baseline)	73.0%	63.1%	67.7%
SKIP – fine-tuned on VN only	76.5%	**67.6%**	**71.8%**
– fine-tuned on both VN and CN	72.0%	61.4%	66.3%
– fine-tuned on CN only	74.1%	63.3%	68.3%

Table 3: The top two rows show the reported and re-implementation results of the KOALA model. The bottom three rows demonstrate the results of our three main experimental settings, where the knowledge encoder used in model training is obtained by fine-tuning on VN (VerbNet) only, CN (ConceptNet) only, or both. These are all evaluations on the ProPara dataset.

of semantic knowledge in developing our knowledge encoder. SKIP performed better compared to the baseline in the experimental setting where the source of knowledge for developing the knowledge encoder was only VerbNet event semantics. Note that we use both entity and event knowledge during the final training stage, and it is only the changes in knowledge source for LM fine-tuning to obtain different knowledge encoders that leads to the best experimental results.

5 Discussion

Our experimental results were interesting in two ways. First, the fact that LM fine-tuning on both VerbNet and ConceptNet lowers the performance compared to fine-tuning on only one knowledge source could be an indication that, given the size of the data, two different sources of knowledge seems to confuse the knowledge encoder more than helping it. Secondly, comparing fine-tuning on VerbNet only vs. ConceptNet only, the former proved to be more effective. This might indicate that knowledge of event semantics may better help the model track entity states and locations during a process, just as we had initially hypothesized based on lexical semantic theories. While entity-centric knowledge may give the model a better understanding of entities and their properties, such as their typical location, state changes are eventive concepts and often lexically encoded in verbs. Since VerbNet provides explicit labels for transitions between entity states, a successful VerbNet parse ensures explicit symbolic knowledge which clarifies the types of state change lexically encoded in verbs.

5.1 Error Analysis

An error analysis on the test set showed that 52.49% of the state change type misclassifications were in fact correct model predictions and incorrect gold annotations, with a further 6.69% examples where both the gold and predicted labels were incorrect. To illustrate, given the two subsequent time steps 'Animals eat plants.' and 'Animals make waste.', for the target entity 'plants', the gold labels include two `Move` events, one at each time step: first from an unknown location to 'animal', and then from 'animal' to an unknown location. In contrast, SKIP predicts a `Destroy` event at the end of the first time-step. Arguably, an entity that is eaten and converted to waste is destroyed, because it has lost its physical integrity, such as a glass that breaks. What returns to nature is not a plant anymore, but waste. This assumption is also confirmed elsewhere in the data. For example, in the sentence 'They absorb nitrates from the soil into their roots.', the gold label for the entity 'nitrates' is `Destroy`. This both suggests inconsistency in human annotation, and the accuracy of SKIP.

Overall, the error analysis demonstrates that the annotation task for entity state tracking is quite complex and challenging, and obtaining acceptable inter-annotator agreement is hard. A knowledge-aware model such as SKIP could be quite beneficial for annotation quality control.

5.2 Purely Symbolic Entity State Tracking Model

LEXIS was designed based on an approach to simulate the cognitive construal of events by humans. This approach is inherently domain-independent and can be readily adapted to other natural language domains or NLP tasks. As an example model founded on this approach, LEXIS relies on the same informative subevents and semantic features from VerbNet that benefited SKIP. In addition, PropBank SRL is used as a backoff for gaps in VerbNet parses. For more details on an earlier version of LEXIS, see (Kazeminejad et al., 2021a)[10].

In addition to the ProPara dataset, we also evaluated LEXIS on the Recipes dataset, which contains 866 human-annotated recipes, with an 80/10/10 data split, with each recipe containing an average of 8.8 sentences. Recipes state change types include changes in `composition`, `cookedness`, `temperature`, `rotation`, `shape`, `cleanliness`, and `accessibility`, as well as `location`. Apparently, there is very little overlap with ProPara state change types of interest. Neither are these state change types normally found in VerbNet. However, we were able to use the recently developed semantic layer added to the VerbNet lexicon that includes more fine-grained semantic features specific to each verb, hence called verb-specific features (Kazeminejad et al., 2022). For instance, the `Other_cos-45.4` class with more than 300 verb members is generally about some physical change of state occurring to a `Patient` argument. These semantic components provide details such as the physical property that is changing (e.g. temperature, speed, intensity, etc.), or the final state of the `Patient` entity (e.g. ±clean, ±open, etc) that LEXIS can use to predict state change types.

LEXIS also uses spaCy (Honnibal et al., 2020) dependency parsing and POS tagging for conjunction analysis, compound identification, extracting objects of prepositions and heads of noun phrases. ConceptNet was used to identify whether an entity is ontologically considered locative, and also to perform fuzzy search (using the spaCy large model) to find the most likely typical location if not explicitly mentioned in a given sentence. We also used fast-coref (Toshniwal et al., 2021), a high-performing generalizable domain-independent coreference resolution module, to identify co-referring entities given a paragraph, and substitute pronominal forms with their content word counterpart. Finally, we used the the logical rule of location transitivity to enable the model to update entity locations accordingly.

On the ProPara dataset, LEXIS achieves an overall F1 score of 55.6% on the test set.

P	R	F1
72.8	45.0	55.6

Table 4: LEXIS results on the ProPara dataset

On the Recipes dataset, LEXIS achieves a new state-of-the-art both in F1 score and accuracy (see Table 5).

Model	P	R	F1	Acc
Lexis	67.9	**72.4**	**70.1**	**94.6**
SGR*	**69.3**	50.5	54.8	-
KOALA	60.1	52.6	56.1	-
REAL**	55.2	52.9	54.1	-
IEN†	58.5	47.0	52.2	-
NCET†	56.5	46.4	50.9	-
NPN‡	-	-	44.64	55.05

Table 5: LEXIS evaluation results on the test set of the Recipes dataset. * (Tang et al., 2022); ** (Huang et al., 2021); † (Tang et al., 2020); ‡ (Bosselut et al., 2017).

A series of ablation tests on the ProPara dataset showed that the best model performance was achieved when all the proposed knowledge components were included in the model. In addition, following VerbNet and PropBank parses which had the greatest impact[11], the single component with the most significant impact on LEXIS results used the verb-specific features (the semantic layer recently added to VerbNet), the removal of which lowered model performance by 3.5% (F1).

In addition, an error analysis of the model showed that within the 24.5% prediction mis-

[10]However, keep in mind that the latest version of this system that is referenced here is yet to be published.

[11]Note that the first version of LEXIS (Kazeminejad et al., 2021b) only used VerbNet parses.

matches, only 7.18% were due to cross-label confusion. For the main part, the mismatches were either false negatives or false positives, with the false negatives being about two times the number of false positives. This is due to the design of the model which tends to avoid labeling if there is any ambiguity or uncertainty. In other words, the model is deterministic by design.

Regarding explainability, LEXIS contains an explanation module which traces back on the prediction path and explains every step in making decisions, including the provenance of that decision. For instance, for the sentence 'They are buried in sediment', LEXIS predicts a `Move` event for the entity 'plants', from an unknown location to 'sediment'. Here is what the explanation module generates:

The verb 'bury' is in `put-9.1-1` VerbNet class. *(provenance: VerbNet parser).*
'they' moves to 'sediment'. *(provenance: VerbNet parser).*
'they' refers to 'plants'. *(provenance: fast-coref).*
'plants' move to 'sediment'. *(provenance: substitution).*

6 Conclusions and Future Work

We presented a method to extract event semantic knowledge and encode it in neural architectures for NLP applications where event semantics theoretically promises to enhance the predictive power of the model. We showed that this method was effective in SKIP – our neurosymbolic model designed for procedural text understanding. Our error analysis demonstrated that SKIP can be relied on to perform annotation quality control. Furthermore, LEXIS, our purely symbolic entity state tracking model designed based on our domain-independent approach, achieved a new state-of-the-art on the Recipes dataset. We explained why this approach is domain-independent and can be adapted to other domains and NLP tasks.

In future work, we would like to expand our neurosymbolic model to use other sources of linguistic knowledge that proved useful in LEXIS ablation tests. It would also be interesting to assess the success of this approach in other NLU tasks, such as causal inference and textual entailment, where event semantic knowledge is again theoretically important.

Limitations

Since our methodology relies heavily on the VerbNet lexicon and parser, the inherent limitations and shortcomings of them percolate into our model as well. VerbNet classes are designed to generalize over and abstract away from some semantic aspects of verbs in order to achieve meaningful classes. Therefore, we can rely on VerbNet only when the type of semantic knowledge we intend to obtain is included in existing VerbNet semantic predicates. For example, ProPara state change types have counterparts in VerbNet semantic predicates, while the Recipes dataset state change types do not. As explained in 5.2, we resorted to verb-specific features to obtain the type of semantic knowledge needed to predict state changes for Recipes.

VerbNet's coverage imposes a second limitation. Some verbs are missing from the lexicon (e.g. 'migrate'), leading to empty parses. Some other verbs may exist in the lexicon but a certain sense of them is missing. For example, at the time of developing the VerbNet labeled data, the locative sense of the verb 'be' was missing from the lexicon, and by extension from the labeled data. In such cases, the parser assigns that verb to an alternative class with a different sense of the same verb lemma (in this case to `seem-109-1-1`).

Finally, the amount of VerbNet training data is relatively small (compared to PropBank (Kingsbury and Palmer, 2002) or AMR (Banarescu et al., 2013)), leading to misclassifications due to sparse data. All of these limitations can be improved by expanding the coverage of the VerbNet lexicon, and expanding and updating the VerbNet labeled data accordingly.

Acknowledgements

We gratefully acknowledge the support of DARPA KAIROS Program No. FA8750-19-2-1004. Any opinions, findings, and conclusions or recommendations expressed in this material are those of the authors and do not necessarily reflect the views of DARPA or the U.S. government.

References

Aida Amini, Antoine Bosselut, Bhavana Dalvi Mishra, Yejin Choi, and Hannaneh Hajishirzi. 2020. Procedural reading comprehension with attribute-aware context flow. In *Automated Knowledge Base Construction*.

Laura Banarescu, Claire Bonial, Shu Cai, Madalina Georgescu, Kira Griffitt, Ulf Hermjakob, Kevin Knight, Philipp Koehn, Martha Palmer, and Nathan Schneider. 2013. Abstract meaning representation for sembanking. In *Proceedings of the 7th linguistic annotation workshop and interoperability with discourse*, pages 178–186.

Yonatan Bisk, Rowan Zellers, Jianfeng Gao, Yejin Choi, et al. 2020. Piqa: Reasoning about physical commonsense in natural language. In *Proceedings of the AAAI conference on artificial intelligence*, volume 34, pages 7432–7439.

Antoine Bosselut, Omer Levy, Ari Holtzman, Corin Ennis, Dieter Fox, and Yejin Choi. 2017. Simulating action dynamics with neural process networks. *arXiv preprint arXiv:1711.05313*.

Susan Windisch Brown, Julia Bonn, James Gung, Annie Zaenen, James Pustejovsky, and Martha Palmer. 2019. Verbnet representations: Subevent semantics for transfer verbs. In *Proceedings of the First International Workshop on Designing Meaning Representations*, pages 154–163.

Susan Windisch Brown, Julia Bonn, Ghazaleh Kazeminejad, Annie Zaenen, James Pustejovsky, and Martha Palmer. 2022. Semantic representations for nlp using verbnet and the generative lexicon. *Frontiers in artificial intelligence*, 5.

Susan Windisch Brown, James Pustejovsky, Annie Zaenen, and Martha Palmer. 2018. Integrating generative lexicon event structures into verbnet. In *Proceedings of the Eleventh International Conference on Language Resources and Evaluation (LREC 2018)*.

William Croft. 2015. Force dynamics and directed change in event lexicalization and argument realization. In *Cognitive science perspectives on verb representation and processing*, pages 103–129. Springer.

William Croft. 2017. The structure of events and the structure of language. In *The new psychology of language*, pages 67–92. Routledge.

Rajarshi Das, Tsendsuren Munkhdalai, Xingdi Yuan, Adam Trischler, and Andrew McCallum. 2018. Building dynamic knowledge graphs from text using machine reading comprehension. *arXiv preprint arXiv:1810.05682*.

Walter De Mulder. 2021. Force dynamics. In *The Routledge Handbook of Cognitive Linguistics*, pages 228–241. Routledge.

Xinya Du, Bhavana Dalvi, Niket Tandon, Antoine Bosselut, Wen-tau Yih, Peter Clark, and Claire Cardie. 2019. Be consistent! improving procedural text comprehension using label consistency. In *Proceedings of the 2019 Conference of the North American Chapter of the Association for Computational Linguistics: Human Language Technologies, Volume 1 (Long and Short Papers)*, pages 2347–2356.

Hossein Rajaby Faghihi and Parisa Kordjamshidi. 2021. Time-stamped language model: Teaching language models to understand the flow of events. In *Proceedings of the 2021 Conference of the North American Chapter of the Association for Computational Linguistics: Human Language Technologies*, pages 4560–4570.

Artur d'Avila Garcez, Marco Gori, Luis C Lamb, Luciano Serafini, Michael Spranger, and Son N Tran. 2019. Neural-symbolic computing: An effective methodology for principled integration of machine learning and reasoning. *arXiv preprint arXiv:1905.06088*.

James Gung. 2020. *Abstraction, Sense Distinctions and Syntax in Neural Semantic Role Labeling*. Ph.D. thesis, University of Colorado at Boulder.

James Gung and Martha Palmer. 2021. Predicate representations and polysemy in verbnet semantic parsing. In *Proceedings of the 14th International Conference on Computational Semantics (IWCS)*, pages 51–62.

Aditya Gupta and Greg Durrett. 2019. Tracking discrete and continuous entity state for process understanding. In *Proceedings of the Third Workshop on Structured Prediction for NLP*, pages 7–12.

Kyle Hamilton, Aparna Nayak, Bojan Božić, and Luca Longo. 2022. Is neuro-symbolic ai meeting its promise in natural language processing? a structured review. *arXiv preprint arXiv:2202.12205*.

Matthew Honnibal, Ines Montani, Sofie Van Landeghem, and Adriane Boyd. 2020. spaCy: Industrial-strength Natural Language Processing in Python.

Hao Huang, Xiubo Geng, Jian Pei, Guodong Long, and Daxin Jiang. 2021. Reasoning over entity-action-location graph for procedural text understanding. In *Proceedings of the 59th Annual Meeting of the Association for Computational Linguistics and the 11th International Joint Conference on Natural Language Processing (Volume 1: Long Papers)*, pages 5100–5109.

Ghazaleh Kazeminejad. 2023. *Computational Lexical Resources for Explainable Natural Language Understanding*. Ph.D. thesis, University of Colorado at Boulder.

Ghazaleh Kazeminejad, Martha Palmer, Susan Windisch Brown, and James Pustejovsky. 2022. Componential analysis of english verbs. *Frontiers in Artificial Intelligence*, 5.

Ghazaleh Kazeminejad, Martha Palmer, Tao Li, and Vivek Srikumar. 2021a. Automatic entity state annotation using the verbnet semantic parser. In *Proceedings of The Joint 15th Linguistic Annotation Workshop (LAW) and 3rd Designing Meaning Representations (DMR) Workshop*, pages 123–132.

Ghazaleh Kazeminejad, Martha Palmer, Tao Li, and Vivek Srikumar. 2021b. Automatic entity state annotation using the VerbNet semantic parser. In *Proceedings of the Joint 15th Linguistic Annotation Workshop (LAW) and 3rd Designing Meaning Representations (DMR) Workshop*, pages 123–132, Punta Cana, Dominican Republic. Association for Computational Linguistics.

Jacob Devlin Ming-Wei Chang Kenton and Lee Kristina Toutanova. 2019. Bert: Pre-training of deep bidirectional transformers for language understanding. In *Proceedings of NAACL-HLT*, pages 4171–4186.

Paul R Kingsbury and Martha Palmer. 2002. From treebank to propbank. In *LREC*, pages 1989–1993.

Inderjeet Mani and James Pustejovsky. 2012. *Interpreting motion: Grounded representations for spatial language*. 5. Oxford University Press.

Bhavana Dalvi Mishra, Lifu Huang, Niket Tandon, Wen-tau Yih, and Peter Clark. 2018. Tracking state changes in procedural text: a challenge dataset and models for process paragraph comprehension. *arXiv preprint arXiv:1805.06975*.

Bhavana Dalvi Mishra, Niket Tandon, Antoine Bosselut, Wen-tau Yih, and Peter Clark. 2019. Everything happens for a reason: Discovering the purpose of actions in procedural text. *arXiv preprint arXiv:1909.04745*.

James Pustejovsky and Jessica L Moszkowicz. 2011. The qualitative spatial dynamics of motion in language. *Spatial Cognition & Computation*, 11(1):15–44.

Danilo Ribeiro, Thomas Hinrichs, Maxwell Crouse, Kenneth Forbus, Maria Chang, and Michael Witbrock. 2019. Predicting state changes in procedural text using analogical question answering. In *7th Annual Conference on Advances in Cognitive Systems*.

Karin Kipper Schuler. 2005. *VerbNet: A broad-coverage, comprehensive verb lexicon*. University of Pennsylvania.

Robyn Speer, Joshua Chin, and Catherine Havasi. 2017. Conceptnet 5.5: An open multilingual graph of general knowledge. In *Thirty-first AAAI conference on artificial intelligence*.

Leonard Talmy. 1988. Force dynamics in language and cognition. *Cognitive science*, 12(1):49–100.

Niket Tandon, Bhavana Dalvi, Keisuke Sakaguchi, Peter Clark, and Antoine Bosselut. 2019. Wiqa: A dataset for "what if..." reasoning over procedural text. In *Proceedings of the 2019 Conference on Empirical Methods in Natural Language Processing and the 9th International Joint Conference on Natural Language Processing (EMNLP-IJCNLP)*, pages 6076–6085.

Jialong Tang, Hongyu Lin, Meng Liao, Yaojie Lu, Xianpei Han, Le Sun, Weijian Xie, and Jin Xu. 2022. Procedural text understanding via scene-wise evolution. In *Proceedings of the AAAI Conference on Artificial Intelligence*, volume 36, pages 11367–11375.

Jizhi Tang, Yansong Feng, and Dongyan Zhao. 2020. Understanding procedural text using interactive entity networks. In *Proceedings of the 2020 Conference on Empirical Methods in Natural Language Processing (EMNLP)*, pages 7281–7290.

Shubham Toshniwal, Patrick Xia, Sam Wiseman, Karen Livescu, and Kevin Gimpel. 2021. On generalization in coreference resolution. In *Proceedings of the Fourth Workshop on Computational Models of Reference, Anaphora and Coreference*, pages 111–120.

Zhihan Zhang, Xiubo Geng, Tao Qin, Yunfang Wu, and Daxin Jiang. 2021. Knowledge-aware procedural text understanding with multi-stage training. In *Proceedings of the Web Conference 2021*, pages 3512–3523.

Leveraging Active Learning to Minimise SRL Annotation Across Corpora

Skatje Myers
University of Colorado at Boulder
skatje.myers@colorado.edu

Martha Palmer
University of Colorado at Boulder
mpalmer@colorado.edu

Abstract

In this paper we investigate the application of active learning to semantic role labeling (SRL) using Bayesian Active Learning by Disagreement (BALD). Our new predicate-focused selection method quickly improves efficiency on three different specialised domain corpora. This is encouraging news for researchers wanting to port SRL to domain specific applications. Interestingly, with the large and diverse *OntoNotes* corpus, the sentence selection approach, that collects a larger number of predicates, taking more time to annotate, fares better than the predicate approach. In this paper, we analyze both the selections made by our two selections methods for the various domains and the differences between these corpora in detail.

1 Introduction

The majority of natural language processing (NLP) systems are reliant on manual annotations to train supervised models. Although semi-supervised and unsupervised methods are frequently employed to help adapt models to new domains, human annotation remains the gold standard for quality input. Due to the high cost of human annotation, especially if the task requires expert knowledge, and the time-intensive process, this can be daunting for many applications.

Active learning (AL) has been shown to reduce annotation requirements for a variety of NLP tasks (Zhang et al., 2022) by selecting more informative instances that are most likely to fill gaps in the model's knowledge.

In this paper, we focus specifically on the NLP task of semantic role labeling (SRL). The goal of SRL is to identify and label the who, what, and when of predicates in a sentence. This information can be used as features in downstream applications such as information extraction (MacAvaney et al., 2017), machine translation (Marcheggiani et al., 2018), and features prominently in Abstract Meaning Representation (AMR) applications (Banarescu et al., 2013).

In this paper, we propose a new selection strategy tuned for SRL that is based off of previous methods of using model dropout to approximate a Gaussian process (Siddhant and Lipton, 2018). We compare this to prior work on AL selection for SRL (Myers and Palmer, 2021) on four corpora in a variety of domains: ecology, earthquakes, clinical notes, and the large multi-genre *OntoNotes* corpus.

Since sentences in most domains typically contain multiple predicates, there are often redundancies in choosing predicates to annotate on the sentence level. Although a sentence may contain a particularly informative predicate, annotating high-frequency verbs such as "be" that co-occur in the sentence may not be beneficial. We instead use a method to select specific predicate-argument structures and compare the impact on performance as compared to selecting whole sentences instead.

This method is a natural extension that allows us to even better leverage the focused annotation that active learning offers by using a more granular approach. While we find consistent early benefit in the more domain-specific corpora, this finer-grained approach proves to be slower for the more diverse *OntoNotes*.

We also explore the statistical differences between these corpora, the selections our algorithm makes, and test a variety of selection batch sizes in order to shed light on expectations for use in future domains.

2 Background

Proposition Bank (PropBank) (Palmer et al., 2005) is verb-oriented semantic representation consisting of a predicate and its arguments. Predicates are given a *roleset ID*, which distinguishes the sense of the word, such as play.01 (*to play a game*) or play.02 (*to play a role*). Each roleset has its own list of permissible semantic roles, or arguments, for

*Proceedings of the The 12th Joint Conference on Lexical and Computational Semantics (*SEM 2023)*, pages 399–408
July 13-14, 2023 ©2023 Association for Computational Linguistics

play.01	
play a game	
ARG0	player
ARG1	game
ARG2	equipment
ARG3	opponent

Table 1: PropBank roleset for *play.01*

that predicate, such as ARG0 (typically the agent of the action). Additionally, all rolesets support the use of a set of modifier arguments such as location (ARGM-LOC) and direction (ARGM-DIR). These arguments are annotated for the constituent spans of the sentence. For example:

[$_{\text{ARG0}}$ I] [$_{\text{Pred}}$ played] [$_{\text{ARG1}}$ chess] [$_{\text{ARG3}}$ against him].

Active learning is an iterative process by which data is selected for annotation using the model's own confidence. After initially training the model on a small amount of annotated data (referred to as the seed set), each unlabeled instance is predicted by the model and those that the model is least certain about (conventionally, by the model's outputs) are presumed to be more informative to learn from than those that the model has high certainty about. The uncertain instances can then be manually annotated and added into the training pool for the next training iteration. This process can repeast until either the performance is no longer significantly increasing or time/budget has been exhausted.

Previous work has shown that neural networks tend to be overconfident in their predictions, owing to their nonlinearity and tendency to overfit (Gal and Ghahramani, 2016)(Dong et al., 2018). Therefore, more recent work (Siddhant and Lipton, 2018) (Shen et al., 2017) has explored using Bayesian Active Learning by Disagreement (Houlsby et al., 2011) (BALD) rather than model outputs as a way of selecting informative instances for active learning for SRL and other NLP tasks. By using dropout during prediction, multiple forward passes can be treated as Monte Carlo draws from a stochastic model. The instances that have more disagreement amongst the predictions are considered to be more informative for the model to learn from.

Myers and Palmer (2021) applied BALD to SRL by calculating disagreement among five forward passes of the trained model using dropout, breaking down agreement scores by individual argument labels. We describe this in more detail in Section 4.1. The active learner used two alternative methods to select sentences: 1) using the average disagreement score amongst all predicates in the sentence (BALD-AP) or 2) by choosing the sentences that contain the single lowest scoring predicate (BALD-LSP). Since BALD-LSP performed best, we compare our predicate-focused BALD strategy against this method on both corpora used previously (*OntoNotes* and *THYME Colon*) as well as two new geoscience corpora from the ClearEarth project (Duerr et al., 2016).

3 Data

We aim to provide a demonstration of active learning for SRL across a variety of domains and sublanguages (Kittredge, 1982). Some knowledge domains exhibit narrow lexical, syntactic, and semantic structures that distinguish them from more general-purpose domains. This can lower performance dramatically when testing with an off-the-shelf general purpose model. Special techniques that take these domain specific-structures into account are needed for adapting NLP tools to these domains, as illustrated below.

THYME Colon is comprised of unstructured clinical notes relating to treatment of colon cancer (Albright et al., 2013). This corpus contains specialised medical vocabulary for a narrow domain and a large number of formulaic sentences, such as the following example:

> Pathology demonstrated a tubular adenoma with moderate dysplasia.

This contains medical terminology (tubular adenoma, dysplasia) as well as a non-standard use of *demonstrate*, which includes the shortening of *The pathology report* to simply *pathology*. This particular framing re-occurs frequently in THYME Colon, sometimes with *show* or *reveal* instead, and occasionally including the word *report* as in *pathology report*.

We also used two distinct geoscience domains from the ClearEarth project (Duerr et al., 2016):

- *Earthquakes* consists of 41k tokens of text from Wikipedia and education texts, and a glossary. This text includes specialised scientific language relating to earthquakes and plate tectonics, but also discussion of the history of the field at a high school reading level and content related to disasters. For example: *The ways that plates interact depend on their relative motion and whether oceanic or continental crust is at the edge of the lithospheric plate.*

- *Ecology* consists of 83k tokens of text from Wikipedia, educational websites, an ecology glossary, and Encyclopedia of Life. The scientific content covers genetics, evolution, reproduction, and food chains. For examples: *Anguis fragilis is an example of ovo-viviparity.* and *Alternatively, transcription factors can bind enzymes that modify the histones at the promoter.*

OntoNotes 5.0 (Weischedel et al., 2013) spans multiple genres, largely consisting of news sources, but also including telephone conversations, text from the New Testament, weblogs, and Usenet. This popular corpus serves as a broad purpose corpus for us, as opposed to the other more specialised domains.

We use a version of *OntoNotes* that does not include files that had no manual PropBank annotation performed. There still exist sentences within this version of the data that had only partial annotation, but we consider this to have a relatively small impact on performance.

Evaluation was performed on the standard test subset for each respective corpus.

4 Methods

We simulated active learning using AllenNLP's (Gardner et al., 2018) implementation of a state-of-the-art BERT-based SRL model (Shi and Lin, 2019).

In order to simulate active learning on each of these corpora, we partitioned the training subset of each corpus into 200 random sentences for seeding the learner, with the remainder used as the initial "unlabeled" pool for selection. The initial 200 seed sentences were the same across the three selection methods tested for each respective corpus.

After initially training on the seed set, we then select a batch of either 100 predicates or a number of sentences containing approximately 100 predicates to add to the training pool using the BALD PREDICATES or BALD SENTENCES strategy described below in Section 4.1 or by choosing 100 random predicates to simulate a passive learning approach. Results are reported on the test subset of the respective corpora and the model was retrained with the extended training pool. We continue iterations of selection and re-training until either all the data has been selected and moved into the training pool, or the experiment performances have sufficiently plateaued.

Our training procedure for this model used 25 epochs or stopped early with a patience of 5 based on the validation data for the relevant corpus.

4.1 Selection Methods

We use the BALD-LSP method tuned for SRL as described in Myers and Palmer (2021), which we will refer to in this paper as BALD SENTENCES for comparison.

After a model is trained, this method uses 10% dropout during 5 forward passes in order to generate multiple predictions for each instance in the unlabeled pool. For each predicate-argument structure in a sentence and each argument label type present in the predictions, we calculate how many of the 5 predictions do not match the mode predicted span. If all five predictions have different spans for an ARG1, for example, then this results in the highest possible disagreement score for ARG1.

After disagreement scores are calculated for each argument label, these scores are averaged to produce a score for the predicate. If there is only one predicate in a sentence, this is the score for the sentence. If a sentence has multiple predicates, the sentence is assigned the score of the predicate that had the most disagreement. The sentences with the highest scores are selected to be included in the next round of training.

Our BALD PREDICATES method is a more granular extension of this previous work. We use the same idea of scoring individual argument spans based on agreement and averaging them into a single score for a given predicate instance, but we do not combine the scores of all predicates within a given sentence. We instead use the score to choose specific predicate instances to add to the training pool

We also compare these two active learning methods against a passive baseline of selecting random predicate instances.

5 Results

We present the learning curves of the different selection methods for the four corpora are presented

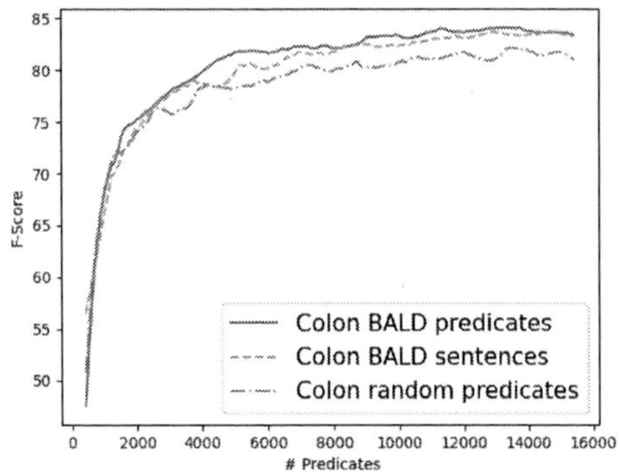

Figure 1: Performance of selection method by approximate number of predicates in the training pool on *THYME Colon* dataset.

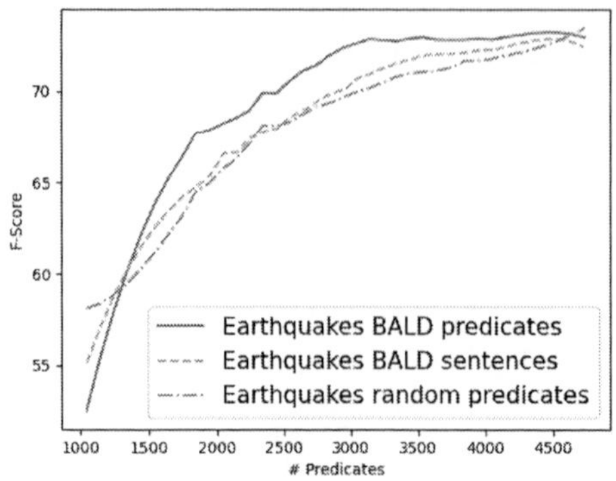

Figure 3: Performance of selection method by approximate number of predicates in the training pool on *ClearEarth Earthquakes* dataset.

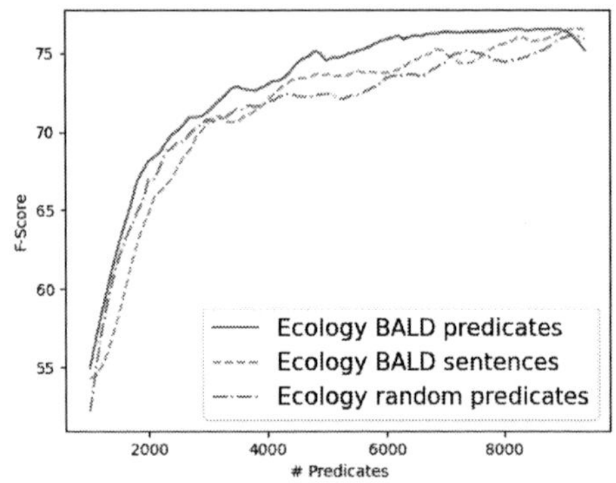

Figure 2: Performance of selection method by approximate number of predicates in the training pool on *ClearEarth Ecology* dataset.

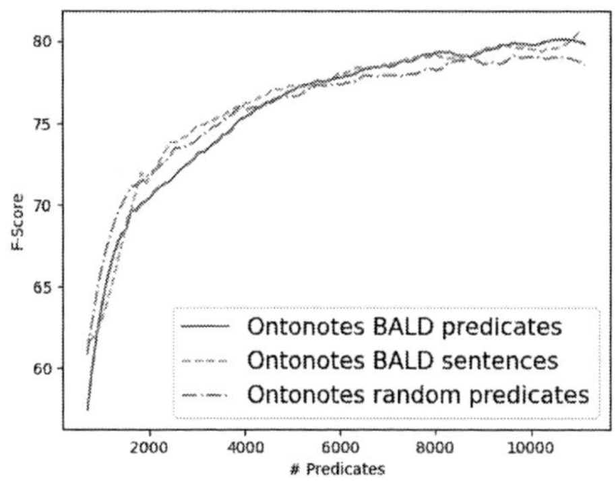

Figure 4: Performance of selection method by approximate number of predicates in the training pool on *OntoNotes*.

in Figures 1, 2, 3, and 4. Natural variability in training the model produces some amount of noise, most prominently during the early iterations. In order to improve readability of these learning curves, we applied a Savitzky–Golay filter using a window of 15 data points and using a cubic polynomial.

We see consistent benefits of the BALD PREDICATES method at different points depending on the corpus.

For *Colon*, *Ecology*, and *Earthquakes* we begin to see consistent improvement for the BALD PREDICATES method over the other methods by approximately 1,500-2,000 predicates. On the other hand, for *OntoNotes*, it only catches up to random selection around 4,500 predicates and begins to improve over it around 7,000 predicates. For this corpus, BALD SENTENCES performs better.

6 Analysis of Selections

In order to better understand the differences between the selection processes used and their variance across datasets, we examine the selections within each batch.

6.1 Diversity

By selecting multiple predicates or sentences in each iteration, we expect that there may be redundancies. For example, if the model has never seen a given predicate, it will likely have low confidence in its predictions for it. We present a study of the diversity of the selections over time.

We first observe the amount of redundancy within BALD PREDICATES. This method is choosing multiple instances of the same predicate lemma, as observed in Figure 5. In the two *ClearEarth* corpora we have analysed in this regard, which both ran to completion on the training data, approximately 25 of the 100 predicates are duplicates in the early phase of active learning and with redundancy getting worse as the process gets closer to completion. The results for *Colon* contain approximately similar amounts of redundancy for the duration we trained it.

While there may sometimes be value in selecting the same lemma in order to obtain multiple senses of the same predicate, minimising this could prove beneficial. Future work could be done to study the effect of limiting the selection batch to unique lemmas.

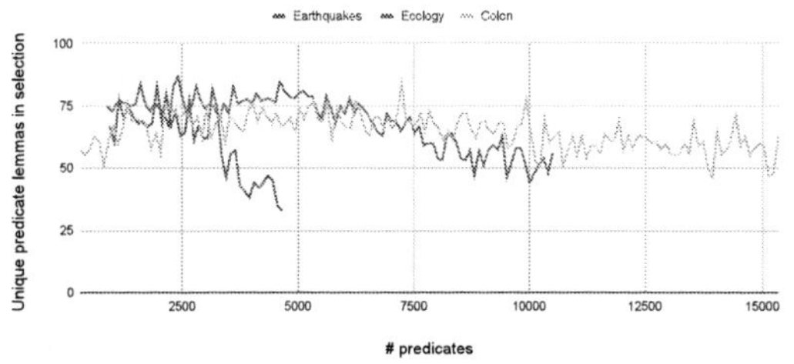

Figure 5: Number of unique predicate lemmas selected in each batch by the BALD PREDICATES method over iterations.

Additionally, the BALD PREDICATES method is capable of selecting multiple instances from the same sentence. While this may be beneficial, it's also possible that learning from just one predicate in the sentence will provide information that can improve agreement on other instances in the sentence.

We have found that for *Colon*, a randomly selected batch of 100 predicates contains 3 duplicate sentences on average, while the selections by BALD PREDICATES contain only 1 duplicate on average. For the *Ecology* corpus, both methods pick 3 duplicate sentences on average. This appears indicative that this is not a significant factor that necessitates correction.

Furthermore, we are interested in the sentence-level semantic redundancies within batches. Using the pre-trained all-mpnet-base-v2 model (Song et al., 2020), we can calculate the average pairwise cosine similarity between the unique sentences within batches. In Figure 6, we find that both active learning methods contain more sentence-level similarity on average (0.26) than what is chosen through random selection (0.19) from the *THYME Colon* corpus.

We can see clear signs of the active learner choosing sentences that would be wasteful to have

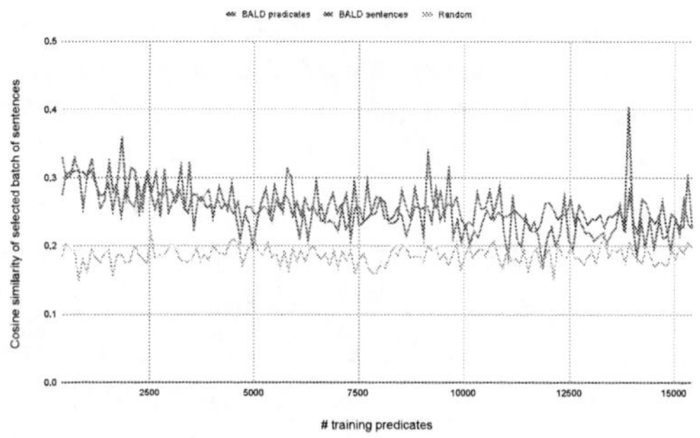

Figure 6: Average pairwise cosine similarity of selected sentences in each batch over iterations on *THYME Colon*.

annotated. In one such batch, BALD SENTENCES selected 29 out of the 52 sentences where the sentences were all of the same basic form, but with varying AJCC cancer staging designations:

With available material: AJCC ypT1N0MX
With available surgical material [AJCC pT3N2Mx]

On the other hand, the difference in selection diversity is less pronounced on the other datasets. In Figure 7, we show the similarity in the selections on *ClearEarth Ecology*, where all methods average 0.20 across the iterations.

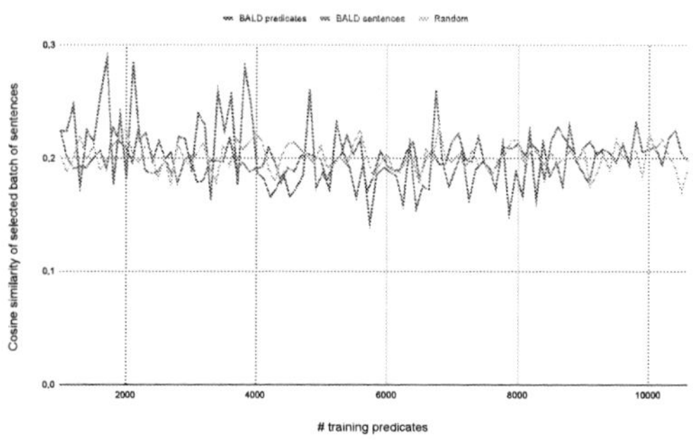

Figure 7: Average pairwise cosine similarity of selected sentences in each batch over iterations on *ClearEarth Ecology*.

6.2 Vocabulary Coverage

We hypothesised that a contributor to BALD PREDICATES's performance may be a rapid coverage of vocabulary, as predicates that involve unseen vocabulary could result in more disagreement. In Figure 8, we show the percentage of the unique vocabulary of the training set that is within the training pool as selections are made.

Across the datasets, we see varying results in how much BALD PREDICATES expedites vocabulary coverage. We find that BALD PREDICATES is not tending to choose unseen vocabulary compared to selecting predicates randomly for *Ecology*. On the other hand, active learning greatly accelerates this for *Ontonotes*, even after performance has largely plateaued. For *THYME Colon*, active learning provides an initial boost to vocabulary, but around the time that the performance plateaus, this decelerates below random.

6.3 Disagreement

For BALD PREDICATES, we calculate an average disagreement score for each selected batch. While early batches primarily contain predicates for which all predictions are in full disagreement, we see this disagreement trend downwards as performance plateaus. This is presented in Figure 9.

Although performance on *OntoNotes* has largely plateaued around an F-score of 79 by 7.5k training predicates, we know that training this model on the full dataset yields another 4 points. Since the disagreement scores of batches chosen by BALD PREDICATES is still over 70%, this seems indicative of the additional further performance to be gained, albeit at a slow pace that gets little value for the effort. In contrast, *Colon* plateaued around 82, but the benefits of annotating the remaining 50k predicates only provides an additional increase of 1 point. With the disagreement score having fallen below 45%, this points toward an appropriate stopping point.

7 Corpus Analysis

Although the new predicate selection method offers immediate benefit over BALD SENTENCES for the three sublanguage corpora, this is inconsistent with the result on *OntoNotes*, where selecting BALD SENTENCES is more advantageous until about 7k predicates. In order to better understand the possible reasons for this, we compare the make-up and distribution of the corpora. These statistics are presented in Table 2.

We use PropBank roleset ID's as our measure of polysemy, since we have gold standard annotation for them in all 4 corpora. Note that PropBank sense distinctions are fairly coarse-grained and were generally only created when there were differences between senses with respect to the semantic roles. VerbNet (Schuler, 2005), FrameNet (Baker et al., 1998) and WordNet (Miller, 1995) would all give much higher polysemy counts.

The largest and most diverse corpus in our experiments is *OntoNotes*, although we find that in terms of ratio of total tokens to predicates, unique rolesets, and unique tokens, *OntoNotes* is statistically more similar to the *THYME Colon Cancer* corpus than to either of the *ClearEarth* corpora. *OntoNotes* and *Colon* contain approximately one unique roleset per 376-403 tokens, whereas *Earthquakes* and *Ecology* contain one per 39 and 60 tokens, respectively.

Since *OntoNotes* covers a wider diversity of text types, it's unsurprising that it contains a much more diverse set of senses compared to the other corpora. While a lemma like "take" shows up with 25 different senses in *OntoNotes*, it only shows up in 8 senses in *Colon*.

For *OntoNotes*, only 30% of predicate occurrences are monosemous within the context of the corpus, whereas this figure is between 54%-61% for the other three corpora. 6% of the unique predicate lemmas within *OntoNotes* are seen in 3 or more rolesets, while this is true of only 2% of the set of lemmas in each of the other corpora.

We believe this polysemy factor may contribute to the predicate selection method being disproportionately slower to improve the learning curve on *OntoNotes* compared to the more focused domain corpora. BALD PREDICATES may be disadvantaged by more frequently choosing these rare senses even though they make up proportionally less of the training data and provide less value in terms of performance, but further investigation is needed.

	OntoNotes	Colon	Earthquakes	Ecology
Tokens	2.2 mil	522k	41k	83k
Unique tokens per token	44.55	36.88	8.42	10.43
Predicates	301k	57k	7.5k	15k
Tokens per predicate	7.41	9.11	39.63	60.45
Avg sentence length	18.74	11.33	23.39	24.48
Unique rolesets	5535	1389	1046	1376
Tokens per roleset	403	376	39	60
Predicate lemmas with 1 roleset	3829 (83.33%)	1340 (90.24%)	985 (91.20%)	1416 (92.73%)
Predicate lemmas with 2 rolesets	494 (10.75%)	112 (7.54%)	73 (6.76%)	80 (5.24%)
Predicate lemmas with 3+ rolesets	272 (5.92%)	33 (2.22%)	22 (2.04%)	31 (2.03%)
Monosemous predicate occurences	29.95%	55.02%	53.53%	60.94%

Table 2: Statistics about the four corpora.

8 Batch Sizes

Each iteration of active learning includes selecting an arbitrary number of instances to query. The number may be static, or dynamic with larger batches

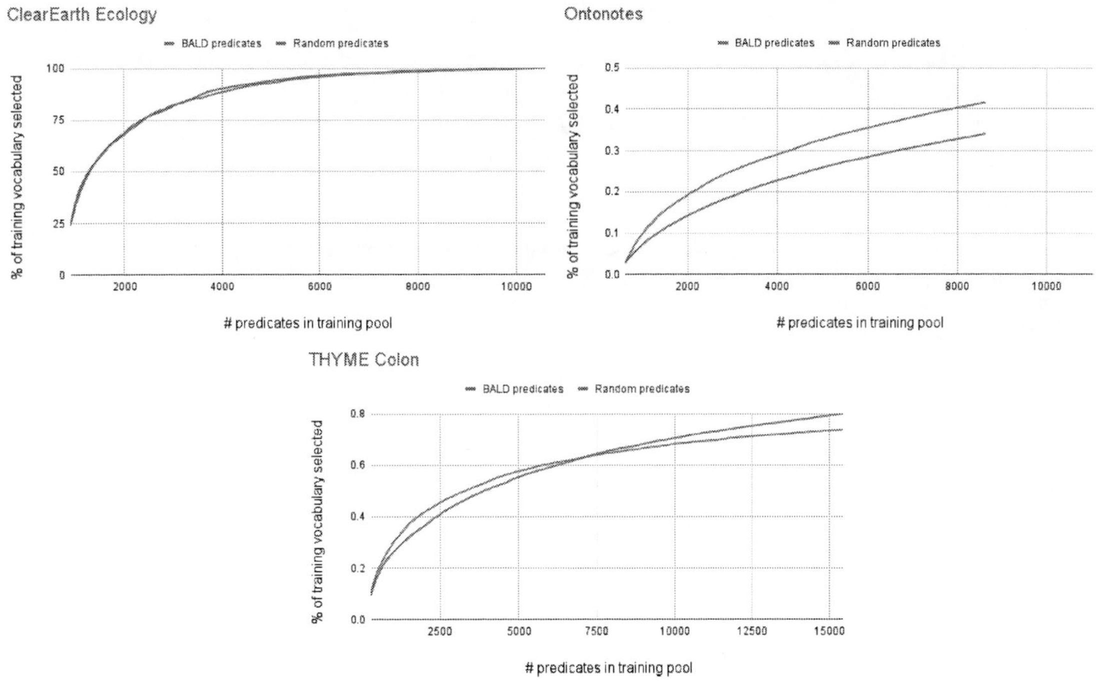

Figure 8: Percent coverage of training vocabulary in by number of predicates in training pool.

being selected in the early training process and smaller batches later on.

To maximally benefit from the model's feedback, in an ideal setup, each iteration would query for only one new instance, thereby minimizing the likelihood of selecting a batch of sentences with redundant information (Schohn and Cohn, 2000). Unfortunately, this leads to the process of active learning being significantly slower due to needing to re-train a model more often. Additionally, annotating a sentence at a time with long breaks in between may cost additional time on the part of the annotator due to mental context-switching and needing to load up appropriate software and resources. It would be more efficient for them to be able to annotate numerous examples in a row.

Our previous experiments testing the BALD PREDICATES method show positive results when selecting 100 predicates in a batch. This small batch size requires about 60 iterations before the learning curve plateaus for the Colon corpus. We examine the effect of larger batches on the learning curves for the *THYME Colon* and the two *ClearEarth* corpora.

8.1 Results

We used the BALD PREDICATES selection strategy with varying sizes of 100, 500, and 1000 query instances. These results are presented for three datasets in Figure 10, using datapoints on intervals of 1000 predicates.

Interestingly, changing the batch size has differing impacts on the datasets we examined this for. The *THYME Colon* corpus suffers very little from scaling all the way to 1000 predicates per selection batch. The results on Earthquakes show the clearest need for small batch sizes, while Ecology exhibits shifting performance over the course of iterations.

9 Conclusion and Future Work

In this paper, we've demonstrated that active learning can reduce annotation requirements for semantic role labeling across multiple domains by employing Bayesian Active Learning by Disagreement and using dropout to provide variability in predictions from the model. These predictions can be used to estimate the model's confidence in its predictions and select informative training instances to annotate.

Selecting predicate instances through the BALD PREDICATES method offers significant improvement in efficiency for *THYME Colon*, *ClearEarth Earthquakes* and *Ecology*, which have very focused domains. This method does not provide the same performance increase on the more general *OntoNotes* over the previous BALD SENTENCES, which selects whole sentences.

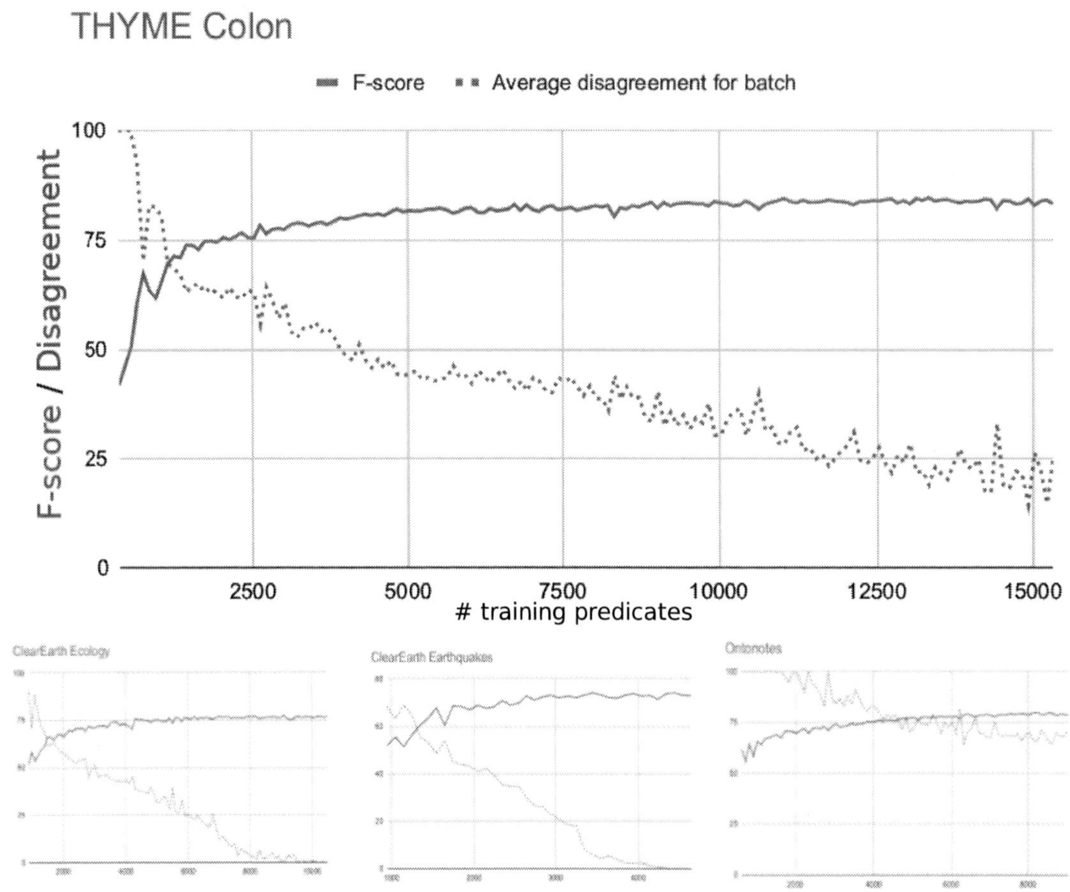

Figure 9: Average disagreement in selected batches decreases as iterations continue, while F-score increases and plateaus.

We have provided a statistical comparison of these corpora and offered some possible reasons for the divergence in performance, including a notable difference in polysemy within *OntoNotes* compared to the rest of the corpora.

Additionally, we examined the diversity of the selected predicates and sentences for BALD PREDICATES. Although these results vary across the different datasets, it indicates a couple potential avenues of future improvement. Reducing sentence-level semantic similarity seems of particular relevance to the *THYME Colon* corpus. We have also identified redundancies in the predicates chosen in each batch by BALD PREDICATES.

We also presented the change in model prediction disagreements over iterations as compared to model performance, which could be beneficial to determine when the costs of further annotation outweigh the additional gains that the model can provide.

Since the choice of how many selections to take on each iteration cannot be tuned for in real-world use of active learning, we have attempted to shed light on the levels of impact to expect on several different corpora, which vary in how sensitive they are to larger batches. We find that further investigation is needed to determine the most significant factors causing these differences so that future applications of active learning to SRL can predict the most ideal selection batch size that balances performance against training time for their target domain.

Limitations

While it reduces annotation costs, AL can be computationally intensive and its success is correlated to the number of training iterations. Whether this will be a net savings for a given project may vary from case to case, depending on computing resource availability and annotator costs. The work-

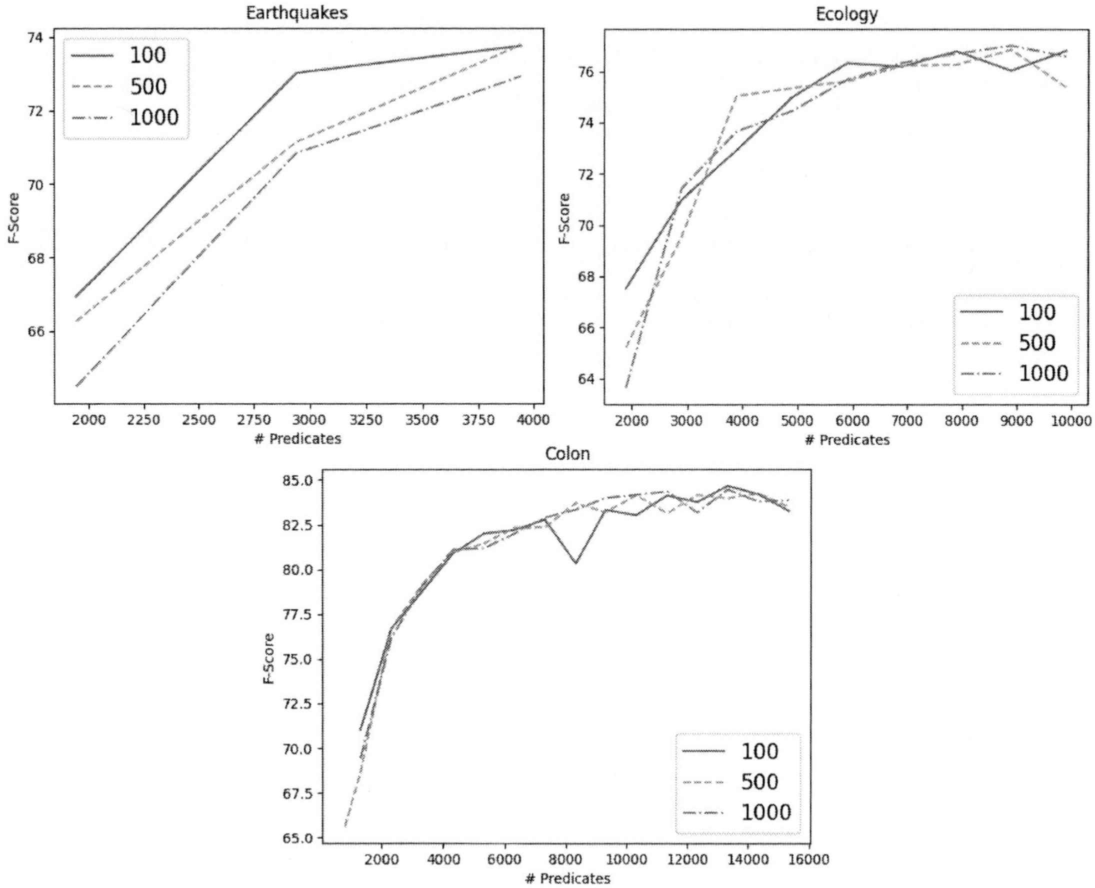

Figure 10: Performance of using BALD PREDICATES, selecting varying numbers of predicates per iteration.

flow of annotating and re-training may not be feasible in the budgetary constraints that inherently make AL desirable over randomly annotating training data.

Partial SRL annotation of sentences or documents may not be desirable in projects that simultaneously annotate other things, such as AMRs or coreference, which rely on whole-sentence or whole-document annotation.

Acknowledgments

We gratefully acknowledge the support of a sub-award from RPI on DARPA KAIROS Program No. FA8750-19-2-1004, a sub-award from Harvard Children's on NIH: 5R01LM010090-09 (THYME-3, Temporal Relation Discovery for Clinical Text), and NSF ACI 1443085: DIBBS (Porting Practical NLP and ML Semantics from Biomedicine to the Earth, Ice and Life Sciences). Any opinions, findings, and conclusions or recommendations expressed in this material are those of the authors and do not necessarily reflect the views of DARPA, NSF, NIST, or the U.S. government.

References

Daniel Albright, Arrick Lanfranchi, Anwen Fredriksen, IV Styler, William F, Colin Warner, Jena D Hwang, Jinho D Choi, Dmitriy Dligach, Rodney D Nielsen, James Martin, Wayne Ward, Martha Palmer, and Guergana K Savova. 2013. Towards comprehensive syntactic and semantic annotations of the clinical narrative. *Journal of the American Medical Informatics Association*, 20(5):922–930.

Collin F Baker, Charles J Fillmore, and John B Lowe. 1998. The berkeley framenet project. In *COLING 1998 Volume 1: The 17th International Conference on Computational Linguistics*.

Laura Banarescu, Claire Bonial, Shu Cai, Madalina Georgescu, Kira Griffitt, Ulf Hermjakob, Kevin Knight, Philipp Koehn, Martha Palmer, and Nathan Schneider. 2013. Abstract meaning representation for sembanking. In *Proceedings of the 7th linguistic annotation workshop and interoperability with discourse*, pages 178–186.

Li Dong, Chris Quirk, and Mirella Lapata. 2018. Confidence modeling for neural semantic parsing. In *Proceedings of the 56th Annual Meeting of the Association for Computational Linguistics (Volume 1: Long Papers)*, pages 743–753, Melbourne, Australia. Association for Computational Linguistics.

R. Duerr, A. Thessen, C. J. Jenkins, M. Palmer, S. Myers, and S. Ramdeen. 2016. The ClearEarth Project: Preliminary Findings from Experiments in Applying the CLEARTK NLP Pipeline and Annotation Tools Developed for Biomedicine to the Earth Sciences. In *AGU Fall Meeting Abstracts*, volume 2016, pages IN11B–1625.

Yarin Gal and Zoubin Ghahramani. 2016. Dropout as a bayesian approximation: Representing model uncertainty in deep learning. In *Proceedings of the 33rd International Conference on International Conference on Machine Learning - Volume 48*, ICML'16, page 1050–1059. JMLR.org.

Matt Gardner, Joel Grus, Mark Neumann, Oyvind Tafjord, Pradeep Dasigi, Nelson F. Liu, Matthew Peters, Michael Schmitz, and Luke Zettlemoyer. 2018. AllenNLP: A deep semantic natural language processing platform. In *Proceedings of Workshop for NLP Open Source Software (NLP-OSS)*, pages 1–6, Melbourne, Australia. Association for Computational Linguistics.

Neil Houlsby, Ferenc Huszár, Zoubin Ghahramani, and Máté Lengyel. 2011. Bayesian active learning for classification and preference learning. *arXiv preprint arXiv:1112.5745*.

Richard Kittredge. 1982. Sublanguages. *American Journal of Computational Linguistics*, 8(2):79–84.

Sean MacAvaney, Arman Cohan, and Nazli Goharian. 2017. GUIR at SemEval-2017 task 12: A framework for cross-domain clinical temporal information extraction. In *Proceedings of the 11th International Workshop on Semantic Evaluation (SemEval-2017)*, pages 1024–1029, Vancouver, Canada. Association for Computational Linguistics.

Diego Marcheggiani, Jasmijn Bastings, and Ivan Titov. 2018. Exploiting semantics in neural machine translation with graph convolutional networks. In *Proceedings of the 2018 Conference of the North American Chapter of the Association for Computational Linguistics: Human Language Technologies, Volume 2 (Short Papers)*, pages 486–492, New Orleans, Louisiana. Association for Computational Linguistics.

George A Miller. 1995. Wordnet: a lexical database for english. *Communications of the ACM*, 38(11):39–41.

Skatje Myers and Martha Palmer. 2021. Tuning deep active learning for semantic role labeling. In *Proceedings of the 14th International Conference on Computational Semantics (IWCS)*, pages 212–221, Groningen, The Netherlands (online). Association for Computational Linguistics.

Martha Palmer, Daniel Gildea, and Paul Kingsbury. 2005. The Proposition Bank: An annotated corpus of semantic roles. *Computational Linguistics*, 31(1):71–106.

Greg Schohn and David Cohn. 2000. Less is more: Active learning with support vector machines. In *Proceedings of the Seventeenth International Conference on Machine Learning*, ICML '00, page 839–846, San Francisco, CA, USA. Morgan Kaufmann Publishers Inc.

Karin Kipper Schuler. 2005. *VerbNet: A broad-coverage, comprehensive verb lexicon*. University of Pennsylvania.

Yanyao Shen, Hyokun Yun, Zachary Lipton, Yakov Kronrod, and Animashree Anandkumar. 2017. Deep active learning for named entity recognition. In *Proceedings of the 2nd Workshop on Representation Learning for NLP*, pages 252–256, Vancouver, Canada. Association for Computational Linguistics.

Peng Shi and Jimmy Lin. 2019. Simple BERT models for relation extraction and semantic role labeling. *arXiv preprint arXiv:1904.05255*.

Aditya Siddhant and Zachary C. Lipton. 2018. Deep Bayesian active learning for natural language processing: Results of a large-scale empirical study. In *Proceedings of the 2018 Conference on Empirical Methods in Natural Language Processing*, pages 2904–2909, Brussels, Belgium. Association for Computational Linguistics.

Kaitao Song, Xu Tan, Tao Qin, Jianfeng Lu, and Tie-Yan Liu. 2020. Mpnet: Masked and permuted pre-training for language understanding. *arXiv preprint arXiv:2004.09297*.

Ralph Weischedel, Martha Palmer, Mitchell Marcus, Eduard Hovy, Sameer Pradhan, Lance Ramshaw, Nianwen Xue, Ann Taylor, Jeff Kaufman, Michelle Franchini, Mohammed El-Bachouti, Robert Belvin, and Ann Houston. 2013. OntoNotes Release 5.0.

Zhisong Zhang, Emma Strubell, and Eduard Hovy. 2022. A survey of active learning for natural language processing. In *Proceedings of the 2022 Conference on Empirical Methods in Natural Language Processing*, pages 6166–6190, Abu Dhabi, United Arab Emirates. Association for Computational Linguistics.

Estimating Semantic Similarity between In-Domain and Out-of-Domain Samples

Rhitabrat Pokharel and **Ameeta Agrawal**
Department of Computer Science
Portland State University
{pokharel,ameeta}@pdx.edu

Abstract

Prior work typically describes out-of-domain (OOD) or out-of-distribution (OODist) samples as those that originate from dataset(s) or source(s) different from the training set but for the same task. When compared to in-domain (ID) samples, the models have been known to usually perform poorer on OOD samples, although this observation is not consistent. Another thread of research has focused on OOD detection, albeit mostly using supervised approaches. In this work, we first consolidate and present a systematic analysis of multiple definitions of OOD and OODist as discussed in prior literature. Then, we analyze the performance of a model under ID and OOD/OODist settings in a principled way. Finally, we seek to identify an unsupervised method for reliably identifying OOD/OODist samples without using a trained model. The results of our extensive evaluation using 12 datasets from 4 different tasks suggest the promising potential of unsupervised metrics in this task.

1 Introduction

What happens when you train a machine learning model on a dataset and use it to predict a sample whose source is unknown? Would you fully rely on the model's prediction on the test sample? Basically, this situation is encountered in most real-world scenarios where the test sample may differ considerably from the training samples. Recent works show that models perform poorer on the samples that come from a different distribution (Gokhale et al., 2022). In many real-world scenarios, such as health and law, false predictions or misclassified results could have significant consequences, and as such identifying out-of-domain or out-of-distribution data beforehand is critical.

Previous works have defined OOD and OODist data in different ways or used them interchangeably. Early works define data that comes from a related but different domain as OOD (Dai et al., 2007), whereas OODist data has been defined as the data that might have been collected at a different time (Ovadia et al., 2019). In recent studies, (Chrysostomou and Aletras, 2022) use the term OOD to describe different datasets for the same task (e.g., SST, IMDb, and Yelp for sentiment classification), whereas (Lin et al., 2022) use OODist to describe the datasets that are not in the training set, including those that are subsets of the same dataset (e.g., PDTB 2.0 (Carlson et al., 2002)). In this paper, we first present a focused analysis of all the various terminologies used in this context in recent works.

Another thread of research has focused on identifying OOD/OODist samples, mostly through supervised methods (Varshney et al., 2022; Chiang and Lee, 2022; Gokhale et al., 2022). However, considering that trained models may not always be available, we take a complementary approach in this work to identify metric(s) that may be able to support OOD detection in an *unsupervised* manner.

The first part of our methodology focuses on establishing to what extent performance (e.g., accuracy) can inform the detection of OOD samples[1]. Our results indicate that indeed performance can serve as a reliable metric for estimating OODness, however, this requires a supervised model. To address this limitation, in the second part of this work, we explore several unsupervised metrics for estimating semantic similarity between the training and test samples. We hypothesize that an unsupervised metric which sufficiently correlates with performance, may be considered as a feasible alternative for detecting OOD samples.

The major contributions of this paper are:

- an in-depth exploration of the usage of the terms OOD and OODist in recent works;
- a systematic assessment of the effectiveness

[1] As formally distinguishing between the two terms remains beyond the scope of this paper, in this work we use the terms OOD and OODist interchangeably.

*Proceedings of the The 12th Joint Conference on Lexical and Computational Semantics (*SEM 2023)*, pages 409–416
July 13-14, 2023 ©2023 Association for Computational Linguistics

Paper	Setup	Term	Metrics	Task
Chrysostomou and Aletras (2022)	A	OOD	-	Sentiment classification
Le Berre et al. (2022)	A	OOD	Accuracy	MCQ
Lin et al. (2022)	A	OODist	-	Extractive QA
Nejadgholi et al. (2022)	A	OOD	AUC, F1	Sentiment classification
Chiang and Lee (2022)	A	OODist	Cosine similarity, Confidence score, Probability distribution	Sentiment classification
Mishra and Arunkumar (2022)	A	OODist	NLI diagnostics	NLI
Varshney et al. (2022)	A	OOD	Accuracy	NLI, Duplicate detection, Sentiment analysis, MCQ, Commonsense Reasoning
Omar et al. (2022)	A	OODist	Accuracy, Success rate, Error rate, Diversity, Fairness, IBP tightness, Robustness	Classification, Paraphrasing, NLI
Adila and Kang (2022)	A	OODist	Confidence, Variability	NLI
Singhal et al. (2022)	A	OOD	Accuracy	NLI, Phrase identification
Agrawal et al. (2022)	A	OOD	Accuracy	Visual QA
Aghazadeh et al. (2022)	A, B	OODist	Accuracy	Metaphorical knowledge
Chen et al. (2023)	A, B	OODist	Accuracy	Sentiment analysis, Toxicity detection, News Classification, Dialogue Intent Classification
Mai et al. (2022)	B	OODist	-	Anomaly detection
Garg et al. (2022)	B	OOD	Accuracy	Rating generation, Toxicity classification
Jin et al. (2021)	B	OOD	False Positive Ratio, AUROC, AUPR	Text Classification
Atwell et al. (2022)	C	OOD	h-discrepancy	Discourse parsing
Gokhale et al. (2022)	C	OOD	Accuracy, EM	NLI, QA, Image classification

Table 1: A survey of recent works using various setups to study OODist or OOD settings. Here, **A** describes the cases where the train set is from one dataset, and the test set from another dataset; **B** describes the scenario where the train and test sets are two subsets of the same dataset; and **C** is a combination of both A and B. The "Metrics" column represents the metrics, while the "Task" column lists the tasks studied in these papers. Note that several papers whose setup can be described as **A** use different terms.

of performance in estimating OODness, and an investigation of unsupervised approaches for identifying OODness;

- an extensive evaluation across four different tasks using a total of twelve datasets; we will also make our code available for facilitating reproducibility.

2 Related Work

Prior research has often used the terms OOD and OODist interchangeably. In some works, dataset X is described to be OODist to dataset Y if they are different datasets, but support the same task (Lin et al., 2022; Aghazadeh et al., 2022; Chiang and Lee, 2022; Mishra and Arunkumar, 2022; Omar et al., 2022; Adila and Kang, 2022), while in other works, the term OOD is used to describe the similar

Task	Datasets	train/ val/ test
Sentiment	IMDb, SST2, Yelp	3310/ 428/ 909
MCQ	SCIQ, CS, QASC	8134/ 926/ 920
Extractive QA	SQUAD, News, Trivia	61688/ -/ 4212
NLI	MNLI, WNLI, QNLI	635/ 71/ 146

Table 2: Task and dataset details

setting (Chrysostomou and Aletras, 2022; Le Berre et al., 2022; Nejadgholi et al., 2022; Varshney et al., 2022). Beyond that, while some consider different subsets of the same dataset to be OODist (Mai et al., 2022; Garg et al., 2022; Jin et al., 2021), others refer to these as OOD to describe distributionally different datasets (Atwell et al., 2022; Gokhale et al., 2022).

When it comes to detecting OOD or OODist samples, using the model's accuracy (Le Berre et al., 2022; Aghazadeh et al., 2022; Gokhale et al., 2022; Omar et al., 2022), input features, hidden features representations, and output probability distribution of the network layers (Chiang and Lee, 2022), or AUC and F1 score (Nejadgholi et al., 2022) have been well-studied. Table 1 presents a brief summary of some recent works.

3 Method

3.1 Problem Definition

Given two datasets, $\mathcal{X} = \{x_1, ..., x_m\}$ and $\mathcal{Y} = \{y_1, ..., y_m\}$, the goal is to assess the correlation between the performance of the two datasets under ID/OOD settings and their (semantic) similarity. The performance is measured by training a model on one of the datasets, say, $\mathcal{X}_{train}$ and testing it on the test set $\mathcal{X}_{test}$ which represents the ID setting, and $\mathcal{Y}_{test}$ representing the OOD setting. The ID similarity is computed by averaging the similarity between the instances of $\mathcal{X}_{train}$ and $\mathcal{X}_{test}$, while OOD similarity is measured between $\mathcal{X}_{train}$ and $\mathcal{Y}_{test}$.

3.2 Datasets

We study four different tasks using a total of 12 datasets (3 datasets for per task). We include the most common tasks that have been used in prior work.

(i) Sentiment Analysis: given a text, classify its sentiment as negative or positive.

(ii) Multiple Choice Question Answering (MCQ): given a question and a context, select the correct answer from a pool of possible answers.

(iii) Extractive Question Answering (QA): given a question and a context, find the answer to the question from the context.

(iv) Natural Language Inference (NLI): given a premise and a hypothesis, determine whether the hypothesis contradicts, entails, or is neutral with respect to the premise.

Table 2 presents the details of the datasets and the tasks. For sentiment classification, we use IMDb (Maas et al., 2011), SST2 (Socher et al., 2013), and Yelp (Zhang et al., 2015) datasets. We experiment with SCIQ (Welbl et al., 2017), CommonsenseQA (CS) (Talmor et al., 2019), and QASC (Khot et al., 2020) for the MCQ task. For the Extractive QA task, SQUAD, News, and Trivia (Fisch et al., 2019) datasets are selected from the MRQA dataset (note that since these datasets do not have a separate test set, we use the validation data as the test set). The NLI datasets include MNLI, QNLI, and WNLI from the GLUE benchmark (Wang et al., 2018). All the other datasets were accessed from the HuggingFace repository[2].

Data preparation: Prior work has largely overlooked the effect of an important aspect – dataset size – in such studies. As such, we control the dataset size as a variable in our study by maintaining the size of all train, validation (when available), and test splits for all three datasets per task by downsampling them to match the size of the **smallest dataset in each set**. For instance, all the splits of all three sentiment analysis datasets are downsampled to be of equal size. Additionally, we balance the number of instances for each class when possible (e.g., in the sentiment datasets).

3.3 Metrics

We use three categories of metrics, one for measuring the performance of the model, another for estimating the similarity between the two datasets,

[2]https://huggingface.co/datasets/

and the third for computing the correlation between performance and similarity.

Performance Metrics. We report accuracy for the classification tasks, i.e., sentiment analysis, MCQ, and NLI tasks, and F1 score for extractive Question Answering task to measure the correctness of model predictions.

Similarity Metrics. To estimate the closeness among the ID and OOD datasets, we use metrics related to semantic similarity (higher value means the samples are from nearby distributions) and semantic distance (higher value indicates less similarity). These include: ***(i) Cosine Similarity***: measures the distance between the samples from two sources[3]. ***(ii) Mauve Score***: measures the similarity between two texts[4] (Pillutla et al., 2021). ***(iii) Wasserstein Distance (Wstn)***: measures the distance between the two distributions and if the distributions overlap enough, then they are close to each other[5] (Weng, 2019). ***(iv) Jensen Shannon Distance (JSD)***: quantifies the similarity between two probability distributions, where the smaller the value, the closer the distributions[6] (Manning and Schutze, 1999).

Correlation Metrics. Lastly, we use two commonly used correlation metrics – Kendall Tau and Pearson[7] (we also experimented with Spearman which gave similar results), with the goal of understanding the relationship between performance and similarity of datasets under ID/OOD settings.

3.4 Measuring Performance and Similarity

For measuring the performance, we fine-tune a BERT `base` uncased model for 2 epochs on each $\mathcal{X}_{train}$ and test it on $\mathcal{X}_{test}$ (ID) and $\mathcal{Y}_{test}$ (OOD). For estimating the similarity between the ID and OOD datasets, we randomly sample two sets of 20 instances, $\mathcal{X}_{train20}$ and $\mathcal{Y}_{test20}$, and estimate pairwise similarity between all of these samples, obtaining a total of 400 similarity scores which are then averaged to compute the similarity.

4 Results and Discussion

Performance analysis: Table 3 presents the results of the performance experiments, where we observe that the model performance under ID settings is generally better than under OOD settings, except for three exceptions, suggesting that performance can indeed serve as a reasonably dependable met-

Trained on	Tested on	Performance
IMDb-train	IMDb-test	0.90
	Yelp-test	0.87
	SST2-test	0.17
SST2-train	SST2-test	0.89
	IMDb-test	0.21
	Yelp-test	0.16
Yelp-train	Yelp-test	0.93
	IMDb-test	0.86
	SST2-test	0.19
SCIQ-train	SCIQ-test	0.64
	QASC-test	0.18
	CS-test	0.34
CS-train	CS-test	0.49
	SCIQ-test	0.58
	QASC-test	0.84
QASC-train	QASC-test	0.92
	SCIQ-test	0.51
	CS-test	0.48
SQUAD-train	SQUAD-test	0.86
	News-test	0.51
	Trivia-test	0.55
News-train	News-test	0.66
	SQUAD-test	0.77
	Trivia-test	0.56
Trivia-train	Trivia-test	0.66
	SQUAD-test	0.52
	News-test	0.31
MNLI-train	MNLI-test	0.57
	WNLI-test	0.56
	QNLI-test	0.54
WNLI-train	WNLI-test	0.42
	MNLI-test	0.26
	QNLI-test	0.47
QNLI-train	QNLI-test	0.83
	MNLI-test	0.43
	WNLI-test	0.56

Table 3: Performance results under different ID/OOD settings. Instances where ID performance is better than OOD performance are indicated in blue.

[3]We estimate this using `word2vec` embeddings.

[4]We use the default embeddings (GPT-2) `https://pypi.org/project/mauve-text/`.

[5]We use the universal sentence encoder for estimating this.

[6]We used `word2vec` embeddings.

[7]`https://pandas.pydata.org/docs/reference/api/pandas.DataFrame.corr.html`

ric for detecting OOD. However, this requires a supervised model, which motivates us to explore unsupervised approaches for estimating OODness. It is worth noting that while Garg et al. (2022) found that OOD accuracy is less than the ID accuracy, this observation does not always hold true according to our analysis.

Correlation between performance and similarity: Figure 1 presents the heatmap visualizing the correlation (Kendall and Pearson) between performance and similarity metrics, across all 12 datasets for the four tasks (the full set of results is included in Appendix A). In looking at the results, we observe that according to Kendall Tau correlation analysis, Wasserstein distance (Wstn) shows the most consistent correlation (in 10 out of 12 cases), whereas according to Pearson correlation, both Wasserstein and Cosine are acceptable metrics (in 9 out of 12 cases). In all the scenarios, however, JSD is clearly the least correlated metric. This suggests the potential of unsupervised approaches in estimating OOD samples.

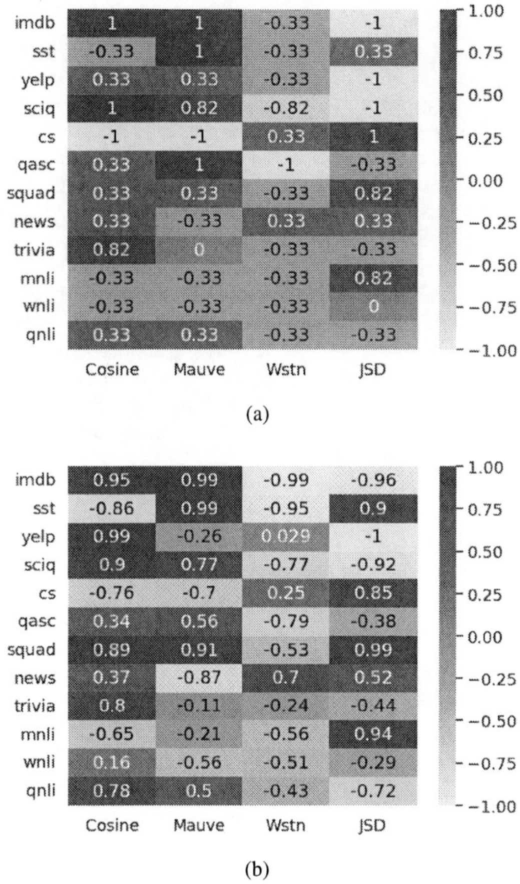

Figure 1: (a) Kendall and (b) Pearson correlation between performance and dataset similarity, evaluated over 12 datasets with each serving as an ID dataset once. For Cosine and Mauve, darker shades are desirable, whereas for Wstn and JSD, lighter shades indicate better correlation.

5 Conclusion

In this work, we aim to identify unsupervised approaches for identifying OOD samples. We conducted an in-depth analysis of different unsupervised similarity metrics and estimated their correlation with performance of a model under ID/OOD settings. Our findings indicate that Wasserstein distance presents a promising metric for determining OOD samples. The natural question of how to determine the appropriate threshold, however, remains to be explored in future work. Another direction worth exploring is to verify the robustness of these similarity metrics when estimated using different embeddings.

Limitations

While our analysis suggests some promising results, we acknowledge some limitations of this work such as:

- on some datasets, the ID performance was observed to be less than the OOD performance, and further investigation is needed to study this observation in detail and bring additional insights.
- all the analysis in this study focuses on datasets in English language, and it will be interesting to investigate whether our findings will generalize to other languages.

Acknowledgements

We are thankful to the anonymous reviewers for their valuable feedback.

References

Dyah Adila and Dongyeop Kang. 2022. Understanding out-of-distribution: A perspective of data dynamics. In *Proceedings on "I (Still) Can't Believe It's Not Better!" at NeurIPS 2021 Workshops*, volume 163 of *Proceedings of Machine Learning Research*, pages 1–8. PMLR.

Ehsan Aghazadeh, Mohsen Fayyaz, and Yadollah Yaghoobzadeh. 2022. Metaphors in pre-trained language models: Probing and generalization across datasets and languages.

Aishwarya Agrawal, Ivana Kajić, Emanuele Bugliarello, Elnaz Davoodi, Anita Gergely, Phil Blunsom, and Aida Nematzadeh. 2022. Rethinking evaluation practices in visual question answering: A case study on out-of-distribution generalization. *arXiv preprint arXiv:2205.12191*.

Katherine Atwell, Anthony Sicilia, Seong Jae Hwang, and Malihe Alikhani. 2022. The change that matters in discourse parsing: Estimating the impact of domain shift on parser error. In *Findings of the Association for Computational Linguistics: ACL 2022*, pages 824–845, Dublin, Ireland. Association for Computational Linguistics.

Lynn Carlson, Mary Ellen Okurowski, and Daniel Marcu. 2002. *RST discourse treebank*. Linguistic Data Consortium, University of Pennsylvania.

Sishuo Chen, Wenkai Yang, Xiaohan Bi, and Xu Sun. 2023. Fine-tuning deteriorates general textual out-of-distribution detection by distorting task-agnostic features. *arXiv preprint arXiv:2301.12715*.

David Cheng-Han Chiang and Hung-Yi Lee. 2022. Understanding, detecting, and separating out-of-distribution samples and adversarial samples in text classification. *CoRR*, abs/2204.04458.

George Chrysostomou and Nikolaos Aletras. 2022. An empirical study on explanations in out-of-domain settings.

Wenyuan Dai, Gui-Rong Xue, Qiang Yang, and Yong Yu. 2007. Co-clustering based classification for out-of-domain documents. In *Proceedings of the 13th ACM SIGKDD international conference on Knowledge discovery and data mining*, pages 210–219.

Adam Fisch, Alon Talmor, Robin Jia, Minjoon Seo, Eunsol Choi, and Danqi Chen. 2019. MRQA 2019 shared task: Evaluating generalization in reading comprehension. In *Proceedings of 2nd Machine Reading for Reading Comprehension (MRQA) Workshop at EMNLP*.

Saurabh Garg, Sivaraman Balakrishnan, Zachary C Lipton, Behnam Neyshabur, and Hanie Sedghi. 2022. Leveraging unlabeled data to predict out-of-distribution performance. *arXiv preprint arXiv:2201.04234*.

Tejas Gokhale, Swaroop Mishra, Man Luo, Bhavdeep Sachdeva, and Chitta Baral. 2022. *Generalized but not Robust?* comparing the effects of data modification methods on out-of-domain generalization and adversarial robustness. In *Findings of the Association for Computational Linguistics: ACL 2022*, pages 2705–2718, Dublin, Ireland. Association for Computational Linguistics.

Di Jin, Shuyang Gao, Seokhwan Kim, Yang Liu, and Dilek Hakkani-Tür. 2021. Towards textual out-of-domain detection without in-domain labels. *IEEE/ACM Transactions on Audio, Speech, and Language Processing*.

Tushar Khot, Peter Clark, Michal Guerquin, Peter Jansen, and Ashish Sabharwal. 2020. Qasc: A dataset for question answering via sentence composition. *arXiv:1910.11473v2*.

Guillaume Le Berre, Christophe Cerisara, Philippe Langlais, and Guy Lapalme. 2022. Unsupervised multiple-choice question generation for out-of-domain Q&A fine-tuning. In *Proceedings of the 60th Annual Meeting of the Association for Computational Linguistics (Volume 2: Short Papers)*, pages 732–738, Dublin, Ireland. Association for Computational Linguistics.

Bill Yuchen Lin, Sida Wang, Xi Lin, Robin Jia, Lin Xiao, Xiang Ren, and Scott Yih. 2022. On continual model refinement in out-of-distribution data streams. In *Proceedings of the 60th Annual Meeting of the Association for Computational Linguistics (Volume 1: Long Papers)*, pages 3128–3139, Dublin, Ireland. Association for Computational Linguistics.

Andrew L. Maas, Raymond E. Daly, Peter T. Pham, Dan Huang, Andrew Y. Ng, and Christopher Potts. 2011. Learning word vectors for sentiment analysis. In *Proceedings of the 49th Annual Meeting of the Association for Computational Linguistics: Human Language Technologies*, pages 142–150, Portland, Oregon, USA. Association for Computational Linguistics.

Kimberly T. Mai, Toby Davies, and Lewis D. Griffin. 2022. Self-supervised losses for one-class textual anomaly detection.

Christopher Manning and Hinrich Schutze. 1999. *Foundations of statistical natural language processing*. MIT press.

Swaroop Mishra and Anjana Arunkumar. 2022. A proposal to study "is high quality data all we need?".

Isar Nejadgholi, Kathleen Fraser, and Svetlana Kiritchenko. 2022. Improving generalizability in implicitly abusive language detection with concept activation vectors. In *Proceedings of the 60th Annual Meeting of the Association for Computational Linguistics (Volume 1: Long Papers)*, pages 5517–5529, Dublin, Ireland. Association for Computational Linguistics.

Marwan Omar, Soohyeon Choi, DaeHun Nyang, and David Mohaisen. 2022. Robust Natural Language Processing: Recent Advances, Challenges, and Future Directions. *arXiv e-prints*, page arXiv:2201.00768.

Yaniv Ovadia, Emily Fertig, Jie Ren, Zachary Nado, David Sculley, Sebastian Nowozin, Joshua Dillon, Balaji Lakshminarayanan, and Jasper Snoek. 2019.

Can you trust your model's uncertainty? evaluating predictive uncertainty under dataset shift. *Advances in neural information processing systems*, 32.

Krishna Pillutla, Swabha Swayamdipta, Rowan Zellers, John Thickstun, Sean Welleck, Yejin Choi, and Zaid Harchaoui. 2021. MAUVE: Measuring the gap between neural text and human text using divergence frontiers. In *Advances in Neural Information Processing Systems*.

Prasann Singhal, Jarad Forristal, Xi Ye, and Greg Durrett. 2022. Assessing out-of-domain language model performance from few examples. *arXiv preprint arXiv:2210.06725*.

Richard Socher, Alex Perelygin, Jean Wu, Jason Chuang, Christopher D. Manning, Andrew Ng, and Christopher Potts. 2013. Recursive deep models for semantic compositionality over a sentiment treebank. In *Proceedings of the 2013 Conference on Empirical Methods in Natural Language Processing*, pages 1631–1642, Seattle, Washington, USA. Association for Computational Linguistics.

Alon Talmor, Jonathan Herzig, Nicholas Lourie, and Jonathan Berant. 2019. CommonsenseQA: A question answering challenge targeting commonsense knowledge. In *Proceedings of the 2019 Conference of the North American Chapter of the Association for Computational Linguistics: Human Language Technologies, Volume 1 (Long and Short Papers)*, pages 4149–4158, Minneapolis, Minnesota. Association for Computational Linguistics.

Neeraj Varshney, Swaroop Mishra, and Chitta Baral. 2022. ILDAE: Instance-level difficulty analysis of evaluation data. In *Proceedings of the 60th Annual Meeting of the Association for Computational Linguistics (Volume 1: Long Papers)*, pages 3412–3425, Dublin, Ireland. Association for Computational Linguistics.

Alex Wang, Amanpreet Singh, Julian Michael, Felix Hill, Omer Levy, and Samuel R Bowman. 2018. Glue: A multi-task benchmark and analysis platform for natural language understanding. *arXiv preprint arXiv:1804.07461*.

Johannes Welbl, Nelson F Liu, and Matt Gardner. 2017. Crowdsourcing multiple choice science questions. *arXiv preprint arXiv:1707.06209*.

Lilian Weng. 2019. From gan to wgan. *ArXiv*, abs/1904.08994.

Xiang Zhang, Junbo Zhao, and Yann LeCun. 2015. Character-level Convolutional Networks for Text Classification. *arXiv:1509.01626 [cs]*.

A Experimental Results

Trained	Tested	Model Accuracy	Cosine	Mauve	Wstn	JSD
IMDb	IMDb	0.90	0.92	1	0.004	0.21
IMDb	Yelp	0.87	0.87	0.91	0.0039	0.26
IMDb	SST2	0.17	0.78	0.42	0.0052	0.36
SST2	SST2	0.89	0.66	0.99	0.0032	0.46
SST2	IMDb	0.21	0.77	0.22	0.0051	0.38
SST2	Yelp	0.16	0.72	0.004	0.0046	0.41
Yelp	Yelp	0.93	0.86	0.98	0.0036	0.26
Yelp	IMDb	0.86	0.87	0.76	0.0041	0.27
Yelp	SST2	0.19	0.73	0.94	0.0038	0.4
SCIQ	SCIQ	0.64	0.82	1	0.004	0.33
SCIQ	QASC	0.18	0.66	0.01	0.008	0.46
SCIQ	CS	0.34	0.78	1	0.004	0.37
CS	CS	0.49	0.71	0.94	0.003	0.45
CS	SCIQ	0.58	0.62	0.01	0.007	0.48
CS	QASC	0.84	0.61	0.004	0.005	0.49
QASC	QASC	0.92	0.75	1	0.003	0.4
QASC	SCIQ	0.51	0.78	0.99	0.004	0.38
QASC	CS	0.48	0.66	0.004	0.006	0.48
SQUAD	SQUAD	0.86	0.84	0.99	0.0037	0.34
SQUAD	NEWS	0.51	0.82	0.32	0.0041	0.33
SQUAD	TRIVIA	0.55	0.81	0.04	0.0059	0.33
NEWS	NEWS	0.66	0.89	0.91	0.0036	0.23
NEWS	SQUAD	0.77	0.86	0.11	0.0046	0.31
NEWS	TRIVIA	0.56	0.84	0.89	0.0039	0.27
TRIVIA	TRIVIA	0.66	0.88	0.99	0.0031	0.23
TRIVIA	SQUAD	0.52	0.82	0.04	0.0062	0.34
TRIVIA	NEWS	0.31	0.82	0.99	0.0042	0.29
MNLI	MNLI	0.57	0.72	0.97	0.0035	0.43
MNLI	WNLI	0.56	0.71	0.27	0.0032	0.43
MNLI	QNLI	0.54	0.73	0.99	0.0037	0.42
WNLI	WNLI	0.42	0.74	0.79	0.0032	0.41
WNLI	MNLI	0.26	0.68	0.66	0.0036	0.46
WNLI	QNLI	0.47	0.67	0.004	0.0035	0.46
QNLI	QNLI	0.83	0.75	0.97	0.0036	0.41
QNLI	MNLI	0.43	0.64	0.66	0.0039	0.45
QNLI	WNLI	0.56	0.58	0.01	0.0034	0.48

Table 4: The results for the sentiment, MCQ, extractive QA, and NLI datasets.

Query Generation Using GPT-3 for CLIP-Based Word Sense Disambiguation for Image Retrieval

Xiaomeng Pan, Zhousi Chen, Mamoru Komachi[*]
Tokyo Metropolitan University
{pan-xiaomeng@ed., chen-zhousi@ed., komachi@}tmu.ac.jp

Abstract

In this study, we propose using the GPT-3 as a query generator for the backend of CLIP as an implicit word sense disambiguation (WSD) component for the *SemEval 2023* shared task *Visual Word Sense Disambiguation* (VWSD). We confirmed previous findings — human-like prompts adapted for WSD with quotes benefit both CLIP and GPT-3, whereas plain phrases or poorly templated prompts yield the worst results. Our code is available at `https://github.com/pxm427/WSD-for-IR`.

1 Introduction

The *SemEval 2023* shared task VWSD[1] combines WSD and Image Retrieval (IR), which aims to select a correct image among ten candidates using a phrase containing ambiguous words. Neural models are likely to be attracted by frequent tokens, labels, and senses of ambiguous words, particularly in limited contexts. We determined that CLIP (Radford et al., 2021) fails to find the correct images using phrases with the ambiguous words of frequent senses even enhanced with contrastive learning on large-scale data.

As shown in Figure 1, given phrase *"Andromeda tree"*, the pretrained CLIP selected incorrect images that focused on either constellation "Andromeda" or part of "tree", neglecting the phrase's meaning entirely. This sample demonstrates ambiguity as a challenge for state-of-the-art neural models. Therefore, we exploited GPT-3 (Brown et al., 2020), a large language model (LLM), for its pretrained knowledge as implicit sense disambiguation and phrase context enrichment for this task.

Prompt engineering boosts model performance and plays a crucial role in applying LLMs to many NLP tasks, which lessens training and testing discrepancies resulting from human-like languages

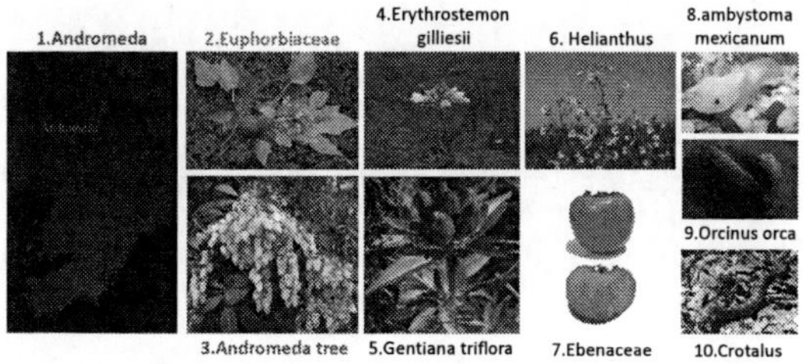

Figure 1: CLIP ranks ten images with respective relevance to the phrase *"Andromeda tree"*, which consists of ambiguous word *"Andromeda"* and limited context *"tree"*. The goal is to select the correct image from ten images of different relevance corresponding to the intended meaning of *"Andromeda tree"*. Note that the first (blue) and second (green) images ranked higher than the correct third image (red).

(Liu et al., 2023). A prompt refers to a text or a set of instructions that guides the model to generate a specific type of response or output. A prompt can be a question, statement, keyword, or sequence of words that provide context and information to the model. Recent research on prompt techniques demonstrates that well-designed prompts spur the potential of neural models without modifying their parameters (Jin et al., 2022). We are curious about how prompts can improve the performance of CLIP on VWSD.

Our main contributions are as follows:

1. We explored different templates for queries and observed their effects on VWSD. The quotes and highlighting ambiguity are effective.

2. We adopted GPT-3 as a key VWSD component to generate queries, which improved the performance in terms of accuracy.

3. We demonstrated that our prompt techniques are effective for finetuning CLIP.

[*] Now at Hitotsubashi University

[1] `https://raganato.github.io/vwsd/`

*Proceedings of the The 12th Joint Conference on Lexical and Computational Semantics (*SEM 2023)*, pages 417–422
July 13-14, 2023 ©2023 Association for Computational Linguistics

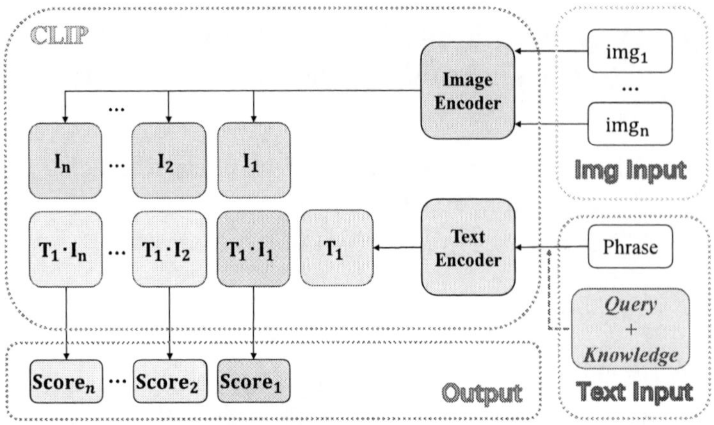

Figure 2: Overview of our method. The left part framed by a brown dotted line is the structure of CLIP, and the right part framed by a blue dotted line and a gray dotted line are our Text and Image Inputs. The bottom part framed by a purple dotted line is our Output.

2 Method

Each VWSD phrase contains an indication of the ambiguous word(s). As illustrated in Figure 2, we first introduce a baseline CLIP that takes text input as either VWSD short phrases or a longer query enhanced with templates for ambiguous words. Then, we leverage GPT-3 to further enrich these queries for CLIP.

CLIP with phrase and queries In a shared feature space, CLIP provides a joint embedding representation for each $(image,\ text)$ pair. The joint embedding representation allows for semantic similarity comparisons between images and text, that is

$$similarity\ score = \text{CLIP}(E_{image}, E_{text})\,,$$

where E_{image} and E_{text} are the embeddings obtained from its image and text encoders, respectively. We focus on $text$ input for VWSD.

$text$ takes the form of either a single VWSD **phrase** or list of **queries** that bears the phrase and indication of the ambiguous words in the phrase. Table 1 lists our nine templates for creating the queries. Take "*Andromeda tree*" as an example; "*Andromeda*" fits the slot **[ambiguous word(s)]** and "tree" fits **[rest of word(s)]**. Template #1 appears to be logically contradicted with #2. This is because some ambiguous words in the phrase do not fit slot **[ambiguous word(s)]**, but fits slot **[rest of word(s)]**. Moreover, template #3 is for both ambiguous words and rest of words to improve the coverage. These different templates semantically fit different phrases in VWSD, and their performance with CLIP are similar. We select the maximum of the *similarity scores* from all the queries, and we want the image with the highest score.

Query Enrichment with GPT-3 GPT-3 is a powerful language model that can perform various NLP tasks such as language generation, text classification, and question answering. It was designed to improve upon the limitations of previous language models by training a large-scale neural network on massive amounts of text data. This allows GPT-3 to understand the context and generate coherent and contextually relevant responses to text-based inputs, making it useful for a wide range of NLP applications. Additionally, GPT-3 can be finetuned on specific NLP tasks to further enhance its ability to perform various language-related tasks.

As shown in Table 2, we induce additonal **knowledge** from GPT-3 by posing different questions for VWSD phrases which was used to finetune the CLIP: 1) a direct query, 2) a query with double quotes to highlight the phrase, and 3) adding an explicit phrase to separate the phrase ambiguity (i.e., ambiguous word(s)) from others based on 2). These three types are concatenated to the original phrase as a query to finetune CLIP for better performance.

3 Experiments

3.1 Settings

In this study, we used data resources including images and phrases released by SemEval-2023 Task 1. Here, we chose only the English version from

#	Query template for CLIP
1	**[phrase]** is **[ambiguous word(s)]**, but **[rest of word(s)]**.
2	**[phrase]** is really **[ambiguous word(s)]**, but **[rest of word(s)]**.
3	**[phrase]** is not **[ambiguous word(s)]**, but **[rest of word(s)]**.
4	**[phrase]** is not really **[ambiguous word(s)]**, but **[rest of word(s)]**.
5	**[phrase]** is apparently **[ambiguous word(s)]**, but indeed **[rest of word(s)]**.
6	Actually, **[phrase]** is apparently **[ambiguous word(s)]**, but indeed **[rest of word(s)]**.
7	In fact, **[phrase]** is apparently **[ambiguous word(s)]**, but indeed **[rest of word(s)]**.
8	**[phrase]** is not only **[ambiguous word(s)]**, but **[rest of word(s)]**.
9	**[phrase]** is not really **[rest of word(s)]**, but **[ambiguous word(s)]**.

Table 1: Nine query templates for CLIP.

Prompt Type	Question for GPT-3	Answer as Knowledge for CLIP
Direct	What is the *Andromeda tree*?	Andromeda tree is a species of evergreen shrub that belongs to the genus Pieris ...
Double quotes	What is the *"Andromeda tree"*?	The Andromeda tree is a species of flowering evergreen shrub native to ...
Explicit phrase	Instead of *"Andromeda"* and *"tree"*, what is the *"Andromeda tree"*?	The Andromeda Tree is a species of evergreen shrub or small tree native to ...

Table 2: Three types of prompts for inducing GPT-3 knowledge: direct query, double quotes for a phrase, and explicit phrase to separate ambiguous word(s).

Model	Prompt Type	Dev		Test
CLIP with phrase only	N/A	71.50	58.53	—
CLIP finetuned with nine queries and GPT-3 knowledge	Direct	90.60	56.16	56.80 (ensemble)
		90.20	55.29	
	Double quotes	93.20	65.44	65.87 (ensemble)
		93.00	65.23	
	Explicit phrase	92.20	66.09	65.01 (ensemble)
		91.80	**66.95**	

Table 3: **Dev** and **Test** accuracy results based on data from *SemEval 2023*. To exclude the effects of randomness, we conducted the experiments twice for each prompt type. **Model** represents different versions in our experiments, where the **baseline** is CLIP (phrase). **Prompt Type** indicates the different prompt types used as mentioned in Table 2.

all the language versions (English, Farsi, Italian). We divided the official training data into a *training set (11,869)* and *development set (500)*. Finally, we evaluated our finetuned models on the *test data (463)*, whose contents are different from the training data.

We employed pretrained CLIP as our baseline to calculate the similarity score between the image and text. In the baseline, we used only a phrase as the input of the text component, and the performance is not good. We further finetuned the CLIP to improve the performance by expanding the phrases to queries, and even enriching queries with GPT-3.

For training, we set the batch size to 100 with 10 epochs and used a learning rate of 1e-7. For GPT-3,

Nine Queries	GPT-3 Knowledge	Finetuning	Dev	Test	Better	Worse
			71.50	58.53	0	0
√			72.40	61.12	64	46
√	√		80.40	64.58	90	56
√		√	88.20	61.34	92	74
√	√	√	**92.20**	**66.09**	107	60

Table 4: Accuracy of ablation experiments testing on **Dev** and **Test**. Table 4 presents the number of **Test** samples becoming **Better** and **Worse** after finetuning. Here, only Prompt Type *Explicit Phrase* is used.

we chose *text-davinci-003*, which was considered the most capable GPT-3 model. *text-davinci-003* exhibited a better performance with a higher quality, longer output, and better instruction-following than the other models.

3.2 Results & Analysis

Table 3 lists the results based on the baseline model and finetuned models using different prompt types.

As shown in Table 3, the accuracy of the finetuned models on *Dev* and *Test* performed better than the baseline model. This proves that finetuning can improve the performance of CLIP. All the results on the *Test* were much lower than those on the *Dev*. This may be because the *Dev* data was obtained from the training dataset, which is thematically different from the *Test* dataset.

For different prompt types, the accuracy on the *Dev* varied. The finetuned CLIP adapting prompt type *Direct* had the lowest overall performance with 90.20, and prompt type *Double quotes* had the highest overall performance with 93.20. A speculative reason for this was the lower knowledge quality when selecting the prompt type *Direct* because GPT-3 tended to not consider the phrase entirely when asking directly, thereby generating inaccurate knowledge. For prompt type *Explicit phrase*, it could reach a point of 92.20.

On the *Test*, including the baseline, prompt type *Explicit phrase* exhibited the best performance, which could reach up to 66.95. This indicates that the knowledge generated by GPT-3 was beneficial. Conversely, the performance of prompt type *Direct* was worse than the baseline, which may indicate that poor knowledge can introduce negative effects.

Finally, we conducted ensemble experiments between each prompt type. The results demonstrated an improvement in accuracy for all prompt types except *Explicit phrase*.

3.3 Ablation Study

To investigate the benefit of the effect of queries, knowledge from GPT-3, and finetuning, we conducted ablation experiments. We counted the number of answers that improved or worsened in terms of the change of the gold answer rank. Table 4 shows that samples that improve are increasing.

Query templates. As shown in Table 4, the baseline results were the lowest: 71.50 and 58.53 on *Dev* and *Test*, respectively. This is because the *phrase* was too short to carry meaningful information. Therefore, when creating a sentence including a target *phrase* as a query, more contextual information can be obtained. Consequently, the score increased by 0.9 and 2.59 on *Dev* and *Test*, respectively, compared with the baseline.

Prompt engineering. To better use of the information in context, we have added knowledge from GPT-3 based on the prompts. The score particularly increased to 80.40 on *Dev*, which proves that adding knowledge from GPT-3 improves the performance.

Finetuning. In the finetuning section, we first finetuned CLIP with only *queries*. After finetuning, the accuracy on *Dev* increased by 15.80 compared with *CLIP with queries*, which proves the importance of finetuning. Paying attention to the results on *Test* in CLIP with queries and GPT-3 knowledge is also important. Table 4 shows the score of 64.58 was 3.24 points higher than the result of *CLIP finetuned with queries*. This is partially explained by the knowledge from GPT-3 being partially effective. We further finetuned CLIP with prompts and GPT-3. The best performance reached scores of 92.20 and 66.09 on *Dev* and *Test*, repectively, which illustrates the usefulness of GPT-3.

4 Related Work

4.1 Knowledge generated from LLMs

Unlike *WordNet* (Miller, 1994) and *SemCor* (Miller et al., 1993), recent large-scale language models (LLMs) provide an easy explanation for ambiguous words. In particular, LLMs are well suited for disambiguation tasks. For example, BERT (Devlin et al., 2019) and RoBERTa (Liu et al., 2019) have a general language understanding ability that has been demonstrated to capture word senses (Coenen et al., 2019).

Recently, Brown et al. (2020) proposed Generative Pretrained Transformer-3 (GPT-3), an LLM trained on a massive amount of data, for various NLP tasks such as dialogue generation (Zheng and Huang, 2021; Lee et al., 2022). It demonstrates an understanding of logical reasoning and external knowledge, which has made it applicable GPT-3 to solving complex problems involving cause-and-effect relationships (Liu et al., 2022). When provied with a proper prompt or asked a human-like question, a pretrained GPT-3 model responds with fluent and relevant text as an answer, which shows passable "logic" and details for disambiguation. The quality of the answer depends on the prompt and question. However, to the best of our knowledge, no research has been conducted on VWSD using LLMs. In this study, we rely on LLM output as external knowledge for VWSD.

4.2 Image Retrieval

Recently, IR has undergone dramatic shifts from approaches handcrafted with global and local descriptors, to convolutional neural networks (He et al., 2016) with adaptive local descriptors, to recent non-convolutional models with one global descriptor, such as a Vision Transformer (Dosovitskiy et al., 2021, ViT). Experimental evaluations (Gkelios et al., 2021) show that ViT achieves competitive results at a low complexity and even finetuning is not required, which makes it an attractive choice as a baseline model for IR.

Recently, researchers began leveraging natural language descriptions in computer vision to improve performance. He and Peng (2017) and Liang et al. (2020) showcased the utilization of natural language descriptions and explanations to enhance the fine-grained visual classification of birds. Radford et al. (2021) presented CLIP in a zero-shot setting, which demonstrated the model's substantial potential for widely-applicable tasks such as IR (Mori et al., 1999).

5 Conclusion and Future Work

We explored the effects of a query on VWSD and used GPT-3 as a key to generate queries. After finetuning CLIP with queries generated from GPT-3, we determined that queries generated by GPT-3 using prompts improved the performance in terms of accuracy.

In the future, we plan to apply some other multimodal models and compare the results with those of existing works. We also intend to adopt GPT-4 [2] to generate knowledge considering both textual and visual cues for VWSD.

References

Tom B. Brown, Benjamin Mann, Nick Ryder, Melanie Subbiah, Jared Kaplan, Prafulla Dhariwal, Arvind Neelakantan, Pranav Shyam, Girish Sastry, Amanda Askell, Sandhini Agarwal, Ariel Herbert-Voss, Gretchen Krueger, Tom Henighan, Rewon Child, Aditya Ramesh, Daniel M. Ziegler, Jeffrey Wu, Clemens Winter, Christopher Hesse, Mark Chen, Eric Sigler, Mateusz Litwin, Scott Gray, Benjamin Chess, Jack Clark, Christopher Berner, Sam McCandlish, Alec Radford, Ilya Sutskever, and Dario Amodei. 2020. Language models are few-shot learners. *CoRR*, abs/2005.14165.

Andy Coenen, Emily Reif, Ann Yuan, Been Kim, Adam Pearce, Fernanda B. Viégas, and Martin Wattenberg. 2019. Visualizing and measuring the geometry of BERT. *CoRR*, abs/1906.02715.

Jacob Devlin, Ming-Wei Chang, Kenton Lee, and Kristina Toutanova. 2019. BERT: Pre-training of deep bidirectional transformers for language understanding. In *Proceedings of the 2019 Conference of the North American Chapter of the Association for Computational Linguistics: Human Language Technologies, Volume 1 (Long and Short Papers)*, pages 4171–4186, Minneapolis, Minnesota. Association for Computational Linguistics.

Alexey Dosovitskiy, Lucas Beyer, Alexander Kolesnikov, Dirk Weissenborn, Xiaohua Zhai, Thomas Unterthiner, Mostafa Dehghani, Matthias Minderer, Georg Heigold, Sylvain Gelly, Jakob Uszkoreit, and Neil Houlsby. 2021. An Image is Worth 16x16 Words: Transformers for Image Recognition at Scale. In *9th International Conference on Learning Representations*.

Socratis Gkelios, Yiannis S. Boutalis, and Savvas A. Chatzichristofis. 2021. Investigating the Vision Transformer Model for Image Retrieval Tasks. In *17th International Conference on Distributed Computing in Sensor Systems*, pages 367–373.

[2] `https://arxiv.org/abs/2303.08774`

Kaiming He, Xiangyu Zhang, Shaoqing Ren, and Jian Sun. 2016. Deep Residual Learning for Image Recognition. In *2016 IEEE Conference on Computer Vision and Pattern Recognition*, pages 770–778.

Xiangteng He and Yuxin Peng. 2017. Fine-graind Image Classification via Combining Vision and Language. *CoRR*, abs/1704.02792.

Woojeong Jin, Yu Cheng, Yelong Shen, Weizhu Chen, and Xiang Ren. 2022. A good prompt is worth millions of parameters: Low-resource prompt-based learning for vision-language models. In *Proceedings of the 60th Annual Meeting of the Association for Computational Linguistics (Volume 1: Long Papers)*, pages 2763–2775, Dublin, Ireland. Association for Computational Linguistics.

Young-Jun Lee, Chae-Gyun Lim, and Ho-Jin Choi. 2022. Does GPT-3 generate empathetic dialogues? a novel in-context example selection method and automatic evaluation metric for empathetic dialogue generation. In *Proceedings of the 29th International Conference on Computational Linguistics*, pages 669–683, Gyeongju, Republic of Korea. International Committee on Computational Linguistics.

Weixin Liang, James Zou, and Zhou Yu. 2020. ALICE: Active learning with contrastive natural language explanations. In *Proceedings of the 2020 Conference on Empirical Methods in Natural Language Processing (EMNLP)*, pages 4380–4391, Online. Association for Computational Linguistics.

Jiacheng Liu, Alisa Liu, Ximing Lu, Sean Welleck, Peter West, Ronan Le Bras, Yejin Choi, and Hannaneh Hajishirzi. 2022. Generated knowledge prompting for commonsense reasoning. In *Proceedings of the 60th Annual Meeting of the Association for Computational Linguistics (Volume 1: Long Papers)*, pages 3154–3169, Dublin, Ireland. Association for Computational Linguistics.

Pengfei Liu, Weizhe Yuan, Jinlan Fu, Zhengbao Jiang, Hiroaki Hayashi, and Graham Neubig. 2023. Pretrain, Prompt, and Predict: A Systematic Survey of Prompting Methods in Natural Language Processing. *ACM Computing Surveys*, 55(9):195:1–195:35.

Yinhan Liu, Myle Ott, Naman Goyal, Jingfei Du, Mandar Joshi, Danqi Chen, Omer Levy, Mike Lewis, Luke Zettlemoyer, and Veselin Stoyanov. 2019. Roberta: A robustly optimized BERT pretraining approach. *CoRR*, abs/1907.11692.

George A. Miller. 1994. WordNet: A lexical database for English. In *Human Language Technology: Proceedings of a Workshop held at Plainsboro, New Jersey, March 8-11, 1994*.

George A. Miller, Claudia Leacock, Randee Tengi, and Ross T. Bunker. 1993. A semantic concordance. In *Human Language Technology: Proceedings of a Workshop Held at Plainsboro, New Jersey, March 21-24, 1993*.

Yasuhide Mori, Hironobu Takahashi, and Ryu ichi Oka. 1999. Image-to-word transformation based on dividing.

Alec Radford, Jong Wook Kim, Chris Hallacy, Aditya Ramesh, Gabriel Goh, Sandhini Agarwal, Girish Sastry, Amanda Askell, Pamela Mishkin, Jack Clark, Gretchen Krueger, and Ilya Sutskever. 2021. Learning transferable visual models from natural language supervision. *CoRR*, abs/2103.00020.

Chujie Zheng and Minlie Huang. 2021. Exploring prompt-based few-shot learning for grounded dialog generation. *CoRR*, abs/2109.06513.

Functional Distributional Semantics at Scale

Chun Hei Lo[1] **Hong Cheng**[1] **Wai Lam**[1] **Guy Emerson**[2]
[1]The Chinese University of Hong Kong [2]University of Cambridge
{chlo, hcheng, wlam}@se.cuhk.edu.hk gete2@cam.ac.uk

Abstract

Functional Distributional Semantics is a linguistically motivated framework for modelling lexical and sentence-level semantics with truth-conditional functions using distributional information. Previous implementations of the framework focus on subject–verb–object (SVO) triples only, which largely limits the contextual information available for training and thus the capability of the learnt model. In this paper, we discuss the challenges of extending the previous architectures to training on arbitrary sentences. We address the challenges by proposing a more expressive lexical model that works over a continuous semantic space. This improves the flexibility and computational efficiency of the model, as well as its compatibility with present-day machine-learning frameworks. Our proposal allows the model to be applied to a wider range of semantic tasks, and improved performances are demonstrated from experimental results.

1 Introduction

Functional Distributional Semantics (FDS; Emerson and Copestake, 2016; Emerson, 2018) aims to capture the truth-conditional aspects of words through learning from distributional information of a corpus. Whilst truth-conditional semantics deals with predications over discrete entities, FDS aims to generalize about predications over a space of *entity representations* with probabilistic semantics.

Contrasted with most distributional methods which map words to vectors, FDS can model various aspects of meaning in a linguistically rigorous manner. For example, vagueness is represented by the probabilistic nature of predications, and hypernymy, defined formally as the subsumption of the extensions between two word senses, can be represented by the subsumption of regions of space (Emerson, 2020b).

Going beyond simple vector spaces, some models of distributional semantics represent words as tensors for composition (e.g., Coecke et al., 2010; Baroni et al., 2014), as static distributions for uncertainty and entailment (e.g., Vilnis and McCallum, 2015), as posterior distributions for context-specific meaning (e.g., Bražinskas et al., 2018), and as regions for set-theoretic properties (e.g., Dasgupta et al., 2022). Among them, only a region-based approach favours logical interpretations (for a discussion, see: Emerson, 2020b, 2023).

In order to be computationally tractable, most models of distributional semantics are trained based on instances defined by context windows (e.g., Mikolov et al., 2013a; Pennington et al., 2014) or incomplete linguistic structures such as immediate dependencies (e.g., Levy and Goldberg, 2014; Czarnowska et al., 2019). All previous instances of FDS (further discussed in §2) are only trained on SVO triples. Consequently, these models underutilize much contextual information.

We hope to extend FDS learning to arbitrary sentences, but not larger linguistic units (e.g., paragraphs), for handling them requires non-trivial extensions such as robust coreference resolution, which is beyond the scope of this work. To this end, we propose to adopt a continuous semantic space and a more expressive lexical model in place of the previous world model on a discrete space. Our new formulation provides a computationally efficient and linguistically principled solution to applying FDS to arbitrary sentences. Furthermore, this also situates the framework closer to modern machine learning models which are mostly built upon continuous latent spaces, thus favouring comparisons among and integration with them. For example, Liu and Emerson (2022) integrated a pre-trained computer vision model with a continuous space to FDS, applying it to annotated images. Joint learning of the visually-grounded and corpus-based models was however left as future work due to the incompatibility of latent spaces.

In this paper, we first give an introduction to FDS

*Proceedings of the The 12th Joint Conference on Lexical and Computational Semantics (*SEM 2023)*, pages 423–436
July 13-14, 2023 ©2023 Association for Computational Linguistics

in §2, explaining why it is difficult for previous implementations to scale up. Then, we present in detail the proposed formulation and how to train the model in §3–§4. Finally, we demonstrate how our model can be applied to a number of semantic evaluation data sets and present the results in §5.

2 Functional Distributional Semantics

The core idea of Functional Distributional Semantics is that a sentence refers to a set of entities, and a word is a predicate that is true or false of entities. Compared to other approaches to distributional semantics, it aligns more with model-theoretic semantics, which approaches meaning in the same way in terms of a *model structure*.

However, fixing a specific set of entities would make it impossible to generalize to new situations. In order for the model to be learnable, predicates do not directly take entities as input, but rather entity representations, referred to as *pixies* for brevity. A predicate is represented as a function from pixies to probabilities of truth. This allows the model to account for vagueness.

FDS does not submit to a fixed interpretation of pixies nor process of obtaining them. Rather, pixies are introduced to merely convey information of latent entities. In the work of Liu and Emerson (2022), pixies are dimensionality-reduced vectors obtained from a pretrained network. In this work, they are learnt to best represent entities according to our particular formulation by probabilistic graphical models, which are introduced below and in detail in §4.

2.1 Probabilistic Graphical Models

The framework is formalized in terms of a family of probabilistic graphical models, each of which generates predicates in a semantic graph. It consists of the *world model*, which handles the joint distribution of pixies, and the *lexical model*, which handles truth-conditional semantics. Given an *argument structure* (predicate–argument structure minus predicates, i.e., a directed graph with labelled edges and unlabelled nodes), a predicate can be generated for each node, in three steps. First, a pixie is generated for each node, which together represent the entities to be described. Then, a truth value in $\{\top, \bot\}$ is generated for each entity and each predicate in the vocabulary $\mathcal{V}$. Finally, a single predicate is generated for each entity. This is shown in Fig. 1, for the simple predicate–argument structure of an SVO triple. Different argument structures have different graphical models.

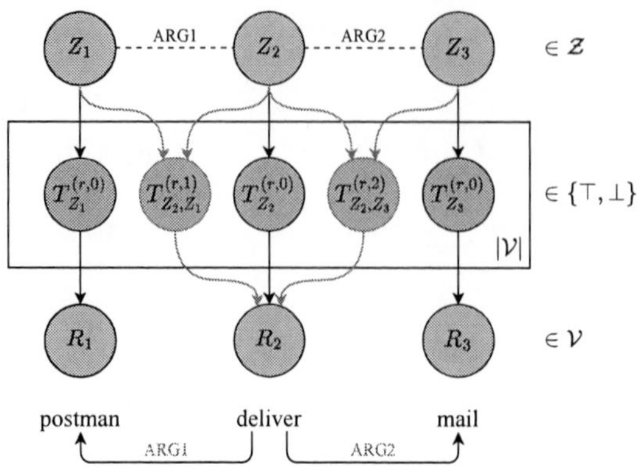

Figure 1: Probabilistic graphical model of FDS for generating words in an SVO triple (e.g., '*postman deliver mail*'). The Z nodes are pixie-valued random variables; T nodes are truth-valued; R nodes are predicate-valued. Only the R nodes are observed (e.g., R_1=*postman*, R_2=*deliver*, R_3=*mail*). This figure contrasts two positions where argument information can be used. In previous work, argument information (i.e., ARG1 and ARG2) only contributes to the world model (in dashed lines). In our formulation, it only contributes to the lexical model (in green lines).

In previous work, $\mathcal{Z}$ is sparse binary-valued vectors, and the joint distribution of pixies is determined by a Cardinality Restricted Boltzmann Machine (CaRBM) using the argument structure. The lexical model comprises unary semantic functions, each of which maps one pixie to the probability that the predicate is true of the pixie.

In §3, we will propose to move the information about the predicate–argument structure from the world model to the lexical model and set $\mathcal{Z} = \mathbb{R}^d$. Concretely, the dependencies among pixies are removed and extra truth-valued random variables $T^{(r,a)}_{Z_i,Z_j}$ are added (also shown in Fig. 1).

2.2 Model Learning from DMRS

The model is trained on graphs of Dependency Minimal Recursion Semantics (DMRS; Copestake et al., 2005; Copestake, 2009). A DMRS graph is derived using the broad-coverage English Resource Grammar (ERG; Flickinger, 2000, 2011), providing a compact representation of the predications expressed by a sentence. Figs. 1 and 2 show three simplified DMRS graphs (with quantifiers and scope removed). Model parameters are optimized in an unsupervised manner to maximize the likelihood of generating the observed predicates given the argument structure of a DMRS graph.

In principle, the formalism of semantic graphs for learning is not restricted to DMRS, but any that include predicate–argument structures. Bender et al. (2015) argued that deriving semantic graphs compositionally and automatically using a broad-coverage grammar is more scalable and consistent than manual annotation, as is common for other formalisms such as Abstract Meaning Representation (AMR; Banarescu et al., 2013).

In §2.3–§2.4, we discuss the linguistic and computational challenges of training previous FDS models on more complex sentences.

2.3 Linguistic Challenges

Vocabulary. Addressing SVO triples only requires training and testing on nouns and verbs. With arbitrary sentences, the vocabulary of predicates expands to (1) adjectives, adverbs and adpositions, which are also predicates, (2) conjunctions, which not only contribute to extensional logic operations (e.g., *and*, *or* and *else*) but also intensional, modal or temporal ones (e.g., *until*, *if* and *since*), and (3) quantifiers. In addition, scope-taking predicates like quantifiers and conjunctions are barely meaningful when the scopes of them are underspecified. Therefore, it is not straightforward to apply the framework to arbitrary sentences without further linguistic assumptions.

Overloaded Argument Roles. The world model with CaRBM uses shared weights for argument roles of different predicates. However, argument roles are overloaded in DMRS. For example, ARG1 of the inchoative predicate `_break_v_1` and causative `_break_v_cause` specify what is broken and what breaks something, respectively. Consequently, predicate-specific thematic interpretations of argument roles are missed out. Argument roles also vary across different parts of speech: the ARG1 of nouns mostly denotes their prepositional complements, that of verbs denotes the agent, and that of an adjective denotes the element to be modified. Dealing with a larger vocabulary of predicates magnifies the problem with the coarse generalization by the undirected graphical models.

2.4 Computational Challenges

With Discrete Pixie Space. Training the model requires computing the likelihood of the observed data, thus the prior of the latent variables. However, it is intractable to compute the probability of a set of pixies in the discrete CaRBM because it requires normalizing over all possible sets of pixie values. Emerson (2020a) approximated the probability using belief propagation methods (Yedidia et al., 2003), which is still computationally expensive. This problem only gets worse when considering larger semantic graphs.

With Continuous Pixie Space. Switching to more tractable continuous distributions makes normalization easier. Nevertheless, the problem is still not simple. Fabiani (2022) explored the use of a continuous space, using a Gaussian Markov Random Field for the world model, and parameterizing the inverse covariance matrix according to the argument roles. Such a matrix has a size of $nd \times nd$ for a DMRS graph with n predicates with pixie dimension d. The complexity of computing its determinant scales to $\mathcal{O}(d^3n^3)$, which is feasible for simple graphs such as SVO triples but computationally prohibitive for larger graphs.

3 Enriching the Lexical Model

In this section, we describe our enriched lexical model and explain how it provides a solution to the linguistic and computational challenges mentioned.

3.1 Neo-Davidsonian Event Semantics

We follow Neo-Davidsonian event semantics (Davidson, 1967; Parsons, 1990) as with previous work, assuming that verbal and adjectival predicates refer to events. For example, to evaluate the claim that 'x *eats* y', we decompose it into three claims: e is an eating event, the ARG1 of this eating event is x, and the ARG2 of this eating event is y.

The event argument naturally allows FDS to be applied to not just nouns and verbs but arbitrary sentences with various types of modifications. For example, for x *eats* y *very quickly*, we have $\text{eat}(e_1, x, y) \wedge \text{quick}(e_2, e_1) \wedge \text{very}(e_3, e_2)$.

3.2 Semantic Functions

As mentioned in §2.1, we introduce truth-valued random variables for argument roles. The probability of truth is determined by either a unary function, as in (1), or a binary function, as in (2), over continuous-valued pixies.

$$P\left(T_{Z_e}^{(r,0)}{=}\top \,\middle|\, z_e\right) = t^{(r,0)}(z_e) \quad (1)$$

$$P\left(T_{Z_e,Z_x}^{(r,a)}{=}\top \,\middle|\, z_e, z_x\right) = t^{(r,a)}(z_e, z_x) \quad (2)$$

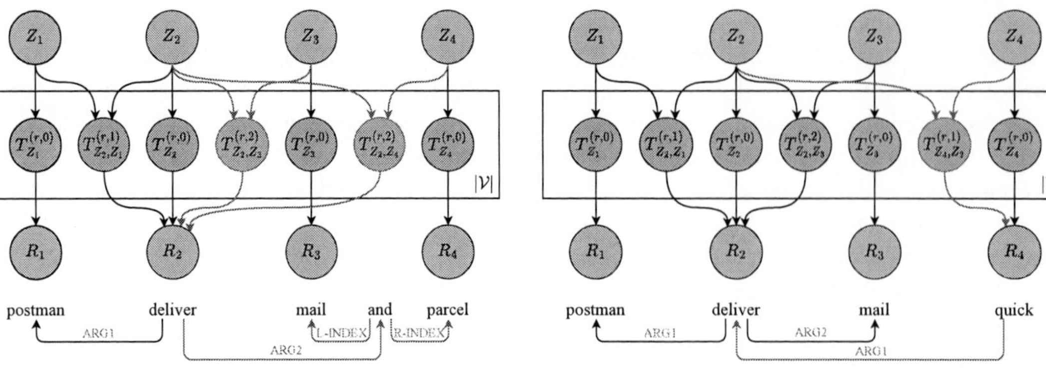

Figure 2: Probabilistic graphical models which can generate the two sentences '*A postman delivers mail and parcels*' (left) and '*A postman delivers mail quickly*' (right) respectively, illustrating how the example in Fig. 1 can be extended with a coordinating conjunction and an adverb. Blue and red lines show the correspondence between dependencies in the graphical models and DMRS argument structures.

We may interpret $t^{(r,0)}(z_e)$ as the probability that r is true of the entity e (represented by z_e) and $t^{(r,a)}(z_e, z_x)$ as the probability that the a-th argument role of r holds between e and x (represented by z_e and z_x). For example, given a predicate r that takes two arguments (e.g., the transitive '*eat*'), the probability of the predication being true is:

$$P\left(T^{(r,0)}_{Z_e} \wedge T^{(r,1)}_{Z_e,Z_x} \wedge T^{(r,2)}_{Z_e,Z_y} = \top \,\middle|\, z_e, z_x, z_y\right) = t^{(r,0)}(z_e)t^{(r,1)}(z_e, z_x)t^{(r,2)}(z_e, z_y) \tag{3}$$

In the same spirit as Paperno et al. (2014)'s proposal, this decomposition of arity-dependent predicates allows dropped arguments to be handled naturally. For the example '*y is eaten*', we have:

$$P\left(T^{(r,0)}_{Z_e} \wedge T^{(r,2)}_{Z_e,Z_y} = \top \,\middle|\, z_e, z_y\right) = t^{(r,0)}(z_e)t^{(r,2)}(z_e, z_y) \tag{4}$$

3.3 Addressing the Challenges

Lexical Model beyond Nouns and Verbs. In our lexical model, nouns, verbs, adjectives, and adverbs all introduce truth-valued random variables but not adpositions, whose uses are considered too flexible to be modelled by our implementation (discussed in §4.3). Proper nouns that mostly denote distinct entities are discarded and arguments that take proper nouns are dropped, as it results in an unreasonably large vocabulary otherwise. We also discard pronouns which require coreferences. Argument roles are propagated through coordinating conjunctions: if a predicate takes a coordinating conjunction as an argument, the argument role is applied to each conjunct. We also neglect quantifiers and modal verbs. Fig. 2 illustrates how the example in Fig. 1 can be extended with additional truth-valued random variables to handle coordinating conjunctions and adverbs. The proposed lexical model thus addresses the vocabulary challenge and also provides a workaround to the problem with overgeneralization of arguments in §2.3.

Computational Efficiency. The information of the predicate–argument structure, which was previously encoded in the world model via dependencies between pixies, is now embedded in the design of the semantic functions. As discussed in §2.4, the main computational challenge in FDS is normalizing joint distributions for sets of pixies. In contrast, the computational cost of binary semantic functions can be kept essentially the same as for unary functions, as discussed further in §4.3. By offloading the complexity from the world model to the lexical model, we can use a simple prior distribution that is trivially normalized, as discussed further in §4.5.

Summary. As compared to previous implementations, our proposal makes FDS more scalable by covering a much broader class of predicates, drastically reducing the computational complexity, and providing a more appropriate treatment of predicate-specific argument roles for richer sentence structures.

4 Variational Autoencoder

As mentioned in §2.2, each training instance is a DMRS graph, which can be characterised in terms of n predicates $R = \{r_1, \ldots, r_n\}$, and the argument structure $A = \left\{(i, j, a) : r_i \xrightarrow{\text{ARG}a} r_j\right\}$.

To optimize the parameters θ of the generative

model, we use a variational autoencoder (VAE) (Kingma and Welling, 2014; Rezende et al., 2014). The intractable true posterior distributions $p_\theta(z \mid R, A)$ over the pixies $z = \{z_1, \ldots, z_n\}$ are first approximated by tractable distributions chosen a priori (discussed in §4.1). Instead of directly performing maximum likelihood estimation on the observed DMRS graphs, the lower bound in (5) is maximized following the β-VAE (Higgins et al., 2017), using a probabilistic encoder q_ϕ (discussed in §4.2) and decoder p_θ (discussed in §4.3). §4.4 and §4.5 reformulate the two terms in (5) respectively based on empirical insights for training stability. Parameters of the encoder and decoder are thus jointly learnt via gradient descent.

$$\begin{aligned}\mathcal{L}_{\phi,\theta}(R \mid A) = \mathbb{E}_{q_\phi(z \mid R,A)}\left[\ln P_\theta(R \mid z, A)\right] \\ - \beta D_{\mathrm{KL}}\left(q_\phi(z \mid R, A) \parallel p_\theta(z \mid A)\right)\end{aligned} \tag{5}$$

4.1 Approximate Posterior Distributions

Given an observed DMRS graph with n latent pixies Z_i, the approximate posterior is partitioned into n independent Gaussians with spherical covariance. Gaussian distributions provide convenient closed forms for analytical computation. For instance, sampling of pixies can be avoided in §4.3. For each Z_i, the encoder q_ϕ predicts a mean vector μ_{Z_i} and a variance $\sigma^2_{Z_i}$. This gives the distribution in (6), where $\mathcal{N}$ is the Gaussian density function.

$$q_\phi(z \mid R, A) = \prod_{i=1}^{n} \mathcal{N}(z_i; \mu_{Z_i}, \sigma^2_{Z_i} I) \tag{6}$$

4.2 Amortized Variational Inference

We devise an encoder that uses both the local predicate–argument structure and global topical information from the whole sentence. For example, the encoder should predict different pixie distributions for '*deliver*' in the contexts of Fig. 2 (delivering mail) and Fig. 3 (delivering a song). The encoder architecture is described by (7), (8), (9) and illustrated in Fig. 3. It is similar to the encoder of Bražinskas et al. (2018), but leverages argument structure. It can also be seen as a simple instantiation of Deep Sets (Zaheer et al., 2017) or a graph-convolutional network (GCN) with complement edges (De Cao et al., 2019). The mean μ_{Z_i} and log variance $\ln \sigma^2_{Z_i}$ are inferred based on a hidden layer $h^{(Z_i)}$, where the logarithm ensures a positive variance. The input embeddings $e^{(r,a)}$ represent predicates standing in particular relation to the target predicate, as detailed in Fig. 3. f can be

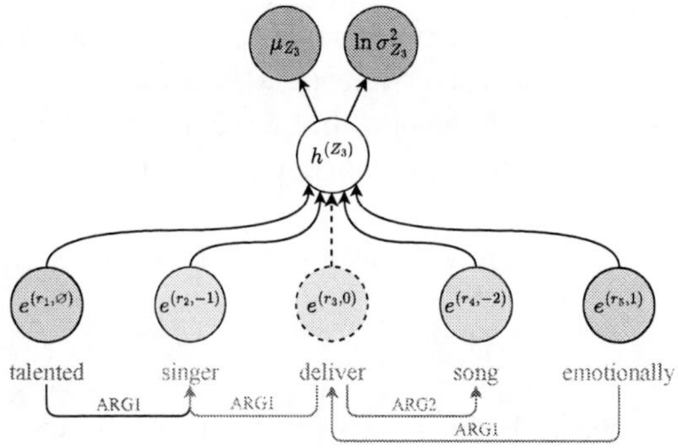

Figure 3: An encoder for inferring the posterior distribution of the pixie of *deliver* in the sentence *talented singer deliver song emotionally*. The inputs represent context predicates standing in particular relation to the target predicate. The embedding $e^{(r,a)}$ represents the predicate r with relation a, where negative a indicates an argument role of the target predicate, positive a an argument role of a context predicate, 0 the target predicate itself, and $\varnothing$ the absence of a direct argument role. The embedding with dropout is shown in dashed lines.

the identity function or a non-linear function, e.g., the hyperbolic tangent. We perform experiments on both choices.

$$h^{(Z_i)} = f\left(\frac{1}{n}\sum_{j=1}^{n} e^{(r_j, a_{j,i})}\right) \tag{7}$$

$$\mu_{Z_i} = W^\top h^{(Z_i)} + c_1 \tag{8}$$

$$\ln \sigma^2_{Z_i} = w^\top h^{(Z_i)} + c_2 \tag{9}$$

During VAE training, the parameters of $t^{(r_i,0)}$ and $e^{(r_i,0)}$ will be optimized to maximize $t^{(r_i,0)}(z_i)$. There is a chance that the distributions of pixies are inferred purely from the embedding of intrinsic arguments and the remaining embeddings are trivially optimized to very small values. To prevent such a learning shortcut, we apply dropout to the embeddings $e^{(r_i,0)}$ with a certain probability where $h^{(Z_i)}$ aggregates without it.

In contrast to our work, Emerson (2020a) used a two-layer GCN as the encoder. Scaling a GCN to larger graphs requires a deeper network to incorporate long-distance, yet crucial topical information. However, a deeper network is computationally expensive and hard to train. We believe that it is worthwhile to start with a simpler and more efficient architecture for our new formulation.

4.3 Probabilistic Decoder

The generative model can be seen as a probabilistic decoder. It consists of the unary and binary semantic functions of predicates. The functions are implemented as linear classifiers in (10) and (11), where S denotes the sigmoid function and $z_{i,j}$ denotes the concatenation of z_i and z_j.

$$t^{(r_i,0)}(z_i) = S\left({v^{(r_i,0)}}^\top z_i + b^{(r,0)}\right) \quad (10)$$

$$t^{(r_i,a)}(z_i, z_j) = S\left({v^{(r_i,a)}}^\top z_{i,j} + b^{(r_i,a)}\right) \quad (11)$$

Linear classifiers provide a number of advantages over complex ones, albeit less expressive. First, they are computationally less expensive. Second, the frequency of word occurrence in a corpus has a long tail, so there are inadequate instances for training more powerful classifiers for the rare predicates. Last but not least, since the pixies are normally distributed given the observation as defined in §4.2, we may use the probit approximation (Murphy, 2012, §8.4.4.2) for computing the expectation of (1) and (2) over the approximate posterior. (12) shows such approximation for the unary semantic function.[1] Computing the first term in (5) otherwise requires sampling, which is more computationally expensive and can result in poor estimations when the variance is high.

$$\mathbb{E}_{q_\phi}\left[t^{(r,0)}(z_i)\right] \approx S\left(\frac{{v^{(r,0)}}^\top \mu_{Z_i} + b^{(r,0)}}{(1 + \frac{\pi}{8}\sigma^2_{Z_i})^{\frac{1}{2}}}\right) \quad (12)$$

4.4 Contrastive Objective on Truth

The first term of (5) requires computing the probability of generating the observed predicates R given the distributions of pixies z and the argument structure A. In previous work, such a probability is set to be proportional to the probabilities of truth of the predications. Consequently, training on this objective only considers the relative probabilities of truth but not absolute probabilities. Truth regularization was introduced to increase the absolute probabilities for better interpretability (Emerson, 2020a). However, both improved and deteriorated model performances were reported by Liu and Emerson (2022) with such regularization. Moreover, we find from experiments that training using the original objective is unstable and requires careful tuning of the regularization coefficient, which furthermore is sensitive to the value of β.

Instead of maximizing the relative probabilities, we propose a contrastive objective on absolute probabilities of truth: we aim to maximize the truth of the observed predicate and the falsehood of negatively sampled predicates, analogous to Skip-gram negative sampling (Mikolov et al., 2013b).

The objective is given in (13) and (14), for unary and binary semantic functions respectively. Each term C_i or $C_{i,j,a}$ corresponds to a truth value node in Fig. 1 and 2, and $N(i)$ denotes the negative samples for the predicate r_i.

$$\begin{aligned} C_i = &\ln \mathbb{E}_{q_\phi}\left[t^{(r_i,0)}(z_i)\right] \\ &+ \sum_{r' \in N(i)} \ln \mathbb{E}_{q_\phi}\left[1 - t^{(r',0)}(z_i)\right] \end{aligned} \quad (13)$$

$$\begin{aligned} C_{i,j,a} = &\ln \mathbb{E}_{q_\phi}\left[t^{(r_i,a)}(z_i, z_j)\right] \\ &+ \sum_{r' \in N(i)} \ln \mathbb{E}_{q_\phi}\left[1 - t^{(r',a)}(z_i, z_j)\right] \end{aligned} \quad (14)$$

Underlying this objective is the assertion that randomly drawn predicates are usually false of the inferred pixies. This objective departs from the generative model in §2.2 and directly operates on probabilities of truth instead of generation probabilities. The proposed objective achieves a very similar goal as the original one, i.e., to maximize the probabilities of truth of the observed predicates and minimizes those of the unobserved, while truth regularization is unnecessary and changes in β do not lead to instability.

For each observed predicate, we draw K samples from the unigram distribution. However, we restrict the distribution to predicates that are compatible with the observed argument roles. Each predicate has a set of possible argument roles (those that appear somewhere in the training data). We restrict to predicates whose possible argument roles are a superset of the observed roles.

4.5 Alternative Variance Regularization

Since we have removed the dependencies among pixies and we have no prior knowledge about the latent space, the KL term in (5) is not informative. In fact, we empirically find that it can even be harmful: (1) adopting a standard normal prior with $\beta > 0$ always yields worse performance on the development set (discussed in §5.2) than when $\beta = 0$, and (2) when $\beta = 0$, the inferred variance occasionally takes very large values when f is the identity function, rendering inference uninformative.

We devise an alternative regularization term (15) that replaces the KL divergence in (5), where d is the dimensionality. This term is derived from the

[1] For brevity, we use $\mathbb{E}_{q_\phi}$ to denote $\mathbb{E}_{q_\phi(z|R,S)}$ hereafter.

KL divergence of q_ϕ from a standard normal distribution, which pulls variances to one but neglects the means. This way, the variance is still regularized to avoid extreme values, while not imposing a strong belief about the expected locations of pixies.

$$\mathcal{D} = \frac{d}{2} \sum_{i=1}^{n} \left(\sigma_{Z_i}^2 - \ln \sigma_{Z_i}^2 \right) \quad (15)$$

For each instance, the final training objective to maximize is reformulated to (16).

$$\tilde{\mathcal{L}}_{\phi,\theta}(R \mid A) = \sum_{i=1}^{n} \mathcal{C}_i + \sum_{(i,j,a) \in A} \mathcal{C}_{i,j,a} - \beta \mathcal{D} \quad (16)$$

5 Experiments

Evaluating a semantic model is not an easy task. We focus on tasks that involve semantic composition and contextualized meaning. In particular, we select RELPRON (Rimell et al., 2016) and GS2011 (Grefenstette and Sadrzadeh, 2011) (and GS2013 (Grefenstette and Sadrzadeh, 2015), a re-annotated version of GS2011), the two data sets evaluated by Emerson (2020a). This allows a direct comparison between our approaches. In addition, our proposed approach formally incorporates adjectives, which gives us the opportunity to evaluate on GS2012 (Grefenstette, 2013). Our implementation is available online.[2]

5.1 Training Data

The data we train on is DMRS graphs extracted from Wikiwoods[3] (Flickinger et al., 2010; Solberg, 2012) using Pydelphin[4] (Copestake et al., 2016). Wikiwoods provides linguistic analyses of 55m sentences (900m tokens) in English Wikipedia. Each sentence was parsed by the PET parser (Callmeier, 2001; Toutanova et al., 2005) using the 1212 version of the ERG, and the parses are ranked by a ranking model trained on WeScience (Ytrestøl et al., 2009). The preprocessed data consists of DMRS graphs of 36m sentences, where 254m tokens are involved in training (preprocessing details described in §A.1). We preprocess the evaluation data into DMRS graphs following ERG analyses.

5.2 Model Configurations

We test for two model configurations: $\text{FDSAS}_{\text{tanh}}$ and FDSAS_{id}. They differ in activation functions

[2]https://github.com/aaronlolo326/TCSfromDMRS

[3]http://ltr.uio.no/wikiwoods/1212/

[4]https://github.com/delph-in/pydelphin

Model	MAP	
	Dev.	Test
Vector addition (add.) (Rimell et al., 2016)	0.496	0.472
Sim. Practical Lexical Function (Rimell et al., 2016)	0.496	0.497
Vector add. (Czarnowska et al., 2019)	0.485	0.475
Dependency vector add. (Czarnowska et al., 2019)	0.497	0.439
Pixie Autoencoder (PixieAE) (Emerson, 2020a)	0.261	0.189
Ensemble of PixieAE & vector add. (Emerson, 2020a)	0.532	0.489
$\text{BERT}_{\text{BASE}}$ (tuned template with full stop)	0.677	0.667
$\text{BERT}_{\text{BASE}}$ (tuned template without full stop)	0.302	0.200
$\text{FDSAS}_{\text{tanh}}$	0.486	0.477
FDSAS_{id}	0.657	0.580

Table 1: Results on RELPRON.

(discussed in §4.2). Each of them comprises 54m parameters. All other hyperparameters are simply fixed (reported in §A.2). Since only RELPRON provides a development set but not GS2011, GS2013, or GS2012, each of our models is tuned on the development set of RELPRON (described in §A.2) and have their outputs averaged over three random seeds. For fair comparisons, we only report results of previous works that train their models on a corpus in an unsupervised manner. We select the best result from each of their models.

5.3 Evaluation on Semantic Composition

RELPRON is a data set of subject and object relative clauses. It consists of terms (e.g., '*telescope*'), paired with up to 10 corresponding properties (e.g., '*device that astronomer use*'). Each property comes in lemmatized words. The development set contains 65 terms and 518 properties and the test set contains 73 terms and 569 properties. The task is to rank all properties for each term so that the correct ones come before the incorrect ones. Performance is measured using Mean Average Precision (MAP).

5.3.1 Using FDS

Following Emerson (2020a), for each property, the encoder is used to compose from the relative clause and infer the pixie distribution of the target subject or object. Then, for each term, we rank the properties by the log of the expected probability that the term is true of the target pixie. This is obtained by applying the semantic function of the term to the inferred pixie distribution using (12).

5.3.2 Results

As a baseline, we adopt $\text{BERT}_{\text{BASE}}$ (Devlin et al., 2019), a language model with 110m parameters, using the Transformers library (Wolf et al., 2019). It performs masked prediction on a cloze sentence, e.g., '*[CLS] a device that an astronomer uses is a*

[MASK]. [SEP]'. As RELPRON properties are lemmatized and contain no articles, they must be converted into cloze sentences using a template. Experimenting with different cloze templates, the best one on the development set uses singular nouns, the article *a/an*, an inflected verb (using Pattern (Smedt and Daelemans, 2012)), and a full stop.

Table 1 shows the results on RELPRON. Our best model outperforms all existing work, except the $\text{BERT}_{\text{BASE}}$ baseline. Nevertheless, it is important to note that $\text{BERT}_{\text{BASE}}$ has twice as many parameters and is trained on ten times more tokens compared to each of our models. As mentioned by Emerson (2020a), vector space models are good at capturing topical relatedness, whereas the PixieAE uses FDS and learns different information. Our large improvement over Emerson's ensemble model suggests that our formulation manages to combine the best of both worlds.

The $\text{BERT}_{\text{BASE}}$ baseline achieves a new state of the art. Nevertheless, our experiments show BERT's sensitivity to the template. While Emerson (2020a) discussed template tuning for BERT, they did not mention punctuation, which we find to be crucial for high performance. Aligning with Kementchedjhieva et al. (2021)'s observation, we found that BERT often generates a full stop with over 90% probability when the template does not end with one, although the [SEP] token already indicates the end of a sentence. This shows that ending the sequence with a full stop is more important to BERT than grammaticality. Performance is also degraded if either of the [CLS] or [SEP] tokens are missing. In contrast, FDS models operate on DMRS, abstracting over punctuation and inflection, and extra tuning of templates is unnecessary.

Rimell et al. (2016) also designed RELPRON to have *confounders*, non-corresponding terms and properties with lexical overlap, e.g., '*soil*' with '*activity that soil support*' (which corresponds to '*farming*') and '*fuel*' with '*phenomenon that require fuel*' (which corresponds to '*propulsion*'). There are 33 confounders in the test set and Emerson (2020a) reported that a vector addition model incorrectly ranked all the confounding properties in the top 4 for the overlapping term. In contrast, $\text{FDSAS}_{\text{tanh}}$, FDSAS_{id} and $\text{BERT}_{\text{BASE}}$ rank them 65st, 70th and 70th on average respectively.

5.4 Evaluation on Verb Disambiguation

GS2011 tests if a model is able to disambiguate ambiguous transitive verbs given the context of a subject and an object noun. It comprises 199 entries and 2,500 judgements by 25 annotators. Each entry of the data set provides an SVO triple (e.g., '*service meet need*') from the British National Corpus (BNC) and a transitive landmark verb (e.g., '*visit*' and '*satisfy*') from WordNet (Miller, 1995). Using a score from 1 to 7, the annotators rate the semantic similarity of the verb pair when each of the verbs takes the given subject and object. We also report the results on GS2013, the re-annotated version of GS2011 with a total of 9,950 judgements, where each pair is annotated by 50 annotators.

GS2012 also tests for verb disambiguation. It additionally includes an adjective for both the subject and object in the entries of GS2011 (e.g., '*social service meet educational need*'). It comprises 194 entries and 9,700 judgements by 50 annotators. A good model is expected to utilize the adjectives for better contextualization.

For each of these data sets, we measure the correlation of models' predictions with either separate or averaged annotators' judgements using Spearman's ρ. We compute the inter-annotator agreements (IAAs) by averaging the Spearman's ρ of each annotator's judgement against the other annotators'. IAA is believed to provide the theoretical maximum value for any model's performance.

5.4.1 Using FDS

We follow Emerson (2020a) that a score between a verb pair is the log of the expected probability that the landmark verb is true of the other verb pixie.

5.4.2 Results

We adopt $\text{BERT}_{\text{BASE}}$ as a baseline using the best template tuned on the development set of RELPRON. Tables 2, 3 and 4 show the results.

Care must be taken when comparing the face values of correlations for two reasons. First, models are trained on data of different sizes and sources. Hashimoto and Tsuruoka (2015) mentioned that their models trained on 1.9m sentences of BNC yield comparable results to those trained on 33m sentences from Wikipedia, which might be due to GS2011 being produced based on BNC. Training on a different corpus (e.g., Wikipedia) can better reflect how well a model generalizes. Hashimoto and Tsuruoka (2016) showed that models trained on

Model	Training Data			ρ	
	Sources	#Sentence (m)	#Token (m)	Separate	Averaged
Kartsaklis and Sadrzadeh (2013); Grefenstette (2013); Van de Cruys et al. (2013); Polajnar et al. (2015); Fried et al. (2015); Tian et al. (2016); Emerson and Copestake (2017)				< 0.4	< 0.5
Hashimoto et al. (2014)	B	6	-	0.41	0.50
Hashimoto and Tsuruoka (2015)	W	80 [33]	-	-	0.614
Hashimoto and Tsuruoka (2016) (Ensemble)	W+B	86 [35]	-	0.524	0.680
Gupta et al. (2015)	W+B+U	-	-	0.406	-
Gamallo (2019)	W+B	-	2,500	0.46	-
Wijnholds et al. (2020)	U	130	3,200	-	0.54
Emerson (2020a) (PixieAE)	W	55 [31]	900 [72]	0.406	0.504
$\text{BERT}_{\text{BASE}}$	W+O	-	3,300	0.394	0.519
$\text{FDSAS}_{\text{tanh}}$	W	55 [36]	900 [254]	0.438	0.553
FDSAS_{id}	W	55 [36]	900 [254]	0.444	0.552
Inter-annotator agreement				0.578	0.739

Table 2: Results on GS2011. Sources: W: Wikipedia, B: BNC, U: ukWaC (Baroni et al., 2009), O: BookCorpus (Zhu et al., 2015). Numbers of sentences and tokens are for raw data. In brackets are numbers after preprocessing; for our models, we report the number of tokens contributing to semantic functions. '-' means not reported.

Model	Training Data		ρ	
	#Snt. (m)	#Token (m)	Sep.	Avg.
Grefenstette and Sadrzadeh (2015)	-	-	0.26	-
Tilk et al. (2016)	138	-	0.34	-
Hong et al. (2018)	-	2,000	0.367	-
$\text{BERT}_{\text{BASE}}$	-	3,300	0.426	0.562
$\text{FDSAS}_{\text{tanh}}$	55 [36]	900 [254]	0.439	0.573
FDSAS_{id}	55 [36]	900 [254]	0.457	0.601
Inter-annotator agreement			0.587	0.777

Table 3: Results on GS2013.

Model	Training Data		ρ	
	#Snt. (m)	#Token (m)	Sep.	Avg.
Grefenstette and Sadrzadeh (2015)	-	-	0.27	-
Tian et al. (2016)	-	-	0.33	-
Gupta et al. (2015)	-	-	0.357	-
Paperno et al. (2014)	-	2,800	0.36	-
$\text{BERT}_{\text{BASE}}$	-	3,300	0.404	0.608
$\text{FDSAS}_{\text{tanh}}$	55 [36]	900 [254]	0.444	0.655
FDSAS_{id}	55 [36]	900 [254]	0.449	0.660
Inter-annotator agreement			0.459	0.687

Table 4: Results on GS2012.

Wikipedia and BNC produce disagreeing outputs, and ensembling them is useful as seen in Table 2.

Second, there is no development set. It is not easy to conclude from a large number of model variants with high variances in test set results. For instance, Hashimoto et al. (2014) reported results for 10 settings, where 8 and 9 out of 10 have $\rho < 0.35$ for separate and averaged judgements respectively. Gamallo (2019) presented 11 model variants and FDSAS_{id} only loses to one of them.

All models trained on substantially more data lose to our models across three data sets, except Gamallo (2019)'s. Bootstrap tests on separate judgements across three data sets show that FDSAS_{id} outperforms $\text{BERT}_{\text{BASE}}$ significantly ($p < 0.02$). We also improve over the PixieAE that adopted FDS on GS2011. FDSAS_{id} performs nearly on par with IAA on GS2012, showing that our approach appropriately handles adjectives.

Trained on similar sources and comparable numbers of sentences, Hashimoto and Tsuruoka (2015)'s model outperforms ours by a considerable margin. They concluded that the use of verb matrices allows direct interaction between verbs and their arguments which helps with verb disambiguation. In contrast, the binary semantic function introduced in (11) allows very limited interaction between the two pixies z_0 and z_a, which in the verb disambiguation case correspond to the verb and argument entities respectively. Two advantages of this formulation are that the number of parameters required grows just linearly with respect to the pixie dimension, and the probit approximation in (12) is still applicable. Increasing the expressiveness of the function while keeping a reasonable number of model parameters is an interesting avenue for future work.

6 Conclusion

We analyzed the linguistic and computational challenges of Functional Distributional Semantics and presented a new formulation where we have improved: applicability to diverse natural language structures, computational efficiency, compatibility with contemporary models, and performances on a range of semantic tasks. We believe this work bridges truth-conditional semantics to practical distributional semantics at scale.

Limitations

From a linguistic perspective, we only handle the extensional fragment of natural language. Consequently, modality and temporal information are excluded from the framework. Nevertheless, we train on encyclopediac text which is believed to be a reasonable domain for the extensional restriction.

From a computational perspective, although the reformulated model is already more computationally efficient than previous implementations of FDS, the variable sizes and topologies of input graphs make efficient batching difficult. It is thus not maximally optimized for training on GPUs (statistics are given in §A.3). We currently set the batch size to 1 and perform gradient accumulation to attain a larger effective batch size.

The framework is now only applicable to English because the training data is DMRS graphs parsed from texts using the English Resource Grammar (ERG). This implies: (1) sentences not parsable by the grammar are not available for training, (2) the correct parse for each sentence may not be ranked top by the parser, and (3) for the model to be applicable to other languages, we either need a broad-coverage grammar on these languages for parsing texts to semantic graphs, or adequate semantic dependency graphs of sentences already annotated in these languages. Still, the ERG is a broad-coverage grammar so (1) is largely mitigated.

Ethics Statement

We anticipate no ethical issues directly stemming from our experiments. However, as with all distributional semantic models, our trained model is likely to have picked up social biases present in the training corpus. Any real-world application of a trained model would need to mitigate risks due to such biases.

Acknowledgements

We thank the reviewers, as well as Eric Chamoun, Michael Schlichtkrull and Justin Tang, for their thoughtful feedback and suggestions.

References

Laura Banarescu, Claire Bonial, Shu Cai, Madalina Georgescu, Kira Griffitt, Ulf Hermjakob, Kevin Knight, Philipp Koehn, Martha Palmer, and Nathan Schneider. 2013. Abstract Meaning Representation for sembanking. In *Proceedings of the 7th Linguistic Annotation Workshop and Interoperability with Discourse*, pages 178–186, Sofia, Bulgaria. Association for Computational Linguistics.

Marco Baroni, Raffaela Bernardi, and Roberto Zamparelli. 2014. Frege in space: A program of compositional distributional semantics. *Linguistic Issues in Language Technology (LiLT)*, 9.

Marco Baroni, Silvia Bernardini, Adriano Ferraresi, and Eros Zanchetta. 2009. The WaCky wide web: a collection of very large linguistically processed web-crawled corpora. *Language resources and evaluation*, 43(3):209–226.

Emily M. Bender, Dan Flickinger, Stephan Oepen, Woodley Packard, and Ann Copestake. 2015. Layers of interpretation: On grammar and compositionality. In *Proceedings of the 11th International Conference on Computational Semantics*, pages 239–249, London, UK. Association for Computational Linguistics.

Arthur Bražinskas, Serhii Havrylov, and Ivan Titov. 2018. Embedding words as distributions with a Bayesian skip-gram model. In *Proceedings of the 27th International Conference on Computational Linguistics*, pages 1775–1789, Santa Fe, New Mexico, USA. Association for Computational Linguistics.

Ulrich Callmeier. 2001. Efficient parsing with large-scale unification grammars. Master's thesis, Universität des Saarlandes, Saarbrücken, Germany.

Bob Coecke, Mehrnoosh Sadrzadeh, and Stephen Clark. 2010. Mathematical foundations for a compositional distributional model of meaning. *Linguistic Analysis*, 36, A Festschrift for Joachim Lambek:345–384.

Ann Copestake. 2009. **Invited Talk:** slacker semantics: Why superficiality, dependency and avoidance of commitment can be the right way to go. In *Proceedings of the 12th Conference of the European Chapter of the ACL (EACL 2009)*, pages 1–9, Athens, Greece. Association for Computational Linguistics.

Ann Copestake, Guy Emerson, Michael Wayne Goodman, Matic Horvat, Alexander Kuhnle, and Ewa Muszyńska. 2016. Resources for building applications with dependency Minimal Recursion Semantics. In *Proceedings of the Tenth International Conference on Language Resources and Evaluation (LREC'16)*, pages 1240–1247, Portorož, Slovenia. European Language Resources Association (ELRA).

Ann Copestake, Dan Flickinger, Carl Pollard, and Ivan A. Sag. 2005. Minimal Recursion Semantics: An introduction. *Research on Language and Computation*, 3(2-3):281–332.

Paula Czarnowska, Guy Emerson, and Ann Copestake. 2019. Words are vectors, dependencies are matrices: Learning word embeddings from dependency graphs. In *Proceedings of the 13th International Conference on Computational Semantics - Long Papers*, pages 91–102, Gothenburg, Sweden. Association for Computational Linguistics.

Shib Dasgupta, Michael Boratko, Siddhartha Mishra, Shriya Atmakuri, Dhruvesh Patel, Xiang Li, and Andrew McCallum. 2022. Word2Box: Capturing set-theoretic semantics of words using box embeddings. In *Proceedings of the 60th Annual Meeting of the Association for Computational Linguistics (Volume 1: Long Papers)*, pages 2263–2276, Dublin, Ireland. Association for Computational Linguistics.

Donald Davidson. 1967. The logical form of action sentences. In Nicholas Rescher, editor, *The Logic of Decision and Action*, chapter 3, pages 81–95. University of Pittsburgh Press. Reprinted in: Davidson (1980/2001), *Essays on Actions and Events*, Oxford University Press.

Nicola De Cao, Wilker Aziz, and Ivan Titov. 2019. Question answering by reasoning across documents with graph convolutional networks. In *Proceedings of the 2019 Conference of the North American Chapter of the Association for Computational Linguistics: Human Language Technologies, Volume 1 (Long and Short Papers)*, pages 2306–2317, Minneapolis, Minnesota. Association for Computational Linguistics.

Jacob Devlin, Ming-Wei Chang, Kenton Lee, and Kristina Toutanova. 2019. BERT: Pre-training of deep bidirectional transformers for language understanding. In *Proceedings of the 2019 Conference of the North American Chapter of the Association for Computational Linguistics (NAACL): Human Language Technologies, Volume 1 (Long and Short Papers)*, pages 4171–4186.

Guy Emerson. 2018. *Functional Distributional Semantics: Learning Linguistically Informed Representations from a Precisely Annotated Corpus*. Ph.D. thesis, University of Cambridge.

Guy Emerson. 2020a. Autoencoding pixies: Amortised variational inference with graph convolutions for functional distributional semantics. In *Proceedings of the 58th Annual Meeting of the Association for Computational Linguistics*, pages 3982–3995, Online. Association for Computational Linguistics.

Guy Emerson. 2020b. What are the goals of distributional semantics? In *Proceedings of the 58th Annual Meeting of the Association for Computational Linguistics*, pages 7436–7453, Online. Association for Computational Linguistics.

Guy Emerson. 2023. Probabilistic lexical semantics: From Gaussian embeddings to Bernoulli Fields. In Jean-Philippe Bernardy, Rasmus Blanck, Stergios Chatzikyriakidis, Shalom Lappin, and Aleksandre Maskharashvili, editors, *Probabilistic Approaches to Linguistic Theory*, pages 65–122. CSLI Publications.

Guy Emerson and Ann Copestake. 2016. Functional distributional semantics. In *Proceedings of the 1st Workshop on Representation Learning for NLP*, pages 40–52, Berlin, Germany. Association for Computational Linguistics.

Guy Emerson and Ann Copestake. 2017. Semantic composition via probabilistic model theory. In *IWCS 2017 - 12th International Conference on Computational Semantics - Long papers*.

Primož Fabiani. 2022. Gaussian pixie autoencoder: Introducing functional distributional semantics to continuous latent spaces. Technical report, University of Cambridge, Computer Laboratory.

Dan Flickinger. 2000. On building a more efficient grammar by exploiting types. *Natural Language Engineering*, 6(1):15–28.

Dan Flickinger. 2011. Accuracy vs. robustness in grammar engineering. In Emily M. Bender and Jennifer E. Arnold, editors, *Language from a Cognitive Perspective: Grammar, Usage, and Processing*, chapter 3, pages 31–50. Center for the Study of Language and Information (CSLI) Publications.

Dan Flickinger, Stephan Oepen, and Gisle Ytrestøl. 2010. WikiWoods: Syntacto-semantic annotation for English Wikipedia. In *Proceedings of the Seventh International Conference on Language Resources and Evaluation (LREC'10)*, Valletta, Malta. European Language Resources Association (ELRA).

Daniel Fried, Tamara Polajnar, and Stephen Clark. 2015. Low-rank tensors for verbs in compositional distributional semantics. In *Proceedings of the 53rd Annual Meeting of the Association for Computational Linguistics and the 7th International Joint Conference on Natural Language Processing (Volume 2: Short Papers)*, pages 731–736, Beijing, China. Association for Computational Linguistics.

Pablo Gamallo. 2019. A dependency-based approach to word contextualization using compositional distributional semantics. *Journal of Language Modelling*, 7(1):99–138.

Edward Grefenstette. 2013. *Category-theoretic quantitative compositional distributional models of natural language semantics*. Ph.D. thesis, Oxford University, UK.

Edward Grefenstette and Mehrnoosh Sadrzadeh. 2011. Experimental support for a categorical compositional distributional model of meaning. In *Proceedings of the 2011 Conference on Empirical Methods in Natural Language Processing*, pages 1394–1404, Edinburgh, Scotland, UK. Association for Computational Linguistics.

Edward Grefenstette and Mehrnoosh Sadrzadeh. 2015. Concrete models and empirical evaluations for the categorical compositional distributional model of meaning. *Computational Linguistics*, 41(1):71–118.

Abhijeet Gupta, Jason Utt, and Sebastian Padó. 2015. Dissecting the practical lexical function model for compositional distributional semantics. In *Proceedings of the Fourth Joint Conference on Lexical and Computational Semantics*, pages 153–158, Denver, Colorado. Association for Computational Linguistics.

Kazuma Hashimoto, Pontus Stenetorp, Makoto Miwa, and Yoshimasa Tsuruoka. 2014. Jointly learning word representations and composition functions using predicate-argument structures. In *Proceedings of the 2014 Conference on Empirical Methods in Natural Language Processing (EMNLP)*, pages 1544–1555, Doha, Qatar. Association for Computational Linguistics.

Kazuma Hashimoto and Yoshimasa Tsuruoka. 2015. Learning embeddings for transitive verb disambiguation by implicit tensor factorization. In *Proceedings of the 3rd Workshop on Continuous Vector Space Models and their Compositionality*, pages 1–11, Beijing, China. Association for Computational Linguistics.

Kazuma Hashimoto and Yoshimasa Tsuruoka. 2016. Adaptive joint learning of compositional and non-compositional phrase embeddings. In *Proceedings of the 54th Annual Meeting of the Association for Computational Linguistics (Volume 1: Long Papers)*, pages 205–215, Berlin, Germany. Association for Computational Linguistics.

Irina Higgins, Loic Matthey, Arka Pal, Christopher Burgess, Xavier Glorot, Matthew Botvinick, Shakir Mohamed, and Alexander Lerchner. 2017. beta-VAE: Learning basic visual concepts with a constrained variational framework. In *Proceedings of the 5th International Conference on Learning Representations (ICLR)*.

Xudong Hong, Asad Sayeed, and Vera Demberg. 2018. Learning distributed event representations with a multi-task approach. In *Proceedings of the Seventh Joint Conference on Lexical and Computational Semantics*, pages 11–21, New Orleans, Louisiana. Association for Computational Linguistics.

Dimitri Kartsaklis and Mehrnoosh Sadrzadeh. 2013. Prior disambiguation of word tensors for constructing sentence vectors. In *Proceedings of the 2013 Conference on Empirical Methods in Natural Language Processing*, pages 1590–1601, Seattle, Washington, USA. Association for Computational Linguistics.

Yova Kementchedjhieva, Mark Anderson, and Anders Søgaard. 2021. John praised Mary because _he_? implicit causality bias and its interaction with explicit cues in LMs. In *Findings of the Association for Computational Linguistics: ACL-IJCNLP 2021*, pages 4859–4871, Online. Association for Computational Linguistics.

Diederik P. Kingma and Max Welling. 2014. Auto-encoding variational Bayes. In *Proceedings of the 2nd International Conference on Learning Representations (ICLR)*.

Omer Levy and Yoav Goldberg. 2014. Dependency-based word embeddings. In *Proceedings of the 52nd Annual Meeting of the Association for Computational Linguistics (Volume 2: Short Papers)*, pages 302–308, Baltimore, Maryland. Association for Computational Linguistics.

Yinhong Liu and Guy Emerson. 2022. Learning functional distributional semantics with visual data. In *Proceedings of the 60th Annual Meeting of the Association for Computational Linguistics (Volume 1: Long Papers)*, pages 3976–3988, Dublin, Ireland. Association for Computational Linguistics.

Tomas Mikolov, Kai Chen, Greg Corrado, and Jeffrey Dean. 2013a. Efficient estimation of word representations in vector space. In *Proceedings of the 1st International Conference on Learning Representations (ICLR), Workshop Track*.

Tomas Mikolov, Ilya Sutskever, Kai Chen, Greg S Corrado, and Jeff Dean. 2013b. Distributed representations of words and phrases and their compositionality. In *Advances in Neural Information Processing Systems*, volume 26. Curran Associates, Inc.

George A Miller. 1995. WordNet: a lexical database for English. *Communications of the ACM*, 38(11):39–41.

Kevin P. Murphy. 2012. *Machine Learning: A Probabilistic Perspective*. Massachusetts Institute of Technology (MIT) Press.

Denis Paperno, Nghia The Pham, and Marco Baroni. 2014. A practical and linguistically-motivated approach to compositional distributional semantics. In *Proceedings of the 52nd Annual Meeting of the Association for Computational Linguistics (Volume 1: Long Papers)*, pages 90–99, Baltimore, Maryland. Association for Computational Linguistics.

Terence Parsons. 1990. *Events in the Semantics of English: A Study in Subatomic Semantics*. Current Studies in Linguistics. Massachusetts Institute of Technology (MIT) Press.

Adam Paszke, Sam Gross, Francisco Massa, Adam Lerer, James Bradbury, Gregory Chanan, Trevor Killeen, Zeming Lin, Natalia Gimelshein, Luca Antiga, Alban Desmaison, Andreas Kopf, Edward Yang, Zachary DeVito, Martin Raison, Alykhan Tejani, Sasank Chilamkurthy, Benoit Steiner, Lu Fang, Junjie Bai, and Soumith Chintala. 2019. Pytorch: An imperative style, high-performance deep learning library. In *Advances in Neural Information Processing Systems*, volume 32. Curran Associates, Inc.

Jeffrey Pennington, Richard Socher, and Christopher D Manning. 2014. Glove: Global vectors for word representation. In *Proceedings of the 2014 Conference on Empirical Methods in Natural Language Processing (EMNLP)*, pages 1532–1543.

Tamara Polajnar, Laura Rimell, and Stephen Clark. 2015. An exploration of discourse-based sentence spaces for compositional distributional semantics. In *Proceedings of the First Workshop on Linking Computational Models of Lexical, Sentential and Discourse-level Semantics*, pages 1–11, Lisbon, Portugal. Association for Computational Linguistics.

Danilo Jimenez Rezende, Shakir Mohamed, and Daan Wierstra. 2014. Stochastic backpropagation and approximate inference in deep generative models. In *Proceedings of the 31st International Conference on Machine Learning (ICML)*, pages 1278–1286.

Laura Rimell, Jean Maillard, Tamara Polajnar, and Stephen Clark. 2016. RELPRON: A relative clause evaluation data set for compositional distributional semantics. *Computational Linguistics*, 42(4):661–701.

Tom De Smedt and Walter Daelemans. 2012. Pattern for Python. *Journal of Machine Learning Research (JMLR)*, 13:2063–2067.

Lars Jørgen Solberg. 2012. A corpus builder for wikipedia. Master's thesis, University of Oslo.

Ran Tian, Naoaki Okazaki, and Kentaro Inui. 2016. Learning semantically and additively compositional distributional representations. In *Proceedings of the 54th Annual Meeting of the Association for Computational Linguistics (Volume 1: Long Papers)*, pages 1277–1287, Berlin, Germany. Association for Computational Linguistics.

Ottokar Tilk, Vera Demberg, Asad Sayeed, Dietrich Klakow, and Stefan Thater. 2016. Event participant modelling with neural networks. In *Proceedings of the 2016 Conference on Empirical Methods in Natural Language Processing*, pages 171–182, Austin, Texas. Association for Computational Linguistics.

Kristina Toutanova, Christopher D. Manning, Dan Flickinger, and Stephan Oepen. 2005. Stochastic HPSG parse disambiguation using the Redwoods corpus. *Research on Language and Computation*, 3(1):83–105.

Tim Van de Cruys, Thierry Poibeau, and Anna Korhonen. 2013. A tensor-based factorization model of semantic compositionality. In *Proceedings of the 2013 Conference of the North American Chapter of the Association for Computational Linguistics: Human Language Technologies*, pages 1142–1151, Atlanta, Georgia. Association for Computational Linguistics.

Luke Vilnis and Andrew McCallum. 2015. Word representations via Gaussian embedding. In *Proceedings of the 3rd International Conference on Learning Representations (ICLR)*.

Gijs Wijnholds, Mehrnoosh Sadrzadeh, and Stephen Clark. 2020. Representation learning for type-driven composition. In *Proceedings of the 24th Conference on Computational Natural Language Learning*, pages 313–324, Online. Association for Computational Linguistics.

Thomas Wolf, Lysandre Debut, Victor Sanh, Julien Chaumond, Clement Delangue, Anthony Moi, Pierric Cistac, Tim Rault, Rémi Louf, Morgan Funtowicz, and Jamie Brew. 2019. HuggingFace Transformers: State-of-the-art natural language processing. Unpublished manuscript, arXiv preprint 1910.03771.

Jonathan S. Yedidia, William T. Freeman, and Yair Weiss. 2003. Understanding Belief Propagation and its generalizations. In Gerhard Lakemeyer and Bernhard Nebel, editors, *Exploring Artificial Intelligence in the New Millennium*, chapter 8, pages 239–269. Morgan Kaufmann Publishers.

Gisle Ytrestøl, Dan Flickinger, and Stephan Oepen. 2009. Extracting and annotating Wikipedia subdomains: Towards a new eScience community resource. In *Proceedings of the 7th International Workshop on Treebanks and Linguistic Theories*, pages 185–197.

Manzil Zaheer, Satwik Kottur, Siamak Ravanbakhsh, Barnabas Poczos, Russ R Salakhutdinov, and Alexander J Smola. 2017. Deep sets. *Advances in neural information processing systems*, 30.

Yukun Zhu, Ryan Kiros, Rich Zemel, Ruslan Salakhutdinov, Raquel Urtasun, Antonio Torralba, and Sanja Fidler. 2015. Aligning books and movies: Towards story-like visual explanations by watching movies and reading books. In *Proceedings of the 2015 IEEE International Conference on Computer Vision (ICCV)*, pages 19–27.

A Training Details

A.1 Preprocessing

Predicates in DMRS can be divided into two classes, namely abstract predicates and surface predicates. Abstract predicates constitute a very small class. They mostly represent grammatical constructions (e.g., apposition and passivization) and are ignored in this work. On the other hand, surface predicates are exclusively introduced by lexical entries, which include nouns, verbs, adjectives, adverbs, adpositions, conjunctions and overt quantifiers. As in previous work, we assume an extensional model structure with entities being existentially quantified, so we ignore predications that take scopal arguments., e.g., quantifiers and modal verbs. Furthermore, the predicates are lemmas. Derivational and morphological distinctions of word-forms are thus disregarded in the framework. This alleviates data sparsity and aligns to the extensional assumption without further temporal information from inflections, such as tense and aspect.

To keep a reasonable size of vocabulary, we filter out the semantic functions that occur fewer than 100 times and keep only the 100,000 most frequent embeddings for the encoder. After that, we further remove the DMRS graphs with only one distinct predicate. A total of 60,081 semantic functions of 41,046 predicates are trained.

A.2 Hyperparameters and Tuning

For the common hyperparameter values among all models, we set the probability of dropout in the encoder to 0.5, and model parameters are optimized with gradient descent using the Adam optimizer.

For $\text{FDSAS}_{\text{tanh}}$ and FDSAS_{id}, we set K to 32, d to 300, and the dimension of the encoder's embedding to 300. We set β to 0 for $\text{FDSAS}_{\text{tanh}}$ and β for FDSAS_{id} to 0.01. The initial learning rates of both the parameters in the encoder and semantic functions are set to 0.001. The learning rates are multiplied by 0.8 per each epoch. We perform gradient accumulation over 128 batches of size 1. We trained with distributed data parallelism using 3 GPUs, so the effective batch size is 384 and the effective learning rates are 0.000333.

As mentioned in §5.3.2, the performance of $\text{FDSAS}_{\text{tanh}}$ peaks early and plateaus on the development set of RELPRON within 2 epochs whereas FDSAS_{id} is still improving after 6 epochs. Since we train models in an unsupervised manner and the only development set we have is from RELPRON, we have to ensure that training is not stopped prematurely based on the development set for evaluation on all other test sets.

To ensure sufficient time for training, we set a minimum number of epochs to be trained for each of our models, and apply early stopping by taking the performance on the development set of RELPRON at the end of it as a benchmark. Concretely, if a later checkpoint performs better than the benchmark on the development set of REPLRON, we select such a checkpoint for evaluations. To take care of different training dynamics, we set $\text{FDSAS}_{\text{tanh}}$ to train for a minimum of 3 epochs and FDSAS_{id} for a minimum of 7 epochs, before performing the early stops.

A.3 Computational Configurations

All models are implemented in PyTorch (Paszke et al., 2019) trained with distributed data parallelism on three NVIDIA GeForce GTX 1080 Ti for a single run. Training a run of $\text{FDSAS}_{\text{tanh}}$ and FDSAS_{id} model takes about 540 and 1260 GPU hours respectively.

FEED PETs: Further Experimentation and Expansion on the Disambiguation of Potentially Euphemistic Terms

Patrick Lee, Iyanuoluwa Shode , Alain Chirino Trujillo, Yuan Zhao, Olumide Ebenezer Ojo, Diana Cuevas Plancarte, Anna Feldman, Jing Peng
Montclair State University
New Jersey, USA
{leep6,shodei1,chirinotruja1,zhaoy2,ojoo,cuevasplancd1,feldmana,pengj}
@montclair.edu

Abstract

Transformers have been shown to work well for the task of English euphemism disambiguation, in which a potentially euphemistic term (PET) is classified as euphemistic or non-euphemistic in a particular context. In this study, we expand on the task in two ways. First, we annotate PETs for vagueness, a linguistic property associated with euphemisms, and find that transformers are generally better at classifying vague PETs, suggesting linguistic differences in the data that impact performance. Second, we present novel euphemism corpora in three different languages: Yoruba, Spanish, and Mandarin Chinese. We perform euphemism disambiguation experiments in each language using multilingual transformer models mBERT and XLM-RoBERTa, establishing preliminary results from which to launch future work.

1 Introduction

Detecting and interpreting figurative language is a rapidly growing area in Natural Language Processing (NLP) (Chakrabarty et al., 2022; Liu and Hwa, 2017). Unfortunately, little work has been done on euphemism processing. Euphemisms are expressions that soften the message they convey. They are culture-specific and dynamic: they change over time. Therefore, dictionary-based approaches are ineffective (Bertram, 1998; Holder, 2002; Rawson, 2003). Euphemisms are often ambiguous: their figurative and non-figurative interpretation is often context-dependent; see Table 1 for examples. Thus, existing work refers to these expressions as potentially euphemistic terms (PETs). State-of-the-art language models such as transformers perform well on many major NLP benchmarks. Recently, an attempt has been made to determine how these models perform in the euphemism disambiguation task (Lee et al., 2022a), in which an input text is classified as containing a euphemism or not. The described systems report promising results; however, without further analysis and experimentation, it is unclear what transformers are capturing in order to perform the disambiguation, and the full extent of their ability in other languages.

To address this, the present study describes two experiments to expand upon the euphemism disambiguation task. In the first, we investigate a pragmatic property of euphemisms, vagueness, and use human annotations to distinguish between PETs which are more vague (vague euphemistic terms, or VETs) versus less vague. We then experiment with transformers' abilities to disambiguate examples containing VETs versus non-VETs, and find that performance is generally higher for VETs. While we are unable to ascertain the exact reason for this discrepancy, we analyze the potential implications of the results and propose follow-up studies. In the second experiment, we create novel euphemism corpora for three other languages: Yorùbá, (Latin American and Castilian) Spanish, and Mandarin Chinese. Similarly to the English data, examples are obtained using a seed list of PETs, and include both euphemistic and non-euphemistic instances. We run initial experiments using multilingual transformer models mBERT and XLM-RoBERTa, testing their ability to classify them. The results establish preliminary baselines from which to launch future multilingual and cross-lingual work in euphemism processing.

2 Previous Work

In the past few years, there has been an interest in the NLP community in computational approaches to euphemisms. Felt and Riloff (2020) present the first effort to recognize euphemisms and dysphemisms (derogatory terms) using NLP. The authors use the term *x-phemisms* to refer to both. They used a weakly supervised algorithm for semantic lexicon induction (Thelen and Riloff, 2002) to generate lists of near-synonym phrases for three sensitive topics (lying, stealing, and firing). The important product of this work is a gold-standard

*Proceedings of the The 12th Joint Conference on Lexical and Computational Semantics (*SEM 2023)*, pages 437–448
July 13-14, 2023 ©2023 Association for Computational Linguistics

Non-euphemistic	Euphemistic
Asked to choose between jobs and the environment, a majority – at least in our warped, first-past-the-post system – will pick jobs.	This summer, the budding talent agent was between jobs and free to babysit pretty much any time.
Managers and scientists switch between jobs in private industry and government in USA in a manner perhaps not yet noticeable in India.	The couple say that they employ some great baristas and are looking to train more as the business expands, they emphasise that it is a job offering a great career and not just for students and those between jobs.

Table 1: Euphemistic and non-euphemistic interpretations are context-sensitive.
Ambiguity of between jobs (Retrieved from the News on the Web Corpus, October 6, 2021)

dataset of human x-phemism judgements showing that sentiment connotation and affective polarity are useful for identifying x-phemisms, but not sufficient.

While the performance of Felt and Riloff (2020)'s system is relatively low and the range of topics is very narrow, this work inspired other research on euphemism detection. Thus, Zhu et al. (2021) define two tasks: 1) euphemism detection (based on the input keywords, produce a list of candidate euphemisms) 2) euphemism identification (take the list of candidate euphemisms produced in (1) and output an interpretation). The authors selected sentences matched by a list of keywords, created masked sentences (mask the keywords in the sentences) and applied the masked language model proposed in BERT (Devlin et al., 2018) to filter out generic (uninformative) sentences and then generated expressions to fill in the blank. These expressions are ranked by relevance to the target topic.

Gavidia et al. (2022) present the first corpus of potentially euphemistic terms (PETs) along with example texts from the GloWbE corpus. They also present a subcorpus of texts where these PETs are not being used euphemistically. Gavidia et al. (2022) find that sentiment analysis on the euphemistic texts supports that PETs generally decrease negative and offensive sentiment. They observe cases of disagreement in an annotation task, where humans are asked to label PETs as euphemistic or not in a subset of our corpus text examples. The disagreement is attributed to a variety of potential reasons, including if the PET was a commonly accepted term (CAT). This work is followed by Lee et al. (2022b) who present a linguistically driven proof of concept for finding potentially euphemistic terms, or PETs. Acknowledging that PETs tend to be commonly used expressions for a certain range of sensitive topics, they make use of distributional similarities to select and filter phrase candidates from a sentence and rank them using a set of simple sentiment-based metrics.

With regards to the euphemism disambiguation task, in which terms are classified as euphemistic or non-euphemistic, a variety of BERT-based approaches featured in the 3rd Workshop on Figurative Language Processing have shown promising results. Keh et al. (2022) and Kesen et al. (2022) both show that supplying the classifier with information about the term itself, such as embeddings and its literal (non-euphemistic) meaning, significantly boost performance, among other enhancements. In a zero-shot experiment, Keh (2022) shows that BERT can disambiguate PETs unseen during training (albeit at a lower success rate), suggesting that some form of general knowledge is learned, though it is unclear what.

3 VET Experiments

In this section, we discuss the concept of Vague Euphemistic Terms (VETs), and subsequent experiments. The linguistics literature often describes euphemisms as either 'more ambiguous' or 'vaguer' than the non-euphemistic expressions they substitute (Burridge, 2012; Williamson, 2002; Égré and Klinedinst, 2011; Russell, 1923; Di Carlo, 2013). We understand ambiguity as a countable property, when an expression can have a certain number of senses; whereas vagueness is not countable, a continuum of meaning or theoretically an infinite number of interpretations. However, we note that these qualities are on a "spectrum", and may not be equal for all euphemisms. See below for examples of some euphemisms which may be considered to be VETs, and others, non-VETs:

VAGUE: The funds will be used to help <neutralize> threats to the operation and ensure our success. (Counter? Peacefully or violently? Kill? Some other form of removing power?)

Non-euphemistic	Euphemistic
pregnant woman	woman in a certain condition
aged care institution	home, hostel, house, cottage, village, residence
old age	certain age
false statements	alternative facts
war	special military operation/campaign
we have to change and do something we aren't used to	we must reach beyond our fears
being out of work	being in transition
a lack of consistent access to enough food for an active healthy life	food insecurity
prison	correctional facility
blind	visually challenged, visually impaired

Table 2: Euphemisms are vaguer than the expressions they substitute.

VAGUE: They were really starting to like each other, but did not know if they were ready to <go all the way> yet. (Start dating? Have sexual intercourse? Begin or complete some other process?)
NONVAGUE: As part of their restructuring, the company will <lay off> part of their workforce by next week.
NONVAGUE: There is always gossip about who <slept with> who on the front page of the magazine.

Additionally, Gavidia et al. (2022); Lee et al. (2022b) observed that there are different kinds of potentially euphemistic terms (PETs). One distinction they suggest is 'commonly accepted terms' (CATs), which are so commonly used in a particular domain that they may have less pragmatic purpose (intention to be vague/neutral/indirect/etc.) than other euphemisms. Some examples of PETs which may be CATs are "elderly", "same-sex", and "venereal disease". Humans may disagree on whether these terms are euphemistic in context, since CATs may be viewed as "default terms" rather than a deliberate attempt to be euphemistic. Notably, since many of the PETs under investigation are established expressions, we expect a fair amount to be non-vague; i.e., modern speakers of the language should precisely understand what the term means.

The differences described above may be a factor in computational attempts to work with euphemisms; e.g., some examples may be harder to disambiguate. To investigate this, we assess transformers' performances on examples annotated to be "vague" versus those that are "non-vague". However, defining and determining the relative vagueness of an expression is not a trivial task. Below, we describe our methodology for obtaining vagueness labels, experimental results and follow-up analyses.

3.1 Methodology

3.1.1 Vagueness Labels

To examine correlations between model performance and vagueness, we first aim to label each PET with a binary label (0 for non-vague, and 1 for vague). Existing computational methods for measuring vagueness are primarily lexically driven, using a dictionary of "vague terms", such as "approximately" or gradable adjectives like "tall" (Guélorget et al., 2021; Lebanoff and Liu, 2018), and do not fit our use case. Thus, we consider human-annotation approaches. However, in discussions with authors and annotators, we found that there was significant disagreement on what is meant by "vagueness", and how it should be defined for this task. Lacking clear instructions for explicitly annotating vagueness, we opted for an indirect annotation task. In this task, we asked annotators to replace the PET with a more direct paraphrase (if possible), and use similarities in annotators' paraphrases as a proxy for "vagueness". Intuitively, if annotators give dissimilar responses for a particular PET, then this indicates the PET is open to multiple interpretations, and thus a VET.

The way we computed the labels was as follows:

1. We supply annotators with a randomly selected example of each PET from the Euphemism Corpus; if a PET was ambiguous, both a euphemistic and a non-euphemistic example was supplied, resulting in an annotation task of 188 examples. A total of 6 linguistically-trained annotators were recruited. Annotators were then supplied with these instructions:

"For this task, you will read through text samples and decide how to paraphrase a certain word/phrase in the text. Each row will contain some text in the "text" column containing a particular word/phrase within angle brackets

Text	Euph Label	Paraphrases	Cos Sim	Vague Label
The violent Indian <Freedom Fighters> who fought the British were very much this. [...]	1	revolutionaries, reformers, anti-government activists, insurrectionists, terrorists, terrorists	0.53	1
[...] He's <passed away> but he started out as [...]	1	dead, died, died, died, died, died	0.924	0
[...] were electrocuted for <passing on> nuclear information to Soviet Russia [...] [...]	0	smuggling, leaking, illegally spreading, giving, passing on, giving away	0.330	1
At home, I wasn't allowed to watch certain movies until I had reached <a certain age>. [...]	0	an old enough age, a certain age, grown mature enough, maturity, adulthood, a certain age	0.608	0

Table 3: Sample of annotation results. The "Paraphrases" column shows the six annotators' responses, and the "Cos Sim" column shows the cosine similarity scores between embeddings of the responses.

< >. In the "paraphrase" column, please try to replace the word/phrase with a more direct interpretation. If you can't think of one, then answer with the original word/phrase."

2. Sentence-BERT (Reimers and Gurevych, 2019) was then used to generate embeddings of the annotators' responses. The cosine similarities between the embeddings were computed for each example and acted as an automatic measure of similarity between responses. See Table 3 for sample responses and the respective cosine similarity scores between them.

3. While this transformer-based similarity score generally captured semantic similarity well for strong cases of similarity or dissimilarity (e.g., see rows 2 and 3 of Table 3), we found that there were several "borderline cases" in which the score did not accurately reflect the semantic similarity between responses. For instance, annotators sometimes "over-paraphrased" non-euphemistic examples, providing responses with significant lexical differences (e.g., the non-euphemistic usage of the word "expecting" was paraphrased as "expecting", "anticipating", "foreseeing", etc.), that led to a low cosine score, despite being semantically similar to human judgment. Therefore, based on an examination of such borderline cases, we used the automatic method to assign a label of 0 (non-vague) to examples with a cosine score greater than 0.65, a label of 1 (vague) to examples with a score lower than 0.50, and manually annotated all examples in between. See Table 3 for sample responses, and the label they resulted in.

4. Lastly, these labels were generalized to the rest of the dataset under the assumption that euphemistic and non-euphemistic PETs are either vague or non-vague, regardless of context. For example, the euphemistic uses of "passed away" or "lay off" are usually non-vague, while "neutralize" and "special needs" are usually vague. Table 4 shows the final distribution of vagueness labels in our dataset when using this procedure.

It should be noted that this is an experimental procedure for approximating human labels of vagueness, in lieu of a more established method. In particular, the generalization that all PETs are vague or not regardless of context is a strong assumption. We leave exploring alternate methods of annotating vagueness for future work.

	Vague	Non-Vague
Euphemistic	408	975
Non-Euphemistic	361	208

Table 4: Number of vague vs. non-vague examples in the dataset

3.1.2 Data and Model

The euphemism dataset used for the experiments is the one created by Gavidia et al. (2022). A few modifications were made to several examples we believed to be misclassified. The final dataset contained 1952 examples, of which 1383 are euphemistic and 569 are non-euphemistic, spanning 128 different PETs.

The model used for all experiments was RoBERTa-base (Liu et al., 2019). RoBERTa was fine-tuned on the data using 10 epochs, a learning rate of 1e-5, a batch size of 16; all other hyperparameters were at default values.

Using the vagueness labels, we run classification tests in which RoBERTa is fine-tuned on both vague and non-vague examples, and then tested on both vague and non-vague examples. Then, we compute performance metrics separately for vague and non-vague examples in the test set for comparison. In the training and test sets, the data was split as evenly as possible across all labels of interest to help eliminate the impact of class imbalance on output metrics. Specifically, samples were randomly selected using the size of the smallest subgroup (vague-euphemistic, nonvague-euphemistic, etc.), and then evenly distributed into training and test sets using an 80-20 split. For example, for the vagueness data shown in Table 4, 208 is the size of the smallest subgroup, so 208 examples were randomly selected from all other subgroups for a total of 832 examples (664 train and 168 test); i.e., there were equal amounts of vague-euphemistic, vague-non-euphemistic, etc. examples in both training and test sets. Additionally, the number of unique/ambiguous PETs was approximately the same in all data splits.

3.2 Experimental Results and Observations

Table 5 shows the results of the VET experiment, which are metrics (Macro-F1, Precision, and Recall) averaged across 10 different classification runs. As aforementioned, in order to look at the effect of vagueness, we compute metrics for vague and nonvague examples separately; the first row shows the average metrics for the vague test examples in each run, while the second row shows metrics for the non-vague test examples. We observe that the performances are better for the examples marked as vague, rather than non-vague, suggesting that this is a meaningful distinction between examples.

	F1	P	R
Vague	0.853	0.856	0.854
Non-vague	0.793	0.805	0.795

Table 5: Results from the vagueness experiments.

As a consequence of the annotation procedure, the immediate conclusion is that examples containing non-vague PETs (i.e., those which annotators interpreted similarly) are somehow harder to classify, while those containing VETs are easier. However, a concrete explanation of this result remains elusive. An initial hypothesis was that non-vague PETs may be more likely to be PETs which annotators disagreed on in the original dataset (Gavidia et al., 2022), but this was not necessarily the case.

An error analysis of the most frequently misclassified examples leads us to a potential cause for the comparatively poor performance of the non-vague examples. We noted that a significant proportion of misclassified examples were non-euphemistic examples (which had been consistently misclassified as euphemistic by BERT). PETs in these examples appeared to co-occur with a relatively high number of "sensitive words" - words relating to sensitive topics that people may typically use euphemisms for, such as death, politics, and so on. If certain "sensitive words" are typically associated with euphemistic examples, then examples where this is not the case may mislead the classifier. In an attempt to quantify this, we use the following procedure:

1. Using a list of sensitive topics previously used for euphemism work as a starting point (Lee et al., 2022b), we come up with "sensitive word list" comprising of a list of 22 words we believe to represent a range of "sensitive topics". See Appendix A for the full list.

2. For each example, we go through each word and compute the cosine similarity with the words in our "sensitive word list" using Word2Vec (Mikolov et al., 2013). For every comparison that yields a similarity score > 0.5, we add a point to this example's "sensitivity score".

3. We then isolate the examples which were misclassified 10 or more times in the experiments, and repeat the above.

Table 6 below shows the results of this procedure. Each row shows a particular subgroup (e.g., the first row is for the euphemistic, vague examples), the number of examples in the subgroup, and the mean "sensitivty score" for examples in the subgroup. The last column shows the score normalized by the number of words in each example.

Euph	Vague	Data-set	Size	Mean Score	Norm Score
1	1	Full	408	**7.94**	**0.126**
1	0	Full	975	7.78	0.13
0	1	Full	361	5.59	0.094
0	0	Full	208	**5.56**	**0.095**
1	1	Err	21	**3.57**	**0.056**
1	0	Err	42	4.36	0.076
0	1	Err	45	7.09	0.114
0	0	Err	35	**8.26**	**0.13**

Table 6: Average sensitivity scores for each subgroup of the full corpus (top 4 rows) versus frequently misclassified examples (bottom 4 rows).

The first 4 rows of the dataset show that for the full corpus, sensitivity scores are higher for euphemistic examples than for non-euphemistic, regardless of vagueness. This suggests that, although euphemisms are milder alternatives to sensitive words, they tend to co-occur with other sensitive words in the context.

In contrast, we observe that this trend is reversed for the frequently misclassified examples (bottom 4 rows). That is, the misclassified euphemistic examples have an unusually low sensitivity score, while non-euphemistic examples have an unusually high score. If BERT has associated sensitive words with the euphemistic label, then it may be "confused" by non-euphemistic examples which have a high occurrence of them, and vice versa. Intuitively, we speculate that this happens more frequently with non-vague examples, because usage of a non-vague PET may correlate with decreased pragmatic intent.

Overall, there appears to be a correlation between the sensitivity score and misclassifed examples. Unfortunately, follow-up experiments involving model interpretability and ablation did not yield concrete results, so we cannot yet claim that BERT is "paying attention" to sensitive words. We leave a more comprehensive investigation to future work. However, the vagueness distinction between PETs indicates that there are linguistic differences between examples that have a concrete impact on model performance. Future work includes investigating other pragmatic features of euphemisms in a similar fashion, such as indirectness or politeness, and in other languages besides English.

4 Multilingual Experiments

Euphemism disambiguation thus far has focused on American English. In this section, we describe euphemism disambiguation experiments run on multilingual data. For each of the different languages, native speakers and language experts created a list of PETs, collected example texts for each PET, and annotated each text for whether the PET was being used euphemistically given the context. We then test the classification abilities of multilingual transformer models. The results are intended to show whether multilingual transformer models have the potential to disambiguate euphemisms in languages other than English, and establish preliminary baselines for the task.

4.1 Datasets

The data collection and annotation for each language is described below. Note that, while inter-annotator agreement is reported by (Gavidia et al., 2022), we did not have enough annotators to report agreement for each language. However, we assume that the agreement for other languages will be similar to American English, and leave more precise metrics for future work with more annotators.

4.1.1 Mandarin Chinese

Euphemisms are widely used in Chinese Mandarin in both formal and informal contexts, and in spoken and written language. It has been a social norm to use euphemisms to express respect and sympathy, and also to avoid certain taboos and controversies. For example, Chinese speakers are accustomed to use euphemisms to talk about topics such as death, sexual activities and disabilities, as explicit and direct narratives can be considered inappropriate or disrespectful.

In collecting the PETs, terms used by mainly ancient Chinese were excluded since the corpus is contemporary. Also, the PETs were restricted to single words and multi-word expressions, rather than sentences (Zhang, 2019). The euphemistic terms are generated based on the language knowledge of the collector, who is a native speaker of Mandarin Chinese. For the source corpus, we referred to an online Chinese corpus made by Bright Xu (username: brightmart) on Github (brightmart,

Non-euphemistic	Euphemistic
放在手机上看又不方便。 / It is not convenient to read it on the phone.	吃饭时，一人说去方便一下。 / During the meal, a person went to use the bathroom.
方便了秦始皇的全国巡游。 / It made the nation-wide tour convenient for Qin Shi Huang.	于是选择了就近的河边方便一下。 / So he chose to relieve himself right by the river.

Table 7: Examples of euphemistic and non-euphemistic sentences in Mandarin Chinese

Non-euphemistic	Euphemistic
Es perfecta para divertirse, pasar un buen rato y dejarte llevar por una historia sin más pretensión. / It is perfect to have some fun, have a good time and to let yourself carry by an unpretentious story.	Con el propósito evidente de pasar un buen rato con ella. La chica no era muy brillante, pero lo que le faltaba de inteligencia le sobraba en curvas. / With the clear purpose of having a good time with her. The girl was not that brilliant, but her curves overshadowed her intelligence.
Que los pocos recursos disponibles estaban comprometidos para pagar las deudas ocultas. /That the few resources are destined to pay off the hidden debt.	Para que jóvenes de pocos recursos logren alcanzar su profesionalización en las aulas. /So that poor young students find a way to become professionals at school.

Table 8: Examples of euphemistic and non-euphemistic sentences in Spanish

Non-euphemistic	Euphemistic
Táiwò, ẹ́gbọn Fùnkẹ̀ rí àlejò rẹ́ lánà tó wá láti ìlú Èkó. Taiwo, Funke's elder sibling saw her visitor who came from Lagos yesterday.	Obìnrin tí kò rí àlejò rẹ́. The woman who does not see her menstruation.
A kò gbọdọ̀ dákẹ̀. We should not be quiet.	Ẹ sara gírí, bàbá ti dákẹ́. Be brave, father is dead.

Table 9: Examples of euphemistic and non-euphemistic sentences in Yorùbá

2019). The particular corpus used was 新闻语料json版 (news2016zh) which consists of 2.5 million news articles from 63,000 media from 2014 to 2016, including title, keyword, summary and text body.

See Table 7 for examples of Chinese PETs. For example, 方便 means "to use the bathroom / to relieve oneself" when used euphemistically; and means "convenient" when used non-euphemistically.

4.1.2 Spanish

Spanish, a Romance language, is the second most spoken language in the world (Lewis, 2009). For the sake of building a wide and robust corpus, it was paramount considering all different dialects of Spanish. Some of the countries considered are: Equatorial New Guinea, Puerto Rico, Argentina, Spain, Chile, Cuba, Mexico, Bolivia, Ecuador, Paraguay, Dominican Republic, Venezuela, Costa Rica, Colombia, Nicaragua, Honduras, Guatemala, Perú, El Salvador, Uruguay, and Panama.

Euphemisms are highly used in Spanish on a daily basis. Topics related to politics, employment, sexual activities or even death are widely communicated with euphemistic terms. First, a list of potentially euphemistic terms (PETs) was created using a dictionary of euphemisms as main reference (Garcia, 2000; Rodríguez and Estrada, 1999). For extracting PETs, we relied heavily on the Real Academia Española (Real Spanish Academy)[1]. The corpus we collected contains sentences with PETS, PET label (euphemistic/non-euphemistic), data source and country of origin. For example: "Pasar un buen rato" meaning "to have/spend a good time" can be used as both, euphemistically and non-euphemistically. This term could be used to express involvement on a sexual activity or to spend a good time with a friend, family or an acquainted. Furthermore, the phrase "Dar a luz" meaning "to give birth" is another example that comprises both uses. Women naturally give birth to babies but women can also give birth to wonderful ideas, so as any other human being. See more examples in Table 8.

4.1.3 Yorùbá

Yorùbá is one of the major languages of Nigeria, the most populous country on the African continent (Okanlawon, 2016). With over 50 million language users as speakers, it is the third most spoken language in Africa (Shode et al., 2022). There

[1] https://apps2.rae.es/CORPES/view/inicioExterno.view

Language	Total Examples	Euph Examples	Non-Euph Examples	Total PETs	Always-Euph PETs	Ambiguous PETs
American English	1952	1383	569	129	71	58
Mandarin Chinese	1552	1134	418	70	46	24
Spanish	961	564	397	80	33	47
Yorùbá	1942	1281	661	129	62	69

Table 10: Statistics of multilingual datasets used for euphemism disambiguation experiments.

Language	mBERT			XLM-RoBERTa-base			XLM-RoBERTa-large		
	F1	P	R	F1	P	R	F1	P	R
American English	0.819	0.876	0.933	0.765	0.852	0.894	0.854	0.907	0.930
Mandarin Chinese	0.901	0.952	0.938	0.884	0.921	0.960	0.952	0.967	0.982
Spanish	0.747	0.781	0.816	0.765	0.799	0.819	0.776	0.813	0.826
Yorùbá	0.729	0.801	0.859	0.683	0.771	0.843	0.667	0.768	0.814

Table 11: Results of euphemism disambiguation experiments on the multilingual datasets.

are many different dialects of Yoruba spoken by Yoruba people in Nigeria, Benin, and Togo, all of which are tonal (change depending on tone) and agglutinative (words are made up of linearly sequential morphemes) in nature.

Euphemisms are often used in everyday Yorùbá language conversations. Speakers use them to communicate sensitive topics like death and physical or mental health in a more socially acceptable manner, and to show reverence for certain people or occupations such as elders of the night which refer to witches and wizards, prostitutes, and so on. Euphemisms in Yorùbá are used to soften the harshness of situations; to report the death of an individual, speakers of the language mostly use indirect or subtle sentences instead of saying it directly.

In NLP research, Yorùbá is considered as a low resourced language because of the limited availability of data in digital formats. There is no corpus dedicated to Yorùbá euphemisms available online so PETs were collected from different sources such as news websites like BBC Yorùbá, Alaroye, religious sources including Yorùbá Bible, `JW.org`, transcribed Muslim and Christian sermons, Yorùbá wikipedia, Yorùbá Web corpus (YorubaWaC), blogposts, journals, research works, books, Global Voices, Nigerian song lyrics, written texts written by Yorùbá native speakers and social media platforms such as tweets, Facebook public posts, and Nairaland. Some samples of PETs are listed in Table 9.

4.2 Methodology

From each language dataset, a maximum of 40 euphemistic and non-euphemistic examples per PET were randomly chosen to be in the experimental dataset. This was done to in an effort to ensure an overall balance of PETs in the data and reduce skewed label proportions for each PET. We also include American English data, sampled in the same manner, to provide a basis of comparison. The final statistics for each dataset are shown in Table 10.

We test three multilingual transformer models: mBERT (Devlin et al., 2018), XLM-RoBERTa and XLM-RoBERTa-large (Conneau et al., 2020). The hyperparameters used were the same as those described in 3.1.2. A stratified 5-fold split is used to create 5 different train-test splits of each dataset, which includes every example while preserving the 80-20 ratio used in previous experiments.

4.3 Results and Observations

Table 11 shows the performance of each model. The metrics reported are macro-F1 (F1), precision (P), and recall (R), averaged across 5 experiments.

We note several things about the results: (1) All languages performed at least decently, indicating that multilingual BERT models pick up on something to disambiguate euphemisms in each language. (2) As expected, XLM-RoBERTa-large generally performed better than XLM-RoBERTa-base, which consistently performed worse than mBERT. (3) Because of differences in each language's dataset, the results are not directly comparable. We aim to make the experimental setup more consistent for future work, but some present inconsistencies include:

- The Chinese data is the only one in which the PET is consistently "identified" (i.e. surrounded) by angle brackets <>, which the classifier may have used to its advantage. (Empirically, we notice that such "identifiers" improve performance.)

- The proportion of non-euphemistic examples to the entire dataset was the smallest for Chinese (27%), followed by English (29%), Yorùbá (34%) and Spanish (41%). This, along with the number of ambiguous PETs, may reflect the relative "difficulty" of disambiguation for each language.

- While mBERT is pretrained on Yorùbá data, the XLM-RoBERTa models are not. Thus, any sort of disambiguation capabilities shown by the XLM-RoBERTa models are notable.

5 Conclusion and Future Work

This study presents an expansion of the euphemism disambiguation task. We describe our method for annotating vagueness, and show that this kind of pragmatic distinction may reveal interesting trends in BERT's ability to perform NLU. Namely, BERT performs better for PETs labeled as VETs, which leads us to the potential result that BERT may be associating the presence of "sensitive words" to euphemisms. Corroborating this result and exploring additional properties of euphemisms are left for future work.

The multilingual results show that BERT models can already disambiguate euphemisms in multiple languages to some extent, and establish a baseline from which to improve results. While continuously expanding the multilingual corpora is a must, a number of modeling aspects can be investigated as well. For instance, error analyses can be run to reveal potential misclassification trends in each language, and data and modeling improvements that were shown to work for American English can be attempted on other languages. In general, such investigations may be used to suggest useful cross-lingual features for PET disambiguation, and more broadly, universal properties of euphemisms.

Limitations

Euphemisms are culture and dialect-specific, and we do not necessarily investigate the full range of euphemistic terms and topics covered by our selected languages. Even for "English", for instance, we do not explore euphemisms unique to "British English", though that warrants a study of its own. Additionally, as aforementioned, differences in the multilingual dataset render the results not directly comparable. For example, there are few large, structured corpora of Yorùbá, so the data was taken from a variety of sources, as opposed to the other languages. Additional limitations prevent some analyses, such as limited ability to identify the PET in Yorùbá due to loss of diacritics.

Ethics Statement

The authors foresee no ethical concerns with the work presented in this paper.

Acknowledgements

This material is based upon work supported by the National Science Foundation under Grant numbers: 2226006 and 1704113.

References

Anne Bertram. 1998. *NTC's Dictionary of Euphemisms*. NTC, Chicago.

brightmart. 2019. nlp_chinese_corpus: release version 1.0 (v1.0).

Kate Burridge. 2012. Euphemism and language change: The sixth and seventh ages. *Lexis. Journal in English Lexicology*, (7).

Tuhin Chakrabarty, Arkadiy Saakyan, Debanjan Ghosh, and Smaranda Muresan. 2022. Flute: Figurative language understanding through textual explanations. In *Proceedings of the 2022 Conference on Empirical Methods in Natural Language Processing*, pages 7139–7159.

Alexis Conneau, Kartikay Khandelwal, Naman Goyal, Vishrav Chaudhary, Guillaume Wenzek, Francisco Guzmán, Edouard Grave, Myle Ott, Luke Zettlemoyer, and Veselin Stoyanov. 2020. Unsupervised cross-lingual representation learning at scale. In *Proceedings of the 58th Annual Meeting of the Association for Computational Linguistics*, pages 8440–8451, Online. Association for Computational Linguistics.

Jacob Devlin, Ming-Wei Chang, Kenton Lee, and Kristina Toutanova. 2018. BERT: Pre-training of deep bidirectional transformers for language understanding. *arXiv preprint arXiv:1810.04805*.

Giuseppina Scotto Di Carlo. 2013. *Vagueness as a political strategy: Weasel words in security council resolutions relating to the second gulf war.* Cambridge Scholars Publishing.

Paul Égré and Nathan Klinedinst. 2011. Introduction: Vagueness and language use. In *Vagueness and Language Use*, pages 1–21. Springer.

Christian Felt and Ellen Riloff. 2020. Recognizing euphemisms and dysphemisms using sentiment analysis. In *Proceedings of the Second Workshop on Figurative Language Processing*, pages 136–145.

José Manuel Lechado Garcia. 2000. *Diccionario de eufemismos (Dictionary of euphemisms and euphemistic expressions of current Spanish).* Verbum, Madrid.

Martha Gavidia, Patrick Lee, Anna Feldman, and JIng Peng. 2022. CATs are fuzzy PETs: A corpus and analysis of potentially euphemistic terms. In *Proceedings of the Thirteenth Language Resources and Evaluation Conference*, pages 2658–2671, Marseille, France. European Language Resources Association.

Paul Guélorget, Benjamin Icard, Guillaume Gadek, Souhir Gahbiche, Sylvain Gatepaille, Ghislain Atemezing, and Paul Égré. 2021. Combining vagueness detection with deep learning to identify fake news. *CoRR*, abs/2110.14780.

R. W. Holder. 2002. *How Not To Say What You Mean: A Dictionary of Euphemisms.* Oxford University Press, Oxford.

Sedrick Scott Keh. 2022. Exploring Euphemism Detection in Few-Shot and Zero-Shot Settings. In *Proceedings of the 3rd Workshop on Figurative Language Processing.* Association for Computational Linguistics.

Sedrick Scott Keh, Rohit K. Bharadwaj, Emmy Liu, Simone Tedeschi, Varun Gangal, and Roberto Navigli. 2022. EUREKA: EUphemism recognition enhanced through knn-based methods and augmentation. In *Proceedings of the 3rd Workshop on Figurative Language Processing.* Association for Computational Linguistics.

Ilker Kesen, Aykut Erdem, Erkut Erdem, and Iacer Calixto. 2022. Detecting Euphemisms with Literal Descriptions and Visual Imagery. In *Proceedings of the 3rd Workshop on Figurative Language Processing.* Association for Computational Linguistics.

Logan Lebanoff and Fei Liu. 2018. Automatic detection of vague words and sentences in privacy policies. *arXiv preprint arXiv:1808.06219.*

Patrick Lee, Anna Feldman, and Jing Peng. 2022a. A report on the euphemisms detection shared task. In *Proceedings of the 3rd Workshop on Figurative Language Processing (FLP)*, Abu Dhabi, United Arab Emirates (Hybrid). Association for Computational Linguistics.

Patrick Lee, Martha Gavidia, Anna Feldman, and Jing Peng. 2022b. Searching for PETs: Using distributional and sentiment-based methods to find potentially euphemistic terms. In *Proceedings of the Second Workshop on Understanding Implicit and Underspecified Language*, pages 22–32, Seattle, USA. Association for Computational Linguistics.

M. Paul Lewis, editor. 2009. *Ethnologue: Languages of the World*, sixteenth edition. SIL International, Dallas, TX, USA.

Changsheng Liu and Rebecca Hwa. 2017. Representations of context in recognizing the figurative and literal usages of idioms. In *Proceedings of the Thirty-First AAAI Conference on Artificial Intelligence*, AAAI'17, page 3230'Ă'Ş3236. AAAI Press.

Yinhan Liu, Myle Ott, Naman Goyal, Jingfei Du, Mandar Joshi, Danqi Chen, Omer Levy, Mike Lewis, Luke Zettlemoyer, and Veselin Stoyanov. 2019. Roberta: A robustly optimized bert pretraining approach. *arXiv preprint arXiv:1907.11692.*

Tomas Mikolov, Kai Chen, Greg Corrado, and Jeffrey Dean. 2013. Efficient estimation of word representations in vector space. *arXiv preprint arXiv:1301.3781.*

Jolaade Okanlawon. 2016. *An Analysis of the Yoruba Language with English: Phonetics, Phonology, Morphology, and Syntax.* Northeastern University.

Hugh Rawson. 2003. *Dictionary of euphemisms and other doublespeak: Being a compilation of linguistic fig leaves and verbal flourishes for artful users of the English language.* Pittsford: Castle Books.

Nils Reimers and Iryna Gurevych. 2019. Sentence-bert: Sentence embeddings using siamese bert-networks. *arXiv preprint arXiv:1908.10084.*

Mauro Rodríguez and Mauro Rodríguez Estrada. 1999. *Creatividad lingüística: diccionario de eufemismos.* Editorial Pax México.

Bertrand Russell. 1923. Vagueness. *The Australasian Journal of Psychology and Philosophy*, 1(2):84–92.

Iyanuoluwa Shode, David Ifeoluwa Adelani, and Anna Feldman. 2022. yosm: A new yoruba sentiment corpus for movie reviews. *arXiv preprint arXiv:2204.09711.*

Michael Thelen and Ellen Riloff. 2002. A bootstrapping method for learning semantic lexicons using extraction pattern contexts. In *Proceedings of the 2002 conference on empirical methods in natural language processing (EMNLP 2002)*, pages 214–221.

Timothy Williamson. 2002. *Vagueness.* Routledge.

Qiaoge Zhang. 2019. 汉语委婉语语用功能探析 On the Pragmatic Functions of Chinese Euphemism. 中国高校人文社会科学信息网 .

Wanzheng Zhu, Hongyu Gong, Rohan Bansal, Zachary Weinberg, Nicolas Christin, Giulia Fanti, and Suma Bhat. 2021. Self-supervised euphemism detection and identification for content moderation. *arXiv preprint arXiv:2103.16808*.

A List of Words used to Represent Sensitive Topics

Listed below are the 22 "sensitive words" used to compute a sensitivity score for each example in the corpus:

['politics', 'death', 'kill', 'crime', 'drugs', 'alcohol', 'fat', 'old', 'poor', 'cheap', 'sex', 'sexual', 'employment', 'job', 'disability', 'pregnant', 'bathroom', 'sickness', 'race', 'racial', 'religion', 'government']

Monolingual Phrase Alignment as Parse Forest Mapping

Sora Kadotani*
NTT Human Informatics Laboratories,
NTT Corporation, Japan
sora.kadotani@ntt.com

Yuki Arase
Osaka University, Japan
Artificial Intelligence Research Center,
AIST, Japan
arase@ist.osaka-u.ac.jp

Abstract

We tackle the problem of monolingual phrase alignment conforming to syntactic structures. The existing method formalises the problem as unordered *tree* mapping; hence, the alignment quality is easily affected by syntactic ambiguities. We address this problem by expanding the method to align parse *forests* rather than 1-best trees, where syntactic structures and phrase alignment are simultaneously identified. The proposed method achieves efficient alignment by mapping forests on a packed structure. The experimental results indicated that our method improves the phrase alignment quality of the state-of-the-art method by aligning forests rather than 1-best trees.

1 Introduction

Monolingual phrase alignment, which identifies semantically corresponding phrase pairs in sentences, is a fundamental technique useful for paraphrase recognition (Das and Smith, 2009), textual entailment recognition (MacCartney et al., 2008; Heilman and Smith, 2010), question answering (Wang and Manning, 2010), and interpreting semantic textual similarity (Agirre et al., 2015; Li and Srikumar, 2016). Its ability to declare overlapping information across sentences is also useful for summarisation (Brook Weiss et al., 2021) and for interactive document exploration (Shapira et al., 2017; Hirsch et al., 2021). There are two approaches to phrase alignment: one aligns chunks of arbitrary spans (e.g., n-grams) (Yao et al., 2013; Ouyang and McKeown, 2019; Lan et al., 2021) while the other targets on syntactic phrases (Arase and Tsujii, 2017, 2020). In this study, we take the latter approach to identify phrasal paraphrases conforming to syntactic structures that allow modelling sentences based on syntax (Socher et al., 2013; Tai et al., 2015).

*This work was completed at Osaka University.

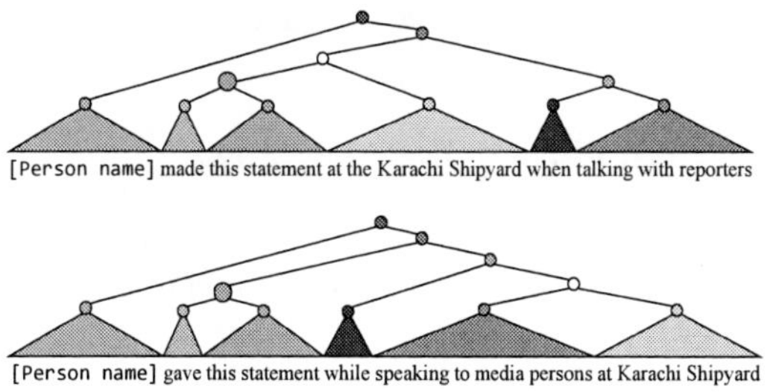

Figure 1: Phrase alignment example by the proposed method (corresponding nodes are colour-coded). Our method aligns a source (top) and target (bottom) parse forests simultaneously determining their structures.

The current state-of-the-art syntactic phrase alignment (Arase and Tsujii, 2020) has formulated the phrase alignment as the unordered tree mapping problem between trees of source and target sentences.[1] Their method realised an efficient alignment with a solid theoretical background by adopting the constrained tree edit distance algorithm (Zhang, 1996), which aligns syntactic *trees*. However, their experiments were limited to using manually assigned gold syntactic trees, disregarding the effects of syntactic ambiguities that cause parse errors in practical parsers.

We address this problem by expanding the method proposed by Arase and Tsujii (2020) to align parse *forests*. Specifically, our method considers the likelihood of both syntactic structures and phrase alignment, i.e., it simultaneously identifies the syntactic structures of input sentence pairs and phrase alignment within. Figure 1 illustrates phrase alignment by our method, where the trees show syntactic structures of the source (top) and target (bottom). The alignment is colour-coded; the same colour nodes are pairs. For example, the pair of orange nodes represent that verb phrases 'made this statement' and 'gave this statement' are paraphrases. Remarkably, in the source tree, the

[1]We refer to one sentence of a pair as a source and another as a target for the sake of explanation.

*Proceedings of the The 12th Joint Conference on Lexical and Computational Semantics (*SEM 2023)*, pages 449–455
July 13-14, 2023 ©2023 Association for Computational Linguistics

prepositional phrase 'at the Karachi Shipyard' (the pink node) is correctly attached to the preceding verb phrase (the orange node) because the attachment ambiguity is resolved by referring to the target. In contrast, the 1-best tree failed to derive this structure.

The experimental results on the standard corpus indicated that the proposed method improves the phrase alignment quality of the state-of-the-art aligning 1-best parse trees. We also conducted a manual analysis that revealed attachment errors can be addressed by forest alignment.

2 Preliminary: Tree Alignment

Arase and Tsujii (2020) has formulated phrase alignment as the unordered tree mapping. They adopted the constrained tree edit distance (CTED) algorithm (Zhang, 1996) to identify optimal mappings of phrases in polynomial time. The CTED algorithm is based on dynamic programming; hence their method recursively aligns phrases from leaves to root nodes of source and target syntactic trees.

In the alignment algorithm, alignment of node i and j, denoted as $\langle i, j\rangle$, incurs a cost defined by a function $\gamma(\langle i, j\rangle) \rightarrow \mathbb{R}$. In their method, the cost function is the cosine distance between phrase vectors of spans covered by i and j, where the vectors are computed by pooling token representations obtained by a fine-tuned pre-trained language model. A phrase is allowed not to have correspondence, i.e., *null* alignment, which is modelled as alignment to an empty node τ_ϕ. The cost of null alignment is predetermined and given as a hyperparameter λ_ϕ.

We denote T_i as the subtree rooted at node i. If we delete the node i from T_i, there remain a set of subtrees whose root nodes have been the children of i: $\{i_\ell | i_1, \cdots, i_{n_i}\}$, where n_i is the number of the children. When we do not assume the order among these subtrees, they constitute an *unordered* forest, denoted as F_i. The CTED algorithm recursively computes the minimum cost to align subtrees of T_i^s and T_j^t as follows.

$$D(T_i^s, T_j^t) = \min \begin{cases} D(\tau_\phi, T_j^t) + \min_{1\le k\le n_j} \{D(T_i^s, T_{j_k}^t) - D(\tau_\phi, T_{j_k}^t)\}, \\ D(T_i^s, \tau_\phi) + \min_{1\le \ell\le n_i} \{D(T_{i_\ell}^s, T_j^t) - D(T_{i_\ell}^s, \tau_\phi)\}, \\ D(F_i^s, F_j^t) + \gamma(\langle i, j\rangle). \end{cases} \quad (1)$$

Specifically, Equation (1) computes the minimum cost among the cases regarding the alignment of i and j, i.e., $\langle \tau_\phi, j\rangle$, $\langle i, \tau_\phi\rangle$, and $\langle i, j\rangle$, which correspond to the first, second, and the third expressions, respectively. Notice that the last case (i.e., $\langle i, j\rangle$) requires the alignment cost of forests under these nodes, i.e., F_i^s and F_j^t. The cost to align F_i^s and F_j^t is computed as follows.

$$D(F_i^s, F_j^t) = \min \begin{cases} D(\tau_\phi, F_j^t) + \min_{1\le k\le n_j} \{D(F_i^s, F_{j_k}^t) - D(\tau_\phi, F_{j_k}^t)\}, \\ D(F_i^s, \tau_\phi) + \min_{1\le \ell\le n_i} \{D(F_{i_\ell}^s, F_j^t) - D(F_{i_\ell}^s, \tau_\phi)\}, \\ \min_{\mathcal{M}(i,j)} \gamma(\mathcal{M}(i, j)). \end{cases} \quad (2)$$

Here, the first two expressions correspond to null alignment. The third expression identifies the constrained edit distance mapping between F_i^s and F_j^t, denoted as $\mathcal{M}(i, j)$, of the minimum cost. It can be efficiently solved as the minimum cost maximum flow problem on a graph constructed based on these forests. For more details of the alignment algorithm, please refer to (Arase and Tsujii, 2020).

Some phrases may have long-distance correspondences (Heilman and Smith, 2010; Arase and Tsujii, 2017) that cannot be monotonically composed of alignment of descendant nodes, which hence cannot be identified by the CTED algorithm. Arase and Tsujii (2020) align such phrases by heuristic-based post-processing.

3 Proposed Method: Forest Alignment

We expand the alignment method proposed by Arase and Tsujii (2020) to align parse forests instead of trees. The syntactic structures of the input sentence pair are determined simultaneously with phrase alignment. A naive approach to align forests is considering combinations of all candidate trees and then finding the best one. However, this procedure is prohibitively computationally expensive considering the number of valid tree structures. We achieve efficient forest alignment by expanding the CTED algorithm to perform tree mapping on a packed forest structure (Miyao and Tsujii, 2008).

Syntactic Plausibility Studies on parallel parsing (Burkett et al., 2010; Choe and McClosky, 2015) have shown that syntactic ambiguity can be resolved by referring to sentences parsed in parallel with each other. Inspired by these studies, we consider the likelihood of parsing in the alignment cost function. Specifically, Equation (2) is expanded to consider the parsing likelihoods:

$$\hat{D}(F_i^s, F_j^t) = D(F_i^s, F_j^t) - \lambda_s \frac{S(T_i^s)+S(T_j^t)}{2}, \quad (3)$$

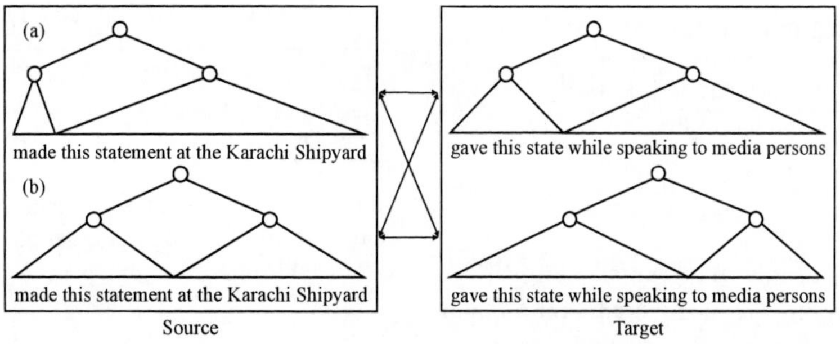

Figure 2: Packed forest structure efficiently stores possible forests under the same nodes.

where $S(\cdot)$ indicates the likelihood of a subtree obtained from a syntactic parser, and λ_s is a hyper-parameter that balances both terms.

Alignment on Packed Forests The packed forest structure corresponds to the packed charts in the CFG parsing and can represent an exponential number of trees with a polynomial number of nodes. Specifically, a packed forests under the node i, $\text{PF}^i = \{F_k^i\}_k$, stores different possible syntactic structures (forests) under i. Figure 2 shows examples. Each box corresponds to a node where different possible structures are stored. In the left box, the source can be composed by combining (a) a verb phrase 'made' and noun phrase 'this statement at the Karachi Shipyard' and (b) a verb phrase 'made this statement' and prepositional phrase 'at the Karachi Shipyard'.

Algorithm 3.1 illustrates our alignment mechanism. It computes the cost to align all combinations of possible structures on the packed forests and memorizes only the one with the minimum cost. That is, only the pair with the minimum cost needs to be considered in the alignment of the upper nodes. In the examples in Figure 2, there are 2 possible structures in the source and target. The proposed method computes the costs of the 2×2 combinations and stores only the minimum cost and the corresponding structures.

Algorithm 3.1 Packed forest mapping

Input: Packed (unordered) forests under the node i and j: $\text{PF}^{s,i}$ and $\text{PF}^{t,j}$

$c_m \leftarrow \infty$ ▷ Minimum cost
$\text{MF} \leftarrow \emptyset$ ▷ Pair of forests
for all $F_k^{s,i} \in \text{PF}^{s,i}$ **do**
  for all $F_\ell^{t,j} \in \text{PF}^{t,j}$ **do**
    $c \leftarrow \hat{D}(F_k^{s,i}, F_\ell^{t,j})$ ▷ Eq. (3)
    if $c < c_m$ **then**
      $c_m \leftarrow c$
      $\text{MF} \leftarrow \{F_k^{s,i}, F_\ell^{t,j}\}$
Compute $D(T_i^s, T_j^t)$ with c_m, MF ▷ Eq. (1)

4 Experiment

We evaluate the performance of syntactic phrase alignment of the proposed method compared to the previous state-of-the-art.

4.1 Evaluation Corpus

As an evaluation corpus, we used Syntactic Phrase Alignment Dataset for Evaluation (SPADE) (Arase and Tsujii, 2018).[2] SPADE consists of English paraphrase sentence pairs assigned by their gold constituency trees annotated by linguistic professionals and phrase alignment identified by three native and near-native English speakers. It provides 50 sentence pairs as a development (dev) set and 151 sentence pairs as a test set. While these numbers of sentences may look small, the numbers of phrase pairs are sufficiently large to have statistically meaningful observations, i.e., $8,708$ phrase pairs and $25,709$ phrase pairs in the dev and test sets, respectively. Remind that our method does not require training; only its hyper-parameters should be tuned using the dev set.

4.2 Evaluation Metrics

Metrics for Alignment Quality Alignment recall (**ALIR**), alignment precision (**ALIP**), and alignment F-measure (**ALIF**) are the standard evaluation metrics defined by SPADE. ALIR evaluates how gold-standard alignment can be replicated by automatic alignment, and ALIP measures how automatic alignment overlaps with alignment pairs

[2] https://catalog.ldc.upenn.edu/LDC2018T09

identified by at least one annotator.

$$\text{ALIR} = \frac{|\{h|h \in \mathcal{H} \wedge h \in \mathcal{G} \cap \mathcal{G}'\}|}{|\mathcal{G} \cap \mathcal{G}'|}, \quad (4)$$

$$\text{ALIP} = \frac{|\{h|h \in \mathcal{H} \wedge h \in \mathcal{G} \cup \mathcal{G}'\}|}{|\mathcal{H}|}, \quad (5)$$

where $\mathcal{H}$ is a set of identified pairs, $\mathcal{G}$ and $\mathcal{G}'$ are those obtained by two respective annotators, and the operator $|\cdot|$ counts the elements in a set. ALIF computes the harmonic mean of ALIR and ALIP. Because SPADE provides alignment pairs by three annotators, there are three combinations for $\mathcal{G}$ and $\mathcal{G}'$. The final ALIR, ALIP, and ALIF values are calculated by taking the averages.

Note that these evaluation metrics count null alignment pairs also; hence, ALIP performs differently from the general precision in that stricter models will have lower ALIP scores. This is because a stricter model aligning only a small number of phrases ($\neq \tau_\phi$) increases the number of null alignment pairs, making $|\mathcal{H}|$ larger.

Metric for Phrase Structure We also evaluated the correctness of phrase structures as the phrase span matching ratio (**PSMR**) against the gold trees. Specifically, PSMR computes the ratio of gold spans that exactly match with the spans in aligned trees. We compute the macro-average of PSMR of all source and target sentences.

4.3 Baseline

We compared our method to the state-of-the-art (Arase and Tsujii, 2020) on the SPADE corpus (denoted as **TreeAligner** hereafter). Their original experiments aligned gold syntactic trees annotated in SPADE. To replicate a realistic scenario where gold syntactic structures are unavailable, we used an off-the-shelf syntactic parser, namely, Enju (Miyao and Tsujii, 2008).[3] We evaluated TreeAligner by inputting the 1-best trees obtained by Enju as the baseline. In contrast, the proposed method (denoted as **ForestAligner** hereafter) takes parse forests in the packed representation obtained by Enju as input.

4.4 Model Settings

For replicating TreeAligner, we used the released codes of the authors.[4] We implemented our ForestAligner based on them using Pytorch[5]. As the phrase representation model in both TreeAligner and ForestAligner, we commonly used the bidirectional encoder representations from transformers (BERT) (Devlin et al., 2019) fine-tuned by Arase and Tsujii (2020)[6]. After inputting a sentence pair, a phrase representation was obtained by mean-pooling the token representations consisting of the corresponding phrase.

The hyperparameters were tuned to maximise the evaluation metrics on the SPADE dev set. For TreeAligner, the hyperparameter of the null alignment cost, λ_ϕ, was set to 0.75 to maximise ALIF on the dev set. For ForestAligner, λ_ϕ and λ_s were set to 0.80 and 3.0×10^{11},[7] respectively, to maximise the arithmetic mean of ALIF and PSMR on the dev set.

	Structure	ALIR	ALIP	ALIF	PSMR
TreeAligner	Gold tree	88.2	86.6	87.4	100.0
TreeAligner	1-best tree	79.8	76.7	78.2	93.1
ForestAligner	Forest	**81.1**	**79.3**	**80.2**	**93.4**

Table 1: Experimental results on the SPADE test set (%) (the performance of TreeAligner on the gold trees were borrowed from the original paper.)

4.5 Results

Table 1 shows the experimental results. The ALIR, ALIP, and ALIF scores of TreeAligner significantly dropped when aligning 1-best trees compared to the case of aligning gold trees (the first row). Our ForestAligner improved ALIR by 1.3%, ALIP by 2.6%, and ALIF by 2.0% compared to TreeAligner with 1-best trees, which confirms the effectiveness of forest alignment.

For PSMR, ForestAligner moderately improved TreeAligner by 0.3%, which shows the parse errors in 1-best trees can be fixed through forest alignment. To investigate what kind of parse errors were addressed and newly introduced by forest alignment, we randomly sampled 40 sentence pairs where the PSMR score increased (20 sentences) and decreased (20 sentences) compared to TreeAligner. One of the authors observed resultant trees and manually categorised them into error types. Table 2 shows the results, indicating

[3] https://mynlp.is.s.u-tokyo.ac.jp/enju/

[4] https://github.com/yukiar/phrase_alignment_cted

[5] https://pytorch.org/ (version 1.7.1)

[6] https://zenodo.org/record/4686663#.YpcR2S_3LJQ (Model: BERT1F_TripletMarginLoss_margin-1.0_lr-3e-05_mean_100_ft-bert-base-uncased.pkl)

[7] The λ_s takes a large value due to different ranges of alignment cost and parsing likelihood. It was searched in the range of 1.0×10^{11} to 9.0×10^{11}.

Error type	Improved	Deteriorated
PP attachment	8	8
NP attachment	5	1
Modifier attachment	1	4
Coordination	2	2
Other	4	5

Table 2: Error analysis of syntactic structures

ForestAligner tends to fix noun phrase attachment errors while increases modifier attachment errors. The prepositional phrase attachment is a mixture of both improvements and deterioration.

Figure 1 illustrates alignment results by ForestAligner. For the source sentence, the correct structure of composing a phrase 'made this statement at the Karachi Shipyard' with a child verb phrase 'made this statement' (the orange node) and prepositional phrase 'at the Karachi Shipyard' (the pink node) were identified. In contrast, in the 1-best tree, the prepositional phrase was wrongly attached to a noun phrase of 'this statement' to compose a phrase 'this statement at the Karachi Shipyard', which prevented alignment of 'made this statement' and 'gave this statement' (the orange node pair).

5 Discussion: Alignment of Less-Similar Sentences

As discussed in Section 1, phrase alignment is coveted by various applications like paraphrase and textual entailment recognition and question answering. Such applications are different from SPADE, i.e., alignment of paraphrases, in that they require alignment of *less-similar* sentences, too. It is not a trivial difference as it sounds.

As a preliminary experiment, we aligned the test set[8] of the semantic textual similarity (STS) benchmark (Cer et al., 2017) and converted alignment costs into similarity scores. Specifically, we normalised the root-level alignment costs by sentence lengths[9] and scaled them to be compatible with the STS labels, i.e., from 0 (dissimilar) to 5 (equivalent). As a result, Pearson's correlation coefficient of the predicted scores and human labels was limited to 0.51, which is comparable to estimating sentence-level similarity using static word embeddings.[10]

[8]We excluded 7 sentence pairs that Enju failed to output.

[9]Alignment costs obviously depend on sentence lengths.

[10]https://ixa2.si.ehu.eus/stswiki/index.php/STSbenchmark

Human label	$[0,1)$	$[1,2)$	$[2,3)$	$[3,4)$	$[4,5]$
Prediction	3.7	3.6	3.6	3.3	4.0

Table 3: Average similarity scores per human labels converted from ForestAligner's alignment costs

Table 3 shows the average similarity scores per human label. While ForestAligner outputs a noticeably high score on the most similar sentence pairs, other scores are almost uniform on less similar sentences. We conjecture that one of the factors causing this phenomenon is the lack of exposure to less-similar examples during development. The same can happen on existing phrase alignment methods trained on annotated corpora consisting of paraphrasal or highly similar sentence pairs (Thadani et al., 2012; Lan et al., 2021). The distributions of alignment pairs are largely different in semantically similar and less-similar sentences, where alignment is dense in the former but sparse in the latter. Hence, alignment methods trained only on similar sentences may tend to align phrases that should be unaligned.

While there are only a few corpora annotating alignment on less-similar sentences (Ernst et al., 2021), this direction is worth exploring to apply alignment techniques in practical applications. In future work, we will create corpora of this kind and explore robust phrase alignment on both similar and less-similar sentences.

Acknowledgements

We sincerely appreciate the anonymous reviewers for their insightful comments and suggestions to improve the paper. This work was supported by JSPS KAKENHI Grant Number JP21H03564.

References

Eneko Agirre, Carmen Banea, Claire Cardie, Daniel Cer, Mona Diab, Aitor Gonzalez-Agirre, Weiwei Guo, Iñigo Lopez-Gazpio, Montse Maritxalar, Rada Mihalcea, German Rigau, Larraitz Uria, and Janyce Wiebe. 2015. SemEval-2015 task 2: Semantic textual similarity, English, Spanish and pilot on interpretability. In *Proceedings of the International Workshop on Semantic Evaluation (SemEval)*, pages 252–263.

Yuki Arase and Junichi Tsujii. 2017. Monolingual phrase alignment on parse forests. In *Proceedings of the Conference on Empirical Methods in Natural Language Processing (EMNLP)*, pages 1–11.

Yuki Arase and Junichi Tsujii. 2018. SPADE: Evaluation dataset for monolingual phrase alignment. In *Proceedings of the Language Resources and Evaluation Conference (LREC)*.

Yuki Arase and Jun'ichi Tsujii. 2020. Compositional phrase alignment and beyond. In *Proceedings of the Conference on Empirical Methods in Natural Language Processing (EMNLP)*, pages 1611–1623.

Daniela Brook Weiss, Paul Roit, Ayal Klein, Ori Ernst, and Ido Dagan. 2021. QA-align: Representing cross-text content overlap by aligning question-answer propositions. In *Proceedings of the Conference on Empirical Methods in Natural Language Processing (EMNLP)*, pages 9879–9894.

David Burkett, John Blitzer, and Dan Klein. 2010. Joint parsing and alignment with weakly synchronized grammars. In *Proceedings of the Annual Conference of the North American Chapter of the Association for Computational Linguistics (NAACL)*, pages 127–135.

Daniel Cer, Mona Diab, Eneko Agirre, Iñigo Lopez-Gazpio, and Lucia Specia. 2017. SemEval-2017 task 1: Semantic textual similarity multilingual and crosslingual focused evaluation. In *Proceedings of the International Workshop on Semantic Evaluation (SemEval)*, pages 1–14.

Do Kook Choe and David McClosky. 2015. Parsing paraphrases with joint inference. In *Proceedings of the Joint Conference of the Annual Meeting of the Association for Computational Linguistics and the International Joint Conference on Natural Language Processing (ACL-IJCNLP)*, pages 1223–1233.

Dipanjan Das and Noah A. Smith. 2009. Paraphrase identification as probabilistic quasi-synchronous recognition. In *Proceedings of the Joint Conference of the Annual Meeting of the Association for Computational Linguistics and the International Joint Conference on Natural Language Processing (ACL-IJCNLP)*, pages 468–476.

Jacob Devlin, Ming-Wei Chang, Kenton Lee, and Kristina Toutanova. 2019. BERT: Pre-training of deep bidirectional transformers for language understanding. In *Proceedings of the Annual Conference of the North American Chapter of the Association for Computational Linguistics: Human Language Technologies (NAACL-HLT)*, pages 4171–4186.

Ori Ernst, Ori Shapira, Ramakanth Pasunuru, Michael Lepioshkin, Jacob Goldberger, Mohit Bansal, and Ido Dagan. 2021. Summary-source proposition-level alignment: Task, datasets and supervised baseline. In *Proceedings of the Conference on Computational Natural Language Learning (CoNLL)*, pages 310–322.

Michael Heilman and Noah A. Smith. 2010. Tree edit models for recognizing textual entailments, paraphrases, and answers to questions. In *Proceedings of the Annual Conference of the North American Chapter of the Association for Computational Linguistics: Human Language Technologies (NAACL-HLT)*, pages 1011–1019.

Eran Hirsch, Alon Eirew, Ori Shapira, Avi Caciularu, Arie Cattan, Ori Ernst, Ramakanth Pasunuru, Hadar Ronen, Mohit Bansal, and Ido Dagan. 2021. iFacetSum: Coreference-based interactive faceted summarization for multi-document exploration. In *Proceedings of the Conference on Empirical Methods in Natural Language Processing: System Demonstrations*, pages 283–297.

Wuwei Lan, Chao Jiang, and Wei Xu. 2021. Neural semi-Markov CRF for monolingual word alignment. In *Proceedings of the Joint Conference of the Annual Meeting of the Association for Computational Linguistics and the International Joint Conference on Natural Language Processing (ACL-IJCNLP)*, pages 6815–6828.

Tao Li and Vivek Srikumar. 2016. Exploiting sentence similarities for better alignments. In *Proceedings of the Conference on Empirical Methods in Natural Language Processing (EMNLP)*, pages 2193–2203.

Bill MacCartney, Michel Galley, and Christopher D. Manning. 2008. A phrase-based alignment model for natural language inference. In *Proceedings of the Conference on Empirical Methods in Natural Language Processing (EMNLP)*, pages 802–811.

Yusuke Miyao and Jun'ichi Tsujii. 2008. Feature forest models for probabilistic HPSG parsing. *Computational Linguistics (CL)*, 34(1):35–80.

Jessica Ouyang and Kathy McKeown. 2019. Neural network alignment for sentential paraphrases. In *Proceedings of the Annual Meeting of the Association for Computational Linguistics (ACL)*, pages 4724–4735.

Ori Shapira, Hadar Ronen, Meni Adler, Yael Amsterdamer, Judit Bar-Ilan, and Ido Dagan. 2017. Interactive abstractive summarization for event news tweets. In *Proceedings of the Conference on Empirical Methods in Natural Language Processing: System Demonstrations*, pages 109–114.

Richard Socher, Alex Perelygin, Jean Wu, Jason Chuang, Christopher D. Manning, Andrew Ng, and Christopher Potts. 2013. Recursive deep models for semantic compositionality over a sentiment treebank. In *Proceedings of the Conference on Empirical Methods in Natural Language Processing (EMNLP)*, pages 1631–1642.

Kai Sheng Tai, Richard Socher, and Christopher D. Manning. 2015. Improved semantic representations from tree-structured long short-term memory networks. In *Proceedings of the Joint Conference of the Annual Meeting of the Association for Computational Linguistics and the International Joint Conference on Natural Language Processing (ACL-IJCNLP)*, pages 1556–1566.

Kapil Thadani, Scott Martin, and Michael White. 2012. A joint phrasal and dependency model for paraphrase alignment. In *Proceedings of the International Conference on Computational Linguistics (COLING)*, pages 1229–1238.

Mengqiu Wang and Christopher Manning. 2010. Probabilistic tree-edit models with structured latent variables for textual entailment and question answering. In *Proceedings of the International Conference on Computational Linguistics (COLING)*, pages 1164–1172.

Xuchen Yao, Benjamin Van Durme, Chris Callison-Burch, and Peter Clark. 2013. Semi-Markov phrase-based monolingual alignment. In *Proceedings of the Conference on Empirical Methods in Natural Language Processing (EMNLP)*, pages 590–600.

Kaizhong Zhang. 1996. A constrained edit distance between unordered labeled trees. *Algorithmica*, 15(3):205–222.

Empirical Sufficiency Lower Bounds for Language Modeling with Locally-Bootstrapped Semantic Structures

Jakob Prange and **Emmanuele Chersoni**
Department of Chinese and Bilingual Studies, The Hong Kong Polytechnic University
11 Yuk Choi Road, Hung Hom, Kowloon, Hong Kong (China)
first.last@polyu.edu.hk

Abstract

In this work we build upon negative results from an attempt at language modeling with predicted semantic structure, in order to establish empirical lower bounds on what *could* have made the attempt successful.[1] More specifically, we design a concise binary vector representation of semantic structure at the lexical level and evaluate in-depth how good an incremental tagger needs to be in order to achieve better-than-baseline performance with an end-to-end *semantic-bootstrapping language model*. We envision such a system as consisting of a (pretrained) sequential-neural component and a hierarchical-symbolic component working together to generate text with low surprisal and high linguistic interpretability. We find that (a) dimensionality of the semantic vector representation *can* be dramatically reduced without losing its main advantages and (b) lower bounds on prediction quality cannot be established via a single score alone, but need to take the *distributions* of signal and noise into account.

1 Introduction

It is well-established by now that large pretrained Transformer language models (LMs) can obtain detectable knowledge about linguistic structure from raw text distributions (Jawahar et al., 2019; Tenney et al., 2019a, *inter alia*), thus continuing a long line of research in collecting solid empirical evidence for the Distributional Hypothesis (Harris, 1954; Firth, 1957). This is often presented in stark contrast to symbolic linguistic theories and representations, which put more emphasis on higher-level structural principles. In practice, purely neural models have achieved groundbreaking performances in a wide range of NLP tasks (Devlin et al., 2019; Brown et al., 2020) in a much more scalable manner than seems to be possible with symbolic ones. Still, theoretical linguistic questions

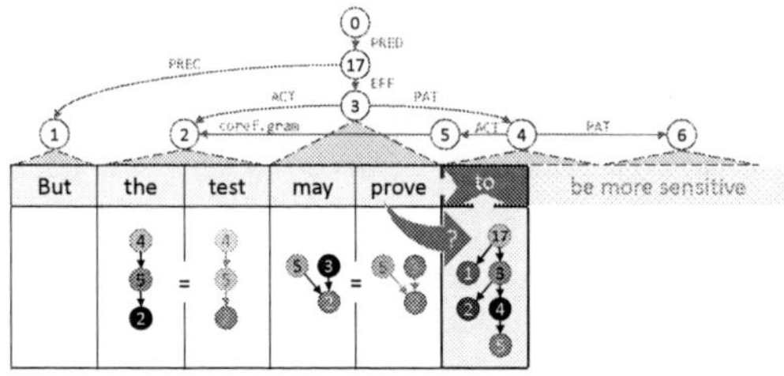

Figure 1: Example of incremental semantic graph slices obtained from a PTG graph and information flow in a (hypothetical) semantic-bootstrapping LM. In this example, the dark-red-shaded token 'to' is the current LM target; the light-yellow-shaded cells to the left and below directly influence the LM decision as in P+22; and the pink arrow marked with ? stands for the intermediate slice prediction step, for which we want to establish sufficiency lower bounds.

about the relationship between neural implementation and higher-level symbolic patterns are far from being answered definitively. A common criticism of purely distributional models is that they generally *lack grounding*, because they do not have access to the external world, while *meaning* is inherently a relation between a linguistic form and a communicative intent about something external to language (Bender and Koller, 2020; Trott et al., 2020; Merrill et al., 2021; Lenci, 2023).[2]

We aim to contribute to this discussion by building upon results by Prange et al. (2022, henceforth P+22), who found that incremental LM perplexity can be significantly improved by providing hierarchical semantic structure as an additional token-level input (fig. 1 and §2.1). Indeed, the integration of symbolic and distributional approaches has long been seen as a possible and necessary step towards the full legitimacy of Distributional Semantic Models (DSMs) as models of meaning (Boleda and Herbelot, 2016; Emerson, 2020), and there is recently

[1]Our experimental code is available at https://github.com/jakpra/SufficiencyLowerBounds.

[2]But see Abdou et al. (2021) for a more optimistic view, backed by empirical results.

*Proceedings of the The 12th Joint Conference on Lexical and Computational Semantics (*SEM 2023)*, pages 456–468
July 13-14, 2023

more and more evidence supporting the benefits of hybrid neuro-symbolic models (e.g., Li and Srikumar, 2019; Li and Rush, 2020), especially for compositional and long-tail generalization (Weißenhorn et al., 2022; Prange et al., 2021) and interpretability (Opitz and Frank, 2022).

P+22's results seem to suggest that at least some aspects of symbolic semantic structure may not be contained in the incremental LM's representation—i.e., that these aspects might constitute an instance of grounding, which is helpful for language understanding, but not fully learnable from text alone. Alternatively, we consider the possibility that the crucial semantic information *could* be learned, extracted, or induced to a sufficient extent, if only explicit supervision were provided at training time. The notion of *sufficiency*, in our case, relates to the potential of improving over a baseline LM (§3). This paints a grand vision of semantic bootstrapping, i.e., a scenario in which the LM first commits to local semantic structure based on the revealed sentence prefix (pink ? arrow in fig. 1) and then uses its prediction to reduce the next token's perplexity. The work by P+22 established *upper bounds* by using an oracle setup where rich semantic structure inputs are known to be correct, not only during training but also at test time. As the main contribution of this work, assuming the local semantic bootstrapping scenario is feasible at all, we look instead for *lower bounds* on what would constitute *sufficient substance and accuracy* in predicted semantic structure for such an improved end-to-end neuro-symbolic LM.

Concretely, we conduct two analyses: First, we make P+22's original formulation of semantic graph slices (SGS) more parsimonious (§5). We extract binary vectors (B-SGS) representing only bare-bones (unlabeled and unanchored) structural relations (§5.2) and find that they are sufficient for improving LM perplexity over a strong baseline in the oracle setting (§5.3). Second, we measure how the language modeling benefits of B-SGS are affected by increasing levels of noise, aiming to emulate various imperfect taggers (§6). Interestingly, a comparison of two different shuffling mechanisms (§6.2) as well as a simple pilot tagger (§6.1) reveals that *how errors are distributed* throughout the data is much more important than overall error rate. Based on our observations, we establish sufficiency lower bounds of B-SGS for use in a semantic bootstrapping LM. We begin by providing the reader with relevant background information from the literature (§2), defining concisely what we mean by *sufficiency lower bounds* (§3), and describing our data set and general experimental setup (§4). Finally, we discuss our findings and limitations within the bigger picture of ongoing research directions (§7).

2 Background

2.1 Language Modeling with Linguistic Graph Slices

P+22 proposed a type of ensemble language model, consisting of a pretrained Transformer and a neural encoder of symbolic linguistic structure, both jointly predicting the next token in a sentence, given the revealed prefix. They extract token-level "slices" from sentence-level graphs.

An incremental linguistic graph **slice** is defined as a connected subgraph minimally including a node directly anchored in the target token (or a preceding token if no such node is available) and extending vertically to include parents, grandparents, and children, horizontally to include left siblings, and diagonally to include children's parents ("co-parents") and parents' siblings ("aunts"). This is illustrated in fig. 1: The original sentence-level graph is shown above the sentence, and extracted token-level slices are shown below. Slices are then **encoded** as fixed-length vectors, including both edge label information and token anchor information. Out of two encoding methods, R-GCN (Schlichtkrull et al., 2018) and a simple concatenation- and averaging-based one, the latter is much faster at roughly equal model size and roughly equal LM quality, so we choose it in our experiments. In essence, the embeddings of all preceding tokens related to the target token in one of the structural ways listed above (parents, siblings, etc), as well as their one-hot-encoded edge labels, are concatenated in a specific pre-defined order. If there are multiple instances of a given relation, or multi-token anchors, their vector representations are averaged. Missing relations are zero-padded. The final slice vector is fed through a simple feed-forward encoder in order to compute logits over the vocabulary, which are finally added to the LM's logits before softmax normalization. The resulting **distribution** is used to compute the loss (during training) or predict the next token (at test time).

In their study, P+22 compared linguistic representations of several different flavors, including syntactic and dependency frameworks. Here we focus on two semantic frameworks, PTG and EDS (§4.1), which structurally go beyond bilexical dependencies, and thus we use the term *semantic graph slice* (SGS). We further extend P+22's work by explicitly comparing their oracle setup against several versions of SGS with varying degrees of richness and correctness, stemming from either signal reduction (§5), automatic prediction (§6.1), or controlled noise induction (§6.2).

2.2 Related Work

Linguistic Analyses of LMs. A large number of studies in the LM literature has been dedicated to the analysis of the linguistic knowledge they encode. A common methodology employs *probing tasks*, where a simple model is asked to solve a task requiring linguistic knowledge using a representation derived from a LM with little or no specific linguistic supervision. If the model is successful, we then can infer that the LM encodes that knowledge (see Linzen et al., 2016; Tenney et al., 2019a,b; Hewitt and Liang, 2019; Liu et al., 2019; Wu et al., 2020; Chersoni et al., 2021; Geiger et al., 2021, *inter alia*). Probes can be particularly insightful when applied *contrastively* to sets of minimal sentence pairs that differ in their grammatical acceptability (Warstadt et al., 2020; Hu et al., 2020; Kim et al., 2019). Our approach of treating semantic structure as an input rather than an output of a neural LM is orthogonal to probing, but can similarly be used for inferences about what kind of knowledge is (not) already encoded in the baseline model. Recently, an interpretability method based on contrastive *explanations* (Jacovi et al., 2021) has been proposed to explain LM predictions on sets of minimal sentence pairs that differ in their grammatical acceptability, showing that the salient tokens for the LM preference of the correct form are quite well aligned with human knowledge of grammatical phenomena (Yin and Neubig, 2022).

Incremental Supertagging and Parsing. Predicting linguistic structure incrementally has been explored especially in the context of strongly-formulated lexico-syntactic grammar formalisms like CCG, in the form of incremental supertagging (Hassan et al., 2009; Ambati et al., 2015; Stanojević and Steedman, 2019, 2020). Having word-level structural categories built in to the formalism has many advantages for both modeling efficiency and linguistic interpretability. But also Penn Treebank-style constituency syntax trees can be parsed incrementally using, e.g., language model grammars (Sartran et al., 2022; Dyer et al., 2016) or word-level beam search (Stern et al., 2017). Finally, another line of work aims to backpropagate linguistic knowledge into the LM itself by optimizing incremental structure prediction as an auxiliary objective (Qian et al., 2021; Glavaš and Vulić, 2021; Kitaev et al., 2022).

Model Explanations and Cognitive Predictions using Linguistic Symbols. Hale et al. (2018) proposed a method relying on probabilistic generative grammars (Dyer et al., 2016) and word-synchronous beam search that allows to extract predictive metrics of processing difficulty, such as surprisal and entropy. The authors showed that, using such metrics as predictors in a regression model, it was possible to predict the amplitude effects of several components of naturalistic EEG. Ek et al. (2019) enhance a LSTM-based LM with syntactic, semantic tags and dependency tree depth features, and reported that the additional linguistic knowledge did not increase the correlation with human ratings in a sentence acceptability task, although syntactic tags and dependency tree depth were helpful for lowering perplexity. Stanojević et al. (2021) used CCG-based predictors to improve a regression model of fMRI time course in six different brain regions, over and above predictors obtained with a simple context-free phrase structure grammar. Finally, Opitz and Frank (2022) presented a technique to partition the BERT sentence embeddings into different sub-embeddings, each one covering meaningful semantic aspects of sentences as represented in the Abstract Meaning Representations (AMR) framework. Experiments on zero-shot sentence and argument similarity tasks proved that the approach maintains a high-level of correlation with human judgements, while making the sentence embeddings interpretable.

3 Sufficiency Lower Bounds

We introduce the concept of *sufficiency*[3] *lower bounds* on the strength of a data signal ξ in order for a system Σ, which takes ξ as an input, to reach a certain performance threshold θ. In this work, the system Σ is a neuro-symbolic LM as proposed

[3]We do not consider *necessity* lower bounds here. I.e., we do not say that data signals of worse substance than our lower bounds cannot be sufficient. We say that distributions of at least lower-bound quality are probably sufficient.

by P+22 (§2.1), ξ is an SGS vector representation (§5) for each (sub)word token in a text corpus D, and θ is the baseline LM performance (measured as surprisal, §4.3). Establishing such bounds is important because ξ's richness may need to be reduced in one way or another—either by theoretical design (because small, simple representations and models are desirable; §5), or by practical necessity (due to unavoidable noise in predicting ξ; §6). A main takeaway from our exploratory study is that it is important to identify (i.e., define or measure) candidate bounds in a way that considers the signal's configuration as a whole, rather than focusing on a single aggregate metric.[4] Approached empirically, this involves computing (multivariate) distributions over ξ as instantiated in a data set D, such that when the system Σ is run on D, the quality of its output is at least θ (i.e., it outperforms a baseline). Simply put, if the signal ξ surpasses the sufficiency lower bound in D, it will likely enable the system Σ to reach performance θ or better.

4 Experimental Setup

4.1 Data

We use the jointly-annotated corpus of the cross-framework meaning representation parsing (MRP) shared tasks (Oepen et al., 2019, 2020), which consists of large parts of the English Wall Street Journal corpus. In particular, we examine two symbolic-structured linguistic representation frameworks, Prague Tectogrammatical Graphs (**PTG**; Sgall et al., 1986; Böhmová et al., 2003; Hajič et al., 2012) and Elementary Dependency Structures (**EDS**; Oepen and Lønning, 2006; Flickinger, 2000; Copestake et al., 2005), each of them focusing on different aspects of semantic predicate-argument structure. EDS derives from Minimal Recursion Semantics (MRS) and thus rather explicitly encodes nominal/referring expressions due to MRS' foundation in variable binding. PTG, on the other hand, is somewhat more guided by syntax and (case-)semantic roles. We use the same training split as P+22, but deviate slightly in using only the first 500 sentences of their development set and reporting most of our results and analyses on this subset. This is because we are reporting incremental results and wish to reserve substantial unseen data for unbiased full evaluation in future work. For comparison, we report a limited amount of aggregate scores over the test set in table 2.

4.2 Model Implementation

Our models (see §2.1 for a conceptual overview) and experiments are implemented in Python, building on P+22's codebase.[5] In addition to standard neural language modeling libraries used therein (PyTorch, huggingface), we also leverage the Pyro-PPL library (Bingham et al., 2018) to implement the variational autoencoder (§6.1).

We follow P+22 in using GPT-2 (Radford et al., 2019, 124M parameters) as the pretrained incremental language model and a simple multilayer perceptron (MLP) to encode and project slice vectors into the vocabulary. These logits are then added to the LM's before taking the softmax to obtain the final next-token prediction distribution. During training, tokens are sampled from a categorical distribution and contribute to the VAE's overall ELBO loss. While this technically is a slight difference to P+22, who used categorical cross-entropy loss, we are able to closely reproduce their reported baseline perplexity on the test set ($\approx 46 \pm 0.1$). As the language modeling baseline we finetune GPT-2 in the target domain (on the raw WSJ text) without any exposure to SGS, as did P+22.

4.3 Evaluation

We measure language modeling performance in terms of surprisal or *perplexity* (PPL), which is computed as the exponential of the model's token-averaged negative log-likelihood (NLL).[6] Whenever we report aggregate performance over all data, we use PPL (tables 2 and 3), but in the detailed analysis of smaller subsets of data we switch to NLL for better readability (fig. 6). For both metrics, lower is better. To evaluate B-SGS correctness, we consider binary micro-accuracy over individual vector dimensions, macro-accuracy over tokens, as well as edge precision, recall, and F1-score.

5 Representation Distillation: What makes semantic structure valuable to language modeling?

Currently well-known as a popular and effective deep learning technique (e.g., Polino et al., 2018; Sanh et al., 2019), distillation (of neural models)

[4] This somewhat circular-looking reasoning warrants full disclosure: We were already proponents of holistic, detailed evaluations over single-number benchmarks before this study, but were still surprised by most of our results, particularly the contrast between §6.1 and §6.2.

[5] `https://github.com/jakpra/LinguisticStructureLM`

[6] See Limitations section for shortcomings of this metric.

aims to reduce redundancy and unwieldiness (§5.1) while retaining core information. Here we apply a similar concept to a family of *symbolic linguistic* representations, SGS. Rather than relying on a blackbox training process to transfer knowledge from a large pretrained model to a smaller model, we manually design a less detailed variant of SGS, which we call B-SGS (§5.2). We use ground-truth B-SGS as additional input to the incremental LM as before and find that it *does* constitute a **lower bound of sufficient richness** (§5.3).

5.1 Unparsimoneousness of Fully Labeled and Anchored SGS

While the very rich SGS representation used by P+22 (which, here, we call F(ull)-SGS; §2.1 and fig. 2 top) proved to be a very potent next token predictor, this power comes at the cost of being rather unwieldy and, as it turns out, redundant.

As input. Recall from §2.1 that, in F-SGS, preceding tokens that are semantically related to each target token (via edges in the graph) are encoded by concatenating their embeddings (in a specific order and with zero-padding to preserve their structural relation, e.g., parent vs. sibling, see §2.1). It is obvious at first glance that this quickly leads to very large slices and models (P+22 report an average influx in models size of 50-60 million parameters for SGS encoding alone). Furthermore, linguistic formalisms vary greatly in the number of semantic relation types (edge labels) they distinguish: e.g., 10 in EDS vs. 72 in PTG. And while this number does not seem to be directly associated with model performance, it still makes the comparison somewhat blurry. In addition to their excessive size, F-SGS vectors also seem to be partially redundant with a pretrained LM, since P+22 found in their ablation experiments that the correct edge label assignment is not essential for achieving high language modeling performance.

As output. In addition to oracle-augmented language modeling, a major use case of SGS we work towards is to incrementally predict them (cf. §1 and §6). This is, however, a non-trivial structured prediction problem. It consists at least of edge prediction and relation classification (cf. Liu et al., 2019). And while on the surface, this is reminiscent of a task that could be solved with an edge-factored parser (Kiperwasser and Goldberg, 2016; Dozat and Manning, 2017), our scenario is much more complex due to the multitude of structural relations

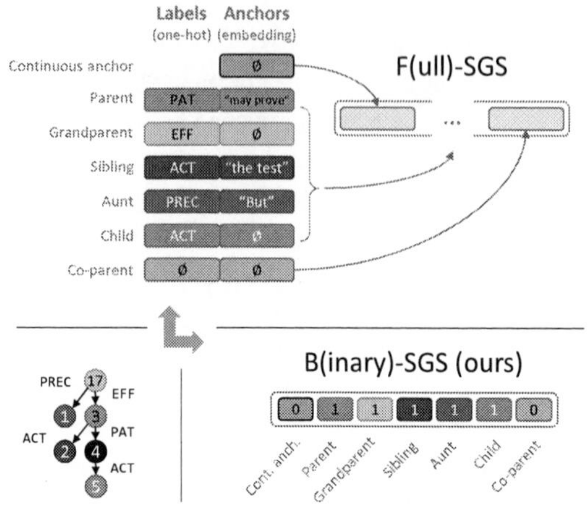

Figure 2: Deriving **F**ull and **B**inary semantic graph slice (SGS) vectors from the PTG subgraph for the token 'to' in fig. 1. The *continuous anchor* dimension would be filled, e.g., in the SGS for the tokens 'test' and 'prove', which each share the rest of their slice with their respective preceding tokens. Node ⑤ in the slice for 'may prove' is an example of a co-parent.

(not just parents), the possibility of multiple parents for each node, abstract nodes not directly anchored in a single token, as well as incrementality. Indeed, it is more akin to supertagging (Bangalore and Joshi, 1999; Clark and Curran, 2004, §2.2) but without the formal guarantees of a mildly context-sensitive grammar formalism like TAG or CCG. In our early exploration with simple multilayer perceptron (MLP) classifiers and a combination of loss functions (categorical cross-entropy for labels; cosine similarity and/or attention loss for token-to-token anchoring), we found it very difficult to train a model to convergence. We suspect that full SGS prediction warrants more complex modeling, optimization, and inference mechanisms, which we leave to future work.

5.2 Reducing SGS to Binary Structural Relations

The challenges described above prompt us to drastically simplify the SGS encoding. We propose to collapse both edge labels and anchor-token embeddings into mere binary indicators of whether an edge of a given *structural* relation type (flat subword continuation, parent, sibling, grandparent, aunt, child, co-parent) exists, resulting in *binary* semantic graph slices, or B-SGS (fig. 2).[7]

[7]While each node may have multiple relatives of the same type (e.g., 2 parents and 3 siblings), a single binary dimension for each type could only indicate the existence of *at least* one

	A	P	P+	O	S	T	C	R
UD	.11	.34	0.	.24	.31	.17	.34	0.
DM	.33	.48	.21	.19	.24	.09	.25	.21
PTG	.43	.75	.07	.69	.42	.41	.41	.10
EDS	.30	.69	.51	.17	.29	.09	.26	.22

Table 1: Relation-wise density of B-SGS vectors in the development set. A: continued anchor, P: parent, P+: 2 or more parents, O: grandparent, S: sibling, T: aunt, C: child, R: co-parent. UD and DM are shown for reference (cf. Liu et al., 2019, §6.1).

Data statistics. We report average density of major SGS dimensions (= relation types) in table 1. Note in particular that EDS and PTG differ substantially in the types of structures they encode, with PTG being denser on average. EDS is quite similar to DM because they are both derived from the same underlying formalism. In contrast to EDS, PTG, and DM graphs, which are generic DAGs, UD graphs are strictly bilexical dependency trees, leading to necessarily empty P+ and R dimensions.

5.3 Validating LM Performance with Oracle B-SGS

Setup. We train for up to 10 epochs, with early stopping based on development set perplexity. See §4 for more details.

Results. Table 2 shows that although B-SGS perplexity is slightly worse than with F-SGS—which is to be expected given the drastic reduction of the input signal—it still clearly outperforms the non-symbolic baseline. This suggests that the most crucial signal contributed by SGS in general is, in fact, the bare-bones hierarchical structure itself. And while P+22's ablation analysis already suggested that the grouping into different edge labels may be less important, it is quite surprising that even the information about *which other tokens* the target token is hierarchically-related to is not necessary to improve language modeling with SGS.

A possible explanation can be found in the fact that the baseline LM already has extensive *gradient* representation of parts-of-speech, syntactic functions, and semantic roles (namely, in its dense hidden states and attention distributions). What it might be lacking, then, is any *discrete* representation, and in particular a commitment to discrete and complex semantic structure seems to be beneficial.

Gold B-SGS is thus a sufficiency lower bound.

such instance. We follow P+22 in allocating additional 'low-resolution' dimensions for certain relation types to indicate the existence of 2 or more relatives. This is illustrated for parents (P+) in table 1 but otherwise omitted (e.g., from fig. 2) for simplicity. Note that a node having multiple parents is distinct and independent from it having one or more *co-parents* (i.e., other parents of the node's children).

	PTG	EDS
Pretrained GPT-2	59.3	
Domain-finetuned (baseline)	46.1	
Gold F-SGS	26.8	24.7
Gold B-SGS (ours)	33.9	28.0

Table 2: Comparing test set LM perplexity (lower is better) with our **Bin**ary slices against **F**ully labeled/anchored ones (P+22).

6 Noise Robustness: How accurate should bootstrapped semantic structure be in order to improve a LM?

In a pilot experiment, we integrate into the P+22 model B-SGS *prediction*. As illustrated in fig. 3, this is an intermediate step, the output of which is now used as input to next-token prediction instead of the ground truth slice. We find that while our relatively simple model (§6.1) produces B-SGS outputs of seemingly reasonable overall quality (in terms of micro-accuracy and F-score), they are *not* sufficient for supporting LM performance. This prompts us to actively search for **lower bounds of sufficient correctness** by artificially inducing various types and levels of noise into gold B-SGS inputs (§6.2). We do find several bounds, but learn that what makes them sufficient has less to do with their single-number correctness and more with intricate details of their overall noise distribution (§6.3).

6.1 Pilot Prediction

Setup. Since we are interested in lower bounds and we are running an exploratory study, we do not perform extensive model engineering. The following description is purely intended for clarity and replicability rather than as a state-of-the-art model proposal. We decide on a variational autoencoder (VAE; Kingma and Welling, 2013), where sampling from the latent space mediates between the LM's hidden state and the sigmoid-activated B-SGS dimensions (fig. 3). This setup is motivated by the high uncertainty involved in the task (we predict the symbolic structure of a token that has not been observed yet, and there may be much genuine ambiguity). All encoders, decoders, and projectors within the VAE, besides GPT-2, are simple

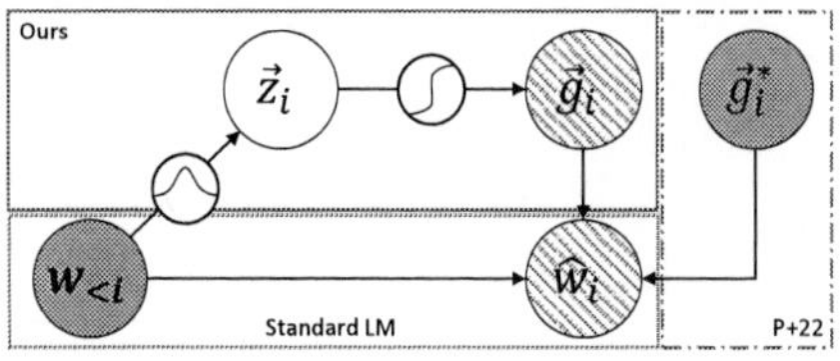

Figure 3: Our simple variational autoencoder model. We project the encoding of observed (solidly shaded) previous words $\mathbf{w}_{<i}$ into latent space and sample hidden states $\vec{z}_i$. Predicted graph slices $\vec{g}_i$ and target tokens $\hat{w}_i$ are supervised during training but unobserved at test time. P+22 used ground truth slices $\vec{g}_i^*$ instead of predicted ones. The standard LM is a component in both versions.

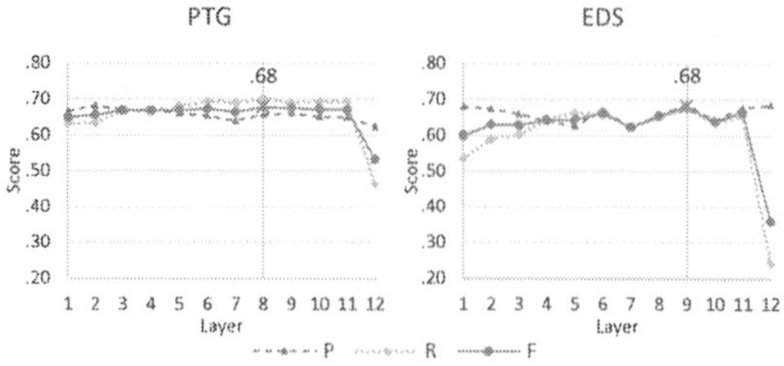

Figure 4: Graph slice prediction performance on the development set by LM layer. P = precision (proportion predicted edges correct), R = recall (gold edges predicted), F = F1-score (harmonic mean of P and R).

feed-forward MLPs. B-SGS prediction is trained deterministically with binary cross-entropy loss.[8] We train the slice predictor for up to 10 epochs with early stopping based on dev set F-score, and then train the SGS-augmented LM as before.

Results. As shown in fig. 4, SGS prediction performance is best in layers 8 (PTG) and 9 (EDS). This is in line with previous studies on probing semantic structure (e.g., Liu et al., 2019; Jawahar et al., 2019; Tenney et al., 2019a), which obtained the best performances in middle/high layers. However, even these best predictions cannot outperform the finetuned LM baseline in the augmented language modeling setting (compare black solid and red dashed lines in fig. 5).

Validation. Prediction micro-accuracies (.84 for PTG, .90 for EDS; last row table 3) are in the same order of magnitude as Liu et al. (2019)'s binary edge prediction results for UD and DM, two representation frameworks featured in the literature much more frequently than PTG and EDS. Although there are many differences in task and experimental setup (dependencies vs. constituencies, single-parent vs. B-SGS prediction; cf. table 1), we find this to be a valuable sanity check for both us and the reader in lieu of a proper baseline.

6.2 Artificial Noise

Why is our pilot system not sufficient? Maybe prediction accuracy just needs to be better? We investigate by using shuffled gold B-SGS as inputs to the LM and systematically altering several characteristics of the shuffling routine. This style of control task is inspired by Hewitt and Liang (2019); Dubossarsky et al. (2018).

We consider two different shuffling mechanisms: (a) Shuffling the node-to-word **anchor** mapping of graphs before vector extraction (i.e., which slice corresponds to which word token, cf. P+22). This guarantees well-formed graphs but may be too optimistic since we only shuffle within each sentence. Thus we also consider a more aggressive option: (b) Randomly switching **bits** (= whether or not a given edge type exists) in the slice vectors extracted from gold graphs.

For both, we also produce *varying degrees* of noise. Namely, whenever we are about to shuffle a graph anchor or vector bit, we decide to instead retain the correct assignment with probability p_{Gold}.

Results. Table 3 shows how the different shuffling conditions affect B-SGS correctness. As expected, within-sentence graph anchor shuffling is generally much more optimistic than bit-switching. By definition, p_{Gold} directly determines micro-accuracy in bit-switched slices, whereas in anchor-shuffled slices, p_{Gold} is more closely correlated with macro-accuracy. LM perplexity of each condition is shown in fig. 5. Note that the signal strength of bit-switching is symmetric around .5. This is an intuitive corollary of it being a binary signal (though macro-accuracy and F-score naturally continue to decline with $p_{Gold} < .5$, as shown exemplarily for values .1 and 0.).

First, we identify conditions that beat the domain-finetuned LM baseline from fig. 5, and then consult table 3 to find their corresponding slice quality. This results in the following sufficiency lower bounds (marked with asterisks in table 3): **Shuffled graphs** with $p_{Gold} \in \{.9, .8, .7, .6, .5\}$ for both PTG and EDS as well as $p_{Gold} \in \{.4, .3, .2, .1, 0.\}$ for EDS; and **bit-switched vec-**

[8] We also experimented with Bernoulli sampling, but to no success.

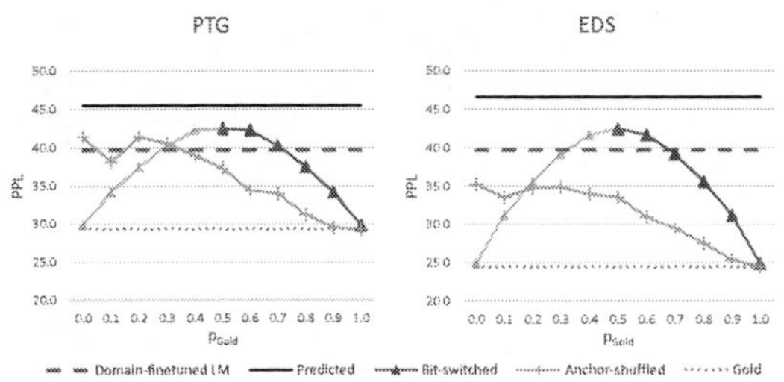

Figure 5: Dev set perplexity (lower is better) of noise-interpolated B-SGS LMs.

	PTG				EDS			
	MaA	MiA	F	LB	MaA	MiA	F	LB
Gold	1.00	1.00	1.00	*	1.00	1.00	1.00	*
Shuffled graph anchors								
$p_{Gold} = .9$	>.99	>.99	>.99	*	.95	.99	.97	*
$p_{Gold} = .8$	.88	.97	.94	*	.81	.97	.91	*
$p_{Gold} = .7$	.60	.93	.86	*	.65	.95	.84	*
$p_{Gold} = .6$	.54	.92	.83	*	.53	.93	.76	*
$p_{Gold} = .5$	.36	.87	.72	*	.34	.88	.63	*
$p_{Gold} = .4$	.23	.83	.64	?	.25	.87	.56	*
$p_{Gold} = .3$	.18	.81	.60	–	.19	.85	.49	*
$p_{Gold} = .2$	.12	.80	.56	–	.17	.84	.48	*
$p_{Gold} = .1$	.10	.79	.55	?	.14	.83	.44	*
$p_{Gold} = 0.$	.08	.78	.53	–	.13	.82	.41	*
Bit-switched vectors								
$p_{Gold} = .9$	.17	.90	.81	*	.17	.90	.75	*
$p_{Gold} = .8$	.02	.80	.66	*	.02	.80	.58	*
$p_{Gold} = .7$	<.01	.70	.53	?	<.01	.70	.44	?
$p_{Gold} = .6$	<.01	.60	.42	–	<.01	.60	.34	–
$p_{Gold} = .5$	0.	.50	.32	–	0.	.50	.26	–
⋮				⋮				⋮
$p_{Gold} = .1$	0.	.10	.05	*	0.	.11	.05	*
$p_{Gold} = 0.$	0.	<.01	<.01	*	0.	.01	.02	*
Predicted	.18	.84	.68	–	.29	.90	.68	–

Table 3: Correctness F1-score (F), accuracy at the macro (token-level, MaA) and micro (bit-level, MiA) levels) of B-SGS with various levels of noise (measured on the dev set). The LB columns indicate whether a condition is a sufficiency lower bound (*=yes, ?=maybe, −=no), i.e., if its corresponding PPL beats the baseline (fig. 5).

tors with $p_{Gold} \in \{.9, .8, .2, .1, 0.\}$, which can be generalized $|p_{Gold} - .5| \geq .3$.

6.3 Detailed Analysis

Unexpectedly, shuffled slices with clearly worse overall accuracy than predicted ones (table 3) sill yield much better perplexity (fig. 5). This leads us to the following hypotheses which we address in order. For brevity, we focus only the comparison between *predicted* and *bit-switched with* $p_{Gold} = .8$, because this condition seems to be a good trade-off between matching or slightly beating the PPL baseline and realism in terms of closeness to predicted in terms of overall accuracy. Consider fig. 6.

Hypothesis: The noise of shuffled slices is uniformly distributed over tokens whereas the noise of predicted slices is distributed similarly as baseline LM surprisal.

Average F-score of predicted B-SGS does indeed decrease as baseline LM surprisal increases (fig. 6b). However, contrary to our expectation, the *same* is true for the F-score of uniformly shuffled slices (fig. 6d)! Thus, the distribution of F-score means over suprisal bins alone does not explain the difference.

Hypothesis: Due to high-surprisal tokens having low B-SGS correctness, we create a noisy feedback loop which worsens LM surprisal in particular for already high-surprisal words (open-class content words) without gaining enough advantage on low-surprisal words.

We find quite the opposite: Both predicted and shuffled slices help in particular for very-high-surprisal tokens, despite the higher average slice noise (fig. 6c+e). In contrast, predicted slices tend to slightly increase surprisal for low-surprisal tokens. And since low-BL-surprisal tokens make up the vast majority of the data (fig. 6a), this slight increase might be enough to confuse the LM beyond baseline. Another crucial factor might be *variance* in slice correctness, which is generally much higher in predicted slices than in shuffled ones (fig. 6b+d).

Most affected words. We manually inspect the data to get an idea of how predicted B-SGS benefits the LM the most. The top 10 tokens in terms of both baseline NLL and Δ NLL (bottom right region of fig. 6c) are dominated by (recurring) named entities and dates, which are likely just an artifact of overfitting. After filtering these out, we find that the highest-baseline-NLL tokens are mostly nouns, adjectives, and verbs that are either rare themselves (e.g., *hopscotched*, *instrumentation*) or used in a rare construction (*paying thin* ***compliments***). In contrast, both PTG and EDS B-SGS reduce NLL the most for verbs, particularly in participle constructions (*dividing*, *has* ***begged***, *will be* ***relocated***).

7 Discussion and Conclusions

We proposed a general framework for semantically-enriched language modeling. Our proposal aims to provide a new perspective on qualitative distributional linguistic analysis, expanding upon prior work in linguistic analysis of neural models in sev-

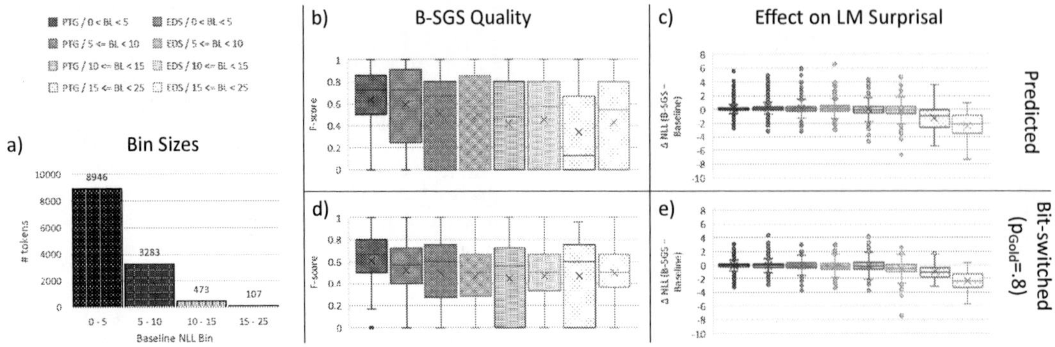

Figure 6: Box-and-whiskers plots of distributions over dev set tokens of B-SGS quality (F1-score) and effect on LM surprisal (Δ NLL), binned by baseline (BL) NLL. $\times$ markers are means and lines within boxes are medians.

eral ways (§7.1). We implemented and tested this framework with GPT-2 and semantic graph slices (SGS) from two formalisms, finding interesting patterns with potential impact for meaning representation design and low-resource modeling (§7.2).

7.1 General Framework

Probing and related methods evaluate language models based on their ability to predict linguistic representations from text. Although this is a relatively practical setup which has already produced many fascinating and replicable findings, it has the disadvantage that results need to be interpreted relative to both the linguistic framework governing the output and the specific probing architecture. In contrast, the approach of Prange et al. (2022) takes linguistic representations as an input and evaluates the language model directly on its native language modeling task. The main problem with their oracle setup is that it is unrealistic to have ground truth linguistic structures available at test time.

We argue for unifying the advantages of both directions, by considering what is in essence a concatenation of the two: a pipeline in which the output of a structure prediction model (similar to probing, except that it may be supervised) is fed back into the LM, enabling comparable evaluation on the raw text itself. This makes it possible to identify shortcomings of the LM and/or benefits of the linguistic representation quantitatively and qualitatively, by modifying either the probing architecture or the linguistic representation itself until LM performance starts or stops improving. The *lower bounds* of this continuum in particular (in contrast to upper bounds) have many theoretical and practical implications, since they separate the wheat from the chaff when it comes to the efficiency/effectiveness trade-off for model and representation. Our definition of sufficiency lower bounds in terms of the signal's data distribution in §3 is intentionally kept high-level and flexible to stimulate adaptations of the idea for a variety of use cases. While here we take an exclusively empirical approach, the framework may lend itself to formally-provable accounts as well.

7.2 Concrete Take-aways

In our experiments with GPT-2 (§5 and §6), we were able to crystallize the simple (unlabeled and unanchored) discrete hierarchical semantic structure of PTG and EDS as both beneficial to language modeling and robust to certain types of noise. We also found, though, that measuring prediction quality via a single aggregate score hides important aspects of the distributions of signal and noise, to the extent of potentially nullifying LM improvements. While the respective structures of PTG and EDS differ from each other in terms of density, relations encoded (§5.2), prediction accuracy (§6.1), and LM benefit (§6.2), the types of words they help the LM with the most are similar (§6.3).

As a nice side-effect from §5, removing the explicit token anchoring from SGS also makes it more applicable to unanchored semantic representations such as AMR (Banarescu et al., 2013). Note, however, that we still need some source of basic anchoring information (e.g., from an automatic aligner) in order to assign a slice to each token.

Finally, based on our findings in §6.3 that rare high-surprisal words most positively affected by even noisily SGS-enhanced language modeling, we are hopeful that our method may be particularly helpful for the Zipfian tail at a small cost to the majority of data.

Limitations

No guarantees. As stated in §3 and substantiated in §6, sufficiency lower bounds tend to be non-trivial, multifaceted configurations. We explore this to some extent (we find, e.g., that overall correctness scores alone, without variance, are *not* reliable identifiers of sufficiency lower bounds), but not exhaustively. To make stronger guarantees rather than just optimism, we need to precisely define when a candidate distribution is 'similar enough' to a known lower bound (e.g., via goodness-of-fit).

Practicability of semantic bootstrapping. We do not present a complete working system yet. It could be that sufficiently distributed performance can only be achieved with more intricate structured decoding mechanisms (e.g., Viterbi or beam search), which would negatively affect running time and thus usability as an end-to-end LM.

Limited evaluation of LM quality. Our evaluation of LM quality has been limited to the effects of the predicted graph slices on the perplexity metric. Alternative evaluations adopting psycholinguistically-inspired metrics, such as the correlation with human norms collected from cloze completion tasks, might yield different results (Hao et al., 2020).

Acknowledgements

We thank the anonymous reviewers for their extremely insightful and constructive feedback and questions, as well as Nathan Schneider and Chu-Ren Huang for helpful early discussions. This work has been supported by Hong Kong PolyU grant 1-YWBW.

References

Mostafa Abdou, Artur Kulmizev, Daniel Hershcovich, Stella Frank, Ellie Pavlick, and Anders Søgaard. 2021. Can language models encode perceptual structure without grounding? a case study in color. In *Proceedings of the 25th Conference on Computational Natural Language Learning*, pages 109–132, Online. Association for Computational Linguistics.

Bharat Ram Ambati, Tejaswini Deoskar, Mark Johnson, and Mark Steedman. 2015. An incremental algorithm for transition-based CCG parsing. In *Proceedings of the 2015 Conference of the North American Chapter of the Association for Computational Linguistics: Human Language Technologies*, pages 53–63, Denver, Colorado. Association for Computational Linguistics.

Laura Banarescu, Claire Bonial, Shu Cai, Madalina Georgescu, Kira Griffitt, Ulf Hermjakob, Kevin Knight, Philipp Koehn, Martha Palmer, and Nathan Schneider. 2013. Abstract Meaning Representation for sembanking. In *Proceedings of the 7th Linguistic Annotation Workshop and Interoperability with Discourse*, pages 178–186, Sofia, Bulgaria. Association for Computational Linguistics.

Srinivas Bangalore and Aravind K. Joshi. 1999. Supertagging: An approach to almost parsing. *Computational Linguistics*, 25(2):237–265.

Emily M. Bender and Alexander Koller. 2020. Climbing towards NLU: On meaning, form, and understanding in the age of data. In *Proceedings of the 58th Annual Meeting of the Association for Computational Linguistics*, pages 5185–5198, Online. Association for Computational Linguistics.

Eli Bingham, Jonathan P. Chen, Martin Jankowiak, Fritz Obermeyer, Neeraj Pradhan, Theofanis Karaletsos, Rohit Singh, Paul Szerlip, Paul Horsfall, and Noah D. Goodman. 2018. Pyro: Deep Universal Probabilistic Programming. *Journal of Machine Learning Research*.

Alena Böhmová, Jan Hajič, Eva Hajičová, and Barbora Hladká. 2003. The Prague Dependency Treebank: A three-level annotation scenario. In Anne Abeillé, editor, *Treebanks: Building and Using Parsed Corpora*, Text, Speech and Language Technology, pages 103–127. Springer Netherlands, Dordrecht.

Gemma Boleda and Aurélie Herbelot. 2016. Formal distributional semantics: Introduction to the special issue. *Computational Linguistics*, 42(4):619–635.

Tom Brown, Benjamin Mann, Nick Ryder, Melanie Subbiah, Jared D Kaplan, Prafulla Dhariwal, Arvind Neelakantan, Pranav Shyam, Girish Sastry, Amanda Askell, et al. 2020. Language models are few-shot learners. *Advances in neural information processing systems*, 33:1877–1901.

Emmanuele Chersoni, Enrico Santus, Chu-Ren Huang, and Alessandro Lenci. 2021. Decoding Word Embeddings with Brain-based Semantic Features. *Computational Linguistics*, 47(3):663–698.

Stephen Clark and James R. Curran. 2004. The importance of supertagging for wide-coverage CCG parsing. In *COLING 2004: Proceedings of the 20th International Conference on Computational Linguistics*, pages 282–288, Geneva, Switzerland. COLING.

Ann Copestake, Dan Flickinger, Carl Pollard, and Ivan A Sag. 2005. Minimal recursion semantics: An introduction. *Research on language and computation*, 3(2):281–332.

Jacob Devlin, Ming-Wei Chang, Kenton Lee, and Kristina Toutanova. 2019. BERT: Pre-training of deep bidirectional transformers for language understanding. In *Proceedings of the 2019 Conference of the North American Chapter of the Association for*

Computational Linguistics: Human Language Technologies, Volume 1 (Long and Short Papers), pages 4171–4186, Minneapolis, Minnesota. Association for Computational Linguistics.

Timothy Dozat and Christopher D. Manning. 2017. Deep biaffine attention for neural dependency parsing. In *International Conference on Learning Representations*.

Haim Dubossarsky, Eitan Grossman, and Daphna Weinshall. 2018. Coming to your senses: on controls and evaluation sets in polysemy research. In *Proceedings of the 2018 Conference on Empirical Methods in Natural Language Processing*, pages 1732–1740, Brussels, Belgium. Association for Computational Linguistics.

Chris Dyer, Adhiguna Kuncoro, Miguel Ballesteros, and Noah A. Smith. 2016. Recurrent neural network grammars. In *Proceedings of the 2016 Conference of the North American Chapter of the Association for Computational Linguistics: Human Language Technologies*, pages 199–209, San Diego, California. Association for Computational Linguistics.

Adam Ek, Jean-Philippe Bernardy, and Shalom Lappin. 2019. Language modeling with syntactic and semantic representation for sentence acceptability predictions. In *Proceedings of the 22nd Nordic Conference on Computational Linguistics*, pages 76–85, Turku, Finland. Linköping University Electronic Press.

Guy Emerson. 2020. What are the goals of distributional semantics? In *Proceedings of the 58th Annual Meeting of the Association for Computational Linguistics*, pages 7436–7453, Online. Association for Computational Linguistics.

John R Firth. 1957. A synopsis of linguistic theory, 1930-1955. *Studies in linguistic analysis*.

Dan Flickinger. 2000. On building a more effcient grammar by exploiting types. *Natural Language Engineering*, 6(1):15–28.

Atticus Geiger, Hanson Lu, Thomas Icard, and Christopher Potts. 2021. Causal abstractions of neural networks. In *Proc. of NeurIPS*.

Goran Glavaš and Ivan Vulić. 2021. Is supervised syntactic parsing beneficial for language understanding tasks? an empirical investigation. In *Proceedings of the 16th Conference of the European Chapter of the Association for Computational Linguistics: Main Volume*, pages 3090–3104, Online. Association for Computational Linguistics.

Jan Hajič, Eva Hajičová, Jarmila Panevová, Petr Sgall, Ondřej Bojar, Silvie Cinková, Eva Fučíková, Marie Mikulová, Petr Pajas, Jan Popelka, Jiří Semecký, Jana Šindlerová, Jan Štěpánek, Josef Toman, Zdeňka Urešová, and Zdeněk Žabokrtský. 2012. Announcing Prague Czech-English Dependency Treebank 2.0. In *Proceedings of the Eighth International Conference on Language Resources and Evaluation (LREC'12)*, pages 3153–3160, Istanbul, Turkey. European Language Resources Association (ELRA).

John Hale, Chris Dyer, Adhiguna Kuncoro, and Jonathan Brennan. 2018. Finding syntax in human encephalography with beam search. In *Proceedings of the 56th Annual Meeting of the Association for Computational Linguistics (Volume 1: Long Papers)*, pages 2727–2736, Melbourne, Australia. Association for Computational Linguistics.

Yiding Hao, Simon Mendelsohn, Rachel Sterneck, Randi Martinez, and Robert Frank. 2020. Probabilistic Predictions of People Perusing: Evaluating Metrics of Language Model Performance for Psycholinguistic Modeling. In *Proceedings of the EMNLP Workshop on Cognitive Modeling and Computational Linguistics*.

Zellig S Harris. 1954. Distributional structure. *Word*, 10(2-3):146–162.

Hany Hassan, Khalil Sima'an, and Andy Way. 2009. Lexicalized semi-incremental dependency parsing. In *Proceedings of the International Conference RANLP-2009*, pages 128–134, Borovets, Bulgaria. Association for Computational Linguistics.

John Hewitt and Percy Liang. 2019. Designing and interpreting probes with control tasks. In *Proceedings of the 2019 Conference on Empirical Methods in Natural Language Processing and the 9th International Joint Conference on Natural Language Processing (EMNLP-IJCNLP)*, pages 2733–2743, Hong Kong, China. Association for Computational Linguistics.

Jennifer Hu, Jon Gauthier, Peng Qian, Ethan Wilcox, and Roger Levy. 2020. A systematic assessment of syntactic generalization in neural language models. In *Proceedings of the 58th Annual Meeting of the Association for Computational Linguistics*, pages 1725–1744, Online. Association for Computational Linguistics.

Alon Jacovi, Swabha Swayamdipta, Shauli Ravfogel, Yanai Elazar, Yejin Choi, and Yoav Goldberg. 2021. Contrastive explanations for model interpretability. In *Proceedings of the 2021 Conference on Empirical Methods in Natural Language Processing*, pages 1597–1611, Online and Punta Cana, Dominican Republic. Association for Computational Linguistics.

Ganesh Jawahar, Benoît Sagot, and Djamé Seddah. 2019. What does BERT learn about the structure of language? In *Proceedings of the 57th Annual Meeting of the Association for Computational Linguistics*, pages 3651–3657, Florence, Italy. Association for Computational Linguistics.

Najoung Kim, Roma Patel, Adam Poliak, Patrick Xia, Alex Wang, Tom McCoy, Ian Tenney, Alexis Ross, Tal Linzen, Benjamin Van Durme, Samuel R. Bowman, and Ellie Pavlick. 2019. Probing what different NLP tasks teach machines about function word comprehension. In *Proceedings of the Eighth Joint Conference on Lexical and Computational Semantics (*SEM 2019)*, pages 235–249, Minneapolis, Minnesota. Association for Computational Linguistics.

Diederik P Kingma and Max Welling. 2013. Auto-encoding variational bayes. *arXiv preprint arXiv:1312.6114*.

Eliyahu Kiperwasser and Yoav Goldberg. 2016. Simple and accurate dependency parsing using bidirectional LSTM feature representations. *Transactions of the Association for Computational Linguistics*, 4:313–327.

Nikita Kitaev, Thomas Lu, and Dan Klein. 2022. Learned incremental representations for parsing. In *Proceedings of the 60th Annual Meeting of the Association for Computational Linguistics (Volume 1: Long Papers)*, pages 3086–3095, Dublin, Ireland. Association for Computational Linguistics.

Alessandro Lenci. 2023. Understanding natural language understanding systems. a critical analysis. Preprint arXiv:2303.04229.

Tao Li and Vivek Srikumar. 2019. Augmenting neural networks with first-order logic. In *Proceedings of the 57th Annual Meeting of the Association for Computational Linguistics*, pages 292–302, Florence, Italy. Association for Computational Linguistics.

Xiang Lisa Li and Alexander Rush. 2020. Posterior control of blackbox generation. In *Proceedings of the 58th Annual Meeting of the Association for Computational Linguistics*, pages 2731–2743, Online. Association for Computational Linguistics.

Tal Linzen, Emmanuel Dupoux, and Yoav Goldberg. 2016. Assessing the ability of LSTMs to learn syntax-sensitive dependencies. *Transactions of the Association for Computational Linguistics*, 4:521–535.

Nelson F. Liu, Matt Gardner, Yonatan Belinkov, Matthew E. Peters, and Noah A. Smith. 2019. Linguistic knowledge and transferability of contextual representations. In *Proceedings of the 2019 Conference of the North American Chapter of the Association for Computational Linguistics: Human Language Technologies, Volume 1 (Long and Short Papers)*, pages 1073–1094, Minneapolis, Minnesota. Association for Computational Linguistics.

William Merrill, Yoav Goldberg, Roy Schwartz, and Noah A. Smith. 2021. Provable limitations of acquiring meaning from ungrounded form: What will future language models understand? *Transactions of the Association for Computational Linguistics*, 9:1047–1060.

Stephan Oepen, Omri Abend, Lasha Abzianidze, Johan Bos, Jan Hajic, Daniel Hershcovich, Bin Li, Tim O'Gorman, Nianwen Xue, and Daniel Zeman. 2020. MRP 2020: The second shared task on cross-framework and cross-lingual meaning representation parsing. In *Proceedings of the CoNLL 2020 Shared Task: Cross-Framework Meaning Representation Parsing*, pages 1–22, Online. Association for Computational Linguistics.

Stephan Oepen, Omri Abend, Jan Hajic, Daniel Hershcovich, Marco Kuhlmann, Tim O'Gorman, Nianwen Xue, Jayeol Chun, Milan Straka, and Zdenka Uresova. 2019. MRP 2019: Cross-framework meaning representation parsing. In *Proceedings of the Shared Task on Cross-Framework Meaning Representation Parsing at the 2019 Conference on Natural Language Learning*, pages 1–27, Hong Kong. Association for Computational Linguistics.

Stephan Oepen and Jan Tore Lønning. 2006. Discriminant-based MRS banking. In *Proceedings of the Fifth International Conference on Language Resources and Evaluation (LREC'06)*, Genoa, Italy. European Language Resources Association (ELRA).

Juri Opitz and Anette Frank. 2022. SBERT studies meaning representations: Decomposing sentence embeddings into explainable semantic features. In *Proceedings of the 2nd Conference of the Asia-Pacific Chapter of the Association for Computational Linguistics and the 12th International Joint Conference on Natural Language Processing (Volume 1: Long Papers)*, pages 625–638, Online only. Association for Computational Linguistics.

Antonio Polino, Razvan Pascanu, and Dan Alistarh. 2018. Model compression via distillation and quantization. In *International Conference on Learning Representations*.

Jakob Prange, Nathan Schneider, and Lingpeng Kong. 2022. Linguistic frameworks go toe-to-toe at neuro-symbolic language modeling. In *Proceedings of the 2022 Conference of the North American Chapter of the Association for Computational Linguistics: Human Language Technologies*, pages 4375–4391, Seattle, United States. Association for Computational Linguistics.

Jakob Prange, Nathan Schneider, and Vivek Srikumar. 2021. Supertagging the long tail with tree-structured decoding of complex categories. *Transactions of the Association for Computational Linguistics*, 9:243–260.

Peng Qian, Tahira Naseem, Roger Levy, and Ramón Fernandez Astudillo. 2021. Structural guidance for transformer language models. In *Proceedings of the 59th Annual Meeting of the Association for Computational Linguistics and the 11th International Joint Conference on Natural Language Processing (Volume 1: Long Papers)*, pages 3735–3745, Online. Association for Computational Linguistics.

Alec Radford, Jeffrey Wu, Rewon Child, David Luan, Dario Amodei, Ilya Sutskever, et al. 2019. Language models are unsupervised multitask learners. OpenAI blog.

Victor Sanh, Lysandre Debut, Julien Chaumond, and Thomas Wolf. 2019. Distilbert, a distilled version of bert: smaller, faster, cheaper and lighter. Preprint arXiv:1910.01108.

Laurent Sartran, Samuel Barrett, Adhiguna Kuncoro, Miloš Stanojević, Phil Blunsom, and Chris Dyer. 2022. Transformer Grammars: Augmenting Transformer Language Models with Syntactic Inductive Biases at Scale. *Transactions of the Association for Computational Linguistics*, 10:1423–1439.

Michael Schlichtkrull, Thomas N. Kipf, Peter Bloem, Rianne van den Berg, Ivan Titov, and Max Welling. 2018. Modeling relational data with graph convolutional networks. In *The Semantic Web*, pages 593–607, Cham. Springer International Publishing.

Petr Sgall, Eva Hajicová, and Jarmila Panevová. 1986. The meaning of the sentence and its semantic and pragmatic aspects. academia.

Miloš Stanojević, Shohini Bhattasali, Donald Dunagan, Luca Campanelli, Mark Steedman, Jonathan Brennan, and John Hale. 2021. Modeling incremental language comprehension in the brain with Combinatory Categorial Grammar. In *Proceedings of the Workshop on Cognitive Modeling and Computational Linguistics*, pages 23–38, Online. Association for Computational Linguistics.

Miloš Stanojević and Mark Steedman. 2019. CCG parsing algorithm with incremental tree rotation. In *Proceedings of the 2019 Conference of the North American Chapter of the Association for Computational Linguistics: Human Language Technologies, Volume 1 (Long and Short Papers)*, pages 228–239, Minneapolis, Minnesota. Association for Computational Linguistics.

Miloš Stanojević and Mark Steedman. 2020. Max-margin incremental CCG parsing. In *Proceedings of the 58th Annual Meeting of the Association for Computational Linguistics*, pages 4111–4122, Online. Association for Computational Linguistics.

Mitchell Stern, Daniel Fried, and Dan Klein. 2017. Effective inference for generative neural parsing. In *Proceedings of the 2017 Conference on Empirical Methods in Natural Language Processing*, pages 1695–1700, Copenhagen, Denmark. Association for Computational Linguistics.

Ian Tenney, Dipanjan Das, and Ellie Pavlick. 2019a. BERT rediscovers the classical NLP pipeline. In *Proceedings of the 57th Annual Meeting of the Association for Computational Linguistics*, pages 4593–4601, Florence, Italy. Association for Computational Linguistics.

Ian Tenney, Patrick Xia, Berlin Chen, Alex Wang, Adam Poliak, R Thomas McCoy, Najoung Kim, Benjamin Van Durme, Sam Bowman, Dipanjan Das, and Ellie Pavlick. 2019b. What do you learn from context? probing for sentence structure in contextualized word representations. In *Proc. of ICLR*.

Sean Trott, Tiago Timponi Torrent, Nancy Chang, and Nathan Schneider. 2020. (Re)construing meaning in NLP. In *Proceedings of the 58th Annual Meeting of the Association for Computational Linguistics*, pages 5170–5184, Online. Association for Computational Linguistics.

Alex Warstadt, Alicia Parrish, Haokun Liu, Anhad Mohananey, Wei Peng, Sheng-Fu Wang, and Samuel R. Bowman. 2020. BLiMP: The benchmark of linguistic minimal pairs for English. *Transactions of the Association for Computational Linguistics*, 8:377–392.

Pia Weißenhorn, Lucia Donatelli, and Alexander Koller. 2022. Compositional generalization with a broad-coverage semantic parser. In *Proceedings of the 11th Joint Conference on Lexical and Computational Semantics*, pages 44–54, Seattle, Washington. Association for Computational Linguistics.

Zhiyong Wu, Yun Chen, Ben Kao, and Qun Liu. 2020. Perturbed masking: Parameter-free probing for analyzing and interpreting BERT. In *Proceedings of the 58th Annual Meeting of the Association for Computational Linguistics*, pages 4166–4176, Online. Association for Computational Linguistics.

Kayo Yin and Graham Neubig. 2022. Interpreting language models with contrastive explanations. In *Proceedings of the 2022 Conference on Empirical Methods in Natural Language Processing*, pages 184–198, Abu Dhabi, United Arab Emirates. Association for Computational Linguistics.

Probing neural language models for understanding of words of estimative probability

Damien Sileo[1] and Marie-Francine Moens[2]

[1]Univ. Lille, Inria, CNRS, Centrale Lille, UMR 9189 - CRIStAL, F-59000 Lille, France
[2]Department of Computer Science, KU Leuven, Belgium
damien.sileo@inria.fr

Abstract

Words of Estimative Probability (WEP) are phrases used to express the plausibility of a statement. Examples include terms like *probably, maybe, likely, doubt, unlikely*, and *impossible*. Surveys have shown that human evaluators tend to agree when assigning numerical probability levels to these WEPs. For instance, the term *highly likely* equates to a median probability of 0.90 ± 0.08 according to a survey by Fagen-Ulmschneider (2015). In this study, our focus is to gauge the competency of neural language processing models in accurately capturing the consensual probability level associated with each WEP. Our first approach is utilizing the UNLI dataset (Chen et al., 2020), which links premises and hypotheses with their perceived joint probability p. From this, we craft prompts in the form: "[PREMISE]. [WEP], [HYPOTHESIS]." This allows us to evaluate whether language models can predict if the consensual probability level of a WEP aligns closely with p. In our second approach, we develop a dataset based on WEP-focused probabilistic reasoning to assess if language models can logically process WEP compositions. For example, given the prompt "[EVENTA] *is likely*. [EVENTB] *is impossible*.", a well-functioning language model should not conclude that [EVENTA&B] is likely. Through our study, we observe that both tasks present challenges to out-of-the-box English language models. However, we also demonstrate that fine-tuning these models can lead to significant and transferable improvements.

1 Introduction

Expression of uncertainty is an important part of communication. Formal statistics are the rigorous way to quantify uncertainty but do not fit all communication styles. Words of estimative probability (WEP) such as *maybe* and *believe* are adverbs or verbs that are informal alternatives. Kent (1964) noted the importance of clarifying WEP meaning for intelligence analysis in the Central Intelligence Agency, and provided guidelines for mapping WEP to numerical probabilities. Several studies then measured the human perceptions of probability words and discovered some agreement with Kent (1964)'s guidelines. In this work, we use the scale derived from a survey (Fagen-Ulmschneider, 2015), which is the largest and most recent WEP perception survey available. 123 participants were asked to label WEP with numerical probabilities. We use the median of the participant answers to assign a consensual value to each WEP. Associated probabilities for the 19 WEP we use are available in Appendix A, table 2.

Here, we assess whether neural language models learn the consensual probability judgment of WEP from language modeling pretraining. We develop datasets and a methodology to probe neural language model understanding of WEP. The first dataset leverages previously annotated probability scores between a premise and a hypothesis, in order to measure a language model's ability to capture the agreement between numerical probabilities and WEP-expressed probabilities. The second dataset is based on compositions of facts with WEP-expressed probabilities, and measures verbal probabilistic reasoning in language models.

Our contributions are as follows: (i) two datasets and methods to measure understanding of WEP; and (ii) evaluation of the ability of neural language models (GPT2, RoBERTa-trained on MNLI) to tackle WEP-related problems, showing that off-the-shelf models are very little influenced by them, even though fine-tuning on our constructed datasets quickly leads to high accuracies. The code and generated datasets are publicly available[1]

[1]/hf.co/.../probability_words_nli

*Proceedings of the The 12th Joint Conference on Lexical and Computational Semantics (*SEM 2023)*, pages 469–476
July 13-14, 2023 ©2023 Association for Computational Linguistics

2 Related work

Our work probes a particular aspect of language understanding. We do not analyze the inside of the models (Rogers et al., 2020). We focus on the models' ability to perform controlled tasks (Naik et al., 2018; Richardson et al., 2020) involving WEP. WEP were studied in the context of intelligence analysis and linguistics, our work is the first to look at them through natural language processing (NLP) models. Our study also pertains to NLP analyses of logical reasoning and probability problems, and to uncertainty in natural language inference tasks.

Linguistics study of WEP Kent (1964)'s seminal work was the first to link WEP and numerical probability estimates, with intelligence analysis motivations (Dhami and Mandel, 2021) and a prescriptivist approach. This inspired further quantifications of human perceptions of WEP, in the context of medical reports (O'Brien, 1989; Ott, 2021) and weather reports (Lenhardt et al., 2020). Fagen-Ulmschneider (2015) proposed the largest survey up to date with 123 participants about general-domain WEP perception.

Logical and probabilistic reasoning Another strand of work probes NLP text encoders capabilities, notably reasoning abilities. Weston et al. (2015) probed understanding of specific problems like negation, spatial and temporal reasoning with the bAbI dataset. Richardson et al. (2020) probe understanding of first-order logic reasoning, Sileo and Lernould (2023) probe epistemic logic reasoning. Our work is the first to address probabilistic logic, alongside Dries et al. (2017); Suster et al. (2021) who construct a dataset of natural language probability problems, e.g., *"A bag has 4 white and 8 blue marbles. You pull out one marble and it is blue. You pull out another marble, what is the probability of it being white?"*. They also rely on the ProbLog solver (De Raedt et al., 2007), but focus on numeric probability problems. By contrast, our work targets WEP, and textual probabilistic logical reasoning.

Natural language inference, uncertainty, modality, evidentiality Uncertainty was also studied in the context of natural language inference tasks. Zhou et al. (2022) study the disagreement across annotators when labeling entailment relationships. Zhang et al. (2017) annotate graded entailment with 5 probability levels, and the UNLI dataset (Chen et al., 2020) go further by annotating numerical probabilities. Our work also pertains to the study of modality (Palmer, 1992; Saurí et al., 2006) and more particularly evidentiality (Su et al., 2010), but where previous work focused on WEP.

3 Probing WEP understanding

3.1 Verbalization and distractor generation

Our goal is to measure the understanding of WEP. One requirement of WEP understanding is capturing the consensual probability level. To test that, we use contexts (PREMISE) paired with a conclusions (HYPOTHESIS). The likelihood of a conclusion, p, depends on the associated context. One example from UNLI (Chen et al., 2020), which annotates that, is (*A man in a white shirt taking a picture* , *A man takes a picture* , 1.0).

We convert a triplet (PREMISE, HYPOTHESIS, p) to the following verbalization:

$$\text{PREMISE. } T_p(\text{HYPOTHESIS}). \quad (1)$$

where T_p is a text template assigned to the probability p. To select a template, we find the WEP whose associated median probability (see table 2) is the closest to p. We then use handcrafted templates to construct a modal sentence from the selected WEP and the hypothesis, e.g., "*It is **certain** that **a man takes a picture***". Table 3 in appendix B displays the templates that we associate with each WEP.

We also generate an invalid verbalization by randomly selecting an incorrect WEP (a WEP whose consensual probability differs from p by at least 40%)[2], e.g., *It is unlikely that a man takes a picture*. We hypothesize that language models and entailment recognition models should give a higher score (respectively likelihood and entailment probability) to the correct valid verbalization than to the invalid verbalization of p.

3.2 WEP-UNLI: probability/WEP matching

The UNLI dataset annotates (PREMISE, HYPOTHESIS) pairs from the SNLI dataset (Bowman et al., 2015) with joint probability scores p, totaling 55k training examples, 3k/3k validation/test examples. We use these examples to generate WEP-understanding dataset with verbalization validity prediction as shown in the previous subsection.

[2]This threshold ensures sufficient distance, while also ensuring that each WEP has at least one possible distractor.

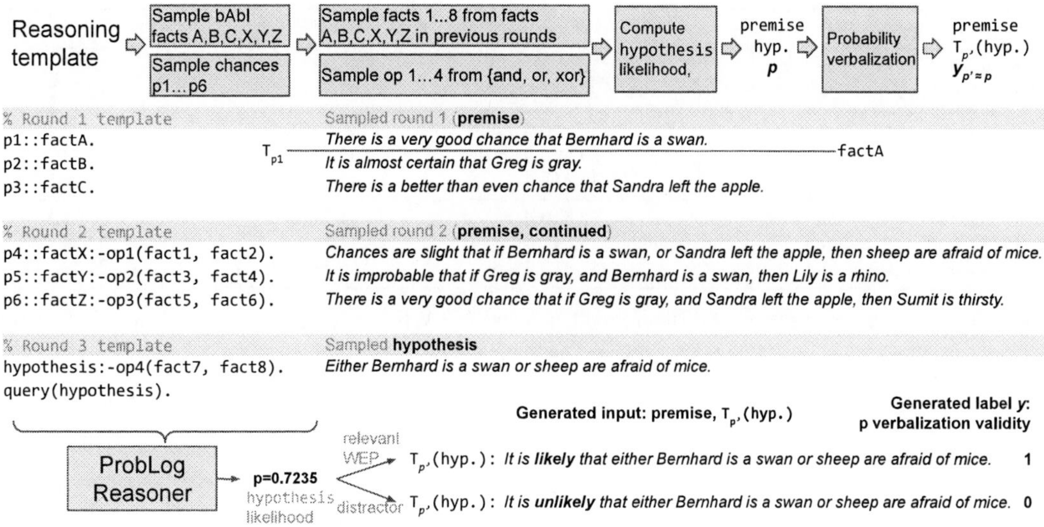

Figure 1: WEP-reasoning task constructions, with 2 hops. We sample randomly concrete facts $fact_i$ and probabilities p_i then build modal sentences with verbalization templates. We randomly sample logical operators to compose the modal sentences from the previous rounds to construct a premise, then a hypothesis, and we use a probabilistic soft logic solver to compute the hypothesis probability. We then correctly and incorrectly verbalize this probability. This process generates data for the task of probability verbalization validity. 1 hop reasoning skips the second round: `fact7` and `fact8` are sampled from {`factA`,`factB`,`factC`}

3.3 WEP-Reasoning: WEP compositions

Here, our goal is to assess models' ability to reason over combinations of probabilistic statements. We construct synthetic (PREMISE, HYPOTHESIS, p) examples from random factoids extracted from the bAbI dataset (Weston et al., 2015). Figure 1 illustrates the construction of WEP-reasoning examples:

We randomly sample initial facts and associated probability levels, and we verbalize them with the previously mentioned templates from Table 3 (Round 1). We further compose them with randomly sampled logical operators (and, or, xor). We then generate a hypothesis with logical combinations of the previous round. Finally, we feed the constructed premise and hypothesis to a probabilistic soft reasoning engine in order to derive the likelihood of the hypothesis given the premise. We rely on the ProbLog (De Raedt et al., 2007) reasoner which implements Dantsin (1992) semantics.

To evaluate different complexities of reasoning, we propose two variants: **2-hop reasoning**, where facts in Round 2 combine facts from Round 1, and the final hypothesis combines facts from Round 2. and **1-hop reasoning** where facts from the hypothesis combine Round 1 facts (Round 2 is skipped).

Since we want to sample more than two facts and we cannot a priori use text from the UNLI dataset, because UNLI only provides entailment likelihood for specific pairs. Combining several sentences could cause unaccounted interference. Therefore, we sample subject/verb/object factoids from the bAbI (Weston et al., 2015) datasets instead, which is built with handwritten arbitrary factoids such as *John went to the kitchen*. To sample multiple factoids, we prevent any overlap of concepts (verb, subject, object) between any pair of facts to make the facts independent of one another.

We sample probability levels from the list of medians of all WEP to prevent sampling the levels that too distant from a known WEP. When we assign a WEP to a probability level, we assume that the correct semantics is the consensual one, but humans differs slightly from this consensus. Still, when adding random perturbations of 20% to sampled $p_{1...6}$, the hypothesis probability is perturbed by less than 40% for 98% of examples.

We generate 5k examples using the template depicted in Figure 1, and use $10\%/10\%$ of the data for the validation/test splits. Appendix C shows the distribution of correct WEP for each dataset.

4 Experiments

We conduct verbalization validity prediction (binary classification task of WEP correctness detection between two candidates) under two settings.

	WEP-Reasoning (1 hop)	WEP-Reasoning (2 hops)	WEP-UNLI
Chance	50.0	50.0	50.0
Human baseline	97.0±1.0	**93.5±1.5**	**89.5±2.5**
GPT2 likelihood zero-shot	50.1±0.0	50.0±0.0	45.6±0.0
RoBERTa likelihood zero-shot	63.4±0.0	63.2±0.0	53.2±0.0
RoBERTa-MNLI zero-shot	49.2±5.4	41.7±4.2	54.6±3.7
RoBERTa+WEP-Reasoning (1 hop) fine-tuning	**97.8±0.4**	81.6±1.3	61.2±0.4
RoBERTa+WEP-Reasoning (2 hops) fine-tuning	85.0±1.6	**91.1±0.1**	62.3±1.7
RoBERTa+WEP-UNLI fine-tuning	62.4±0.4	64.3±0.1	**84.4±0.5**

Table 1: Test accuracy percentage of different models over the 3 WEP-understanding tasks. The last three rows display the accuracy when fine-tuning on each task, and transferability of the fine-tuned model outside the diagonal.

4.1 Zero-shot models

We use off-the-shelf language models to assign likelihood scores to a context and its conclusion. We evaluate the rate at which valid verbalization is scored higher than invalid verbalization. We refine the scores by also considering the average likelihood per token (Brown et al., 2020; Schick and Schütze, 2021) and calibrated scores (Brown et al., 2020; Zhao et al., 2021) where we divide the score of a PREMISE. T_p(HYPOTHESIS). by the score of T_p(HYPOTHESIS). We evaluate the normalized, length-normalized, and calibrated likelihood on the validation sets of each dataset and select the most accurate method for each dataset and model.

We also consider a pretrained natural language inference model, which is trained to predict entailment scores between a context and a conclusion.

GPT2 We use the pretrained GPT2 base version with 127M parameters (Radford et al., 2019), which is a causal language model trained to estimate text likelihood. We concatenate the premise and hypothesis and compute their likelihood as a plausibility score.

RoBERTa We also use the pretrained RoBERTa base model with 123M parameters (Liu et al., 2019) to score the masked language modeling likelihood of the premise/hypothesis pair.

RoBERTa-MNLI We fine-tune RoBERTa on the MNLI entailment detection dataset (Williams et al., 2018) with standard hyperparameters (see the following subsection).

Human baseline To establish human baseline performance on the constructed dataset, we had two NLP researchers annotate 100 examples randomly sampled from the test set of each dataset, with a multiple-choice question answering setting. Overall inter-annotator agreement is relatively high, with a Fleiss's κ of 0.70/0.68/0.71 for WEP Reasoning 1 hop, 2 hops and WEP-UNLI respectively.

4.2 Fine-tuning and transfer across probes

We fine-tune RoBERTa-base models on our datasets, using standard (Mosbach et al., 2021) hyperparameters[3] (3 epochs, sequence length of 256, learning rate of 2.10^{-5} batch size of 16. We use length-normalization with GPT2 likelihood and calibration with RoBERTa likelihood as they worked best on the validation sets.). We use a multiple-choice-question answering setup (we predict logit scores for the valid and invalid verbalization, combine their score with a softmax, then optimize the likelihood of the valid verbalization). The same format is applied to all tasks, so we can also study the transfer of capacities acquired during fine-tuning of each probe, for instance, between probability matching and compositional reasoning.

4.3 Results and discussion

Table 1 shows the results of our experiments. The very low accuracy of causal and masked language models (first two rows) demonstrates how challenging the WEP-understanding tasks are.

RoBERTa fine-tuned on MNLI dataset performs better than chance for WEP-UNLI. MNLI contains 814 instances of *probably* in the MNLI dataset, but we found little to no evidence of WEP compositions among them, which can explain the results.

Finally, fine-tuning on the dataset of a particular probe leads to high test accuracy on the associated test set. More surprisingly, fine-tuning on one dataset also causes substantial accuracy gain on other probes. This suggests that our datasets can

[3]Deviation from these hyperparameters did not yield significant improvement on the validation sets.

be incorporated in text encoder training in order to improve WEP handling.

5 Conclusion

We investigated WEP understanding in neural language models with new datasets and experiments, showing that WEP processing is challenging but helped by supervision which leads to transferable improvement. Future work could extract WEP probability scales from the UNLI dataset as an alternative to human perception surveys, but our work suggests that this requires language modeling progress.

6 Acknowledgements

This work is part of the CALCULUS project, which is funded by the ERC Advanced Grant H2020-ERC-2017 ADG 788506[4].

References

Samuel R. Bowman, Gabor Angeli, Christopher Potts, and Christopher D. Manning. 2015. A large annotated corpus for learning natural language inference. In *Proceedings of the 2015 Conference on Empirical Methods in Natural Language Processing*, pages 632–642, Lisbon, Portugal. Association for Computational Linguistics.

Tom Brown, Benjamin Mann, Nick Ryder, Melanie Subbiah, Jared D Kaplan, Prafulla Dhariwal, Arvind Neelakantan, Pranav Shyam, Girish Sastry, Amanda Askell, et al. 2020. Language models are few-shot learners. *Advances in neural information processing systems*, 33:1877–1901.

Tongfei Chen, Zhengping Jiang, Adam Poliak, Keisuke Sakaguchi, and Benjamin Van Durme. 2020. Uncertain natural language inference. In *Proceedings of the 58th Annual Meeting of the Association for Computational Linguistics*, pages 8772–8779, Online. Association for Computational Linguistics.

Eugene Dantsin. 1992. Probabilistic logic programs and their semantics. In *Logic Programming*, pages 152–164, Berlin, Heidelberg. Springer Berlin Heidelberg.

Luc De Raedt, Angelika Kimmig, and Hannu Toivonen. 2007. Problog: A probabilistic prolog and its application in link discovery. In *IJCAI*, volume 7, pages 2462–2467. Hyderabad.

Mandeep K Dhami and David R Mandel. 2021. Words or numbers? communicating probability in intelligence analysis. *American Psychologist*, 76(3):549.

[4]https://calculus-project.eu/

Anton Dries, Angelika Kimmig, Jesse Davis, Vaishak Belle, and Luc de Raedt. 2017. Solving probability problems in natural language. In *Proceedings of the Twenty-Sixth International Joint Conference on Artificial Intelligence, IJCAI-17*, pages 3981–3987.

Wade Fagen-Ulmschneider. 2015. Perception of probability words.

Sherman Kent. 1964. Words of estimative probability. *Studies in intelligence*, 8(4):49–65.

Emily D Lenhardt, Rachael N Cross, Makenzie J Krocak, Joseph T Ripberger, Sean R Ernst, Carol L Silva, and Hank C Jenkins-Smith. 2020. How likely is that chance of thunderstorms? a study of how national weather service forecast offices use words of estimative probability and what they mean to the public. *Journal of Operational Meteorology*, 8(5).

Yinhan Liu, Myle Ott, Naman Goyal, Jingfei Du, Mandar Joshi, Danqi Chen, Omer Levy, Mike Lewis, Luke Zettlemoyer, and Veselin Stoyanov. 2019. Roberta: A robustly optimized bert pretraining approach. *arXiv preprint arXiv:1907.11692*.

Marius Mosbach, Maksym Andriushchenko, and Dietrich Klakow. 2021. On the stability of fine-tuning bert: Misconceptions, explanations, and strong baselines. In *International Conference on Learning Representations*.

Aakanksha Naik, Abhilasha Ravichander, Norman Sadeh, Carolyn Rose, and Graham Neubig. 2018. Stress test evaluation for natural language inference. In *Proceedings of the 27th International Conference on Computational Linguistics*, pages 2340–2353, Santa Fe, New Mexico, USA. Association for Computational Linguistics.

B J O'Brien. 1989. Words or numbers? the evaluation of probability expressions in general practice. *The Journal of the Royal College of General Practitioners*, 39 320:98–100.

Douglas E Ott. 2021. Words representing numeric probabilities in medical writing are ambiguous and misinterpreted. *JSLS: Journal of the Society of Laparoscopic & Robotic Surgeons*, 25(3).

F.R. Palmer. 1992. Words and worlds; on the linguistic analysis of modality. (european university studies, series xiv, vol. 191): Richard matthews, frankfurt am main/bern/ new york/paris, peter lang, 1991. 310 pp. sfr 76.00 (pb.). *Lingua*, 88(1):87–90.

Alec Radford, Jeffrey Wu, Rewon Child, David Luan, Dario Amodei, Ilya Sutskever, et al. 2019. Language models are unsupervised multitask learners. *OpenAI blog*, 1(8):9.

Kyle Richardson, Hai Hu, Lawrence Moss, and Ashish Sabharwal. 2020. Probing natural language inference models through semantic fragments. In *Proceedings of the AAAI Conference on Artificial Intelligence*, volume 34, pages 8713–8721.

Anna Rogers, Olga Kovaleva, and Anna Rumshisky. 2020. A primer in BERTology: What we know about how BERT works. *Transactions of the Association for Computational Linguistics*, 8:842–866.

Roser Saurí, Marc Verhagen, and James Pustejovsky. 2006. Annotating and recognizing event modality in text. In *Proceedings of the Nineteenth International Florida Artificial Intelligence Research Society Conference, Melbourne Beach, Florida, USA, May 11-13, 2006*, pages 333–339. AAAI Press.

Timo Schick and Hinrich Schütze. 2021. Exploiting cloze-questions for few-shot text classification and natural language inference. In *Proceedings of the 16th Conference of the European Chapter of the Association for Computational Linguistics: Main Volume*, pages 255–269, Online. Association for Computational Linguistics.

Damien Sileo and Antoine Lernould. 2023. Mindgames: Targeting theory of mind in large language models with dynamic epistemic modal logic. *arXiv preprint arXiv:2305.03353*.

Aarohi Srivastava, Abhinav Rastogi, Abhishek Rao, Abu Awal Md Shoeb, Abubakar Abid, Adam Fisch, Adam R Brown, Adam Santoro, Aditya Gupta, Adrià Garriga-Alonso, et al. 2022. Beyond the imitation game: Quantifying and extrapolating the capabilities of language models. *arXiv preprint arXiv:2206.04615*.

Qi Su, Chu-Ren Huang, and Kai-yun Chen. 2010. Evidentiality for text trustworthiness detection. In *Proceedings of the 2010 Workshop on NLP and Linguistics: Finding the Common Ground*, pages 10–17, Uppsala, Sweden. Association for Computational Linguistics.

Simon Suster, Pieter Fivez, Pietro Totis, Angelika Kimmig, Jesse Davis, Luc de Raedt, and Walter Daelemans. 2021. Mapping probability word problems to executable representations. In *Proceedings of the 2021 Conference on Empirical Methods in Natural Language Processing*, pages 3627–3640, Online and Punta Cana, Dominican Republic. Association for Computational Linguistics.

Jason Weston, Antoine Bordes, Sumit Chopra, Alexander M Rush, Bart Van Merriënboer, Armand Joulin, and Tomas Mikolov. 2015. Towards ai-complete question answering: A set of prerequisite toy tasks. *arXiv preprint arXiv:1502.05698*.

Adina Williams, Nikita Nangia, and Samuel Bowman. 2018. A broad-coverage challenge corpus for sentence understanding through inference. In *Proceedings of the 2018 Conference of the North American Chapter of the Association for Computational Linguistics: Human Language Technologies, Volume 1 (Long Papers)*, pages 1112–1122. Association for Computational Linguistics.

Sheng Zhang, Rachel Rudinger, Kevin Duh, and Benjamin Van Durme. 2017. Ordinal common-sense inference. *Transactions of the Association for Computational Linguistics*, 5:379–395.

Zihao Zhao, Eric Wallace, Shi Feng, Dan Klein, and Sameer Singh. 2021. Calibrate before use: Improving few-shot performance of language models. In *Proceedings of the 38th International Conference on Machine Learning*, volume 139 of *Proceedings of Machine Learning Research*, pages 12697–12706. PMLR.

Xiang Zhou, Yixin Nie, and Mohit Bansal. 2022. Distributed nli: Learning to predict human opinion distributions for language reasoning. In *Findings of the Association for Computational Linguistics: ACL 2022*. Association for Computational Linguistics.

A Associated probabilities

WEP	Median probability judgment
certain	100†
almost certain	95.0 ± 10.9
highly likely	90.0 ± 8.4
very good chance	80.0 ± 10.8
we believe	75.0 ± 15.0
likely	70.0 ± 11.3
probably	70.0 ± 12.9
probable	70.0 ± 14.7
better than even	60.0 ± 9.1
about even	50.0 ± 4.9
probably not	25.0 ± 14.4
we doubt	20.0 ± 16.9
unlikely	20.0 ± 15.0
little chance	10.0 ± 12.2
chances are slight	10.0 ± 10.9
improbable	10.0 ± 17.5
highly unlikely	5.0 ± 17.3
almost no chance	2.0 ± 17.0
impossible	0†

Table 2: Median probability percentage associated to words of estimative probability according to (Fagen-Ulmschneider, 2015). First and last words (†) are taken from (Kent, 1964).

B WEP verbalization template

WEP	Verbalization template
about even	*chances are about even that* [FACT]
almost certain	*it is almost certain that* [FACT]
almost no chance	*there is almost no chance that* [FACT]
better than even	*there is a better than even chance that* [FACT]
certain	*it is certain that* [FACT]
chances are slight	*chances are slight that* [FACT]
highly likely	*it is highly likely that* [FACT]
highly unlikely	*it is highly unlikely that* [FACT]
impossible	*it is impossible that* [FACT]
improbable	*it is improbable that* [FACT]
likely	*it is likely that* [FACT]
little chance	*there is little chance that* [FACT]
probable	*it is probable that* [FACT]
probably	*it is probably the case that* [FACT]
probably not	*it is probably not the case that* [FACT]
unlikely	*it is unlikely that* [FACT]
very good chance	*there is a very good chance that* [FACT]
we believe	*we believe that* [FACT]
we doubt	*we doubt that* [FACT]

Table 3: Templates used to convert a fact and a WEP expressed uncertainty into a modal sentence.

C WEP frequencies on the generated datasets

WEP-reasoning	(1 hop)	WEP-Reasoning	(2 hops)	WEP-USNLI	
WEP	frequency	WEP	frequency	WEP	frequency
about even	11.1	*impossible*	13.2	*impossible*	25.6
probably not	9.7	*about even*	10.8	*better than even*	10.7
better than even	7.7	*probably not*	9.0	*certain*	7.2
we believe	7.1	*highly unlikely*	8.2	*about even*	6.9
highly likely	6.4	*almost no chance*	8.0	*almost certain*	6.7
certain	6.0	*better than even*	6.6	*highly likely*	6.0
highly unlikely	5.9	*we believe*	4.3	*very good chance*	5.9
almost no chance	5.8	*highly likely*	4.0	*almost no chance*	5.0
impossible	5.3	*very good chance*	4.0	*we believe*	4.1
almost certain	5.1	*we doubt*	4.0	*highly unlikely*	4.1
very good chance	4.7	*improbable*	3.9	*probably not*	3.4
chances are slight	3.6	*chances are slight*	3.9	*likely*	2.5
little chance	3.5	*unlikely*	3.6	*probable*	2.4
probable	3.2	*little chance*	3.5	*probably*	2.4
unlikely	3.1	*almost certain*	2.9	*unlikely*	1.5
likely	3.1	*certain*	2.7	*little chance*	1.5
probably	3.0	*likely*	2.5	*chances are slight*	1.5
we doubt	2.9	*probable*	2.4	*improbable*	1.4
improbable	2.9	*probably*	2.2	*we doubt*	1.4

Table 4: Validation set frequency of WEP in the correct answer of each dataset (percentages).

Arithmetic-Based Pretraining – Improving Numeracy of Pretrained Language Models

Dominic Petrak[†] , **Nafise Sadat Moosavi**[‡], **Iryna Gurevych**[†]

[†]Ubiquitous Knowledge Processing Lab (UKP Lab),
Department of Computer Science and Hessian Center for AI (hessian.AI),
Technical University of Darmstadt, Germany
`https://www.ukp.tu-darmstadt.de`
[‡]Department of Computer Science, The University of Sheffield, UK

Abstract

State-of-the-art pretrained language models tend to perform below their capabilities when applied out-of-the-box on tasks that require understanding and working with numbers. Recent work suggests two main reasons for this: (1) popular tokenisation algorithms have limited expressiveness for numbers, and (2) common pretraining objectives do not target numeracy. Approaches that address these shortcomings usually require architectural changes or pretraining from scratch. In this paper, we propose a new extended pretraining approach called Arithmetic-Based Pretraining that jointly addresses both in one extended pretraining step without requiring architectural changes or pretraining from scratch. Arithmetic-Based Pretraining combines contrastive learning to improve the number representation, and a novel extended pretraining objective called Inferable Number Prediction Task to improve numeracy. Our experiments show the effectiveness of Arithmetic-Based Pretraining in three different tasks that require improved numeracy, i.e., reading comprehension in the DROP dataset, inference-on-tables in the InfoTabs dataset, and table-to-text generation in the WikiBio and SciGen datasets[1].

1 Introduction

Numbers are ubiquitous in natural language. Therefore, understanding and working with numbers (usually referred to as numeracy) is a critical capability for pretrained language models such as BART (Lewis et al., 2020) or T5 (Raffel et al., 2019), cornerstones of modern NLP, in order to utilize quantitative information for various NLP tasks. Recent works question whether these models meet this requirement out-of-the-box (Wallace et al., 2019; Zhang et al., 2020): Common pretraining objectives such as the denoising autoencoder of BART (Lewis et al., 2020), the masked language modeling objective of BERT (Devlin et al., 2019), or the span-corruption objective of T5 (Raffel et al., 2019), are designed for understanding structure and semantic meaning of language and not to learn working with numbers. Furthermore, commonly used subword-based tokenisation algorithms such as Byte Pair Encoding (Sennrich et al., 2016) or WordPiece (Wu et al., 2016) are designed to handle patterns that are frequently observed during training, which is disadvantageous for numbers. For instance, 0.72 and 0.73 are two similar numbers. They should be processed similarly, but according to their frequency in the pretraining data they might be tokenised very differently, e.g., [0, ., 72] and [0, ., 7, 3], which will have an impact on their representation in embedding space. To address these shortcomings, various approaches have been proposed recently. However, most of them introduce additional components or rely on predefined features that limit their application, e.g., they are only applicable in a specific task like reading comprehension (Andor et al., 2019; Geva et al., 2020) or require architectural changes (Herzig et al., 2020).

In this paper, we propose a new extended pretraining approach called Arithmetic-Based Pretraining that targets both shortcomings for pretrained language models in one extended pretraining step without introducing new components or requiring pretraining from scratch. It consists of:

- A contrastive loss that combines subword-based with character-level tokenisation to improve the representation of numbers.
- A denoising pretraining objective, called the Inferable Number Prediction Task, to improve the model's capability of working with numbers.

Our experiments show that Arithmetic-Based Pretraining has a positive impact on BART (Lewis

[1]Code, data, and models trained using Arithmetic-Based Pretraining are available here: `https://github.com/UKPLab/starsem2023-arithmetic-based-pretraining`.

*Proceedings of the The 12th Joint Conference on Lexical and Computational Semantics (*SEM 2023)*, pages 477–493
July 13-14, 2023 ©2023 Association for Computational Linguistics

et al., 2020), T5 (Raffel et al., 2019) and Flan-T5 (Chung et al., 2022) in various tasks. It improves the accuracy in case of reading comprehension and inference-on-tables, and the factual correctness in case of table-to-text generation.

2 Related Work

Number Representations in Language Models. State-of-the-art language models like BART (Lewis et al., 2020) or T5 (Raffel et al., 2019) use subword-based tokenisation algorithms (such as Byte Pair Encoding (Sennrich et al., 2016)) to build vocabularies based on frequently observed sequences in a text corpus. While this is effective for common words, it is problematic for numbers. In an extensive study, Wallace et al. (2019) shows that models using character-level tokenisation, such as ELMo (Peters et al., 2018), usually achieve better results in numerical probing tasks and extrapolate better to unseen numbers compared to models using subword-based tokenisation. Thawani et al. (2021), Peng et al. (2021) and Zhang et al. (2020) report similar findings. In our work, we use the character-level tokenisation for numbers to address this shortcoming in BART, T5, and Flan-T5 (Chung et al., 2022).

Approaches for Improving Numeracy. Numeracy requires to understand and work with numbers, i.e., to do artihmetic operations, in order to generate the expected result. To improve this capability, recent approaches propose pretraining from scratch or architectural changes to tailor pretrained language models towards specific tasks. TAPAS (Herzig et al., 2020) targets question answering with tabular data. It is pretrained from scratch and extends BERT (Devlin et al., 2019) by introducing additional embeddings for capturing tabular structure. GenBERT (Geva et al., 2020) reuses a pretrained BERT model and adds a decoder on top. It is then further trained using math word problems and arithmetic operations for (1) incorporating the character-level tokenisation for numbers, and (2) to improve the numerical reasoning skills. It achieves state-of-the-art results in the DROP (Dua et al., 2019) and SQUAD (Rajpurkar et al., 2016) datasets. Andor et al. (2019) also reuses the pretrained BERT model and targets reading comprehension. They add a new layer on top that predicts and executes arithmetic operations. Suadaa et al. (2021) target table-to-text generation and propose a framework that uses the template-guided text generation from Kale and Rastogi (2020) to inject pre-executed numerical operations into the pretrained GPT-2 (Radford et al., 2019) and T5 (Raffel et al., 2019) models.

In their experiments, all of these works show that much of their performance improvements are due to specific design decisions or multi-level pretraining setups which result in new or task-specific models. With Arithmetic-Based Pretraining, we propose an approach that improves a model's numeracy with just one extended pretraining step and without changing its architecture.

Domain-Adaptive Pretraining. The idea of domain-adaptive pretraining is to bridge the gap between the vocabulary of a model's original pretraining corpus and the target domain by continuing pretraining using in-domain data (Gururangan et al., 2020). In this work, we propose the Inferable Number Prediction Task which is similar to domain-adaptive pretraining if the data used is from the same domain as that of finetuning. However, we show that this is not the only reason for performance improvements (Section 5.3).

Contrastive Learning. Contrastive learning is a general way to learn to map vector representations of similar data points (usually called *anchor* and *positive*) close to each other while pushing non-similar data points apart. In NLP, it is commonly used for learning sentence representations (Kim et al., 2021; Giorgi et al., 2021) or semantic similarities (Wang et al., 2021). In this work, we use contrastive learning to improve the representation of numbers.

3 Arithmetic-Based Pretraining

In this section, we propose Arithmetic-Based Pretraining. It combines different tokenisation algorithms, i.e., character-level and subword-based, with contrastive learning to improve the representation of numbers in pretrained language models (Section 3.1), while training on the Inferable Number Prediction Task (Section 3.2) to improve the capability of working with numbers. Section 3.3 describes the joint loss function.

3.1 Contrastive Learning

We propose to use a contrastive loss as additional training signal to improve the representation of numbers. For example, the model should learn a similar representation for the number 108.89, whether it is initially tokenised as [1, 0, 8, ., 8, 9] (character-level) or [10, 8, ., 89] (subword-based). If a number frequently occurs in the pretraining corpus, its corresponding subword-based encoding may be more informative. If this is not the case, its character-level tokenisation may be more informative. Therefore, our motivation is to benefit from both embedding spaces for learning better number representations. For implementation, we use the Multiple Negative Ranking Loss as proposed by Henderson et al. (2017)[2]:

$$\mathcal{L}_C = -\frac{1}{N}\sum_{i=1}^{N} \frac{e^{\text{sim}(\text{avg}(\hat{p}_i),\text{avg}(\hat{p\prime}_i))}}{\sum_j e^{\text{sim}(\text{avg}(\hat{p}_i),\text{avg}(\hat{p}_{neg}))}} \quad (1)$$

For the contrastive loss, we consider all numbers in the batch independently of the input sequences. Each number is used twice, once in character-level tokenisation (anchor), and once in subword-based tokenisation[3]. Assume p is a list of all numbers in the batch in character-level tokenisation. $p\prime$ is a list of all numbers in the batch in subword-based tokenisation. We consider p_i and $p\prime_i$ as a positive pair. Every other number in p and $p\prime$ is considered as negative sample to p_i (denoted as p_{neg}). $\hat{p_i}$, $\hat{p\prime}_i$, and $\hat{p}_{neg}$ are the corresponding embeddings after the encoder pass. sim represents the cosine similarity and avg represents the mean-average of the embedding. Averaging is a simple and effective form of aggregation which is necessary at this point, as the numbers are split into multiple tokens during tokenisation.

3.2 The Inferable Number Prediction Task

The Inferable Number Prediction Task is a variation of the classic masked language modeling objective (Devlin et al., 2019), but aims on improving a model's capability on working with numbers by focusing on data that requires arithmetic operations. The task consists of input C and the corresponding target sequence D. C consists of a pair of text sequences, C_1 and C_2, that are separated with a special character. C_2 equals to D, but contains a masked number that can be inferred from C_1. Given C, the task is to reconstruct D by correctly predicting the masked number in C_2[4]. For instance, for the task of table-to-text generation, C consists of the linearized form of the input table (C_1) and its description with one masked number (C_2). We select data with the following criteria:

- D (C_2 in C) and C_1 should have at least one overlapping entity, e.g., D should contain at least one of the entities that appear in the row or column headers of C_1 if C_1 is a table. This ensures that D is relevant to the information given in C_1.
- D (C_2 in C) should contain at least one number that either occurs in C_1 or is inferable by summation, subtraction, multiplication, division or ordering. This ensures that the masked number in C_2 is arithmetically related to the numbers given in C_1.

Next, we reduce C to the necessary information. If C_1 is an extensive text or paragraph, we apply each of these heuristics to each of the sentences and retain only the matching ones (the same applies to C_2). If C_1 is a table, we remove rows and columns that do not share entities with C_2 (see Appendix B for further details and illustrations).

For training, we use the cross-entropy loss function:

$$\mathcal{L}_{INP}(x,y) = \frac{1}{N}\sum_{n=1}^{N} -\log\left(\frac{e^{(x_{n},y_{n})}}{\sum_{k=1}^{K} e^{(x_{n,k})}}\right) \quad (2)$$

where x represents the logits of the predicted input sequence, and $y = y_1, ..., y_N$ represents the indices of the tokens of the output sequence. N is the size of the target sequence. x_{n,y_n} is the logit of the x_n token corresponding to the output token y_n. K is the size of the model's vocabulary.

3.3 Joint Loss Function

We combine the contrastive loss $\mathcal{L}_C$ (Equation 1) and the loss for the Inferable Number Prediction Task $\mathcal{L}_{INP}$ (Equation 2) as weighted sum in a joint loss function:

$$\mathcal{L} = \frac{\mathcal{L}_C}{2} + \frac{\mathcal{L}_{INP}}{2} \quad (3)$$

[2]We use the implementation from the sentence-transformer library (Reimers and Gurevych, 2019).

[3]Note that we use both only for Arithmetic-Based Pretraining. For finetuning and during inference, we only use character-level tokenisation for numbers.

[4]Preliminary experiments revealed that just reconstructing the masked number, without its context, has a negative impact on a model's text generation capabilities.

4 Experimental Setup

We implement our approach using Python 3.10, PyTorch (Paszke et al., 2019) and Huggingface (Wolf et al., 2020). As pretrained language models, we use the large variant of BART (Lewis et al., 2020) and the base variant of T5 (Raffel et al., 2019) and Flan-T5 (Chung et al., 2022) as provided by the Huggingface platform (see Appendix A for details on hyperparameters)[5]. All models are pretrained Transformer-based encoder-decoder models, but different in size. BART-large consists of a total of 24 layers and 406M parameters. T5-base and Flan-T5-base consist of 12 layers and 220M parameters. Flan-T5 is based on T5, but trained on more tasks, e.g., arithmetic reasoning, and chain-of-thought data (instructions). It significantly improves the results of the original model in many tasks (Chung et al., 2022). We conduct all experiments on a Tesla V100-SXM3 GPU with 32 GB memory. For experiments using table-to-text datasets, we represent tables as linearized sequence. We report the results of the best single runs.

4.1 Original Datasets

Reading Comprehension. The task of reading comprehension is to answer a question by reasoning over a related text passage. DROP (Dua et al., 2019) is such a dataset. It contains over 96,567 open-domain question-answer pairs and 6,735 paragraphs. According to the authors, 59.1% of answers consist of numbers and therefore implicitly require performing arithmetic operations to be predicted correctly. Each paragraph consists of 9.19% numbers on average. We split the dev data into two equally-sized subsets and use one for testing. Each subset contains 4,828 question-answer pairs.

Inference-on-Tables. Given a premise and a hypothesis, natural language inference (NLI) is the task of deciding whether the hypothesis is entailed, contradictory, or neutral to the premise. InfoTabs (Gupta et al., 2020) extends NLI to using semi-structured data, i.e., tables, as hypothesis. It consists of 23,738 hypothesis for 2,540 Wikipedia infoboxes from a variety of domains and provides three different test sets: in-domain, cross-domain, and an adversarial test set. The cross-domain test set uses premises from domains not used for training. The adversarial test set uses a different set of source tables. Furthermore, the wording of hypotheses was slightly changed by expert annotators. According to the authors, InfoTabs requires numerical and temporal reasoning (which implicitly requires performing arithmetic operations) across multiple rows and to a large extent. Each table consists on average of 13, 89% numbers.

Table-to-Text Generation. Table-to-text generation is the task of summarizing tabular data (which is often numerical) in a descriptive text. It requires to implicitly perform arithmetic operations such as ordering, summation or subtraction, or to capture magnitudes. SciGen (Moosavi et al., 2021) is a table-to-text generation dataset that requires to generate descriptions for scientific tables[6]. It is designed for arithmetic reasoning and consists of 53,136 table-description pairs. Each table consists of 41.55% numbers on average.

WikiBio (Lebret et al., 2016) is a dataset from the biographical domain. It consists of 728,321 table-description pairs. The task is to reproduce the first paragraph of biographical Wikipedia articles, given the corresponding infobox. According to the authors, dates, ages, and other quantities play an important role. Each table consists of 16.83% numbers on average. However, most values can be directly copied from the tables and do not require arithmetic operations.

4.2 Preprocessing for the Inferable Number Prediction Task

To fulfill the requirements of the Inferable Number Prediction Task, we apply the criterias described in Section 3.2 to all datasets in an offline preprocessing step. In case of InfoTabs (Gupta et al., 2020), we only use the data labeled with entailed in order to exclude contradictions (see Appendix B for examples and illustrations). Table 1 shows the resulting datasets.

	Train	Dev	Test
SciGen	4,859	1,473	55
WikiBio	412,053	51,424	51,657
DROP	8,336	849	850
InfoTabs	1,981	1,800	1,800

Table 1: Data distribution for the Inferable Number Prediction Task after applying the criterias to the original dataset splits.

[5]We could not use the large variant of T5 and Flan-T5 due to hardware limitations (each model has 770M parameters).

[6]NumericNLG (Suadaa et al., 2021) is a similar dataset. As SciGen (Moosavi et al., 2021) provides more unsupervised training pairs that we can use for Arithmetic-Based Pretraining, we use SciGen in our experiments.

We also find that the resulting datasets have slightly different number-to-word ratios. In the case of DROP (Dua et al., 2019) and InfoTabs, preprocessing increases the portion of numbers up to 18.98% and 17.25% in paragraphs and tables. In the case of WikiBio (Lebret et al., 2016) the ratio remains unchanged and in the case of SciGen (Moosavi et al., 2021) it reduces the numbers per table to 33.88%.

	OCC	ORD	SUM	SUB	MUL	DIV
DROP	0.41	0.32	0.04	0.07	0.13	0.02
InfoTabs	0.23	0.34	0.05	0.17	0.15	0.06
SciGen	0.11	0.06	0.03	0.12	0.41	0.27
WikiBio	0.24	0.38	0.03	0.10	0.20	0.03

Table 2: Distribution of arithmetic operations in the preprocessed datasets.

Table 2 shows the ratio of samples per dataset that we have identified as being inferable by arithmetic operiations, i.e., occurence (OCC), ordering (ORD), summation (SUM), subtraction (SUB), multiplication (MUL) or division (DIV). Appendix C provides a detailed analysis.

5 Evaluation

In this section, we evaluate the impact of Arithmetic-Based Pretraining on downstream applications with BART (Lewis et al., 2020), T5 (Raffel et al., 2019) and Flan-T5 (Chung et al., 2022) using in-domain data (Section 5.2), and out-of-domain data (Section 5.3). For Arithmetic-Based Pretraining, we use the preprocessed subsets of the original datasets as described in Section 4.2.

5.1 Evaluation Metrics

For inference-on-tables, we evaluate the results using Exact Match (EM score). For reading comprehension, we additionally use F1 score. The EM score evaluates the prediction accuracy, i.e., if the prediction exactly matches the target. It is the preferred metric for these tasks (Dua et al., 2019; Gupta et al., 2020). The F1 score reports the overlap between the prediction and the target. This results in partial reward in cases where the prediction is partially correct. In case of table-to-text generation, we conduct a human evaluation. This is due to the shortcomings of common automatic metrics for this task, as they are hardly able to assess the correctness of information not directly contained in the source data, i.e., information obtained by reasoning (Moosavi et al., 2021; Chen et al., 2020b; Suadaa et al., 2021). We provide the results of the automatic metrics in Appendix D.

For all experiments, *Baseline* represents the BART (Lewis et al., 2020), T5 (Raffel et al., 2019), and Flan-T5 (Chung et al., 2022) model directly finetuned on the corresponding dataset without Arithmetic-Based Pretraining. *Ours* represents these models with Arithmetic-Based Pretraining. We highlight statistically significant improvements of Ours over the respective baseline in the tables (independent two-sample t-test, $p \leq 0.05$).

5.2 In-Domain Pretraining

This section discusses the results on downstream tasks when using models that are pretrained using Arithmetic-Based Pretraining with in-domain data. For comparison, we will also report the results of the specialised state-of-the-art model for each task.

Reading Comprehension. Table 3 shows the results achieved on DROP (Dua et al., 2019).

		EM	F1
BART	Baseline	36.00	39.26
	Ours	**45.60**	**49.50**
T5	Baseline	10.40	14.60
	Ours	11.00	15.20
Flan-T5	Baseline	46.34	94.41
	Ours	**72.18**	**97.65**
QDCAT		85.46	88.38

Table 3: Evaluation on the DROP dataset. Our approach outperforms the baseline in all cases.

In all cases, Arithmetic-Based Pretraining improves the results over the baseline. Based on our analysis of the test results, i.e., by comparing the predictions of Baseline with Ours, we find that our approach reduces the incorrectly predicted numbers by 14.27% in case of BART (Lewis et al., 2020), 16.62% in case of T5 (Raffel et al., 2019), and 30.56% in case of Flan-T5 (Chung et al., 2022). The results achieved with Flan-T5 even outperform the results reported by Geva et al. (2020) for GenBERT (EM 68.6)[7]. Regarding the performance differences between BART and T5, we attribute this to the difference in model size. In this context, the performance difference between BART and Flan-T5 is particularly interesting. We attribute this to the fact that among other things, Flan-T5 was trained in arithmetic reasoning. QDCAT (Chen

[7]We also did preliminary experiments with the math word problems dataset provided by Geva et al. (Geva et al., 2020) as a first pretraining task but found that this does not improve the results (see Appendix G).

et al., 2020a) is the current state-of-the-art in the DROP task. It was built for reading comprehension and is based on RoBERTa (Liu et al., 2019), but adds an additional question-conditioned reasoning step on top (using a graph-attention network).

Inference-on-Tables. Table 4 presents the prediction accuracies (EM score) achieved on the InfoTabs (Gupta et al., 2020) dataset.

		In-Domain	Cross-Domain	Adversarial
BART	Baseline	33.30	23.67	27.68
	Ours	**67.20**	**54.40**	**57.20**
T5	Baseline	32.00	11.76	13.00
	Ours	32.30	**18.07**	**15.25**
Flan-T5	Baseline	27.23	25.14	29.17
	Ours	**34.04**	26.14	29.04
BPR		78.42	71.97	70.03

Table 4: Evaluation on the InfoTabs dataset. Our approach significantly improves the results on the in-domain data.

Similarly to reading comprehension, Arithmetic-Based Pretraining significantly improves EM scores in all cases. This applies especially to the in-domain test set. For the other two test sets, our approach also shows improvements over the baselines (mostly for BART (Lewis et al., 2020)), indicating to improve the model's robustness and capability to extrapolate to unseen data. We attribute performance differences to model sizes. Furthermore, analysis of the in-domain test results shows that T5 and Flan-T5 are biased toward predicting entailment. Since we observe this in both Baseline and Ours, we do not attribute this to how the data was preprocessed for the Inferable Number Prediction Task (Section 4.2). This is different for BART. An analysis of the in-domain test results shows that the model correctly predicts 60.30% of entailments, 75.50% of contradictions, and 65.83% of neutrals. BPR (Neeraja et al., 2021) is the current state-of-the-art in the InfoTabs task. It is based on BERT (Devlin et al., 2019) but built for inference over tabular data. It provides an improved representation of the input data, is pretrained on MultiNLI (Williams et al., 2018), and incorporates external knowledge.

Table-to-Text Generation. For human evaluation[8], we follow the approach used by Moosavi et al. (2021) for evaluating the results on SciGen. As this is very time-consuming, we only analyse 100 random table-description pairs from each, the SciGen and WikiBio (Lebret et al., 2016) dataset, and also only from the BART (Lewis et al., 2020) experiments. For SciGen, we use the results from the large split experiment[9].

For annotation, we break down each generated output to its corresponding statements (facts). We create one CSV file for each dataset that contains these statements in random order. This way, the annotator can not see whether a statement was generated by Ours (BART with Arithmetic-Based Pretraining) or Baseline (BART without Arithmetic-Based Pretraining). Alongside with the generated statements, this CSV file contains the original tables and gold descriptions. The annotator then decides for each of the statements whether it belongs to one of the following labels:

- *Entailed*: The statement is entailed in the gold description, e.g., a fact that is mentioned either in a similar or different wording in the description.
- *Extra*: The statement is not entailed in the gold description but is factually correct based on the table's content.
- *Incorrect*: The statement is relevant to the table, i.e., it contains relevant entities but is factually incorrect. For instance, the statement says *system A outperforms system B by 2 points* while based on the table system A has a lower performance than system B.
- *Hallucinated*: The statement is not relevant to the table.

Based on these labels, we then compute the recall (#entailed/#gold), precision (#entailed/#generated), correctness ((#entailed + #extra)/#generated), and hallucination (#hallucinated/#generated) scores for the generated facts. #gold and #generated refers to the respective number of included statements, not complete sequences. Table 5 shows the results.

Arithmetic-Based Pretraining improves the precision, recall, and correctness for both SciGen and WikiBio. In case of WikiBio, it improves the precision by 0.06 points, suggesting that generated

[8]The human evaluation was conducted by one of the authors.

[9]For SciGen, BART is the current state-of-the-art, and the baseline results of our human evaluation are comparable with those reported by Moosavi et al. (2021). We are not aware of a comparable human evaluation for WikiBio. Appendix D shows a comparison of automatic metrics for both datasets.

	Prec.	Rec.	Cor.	Hall.
SciGen				
Baseline	0.08	0.02	0.31	0.29
Ours	0.09	0.03	**0.40**	0.33
WikiBio				
Baseline	0.22	0.07	0.33	0.03
Ours	**0.28**	**0.09**	**0.46**	0.02

Table 5: Results of the human evaluation. In both cases, our approach improves the correctness of the generated facts.

	EM	F1
DROP		
DROP (in-domain)	45.60	49.50
Wikibio → DROP	6.00	33.50
InfoTabs → DROP	35.50	39.63
SciGen → DROP	**47.70**	**51.60**
InfoTabs		
InfoTabs (in-domain)	**67.20**	-
WikiBio → InfoTabs	33.15	-
DROP → InfoTabs	32.80	-
SciGen → InfoTabs	64.70	-

Table 6: Results of the out-of-domain pretraining (see Tables 3 and 4 for the in-domain experiments).

statements are more concise and closer to the target description. It also improves the ratio of statements that are factually correct by 0.13 points. In case of SciGen, the baseline results reflect the results reported by Moosavi et al. (2021), who also used the large variant of BART for their experiments. Ours improves the results in almost every aspect (especially in case of factual correctness, where it improves the results by 0.09 points). However, we observe a slight increase in hallucinations, which is a minor deterioration. We found that while Baseline seems to generate descriptions close to the target, Ours is somewhat more oriented towards the tabular values, whereby these values are used out-of-context in some cases which might be the reason for this deterioration. Nevertheless, all models generate fluent and valid-looking descriptions (see Appendix H for examples). This suggests that Arithmetic-Based Pretraining has no negative impact on a model's text generation capability. This is also supported by the results achieved using automatic metrics (see Appendix D).

5.3 Out-of-Domain Pretraining

To investigate whether the effectiveness of Arithmetic-Based Pretraining is a result of using in-domain data for pretraining (domain-adaptive pretraining) or improved numeracy, we evaluate our approach using out-of-domain data for pretraining. We focus on BART (Lewis et al., 2020) for this experiment and perform Arithmetic-Based Pretraining on a different dataset before finetuning on DROP (Dua et al., 2019) and InfoTabs (Gupta et al., 2020). For instance, for the DROP experiments, we pretrain models on WikiBio (Lebret et al., 2016), SciGen (Moosavi et al., 2021), and InfoTabs, which all include data from a different domain, before finetuning. For SciGen, we use the large split in this experiment.

Table 6 shows the results. Overall, the models pretrained using SciGen achieve the best out-of-domain results in both cases. In case of DROP, the results even exceed the ones achieved with in-domain pretraining. We find that the extent to which the pretraining dataset requires understanding and working with numbers has a major impact on the downstream performance (the more, the greater the impact). Among the datasets used, SciGen is in particular designed for the task of text generation based on arithmetic reasoning. It has a high number-to-word ratio and the subset used for pretraining on the Inferable Number Prediction Task (see Section 3.2) predominantly depends on arithmetic operations such as multiplications or divisions (see Table 2) instead of lookups or orderings (like in the other datasets).

6 Ablation Study

In this section, we investigate the impact of Arithmetic-Based Pretraining on the numeracy of a pretrained language model. Due to the shortcomings of automatic metrics in table-to-text generation (see Section 5.1) and because we want to be able to compare and discuss the impact of each component across datasets, we use the Inferable Number Prediction task for this and evaluate the number of correctly predicted context-related masked numbers (please see Appendix E for ablation experiments in downstream tasks)[10]. We use the preprocessed subsets of the original datasets for the Inferable Number Prediction Task (see Section 4.2). For evaluation, we use Exact Match (EM score) and F1 score (see Section 5.1). Table 7 shows the results.

We consider the large variant of BART (Lewis et al., 2020) with its default tokenisation (DT) and masking procedure (DM) as baseline for this

[10]In case of the contrastive loss, we also experiment with other number representations (see Appendix F).

	EM	F1
WikiBio		
BART	29.69	48.12
CLT + INP	**43.13**	**69.97**
Ours	**77.38**	**74.69**
SciGen		
BART	7.04	32.21
DT + INP	7.20	**35.11**
CLT + INP	**12.26**	**36.78**
Ours	**24.68**	**45.81**
Ours - INP	**21.49**	**40.51**
InfoTabs		
BART	12.43	22.17
DT + INP	**23.20**	**46.17**
CLT + INP	**59.09**	**73.88**
Ours	**60.45**	**74.33**
Ours - INP	**59.66**	**72.71**
DROP		
BART	7.20	7.20
DT + INP	6.33	**55.51**
CLT + INP	**29.40**	**66.43**
Ours	**30.58**	**67.07**
Ours - INP	**25.37**	**59.83**

Table 7: Ablation study on the Inferable Number Prediction Task. We conduct DT + INP and Ours - INP once for each task and with SciGen (Moosavi et al., 2021) as representative for table-to-text generation.

experiment. *DT + INP* uses the default tokenisation but our masking procedure (INP). *CLT + INP* then uses the character-level tokenisation for numbers (CLT). *Ours* finally combines CLT and INP with the contrastive loss (CL) as supporting signal to improve the representation of numbers. As last ablation, *Ours - INP* combines CLT with the contrastive loss but uses DM instead of INP and shows the contribution of our masking procedure to the effectiveness of Arithmetic-Based Pretraining.

In comparison with BART, DT + INP shows that our masking procedure improves the results across all tasks. This is most significant in case of InfoTabs (up to 10.77 points in EM score). In case of DROP, it raises the F1 score from 7.20 to 55.51 points, meaning that there is a significantly larger overlap between predicted numbers and target numbers. Using character-level instead of default tokenisation for numbers (CLT + INP) again improves the results across all datasets, indicating improved capabilities for arithmetic operations. Compared to DT + INP, it improves the EM score by 35.89 points in case of InfoTabs, and by 23.07 points in case of DROP. Ours further improves the results across all datasets. This is most significant in case of the table-to-text datasets, where it improves the EM score by 34.25 points in case of WikiBio (Lebret et al., 2016), and 12.42 points in case of SciGen (Moosavi et al., 2021). Since we create the pairs for the contrastive loss batch-wise, i.e., we consider all numbers in a batch independently from the samples (see Section 3.1), an advantageous number-to-word ratio favors a good positive-negative pair ratio for the contrastive loss, as in the case of SciGen which has the highest number to word ratio in input tables (33.88%, see also Section 4.1). This is counteracted by WikiBio which has a lower number-to-word ratio (16.32%). However, with 728,321 samples, Wikibio is the largest dataset. We therefore assume that more data compensates for a poor number-to-word ratio. Ours - INP deteriorates the EM score by 5.21 points in case of DROP, 3.19 points in case of SciGen, and 0.79 points in case of InfoTabs. This shows the contribution of our masking procedure to the effectiveness of Arithmetic-Based Pretraining.

7 Conclusions

In this paper, we propose Arithmetic-Based Pretraining, an approach for jointly addressing the shortcomings of pretrained language models in understanding and working with numbers (usually referred to as numeracy). In contrast to existing approaches, Arithmetic-Based Pretraining does not require architectural changes or pretraining from scratch. It uses contrastive learning to improve number representation and a novel extended pretraining objective, the Inferable Number Prediction Task, to improve numeracy in just one extended pretraining step. Our experiments show performance improvements due to better numeracy in three different state-of-the-art pretrained language models, BART, T5, and Flan-T5, across various tasks and domains, including reading comprehension (DROP), inference-on-tables (InfoTabs), and table-to-text generation (SciGen and WikiBio). We show that the effectiveness of our approach is not limited to in-domain pretraining, but rather depends on the extent to which the dataset used in the Inferable Number Prediction Task requires understanding numbers. For example, pretraining on the SciGen dataset improves the results achieved on DROP. Our ablation studies show that contrastive learning and the Inferable Number Prediction Task are key to improving the numeracy of the examined models.

8 Limitations

Our work is subject to some limitations. First of all, due to hardware limitations, we could not use the large variant of T5 (Raffel et al., 2019) and Flan-T5 (Chung et al., 2022) in a setting comparable to our BART-large experiments. Furthermore, BART (Lewis et al., 2020) restricts the maximum length of input sequences to 1024 characters[11]. For better comparability, we also use T5 and Flan-T5 accordingly. This limitation is due to the increased computational complexity of longer input sequences, but it is problematic with table-to-text generation datasets. For example, SciGen (Moosavi et al., 2021) consists in large parts of tables that exceed this sequence length when represented as a linearized sequence. While we have tried to take this into account by reducing the input data to necessary information, it was not guaranteed that the model always sees the complete information, which certainly has a negative impact on the evaluation results achieved on the downstream tasks. We guess that the results would have been more expressive if we would have used a different representation for tables, or focused on models that do not have this sequence length limitation.

Another limitation of our work concerns the impact of contrastive learning. According to Henderson et al. (2017), the impact of contrastive loss is favored by large batch sizes. Due to hardware limitations, we were only able to use small batch sizes (see Appendix A). The models might have adapted better if we would had the possibility to train with larger batch sizes. Regarding the weighting of contrastive and masked loss in the joint loss function, we only use equal weighting for our experiments, since we found that this already leads to good results, and due to the already large number of experiments conducted in this paper, we did not experiment with other weightings. However, optimizing this hyperparameter could further improve the results.

Evaluation is also a critical point. Although metrics such as PARENT (Dhingra et al., 2019) try to measure the factual correctness of generated descriptions, it requires a more individual examination in many cases. Especially in such highly specialized scenarios such as SciGen. Therefore, we conduct a human evaluation in order to analyse the impact of our Arithmetic-Based Pretraining on the downstream tasks. However, due to limited resources, we were only able to conduct a small-scale human evaluation. At this point, we would also like to mention that our evaluation setup in general is subject to limitations. As an extended pretraining approach, Arithmetic-Based Pretraining might have a negative impact on a model's general applicability, i.e., downstream performance in tasks used for pretraining, e.g., translation in case of T5, or other non-number related tasks commonly used in model benchmarking, such as question answering, text classification, or sentiment analysis. We only examined the impact on text generation as part of our human evaluation and with automatic metrics (see Appendix D). However, since (1) the Inferable Number Prediction Task (Section 3.2) is a variation of the widely used masked language modeling objective (Devlin et al., 2019), and (2) character-level tokenisation does not introduce new embeddings into a pretrained language model, we don't expect a negative impact here.

Another limitation concerns the evaluation of the Inferable Number Prediction Task on a model's numeracy. Since it is not reliably traceable whether and which arithmetic operation was used by a model to come to a specific result, we can only infer improved capabilities for arithmetic operations by performance improvements in the Inferable Number Prediction Task. We cannot clearly distinguish performance improvements on specific arithmetic operations.

[11]https://huggingface.co/docs/transformers/model_doc/bart#transformers.BartConfig, last accessed on 10/02/23.

9 Acknowledgements

This research work has been funded by the German Federal Ministry of Education and Research and the Hessian Ministry of Higher Education, Research, Science and the Arts within their joint support of the National Research Center for Applied Cybersecurity ATHENE. It also received funding from the German Research Foundation (DFG) under grant № EC 503/1-1 and GU 798/21-1.

References

Daniel Andor, Luheng He, Kenton Lee, and Emily Pitler. 2019. Giving BERT a calculator: Finding operations and arguments with reading comprehension. In *Proceedings of the 2019 Conference on Empirical Methods in Natural Language Processing and the 9th International Joint Conference on Natural Language Processing (EMNLP-IJCNLP)*, pages 5947–

5952, Hong Kong, China. Association for Computational Linguistics.

Kunlong Chen, Weidi Xu, Xingyi Cheng, Zou Xiaochuan, Yuyu Zhang, Le Song, Taifeng Wang, Yuan Qi, and Wei Chu. 2020a. Question directed graph attention network for numerical reasoning over text. In *Proceedings of the 2020 Conference on Empirical Methods in Natural Language Processing (EMNLP)*, pages 6759–6768, Online. Association for Computational Linguistics.

Wenhu Chen, Jianshu Chen, Yu Su, Zhiyu Chen, and William Yang Wang. 2020b. Logical natural language generation from open-domain tables. In *Proceedings of the 58th Annual Meeting of the Association for Computational Linguistics*, pages 7929–7942, Online. Association for Computational Linguistics.

Hyung Won Chung, Le Hou, Shayne Longpre, Barret Zoph, Yi Tay, William Fedus, Yunxuan Li, Xuezhi Wang, Mostafa Dehghani, Siddhartha Brahma, Albert Webson, Shixiang Shane Gu, Zhuyun Dai, Mirac Suzgun, Xinyun Chen, Aakanksha Chowdhery, Alex Castro-Ros, Marie Pellat, Kevin Robinson, Dasha Valter, Sharan Narang, Gaurav Mishra, Adams Yu, Vincent Zhao, Yanping Huang, Andrew Dai, Hongkun Yu, Slav Petrov, Ed H. Chi, Jeff Dean, Jacob Devlin, Adam Roberts, Denny Zhou, Quoc V. Le, and Jason Wei. 2022. Scaling instruction-finetuned language models.

Jacob Devlin, Ming-Wei Chang, Kenton Lee, and Kristina Toutanova. 2019. BERT: Pre-training of deep bidirectional transformers for language understanding. In *Proceedings of the 2019 Conference of the North American Chapter of the Association for Computational Linguistics: Human Language Technologies, Volume 1 (Long and Short Papers)*, pages 4171–4186, Minneapolis, Minnesota. Association for Computational Linguistics.

Bhuwan Dhingra, Manaal Faruqui, Ankur Parikh, Ming-Wei Chang, Dipanjan Das, and William Cohen. 2019. Handling divergent reference texts when evaluating table-to-text generation. In *Proceedings of the 57th Annual Meeting of the Association for Computational Linguistics*, pages 4884–4895, Florence, Italy. Association for Computational Linguistics.

Dheeru Dua, Yizhong Wang, Pradeep Dasigi, Gabriel Stanovsky, Sameer Singh, and Matt Gardner. 2019. DROP: A reading comprehension benchmark requiring discrete reasoning over paragraphs. In *Proceedings of the 2019 Conference of the North American Chapter of the Association for Computational Linguistics: Human Language Technologies, Volume 1 (Long and Short Papers)*, pages 2368–2378, Minneapolis, Minnesota. Association for Computational Linguistics.

Mor Geva, Ankit Gupta, and Jonathan Berant. 2020. Injecting numerical reasoning skills into language models. In *Proceedings of the 58th Annual Meeting of the Association for Computational Linguistics*, pages 946–958, Online. Association for Computational Linguistics.

John Giorgi, Osvald Nitski, Bo Wang, and Gary Bader. 2021. DeCLUTR: Deep contrastive learning for unsupervised textual representations. In *Proceedings of the 59th Annual Meeting of the Association for Computational Linguistics and the 11th International Joint Conference on Natural Language Processing (Volume 1: Long Papers)*, pages 879–895, Online. Association for Computational Linguistics.

Vivek Gupta, Maitrey Mehta, Pegah Nokhiz, and Vivek Srikumar. 2020. INFOTABS: Inference on tables as semi-structured data. In *Proceedings of the 58th Annual Meeting of the Association for Computational Linguistics*, pages 2309–2324, Online. Association for Computational Linguistics.

Suchin Gururangan, Ana Marasović, Swabha Swayamdipta, Kyle Lo, Iz Beltagy, Doug Downey, and Noah A. Smith. 2020. Don't stop pretraining: Adapt language models to domains and tasks. In *Proceedings of the 58th Annual Meeting of the Association for Computational Linguistics*, pages 8342–8360, Online. Association for Computational Linguistics.

Matthew Henderson, Rami Al-Rfou, Brian Strope, Yun-Hsuan Sung, László Lukács, Ruiqi Guo, Sanjiv Kumar, Balint Miklos, and Ray Kurzweil. 2017. Efficient natural language response suggestion for smart reply. *arXiv preprint arXiv:1705.00652*.

Jonathan Herzig, Pawel Krzysztof Nowak, Thomas Müller, Francesco Piccinno, and Julian Eisenschlos. 2020. TaPas: Weakly supervised table parsing via pre-training. In *Proceedings of the 58th Annual Meeting of the Association for Computational Linguistics*, pages 4320–4333, Online. Association for Computational Linguistics.

Mihir Kale and Abhinav Rastogi. 2020. Template guided text generation for task-oriented dialogue. In *Proceedings of the 2020 Conference on Empirical Methods in Natural Language Processing (EMNLP)*, pages 6505–6520, Online. Association for Computational Linguistics.

Taeuk Kim, Kang Min Yoo, and Sang-goo Lee. 2021. Self-guided contrastive learning for BERT sentence representations. In *Proceedings of the 59th Annual Meeting of the Association for Computational Linguistics and the 11th International Joint Conference on Natural Language Processing (Volume 1: Long Papers)*, pages 2528–2540, Online. Association for Computational Linguistics.

Rémi Lebret, David Grangier, and Michael Auli. 2016. Neural text generation from structured data with application to the biography domain. In *Proceedings of the 2016 Conference on Empirical Methods in Natural Language Processing*, pages 1203–1213, Austin, Texas. Association for Computational Linguistics.

Mike Lewis, Yinhan Liu, Naman Goyal, Marjan Ghazvininejad, Abdelrahman Mohamed, Omer Levy, Veselin Stoyanov, and Luke Zettlemoyer. 2020. BART: Denoising sequence-to-sequence pre-training for natural language generation, translation, and comprehension. In *Proceedings of the 58th Annual Meeting of the Association for Computational Linguistics*, pages 7871–7880, Online. Association for Computational Linguistics.

Yinhan Liu, Myle Ott, Naman Goyal, Jingfei Du, Mandar Joshi, Danqi Chen, Omer Levy, Mike Lewis, Luke Zettlemoyer, and Veselin Stoyanov. 2019. Roberta: A robustly optimized bert pretraining approach.

Nafise Moosavi, Andreas Rücklé, Dan Roth, and Iryna Gurevych. 2021. Scigen: a dataset for reasoning-aware text generation from scientific tables. In *Proceedings of the Neural Information Processing Systems Track on Datasets and Benchmarks*, volume 1.

J. Neeraja, Vivek Gupta, and Vivek Srikumar. 2021. Incorporating external knowledge to enhance tabular reasoning. In *Proceedings of the 2021 Conference of the North American Chapter of the Association for Computational Linguistics: Human Language Technologies*, pages 2799–2809, Online. Association for Computational Linguistics.

Kishore Papineni, Salim Roukos, Todd Ward, and Wei-Jing Zhu. 2002. Bleu: a method for automatic evaluation of machine translation. In *Proceedings of the 40th Annual Meeting of the Association for Computational Linguistics*, pages 311–318, Philadelphia, Pennsylvania, USA. Association for Computational Linguistics.

Adam Paszke, Sam Gross, Francisco Massa, Adam Lerer, James Bradbury, Gregory Chanan, Trevor Killeen, Zeming Lin, Natalia Gimelshein, Luca Antiga, Alban Desmaison, Andreas Kopf, Edward Yang, Zachary DeVito, Martin Raison, Alykhan Tejani, Sasank Chilamkurthy, Benoit Steiner, Lu Fang, Junjie Bai, and Soumith Chintala. 2019. Pytorch: An imperative style, high-performance deep learning library. *Advances in Neural Information Processing Systems 32*, pages 8024–8035.

Shuai Peng, Ke Yuan, Liangcai Gao, and Zhi Tang. 2021. Mathbert: A pre-trained model for mathematical formula understanding. *arXiv preprint arXiv:2105.00377*.

Matthew E. Peters, Mark Neumann, Mohit Iyyer, Matt Gardner, Christopher Clark, Kenton Lee, and Luke Zettlemoyer. 2018. Deep contextualized word representations. In *Proceedings of the 2018 Conference of the North American Chapter of the Association for Computational Linguistics: Human Language Technologies, Volume 1 (Long Papers)*, pages 2227–2237, New Orleans, Louisiana. Association for Computational Linguistics.

Alec Radford, Jeffrey Wu, Rewon Child, David Luan, Dario Amodei, Ilya Sutskever, et al. 2019. Language models are unsupervised multitask learners. *OpenAI blog*, 1(8):9.

Colin Raffel, Noam Shazeer, Adam Roberts, Katherine Lee, Sharan Narang, Michael Matena, Yanqi Zhou, Wei Li, and Peter J. Liu. 2019. Exploring the limits of transfer learning with a unified text-to-text transformer.

Pranav Rajpurkar, Jian Zhang, Konstantin Lopyrev, and Percy Liang. 2016. SQuAD: 100,000+ questions for machine comprehension of text. In *Proceedings of the 2016 Conference on Empirical Methods in Natural Language Processing*, pages 2383–2392, Austin, Texas. Association for Computational Linguistics.

Clément Rebuffel, Marco Roberti, Laure Soulier, Geoffrey Scoutheeten, Rossella Cancelliere, and Patrick Gallinari. 2021. Controlling hallucinations at word level in data-to-text generation.

Nils Reimers and Iryna Gurevych. 2019. Sentence-BERT: Sentence embeddings using Siamese BERT-networks. In *Proceedings of the 2019 Conference on Empirical Methods in Natural Language Processing and the 9th International Joint Conference on Natural Language Processing (EMNLP-IJCNLP)*, pages 3982–3992, Hong Kong, China. Association for Computational Linguistics.

Thibault Sellam, Dipanjan Das, and Ankur Parikh. 2020. BLEURT: Learning robust metrics for text generation. In *Proceedings of the 58th Annual Meeting of the Association for Computational Linguistics*, pages 7881–7892, Online. Association for Computational Linguistics.

Rico Sennrich, Barry Haddow, and Alexandra Birch. 2016. Neural machine translation of rare words with subword units. In *Proceedings of the 54th Annual Meeting of the Association for Computational Linguistics (Volume 1: Long Papers)*, pages 1715–1725, Berlin, Germany. Association for Computational Linguistics.

Lya Hulliyyatus Suadaa, Hidetaka Kamigaito, Kotaro Funakoshi, Manabu Okumura, and Hiroya Takamura. 2021. Towards table-to-text generation with numerical reasoning. In *Proceedings of the 59th Annual Meeting of the Association for Computational Linguistics and the 11th International Joint Conference on Natural Language Processing (Volume 1: Long Papers)*, pages 1451–1465, Online. Association for Computational Linguistics.

Avijit Thawani, Jay Pujara, Filip Ilievski, and Pedro Szekely. 2021. Representing numbers in NLP: a survey and a vision. In *Proceedings of the 2021 Conference of the North American Chapter of the Association for Computational Linguistics: Human Language Technologies*, pages 644–656, Online. Association for Computational Linguistics.

Eric Wallace, Yizhong Wang, Sujian Li, Sameer Singh, and Matt Gardner. 2019. Do NLP models know numbers? probing numeracy in embeddings. In *Proceedings of the 2019 Conference on Empirical Methods in Natural Language Processing and the 9th International Joint Conference on Natural Language Processing (EMNLP-IJCNLP)*, pages 5307–5315, Hong Kong, China. Association for Computational Linguistics.

Dong Wang, Ning Ding, Piji Li, and Haitao Zheng. 2021. CLINE: Contrastive learning with semantic negative examples for natural language understanding. In *Proceedings of the 59th Annual Meeting of the Association for Computational Linguistics and the 11th International Joint Conference on Natural Language Processing (Volume 1: Long Papers)*, pages 2332–2342, Online. Association for Computational Linguistics.

Adina Williams, Nikita Nangia, and Samuel Bowman. 2018. A broad-coverage challenge corpus for sentence understanding through inference. In *Proceedings of the 2018 Conference of the North American Chapter of the Association for Computational Linguistics: Human Language Technologies, Volume 1 (Long Papers)*, pages 1112–1122, New Orleans, Louisiana. Association for Computational Linguistics.

Thomas Wolf, Lysandre Debut, Victor Sanh, Julien Chaumond, Clement Delangue, Anthony Moi, Pierric Cistac, Tim Rault, Rémi Louf, Morgan Funtowicz, Joe Davison, Sam Shleifer, Patrick von Platen, Clara Ma, Yacine Jernite, Julien Plu, Canwen Xu, Teven Le Scao, Sylvain Gugger, Mariama Drame, Quentin Lhoest, and Alexander M. Rush. 2020. Transformers: State-of-the-art natural language processing. In *Proceedings of the 2020 Conference on Empirical Methods in Natural Language Processing: System Demonstrations*, pages 38–45, Online. Association for Computational Linguistics.

Yonghui Wu, Mike Schuster, Zhifeng Chen, Quoc V Le, Mohammad Norouzi, Wolfgang Macherey, Maxim Krikun, Yuan Cao, Qin Gao, Klaus Macherey, et al. 2016. Google's neural machine translation system: Bridging the gap between human and machine translation. *arXiv preprint arXiv:1609.08144*.

Xikun Zhang, Deepak Ramachandran, Ian Tenney, Yanai Elazar, and Dan Roth. 2020. Do language embeddings capture scales? In *Findings of the Association for Computational Linguistics: EMNLP 2020*, pages 4889–4896, Online. Association for Computational Linguistics.

Wei Zhao, Maxime Peyrard, Fei Liu, Yang Gao, Christian M. Meyer, and Steffen Eger. 2019. MoverScore: Text generation evaluating with contextualized embeddings and earth mover distance. In *Proceedings of the 2019 Conference on Empirical Methods in Natural Language Processing and the 9th International Joint Conference on Natural Language Processing (EMNLP-IJCNLP)*, pages 563–578, Hong Kong, China. Association for Computational Linguistics.

A Hyperparameters for Experiments

Table 8 shows the hyperparameter configuration for our experiments. In order to not train longer than necessary, we have determined the optimal number of epochs for each experiment by using early stopping with a patience of 10. For the downstream tasks, we have used the MoverScore (Zhao et al., 2019) with the table-to-text generation datasets. For DROP (Dua et al., 2019) and InfoTabs (Gupta et al., 2020), we have used the EM score. All models were trained for the same amount of epochs.

	Batch Size	Epochs	Learning Rate
Inferable Number Prediction Task			
SciGen	8	50	3e-5
WikiBio	8	3	3e-5
InfoTabs	8	21	3e-5
DROP	8	48	3e-5
Downstream Tasks			
SciGen	8	27	3e-5
WikiBio	8	9	3e-5
InfoTabs	8	14	3e-5
DROP	8	10	3e-5

Table 8: Hyperparameter Configuration.

B Inferable Number Prediction Task – Example Input Data

For table-to-text generation, Figure 1 shows an example of a (linearized) table from SciGen (Moosavi et al., 2021) with its caption as C_1, concatenated to its masked description C_2 using *</s>*. *<s>* and *</s>* are special tokens used by BART (Lewis et al., 2020) to represent the beginning and ending of a sequence. In case of WikiBio (Lebret et al., 2016), the input data is represented accordingly.

<s> <R> <C> Model <C> F1 Score <C> Accuracy <R> <C> Our Approach <C> 76.58 <C> 88.55 <R> <C> Their Approach <C> 65.78 <C> 74.32 <CAP> Comparison between us and them. </s> Our approach achieves an F1 score **<mask>** points higher than their approach. </s>

⇒ Our approach achieves an F1 score **10.8** points higher than their approach.

Figure 1: Illustration of a linearized table that is used for the Inferable Number Prediction Task. *<R>*, *<C>* and *<CAP>* symbolize the beginning of a new row, cell, and the table's caption.

For DROP (Dua et al., 2019), Figure 2 shows an example. It consists of the paragraph C_1, and a question C_2. The question contains a number (2) that also occurs in the paragraph.

<s> He lied on the ground, motionless, for about 7 minutes before he was taken off the field on a cart. Dallas lead 12-10 with under 2 minutes to go. Dallas tried to come back, but Seattle forced a turnover on downs to end the game. </s> With less than **<mask>** minutes to go, how many points ahead was Dallas? </s>

→ With less than **2** minutes to go, how many points ahead was Dallas?

Figure 2: Illustration of an input sample for the Inferable Number Prediction Task using DROP.

Figure 3 shows an example for the InfoTabs (Gupta et al., 2020) datasets. It is basically the same as for the table-to-text generation datasets, but uses the hypothesis as C_2.

<s><R> <C> title <C> Country <C> Single match <C> Season <R> <C> India vs Pakistan 1999 <C> India <C> 465,000 (Five-day Test) India v. Pakistan at Eden Gardens, Kolkata, 16-20 February 1999 <C> 1,592,543 (Total), 26,528 per match, 2017 IPL </s> India faced Pakistan in a five day match in **<mask>**. </s>

→ India faced Pakistan in a five day match in **1999**.

Figure 3: Illustration of an input sample for the Inferable Number Prediction Task using InfoTabs.

C Inferable Number Prediction Task – Dataset Details

In this section, we want to provide more details on the distribution of arithmetic operations across datasets used for the Inferable Number Prediction Task. Table 9 shows the ratio of each arithmetic operation on the overall number of samples for each split for the InfoTabs (Gupta et al., 2020) dataset.

	OCC	ORD	SUM	SUB	MUL	DIV
Train	0.24	0.35	0.05	0.16	0.15	0.05
Dev	0.15	0.34	0.07	0.18	0.20	0.06
Test	0.22	0.16	0.09	0.23	0.23	0.07

Table 9: Ratio of arithmetic operations for each split of the InfoTabs dataset.

Table 10 shows this ratio for the DROP (Dua et al., 2019) dataset.

	OCC	ORD	SUM	SUB	MUL	DIV
Train	0.41	0.32	0.4	0.07	0.13	0.03
Dev	0.42	0.31	0.05	0.05	0.14	0.03
Test	0.43	0.30	0.04	0.05	0.15	0.03

Table 10: Ratio of arithmetic operations for each split of the DROP dataset.

Table 11 shows this ratio for the SciGen (Moosavi et al., 2021) dataset.

	OCC	ORD	SUM	SUB	MUL	DIV
Train	0.11	0.06	0.04	0.12	0.40	0.27
Dev	0.11	0.05	0.04	0.12	0.43	0.25
Test	0.15	0.09	0.02	0.19	0.43	0.13

Table 11: Ratio of arithmetic operations for each split of the SciGen dataset.

Table 12 shows this ratio for the WikiBio (Lebret et al., 2016) dataset.

	OCC	ORD	SUM	SUB	MUL	DIV
Train	0.25	0.38	0.03	0.10	0.20	0.03
Dev	0.25	0.38	0.03	0.10	0.19	0.04
Test	0.25	0.38	0.03	0.11	0.20	0.03

Table 12: Ratio of arithmetic operations for each split of the SciGen dataset.

D Evaluation Using Automatic Metrics

This section presents the evaluation of our results on table-to-text datasets using automatic metrics. For this, we use a variety of metrics commonly used for this task, i.e., *BLEU* (Papineni et al., 2002), *MoverScore* (Zhao et al., 2019), *BLEURT* (Sellam et al., 2020), and *PARENT* (Dhingra et al., 2019). While BLEU calculates the concordance between the predicted description and the actual target on word-level, MoverScore and BLEURT measure the semantic concordance between the predicted description and the target using BERT (Devlin et al., 2019). BLEURT also takes the fluency of the predictions into account. PARENT estimates the factual correctness by comparing the predicted description to the original table and the target description, and especially rewards correct information that is contained in the table but not in the target. It has a higher correlation with human judgment. Table 13 reports the results. We highlight statistically significant improvements of our approach over the respective baseline in the tables (independent two-sample t-test, $p \leq 0.05$).

			MoverS	BLEU	BLEURT	PARENT
SciGen						
BART	Baseline	Few	52.48	4.60	-0.63	3.38
		Medium	53.76	4.26	-0.69	3.72
		Large	53.43	4.87	-0.70	3.68
	Ours	Few	**53.30**	1.73	-0.76	3.81
		Medium	**53.40**	2.71	-0.78	3.45
		Large	**55.00**	**9.30**	-0.76	3.82
	BART (Moosavi et al.)	Large	14.00	5.04	-0.71	-
T5	Baseline	Few	52.30	2.96	-0.94	6.39
		Medium	51.79	2.67	-0.95	4.08
		Large	53.00	3.40	-0.70	5.18
	Ours	Few	52.00	2.83	-0.98	4.32
		Medium	52.00	2.51	-0.86	4.70
		Large	53.40	2.96	-0.89	**6.72**
	BART (Moosavi et el.)	Large	6.00	3.38	-0.79	-
Flan-T5	Baseline	Few	53.03	2.76	-0.67	7.89
		Medium	53.56	3.03	-0.68	6.14
		Large	54.15	3.54	-0.65	7.94
	Ours	Few	**54.22**	3.14	-0.65	8.54
		Medium	**54.76**	3.25	-0.71	**8.12**
		Large	**55.12**	3.34	-0.61	**9.32**
WikiBio						
BART	Baseline		61.50	17.98	-0.64	45.18
	Ours		**62.78**	18.54	-0.27	44.32
T5	Baseline		60.30	17.94	-0.86	43.97
	Ours		60.10	20.00	-0.22	**45.25**
Flan-T5	Baseline		59.81	17.56	-0.78	44.67
	Ours		**62.51**	**21.11**	**-0.18**	**46.10**
	MBD		-	41.56	-	56.16

Table 13: Evaluation of our results on table-to-text datasets using automatic metrics. *Baseline* presents the results of the BART-large and Flan-T5-base models without Arithmetic-Based Pretraining. *Ours* shows the results of these models with Arithmetic-Based Pretraining.

The results show that Arithmetic-Based Pretraining slightly improves the performance in most experiments (based on PARENT and MoverScore), and has no negative impact text generation capabilities. However, as outlined in Section 5.1, none of these metrics can really assess the correctness of a fact that might be reasoned from the source data (Moosavi et al., 2021; Chen et al., 2020b; Suadaa et al., 2021). PARENT tries to address this, which is why this metric is the most appropriate one. Like BLEURT, Moverscore measures the semantic concordance between target and prediction. The advantage of MoverScore is that it is easier to interpret.

In case of SciGen, even our baseline results for BART (Lewis et al., 2020) are better than reported by Moosavi et al. (2021). We attribute this to different training hyperparameters (they did not report hyperparameters). While BART (Lewis et al., 2020) and T5 (Raffel et al., 2019) are state-of-the-art in SciGen (Moosavi et al., 2021), MBD (Rebuffel et al., 2021) is the state-of-the-art in WikiBio (Lebret et al., 2016). It is a multi-branch decoder that was build to reduce the hallucination in data-to-text tasks.

E Ablation Study – Downstream Tasks

This section shows the results of our downstream ablation experiments. For experiments, we use the same setup as described in Section 6, i.e., we consider the large variant of BART (Lewis et al., 2020) with its default tokenisation (DT) and masking procedure (DM) as baseline for this experiment. Additionally, we finetune the models in the downstream task (using the hyperparameters described in Appendix A). For evaluation, we use the respective test splits (in-domain in case of InfoTabs (Gupta et al., 2020)). Table 14 and Table 15 show the results of our ablation experiments in downstream tasks. We conduct the same experiments as for the general ablation study (Section 6): *DT + INP* uses the default tokenisation but our masking procedure (the Inferable Number Prediction Task, Section 3.2), *CLT + INP* uses the character-level tokenisation for numbers (CLT), *Ours* combines CLT and INP with the contrastive loss (CL), and *Ours - INP* combines CLT with the contrastive loss but uses DM instead of INP. Overall, the results reflect the findings described in Section 6. We highlight statistically significant improvements of our approach over the respective baseline in the tables (independent two-sample t-test, $p \leq 0.05$).

	MoverScore	BLEU
WikiBio		
BART	61.50	17.98
DT + INP	61.74	17.31
CLT + INP	**62.01**	**18.42**
Ours	**62.78**	**18.54**
Ours - INP	**62.15**	**18.25**
SciGen		
BART	53.43	4.87
DT + INP	53.76	4.65
CLT + INP	**54.12**	**6.45**
Ours	**55.00**	**9.30**
Ours - INP	**54.87**	**7.32**

Table 14: Downstream ablation study for SciGen and WikiBio.

According to automatic metrics, the impact on table-to-text generation is rather limited. We suspect that this is partly due to their shortcomings in assessing the correctness of information not directly included in the source data (see also Section 5.1). DT + INP shows that pretraining using our masking procedure slightly improves the results in both cases. Using the character-level tokenisation for numbers further improves the results (CLT + INP). In case of SciGen, the comparison between Ours and Ours - INP suggests that using the character-level tokenisation and contrastive learning to improve the number representation has more impact than pretraining using INP. In case of WikiBio, the differences are rather negligible (although Ours outperforms the baseline). This might be due to the characteristics of the dataset. As described in Section 4.1, WikiBio rather requires copying numbers from input tables to output text, than inferring context-related numbers (which is different in the other datasets).

	EM	F1
DROP		
BART	36.00	39.26
DT + INP	**39.87**	**43.77**
CLT + INP	**42.19**	**46.09**
Ours	**45.60**	**49.50**
Ours - INP	**43.68**	**47.45**
InfoTabs		
BART	33.30	-
DT + INP	**48.21**	-
CLT + INP	**61.56**	-
Ours	**67.20**	-
Ours - INP	**62.56**	-

Table 15: Downstream ablation study for DROP and InfoTabs

In case of DROP (Dua et al., 2019) and InfoTabs (Gupta et al., 2020), the results are more expressive. In both cases, we find that just using INP (DT + INP) as an extended pretraining task already brings a significant improvement over the baselines. This is further improved by using character-level tokenisation for numbers (CLT + INP) and contrastive learning (Ours). Ours - INP shows that in both cases, INP has a significant impact on performance improvements.

F Experiments using other Contrastive Representations

Regarding the contrastive representation, we also experiment with number representations other than the default subword-level one in order to improve the representation of numbers using the character-level tokenisation, i.e., exponent-mantissa (Zhang et al., 2020), a verbalized representation, and a combination of all of them using the Inferable Number Prediction Task. We focus on BART (Lewis et al., 2020) (the large variant) for this experiment. We conduct this experiment using the large split of the SciGen dataset (Moosavi et al., 2021). Table 16 shows the results.

None of the other representations improves the results over using the default subword-level tokenisation.

Experiment	EM	F1
BART (verb. repr.)	15.69	41.01
BART (exp.-mant. repr)	18.13	36.78
BART (subword-based tok.)	**24.68**	**45.81**
BART (combined)	17.92	38.43

Table 16: Comparison of results when using different representations for incorporating the character-level tokenisation.

G Preliminary Math Experiments

With GenBERT, Geva et al. (2020) propose to start pretraining with math word problems in order to improve the model's number understanding and capabilities for arithmetic operations. Therefore, following this idea would be an obvious step in order to improve the numeracy of general purpose pretrained language models. Table 17 shows the results of a preliminary experiment using GenBERT's math word problems dataset (MWP), BART (Lewis et al., 2020), and SciGen (Moosavi et al., 2021) on the Inferable Number Prediction Task. We highlight statistically significant improvements of our approach over the respective baseline in the tables (independent two-sample t-test, $p \leq 0.05$).

Experiment	EM	F1
Baseline	7.20	35.11
MWP-pretrained Baseline	**15.19**	34.18
MWP-pretrained Baseline + CLT	**22.94**	**42.55**
MWP-pretrained Baseline + CLT + CL	**22.78**	**43.14**
Ours	**24.68**	**45.81**

Table 17: Results achieved on the Inferable Number Prediction Task with and without pretraining using math word problems.

Baseline refers to the BART-large model. *MWP-pretrained Baseline* shows the results for Baseline, but further pretrained on MWP. *MWP-pretrained Baseline + CLT* represents the results for the MWP-pretrained Baseline, but uses the character-level representation (CLT) for numbers instead of BART's default tokenisation. Accordingly, *MWP-pretrained Baseline + CLT + CL* incorporates the contrastive loss (CL) as additional training signal. The results show that pretraining using math word problems as a first step, in general, improves the results for the Inferable Number Prediction Task, but not over using Arithmetic-Based Pretraining

(*Ours*).

In case of SciGen, the Inferable Number Prediction Task, only uses samples with target descriptions that contain numbers that are inferable from the input table by lookup or arithmetic operations (see Section 4.2). Therefore, even though it is a synthetic task, the results give insights on how effective pretraining on math word problems is for improving a model's numeracy.

H Examples from the Human Evaluation

Figure 4 shows two sample generations from our approach and the BART (Lewis et al., 2020) baseline from the SciGen (Moosavi et al., 2021) experiment using the medium split. Both read fluent and plausible.

Example 1

Our Approach

Observe that E2E and WebNLG char. had similar overall performance in terms of content errors and overall correctness. As expected, the phrasal errors corrected by the parser do not affect the performance of the system, except for spelling errors, which are in line with the automatic evaluation results reported by WMT Workshop on SemEval 2017.

Baseline

In terms of linguistic errors , the overall correctness of the e2e system is higher than that of the WebNLG system . however , the content errors of the two systems are very different , with content errors ranging from 4.4% (WebNLG char . dropped) to 55.6% (E2E word). The linguistic errors of both systems are similar, with spelling mistakes and punctuation errors accounting for most of the linguistic errors.

Example 2

Our Approach

Embeddings show to be very similar to one another – removing the closest kernel leads to worse performance. We hypothesize that this is due to a mismatch between training and test data. Word2Vec embeddings have the highest cosine similarities.

Baseline

Word2Vec shows the cosine similarity between event entity pairs. KCE lists their closest kernel mean after training. We can see that Word2Vec embeddings have the highest cosine similarities to all event pairs after training, with the exception of two event pairs ("assault" and "kill"). We can also see that event pairs marked with "attack" , "assault", or "scare" have similar cosine scores after training; however, after the model finishes training, their cosine score for "hate speech" is lower than for all other event pairs.

Figure 4: Generation from our approach and the BART baseline from the SciGen experiment using the medium split.

Robust Integration of Contextual Information for Cross-Target Stance Detection

Tilman Beck[*1], **Andreas Waldis**[*1,2], **Iryna Gurevych**[1]
[1]Ubiquitous Knowledge Processing Lab (UKP Lab)
Department of Computer Science and Hessian Center for AI (hessian.AI)
Technical University of Darmstadt
[2]Information Systems Research Lab
Department of Computer Science, Lucerne University of Applied Sciences and Arts
www.ukp.tu-darmstadt.de www.hslu.ch

Abstract

Stance detection deals with identifying an author's stance towards a target. Most existing stance detection models are limited because they do not consider relevant contextual information which allows for inferring the stance correctly. Complementary context can be found in knowledge bases but integrating the context into pretrained language models is non-trivial due to the graph structure of standard knowledge bases. To overcome this, we explore an approach to integrate contextual information as text which allows for integrating contextual information from heterogeneous sources, such as structured knowledge sources and by prompting large language models. Our approach can outperform competitive baselines on a large and diverse stance detection benchmark in a cross-target setup, i.e. for targets unseen during training. We demonstrate that it is more robust to noisy context and can regularize for unwanted correlations between labels and target-specific vocabulary. Finally, it is independent of the pretrained language model in use.[1]

1 Introduction

Given a text and a target the text is directed at, stance detection (SD) aims to predict whether the text contains a positive or negative stance towards the target or is unrelated. We provide an example in Figure 1. In contrast to formal polls, stance detection (SD) provides a scalable alternative to assess opinions expressed in unstructured texts. However, in contrast to predicting the polarity of a text (i.e., sentiment analysis), SD is more challenging because it requires establishing the relation towards a target which is rarely mentioned in the text (Augenstein et al., 2016).

Further, to infer the correct stance, often the text alone is not sufficient and contextual information needs to be taken into account (Du Bois, 2007). In contrast, most stance classification models are expected to make a correct prediction given the text and target only. This can lead to overly relying on label correlations with target-specific vocabulary (Reuver et al., 2021; Thorn Jakobsen et al., 2021). In our example (Figure 1), it is challenging to follow the reasoning of the text if the meaning of *school spirit* is left unclear.

Target: School Uniforms
Label: Pro
Text: Creates a sense of school spirit.
Context: ['school spirit is the enthusiasm and pride felt by the students of a school', 'a strong sense of school spirit is a positive and uplifting influence on the school and its students']

Figure 1: Example for Stance Detection from the UKP ArgMin dataset (Stab et al., 2018). The context is not part of the original dataset and was extracted from a large language model via prompting.

Consequently, providing external knowledge as an additional signal to stance classification has been proposed as a remedy. However, lacking a general solution, previous work applies knowledge integration only for a specific text domain like social media (Allaway et al., 2021; Clark et al., 2021). Nevertheless, SD algorithms are applied on a multitude of different text sources like social media (ALD), news (Hanselowski et al., 2019) or debating fora (Hasan and Ng, 2013; Chen et al., 2019) and on diverse targets such as persons (Sobhani et al., 2017; Li et al., 2021), products (Somasundaran and Wiebe, 2010), or controversial topics (Stab et al., 2018; Jo et al., 2021a), among other things. In addition, existing approaches (Zhang et al., 2020; Paul et al., 2020) often depend on the structure of the external knowledge source used. However, a single source of knowledge will likely not suffice for all different scenarios and adapting

* Equal contribution.

[1]Data and code at `https://github.com/UKPLab/arxiv2022-context-injection-stance`

*Proceedings of the The 12th Joint Conference on Lexical and Computational Semantics (*SEM 2023)*, pages 494–511
July 13-14, 2023 ©2023 Association for Computational Linguistics

the model architecture to the structure of a specific knowledge source (e.g. graph-based) limits its applicability.

This work proposes a flexible and robust approach to integrate contextual information by encoding it as text. It is better aligned to the encoding schema of a pre-trained language model (PLM) and circumvents any dependency on the structure of a particular knowledge source. It also allows for using any context source that best fits the data's text domain or mixing contextual information from multiple sources. In detail, we propose a dual-encoder architecture (INJECT), which encodes the input text and context information separately while facilitating information exchange between both via attention. We investigate extracting contextual information from various sources using different extraction strategies. We evaluate our approach across a benchmark of 16 stance detection datasets exhibiting different characteristics concerning text source, size, and label imbalance.

First, we demonstrate that existing state-of-the-art approaches outperform standard baselines only on the domains they have been tuned for - but perform worse on average. When integrating context via INJECT, we observe improvements on average and provide an analysis demonstrating the robustness of our approach. In summary, we make the following contributions:

- We show that the performance of existing state-of-the-art approaches does not transfer across a large and diverse benchmark of 16 SD datasets compared to a standard baseline.
- We propose the INJECT architecture to integrate contextual information for cross-target stance detection. Our approach leads to performance improvements across the benchmark and is independent of the underlying pre-trained language model.
- We compare different sources for extracting contextual information and their effectiveness for stance detection. We extract context from structured knowledge bases by prompting a large pre-trained language model.
- An analysis highlights our approach's benefits compared to a more direct integration via appending the context to the input. Our approach regularizes the influence of correlations of target-specific vocabulary and is robust to noisy contexts.

2 Related Work

Many tasks in NLP benefit from access to external knowledge such as natural language inference (Chen et al., 2018), machine translation (Shi et al., 2016) or argument mining (Lauscher et al., 2022). Within the era of PLMs, many approaches rely on extensive pretraining using data from knowledge bases (Peters et al., 2019; Zhang et al., 2019) (KB) or supervision from knowledge completion tasks (Wang et al., 2021; Rozen et al., 2021).

Early works leveraged sentiment lexicons (Bar-Haim et al., 2017b) or combinations thereof (Zhang et al., 2020) to improve SD classification performance. Other contextual components like author information (Li et al., 2018; Sasaki et al., 2018; Lukasik et al., 2019), dissemination features of social media (Lai et al., 2018; Veyseh et al., 2017) such as retweets or structural discourse elements (Nguyen and Litman, 2016; Opitz and Frank, 2019) have been shown to play an important role for stance detection. Similarly to the aforementioned approaches, the focus in SD has shifted towards combining structural KBs and PLMs. Kawintiranon and Singh (2021) identify label-relevant tokens and prioritize those during masked language modeling. This approach risks overfitting on target-specific tokens because stance is often expressed using target-specific terminology - an issue which is particularly problematic for argumentative sentences (Thorn Jakobsen et al., 2021). Clark et al. (2021) apply a knowledge infusion method for PLMs by filtering Wikipedia triplets for contextual knowledge. Popat et al. (2019) extend BERT by introducing a consistency constraint to learn agreement between the text and its target. Jo et al. (2021b) presents a variant of BERT pre-trained using a variety of supervised tasks resembling logical mechanisms. Paul et al. (2020) extract relevant concepts from ConceptNet using graph-based ranking methods to improve argument relation classification. Likewise, Liu et al. (2021) uses ConceptNet to identify relevant concept-edge pairs and integrate them via a graph neural network during training. Finally, Hardalov et al. (2021) used label embeddings to improve SD multi-dataset learning and recently showed (Hardalov et al., 2022) that sentiment-based pretraining improves multi-lingual stance detection.

In summary, most existing approaches integrate knowledge through extensive pretraining on knowledge-rich data. This does not guarantee improvement of the downstream task they are intended for and requires additional experiments. Another line of work introduces architectural dependencies on the structure of the knowledge source, thereby limiting their usage to tasks and domains for which the knowledge source is applicable. In contrast, our approach does not require further pre-training but directly learns to integrate contextual information during supervised training. The usefulness of the context is, therefore, directly measurable. Further, our proposed approach integrates context in natural language, thereby decoupling it from the structure of the context source. It is better aligned with the encoding mechanism of pre-trained language models and enables the integration of contextual information from various sources.

3 Methodology

Our goal is twofold: (1) we aim to integrate contextual information independent of the context source and (2) in a way that is robust to noisy and irrelevant content in the context. We propose INJECT, a dual encoder approach to integrate contextual sentences using the cross-attention mechanism introduced by Vaswani et al. (2017). The general intuition is that information can flow from input to context and vice versa, thereby regularizing the attention in both encoders. Thus, the context provides further information to reweigh the prediction importance of individual tokens in the input.

3.1 Contextual information

With regards to stance detection, we define *contextual information* (or short *context*) as the sum of all information which, given the text and its target, renders the conclusion of the stance plausible. The context for each dataset instance is retrieved beforehand and is provided as text to the model. Formally, we describe context $\mathbf{c} \in \mathbf{C}$ where $\mathbf{c}$ is a list containing m texts which provide contextual information on the input text $\mathbf{x}$. See Figure 1 for an example ($m = 2$). The length of these texts is upper bounded by the maximum sequence length of the encoder model.

3.2 Context integration via INJECT

Figure 2 provides a high-level visualization of our proposed INJECT architecture. It consists of two modules: input- and context-encoder. The input encoder processes input and target $I = (X, T)$

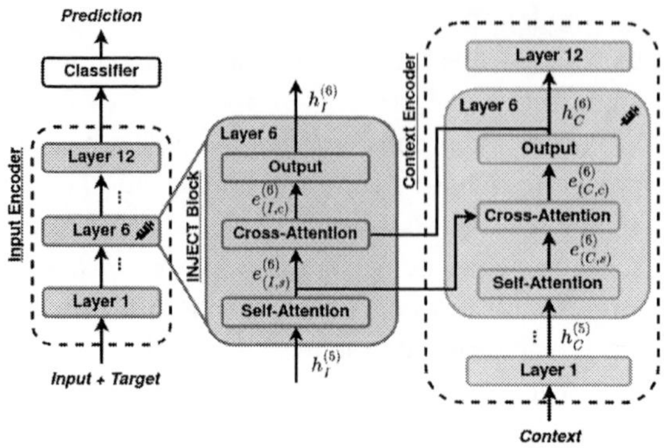

Figure 2: Visualization of the INJECT architecture. It consists of two modules - input encoder and context encoder. The context encoder encodes contextual information, and both encoders are interwoven using an INJECT-block based on the cross-attention mechanism.

while the context encoder processes the context sentences C. The encoders exchange information using inject blocks ($IB^{(j)}$) which are injected on layer j of both encoders. j is a hyperparameter tuned using the dataset's development set. All other layers are standard transformer blocks. An IB block is technically similar to a self-attention block but receives different inputs for key K, value V, and query Q. In detail, the inject block of the context-encoder (on layer j) receives the output from the self-attention $e^{(j)}_{(I,s)}$ on layer j of the input-encoder as key and value and the output of its own self-attention $e^{(j)}_{(C,s)}$ on layer j as query:

$$IB^{(j)}(K{=}e^{(j)}_{(I,s)}, V{=}e^{(j)}_{(I,s)}, Q{=}e^{(j)}_{(C,s)})$$

Afterward, it is forwarded to get the new hidden state $h^{(i)}_C$ of the context. Next, we back-inject the context into the input-encoder by feeding $h^{(i)}_C$ as key and value in its inject block:

$$IB^{(j)}(K{=}h^{(j)}_C, V{=}h^{(j)}_C, Q{=}e^{(j)}_{(I,s)})$$

Next, the hidden state $h^{(i)}_I$ at layer j of the input encoder is produced by processing the cross-attention output $e^{(j)}_{(I,c)}$. Finally, we add a classification head to the input encoder, which consists of a pooling layer, a dropout, and a linear classification layer. The parameters of both modules are optimized using the standard cross-entropy loss.

Our architecture is flexible regarding the number of context sentences that can be encoded (parameter m). In the case of multiple sentences, we average the cross-attention for all of them. Due to the dual encoders, INJECT is computationally more efficient than context integration via concatenation, as we explain in the Appendix A.7.

3.3 Context integration via concatenation

An alternative approach would be to append contextual information to the input text such that the model can exploit context directly using the self-attention mechanism. Technically, this is implemented by separating the input and context using the model-specific separation token (e.g., `text + [SEP] + context` for BERT)[2].

We see two major drawbacks of this approach. First, integrating irrelevant context will hurt downstream performance due to its direct influence on attention. Second, it is limited by the maximum sequence length of the model in use.

4 Context integration for stance detection

Task In stance detection, given an input text $\mathbf{x} \in \mathbf{X}$ and its corresponding target $\mathbf{t} \in \mathbf{T}$, the goal is to identify the correct label $\mathbf{y} \in \mathbf{Y}$ from a predefined set of stance descriptions. We further provide a set of contextual sentences C. The retrieval of C is explained in the next section.

4.1 Context retrieval

The INJECT model expects the context in natural language form and is therefore flexible with regard to the source of contextual information. To showcase, we evaluate different context sources that we deem relevant for inferring stance relations: (1) a structured knowledge base which stores knowledge as entity-relationship triplets, (2) a set of causal relations extracted from an encyclopedia, and (3) prompting a large pretrained language model using predefined question templates. The latter provides an intuitive interface to prompt for relevant sample-specific context, especially without suitable knowledge bases.

We neither expect these sources always to provide *perfect* contextual information nor to be suitable for all of the heterogeneous stance detection applications (see §5.1). However, our proposed architecture is designed to be robust, i.e., it utilizes beneficial context and ignores irrelevant information. In the following, we describe each approach in detail.

[2]In case of two input texts, the context is concatenated to the second input text.

ConceptNet Oftentimes, commonsense knowledge is beneficial to infer the stance towards a target correctly and has been shown to complement stance classification (Liu et al., 2021). Therefore, we use ConceptNet (Speer et al., 2017), a directed graph whose nodes are concepts and whose edges are assertions of commonsense about these concepts. For every edge, ConceptNet provides a textual description of the type of node relationship. Further, ConceptNet provides a weight factor for every edge computed based on the edge frequency within the ConceptNet training corpus.

Our approach uses the English subset of ConceptNet to get context sentences. We filter out concepts that are part of English stopwords [3] and ignore relations without descriptions. In total, we consider 400k nodes connected through approximately 600k edges. To retrieve the context, we use all tokens of the input text to search for string matches within the ConceptNet concepts. We consider only paths of length one where the start- and/or end-concept are contained in the input text. Finally, we sort the paths based on their weight (provided by ConceptNet) and convert every path into a context candidate by joining the descriptions of all its edges, as done in previous work (Lauscher et al., 2020).

CauseNet Causal relations, as a more specific example of commonsense knowledge, are often beneficial for understanding opinionated expressions (Sasaki et al., 2016) but rarely formulated in the text. To explain such relations, we investigate CauseNet (Heindorf et al., 2020), a KB of claimed causal relations extracted from the ClueWeb12 corpus and Wikipedia. We use the causal relations contained in the high-precision subset[4] of CauseNet, consisting of 80,223 concepts and 199,806 relations. We ignore concepts shorter than three characters or consisting of a modal verb (see Appendix A.6.1). We encode all relations using a sentence encoder (Reimers and Gurevych, 2019) using BERT-base-uncased weights. For each sample in a dataset, we retrieve the most relevant relations by ranking based on the cosine similarity between the encoded sample and all relations.

Pretrained language model Large PLMs can be queried as KBs using natural language prompts (Petroni et al., 2019; Heinzerling and Inui,

[3]As in NLTK (Bird, 2006)
[4]see `https://causenet.org/`

2021). We adopt this paradigm and generate context candidates by prompting a PLM to provide more information on either the target, parts of the input, or a combination of both. Precisely, we extract noun-phrases from the input sentence of a length of up to three words using the Stanford CoreNLP tool (Manning et al., 2014), ignoring stopwords and filtering noun-phrases that are equal to the target. Then, we create prompts using the following templates for single inputs a (e.g., target or noun-phrase)

$$P_1(a) = \text{define } a$$
$$P_2(a) = \text{what is the definition of } a$$
$$P_3(a) = \text{explain } a$$

and combination of inputs (a, b).

$$P_4(a, b) = \text{relation between } a \text{ and } b$$
$$P_5(a, b) = \text{how is } a \text{ related to } b$$
$$P_6(a, b) = \text{explain } a \text{ in terms of } b$$

The single-input approach is referred to as `T0pp-NP`, and the second approach as `T0pp-NP-T`. We found those prompts to generate the most meaningful contexts across different targets and noun-phrases (see Appendix A.6.2 for more details). The prompts can then generate outputs using any pre-trained sequence-to-sequence model.

We make use of T0pp[5] (Sanh et al., 2022), which is based on a pre-trained encoder-decoder (Raffel et al., 2020) and was fine-tuned using multiple diverse prompts generated using a large set of supervised datasets. We set the output sequence length to 40 words and sort the generated outputs by the length in descending order because we sometimes observe T0pp degenerate into producing single words. We filter those candidates where more than half of the generated words are repetitions. Finally, we remove all special tokens from the candidates. We found using two context sentences ($m = 2$) most beneficial in preliminary experiments.

5 Experiments

5.1 Datasets

We use a SD benchmark (Schiller et al., 2021; Hardalov et al., 2021), which covers 16 English datasets for research on (cross-domain) stance detection. We use this benchmark (Table 1) because it shows a large diversity regarding text sources, the number of targets, the number of annotated instances, and label imbalance. Thus, it provides a suitable testbed to evaluate the effectiveness of our context injection approach. More information about the details of each dataset can be found in the Appendix A.2.

5.2 Experimental details

Evaluation Our results are evaluated in a cross-target fashion (Augenstein et al., 2016; Xu et al., 2018), i.e., the setup is organized such that instances of a specific target are only contained in the training, development, or test split. We point out that our results are not directly comparable to Hardalov et al. (2021) as they perform experiments in a cross-domain fashion, i.e., their goal is to evaluate transfer learning effects by training on *all* but one dataset, which is used for testing. In contrast, we use *one* dataset per experiment to study the usefulness of context integration.

Baselines We compare INJECT to the following baselines. `BERT` is provided only the input, whereas `BERT+Target` is provided with both input and target using the model-specific separator token. (`BERT⊕X`) refers to `BERT+Target` with the retrieved context being appended, where X refers to context sources used (`ConceptNet`, `CauseNet`, `T0pp-NP` and `T0pp-NP-T`). We also test a combination of all context sources (`All`) and integration of random context (`Random`). To the best of our knowledge, no prior work has evaluated context integration for cross-target SD on the full benchmark. Thus, we compare with `TGA-Net` (Allaway and McKeown, 2020), `STANCY` (Popat et al., 2019), and `JointCL` (Liang et al., 2022) three state-of-the-art methods for SD which have been proposed for subsets of the benchmark. `TGA-Net` uses clustering to identify generalized topic representations. `STANCY` applies contrastive learning to learn embeddings where texts supporting a target are closer and opposing texts are more distant to their targets. `JointCL` use a prototypical graph for target-aware token representations. All of them require target information, which is not available for semeval19. In addition, we found `JointCL` is not working on fnc1 due to its long input texts. In these cases, we use the corresponding `BERT-Target` score for macro-F_1 avg. calcula-

[5] See `https://huggingface.co/bigscience/T0pp`. We also did experiments using T5 directly but found the outputs to be inferior to T0pp.

Dataset	Target	Type	Labels	Source
arc (Habernal et al., 2018)	Headline	User Post	unrelated (75%), disagree (10%), agree (9%), discuss (6%)	Debates
iac1 (Walker et al., 2012)	Topic	Debating Thread	pro (55%), anti (35%), other (10%)	Debates
perspectrum (Chen et al., 2019)	Claim	Perspective Sent.	support (52%), undermine (48%)	Debates
poldeb (Somasundaran and Wiebe, 2010)	Topic	Debate Post	for (56%), against (44%)	Debates
scd (Hasan and Ng, 2013)	None (Topic)	Debate Post	for (60%), against (40%)	Debates
emergent (Ferreira and Vlachos, 2016)	Headline	Article	for (48%), observing (37%), against (15%)	News
fnc1 (Pomerleau and Rao, 2017)	Headline	Article	unrelated (73%), discuss (18%), agree (7%), disagree (2%)	News
snopes (Hanselowski et al., 2019)	Claim	Article	agree (74%), refute (26%)	News
mtsd (Sobhani et al., 2017)	Person	Tweet	against (42%), favor (35%), none (23%)	Social Media
rumor (Qazvinian et al., 2011)	Topic	Tweet	endorse (35%), deny (32%), unrelated (18%), question (11%), neutral (4%)	Social Media
semeval2016t6 (Mohammad et al., 2016)	Topic	Tweet	against (51%), none (24%), favor (25%)	Social Media
semeval2019t7 (Gorrell et al., 2019)	None (Topic)	Tweet	comment (72%), support (14%), query (7%), deny (7%)	Social Media
wtwt (Conforti et al., 2020)	Claim	Tweet	comment (41%), unrelated (38%), support (13%), refute (8%)	Social Media
argmin (Stab et al., 2018)	Topic	Sentence	argument against (56%), argument for (44%)	Various
ibmcs (Bar-Haim et al., 2017a)	Topic	Claim	pro (55%), con (45%)	Various
vast (Allaway and McKeown, 2020)	Topic	User Post	con (39%), pro (37%), neutral (23%)	Various

Table 1: Stance Detection Benchmark datasets and their characteristics (sorted by source, then alphabetically). This table is based on Hardalov et al. (2021).

	macro-F_1avg.	arc	iac1	perspectrum	poldeb	scd	emergent	fnc1	snopes	mtsd	rumor	semeval16	semeval19	wtwt	argmin	ibmcs	vast
BERT	48.3±0.7	21.5	35.6	64.6	**51.3**	56.7	78.3	27.2	68.7	40.4	44.6	63.5	53.7	25.5	59.6	50.7	32.2
BERT+Target	56.8±0.8	62.5	36.3	**76.0**	49.8	57.9	78.0	72.9	69.7	41.2	40.5	64.8	53.7	55.2	60.3	52.0	36.1
STANCY	56.2±0.5	62.6	36.9	75.2	50.2	57.9	78.3	**74.3**†	**69.9**	40.3	32.9	64.9	–	54.0	60.0	52.5	36.1
TGA-Net	46.8±1.4	57.2	33.9	57.5	42	49.8	59.0	46.2	57.1	37.7	16.0	59.5	–	19.0	50.1	47.9	**62.7**†
JointCL	50.9±1.8	28.6	35.8	69.6	27.2	47.1	**78.9**	–	69.7	**55.1**†	51.5†	**67.5**†	–	**65.1**†	35.3	35.3	31.4
BERT⊕ConceptNet	55.7±0.6	61.4	**39.3**†	74.2	49.2	57.6	76.4	72.1	69.4	41.1	44.6	63.5	53.3	43.5	60.2	50.0	35.1
BERT⊕CauseNet	54.9±1.3	60.6	35.0	74.4	50.0	58.0	75.0	70.9	69.2	43.2	39.1	61.1	54.3	44.5	59.4	47.3	36.0
BERT⊕T0pp-NP	55.7±1.0	61.3	37.2	74.0	49.8	54.5	77.2	71.9	69.4	42.1	41.3	62.4	52.2	50.9	60.2	51.1	35.4
BERT⊕T0pp-NP-T	56.2±0.8	61.4	36.7	73.3	48.8	58.2	77.5	72.1	69.8	40.6	44.5	61.9	53.5	54.2	59.3	52.2	34.4
BERT⊕All	55.5±1.3	61.5	38.2	74.3	49.5	56.2	75.7	70.9	68.8	43.5	42.7	62.4	**55.3**†	42.9	60.3	50.6	35.5
BERT⊕Random	54.5±1.1	61.3	36.3	74.5	49.7	48.3	74.8	72.1	69.6	38.4	38.2	61.8	53.8	49.6	59.0	48.2	36.1
BERT⊗ConceptNet	57.2±1.0	62.7	36.5	75.6	49.3	**58.3**	77.8	73.8	69.0	41.9	47.9	65.1	54.4	52.5	60.1	53.0	37.4†
BERT⊗CauseNet	57.7±0.9	62.9	36.9	75.5	48.9	58.0	78.1	73.6	69.3	42.4	48.1	65.7†	55.1	54.8	60.7	**53.6**†	39.6†
BERT⊗T0pp-NP	57.5±1.0	62.6	37.2	75.6	48.7	57.2	77.2	73.7	69.6	41.2	49.2†	65.6†	55.1	55.6	60.9	52.9	37.3†
BERT⊗T0pp-NP-T	**57.8±1.0**	62.7	37.2	75.9	49.1	57.9	78.7	74.0†	69.1	41.4	**52.2**†	65.9†	55.0	54.4	**61.0**	53.4†	37.5†
BERT⊗All	57.2±0.9	**63.0**	36.6	75.4	49.7	57.9	78.8	73.3	69.1	42.4	44.3	65.5	54.8	53.6	60.3	53.6†	37.7†
BERT⊗Random	57.3±1.0	62.9	36.8	75.5	49.4	57.9	78.0	73.5	69.6	41.6	45.4	65.8	54.3	54.4	60.5	53.4†	37.5†

Table 2: Overview of the cross-target results across stance detection benchmark datasets. We highlight best performance per evaluation setting and dataset in bold. Statistically significant differences compared to the best performing baseline without access to context (BERT+Target) are indicated by †. Numbers are macro-F_1 scores averaged over ten runs with differently initialized seeds.

tion for a fair comparison.

Training setup We make use of the standard splits given in the benchmark (Hardalov et al., 2021) where possible or create our own (see Appendix A.1). We use macro-F_1 as evaluation metric and average across ten runs with different seeds. Performance is measured after the best-performing epoch based on the development set. We use Mann-Whitney U-Test (Mann and Whitney, 1947) with $p < 0.05$ to test statistical significance. We use the uncased BERT base model (Devlin et al., 2019) for all experiments. We use the same set of hyper-parameters for all model setups. For INJECT, we use the same model architecture for the input and context encoder. We tune the layer j for context integration (see §3.2). We tested layers 3, 6, 9, and 12 on the development set of the benchmark. Layer 12 performed the best and was used for all reported results. More details are in the Appendix A.1.

6 Results

This section shows the effectiveness of INJECT by providing constant improvements using noisy context on the heterogeneous benchmark (Table 2).

First, we note a large performance boost (+8.5pp) when including information about the target when comparing BERT and BERT+Target. While target information improved the performance for individual datasetes (Stab et al., 2018), we generalize this finding for 14 out of 16 SD datasets.

The baselines STANCY, TGA-Net, and JointCL mostly show the best performance for the datasets they have been proposed for. However, on average, they do not perform on par with the strong BERT+Target baseline. STANCY performs slightly worse, probably due to the binary contrastive loss and thereby ignoring multi-label information. TGA-Net underperforms all other approaches except for vast. Using generalized topic representations transfers to a scenario where the number of targets is relatively high (5634) and only a few examples per target exist (mean 2.4), as for vast. JointCL performs best on datasets from social media (semeval16, wtwt, or mtsd), but is outperformed by standard baselines for the rest of the tasks. Thus, this approach can not generalize to datasets with longer text inputs. We conclude that existing state-of-the-art approaches for cross-target stance detection work well for the datasets they have been designed for but do not generalize across the diverse set of datasets that exist in SD.

INJECT outperforms BERT+Target in 13 of 16 cases, while for three datasets (perspectrum, poldeb, snopes) none of the extracted contexts provides benefits, independently of the integration. On average, all context sources lead to performance improvements in combination with INJECT, with T0pp-NP-T being the best. Combining all context sources underperforms the integration of individual context, most probably due to the average function leading to a perturbation of the context. Surprisingly, integration of random context slightly outperforms the strong BERT+Target baseline in ten datasets while degrading the direct integration performance, as expected. We investigate the reasons in our subsequent analysis (§6.3).

6.1 Quality of context

To evaluate the quality of each context source, we looked at the aggregated performance differences with the baseline across each source (Figure 3b). While CauseNet leads to performance improvements for a maximum number of tasks (12), T0pp-NP-T leads the board concerning the total sum of absolute improvements across all datasets. The context quality extracted by prompting a PLM also becomes evident when looking at the performance of BERT⊕. ConceptNet and CauseNet lead to large performance degradation both in number of tasks and absolute numbers.

6.2 Generalization across PLMs

We investigate if the benefits of INJECT transfer to other PLM architectures by evaluating it in combination with RoBERTa (Liu et al., 2019) and ELECTRA (Clark et al., 2020). We follow the same experimental protocol as for BERT A.1, but chose only the best-performing context source (T0pp-NP-T) due to the large number of experiments. The results (Table 3) confirm the previously observed findings that INJECT improves the performance on average across this diverse set of stance detection tasks. We observe similar improvements as with BERT for both models, with the strongest increase (+1.1pp on average) and the best overall performance for ELECTRA.

6.3 Further analysis

As integration with INJECT outperforms direct integration and even performs more robustly when provided with random context, we analyze the regularization provided by the INJECT architecture.

Regularization via INJECT We analyze how INJECT regularizes inputs by examining how models rely on target-specific vocabulary. Such vocabulary is often used to express a stance (Wei and Mao, 2019), but can lead to spurious correlations (Thorn Jakobsen et al., 2021). Therefore, we identify the top 5% label-indicative and target-specific tokens and correlate them with the model attributions using vector-norms (Kobayashi et al., 2020) (see Appendix A.4 for details). Table 4 shows these correlations for six benchmark datasets. For arc, argmin, and rumor we note a general low to negative correlation of BERT+Target. Further, we see BERT⊕T0pp-NP-T and BERT⊗T0pp-NP-T increasing the correlation - giving more attribution to target and label indicative tokens. This behavior is one reason for the bad performance of BERT+Target for these tasks. For rumor, we note a correlation increase of 45.5 for INJECT+T0pp-NP-T, which leads to a clear performance improvement of 11.7pp (Table 2). Thus, INJECT adjusts the low attribution to relevant tokens compared to BERT+Target. On the other hand, we see INJECT+T0pp-NP-T reducing the attribution for ibmcs, mtsd, and wtwt. Given the better performance of INJECT+T0pp-NP-T on ibmcs and mtsd, we conclude that INJECT can reduce potential spurious correlations in this case. For wtwt, INJECT+T0pp-NP-T reduces the correlation but has a performance loss of 0.8pp. Given the niche domain of wtwt (financial mergers and acquisitions on Twitter), identifying relevant context is more challenging using standard context sources.

Dataset characteristics We investigate which dataset characteristics are indicative of perfor-

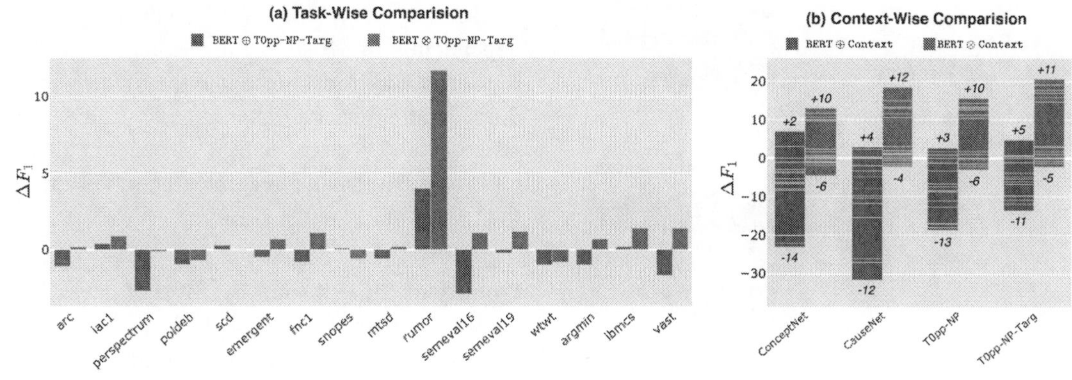

Figure 3: In (a), we compare the relative performance change ΔF_1 of `BERT⊕TOpp-NP-T` (blue) or `BERT⊗TOpp-NP-T` (red) compared to `BERT+Target` for every task. Within (b), we show the aggregated relative performance change of `BERT⊕`(blue) and `BERT⊗`(red) compared to `BERT+Target` per context source. In addition, we count the number of tasks exhibiting performance improvement and deterioration above and below the bars, respectively.

	macro-F$_1$avg.	arc	iac1	perspectrum	poldeb	scd	emergent	fnc1	snopes	mtsd	rumor	semeval16	semeval19	wtwt	argmin	ibmcs	vast
`BERT+Target`	56.8±0.8	62.5	36.3	**76.0**	**49.8**	57.9	78.0	72.9	69.7	41.2	40.5	64.8	53.7	**55.2**	60.3	52.0	36.1
`BERT⊖TOpp-NP-T`	56.2±0.8	61.4	36.7	73.3	48.8	**58.2**	77.5	72.1	**69.8**	40.6	44.5	61.9	53.5	54.2	59.3	52.2	34.4
`BERT⊗TOpp-NP-T`	**57.8±1.0**	**62.7**	**37.2**	75.9	49.1	57.9	**78.7**	**74.0**†	69.1	**41.4**	**52.2**†	**65.9**†	**55.0**	54.4	**61.0**	**53.4**†	**37.5**†
`RoBERTa+Target`	61.6±0.6	60.4	32.9	85.1	49.6	**62.3**	**79.0**	**77.3**	**74.9**	61.2	49.9	70.3	57.8	**64.2**	60.9	62.9	37.0
`RoBERTa⊕TOpp-NP-T`	60.8±0.8	61.7	**35.1**	84.1	**50.6**	62.1	77.8	77.0	73.9	55.2	**51.3**	68.2	57.8	63.4	**61.6**	57.9	35.6
`RoBERTa⊗TOpp-NP-T`	**61.9±0.7**	**62.9**†	33.4	**85.4**	49.6	59.5	78.5	**77.3**	74.6	**64.4**	51.2	**70.5**	**58.0**	62.2	61.1	**63.5**	**38.5**†
`ELECTRA+Target`	62.0±0.9	59.5	35.2	89.2	45.7	61.7	77.4	73.8	75.4	66.9	50.0	**70.1**	55.0	63.7	60.2	71.6	36.2
`ELECTRA⊕TOpp-NP-T`	61.6±0.7	59.6	**35.5**	87.5	**47.8**	**62.1**	77.4	73.8	74.0	64.7	53.1	67.2	54.1	**65.3**	60.6	68.4	35.2
`ELECTRA⊗TOpp-NP-T`	**63.1±0.6**	**62.5**†	35.4	**89.3**	47.4	60.4	**78.2**	**76.2**†	**75.7**	**68.9**†	**54.7**	70.0	**57.1**	63.7	**60.7**	**71.7**	**37.2**

Table 3: Comparing context integration using different PLM architectures in a cross-target setup across stance detection benchmark datasets. We highlight the best performance per model architecture and dataset in bold. Statistically significant differences compared to the best-performing baseline without access to context (`BERT+Target`) are indicated by †. Numbers are macro-F$_1$ scores averaged over three runs with differently initialized seeds (see Appendix A.1 for experimental details.)

model	arc	rumor	argmin	ibmcs	mtsd	wtwt
`BERT+Target`	-6.3	-14.1	6.9	27.0	64.5	11.6
`BERT⊕TOpp-NP-T`	4.5	31.0	16.2	25.7	48.9	5.3
`BERT⊗TOpp-NP-T`	8.8	31.4	9.8	22.7	33.8	6.4

Table 4: Pearson correlation between self-attention and target-label-specific tokens for the baseline model `BERT+Target` and the context integration approaches (`BERT⊕` and `BERT⊗`) using the best performing context source (`TOpp-NP-T`). A larger correlation indicates stronger attention attribution.

mance improvements using INJECT. Thus, we compute the Pearson correlation of various dataset characteristics and the performance differences between the baseline and the average of the INJECT variants. Details about how we calculate dataset characteristics are provided in the Appendix A.5. The results are visualized in Figure 4. Independent of the context source, we observe beneficial improvements using INJECT if datasets exhibit characteristics leading to performance instabilities. This is indicated by positive correlations with an increasing number of labels and label imbalance. Further, we measure text understanding difficulty using the Flesch reading-ease score (FRES) by Flesch (1948). Interestingly, INJECT can better deal with datasets exposing a high variability of FRES within their instances (mean-flesch, std-flesch). These factors generally contribute to training instabilities where INJECT is more robust. This observation is confirmed by the strong positive correlation of the variance across random initializations and INJECT performance.

Robustness We investigate robustness across all benchmark datasets for the `TOpp-NP-T` context by visualizing the performance differences to the baseline (`BERT+Target`) in Figure 3a. In the case of performance improvements, INJECT consistently outperforms direct context integration. If there is no improvement for both integration ap-

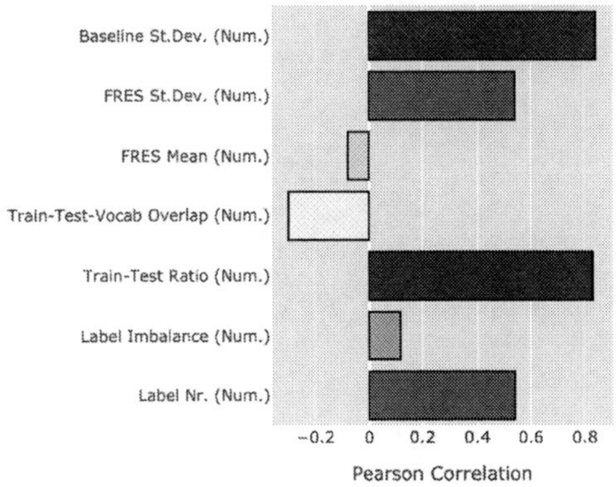

Figure 4: Pearson correlation of various dataset characteristics with performance difference compared to the baseline.

proaches, the performance loss is less pronounced for INJECT with only one exception (snopes). To substantiate this finding, we contrast both context integration approaches in a scenario with both *ideal* context, i.e., the contextual information is guaranteed to be beneficial in predicting the correct class and random context. Our results demonstrate INJECT successfully leveraging the contextual information while not outperforming direct integration in the case of ideal context. However, when given irrelevant context, INJECT is closer to context-free baseline performance. Details about the experiments are provided in the Appendix §A.3. In summary, we conclude that context integration is more robust regarding noisy context.

7 Conclusion

We propose INJECT, a dual-encoder approach to integrate contextual information for stance detection based on cross-attention. While state-of-the-art approaches perform mostly well on the datasets they have been proposed for, we evaluate our approach across a large and diverse benchmark in a cross-target setting and observe improvements compared using three different sources for extracting contextual information. We show that the context integrated via INJECT improves stance detection and is beneficial for generalization on targets not seen during training. In future, we plan to explore more sophisticated ways of prompting large pre-trained language models for helpful context.

Ethical Considerations and Limitations

Quality of the context The performance improvement for contextual information injection is bounded by the quality of the context source. Independently of the source in use, it is possible to introduce additional noise into the training procedure. While this is a rather generic problem, our proposed architecture seems to be better at filtering noisy context than a direct integration via appending to the input.

Quality of context source Most of the existing knowledge bases provide high-quality and curated knowledge. In contrast, when prompting a large language model for knowledge, we are also exposed to the risk that we extract the biases (e.g. false facts or stereotypical biases) that the model has learned during pretraining. In our experiments, we use the T0pp language model where biases have been reported to exist[6]. These biases can potentially influence the prediction performance unintendedly, especially as in many SD datasets, the annotated targets are often controversial. While investigating such effects is out of scope for this work, we consider such an evaluation inevitable before deploying our proposed model to any data outside (academic) research context.

Limitations As described in §3, our proposed approach uses two parallel encoder models (input and context). It thus requires twice as many parameters as the baseline model we compare to, thereby enforcing additional hardware demands. We consider our approach as a proof-of-concept on how to integrate contextual knowledge without amplifying a model's exploitation of spurious correlations. We plan to make our architecture more parameter-efficient by investigating more recent approaches for parameter sharing, e.g. with the use of adapters (Houlsby et al., 2019).

Moreover, we acknowledge the strong influence of wording in prompts on the output of a language model, as has been reported in the literature (Jiang et al., 2020; Schick and Schütze, 2021). We experienced similar effects during preliminary experiments and pointed out that we did not find a one-size-fits-all solution which works equally well across the diverse set of SD benchmark datasets. Therefore, special care must be taken when extracting contextual information from large language models using prompting.

[6] More details at `https://huggingface.co/bigscience/T0pp?`

Acknowledgements

We thank Leonardo F. R. Ribeiro, Haritz Puerto, Nico Daheim and the anonymous ARR reviewers for their valuable feedback. This work has been funded by the German Research Foundation (DFG) as part of the Research Training Group KRITIS No. GRK 2222 and by the German Federal Ministry of Education and Research (BMBF) under the promotional reference 01UP2229B (KoPoCoV) as well as by the Hasler Foundation Grant No. 21024.

References

Stance detection on social media: State of the art and trends. *Information Processing & Management*, 58(4).

Emily Allaway and Kathleen McKeown. 2020. Zero-Shot Stance Detection: A Dataset and Model using Generalized Topic Representations. In *Proceedings of the 2020 Conference on Empirical Methods in Natural Language Processing (EMNLP)*, pages 8913–8931, Online. Association for Computational Linguistics.

Emily Allaway, Malavika Srikanth, and Kathleen McKeown. 2021. Adversarial learning for zero-shot stance detection on social media. In *Proceedings of the 2021 Conference of the North American Chapter of the Association for Computational Linguistics: Human Language Technologies*, pages 4756–4767, Online. Association for Computational Linguistics.

Isabelle Augenstein, Tim Rocktäschel, Andreas Vlachos, and Kalina Bontcheva. 2016. Stance detection with bidirectional conditional encoding. In *Proceedings of the 2016 Conference on Empirical Methods in Natural Language Processing*, pages 876–885, Austin, Texas. Association for Computational Linguistics.

Roy Bar-Haim, Indrajit Bhattacharya, Francesco Dinuzzo, Amrita Saha, and Noam Slonim. 2017a. Stance classification of context-dependent claims. In *Proceedings of the 15th Conference of the European Chapter of the Association for Computational Linguistics: Volume 1, Long Papers*, pages 251–261, Valencia, Spain. Association for Computational Linguistics.

Roy Bar-Haim, Lilach Edelstein, Charles Jochim, and Noam Slonim. 2017b. Improving claim stance classification with lexical knowledge expansion and context utilization. In *Proceedings of the 4th Workshop on Argument Mining*, pages 32–38, Copenhagen, Denmark. Association for Computational Linguistics.

Vasant P. Bhapkar. 1966. A note on the equivalence of two test criteria for hypotheses in categorical data. *Journal of the American Statistical Association*, 61:228–235.

Steven Bird. 2006. NLTK: The Natural Language Toolkit. In *Proceedings of the COLING/ACL 2006 Interactive Presentation Sessions*, pages 69–72, Sydney, Australia. Association for Computational Linguistics.

Oana-Maria Camburu, Tim Rocktäschel, Thomas Lukasiewicz, and Phil Blunsom. 2018. e-snli: Natural language inference with natural language explanations. In S. Bengio, H. Wallach, H. Larochelle, K. Grauman, N. Cesa-Bianchi, and R. Garnett, editors, *Advances in Neural Information Processing Systems 31*, pages 9539–9549. Curran Associates, Inc.

Qian Chen, Xiaodan Zhu, Zhen-Hua Ling, Diana Inkpen, and Si Wei. 2018. Neural natural language inference models enhanced with external knowledge. In *Proceedings of the 56th Annual Meeting of the Association for Computational Linguistics (Volume 1: Long Papers)*, pages 2406–2417, Melbourne, Australia. Association for Computational Linguistics.

Sihao Chen, Daniel Khashabi, Wenpeng Yin, Chris Callison-Burch, and Dan Roth. 2019. Seeing things from a different angle:discovering diverse perspectives about claims. In *Proceedings of the 2019 Conference of the North American Chapter of the Association for Computational Linguistics: Human Language Technologies, Volume 1 (Long and Short Papers)*, pages 542–557, Minneapolis, Minnesota. Association for Computational Linguistics.

Kevin Clark, Minh-Thang Luong, Quoc V. Le, and Christopher D. Manning. 2020. ELECTRA: Pre-training text encoders as discriminators rather than generators. In *8th International Conference on Learning Representations, ICLR 2020, Addis Ababa, Ethiopia, April 26-30, 2020*.

Thomas Clark, Costanza Conforti, Fangyu Liu, Zaiqiao Meng, Ehsan Shareghi, and Nigel Collier. 2021. Integrating transformers and knowledge graphs for Twitter stance detection. In *Proceedings of the Seventh Workshop on Noisy User-generated Text (W-NUT 2021)*, pages 304–312, Online. Association for Computational Linguistics.

Costanza Conforti, Jakob Berndt, Mohammad Taher Pilehvar, Chryssi Giannitsarou, Flavio Toxvaerd, and Nigel Collier. 2020. Will-they-won't-they: A very large dataset for stance detection on Twitter. In *Proceedings of the 58th Annual Meeting of the Association for Computational Linguistics*, pages 1715–1724, Online. Association for Computational Linguistics.

Jacob Devlin, Ming-Wei Chang, Kenton Lee, and Kristina Toutanova. 2019. BERT: Pre-training of deep bidirectional transformers for language understanding. In *Proceedings of the 2019 Conference of the North American Chapter of the Association for Computational Linguistics: Human Language Technologies, Volume 1 (Long and Short Papers)*, pages 4171–4186, Minneapolis, Minnesota. Association for Computational Linguistics.

John W Du Bois. 2007. The stance triangle. *Stancetaking in discourse: Subjectivity, evaluation, interaction*, 164(3):139–182.

William Ferreira and Andreas Vlachos. 2016. Emergent: a novel data-set for stance classification. In *Proceedings of the 2016 Conference of the North American Chapter of the Association for Computational Linguistics: Human Language Technologies*, pages 1163–1168, San Diego, California. Association for Computational Linguistics.

Rudolph Flesch. 1948. A new readability yardstick. *Journal of applied psychology*, 32(3):221.

Genevieve Gorrell, Elena Kochkina, Maria Liakata, Ahmet Aker, Arkaitz Zubiaga, Kalina Bontcheva, and Leon Derczynski. 2019. SemEval-2019 task 7: RumourEval, determining rumour veracity and support for rumours. In *Proceedings of the 13th International Workshop on Semantic Evaluation*, pages 845–854, Minneapolis, Minnesota, USA. Association for Computational Linguistics.

Ivan Habernal, Henning Wachsmuth, Iryna Gurevych, and Benno Stein. 2018. The argument reasoning comprehension task: Identification and reconstruction of implicit warrants. In *Proceedings of the 2018 Conference of the North American Chapter of the Association for Computational Linguistics: Human Language Technologies, Volume 1 (Long Papers)*, pages 1930–1940, New Orleans, Louisiana. Association for Computational Linguistics.

Andreas Hanselowski, Christian Stab, Claudia Schulz, Zile Li, and Iryna Gurevych. 2019. A richly annotated corpus for different tasks in automated fact-checking. In *Proceedings of the 23rd Conference on Computational Natural Language Learning (CoNLL)*, pages 493–503, Hong Kong, China. Association for Computational Linguistics.

Momchil Hardalov, Arnav Arora, Preslav Nakov, and Isabelle Augenstein. 2021. Cross-domain label-adaptive stance detection. In *Proceedings of the 2021 Conference on Empirical Methods in Natural Language Processing*, pages 9011–9028, Online and Punta Cana, Dominican Republic. Association for Computational Linguistics.

Momchil Hardalov, Arnav Arora, Preslav Nakov, and Isabelle Augenstein. 2022. Few-shot cross-lingual stance detection with sentiment-based pre-training. In *Thirty-Sixth AAAI Conference on Artificial Intelligence, AAAI 2022, Thirty-Fourth Conference on Innovative Applications of Artificial Intelligence, IAAI 2022, The Twelveth Symposium on Educational Advances in Artificial Intelligence, EAAI 2022 Virtual Event, February 22 - March 1, 2022*, pages 10729–10737. AAAI Press.

Kazi Saidul Hasan and Vincent Ng. 2013. Stance classification of ideological debates: Data, models, features, and constraints. In *Proceedings of the Sixth International Joint Conference on Natural Language Processing*, pages 1348–1356, Nagoya, Japan. Asian Federation of Natural Language Processing.

Stefan Heindorf, Yan Scholten, Henning Wachsmuth, Axel-Cyrille Ngonga Ngomo, and Martin Potthast. 2020. Causenet: Towards a causality graph extracted from the web. In *Proceedings of the 29th ACM International Conference on Information I& Knowledge Management*, CIKM'20, page 3023–3030, New York, NY, USA. Association for Computing Machinery.

Benjamin Heinzerling and Kentaro Inui. 2021. Language models as knowledge bases: On entity representations, storage capacity, and paraphrased queries. In *Proceedings of the 16th Conference of the European Chapter of the Association for Computational Linguistics: Main Volume*, pages 1772–1791, Online. Association for Computational Linguistics.

Neil Houlsby, Andrei Giurgiu, Stanislaw Jastrzebski, Bruna Morrone, Quentin de Laroussilhe, Andrea Gesmundo, Mona Attariyan, and Sylvain Gelly. 2019. Parameter-efficient transfer learning for NLP. In *Proceedings of the 36th International Conference on Machine Learning, ICML 2019, 9-15 June 2019, Long Beach, California, USA*, volume 97 of *Proceedings of Machine Learning Research*, pages 2790–2799. PMLR.

Zhengbao Jiang, Frank F. Xu, Jun Araki, and Graham Neubig. 2020. How Can We Know What Language Models Know? *Transactions of the Association for Computational Linguistics*, 8:423–438.

Yohan Jo, Seojin Bang, Chris Reed, and Eduard Hovy. 2021a. Classifying Argumentative Relations Using Logical Mechanisms and Argumentation Schemes. *Transactions of the Association for Computational Linguistics*, 9:721–739.

Yohan Jo, Seojin Bang, Chris Reed, and Eduard Hovy. 2021b. Classifying argumentative relations using logical mechanisms and argumentation schemes. *Transactions of the Association for Computational Linguistics*, 9:721–739.

Kornraphop Kawintiranon and Lisa Singh. 2021. Knowledge enhanced masked language model for stance detection. In *Proceedings of the 2021 Conference of the North American Chapter of the Association for Computational Linguistics: Human Language Technologies*, pages 4725–4735, Online. Association for Computational Linguistics.

Goro Kobayashi, Tatsuki Kuribayashi, Sho Yokoi, and Kentaro Inui. 2020. Attention is not only a weight: Analyzing transformers with vector norms. In *Proceedings of the 2020 Conference on Empirical Methods in Natural Language Processing (EMNLP)*, pages 7057–7075, Online. Association for Computational Linguistics.

Mirko Lai, Viviana Patti, Giancarlo Ruffo, and Paolo Rosso. 2018. Stance evolution and twitter interactions in an italian political debate. In *Natural Language Processing and Information Systems*, pages 15–27, Cham. Springer International Publishing.

Anne Lauscher, Olga Majewska, Leonardo F. R. Ribeiro, Iryna Gurevych, Nikolai Rozanov, and Goran Glavaš. 2020. Common sense or world knowledge? investigating adapter-based knowledge injection into pretrained transformers. In *Proceedings of Deep Learning Inside Out (DeeLIO): The First Workshop on Knowledge Extraction and Integration for Deep Learning Architectures*, pages 43–49, Online. Association for Computational Linguistics.

Anne Lauscher, Henning Wachsmuth, Iryna Gurevych, and Goran Glavaš. 2022. Scientia potentia est—on the role of knowledge in computational argumentation. *Transactions of the Association for Computational Linguistics*, 10:1392–1422.

Chang Li, Aldo Porco, and Dan Goldwasser. 2018. Structured representation learning for online debate stance prediction. In *Proceedings of the 27th International Conference on Computational Linguistics*, pages 3728–3739, Santa Fe, New Mexico, USA. Association for Computational Linguistics.

Yingjie Li, Tiberiu Sosea, Aditya Sawant, Ajith Jayaraman Nair, Diana Inkpen, and Cornelia Caragea. 2021. P-stance: A large dataset for stance detection in political domain. In *Findings of the Association for Computational Linguistics: ACL-IJCNLP 2021*, pages 2355–2365, Online. Association for Computational Linguistics.

Bin Liang, Qinglin Zhu, Xiang Li, Min Yang, Lin Gui, Yulan He, and Ruifeng Xu. 2022. JointCL: A joint contrastive learning framework for zero-shot stance detection. In *Proceedings of the 60th Annual Meeting of the Association for Computational Linguistics (Volume 1: Long Papers)*, pages 81–91, Dublin, Ireland. Association for Computational Linguistics.

Rui Liu, Zheng Lin, Yutong Tan, and Weiping Wang. 2021. Enhancing zero-shot and few-shot stance detection with commonsense knowledge graph. In *Findings of the Association for Computational Linguistics: ACL-IJCNLP 2021*, pages 3152–3157, Online. Association for Computational Linguistics.

Yinhan Liu, Myle Ott, Naman Goyal, Jingfei Du, Mandar Joshi, Danqi Chen, Omer Levy, Mike Lewis, Luke Zettlemoyer, and Veselin Stoyanov. 2019. Roberta: A robustly optimized BERT pretraining approach. *CoRR*, abs/1907.11692.

Ilya Loshchilov and Frank Hutter. 2019. Decoupled weight decay regularization. In *7th International Conference on Learning Representations, ICLR 2019, New Orleans, LA, USA, May 6-9, 2019*. OpenReview.net.

Michal Lukasik, Kalina Bontcheva, Trevor Cohn, Arkaitz Zubiaga, Maria Liakata, and Rob Procter. 2019. Gaussian processes for rumour stance classification in social media. *ACM Trans. Inf. Syst.*, 37(2):20:1–20:24.

Henry B Mann and Donald R Whitney. 1947. On a test of whether one of two random variables is stochastically larger than the other. *The annals of mathematical statistics*, pages 50–60.

Christopher Manning, Mihai Surdeanu, John Bauer, Jenny Finkel, Steven Bethard, and David McClosky. 2014. The Stanford CoreNLP natural language processing toolkit. In *Proceedings of 52nd Annual Meeting of the Association for Computational Linguistics: System Demonstrations*, pages 55–60, Baltimore, Maryland. Association for Computational Linguistics.

Saif Mohammad, Svetlana Kiritchenko, Parinaz Sobhani, Xiaodan Zhu, and Colin Cherry. 2016. SemEval-2016 task 6: Detecting stance in tweets. In *Proceedings of the 10th International Workshop on Semantic Evaluation (SemEval-2016)*, pages 31–41, San Diego, California. Association for Computational Linguistics.

Huy Nguyen and Diane Litman. 2016. Context-aware argumentative relation mining. In *Proceedings of the 54th Annual Meeting of the Association for Computational Linguistics (Volume 1: Long Papers)*, pages 1127–1137, Berlin, Germany. Association for Computational Linguistics.

Juri Opitz and Anette Frank. 2019. Dissecting content and context in argumentative relation analysis. In *Proceedings of the 6th Workshop on Argument Mining*, pages 25–34, Florence, Italy. Association for Computational Linguistics.

Debjit Paul, Juri Opitz, Maria Becker, Jonathan Kobbe, Graeme Hirst, and Anette Frank. 2020. Argumentative relation classification with background knowledge. In *Computational Models of Argument - Proceedings of COMMA 2020, Perugia, Italy, September 4-11, 2020*, volume 326 of *Frontiers in Artificial Intelligence and Applications*, pages 319–330. IOS Press.

F. Pedregosa, G. Varoquaux, A. Gramfort, V. Michel, B. Thirion, O. Grisel, M. Blondel, P. Prettenhofer, R. Weiss, V. Dubourg, J. Vanderplas, A. Passos, D. Cournapeau, M. Brucher, M. Perrot, and E. Duchesnay. 2011. Scikit-learn: Machine learning in Python. *Journal of Machine Learning Research*, 12:2825–2830.

Matthew E. Peters, Mark Neumann, Robert Logan, Roy Schwartz, Vidur Joshi, Sameer Singh, and Noah A. Smith. 2019. Knowledge enhanced contextual word representations. In *Proceedings of the 2019 Conference on Empirical Methods in Natural Language Processing and the 9th International Joint Conference on Natural Language Processing (EMNLP-IJCNLP)*, pages 43–54, Hong Kong, China. Association for Computational Linguistics.

Fabio Petroni, Tim Rocktäschel, Sebastian Riedel, Patrick Lewis, Anton Bakhtin, Yuxiang Wu, and

Alexander Miller. 2019. Language models as knowledge bases? In *Proceedings of the 2019 Conference on Empirical Methods in Natural Language Processing and the 9th International Joint Conference on Natural Language Processing (EMNLP-IJCNLP)*, pages 2463–2473, Hong Kong, China. Association for Computational Linguistics.

Dean Pomerleau and Delip Rao. 2017. Fake news challenge stage 1 (FNC-I): Stance detection.

Kashyap Popat, Subhabrata Mukherjee, Andrew Yates, and Gerhard Weikum. 2019. STANCY: Stance classification based on consistency cues. In *Proceedings of the 2019 Conference on Empirical Methods in Natural Language Processing and the 9th International Joint Conference on Natural Language Processing (EMNLP-IJCNLP)*, pages 6413–6418, Hong Kong, China. Association for Computational Linguistics.

Vahed Qazvinian, Emily Rosengren, Dragomir R. Radev, and Qiaozhu Mei. 2011. Rumor has it: Identifying misinformation in microblogs. In *Proceedings of the 2011 Conference on Empirical Methods in Natural Language Processing*, pages 1589–1599, Edinburgh, Scotland, UK. Association for Computational Linguistics.

Colin Raffel, Noam Shazeer, Adam Roberts, Katherine Lee, Sharan Narang, Michael Matena, Yanqi Zhou, Wei Li, and Peter J. Liu. 2020. Exploring the limits of transfer learning with a unified text-to-text transformer. *Journal of Machine Learning Research*, 21(140):1–67.

Nils Reimers and Iryna Gurevych. 2019. Sentence-BERT: Sentence embeddings using Siamese BERT-networks. In *Proceedings of the 2019 Conference on Empirical Methods in Natural Language Processing and the 9th International Joint Conference on Natural Language Processing (EMNLP-IJCNLP)*, pages 3982–3992, Hong Kong, China. Association for Computational Linguistics.

Myrthe Reuver, Suzan Verberne, Roser Morante, and Antske Fokkens. 2021. Is stance detection topic-independent and cross-topic generalizable? - a reproduction study. In *Proceedings of the 8th Workshop on Argument Mining*, pages 46–56, Punta Cana, Dominican Republic. Association for Computational Linguistics.

Ohad Rozen, Shmuel Amar, Vered Shwartz, and Ido Dagan. 2021. Teach the rules, provide the facts: Targeted relational-knowledge enhancement for textual inference. In *Proceedings of *SEM 2021: The Tenth Joint Conference on Lexical and Computational Semantics*, pages 89–98, Online. Association for Computational Linguistics.

Victor Sanh, Albert Webson, Colin Raffel, Stephen Bach, Lintang Sutawika, Zaid Alyafeai, Antoine Chaffin, Arnaud Stiegler, Arun Raja, Manan Dey, M Saiful Bari, Canwen Xu, Urmish Thakker, Shanya Sharma Sharma, Eliza Szczechla, Taewoon Kim, Gunjan Chhablani, Nihal Nayak, Debajyoti Datta, Jonathan Chang, Mike Tian-Jian Jiang, Han Wang, Matteo Manica, Sheng Shen, Zheng Xin Yong, Harshit Pandey, Rachel Bawden, Thomas Wang, Trishala Neeraj, Jos Rozen, Abheesht Sharma, Andrea Santilli, Thibault Fevry, Jason Alan Fries, Ryan Teehan, Teven Le Scao, Stella Biderman, Leo Gao, Thomas Wolf, and Alexander M Rush. 2022. Multitask prompted training enables zero-shot task generalization. In *International Conference on Learning Representations*.

Akira Sasaki, Kazuaki Hanawa, Naoaki Okazaki, and Kentaro Inui. 2018. Predicting stances from social media posts using factorization machines. In *Proceedings of the 27th International Conference on Computational Linguistics*, pages 3381–3390, Santa Fe, New Mexico, USA. Association for Computational Linguistics.

Akira Sasaki, Junta Mizuno, Naoaki Okazaki, and Kentaro Inui. 2016. Stance classification by recognizing related events about targets. In *2016 IEEE/WIC/ACM International Conference on Web Intelligence (WI)*, pages 582–587. IEEE.

Timo Schick and Hinrich Schütze. 2021. Exploiting cloze-questions for few-shot text classification and natural language inference. In *Proceedings of the 16th Conference of the European Chapter of the Association for Computational Linguistics: Main Volume*, pages 255–269, Online. Association for Computational Linguistics.

Benjamin Schiller, Johannes Daxenberger, and Iryna Gurevych. 2021. Stance detection benchmark: How robust is your stance detection? *KI-Künstliche Intelligenz*, pages 1–13.

Chen Shi, Shujie Liu, Shuo Ren, Shi Feng, Mu Li, Ming Zhou, Xu Sun, and Houfeng Wang. 2016. Knowledge-based semantic embedding for machine translation. In *Proceedings of the 54th Annual Meeting of the Association for Computational Linguistics (Volume 1: Long Papers)*, pages 2245–2254, Berlin, Germany. Association for Computational Linguistics.

Parinaz Sobhani, Diana Inkpen, and Xiaodan Zhu. 2017. A dataset for multi-target stance detection. In *Proceedings of the 15th Conference of the European Chapter of the Association for Computational Linguistics: Volume 2, Short Papers*, pages 551–557, Valencia, Spain. Association for Computational Linguistics.

Swapna Somasundaran and Janyce Wiebe. 2010. Recognizing stances in ideological on-line debates. In *Proceedings of the NAACL HLT 2010 Workshop on Computational Approaches to Analysis and Generation of Emotion in Text*, pages 116–124, Los Angeles, CA. Association for Computational Linguistics.

Robyn Speer, Joshua Chin, and Catherine Havasi. 2017. Conceptnet 5.5: An open multilingual graph of general knowledge. In *Proceedings of the Thirty-First*

AAAI Conference on Artificial Intelligence, AAAI'17, page 4444–4451. AAAI Press.

Christian Stab, Tristan Miller, Benjamin Schiller, Pranav Rai, and Iryna Gurevych. 2018. Cross-topic argument mining from heterogeneous sources. In *Proceedings of the 2018 Conference on Empirical Methods in Natural Language Processing*, pages 3664–3674, Brussels, Belgium. Association for Computational Linguistics.

Terne Sasha Thorn Jakobsen, Maria Barrett, and Anders Søgaard. 2021. Spurious correlations in cross-topic argument mining. In *Proceedings of *SEM 2021: The Tenth Joint Conference on Lexical and Computational Semantics*, pages 263–277, Online. Association for Computational Linguistics.

Ashish Vaswani, Noam Shazeer, Niki Parmar, Jakob Uszkoreit, Llion Jones, Aidan N Gomez, Łukasz Kaiser, and Illia Polosukhin. 2017. Attention is all you need. *Advances in neural information processing systems*, 30.

Amir Pouran Ben Veyseh, Javid Ebrahimi, Dejing Dou, and Daniel Lowd. 2017. A Temporal Attentional Model for Rumor Stance Classification. In *Proceedings of the 2017 ACM on Conference on Information and Knowledge Management*, CIKM '17, pages 2335–2338, New York, NY, USA. Association for Computing Machinery.

Marilyn Walker, Jean Fox Tree, Pranav Anand, Rob Abbott, and Joseph King. 2012. A corpus for research on deliberation and debate. In *Proceedings of the Eighth International Conference on Language Resources and Evaluation (LREC'12)*, pages 812–817, Istanbul, Turkey. European Language Resources Association (ELRA).

Ruize Wang, Duyu Tang, Nan Duan, Zhongyu Wei, Xuanjing Huang, Jianshu Ji, Guihong Cao, Daxin Jiang, and Ming Zhou. 2021. K-Adapter: Infusing Knowledge into Pre-Trained Models with Adapters. In *Findings of the Association for Computational Linguistics: ACL-IJCNLP 2021*, pages 1405–1418, Online. Association for Computational Linguistics.

Penghui Wei and Wenji Mao. 2019. Modeling Transferable Topics for Cross-Target Stance Detection. In *Proceedings of the 42nd International ACM SIGIR Conference on Research and Development in Information Retrieval*, SIGIR'19, pages 1173–1176, New York, NY, USA. Association for Computing Machinery.

Chang Xu, Cécile Paris, Surya Nepal, and Ross Sparks. 2018. Cross-target stance classification with self-attention networks. In *Proceedings of the 56th Annual Meeting of the Association for Computational Linguistics (Volume 2: Short Papers)*, pages 778–783, Melbourne, Australia. Association for Computational Linguistics.

Bowen Zhang, Min Yang, Xutao Li, Yunming Ye, Xiaofei Xu, and Kuai Dai. 2020. Enhancing cross-target stance detection with transferable semantic-emotion knowledge. In *Proceedings of the 58th Annual Meeting of the Association for Computational Linguistics*, pages 3188–3197, Online. Association for Computational Linguistics.

Zhengyan Zhang, Xu Han, Zhiyuan Liu, Xin Jiang, Maosong Sun, and Qun Liu. 2019. ERNIE: Enhanced language representation with informative entities. In *Proceedings of the 57th Annual Meeting of the Association for Computational Linguistics*, pages 1441–1451, Florence, Italy. Association for Computational Linguistics.

A Appendix

A.1 Experimental Details

- All models are trained using five epochs, batch size of 16, a learning rate of 0.00002, a warmup-up ratio of 0.2 with linear scheduling, and AdamW (Loshchilov and Hutter, 2019) as optimizer. The hyperparameters tuned during training are described in the main paper (see §5.2).

- We use CUDA 11.6, Python v3.8.10, torch v1.10.0, and transformers v4.13.0 as software environment and a mixture of NVIDIA P100, V100, A100, A6000 as GPU hardware.

- We load all pretrained language models from HuggingFace model hub. In detail, we use the following model tags: `bert-base-uncased` for BERT, `google/electra-base-discriminator` for ELECTRA, and `roberta-base` for RoBERTa.

- We use the captum library (v0.5.0) to calculate the vector-norms for approximating token-attributions (Kobayashi et al., 2020) in §6.3.

- We use the statsmodel library (v0.13.2) to calculate statistical significant differences using the Bhapkar test (Bhapkar, 1966) with $p < 0.05$.

- We use sklearn (Pedregosa et al., 2011) for computing evaluation metrics (e.g. macro-F1).

- We measured the average training runtime of models on the argmin dataset as a reference. `BERT+Target` and `BERT+ConceptNet` needed 618 seconds whereas `INJECT` needed 400 seconds.

- We use the seeds $[0, 1, 2, 3, 4, 5, 6, 7, 8, 9]$.

A.2 Datasets

We provide details about the individual split proportions for the cross-target evaluation setup in Table 5. For more information on each individual dataset, we refer to Schiller et al. (2021) and Hardalov et al. (2021).

Dataset	Train	Dev	Test	Total
arc	12,382	1,851	3,559	17,792
argmin	6,845	1,568	2,726	11,139
emergent	1,638	433	524	2,595
fnc1	42,476	7,496	25,413	75,385
iac1*	4,221	453	923	5,597
ibmcs	935	104	1,355	2,394
mtsd	6,227	1,317	1,366	8,910
perspectrum	6,978	2,071	2,773	11,822
poldeb	4,753	1,151	1,230	7,134
rumor*	6,093	299	505	7,106 (10,237)
scd	3,251	624	964	4,839
semeval2016t6	2,497	417	1,249	4,163
semeval2019t7*	5,205	1,478	1,756	8,439 (8,529)
snopes	14,416	1,868	3,154	19,438
vast	13,477	2,062	3,006	18,545
wtwt	25,193	7,897	18,194	51,284

Table 5: Number of examples per data split for the cross-target evaluation setting. For datasets marked with *, not all tweets could be downloaded or we discovered empty instances which we excluded (in comparison to the numbers provided by Hardalov et al. (2021)); for mtsd, we received the full dataset by the original authors; the original number of tweets is in parentheses.

A.3 Evaluation with ideal context

To evaluate our goal of robust integration of contextual information using INJECT, we contrast both context integration approaches in a scenario with both *ideal* context, i.e. the contextual information is guaranteed to be beneficial in predicting the correct class, and random context. To showcase, we use the e-SNLI (Camburu et al., 2018) corpus for natural language inference and the Snopes (Hanselowski et al., 2019) corpus for claim verification. We use the provided explanations (e-SNLI, m=1) and evidences (Snopes, m=10) as ideal context, respectively. As random (but syntactically correct) context, we randomly extract sentences from the Gutenberg corpus[7] included in NLTK (Bird, 2006). Table 6 compares a BERT baseline without context, BERT with context integration via concatenation (BERT$\oplus$), and integration via INJECT (BERT$\otimes$).

The results demonstrate INJECT successfully leveraging the contextual information while not outperforming direct integration in the case of ideal context. However, when provided with irrelevant context, INJECT is closer to the context-free baseline performance.

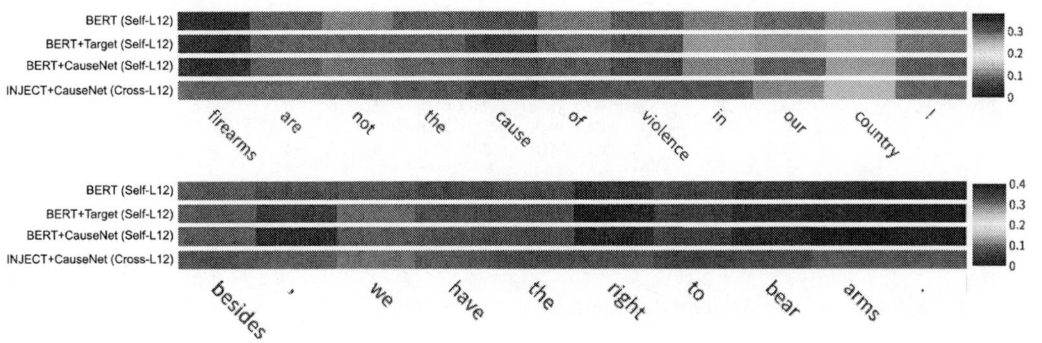

Figure 5: Two examples of the argmin dataset. The first is an argument against gun control, while the second supports it. It shows the token-level attribution for BERT, BERT+Target, BERT+CauseNet, and INJECT+CauseNet.

	e-SNLI (Ideal)	e-SNLI (Random)	Snopes (Ideal)	Snopes (Random)
BERT	90.33	90.33	51.8	51.8
BERT⊕	98.70	90.08	78.0	49.7
BERT⊗	98.35	90.52	75.8	51.1

Table 6: Comparison of context integration via concatenation (BERT⊕) and INJECT (BERT⊗) on e-SNLI and Snopes. Original dataset splits are used. Scores are macro-F1 averaged across three seeds.

A.4 Identification of target-specific label correlations

We examine internal processes in the model architecture by analyzing how relevant a token is compared to how much a model attributes to the token. In detail, we calculate for the 5% most relevant tokens for target and label the correlation of this relevance and the model attribution on them.

Token Relevance We consider the probability of a token to appear in combination with a label l and target t. A higher probability indicates that a token is more likely to occur within a label-target combination.

In detail, we first calculate the relevance as the maximum log-odds-ratio $r_{(w,(l_i,t_j))}$ (Kawintiranon and Singh, 2021) over all possible combinations of labels $L = \{l_1, ..., l_n\}$ and targets $T = \{t_1, ..., t_k\}$ for a given token w. We define $o_{(w,(l,t))}$ (Equation 1) as the probability of token t appearing in combination with label l and target t, with $c(w,(l,t))$ denoting the counts of w in texts with label l and target t. Next, we calculate the maximum log odds-ratio $r_{(t,(L,T))}$ as in Equation 2. This tells us how specific a token w is at max. for a label-target combination.

[7]http://www.gutenberg.org/

$$o_{(w,(l_i,t_j))} = \frac{c(w,(l_i,t_j))}{c(\neg w,(l_i,t_j))} \quad (1)$$

$$r_{(w,(L,T))} = \max_{(l_i,t_j)\in L\times T} log(\frac{o_{(w,(l_i,t_j))}}{o_{(w,\neg(l_i,t_j))}}) \quad (2)$$

Token Attributions To approximate a token's attribution, we calculate the vector-norms (Kobayashi et al., 2020) for the output of the 12th layer.

We provide anecdotal examples in Figure 5 along with their token-level attribution of the 12th layer from (BERT, BERT+Target, BERT+CauseNet) and INJECT+CauseNet. For the first three, we use the self-attention and for the latter one the cross-attention. In the first example, INJECT+CauseNet made the right prediction while all BERT-based models failed and vice-versa for the second one. In both examples, we see lower attribution for target-specific terms like *firearms* or *arms* and higher attribution for terms with general use like *besides*, *cause*, or *to*. INJECT+CauseNet makes the correct prediction while BERT+Target failed due to its high attribution to *firearms* - an example of a spurious correlation. However, in some cases this can also lead to erroneous predictions as in the second example where INJECT+CauseNet gives less importance to the specific - and in this case important - tokens of the sentences (*right to bear arms*).

A.5 Dataset Characteristics

In Table 7, we provide relevant dataset characteristics for each dataset in the stance detection benchmark. To compute label imbalance, we first calculate the mean and standard deviation of the number of instances per label. The label imbalance is then

	arc	iac1	perspectrum	poldeb	scd	emergent	fnc1	snopes	mtsd	rumor	semeval16	semeval19	wtwt	argmin	ibmcs	vast
Number of Labels	4	3	2	2	2	3	4	2	3	5	3	4	4	2	2	2
Label Imbalance	1,16	0,55	0,03	0,11	0,20	0,41	1,13	0,48	0,23	0,61	0,37	1,09	0,58	0,11	0,11	0,22
Train-Test-ratio	3.48	4.57	2.52	3.86	3.37	3.13	1.67	4.57	4.56	12.48	2	2.96	1.38	2.51	0.69	4.48
Train-Test-Vocabulary Overlap	16461	16939	2875	7553	5171	861	11244	8092	4876	818	2666	3248	7836	4454	1361	6271
FRES Mean	63.07	70.27	53.12	65.11	70.70	66.37	61.44	61.36	71.43	58.08	67.43	58.62	48.41	51.73	39.94	63.19
FRES St.Dev.	14.2	13.6	29.6	37.4	29.5	21.5	10.3	26.3	17.5	57.7	22.2	49.3	26.8	22.8	29.4	14.1
Baseline St.Dev.	0.8	2.9	0.8	2.8	1.7	1.5	1.3	0.8	2.1	9.8	0.6	2.6	4.1	1.4	1.5	1

Table 7: Overview of the dataset-characteristic for each dataset.

defined as the division of the standard deviation by the mean.

A.6 Knowledge

The information about the average length of the retrieved contextual knowledge is given in Table 8. We observe substantially longer paragraphs extracted from CauseNet which is not surprising as CauseNet consists of passages extracted from Wikipedia.

A.6.1 CauseNet

We ignore concepts which are shorter than 3 characters or consist of one of the following modal verbs ("must", "shall", "will", "should", "would", "can", "could", "may", "might").

A.6.2 Prompts

We manually evaluated the following prompts for both single and combination inputs. As reported in related work (Jiang et al., 2020; Schick and Schütze, 2021), the generated text is sensible to wording and punctuation in the prompt. We made similar experiences and removed all punctuation at the end of the prompt to prevent the model from generating outputs of short length.

A.7 On Efficiency of INJECT

From an efficiency point-of-view, INJECTprocesses a text and corresponding contexts more efficiently than via SEP integration. This is because there is no self-attention over *input* and *context* jointly where the attention dimension is $d_{sep} = (\text{len}(input) + \text{len}(context)) \times (\text{len}(input) + \text{len}(context))$. For INJECT, in contrast, input and context are processed in separate encoders with attention dimensions $d_{input} = \text{len}(input) \times \text{len}(input)$ and $d_{context} = \text{len}(context) \times \text{len}(context)$ on every layer. Just in the INJECT-layer, there are two additional attention blocks with dimensions $d_{\textit{cross context}} = \text{len}(input) \times \text{len}(context)$ and $d_{\textit{cross input}} = \text{len}(context) \times \text{len}(input)$.

Knowledge Source	arc	iac1	perspectrum	poldeb	scd	emergent	fnc1	snopes	mtsd	rumor	semeval16	semeval19	wtwt	argmin	ibmcs	vast
`ConceptNet`	5.1	5.1	5.5	5.1	5.2	5.5	5.1	5.5	5.6	6.0	5.5	5.6	5.6	5.3	5.3	5.1
`CauseNet`	91.2	112.1	20.5	78.4	69.8	34.1	137.6	40.3	56.4	50.6	52.1	47.0	43.0	36.4	23.7	89.5
`T0pp-NP`	13.1	13.1	13.0	12.9	12.5	13.3	14.1	13.6	12.9	13.1	12.4	13.0	12.5	12.5	13.5	13.1
`T0pp-NP-T`	9.9	12.7	10.5	12.1	11.9	11.6	16.7	11.9	14.0	13.6	12.7	9.4	11.1	12.7	11.7	12.2

Table 8: Average length for each combination of knowledge extraction method and dataset.

Prompt	Usage
define a	✓
what is a	
describe a	
what is the definition of a	✓
explain a	✓
relation between a and b	✓
how is a related to b	✓
explain a in terms of b	✓

Table 9: Prompts which have been evaluated for generating contextual knowledge for stance detection.

Adverbs, Surprisingly

Dmitry Nikolaev[1] **Collin F. Baker**[2] **Miriam R.L. Petruck**[3] **Sebastian Padó**[1]
[1] IMS, University of Stuttgart, Germany
[2] International Computer Science Institute, Berkeley, USA
[3] FrameNet
Corresponding Author: dnikolaev@fastmail.com

Abstract

This paper begins with the premise that adverbs are neglected in computational linguistics. This view derives from two analyses: a literature review and a novel adverb dataset to probe a state-of-the-art language model, thereby uncovering systematic gaps in accounts for adverb meaning. We suggest that using Frame Semantics for characterizing word meaning, as in FrameNet, provides a promising approach to adverb analysis, given its ability to describe ambiguity, semantic roles, and null instantiation.

1 Introduction

Adverbs are the part of speech (POS) that has seen the least attention in (computational) linguistics, likely due to its challenging nature (Conlon and Evens, 1992). As Huddleston and Pullum (2002, 563) state, "the adverb is a [...] residual category [...] to which words are assigned if they do not satisfy the more specific criteria for nouns, verbs, adjectives, prepositions, and conjunctions."

Syntactically, they modify many POSs, except nouns (*eat porridge quickly, hardly noticeable*), or even complete clauses (*Probably, I'll come tomorrow*). They are semantically varied (Thomason and Stalnaker, 1973), ranging from intensifiers/modifiers (*absolutely*, *beautifully*) to temporal and spatial specifications (*yesterday, forward*), to so-called *speaker-oriented adverbs* yielding inferences about speaker attitudes, beliefs, and evaluations. Finally, adverbs can occupy different positions in sentences, creating complex issues of scoping and ambiguity (Alexiadou, 2004; Payne et al., 2010). Consider the following sentences:[1]

(1) a. Happily, they watched TV until dinner.
b. They happily watched TV until dinner.
c. They watched TV happily until dinner.
d. They watched TV until dinner happily.

[1] Huddleston and Pullum (2002, 575)

While language users tend to interpret Ex. 1b–1d as describing the TV watchers' mental state, Ex. 1a is ambiguous and can also be read as a positive evaluation of the situation by the speaker.

In sum, adverbs provide crucial information not just about the where and how of events, but also about attitudes and evaluations. However, relatively little research on adverbs exists in computational linguistics, although lexical factors are generally recognized as central for many NLP tasks (Berger et al., 2000). Lexical information is generally represented either in online dictionaries or by embeddings extracted from corpora (Turney and Pantel, 2010; Devlin et al., 2019; Peters et al., 2018). As a dictionary, WordNet (Miller et al., 1990) lists adverbs but only provides a relatively impoverished account, while lexicons for sentiment analysis (Benamara et al., 2007; Dragut and Fellbaum, 2014) and hedging detection (Jeon and Choe, 2009; Islam et al., 2020) only consider specific subtypes of adverbs as to how they modulate the intensity of adjectives. On the distributional side, adverbs have been considered from a derviational perspective (Lazaridou et al., 2013); yet, they are rarely scrutinized in detail. Among the standard benchmarks, only GLUE (Wang et al., 2018) and BLiMP (Warstadt et al., 2020) cover adverbs, and then only marginally. The same is true of approaches that combine dictionaries and embeddings (Faruqui et al., 2015). As a consequence, SOTA language models consistently struggle with adverb meaning, as Section 2.2 will demonstrate empirically.

This paper argues that Frame Semantics (Fillmore, 1985), as realized in FrameNet (FN) (Ruppenhofer et al., 2016), provides an efficacious framework to articulate the relevant aspects of adverb meaning. Specifically, as Ex. 1 illustrates, lexical ambiguity is captured in terms of frame ambiguity. Moreover, inferences about the arguments of adverbs, typically filled by the speaker and the lexical unit that the adverb modifies, can be cap-

*Proceedings of the The 12th Joint Conference on Lexical and Computational Semantics (*SEM 2023)*, pages 512–526
July 13-14, 2023 ©2023 Association for Computational Linguistics

tured and characterized via the frame elements (i.e. semantic roles) of the frame. Notably, FrameNet mechanisms will account for null-instantiated roles, allowing it to hint at unexpressed content in cases like Example 2b (v. Section 4.2 for details).

(2) a. [SPEAKER The Minister] **reported** [MESSAGE that the cost had exploded].

b. [MESSAGE The cost had] **reportedly** [MESSAGE exploded].

In such cases specifically, FrameNet considerations of frame element realization help to explain the absence of the SPEAKER semantic role in 2b.

Plan of the Paper. Section 2 defines the scope of this paper (speaker-oriented adverbs) and shows the lack of accounts for adverbs in NLP through a literature review. Section 3 presents a probing dataset for speaker-oriented adverbs on the basis of which it demonstrates empirically that current large language models do not provide accounts for adverb meaning. Section 4 provides general background information on FrameNet, gives details on the framework's approach to the description of adverb meaning, and suggests its use to improve NLP models. Section 5 concludes the paper.

2 Scope and Motivation

2.1 Scope

Given the variety and heterogeneity of adverbs, we restrict the empirical scope of this paper to a subclass of them – even though we believe that the conceptual points apply to adverbs generally. We focus on *speaker-oriented adverbs* (Ernst, 2009). This broad class of adverbs, itself comprises several subtypes brought together by their giving rise to a range of inferences about attitudes and beliefs of the speaker, such as epistemic beliefs (Ex. 3), evaluations (Ex. 1 and 4), and speech acts (Ex. 5):

(3) Peter says: "Paul is **certainly** right".
$\models$ Peter is certain that Paul is right.

(4) Peter says: "**Unfortunately**, Paul arrived".
$\models$ Peter is unhappy that Paul arrived.

(5) Peter says: "**Frankly**, Paul annoys me."
$\models$ Peter voices his frank opinion.

Structurally, these entailments are similar to entailments that arise from implicative verbs (Karttunen, 1971). As sources of information about how speakers assess states of affairs, they are highly relevant for tasks like opinion mining (Pang and Lee, 2008) and stance detection (Thomas et al., 2006). However, while implicative verbs have received considerable attention in the context of textual entailment (Karttunen, 2012; Lotan et al., 2013), speaker-oriented adverbs have not.

2.2 Treatment of Adverbs in Computational Linguistics

This section summarizes work on adverbs in computational linguistics in the four most relevant areas: WordNets, applications, distributional modeling, and semantic annotation. Section 3 covers large language models separately.

WordNets. Princeton WordNet (WN, version 1.3) (Miller et al., 1990) covers about 4,500 English adverbs, comprising both single words and adverbial multi-word expressions like *a priori*. The information recorded includes senses (although most adverbs are monosemous) and semantic relations: almost all single-word adverbs are linked to the adjectives from which they are derived,and some adverbs have antonyms. However, WN has no information on the adverbs' syntactic or semantic behavior. The approach of corresponding WordNet resources varies substantially: GermaNet, for German, does not treat adverbs at all (Hamp and Feldweg, 1997). In contrast, plWordNet (Maziarz et al., 2016) provides a considerably richer description of adverbs, notably regarding lexical relations, but is only available for Polish.

NLP applications. Apparently, sentiment and emotion analysis are the NLP applications that have paid the most attention to adverbs (Benamara et al., 2007; Dragut and Fellbaum, 2014; Chauhan et al., 2020). Hedge detection, that is, the recognition of expressions that modulate speaker confidence in their statements boasts additional work on adverbs (Jeon and Choe, 2009; Islam et al., 2020). However, these studies, are generally limited to two specific subtypes: scalar adverbs that modify sentiment strength (intensifiers/minimizers: *very/hardly nice*) and adverbs that modify confidence (*certainly/apparently*). Haider et al. (2021) also considers locative and temporal adverbs. Confidence-modifying adverbs form a subtype of the speaker-oriented adverbs addressed here, but existing studies do not offer a general account of these adverbs beyond the requirements of specific tasks.

Studies on structured sentiment and emotion analysis (Barnes et al., 2021; Kim and Klinger, 2018) assume a different perspective. These works concentrate on defining and modeling the relations between sentiment- and emotion- introducing expressions and their semantic arguments, such as the experiencer of the affect and its target. As the comparison with Example 2 shows, these relations are at times tied to adverb meanings. However, we are not aware of studies in this area that deal specifically with adverbs.

Distributional modeling. A number of studies investigated the interplay between word embeddings and morphology, analyzing similarity by parts of speech (Cotterell and Schütze, 2015) or investigating meaning shifts corresponding to morphological derivation (Lazaridou et al., 2013; Padó et al., 2016). Typically, these studies include adverbs, and not surprisingly find that adverbs behave highly inconsistently.

Semantic annotation. In principle, frameworks for the annotation of (semantic) argument structure are promising sources for information about adverb meaning, but they differ widely in the information that they offer. The PropBank (Palmer et al., 2005) annotation scheme offers a range of modifier roles (ARGM) for the annotation of modifiers, including adverbs. However, the most fitting of these roles, ARGM-ADV, is a "catch-all" category. In addition, the PropBank analysis does not treat adverbs as predicates in their own right and does not assign roles to them. Thus, ***fortunately**, she accepted* and ***even** she accepted* would receive the same analysis.

In contrast, UCCA (Abend and Rappoport, 2013) explicitly splits adverbs into adverbial modifiers proper (D) and ground elements (G), where the latter expresses the speaker's attitude toward the event. However, UCCA does not make the structural relations explicit either.

AMR (Banarescu et al., 2013) offers a more nuanced approach: many adverbs are mapped to their underlying predicates and endowed with complete argument structure,[2] while others are interpreted as degree, manner, or time modifiers. However, no provision exists in the representation for speaker-oriented adverbs. To illustrate, the AMR annotation of *thankfully, she accepted the present* either treats the adverb as describing a general state of affairs (*it is good that she accepted*) or simply omits it.

Finally, Frame Semantics (Fillmore, 1985) offers the conceptual infrastructure to improve on these treatments and avoid their limitations. Section 4 provides justification of this understanding.

3 Case Study: Modeling Adverb Meaning as Natural Language Inference

One possibility, so far not mentioned, is that the knowledge inherent in large neural language models might provide a sufficient account of the meaning of (speaker-oriented) adverbs. In that case, at least from the NLP perspective, no (new) specific treatment would be required. However, this state of affairs is not the case, as we show below.

3.1 Creating Probing Datasets

To operationalize "a sufficient account," we ask language models to distinguish between valid and invalid inferences along the lines of Examples 3–5. As input data, we constructed probing examples with inferences for speaker-oriented adverbs.

We examined four classes of adverbs, motivated by current FrameNet frames containing adverbs (see Section 4.3 for details). These are: likelihood adverbs (e.g. *undoubtedly*, *probably*); unattributed-information adverbs (*reportedly*, *allegedly*, *supposedly*); degree adverbs (*at least*, *approximately*); and obviousness adverbs (*blatantly*, *conspicuously*).

We built the datasets from combinations of premises and hypotheses containing such adverbs, formulated as templates with sets of fillers for the adverbs and different participant positions. In this manner, we assessed the LM's capabilities irrespective of specific word choice. We paired each premise with two to four unambiguous hypotheses depending on the adverb class. The premise either implies or contradicts the hypothesis. Table 1 shows an example. Hypothesis 1 negates the premise and constitutes a contradiction. Hypothesis 2 is a valid inference about speaker evaluation; and Hypothesis 3 is a valid inference about the uncertainty inherent in the premise.

We report studies on two datasets with different emphases. We designed the first to be *naturalistic*, based on existing sentences for adverbs in FrameNet. Given the limited size of this dataset, we also created a larger *synthetic* dataset with simpler, more varied, sentences. The Appendix lists full details on both datasets.

Naturalistic Dataset. As stated, we created this dataset based on sentences in the FrameNet database containing adverbs of the four classes enumerated above. We "templatized" the sentences

[2] For example, AMR treats *sing* in *sing beautifully* as the first argument of `beautiful-02`.

Premise	The celebration had been postponed, **ostensibly** because of the Gulf War
Hyp 1	The Gulf War **ostensibly** had no effect on the celebration (CONTRADICTION)
Hyp 2	Someone said that the celebration was postponed because of the Gulf War (ENTAILMENT)
Hyp 3	The Gulf War may have had no effect on the celebration (ENTAILMENT)

Table 1: Naturalistic dataset: Probing items

Premise	SUBJ1 said that SUBJ2 **ADV** opposed ACTION
Hyp 1	SUBJ1 said that SUBJ2 may have opposed ACTION (ENTAILMENT)
Hyp 2	SUBJ1 is not sure that SUBJ2 opposed ACTION (ENTAILMENT)
Hyp 3	SUBJ1 is sure that SUBJ2 opposed ACTION (CONTRADICTION)
Hyp 4	SUBJ1 is sure that SUBJ2 did not support ACTION (CONTRADICTION)

Table 2: Synthetic dataset: Probing items

by treating the position of the adverb as a slot that can be filled by all semantically congruent adverbs from the respective class. In sentences where the subject is a personal name, we also treated the subject position as a slot, which we filled with twenty female and male names popular in the United States. Because the low number of sentences of the each type in the FrameNet database, and most templates have only one slot, viz. the adverb, the size of this dataset is limited. See Table 3 for example counts by adverb class.

Synthetic Dataset. The goal of this dataset was to test if the performance of the model is robust with regard to the replacement of the main-event description and varying syntactic complexity of the premises and hypotheses. It covers three of the four adverb classes: unattributed-information, degree, and obviousness, where the templates from the first dataset were most restricted. In these templates, subjects are always exchangeable. In addition, we also varied the description of the main action or relation described the sentence.

Table 2 shows the template set for unattributed-information adverbs. The set of adverbs for this class comprises *reportedly*, *allegedly*, *supposedly*, *apparently*, and *ostensibly*. Fillers of the ACTION slot include both gerund phrases (e.g. *selling the house*) and noun phrases (e.g. *the wedding*). Entailments and contradictions are produced in pairs. For entailments, we test two valid inferences triggered by the adverb. For contradictions, we test embedded clauses with and without negation. Table 5 shows the example count for each input type.

3.2 Probing Setup: NLI models

Arguably the best match for these types of datasets are the family of language models optimized for the task of natural-language inference (Storks et al., 2019). Concretely, we evaluated the series of NLI models released by Nie et al. (2020), the SNLI or Stanford Natural Language Inference models. These models carry out a three-way classification between ENTAILMENT, CONTRADICTION, and NEUTRAL. The author fine-tuned their models on a data set created in an iterative, adversarial, human-in-the-loop fashion, designed to remedy the shortcomings of previous NLI datasets (Belinkov et al., 2019). Preliminary experiments with different available base architectures (RoBERTa, ALBERT, BART, ELECTRA, and XLNet) showed that RoBERTa-large[3] was the best-performing variant. Thus, we used this model for evaluations. We used our probing datasets solely for evaluation, not for further fine-tuning.

For analysis, we checked the labels that the model predicted with their corresponding probabilities. In several cases, we performed additional tests to verify whether the adverbs or other properties of the sentence determined the model predictions.

3.3 Evaluation on a Naturalistic Dataset

3.3.1 Overall results

Table 3 shows overall results of the SNLI model on the naturalistic dataset for the four adverb classes. The adverb classes are not strictly comparable because they are represented by different input sentences (as described above), which include all types of lexical and syntactic confounds. Nevertheless, our experiments showed two consistent results: (i) the model cannot correctly draw inferences based on some set of adverbs on which it fails; (ii) the presence of adverbs increases the difficulty for the model to draw correct inferences in general. What follows is a survey of the evidence for these two claims.

3.3.2 Failure to Understand Adverbs

Degree adverbs. The model does not understand that *at least as big* is incompatible with *smaller*.

[3] ynie/roberta-large-snli_mnli_fever_anli_R1_R2_R3-nli

Adverb class	Error rate (%)	# sentences
Likelihood	2	5,880
Unattributed information	6	90
Degree	25	35
Obviousness	23	16

Table 3: Naturalistic dataset: SNLI model error rates by adverb class

While it correctly labels the pair *Lantau covers nearly twice the area of Hong Kong Island – Lantau is at least as big as Hong Kong Island* as ENTAILMENT and the same premise with *Lantau is much smaller than Hong Kong Island* as CONTRADICTION, it considers that this premise also entails *Hong Kong Island is at least as big as Lantau*, which is also a straightforward contradiction.

The quantifier–adverb combination *almost every* constitutes another weak point of the model. While it correctly labels the pair ***Almost all** assignments are challenging in different ways* vs. *Most of the assignments are difficult*, it labels ***Almost every** assignment is a challenge in a different way* vs. the same as NEUTRAL.[4]

Unattributed-information adverbs. The correct analysis of these adverbs is subtle since valid inferences may be expressed in ways that differ from the premise both lexically and syntactically.

Sometimes the model answers incorrectly with extremely high confidence. The example from Table 1 is a case in point. *The Gulf War ostensibly had no effect on the celebration* is always correctly labeled as CONTRADICTION. The *Someone said...* hypothesis is also correctly labelled as ENTAILMENT with **any** adverb in the premise. Strikingly, the model gives the same result when the adverb is omitted. This suggests that the model does not take the adverb in the premise into account.

The experiments with Hypothesis 3 (cf. Table 1) corroborated that understanding: regardless of the combination of the adverb in the premise and the hypothesis, the model confidently marks the pair as CONTRADICTION or NEUTRAL with almost zero probability attached to the prediction of ENTAILMENT. This finding shows that while the model may be able to draw a positive inference from the hearsay adverb (the reported event may have happened), it is completely unaware of the possibility of the negative inference, i.e. that the reported event may not have taken place: 12 times out of 16, the model confidently predicts CONTRADICTION.

[4]The model answers correctly only when there is a larger lexical overlap, as in *Most of the assignments are challenging*.

3.3.3 Adverbs Complicate Inference

In another analysis, we investigate the impact of the sentences' structural complexity on prediction quality. We frequently found that the model correctly inferred when the hypothesis is structurally simple or no adverb is given, but failed when the hypothesis had an embedded clause and the premise had an adverb. Table 4 shows a concrete example, which permits three observations:

1. The model is sensitive to whether the hypothesis contains an embedded clause: the confidence for the correct prediction drops from $\approx$1 to $\approx$0.8 for all verbs in the no-adverb case.
2. The presence of the adverb is not noticeable with structurally simple hypotheses: the confidence in the correct answer remains $>$0.9.
3. The combination of an adverb and an embedded clause can derail the model – paradoxically most so for the verb *support*, where the model was most confident without an adverb.

Furthermore, note that an adverb can force the model to change its decision even in the presence of a strong lexical cue. Given the hypothesis *The students were obviously drunk*, the model correctly identifies *The students abhor/forswore/renounced alcohol* as CONTRADICTION. While the model labels *The students abjured alcohol* as ENTAILMENT, (perhaps) because of an incorrect analysis of the verb, when we change the hypothesis to *The students were **conspicuously** drunk*, the model confidently and correctly labels *The students abjured alcohol* as CONTRADICTION.

3.4 Evaluation on a Synthetic Dataset

The results for the application of same model on the larger synthetic dataset are shown in Table 5. They demonstrate that in general the task of drawing correct inferences from adverbs is very difficult for the model. Instead, the model tends to consistently predict the same relation (entailment / neutral / contradiction) for all sentences for an adverb class. It is able to correctly predict inference for the quantity degree class (*at least two dozen people* $\models$ *many people* and $\not\models$ *nobody*). However, even syntactically trivial entailments and contradictions in other classes lead to systematic failures. E.g., while the model can correctly identify the inference *James said that Mary reportedly opposed the wedding* $\models$ *James said that Mary may have opposed the wed-*

Verb	Prediction	Hypothesis	obviously	clearly	publicly	blatantly	no adverb
aid	Entailment	Simple	0.94	0.94	0.95	0.96	0.97
		Complex	0.60	0.62	0.70	0.71	0.85
	Neutral	Simple	0.05	0.05	0.05	0.04	0.02
		Complex	0.39	0.38	0.29	0.27	0.15
help	Entailment	Simple	0.92	0.92	0.92	0.95	0.97
		Complex	0.53	0.52	0.58	0.61	0.77
	Neutral	Simple	0.07	0.08	0.08	0.05	0.03
		Complex	0.47	0.47	0.41	0.38	0.22
support	Entailment	Simple	0.99	0.99	0.99	0.99	0.99
		Complex	0.41	0.43	0.57	0.39	0.85
	Neutral	Simple	0.01	0.01	0.01	0.01	0
		Complex	**0.55**	**0.53**	0.40	**0.40**	0.15

Table 4: Prediction of NLI model given *Castro ADV backed the rebels* as premise and *Castro VERBed the rebels* or *Castro tried to VERB the rebels* as hypothesis (*simple* and *complex* respectively). Boldface indicates wrong model predictions; underline indicates "borderline correct" cases where an incorrect label received a probability $> 40\%$.

Semantic type	Test	Entailment	Neutral	Contradiction	Error rate (%)	# sentences
Unattributed information	Entailment 1	70,188	12	0	≈ 0	70,200
	Entailment 2	134	70,066	0	≈ 100	70,200
	Contradiction 1	7,940	62,260	0	100	70,200
	Contradiction 2	567	69,633	0	100	70,200
Degree (properties of people)	Entailment	31,200	0	0	0	31,200
	Contradiction	12,390	3,980	14,830	52	31,200
Degree (properties of objects)	Entailment	840	0	0	0	840
	Contradiction	547	0	293	65	840
Degree (quantities)	Entailment	38,400	0	0	0	38,400
	Contradiction	0	0	38,400	0	38,400
Obviousness	Entailment 1	54,600	0	0	0	54,600
	Entailment 2	33,217	21,383	0	39	54,600
	Contradiction 1	61	0	54,539	≈ 0	54,600
	Contradiction 2	0	1,615	52,985	3	54,600

Table 5: Synthetic dataset: Model predictions (cells with correct predictions have gray background) for each template class and error rates.

ding, it fails on the entailment of the type *James* ***is not sure*** *that Mary opposed the wedding*.

Similarly, with obviousness adverbs, while the examples of the type *James blatantly criticized Mary* $\models$ *James disparaged Mary* are easy for the model, entailments like *James tried to disparage Mary* leads to near-chance performance. In the domain of adverb-modulated relations, while the model seems to do well on entailments (*James is at least twice as rich as Mary* $\models$ *James's net worth is at least as big as Mary's*), in fact it does not understand that the relation is not symmetric and therefore cannot correctly identify contradictions (*Mary's net worth is at least as big as James's*).

3.5 Discussion

Taken together, these experiments demonstrate systematic shortcomings in the ability of current large language models to account for adverb meaning, either glossing over them completely or making rather random inferences about their meaning. Arguably, this study only looked at a specific type of language model and other types of language models would fare better. However, converging evidence from the literature exists.

For instance, Nikolaev and Padó (2023) analyzed sentence transformers, which might be expected to provide the most nuanced understanding of adverbs. Instead, the study found that the sentences' main participants (subjects and objects) primarily determine the semantic similarity of sentence pairs, which is largely independent of adverbs. The paper argues that this behavior arises from the structure of the training data for sentence transformers (online conversations, duplicate questions on WikiAnswers), where sentence pairs labelled as semantically similar often have similar sets of main participants (subjects and objects) and can vary widely in other respects.

If a similar bias is at play in the NLI models in the present study, creating larger, richer training sets that involve adverbs in a systematic manner is a way forward. However, given the relative scarcity of adverbs and their complex behavior (cf. Section 1), it seems unlikely that this effect will emerge naturally by pre-training on ever larger datasets. Instead, the evidence provided here indicates that adverb data must be created intentionally. The following section outlines a proposal to do so.

4 Describing Adverbs in FrameNet

This section will provide a brief background to FrameNet (Section 4.1), show how FrameNet can be useful for the analysis of adverbs (Section 4.2), survey the data on adverbs contained in the current version of the dataset (Section 4.3), and propose concrete directions for next steps (Section 4.4).

4.1 Background to FrameNet

FrameNet (*FN*, Ruppenhofer et al. 2016) is a research and resource-development project in corpus-based computational lexicography grounded in the theory of *Frame Semantics* (Fillmore, 1985).

At the heart of the work is the *semantic frame*, a script-like knowledge structure that facilitates inferencing within and across events, situations, states-of-affairs, relations, and objects. FN defines a semantic frame in terms of its *frame elements* (*FEs*), or participants (and other concepts) in the scene that the frame captures; a *lexical unit* (LU) is a pairing of a lemma and a frame, characterizing that LU in terms of the frame that it evokes. FN frames may include more than one POS, and FrameNet does not claim that the LUs of a frame are synonymous, merely that they are semantically similar in referring to the same situation. Additionally, FN distinguishes between core FEs and non-core FEs; the former uniquely define a frame and the later identify concepts that characterize events or situations more generally, such as time and place. To illustrate, Example 6 shows annotation for the verb *BUY*, defined in the `Commerce_buy` frame, with the FEs BUYER, SELLER, GOODS, and MONEY.[5]

(6) [Chuck $_{\text{BUYER}}$] **BOUGHT** [a car $_{\text{GOODS}}$] [from Jerry $_{\text{SELLER}}$] [for \$2,000 $_{\text{MONEY}}$]

FrameNet annotators label approximately 20 sentences for each LU in each frame; and automatic processes tabulate the results to produce *valence* descriptions, or *semantic-syntactic combinatorial possibilities* of each LU. These also include *null-instantiated* core FEs, i.e. FEs that uniquely define a frame, even when not realized linguistically. Such valence descriptions provide information about meaning-form mappings that are important for natural-language understanding. FrameNet data, or semantic parsers built from them, have proven useful for tasks such as recognizing paraphrases (Ellsworth and Janin, 2007), drawing inferences (Ben Aharon et al., 2010), machine translation (Zhai et al., 2013), question answering (Khashabi et al., 2018), or paraphrasing (Wang et al., 2019).

At present, the FrameNet database (Release 1.7) holds 1,224 frames, defined in terms of 10,478 frame-specific FEs, and 13,686 LUs. Of those lexical units, 61% have *lexicographic* annotation, i.e. annotation for one target lemma per sentence.

4.2 FrameNet for the Analysis of Adverbs

We now outline how the descriptive devices of FrameNet, as outlined in Section 4.1, can capture the relevant facts about adverb meaning and address the core challenges of adverb classes, ambiguity, inferences, and null instantiation of roles.

Frames. Since frame definitions encompass much of the meaning of each LU, many FN frames already offer fine-grained, semantically motivated descriptions of adverb classes. For example, the `Emotion_directed` frame captures the semantic similarity of *happy*, *happily*, *happiness*, *sad*, and *sadly* and offers a starting point for the description of emotion-related adverbs, by exploiting the fact that these adverbs evoke the same background knowledge as the corresponding LUs of other parts of speech (Ruppenhofer et al., 2016).

When a lemma is ambiguous, each sense gets mapped to a different frame; each mapping is a separate lexical unit (LU). For instance, Example 1 in Section 1 includes the lemma *happily*, which is ambiguous: In Example 1a, *happily* is defined in the `Luck` frame (along with *fortunately* and *luckily*). The definition of this frame indicates that there is someone, the PROTAGONIST, for whom a particular state of affairs is surprisingly good or

[5]This paper uses the following typographical conventions: frame names appear in `typewriter font`; FE names are in SMALL CAPS; and lexical units are in **BOLD CAPS.**

bad. But this sentence does not express the PROTAGONIST; this is a case of null instantiation or NI (see below for details). The other three sentences, Examples 1b–1d, illustrate *happily* in the `Emotion_directed` frame. This involves an emotional response of someone, the EXPERIENCER, to a stimulus, the STIMULUS FE (here, watching TV), which evokes the emotional response, specifically happiness (recoverable from the definition of the LU *happily*). In these examples, the EXPERIENCER is explicit, so no inference is required (although coreference resolution will be required to resolve the referent of *they*). Example 7 shows the annotations of the sentences in the `Luck` frame (Ex. 7a) and in the `Emotion_directed` frame (Ex. 7b):

(7) a. HAPPILY, [they watched TV until dinner $_{\text{STATE\_OF\_AFFAIRS}}$] PROTAGONIST: NI.
b. [They $_{\text{EXPERIENCER}}$] HAPPILY [watched TV until dinner $_{\text{STIMULUS}}$].

Frame Elements. In FrameNet, frame elements are associated with (classes of) inferences (Chang et al., 2002). Such inferences can capture important aspects of adverb meaning, as we have shown in Section 2. The valence patterns for the two senses of *happily* shown above lead to different inferences via the two sets of frame elements:

`Luck`: A STATE_OF_AFFAIRS is evaluated as good (or bad) [...] for a particular PROTAGONIST.

`Emotion_directed`: An EXPERIENCER [feels or experiences] a particular emotional response to a STIMULUS or about a TOPIC.

While such natural language descriptions were traditionally hard to formalize, the recent advances in "prompting" language models (Shin et al., 2020) have reestablished natural language descriptions as sufficient in many conditions (cf. also our template-based probing dataset in Section 3).

Null instantiation. FrameNet annotates information about the conceptually required "core" semantic roles of a frame even if absent from the text. FN distinguishes three types of null instantiation, one licensed by a construction and the others licensed lexically. FrameNet includes approximately 55,700 NI labels in its annotations; and roughly one-quarter of these omissions are licensed constructionally, with the remaining 75% licensed lexically (Petruck, 2019).

This capability of FrameNet is particularly important for adverbs, notably speaker-oriented adverbs. By definition, these adverbs welcome inferences about the speaker, who is typically not realized unless the statement is part of reported speech or thought: *The father thought: "Happily they are all watching TV."*

Returning to Example 2 (above), 2a illustrates an instantiated SPEAKER and 2b illustrates a *null-instantiated* SPEAKER, a fact that FN records in its database. No other lexical resource used extensively in computational linguistics records such information.

4.3 Current Status of Adverbs in FrameNet

Currently, FrameNet (Release 1.7) contains 217 adverb LUs. Of these adverbs, 158 have annotation, with a total of 2,475 annotations of adverbs on sentences in the database, yielding a mean of 16 annotations per LU. However, like many linguistic phenomena, the annotations exhibit a highly skewed (Zipfian) distribution: 41 of the 158 LUs have only one annotation while nine have more than 50 annotations each. In line with its general principles, FrameNet chose not to define one single frame to capture all speaker-oriented adverbs, instead defining each such adverb according to the specific frame it evokes. At the same time, the class of speaker-oriented adverbs is arguably recoverable from the union of a set of frames all of which support inferences about the speaker by way of describing the speaker through a certain frame element. In this way, the existing frames and their annotations provide a suitable basis for creating data for this (and future) research.

Table 6 shows the four FrameNet frames used to suggest adverbs for the experiment described in Section 3 together with the adverbs listed, illustrative example sentences, and their definitions.

4.4 Next Steps

As the numbers show (Section 4.3), FrameNet has not attended to adverbs either. Perhaps this fact represents a principal incompatibility: the description of adverbs may not welcome using concepts that FN developed for traditional predicates with clear-cut valence. Yet, we believe that including adverbs in FrameNet both follows the spirit of what Fillmore (1985) called "semantics of understanding" and is in line with FrameNet practice. Still, it will require work on two principal levels: theoretical development and practical lexicographic analysis.

Frame name	Adverbial lexical units & example sentence	Definition
`Unattributed information`	*allegedly.adv, ostensibly.adv, purportedly.adv, reportedly.adv, supposedly.adv* **Ex.** One person was REPORTEDLY killed...	A speaker presents a REPORTED FACT as deriving from statements (made directly to them or to others) of third parties.
`Likelihood`	*certainly, likely, probably, possibly* **Ex.** This will LIKELY not be enough to stop...	This frame concerns the likelihood of a HYPOTHETICAL EVENT occurring, the only core frame element in the frame.
`Obviousness`	*audibly.adv, clearly.adv, evidently.adv, noticeably.adv, obviously.adv, visibly.adv* **Ex.** It is CLEARLY desirable to permit the gifted youngsters to flourish.	A PHENOMENON is portrayed in terms of the DEGREE of likelihood that it will be perceived and known, given the (usually implicit) EVIDENCE, PERCEIVER, and CIRCUMSTANCES in which it is considered.
`Degree`	*a little (bit).adv, a lot.adv, absolutely.adv, as hell.adv, far.adv, fully.adv, in part.adv, kind of.adv, so.adv, somewhat.adv, that.adv, totally.adv, very.adv, way.adv* **Ex.** I had ABSOLUTELY nothing to say.	LUs in this frame modify a GRADABLE ATTRIBUTE and describe intensities at the extreme positions on a scale.

Table 6: FrameNet Frames characterizing Speaker-Oriented Adverbs

At the theoretical level, the FrameNet approach has seen constant development over the 25 years of the project's existence. In initial verb-centered frames, nominals tended to fill FEs, with additional attributes realized as adverbs. Next, FN added deverbal nouns to frames, which largely take the same frame elements. To expand to other types of nouns, like natural kinds and artifacts, FrameNet broadened the concept of FE to encompass *qualia* such as substance or purpose (Pustejovsky, 1991). Layering the annotation of nouns as FEs of verbs, and modifiers of nouns as *their* FEs provided a richer semantic representation. Next, FrameNet included adjectives as frame-evoking elements, permitting generalizations over domains like speed or temperature. While most aspects of adverbs description are already present in FrameNet (cf. above), theoretical analysis must make precise the implications of annotating null instantiated adverbial frame elements at scale.

At the practical level, the time is ripe to add many more adverbs to appropriate existing frames and to create new frames for adverbs as needed. The principles of annotating naturally occurring text and extracting valence descriptions for LUs established on the other parts of speech carry over to adverbs. The combination of valence descriptions and annotated instances constitute essential inputs to characterize inferences.

Clearly, the more annotation, the better, but large-scale expert annotation is slow and resource-intensive. Using crowdsourcing, which permits parallelizing (thus, speeding up) annotation, is a possible mitigation. Fossati et al. (2013) and Feizabadi and Padó (2014) demonstrated success with crowdsourcing for frame-semantic annotation when the task is narrowed down appropriately. Substantial promise exists to extract adverb annotation automatically from comparable corpora (Roth and Frank, 2015) and paraphrasing models (Wang et al., 2019). Even for the core task of FrameNet analysis, defining frames, Ustalov et al. (2018) proposed automatic methods. Still, full automation remains hard, given concerns of quality and consistency.

5 Conclusion

Conlon and Evens (1992) stated that adverbs are under-researched in computational linguistics; this statement is still true. Adverbs have received attention only in two applications: sentiment analysis and hedging detection. The large language models used here show systematic gaps in capturing adverb meaning. The problem is **not** solved.

We propose that Frame Semantics, as embodied in FrameNet, along with improved techniques to mitigate the annotation effort to extend FN with new frames and annotations, can capture the meaning and implicatures of adverbs. Considering frames as lexical constructions (Fillmore, 2008), this proposal fits well with recent work to combine language models and construction grammar (Weissweiler et al., 2023).

Multiple ways exist for computational modeling to use such a resource, e.g., by extending the coverage of semantic role labellers to a larger range of adverbs, or by fine-tuning language models on large annotated datasets for which our probing dataset can serve as a blueprint.

Limitations

We only used English data in the study, so we cannot guarantee that the findings will generalize to other languages (cf. Bender 2019). The English NLI datasets are, as usual, larger than for other languages, so we should expect models targeting other languages to have worse performance. We do, however, believe that the challenges of adverbs are comparable in other languages, particularly in typologically similar languages.

Ethics Statement

The paper argues for a new approach to the treatment of adverbs in the development of resources and applications in NLP. We consider better understanding of language by computational models as not posing a significant societal risk in itself. The dataset used for the computational experiment in Section 3 was created based on the data contained in the publicly available FrameNet corpus and, as far as we are aware, does not contain sensitive elements. Implementation of our proposed methodology has the same risks as any data-driven approach in computational linguistics, but we assume that we cannot safeguard against its possible misuse due to its very general nature.

References

Omri Abend and Ari Rappoport. 2013. Universal Conceptual Cognitive Annotation (UCCA). In *Proceedings of the 51st Annual Meeting of the Association for Computational Linguistics (Volume 1: Long Papers)*, pages 228–238, Sofia, Bulgaria. Association for Computational Linguistics.

Artemis Alexiadou. 2004. Adverbs across frameworks. *Lingua*, 114(6):677–682.

Laura Banarescu, Claire Bonial, Shu Cai, Madalina Georgescu, Kira Griffitt, Ulf Hermjakob, Kevin Knight, Philipp Koehn, Martha Palmer, and Nathan Schneider. 2013. Abstract meaning representation for sembanking. In *Proceedings of the 7th Linguistic Annotation Workshop and Interoperability with Discourse*, pages 178–186.

Jeremy Barnes, Robin Kurtz, Stephan Oepen, Lilja Øvrelid, and Erik Velldal. 2021. Structured sentiment analysis as dependency graph parsing. In *Proceedings of the 59th Annual Meeting of the Association for Computational Linguistics and the 11th International Joint Conference on Natural Language Processing (Volume 1: Long Papers)*, pages 3387–3402, Online. Association for Computational Linguistics.

Yonatan Belinkov, Adam Poliak, Stuart Shieber, Benjamin Van Durme, and Alexander Rush. 2019. Don't take the premise for granted: Mitigating artifacts in natural language inference. In *Proceedings of the 57th Annual Meeting of the Association for Computational Linguistics*, pages 877–891, Florence, Italy. Association for Computational Linguistics.

Roni Ben Aharon, Idan Szpektor, and Ido Dagan. 2010. Generating entailment rules from FrameNet. In *Proceedings of the ACL 2010 Conference Short Papers*, pages 241–246, Uppsala, Sweden. Association for Computational Linguistics.

Farah Benamara, Carmine Cesarano, Antonio Picariello, Diego Reforgiato Recupero, and V. S. Subrahmanian. 2007. Sentiment analysis: Adjectives and adverbs are better than adjectives alone. In *Proceedings of ICWSM*.

Emily Bender. 2019. The #benderrule: On naming the languages we study and why it matters. *The Gradient*.

Adam Berger, Rich Caruana, David Cohn, Dayne Freitag, and Vibhu Mittal. 2000. Bridging the lexical chasm: Statistical approaches to answer-finding. In *Proceedings of the 23rd Annual International ACM SIGIR Conference on Research and Development in Information Retrieval*, page 192–199, New York, NY, USA. Association for Computing Machinery.

Nancy Chang, Srini Narayanan, and Miriam R.L. Petruck. 2002. Putting frames in perspective. In *COLING 2002: The 19th International Conference on Computational Linguistics*.

U.A. Chauhan, M.T. Afzal, A. Shahid, M. Abdar, M.E. Basiri, and X. Zhou. 2020. A comprehensive analysis of adverb types for mining user sentiments on Amazon product reviews. *World Wide Web*, 23:1811–1829.

Sumali Pin-Ngern Conlon and Martha Evens. 1992. Can computers handle adverbs? In *COLING 1992 Volume 4: The 14th International Conference on Computational Linguistics*.

Ryan Cotterell and Hinrich Schütze. 2015. Morphological word-embeddings. In *Proceedings of the 2015 Conference of the North American Chapter of the Association for Computational Linguistics: Human Language Technologies*, pages 1287–1292, Denver, Colorado. Association for Computational Linguistics.

Jacob Devlin, Ming-Wei Chang, Kenton Lee, and Kristina Toutanova. 2019. BERT: Pre-training of deep bidirectional transformers for language understanding. In *Proceedings of the 2019 Conference of the North American Chapter of the Association for Computational Linguistics: Human Language Technologies, Volume 1 (Long and Short Papers)*, pages 4171–4186, Minneapolis, Minnesota. Association for Computational Linguistics.

Eduard Dragut and Christiane Fellbaum. 2014. The role of adverbs in sentiment analysis. In *Proceedings of Frame Semantics in NLP: A Workshop in Honor of Chuck Fillmore (1929-2014)*, pages 38–41, Baltimore, MD, USA. Association for Computational Linguistics.

Michael Ellsworth and Adam Janin. 2007. Mutaphrase: Paraphrasing with FrameNet. In *Proceedings of the ACL-PASCAL Workshop on Textual Entailment and Paraphrasing*, pages 143–150, Prague. Association for Computational Linguistics.

Thomas Ernst. 2009. Speaker-oriented adverbs. *Natural Language and Linguistic Theory*, 27:497–544.

Manaal Faruqui, Jesse Dodge, Sujay Kumar Jauhar, Chris Dyer, Eduard Hovy, and Noah A. Smith. 2015. Retrofitting word vectors to semantic lexicons. In *Proceedings of the 2015 Conference of the North American Chapter of the Association for Computational Linguistics: Human Language Technologies*, pages 1606–1615, Denver, Colorado. Association for Computational Linguistics.

Parvin Sadat Feizabadi and Sebastian Padó. 2014. Crowdsourcing annotation of non-local semantic roles. In *Proceedings of the 14th Conference of the European Chapter of the Association for Computational Linguistics, volume 2: Short Papers*, pages 226–230, Gothenburg, Sweden. Association for Computational Linguistics.

Charles J Fillmore. 1985. Frames and the Semantics of Understanding. *Quaderni di Semantica*, IV(2):222–254.

Charles J Fillmore. 2008. Border conflicts: Framenet meets Construction Grammar. In *Proceedings of the XIII. EURALEX international congress*, volume 4968, pages 49–68, Barcelona, Spain.

Marco Fossati, Claudio Giuliano, and Sara Tonelli. 2013. Outsourcing FrameNet to the crowd. In *Proceedings of the 51st Annual Meeting of the Association for Computational Linguistics (Volume 2: Short Papers)*, pages 742–747, Sofia, Bulgaria. Association for Computational Linguistics.

Sajjad Haider, Muhammad Tanvir Afzal, Muhammad Asif, Hermann Maurer, Awais Ahmad, and Abdelrahman Abuarqoub. 2021. Impact analysis of adverbs for sentiment classification on Twitter product reviews. *Concurrency and Computation: Practice and Experience*, 33(4):e4956. E4956 CPE-18-0194.R2.

Birgit Hamp and Helmut Feldweg. 1997. GermaNet - a lexical-semantic net for German. In *Automatic Information Extraction and Building of Lexical Semantic Resources for NLP Applications*.

Rodney Huddleston and Geoffrey K. Pullum. 2002. *The Cambridge Grammar of the English Language*. Cambridge University Press.

Jumayel Islam, Lu Xiao, and Robert E. Mercer. 2020. A lexicon-based approach for detecting hedges in informal text. In *Proceedings of the Twelfth Language Resources and Evaluation Conference*, pages 3109–3113, Marseille, France. European Language Resources Association.

Jieun Jeon and Jae-Woong Choe. 2009. A key word analysis of English intensifying adverbs in male and female speech in ICE-GB. In *Proceedings of the 23rd Pacific Asia Conference on Language, Information and Computation, Volume 1*, pages 210–219, Hong Kong. City University of Hong Kong.

Lauri Karttunen. 1971. Implicative verbs. *Language*, 47(2):340–358.

Lauri Karttunen. 2012. Simple and phrasal implicatives. In **SEM 2012: The First Joint Conference on Lexical and Computational Semantics – Volume 1: Proceedings of the main conference and the shared task, and Volume 2: Proceedings of the Sixth International Workshop on Semantic Evaluation (SemEval 2012)*, pages 124–131, Montréal, Canada. Association for Computational Linguistics.

Daniel Khashabi, Tushar Khot, Ashish Sabharwal, and Dan Roth. 2018. Question answering as global reasoning over semantic abstractions. In *Proceedings of the 32nd AAAI Conference on Artificial Intelligence*, New Orleans, LA, USA.

Evgeny Kim and Roman Klinger. 2018. Who feels what and why? annotation of a literature corpus with semantic roles of emotions. In *Proceedings of the 27th International Conference on Computational Linguistics*, pages 1345–1359, Santa Fe, New Mexico, USA. Association for Computational Linguistics.

Angeliki Lazaridou, Marco Marelli, Roberto Zamparelli, and Marco Baroni. 2013. Compositional-ly derived representations of morphologically complex words in distributional semantics. In *Proceedings of the 51st Annual Meeting of the Association for Computational Linguistics (Volume 1: Long Papers)*, pages 1517–1526, Sofia, Bulgaria. Association for Computational Linguistics.

Amnon Lotan, Asher Stern, and Ido Dagan. 2013. TruthTeller: Annotating predicate truth. In *Proceedings of the 2013 Conference of the North American Chapter of the Association for Computational Linguistics: Human Language Technologies*, pages 752–757, Atlanta, Georgia. Association for Computational Linguistics.

Marek Maziarz, Stan Szpakowicz, and Michal Kalinski. 2016. Adverbs in plWordNet: Theory and implementation. In *Proceedings of the 8th Global WordNet Conference (GWC)*, pages 209–217, Bucharest, Romania. Global Wordnet Association.

George Miller, Richard Beckwith, Christiane Fellbaum, Derek Gross, and Katherine Miller. 1990. Five papers on WordNet. *International Journal of Lexicography*, 3(4):235–312.

Yixin Nie, Adina Williams, Emily Dinan, Mohit Bansal, Jason Weston, and Douwe Kiela. 2020. Adversarial NLI: A new benchmark for natural language understanding. In *Proceedings of the 58th Annual Meeting of the Association for Computational Linguistics*, pages 4885–4901, Online. Association for Computational Linguistics.

Dmitry Nikolaev and Sebastian Padó. 2023. Representation biases in sentence transformers. In *Proceedings of the 17th Conference of the European Chapter of the Association for Computational Linguistics*, pages 3701–3716, Dubrovnik, Croatia. Association for Computational Linguistics.

Sebastian Padó, Aurélie Herbelot, Max Kisselew, and Jan Šnajder. 2016. Predictability of distributional semantics in derivational word formation. In *Proceedings of COLING 2016, the 26th International Conference on Computational Linguistics: Technical Papers*, pages 1285–1296, Osaka, Japan. The COLING 2016 Organizing Committee.

Martha Palmer, Daniel Gildea, and Paul Kingsbury. 2005. The proposition bank: An annotated corpus of semantic roles. *Computational linguistics*, 31(1):71–106.

Bo Pang and Lillian Lee. 2008. Opinion mining and sentiment analysis. *Foundations and Trends in Information Retrieval*, 2(1-2):1–135.

John Payne, Rodney Huddleston, and Geoffrey K. Pullum. 2010. The distribution and category status of adjectives and adverbs. *Word Structure*, 3(1):31–81.

Matthew E. Peters, Mark Neumann, Mohit Iyyer, Matt Gardner, Christopher Clark, Kenton Lee, and Luke Zettlemoyer. 2018. Deep contextualized word representations. In *Proceedings of the 2018 Conference of the North American Chapter of the Association for Computational Linguistics: Human Language Technologies, Volume 1 (Long Papers)*, pages 2227–2237, New Orleans, Louisiana. Association for Computational Linguistics.

Miriam R L Petruck. 2019. Meaning representation of null instantiated semantic roles in FrameNet. In *Proceedings of the First International Workshop on Designing Meaning Representations*, pages 121–127, Florence, Italy. Association for Computational Linguistics.

James Pustejovsky. 1991. The Generative Lexicon. *Computational Linguistics*, 17(4):409–441.

Michael Roth and Anette Frank. 2015. Inducing implicit arguments from comparable texts: A framework and its applications. *Computational Linguistics*, 41(4):625–664.

Josef Ruppenhofer, Michael Ellsworth, Miriam R. L. Petruck, Christopher R. Johnson, Collin F. Baker, and Jan Scheffczyk. 2016. *FrameNet II: Extended Theory and Practice*. ICSI: Berkeley.

Taylor Shin, Yasaman Razeghi, Robert L. Logan IV, Eric Wallace, and Sameer Singh. 2020. AutoPrompt: Eliciting Knowledge from Language Models with Automatically Generated Prompts. In *Proceedings of the 2020 Conference on Empirical Methods in Natural Language Processing (EMNLP)*, pages 4222–4235, Online. Association for Computational Linguistics.

Shane Storks, Qiaozi Gao, and Joyce Y. Chai. 2019. Commonsense reasoning for natural language understanding: A survey of benchmarks, resources, and approaches. *CoRR*, abs/1904.01172.

Matt Thomas, Bo Pang, and Lillian Lee. 2006. Get out the vote: Determining support or opposition from congressional floor-debate transcripts. In *Proceedings of the 2006 Conference on Empirical Methods in Natural Language Processing*, pages 327–335, Sydney, Australia. Association for Computational Linguistics.

Richmond H. Thomason and Robert C. Stalnaker. 1973. A semantic theory of adverbs. *Linguistic Inquiry*, 4(2):195–220.

Peter D Turney and Patrick Pantel. 2010. From Frequency to Meaning: Vector Space Models of Semantics. *Journal of Artificial Intelligence Research*, 37(1):141–188.

Dmitry Ustalov, Alexander Panchenko, Andrey Kutuzov, Chris Biemann, and Simone Paolo Ponzetto. 2018. Unsupervised semantic frame induction using triclustering. In *Proceedings of the 56th Annual Meeting of the Association for Computational Linguistics (Volume 2: Short Papers)*, pages 55–62, Melbourne, Australia. Association for Computational Linguistics.

Alex Wang, Amanpreet Singh, Julian Michael, Felix Hill, Omer Levy, and Samuel Bowman. 2018. GLUE: A multi-task benchmark and analysis platform for natural language understanding. In *Proceedings of the 2018 EMNLP Workshop BlackboxNLP: Analyzing and Interpreting Neural Networks for NLP*, pages 353–355, Brussels, Belgium. Association for Computational Linguistics.

Su Wang, Rahul Gupta, Nancy Chang, and Jason Baldridge. 2019. A task in a suit and a tie: paraphrase generation with semantic augmentation. In *Proceedings of the 32nd AAAI Conference on Artificial Intelligence*, Honolulu, HI, USA.

Alex Warstadt, Alicia Parrish, Haokun Liu, Anhad Mohananey, Wei Peng, Sheng-Fu Wang, and Samuel R. Bowman. 2020. Blimp: The benchmark of linguistic minimal pairs for English. *Transactions of the Association for Computational Linguistics*, 8:377–392.

Leonie Weissweiler, Taiqi He, Naoki Otani, David R. Mortensen, Lori Levin, and Hinrich Schütze. 2023. Construction grammar provides unique insight into neural language models. In *Georgetown University Round Table Workshop on CxGs+NLP*.

Feifei Zhai, Jiajun Zhang, Yu Zhou, and Chengqing Zong. 2013. Handling ambiguities of bilingual predicate-argument structures for statistical machine translation. In *Proceedings of the 51st Annual Meeting of the Association for Computational Linguistics (Volume 1: Long Papers)*, pages 1127–1136, Sofia, Bulgaria. Association for Computational Linguistics.

A Details on the Naturalistic Dataset

The probing dataset includes a series of template classes. Each template class corresponds to an adverb class and contains several NLI templates with slots for adverbs and, when the structure permits it, also for the subject. In testing, we used all pairs of adverbs from the relevant class to instantiate the premise and the hypothesis. When a variable for subject exists in the premise, we used the same subject in the hypotheses.

A.1 Likelihood Adverbs

Adverbs: *undoubtedly, surely, positively, likely, certainly, definitely, totally.*

Fillers for the subject slot: *Barbara, Charles, David, Elizabeth, James, Jennifer, Jessica, John, Joseph, Karen, Linda, Mary, Michael, Patricia, Richard, Robert, Sarah, Susan, Thomas, William.*

1. **Premise:** *SUBJ is ADV gonna have to check it tomorrow afternoon again.*
   Entailment: *SUBJ is ADV going to have to check it again.*
   Contradiction: *SUBJ ADV won't need to check it again.*

2. **Premise:** *SUBJ can ADV find bargains in Tunis.*
   Entailment: *SUBJ will ADV find good deals in Tunis.*
   Contradiction: *SUBJ will ADV discover that everything is expensive in Tunis.*

3. **Premise:** *His friend, SUBJ, is ADV a foreigner.*
   Entailment: *SUBJ ADV is from another country.*
   Contradiction: *SUBJ ADV is a native here.*

A.2 Unattributed-information adverbs

Adverbs: *reportedly, allegedly, supposedly, apparently, ostensibly.*

1. **Premise:** *The German government ADV opposed the quotas.*
   Entailments: *The German government ADV was against the quotas*; *The German government may have supported the quotas.*
   Contradiction: *The German ADV supported more quotas.*

2. **Premise:** *The celebration had been postponed, ADV because of the Gulf War.*
   Entailments: *Someone said that the celebration was postponed because of the Gulf War*; *The Gulf War may have had no effect on the celebration.*
   Contradiction: *The Gulf War ADV had no effect on the celebration.*

A.3 Degree Adverbs

Adverbs: *at least, at a minimum, nearly, approximately.*

1. **Premise:** *Lantau covers ADV twice the area of Hong Kong Island.*
   Entailment: *Lantau is at least as big as Hong Kong Island.*
   Contradiction: *Hong Kong Island is at least as big as Lantau.*

2. **Premise:** *At the moment ADV 140 persons are working to curtail the fire.*
   Entailment: *Many people are fighting the fire.*
   Contradiction: *Nobody is fighting the fire.*

A.4 Obviousness Adverbs

Adverbs: *blatantly, obviously, clearly, ostentatiously, noticeably, visibly, conspicuously.*

1. **Premise:** *Castro ADV backed the rebels.*
   Entailments: *Castro helped the rebels*; *Castro tried to help the rebels.*
   Contradiction: *Castro tried to stop the rebels.*

2. **Premise:** *The students were ADV drunk.*
   Entailment: *The students were surely drinking too much.*
   Contradiction: *The students renounced alcohol.*

B Details on the Synthetic Dataset

B.1 Fillers for the human-subject slot

James, Mary, Robert, Patricia, John, Jennifer, Michael, Linda, David, Elizabeth, William, Barbara, Richard, Susan, Joseph, Jessica, Thomas,

Sarah, Charles, Karen, Li, Wei, Fang, Xiuying, Na, Priya, Rahul, Divya, Abhishek, Ishita, Melokuhle, Omphile, Iminathi, Lisakhanya, Lethabo, Ivaana, Malik, Pipaluk, Aputsiaq, Nivi.

B.2 Unattributed-information adverbs

Adverbs: *reportedly, allegedly, supposedly, apparently, ostensibly.*

Actions: *the wedding, the marriage, buying the house, selling the car, moving away, staying in Canberra, delaying the funeral, the arrangement, the lawsuit.*

Premise: *SUBJ1 said that SUBJ2 ADV opposed ACTION.*

Entailments:

1. *SUBJ1 said that SUBJ2 may have opposed ACTION.*
2. *SUBJ1 is not sure that SUBJ2 opposed ACTION.*

Contradictions:

1. *SUBJ1 is sure that SUBJ2 opposed ACTION.*
2. *SUBJ1 is sure that SUBJ2 did not support ACTION.*

B.3 Degree adverbs

Adverbs: *at least, at a minimum, nearly, approximately.*

B.3.1 Properties of people

Properties: *net worth, knowledge, manners, fan base, culpability.*[6]

Adjectives:

- **Adjective 1**: *rich, erudite, polite, popular, guilty.*
- **Adjective 2**: *big, extensive, good, large, high.*

Premise: *SUBJ1 is ADV twice as ADJ1 as SUBJ2.*

Entailment: *SUBJ1's PROPERTY is/are at least as ADJ2 as SUBJ2's.*

Contradiction: *SUBJ2's PROPERTY is/are at least as ADJ2 as SUBJ1's.*

B.3.2 Properties of objects

Subjects: *the truck, the house, the hotel, the ship, the wagon, the car, the tree.*

Properties: *age, weight, height, width, price.*

Adjectives:

- **Adjective 1**: *old, heavy, tall, wide, expensive.*
- **Adjective 2**: *great, big, big, big, high.*

Premise: *SUBJ1 is ADV twice as ADJ1 as SUBJ2.*

Entailment: *The PROPERTY of SUBJ1 is at least as ADJ2 as that of SUBJ2.*

Contradiction: *The PROPERTY of SUBJ2 is at least as ADJ2 as that of SUBJ1.*

B.3.3 Quantities

Times: *at the moment, now, these days, this month, this week.*[7]

Numbers: *two dozen, thirty, fifty, 140.*

Related-person groups: *friends, relatives, acquaintances, coworkers.*

Activities: *working on this, helping with the move, coming to visit us.*

Premise: *TIME ADV NUMBER of SUBJ's RELATED_PERSONS are ACTIVITY.*

Entailment: *Many people are ACTIVITY.*

Contradiction: *Nobody is ACTIVITY.*

B.4 Obviousness adverbs

Adverbs: *blatantly, obviously, clearly, ostentatiously, noticeably, visibly, conspicuously.*

Actions: [8]

- **Action 1**: *backed, supported, criticized, provoked, brainwashed.*

[6]Unlike in case with adverbs and subject-slot fillers, where all combinations are used, properties and adjectives in this and the next subclass are used in parallel. I.e., when the *i*'th adjective from the first list is used in the premise, the corresponding *i*'th property and adjective from the second list will be used in the hypotheses.

[7]Similarly to the two previous subclasses, times, numbers, activities, and related-person groups in this subclass are used in parallel. I.e., when the *i*'th time, number, related-person group, and activity are used in the premise, the corresponding *i*'th activity will be used in the hypotheses.

[8]Similarly to adjectives and properties in the case of degree adverbs above, actions of different types are used in parallel. I.e., when the *i*'th element from the first list is used in the premise, corresponding *i*'th elements from other lists will be used in the hypotheses.

- **Action 2, past**: *helped, encouraged, disparaged, incited, indoctrinated.*
- **Action 2, infinitive**: *help, encourage, disparage, incite, indoctrinate.*
- **Action 3, past**: *stopped, deterred, praised, calmed, deprogrammed.*
- **Action 3, infinitive**: *stop, deter, praise, calm, deprogram.*

Premise: *SUBJ1 ADV ACTION1 SUBJ2.*

Entailments:

1. *SUBJ1 ACTION2_PAST SUBJ2.*
2. *SUBJ1 tried to ACTION2_INF SUBJ2.*

Contradictions:

1. *SUBJ1 ACTION3_PAST SUBJ2.*
2. *SUBJ1 tried to ACTION3_INF SUBJ2.*

Can Sequence-to-Sequence Transformers Naturally Understand Sequential Instructions?

Xiang Zhou[1*] **Aditya Gupta**[2] **Shyam Upadhyay**[2] **Mohit Bansal**[1] **Manaal Faruqui**[2]
[1]UNC Chapel Hill [2]Google
{xzh, mbansal}@cs.unc.edu
{gaditya, shyamupa, mfaruqui}@google.com

Abstract

While many real-life tasks require reasoning over multi-step sequential instructions, collecting fine-grained annotations for each intermediate step can be prohibitively expensive. In this work, we study how general pretrained sequence-to-sequence transformers perform under varying types of annotation for sequential instruction understanding. We conduct experiments using T5 (Raffel et al., 2020) on a commonly-used multi-step instruction understanding dataset SCONE (Long et al., 2016) that includes three sub-tasks. First, we show that with only gold supervision for the final step of a multi-step instruction sequence, depending on the sequential properties of different tasks, transformers may exhibit extremely bad performance on intermediate steps, in stark contrast with their performance on the final step. Next, we explore two directions to relieve this problem. We show that with the same limited annotation budget, using supervision uniformly distributed across different steps (instead of only final-step supervision), we can greatly improve the performance on intermediate steps with a drop in final-step performance. Further, we explore a contrastive learning approach to provide training signals on intermediate steps with zero intermediate gold supervision. This, however, achieves mixed results. It significantly improves the model's bad intermediate-step performance on one subtask, but also shows decreased performance on another subtask.

1 Introduction

Transformer-based sequence-to-sequence models (Vaswani et al., 2017; Raffel et al., 2020) have shown remarkable performance on many natural language understanding tasks including semantic parsing (Yu et al., 2018), dialog state tracking (Budzianowski et al., 2018), procedure text understanding (Dalvi et al., 2018) etc. However, much of this success relies on fine-grained annotations. For example, many instruction-following datasets (Long et al., 2016) contain the corresponding parse or label for every single instruction showing their immediate effects. However, such data can be hard to collect in practice because even seemingly simple and straightforward tasks can involve multiple steps,[1] making the collection of detailed annotations expensive and time-consuming.

For these scenarios, many earlier works applied task-specific methods to provide additional inductive biases about the sequential nature of these instructions (Suhr and Artzi, 2018; Muhlgay et al., 2019). These methods need substantial prior knowledge and can be harder to generalize to new domains.[2] In this work, first, we provide a case study to explore whether transformer-based seq2seq models trained only using end-step supervision (i.e., gold supervision is given only at the very end of the entire sequence) can naturally handle these sequential instructions without task-aware specific architecture changes. We conduct experiments on the SCONE dataset (Long et al., 2016) including three different subtasks. The input of each example contains a sequence of instructions. During training, the model *only* observes the final state (label) after executing all the instructions, while for evaluation, the model needs to predict both the final states and all the intermediate states. We use T5 (Raffel et al., 2020) as our baseline model. Interestingly, we observe mixed trends on the three different subtasks of SCONE depending on their different sequential properties. On two out of three tasks (SCENE and TANGRAMS), T5 models demonstrate good performance on the intermediate steps.

*Work partially conducted during an internship at Google.

[1]For example, map instructions for how to reach the closest supermarket may involve a number of turns, cooking instructions may involve adding multiple different spices, etc.

[2]The prior knowledge is usually injected by either knowing the exact parses or grounded actions of each instruction, or by using a world simulator that can execute the instructions and facilitates RL-based approaches.

*Proceedings of the The 12th Joint Conference on Lexical and Computational Semantics (*SEM 2023)*, pages 527–534
July 13-14, 2023 ©2023 Association for Computational Linguistics

On ALCHEMY, however, the performance on intermediate steps is extremely bad, in stark contrast with their decent performance on final steps. Such behavior reveals that the model does not learn to understand the instructions sequentially and is not maintaining a correct intermediate state. Therefore, while these models may do well on instructions similar to the training examples, they can also fail miserably on instructions shorter or longer than the instructions they are trained on.

Hence, we next explore two potential mitigations to this problem. We first study an alternative labeling schema. We find that if the *same amount* of labels are uniformly sampled across multiple steps instead of only coming from the last step, the model can have substantially better performance at intermediate steps, despite a drop of the performance on the final step. This can be a favorable behavior if the target application has more focus on intermediate steps. However, re-collecting labels may not always be practical. Therefore, for scenarios where only final-step labels are accessible, we also explore a contrastive learning based approach to improve the intermediate-state performance without additional gold labels. Specifically, we use a contrastive learning loss to encourage an alignment between the change in the predicted states and the most recent instruction, and provide useful training signals on the intermediate steps. However, we see mixed results from this approach. While it can significantly improve the low intermediate-step performance on ALCHEMY, it decreases performance on SCENE and does not further improve other models that already have decent performance. Finally, we discuss the limitation of this approach and point out that the lack of precise regularization to capture the fine-grained state differences may be the reason behind the mixed results, which makes it hard to further improve strong baselines already showing sequential understanding abilities (as in SCENE).

2 Background and Baseline Performances

Problem and Evaluation Setup. We focus on sequential instruction following tasks, more specifically, state tracking or state prediction with multi-step instructions. Given an initial state and a sequence of instructions, the model needs to predict the states after the execution of each instruction. Formally, the training set $D^{train} = \{(inst^i_{j=1..m}, state^i_0, state^i_m)|^n_{i=1}\}$ contains n examples. Each example consists of a sequence of m instructions and two states, the initial state $state_0$, and the final state $state_m$ after executing all the m instructions. The training objective is to predict the final state $state_m$ given the initial state and all the previous instructions. The evaluation sets $D^{eval} = \{(inst^i_{j=1..m}, state^i_{j=0..m})|^{n'}_{i=1}\}$ contain not only the initial and the final state, but also all the intermediate states $state_j$ after every instruction $inst_j$. This allows us to evaluate the models' performance in two ways: (1) the exact-match accuracy at the final state (**acc_{final}**), similar to the training setup; and (2) the exact-match accuracy at all the states from $state_1$ to $state_m$ (**acc_{all}**).

Dataset. We use the SCONE dataset as it contains three different subtasks: ALCHEMY, SCENE and TANGRAMS (Long et al., 2016), and covers a diverse set of different states and instructions. For every example in these three subtasks, the instruction contains 5 steps. See Appendix A for examples and a detailed dataset introduction.

Baseline Performances with Final-Step Supervision. We use T5-base (Raffel et al., 2020) as our main model.[3] At each step, to get the prediction of $state_i$, the model will receive an input containing the concatenation of the initial state $state_0$ and all the instructions from $inst_1$ till $inst_i$. More hyperparameter and preprocessing details are in Appendix A and B. The performance is shown in Table 1. First, if we follow the traditional setup for previous papers to use gold labels across all the steps (the first row), fine-tuned T5 models without any task-specific tricks can already achieve strong performance on **acc_{final}**, reaching competitive performance on all three subtasks compared to all previous methods (including Shi et al. (2022) who also uses pre-trained Transformer-based models) using similar supervision, and the performance on ALCHEMY is even higher. By using all the gold labels across steps, the performances are substantially higher than the results only using final-step supervision. This observation is also connected to the observation in Wies et al. (2023) and Yu et al. (2023), where they notice the decomposition of complex tasks makes learning easier. When we only use final-step supervision (the second row), both **acc_{all}** and **acc_{final}** decrease substantially. However, the trends on different subtasks are different. On SCENE and TANGRAMS, the **acc_{all}** is equal or

[3]Preliminarily, we also conduct our experiments on other scales of T5 (i.e., T5-small and T5-large), but they do not show better performance on our tasks.

Models	Supervision	ALCHEMY		SCENE		TANGRAMS	
		$\mathbf{acc}_{\text{final}}$	$\mathbf{acc}_{\text{all}}$	$\mathbf{acc}_{\text{final}}$	$\mathbf{acc}_{\text{all}}$	$\mathbf{acc}_{\text{final}}$	$\mathbf{acc}_{\text{all}}$
T5-base	All steps	$77.0_{\pm 0.9}$	$86.6_{\pm 0.5}$	$72.9_{\pm 1.8}$	$84.9_{\pm 0.7}$	$60.1_{\pm 2.4}$	$79.0_{\pm 0.8}$
T5-base	Final step	$70.0_{\pm 1.7}$	$58.0_{\pm 3.8}$	$60.5_{\pm 2.9}$	$71.7_{\pm 3.8}$	$14.2_{\pm 4.5}$	$22.3_{\pm 6.2}$
+CL	Final step	$70.7_{\pm 2.4}$	$72.4_{\pm 4.4}$	$62.5_{\pm 2.3}$	$60.8_{\pm 2.0}$	$14.7_{\pm 6.7}$	$29.0_{\pm 12.1}$
T5-base	Uniformly sampled steps	$62.8_{\pm 3.0}$	$80.0_{\pm 1.3}$	$54.3_{\pm 1.5}$	$75.2_{\pm 0.8}$	$23.7_{\pm 3.2}$	$60.2_{\pm 2.5}$
Shi et al. (2022)	All steps	75.4	-	72.3	-	60.0	-
Suhr and Artzi (2018)	All steps	62.7	-	62.0	-	62.4	-
Yeh and Chen (2019)	All steps+Annotated programs	76.1	-	75.1	-	72.5	-

Table 1: Model performance on the SCONE dataset. The numbers in this table are mean and std over 10 runs.

Task	Instructions
ALCHEMY	Instruction i: *throw out the right most orange chemical* Instruction $i+1$: *throw out 2 units of the purple chemical*
SCENE	Instruction i: *he disappears* Instruction $i+1$: *the person in all orange moves one step right*
TANGRAMS	Instruction i: *remove the first figure* Instruction $i+1$: *swap the first and third figures*

Table 2: Example instructions from the three subsets in SCONE. Due to the heavy use of coreference, changing the order of instructions in SCENE and TANGRAMS can lead to different results, while a larger number of examples in ALCHEMY are interchangeable as they may refer to independent actions for different beakers.

higher than $\mathbf{acc}_{\text{final}}$, showing that the models already have a tendency to track the semantics on intermediate steps and early steps are easier than later steps. On the contrary, the $\mathbf{acc}_{\text{all}}$ performance on ALCHEMY is substantially lower than $\mathbf{acc}_{\text{final}}$. Such low performance indicates that after training on the ALCHEMY, despite the decent $\mathbf{acc}_{\text{final}}$, the model does not always maintain a correct state in the intermediate steps.

Why are the trends different across subtasks? The three subtasks in SCONE are designed to focus on different linguistic phenomena (Long et al., 2016). Here, we argue these different designs cause T5 to correctly understand the sequential nature of the instructions on SCENE and TANGRAMS and achieve good $\mathbf{acc}_{\text{all}}$, but not on ALCHEMY. Due to the focus on the coreference across steps (see Table 2 and dataset descriptions in Appendix A), instructions in SCENE and TANGRAMS are more sensitive in their order, because switching the order of instructions can break the coreference and lead to different outcomes. Specifically, only 39% of the instruction pairs in ALCHEMY are non-interchangeable in their orders, compared to 62% in SCENE and 85% in TANGRAMS.[4] These non-interchangeable instructions encourage the model to keep tracking the state change in a correct sequential way. Otherwise, as in ALCHEMY, the model may not have a strong incentive to follow the order of the instructions and understand them sequentially. Nonetheless, our finding here is *not* a dataset design problem, as many real-life instructions can have the same property, but more about analyzing the effect of differing dataset properties. Additionally, these results can be seen as empirical evidence about how or whether fine-tuned seq2seq models form internal meaning representations when only final-supervision is given, complementing the study by Li et al. (2021). Models with internal meaning representations should have higher $\mathbf{acc}_{\text{all}}$ than $\mathbf{acc}_{\text{final}}$ as representations at later steps are built on representations at earlier steps so they will be more error-prone. Therefore, our experiments imply that the exact behavior may depend on the nature of the fine-tuning tasks. On ALCHEMY, the model shows no significant evidence of maintaining a reliable meaning representation, while on the other two tasks, the model shows hints of maintaining a meaning representation even with final step supervision.

3 Intermediate State Prediction with Uniformly Sampled Annotations

One of the major reasons behind the poor performance in Sec. 2 is that all the gold labels are at the final step, so for the intermediate steps, there is no strong supervision to ensure a desirable behavior. While for many applications, final-step labels are indeed more natural to collect, in this section, we explore if a better annotation strategy can improve the performance with the *same amount of labeling budget*. Specifically, we replace the final-step-only supervision with the same amount of supervision

[4]These statistics are manually estimated by the authors from 100 randomly-sampled instruction pairs from each task.

distributed uniformly across different steps. Such labels can reduce the gap between training and evaluation, and the model can receive supervision at intermediate steps. The results with such uniformly sampled labels are shown in the fourth row of Table 1. Compared to the final-step supervision results, we notice a substantial improvement on $\mathbf{acc_{all}}$ on all three subtasks, but there is a drop on $\mathbf{acc_{final}}$ on two subtasks (ALCHEMY and SCENE). Therefore, the preference between uniformly-distributed labels and end-step only labels depends on the final target. Additionally, there still exist many applications where the intermediate labels are difficult to collect or there is no budget to re-annotate labels. For those cases, we next describe our exploration to improve $\mathbf{acc_{all}}$ without additional gold labels.

4 Intermediate State Prediction with Contrastive Learning

Method. In Sec. 2, our baseline T5 predicts all the intermediate states independently, similar to the re-translation strategy (Arivazhagan et al., 2020) in streaming MT. However, it ignores the strong correlation of predictions over different steps, which partially leads to weak intermediate-step results. Next, we use contrastive learning to leverage such correlation without gold labels.

We first introduce the notations. We denote the function learned by the seq2seq transformer as $f(state_0, inst_1, \ldots, inst_i) = p_i^{state}$. Here $state_i$ and $inst_i$ are input tokens representing the state representation at step i and the instruction at step i respectively. p_i^{state} is the model prediction of the state at step i, which is a sequence of categorical distributions. The length of the sequence is the total number of tokens of the state representation, and each categorical distribution is over the vocabulary. For two consecutive steps, the seq2seq model produces two predictions p_i^{state} and p_{i+1}^{state}.

Our main intuition is to leverage the observation that *"There is a strong correlation between **the change in two consecutive states** and **the instruction of that step**."* To implement this idea, we compute two sets of vectors, one for the difference in consecutive states, and the other to represent the instruction. Then we use contrastive learning to encourage matching between these two sets of embeddings. Concretely, we start from the model predicted distribution p_i^{state}. We map the distribution back to the embedding space by computing $e_i^{state} = Ep_i^{state}$ where E is the

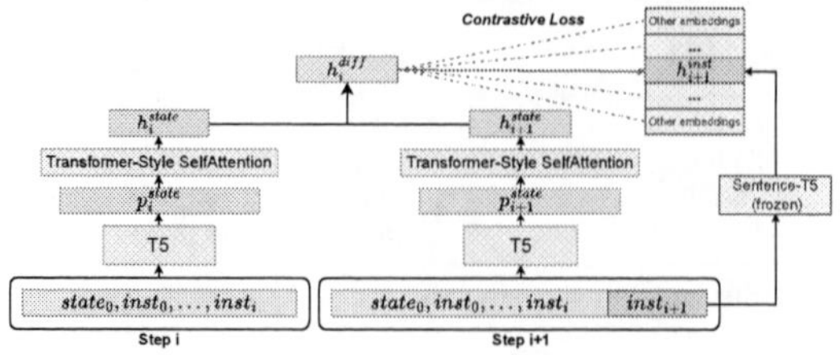

Figure 1: Contrastive learning encourages matching between state differences and corresponding instructions.

input embedding matrix of the seq2seq model. Then, we compute a vector h_i^{state} to represent each state by computing the transformer-style multi-layer self-attention between the embeddings e_i^{state} and an additional learnable vector h^s. $h_i^{state} = \mathrm{SelfAtt}([h^s, e_i^{state}])$. Now, with two state embeddings for two consecutive steps, we can compute a difference vector that captures the difference in consecutive states following Conneau et al. (2017): $h_i^{diff} = \mathrm{MLP}(h_i^{state}, h_{i+1}^{state}, |h_i^{state} - h_{i+1}^{state}|, h_i^{state} \odot h_{i+1}^{state})$. For the instruction vector, we directly feed the latest instruction $inst_{i+1}$ to an off-the-shelf sentence-T5 model (Ni et al., 2022).[5] With these two set of embeddings, we compute a contrastive matching loss (Gao et al., 2021): $\mathcal{L}_{cont} = \frac{\exp(\mathrm{sim}(h_i^{diff}, h_{i+1}^{inst}))}{\sum_{\text{all } inst \text{ in the batch}} \exp(\mathrm{sim}(h_i^{diff}, h^{inst}))}$, where sim is the similarity function, and we use all the other in-batch examples as negative examples. An illustration of this idea is at Fig. 1. The total training loss will be the sum of both standard MLE loss and the contrastive loss, $\mathcal{L}_{total} = \mathcal{L}_{MLE} + \mathcal{L}_{cont}$.

Results. The results for our contrastive learning method are in the "+CL" row of Table 1. We see opposite trends on ALCHEMY and SCENE. On ALCHEMY, we can see a substantial increase on $\mathbf{acc_{all}}$, improving it from the extremely low accuracy of 58.0% to 72.4%, which is comparable to its $\mathbf{acc_{final}}$, and making its behavior similar to other tasks. We can also observe a small improvement on the TANGRAMS subtask. However, such improvement does not translate to other settings where the $\mathbf{acc_{all}}$ performance is already decent and is comparable to $\mathbf{acc_{final}}$. For instance, on SCENE, adding our contrastive learning method does not improve either $\mathbf{acc_{final}}$ or $\mathbf{acc_{all}}$, and leads to a drop on $\mathbf{acc_{final}}$. We also do not observe additional gain by combining contrastive learning with the uniformly sampled annotation described in Sec. 3. We conjec-

[5] Preliminarily, we tried to extract embeddings from our model itself, but observe no substantial improvement.

ture such mixed results may result from a lack of more fine-grained control on h_i^{diff}, as the current implementation may allow h_i^{diff} to encode irrelevant features from one of the consecutive steps. This lack of more precise regularization makes it hard to further improve strong baselines already showing sequential understanding abilities (e.g., on SCENE). See Appendix C for more discussions.

5 Related Works

Our work focuses on sequential instruction understanding. Many earlier works in this direction rely on a pre-defined action set or a world simulator that facilitates the inference of the semantics of each sentence (Long et al., 2016; Guu et al., 2017; Suhr and Artzi, 2018; Muhlgay et al., 2019). Neural models can bring additional improvement, especially with specifically designed architectures (Huang et al., 2018; Yeh and Chen, 2019) or training methods (Fried et al., 2018; Shi et al., 2022). Our work advances this direction by examining transformer seq2seq models in limited supervision settings, and providing solutions for undesirable behaviors. Many other tasks (Anderson et al., 2018; Dalvi et al., 2018; Kiddon et al., 2015) also require understanding the sequential relationship between sentences. The contrastive learning component can also be viewed as a way to relieve the reward sparsity problem, similar to the effect of forward modeling (Pathak et al., 2017). Pretrained transformers have been applied to many different tasks. However, it is unclear how they process sequences inherently. Li et al. (2021) study whether language models implicitly build meaning representations. Our empirical results provide evidence of different behaviors in different datasets.

6 Conclusion

We study seq2seq transformers for sequential instruction following. Depending on data properties, if only final-supervision is given, transformers may naturally perform well on intermediate steps, but can also fail miserably. We explore two potential remedies, one with uniformly sampled supervision, and the other with contrastive learning.

Acknowledgments

We thank the reviewers for their helpful comments. This work was partially supported by NSF-CAREER Award 1846185, ONR Grant N00014-18-1-2871, and DARPA Machine Commonsense (MCS) Grant N66001-19-2-4031. The views are those of the authors and not of the funding agency.

Limitations

The main limitation of this work is a limited choice of models and datasets. In our work, we mainly tested with T5-base models. We expect our claims to hold on models with similar scales, but models with significantly more parameters (e.g., GPT-3) may demonstrate different fine-tuning behaviors. Additionally, we observe different behaviors on three subtasks on SCONE, so in order to generalize our finding to other datasets and predict the intermediate step performance, one needs to judge whether the new dataset is more similar to ALCHEMY or more similar to SCENE and TANGRAMS, which may not be straightforward for some applications.

Ethics Statement

Our work studies transformer-based seq2seq models for sequential instruction following tasks. Our experiment is conducted on synthetic domains in the SCONE (Long et al., 2016) dataset, and aims to have a better understanding of transformer models. We do not foresee any ethical risk for this work.

References

Peter Anderson, Qi Wu, Damien Teney, Jake Bruce, Mark Johnson, Niko Sünderhauf, Ian Reid, Stephen Gould, and Anton Van Den Hengel. 2018. Vision-and-language navigation: Interpreting visually-grounded navigation instructions in real environments. In *Proceedings of the IEEE Conference on Computer Vision and Pattern Recognition*, pages 3674–3683.

Naveen Arivazhagan, Colin Cherry, Wolfgang Macherey, and George Foster. 2020. Re-translation versus streaming for simultaneous translation. In *Proceedings of the 17th International Conference on Spoken Language Translation*, pages 220–227.

James Bradbury, Roy Frostig, Peter Hawkins, Matthew James Johnson, Chris Leary, Dougal Maclaurin, George Necula, Adam Paszke, Jake VanderPlas, Skye Wanderman-Milne, and Qiao Zhang. 2018. JAX: Composable transformations of Python+NumPy programs.

Paweł Budzianowski, Tsung-Hsien Wen, Bo-Hsiang Tseng, Iñigo Casanueva, Stefan Ultes, Osman Ramadan, and Milica Gašić. 2018. MultiWOZ - a large-scale multi-domain Wizard-of-Oz dataset for task-oriented dialogue modelling. In *Proceedings of the 2018 Conference on Empirical Methods in Natural*

Language Processing, pages 5016–5026, Brussels, Belgium. Association for Computational Linguistics.

Alexis Conneau, Douwe Kiela, Holger Schwenk, Loïc Barrault, and Antoine Bordes. 2017. Supervised learning of universal sentence representations from natural language inference data. In *Proceedings of the 2017 Conference on Empirical Methods in Natural Language Processing*, pages 670–680, Copenhagen, Denmark. Association for Computational Linguistics.

Bhavana Dalvi, Lifu Huang, Niket Tandon, Wen-tau Yih, and Peter Clark. 2018. Tracking state changes in procedural text: a challenge dataset and models for process paragraph comprehension. In *Proceedings of the 2018 Conference of the North American Chapter of the Association for Computational Linguistics: Human Language Technologies, Volume 1 (Long Papers)*, pages 1595–1604, New Orleans, Louisiana. Association for Computational Linguistics.

Daniel Fried, Jacob Andreas, and Dan Klein. 2018. Unified pragmatic models for generating and following instructions. In *Proceedings of the 2018 Conference of the North American Chapter of the Association for Computational Linguistics: Human Language Technologies, Volume 1 (Long Papers)*, pages 1951–1963, New Orleans, Louisiana. Association for Computational Linguistics.

Tianyu Gao, Xingcheng Yao, and Danqi Chen. 2021. SimCSE: Simple contrastive learning of sentence embeddings. In *Proceedings of the 2021 Conference on Empirical Methods in Natural Language Processing*, pages 6894–6910, Online and Punta Cana, Dominican Republic. Association for Computational Linguistics.

Kelvin Guu, Panupong Pasupat, Evan Liu, and Percy Liang. 2017. From language to programs: Bridging reinforcement learning and maximum marginal likelihood. In *Proceedings of the 55th Annual Meeting of the Association for Computational Linguistics (Volume 1: Long Papers)*, pages 1051–1062, Vancouver, Canada. Association for Computational Linguistics.

Hsin-Yuan Huang, Eunsol Choi, and Wen-tau Yih. 2018. Flowqa: Grasping flow in history for conversational machine comprehension. In *International Conference on Learning Representations*.

Chloé Kiddon, Ganesa Thandavam Ponnuraj, Luke Zettlemoyer, and Yejin Choi. 2015. Mise en place: Unsupervised interpretation of instructional recipes. In *Proceedings of the 2015 Conference on Empirical Methods in Natural Language Processing*, pages 982–992, Lisbon, Portugal. Association for Computational Linguistics.

Belinda Z. Li, Maxwell Nye, and Jacob Andreas. 2021. Implicit representations of meaning in neural language models. In *Proceedings of the 59th Annual Meeting of the Association for Computational Linguistics and the 11th International Joint Conference on Natural Language Processing (Volume 1: Long Papers)*, pages 1813–1827, Online. Association for Computational Linguistics.

Reginald Long, Panupong Pasupat, and Percy Liang. 2016. Simpler context-dependent logical forms via model projections. In *Proceedings of the 54th Annual Meeting of the Association for Computational Linguistics (Volume 1: Long Papers)*, pages 1456–1465, Berlin, Germany. Association for Computational Linguistics.

Dor Muhlgay, Jonathan Herzig, and Jonathan Berant. 2019. Value-based search in execution space for mapping instructions to programs. In *Proceedings of the 2019 Conference of the North American Chapter of the Association for Computational Linguistics: Human Language Technologies, Volume 1 (Long and Short Papers)*, pages 1942–1954, Minneapolis, Minnesota. Association for Computational Linguistics.

Jianmo Ni, Gustavo Hernandez Abrego, Noah Constant, Ji Ma, Keith Hall, Daniel Cer, and Yinfei Yang. 2022. Sentence-t5: Scalable sentence encoders from pretrained text-to-text models. In *Findings of the Association for Computational Linguistics: ACL 2022*, pages 1864–1874, Dublin, Ireland. Association for Computational Linguistics.

Deepak Pathak, Pulkit Agrawal, Alexei A Efros, and Trevor Darrell. 2017. Curiosity-driven exploration by self-supervised prediction. In *International conference on machine learning*, pages 2778–2787. PMLR.

Colin Raffel, Noam Shazeer, Adam Roberts, Katherine Lee, Sharan Narang, Michael Matena, Yanqi Zhou, Wei Li, and Peter J Liu. 2020. Exploring the limits of transfer learning with a unified text-to-text transformer. *Journal of Machine Learning Research*, 21:1–67.

Adam Roberts, Hyung Won Chung, Anselm Levskaya, Gaurav Mishra, James Bradbury, Daniel Andor, Sharan Narang, Brian Lester, Colin Gaffney, Afroz Mohiuddin, Curtis Hawthorne, Aitor Lewkowycz, Alex Salcianu, Marc van Zee, Jacob Austin, Sebastian Goodman, Livio Baldini Soares, Haitang Hu, Sasha Tsvyashchenko, Aakanksha Chowdhery, Jasmijn Bastings, Jannis Bulian, Xavier Garcia, Jianmo Ni, Andrew Chen, Kathleen Kenealy, Jonathan H. Clark, Stephan Lee, Dan Garrette, James Lee-Thorp, Colin Raffel, Noam Shazeer, Marvin Ritter, Maarten Bosma, Alexandre Passos, Jeremy Maitin-Shepard, Noah Fiedel, Mark Omernick, Brennan Saeta, Ryan Sepassi, Alexander Spiridonov, Joshua Newlan, and Andrea Gesmundo. 2022. Scaling up models and data with `t5x` and `seqio`. *arXiv preprint arXiv:2203.17189*.

Qi Shi, Qian Liu, Bei Chen, Yu Zhang, Ting Liu, and Jian-Guang Lou. 2022. LEMON: Language-based environment manipulation via execution-guided pretraining. In *Findings of the Association for Computational Linguistics: EMNLP 2022*, pages 471–485, Abu Dhabi, United Arab Emirates. Association for Computational Linguistics.

Alane Suhr and Yoav Artzi. 2018. Situated mapping of sequential instructions to actions with single-step reward observation. In *Proceedings of the 56th Annual Meeting of the Association for Computational Linguistics (Volume 1: Long Papers)*, pages 2072–2082, Melbourne, Australia. Association for Computational Linguistics.

Ashish Vaswani, Noam Shazeer, Niki Parmar, Jakob Uszkoreit, Llion Jones, Aidan N Gomez, Łukasz Kaiser, and Illia Polosukhin. 2017. Attention is all you need. *Advances in neural information processing systems*, 30.

Noam Wies, Yoav Levine, and Amnon Shashua. 2023. Sub-task decomposition enables learning in sequence to sequence tasks. In *The Eleventh International Conference on Learning Representations*.

Yi-Ting Yeh and Yun-Nung Chen. 2019. FlowDelta: Modeling flow information gain in reasoning for conversational machine comprehension. In *Proceedings of the 2nd Workshop on Machine Reading for Question Answering*, pages 86–90, Hong Kong, China. Association for Computational Linguistics.

Hangyeol Yu, Myeongho Jeong, Jamin Shin, Hyeongdon Moon, Juneyoung Park, and Seungtaek Choi. 2023. Towards zero-shot functional compositionality of language models.

Tao Yu, Rui Zhang, Kai Yang, Michihiro Yasunaga, Dongxu Wang, Zifan Li, James Ma, Irene Li, Qingning Yao, Shanelle Roman, Zilin Zhang, and Dragomir Radev. 2018. Spider: A large-scale human-labeled dataset for complex and cross-domain semantic parsing and text-to-SQL task. In *Proceedings of the 2018 Conference on Empirical Methods in Natural Language Processing*, pages 3911–3921, Brussels, Belgium. Association for Computational Linguistics.

A Dataset

In this section, we provide a detailed description of the dataset we use in our experiments and the preprocessing steps. The experiment in this paper focuses on the SCONE (Long et al., 2016) dataset. The SCONE dataset contains three subtasks: ALCHEMY, SCENE, and TANGRAMS. Each subtask focuses on a different domain and highlights different linguistic properties. The ALCHEMY task includes instructions about mixing colored chemicals in 7 beakers, and focuses on the ellipsis phenomenon. The SCENE task includes descriptions about people's movement in a scene, and focuses on object coreference. The TANGRAMS task includes instructions to manipulate tangram pieces, and focuses on action coreference. Table 3 shows the dataset statistics of all three datasets. The only data filtering we used in this work is that we removed a few examples from the TANGRAMS task where it does not contain 5 complete instructions. Other than that, we use all the examples in the original dataset.

Task	Train	Dev	Test
ALCHEMY	3567	245	899
SCENE	3352	198	1035
TANGRAMS	4159	198	990

Table 3: Dataset statistics for the SCONE (Long et al., 2016) dataset. The numbers in this Table are the number of examples. Each example will contain 5 steps.

State Representation Linearization Pretrained Transformers, including T5s used in this paper, are shown to be sensitive to the output format. Therefore, we convert the original output format in SCONE into a more readable text description. An example for each subtask can be seen in Table 4.

B Implementation Details

All the models used in this work are implemented using JAX (Bradbury et al., 2018) and the T5x (Roberts et al., 2022) framework. For all the experiments, we finetune the T5-v1.1-base model. We use a batch size of 128, a constant learning rate of 0.0001, and a dropout rate of 0.1. For the ALCHEMY task, we finetune for 100k steps. For the SCENE and TANGRAMS tasks, we notice the model converges faster, so we finetune for 50k steps. For the contrastive learning experiments, the instruction embeddings are extracted using sentence-T5-base (Ni et al., 2022) models. We use cosine similarity as the similarity function in the contrastive loss. All our experiments are conducted on Google v3 TPUs.

C More Discussions about Contrastive Learning Results

In Sec. 4, we notice that while our contrastive learning approach can improve the low $\textbf{acc}_{\textbf{all}}$ on ALCHEMY, it fails to consistently improve in other settings, especially when the baseline performance is already decent on the SCENE subtask. One of our observations that may prevent contrastive learning from further improvement is the tendency for the contrastive loss to overfit during the training. In our experiments, we often observe a significant gap between the contrastive matching accuracy on the training set and on the development set. This problem is very likely to be caused by the lack of regularization in the current implementation of the

Task	Example state	Example instructions
ALCHEMY	1: empty empty empty empty, 2: empty empty empty empty, 3: empty empty empty empty, 4: empty empty empty empty, 5: orange empty empty empty, 6: orange orange orange empty, 7: green green green green	Instruction 1: pour the last orange beaker into beaker two Instruction 2: then into the first ...
SCENE	1: red empty, 2: empty empty, 3: empty empty, 4: empty empty, 5: green empty, 6: green orange, 7: yellow orange, 8: empty empty, 9: yellow empty, 10: empty empty	Instruction 1: the man in the red hat takes a step to the right Instruction 2: he's joined on his left by a person wearing a blue shirt ...
TANGRAMS	1: two, 2: one, 3: four, 4: zero, 5: three	Instruction 1: delete the second object from the left Instruction 2: undo that ...

Table 4: Example linearized states and instructions used in this work for three subtasks of SCONE. For graphic demonstrations of these states and instructions, please visit `https://nlp.stanford.edu/projects/scone/`

difference vector. In our current implementation, the only constraint the difference vector have is that it needs to be a function of consecutive states, i.e. $h_i^{diff} = f(h_i^{state}, h_{i+1}^{state})$. While this implementation can capture the difference between the states, and can help when the model's performance is bad (as empirically verified on ALCHEMY), it can also capture many irrelevant features, which helps reduce the contrastive matching loss, but does not help the model to correct its prediction on intermediate steps. In our experiments, we have also tried several approaches to resolve this problem, including having hard negatives in contrastive learning, having an auto-encoder style reconstruction loss, etc. But none of these methods solves this problem effectively. Hence, we leave a more in-depth exploration of this direction for future work.

Author Index

Association for Computational Linguistics
209 N. Eighth Street
Stroudsburg, Pennsylvania 18360

ISBN 978-1-7138-8234-3

CURRAN ASSOCIATES INC.
proceedings.com